Introduction to the Theory and Practice of Econometrics

Introduction to the Theory and Practice of Econometrics

Second Edition

George G. Judge
University of California, Berkeley

R. Carter Hill
Louisiana State University

William E. Griffiths
University of New England

Helmut Lütkepohl
Christian-Albrechts-Universität Kiel

Tsoung-Chao Lee
University of Connecticut

WILEY

JOHN WILEY & SONS

New York Chichester Brisbane Toronto Singapore

Library of Congress Cataloging in Publication Data:

Introduction to the theory and practice of econometrics / George G.
Judge ... [et al.]. — 2nd ed.
p. cm.
Includes index.
ISBN 0-471-62414-4
1. Econometrics. I. Judge, George G.
HB 139.I58 1988
330'.028—dc19

87-28569
CIP

Printed in the United States of America

10 9 8 7 6 5 4 3 2

To

Lisa and Laura Judge
Mima Hill
JoAnn, Jill, David and Wendy Griffiths
Hilde and Karlheinz Lütkepohl
Nancy, Tony and Jean Lee

Preface to Second Edition

In revising the first edition of ITPE, our objective was to make changes in the content, organization, and exposition so that it is a friendly book for both the instructor and the student. The scope of the book is not greatly changed from the first edition. However, (1) by adding some new material we have made the book more self-contained, (2) by changing the organization and exposition we have tried to make the book serve wider introductory- and intermediate-level audiences, (3) by carrying through meaningful examples in each chapter we have tried to improve the interweaving of theory and practice, and (4) by providing a Computer Handbook the computer is made an important part of the teaching–learning process.

As in the first edition, the linkage between the economic process thought to underlie data generation and the statistical model reflecting the corresponding sampling process serves as a unifying theme throughout the book as we progress from the simple to the complex ways of modeling economic data. Also as in the first edition, to ensure the student fully appreciates the sampling theory approach to inference, Monte Carlo sampling procedures are introduced in the Exercises for most of the chapters to illustrate important sampling concepts.

To demonstrate how standard econometric software can be used to implement the procedures outlined in the text, a Computer Handbook containing the applications and Monte Carlo exercises in each chapter has been developed. This Computer Handbook should make possible a "hands on" experience with micro or main frame computers through the use of the widely available SHAZAM and SAS software packages. A corresponding GAUSS manual is being developed separately.

The book is more self-contained than the first edition in that it contains chapters on the basic concepts of classical and Bayesian inference and an extensive appendix on linear algebra. Therefore, introductory knowledge in these areas, although beneficial, is not necessary.

Some of the specific changes relative to the first edition are

1. The early chapters are devoted to a discussion of the basic concepts of classical and Bayesian inference. For most students, these chapters are intended as a review or reference point for some of the basic definitions and concepts of statistical inference.

2. The discussion of the linear-statistical (regression) model is started with two unknown location parameters, and the analysis is carried through with both summation and matrix-vector notation.
3. A linear algebra appendix is included that serves the needs of each chapter (for example, the operations of vectors and matrices and the matrix algebra relevant to normal distribution theory).
4. Relative to the first edition, we have combined some of the chapters and changed the order in which some of the topics are developed. For example, we have included autocorrelation and heteroskedasticity in the chapter concerned with Aitken estimation with an unknown covariance matrix.
5. One or more applied examples are presented in each chapter that can be reproduced by the student.
6. Asymptotics have been introduced in the early chapters, and this concept is made use of throughout this book.
7. A Computer Handbook is provided that makes the computer an integral part of the teaching–learning process for each chapter. Both micro and mainframe computers are used along with SHAZAM and SAS econometric software packages. A corresponding manual for the GAUSS software package is also being developed.

As with the first edition, the objectives of the book are multiple. The first third of the book reviews statistical concepts and introduces the linear statistical model and its uses. The remainder of the book introduces the student to econometric problems that arise when we take into account that economic data are generated from a system of relations that are dynamic, stochastic, and simultaneous and that statistical procedures change as we change the statistical model, the amount and type of information used, and the measure of performance. These topics, although not treated in depth, in each case identify the general problem area and suggest one or more ways of mitigating its statistical impact. For a more in depth treatment of each problem area, the student is referred to a particular chapter in the second edition of *The Theory and Practice of Econometrics.*

As the book is designed, it may be used (1) as a one-semester/quarter course that introduces the undergraduate student to classical and Bayesian statistics and to the general linear-statistical (regression) model, (2) as a one- or two-semester/quarter course in undergraduate econometrics, (3) as a one- or two-semester/quarter course in intermediate econometrics at the graduate level, (4) as a problems course in econometrics at the undergraduate or graduate level, and (5) as a review or refresher course in statistical inference and econometrics.

The criticisms and suggestions we have received from colleagues and students who used the first edition were very helpful in eliminating errors and in determining the contents and organization of this volume. We cannot acknowledge each of the individual contributions, but we do want to indicate our debt to those behind-the-scenes colleagues and to each we offer our sincere thanks.

Ken White has not only taken the leadership in developing the Computer Handbook, but he has also contributed to the content of many of the chapters. To Ken we owe a special thanks, and we are pleased to see his name associated with the book.

In addition the following have made substantive contributions: Larry Marsh, Minbo Kim, James Chalfont and Shirley Haun.

For a book of this nature, skilled technical typists are a necessity. In this context we would like to recognize and thank members of the Giannini Foundation Word Processing Center, Jerry Rowley, Mary Jo Neathery, Shirley DeJean, Val Boland, and Marlene Youman. Partial support for this work was provided by a National Science Foundation grant.

George G. Judge
R. Carter Hill
William Griffiths
Helmut Lütkepohl
Tsoung-Chao Lee

April 1987

Preface
To First Edition

The descriptive and prescriptive goals of understanding, predicting, and controlling economic processes and institutions requires that the student in economics and business makes use of an array of statistical models and measurement procedures. An operational knowledge in this area calls for (1) an understanding of the basic concepts of the calculus, linear algebra, and statistical inference; (2) having an array of statistical models that are consistent with the alternative ways in which economic data are generated; and (3) given the statistical model, a set of procedures or rules that permits the data to be used in an "optimal" way.

Many undergraduate textbooks in statistics and econometrics treat these topics in a disjoint way. Thus a student may first learn about probability and distribution theory, then about estimation and hypothesis testing from a sampling theory or Bayesian approach, and finally turn to the area of econometrics or the application of these tools to a particular subject matter area. Often this approach leaves the student without a clear understanding of the alternative approaches to statistical inference, the connection between statistical theory and econometric practice and, from a research standpoint, how one would go about producing new econometric knowledge. In this book the objective is to interweave inferential approaches and theory and practice. Therefore, for example, the basic statistical and linear algebra concepts are introduced as they are needed to give life to the statistical model under study.

Also, because there is limited opportunity to experiment in economics, most econometric applications start with a tentative theory or hypothesis, a sample of data, and the goal of learning something about the phenomena under study from the limited set of observations. Therefore, a sample of data that may be used to investigate a particular economic hypothesis is presented to motivate the analysis of each of the statistical models presented. This linkage between the economic process that is thought to have generated the data and a particular statistical model is a unifying theme throughout the book. We progress from the special case of investigating the possibilities for determining the location and scale parameters for a population from a sample of observations to investigating a complex simultaneous system of structural equations under general stochastic assumptions. To ensure that the reader understands the basic concepts and conclusions as they relate to linear statistical models, simple special case models are evaluated, and then the analysis is repeated for the general case.

To make certain that the student fully appreciates the sampling theory approach to inference, Monte Carlo experiments and results that illustrate important sampling concepts and properties are introduced in many chapters. Exercises that improve manipulative skills and samples of data from a Monte Carlo experiment for a particular statistical model form the basis for student exercises in each chapter. In this way students can obtain hands-on experience with the computer *and* verify empirically the sampling characteristics that have been analytically derived.

The book is self-contained in the sense that statistical concepts and linear algebra are introduced when they are needed and are most relevant for analysis and inference. Applications of calculus are presented in such a way that the ideas are transmitted even though the underlying concepts may be unfamiliar. Introductory knowledge in these areas, although beneficial, is not necessary.

The objectives of the book are multiple. The first half of the book gives the student a solid introduction to the formulation and use of linear statistical models. The second half introduces the student to the econometric problems that arise when we take into account the facts that economic data are stochastic, dynamic, and simultaneous and that the optimal statistical procedure sometimes changes as we change the statistical model, the amount and type of information used, and the measure of performance. These topics, although not treated in great depth, identify the general problem area and suggest one or more procedures for mitigating the statistical impact of the econometric evil in question. For a more complete treatment of each of the problems covered in the last half of the book, the reader should refer to our other book, *The Theory and Practice of Econometrics* (Wiley, 1980).

As written, this book is designed to serve multiple uses by varying the sections used or the sequence of chapters.

Each instructor will, of course, emphasize different aspects of the econometric puzzle. Our purpose has been to put together a book that is rich enough in the basic ingredients to permit instructors and students to select the menu that will satisfy their individual needs.

After we completed *The Theory and Practice of Econometrics* it seemed appropriate that we should undertake the writing of an introductory text that would be the foundation for econometric practice. The resulting set of words and symbols represents the combined judgments that have come from teaching a range of mathematics, statistics, economics, and econometrics courses over the last three decades. Students' and colleagues' ideas have been very important in the organization, readability, and possible usefulness of the book. In particular we thank Albert Link, Auburn University, Malcolm Dowling, University of Colorado, and Peter

Zadrozny, New York University, for their early input and suggestions. The final product owes a great debt to the careful and detailed recommendations of Keith Johnson, New York University, E. P. Howrey, University of Michigan, and Gregg Duncan, Washington State University. Rich Esposito, the economics editor at Wiley, made substantive contributions at each stage of the project. Mary Halloran contributed her superb talents to solving the problems of style and format and the production of the book.

For a book of this nature a skilled technical typist is a necessity. Dixie Trinkle is not only a skilled typist, but her patience and emphasis on accuracy and consistency made the task of going from the handwritten copy to the final manuscript a pleasure. Others who helped with the typing include Shirley Williams, Judy Griffin, Sylvia Graves, Carline Lancaster, Linda McKellar, and Rosean Swan. Partial support of this work was provided by a National Science Foundation grant.

George G. Judge
R. Carter Hill
William Griffiths
Helmut Lütkepohl
Tsoung-Chao Lee

May 1981

CONTENTS

Statistical Tables

CHAPTER 1

Introduction

1.1 The Nature of Econometrics

This book is concerned with the problem of measurement in economics, and it is directed toward developing, reviewing, and synthesizing some of the analytical methods that may be employed to analyze and learn from economic data. Over the last half-century, a great many achievements have been realized through a systematic use of economic data in conjunction with economic and statistical models and the sampling theory and Bayesian approaches to inference. These productive efforts have given content to both the theory and the practice of econometrics.

Economic theory is concerned with explaining the relationships among economic variables and using that information within a general theory of choice to explain production, allocation, and distribution decisions for a system that must operate within the implications of scarcity. On the other hand, statistical inference is concerned with drawing conclusions from limited data or bits of information, and the existence of this type of scarcity has led to the development of a general theory for dealing with decision problems under conditions of uncertainty. Consequently, both economics and statistical inference are concerned with generating information that may be used to improve decision making or strategy formation.

If the goal is to select the best decision from a set of economic choices, it is usually not enough to know that economic variables are related. In addition, we must also know the direction of the relation and, in many cases, the magnitudes involved. Toward this end, econometrics, using economic theory, mathematical economics, and statistical inference as analytical foundation stones and economic data as the information base, provides a basis for (1) modifying, refining, or possibly refuting conclusions contained in the body of knowledge known as economic theory, and (2) attaching signs, numbers, and reliability statements to the coefficients of variables in economic relationships so that this information can be used as a basis for decision making and choice.

Progress in economics in general and econometrics in particular depends on at least three related activities:

1. Development of tools to facilitate both the formulation and the testing of possible economic generalizations.

2. Collection, or generation and accumulation, of observations on economic processes and institutions.
3. Application of the tools and the observations to enlarge the body of established generalizations about economic affairs.

Given a basis for organizing knowledge, and given the usefulness or indeed the necessity of quantitative economic knowledge, the next important question involves how to go about searching for it. If all economists had IQs that were 300 standard deviations above the mean, this question might be of limited importance. However, many of us do not fit into this category, and the question of how to get on the efficient search turnpike is a real one.

1.2 The Search for Quantitative Economic Knowledge

1.2.1 Postulation

Much of the knowledge in economics is gained by a process of abstraction. Economic systems, like mathematical systems such as the number system, are invented, not discovered. Therefore, we start with the phenomena the scientist seeks to understand, and we develop a mathematical system or theory that consists of a set of assertions from which consequences are derived by using the rules of logic. The model of reality that results reflects an attempt to reconstruct in a simplified way the mechanism thought to lie behind the phenomena under study by the scientist. Therefore, the model represents the outcome of the process of abstraction, whereby tentative explanations are formulated. These tentative explanations, which are formulated as propositions, provide the hypothesis that may be tested. Consequently, the postulation process by which certain components of the phenomena under study are mapped into a formal deductive system with real-world interpretations tells us nothing about the truth or falsity of the conclusions. It only gives us the possibilities, provided that we have correctly made use of logic. In economics, partial equilibrium, general equilibrium, and aggregative economics are three systems methods that have been developed and used to organize knowledge and that form one basis for drawing economic conclusions.

The use of postulation and logic to obtain knowledge may be viewed, following Thrall, Coombs, and Raiffa, through the flow diagram shown in Figure 1.1.

The conclusions about economic processes and institutions reached by this process are usually labeled economic theory. Within this context the area of mathematical economics uses the methods of mathematics (1) to help us express

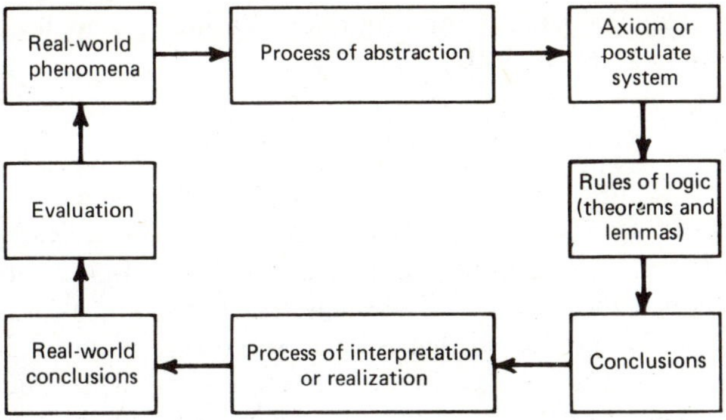

Figure 1.1 The postulation approach.

both the postulates and the conclusions of economic theory with clarity and consistency, (2) to facilitate drawing conclusions that might otherwise be obscured; and (3) to state the conclusions or propositions in such a form that they provide the basis for econometric analysis and testing.

Examples of conclusions reached in the economic sphere, by use of the postulation route, abound in introductory and upper-level courses in micro and macro theory. For example, in macroeconomic statics the basic postulate is as follows:

Equilibrium exists if and only if prices and quantities are such that

(i) Each commodity has market excess demand equal to zero.

(ii) Each commodity has excess flow demand equal to zero.

From our standpoint, interest would center on the allocative and distributive implications or conclusions that would flow from this postulate and thus provide a framework for testing. Alternatively, in the micro theory of consumer choice the level of consumption of a superior good is posited as a function of the price of the commodity, the price of competing and complementary commodities, and income. This then specifies the set of variables thought relevant in conditioning the level of consumption and gives some indication of the direction of the relationship among the variables. That is, we would expect the price coefficient to be negative and the income coefficient to be positive. As a final example, in the theory of the firm the output of a firm is specified to be a function of the level of one or more inputs, and some insights are given in terms of the form of the relationship. Each insight provides an example of economic knowledge reached via postulation. Other routes that have been proposed and possibly tried as a basis for going from phenomena to conclusions are revelation, magic, mysticism, and intuition. Various claims have been made about the role and success of each.

1.2.2 Experimentation

Since postulation only provides a range of possible conclusions and indicates nothing about the real-world truth content, the urge is strong to find a way to sort out fact from fiction or reduce the number of alternatives. Therefore, as was recognized early, one way to obtain knowledge is to observe the outcome of experiments that yield reproducible knowledge. In this process, a theoretical model is proposed and the uncontrolled elements are handled by the use of probability. In essence the postulation route to knowledge provides the theoretical model that may be used in the experimental search process or in alternatively learning from passively generated data.

The process by which choices between the tentative explanations, reached by postulation, may be made and theoretical parameters converted to useful information for decision purposes may be viewed as shown in Figure 1.2. Thus measurement provides one basis for choosing between the model alternatives and permits us to say, relative to the relationship between economic variables, something about how much, or at least the probability of how much. Disagreement between the statistical conclusions and those reached by postulation provide a basis for reevaluating the economic and experimental models and starting the search process again.

Given these knowledge-search processes, the task of econometrics is to use postulation and experimentation to generate information that may be used to reach conclusions of both a descriptive and a prescriptive nature about economic processes and institutions.

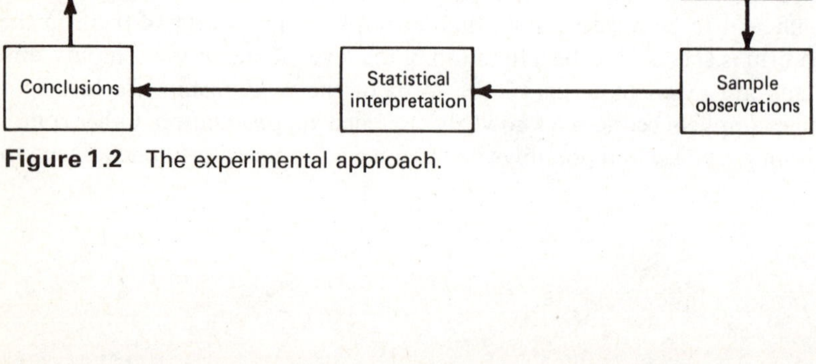

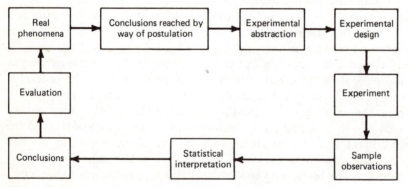

Figure 1.2 The experimental approach.

1.3 The Nonexperimental Model-Building Restriction

Economic theory, through a formal deductive system, provides the basis for experimental abstraction and the experimental design, but society in most cases carries out the experiment, possibly using its own design. Therefore, the economic researcher observes the outcome of society's experiment or performance but has little or no impact on the experimental design and the observations generated. This means that the economist is often asked to estimate the impact of a change in the mechanism that produces the data when there is limited or no possibility of producing the data beforehand in a laboratory experiment. Thus, by the passive nature of the data, economic researchers are, to a large extent, restricted in their knowledge search to the process of nonexperimental model building. As shown in Figure 1.2, we start with the observations and the experimental design, but the experiment is outside of the researcher's control.

Unfortunately, postulation typically provides many admissible economic and thus statistical models that do not contradict our perceived knowledge of human behavior or the economic and institutional process through which these data are generated. Therefore, in most econometric work, there is uncertainty as to the economic and statistical model that is used for estimation and inference purposes and the sampling model that actually was the basis for the data generation.

When econometric models are correctly specified, statistical theory provides well-defined procedures for obtaining point and interval estimates and evaluating the performance of various linear and usually unbiased estimators. However, uncertainties usually exist about the correct underlying economic and statistical models, such as the variables that should appear in the design matrix, the algebraic form of the relation or the type of nonlinearities that should be considered, the dynamic or lag structure between the economic variables, and the stochastic assumptions underlying the statistical model. In many cases, these uncertainties lead to models that are incorrectly specified and thus invalidate the sampling results that are traditionally claimed and generate estimators with unknown sampling performance. Consequently, to a large extent, econometrics is concerned with efficient procedures for identifying or mitigating the impacts of model misspecification.

The nonexperimental restriction also means that in addition to being efficient in using the data that are available, one must, in many cases, use nonsample information in order to support the parameter space adequately. Thus, much of econometrics is concerned with how to sort out and make use of this nonsample information in conjunction with the sample observations. In fact, much of the success in handling many of the problems in this book springs from how effectively this prior information is used. Therefore, in econometric work, as one goes from the conceptual model to the observed data and from prior information to the estimated relations, many interrelated questions face the researcher.

1.4 Objectives of the Book

Given a rich heritage of economic and statistical models that provide the tools to facilitate both the collection, generation, and accumulation of sample observations and the formulation and testing of possible economic generalizations on economic processes and institutions, the purpose of this book is to provide you with a basis for (1) specifying statistical models that may be compatible with the sampling scheme underlying the data under analysis; (2) developing alternative approaches to estimation and inference and demonstrating rules that may be used to obtain information or to learn from the sample observations; (3) gauging the sampling performance of the alternative rules for using the sample observations; and (4) drawing inferential conclusions and developing econometric procedures consistent with the nonexperimental nature of economic data. In particular, the purposes of this book are

1. To consider a range of traditional and nontraditional estimating and hypothesis-testing rules, within both a sampling theory and a Bayesian framework.

2. To question, in some cases, the use of conventional statistical properties in evaluating the performance of estimators and to use a decision theory framework for evaluating estimator performance.

3. To indicate the statistical consequences of traditional and ad hoc rules for hypothesis testing and model selection.

4. To recognize that econometricians may, to a large extent, work with false models and to suggest procedures to cope with this fact of econometric life.

5. To recognize that much information exists other than sample information and to propose and evaluate procedures that combine both sample and this other information.

6. To provide an up-to-date treatment of some of the most important questions and statistical models encountered in attempting to learn from economic data.

1.5 Organization of the Book

In specifying and analyzing an array of statistical models that may be consistent with economic data-generating processes, we have organized the book into six parts. In Part 1 some of the concepts that form the basis for statistical inference are introduced and reviewed. Both the sampling theory and Bayesian approaches to inference are considered, and one of the trickier areas of statistical methodology, asymptotics, is introduced.

In Part 2 the classical linear statistical (regression) model is specified; sampling theory and Bayesian theory form the basis for inference relating to the unknown location and scale parameters.

In Part 3, with a view toward specifying statisical models that are consistent with the characteristics of economic data, we start asking "What if" type of questions. What if the stochastic characteristics of the equation errors are such that they cannot be assumed to be independently and identically distributed? What if the underlying sampling process is unknown? What if the underlying constant location parameter vector assumption is not viable? What if we have both cross-section and time-series data, and what if we have sets of regression equations that are error related? Finally, what if the statistical models are nonlinear in the parameters and/or the right-hand variables are stochastic rather than fixed?

In Part 4 statistical models that are consistent with the simultaneous and stochastic nature of economic data are specified and alternative identification and estimation rules for coping with this type of feedback-sampling mechanism are analyzed and evaluated.

In Part 5 the dynamic-stochastic content of economic data is recognized and univariate and multivariate time series models and finite and infinite distributed lag models are reviewed and statistically analyzed.

Part 6 recognizes (1) that some economic data should be modeled by discrete rather than continuous random variables, (2) the need for statistical models and inference rules that take into account the existence of both sample and nonsample information, (3) that not all statistical models used in practice have design matrices with the correct column dimensions and that some design matrices are ill conditioned, and, finally, (4) that the error distributions are generally unknown and the possibility of developing estimation rules that are robust over a range of error specifications is pursued.

In the Appendix to the book, the linear algebra relevant to normal distribution theory and to the specification and analysis of an array of statistical models is developed.

Given an understanding of the concepts, statistical models, and approaches to inference developed in Parts 1 and 2, the sequence in which the other chapters are covered can be tailored to fit the desires of the instructor and the needs of the students. Given this overview, let us turn to the problems of inference from a sample of data.

PART 1

The Foundations of Statistical Inference

In the following three chapters, we review the basic concepts underlying the sampling theory and Bayesian approaches to inference. Building on the statistical concepts of probability and distribution theory, point and interval estimation and hypothesis testing are first developed within a classical statistics framework that uses sample information in making inferences about the unknown parameters. In contrast, under Bayesian inference, unknown parameters are treated as random variables, and loss functions, nonsample information (prior distributions), and posterior distributions are introduced and used as a basis for defining estimation rules and gauging performance.

CHAPTER 2

Probability and Distribution Theory

2.1 Introduction

In this chapter we lay the foundation for the discussion of statistical inference contained in Chapter 3. That foundation is probability and distribution theory, which we present concisely here to serve as a review of and reference for basic concepts. In Section 2.2 we discuss the notion of probability of events associated with random experiments. Section 2.3 contains the definitions of univariate and multivariate random variables and their probability distributions. In Section 2.4 mathematical expectation is defined for random variables and functions of random variables. Section 2.5 contains a discussion of the properties of some special probability distributions, including the normal probability distribution. Section 2.6 contains a summary and guide to further reading.

2.2 Probability

The term *probability* is loosely used by many persons to indicate the measure of one's belief in the occurrence of an uncertain future event. Despite its common usage, however, there is no single definition of the term probability that is universally accepted. Three different interpretations will be described in this section, each of which can be usefully applied to practical problems. An axiomatic approach to probability theory is then presented that is rich enough to include each of the interpretations of probability.

2.2.1 Experiments, Sample Spaces, and Events

A feature we commonly associate with the scientific method is experimentation. A scientist performs a controlled (repeatable) experiment and observes an outcome, which cannot be predicted with certainty prior to the experiment. This kind of experiment is called a *random experiment*. Each conceivable outcome is a *sample point*, and the set of all possible outcomes is defined as the *sample space* of the experiment. The word "sample" is included as a reminder of the random nature of the experiment and that a given outcome is just one of the possible outcomes. We are often interested in one or more subsets of the sample space, which are defined to be *events.*

Example 2.1 Let the experiment be the roll of a single die. The sample space of the experiment is $S = \{1, 2, 3, 4, 5, 6\}$, which contains all the possible outcomes of the experiment. Each outcome is a sample point, and this sample space has a *finite* number of elements. $A_1 = \{2, 4, 6\}$ is a subset of S and defines the event of obtaining an even outcome. $A_2 = \{4\}$ defines the event of rolling a 4. If a roll produces a 2 or 4 or 6, then the event A_1 is said to occur. If a 4 is rolled, then the events A_1 and A_2 both occur. ■

Example 2.2 Consider the experiment of flipping a coin until a head appears. The sample space for this experiment is

$$S = \{\text{H, TH, TTH, TTTH, TTTTH}, \ldots\}$$

since the first head could occur on the first, second, third, fourth,... flip. This sample space has infinitely many sample points, but the elements can be put into a one-to-one correspondence with the positive whole numbers, and, in this sense, the sample space is *countable* or *countably infinite.* If a sample space contains a finite number of elements, or an infinite though countable number of elements, it is said to be *discrete.* ■

Example 2.3 Consider the agricultural experiment of growing soybeans on an acre of land under a well-defined set of conditions, then recording the yield in bushels (x). The sample space here is $S = \{x | x \geq 0\}$, since the outcome of this experiment could be any nonnegative number of bushels. This sample space is *continuous* since it contains an interval of the real number line, and it has an uncountably infinite number of elements. Examples of events are $A_1 = \{x | x \leq 100\}$ and $A_2 = \{x | 20 < x < 50\}$, the former indicating the event of a yield less than or equal to 100 bushels and the latter of obtaining between 20 and 50 bushels. ■

Within this framework we can discuss the term probability. The *classical* interpretation of probability is based on the notion of *mutually exclusive and equally likely* experimental outcomes. If the sample space consists of n mutually exclusive and equally likely outcomes, then the probability of any single outcome, or sample point, is $1/n$. The probability of an event in such a setting is simply the sum of the probabilities of the sample points that result in the occurrence of the event. In Example 2.1, if the die is fair, or unbiased, the probability of any single outcome on a single toss is $\frac{1}{6}$. If $A = \{1, 2, 3\}$, then the probability of the event A occurring is $\frac{1}{2}$, or $P(A) = \frac{1}{2}$.

Note that for this interpretation of probability no actual experiment need ever take place. It is possible to conceive the experiment and proceed logically on the assumption of a fair die. Despite its appeal and simplicity, the classical interpretation of probability has serious weaknesses once one leaves the realm of well-defined games of chance with fair die, coins, cards, or such. For example, what is the probability of the event of rolling a 1, 2, or 3 with a single die if it is *not* fair? Or how would we answer questions like: What is the probability that a child born in New Orleans will contract cancer before the age of 40? Or, what is the probability of rain tomorrow?

To deal with these sorts of questions, we can consider broader notions of probability. One is the *relative frequency* interpretation of probability. Consider an experiment that has sample space S; let A be an event defined on S. Suppose we repeat the experiment N times and observe that the event A occurs f times. Then the ratio f/N is the relative frequency of A in these N trials of the experiment. The probability of event A is then the limit of this relative frequency as $N \to \infty$. This definition depends on the fact that the experiment can be repeated under essentially the identical conditions, at least conceptually. Classical, statistical theory is based on the notion of repeated sampling or experimentation and thus is associated with this concept of probability. An advantage of this interpretation is that it does not require equally likely sample points and is a meaningful measure of one's belief in the occurrence of an event that is associated with a repeatable experiment. For most purposes in the remainder of this book, the relative frequency interpretation of probability is satisfactory.

There are many situations, however, when the relative frequency interpretation is difficult to adopt. For example, when the weather forecaster announces that the probability of rain tomorrow is 80%, it is not likely to be a limiting relative frequency. Instead, it is a *personal* or *subjective* probability of the event that reflects a degree of belief. Hence it could be interpreted as a willingness to bet on the outcome (rain tomorrow) so that the payoffs are in the ratio $0.8/(1 - 0.8) = 4{:}1$. Furthermore, if the chance of rain tomorrow is 0.8, then on either side of the bet, the expected winnings are zero. Subjective probabilities are based on any and all information available to each person about the uncertainties related to the outcome of the event and will differ from person to person. The concept of subjective probability provides the foundation for the Bayesian approach to statistics discussed in Chapters 4 and 7.

In the remainder of this chapter we consider mathematical properties of probabilities. Any one of the foregoing probability concepts, or interpretations, can be used in applications, as long as it is consistent with the rules we develop.

2.2.2 Probability of Events

Given the correspondence between events and sets of points, recall the following definitions from set theory.

1. A is a subset of B, denoted $A \subset B$, if every point in A is also in B. Note that $A \subset A$, a set is always a subset of itself.
2. The *null* or *empty* set, ϕ, is the set consisting of no points, and thus ϕ is a subset of every set.
3. The *union* of sets A and B, denoted $A \cup B$, is the set of all points in A or B or both.
4. The *intersection* of A and B, denoted $A \cap B$, is the set of all points in both A and B.
5. If $A \subset S$ (the sample space) then the *complement of A* relative to S, denoted by $\bar{A}$, is the set of points in S, but not in A.
6. If A and B have no points in common, so $A \cap B = \phi$, then they are *mutually exclusive* or *disjoint*.

With these ideas from set theory we can now place mathematical restrictions on a type of function P, called a probability measure, that can be used to calculate probabilities of events. Intuitively, given the interpretation of probability as a limiting relative frequency, probabilities should have the usual properties of proportions. That is: (1) a probability should be a number between 0 and 1 because a proportion is that kind of number; (2) since the sample space S is an event itself and includes all possible outcomes, the probability of the event S should be 1; and (3) if two events A and B are disjoint, then the probability of their union should be equal to the sum of their probabilities since the proportion of the time that A or B occurs will be equal to the proportion of the time A occurs plus the proportion of the time B occurs. This idea clearly extends to more than two disjoint sets.

To summarize, a probability measure P (also a probability distribution or just a probability) on a sample space S must satisfy the following *Axioms of Probability*:

$$\text{For any event } A \subset S,\ 0 \le P(A) \le 1 \tag{2.2.1}$$

$$P(S) = 1 \tag{2.2.2}$$

$$P(A_1 \cup A_2 \cup \cdots) = P(A_1) + P(A_2) + \cdots \tag{2.2.3}$$

for every finite or infinite sequence of disjoint events $A_1, A_2, \ldots$

Using these axioms, the following properties of probability can be proved

$$P(\phi) = 0 \tag{2.2.4}$$

$$\text{For any } A \subset S,\ P(\bar{A}) = 1 - P(A) \tag{2.2.5}$$

$$\text{If } A \subset B,\ P(A) \leq P(B) \tag{2.2.6}$$

$$P(A \cup B) = P(A) + P(B) - P(A \cap B) \tag{2.2.7}$$

2.2.3 Conditional Probability and Independent Events

In the application of probability theory, situations frequently arise when we want to know the probability of an event (A) *given* that some other event (B) has occurred or is certain to occur. The effect of *conditioning* one event on the occurrence of another is to reduce the size of the sample space that is relevant for A, thus (usually) affecting the probability of A occurring. The conditional probability of event A given that event B will occur or has occurred is written $P(A|B)$.

Example 2.4 A single die is tossed. Let $A = \{1\}$ and $B = \{1, 3, 5\}$. Then $P(A) = \frac{1}{6}$, which is an *unconditional* probability. But, $P(A|B) = \frac{1}{3}$, the conditional probability of rolling a 1 *given* that an odd number is obtained is $\frac{1}{3}$. The effect of the given information is to reduce the sample space of the experiment from $S = \{1, 2, 3, 4, 5, 6)$ to the set B. ■

We can state the following property of conditional probability: If A and B are events in S, then the conditional probability of event A, given that event B has occurred, is

$$P(A|B) = \frac{P(A \cap B)}{P(B)} \tag{2.2.8}$$

provided $P(B) > 0$. It is straightforward to show that this definition of conditional probability obeys the axioms of probability and thus is a legitimate probability measure.

Note that (2.2.8) in product form is

$$P(A \cap B) = P(A|B)P(B) = P(B|A)P(A) \tag{2.2.9}$$

More generally, if $A_1, A_2, \ldots A_n$ are events such that $P(A_1) > 0$, $P(A_1 \cap A_2) > 0, \ldots, P(A_1 \cap A_2 \cap \cdots \cap A_{n-1}) > 0$, then

$$P(A_1 \cap A_2 \cap \cdots \cap A_n) = P(A_1)P(A_2|A_1)P(A_3|A_1 \cap A_2)\ldots P(A_n|A_1 \cap A_2 \cap A_3 \cap \cdots \cap A_{n-1}) \tag{2.2.10}$$

This definition of conditional probability leads to the definition of *independence of events*. Suppose that $P(A|B) = P(A)$. This would imply that *knowing* that event B occurred has no effect on the chance of event A occurring. It would be reasonable then to say that events A and B are independent events. Using this definition with the multiplication rule (2.2.9) leads to a formal definition of independence. Two events A and B are independent when

$$P(A \cap B) = P(A|B)P(B) = P(A)P(B) \tag{2.2.11}$$

Otherwise A and B are said to be dependent. Clearly if (2.2.11) is true, then $P(B|A) = P(B)$ as well. This definition extends to more than two events, for example, events A, B, and C are independent if $P(A \cap B \cap C) = P(A)P(B)P(C)$.

Example 2.5 Consider the experiment of tossing a coin three times. The sample space is $S = \{\text{HHH, HHT, HTH, THH, HTT, THT, TTH, TTT}\}$. Assume each of the outcomes is equally likely and define

$$A = \{\text{Head on each of the first 2 tosses}\}$$
$$B = \{\text{Tail occurs on the 3rd toss}\}$$
$$C = \{\text{Exactly 2 tails occur in the 3 tosses}\}$$

Events A and B are independent since

$$A = \{\text{HHH, HHT}\} \qquad P(A) = \tfrac{1}{4}$$
$$B = \{\text{HHT, HTT, THT, TTT}\} \qquad P(B) = \tfrac{1}{2}$$
$$A \cap B = \{\text{HHT}\} \qquad P(A \cap B) = \tfrac{1}{8}$$

so $P(A \cap B) = P(A)P(B)$, and $P(A|B) = P(A)$ and $P(B|A) = P(B)$. Events B and C are dependent since

$$C = \{\text{HTT, THT, TTH}\} \qquad P(C) = \tfrac{3}{8}$$
$$B \cap C = \{\text{HTT, THT}\} \qquad P(B \cap C) = \tfrac{1}{4}$$

and $P(B \cap C) \neq P(B)P(C)$. ■

2.2.4 Bayes' Rule

Let S denote the sample space of some experiment. The disjoint events $A_1, A_2, \ldots, A_n$ are a *partition* of S if $A_1 \cup A_2 \cup \cdots \cup A_n = S$ and $P(A_i) > 0$ for each i. If

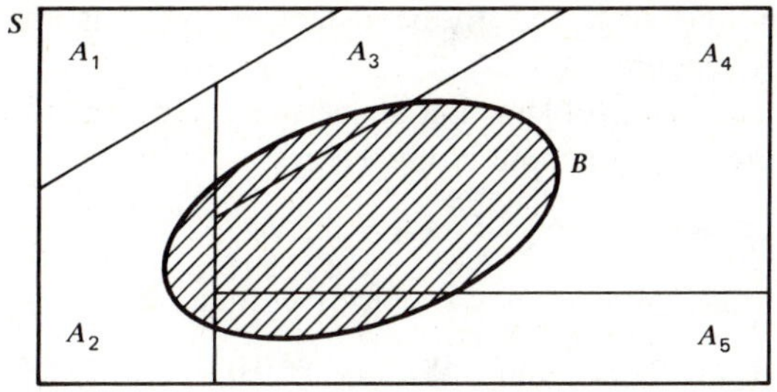

Figure 2.1 The intersection of B with the events $A_1, \ldots, A_5$.

B is any event in S so that $P(B) > 0$, then it will be true that

$$B = (A_1 \cap B) \cup (A_2 \cap B) \cup \cdots \cup (A_n \cap B)$$

This equality is illustrated in the Venn diagram, Figure 2.1.

Since the events $A_i \cap B$ are disjoint

$$P(B) = \sum_{i=1}^{n} P(A_i \cap B)$$

Also, if $P(A_i) > 0$, then $P(A_i \cap B) = P(B|A_i)P(A_i)$, so

$$P(B) = \sum_{i=1}^{n} P(B|A_i)P(A_i) \tag{2.2.12}$$

which is called the *law of total probability.*

The formation of a partition of S means that when the experiment is performed then exactly one of the events A_i will occur. Situations arise in which we would like to determine the probability of the event A_i *given* that the event B occurs. The solution to this problem is given by *Bayes' theorem,*

$$\begin{aligned} P(A_i|B) &= \frac{P(A_i \cap B)}{P(B)} = \frac{P(B|A_i)P(A_i)}{P(B)} \\ &= \frac{P(B|A_i)P(A_i)}{\sum_{i=1}^{n} P(B|A_i)P(A_i)} \end{aligned} \tag{2.2.13}$$

Example 2.6 Three different machines are used to produce chocolate chip cookies by Mima's Cookie Company, which promises to have at least six chips in every cookie. Suppose machine No. 1 produces 20% of Mima's cookies, No. 2 produces 30%, and No. 3 produces 50%. Also suppose that the machines represent different vintages of capital so that 1% of the cookies produced by machine No. 1 are defective, in the sense that they have less than six chips, 2% of those produced by machine No. 2 are defective, and 3% of those produced by No. 3 are defective. If one cookie is chosen at random and observed to be defective, what is the probability that it was produced by machine No. 2?

We apply Bayes' theorem to solve this problem. Let A_i be the event that the randomly chosen cookie was produced by machine No. i. Then

$$P(A_1) = 0.2, P(A_2) = 0.3, \quad \text{and} \quad P(A_3) = 0.5$$

Also, if B is the event that a randomly drawn cookie is defective, then

$$P(B|A_1) = 0.01, P(B|A_2) = 0.02, \quad \text{and} \quad P(B|A_3) = 0.03$$

Applying (2.2.13) we have

$$P(A_2|B) = \frac{P(A_2)P(B|A_2)}{\sum_{i=1}^{n} P(A_i)P(B|A_i)} = \frac{(0.3)(0.02)}{(0.2)(0.01) + (0.3)(0.02) + (0.5)(0.03)}$$

$$= 0.26 \quad \blacksquare$$

Bayes' theorem has an interesting interpretation that we will use extensively in Chapters 4 and 7. The probabilities $P(A_i)$ can be called "prior" probabilities since they represent the probabilities of the different machines in Example 2.6 producing a randomly selected cookie *before* that cookie is checked to see if it is defective. The conditional probability $P(A_i|B)$ is called a "posterior" probability since it represents our (revised) assignment of probabilities *after* the sample evidence of the defective cookie is obtained. Thus we can restate Bayes' theorem (2.2.13) verbally as *the posterior probability of an event A_i is proportional to the probability of the sample evidence after A_i times the prior probability of A_i*.

2.3 Random Variables and Probability Distributions

2.3.1 Random Variables and Values of Random Variables

In many applications of probability theory (including those in this book) the primary concern is with numerical values assigned to outcomes of an experiment. For example, in Example 2.6 we were interested in the *number* of chocolate chips in a randomly drawn cookie (the experiment). We might have been interested in the *weight* of the cookie or the *calorie* content of the cookie. In each of these cases, we are interested in numbers that are associated with the outcomes of a random experiment. We can define variables for each of these measurements. Let

$$X_1 = \text{the number of chips in a randomly drawn cookie}$$

$$X_2 = \text{the weight of a randomly drawn cookie}$$

$$X_3 = \text{the number of calories in a randomly drawn cookie}$$

The "measurement" could even be of a qualitative nature, such as

$$X_4 = \begin{cases} 1 \text{ if the randomly drawn cookie is whole} \\ 0 \text{ if the randomly drawn cookie is broken} \end{cases}$$

Each of the variables X_1, X_2, X_3, and X_4 is a *random variable* since its value is unknown until an experiment is performed. More specifically, a random variable is a real-valued function that assigns a number to each sample point (outcome) in the sample space of an experiment.

It is important to distinguish between the *rule* or *function* that assigns the numbers to each sample point and the numerical values themselves. In this chapter we distinguish between the two by writing random variables as upper case letters, X, and the values of the random variable by lower case letters, x. So statements like $P(X = x)$ or $P(X < 3)$ mean the probability that the random variable X takes the value x or takes a value less than 3, respectively. In later chapters this symbolic difference will not be made and a symbol's context will make it clear whether it represents a random variable or the value of a random variable. To reiterate, prior to an experiment we know what values the random variable X *might* take, but the value that X does take, x, is not known until after the experiment has been performed.

2.3.2 Discrete and Continuous Random Variables

The examples just suggested illustrate that random variables can be discrete or continuous. The random variable X_4 is discrete since it can only take two values, and X_1 is discrete since it can take only a countable number of values. The random variables X_2 and X_3 can take any positive real value and are continuous. More formally, a *discrete random variable* is one whose set of possible values is finite or countably infinite. A *continuous random variable* is one that may assume all values in at least one interval of the real number line.

We will assume that we have a probability measure P defined on the sample space S that is associated with some experiment. It should not be surprising that we can use the assigned probability measure to make probabilistic statements about the possible values of a random variable X. That is, we can construct a *probability distribution* or *probability density function* (abbreviated p.d.f.) for X that will literally tell us how the probability mass (total mass of 1) is distributed (i.e., allocated or spread out) across the values x that X can take. This p.d.f. can be used, for example, to compute the probability that X takes certain values or falls in a given range.

2.3.3 Probability Distributions for Discrete Random Variables

For a discrete random variable X, a probability density function (also sometimes called a probability function) is defined to be the function $f(x)$ such that for any real number x, which is a value that X can take, $f(x) = P(X = x)$. Consequently, $0 \leq f(x) \leq 1$. If x is not one of the values that X can take, then $f(x) = 0$. Also, if the sequence $x_1, x_2, x_3, \ldots$ includes *all* the values that X can take then $\sum_{i=1}^{\infty} f(x_i) = 1$. In some texts, the word "density" is reserved for continuous random variables, but we will not follow that practice.

The actual nonzero values of $f(x)$ are *induced* from the probability measure associated with the sample space for the experiment in question. To illustrate this concept, consider the following example.

Example 2.7 Let the experiment be the tossing of a fair coin twice. The sample space is $S = \{\text{HH, HT, TH, TT}\}$. Assume each of the outcomes is equally likely and consider the random variable X = number of heads obtained. The p.d.f. for X can be represented as a table or bar graph as illustrated here.

x	$f(x)$
0	$\frac{1}{4}$
1	$\frac{1}{2}$
2	$\frac{1}{4}$

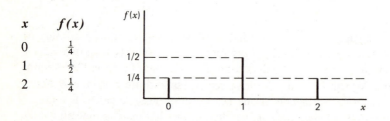

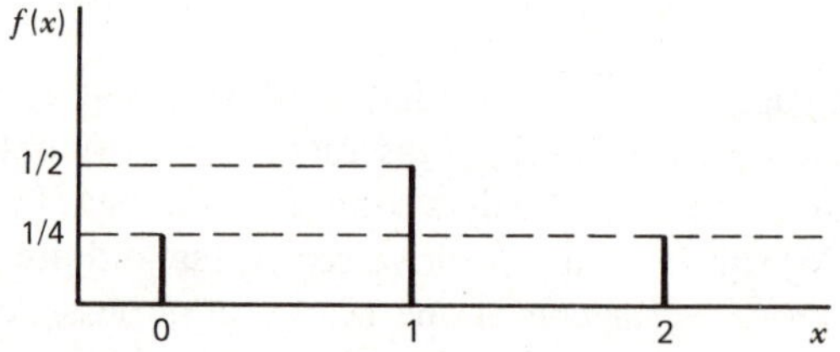

The values $f(x)$ are obtained by computing the probabilities of the events associated with the values of the random variable; for example, $f(0) = \frac{1}{4} = P(X = 0) = P(A)$ where $A = \{\text{TT}\}$. ■

A function closely related to the probability density function of a random variable is the corresponding *distribution function* or *cumulative distribution function* (abbreviated c.d.f.). The c.d.f. of a random variable X is defined for each real number x as

$$F(x) = P(X \leq x) \quad \text{for} \quad -\infty < x < \infty \tag{2.3.1}$$

That is, $F(x)$ is the probability that the random variable X takes a value less than or equal to x. For a discrete random variable X, $F(x) = \sum_{t \leq x} f(t)$, where this summation notation means sum all the values of the p.d.f. $f(t)$ for the values the random variable can take less than or equal to the specified value.

Example 2.8 Consider the experiment of tossing a coin 4 times and let X = number of heads obtained. Then

x	$f(x)$
0	$\frac{1}{16}$
1	$\frac{4}{16}$
2	$\frac{6}{16}$
3	$\frac{4}{16}$
4	$\frac{1}{16}$

and

$$F(x) = \begin{cases} 0 & \text{for } x < 0 \\ \frac{1}{16} & \text{for } 0 \leq x < 1 \\ \frac{5}{16} & \text{for } 1 \leq x < 2 \\ \frac{11}{16} & \text{for } 2 \leq x < 3 \\ \frac{15}{16} & \text{for } 3 \leq x < 4 \\ 1 & \text{for } x \geq 4 \end{cases}$$

Note that $F(x)$ is defined for all real numbers, thus $F(2.5) = \frac{11}{16} = P(X \leq 2.5)$, even though X cannot actually take the value 2.5. The graph of $F(x)$ is given here.

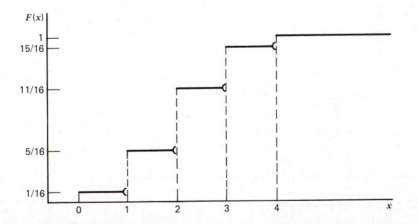

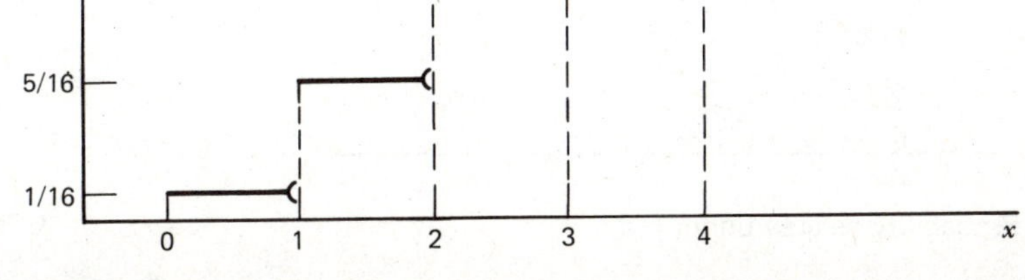

■

For discrete random variables, the c.d.f. is a step function and is right-continuous. Furthermore, it has the properties that $F(-\infty) = 0$, $F(\infty) = 1$, and if $a < b$, then $F(a) \leq F(b)$ for any real numbers a and b. If the discrete random variable X can take the values $-\infty < x_1 < x_2 < \cdots < x_n < \infty$, then $f(x_1) = F(x_1)$ and $f(x_i) = F(x_i) - F(x_{i-1})$ for $i = 2, \ldots, n$.

2.3.4 Probability Distributions for Continuous Random Variables

A continuous random variable X can take any value in at least one interval on the real number line. Suppose X can take all possible values $a \leq x \leq b$. Since the possible values of X are uncountable, the probability that X takes any particular value is zero! Thus, unlike the situation for discrete random variables, the p.d.f. of a continuous random variable, say $f(x)$, will *not* give the probability that X takes the value x. Instead, the p.d.f. $f(x)$ of a continuous random variable X will be such that areas under $f(x)$ will give probabilities associated with the corresponding intervals on the horizontal axis. More specifically, a function with values $f(x)$, defined over all real x, is a p.d.f. for the continuous random variable X if

(*i*) $f(x) \geq 0$ for all x

(*ii*) $$\int_{-\infty}^{\infty} f(x)\,dx = 1 \tag{2.3.2}$$

(*iii*) For any a, b with $-\infty < a < b < \infty$

$$P(a \leq X \leq b) = \int_a^b f(x)\,dx$$

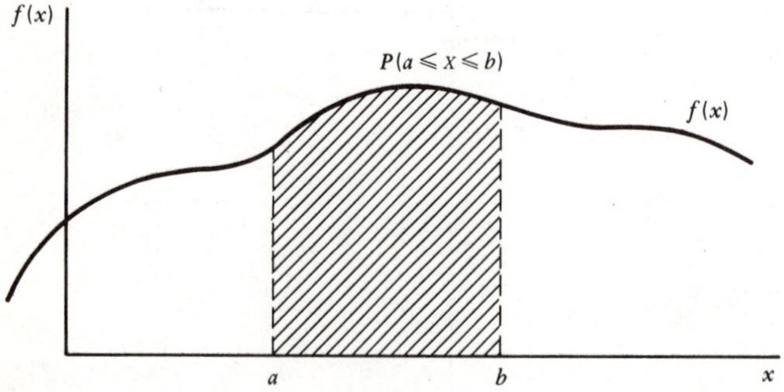

Figure 2.2 Probability as area under p.d.f.

Graphically then, probabilities are areas as illustrated in Figure 2.2. The shaded area is $P(a \leq X \leq b)$. It is also $P(a < X < b)$ and $P(a < X \leq b)$ and $P(a \leq X < b)$, since all these intervals differ only by one or two points that have probability zero.

The cumulative distribution function for a continuous random variable X is given by

$$F(x) = P(X \leq x) = \int_{-\infty}^{x} f(t)\,dt \quad \text{for} \quad -\infty < x < \infty \tag{2.3.3}$$

where $f(t)$ is the value of the p.d.f. at t. Note that $F(-\infty) = 0$, $F(\infty) = 1$, and when $a < b$, $F(a) \leq F(b)$. Furthermore,

$$P(a \leq X \leq b) = F(b) - F(a) \tag{2.3.4}$$

and

$$f(x) = dF(x)/dx = F'(x) \tag{2.3.5}$$

where the derivative exists.

Example 2.9 Let x be a continuous random variable with p.d.f.

$$f(x) = \begin{cases} 3e^{-3x} & x > 0 \\ 0 & \text{otherwise} \end{cases}$$

which is represented graphically as

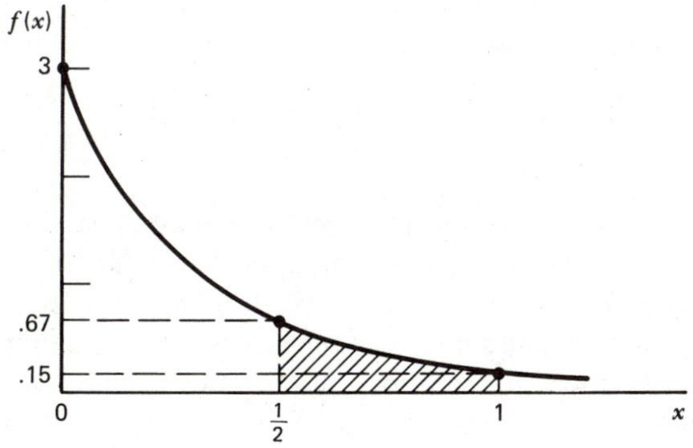

For this p.d.f., $f(x) \geq 0$ for all x and

$$\int_{-\infty}^{\infty} f(x)\,dx = \int_{0}^{\infty} 3e^{-3x}\,dx = 3 \cdot \lim_{t \to \infty} \left. \frac{e^{-3x}}{-3} \right|_0^t = 1$$

We can compute the probability that X falls between 0.5 and 1 as

$$P(0.5 \leq X \leq 1) = \int_{.5}^{1} 3e^{-3x}\,dx = -e^{-3} + e^{-1.5} = 0.173$$

The c.d.f. is obtained by integrating the p.d.f. For $x > 0$,

$$F(x) = \int_{-\infty}^{x} f(t)\, dt = \int_{0}^{x} 3e^{-3t}\, dt = -e^{-3t}\Big|_{0}^{x} = 1 - e^{-3x}$$

So,

$$F(x) = \begin{cases} 0 & x \leq 0 \\ 1 - e^{-3x} & x > 0 \end{cases}$$

A sketch of the c.d.f. is given here.

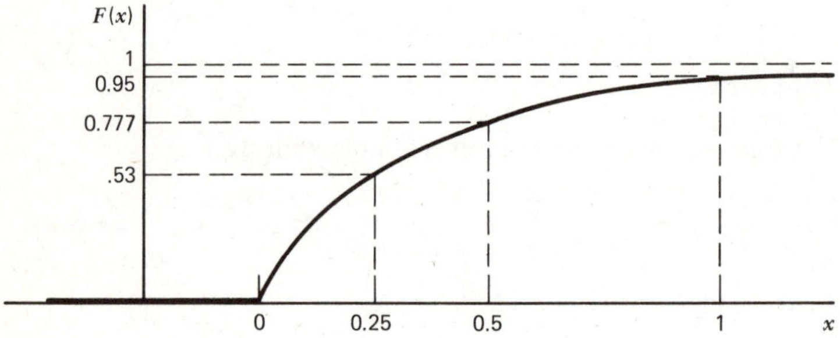

Then $P(0.5 \leq X \leq 1)$ can also be computed as

$$F(1) - F(0.5) = (1 - e^{-3}) - (1 - e^{-1.5}) = 0.173 \quad \blacksquare$$

Given the functions $f(x)$ and $F(x)$, the computation of probabilities is very elegant. One must ask, of course, where, in any actual application, do these functions come from? The answer is that there are many special distributions that are widely used in probability and statistics and have mathematical properties that are well understood. Each is well suited for certain types of experiments and random variables. Part of the "art of statistics" is choosing a functional form $f(x)$ that adequately, yet parsimoniously, represents the random elements in the situation at hand.

2.3.5 Multivariate Distributions

It is possible, as we have seen, to define many different random variables for any given experiment. The random variables X_1, X_2, X_3, and X_4 associated with the cookie example are an illustration. If we ask questions about the values that two or more of these random variables take at *the same time*, or jointly, then we are extending the notion of a probability distribution or p.d.f. to the *multivariate case*. As an example of such a question, we might ask for the probability that the number of chips in a cookie is equal to four and the cookie is broken. That is,

$$P(X_1 = 4 \quad \text{and} \quad X_4 = 0) = P(X_1 = 4, X_4 = 0)$$

Another situation where a multivariate distribution is important is when the random variables represent repeated trials of (or repeated samples from) an experiment. That is, suppose the measurement we are interested in is the number of chips in a randomly drawn cookie. Let X_i be the number of chips in the ith randomly drawn cookie, for $i = 1, \ldots, n$. Then we can ask questions about the (joint) probability that, say, $X_1 = 6$, $X_2 = 6, \ldots, X_n = 6$ in the n trials of the experiment.

If X and Y are discrete random variables, then the function $f(x, y) = P(X = x, Y = y)$, defined for each pair of values (x, y) that X and Y can take, is called the *joint probability distribution* or *joint probability density function* of X and Y. The function $f(x, y)$ must satisfy $f(x, y) \geq 0$ for (x, y) in its domain and $\sum_x \sum_y f(x, y) = 1$ where the double sum is over all pairs (x, y) in the domain of $f(x, y)$. If A and B are sets of values of x and y, respectively, then

$$P(X \in A, Y \in B) = \sum_{x \in A} \sum_{y \in B} f(x, y), \quad (x, y) \in R^2 \tag{2.3.6}$$

where R^2 denotes the real two-dimensional plane.

Example 2.10 Consider a population of T persons. Suppose we are interested in the two-way classification of persons by sex (male = M, or female = F) and smoking habit (smoking = S or nonsmoking = N). Suppose in these T persons there are a male smokers, b female smokers, c male nonsmokers, and d female nonsmokers, so $a + b + c + d = T$. If we define two discrete random variables on this population as

$$X = \begin{cases} 1 & \text{if a randomly drawn person is female} \\ 0 & \text{if a randomly drawn person is male} \end{cases}$$

$$Y = \begin{cases} 1 & \text{if a randomly drawn person is a smoker} \\ 0 & \text{if a randomly drawn person is a nonsmoker} \end{cases}$$

Then the joint p.d.f. of X and Y is

		x: 1	x: 0
y	1	$\frac{b}{T}$	$\frac{a}{T}$
	0	$\frac{d}{T}$	$\frac{c}{T}$

Thus, for example, $P(X = 1, Y = 0) = d/T$. ■

If X and Y are continuous random variables, then the bivariate function $f(x, y)$ with values defined for $(x, y) \in R^2$ is a joint p.d.f. for X and Y if

$$P[(X, Y) \in A] = \iint_A f(x, y)\, dx\, dy \tag{2.3.7}$$

for any region $A \in R^2$ that represents an event. The function $f(x, y)$ must have the properties that $f(x, y) \geq 0$ and

$$\int_{-\infty}^{\infty} \int_{-\infty}^{\infty} f(x, y)\, dx\, dy = 1$$

The corresponding joint cumulative distribution function for the continuous random variables X and Y is

$$F(x, y) = P(X \leq x, Y \leq y) = \int_{-\infty}^{y} \int_{-\infty}^{x} f(s, t)\, ds\, dt$$

for $(x, y) \in R^2$. Analogous to $f(x) = dF(x)/dx$ is

$$f(x, y) = \frac{\partial^2 F(x, y)}{\partial x\, \partial y} \tag{2.3.8}$$

if the partial derivatives exist.

Example 2.11 Consider the joint p.d.f. for two continuous random variables X and Y,

$$f(x, y) = \begin{cases} e^{-(x+y)} & x > 0, y > 0 \\ 0 & \text{otherwise} \end{cases}$$

The graph of $f(x, y)$ follows.

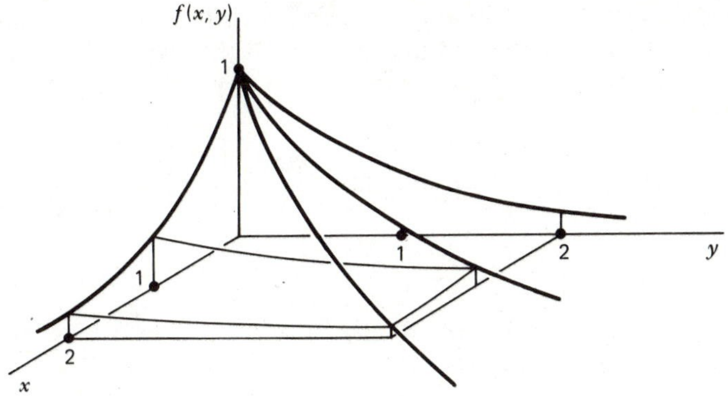

Using $f(x, y)$, we can calculate $P(1 \le X \le 2, 0 \le Y \le 2)$ as

$$\int_{y=0}^{2}\int_{x=1}^{2} f(x, y)\, dx\, dy = \int_{y=0}^{2}\int_{x=1}^{2} e^{-(x+y)}\, dx\, dy$$
$$= (e^{-1} - e^{-2})(e^{0} - e^{-2}) \doteq 0.2$$

Graphically, the probability is given by the volume under the graphed surface in the figure. ■

The definitions and concepts we have presented and illustrated for the bivariate case extend to the general multivariate case straightforwardly.

2.3.6 Marginal Distributions

To introduce the concept of a marginal distribution, reconsider Example 2.10. Suppose we simply want to know the probability distribution of X, say $g(x)$. How can we use the joint p.d.f. for X and Y to obtain $g(x)$? The discrete random variable X can take the values 1 and 0, and

$$g(1) = P(X = 1) = f(1, 1) + f(1, 0) = b/T + d/T = \sum_{y=0}^{1} f(1, y)$$

$$g(0) = P(X = 0) = f(0, 1) + f(0, 0) = a/T + c/T = \sum_{y=0}^{1} f(0, y)$$

Or more compactly, $g(x) = \sum_y f(x, y)$, meaning that the p.d.f. of X, $g(x)$ is obtained by summing the joint p.d.f. of X and Y over *all* values of Y for each value x of X.

The p.d.f $g(x)$ is called a marginal distribution because if we obtain the row and column sums of $f(x, y)$, and display them in the *margins* of the table, we have

		x = 1	x = 0	$h(y)$
y	1	$\frac{b}{T}$	$\frac{a}{T}$	$\frac{a+b}{T}$
	0	$\frac{d}{T}$	$\frac{c}{T}$	$\frac{c+d}{T}$
$g(x)$		$\frac{b+d}{T}$	$\frac{a+c}{T}$	

So $g(x)$ is given by the row totals. Similarly, the p.d.f. of Y, $h(y)$, is given by the column totals and in general $h(y) = \sum_x f(x, y)$. These probability density functions, obtained from the joint p.d.f., are the *marginal probability density functions* of X and Y.

If X and Y are continuous, the summation signs are replaced by integrals and we get

$$g(x) = \int_{-\infty}^{\infty} f(x, y)\, dy, \qquad -\infty < x < \infty$$

and

$$h(y) = \int_{-\infty}^{\infty} f(x, y)\, dx, \qquad -\infty < y < \infty$$

as the marginal probability density functions for X and Y.

Example 2.12 Given the joint density

$$f(x, y) = \begin{cases} \frac{2}{3}(x + 2y) & 0 < x < 1, 0 < y < 1 \\ 0 & \text{otherwise} \end{cases}$$

$$g(x) = \int_{-\infty}^{\infty} f(x, y)\, dy = \int_0^1 \frac{2}{3}(x + 2y)\, dy = \frac{2}{3}(x + 1), \qquad 0 < x < 1$$

$$= \begin{cases} 2(x + 1)/3 & 0 < x < 1 \\ 0 & \text{otherwise} \end{cases}$$

Similarly,

$$h(y) = \int_{-\infty}^{\infty} f(x, y)\, dy = \int_0^1 \frac{2}{3}(x + 2y)\, dx = \frac{1}{3}(1 + 4y), \qquad 0 < y < 1$$

$$= \begin{cases} (1 + 4y)/3 & 0 < y < 1 \\ 0 & \text{otherwise} \end{cases} \quad \blacksquare$$

2.3.7 Conditional Distributions and Independent Random Variables

In Section 2.2 we defined the conditional probability of event A given event B as $P(A|B) = P(A \cap B)/P(B)$ if $P(B) > 0$. If X and Y are discrete random variables, then we can write

$$P(X = x | Y = y) = \frac{P(X = x, Y = y)}{P(Y = y)} = \frac{f(x, y)}{h(y)} = f(x|y)$$

provided $P(Y = y) = h(y) \neq 0$, where $f(x, y)$ is the joint p.d.f. of X and Y, $h(y)$ is the p.d.f. of Y at y, and $f(x|y)$ is the probability distribution of X given that Y is fixed at the value y. The function $f(x|y)$ is called the *conditional* probability density function of X given $Y = y$.

Example 2.13 Referring to Example 2.10 again, we can find $f(x|1)$ as

$$f(x|1) = \begin{cases} f(0|1) = \dfrac{f(0, 1)}{h(1)} = \dfrac{a/T}{(a + b)/T} = \dfrac{a}{a + b} \\[2ex] f(1|1) = \dfrac{f(1, 1)}{h(1)} = \dfrac{b/T}{(a + b)/T} = \dfrac{b}{a + b} \end{cases}$$

This conditional p.d.f. gives the probability of drawing a female or a male given that the person is a smoker. ■

If X and Y are continuous random variables, then

$$f(x|y) = \frac{f(x, y)}{h(y)}, \quad h(y) \neq 0, \quad -\infty < x < \infty$$

is the conditional p.d.f. of X given $Y = y$.

Example 2.14 Using the joint p.d.f. in Example 2.12, let us compute $P(X \leq \frac{1}{2} | Y = \frac{1}{2})$.

$$f(x|y) = \frac{f(x, y)}{h(y)} = \frac{\frac{2}{3}(x + 2y)}{\frac{1}{3}(1 + 4y)} = \frac{2x + 4y}{1 + 4y}$$

So $f(x|\frac{1}{2}) = \frac{2}{3}(x+1)$.

$$\therefore \quad P\left(X \le \frac{1}{2} \middle| Y = \frac{1}{2}\right) = \int_0^{1/2} \frac{2}{3}(x+1)\,dx = \frac{5}{12} \qquad \blacksquare$$

Having defined the idea of a conditional p.d.f., we can now define the *independence of random variables* in the same way as we defined independent events. Namely, if

$$f(x|y) = g(x) \tag{2.3.9}$$

so that knowing that $Y = y$ does not affect the probability distribution of X then it is reasonable to say that X is independent of Y, and vice versa. If (2.3.9) holds, then

$$f(x, y) = f(x|y)h(y) = g(x)h(y) \tag{2.3.10}$$

We can then formally define X and Y to be statistically independent if and only if

$$f(x, y) = g(x)h(y) \tag{2.3.11}$$

for all values (x, y) of (X, Y) in the sample space.

Example 2.15 In Example 2.14 X and Y are not independent using (2.3.11). However, in Example 2.11, $g(x) = e^{-x}$, $x > 0$, and $h(y) = e^{-y}$ for $y > 0$ and X and Y are statistically independent. ■

If $X_1, X_2, \ldots, X_n$ have joint p.d.f. $f(x_1, x_2, \ldots, x_n)$, then the random variables $X_1, \ldots, X_n$ are *mutually stochastically independent* if and only if $f(x_1, \ldots, x_n) = f(x_1) \cdot f(x_2) \cdot \cdots \cdot f(x_n)$. Using this definition of stochastic independence, we can define a *random sample*. Suppose we repeat an experiment n times, and let $X_1, X_2, \ldots, X_n$ be random variables representing a certain measurement or values for those n trials. Then $X_1, \ldots, X_n$ constitute a random sample if they are independent and identically distributed. That is,

$$f(x_1, \ldots, x_n) = f(x_1) \cdot \cdots \cdot f(x_n)$$

and

$$f(x_1) = f(x_2) = \cdots = f(x_n) = f(x)$$

2.3.8 Distributions of Functions of Random Variables

There will be many instances when we wish to find probabilities of events associated with one or more functions of random variables rather than with the original random variables themselves. Since a function of random variables is random itself, one way to accomplish the task would be to determine the p.d.f. of the function(s) and use it to compute the probabilities. In certain circumstances this can be done, and there are several ways of going about the problem, each of which can be useful. See Mendenhall and Schaeffer (1973, Chapter 6) for a survey. We present one of the techniques and only for continuous random variables, the *change-of-variable* technique, that has wide applicability in econometrics. We introduce the idea with an example.

Example 2.16 Let X be a continuous random variable with p.d.f.

$$f(x) = \begin{cases} 2x & 0 < x < 1 \\ 0 & \text{otherwise} \end{cases}$$

Let $Y = g(X) = 2X$ be another random variable; we wish to compute probabilities of Y falling in certain intervals. One solution is to compute probabilities for Y based on the probability of the corresponding event for X. Thus

$$P(0 < Y < 1) = P(0 < X < \tfrac{1}{2}) = \tfrac{1}{4}$$

Although this is reasonable and simple to do in this case, it will not always be so easy. It is preferable to actually determine the p.d.f. of Y, say $h(y)$, and use it to compute probabilities for Y. Since $X = Y/2$, one might be tempted to substitute this in the p.d.f. $f(x)$ to obtain

$$h(y) = \begin{cases} 2(y/2) & 0 < y < 2 \\ 0 & \text{otherwise} \end{cases}$$

This substitution clearly does not lead to a satisfactory solution since the total area under $h(y)$ over the interval $0 < y < 2$ is 2 and thus $h(y)$ as it is does not satisfy the basic properties of a p.d.f. Furthermore, using $h(y)$ as it is leads to a computation of the probability of Y falling in the (0, 1) interval as $\frac{1}{2}$, which we know is incorrect.

The problem is that we must adjust the height of $h(y)$ to account for the fact that the domain of Y is larger than that for X. In fact, a change in Y of one unit corresponds to a change in X of $\frac{1}{2}$ unit, and if we adjust $h(y)$ by that factor we have

$$h(y) = \begin{cases} 2(y/2)(\tfrac{1}{2}) = (y/2) & 0 < y < 2 \\ 0 & \text{otherwise} \end{cases}$$

You can verify that using this p.d.f. leads to correct computation of probabilities for Y. The adjustment factor of $\frac{1}{2}$ spreads the unit probability mass of X over the domain of Y so that the areas under $f(x)$ correspond to the areas under $h(y)$ for equivalent events. See Figure 2.3 for a graphical illustration of this.

Another perspective on this *change of variable* technique can be obtained by examining the integral representation for the probability that Y falls in the interval

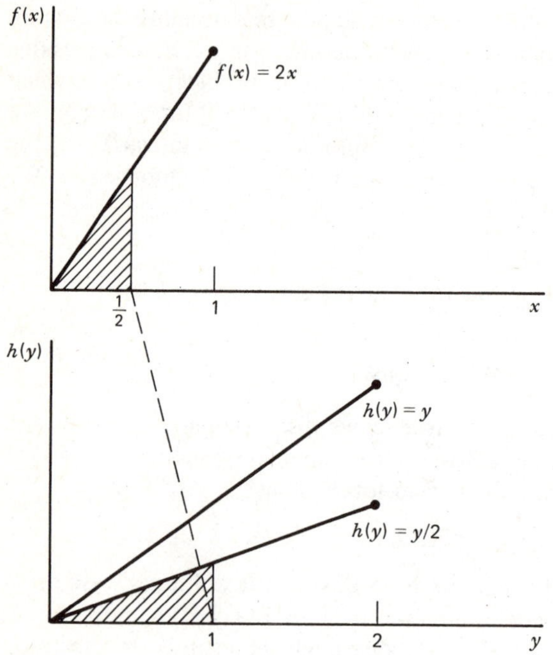

Figure 2.3 Illustration of the change of variable technique.

(0, 1), $P[0 < Y < 1] = \int_0^1 h(y)\,dy$. Now the question is, how can we adjust the integral representation of the probability of the equivalent X-event.

$$P[0 < Y < 1] = P[0 < X < \tfrac{1}{2}]$$
$$= \int_{x=0}^{1/2} f(x)\,dx = \int_{x=0}^{1/2} 2x\,dx$$

but $x = y/2$ and $dx = (1/2)\,dy$, so

$$P[0 < Y < 1] = \int_{(1/2)y=0}^{1} 2(\tfrac{1}{2}y)(\tfrac{1}{2}\,dy) = \int_{y=0}^{1} \frac{1}{2}\,y\,dy$$

Thus the adjustment factor ($\frac{1}{2}$) that we obtained intuitively appears here in the relation of the differential of x to that of y. The mathematical name for the adjustment factor is the *Jacobian of the transformation* (actually its absolute value, as we will see); its function is to make the integral expression in terms of x equal that in terms of y. In fact, the basis of this statistical technique, as its name implies, is the calculus procedure for making a change of variable in an integral. ■

We now state the change of variable technique, for a single continuous random variable, more precisely. Let X be a continuous random variable with p.d.f. $f(x)$. Let $Y = g(X)$ represent a function of X that is one-to-one. That is, for each value of X there is exactly one value for Y and vice versa. In this case that means that the function $g(X)$ must be *monotonic*, strictly increasing or strictly decreasing. This condition ensures that we can solve $Y = g(X)$ for X. That is, we can solve for the *inverse function* of $g(\cdot)$, say $X = w(Y)$. Then the p.d.f. of Y, $h(y)$, is given by

$$h(y) = f[w(y)] \cdot |\partial w(y)/\partial y| \tag{2.3.12}$$

This expression means that to find the p.d.f. of Y you must solve $y = g(x)$ for x and substitute this for x in $f(x)$, and then multiply by the absolute value of the derivative $\partial w(y)/\partial y$. The derivative in this context is the Jacobian of the transformation and $|\partial w(y)/\partial y|$ is the absolute value of the Jacobian. This scale factor is the adjustment factor that makes the probabilities (i.e., integrals) come out right. You should check to see that $|\partial w(y)/\partial y| = \frac{1}{2}$ in Example 2.16.

Example 2.17 Let X be a continuous random variable with p.d.f.

$$f(x) = \begin{cases} 2x & 0 < x < 1 \\ 0 & \text{otherwise} \end{cases}$$

Define the set S as $S = \{x | 0 < x < 1\}$. Let $Y = g(x) = 8x^3$ and $T = \{y | 0 < y < 8\}$. This transformation is one-to-one. The inverse transformation is

$$x = w(y) = (\tfrac{1}{8}y)^{1/3} = \tfrac{1}{2}y^{1/3}$$

and

$$\frac{\partial w(y)}{\partial y} = \tfrac{1}{6}y^{-2/3}$$

which exists for all y in T. Then, using (2.3.12) we have

$$\begin{aligned} h(y) &= f[w(y)] \cdot |\partial w(y)/\partial y| \\ &= 2(\tfrac{1}{2}y^{1/3}) \cdot |\tfrac{1}{6}y^{-2/3}| \\ &= \tfrac{1}{6}y^{-1/3} \qquad 0 < y < 8 \qquad \blacksquare \end{aligned}$$

The same sort of procedures can be used in the general multivariate situation. We first state the general result and then give examples. Let $X_1, \ldots, X_n$ be random variables that have a continuous joint distribution and joint p.d.f. $f(x_1, \ldots, x_n)$. Let $Y_1, \ldots, Y_n$ be n new random variables defined as

$$Y_i = g_i(X_1, \ldots, X_n) \qquad i = 1, \ldots, n \tag{2.3.13}$$

The functions $g_i(\cdot)$ will be assumed to have certain properties; namely, they will be assumed to define a one-to-one transformation. Specifically, let S be a subset of R^n, possibly the entire space, such that

$$P[(X_1, \ldots, X_n) \in S] = 1$$

Let T denote the subspace of R^n that is the image of S under the transformation (2.3.13). That is, as the values of $(X_1, \ldots, X_n)$ vary over the set S, the values of $(Y_1, \ldots, Y_n)$ vary over the set T. We assume the transformation from S to T is one-to-one, so that corresponding to each value of $(Y_1, \ldots, Y_n)$ in T there is a *unique* value of $(X_1, \ldots, X_n)$ in S such that (2.3.13) is satisfied. The assumption that the transformation is one-to-one ensures that there is an inverse transformation for $(y_1, \ldots, y_n)$ in T such that

$$x_i = w_i(y_1, \ldots, y_n), \quad i = 1, \ldots, n \tag{2.3.14}$$

where the n equations (2.3.14) define the inverse transformation from T to S.

Next we assume that the partial derivatives $\partial w_i/\partial y_j$ exist for all i, j at every point $(y_1, \ldots, y_n)$ in T. We then define the *Jacobian* of the transformation (2.3.13)

$$J = \det \begin{bmatrix} \partial w_1/\partial y_1 & \cdots & \partial w_1/\partial y_n \\ \vdots & \ddots & \vdots \\ \partial w_n/\partial y_1 & \cdots & \partial w_n/\partial y_n \end{bmatrix} \tag{2.3.15}$$

where "det" denotes the determinant of the matrix. See the matrix appendix, Section A.5, for a discussion of determinants. Then the joint p.d.f. of the n random variables $Y_1, \ldots, Y_n$ can be derived using a theorem from advanced calculus on changing variables in a multiple integral. See Friedman (1971, p. 276). The result is as follows. The joint p.d.f. of $Y_1, \ldots, Y_n$ is

$$h(y_1, \ldots, y_n) = f(w_1, \ldots, w_n)|J| \tag{2.3.16}$$

for $(y_1, \ldots, y_n)$ in T and 0 otherwise. Equation (2.3.16) means that each x_i in the function $f(x_1, \ldots, x_n)$ is replaced by $x_i = w_i\,(y_1, \ldots, y_n)$ and the result is multiplied by the absolute value of the Jacobian of the transformation.

Example 2.18 Let X_1 and X_2 have joint p.d.f.

$$f(x_1, x_2) = \begin{cases} 1 & 0 < x_1 < 1, 0 < x_2 < 1 \\ 0 & \text{otherwise} \end{cases}$$

Consider the two random variables $Y_1 = X_1 + X_2$, $Y_2 = X_1 - X_2$. We wish to find the joint p.d.f. of Y_1 and Y_2. The random variables X_1 and X_2 are defined on the two-dimensional space S depicted in Figure 2.4*a*.

The one-to-one transformation $y_1 = x_1 + x_2$, $y_2 = x_1 - x_2$ maps S onto the space T depicted in Figure 2.4*b*. You should verify that the area of T is twice that of S.

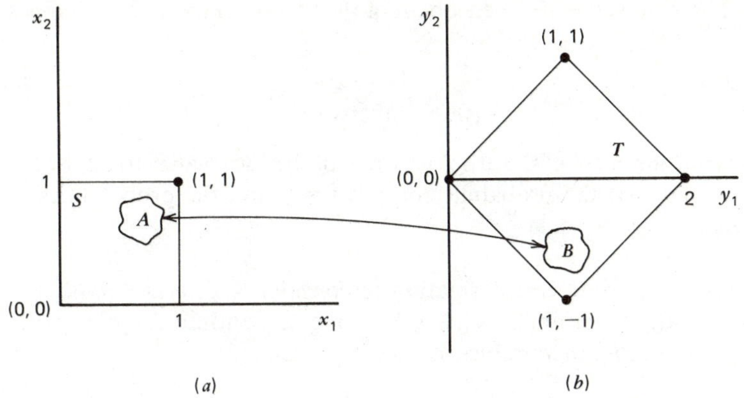

Figure 2.4

Now let A be a subset of S and B the set onto which A is mapped by the one-to-one transformation. So the events $(X_1, X_2) \in A$ and $(Y_1, Y_2) \in B$ are equivalent. Therefore,

$$P[(Y_1, Y_2) \in B] = P[(X_1, X_2) \in A]$$
$$= \iint_A f(x_1, x_2)\, dx_1\, dx_2$$

We can perform a change of variables of integration by solving for x_1 and x_2 as

$$x_1 = w_1(y_1, y_2) = (y_1 + y_2)/2$$
$$x_2 = w_2(y_1, y_2) = (y_1 - y_2)/2$$

For this multivariate case, the Jacobian is the (2×2) *determinant*

$$J = \begin{vmatrix} \partial w_1/\partial y_1 & \partial w_1/\partial y_2 \\ \partial w_2/\partial y_1 & \partial w_2/\partial y_2 \end{vmatrix} = \begin{vmatrix} \frac{1}{2} & \frac{1}{2} \\ \frac{1}{2} & -\frac{1}{2} \end{vmatrix} = -\tfrac{1}{2}$$

so

$$P[(Y_1, Y_2) \in B] = \iint_B h(y_1, y_2)\, dy_1\, dy_2$$
$$= \iint_B f[w_1(y_1, y_2), w_2(y_1, y_2)]|J|\, dy_1\, dy_2$$
$$= \iint_B 1 \cdot \tfrac{1}{2}\, dy_1\, dy_2$$

where $|J|$ is the absolute value of the Jacobian of the transformation. This implies that the joint p.d.f. of (Y_1, Y_2) is

$$h(y_1, y_2) = \begin{cases} \frac{1}{2} & (y_1, y_2) \in T \\ 0 & \text{otherwise} \end{cases}$$

Note once again that the effect of the absolute value of the Jacobian is to adjust the height of the p.d.f. so that the probability of T is unity and the probabilities of equivalent events are equal. ■

Example 2.19 An important transformation to consider is a *linear transformation.* Let the n random variables $X_1, \ldots, X_n$ have a continuous joint p.d.f. $f(x_1, \ldots, x_n)$. Let the n random variables $Y_1, \ldots, Y_n$ be defined by

$$\begin{aligned} Y_1 &= a_{11}X_1 + a_{12}X_2 + \cdots + a_{1n}X_n \\ Y_2 &= a_{21}X_1 + a_{22}X_2 + \cdots + a_{2n}X_n \\ &\vdots \\ Y_n &= a_{n1}X_1 + a_{n2}X_2 + \cdots + a_{nn}X_n \end{aligned}$$

which in matrix terms (see Section A.3) is

$$\mathbf{Y} = A\mathbf{X}$$

where $\mathbf{Y}' = (Y_1, \ldots, Y_n)$, $\mathbf{X}' = (X_1, \ldots, X_n)$, and

$$A = \begin{bmatrix} a_{11} & a_{12} & \cdots & a_{1n} \\ a_{21} & a_{22} & \cdots & a_{2n} \\ \vdots & \vdots & & \vdots \\ a_{n1} & a_{n2} & \cdots & a_{nn} \end{bmatrix}$$

If A is nonsingular (see Section A.8), then the linear transformation is one-to-one and the inverse transformation exists and is

$$\mathbf{X} = A^{-1}\mathbf{Y}$$

where A^{-1} is the matrix inverse of A (see Section A.7). Then the Jacobian is

$$\det\left(\frac{\partial \mathbf{X}}{\partial \mathbf{Y}'}\right) = \det(A^{-1}) = \frac{1}{\det(A)}$$

(See Section A.17 for the definition of matrix differentiation.) Therefore,

$$h(\mathbf{Y}) = f(A^{-1}\mathbf{Y})\left|\frac{1}{\det(A)}\right| \qquad \text{for } \mathbf{Y} \in R^n \qquad ■$$

For other examples see, for example, Hogg and Craig (1978, pp. 132–141) or DeGroot (1975, pp. 133–140).

2.4 Mathematical Expectation

In order to study random variables and their probability distributions, it is useful to define the concept of mathematical expectation of a random variable and of functions of a random variable; these definitions are given in this section.

2.4.1 Expected Value of a Random Variable

Consider the experiment of rolling a single die. Let X be the value that shows on the die. The probability distribution of X is

x	1	2	3	4	5	6
$f(x)$	$\frac{1}{6}$	$\frac{1}{6}$	$\frac{1}{6}$	$\frac{1}{6}$	$\frac{1}{6}$	$\frac{1}{6}$

What would the *average* value of X be if the experiment were repeated an infinite number of times? Intuitively, you would expect $X = 1$ on $\frac{1}{6}$ of the throws, $X = 2$ on $\frac{1}{6}$ of the throws, and so on. So, *on the average*, the value of X is

$$1 \cdot \tfrac{1}{6} + 2 \cdot \tfrac{1}{6} + 3 \cdot \tfrac{1}{6} + 4 \cdot \tfrac{1}{6} + 5 \cdot \tfrac{1}{6} + 6 \cdot \tfrac{1}{6} = 3.5.$$

That is, 3.5 is the average value of X that occurs in infinitely many trials of the experiment. This average is the *expected value* of the random variable X, despite the fact that X cannot actually take the value 3.5.

If X is a discrete random variable and $f(x)$ is its p.d.f., then the expected value of X is

$$E[X] = \sum_{x} x f(x) \tag{2.4.1}$$

Examining (2.4.1) it is clear that the expected value of X is a weighted average of the values that X can take, with the weights being the probabilities of each value's occurrence.

Correspondingly, if X is a continuous random variable with p.d.f. $f(x)$, then the expected value of X is

$$E[X] = \int_{-\infty}^{\infty} x f(x)\, dx \tag{2.4.2}$$

Definitions (2.4.1) and (2.4.2) assume that the sum or integral exists.

Example 2.20 Suppose X is a continuous random variable with p.d.f.

$$f(x) = \begin{cases} 1/(b-a) & a \le x \le b \\ 0 & \text{otherwise} \end{cases}$$

Then

$$E[X] = \int_{-\infty}^{\infty} xf(x)\,dx$$

$$= \int_a^b x \cdot \frac{1}{b-a}\,dx$$

$$= (b+a)/2$$

The random variable X in this example is said to be *uniformly distributed* on the interval $[a, b]$. The expected value of X is the midpoint of the interval. ■

The expected value of X, $E[X]$, is also called the *mean* of X or the mean of the distribution of X. It is a measure of the average value of X and a measure of the center of the probability distribution. In fact, $E[X]$ can be regarded as the *center of gravity* of the probability distribution. That is, if the x-axis is a weightless rod on which the weights $f(x_i)$ are placed at each point x_i, then the rod will be balanced if it is supported at $E[X]$. It follows that if a p.d.f. is symmetric with respect to a value x_0 on the x-axis, then $E[X] = x_0$ if it exists. Two other common measures of the center of the distribution are the *median*, which is the value of the random variable below which 50% of the probability mass falls, and the *mode*, which is the value of the random variable at which its p.d.f. attains the maximum value.

2.4.2 Expectation of a Function of a Single Variable

In many problems that we will encounter we will be interested not only in $E[X]$ but also in the mathematical expectation of functions of X, say $g(X)$. These expectations are given by

$$E[g(X)] = \sum_x g(x)f(x) \tag{2.4.3}$$

for discrete random variables and

$$E[g(X)] = \int_{-\infty}^{\infty} g(x)f(x)\,dx \tag{2.4.4}$$

for continuous random variables.

Example 2.21 Consider Example 2.20 and let $g(X) = X^2$. Then

$$E[g(X)] = E[X^2] = \int_{-\infty}^{\infty} g(x)f(x)\,dx$$

$$= \int_a^b x^2 \frac{1}{b-a}\,dx$$

$$= \tfrac{1}{3}(b^2 + ba + a^2) \qquad \blacksquare$$

Using the definition of the expectation of a single random variable, it is easy to obtain the following useful result: if a and b are constants then

$$E[aX + b] = aE[X] + b \tag{2.4.5}$$

which implies

$$E[aX] = aE[X] \tag{2.4.6}$$

and

$$E[b] = b \tag{2.4.7}$$

2.4.3 Expectations of Functions of Several Random Variables

We may evaluate the expectation of functions of several random variables in much the same way. Suppose $Y = g(X_1, \ldots, X_n)$ and let $f(x_1, \ldots, x_n)$ be the joint p.d.f. of the continuous random variables $X_1, \ldots, X_n$. Then

$$E[Y] = \int_{-\infty}^{\infty} \cdots \int_{-\infty}^{\infty} g(x_1, \ldots, x_n) f(x_1, \ldots, x_n)\,dx_1 \ldots dx_n \tag{2.4.8}$$

If the random variables were discrete, the integrals would be replaced by sums. Using this definition, the following useful results can be obtained.

(*i*) Let $a_0, a_1, \ldots, a_n$ be constants, then

$$E[a_0 + a_1X_1 + \cdots + a_nX_n] = a_0 + a_1E[X_1] + \cdots + a_nE[X_n] \tag{2.4.9}$$

(*ii*) Let $X_1, \ldots, X_n$ be independent random variables such that $E[X_i]$ exists, then

$$E[X_1 X_2 \ldots X_n] = E[X_1] \cdot \cdots \cdot E[X_n] \tag{2.4.10}$$

2.4.4 Moments

Among the mathematical expectations that are of special importance are the *moments* of a random variable. They are defined as follows: the *rth moment* of the random variable X *about the origin* is denoted μ'_r and is $E[X^r]$. Note that for $r = 1$, $\mu'_1 = E[X]$ is the mean of X and is often simply denoted as μ. The term "moments" comes from physical interpretations of mathematical expectations, such as the fact that μ'_1 is the center of gravity.

The *rth moment about the mean* of X is $\mu_r = E[(X - \mu)^r]$. If $r = 2$, $\mu_2 = E[(X - \mu)^2]$ is called the *variance* of the distribution of X, or just the variance of X. It is often denoted as σ^2 or var (X). The positive square root of σ^2, σ is called the *standard deviation* of X. It is useful to note that

$$\sigma^2 = E[(X - E[X])^2] = E[X^2] - (E[X])^2 \tag{2.4.11}$$

In order to motivate an interpretation of the variance of X, recall that the distance between two points x_1 and x_2 on the real line is $d = \sqrt{(x_1 - x_2)^2}$. If we let one of these points be the value x of the random variable X and the other be $\mu = E[X]$, then $d = \sqrt{(x - \mu)^2}$, and the squared distance is $(x - \mu)^2$. Therefore $E[(X - \mu)^2]$ is interpreted as the average of the squared distance between the value of the random variable X and $E[X]$ when the experiment is repeated infinitely many times. The larger the value of σ^2, the greater the average squared distance between the values of the random variable and $E[X]$, and thus the more likely a value of X far from its mean is to occur. We can represent this graphically by comparing the probability distributions of two random variables X and Y that have the same mean but $\text{var}(X) > \text{var}(Y)$.

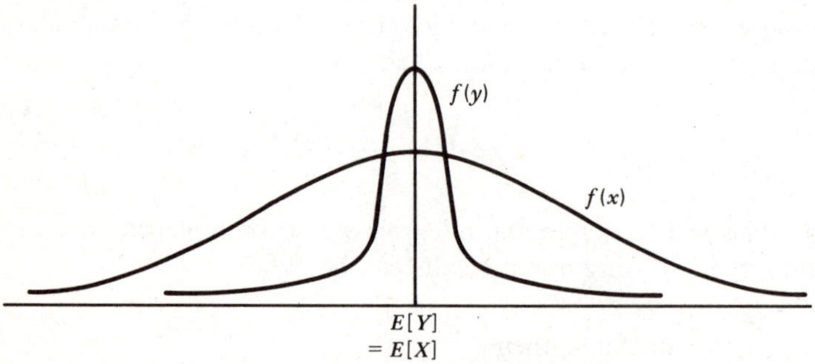

The probability mass of X is more "spread-out" than that of Y. Thus the variance of X is a measure of the dispersion of the probability mass of X about its mean. The greater the value of var (X), the wider the dispersion of the values of X about its mean.

Product moments for two or more random variables are similarly defined. The rth and sth product moment about the origin of the random variables X and Y is $\mu'_{rs} = E[X^r Y^s]$. The rth and sth product moment about the means of X and Y is $\mu_{rs} = E[(X - E[X])^r(Y - E[Y])^s]$. Of special interest is μ_{11}, which is called the *covariance* between X and Y, and denoted σ_{xy} or $\text{cov}(X, Y)$,

$$\sigma_{xy} = E[(X - E[X])(Y - E[Y])] = E[XY] - E[X]E[Y] \tag{2.4.12}$$

The covariance between two random variables is a measure of the association between them. Examining (2.4.12) and interpreting $E[\cdot]$ as "the average in infinitely many trials," we see that $\text{cov}(X, Y) > 0$ if X and Y jointly tend to be greater than their means, or less than their means—on average. $\text{Cov}(X, Y)$ can also be 0 or negative with obvious meaning. To see that $\text{cov}(X, Y)$ measures *linear* association, let us define a related measure, the *correlation* between X and Y, denoted ρ_{xy} and defined as

$$\rho_{xy} = \frac{\text{cov}(X, Y)}{\sqrt{\text{var}(X)}\sqrt{\text{var}(Y)}} \tag{2.4.13}$$

The correlation between X and Y has the property that it is a pure number and falls between -1 and 1. If $\text{cov}(X, Y) = 0$ then $\rho_{xy} = 0$. Consequently, if X and Y are independent then, from (2.4.12), $\rho_{xy} = 0$. If $Y = a + bX$ for some constants a and b ($\neq 0$), then $|\rho_{xy}| = 1$, and X and Y are said to be perfectly correlated. The more nearly the values of X and Y are linearly related, the larger $|\rho_{xy}|$.

Using these definitions we can state the following results: If $a_0, \ldots, a_n$ are constants and $X_1, \ldots, X_n$ are random variables, then

$$\text{var}(a_0 + a_1X_1 + \cdots + a_nX_n) = \sum_{i=1}^{n} a_i^2 \,\text{var}(X_i) + 2\sum\sum_{i<j} a_i a_j \,\text{cov}(X_i, X_j) \tag{2.4.14}$$

Two special cases of (2.4.14) are especially useful,

$$\text{var}(a_0 + a_1X_1) = a_1^2 \,\text{var}(X_1) \tag{2.4.15}$$

and

$$\text{var}(X_1 \pm X_2) = \text{var}(X_1) + \text{var}(X_2) \pm 2\,\text{cov}(X_1, X_2) \tag{2.4.16}$$

Note that if the X_i's are statistically independent, then the covariance terms drop out of (2.4.14) and (2.4.16).

2.4.5 Chebyshev's Theorem

A useful result that holds for all random variables that have a mean and a variance is *Chebyshev's theorem* or *inequality*. It illustrates how the variance and standard deviation are related to the dispersion of the probability mass and is very useful for many theoretical proofs in statistics. If X is a random variable with mean μ and variance σ^2, then

$$P(|X - \mu| < k\sigma) \geq 1 - 1/k^2 \tag{2.4.17}$$

or

$$P(|X - \mu| \geq k\sigma) < 1/k^2 \tag{2.4.18}$$

For example, using (2.4.18), the probability that the value of a random variable falls more than three standard deviations from its mean is less than $\frac{1}{9}$. The probability will be much less than $\frac{1}{9}$ for many random variables, but the Chebyshev inequality is valuable because it provides a bound for *all* random variables.

2.4.6 Expectations Involving Multivariate Random Variables*

In this book we will frequently be interested in expectations involving multivariate random variables. Let $\mathbf{X}$ denote the vector of random variables (hence $\mathbf{X}$ is a random vector)

$$\mathbf{X} = \begin{bmatrix} X_1 \\ X_2 \\ \vdots \\ X_n \end{bmatrix}$$

where $E[X_i] = \mu_i$, $\text{var}(X_i) = \sigma_i^2$ and $\text{cov}(X_i, X_j) = \sigma_{ij}$. Then,

$$E[\mathbf{X}] = \begin{bmatrix} E[X_1] \\ E[X_2] \\ \vdots \\ E[X_n] \end{bmatrix} = \begin{bmatrix} \mu_1 \\ \mu_2 \\ \vdots \\ \mu_n \end{bmatrix} = \boldsymbol{\mu} \tag{2.4.19}$$

That is, the *expected value of a random vector* is the vector of expectations.

* This section requires knowledge of matrix algebra.

We can define a *covariance matrix* for the random vector **X** as follows:

$$\begin{aligned}
\operatorname{cov}(\mathbf{X}) &= E[(\mathbf{X} - E[\mathbf{X}])(\mathbf{X} - E[\mathbf{X}])'] \\
&= E\begin{bmatrix} (X_1-\mu_1)^2 & (X_1-\mu_1)(X_2-\mu_2) & \cdots & (X_1-\mu_1)(X_n-\mu_n) \\ (X_2-\mu_2)(X_1-\mu_1) & (X_2-\mu_2)^2 & \cdots & (X_2-\mu_2)(X_n-\mu_n) \\ \vdots & \vdots & & \vdots \\ (X_n-\mu_n)(X_1-\mu_1) & (X_n-\mu_n)(X_2-\mu_2) & \cdots & (X_n-\mu_n)^2 \end{bmatrix} \\
&= \begin{bmatrix} \operatorname{var}(X_1) & \operatorname{cov}(X_1, X_2) & \cdots & \operatorname{cov}(X_1, X_n) \\ \operatorname{cov}(X_2, X_1) & \operatorname{var}(X_2) & \cdots & \operatorname{cov}(X_2, X_n) \\ \vdots & \vdots & & \vdots \\ \operatorname{cov}(X_n, X_1) & \operatorname{cov}(X_n, X_2) & \cdots & \operatorname{var}(X_n) \end{bmatrix} \qquad (2.4.20) \\
&= \begin{bmatrix} \sigma_1^2 & \sigma_{12} & \cdots & \sigma_{1n} \\ \sigma_{21} & \sigma_2^2 & \cdots & \sigma_{2n} \\ \vdots & \vdots & & \vdots \\ \sigma_{n1} & \sigma_{n2} & \cdots & \sigma_n^2 \end{bmatrix}
\end{aligned}$$

The covariance matrix of **X**, often denoted $\boldsymbol{\Sigma}_x$, is a positive semidefinite matrix with variances on the main diagonal and off-diagonal elements that are covariances. If none of the random variables $X_1, \ldots, X_n$ are degenerate (i.e., if none of them have zero variances), and no exact linear relationships between the X_i exist, then $\boldsymbol{\Sigma}_x$ is positive definite.

Let $\mathbf{a}' = (a_1, \ldots, a_n)$ be a vector of constants. Then,

$$E[\mathbf{a}'\mathbf{X}] = \mathbf{a}'\boldsymbol{\mu} = a_1\mu_1 + \cdots + a_n\mu_n \qquad (2.4.21)$$

and

$$\begin{aligned}
\operatorname{var}(\mathbf{a}'\mathbf{X}) &= \mathbf{a}'\boldsymbol{\Sigma}_x\mathbf{a} \\
&= \sum_{i=1}^{n} a_i^2\sigma_i^2 + 2\sum\sum_{i<j} a_i a_j \sigma_{ij} \qquad (2.4.22)
\end{aligned}$$

Result (2.4.22) can be obtained by expressing

$$\begin{aligned}
\operatorname{var}(\mathbf{a}'\mathbf{X}) = E[\mathbf{a}'\mathbf{X} - E[\mathbf{a}'\mathbf{X}]]^2 &= E[(\mathbf{a}'X - E[\mathbf{a}'\mathbf{X}])(\mathbf{a}'\mathbf{X} - E[\mathbf{a}'\mathbf{X}])'] \\
&= \mathbf{a}'E[(\mathbf{X} - E[\mathbf{X}])(\mathbf{X} - E[\mathbf{X}])']\mathbf{a}
\end{aligned}$$

The next to the last step uses the fact that $\mathbf{a}'\mathbf{X}$ is a (1×1) matrix, or a single variable. The results in (2.4.21) and (2.4.22) should be compared with (2.4.9) and (2.4.14).

Let P be an $(m \times n)$ matrix of constants with $m \leq n$. Then $\mathbf{Z} = P\mathbf{X}$ is an $(m \times 1)$ random vector. Using (2.4.19) to (2.4.22), it follows that

$$E[\mathbf{Z}] = E[P\mathbf{X}] = PE[\mathbf{X}] = P\boldsymbol{\mu} \tag{2.4.23}$$

and

$$\text{cov}(\mathbf{Z}) = \text{cov}(P\mathbf{X}) = P\boldsymbol{\Sigma}_x P' \tag{2.4.24}$$

2.5 Some Special Distributions

In this section we define and discuss some special distributions that are widely used in econometrics. The discrete distributions that will be presented are the Bernoulli, binomial, and the multinomial. The continuous random variables that we will discuss are the normal, the multivariate normal, the gamma, chi-square, t, and F distributions. For more complete discussions of these probability distributions, plus more, see Johnson and Kotz (1970) and mathematical statistics books cited earlier in this chapter.

2.5.1 The Bernoulli Distribution

Consider an experiment in which only two outcomes are possible, such as a head or a tail, or a success or a failure. It is convenient to designate these two outcomes as 0 and 1. Then X is said to have a *Bernoulli distribution* if it can only take the two values 0 or 1 and the probabilities are $P(X = 1) = p$ and $P(X = 0) = 1 - p$, where $0 \leq p \leq 1$. The p.d.f. of this random variable is

$$f(x|p) = \begin{cases} p^x(1-p)^{1-x} & x = 0, 1 \\ 0 & \text{otherwise} \end{cases} \tag{2.5.1}$$

where the notation $f(x|p)$ denotes that the p.d.f. of X depends on the parameter p. It is easy to check that $E[X] = p$ and $\text{var}(X) = p(1 - p)$. This random variable arises in econometrics in *choice models*, where a decision maker must choose between two alternatives, like buying a car or not buying a car.

2.5.2 The Binomial Distribution

If $X_1, \ldots, X_n$ are independent random variables each having a Bernoulli distribution with parameter p, then $X = \sum_{i=1}^n X_i$ is a discrete random variable that is the number of successes (i.e., Bernoulli experiments with outcome $X_i = 1$) in the n

trials of the experiment and X has a *binomial* distribution. This random variable has p.d.f.

$$f(x|n, p) = \begin{cases} \binom{n}{x} p^x(1-p)^{n-x} & x = 0, 1, \ldots, n \\ 0 & \text{otherwise} \end{cases} \tag{2.5.2}$$

where

$$\binom{n}{x} = \frac{n!}{x!(n-x)!}$$

is the number of combinations of n things taken x at a time. This distribution has two parameters, n and p, where n is a positive integer and $0 \leq p \leq 1$. The mean and variance of X are

$$E[X] = \sum_{i=1}^{n} E[X_i] = np$$

$$\text{var}(X) = \sum_{i=1}^{n} \text{var}(X_i) = np(1-p)$$

A related random variable is $Y = X/n$, which is the proportion of successes in n trials of an experiment. Its mean and variance are $E[Y] = p$ and $\text{var}(Y) = p(1-p)/n$.

2.5.3 The Multinomial Distribution

The Bernoulli and binomial distributions can be extended as follows. Consider an experiment that can have $m > 2$ outcomes, and let the probability of each outcome be $p_i > 0$, $i = 1, 2, \ldots, m$, so that $\sum_{i=1}^{m} p_i = 1$. Define m random variables Z_i that take the values 1 or 0 depending on whether an outcome of the ith type occurs or not. For example, consider the experiment of randomly drawing a chocolate chip cookie from a large population of chocolate chip cookies (i.e., a large box) and defining Z_1 to Z_6 as

$$Z_i = \begin{cases} 1 & \text{the number of chips is } i,\ i = 1, \ldots, 5 \\ 0 & \text{otherwise} \end{cases}$$

$$Z_6 = \begin{cases} 1 & \text{the number of chips is 6 or more} \\ 0 & \text{otherwise} \end{cases}$$

Then $\sum_{i=1}^{6} Z_i = 1$, and if $p_i > 0$ is the proportion of each type of cookie in the population then $\sum_{i=1}^{6} p_i = 1$. Consider repeating this experiment n times, or drawing n cookies from the box with replacement. If Z_{ij} is the value of the ith random variable on the jth trial, or draw, then $X_i = \sum_{j=1}^{n} Z_{ij}$ is the number of items that are of type i, $i = 1, \ldots, m$. Note that $\sum_{i=1}^{m} X_i = n$. Then the vector $\mathbf{X}' = (X_1, \ldots, X_m)$ has a *multinomial* distribution with parameters n and $\mathbf{p}' = (p_1, \ldots, p_m)$. The joint p.d.f. of $X_1, \ldots, X_m$ is

$$f(\mathbf{x}|n, \mathbf{p}) = P[\mathbf{X} = \mathbf{x}] = \frac{n!}{x_1!x_2!\ldots x_m!} p_1^{x_1} p_2^{x_2} \cdots p_m^{x_m} \tag{2.5.3}$$

if $x_1, \ldots, x_m$ are nonnegative numbers such that their sum is n and 0 otherwise. Not surprisingly, this distribution appears in econometric applications where choices are made from a limited number of options. An example would be studying the behavior of a commuter who must travel from point A to point B by car, bus, or train. That the multinomial distribution is a generalization of the binomial can be seen by letting $m = 2$.

2.5.4 The Gamma Distribution

The gamma distribution is an example of a distribution that is skewed to the right (i.e., long tail to the right) and is nonnegative. If X is a continuous random variable with p.d.f.

$$f(x|\alpha, \beta) = \frac{1}{\Gamma(\alpha)\beta^\alpha} x^{\alpha-1} e^{-x/\beta}; \quad \alpha, \beta > 0; \quad 0 \leq x < \infty \tag{2.5.4}$$

then is has a *gamma distribution with parameters* α *and* β. In (2.5.4) $\Gamma(\alpha)$ is the gamma function,

$$\Gamma(\alpha) = \int_0^\infty y^{\alpha-1} e^{-y}\, dy$$

In advanced calculus books it is shown that $\Gamma(\alpha) = (\alpha - 1)\Gamma(\alpha - 1)$ and that if $\alpha = n$ and n is an integer, $\Gamma(n) = (n - 1)!$. The mean and variance of a random variable X with a gamma distribution are

$$E[X] = \alpha\beta, \quad \text{var}(X) = \alpha\beta^2$$

Two special cases of the gamma distribution appear frequently in statistics. If $\alpha = 1$, the resulting distribution is called an *exponential* distribution, with parameter β. If $\alpha = r/2$ and $\beta = 2$, the resulting distribution is called a *chi-square* distribution with parameter r and the random variable is denoted $\chi^2_{(r)}$. The parameter r is called the *degrees of freedom* of the random variable. More about the chi-square distribution will be presented later. Other distributions related to the gamma include the *Pareto* and *Weibull* distributions. For more about these and other distributions see Johnson and Kotz (1970).

2.5.5 The Normal Distribution

The normal distribution is the most important distribution in statistics. Physical scientists have observed that experimental outcomes in *many* situations have normal distributions. For example, the normal distribution provides a close approximation to the heights and weights of individuals from homogeneous populations, whether they be a population of people, corn stalks, or mice; or breaking strength of lengths of twine produced by a certain process; or independent errors in measurements of physical quantities. The list goes on and on. An important reason for the predominance of the normal distribution is the central limit theorem, which says that many important functions of observations, like the sample mean, tend to be normally distributed given a large enough sample, no matter what the distribution of the original population. Finally, the normal distribution has many nice mathematical properties that make it convenient to work with.

A continuous random variable X has a *normal distribution with mean* μ *and variance* σ^2 $(-\infty < \mu < \infty, \sigma^2 > 0)$, often denoted $X \sim N(\mu, \sigma^2)$, if X has p.d.f.

$$f(x|\mu, \sigma^2) = \frac{1}{(2\pi\sigma^2)^{1/2}} \exp\left\{-\frac{(x-\mu)^2}{2\sigma^2}\right\} \qquad -\infty < x < \infty \tag{2.5.5}$$

This p.d.f. is "bell-shaped," as represented in Figure 2.5. The p.d.f. is symmetric about the parameter μ, which is the mean, median, and mode of the distribution. The variance of X is the parameter σ^2. For proof that $E[X] = \mu$ and $\text{var}(X) = \sigma^2$ see Hogg and Craig (1978, p. 110). Also, the p.d.f. has points of inflection at $x = \mu \pm \sigma$.

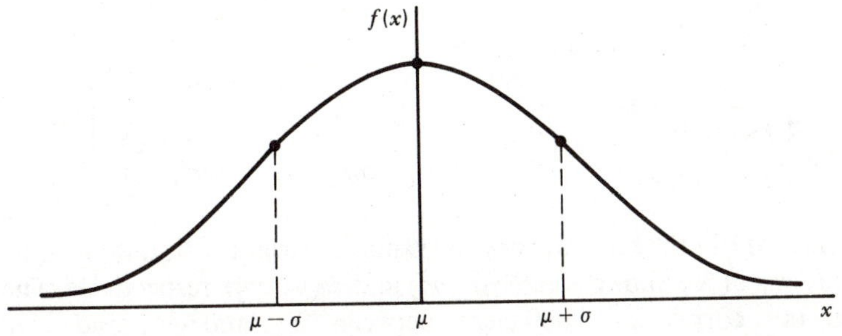

Figure 2.5 The normal distribution

The p.d.f. of a normal random variable does not have a definite integral that has a closed-form expression, so probabilities must be computed numerically. The probabilities can be economically presented in one table using a standard form. To see this, we use the fact that a linear function of a normal random variable is itself normal (see Exercise 2.9). That is, if $X \sim N(\mu, \sigma^2)$ and $Y = aX + b$, where a, b are constants with $a \neq 0$, then $Y \sim N(a\mu + b, a^2\sigma^2)$. Consequently,

$$Z = \frac{1}{\sigma}(X - \mu) \sim N(0, 1)$$

and is called a *standard normal* random variable. If $\Phi(z)$ denotes the c.d.f. of Z evaluated at z, then probability statements about X can be made in terms of X using values of $\Phi(z)$, which appear in Table 1 at the end of the book. For example, if $X \sim N(\mu, \sigma^2)$, then

$$P(a < X < b) = P\left(\frac{a - \mu}{\sigma} < Z < \frac{b - \mu}{\sigma}\right) = \Phi\left(\frac{b - \mu}{\sigma}\right) - \Phi\left(\frac{a - \mu}{\sigma}\right)$$

2.5.6 The Bivariate Normal Distribution

As a link between the univariate normal distribution that we have just considered and the multivariate normal that follows, we will discuss the bivariate normal distribution. Intuitively, the bivariate normal distribution is the joint distribution of two random variables each of which by itself is normally distributed.

Let X_1 and X_2 be random variables with joint p.d.f.

$$f(x_1, x_2 | \mu_1, \mu_2, \sigma_1^2, \sigma_2^2, \rho) = (2\pi)^{-1}[\sigma_1^2\sigma_2^2(1 - \rho^2)]^{-1/2}\exp\{-Q/2\}, \qquad -\infty < x_1, x_2 < \infty \tag{2.5.6}$$

where $\sigma_1 > 0$, $\sigma_2 > 0$, $-1 < \rho < 1$, and

$$Q = \frac{1}{1 - \rho^2}\left[\left(\frac{x_1 - \mu_1}{\sigma_1}\right)^2 - 2\rho\left(\frac{x_1 - \mu_1}{\sigma_1}\right)\left(\frac{x_2 - \mu_2}{\sigma_2}\right) + \left(\frac{x_2 - \mu_2}{\sigma_2}\right)^2\right]$$

$f(x_1, x_2)$ is the joint p.d.f. of the bivariate normal random variables X_1 and X_2. The marginal distributions of X_1 and X_2 are $N(\mu_1, \sigma_1^2)$ and $N(\mu_2, \sigma_2^2)$, respectively. The parameter ρ is the correlation coefficient between X_1 and X_2 and $\rho = \text{cov}(X_1, X_2)/\sigma_1\sigma_2$.

The bivariate normal has many interesting properties. One is that the *conditional distribution* of X_2 given X_1 is also normal. Specifically,

$$f(x_2|x_1) \sim N(b, \sigma_2^2(1-\rho^2)) \tag{2.5.7}$$

and

$$b = \mu_2 + \rho\frac{\sigma_2}{\sigma_1}(x_1 - \mu_1) \tag{2.5.8}$$

The conditional mean $b = E[X_2|X_1]$ is a linear function of x_1. Also, the bivariate normal has the unique property that if $\rho = 0$ then X_1 and X_2 are statistically independent, which is not true of other pairs of random variables in general. To see this note that if $\rho = 0$ then $f(x_2|x_1) = f(x_2) \sim N(\mu_2, \sigma_2^2)$.

It is often convenient to write the p.d.f. of jointly normal random variables in matrix form. If $\mathbf{X}' = (X_1, X_2)$, then (2.5.6) can be rewritten (see Exercise 2.13),

$$f(\mathbf{x}) = (2\pi)^{-1}\,|\Sigma|^{-1/2}\exp\{-\tfrac{1}{2}(\mathbf{x}-\boldsymbol{\mu})'\Sigma^{-1}(\mathbf{x}-\boldsymbol{\mu})\} \tag{2.5.9}$$

where

$$\mathbf{x} = \begin{bmatrix} \mathbf{x}_1 \\ \mathbf{x}_2 \end{bmatrix}, \qquad \boldsymbol{\mu} = \begin{bmatrix} \mu_1 \\ \mu_2 \end{bmatrix}, \qquad \Sigma = \begin{bmatrix} \sigma_1^2 & \sigma_1\sigma_2\rho \\ \sigma_1\sigma_2\rho & \sigma_2^2 \end{bmatrix} = \begin{bmatrix} \sigma_1^2 & \sigma_{12} \\ \sigma_{21} & \sigma_2^2 \end{bmatrix}$$

and $\sigma_{12} = \sigma_1\sigma_2\rho$ is the covariance between X_1 and X_2.

2.5.7 The Multivariate Normal Distribution

To introduce the multivariate normal distribution, let us begin with n independent and identically distributed standard normal random variables; Z_i, $i = 1, \ldots, n$ are independent and $Z_i \sim N(0, 1)$. Since the Z_i are independent, we can obtain their joint p.d.f. as

$$\begin{aligned} f(z_1, \ldots, z_n) = f(\mathbf{z}) &= \prod_{i=1}^{n} f(z_i) \\ &= \prod_{i=1}^{n} (2\pi)^{-1/2}\exp\left\{-\frac{z_i^2}{2}\right\} \\ &= (2\pi)^{-n/2}\exp\left\{-\frac{1}{2}\sum_{i=1}^{n} z_i^2\right\} \\ &= (2\pi)^{-n/2}\exp\left\{-\frac{1}{2}\mathbf{z}'\mathbf{z}\right\} \end{aligned}$$

where $\mathbf{Z}' = (Z_1, \ldots, Z_n)$ is a vector of independent standard normal random variables and $\mathbf{z}$ is the corresponding vector of values. Now consider the transformation $\mathbf{X} = A\mathbf{Z} + \mathbf{b}$, where A is an $(n \times n)$ nonsingular matrix and $\mathbf{b}$ is a $(n \times 1)$ vector of constants. Using the change of variable technique

$$\begin{aligned} g(\mathbf{x}) &= f[A^{-1}(\mathbf{x} - \mathbf{b})]|A|^{-1} \\ &= (2\pi)^{-n/2}|A|^{-1} \exp\{-\tfrac{1}{2}(\mathbf{x} - \mathbf{b})'A'^{-1}A^{-1}(\mathbf{x} - \mathbf{b})\} \end{aligned}$$

Since $E[\mathbf{Z}] = \mathbf{0}$ and $\text{cov}(\mathbf{Z}) = I_n$, $E[\mathbf{X}] = \mathbf{b}$ and $\text{cov}(\mathbf{X}) = AA'$. Letting $\boldsymbol{\mu} = \mathbf{b}$ and $\Sigma = AA'$, we can rewrite $g(\mathbf{x})$ in standard form as

$$g(\mathbf{x}) = (2\pi)^{-n/2}|\Sigma|^{-1/2} \exp\{-\tfrac{1}{2}(\mathbf{x} - \boldsymbol{\mu})'\Sigma^{-1}(\mathbf{x} - \boldsymbol{\mu})\}, \quad \mathbf{x} \in R^n \qquad (2.5.10)$$

which is the *multivariate normal distribution with mean* $\boldsymbol{\mu}$ *and covariance matrix* Σ.

Properties of the multivariate normal distribution include the following powerful result [Anderson (1984, p. 31)]: If $\mathbf{X} \sim N(\boldsymbol{\mu}, \Sigma)$ and D is a $(m \times n)$ matrix of constants, $m \leq n$, then

$$D\mathbf{X} \sim N(D\boldsymbol{\mu}, D\Sigma D') \qquad (2.5.11)$$

Using this general result, we can see that if $\mathbf{X}$, $\boldsymbol{\mu}$ and Σ are partitioned as

$$\mathbf{X} = \begin{bmatrix} \mathbf{X}_1 \\ \mathbf{X}_2 \end{bmatrix}, \qquad \boldsymbol{\mu} = \begin{bmatrix} \boldsymbol{\mu}_1 \\ \boldsymbol{\mu}_2 \end{bmatrix}, \qquad \Sigma = \begin{bmatrix} \Sigma_{11} & \Sigma_{12} \\ \Sigma_{21} & \Sigma_{22} \end{bmatrix}$$

where $\mathbf{X}_1$ is $(m \times 1)$ and $\mathbf{X}_2$ is $(n - m) \times 1$, $\boldsymbol{\mu}$ is conformably partitioned and Σ_{11} is the $(m \times m)$ submatrix of Σ corresponding to $\mathbf{X}_1$, then $\mathbf{X}_1 \sim N(\boldsymbol{\mu}_1, \Sigma_{11})$. To see that it is true, let D be the $(m \times n)$ partioned matrix $D = (I_m|0)$. Then

$$D\mathbf{X} = \begin{bmatrix} X_1 \\ \vdots \\ X_m \end{bmatrix} = \mathbf{X}_1 \sim N(\boldsymbol{\mu}_1, \Sigma_{11}) \qquad (2.5.12)$$

Thus partitions of $\mathbf{X}$ have a multivariate normal distribution themselves.
We can also determine the conditional distribution of $\mathbf{X}_1$ given values of $\mathbf{X}_2$. It is

$$\mathbf{X}_1|\mathbf{X}_2 \sim N(\boldsymbol{\mu}_1 + \Sigma_{12}\Sigma_{22}^{-1}(\mathbf{X}_2 - \boldsymbol{\mu}_2), \Sigma_{11} - \Sigma_{12}\Sigma_{22}^{-1}\Sigma_{21}) \qquad (2.5.13)$$

Using (2.5.13) it can be shown that $\mathbf{X}_1$ and $\mathbf{X}_2$ are mutually independent if and only if $\Sigma_{12} = 0$. That is, normal random variables that are uncorrelated are also statistically independent.

For further discussion of the multivariate normal distribution see Anderson (1984, Chapter 2), Dhrymes (1974, Chapter 1), and Hogg and Craig (1978, Chapter 12).

2.5.8 Distributions Related to the Normal: χ^2, t, F

Many important distributions in statistics are related to the normal and multivariate normal distributions. The three most important of these are the chi-square, (Student's) t, and the F-distributions. These distributions are widely used, along with the normal, as a basis for hypothesis tests and confidence-interval statements in statistics. The t- and F-distributions have not been introduced; we will briefly define them, after exploring the chi-square distribution more thoroughly.

Let us consider the relationship between the chi-square and normal distributions. The square of a standard normal variable has a chi-square distribution with 1 degree of freedom, or, if $Z \sim N(0, 1)$, then $Z^2 \sim \chi^2_{(1)}$ [Hogg and Craig (1978, p. 114)]. Furthermore, if $\chi^2_{(r_1)}, \chi^2_{(r_2)}, \ldots, \chi^2_{(r_n)}$ are mutually stochastically independent chi-square random variables, then [Hogg and Craig (1978, p. 169)]

$$Y = \chi^2_{(r_1)} + \chi^2_{(r_2)} + \cdots + \chi^2_{(r_n)} \sim \chi^2_{(r_1+r_2+\cdots+r_n)} \tag{2.5.14}$$

Consequently, if $Z_1, \ldots, Z_n$ are independent and standard normal random variables then

$$Y = Z_1^2 + Z_2^2 + \cdots + Z_n^2 \sim \chi^2_{(n)} \tag{2.5.15}$$

Percentage points for the chi-square distribution that are useful for hypothesis testing are found in Table 3 at the end of the book.

Let Z be a $N(0, 1)$ random variable and let $\chi^2_{(r)}$ denote a chi-square random variable with r degrees of freedom. Furthermore, let Z and $\chi^2_{(r)}$ be stochastically independent. Then

$$T = \frac{Z}{\sqrt{\chi^2_{(r)}/r}} \tag{2.5.16}$$

has a t-distribution with r degrees of freedom and is denoted $t_{(r)}$. The p.d.f. of the T random variable can be derived using the change-of-variable technique [Hogg and Craig (1978, p. 144)]. The p.d.f. of T is symmetric about 0, $E[T] = 0$, and is bell-shaped but flatter than the $N(0, 1)$ distribution. The variance of the random variable T is $r/(r-2)$ for $r > 2$. As r approaches ∞ the distribution of the T random variable can be closely approximated by that of a $N(0, 1)$ random variable. This relationship will be explored further in the next chapter when convergence in distribution is discussed. Tables of critical values for hypothesis tests that use the t-distribution appear at the end of this book in Table 2.

Next, let $\chi^2_{(r_1)}$ and $\chi^2_{(r_2)}$ be *independent* chi-square random variables with r_1 and r_2 degrees of freedom, respectively. Then,

$$F = \frac{\chi^2_{(r_1)}/r_1}{\chi^2_{(r_2)}/r_2} \tag{2.5.17}$$

has an F-distribution with parameters r_1 and r_2, which are called the numerator and denominator degrees of freedom, respectively. This distribution is denoted $F_{(r_1, r_2)}$. Once again the p.d.f. of this F random variable can be obtained using the change-of-variable technique [Hogg and Craig (1978, pp. 145–146)]. The F-distribution is skewed to the right and nonnegative since the chi-square random variable is nonnegative. Tables of critical values for hypothesis tests based on the F-distribution appear at the end of the book in Table 4.

2.5.9 The Distribution of Quadratic Forms in Multivariate Normal Random Variables

The result in (2.5.15) can be presented in a more general way as follows: If $\mathbf{X} \sim N(\boldsymbol{\mu}, \Sigma)$, then the quadratic form (see Section A.19 for the definition of quadratic forms)

$$Y = (\mathbf{X} - \boldsymbol{\mu})'\Sigma^{-1}(\mathbf{X} - \boldsymbol{\mu}) \sim \chi^2_{(n)}$$

where n is the dimension of the random vector $\mathbf{X}$. To prove this result, let A be the nonsingular matrix such that $A\Sigma A' = I$. (See Section A.11 in the matrix appendix.) Then $A\mathbf{X} \sim N(A\boldsymbol{\mu}, I)$ and $\mathbf{Z} = A(\mathbf{X} - \boldsymbol{\mu}) \sim N(\mathbf{0}, I)$. So $Y = \mathbf{Z}'\mathbf{Z} = Z_1^2 + \cdots + Z_n^2 \sim \chi^2_{(n)}$ using (2.5.15).

In turn, (2.5.15) is a special case of a more general result about the distribution of quadratic forms in normal variables. If M is a $(n \times n)$ symmetric idempotent (i.e., $M \cdot M = M$, see Section A.12) matrix of rank m and $\mathbf{X}$ is a $(n \times 1)$ vector of normal random variables such that $\mathbf{X} \sim N(\mathbf{0}, \sigma^2 I_n)$, then

$$\frac{\mathbf{X}'M\mathbf{X}}{\sigma^2} \sim \chi^2_{(m)} \tag{2.5.18}$$

To prove this result, let A be the orthogonal matrix such that

$$A'MA = \begin{bmatrix} I_m & 0 \\ 0 & 0 \end{bmatrix} \tag{2.5.19}$$

There must be such an A since of the n characteristic roots of M, m are one and the remainder are zero. Define $\mathbf{V} = A'\mathbf{X} \sim N(\mathbf{0}, \sigma^2 I)$ because $A'A = I$. Also $(1/\sigma) \cdot \mathbf{V} \sim N(\mathbf{0}, I)$, therefore $\mathbf{X} = A\mathbf{V}$ and $\mathbf{X}'M\mathbf{X} = \mathbf{V}'A'MA\mathbf{V} = \sum_{i=1}^m v_i^2$ using (2.5.19). Since $(v_i/\sigma) \sim N(0, 1)$ and the v_i are independent of one another, the result in (2.5.18) follows.

A related result deals with the independence of two quadratic forms. If $\mathbf{X} \sim N(\mathbf{0}, \sigma^2 I_n)$ and A and B are real symmetric matrices, then the quadratic forms $\mathbf{X}'A\mathbf{X}$ and $\mathbf{X}'B\mathbf{X}$ are independent if and only if $AB = 0$ [Hogg and Craig (1978, pp. 413–417)]. Also, if B is a matrix and A is symmetric, then the linear form $B\mathbf{X}$ is independent of the quadratic form $\mathbf{X}'A\mathbf{X}$ if and only if $BA = 0$.

2.6 Summary and Guide to Further Reading

In this chapter we have developed basic notions of probability theory, defined random variables, and studied properties of their probability density functions. We have defined mathematical expectation and studied how to determine the p.d.f. of a function of random variables. Finally, we have looked at some specific probability models that are especially useful in econometrics. This survey encompasses all the tools that are necessary to begin the study of econometrics in a good fashion. You will refer back to this chapter many times as you progress through this book, and we encourage you to do so.

Our discussion has necessarily been an abbreviated one. For more complete presentations of the material summarized in this chapter see Hogg and Craig (1978, Chapters 1–3), Freund and Walpole (1980, Chapters 1–6), Hoel (1971, Chapters 2–3), Mood, Graybill, and Boes (1974, Chapters 1–5), Mendenhall, and Schaeffer (1973, Chapters 1–6), or DeGroot (1975, Chapters 1–5). For an interesting exposition of these ideas from the Bayesian perspective see Hey (1983, Chapters 2–4).

2.7 Exercises

2.1 Let X be a continuous random variable with p.d.f. $f(x) = 3x^2/8$ for $0 < x < 2$. Compute $P[0 < X < \frac{1}{2}]$, $P[1 < X < 2]$, and $P[0 < X < \frac{1}{2}$ or $1 < X < 2]$.

2.2 Let X and Y have joint p.d.f.

$$f(x, y) = \begin{cases} 6x^2y & 0 < x < 1, 0 < y < 1 \\ 0 & \text{otherwise} \end{cases}$$

Compute $P[0 < X < \frac{3}{4}, \frac{1}{3} < Y < 2]$.

2.3 Let X be a continuous random variable with p.d.f. $f(x) = 2/x^3$, $1 < x < \infty$, zero elsewhere. Find the c.d.f. of X.

2.4 Let X have p.d.f. $f(x) = 2(1 - x)$, $0 < x < 1$, zero elsewhere. Find $E[X]$, $E[X^2]$, the variance of X, $E[6X + 3X^2]$.

2.5 Let X have p.d.f. $f(x) = \frac{1}{2}(x + 1)$, $-1 < x < 1$, zero elsewhere. Find $E[X]$ and the variance of X.

2.6 Let X have p.d.f. $f(x) = 1/2\sqrt{3}$, $-\sqrt{3} < x < \sqrt{3}$ and zero elsewhere. Compute the exact probability that $|X - E(X)| \geq k\sigma$ if $k = \frac{3}{2}$. Compare the exact value to that obtained using Chebyshev's inequality.

2.7 Let X_1 and X_2 have joint p.d.f.

$$f(x_1, x_2) = \begin{cases} 2 & 0 < x_1 < x_2 < 1 \\ 0 & \text{otherwise} \end{cases}$$

Find $f(x_1)$, $f(x_2)$, $f(x_1|x_2)$, $E[X_1|X_2]$ and $\text{var}(X_1|X_2)$. Compute $P[0 < X_1 < \frac{1}{2}|X_2 = \frac{3}{4}]$ and $P[0 < X_1 < \frac{1}{2}]$.

2.8 Let X, Y have joint p.d.f.

$$f(x, y) = \begin{cases} (x + y) & 0 < x < 1, 0 < y < 1 \\ 0 & \text{elsewhere} \end{cases}$$

Show that the correlation between X and Y is $\rho = -\frac{1}{11}$.

2.9 Let $X \sim N(\mu, \sigma^2)$. Use the change of variable technique to derive the p.d.f. of $Z = (X - \mu)/\sigma$.

2.10 Using the definition of $E[g(X)]$, verify the results in equations (2.4.5), (2.4.6), and (2.4.7).

2.11 Using the definition of $E[g(X_1, \ldots, X_n)]$, verify the results in (2.4.9) and (2.4.10).

2.12 Let X have a Bernoulli distribution with parameter p. Confirm that $E[X] = p$ and $\text{var}(X) = p(1 - p)$.

2.13 Show that the bivariate normal p.d.f. in (2.5.6) can be written in matrix form as (2.5.9).

2.14 Let the random variable X have a uniform distribution (see Example 2.20) in the interval $[a, b]$. Find its variance.

2.15 Let $\mathbf{X} = (X_1, \ldots, X_n)'$ be a vector of multivariate normal random variables with mean vector $\boldsymbol{\mu}$ and covariance matrix Σ. Use (2.5.11) to show the following:

(*a*) If $a_1, \ldots, a_n$ are constants, then $a_1X_1 + \cdots + a_nX_n = \sum_{i=1}^{n} a_iX_i$ has a normal distribution with mean $\sum_{i=1}^{n} a_i\mu_i$ and variance $\sum_{i=1}^{n} \sum_{j=1}^{n} a_ia_j\sigma_{ij}$.

(*b*) If $X_1, \ldots, X_n$ are a random sample from a $N(\beta, \sigma^2)$ population and $a_1, \ldots, a_n$ are constants, then $\sum_{i=1}^{n} a_iX_i$ has a normal distribution with mean $\beta \sum_{i=1}^{n} a_i$ and variance $\sigma^2 \sum_{i=1}^{n} a_i^2$.

2.16 Let X_1 and X_2 be independent random variables each with p.d.f. $f(x) = e^{-x}$, $0 < x < \infty$, and zero elsewhere. Let $Y_1 = X_1 + X_2$, $Y_2 = X_1/(X_1 + X_2)$. Find the joint p.d.f. of Y_1 and Y_2.

2.17 Let X_1 and X_2 be continuous random variables with joint p.d.f.

$$f(x_1, x_2) = \begin{cases} 4x_1x_2 & 0 < x_1, x_2 < 1 \\ 0 & \text{otherwise} \end{cases}$$

Let $Y_1 = X_1/X_2$, $Y_2 = X_1X_2$. Find the joint p.d.f. of Y_1 and Y_2.

2.18 Let X and Y be continuous random variables that are independent. Let $W = XY$ and $U = X$. Find the p.d.f. of W.

2.19 Let $X_1, \ldots, X_n$ have a multivariate normal distribution with mean vector $\boldsymbol{\mu}$ and covariance matrix Σ.

(*a*) Let $Y = \mathbf{a}'\mathbf{X}$ and $Z = \mathbf{b}'\mathbf{X}$, where $\mathbf{X}' = (X_1, \ldots, X_n)$, $\mathbf{a}' = (a_1, \ldots, a_n)$, $\mathbf{b}' = (b_1, \ldots, b_n)$. Show that Y and Z are independent if $\mathbf{a}'\Sigma\mathbf{b} = 0$.

(*b*) Let $X_1, X_2, \ldots, X_{10}$ denote a random sample of size 10 from a distribution that is $N(4, 9)$. If

$$Y_1 = 2X_1 - 4X_6 + 10$$

and

$$Y_2 = X_1 + 3X_2 - 2X_{10}$$

(*i*) What are the distributions of Y_1 and Y_2?

(*ii*) Are Y_1 and Y_2 independent?

2.20 Suppose X_1 and X_2 have a bivariate normal distribution with $\mu_1 = 0$, $\mu_2 = 0$, $\sigma_1^2 = 1$, $\sigma_2^2 = 1$, and correlation coefficient ρ.

(*a*) If $\rho = 0$ and

$$Y_1 = \frac{1}{\sqrt{2}}X_1 + \frac{1}{\sqrt{2}}X_2$$

$$Y_2 = \frac{1}{\sqrt{2}}X_1 - \frac{1}{\sqrt{2}}X_2$$

What is the joint distribution of Y_1 and Y_2?

(*b*) If $\rho = \frac{1}{4}$, what is the conditional distribution of X_2 *given* $X_1 = 2$?

(*c*) If $\rho = 0$, find constants c_1 and c_2 so that

$$E[c_1X_1^2 + c_2X_2^2] = 2$$

$$E[c_1X_1^2 - c_2X_2^2] = 0$$

2.21 Let X_1 and X_2 denote a random sample of size 2 from a distribution that is $N(\mu, \sigma^2)$. Let $Y_1 = X_1 + X_2$ and $Y_2 = X_1 + 2X_2$.

(*a*) Use transformation of variable techniques to show that the joint distribution of Y_1 and Y_2 is bivariate normal with correlation coefficient $3/\sqrt{10}$.

(b) How else (more easily) could you have found the joint distribution of Y_1 and Y_2?

2.22 Let $X_1, X_2, \ldots, X_n$ be a random sample from a $N(0, \sigma^2)$ population. Consider the two random variables

$$\bar{X} = \frac{\sum_{i=1}^{n} X_i}{n} = \left(\frac{1}{n}\right)\mathbf{j}_n'\mathbf{X}$$

and

$$S^2 = \frac{1}{n-1}\sum_{i=1}^{n}(X_i - \bar{X})^2 = \frac{1}{n-1}\mathbf{X}'A\mathbf{X}$$

where $A = [I_n - (1/n)\mathbf{j}_n\mathbf{j}_n']$, $\mathbf{X}' = [X_1, \ldots, X_n]$, $\mathbf{j}_n' = (1, 1, \ldots, 1)_{(1\times n)}$.

(*a*) Show that $(1/(n-1))\sum_{i=1}^{n}(X_i - \bar{X})^2 = (1/(n-1))\mathbf{X}'A\mathbf{X}$.

(*b*) Use results on the independence of linear and quadratic forms in normal variables to show that $\bar{X}$ and S^2 are independent.

(*c*) What are the distributions of $\bar{X}$ and S^2?

2.8 References

Anderson, T. (1984) *An Introduction to Multivariate Statistical Analysis*, 2nd ed. New York: Wiley.

DeGroot, M. (1975) *Probability and Statistics.* Reading, MA: Addison–Wesley.

Dhrymes, P. (1974) *Econometrics: Statistical Foundations and Applications.* New York: Springer-Verlag.

Freund, J., and R. Walpole (1980) *Mathematical Statistics*, 3rd ed. Englewood Cliffs, NJ: Prentice–Hall.

Friedman, A. (1971) *Advanced Calculus.* New York: Holt, Rinehart & Winston.

Hey, J. (1983) *Data in Doubt.* Oxford, Eng: Martin Robertson.

Hoel, P. (1971) *Introduction to Mathematical Statistics*, 4th ed. New York: Wiley.

Hogg, R., and A. Craig (1978) *Introduction to Mathematical Statistics*, 4th ed. New York: Macmillan.

Johnson, N., and S. Kotz (1970) *Distributions in Statistics.* New York: Wiley.

Mendenhall, W., and R. Schaeffer (1973) *Mathematical Statistics with Applications.* North Scituate, MA: Duxbury Press.

Mood, A., F. Graybill, and D. Boes (1974) *Introduction to the Theory of Statistics,* 3rd ed. New York: McGraw-Hill.

CHAPTER 3

Statistical Inference: Estimation and Hypothesis Testing

3.1 Introduction

In Chapter 2 we reviewed the theory and methods of probability. In this chapter we use those tools to study the theory and methods of *statistical inference.* A problem of statistical inference starts with a sample of data—observed values of one or more random variables representing the outcomes of some repeated experiment. The probability distribution of the random variables is *unknown,* and we wish to use the data to learn about the characteristics of that unknown distribution. If the outcome of the experiment can be described by a single number and the experiment is repeated T times, then the sample consists of the T random variables $(Y_1, \ldots, Y_T) = \mathbf{Y}'$. The joint p.d.f. of the sample $\mathbf{Y}$ is assumed to have a known mathematical form $f(\mathbf{y}|\boldsymbol{\theta})$ but depends on one or more parameters $(\theta_1, \ldots, \theta_K) = \boldsymbol{\theta}'$ that are known to fall in a set of possible values, Ω, called the parameter space. The investigator is always assumed to know the mathematical form of $f(\mathbf{y}|\boldsymbol{\theta})$ and the set Ω of possible values of $\boldsymbol{\theta}$. This constitutes a *statistical model* for how the values of the random variables $\mathbf{Y}$ are obtained and is the basis for classical statistical inference and decision theory. Given the statistical model, statistical inference consists of using the sample values for $\mathbf{Y}$ to specify plausible values for $\theta_1, \ldots, \theta_K$ (this is the problem of point estimation) or at least to determine a subset of Ω for which we can assert does, or does not, contain $\boldsymbol{\theta}$ (interval estimation or hypothesis testing). These are the senses in which we wish to use the data to learn about $f(\mathbf{y}|\boldsymbol{\theta})$.

As an example, we may assume that the amount of expenditures by persons with an annual income of \$20,000, from a certain population, follow a normal distribution, $N(\theta, \sigma^2)$, with *unknown* values of location parameter θ and scale parameter σ^2. Parameter estimation then involves using a sample of data on the expenditures by persons with \$20,000 income to make an inference about θ and σ^2. These inferences may take either the form of specific *point estimates* or the form of specifying a range of values, or an *interval estimate.* In either case, we are using the information in the sample of data, in conjunction with our a priori, nonsample information about the distribution, to make a judgement about the values of the unknown parameters.

The hypothesis-testing problem relates to using the data in a way to provide evidence about a conjecture concerning the population. Continuing the example, we may entertain the notion that the mean expenditure level by households with \$20,000 annual income is \$15,000. Using the assumption that the probability distribution of expenditures is normal, we then examine the data, and make a judgment as to whether or not the data appear to be consistent with the conjecture.

Two other components of statistical inference should be recognized. One is the problem of *experimental design*. Statistical inference can be assisted by use of data from a well-planned experiment. In this book, we will not study the theory and methods of experimental design since in *most* economics applications the sample of data is passively generated, or, in other words, is generated by an experiment over which we have no control. What we will do, however, is to illustrate repeatedly that effective statistical inference using such data is based on assumptions that are consistent with the underlying sampling process by which the data are generated.

Another problem that we will address in later chapters of the book is that of making decisions. *Statistical decision theory* applies to situations when the choice set from which we may choose is well defined and the consequences of the decision depend on the values of one or more unknown parameters.

In this chapter we focus on problems of estimation and hypothesis testing. In particular, the plan of this chapter is as follows: In Sections 3.2 and 3.3 we consider point estimation: first, methods of obtaining point estimation rules, including the method of moments, maximum likelihood, and least squares; then criteria by which the estimation rules can be evaluated and compared in small and large samples. In Section 3.4 we consider the problem of interval estimation. Section 3.5 contains a development of classical hypothesis-testing procedures, methods for evaluating testing procedures, and ways to develop statistical tests in small and large samples. In Section 3.6 the link between interval estimation and hypothesis testing is explored, and in Section 3.7 we summarize and make suggestions for further reading.

3.2 Methods For Finding Point Estimators

The purpose of point estimation is to use a sample of data, plus any *a priori* (nonsample) information we have about the probability distribution in question, to provide a value that is in some sense our best estimate of the unknown parameter value. The question we address now is how estimation rules can be obtained. There are many methods that can be used to derive estimators. Most of the methods are based on reasonable and intuitively appealing principles. In this section we present the method of moments, the method of maximum likelihood, and the method of least squares. The Bayesian approach to estimation will be discussed in Chapter 4. All these procedures will be used throughout this book.

Before proceeding, we must carefully define exactly what an estimator is. Let Y be a random variable with p.d.f. $f(y|\theta)$, where θ is a parameter that we would like to estimate. Let $Y_1, \ldots, Y_T$ be a random sample from this population. Then an *estimator* of θ is a function or rule of the form

$$\hat{\theta} = \hat{\theta}(Y_1, \ldots, Y_T) \tag{3.2.1}$$

which signifies that the estimator $\hat{\theta}$ is a function of $Y_1, \ldots, Y_T$. The estimator $\hat{\theta}$ is clearly a random variable since it is a function of random variables. The "hat" (or sometimes a tilde $\sim$) signifies that it is an estimator, or rule for estimating, the parameter θ. When the *values* of the random variables are inserted into (3.2.1), an *estimate* is produced, which is simply the value of the random variable or estimator $\hat{\theta}$. We will not make a notational distinction between *estimators* and *estimates*, despite the fact that one is random and one is not. Note that (3.2.1) does not depend on the unknown parameter θ or any other unknown parameter. An estimator or decision rule is a function of the sample observations that does not depend on any unknown parameters.

Example 3.1 Suppose that we are willing to assume that expenditures by persons with an annual income of \$20,000 are approximately normally distributed with a unknown mean θ but known variance, say $\sigma^2 = \$5000^2$. That is, if Y is the expenditure from a \$20,000 income by a person in this population then

$$Y \sim N(\theta, \sigma^2 = \$5000^2)$$

This statistical model is graphically represented in Figure 3.1.

Let $Y_1, \ldots, Y_T$ be a *random sample* of observations on expenditures from this population. Thus we are asserting, equivalently, that

$$Y_i = \theta + e_i, \quad i = 1, \ldots, T \tag{3.2.2a}$$

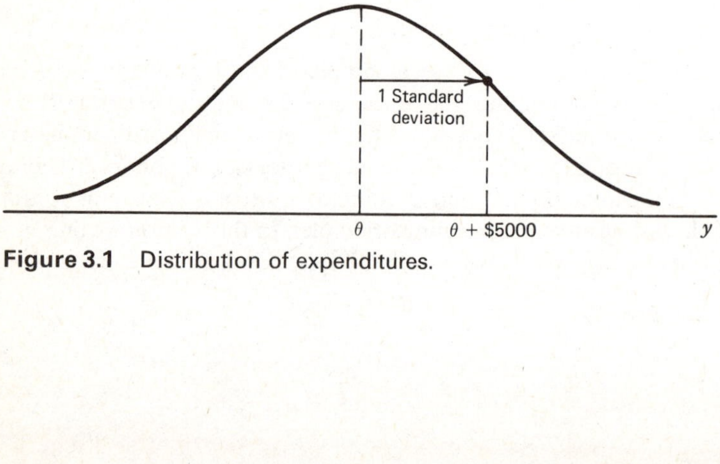

Figure 3.1 Distribution of expenditures.

where the random variable $e_i = Y_i - \theta$ has distribution

$$e_i \sim N(0, \$5000^2) \tag{3.2.2b}$$

and represents the difference between Y_i and its mean. In this case, e_i represents all the factors that influence the level of expenditure, other than income. Equation (3.2.2a) is a *linear* statistical model that represents our maintained hypothesis about the underlying sampling process, or, in other words, how sample observations on expenditure are obtained. Namely, the sample observations are assumed to be experimental outcomes equal to the mean value plus some random disturbance e_i, which has a well-defined distribution.

A common estimator of θ is the arithmetic mean, given by

$$\hat{\theta} = \hat{\theta}(Y_1, \ldots, Y_T) = \sum_{i=1}^{T} Y_i/T = \bar{Y} \tag{3.2.3}$$

Note that the estimator $\hat{\theta}$ in (3.2.3) is a random variable, since the rule says "no matter what the values of Y_i are, sum them and divide by the sample size." If the sample of size $T = 3$ happened to be $y_1 = \$9000$, $y_2 = \$12{,}000$ and $y_3 = \$18{,}000$, then the parameter *estimate* is

$$\hat{\theta} = \sum_{i=1}^{T} y_i/T = \$13{,}000. \qquad \blacksquare$$

Example 3.1 illustrates several important things. First, it introduces the linear statistical model (3.2.2a), which is a model of how we believe the observations on Y are being produced by our experiment. Linear statistical models like (3.2.2a) are specified and analyzed throughout the remainder of this book. Second, the example clarifies the problem of defining what it means to study the properties of estimators, the topic of Section 3.3. How good an *estimate* is $\hat{\theta} = \$13{,}000$? The answer is that it is impossible to tell *without knowing the true value of the parameter* θ. The impossibility of evaluating the *estimate* leads us to the conclusion that we must study, usually in a repeated sampling sense, the properties of the estimation rule that leads to the estimate. Since it is random, we can study its mean, variance, and probability distribution. At this point, however, we will ask: Where did the idea come from that the arithmetic mean of a sample of values can or should be used to estimate a population mean? Specifically, we now examine methods that may be used to obtain point estimators.

3.2.1 The Method of Moments

In Section 2.4.4 we defined the rth moment of a random variable Y about the origin as $\mu'_r = E[Y^r]$. If the p.d.f. of Y is $f(\mathbf{y}|\boldsymbol{\theta})$ where $\boldsymbol{\theta}' = (\theta_1, \ldots, \theta_K)$ is a vector of unknown parameters, then in general μ'_r will be a known function of $\boldsymbol{\theta}$, say $\mu'_r = \mu'_r(\boldsymbol{\theta})$. The idea of the method of moments is to use a random sample of data, $Y_1, \ldots, Y_T$, to compute the sample moments

$$\hat{\mu}'_r = \sum_{i=1}^{T} Y_i^r/T, \qquad r = 1, \ldots, K \tag{3.2.4}$$

and then to equate the sample and true moments $\hat{\mu}'_r = \mu_r(\boldsymbol{\theta})$, and solve the resulting system of K equations (if possible) for the unknown parameters. The resulting estimator, $\hat{\boldsymbol{\theta}}$, is the *method of moments estimator.*

Example 3.2 Let $Y_1, \ldots, Y_T$ be a random sample from a $N(\theta, \sigma^2)$ population. Recall that $E[Y] = \theta = \mu'_1$ and $\sigma^2 = E[Y^2] - (E[Y])^2 = \mu'_2 - (\mu'_1)^2$. Then, equating the sample to population moments,

$$\hat{\mu}'_1 = \sum_{i=1}^{T} Y_i/T = \bar{Y} = \hat{\theta}$$

$$\hat{\mu}'_2 = \sum_{i=1}^{T} Y_i^2/T = \hat{\sigma}^2 + \hat{\theta}^2$$

so

$$\begin{aligned} \hat{\sigma}^2 &= \left(\sum_{i=1}^{T} Y_i^2/T \right) - \bar{Y}^2 \\ &= \frac{1}{T} \sum_{i=1}^{T} (Y_i - \bar{Y})^2 \qquad \blacksquare \end{aligned}$$

Although method of moments estimators are intuitive, there are some difficulties. The method of moments estimators need not be unique, and the method can be difficult to apply in more complicated problems. It also depends on the random variable in question *having* moments, which is not always the case. We consider next a more powerful, general estimation procedure, the method of maximum likelihood.

3.2.2 The Method of Maximum Likelihood

To introduce the notion of maximum likelihood estimation, consider the following example. Let Y be a Bernoulli random variable, as described in Section 2.5.1, with parameter p, which we know, for some reason, can *only* take the values $\frac{1}{4}$ or $\frac{3}{4}$.

Suppose we have a random sample of size $T = 3$ with values $y_1 = 1$, $y_2 = 1$, and $y_3 = 0$. The question is how to use these data to estimate the unknown parameter p, which for this problem boils down to choosing either $p = \frac{1}{4}$ or $p = \frac{3}{4}$. *The method of maximum likelihood will choose that value of the unknown parameter* (p) *that maximizes the probability (likelihood) of randomly drawing the sample that was actually obtained.* Since $f(y|p) = p^y(1-p)^{1-y}$ for $y = 0$ or 1, we can calculate the probability of our random sample from the joint p.d.f. of Y_1, Y_2, and Y_3. It is,

$$f(y_1 = 1, y_2 = 1, y_3 = 0) = f(1, 1, 0) = \prod_{i=1}^{3} p^{y_i}(1-p)^{1-y_i} = p \cdot p \cdot (1-p) \qquad (3.2.5)$$

We are now going to interpret (3.2.5) as a function of p given the sample observations. When we do so, it is called a *likelihood function* and written $l(p|\mathbf{y})$. It is mathematically identical to the joint p.d.f. of the random sample, but it is interpreted as a function of the unknown parameters instead of the values of the random variables, which are assumed to be known. In making inferences or decisions about p after the sample values are observed, all relevant sample information is contained in the likelihood function. Then

$$l(\tfrac{1}{4}|\mathbf{y}) = 0.046$$

and

$$l(\tfrac{3}{4}|\mathbf{y}) = 0.141$$

Thus the probability (or likelihood) of obtaining the sample values we actually have is maximized by choosing $\tilde{p} = \frac{3}{4}$ rather than $\tilde{p} = \frac{1}{4}$, given that these are our only choices, and thus $\tilde{p} = \frac{3}{4}$ is the maximum likelihood estimate of p in this problem. It is, in the sense described, the value of p most likely to have generated our sample.

Of course, it will rarely be the case that the admissible set of parameters contains only two elements. For the Bernoulli distribution, the parameter can take any value in the closed interval zero to one. That is, p can take any value in the parameter space $\Omega = \{p | 0 \le p \le 1\}$. In this situation, there are several ways to proceed. One is to take advantage of the power of modern computers and use numerical techniques (described in Chapter 12) to maximize $l(p|\mathbf{y}) = p^2(1-p)$. For example, in the Figure 3.2 the values of $l(p|\mathbf{y})$ are plotted as a function of p. The function reaches its maximum when the parameter p takes the value 0.67, so the maximum likelihood estimate of p *given this grid search* is $\tilde{p} = 0.67$. Obviously the nature of the numerical technique will actually determine in part the value of p, but in every case we seek the value of the unknown parameter that maximizes (globally) the joint p.d.f. of the random sample, evaluated at the sample values actually obtained.

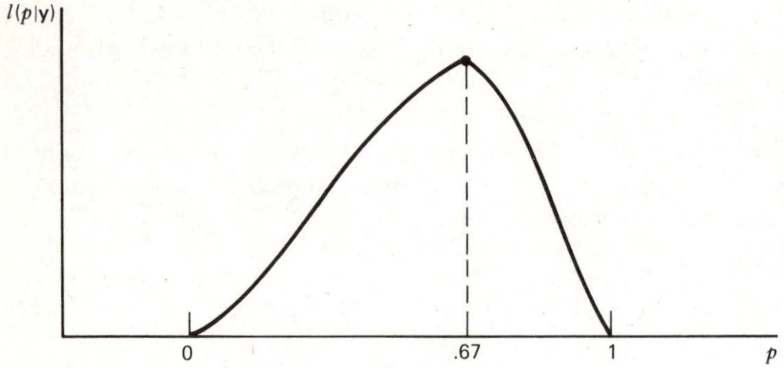

Figure 3.2 Graph of the likelihood function.

A second way to find the value of p that maximizes $l(p|\mathbf{y})$ in this case is to use calculus techniques. A local maximum of a continuous function occurs where its slope is zero and its second derivative is negative. Here,

$$\frac{dl(p|\mathbf{y})}{dp} = 2p - 3p^2, \quad \frac{d^2l(p|\mathbf{y})}{dp^2} = 2 - 6p$$

Setting the first derivative to zero and solving, we see there are two solutions, $\tilde{p} = 0$ and $\tilde{p} = \frac{2}{3}$. The solution $\tilde{p} = 0$ is ruled out since it clearly does not maximize the likelihood function. In fact, if $\tilde{p} = 0$, then we could *not* have drawn the sample since $P(Y = 1) = p$ and thus obtaining a value $y = 1$ would have been impossible. On the other hand, $\tilde{p} = \frac{2}{3}$ satisfies both the first- and second-order conditions for a local maximum and is the maximum likelihood estimate of p. It agrees with our graphical results as well.

To summarize the method of maximum likelihood: the likelihood function $l(\boldsymbol{\theta}|\mathbf{y})$ is algebraically identical to the joint p.d.f. $f(\mathbf{y}|\boldsymbol{\theta})$ of the random sample $Y_1, \ldots, Y_T$, where $\boldsymbol{\theta}$ is a vector of unknown parameters with a true value known to fall in the parameter space Ω. The difference between $l(\boldsymbol{\theta}|\mathbf{y})$ and $f(\mathbf{y}|\boldsymbol{\theta})$ is that $l(\boldsymbol{\theta}|\mathbf{y})$ is interpreted as a function of $\boldsymbol{\theta}$ *given* the values of a random sample $\mathbf{y}$; and the joint p.d.f. $f(\mathbf{y}|\boldsymbol{\theta})$ is a function of $\mathbf{y}$ given particular values of $\boldsymbol{\theta}$. The maximum likelihood estimate of $\boldsymbol{\theta}$ is that value in Ω, say $\tilde{\boldsymbol{\theta}}$, that maximizes $l(\boldsymbol{\theta}|\mathbf{y})$. The value $\tilde{\boldsymbol{\theta}}$ is in general a function of $\mathbf{y}$, say $\tilde{\boldsymbol{\theta}} = \tilde{\boldsymbol{\theta}}(\mathbf{y})$, so the *random variable* $\tilde{\boldsymbol{\theta}} = \tilde{\boldsymbol{\theta}}(\mathbf{Y})$, where $\mathbf{Y} = (Y_1, \ldots, Y_T)'$, is the *maximum likelihood estimator* of $\boldsymbol{\theta}$.

As a practical matter, it is usual practice to maximize the natural logarithm of the likelihood function rather than the likelihood function itself. This is very convenient, since the log-likelihood $L = \ln l(\boldsymbol{\theta}|\mathbf{y})$ is composed of sums rather than products and exponential functions simplify nicely. Since the natural logarithm is a monotonic function, $\ln l(\boldsymbol{\theta}|\mathbf{y})$ and $l(\boldsymbol{\theta}|\mathbf{y})$ attain their maxima at the *same* value of $\boldsymbol{\theta}$.

Let us consider two examples that illustrate how maximum likelihood estimators can be obtained.

Example 3.3 Let $Y_1, \ldots, Y_T$ be a random sample of Bernoulli random variables with

$$f(y_i|p) = p^{y_i}(1-p)^{1-y_i}, \quad i = 1, \ldots, T$$

and $0 \le p \le 1$. Then the log likelihood is

$$\begin{aligned} L = \ln l(p|\mathbf{y}) &= \ln\left[\prod_{i=1}^{T} f(y_i|p)\right] \\ &= \ln[p^{\sum y_i} \cdot (1-p)^{\sum(1-y_i)}] \\ &= \sum y_i \cdot \ln(p) + \sum(1-y_i) \cdot \ln(1-p) \end{aligned}$$

The first and second derivatives are

$$\frac{dL}{dp} = \sum y_i \cdot \frac{1}{p} - \sum (1-y_i) \cdot \frac{1}{1-p}$$

$$\frac{d^2L}{dp^2} = -\sum y_i \cdot \frac{1}{p^2} - \sum (1-y_i) \cdot \frac{1}{(1-p)^2}$$

Equating the first derivative to zero and solving yields $\tilde{p} = \sum y_i/T$, which is the sample mean. Note that d^2L/dp^2 is always negative for $0 < p < 1$, so $\tilde{p}$ yields a global maximum of the log-likelihood function. ■

Example 3.4 Let $Y_1, \ldots, Y_T$ be a random sample from a $N(\beta, \sigma^2)$ population. Thus the unknown parameters are $\boldsymbol{\theta}' = (\beta, \sigma^2)$. The log-likelihood function is

$$\begin{aligned} L = \ln l(\boldsymbol{\theta}|\mathbf{y}) &= \ln\left\{\prod_{i=1}^{T} \frac{1}{\sqrt{2\pi\sigma^2}} \exp\left[-\frac{1}{2}\frac{(y_i-\beta)^2}{\sigma^2}\right]\right\} \\ &= \ln\left\{(2\pi)^{-T/2}(\sigma^2)^{-T/2} \exp\left[-\frac{1}{2}\sum_{i=1}^{T}\frac{(y_i-\beta)^2}{\sigma^2}\right]\right\} \qquad (3.2.6) \\ &= -\frac{T}{2}\ln 2\pi - \frac{T}{2}\ln(\sigma^2) - \frac{1}{2}\sum_{i=1}^{T}\frac{(y_i-\beta)^2}{\sigma^2} \end{aligned}$$

Then the first- and second-order derivatives are

$$
\begin{aligned}
\frac{\partial L}{\partial \beta} &= \frac{1}{\sigma^2}\left(\sum_{i=1}^{T} y_i - T\beta\right) \\
\frac{\partial L}{\partial \sigma^2} &= -\frac{T}{2\sigma^2} + \frac{1}{2\sigma^4}\sum_{i=1}^{T}(y_i - \beta)^2 \\
\frac{\partial^2 L}{\partial \beta^2} &= -\frac{T}{\sigma^2} \\
\frac{\partial^2 L}{\partial (\sigma^2)^2} &= \frac{T}{2\sigma^4} - \frac{1}{\sigma^6}\sum_{i=1}^{T}(y_i - \beta)^2 \\
\frac{\partial^2 L}{\partial \beta\, \partial \sigma^2} &= -\frac{1}{\sigma^4}\left(\sum_{i=1}^{T} y_i - T\beta\right)
\end{aligned}
\tag{3.2.7}
$$

Setting the first-order derivatives to zero, using (3.2.7), we have

$$
\frac{1}{\tilde{\sigma}^2}\left(\sum_{i=1}^{T} y_i - T\tilde{\beta}\right) = 0
$$

$$
\frac{-T}{2\tilde{\sigma}^2} + \frac{1}{2\tilde{\sigma}^4}\sum_{i=1}^{T}(y_i - \tilde{\beta})^2 = 0
$$

and solving

$$
\tilde{\beta} = \sum_{i=1}^{T} \frac{y_i}{T} = \bar{y}
$$

$$
\tilde{\sigma}^2 = \frac{\sum (y_i - \tilde{\beta})^2}{T}
$$

That these unique solutions actually maximize the log-likelihood function can be verified by checking the second-order conditions for a local maximum. That is, the matrix of second-order derivatives must be determined to be negative definite when evaluated at the solutions $\tilde{\beta}$ and $\tilde{\sigma}^2$. This follows since

$$
\begin{bmatrix}
\dfrac{\partial^2 L}{\partial \beta^2} & \dfrac{\partial^2 L}{\partial \beta\, \partial \sigma^2} \\[2ex]
\dfrac{\partial^2 L}{\partial \sigma^2\, \partial \beta} & \dfrac{\partial^2 L}{\partial (\sigma^2)^2}
\end{bmatrix}_{\beta = \tilde{\beta},\, \sigma^2 = \tilde{\sigma}^2}
=
\begin{bmatrix}
-\dfrac{T}{\tilde{\sigma}^2} & 0 \\[2ex]
0 & \dfrac{-T}{2\tilde{\sigma}^4}
\end{bmatrix}
$$

which is negative definite (see matrix appendix Section A.14). ■

3.2.3 Least Squares Estimation

A difficulty with both the method of moments and the method of maximum likelihood is that each requires a specific assumption about the distribution of the random variable in question. Sometimes it is possible to use estimation methods that do not require exact specification of the population distribution. One method that is very useful and popular is the method of least squares. It can be used to estimate central moments of random variables, $\mu'_r = E[Y^r]$. The idea is straightforward. Since the mathematical expectation of a random variable is the mean of the random variable, given the values of a random sample of data $y_1, \ldots, y_T$, it is reasonable to use the "center" of the data y_i^r, $i = 1, \ldots, T$, to estimate μ'_r. One way to define the center of a set of data is to find the value $\hat{\mu}'_r$ that minimizes

$$S = \sum_{i=1}^{T} (y_i^r - \mu'_r)^2 \tag{3.2.8}$$

The value S is the sum of squared differences between y_i^r and the expectation $\mu'_r = E[Y_i^r]$. The value $\hat{\mu}'_r$ that minimizes S for a given set of data values of the random variable is called the *least squares estimate* of μ'_r. If $\hat{\mu}'_r$ is considered a function of the random variables Y_i, then it is the *least squares (LS) estimator.*

Choosing to minimize (3.2.8) is "reasonable" but also arbitrary. Note that the values of Y_i^r that are far away from $E[Y_i^r]$ are weighted heavily since those values are squared. A convincing argument could be made for using

$$S' = \sum_{i=1}^{T} |y_i^r - \mu'_r|$$

as a criterion for finding the center of the values of y_i^r. The resulting estimator is called the *least absolute deviation (LAD) or minimum absolute deviation (MAD)* estimator. These rules will be considered in Chapter 22. The LAD rules are not as popular as the LS rules for several reasons. It is often easier to find the LS rules since S in (3.2.8) is easier to minimize. Second, the LS procedure often produces estimators with desirable properties.

Example 3.5 Let $Y_1, \ldots, Y_T$ be a random sample from a population with mean β and finite variance σ^2. Then the LS estimator of β is obtained by minimizing

$$S = \sum_{i=1}^{T} (y_i - \beta)^2$$

The first-order condition is

$$\frac{dS}{d\beta} = \sum_{i=1}^{T} -2(y_i - \hat{\beta}) = 0$$

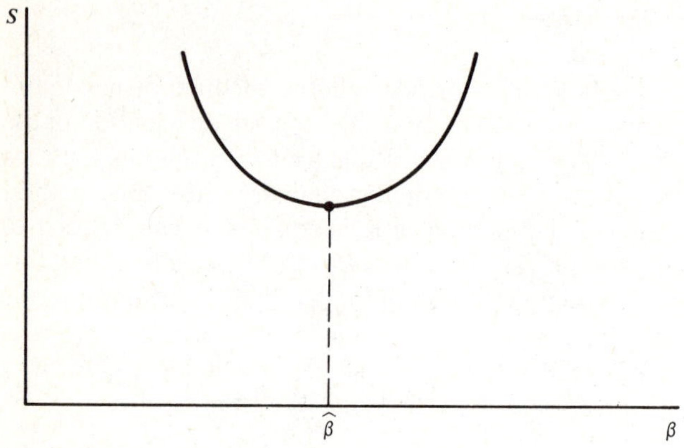

Figure 3.3 The sum of squares parabola.

So $\hat{\beta} = \sum_{i=1}^{T} y_i/T$. You may verify that $\hat{\beta}$ does in fact minimize S by checking the second-order condition. Graphically, the sum of squares S may be viewed as a parabola, as illustrated in Figure 3.3. Finding the LS estimator of β amounts to finding the value of β that corresponds to the minimum point on the parabola. ■

3.2.4 Bayesian Estimation Methods

In any problem of statistical inference it is likely that the investigator has some prior knowledge, either from theoretical results, prior empirical work, or introspection, about the underlying parameters of the problem. That is, suppose observations are to be taken on a random variable Y with p.d.f. $f(y|\theta)$ where θ is an unknown parameter that must lie in the parameter space Ω. The task of statistical inference is to make judgments about the actual value of θ based on a sample of observations. But suppose, *prior* to the sample data actually being collected, the knowledge of the investigator can be summarized by a probability distribution for θ on the set Ω. This *prior distribution*, say $g(\theta)$, expresses all prior information about θ by specifying portions of Ω where θ is relatively likely, or relatively unlikely, to fall. This is not an uncontroversial notion, and in practice it may be difficult to summarize one's prior nonsample information in the form of a prior distribution. Nonetheless, the Bayesian approach provides a powerful methodology for combining sample data with nonsample information. We use this approach frequently throughout this book. Chapters 4 and 7 are wholly devoted to studying the Bayesian methodology, so we refer you to these chapters for details and examples.

3.3 Properties of Point Estimators

In the previous section we developed intuitive and reasonable procedures for obtaining estimation rules, or estimators. We must now examine the properties of estimation rules so that we can understand what they can, and cannot, do for us. As noted earlier, estimators are random variables, so evaluating their properties amounts to studying the properties of their probability distributions. This section is broken into two major parts. The first concerns the "small sample" properties of estimators; that is, those properties that hold for samples of all sizes, even small ones. The second part considers "large sample" or "asymptotic" properties of estimators. These are properties based on samples whose size is assumed to grow to infinity. Such notions are frequently required in econometrics as estimation rules' properties are so complicated that little specific can be said about them without the assumption of very large samples.

3.3.1 Small Sample Properties of Estimators: Single Parameter Case

In this section we consider the small sample properties of an estimator of a single parameter. That is, let Y be a random variable with p.d.f. $f(y|\theta)$, where θ is a parameter that we would like to estimate, and let $Y_1, \ldots, Y_T$ be a sample of observations on Y. Suppose $\hat{\theta} = \hat{\theta}(Y_1, \ldots, Y_T)$ is an estimator of θ. As noted following Example 3.1, we will evaluate the estimator $\hat{\theta}$ in a repeated sampling sense, since to do otherwise requires knowledge of the true parameter θ.

3.3.1a Estimator Performance: Bias and Precision

One classical criterion for evaluating an estimator, and an intuitive property that appeals to many, is unbiasedness. An *unbiased* estimator of a parameter is one with a mathematical expectation that equals the true parameter value. That is, $\hat{\theta}$ is an unbiased estimator of θ if $E[\hat{\theta}] = \theta$. If $E[\hat{\theta}] \neq \theta$, then $\hat{\theta}$ is a *biased* estimator and $E[\hat{\theta}] - \theta = \delta$ is the amount of bias. If the p.d.f. of $\hat{\theta}$ is symmetric and $\hat{\theta}$ is unbiased, then θ is located at the center of the distribution, as illustrated in Figure 3.4.

Recalling the interpretation of mathematical expectation, unbiasedness means that the estimator "on the average" will yield the true parameter value; that is, if the underlying experiment is repeated infinitely many times by drawing samples of size T, the average value of the estimates $\hat{\theta}$ from all those samples will be θ.

Since $\hat{\theta}$ is a random variable, in addition to the mean of the estimator we are also concerned about its variance. Figure 3.5 illustrates the p.d.f.'s of two unbiased estimators $\tilde{\theta}$ and $\hat{\theta}$. The estimator $\hat{\theta}$ has a larger variance than $\tilde{\theta}$, and thus within a

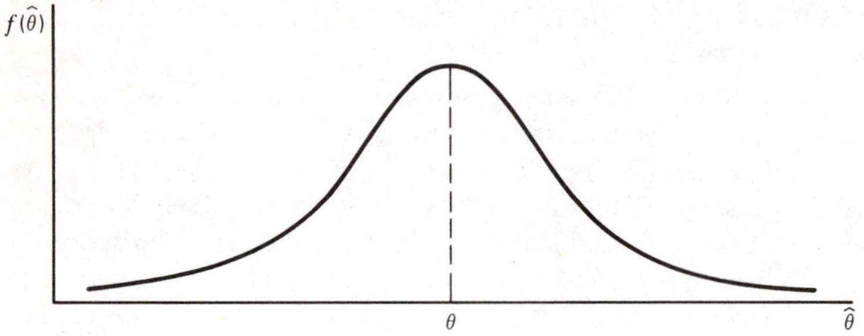

Figure 3.4

sampling context can more frequently lead to estimates that are far from the true parameter θ. Since both estimators are unbiased, we would prefer the estimator $\tilde{\theta}$ to $\hat{\theta}$ since using $\tilde{\theta}$ gives us a higher probability of obtaining an estimate that is *close* to the true parameter value.

Example 3.6 Continuing Example 3.1, let us consider the properties of the sample mean in (3.2.3), $\hat{\theta} = \sum_{i=1}^{T} Y_i/T$. This estimator is unbiased since

$$E[\hat{\theta}] = \sum_{i=1}^{T} E[Y_i/T] = \sum_{i=1}^{T} \theta/T = T\theta/T = \theta$$

The variance of $\hat{\theta}$ can be determined easily using the properties of variance learned in Chapter 2. Since the Y_i are independent (recall that $Y_1, \ldots, Y_T$ constitute a random sample),

$$\text{var}(\hat{\theta}) = \frac{1}{T^2} \sum_{i=1}^{T} \text{var}(Y_i) = T\sigma^2/T^2 = \sigma^2/T$$

A very important additional result is possible to obtain in this example, namely the *exact* distribution of the estimator $\hat{\theta}$. Since the Y_i's are jointly distributed, $\hat{\theta}$ is a

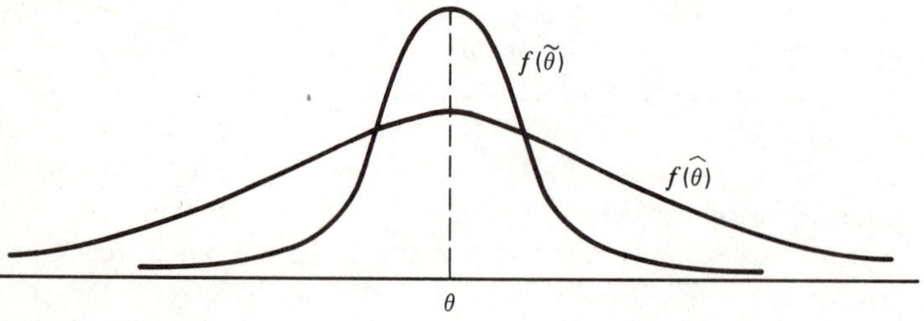

Figure 3.5

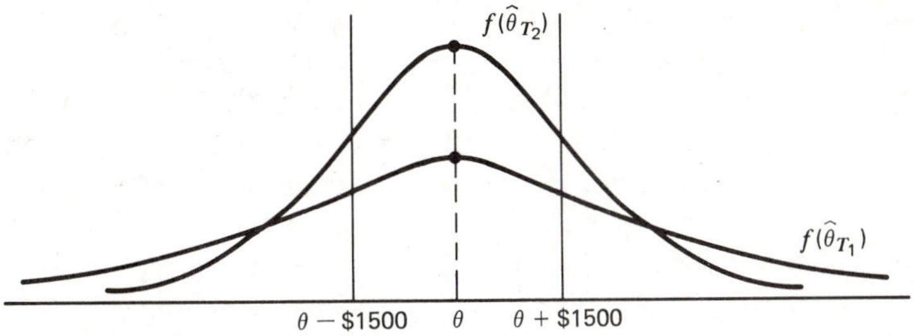

Figure 3.6

linear combination of normal variables, which can be seen if we write it as

$$\hat{\theta} = \frac{1}{T}Y_1 + \frac{1}{T}Y_2 + \cdots + \frac{1}{T}Y_T$$

Then, using the result in (2.5.11) (see Exercise 2.15), we can state that $\hat{\theta}$ has a normal distribution with mean θ and variance σ^2/T. If, as assumed in Example 3.1, $\sigma^2 = \$5000^2$, we can see the effects of using a larger sample size rather than a smaller one. Let $\hat{\theta}_{T_1} = \sum_{i=1}^{T_1} Y_i/T_1$ and $\hat{\theta}_{T_2} = \sum_{i=1}^{T_2} Y_i/T_2$ where $T_1 = 10$ and $T_2 = 20$. Both $\hat{\theta}_{T_1}$ and $\hat{\theta}_{T_2}$ are unbiased, yet $\text{var}(\hat{\theta}_{T_1}) = \sigma^2/T_1 = \$2{,}500{,}000$ and $\text{var}(\hat{\theta}_{T_2}) = \sigma^2/T_2 = \$1{,}250{,}000$. If we define being close to θ as being within \$1500, we can compute the probability that $\hat{\theta}_{T_1}$ and $\hat{\theta}_{T_2}$ fall within \$1500 of the true mean θ, as illustrated in Figure 3.6. Using the properties of the normal distribution as described in Section 2.5.5,

$$P[\theta - 1500 \leq \hat{\theta}_{T_1} \leq \theta + 1500] = 0.66$$

and

$$P[\theta - 1500 \leq \hat{\theta}_{T_2} \leq \theta + 1500] = 0.82.$$

Thus we have a higher chance of being "close" to the true but unknown mean using $\hat{\theta}_{T_2}$, based on the larger sample size, since it has the smaller variance of the two unbiased estimators. ■

Just as unbiasedness alone does not serve as an adequate basis for evaluating an estimator, neither does simply considering the variance. For example, the *estimator* $\hat{\theta} = 5$ has zero variance, yet in general it is not a good estimator since its bias is $\delta = E[\hat{\theta} - \theta] = 5 - \theta$ which can be very large.

3.3.1b Bias versus Precision

What we want, of course, is an estimator that usually yields estimates of the unknown parameter that are "close" to the true parameter value. From the foregoing discussion it is clear that both bias and variance must be taken into account when evaluating an estimator. One way to do this is to consider an estimator's *mean square error*, which is defined as $\text{MSE}(\hat{\theta}) = E[\hat{\theta} - \theta]^2$. It is, within the repeated sampling context, the average squared distance between $\hat{\theta}$ and the true parameter value θ. Furthermore, $(\hat{\theta} - \theta)^2$ measures the *loss* from using $\hat{\theta}$ as an estimator of θ and taking mathematical expectation of this loss yields the average loss or *risk* of using $\hat{\theta}$ to estimate θ. See Section 4.3 for more on these decision theoretic concepts. To see that this measure encompasses both precision and bias note that

$$\begin{aligned} \text{MSE}(\hat{\theta}) &= E[\hat{\theta} - E(\hat{\theta}) + E(\hat{\theta}) - \theta]^2 \\ &= E\{[\hat{\theta} - E(\hat{\theta})] + [E(\hat{\theta}) - \theta]\}^2 \\ &= E[\hat{\theta} - E(\hat{\theta})]^2 + [E(\hat{\theta}) - \theta]^2 + 2E[\hat{\theta} - E(\hat{\theta})][E(\hat{\theta}) - \theta] \end{aligned}$$

The last term is zero since

$$\begin{aligned} E[\hat{\theta} - E(\hat{\theta})][E(\hat{\theta}) - \theta] &= [E(\hat{\theta}) - \theta] \cdot E[\hat{\theta} - E(\hat{\theta})] \\ &= [E(\hat{\theta}) - \theta] \cdot [E(\hat{\theta}) - E(\hat{\theta})] = 0 \end{aligned}$$

So

$$\begin{aligned} \text{MSE}(\hat{\theta}) &= E[\hat{\theta} - E(\hat{\theta})]^2 + [E(\hat{\theta}) - \theta]^2 \\ &= \text{var}(\hat{\theta}) + [\text{bias}(\hat{\theta})]^2 \end{aligned} \tag{3.3.1}$$

The use of mean square error allows us to compare estimators such as $\tilde{\theta}$ and $\hat{\theta}$ whose p.d.f.'s are shown in Figure 3.7. $\hat{\theta}$ is an unbiased estimator whose variance is larger than that of the biased estimator $\tilde{\theta}$. For the purpose of using an estimator that will give estimates close to θ, $\tilde{\theta}$ may be preferred even though it is biased, if it yields a smaller mean squared error.

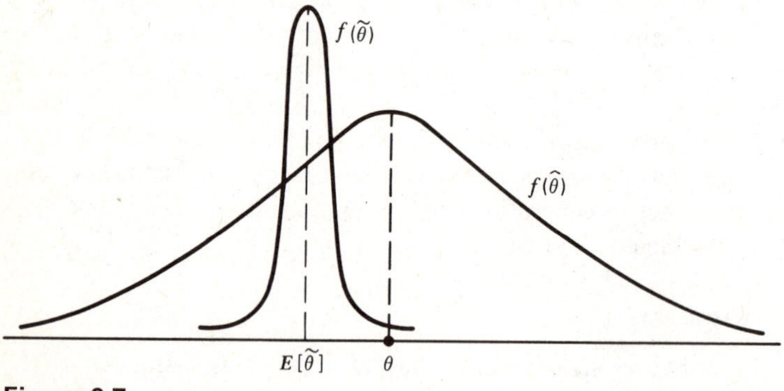

Figure 3.7

3.3.1c Efficiency

Another way to take into account both bias and variance is only to compare estimators that are unbiased. Then the estimator with the smaller variance would be preferred. This approach is widely used and forms the basis of the definition of estimator *efficiency*. An estimator $\hat{\theta}$ is an efficient estimator of θ if $E[\hat{\theta}] = \theta$ and $\text{var}(\hat{\theta}) \leq \text{var}(\tilde{\theta})$, where $\tilde{\theta}$ is any other unbiased estimator of θ. The following important result, known as the *Cramér–Rao inequality*, provides a sufficient but not necessary condition for an estimator to be efficient. Let Y be a random variable with p.d.f. $f(y|\theta)$. If $Y_1, \ldots, Y_T$ is a random sample, then the joint p.d.f. of the T random variables Y_i is

$$f(\mathbf{y}|\theta) = f(y_1, \ldots, y_T|\theta) = \prod_{i=1}^{T} f(y_i|\theta)$$

Recall that if we interpret the joint p.d.f. $f(y_1, \ldots, y_T|\theta)$ as a function of the unknown parameter θ given the values of the random sample, then the resulting function is known as the likelihood function and written as $l(\theta|\mathbf{y}) = l(\theta|y_1, \ldots, y_T)$. It is mathematically identical to the joint p.d.f. but has a different interpretation. Let $L(\theta)$ denote the natural logarithm of the likelihood function. Then the Cramér–Rao inequality states that if $\hat{\theta}$ is any unbiased estimator of θ, and certain regularity conditions hold, then

$$\text{var}(\hat{\theta}) \geq \frac{1}{-E\left[\dfrac{d^2L(\theta)}{d\theta^2}\right]} \tag{3.3.2}$$

For proof, see Theil (1971, pp. 384–386). This result is a very powerful one. It says that if an unbiased estimator $\hat{\theta}$ has variance *equal* to $-1/E[d^2L/d\theta^2]$, which is known as the *Cramér–Rao lower bound* (*CRLB*), then it is *efficient*, since no lower variance is possible for an unbiased estimator. As noted already, this condition is sufficient but not necessary. It is possible that *no* unbiased estimator has variance as small as the CRLB.

Example 3.7 Let us reconsider Example 3.3. The estimator $\tilde{p} = \sum_{i=1}^{T} Y_i/T$ was found to be the maximum likelihood estimator of the unknown parameter p of a Bernoulli random variable. The estimator $\tilde{p}$ can also be shown to be efficient as follows. First, $\tilde{p}$ is unbiased since

$$E[\tilde{p}] = E\left[\sum_{i=1}^{T} Y_i/T\right] = \sum_{i=1}^{T} E[Y_i]/T = Tp/T = p$$

The variance of $\tilde{p}$ is found using the properties of variance as

$$\begin{aligned}\operatorname{var}(\tilde{p}) &= \operatorname{var}\left(\sum_{i=1}^{T} Y_i/T\right) = T^{-2}\sum_{i=1}^{T}\operatorname{var}(Y_i)\\ &= T^{-2}[Tp(1-p)] = p(1-p)/T\end{aligned}$$

The second derivative of the log-likelihood function is given in Example 3.3, and taking its expectation we have

$$\begin{aligned}E\left[\frac{d^2L}{dp^2}\right] &= E\left[-\sum_{i=1}^{T} Y_i\frac{1}{p^2} - \sum_{i=1}^{T}(1-Y_i)\frac{1}{(1-p)^2}\right]\\ &= -\frac{1}{p^2}\sum_{i=1}^{T}E[Y_i] - \frac{1}{(1-p)^2}\sum_{i=1}^{T}E[1-Y_i]\\ &= -\frac{T}{p} - \frac{T}{1-p}\\ &= -\frac{T}{p(1-p)}\end{aligned}$$

Thus the Cramér–Rao lower bound is

$$\frac{1}{-E[d^2L/dp^2]} = \frac{p(1-p)}{T}$$

which is identical to the variance of $\tilde{p}$. Thus we can assert that $\tilde{p}$ is the unbiased estimator with the smallest variance, that is, it is efficient with respect to the class of estimators that are unbiased. Sometimes this is also expressed by saying that $\tilde{p}$ is the best or minimum variance unbiased estimator for p. ■

Example 3.8 Let $Y_1, \ldots, Y_T$ be a random sample from a $N(\beta, \sigma^2)$ population where the variance σ^2 is assumed to be known. The fact that σ^2 is known does not affect the mathematical form of the log-likelihood function, which is given in (3.2.6). It does mean that when maximizing the log-likelihood only β is treated as unknown and so only the derivatives with respect to β in (3.2.7) are relevant to us here. Setting the first derivative to zero and solving, we obtain the ML estimator for β as $\tilde{\beta} = \sum_{i=1}^{T} Y_i/T$, which is the sample mean. This estimator is unbiased since

$$E[\tilde{\beta}] = E\left[\sum_{i=1}^{T} Y_i/T\right] = \frac{1}{T}\sum_{i=1}^{T}E[Y_i] = T\beta/T = \beta$$

and its variance is obtained using the properties of variance as

$$\operatorname{var}(\tilde{\beta}) = \operatorname{var}\left[\sum_{i=1}^{T} Y_i/T\right] = \frac{1}{T^2}\operatorname{var}\left[\sum_{i=1}^{T} Y_i\right]$$

$$= \frac{1}{T^2}\sum_{i=1}^{T} \operatorname{var}(Y_i) = \frac{T\sigma^2}{T^2} = \frac{\sigma^2}{T}$$

The Cramér–Rao lower bound is easily found in this case since the second derivative of the log-likelihood function contains no random terms. It is

$$\frac{1}{-E\left[\dfrac{d^2L}{d\beta^2}\right]} = \frac{\sigma^2}{T}$$

Since the variance of the unbiased estimator $\tilde{\beta}$ is identical to the CRLB, we can assert that $\tilde{\beta}$ is the *best unbiased estimator* for the mean of a normal population, when the variance is known. Recall from Example 3.6 that we also know the exact distribution of the sample mean from a normal distribution, namely, that it is normally distributed itself with mean β and variance σ^2/T. ■

Despite the power of the Cramér–Rao inequality, it is difficult to use in certain instances because it is not a necessary condition for efficiency (we illustrate this in Example 3.10) and because the distribution of the underlying population must be known in order to use it. Given these difficulties in finding the minimum variance unbiased estimator, attention has frequently focused on a more restricted problem. It is often *much* simpler to find the minimum variance estimator among those that are not only unbiased but also *linear functions of the sample observations.* Specifically, let $\hat{\theta}$ be an estimator of an unknown parameter θ and be of the form $\hat{\theta} = a_1 Y_1 + \cdots + a_T Y_T$, where the a_i's are constants. Then $\hat{\theta}$ is defined to be a *linear estimator* since it is a linear function of the sample observations. If $\hat{\theta}$ is unbiased and $\operatorname{var}(\hat{\theta}) \leq \operatorname{var}(\tilde{\theta})$, where $\tilde{\theta}$ is any other linear and unbiased estimator of θ, then $\hat{\theta}$ is the *best linear unbiased estimator* (*BLUE*) of θ. It is often possible to find such an estimator without knowledge of the underlying p.d.f. of Y, as the following example illustrates.

Example 3.9 Let $Y_1, \ldots, Y_T$ be a random sample from a population with mean β and variance σ^2. Then for $\hat{\beta}$ to be a linear estimator it must have the form

$$\hat{\beta} = \sum_{i=1}^{T} a_i Y_i$$

Then

$$E[\hat{\beta}] = \sum_{i=1}^{T} a_i E[Y_i] = \beta \sum_{i=1}^{T} a_i$$

and in order for $\hat{\beta}$ to be unbiased it must be true that $\sum_{i=1}^{T} a_i = 1$. The variance of $\hat{\beta}$ is

$$\operatorname{var}(\hat{\beta}) = \operatorname{var}\left(\sum_{i=1}^{T} a_i Y_i\right) = \sum_{i=1}^{T} a_i^2 \operatorname{var}(Y_i)$$

$$= \sigma^2 \sum_{i=1}^{T} a_i^2$$

Thus to find the best linear unbiased estimator we must choose the constants a_i so that $\sum_{i=1}^{T} a_i^2$ is minimized and $\sum_{i=1}^{T} a_i = 1$. Forming the Lagrangian (where λ is a Lagrange multiplier)

$$L = \sum_{i=1}^{T} a_i^2 - \lambda\left(\sum_{i=1}^{T} a_i - 1\right)$$

The first-order conditions from this constrained minimization problem require that

$$\partial L/\partial a_i = 0, \quad i = 1, \ldots, T$$

and

$$\partial L/\partial \lambda = 0$$

The optimizing values for the a_i's are $a_i = 1/T$, $i = 1, \ldots, T$. So the best linear unbiased estimator of the mean of a population, using a random sample of values, is

$$\hat{\beta} = \sum_{i=1}^{T} a_i Y_i = \sum_{i=1}^{T} (1/T) Y_i = \sum_{i=1}^{T} Y_i/T,$$

which is the sample mean. The variance of this estimator is

$$\operatorname{var}(\hat{\beta}) = \sigma^2 \sum_{i=1}^{T} a_i^2 = \sigma^2 \sum_{i=1}^{T} (1/T^2) = \sigma^2/T \qquad \blacksquare$$

Note that in the previous example we did not need to know the population distribution of Y in order to obtain the best linear unbiased estimator of the population mean. Also note that the sample mean is not only the best linear unbiased estimator of the population mean but it is also the least squares estimator, as illustrated in Example 3.5. *If* we additionally assume that the population is normal, or Bernoulli for that matter, then the sample mean is not only the least squares and best *linear* unbiased estimator of the population mean, but is also the maximum likelihood and best or minimum variance unbiased estimator of the population mean. Knowledge of the distribution of the population allows us to make a stronger efficiency claim, namely that the sample mean is efficient relative to the class of *all* unbiased estimators, whether linear or nonlinear.

One other important consequence of being willing to assume the nature of the population distribution should be pointed out at this time. If no assumption about the distribution of the population is made, then it is impossible to determine the distribution of any estimation rule based on that sample without invoking asymptotic results; that is, without assuming the existence of a large sample of observations. On the other hand, if the population is assumed to have a certain distribution, then sometimes it is possible to determine the exact probability distribution of estimators of unknown parameters. In Example 3.8, for instance, knowledge that the population is normal allows us to use the properties of the normal distribution to assert that the sample mean itself is normally distributed, whatever the size of the sample is. In Section 3.3.3.2 we will see that if no assumption is made about the distribution of the population from which a random sample is drawn other than that it has a finite mean and a finite variance, then the sample mean is "asymptotically" normal, (i.e., approximately normal if the sample size is large.)

3.3.2 Small Sample Properties of Estimators: The Case of Several Parameters

In Section 3.2.1 we examined the small sample properties of an estimator for a single parameter. The fact of the matter is, however, that in the remainder of this book we are generally concerned with statistical models involving several unknown parameters. Example 3.4, in which we estimated the mean and variance of a normal population using the method of maximum likelihood, exemplifies the multiparameter problem. For purposes of a general discussion we assume that we are concerned with a statistical model involving K unknown parameters: $\theta_1, \ldots, \theta_K$. Specifically, let Y be a random variable with p.d.f. $f(y|\boldsymbol{\theta})$ where $\boldsymbol{\theta} = (\theta_1, \ldots, \theta_K)'$ is a $(K \times 1)$ vector of unknown parameters that we wish to estimate. Then let $\hat{\boldsymbol{\theta}} = (\hat{\theta}_1, \ldots, \hat{\theta}_K)'$ be a $(K \times 1)$ vector whose elements $\hat{\theta}_i$ are estimators for the corresponding elements θ_i of $\boldsymbol{\theta}$. In the context of Example 3.4, $\tilde{\boldsymbol{\theta}} = (\tilde{\beta}, \tilde{\sigma}^2)'$ is the estimator for $\boldsymbol{\theta} = (\beta, \sigma^2)'$. The discussion that follows parallels Section 3.2.1 in the development of small sample properties for vectors of estimators.

3.3.2a Estimator Performance: Bias and Precision

If $\boldsymbol{\theta}$ is a $(K \times 1)$ vector of unknown parameters, then the $(K \times 1)$ random vector $\hat{\boldsymbol{\theta}}$ is an unbiased estimator of $\boldsymbol{\theta}$ if $E[\hat{\boldsymbol{\theta}}] = \boldsymbol{\theta}$, where the mathematical expectation of the vector $\hat{\boldsymbol{\theta}}$ is taken element by element (see Section 2.4.5). That is, $\hat{\boldsymbol{\theta}}$ is unbiased for $\boldsymbol{\theta}$ if

$$E[\hat{\boldsymbol{\theta}}] = \begin{bmatrix} E\hat{\theta}_1 \\ E\hat{\theta}_2 \\ \vdots \\ E\hat{\theta}_K \end{bmatrix} = \begin{bmatrix} \theta_1 \\ \theta_2 \\ \vdots \\ \theta_K \end{bmatrix} = \boldsymbol{\theta}$$

If $E[\hat{\boldsymbol{\theta}}] \neq \boldsymbol{\theta}$, then $\hat{\boldsymbol{\theta}}$ is *biased* and $\boldsymbol{\delta} = E[\hat{\boldsymbol{\theta}}] - \boldsymbol{\theta}$ is the *bias vector.*

The precision of $\hat{\boldsymbol{\theta}}$ is measured by its covariance matrix, which is defined as

$$\operatorname{cov}(\hat{\boldsymbol{\theta}}) = E[(\hat{\boldsymbol{\theta}} - E(\hat{\boldsymbol{\theta}}))(\hat{\boldsymbol{\theta}} - E(\hat{\boldsymbol{\theta}}))']$$

$$= \begin{bmatrix} E(\hat{\theta}_1 - E\hat{\theta}_1)^2 & E(\hat{\theta}_1 - E\hat{\theta}_1)(\hat{\theta}_2 - E\hat{\theta}_2) & \cdots & E(\hat{\theta}_1 - E\hat{\theta}_1)(\hat{\theta}_K - E\hat{\theta}_K) \\ E(\hat{\theta}_2 - E\hat{\theta}_2)(\hat{\theta}_1 - E\hat{\theta}_1) & E(\hat{\theta}_2 - E\hat{\theta}_2)^2 & \cdots & E(\hat{\theta}_2 - E\hat{\theta}_2)(\hat{\theta}_K - E\hat{\theta}_K) \\ \vdots & \vdots & \ddots & \vdots \\ E(\hat{\theta}_K - E\hat{\theta}_K)(\hat{\theta}_1 - E\hat{\theta}_1) & E(\hat{\theta}_K - E\hat{\theta}_K)(\hat{\theta}_2 - E\hat{\theta}_2) & \cdots & E(\hat{\theta}_K - E\hat{\theta}_K)^2 \end{bmatrix}$$

$$= \begin{bmatrix} \operatorname{var}(\hat{\theta}_1) & \operatorname{cov}(\hat{\theta}_1, \hat{\theta}_2) & \cdots & \operatorname{cov}(\hat{\theta}_1, \hat{\theta}_K) \\ \operatorname{cov}(\hat{\theta}_2, \hat{\theta}_1) & \operatorname{var}(\hat{\theta}_2) & \cdots & \operatorname{cov}(\hat{\theta}_2, \hat{\theta}_K) \\ \vdots & \vdots & \ddots & \vdots \\ \operatorname{cov}(\hat{\theta}_K, \hat{\theta}_1) & \operatorname{cov}(\hat{\theta}_K, \hat{\theta}_2) & \cdots & \operatorname{var}(\hat{\theta}_K) \end{bmatrix}$$

If $\boldsymbol{\theta}$ is a $(K \times 1)$ vector, then $\operatorname{cov}(\hat{\boldsymbol{\theta}})$ is a $(K \times K)$ positive definite and symmetric matrix (see Section 2.4.6).

An obvious question now arises as to how the precision of two competing estimators of $\boldsymbol{\theta}$ can be compared. That is, if $\hat{\boldsymbol{\theta}}$ and $\tilde{\boldsymbol{\theta}}$ are both estimators of $\boldsymbol{\theta}$, how do we compare $\operatorname{cov}(\hat{\boldsymbol{\theta}})$ and $\operatorname{cov}(\tilde{\boldsymbol{\theta}})$ since they are matrices? We will say that $\operatorname{cov}(\hat{\boldsymbol{\theta}})$ is "smaller than" $\operatorname{cov}(\tilde{\boldsymbol{\theta}})$, in a matrix sense, if $\operatorname{cov}(\tilde{\boldsymbol{\theta}}) - \operatorname{cov}(\hat{\boldsymbol{\theta}})$ is a positive semidefinite matrix. The implications of this definition are threefold. If $\operatorname{cov}(\tilde{\boldsymbol{\theta}}) - \operatorname{cov}(\hat{\boldsymbol{\theta}})$ is a positive semidefinite matrix then

(*i*) $\operatorname{var}(\tilde{\theta}_i) \geq \operatorname{var}(\hat{\theta}_i),\ i = 1, \ldots, K$ (3.3.3a)

(*ii*) $|\operatorname{cov}(\tilde{\boldsymbol{\theta}})| \geq |\operatorname{cov}(\hat{\boldsymbol{\theta}})|$ (3.3.3b)

(*iii*) If $\mathbf{c}$ is any $(K \times 1)$ vector of constants, then
$\operatorname{var}(\mathbf{c}'\tilde{\boldsymbol{\theta}}) = \mathbf{c}'[\operatorname{cov}(\tilde{\boldsymbol{\theta}})]\mathbf{c} \geq \operatorname{var}(\mathbf{c}'\hat{\boldsymbol{\theta}}) = \mathbf{c}'[\operatorname{cov}(\hat{\boldsymbol{\theta}})]\mathbf{c}$ (3.3.3c)

For proof of (3.3.3) see Goldberger (1964, p. 38).

3.3.2b Bias versus Precision

As with the case of a single parameter, we will sometimes be interested in weighing bias versus precision in the case of several parameters. One way to do this is to define the *mean squared error matrix* of an estimator $\hat{\boldsymbol{\theta}}$ for $\boldsymbol{\theta}$ as

$$\begin{aligned}\operatorname{MSE}(\hat{\boldsymbol{\theta}}) &= E[(\hat{\boldsymbol{\theta}} - \boldsymbol{\theta})(\hat{\boldsymbol{\theta}} - \boldsymbol{\theta})'] \\ &= E[\hat{\boldsymbol{\theta}} - E(\hat{\boldsymbol{\theta}})][\hat{\boldsymbol{\theta}} - E(\hat{\boldsymbol{\theta}})]' + [E(\hat{\boldsymbol{\theta}}) - \boldsymbol{\theta}][E(\hat{\boldsymbol{\theta}}) - \boldsymbol{\theta}]' \\ &= \operatorname{cov}(\hat{\boldsymbol{\theta}}) + [\operatorname{bias}(\hat{\boldsymbol{\theta}})][\operatorname{bias}(\hat{\boldsymbol{\theta}})]'\end{aligned} \tag{3.3.4}$$

where $\operatorname{cov}(\hat{\boldsymbol{\theta}})$ is the covariance matrix of the estimator $\hat{\boldsymbol{\theta}}$ and the "squared bias" matrix has elements $[\operatorname{bias}(\hat{\theta}_i)]^2$ on the diagonal and the product $\operatorname{bias}(\hat{\theta}_i) \cdot \operatorname{bias}(\hat{\theta}_j)$ in the ijth off-diagonal positions. A common scalar measure of the mean squared error of an estimator $\hat{\boldsymbol{\theta}}$ is $\operatorname{tr}\{\operatorname{MSE}(\hat{\boldsymbol{\theta}})\} = \sum_{i=1}^{K} \operatorname{MSE}(\hat{\theta}_i) = \sum_{i=1}^{K} \{\operatorname{var}(\hat{\theta}_i) + [\operatorname{bias}(\hat{\theta}_i)]^2\}$ and is often simply called the mean squared error of $\hat{\boldsymbol{\theta}}$ or the average loss or risk incurred when using $\hat{\boldsymbol{\theta}}$ to estimate $\boldsymbol{\theta}$. The concepts of loss and risk are more fully defined in Chapter 4.

3.3.2c Efficiency

The notion of *efficiency* generalizes straightforwardly from the single to the multiparameter case. An estimator $\hat{\boldsymbol{\theta}}$ is efficient for $\boldsymbol{\theta}$ if $\hat{\boldsymbol{\theta}}$ is unbiased *and* $\operatorname{cov}(\tilde{\boldsymbol{\theta}}) - \operatorname{cov}(\hat{\boldsymbol{\theta}})$ is positive semidefinite where $\tilde{\boldsymbol{\theta}}$ is any other unbiased estimator for $\boldsymbol{\theta}$. A multivariate version of the Cramér–Rao inequality provides a sufficient but not necessary condition for $\hat{\boldsymbol{\theta}}$ to be efficient

Let Y be a random variable with p.d.f. $f(y|\boldsymbol{\theta})$ where $\boldsymbol{\theta}' = (\theta_1, \ldots, \theta_K)$. If $Y_1, \ldots, Y_T$ is a random sample, then the joint p.d.f. is

$$f(\mathbf{y}|\boldsymbol{\theta}) = f(y_1, \ldots, y_T|\boldsymbol{\theta}) = \prod_{i=1}^{T} f(y_i|\boldsymbol{\theta})$$

If we interpret the joint p.d.f. as a function of the unknown parameter vector $\boldsymbol{\theta}$ given the values of the random sample $\mathbf{y}$, then the resulting function is the likelihood function and is written $l(\boldsymbol{\theta}|\mathbf{y})$. It is mathematically identical to the joint p.d.f. of the random sample but is a function of $\boldsymbol{\theta}$ instead of $\mathbf{y}$. Let $L(\boldsymbol{\theta})$ denote the logarithm of the likelihood function, then the matrix

$$I(\boldsymbol{\theta}) = -E\left[\frac{\partial^2 L}{\partial \boldsymbol{\theta}\, \partial \boldsymbol{\theta}'}\right]$$

$$= \begin{bmatrix} -E\left(\dfrac{\partial^2 L}{\partial \theta_1^2}\right) & -E\left(\dfrac{\partial^2 L}{\partial \theta_1\, \partial \theta_2}\right) & \cdots & -E\left(\dfrac{\partial^2 L}{\partial \theta_1\, \partial \theta_K}\right) \\ -E\left(\dfrac{\partial^2 L}{\partial \theta_2\, \partial \theta_1}\right) & -E\left(\dfrac{\partial^2 L}{\partial \theta_2^2}\right) & \cdots & -E\left(\dfrac{\partial^2 L}{\partial \theta_2\, \partial \theta_K}\right) \\ \vdots & \vdots & \ddots & \vdots \\ -E\left(\dfrac{\partial^2 L}{\partial \theta_K\, \partial \theta_1}\right) & -E\left(\dfrac{\partial^2 L}{\partial \theta_K\, \partial \theta_2}\right) & \cdots & -E\left(\dfrac{\partial^2 L}{\partial \theta_K^2}\right) \end{bmatrix} \tag{3.3.5}$$

is known as the *information matrix.* Note that although this matrix is written in terms of the log-likelihood function $L(\boldsymbol{\theta})$, the expectations in (3.3.5) are taken assuming the Y_i's are random. The inverse of the information matrix, $[I(\boldsymbol{\theta})]^{-1}$, is the *Cramér–Rao lower bound (CRLB) matrix.* If $\hat{\boldsymbol{\theta}}$ is an unbiased estimator of $\boldsymbol{\theta}$, then $\text{cov}(\hat{\boldsymbol{\theta}}) - \text{CRLB}$ is a positive semidefinite matrix, which is the matrix version of the *Cramér–Rao inequality.* This result is a very powerful one, for it says that if $\hat{\boldsymbol{\theta}}$ is an unbiased estimator with $\text{cov}(\hat{\boldsymbol{\theta}}) = \text{CRLB}$ then $\hat{\boldsymbol{\theta}}$ is *efficient.* Unfortunately, this condition is sufficient but not necessary for efficiency. Furthermore, to establish this result the p.d.f. of Y must be known.

As we noted in Section 3.3.1c, given the difficulty in establishing efficiency, attention is often focused on a narrower, more restricted problem. It is often easier to find an estimator that is efficient with respect to the class of *linear and unbiased* estimators. Furthermore, the search for the *best linear unbiased estimator* can be carried out without the knowledge of the distribution of Y. Although a specific example of best linear unbiased estimation will be deferred until Chapter 5, we will state the definition of such an estimator as follows. If $\boldsymbol{\theta}$ is a $(K \times 1)$ vector of parameters, then $\hat{\boldsymbol{\theta}}$ is a linear estimator of $\boldsymbol{\theta}$ if $\hat{\boldsymbol{\theta}} = A\mathbf{Y}$, where A is a $(K \times T)$ matrix of constants and $\mathbf{Y}$ is a $(T \times 1)$ vector of observations. The linear estimator $\hat{\boldsymbol{\theta}}$ is the best linear unbiased estimator of $\boldsymbol{\theta}$ if it is unbiased and $\text{cov}(\tilde{\boldsymbol{\theta}}) - \text{cov}(\hat{\boldsymbol{\theta}})$ is positive semidefinite, where $\tilde{\boldsymbol{\theta}}$ is any other linear and unbiased estimator of $\boldsymbol{\theta}$.

In addition to knowing that an estimator is unbiased or efficient or best linear unbiased, it is extremely desirable to know the *exact* p.d.f. of the estimator, or its *sampling distribution.* If the p.d.f. of the population is known, it is sometimes possible to determine this distribution for a sample of any size T. If the distribution of the population is not assumed, the distributions of estimators can be determined only with the additional assumption that the sample size is large, which is the subject of the next section. For now, we present a rather extended example in which the distributions of two important estimators are determined.

Example 3.10 Let $Y_1, \ldots, Y_T$ be a random sample from a $N(\beta, \sigma^2)$ population. In Example 3.4 we obtained the maximum likelihood estimators for β and σ^2, and now we investigate their bias, efficiency, and sampling distributions. As a first step, let us obtain the information matrix and the Cramér–Rao lower bound. The information matrix is

$$I(\boldsymbol{\theta}) = -E\begin{bmatrix} \dfrac{\partial^2 L}{\partial \beta^2} & \dfrac{\partial^2 L}{\partial \beta\, \partial \sigma^2} \\ \dfrac{\partial^2 L}{\partial \sigma^2\, \partial \beta} & \dfrac{\partial^2 L}{\partial (\sigma^2)^2} \end{bmatrix} = \begin{bmatrix} \dfrac{T}{\sigma^2} & 0 \\ 0 & \dfrac{T}{2\sigma^4} \end{bmatrix}$$

where we have used the facts that $E[Y_i] = \beta$ and

$$E\{Y_i - E[Y_i]\}^2 = E[Y_i - \beta]^2 = \sigma^2$$

Then

$$\text{CRLB} = [I(\boldsymbol{\theta})]^{-1} = \begin{bmatrix} \dfrac{\sigma^2}{T} & 0 \\ 0 & \dfrac{2\sigma^4}{T} \end{bmatrix}$$

The maximum likelihood estimator of the population mean β is $\tilde{\beta} = \sum_{i=1}^{T} Y_i/T$, which we have already seen is unbiased, has variance σ^2/T, and is, in fact, normally distributed itself. Since this unbiased estimator has variance that equals the CRLB for this parameter, we can assert that $\tilde{\beta}$ is the efficient estimator for β. Also, it is worth remembering that if the distribution of the population is not known the sample mean $\tilde{\beta}$ is still the best linear unbiased estimator of the population mean. Without knowing the distribution of the population, however, we cannot determine the small sample distribution of the sample mean and we cannot assert that it is efficient.

The maximum likelihood estimator of the variance σ^2 is $\tilde{\sigma}^2 = \sum_{i=1}^{T} (Y_i - \tilde{\beta})^2/T$. This estimator is biased, as we will show in the next paragraph, so it cannot be efficient. Instead, we will examine the properties of the estimator $\hat{\sigma}^2 = \sum_{i=1}^{T} (Y_i - \tilde{\beta})^2/(T-1)$, which we will show is an unbiased estimator for σ^2 and thus *may* be efficient. First, we will show that $\hat{\sigma}^2$ is unbiased, and thus that $\tilde{\sigma}^2$ is biased. Then we will determine the sampling distribution of $\hat{\sigma}^2$ and use the properties of that sampling distribution to determine the variance of $\hat{\sigma}^2$, which we can then compare to the CRLB. Sounds great, doesn't it? Let's go to it, and remember, econometrics is *fun*!

The properties of the estimator $\hat{\sigma}^2$ are obtained by using the result (2.5.18) in Chapter 2 about the distribution of quadratic forms in normal variables. Consider $\sum_{i=1}^{T} (Y_i - \tilde{\beta})^2$ and write it as $(\mathbf{Y} - \tilde{\beta}\mathbf{j}_T)'(\mathbf{Y} - \tilde{\beta}\mathbf{j}_T)$, where $\mathbf{Y}$ is a $(T \times 1)$ vector, $\tilde{\beta}$ is a scalar, and $\mathbf{j}_T$ is a $(T \times 1)$ vector all of whose elements are one. You should verify that if $M = I_T - \mathbf{j}_T\mathbf{j}_T'/T$, then $M\mathbf{Y} = \mathbf{Y} - \tilde{\beta}\mathbf{j}_T$, and M is both symmetric and idempotent, that is, $M = M'$ and $MM = M$. The values of $\mathbf{Y}$ can be expressed as $\mathbf{Y} = \mathbf{j}_T\beta + \mathbf{e}$, where $\mathbf{e} = (e_1, \ldots, e_T)'$ is a vector of independent $N(0, \sigma^2)$ random variables, so

$$M\mathbf{Y} = M\mathbf{j}_T\beta + M\mathbf{e} = M\mathbf{e}$$

since $M\mathbf{j}_T = 0$. Finally, then

$$\begin{aligned}\sum_{i=1}^{T} (Y_i - \tilde{\beta})^2 = \sum_{i=1}^{T} (Y_i - \bar{Y})^2 &= (\mathbf{Y} - \tilde{\beta}\mathbf{j}_T)'(\mathbf{Y} - \tilde{\beta}\mathbf{j}_T) \\ &= \mathbf{Y}'M'M\mathbf{Y} = \mathbf{e}'M'M\mathbf{e} \\ &= \mathbf{e}'MM\mathbf{e} = \mathbf{e}'M\mathbf{e}\end{aligned}$$

Since $\mathbf{e} \sim N(\mathbf{0}, \sigma^2 I_T)$, and $\text{tr}(M) = (T-1)$, it follows that $\mathbf{e}'M\mathbf{e}/\sigma^2 \sim \chi^2_{(T-1)}$. Consequently, recalling that the mean of a χ^2 random variable equals its degrees of freedom and its variance is twice its degrees of freedom, $(T-1)\hat{\sigma}^2/\sigma^2 \sim \chi^2_{(T-1)}$ and $\hat{\sigma}^2 \sim (\sigma^2/(T-1)) \cdot \chi^2_{(T-1)}$. So

$$E[\hat{\sigma}^2] = \frac{\sigma^2}{(T-1)} \cdot E[\chi^2_{(T-1)}] = \frac{\sigma^2}{(T-1)} \cdot (T-1) = \sigma^2$$

which shows that $\hat{\sigma}^2$ is unbiased and $\tilde{\sigma}^2$ is biased, and

$$\text{var}(\hat{\sigma}^2) = \left[\frac{\sigma^2}{(T-1)}\right]^2 \text{var}(\chi^2_{(T-1)}) = \frac{\sigma^4}{(T-1)^2} \cdot 2(T-1) = \frac{2\sigma^4}{(T-1)}$$

Note that $\text{var}(\hat{\sigma}^2)$ is greater than the CRLB for an unbiased estimator and thus the efficiency of $\hat{\sigma}^2$ cannot be established using the Cramér–Rao inequality. However, using an alternative approach, that of sufficient statistics, one can indeed show that $\hat{\sigma}^2$ is efficient. ■

Sufficiency is a property of an estimator indicating that it "uses" all the information in the statistical model. An important concept related to the information in a statistical model is that of a *sufficient statistic*. A statistic $\boldsymbol{\tau}(\mathbf{Y})$, which has dimension less than T, is said to be sufficient for $\boldsymbol{\theta}$ if it makes no difference whether we use $\mathbf{Y}$ or $\boldsymbol{\tau}(\mathbf{Y})$ in inferences concerning $\boldsymbol{\theta}$. Formally, $\boldsymbol{\tau}(\mathbf{Y})$ is a sufficient statistic for $\boldsymbol{\theta}$ if the conditional distribution $f(\mathbf{y}|\boldsymbol{\tau}(\mathbf{y}))$ does not depend, in any way, on $\boldsymbol{\theta}$.

Reconsider for a moment the problem of estimating the mean β of a normal population, when the variance is known, from a random sample of size T. Since $\tilde{\beta} = \sum Y_i/T$ is a "very good" estimator of β, it seems reasonable that $\tau(\mathbf{Y}) = \sum Y_i$ is a sufficient statistic for β. All we really need to know from the random sample is $\sum Y_i$, and not $\mathbf{Y}' = (Y_1, \ldots, Y_T)$, in order to make inferences about β. Unfortunately, showing that $\sum Y_i$ is a sufficient statistic using the foregoing definition is not necessarily easy.

An indirect way of showing that $\boldsymbol{\tau}(\mathbf{Y})$ is sufficient for $\boldsymbol{\theta}$ is to use the *factorization criterion*. The statistic $\boldsymbol{\tau}(\mathbf{Y})$ is sufficient for $\boldsymbol{\theta}$ if and only if the joint p.d.f. $f(\mathbf{y}|\boldsymbol{\theta})$ can be factored as

$$f(\mathbf{y}|\boldsymbol{\theta}) = g[\boldsymbol{\tau}(\mathbf{Y})|\boldsymbol{\theta}] \cdot h(\mathbf{y})$$

where $g(.)$ *and* $h(\cdot)$ are nonnegative functions, $g(.)$ depending on $\boldsymbol{\tau}(\mathbf{Y})$ and $\boldsymbol{\theta}$ and $h(\mathbf{y})$ being a function independent of $\boldsymbol{\theta}$. Although this result can be useful, one must know what $\boldsymbol{\tau}(\mathbf{Y})$ is in order to use it.

A sufficient statistic is said to be a *minimal sufficient statistic* if the sample $\mathbf{Y}$ cannot be reduced beyond $\boldsymbol{\tau}(\mathbf{Y})$ without losing sufficiency. Lehmann and Scheffe

(1950) suggest choosing an arbitrary value $\mathbf{y}_0$ in the sample space and forming the ratio

$$f(\mathbf{y}|\boldsymbol{\theta})/f(\mathbf{y}_0|\boldsymbol{\theta}) = g(\mathbf{y}, \mathbf{y}_0|\boldsymbol{\theta})$$

The values of $\mathbf{y}_0$ that make $g(\mathbf{y}, \mathbf{y}_0|\boldsymbol{\theta})$ independent of $\boldsymbol{\theta}$ are the required minimal sufficient statistics.

In the case of estimating the mean and variance of a normal population [Spanos (1986, p. 243)],

$$g(\mathbf{y}, \mathbf{y}_0|\boldsymbol{\theta}) = \exp\{-[\sum Y_i^2 - \sum Y_{io}^2]/2\sigma^2 + \beta[\sum Y_i - \sum Y_{io}]/\sigma^2\}$$

Which shows that $\boldsymbol{\tau}(\mathbf{Y}) = (\sum Y_i, \sum Y_i^2)'$ is a minimal sufficient statistic since for these values of $\mathbf{y}_0$, $g(\mathbf{y}, \mathbf{y}_0|\boldsymbol{\theta}) = 1$. Hence $(\hat{\beta}, \hat{\sigma}^2)$, being simple functions of $\boldsymbol{\tau}(\mathbf{Y})$, are sufficient statistics, too.

The final link in the chain we are building is provided by the Rao-Blackwell theorem. If $\mathbf{Y}$ is a random sample and $\boldsymbol{\tau}(\mathbf{Y})$ is a sufficient statistic for $\boldsymbol{\theta}$, let $\tilde{\boldsymbol{\theta}}$ be an unbiased estimator of $\boldsymbol{\theta}$ that is not a function of $\boldsymbol{\tau}(\mathbf{Y})$ alone. Then $E[\tilde{\boldsymbol{\theta}}|\boldsymbol{\tau}(\mathbf{y})] = \hat{\boldsymbol{\theta}}[\boldsymbol{\tau}(\mathbf{Y})]$ is an unbiased estimator of $\boldsymbol{\theta}$ and $\text{cov}(\tilde{\boldsymbol{\theta}}) - \text{cov}(\hat{\boldsymbol{\theta}})$ is positive semidefinite. This result says that in our search for the best unbiased estimator of $\boldsymbol{\theta}$ we may restrict ourselves to functions of the sufficient statistic. For if we begin with an unbiased estimator of $\boldsymbol{\theta}$ that is not a function of the sufficient statistic alone, then it can always be improved on. The estimators $\hat{\beta}$ and $\hat{\sigma}^2$ are unbiased sufficient statistics, and indeed there are no other unbiased estimators that are functions of the sufficient statistics alone. Thus $\hat{\beta}$ and $\hat{\sigma}^2$ as the unique sufficient unbiased estimators for β and σ^2 must necessarily be minimum variance. This last conclusion is reached by showing that the multivariate normal p.d.f. is a *complete* family. See Hogg and Craig (1978, pp. 353–360) and DeGroot (1975, pp. 298–317) for excellent discussions of these points.

3.3.3 Properties of Estimators: Large Sample Results

In the preceding section we discussed desirable small sample properties of estimators. Unfortunately, there are many situations when the small sample properties of estimators can not be determined exactly, and thus to compare estimators we must study their asymptotic properties, that is, their approximate behavior when the sample size T is large and approaches infinity. In this section we define the properties of consistency, convergence in distribution, and asymptotic efficiency.

3.3.3a Consistency

The property of *consistency* ensures that the estimation rule will produce an estimate that is *close* to the true parameter value with high probability if the sample size is large enough. More precisely, let $\hat{\theta}_T$ be an estimator of θ based on a sample of size T. Then $\hat{\theta}_T$ is a *consistent* estimator of θ if

$$\lim_{T \to \infty} P(|\hat{\theta}_T - \theta| < \epsilon) = 1 \tag{3.3.6}$$

where ϵ is an arbitrarily small positive number. This means that the probability that the value of $\hat{\theta}_T$ falls in the interval $[\theta - \epsilon, \theta + \epsilon]$ can be made arbitrarily close to 1 given a large enough sample size, *no matter how small* ϵ *is*. If (3.3.6) is true, then the sequence of random variables $\hat{\theta}_T$ is said to *converge in probability* to the constant θ; and θ is said to be the *probability limit* of the sequence $\hat{\theta}_T$. This is usually abbreviated as

$$\text{plim } \hat{\theta}_T = \theta$$

Thus the estimator $\hat{\theta}_T$ is consistent for θ if (3.3.6) is true or, equivalently, when plim $\hat{\theta}_T = \theta$.

To see the meaning of (3.3.6), let $Y_1, \ldots, Y_T$ be a random sample from a $N(\beta, \sigma^2)$ population, and consider the estimator of β, $\hat{\beta}_T = \sum_{i=1}^{T} Y_i/T$, which is the sample mean. We know that $\hat{\beta}_T \sim N(\beta, \sigma^2/T)$. If we consider three sample sizes, $T_3 > T_2 > T_1$, the sampling distributions of $\hat{\beta}_T$ might appear as in Figure 3.8. We see that the probability mass in the interval $[\beta - \epsilon, \beta + \epsilon]$ is getting large as the sample size increases from T_1 to T_2 to T_3, and the sampling distribution of $\hat{\beta}_T$ is collapsing about the true parameter β. In fact, since $\lim_{T\to\infty} \text{var}(\hat{\beta}_T) = \lim_{T\to\infty} \sigma^2/T = 0$, the sampling distribution of $\hat{\beta}_T$ becomes degenerate at the true parameter value in the limit, so that all its probability mass occurs at β.

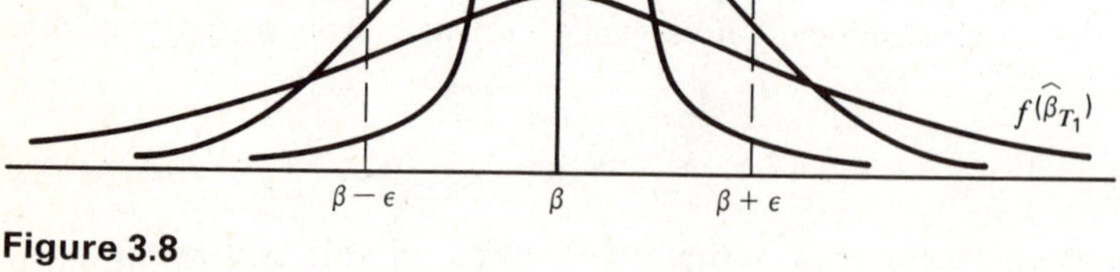

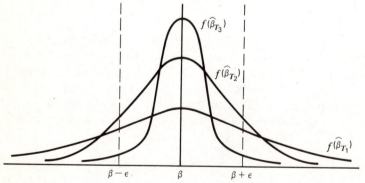

Figure 3.8

Given the foregoing discussion, it should be intuitively reasonable that sufficient, but not necessary, conditions for an estimator $\hat{\theta}_T$ to be consistent for θ are

$$\lim_{T\to\infty} E[\hat{\theta}_T] = \theta \tag{3.3.7a}$$

$$\lim_{T\to\infty} \mathrm{var}(\hat{\theta}_T) = 0 \tag{3.3.7b}$$

If both the conditions in (3.3.7) are satisfied, then the sampling distribution of $\hat{\theta}_T$ will "collapse" on the true parameter value as depicted in Figure 3.8. Since these conditions are sufficient but not necessary, however, it is possible for an estimator to be consistent without the conditions in (3.3.7) holding. Such a case occurs, for example, when the estimator $\hat{\theta}_T$ does not have a mean or variance. By not having a mean or variance, we mean that the integrals like (2.4.2) are infinite. In such cases, it is still possible for the distribution of $\hat{\theta}_T$ to collapse to a single point as $T \to \infty$.

An estimator that satisfies (3.3.7a) is said to be *asymptotically unbiased*. Thus an estimator is consistent if any bias it has goes to zero as the sample size grows and if its variance goes to zero as $T \to \infty$. An example of an estimator that is biased and yet consistent is the following.

Example 3.11 Let $Y_1, \ldots, Y_T$ be a random sample from a $N(\beta, \sigma^2)$ population. Then the maximum likelihood estimator of the population variance σ^2 is $\tilde{\sigma}^2 = \sum (Y_i - \tilde{\beta})^2/T$, where $\tilde{\beta}$ is the sample mean. Although $\tilde{\sigma}^2$ is biased, it is a consistent estimator. To see this result, note that $T\tilde{\sigma}^2/\sigma^2 \sim \chi^2_{(T-1)}$, so $\tilde{\sigma}^2 \sim \sigma^2/T \cdot \chi^2_{(T-1)}$. Therefore $E(\tilde{\sigma}^2) = \sigma^2(T-1)/T$ and $\mathrm{var}(\tilde{\sigma}^2) = 2\sigma^4(T-1)/T^2$. Thus although $\tilde{\sigma}^2$ is biased, it is true that $\lim_{T\to\infty} E[\tilde{\sigma}^2] = \sigma^2$ and $\lim_{T\to\infty} \mathrm{var}[\tilde{\sigma}^2] = 0$, so $\tilde{\sigma}^2$ is consistent. ■

A powerful result involving consistent estimators is *Slutsky's theorem* which says that if $\mathrm{plim}\, \hat{\theta}_T = \theta$ and $g(\hat{\theta}_T)$ is a continuous function of $\hat{\theta}_T$, then $\mathrm{plim}\, g(\hat{\theta}_T) = g(\mathrm{plim}\, \hat{\theta}_T) = g(\theta)$. That is, the probability limit of a continuous function is the function evaluated at the probability limit. This means, for example, that $\tilde{\sigma} = (\tilde{\sigma}^2)^{1/2}$ is a consistent estimator for σ since

$$\mathrm{plim}(\tilde{\sigma}) = \mathrm{plim}(\tilde{\sigma}^2)^{1/2} = (\mathrm{plim}\, \tilde{\sigma}^2)^{1/2} = (\sigma^2)^{1/2} = \sigma$$

Note that a similar result is not true for mathematical expectation. We will employ Slutsky's theorem many times in this book to examine the consistency of estimators.

Before we discuss the next asymptotic property, we simply note that the consistency results just stated in terms of a single parameter carry over to the multiparameter case by appropriately substituting the mean vector for the mean and the covariance matrix for the variance.

3.3.3b Convergence in Distribution

The next asymptotic property we wish to consider is *convergence in distribution.* The idea here is to study the probability distribution of an estimator as the sample size becomes increasingly large. It is remarkable that estimators whose distributions are unknown in small samples can sometimes be shown to have a particular, known distribution in large samples. A well-known example of this is the *central limit theorem*: Let $Y_1, \ldots, Y_T$ be independently and identically distributed random variables with $E[Y_i] = \beta$ and $\text{var}(Y_i) = \sigma^2$; also let $\hat{\beta}_T = \sum_{i=1}^{T} Y_i/T$. Then, $\sqrt{T}(\hat{\beta}_T - \beta)$ converges in distribution to a $N(0, \sigma^2)$ random variable. This result is often written as

$$\sqrt{T}(\hat{\beta}_T - \beta) \xrightarrow{d} N(0, \sigma^2)$$

This remarkable result says that given a random sample of observations from an infinite population with *any* distribution, as long as it has a finite mean and finite variance, then a simple function of the sample mean $\sqrt{T}(\hat{\beta}_T - \beta)$, has a limiting distribution that is normal, in fact $N(0, \sigma^2)$.

A few comments are in order here. The usefulness of this result, and results like it, is that there will be many practical situations when we want to make probability statements about an estimator when the exact small sample distribution of the estimator cannot be determined. *If* a limiting distribution exists, then we can use that limiting distribution as an approximation to the true but unknown distribution *if the sample we have at our disposal is sufficiently large* for us to believe the approximation will be a reasonable one. Thus in the situation described by the central limit theorem, the exact p.d.f. of $\hat{\beta}_T$ is unknown, but if the sample size is large, we might take $\sqrt{T}(\hat{\beta}_T - \beta)$ to be approximately normally distributed with mean 0 and variance σ^2. And if $\sqrt{T}(\hat{\beta}_T - \beta) \mathrel{\dot\sim} N(0, \sigma^2)$ then $\hat{\beta}_T \mathrel{\dot\sim} N(\beta, \sigma^2/T)$, where "$\dot\sim$" implies "approximately distributed." To remind us that this is an asymptotic or large sample approximation, the result is often written as $\hat{\beta}_T \overset{\text{asy}}{\sim} N(\beta, \sigma^2/T)$ and $N(\beta, \sigma^2/T)$ is called the *asymptotic distribution* of $\hat{\beta}_T$.

You may be wondering why the central limit theorem is stated in terms of $\sqrt{T}(\hat{\beta}_T - \beta)$. The reason is that it is awkward to talk about the distribution of $\hat{\beta}_T$ as $T \rightarrow \infty$. In particular, we know that under the conditions of the central limit theorem $\hat{\beta}_T \sim (\beta, \sigma^2/T)$ for any sample of size T. Consequently, as $T \rightarrow \infty$, $\text{var}(\hat{\beta}_T) \rightarrow 0$, and the distribution of $\hat{\beta}_T$ becomes degenerate, a decidedly nonnormal distribution! However, it can be shown that the sequence of random variables $\sqrt{T}(\hat{\beta}_T - \beta)$, as $T \rightarrow \infty$, has a sequence of c.d.f.'s F_T that converge, pointwise, to the c.d.f. F of a $N(0, \sigma^2)$ random variable. That is, $\lim_{T \rightarrow \infty} F_T = F$ at all continuity points of F. This is in fact a definition of the *convergence in distribution* of the sequence of random variables $z_T = \sqrt{T}(\hat{\beta}_T - \beta)$, and z_T is said to have the *limiting distribution F*.

A similar notation and terminology will be used for vectors of estimators. If $\hat{\boldsymbol{\theta}}_T$ is a consistent estimator for $\boldsymbol{\theta}$ and $\sqrt{T}(\hat{\boldsymbol{\theta}}_T - \boldsymbol{\theta})$ converges in distribution to $N(\mathbf{0}, \Sigma)$, then $\hat{\boldsymbol{\theta}}_T$ is said to have the asymptotic distribution $N(\boldsymbol{\theta}, (1/T)\Sigma)$ or $\hat{\boldsymbol{\theta}}_T \overset{\text{asy}}{\sim} N(\boldsymbol{\theta}, \Sigma/T)$.

3.3.3c Asymptotic Efficiency

Finally, we define the concept of *asymptotic efficiency*. Suppose we have two estimators $\hat{\theta}$ and $\tilde{\theta}$ of a parameter θ such that $\sqrt{T}(\hat{\theta} - \theta) \xrightarrow{d} N(0, \sigma_1^2)$ and $\sqrt{T}(\tilde{\theta} - \theta) \xrightarrow{d} N(0, \sigma_2^2)$. If $\sigma_2^2 \geq \sigma_1^2$, then $\hat{\theta}$ is asymptotically efficient *relative to* $\tilde{\theta}$. If $\boldsymbol{\theta}$ is a vector of parameters and $\hat{\boldsymbol{\theta}}$ and $\tilde{\boldsymbol{\theta}}$ are consistent estimators such that $\sqrt{T}(\hat{\boldsymbol{\theta}} - \boldsymbol{\theta}) \xrightarrow{d} N(\mathbf{0}, \Sigma)$ and $\sqrt{T}(\tilde{\boldsymbol{\theta}} - \boldsymbol{\theta}) \xrightarrow{d} N(\mathbf{0}, \Omega)$, then $\hat{\boldsymbol{\theta}}$ is asymptotically efficient *relative to* $\tilde{\boldsymbol{\theta}}$ if $\Omega - \Sigma$ is positive semidefinite.

As in the case with finite sampling efficiency, showing that an estimator is asymptotically efficient relative to any other consistent estimator requires knowledge of the parent distribution, so that the information matrix and the *asymptotic Cramér–Rao lower bound* can be established. Let $\hat{\boldsymbol{\theta}}$ be a consistent estimator of $\boldsymbol{\theta}$ such that $\sqrt{T}(\hat{\boldsymbol{\theta}} - \boldsymbol{\theta}) \xrightarrow{d} N(\mathbf{0}, \Sigma)$. Then the estimator $\hat{\boldsymbol{\theta}}$ is *asymptotically efficient* if

$$\Sigma = \lim_{T \to \infty} \left[\frac{1}{T} I(\boldsymbol{\theta}) \right]^{-1}$$

where $I(\boldsymbol{\theta})$ is the information matrix defined in (3.3.5). Thus both small sample and asymptotic efficiency are established using the Cramér–Rao inequality as a reference point.

We can now state a property of the method of maximum likelihood that is perhaps more important than its intuitive appeal. *Under some fairly general conditions maximum likelihood estimators are consistent, asymptotically normal, asymptotically unbiased, and asymptotically efficient.* That is, if $\hat{\boldsymbol{\theta}}$ is the maximum likelihood estimator of the vector of parameters $\boldsymbol{\theta}$, then

$$\sqrt{T}(\hat{\boldsymbol{\theta}} - \boldsymbol{\theta}) \xrightarrow{d} N\left(\mathbf{0}, \lim_{T \to \infty} \left[\frac{1}{T} I(\boldsymbol{\theta}) \right]^{-1} \right)$$

Consequently, in a problem like Example 3.3 (continued in Example 3.7), where we obtained the maximum likelihood estimator of the parameter p of a Bernoulli population, even though we do not know the small sample distribution of the estimator, we can rely on the fact that it is asymptotically normal to test hypotheses or make confidence interval statements.

Example 3.10 (continued) To illustrate the concept of asymptotic efficiency, let $Y_1, \ldots, Y_T$ be a random sample from a $N(\beta, \sigma^2)$ population. Then the estimator

$$\hat{\beta}_T = \sum_{i=1}^{T} Y_i/T \sim N(\beta, \sigma^2/T)$$

and clearly $\sqrt{T}(\hat{\beta}_T - \beta) \xrightarrow{d} N(0, \sigma^2)$. The estimator

$$\hat{\sigma}^2 = \sum_{i=1}^{T} (Y_i - \hat{\beta}_T)^2/(T-1) \sim \frac{\sigma^2}{T-1} \cdot \chi^2_{(T-1)}$$

has $E[\sigma^2] = \sigma^2$ and $\text{var}(\hat{\sigma}^2) = 2\sigma^4/(T-1)$. Therefore,

$$\begin{aligned}\sqrt{T}(\hat{\sigma}^2 - \sigma^2) &= \sqrt{T}\left[\frac{\sigma^2}{(T-1)} \cdot \chi^2_{(T-1)} - \frac{(T-1)\sigma^2}{T-1}\right] \\ &= \frac{\sqrt{T}(\sigma^2)}{T-1}[\chi^2_{(T-1)} - (T-1)]\end{aligned}$$

has mean 0 and variance

$$\frac{T}{(T-1)^2} \cdot \sigma^4 \cdot 2(T-1) = \frac{T}{T-1} 2\sigma^4$$

Furthermore, it can be shown that $\sqrt{T}(\hat{\sigma}^2 - \sigma^2) \xrightarrow{d} N(0, 2\sigma^4)$ since a $\chi^2_{(T)}$ distribution has an asymptotic distribution that is $N(T, 2T)$. Thus both $\hat{\beta}_T$ and $\hat{\sigma}^2$ are consistent and asymptotically normal estimators. The information matrix for $\boldsymbol{\theta}' = (\beta, \sigma^2)$ is derived in Example 3.10 and is

$$I(\boldsymbol{\theta}) = \begin{bmatrix} T/\sigma^2 & 0 \\ 0 & T/2\sigma^4 \end{bmatrix}$$

Thus the asymptotic CRLB for consistent and asymptotically normal estimators of β and σ^2 is

$$\lim_{T=\infty} [I(\boldsymbol{\theta})/T]^{-1} = \begin{bmatrix} \sigma^2 & 0 \\ 0 & 2\sigma^4 \end{bmatrix}$$

Thus both $\hat{\beta}_T$ and $\hat{\sigma}^2$ are asymptotically efficient, since the variances of their limiting distributions are σ^2 and $2\sigma^4$, respectively, the asymptotic Cramér–Rao lower bounds. Using these results, you might show that $\tilde{\sigma}^2 = \sum (Y_i - \hat{\beta}_T)^2/T$ is also asymptotically efficient, thus illustrating that asymptotically efficient estimators are not unique. ■

3.4 Interval Estimation

In problems where point estimates are required, investigators are, of course, concerned about the "reliability" of the estimate. For those trained in statistics, knowledge of the variance of the estimator (or an estimate of it) plus knowledge of the finite or asymptotic sampling distribution conveys that information. It is sometimes useful, however, when reporting results to give a range of possible values that incorporates both a point estimate and a measure of precision. An *interval estimate* does just that. Interval estimates are usually based on the sampling distribution of an estimator, although Chebyshev's inequality could also be used. We will illustrate using three common examples.

Example 3.12 Let $Y_1, \ldots, Y_T$ be a random sample from a $N(\beta, \sigma^2)$ population where σ^2 is known. Then the maximum likelihood estimator of β is $\hat{\beta} = \sum_{i=1}^{T} Y_i/T \sim N(\beta, \sigma^2/T)$. We can use the sampling distribution of $\hat{\beta}$ to make probability statements. Since

$$z = (\hat{\beta} - \beta)/(\sigma/\sqrt{T}) \sim N(0, 1)$$

it follows that

$$P[-z_{(\alpha/2)} \le z \le z_{(\alpha/2)}] = 1 - \alpha$$

where $z_{(\alpha/2)}$ is the upper-$\alpha/2$ percentile of the $N(0, 1)$ distribution, as illustrated in Figure 3.9. These values are tabulated at the back of the book in Table 1. Substituting for z and rearranging

$$P[-z_{(\alpha/2)} \le z \le z_{(\alpha/2)}] = 1 - \alpha$$

$$P\left[-z_{(\alpha/2)} \le \frac{\hat{\beta} - \beta}{\sigma/\sqrt{T}} \le z_{(\alpha/2)}\right] = 1 - \alpha$$

$$P[\hat{\beta} - z_{(\alpha/2)}(\sigma/\sqrt{T}) \le \beta \le \hat{\beta} + z_{(\alpha/2)}(\sigma/\sqrt{T})] = 1 - \alpha \quad (3.4.1)$$

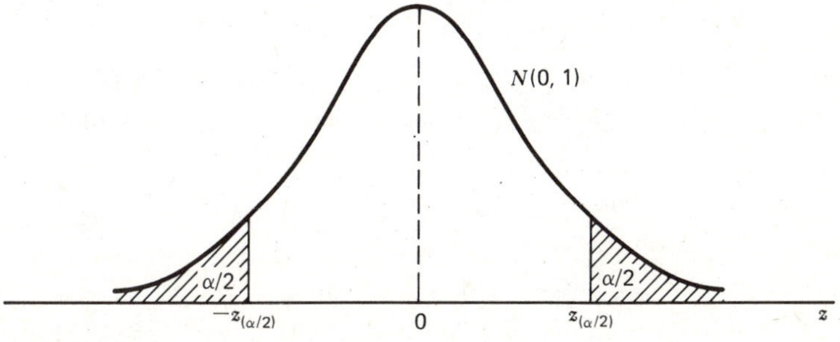

Figure 3.9

The end points of the interval containing β in (3.4.1) are random since $\hat{\beta}$ is random. The random interval $[\hat{\beta} - z_{(\alpha/2)}(\sigma/\sqrt{T}), \hat{\beta} + z_{(\alpha/2)}(\sigma/\sqrt{T})]$ is an *interval estimator of* β and contains the unknown parameter β with probability $1 - \alpha$, which is known as the confidence coefficient for the interval estimator. An *interval estimate* is obtained when the estimator $\hat{\beta}$ is replaced by an estimate based on a particular sample of values. Referring back to Example 3.1, an interval estimate of the *mean* consumption level with confidence coefficient $1 - \alpha = 0.95$ is

$$\$13{,}000 \pm (1.96)(5000/\sqrt{3})$$

or

$$[\$7341.97, \$18{,}658.03]$$

Given the estimation rule, sample size, and prior information about the population, this interval incorporates both our point estimate and the reliability or precision of the estimation rule used. It is *not* true that the interval estimate contains the true parameter with probability 0.95. Such probability statements are correct, from the sampling viewpoint, when in reference to the random interval *estimator* (3.4.1). Instead, we can state that [\$7341.97, \$18,658.03] is a 95% *confidence interval* for β, which means it is one realization of the interval estimator (3.4.1) based on a particular sample. ■

Example 3.13 Let $Y_1, \ldots, Y_T$ be a random sample from a $N(\beta, \sigma^2)$ population. Then we know that

$$\hat{\beta} = \sum Y_i/T = \bar{Y} \sim N(\beta, \sigma^2/T)$$

and

$$\frac{(T-1)\hat{\sigma}^2}{\sigma^2} \sim \chi^2_{(T-1)}$$

where $\hat{\sigma}^2 = \sum (Y_i - \hat{\beta})^2/(T-1)$. From Example 3.10 we also know that $(T-1)\hat{\sigma}^2 = \mathbf{e}'M\mathbf{e}$ where $\mathbf{e} \sim N(\mathbf{0}, \sigma^2 I_T)$ and $M = I_T - \mathbf{j}_T\mathbf{j}_T'/T$ is symmetric and idempotent. Furthermore,

$$\begin{aligned}\hat{\beta} &= \sum Y_i/T \\ &= \sum (\beta + e_i)/T \\ &= \beta + \frac{1}{T}\mathbf{j}_T'\,\mathbf{e}\end{aligned}$$

Consequently, $\hat{\beta}$ and $\hat{\sigma}^2$ are statistically independent since $\mathbf{e}'M\mathbf{e}$ and $\mathbf{j}'_T\mathbf{e}$ are quadratic and linear forms, respectively, in $N(\mathbf{0}, \sigma^2 I)$ random variables such that $\mathbf{j}'_T M = \mathbf{0}$ (see Section 2.5.8). Therefore

$$z = (\hat{\beta} - \beta)/(\sigma/\sqrt{T}) \sim N(0, 1)$$

and

$$(T - 1)\hat{\sigma}^2/\sigma^2 \sim \chi^2_{(T-1)}$$

and the two random variables are independent of one another. Thus, the ratio

$$t = \frac{\dfrac{\hat{\beta} - \beta}{\sigma/\sqrt{T}}}{\left\{\left[\dfrac{(T - 1)\hat{\sigma}^2}{\sigma^2}\right]/(T - 1)\right\}^{1/2}} = \frac{\hat{\beta} - \beta}{\hat{\sigma}/\sqrt{T}} \tag{3.4.2}$$

has a t-distribution with $(T - 1)$ degrees of freedom. This result can be used as a basis for constructing an *interval estimator* for β from a $N(\beta, \sigma^2)$ population when both β and σ^2 are unknown. Specifically, if $t_{(T-1,\alpha/2)}$ is the upper-$\alpha/2$ percentile of a t-distribution with $(T - 1)$ degrees of freedom then

$$P[-t_{(T-1,\alpha/2)} \leq t \leq t_{(T-1,\alpha/2)}] = 1 - \alpha$$

and

$$P[\hat{\beta} - t_{(T-1,\alpha/2)}(\hat{\sigma}/\sqrt{T}) \leq \beta \leq \hat{\beta} + t_{(T-1,\alpha/2)}(\hat{\sigma}/\sqrt{T})] = 1 - \alpha$$

Thus the random interval

$$\hat{\beta} \pm t_{(T-1,\alpha/2)}(\hat{\sigma}/\sqrt{T})$$

contains the unknown parameter β with probability $(1 - \alpha)$. Note that these intervals will have centers and widths that vary from sample to sample, unlike the situation in Example 3.12 where only the center of the random interval changed from sample to sample. ■

Example 3.14 If $Y_1, \ldots, Y_T$ is a random sample from a $N(\beta, \sigma^2)$ population, then an interval estimator for σ^2 can be constructed using the distributional result that $(T - 1)\hat{\sigma}^2/\sigma^2 \sim \chi^2_{(T-1)}$. Let $\chi^2_{(k,C_1)}$ be such that

$$P[\chi^2_{(k)} \leq \chi^2_{(k,C_1)}] = \alpha/2$$

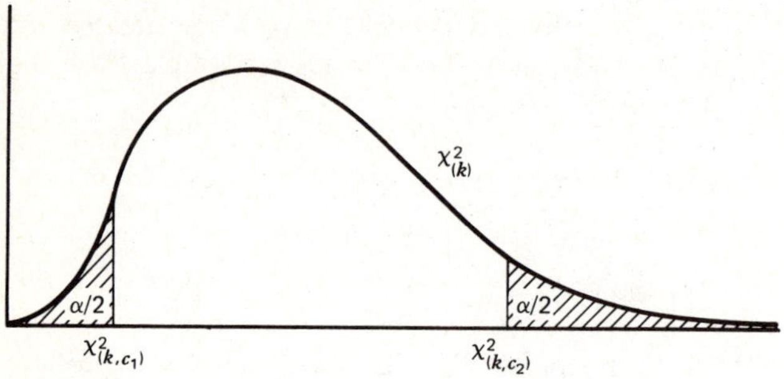

Figure 3.10

and let $\chi^2_{(k,C_2)}$ be such that

$$P[\chi^2_{(k)} \geq \chi^2_{(k,C_2)}] = \alpha/2$$

as illustrated in Figure 3.10.

Then

$$P[\chi^2_{(T-1,C_1)} \leq \chi^2_{(T-1)} \leq \chi^2_{(T-1,C_2)}] = 1 - \alpha$$

and therefore

$$P\left[\chi^2_{(T-1,C_1)} \leq \frac{(T-1)\hat{\sigma}^2}{\sigma^2} \leq \chi^2_{(T-1,C_2)}\right] = 1 - \alpha$$

or

$$P\left[\frac{(T-1)\hat{\sigma}^2}{\chi^2_{(T-1,C_2)}} \leq \sigma^2 \leq \frac{(T-1)\hat{\sigma}^2}{\chi^2_{(T-1,C_1)}}\right] = 1 - \alpha \tag{3.4.3}$$

which provides a basis for making confidence interval statements about σ^2. ■

The foregoing examples present the sampling theory approach to the construction and interpretation of confidence intervals. In the Bayesian approach, both the method of construction and interpretation are somewhat different. This approach will be considered in Chapter 4.

3.5 Hypothesis Testing

In this section we survey important ideas related to the second branch of statistical inference, that of hypothesis testing. We begin by looking at various properties of statistical tests and then at procedures or principles by which test statistics can be obtained. These include the likelihood ratio principle, the Wald test, and the

Lagrange multiplier test. Bayesian testing procedures will be considered in Chapters 4 and 7.

3.5.1 The Elements of a Statistical Test

A statistical test is a decision problem involving an unknown parameter θ that must lie in a certain parameter space Ω. However, Ω can be divided into two disjoint subsets Ω_0 and Ω_1, and we must decide, perhaps using a sample of data, whether θ lies in Ω_0 or Ω_1. Let H_0 denote the null hypothesis that $\theta \in \Omega_0$, and let H_1 denote the alternative hypothesis that $\theta \in \Omega_1$. Since Ω_0 and Ω_1 are disjoint, only one of the hypotheses H_0 and H_1 is true, and by accepting one we are at the same time rejecting the other. Testing a hypothesis then involves accepting either H_0 or H_1 in light of the costs of making an incorrect decision and using whatever data are available as efficiently as possible.

Suppose we observe a random sample of data $\mathbf{Y} = (Y_1, \ldots, Y_T)'$ that has joint p.d.f. $f(\mathbf{y}|\boldsymbol{\theta})$. The set of all possible values of $\mathbf{Y}$ is the sample space of the experiment. A *test procedure* is defined by dividing the sample space into *two* parts, one containing the subset of values of $\mathbf{Y}$ that will lead to H_0 being accepted, and the other being the subset of values of $\mathbf{Y}$ where H_1 will be accepted (and H_0 rejected). The latter subset, where H_0 will be rejected, is called the *critical region* or the *rejection region* of the test.

In practice, a test is carried out using a *test statistic* rather than by considering the T-dimensional sample space of $\mathbf{Y}$. A test statistic is one that has a *known distribution* under the null hypothesis (i.e., assuming H_0 is true) and has some other distribution when H_1 is true. Thus the critical region of a hypothesis test is that set of values of the test statistic for which the null hypothesis will be rejected. Thus the basic elements of every statistical test are: A null hypothesis (H_0) that will be maintained until evidence to the contrary is shown, an alternative hypothesis (H_1) that will be adopted if the null hypothesis is rejected, a test statistic, and a region of rejection or critical region.

Example 3.15 We wish to test a simple null hypothesis about the unknown mean β of a normal population with variance that is known to be $\sigma^2 = 10$. Specifically, let the hypotheses be

$$H_0: \beta = 1$$

$$H_1: \beta \neq 1$$

Given a random sample of size $T = 10$, $Y_1, \ldots, Y_{10}$, we know that

$$\hat{\beta} = \sum_{i=1}^{T} Y_i/T \sim N(\beta, \sigma^2/T) = N(\beta, 1)$$

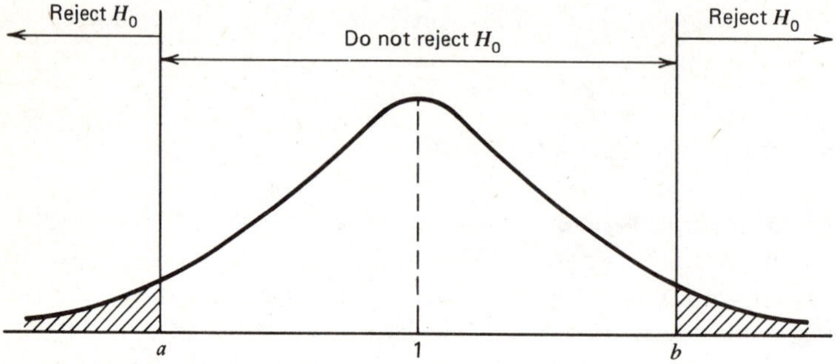

Figure 3.11 Distribution of $\hat{\beta}$ under the null hypothesis.

Under a null hypothesis (i.e., assuming that it is true) $\hat{\beta} \sim N(1, 1)$ is depicted as in Figure 3.11.

To define a critical region, we choose values of $\hat{\beta}$ that will lead us to reject H_0, and accept H_1. An intuitive rule is to select the rejection region to be values of $\hat{\beta}$ that are *unlikely* to occur *if the null hypothesis is true.* Then, if one of the unlikely values does occur, that provides evidence *against* the null hypothesis and would lead us to reject it. In Figure 3.11 if we choose a and b so that

$$P[\hat{\beta} \leq a] = P[\hat{\beta} \geq b] = \alpha/2$$

we can define an unbiased (since equal amounts of probability are in the two tails) test with size α (which represents the probability of rejecting H_0 when it is true) as follows

$$\text{Reject } H_0 \text{ if } \hat{\beta} \leq a \quad \text{or} \quad \hat{\beta} \geq b$$

$$\text{Accept } H_0 \text{ (at least do not reject it) if } a < \hat{\beta} < b$$

For the problem at hand, the test is usually carried out using the test statistic $z = (\hat{\beta} - 1)/(\sigma/\sqrt{T})$, *which has a* $N(0, 1)$ *distribution if* H_0 *is true.* If H_0 is not true, say $\beta = \beta_0 \neq 1$, then $z \sim N(\beta_0 - 1, 1)$. The rejection region for the test is $z \geq z_{(\alpha/2)}$ or $z \leq -z_{(\alpha/2)}$ (or $|z| \geq z_{(\alpha/2)}$), as shown in Figure 3.12. If $\alpha = 0.05$, then $z_{(\alpha/2)} = 1.96$ using Table 1 at the back of the book. In Figure 3.11, this corresponds to values of $a = -0.96$ and $b = 2.96$.

In terms of the test statistic z, the reasoning of the statistical test is as follows. If a sample value of $\hat{\beta}$ is obtained that leads to a calculated value of $|z| \geq z_{(\alpha/2)}$, then we reject H_0 since

(*i*) If the hypothesis is true, the chances of obtaining a value of z in the rejection region are "only" α.

(*ii*) This is an unlikely event, so we conclude that the test statistic is unlikely to have a $N(0, 1)$ distribution.

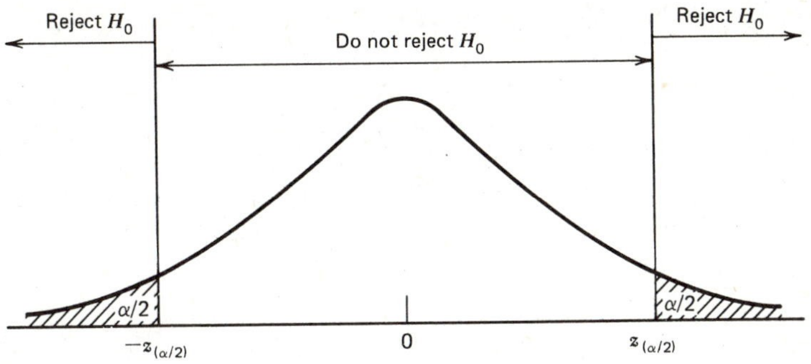

Figure 3.12 Rejection region.

(*iii*) *If* the null hypothesis is true, the test statistic z *does* have a $N(0, 1)$ distribution.

We conclude that the hypothesis is unlikely to be true since the sample evidence does not support it. ■

The problem of how to obtain a suitable test statistic and defining critical region will be considered in Section 3.5.3. A word about formulation of null and alternative hypotheses is in order first. The null hypothesis is usually stated to be the intellectual position that will be maintained unless convincing evidence to the contrary is provided, in which case the alternative is accepted. As an example, in an American court of law an accused person is "innocent until proven guilty." The null hypothesis is that the person is innocent, and the alternative is that the person is guilty. Null hypotheses in economic applications usually take the form of asserting that some parameter, linear combination of parameters, or set of linear combinations of parameters take specified values. The alternative is simply that they do not. That is, if $\boldsymbol{\theta} = (\theta_1, \ldots, \theta_K)'$ is a set of parameters, then the following pairs of null and alternative hypotheses are frequently seen:

(*i*) $H_0: \theta_i = 0$
$H_1: \theta_i \neq 0$

(*ii*) $H_0: \theta_i + \theta_j = 1$
$H_1: \theta_i + \theta_j \neq 1$

(*iii*) $H_0: \theta_1 = 0$ and $\theta_2 = 0$ and $\cdots \theta_K = 0$
H_1: at least one of the equalities in H_0 is false

In case (i) and case (ii), the null hypothesis represents *one* condition on the parameter vector $\boldsymbol{\theta}$ and thus constitutes a single hypothesis. Also, the single hypothesis is said to be a *simple hypothesis* since it specifies a single value for the parameter and linear combination of parameters. The alternative hypothesis in cases (i) and (ii) is simply the negation of H_0 and a specific value is not given. Such a hypothesis is said to be *composite* as it represents more than one specific value for the parameter or linear combination of parameters. In case (iii) the null hypothesis is *joint* since values are specified for several parameters and the question is do all these hypotheses hold simultaneously? The alternative in this case is that any one of the individual hypotheses is false. In addition to these cases, inequality hypotheses are often stated, such as

(*iv*) $H_0: \theta_i \geq 0$
$H_1: \theta_i < 0$

In this case, both the null and alternative hypotheses are composite.

3.5.2 The Power of a Test

Since a hypothesis test involves making a choice, there is a chance that the decision made is an incorrect one. Suppose $H_0: \theta \in \Omega_0$ and $H_1: \theta \in \Omega_1$. Once a test statistic and critical region have been defined, then the probability of rejecting H_0 can be determined for every $\theta \in \Omega$. Let $\Pi(\theta) = P$ [rejecting $H_0|\theta$] where H_0 is rejected when the test statistic falls in the critical region. Then $\Pi(\theta)$ is called the *power function* of the test. Ideally $\Pi(\theta) = 0$ for every value of $\theta \in \Omega_0$ and $\Pi(\theta) = 1$ for every $\theta \in \Omega_1$. This would imply that the test procedure *always* leads to the correct decision. Unfortunately, such perfect tests do not usually exist. Consequently, there is usually a nonzero probability of rejecting H_0 even when it is true (called a Type I error). When testing hypotheses, it is customary to only consider test procedures such that this probability is bounded by a constant α called the *size of the test* or *level of significance* of the test. That is, the size of the test α is the largest value of $\Pi(\theta)$ for any value of θ that makes H_0 true, that is $\theta \in \Omega_0$. Therefore,

$$P[\text{Type I error}] = P[\text{rejecting } H_0|H_0 \text{ true}] \leq \alpha$$

Note that if H_0 is "simple" as in cases (i) to (iii), then only the equality holds.

The second possible error (called Type II error) when testing a hypothesis is to accept a false hypothesis. The probability of a Type II error (often denoted β, not to be confused with a parameter β) is

$$\begin{aligned} \beta &= P[\text{Type II error}] = P[\text{accepting } H_0|H_1 \text{ true}] \\ &= 1 - \Pi(\theta) \qquad \text{for} \quad \theta \in \Omega_1 \end{aligned}$$

It is unfortunately true that no test procedures exist, for a given sample size, that allow *both* Type I and Type II errors to be made arbitrarily small. It is generally true that reducing the size of the test α increases the probability of a Type II error and vice versa. The magnitude of the Type I error is conventionally fixed and usually at a small value, the reason being that it is the probability of rejecting the null hypothesis incorrectly, and that is the error we want to avoid the most. That is, we do not want to reject the null hypothesis, as in the courtroom example, unless convincing evidence to the contrary has been provided. To illustrate these points we continue Example 3.15.

Example 3.15 (continued) When H_0 is true, the power of the test is less than or equal to the size of the test α. In this example, the power of the test equals 0.05 when $\beta = 1$ and the hypothesis is true. To investigate the power when $\beta \neq 1$, we will begin by assuming that, in fact, $\beta = 2$. Then the true distribution of $\hat{\beta}$ is $\hat{\beta} \sim N(2, 1)$ and the true distribution of the test statistic z is $N(1, 1)$.

In Figure 3.13 we compare the true distribution of $\hat{\beta}[N(2, 1)]$ with the distribution under $H_0[N(1, 1)]$. Having defined the critical region of the test, we can compute the power of the test when $\beta = 2$ as

$$\begin{aligned}
\Pi(2) &= P[\hat{\beta} \leq -0.96 \quad \text{or} \quad \hat{\beta} \geq 2.96 | \beta = 2] \\
&= 1 - P\left[\frac{-0.96 - 2}{1} \leq \frac{\hat{\beta} - 2}{1} \leq \frac{2.96 - 2}{1}\right] \\
&= 1 - P[-2.96 \leq z \leq 0.96] \\
&= 0.17
\end{aligned}$$

In Table 3.1 we report the values of the power function $\Pi(\beta)$ for alternative values of β, the true mean of the population, and in Figure 3.14 we graph the power function.

Note that in Figure 3.14 and Table 3.1 that the further β is from the hypothesized value the *greater* is the power of the test. In fact, as $|\beta - 1|$ approaches infinity, the power of the test goes to one. In Table 3.1 we also report the probability of a Type

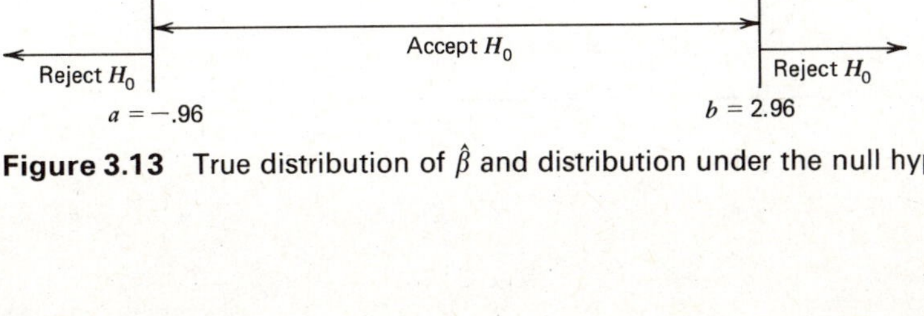

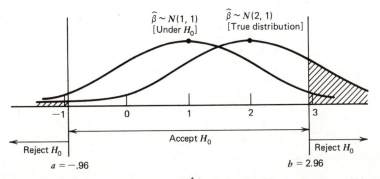

Figure 3.13 True distribution of $\hat{\beta}$ and distribution under the null hypothesis.

Table 3.1 The power function.

β	$\Pi(\beta)$	P[Type II error$\vert\alpha = 0.05$]	$\Pi(\beta)$	P[Type II error$\vert\alpha = 0.10$]
−4	0.9988	1.18×10^{-3}	0.9996	4.0×10^{-4}
−3	0.98	0.02	0.9906	9.36×10^{-3}
−2	0.851	0.149	0.9115	0.0885
−1	0.516	0.484	0.637	0.363
0	0.17	0.83	0.2612	0.7388
1	$\alpha = 0.05$	0.95	$\alpha = 0.10$	0.90
2	0.17	0.83	0.2612	0.7388
3	0.516	0.484	0.637	0.363
4	0.851	0.149	0.9115	0.0885
5	0.98	0.02	0.9906	9.36×10^{-3}
6	0.9988	1.18×10^{-3}	0.9996	4.0×10^{-4}

II error for two different sizes of the test. If $\alpha = 0.10$, then the critical value is $z_{(\alpha/2)} = 1.65$ and the test procedure will reject H_0 when $\hat{\beta} \geq 2.65$ and when $\hat{\beta} \leq 0.65$. Then if $\beta = 2$, for example, the power of the test is

$$\Pi(2) = P[\hat{\beta} \leq -0.65 \quad \text{or} \quad \hat{\beta} \geq 2.65]$$
$$= 1 - P\left[\frac{-0.65 - 2}{1} \leq \frac{\hat{\beta} - 2}{1} \leq \frac{2.65 - 2}{1}\right]$$
$$= 1 - 0.7388 = 0.2612$$

Note that by increasing the amount of Type I error we are prepared to tolerate, the probability of a Type II error diminishes.

As a final note on the power of a test, note that for a given level of significance of the test, α, as the sample size increases (to infinity) the power of the test increases (to one) for every $\beta \neq 1$. The intuition for this is based on the fact that the test is constructed around a consistent estimator. As the sample size increases, the

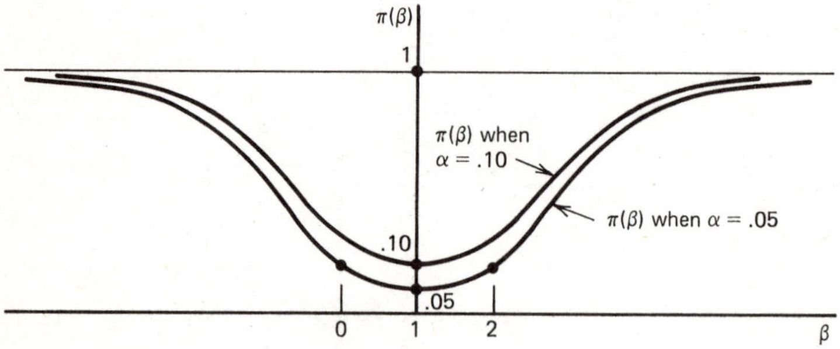

Figure 3.14 Graph of the power function.

sampling distribution of the estimator collapses about the true parameter value, and thus the probability that we would reject a false hypothesis goes to unity. Tests with this property are called *consistent tests.* ■

In Example 3.15 we examined the characteristics of a particular test procedure for a hypothesis concerning the mean of a normal population. The power function was far from the "ideal," where the power is zero when the null is true and one when the null is false. Although ideal tests are not available, we can ask the following question: For a given size test, is there a test procedure (i.e., test statistic and rejection region) that is *uniformly most powerful,* that is, *one* test procedure that has the highest power of any test of similar size for every value of the unknown parameter? If there were such a test, then it would certainly be a good one to use. In fact, such tests do exist for many problems. Unfortunately, for most common situations in economics, such as cases (i) through (iii), there will not be a uniformly most powerful test, although there is one for case (iv). In the next section, we present a general procedure for deriving tests that do have good power characteristics. These are tests based on the likelihood ratio principle.

3.5.3 Likelihood Ratio Tests

In this section we consider a principle by which tests and test statistics can be derived under a variety of null and alternative hypotheses. The likelihood ratio test procedure compares the maximum value of the likelihood function under the assumption that the null hypothesis is correct to the maximum value of the unrestricted likelihood function. A useful way to think about likelihood ratio tests follows. The null hypothesis can be thought of as reducing or restricting the set of possible values for the parameters. This reduced set of possible values restricts the maximum value that the likelihood function can take. Suppose that we obtain unrestricted maximum likelihood estimates of the parameters based on the observed sample and then compare this result to the set of parameters defined by the null hypothesis. If the two resulting estimates were sufficiently close, that would support the conjecture that the hypothesis is true. The meaning of *sufficiently close* can be characterized by examining the values of the likelihood function at each of these sets of estimates. If the values of the likelihood function are close, then the two sets of estimates are close. On the other hand, if the values of the likelihood function differ substantially, the validity of the hypothesis should be questioned.

Consider the random variable $Y \sim N(\beta, \sigma^2)$. The complete (unrestricted) *parameter space* for this random variable is

$$\Omega = \{(\beta, \sigma^2); -\infty < \beta < \infty, 0 < \sigma^2 < \infty\}$$

Let our null hypothesis and alternative hypothesis be

$$H_0: \beta = \beta_0$$

$$H_1: \beta \neq \beta_0$$

Here no conjecture is made about the unknown parameter σ^2. The null hypothesis defines a *subspace* of the unrestricted parameter space Ω. That subspace will be denoted

$$\omega = \{(\beta, \sigma^2); \beta = \beta_0, 0 < \sigma^2 < \infty\}$$

Within the parameter spaces ω and Ω are values of the unknown parameters that maximize the likelihood function. The values of the likelihood functions at those maximum points are denoted $\hat{l}(\omega)$ and $\hat{l}(\Omega)$. The notion of the likelihood ratio procedure is that if the hypothesis is true, the likelihood ratio

$$\lambda = \frac{\hat{l}(\omega)}{\hat{l}(\Omega)} \tag{3.5.1}$$

should be "large," where according to the foregoing argument, $0 \leq \lambda \leq 1$. The *likelihood ratio principle* states that the null hypothesis defining the subspace ω, is rejected if and only if

$$\lambda \leq \lambda_0$$

where λ_0 is a suitably chosen constant. Therefore, an important question is how one should choose λ_0. Since λ is a random variable, and will be our test statistic, the significance level of the test is defined as

$$\alpha = P[\lambda \leq \lambda_0 | H_0 \text{ is true}]$$

and λ_0 is chosen so as to make α equal to the preassigned significance level.

Example 3.16 As an example of the likelihood ratio procedure, let $Y_1, \ldots, Y_T$ be a random sample from a $N(\beta, \sigma_0^2)$ population, where σ_0^2 is known. The null and alternative hypotheses are

$$H_0: \beta = \beta_0$$

$$H_1: \beta \neq \beta_0$$

Thus

$$\Omega = \{(\beta, \sigma^2); -\infty < \beta < \infty, \sigma^2 = \sigma_0^2\}$$

and

$$\omega = \{(\beta, \sigma^2); \beta = \beta_0, \sigma^2 = \sigma_0^2\}$$

The ML estimator of β on Ω is $\hat{\beta} = \sum Y_i/T$ and on ω is simply β_0. The values of the restricted and unrestricted likelihood functions are

$$\hat{l}(\omega) = (2\pi\sigma_0^2)^{-T/2} \exp\left[-\frac{1}{2\sigma_0^2}\sum_{i=1}^{T}(y_i - \beta_0)^2\right]$$

and

$$\hat{l}(\Omega) = (2\pi\sigma_0^2)^{-T/2} \exp\left[-\frac{1}{2\sigma_0^2}\sum_{i=1}^{T}(y_i - \hat{\beta})^2\right]$$

The likelihood ratio is then

$$\begin{aligned}\lambda = \frac{\hat{l}(\omega)}{\hat{l}(\Omega)} &= \frac{\exp[-(1/2\sigma_0^2)\sum_{i=1}^{T}(y_i - \beta_0)^2]}{\exp[-(1/2\sigma_0^2)\sum_{i=1}^{T}(y_i - \hat{\beta})^2]}\\ &= \exp\left\{-\frac{1}{2\sigma_0^2}\left[\sum_{i=1}^{T}(y_i - \beta_0)^2 - \sum_{i=1}^{T}(y_i - \hat{\beta})^2\right]\right\}\end{aligned}$$

but

$$\begin{aligned}\sum_{i=1}^{T}(y_i - \beta_0)^2 &= \sum_{i=1}^{T}[(y_i - \hat{\beta}) + (\hat{\beta} - \beta_0)]^2\\ &= \sum_{i=1}^{T}(y_i - \hat{\beta})^2 + T(\hat{\beta} - \beta_0)^2 + 2(\hat{\beta} - \beta_0)\sum_{i=1}^{T}(y_i - \hat{\beta})\end{aligned}$$

and

$$\sum_{i=1}^{T}(y_i - \hat{\beta}) = 0$$

since $\hat{\beta} = \bar{y}$, so

$$\lambda = \exp\left\{-\frac{T}{2\sigma_0^2}(\hat{\beta} - \beta_0)^2\right\}$$

In this (and in most) examples of tests that use the likelihood ratio principle it is convenient to transform λ to obtain another statistic where the distribution under H_0 is known. Such transformations lead to equivalent tests. Specifically, $\lambda \le \lambda_0$ implies that $\ln \lambda \le \ln \lambda_0$ or

$$-\frac{T}{2\sigma_0^2}(\hat{\beta} - \beta_0)^2 \le \ln \lambda_0$$

which is satisfied if

$$\frac{\hat{\beta} - \beta_0}{\sigma_0/\sqrt{T}} \geq \sqrt{\lambda^*} \qquad \text{and} \qquad \frac{\hat{\beta} - \beta_0}{\sigma_0/\sqrt{T}} \leq -\sqrt{\lambda^*}$$

where $\lambda^* = -2 \ln \lambda_0$. Thus the likelihood ratio test statistic is

$$z = \frac{\hat{\beta} - \beta_0}{\sigma_0/\sqrt{T}}$$

which has a $N(0, 1)$ distribution *if* the hypothesis $H_0\colon \beta = \beta_0$ is true. The value of $\sqrt{\lambda^*}$ is $z_{(\alpha/2)}$. Thus the test presented in Example 3.15 is a likelihood ratio test. ■

In this example the likelihood principle has led us to a test statistic with a well-known distribution. The following series of examples illustrate the use of other well-known distributions in hypothesis tests. These tests can also be obtained by using the likelihood ratio principle, but the algebra will not be presented here.

Example 3.17 The likelihood ratio test about the mean of a normal population when σ^2 is not known is based on the t-distribution. Specifically, given the null hypothesis $H_0\colon \beta = \beta_0$ against $H_1\colon \beta \neq \beta_0$, the unrestricted parameter space is $\Omega = \{(\beta, \sigma^2); -\infty < \beta < \infty, \sigma^2 > 0\}$ and the restricted parameter space is $\omega = \{(\beta, \sigma^2); \beta = \beta_0, \sigma^2 > 0\}$. Then the maximum value of the likelihood function on the restricted parameter space ω is

$$\hat{l}(\omega) = (2\pi\tilde{\sigma}_0^2)^{-T/2} \exp\left[-\frac{1}{2\tilde{\sigma}_0^2} \sum_{i=1}^{T} (y_i - \beta_0)^2\right]$$

where $\tilde{\sigma}_0^2$ is the maximum likelihood estimator of σ^2, $\tilde{\sigma}_0^2 = \sum (y_i - \beta_0)^2/T$. The maximum value of the likelihood function on Ω is

$$\hat{l}(\Omega) = (2\pi\tilde{\sigma}^2)^{-T/2} \exp\left[-\frac{1}{2\tilde{\sigma}^2} \sum_{i=1}^{T} (y_i - \hat{\beta})^2\right]$$

where $\hat{\beta}$ and $\tilde{\sigma}^2$ are the usual maximum likelihood estimators of β and σ^2. Forming the likelihood ratio, applying the likelihood principle, and manipulating the result, we reject the null hypothesis in favor of the alternative when

$$\frac{\hat{\beta} - \beta_0}{\hat{\sigma}/\sqrt{T}} \geq \lambda^* \qquad \text{or} \qquad \frac{\hat{\beta} - \beta_0}{\hat{\sigma}/\sqrt{T}} \leq -\lambda^*$$

where $\hat{\sigma}^2 = \sum (y_i - \hat{\beta})^2/(T - 1)$. The test statistic is recognized to have a t-distribution with $(T - 1)$ degrees of freedom, if $H_0\colon \beta = \beta_0$ is true. Consequently, the value of λ^* can be chosen to be the critical value $t_{(T-1,\alpha/2)}$. These values are found in Table 2 at the back of the book. ■

Example 3.18 Consider testing a hypothesis about the variance of a normal population with mean β and variance σ^2. Let the null hypothesis be $H_0: \sigma^2 = \sigma_0^2$ and the alternative $H_1: \sigma^2 \neq \sigma_0^2$. In this case the unrestricted parameter space is $\Omega = \{(\beta, \sigma^2); -\infty < \beta < \infty, \sigma^2 > 0\}$ and the restricted parameter space is $\omega = \{(\beta, \sigma^2); -\infty < \beta < \infty, \sigma^2 = \sigma_0^2\}$. The likelihood ratio test statistic is

$$\sum_{i=1}^{T} (y_i - \hat{\beta})^2/\sigma_0^2 = \frac{(T-1)\hat{\sigma}^2}{\sigma_0^2}$$

which has a $\chi^2_{(T-1)}$ distribution if $\sigma^2 = \sigma_0^2$. The likelihood ratio principle leads us to reject the null hypothesis at an α level of significance if

$$\frac{(T-1)\hat{\sigma}^2}{\sigma_0^2} \geq \chi^2_{(T-1,C_2)} \qquad \text{or} \qquad \frac{(T-1)\hat{\sigma}^2}{\sigma_0^2} \leq \chi^2_{(T-1,C_1)}$$

where $\chi^2_{(T-1,C_2)}$ and $\chi^2_{(T-1,C_1)}$ are respectively the upper and lower $\alpha/2$ critical values of the $\chi^2_{(T-1)}$ distribution. Critical values for this distribution are given in Table 3 at the back of this book. ■

Example 3.19 Consider the problem of testing the equality of the variances of two normal populations. In particular, suppose the random sample $Y_1, \ldots, Y_{T_1}$ comes from a $N(\beta_1, \sigma_1^2)$ population and $X_1 \ldots, X_{T_2}$ from a $N(\beta_2, \sigma_2^2)$ population, where β_1, σ_1^2, β_2, and σ_2^2 are all unknown. Let the null hypothesis be $H_0: \sigma_1^2 = \sigma_2^2$ and the alternative $H_1: \sigma_1^2 > \sigma_2^2$. The likelihood ratio test statistic is

$$\frac{\sum_{i=1}^{T_1} (y_i - \hat{\beta}_1)^2/(T_1 - 1)}{\sum_{i=1}^{T_2} (x_i - \hat{\beta}_2)^2/(T_2 - 1)} = \frac{\hat{\sigma}_1^2}{\hat{\sigma}_2^2}$$

where $\hat{\beta}_1 = \sum Y_i/T_1$ and $\hat{\beta}_2 = \sum X_i/T_2$. The likelihood ratio principle leads to rejection of the null hypothesis if this test statistic is too large. The distribution of the test statistic is based on the fact that

$$(T_i - 1)\hat{\sigma}_i^2/\sigma_i^2 \sim \chi^2_{(T_i-1)}$$

Thus, if $H_0: \sigma_1^2 = \sigma_2^2$ is true, then the test statistic $\hat{\sigma}_1^2/\hat{\sigma}_2^2$ is the ratio of two χ^2 random variables divided by their degrees of freedom. Furthermore, the χ^2 random variables are independent if the samples are independently collected, so that the test statistic has an F-distribution with $(T_1 - 1)$ and $(T_2 - 1)$ degrees of freedom if H_0 is true. The null hypothesis is rejected in favor of the alternative if

$$\frac{\hat{\sigma}_1^2}{\hat{\sigma}_2^2} \geq F_{(\alpha, T_1-1, T_2-1)}$$

where $F_{(\alpha, T_1-1, T_2-1)}$ is the upper-α percentile of the F-distribution with $(T_1 - 1)$ numerator degrees of freedom and $(T_2 - 1)$ denominator degrees of freedom. Critical values of this distribution are found in Table 4 at the back of the book. ■

Example 3.20 As an example of a *joint* hypothesis test based on the likelihood ratio test procedure, consider the problem of testing the equality of means of two normal populations with variances known to be equal. That is, let $Y_{11}, Y_{12}, \ldots, Y_{1T_1}$ be a random sample from a $N(\beta_1, \sigma^2)$ population and $Y_{21}, Y_{22}, \ldots, Y_{2T_2}$ be an independent random sample from a $N(\beta_2, \sigma^2)$ population, where β_1, β_2, and σ^2 are unknown. Let the joint null hypothesis be

$$H_0: \beta_1 = \beta_1^0, \ \beta_2 = \beta_2^0$$

and the alternative

$$H_1: \beta_1 \neq \beta_1^0 \quad \text{or} \quad \beta_2 \neq \beta_2^0 \quad \text{or both}$$

The likelihood ratio principle leads to a test based on the test statistic

$$u = \frac{[(\hat{\beta}_1 - \beta_1^0)^2 + (\hat{\beta}_2 - \beta_2^0)^2]/2}{\hat{\sigma}^2}$$

where $\hat{\beta}_1 = \sum Y_{1i}/T_1$, $\hat{\beta}_2 = \sum Y_{2i}/T_2$, and $\hat{\sigma}^2$ is a pooled estimator of the common variance and is given by

$$\hat{\sigma}^2 = \frac{\sum_{i=1}^{T_1}(Y_{1i} - \hat{\beta}_1)^2 + \sum_{i=1}^{T_2}(Y_{2i} - \hat{\beta}_2)^2}{T_1 + T_2 - 2}$$

The test statistic u is seen to have a $F_{(\alpha/2, T_1+T_2-2)}$ distribution if H_0 is true by noting that it can be rewritten:

$$u = \frac{\{[(\hat{\beta}_1 - \beta_1^0)/\sigma]^2 + [(\hat{\beta}_2 - \beta_2^0)/\sigma]^2\}/2}{\hat{\sigma}^2/\sigma^2}$$

so that the numerator is one-half the sum of two squared, independent $N(0, 1)$ random variables, and thus has a $\chi^2_{(2)}$ distribution that has been divided by its degrees of freedom. Similarly, the denominator is a $\chi^2_{(T_1+T_2-2)}$ random variable divided by its degrees of freedom and the numerator and denominator can be shown to be independent. The null hypothesis is rejected in favor of the alternative if $u \geq F_{(\alpha/2, T_1+T_2-2)}$. ■

3.5.4 Asymptotic Tests

To this point we have only considered tests based on finite or small sample results. It is possible to use asymptotic results to test hypotheses in cases where an appropriate finite sample test statistic is unavailable. In this section we present three approaches to constructing large sample tests, each one of which can be convenient under appropriate circumstances, and which are asymptotically equivalent. The tests are the likelihood ratio (LR) test, the Wald (W) test, and the Lagrange multiplier (LM) test.

All three test procedures are developed within the framework of maximum likelihood estimation and use the asymptotic normality of the ML estimators. Let $L(\theta)$ be the log-likelihood function, θ a single unknown parameter known to fall in the parameter space Ω, and $\hat{\theta}$ is the (unrestricted) ML estimator of θ. Let the null hypothesis we want to test be $H_0\colon \theta = \theta_0$ against the alternative $H_1\colon \theta \neq \theta_0$. Thus the restricted parameter space ω consists of the single point θ_0 and the ML estimator of θ over ω is $\theta^* = \theta_0$. Then the likelihood ratio (see Section 3.5.3) is

$$\lambda = \frac{\hat{\ell}(\omega)}{\hat{\ell}(\Omega)}$$

Then, it can be shown that if the null hypothesis is true

$$LR = -2 \log \lambda = -2[L(\theta_0) - L(\hat{\theta})] = 2[L(\hat{\theta}) - L(\theta_0)] \tag{3.5.2}$$

is asymptotically distributed as a χ^2 random variable with degrees of freedom J equal to the number of hypotheses, which in this case is one. The null hypothesis is rejected if the value of the test statistic LR is too large, that is, if $LR \geq \chi^2_{(\alpha, J)}$ where $\chi^2_{(\alpha, J)}$ is the upper α-percentile of a $\chi^2_{(J)}$ distribution. In Figure 3.15 we depict a

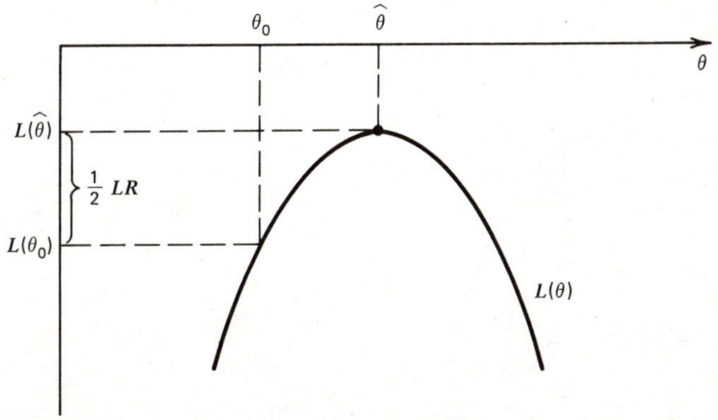

Figure 3.15 A log-likelihood function.

log-likelihood function $L(\theta)$ and note that $LR/2$ is just the difference between the values of the log-likelihood function evaluated at $\hat{\theta}$ and θ_0. The intuition of this asymptotic likelihood ratio test is exactly the same as that described in Section 3.5.3. If the values of $L(\hat{\theta})$ and $L(\theta_0)$ are too far apart, then we reject the null hypothesis and accept the alternative.

In Figure 3.15 it is clear that $LR/2$ will depend on the distance $\hat{\theta} - \theta_0$ and the curvature of $L(\theta)$. In Figure 3.16 we show two log-likelihood functions: $L_A(\theta)$ and $L_B(\theta)$, which attain their maxima at the same value $\hat{\theta}$ but which have different curvatures. The distance $\hat{\theta} - \theta_0$ translates into a larger value of $LR/2$ for the more curved likelihood function $L_B(\theta)$. We measure the curvature of the likelihood function using the negative of its second derivative evaluated at the unrestricted ML estimator $\hat{\theta}$, that is by

$$-\left.\frac{d^2L(\theta)}{d\theta^2}\right|_{\theta=\hat{\theta}}$$

The greater this magnitude, the more curved the log-likelihood function. Then, it would seem, we could construct a reasonable test statistic by weighting the squared distance between $\hat{\theta}$ and θ_0 by the curvature of the log-likelihood function. This is exactly what the Wald test does, as it is based on the test statistic

$$W = (\hat{\theta} - \theta_0)^2\left[-\left.\frac{d^2L(\theta)}{d\theta^2}\right|_{\theta=\hat{\theta}}\right] \tag{3.5.3}$$

If the null hypothesis is true then just like LR, W is distributed $\chi^2_{(1)}$. Large values of W imply large values of LR, and vice versa, and the two tests are asymptotically equivalent. A more common form of the Wald statistic is

$$W = (\hat{\theta} - \theta_0)^2 I(\hat{\theta}) \tag{3.5.4}$$

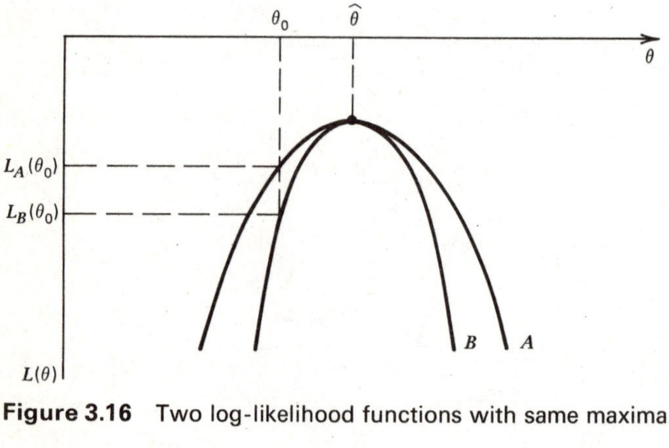

Figure 3.16 Two log-likelihood functions with same maxima.

where $I(\hat{\theta})$ is the information matrix

$$I(\theta) = -E\left[\frac{d^2L(\theta)}{d\theta^2}\right]$$

evaluated at $\hat{\theta}$. These two forms of the Wald statistic are asymptotically equivalent since

$$-\left.\frac{d^2L(\theta)}{d\theta^2}\right|_{\theta=\hat{\theta}}$$

is a consistent estimator for $I(\theta)$.

The Lagrange multiplier test derives from a restricted maximum likelihood estimation using Lagrange multipliers. That is, if we maximize $L(\theta)$ subject to the condition that $\theta = \theta_0$, we would form the Lagrangian function

$$\mathscr{L} = L(\theta) - \lambda(\theta - \theta_0)$$

where λ is a Lagrange multiplier. Differentiating $\mathscr{L}$ with respect to θ and λ and setting to zero yields the restricted ML estimator $\theta^* = \theta_0$ and Lagrange multiplier value $\lambda^* = S(\theta^*) = S(\theta_0)$, where $S(\theta)$ is the slope of the log-likelihood function

$$S(\theta) = \frac{dL(\theta)}{d\theta}$$

Since $\hat{\theta}$ maximizes $L(\theta)$, it satisfies the first-order conditions for a maximum and $S(\hat{\theta}) = 0$. The more the data "agree with" the null hypothesis that $\theta = \theta_0$ the closer θ^* will be to $\hat{\theta}$ and the smaller will be $\lambda^* = S(\theta_0)$. Thus the magnitude of $S(\theta_0)$ measures, in this sense, the distance between $\theta^* = \theta_0$ and $\hat{\theta}$. However, two data sets can yield equal values of $S(\theta_0)$ and imply different values of LR and distances between $\hat{\theta}$ and θ_0, depending on the curvature of $L(\theta)$ at θ_0, as illustrated by Figure 3.17.

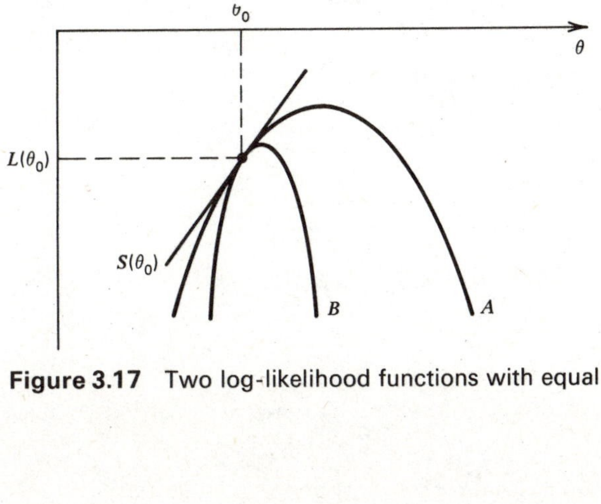

Figure 3.17 Two log-likelihood functions with equal slopes.

Thus to construct a test statistic based on the departure of $S(\theta_0)$ from zero, we should weight $[S(\theta_0)]^2$ by the reciprocal of the curvature of $L(\theta)$ since now more curvature implies smaller differences between θ_0 and $\hat{\theta}$ and smaller values of LR. The Lagrange multiplier test statistic does just that and is written

$$LM = \frac{[S(\theta_0)]^2}{[-d^2L(\theta)/d\theta^2|_{\theta=\theta}]} \tag{3.5.5}$$

or, asymptotically equivalently, as

$$LM = [S(\theta_0)]^2[I(\theta_0)]^{-1} \tag{3.5.6}$$

If the null hypothesis is true, then LM is asymptotically distributed as $\chi^2_{(1)}$ and the test is carried out by rejecting the null hypothesis if LM is too large.

Example 3.21 Let $Y_1, \ldots, Y_T$ be a random sample from a $N(\beta, \sigma^2 = 1)$ population. Then the log-likelihood function is

$$L(\beta) = -\frac{T}{2}\log(2\pi) - \frac{1}{2}\sum_{i=1}^{T}(Y_i - \beta)^2$$

which is quadratic in β and looks like Figure 3.15. Then

$$\frac{dL(\beta)}{d\beta} = \sum_{i=1}^{T}(Y_i - \beta)$$

$$\frac{d^2L}{d\beta^2} = -T$$

Note that $-d^2L/d\beta^2 = I(\beta) = T$ and the larger the sample size the greater the curvature of the likelihood function. The ML estimator of β is $\hat{\beta} = \sum_{i=1}^{T} Y_i/T$, and for the hypothesis $\beta = \beta_0$ the LR test statistic is

$$\begin{aligned} LR &= 2[L(\hat{\beta}) - L(\beta_0)] \\ &= \sum(Y_i - \beta_0)^2 - \sum(Y_i - \hat{\beta})^2 \\ &= T(\hat{\beta} - \beta_0)^2 \end{aligned}$$

The Wald statistic is

$$W = (\hat{\beta} - \beta_0)^2 \cdot I(\hat{\beta}) = T(\hat{\beta} - \beta_0)^2$$

and since

$$S(\beta_0) = \sum(Y_i - \beta_0) = T(\hat{\beta} - \beta_0)$$

we have

$$\begin{aligned} LM &= [S(\beta_0)]^2 \cdot [I(\beta_0)]^{-1} \\ &= T^2(\hat{\beta} - \beta_0)^2 \cdot \frac{1}{T} \\ &= T(\hat{\beta} - \beta_0)^2 \end{aligned}$$

In this case all three test statistics are numerically identical since the likelihood function is a quadratic function. ■

These testing procedures apply straightforwardly to the multiparameter case. If $\boldsymbol{\theta}$ is a $(K \times 1)$ vector of parameters and the joint null hypothesis is

$$H_0\colon \theta_1 = \theta_1^0, \theta_2 = \theta_2^0, \ldots, \theta_K = \theta_K^0 \quad \text{or} \quad H_0\colon \boldsymbol{\theta} = \boldsymbol{\theta}_0$$

and the alternative is that at least one of the hypothesis is incorrect, then

$$LR = -2 \log \lambda = 2[L(\hat{\boldsymbol{\theta}}) - L(\boldsymbol{\theta}_0)]$$

and $LR \xrightarrow{d} \chi^2_{(K)}$ if H_0 is true. The Wald statistic is

$$W = (\hat{\boldsymbol{\theta}} - \boldsymbol{\theta}_0)' I(\hat{\boldsymbol{\theta}})(\hat{\boldsymbol{\theta}} - \boldsymbol{\theta}_0)$$

where $I(\hat{\boldsymbol{\theta}})$ is the information matrix evaluated at the unrestricted ML estimates. The Lagrange multiplier test statistic is

$$LM = S(\boldsymbol{\theta}_0)'[I(\boldsymbol{\theta}_0)]^{-1} S(\boldsymbol{\theta}_0)$$

where $S(\boldsymbol{\theta}) = \partial L(\boldsymbol{\theta})/\partial \boldsymbol{\theta}$ and $LM \xrightarrow{d} \chi^2_{(K)}$ if H_0 is true. For all three test statistics the null hypothesis is rejected if the value of the test statistic is too large.

In addition to testing the "simple" hypothesis $H_0\colon \boldsymbol{\theta} = \boldsymbol{\theta}_0$ in the multivariate case, these test procedures can be extended to develop tests for sets of linear and nonlinear hypotheses about the vector of parameters $\boldsymbol{\theta}$. These extensions will be treated in Chapters 6 and 12.

Finally, it is useful to note that the Wald test procedure can be based on any estimator that is asymptotically normal, not just the ML estimator. If $\hat{\boldsymbol{\theta}} \overset{asy}{\sim} N(\boldsymbol{\theta}, \Sigma_\theta)$, then we can use the result in Section 2.5.8 to show that

$$(\hat{\boldsymbol{\theta}} - \boldsymbol{\theta})' \, \Sigma_\theta^{-1} (\hat{\boldsymbol{\theta}} - \boldsymbol{\theta}) \overset{asy}{\sim} \chi^2_{(K)}$$

Consequently, the null hypothesis that $\boldsymbol{\theta} = \boldsymbol{\theta}_0$ can be tested using the test statistic

$$W = (\hat{\boldsymbol{\theta}} - \boldsymbol{\theta}_0)' \Sigma_\theta^{-1} (\hat{\boldsymbol{\theta}} - \boldsymbol{\theta}_0)$$

which is asymptotically $\chi^2_{(K)}$ if H_0 is true. Thus, for example, if we have a random sample from a population with unknown distribution, we can assert that the sample mean is asymptotically normal by the central limit theorem and use the Wald test statistic to carry out tests about the mean of the population.

3.6 The Relationship between Confidence Intervals and Hypothesis Tests

There is a relationship between confidence intervals and hypothesis tests that is sometimes useful. Suppose we are considering a population that is known to be $N(\beta, 10)$ and we draw a random sample of size $T = 10$, say $Y_1, \ldots, Y_{10}$. Then the maximum likelihood estimator of β is $\hat{\beta} = \sum Y_i/10 \sim N(\beta, 1)$. A 95% confidence interval for β is

$$\hat{\beta} \pm z_{(\alpha/2)}\sigma/\sqrt{T} = \hat{\beta} \pm (1.96)$$

which is represented in Figure 3.18.

Now consider testing the null hypothesis $H_0\colon \beta = \beta_0$ against $H_1\colon \beta \neq \beta_0$. The test statistic is $z = \sqrt{T}(\hat{\beta} - \beta_0)/\sigma = \hat{\beta} - \beta_0$. The hypothesis is rejected if $|z| \geq 1.96$ and not rejected if $|z| < 1.96$. Examining the latter statement, the hypothesis is not rejected if

$$-1.96 < \hat{\beta} - \beta_0 < 1.96$$

or

$$\hat{\beta} - 1.96 < \beta_0 < \hat{\beta} + 1.96$$

That is, it is clear in the hypothesis-testing problem that any value β_0 that falls "inside" the 95% confidence interval will lead to acceptance of the hypothesis at the 0.05 level of significance. Any value of β_0 outside the 95% confidence interval will lead to H_0 being rejected at the level of significance 0.05. Stated in another way, if a $(1 - \alpha) \times 100\%$ confidence interval *covers the hypothesized value*, then the associated hypothesis test will be accepted.

We will use this idea to illustrate the difference in interpretation of joint and individual hypothesis tests. Suppose we are considering random samples from two

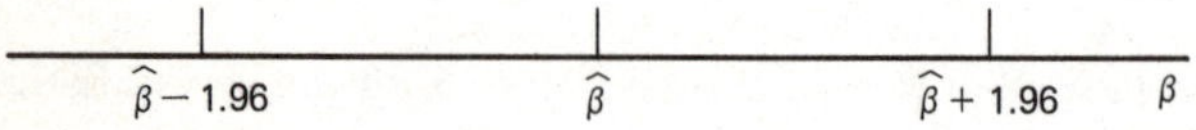

Figure 3.18 A 95% confidence interval for the mean of a population.

different populations: $Y_{1i} \sim N(\beta_1, 10)$ and $Y_{2i} \sim N(\beta_2, 10)$ and we have $T = 10$ observations on each population. Then if $\hat{\beta}_1 = \sum Y_{1i}/10$ and $\hat{\beta}_2 = \sum Y_{2i}/10$ are the maximum likelihood estimators of β_1 and β_2, then their *joint* distribution is

$$\hat{\boldsymbol{\beta}} = \begin{bmatrix} \hat{\beta}_1 \\ \hat{\beta}_2 \end{bmatrix} \sim N\left(\begin{bmatrix} \beta_1 \\ \beta_2 \end{bmatrix}, \begin{bmatrix} 1 & \sigma_{12} \\ \sigma_{21} & 1 \end{bmatrix} \right) = N(\boldsymbol{\beta}, \Sigma)$$

where σ_{12} is the covariance between $\hat{\beta}_1$ and $\hat{\beta}_2$ and in this case is also the correlation between them since both have unit variance. Note that unless $\sigma_{12} = 0$, $\hat{\beta}_1$ and $\hat{\beta}_2$ are not independent.

Individual confidence intervals for β_1 and β_2 are of the form $\hat{\beta}_i \pm 1.96$, $i = 1, 2$. *Joint* confidence intervals are based on the fact that

$$(\hat{\boldsymbol{\beta}} - \boldsymbol{\beta})'\Sigma^{-1}(\hat{\boldsymbol{\beta}} - \boldsymbol{\beta}) \sim \chi^2_{(2)}$$

Here

$$\Sigma^{-1} = \frac{1}{1 - \sigma_{12}^2} \begin{bmatrix} 1 & -\sigma_{12} \\ -\sigma_{12} & 1 \end{bmatrix}$$

So

$$P[(\hat{\boldsymbol{\beta}} - \boldsymbol{\beta})'\Sigma^{-1}(\hat{\boldsymbol{\beta}} - \boldsymbol{\beta}) \leq \chi^2_{(2, C_2)}] = 1 - \alpha$$

or a $(1 - \alpha) \times 100\%$ confidence interval for β_1 or β_2 is the set of their values such that

$$\frac{1}{1 - \sigma_{12}^2} \{(\hat{\beta}_1 - \beta_1)^2 - 2\sigma_{12}(\hat{\beta}_1 - \beta_1)(\hat{\beta}_2 - \beta_2) + (\hat{\beta}_2 - \beta_2)^2\} \leq \chi^2_{(2, C_2)} \tag{3.6.1}$$

Equation (3.6.1) is the equation of an *ellipse* in β_1 and β_2 centered at $\hat{\beta}_1$ and $\hat{\beta}_2$. All points on or inside the ellipse constitute a $(1 - \alpha) \times 100\%$ joint confidence interval for $\boldsymbol{\beta} = (\beta_1, \beta_2)'$. In Figure 3.19 three joint confidence sets are depicted for selected values of σ_{12}. Note that if $\sigma_{12} = 0$ the confidence set is a circle and as σ_{12} gets larger the ellipse becomes more "cigar"-shaped and elongated.

On the vertical and horizontal axes are marked the individual 95% confidence intervals for β_1 and β_2. Now the difference between joint and individual hypothesis tests is clear. An individual hypothesis test is carried out by seeing if the hypothesized value falls in the individual confidence interval. The individual hypotheses do not take into account any information about the other parameter(s). Two individual hypothesis tests do not produce the results of a joint hypothesis test, or vice versa, even when $\sigma_{12} = 0$. In contrast, joint hypothesis statements take

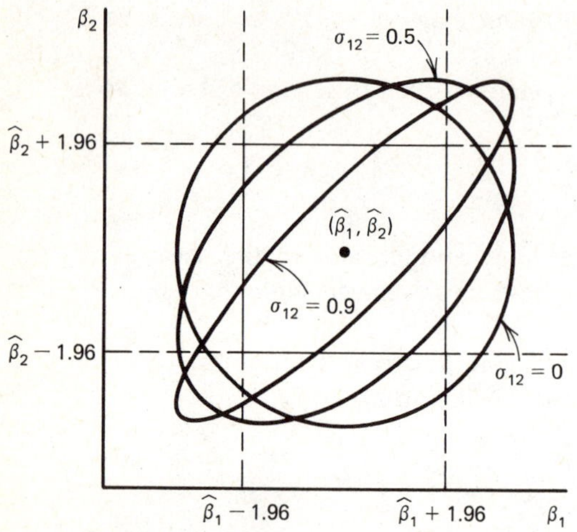

Figure 3.19 Ninety-five percent confidence sets for $\boldsymbol{\beta}$ given σ_{12}, $\hat{\beta}_1 = 0.7$, $\hat{\beta}_2 = 0.5$.

into account the values of several parameters simultaneously. It is clear that neither of these types of tests (or confidence sets) is a substitute for the other and should not be used in that way.

3.7 Summary and Guide to Further Reading

In this chapter we have reviewed the classical approach to statistical inference: point and interval estimation and hypothesis testing. The Bayesian approach to these topics will be presented in Chapter 4. As methods of point estimation we have presented the method of moments, maximum likelihood, and least squares. Although each technique is used throughout the book, for the present and foreseeable future the maximum likelihood technique is the most important. The ML estimators often have good small sample properties and under basic "regularity" conditions also have the desirable large sample properties of consistency, asymptotic normality, and asymptotic efficiency. There are many sources that you can use to supplement your reading on methods and properties of point estimators. A standby for econometricians is Kmenta (1986, Chapter 6). You will also find it useful, now and later, to refer to Kennedy (1985, Chapter 2) and Harvey (1981, pp. 19–24 and Chapter 3). The material in Chapter 3 of Harvey's book is on maximum likelihood estimation and somewhat beyond your current needs, but you will find it a useful reference. In addition to these books aimed at econometricians, most intermediate mathematical statistics books have sections or chapters on point estimation. See DeGroot (1975, Chapter 6 and 7) and Mood, Graybill, and Boes (1974, Chapter 6 and 7). The latter reference is "relatively" technical compared with the others.

Related to point estimation, we have briefly discussed interval estimation and, more completely, hypothesis testing. See Kmenta (1986, Chapter 5), Kennedy (1985, Chapter 4), and Harvey (1981, Chapter 5). Once again, these references cover more than you need to know right now but will be extremely valuable. Among the statistics books, see DeGroot (1975, Chapter 8) and Mood, Graybill, and Boes (1974, Chapters 8 and 9). For an elegant and more complete presentation of the Wald, likelihood ratio, and Lagrange multiplier tests, from which we have borrowed heavily, see Buse (1982).

3.8 Exercises

3.1 Let $Y_1, \ldots, Y_T$ be a random sample from a population with mean β and variance σ^2. Let b^* be an estimator of β given by

$$b^* = \frac{\sum_{i=1}^{T} iY_i}{\sum_{i=1}^{T} i}$$

(*a*) Show that b^* is a linear estimator.

(*b*) Show that b^* is unbiased.

(*c*) Compute the variance of b^*. *Hint*:

$$\sum_{i=1}^{T} i = \frac{T(T+1)}{2} \quad \text{and} \quad \sum_{i=1}^{T} i^2 = \frac{T(T+1)(2T+1)}{6}$$

(*d*) Show that b^* is consistent.

(*e*) Compare b^* to the sample mean $\hat{b} = \sum_{i=1}^{T} Y_i/T$ as an estimator of β.

3.2 We wish to test a hypothesis about the mean β of a normal population that has known variance $\sigma^2 = 81$. We have a random sample of size $T = 9$ and wish to test $H_0\colon \beta = 10$ against $H_1\colon \beta \neq 10$. Compute the power of the usual likelihood ratio test at $\beta = -10, -5, 0, 6$ at $\alpha = 0.05$.

3.3 A random sample of size $T = 4$ is drawn from one of two normal populations that have the same known variance ($\sigma^2 = 3000^2$) but different means (either $\beta = 25{,}000$ or $\beta = 30{,}000$). Compute the power of the likelihood ratio test for $H_0\colon \beta = 25{,}000$ against $H_1\colon \beta = 30{,}000$ at $\alpha = 0.01$, 0.05, and 0.10.

3.4 Let Y be a discrete (geometric) random variable with p.d.f.

$$f(y) = p(1-p)^{y-1}, \quad y = 1, 2, 3, \ldots$$

where p is an unknown parameter. Find the maximum likelihood estimate of p if only one sample observation is available.

3.5 Let $Y_1, \ldots, Y_T$ be a random sample from a population with p.d.f.

$$f(y) = \frac{1}{\Gamma(\alpha)\theta^\alpha} y^{\alpha-1} e^{-y/\theta}, \quad y > 0$$

which is a gamma distribution (which has mean $E[Y] = \alpha\theta$ and variance $\text{var}(Y) = \alpha\theta^2$).

(*a*) Find the maximum likelihood estimator of θ if α is known.

(*b*) Show that the maximum likelihood estimator is unbiased and consistent and efficient.

3.6 Let $Y_1, \ldots, Y_T$ be a random sample from a population with p.d.f.

$$f(y) = \frac{\lambda^y e^{-\lambda}}{y!}, \quad y = 0, 1, 2, \ldots$$

Y is a Poisson random variable and has mean and variance equal to the parameter λ.

(*a*) Find the maximum likelihood estimator of λ.

(*b*) Find the mean and variance of the maximum likelihood estimator of λ and show that it is consistent.

(*c*) What is the asymptotic distribution of the ML estimator of λ.

(*d*) Is the ML estimator efficient in either large or small samples (or both?).

3.7 A random sample of size T is taken from a population with p.d.f.

$$f(y) = (\theta + 1)y^\theta, \quad 0 < y < 1$$

(*a*) Find the estimator of θ using the method of moments.

(*b*) Find the maximum likelihood estimator of θ.

3.8 Let $Y_1, \ldots, Y_T$ be a random sample from a $N(\beta, 1)$ distribution. *Derive* the likelihood ratio test for the hypothesis that $H_0\colon \beta = 0$ against $H_1\colon \beta \neq 0$.

3.9 Consider the linear model for the mean of a population

$$y_i = \beta + e_i$$

In this exercise you will carry out a Monte Carlo experiment that illustrates the statistical properties of the sample mean as an estimator of β. In order to generate the y_i values let $\beta = 5$ and let the random disturbances e_i have a uniform distribution with mean 0 and variance 2. Specifically the p.d.f. of the random disturbance e will be

$$f(e) = \begin{cases} 1/2\sqrt{6} & -\sqrt{6} \leq e \leq \sqrt{6} \\ 0 & \text{otherwise} \end{cases}$$

Your instructor will show you how to generate 100 samples of the e_i's with 10 observations each. Then by adding 5 to these values, 100 samples of size 10 from a uniformly distributed population with mean 5 and variance 2 are generated.

(*a*) Estimate β using the sample mean for all 100 samples. If $\hat{\beta}_i$ is the value of the sample mean in the ith sample, compute $\bar{\hat{\beta}} = \sum_{i=1}^{100} \hat{\beta}_i/100$. This is the empirical analog to the expected value of $\hat{\beta}$. Compare $\bar{\hat{\beta}}$ to the true expected value.

(*b*) Compute the sample variance of the 100 values of the sample mean as $s^2 = \sum_{i=1}^{100} (\hat{\beta}_i - \bar{\hat{\beta}})^2/(100 - 1)$. The value s^2 measures the sampling variability of $\hat{\beta}$. Compare s^2 to its true value.

(*c*) For each sample estimate the variance of the population using $\hat{\sigma}^2 = \sum_{i=1}^{T} (y_i - \bar{y})^2/(T - 1)$. If $\hat{\sigma}_i^2$ is the estimate of σ^2 from the ith sample, compare $\sum_{i=1}^{100} \hat{\sigma}_i^2/100$ to the true value.

(*d*) For each of the 100 samples construct the random variables

$$z = \frac{\hat{\beta} - \beta}{\sigma/\sqrt{T}}$$

where you use the true values of β and σ^2. Construct a frequency diagram for the 100 values of z and compute the percentages that fall in the intervals [-4, -3], [-3, -2], [-2, -1], [-1, 0] and then the same intervals on the positive side. Compare these frequencies to the probabilities of a $N(0, 1)$ random variable falling in those same intervals. Are they close? Why should they be?

(*e*) Repeat (a) and (d), combining your samples into 50 samples of size 20. Comment on any differences that you observe and try to explain them using your knowledge of the properties of the sample mean.

3.10 Repeat Exercise 3.9 using a *normal* random number generator and compare and contrast your results to those obtained in Exercise 3.9. In addition, do the following.

(*a*) Construct 95% confidence intervals for β in each of the samples, first assuming σ^2 is known and then assuming it is unknown. Tally how many contain the true parameter values.

(*b*) For each of the samples compute $z^* = (\hat{\beta} - 7)/(\sigma/\sqrt{T})$, which is the test statistic you would use when testing the hypothesis that $\beta = 7$ if σ^2 were known. Construct the empirical frequency distribution for this statistic and compare it to the $N(0, 1)$ distribution. Are they similar? What is the *true* distribution of z^*?

3.9 References

Buse, A. (1982) "The Likelihood Ratio, Wald and Lagrange Multiplier Tests: An Expository Note." *American Statistician*, 36, 153–157.

DeGroot, M. (1975) *Probability and Statistics.* Reading, MA: Addison–Wesley.

Goldberger, A. (1964) *Econometric Theory.* New York: Wiley.

Harvey, A. C. (1981) *The Econometric Analysis of Time Series.* New York: Halsted Press.

Hogg, R., and A. Craig (1978) *Introduction to Mathematical Statistics.* 4th ed. New York: Macmillan.

Kennedy, P. (1985) *A Guide to Econometrics*, 2nd ed. Cambridge, MA: MIT Press.

Kmenta, J. (1986) *Elements of Econometrics*, 2nd ed. New York: Macmillan.

Lehmann, E., and H. Scheffe (1950) "Complete, Similar Regions, and Unbiased Estimation, Part I." *Sankhya*, 10, 305–340.

Mood, A., F. Graybill, and D. Boes (1974) *Introduction to the Theory of Statistics*, 3rd ed. New York: McGraw-Hill.

Spanos, A. (1986) *Statistical Foundations of Econometric Modelling.* Cambridge, Eng: Cambridge University Press.

Theil, H. (1971) *Principles of Econometrics.* New York: Wiley.

CHAPTER 4

Bayesian Inference

4.1 Introduction

In Chapter 3, estimation and hypothesis testing were treated within a classical, or sampling theory, framework. In this chapter an alternative approach to inference, namely, the Bayesian approach, is presented. We begin by outlining some of the differences between the two approaches.

The term *classical* does not have the unanimous support of all statisticians, but it is usually used to describe inference with at least the following characteristics.

1. Estimators and test procedures are evaluated in terms of their properties in repeated samples.
2. The probability of an event is defined in terms of the limit of the relative frequency of that event.
3. There is no provision for the formal inclusion of nonsample and loss information.

When estimating a parameter within the classical framework, an *unbiased* estimator is considered desirable because, as more and more samples are taken, the average value of the sample estimates tends toward the value of the unknown parameter. In the class of unbiased estimators a *minimum variance* unbiased estimator is preferred because, *on average*, it yields values that are closer (in terms of squared difference) to the real parameter than are those obtained from any other unbiased estimator. Biased estimators are also used if their mean squared error (variance plus bias squared) is low relative to that of other estimators. Methods for interval estimation and hypothesis testing are similarly evaluated in terms of their performance in a large number of repeated samples. Roughly speaking, evaluation takes place within a repeated sampling context because we like to have techniques with a high *probability* of giving the correct result, and probability is defined in terms of the limit of a relative frequency.

In a Bayesian framework, probability is defined in terms of a *degree of belief* (see Section 2.2.1), and although the properties of estimators and tests in repeated samples are of some interest, they do not provide the main basis for inference and estimator choice. The probability of an event is given by an individual's belief in how likely or unlikely the event is to occur. This belief may depend on quantitative and/or qualitative information, but it does not necessarily depend on the relative frequency of the event in a large number of future hypothetical experiments, a characteristic that has led some to comment that Bayesians do it with less frequency.

Because, in a Bayesian context, the definition of probability is subjective, different persons may assign different probabilities to the same event. Another consequence, and one of the main features of Bayesian analysis, is that uncertainty about the value of an unknown parameter can be expressed in terms of a probability distribution. It is assumed that what are likely and unlikely values for a parameter can be formalized by assigning to that parameter a probability density function. In the Bayesian framework, parameters are treated as random variables; not in the sense that different outcomes of an experiment yield different realizations of a parameter, but in the sense that a parameter has associated with it a subjective probability distribution that describes our state of knowledge about that parameter. In the classical framework, because a parameter is fixed in repeated samples, a probability distribution cannot be assigned to the parameter, or, more correctly, it would simply be the trivial distribution where the probability is equal to one at the true parameter value and zero elsewhere. See Leamer (1978, pp. 22–39) and Berger (1985, Chapter 3) for further discussion on subjective probability and for a comparison with other probability definitions.

The Bayesian subjective probability distribution on a parameter summarizes an individual's knowledge about that parameter. The knowledge may exist before observing any sample information, in which case the distribution is called a *prior distribution*, or it may be derived from both prior and sample information, in which case the distribution is called a *posterior distribution.* A distribution that is a posterior distribution in relation to some past sample can be regarded as a prior distribution when viewed in relation to a future sample. In either case, the subjective distribution is the source of all inferences about the unknown parameter, and, in contrast to the classical approach that concentrates on point estimates, attainment of the posterior distribution is often the final objective of any research investigation. The procedure that combines a prior distribution with sample information to form a posterior distribution is known as *Bayes' theorem.*

The discrete version of Bayes' theorem was introduced in Section 2.2.4. In this chapter we are concerned with a version where the prior and posterior distributions are continuous density functions. The first step toward stating this version is to introduce some notation. Let $\boldsymbol{\theta}$ be a vector of parameters in which we are interested, and let $\mathbf{y}$ be a vector of sample observations from the joint density function $f(\mathbf{y}|\boldsymbol{\theta})$. The function $f(\mathbf{y}|\boldsymbol{\theta})$ is algebraically identical to the likelihood function for $\boldsymbol{\theta}$ and contains all the sample information about $\boldsymbol{\theta}$. In the Bayesian framework, where a subjective probability distribution is placed on $\boldsymbol{\theta}$, and, in this sense, $\boldsymbol{\theta}$ is a random vector, $f(\mathbf{y}|\boldsymbol{\theta})$ is regarded as the conditional density function for $\mathbf{y}$, given $\boldsymbol{\theta}$. Furthermore, we can write

$$h(\boldsymbol{\theta}, \mathbf{y}) = f(\mathbf{y}|\boldsymbol{\theta})g(\boldsymbol{\theta}) = g(\boldsymbol{\theta}|\mathbf{y})f(\mathbf{y}) \tag{4.1.1}$$

where h is the joint density function for $\boldsymbol{\theta}$ and $\mathbf{y}$, g denotes a density function for $\boldsymbol{\theta}$, and f denotes a density function for $\mathbf{y}$. Obviously, f and g sometimes denote marginal distributions and sometimes denote conditional distributions, and hence they are not used consistently to denote the same functional form. Nevertheless, in each case the meaning should be clear.

Rearranging (4.1.1) yields

$$g(\boldsymbol{\theta}|\mathbf{y}) = \frac{f(\mathbf{y}|\boldsymbol{\theta})g(\boldsymbol{\theta})}{f(\mathbf{y})} \tag{4.1.2}$$

This expression is known as Bayes' theorem. The posterior density function for $\boldsymbol{\theta}$ is $g(\boldsymbol{\theta}|\mathbf{y})$, since it summarizes all the information about $\boldsymbol{\theta}$ after the sample $\mathbf{y}$ has been observed; $g(\boldsymbol{\theta})$ is the prior density for $\boldsymbol{\theta}$, summarizing the nonsample information about $\boldsymbol{\theta}$. If we recognize that, with respect to $\boldsymbol{\theta}$, $f(\mathbf{y})$ can be regarded as a constant and that $f(\mathbf{y}|\boldsymbol{\theta})$ can be written as the likelihood function $l(\boldsymbol{\theta}|\mathbf{y})$, then (4.1.2) becomes

$$g(\boldsymbol{\theta}|\mathbf{y}) \propto l(\boldsymbol{\theta}|\mathbf{y})g(\boldsymbol{\theta}) \tag{4.1.3}$$

where $\propto$ denotes "proportional to." In words, (4.1.3) can be written as

$$\text{Posterior information} \propto \text{sample information} \times \text{prior information}$$

Thus, the version of Bayes' theorem in (4.1.3) shows us how prior information about $\boldsymbol{\theta}$, expressed in terms of the prior density function $g(\boldsymbol{\theta})$, is modified by the sample information expressed in terms of the likelihood function $l(\boldsymbol{\theta}|\mathbf{y})$, to give our posterior information about $\boldsymbol{\theta}$, expressed in terms of the posterior density function $g(\boldsymbol{\theta}|\mathbf{y})$. Attainment of this posterior density function could be viewed as the end point in any scientific investigation. Alternatively, $g(\boldsymbol{\theta}|\mathbf{y})$ could be one of the essential ingredients in a general decision theory problem, or, more specifically, it could be used to obtain a point or interval estimate or to test hypotheses.

The next section in this chapter (Section 4.2) is concerned with the application of Equation 4.1.3 to the mean of a normal distribution with known variance. In Section 4.4 the assumption of known variance is relaxed and (4.1.3) is applied to both the mean and variance of a normal distribution. In the intervening section (Section 4.3) the decision theory approach to inference is discussed. This approach can be viewed within the repeated sampling context used by classical statistics or within a Bayesian context. The relationship between the two decision theory approaches is examined.

4.2 Bayesian Inference for the Mean of a Normal Distribution (Known Variance)

4.2.1 Posterior Distribution From an Informative Prior

We use an example to introduce the Bayesian approach to inference and to contrast it with the classical approach. Suppose that weekly receipts (in thousands of dollars) at a Louisiana Fried Chicken (LFC) outlet are normally distributed with a mean of β and variance $\sigma^2 = 4$. Denoting weekly receipts by Y, we have $Y \sim N(\beta, \sigma^2 = 4)$. The assumption that the variance is known and equal to 4 is made to keep the example simple; it is relaxed later in the chapter. Let us assume we are interested in purchasing the LFC outlet, and, therefore, that we are interested in gathering information about mean weekly receipts β. In the sampling theory approach we would begin by taking a sample of weekly receipts. Suppose that a sample of size 10 is taken and that it yields the following observations.

$$\begin{aligned}\mathbf{y}' &= (y_1, y_2, \ldots, y_{10})\\ &= (4.74, 7.11, 5.31, 6.28, 6.09, 8.52, 2.78, 7.38, 5.44, 5.72).\end{aligned}$$

Our sampling theory information would then be presented in terms of a point and/or an interval estimate for β. Using any of the estimation rules outlined in Chapter 3, the sample mean would be used as a point estimate, and, in this case, it is given by

$$\hat{\beta} = \sum_{t=1}^{10} y_t/10 = 5.937 \tag{4.2.1}$$

For an interval estimate, say a 95% confidence interval, we have

$$\hat{\beta} \pm 1.96\sigma/\sqrt{T} = 5.937 \pm 1.96 \times 2/\sqrt{10}$$

or

$$(4.697, 7.177) \tag{4.2.2}$$

Thus, roughly speaking, our sample information suggests that mean weekly receipts are about \$5900 but that this mean could be as low as \$4700 or as high as \$7200.

In the Bayesian approach we tackle the problem by first asking whether or not we have any prior information about β and by expressing this information in terms of a subjective p.d.f. for β. Suppose that, from our previous experience in fast chicken outlets, we believe that there is a 0.95 probability that mean weekly receipts lies between \$5000 and \$11,000. That is, in thousands of dollars,

$$P(5 < \beta < 11) = 0.95 \tag{4.2.3}$$

Suppose also that our subjective p.d.f. about likely values of β can be adequately represented by a normal distribution with mean $\bar{\beta}$ and variance $\bar{\sigma}_\beta^2$. That is, $\beta \sim N(\bar{\beta}, \bar{\sigma}_\beta^2)$, or

$$g(\beta) = \frac{1}{\sqrt{2\pi}\,\bar{\sigma}_\beta} \exp\left\{-\frac{1}{2\bar{\sigma}_\beta^2}(\beta - \bar{\beta})^2\right\} \tag{4.2.4}$$

Using properties of the normal distribution, we have

$$P\left(-1.96 < \frac{\beta - \bar{\beta}}{\bar{\sigma}_\beta} < 1.96\right) = 0.95$$

or

$$P(\bar{\beta} - 1.96\bar{\sigma}_\beta < \beta < \bar{\beta} + 1.96\bar{\sigma}_\beta) = 0.95 \tag{4.2.5}$$

From the equivalence of (4.2.3) and (4.2.5) we have

$$\bar{\beta} - 1.96\bar{\sigma}_\beta = 5 \quad \text{and} \quad \bar{\beta} + 1.96\bar{\sigma}_\beta = 11$$

Solving these two equations for $\bar{\beta}$ and $\bar{\sigma}_\beta$ yields

$$\bar{\beta} = 8, \quad \bar{\sigma}_\beta = 1.5306, \quad \text{and} \quad \bar{\sigma}_\beta^2 = 2.3427$$

Thus, if a normal distribution is appropriate to represent out prior views about β, and we believe that $P(5 < \beta < 11) = 0.95$, then $g(\beta)$ is such that $\beta \sim N(8, 2.3427)$. Note that, in addition to (4.2.3), the assumption of a normal distribution implies other probability statements about β. For example,

$$P(\beta > 8) = P(\beta < 8) = 0.5$$

$$P(6 < \beta < 10) = 0.81$$

and

$$P(4 < \beta < 12) = 0.99$$

Before examining how Bayes' theorem is used to combine this prior information with our sample information, some explanatory remarks are in order. First, in the sampling theory or classical approach to inference there is no formal mechanism for incorporating prior information like that we have just described; the formal incorporation of prior knowledge is one of the main distinguishing features of Bayesian inference. Furthermore, in the classical approach it is not possible to make probability statements about unknown parameters as we have done in (4.2.3) and (4.2.5); since the classical approach treats unknown parameters as constants that do not vary in repeated samples and defines probability in terms of the limit of a relative frequency, it makes no sense in this context to make probability statements about unknown parameters. On the other hand, with the subjective probability definition employed by Bayesian inference, such probability statements are permissible. Finally, the prior p.d.f. considered in (4.2.4) conveys some definite prior information about a parameter; priors with this characteristic are often called informative priors to distinguish them from another class of priors known as noninformative priors. Noninformative priors will be considered in the next subsection.

Being Bayesian decision makers, we could decide whether or not to purchase the LFC outlet simply on the basis of our prior information. However, we are likely to make a more informed decision if we can collect additional information, in the form of a sample of weekly receipts, and combine this sample information with our prior information. Such a combination is achieved using Bayes' theorem, which, in this context, is

$$g(\beta|\mathbf{y}) \propto l(\beta|\mathbf{y})g(\beta) \tag{4.2.6}$$

where

$$l(\beta|\mathbf{y}) \propto \exp\left\{-\frac{1}{2\sigma^2}\sum_{t=1}^{T}(y_t-\beta)^2\right\} \tag{4.2.7}$$

and $g(\beta)$ is defined in (4.2.4). In (4.2.7) we have written the likelihood function for β as proportional to the exponent; the omitted term, $(2\pi\sigma^2)^{-T/2}$, can be regarded as a constant of proportionality because σ^2 is assumed known. Before proceeding any further, it is convenient to write

$$\begin{aligned}\sum_{t=1}^{T}(y_t-\beta)^2 &= \sum_{t=1}^{T}[(y_t-\hat{\beta})-(\beta-\hat{\beta})]^2\\ &= T(\beta-\hat{\beta})^2+\sum_{t=1}^{T}(y_t-\hat{\beta})^2\end{aligned} \tag{4.2.8}$$

where $\hat{\beta}$ is the sample mean. The likelihood function then becomes

$$l(\beta|\mathbf{y}) \propto \exp\left\{-\frac{1}{2\sigma^2}\left[T(\beta-\hat{\beta})^2 + \sum_{t=1}^{T}(y_t-\hat{\beta})^2\right]\right\}$$

$$\propto \exp\left\{-\frac{T}{2\sigma^2}(\beta-\hat{\beta})^2\right\} \tag{4.2.9}$$

The last term can be absorbed into the proportionality constant because it does not contain β.

Using (4.2.6) to multiply $l(\beta|\mathbf{y})$ in (4.2.9) by $g(\beta)$ in (4.2.4), and ignoring the constants in (4.2.4), yields the posterior p.d.f. for β

$$g(\beta|\mathbf{y}) \propto \exp\left\{-\frac{1}{2}\left[\frac{T}{\sigma^2}(\beta-\hat{\beta})^2 + \frac{1}{\bar{\sigma}_\beta^2}(\beta-\bar{\beta})^2\right]\right\}$$

After some straightforward but tedious algebra (see Problem 4.1), it is possible to show that

$$\frac{T}{\sigma^2}(\beta-\hat{\beta})^2 + \frac{1}{\bar{\sigma}_\beta^2}(\beta-\bar{\beta})^2 = \frac{1}{\bar{\bar{\sigma}}_\beta^2}(\beta-\bar{\bar{\beta}})^2 - \bar{\bar{\beta}}^2\left(\frac{T}{\sigma^2}+\frac{1}{\bar{\sigma}_\beta^2}\right) + \frac{T\hat{\beta}^2}{\sigma^2} + \frac{\bar{\beta}^2}{\bar{\sigma}_\beta^2} \tag{4.2.10}$$

where

$$\bar{\bar{\beta}} = \frac{\dfrac{T\hat{\beta}}{\sigma^2}+\dfrac{\bar{\beta}}{\bar{\sigma}_\beta^2}}{\dfrac{T}{\sigma^2}+\dfrac{1}{\bar{\sigma}_\beta^2}} = \frac{h_s\hat{\beta}+h_0\bar{\beta}}{h_s+h_0} \tag{4.2.11}$$

$$\bar{\bar{\sigma}}_\beta^2 = \frac{1}{\dfrac{T}{\sigma^2}+\dfrac{1}{\bar{\sigma}_\beta^2}} = \frac{1}{h_s+h_0} = \frac{1}{h_1} \tag{4.2.12}$$

and

$$h_0 = \frac{1}{\bar{\sigma}_\beta^2} \qquad h_s = \frac{T}{\sigma^2} \qquad h_1 = h_0 + h_s \tag{4.2.13}$$

Noting that the last three terms in (4.2.10) do not depend on β, we can write the posterior p.d.f. $g(\beta|\mathbf{y})$ as

$$g(\beta|\mathbf{y}) \propto \exp\left\{-\frac{1}{2\bar{\bar{\sigma}}_\beta^2}(\beta-\bar{\bar{\beta}})^2\right\} \tag{4.2.14}$$

This p.d.f. can be recognized as a normal distribution with mean $\bar{\bar{\beta}}$ and variance $\bar{\bar{\sigma}}_\beta^2$. That is,

$$(\beta \mid \mathbf{y}) \sim N(\bar{\bar{\beta}}, \bar{\bar{\sigma}}_\beta^2) \tag{4.2.15}$$

Note that the term that determines the functional form of the normal distribution is the term in the exponent, as given in (4.2.14). This term is known as the *kernel* of the density function. The remaining term, $(2\pi\bar{\bar{\sigma}}_\beta^2)^{-1/2}$, is simply included to make the function integrate to 1 (or to make the area under the p.d.f. equal to 1). Including this term in (4.2.14) yields

$$g(\beta \mid \mathbf{y}) = \frac{1}{\sqrt{2\pi}\,\bar{\bar{\sigma}}_\beta} \exp\left\{-\frac{1}{2\bar{\bar{\sigma}}_\beta^2}(\beta - \bar{\bar{\beta}})^2\right\} \tag{4.2.16}$$

If we had not ignored constants in the derivation of (4.2.14), and if we had included $f(\mathbf{y})$ in the denominator of Bayes' theorem as appears in (4.1.2), then (4.2.16) would have been obtained exactly, without a need to introduce an "integrating constant." The algebra is much easier, however, if our strategy of just considering the proportional relationships, and introducing the integrating constant at the final stage, is adopted.

Note that we began with a normal prior p.d.f., combined it with the likelihood for a normal distribution, and ended with a normal posterior p.d.f. A prior distribution that, after combination with the likelihood function, yields a posterior distribution of the same form is known as a *conjugate prior*. If this conjugate prior can be chosen as belonging to the class of distributions with the same functional form as the likelihood function (viewed as a function of the unknown parameter —see equation 4.2.9), then the conjugate prior is known as a *natural* conjugate prior. We have just shown that the natural conjugate prior for the mean of a normal distribution with known variance is also a normal distribution. Natural conjugate priors are popular because of their algebraic convenience and because they are rich enough to represent a wide diversity of prior opinions. There are some cases, however, where results can be quite sensitive to the specification of an informative prior, and the natural conjugate prior may not satisfy certain "robustness" criteria. Such issues are well beyond the scope of this book; we refer you to Berger (1985, Chapter 4) for details.

It is instructive to consider the relationship between the posterior mean $\bar{\bar{\beta}}$ and the prior and sample information, as well as the relationship between the posterior variance $\bar{\bar{\sigma}}_\beta^2$ and the prior and sample information. From (4.2.11) we can see that the posterior mean $\bar{\bar{\beta}}$ is a weighted average of the sample mean $\hat{\beta}$ and the prior mean $\bar{\beta}$ with weights given by the precision of each source of information, where precision is defined as the inverse of the variance. The precision of the prior information is $h_0 = 1/\bar{\sigma}_\beta^2$; vague prior information is reflected by a high prior variance $\bar{\sigma}_\beta^2$, a low precision h_0, and, consequently, a low weight on the prior mean $\bar{\beta}$. The precision of the sample information, $h_s = T/\sigma^2$, is, as we will see in the next subsection, the inverse of the variance of β when only sample information is used. It is, of course, also the inverse of the variance of $\hat{\beta}$ in the sampling theory approach. The greater the precision of the sample information, the greater the contribution of the sample mean $\hat{\beta}$ toward the calculation of the posterior mean. The sample information will be more precise, the larger is the sample size T and the smaller is the variance σ^2.

Let us return to the LFC example. From our prior information and the sample of 10 weeks considered earlier, we have $h_0 = 1/2.3427 = 0.4269$ and $h_s = \frac{10}{4} = 2.5$. Thus, the posterior mean is

$$\bar{\bar{\beta}} = \frac{h_s\hat{\beta} + h_0\bar{\beta}}{h_s + h_0} = \frac{2.5 \times 5.937 + 0.4269 \times 8}{2.5 + 0.4269} = 6.238$$

The much greater precision of the sample information relative to the prior information has led to a posterior mean that is relatively close to the sample mean. It appears that we were initially overly optimistic about the earnings of the chicken outlet.

The precision of the posterior information, $h_1 = 1/\bar{\bar{\sigma}}_\beta^2$, is given by the sum of the prior and sample precisions. That is, $h_1 = h_0 + h_s$. Thus the precision (variance) of the posterior distribution will always be greater (less) than both the sample precision (variance) and the prior precision (variance). For our example, we have

$$h_1 = h_0 + h_s = 0.4269 + 2.5 = 2.9269$$

and

$$\bar{\bar{\sigma}}_\beta^2 = 1/h_1 = 1/2.9269 = 0.3417$$

A comparison of the prior and posterior p.d.f.'s for β, which are graphed in Figure 4.1, clearly shows the effect of the sample information. The sample information has moved the distribution to the left, and made it much sharper, reflecting the improved precision in our information.

The presentation of the complete posterior distribution for β, or summary statistics such as the posterior mean and the posterior variance, are conventional ways of presenting information about β collected within the Bayesian inference framework. However, there are also Bayesian counterparts to the conventional sampling theory ways of presenting information such as point estimates, interval estimates, and the outcome of hypothesis tests. After considering the posterior density from a noninformative prior in the next subsection, we will use the LFC example to illustrate Bayesian methods for interval estimation, hypothesis testing, prediction, and point estimation in Sections 4.2.3, 4.2.4, 4.2.5 and 4.3, respectively.

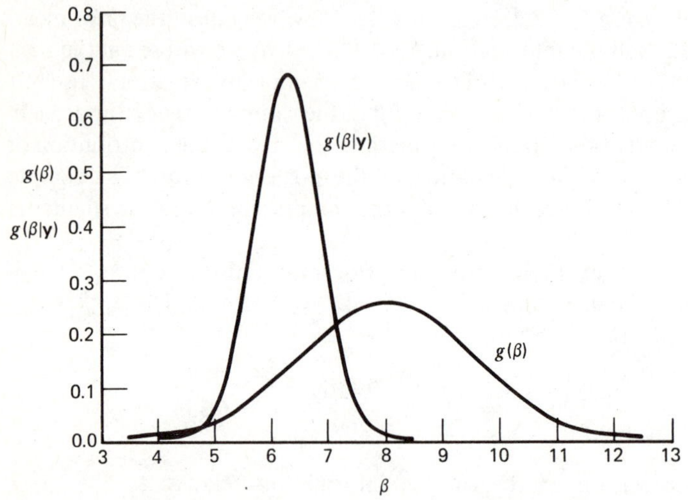

Figure 4.1 Prior and posterior densities for β when σ is known.

4.2.2 Inference From a Noninformative Prior

In the previous subsection we demonstrated how the Bayesian approach to inference can be used to include prior information about an unknown parameter. A natural question to ask is whether the Bayesian approach can be employed when no prior information is available, or whether the absence of prior information leads a researcher to choose the sampling theory approach automatically. It so happens that there is a very well developed theory of Bayesian inference based on what are known as noninformative priors, and there are many statisticians who believe the Bayesian approach to inference is superior to the classical approach, irrespective of whether or not substantial prior information is incorporated. We will, therefore, continue our example of the previous subsection, and examine the question of specifying a noninformative prior for the mean β of a normal distribution with known variance σ^2. For further details about general noninformative priors see Zellner (1971), Box and Tiao (1973), and Berger (1985).

A noninformative prior is a prior distribution that contains no information about a parameter and hence, when it is combined with the likelihood function via Bayes' theorem, it leads to a posterior distribution that is completely dominated by the sample information. There are three main reasons for using noninformative priors. First, there may be circumstances where we have very little information on the parameters (our knowledge is "vague" or "diffuse"), and we would like a prior distribution that reflects this lack of information. Second, although we might have substantial prior information, there may be occasions where it is considered more objective to present a posterior distribution that reflects only sample information, instead of "biasing" it with our own views. Finally, it is sometimes very difficult to formulate an appropriate informative prior distribution, and, although better decision making is likely to result if the prior information is incorporated, an easy way out of the difficulty is to use a noninformative prior.

Returning to our example of the previous subsection, an examination of the posterior mean and the posterior variance of β in (4.2.11) and (4.2.12) indicates that as the prior variance $\bar{\sigma}_\beta^2$ increases, our prior information about β becomes more vague, and it contributes less to the posterior distribution. In fact, taking the limit as $\bar{\sigma}_\beta^2 \to \infty$, we have

$$\bar{\bar{\beta}} = \hat{\beta} \qquad \text{and} \qquad \bar{\bar{\sigma}}_\beta^2 = \frac{\sigma^2}{T} \tag{4.2.17}$$

indicating that, in this limiting case of vague prior information, the posterior mean and variance depend only on sample quantities. Substituting (4.2.17) into the posterior p.d.f. in (4.2.14) yields

$$g(\beta|\mathbf{y}) \propto \exp\left\{-\frac{T}{2\sigma^2}(\beta - \hat{\beta})^2\right\} \tag{4.2.18}$$

From this posterior p.d.f. we have $\beta \sim N(\hat{\beta}, \sigma^2/T)$. Note that this result is similar to the sampling theory result obtained in Chapter 3. In the Bayesian case in (4.2.18), β is treated as the random variable and, after the sample has been realized, $\hat{\beta}$ is regarded as fixed. The sampling theory result is $\hat{\beta} \sim N(\beta, \sigma^2/T)$, where $\hat{\beta}$ is treated as the random variable and β is a fixed parameter.

Given the similarities between the result in (4.2.18) and the sampling theory result, and given that $g(\beta|\mathbf{y})$ in (4.2.18) was obtained by making our prior information more vague ($\bar{\sigma}_\beta^2 \to \infty$), this posterior p.d.f. seems a natural one for reflecting sample information only. Thus, a reasonable noninformative prior would be one that, after using Bayes' theorem, yields the posterior p.d.f. in (4.2.18). At first one might suspect that such a prior can be found by letting $\bar{\sigma}_\beta^2 \to \infty$ in the expression for the prior $g(\beta)$ given in (4.2.4); this strategy parallels the one we adopted to find the posterior p.d.f. However, we note that, as $\bar{\sigma}_\beta^2 \to \infty$, $g(\beta) \to 0$. To find an alternative prior, consider the expression for the likelihood function in (4.2.9), namely

$$l(\beta|\mathbf{y}) \propto \exp\left\{-\frac{T}{2\sigma^2}(\beta - \hat{\beta})^2\right\} \tag{4.2.19}$$

This expression is identical to that for the posterior p.d.f. that we derived in (4.2.18). Thus, if we specify the prior p.d.f. as equal to (or proportional to) any constant, that is,

$$g(\beta) \propto \text{constant} \tag{4.2.20}$$

multiplication of the likelihood by this prior will yield the posterior p.d.f. in (4.2.18). Specifically,

$$\begin{aligned} g(\beta \mid \mathbf{y}) &\propto g(\beta) l(\beta \mid \mathbf{y}) \\ &\propto \text{constant} \exp\left\{ -\frac{T}{2\sigma^2} (\beta - \hat{\beta})^2 \right\} \\ &\propto \exp\left\{ -\frac{T}{2\sigma^2} (\beta - \hat{\beta})^2 \right\} \end{aligned} \tag{4.2.21}$$

Our noninformative prior p.d.f. for β is, therefore, $g(\beta) \propto$ constant. This p.d.f. is a uniform density over the entire real line, $-\infty < \beta < \infty$. It is a reflection of ignorance or vague prior information because it suggests that all values of β are equally likely. A property of $g(\beta)$ that is not shared by conventional density functions is that it does not integrate to unity. That is

$$\int_{-\infty}^{\infty} g(\beta)\, d\beta = \infty \tag{4.2.22}$$

Density functions with this property are termed improper, and $g(\beta)$ is referred to as an *improper prior*. Improper priors are often used for representing ignorance. The fact that they are not integrable is of no consequence for making posterior inferences, providing that they lead (via Bayes' theorem) to posterior densities that are proper. Alternatively, one interpretation of noninformative priors like (4.2.20) is that they are locally uniform [Box and Tiao (1973)]. That is, they are assumed to hold over the region of the parameter space for which the likelihood function is appreciable, but outside this region they taper off to zero, and are therefore proper.

It should be pointed out that the approach we have taken in this subsection could be regarded as back to front. Instead of beginning with a posterior p.d.f. that reflects only sample information, and finding a noninformative prior that yields that posterior p.d.f., it is more conventional to begin with a noninformative prior that reflects ignorance or vague knowledge about a parameter and to derive the posterior p.d.f. that corresponds to this prior. A number of rules for specifying noninformative priors have been suggested in the literature. We refer the interested reader to Zellner (1971), Box and Tiao (1973), and Berger (1985).

If, in the LFC example, we use a noninformative prior for β, then the posterior p.d.f. is

$$(\beta \mid \mathbf{y}) \sim N(\hat{\beta}, \sigma^2/T) = N(5.937, 0.4) \tag{4.2.23}$$

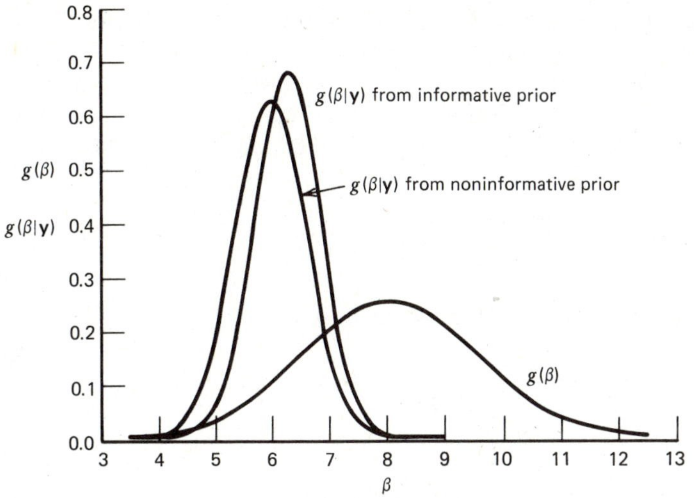

Figure 4.2 Prior and posterior densities for β when σ is known.

A graph of this p.d.f. is presented in Figure 4.2, along with the informative prior and the posterior p.d.f. derived from the informative prior. Including all three densities on the one graph clearly shows the contributions of the prior and the sample information to the posterior p.d.f.

4.2.3 Interval Estimation

As was discussed in Chapter 3, in the classical approach to inference we frequently summarize our knowledge about a parameter by expressing our research results in terms of a confidence interval for that parameter. In the Bayesian approach it is preferable to present the complete posterior density function, but, if this approach is too unwieldly, it may be useful to use an interval estimate as a summary measure.

To obtain a Bayesian interval estimate for a parameter θ, with a probability content of, for example, 0.95, we need two values, a and d, such that

$$P(a < \theta < d) = \int_a^d g(\theta|\mathbf{y})\, d\theta = 0.95 \tag{4.2.24}$$

Values a and d that satisfy (4.2.24) will not be unique, however, and so we need some criterion for choosing between alternative intervals. One possibility is to choose the most likely region by insisting that the value of the posterior density function for every point inside the interval is greater than that for every point outside the interval, which implies $g(a|\mathbf{y}) = g(d|\mathbf{y})$. An interval with this property is known as the *highest posterior density* (HPD) interval, and, if the posterior density is unimodal, it is equivalent to finding the shortest interval (minimizing $d - a$) such that (4.2.24) holds.

For an example, consider the LFCs mean weekly receipts β and the posterior p.d.f. $g(\beta|\mathbf{y})$ specified in (4.2.16). Using the data provided, $(\beta|\mathbf{y}) \sim N(6.238, 0.3417)$. Thus,

$$\frac{\beta - 6.238}{\sqrt{0.3417}} \sim N(0, 1)$$

and, for an HPD interval with probability content 0.95,

$$P\left(-1.96 < \frac{\beta - 6.238}{\sqrt{0.3147}} < 1.96\right) = 0.95$$

or,

$$P(5.092 < \beta < 7.384) = 0.95 \tag{4.2.25}$$

Thus, our 0.95 HPD interval for β is (5.092, 7.384). After observing the sample, there is 0.95 probability that β lies between 5.092 to 7.384. Note the effect of the sample information. Based only on prior information, there was a 0.95 probability that β lies between 5.0 and 11.0.

The 0.95 Bayesian interval in (4.2.25) is not just any 0.95 interval. It will indeed be the 0.95 HPD interval (or the shortest 0.95 interval) because the normal distribution is symmetric about the mean $\bar{\bar{\beta}}$. For nonsymmetric posterior p.d.f.'s computation of the shortest interval can be more involved.

If we had employed the posterior p.d.f. from a noninformative prior, namely $(\beta|\mathbf{y}) \sim N(5.937, 0.4)$, the 0.95 HPD interval would have been (4.697, 7.177). Note that this interval is identical to the 95% confidence interval that was obtained in (4.2.2) using the sampling theory approach. However, the interpretation is different. In the Bayesian framework the statement $P(a < \beta < d) = 1 - \alpha$ means that there is a $(1 - \alpha)$ (subjective) probability that β lies between a and d. In the sampling theory framework, this statement implies that, in any given sample, there is a $(1 - \alpha)$ probability of obtaining a and d such that $a < \beta < d$.

4.2.4 Hypothesis Testing

4.2.4a Hypothesis Testing Using HPD Intervals

One method for testing hypotheses within the Bayesian framework (but not the most common method) is to accept or reject a point null hypothesis depending on whether or not the specified value under H_0 lies within an HPD interval with a preassigned probability content. For example, in terms of the HPD for β given in (4.2.25), we would accept a null hypothesis of the form $H_0: \beta = \beta^*$ if β^* lies in the interval (5.092, 7.384); otherwise we would reject H_0.

This method for testing hypotheses is obviously similar to the sampling theory approach of rejecting a null hypothesis when the hypothesized value for a parameter falls outside a confidence interval. When a noninformative prior and the example of this chapter are employed, the results (but not the interpretations) are identical. There are many examples, however, when the approaches do not yield identical results.

The more conventional Bayesian framework for hypothesis testing is that using posterior odds. It is to this topic that we now turn.

4.2.4b. Posterior Odds and Hypothesis Testing

In the sampling theory approach to hypothesis testing, two hypotheses H_0 and H_1 are set up, an appropriate test statistic is specified, and based on whether or not a value of that test statistic falls within a critical region, each hypothesis is accepted or rejected. With the Bayesian approach, which uses posterior odds, it is more appropriate to speak of "comparing" hypotheses than "testing" hypotheses. In this approach the posterior probabilities of each hypothesis being correct, $P(H_0|\mathbf{y})$ and $P(H_1|\mathbf{y})$, are computed and the *posterior odds ratio*

$$K_{01} = \frac{P(H_0|\mathbf{y})}{P(H_1|\mathbf{y})} \tag{4.2.26}$$

is formed. This ratio gives the odds in favor of H_0 relative to H_1. It is a simple and convenient way of expressing the evidence in favor of one hypothesis relative to another. Unlike the sampling theory approach to hypothesis testing, the Bayesian approach does not require that each of the hypotheses be accepted or rejected. It is sufficient for the evidence on the hypotheses to be summarized in terms of the posterior odds ratio. If a decision to accept or to reject needs to be made, it can be made by defining a loss function that expresses the consequences of making the wrong decision, and by minimizing expected loss where the expectation is with respect to the posterior probabilities on each hypothesis.

Let us consider an example using a one-sided test of the form

$$H_0: \beta \leq 5 \tag{4.2.27a}$$

$$H_1: \beta > 5 \tag{4.2.27b}$$

In the context of the LFC example, such hypotheses might be relevant for our decision concerning whether or not to purchase the chicken outlet. Let us suppose that it is profitable to purchase the outlet if H_1 is true (average weekly earnings are greater than \$5000); otherwise, it is not profitable (H_0 is true). Using the sampling theory procedures outlined in Chapter 3, the first step toward carrying out this test is to calculate a value of the relevant test statistic, namely,

$$z = \frac{\hat{\beta} - 5}{\sigma/\sqrt{T}} = \frac{5.937 - 5}{2/\sqrt{10}} = 1.482 \tag{4.2.28}$$

Using a 5% significance level (or a maximum Type I error of 0.05) the critical value for the test is $z_{(0.05)} = 1.645$. Since $z = 1.482 < 1.645$, the sampling theory approach leads us to accept H_0 and to not purchase the outlet.

To compute the posterior odds in favor of H_0, we use the posterior p.d.f. $(\beta|\mathbf{y}) \sim N(6.238, 0.3417)$. We have

$$\begin{aligned} P(H_0|\mathbf{y}) &= P(\beta \leq 5|\mathbf{y}) \\ &= P\left(Z \leq \frac{5 - 6.238}{\sqrt{0.3417}}\right) \\ &= P(Z \leq -2.12) \\ &= 0.017 \\ P(H_1|\mathbf{y}) &= P(\beta > 5|\mathbf{y}) = 0.983 \end{aligned}$$

Thus, the posterior odds in favor of H_0 are $K_{01} = P(H_0|\mathbf{y})/P(H_1|\mathbf{y}) = 0.017/0.983 = 0.0173$. Alternatively, the posterior odds in favor of H_1 are

$$K_{10} = \frac{P(H_1|\mathbf{y})}{P(H_0|\mathbf{y})} = \frac{0.983}{0.017} = 57.8 \tag{4.2.29}$$

Thus, within the Bayesian framework, we conclude that H_1 is more than 57 times more likely to be true than is H_0.

This example clearly demonstrates how vastly different the outcomes of the two procedures can be. A sampling theorist may criticize the comparison on the grounds that our prior information has "biased" the result. However, if the posterior p.d.f. from a noninformative prior is employed, the posterior odds ratio in favor of H_1 is still 13.5. The sampling theory approach has implicitly assigned a much heavier loss to a Type I error than it has to a Type II error. That is, it assumes the loss associated with purchasing the LFC outlet when $\beta \leq 5$ is much greater than the opportunity cost of not purchasing when $\beta > 5$. In fact, under the assumptions about costs that follow, we can show that the sampling theory approach (with a 5% significance level) assumes the cost of incorrectly purchasing is more than 57.8 times (or 13.5 times for a noninformative prior) greater than the opportunity cost of incorrectly not purchasing.

As was already mentioned, the posterior odds ratio is a convenient method of summarizing the results from a comparison of two hypotheses. However, if a decision to accept or reject each hypothesis needs to be made, we can proceed in the following way.

Let

c_1 = the loss from purchasing the LFC outlet when $\beta \leq 5$

c_2 = the opportunity cost of not purchasing the LFC outlet when $\beta > 5$

Then,

$$\begin{aligned} E[\text{Loss}|\text{do not purchase}] &= 0 \cdot P(\beta \leq 5) + c_2 P(\beta > 5) \\ &= 0.983c_2 \\ E[\text{Loss}|\text{purchase}] &= c_1 P(\beta \leq 5) + 0 \cdot P(\beta > 5) \\ &= 0.017c_1 \end{aligned}$$

We will purchase the outlet if

$$E[\text{Loss}\,|\text{do not purchase}] > E[\text{Loss}|\text{purchase}]$$

That is, if $0.983c_2 > 0.017c_1$, or

$$c_1 < 57.8c_2$$

Thus, the sampling theory approach implicitly assumes the cost of incorrectly purchasing is more than 57.8 times greater than the opportunity cost of incorrectly not purchasing. This figure is 13.5 if the posterior p.d.f. from a noninformative prior is used.

The assumption of c_1 and c_2 being constant is not realistic, but was made to simplify the example. It is more likely that c_1 will be a decreasing function of β defined over the range $-\infty < \beta \leq 5$, and that c_2 will be an increasing function of β defined over the range $5 < \beta < \infty$. Solution of this more realistic version takes us further into decision theory than we wish to travel. The appropriate methodology is covered in most introductory courses on decision theory. See, for example, Jones (1977, Chapter 11).

In this section we have demonstrated how the posterior odds ratio for two hypotheses can be calculated when the hypotheses are "one-sided" as in (4.2.27). In Chapter 7 we will show how the posterior odds ratio is computed for a "point null hypothesis."

4.2.5 Prediction

Suppose that, after purchasing the LFC outlet, we are interested in obtaining information about receipts in some future week, say $(T + 1)$. In the Bayesian framework such information is summarized using a predictive p.d.f. for y_{T+1}. This predictive p.d.f. can tell us the probability of a future week's receipts lying within some specified range.

To derive the predictive p.d.f. for y_{T+1}, it is convenient to write the model generating this observation as

$$y_{T+1} = \beta + e_{T+1} \tag{4.2.30}$$

where $e_{T+1} \sim N(0, \sigma^2 = 4)$. Using all the information on β that was outlined in Section 4.2.1, the posterior p.d.f. derived in that section is relevant and is

$$(\beta|\mathbf{y}) \sim N(6.238, 0.3417) \tag{4.2.31}$$

Since, in (4.2.30), both β and e_{T+1} are normally distributed, it follows that the predictive p.d.f. for y_{T+1} will be normal. Furthermore, e_{T+1} and β can be treated as independent because the posterior p.d.f. for β is based only on past observations $(y_1, y_2, \ldots, y_T)$, which are assumed to be independent of the future observation y_{T+1} (and the future error term e_{T+1}). Thus

$$E[y_{T+1}] = E[\beta] + E[e_{T+1}] = 6.238$$

$$\text{var}[y_{T+1}] = \text{var}[\beta] + \text{var}[e_{T+1}] = 4.3417$$

The predictive p.d.f. for y_{T+1} is, therefore,

$$y_{T+1} \sim N(6.238, 4.3417)$$

and this p.d.f. can be used to make probability statements about likely future values of weekly receipts.

The foregoing example was particularly easy because y_{T+1} was equal to the sum of two independent normal random variables. In the general prediction problem involving some parameter θ, the marginal density $f(y_{T+1}|\mathbf{y})$ is obtained by integrating θ out of the joint density function $f(y_{T+1}, \theta|\mathbf{y})$.

4.3 Point Estimation

The posterior density function for a parameter summarizes all the information that a researcher has about that parameter; thus, once the equation of the posterior density has been derived, this could be regarded as a reasonable point at which to conclude a study. Under some circumstances, however, a researcher needs to make a decision on just one value (or *point estimate*) of a parameter, and in this situation, we need some procedure for determining which value is best. The choice of a "best estimate" will typically depend on the costs or loss to the investigator from using an estimate of a parameter, say $\hat{\theta}$, that is not equal to the true parameter value θ. This loss is likely to be greater the further the estimate is from the true value. The function $L(\theta, \hat{\theta})$ that describes the consequences of basing a decision on the point estimate $\hat{\theta}$ when θ is the true parameter value is known as the loss function. Examples of commonly used loss functions are the quadratic loss function $L_2 = c(\hat{\theta} - \theta)^2$ and the linear loss function $L_1 = c|\hat{\theta} - \theta|$, where, in each case, c is a positive constant.

To obtain a point estimate we need to consider minimizing loss in some sense. The value of $\hat{\theta}$ that minimizes loss for all reasonable loss functions is $\hat{\theta} = \theta$. However, because θ is unknown, it is clearly not a feasible estimate. To overcome this problem we minimize averages (or expected) loss over all possible values of θ, with the different values of θ being weighted by the posterior distribution $g(\theta|\mathbf{y})$. Thus, a Bayesian point estimate is that value of $\hat{\theta}$ that minimizes expected posterior loss, where expected posterior loss is given by

$$E_{\theta|\mathbf{y}}[L(\theta, \hat{\theta})] = \int L(\theta, \hat{\theta})g(\theta|\mathbf{y})\, d\theta \tag{4.3.1}$$

Under the quadratic loss function L_2 the *mean* of the posterior distribution is the Bayesian point estimate that minimizes (4.3.1). With the linear loss function L_1 *the median* of the posterior distribution is the Bayesian point estimate. In the LFC example introduced in Section 4.2.1 the posterior distribution is a normal distribution with

$$\text{Mean} = \text{median} = \bar{\bar{\beta}} = 6.238$$

Thus, in this case, the Bayesian point estimate is 6.238 for both loss functions.

In the next two subsections we prove the foregoing results concerning Bayesian point estimates from quadratic and linear loss functions.

4.3.1 The Bayesian Point Estimator for a Quadratic Loss Function

We seek the value of $\hat{\theta}$ that minimizes

$$E_{\theta|\mathbf{y}}[L_2] = \int c(\hat{\theta} - \theta)^2 g(\theta|\mathbf{y})\, d\theta \tag{4.3.2}$$

Using differentiation under the integral sign (e.g., Spiegel, 1963), we have

$$\frac{d}{d\hat{\theta}}\{E_{\theta|\mathbf{y}}[L_2]\} = \int 2c(\hat{\theta} - \theta)g(\theta|\mathbf{y})\, d\theta$$

which, when equated to zero to obtain the minimizing value for $\hat{\theta}$, yields

$$\hat{\theta}\int g(\theta|\mathbf{y})\, d\theta = \int \theta g(\theta|\mathbf{y})\, d\theta$$

From the properties of a proper density function, the integral on the left is unity, so the point estimate for θ under a quadratic loss function is the mean of the posterior density. Specifically,

$$\hat{\theta} = E[\theta|\mathbf{y}] = \int \theta g(\theta|\mathbf{y})\, d\theta \tag{4.3.3}$$

4.3.2 The Bayesian Point Estimator for a Linear Loss Function

Consider now the linear loss function $L_1 = c|\hat{\theta} - \theta|$. In this case

$$\begin{aligned} E_{\theta|\mathbf{y}}[L_1] &= \int c|\hat{\theta} - \theta| g(\theta|\mathbf{y})\, d\theta \\ &= \int_{-\infty}^{\theta} c(\hat{\theta} - \theta) g(\theta|\mathbf{y})\, d\theta + \int_{\theta}^{\infty} c(\theta - \hat{\theta}) g(\theta|\mathbf{y})\, d\theta \end{aligned}$$

and [see Spiegel (1963, p. 163)]

$$\frac{d}{d\hat{\theta}} \{E_{\theta|\mathbf{y}}[L_1]\} = \int_{-\infty}^{\theta} cg(\theta|\mathbf{y})\, d\theta - \int_{\theta}^{\infty} cg(\theta|\mathbf{y})\, d\theta$$

Equating this derivative to zero gives

$$\int_{-\infty}^{\hat{\theta}} g(\theta|\mathbf{y})\, d\theta = \int_{\hat{\theta}}^{\infty} g(\theta|\mathbf{y})\, d\theta = \tfrac{1}{2} \tag{4.3.4}$$

with the 1/2 term arising because the integrals are equal and their sum is one. Equation 4.3.4 shows that $\hat{\theta}$ is the median of the posterior density function.

4.3.3 Using Decision Theory within a Sampling Theory Framework

Let us now compare the Bayesian approach of obtaining estimators that minimize expected posterior loss with a decision theory approach that can be employed within the sampling theory framework. To use decision theory within a sampling theory framework we begin, as we did for the Bayesian framework, by specifying a loss function $L(\theta, \hat{\theta})$ that reflects the consequences of choosing $\hat{\theta}$ when θ is the real parameter value. Then we assume that a desirable estimator is one that minimizes expected loss *where the expectation is taken with respect to* $\mathbf{y}$. That is, we seek an estimator that minimizes average loss where the average is calculated from the losses that would be obtained from repeated samples. This average loss is known as the *risk function* and is given by

$$\rho(\theta, \hat{\theta}) = E_{\mathbf{y}|\theta}[L(\theta, \hat{\theta}(\mathbf{y}))]$$

$$= \int L(\theta, \hat{\theta}(\mathbf{y}))f(\mathbf{y}|\theta)\, d\mathbf{y} \qquad (4.3.5)$$

where $f(\mathbf{y}|\theta)$ is the joint density function for the sample observations and where, for the moment, we have written $\hat{\theta}(\mathbf{y})$ to emphasize that $\hat{\theta}$ is a function of $\mathbf{y}$, and hence a random variable.

The most popular loss function is the quadratic, in which case the risk function becomes

$$\rho(\theta, \hat{\theta}) = cE_{\mathbf{y}|\theta}[(\hat{\theta} - \theta)^2] = c\int (\hat{\theta} - \theta)^2 f(\mathbf{y}|\theta)\, d\mathbf{y} \qquad (4.3.6)$$

which, apart from the constant c, is the mean square error (MSE) of the estimator $\hat{\theta}$. Thus, in the sampling theory approach, with a quadratic loss function, we would like to choose an estimator that minimizes the MSE. However, it is impossible to find an estimator that minimizes the MSE for all θ in the parameter space. This can easily be proved by noting that the estimator $\hat{\theta} = \theta_0$ is better than any other estimator when $\theta = \theta_0$, but it could be considerably worse than other estimators away from this point. Although this example is unrealistic, it illustrates a situation that frequently arises in practice, namely, that one estimator may have a lower MSE than another for some values in the parameter space but a higher MSE for other values.

As a further example, let us return to the problem of estimating the mean β of a normal distribution and consider the following four alternative estimators for β and their corresponding MSEs (see Problem 4.6).

$$\hat{\beta}(1) = \bar{\beta} \qquad \text{MSE}_1 = (\beta - \bar{\beta})^2$$

$$\hat{\beta}(2) = \sum y_t/T \qquad \text{MSE}_2 = \frac{\sigma^2}{T}$$

$$\hat{\beta}(3) = \bar{\bar{\beta}} \qquad \text{MSE}_3 = \frac{T\sigma^2\bar{\sigma}_\beta^4 + \sigma^4(\bar{\beta} - \beta)^2}{(T\bar{\sigma}_\beta^2 + \sigma^2)^2}$$

$$\hat{\beta}(4) = \sum y_t/T - \bar{\beta} \qquad \text{MSE}_4 = \frac{\sigma^2}{T} + \bar{\beta}^2$$

The first estimator, $\hat{\beta}(1)$, is the prior mean of the natural conjugate prior and, because it does not depend on the sample information, it has zero variance, and its MSE is equal to its bias squared. The second estimator, $\hat{\beta}(2)$, is the sample mean or, equivalently, the posterior mean derived from a noninformative prior. It is

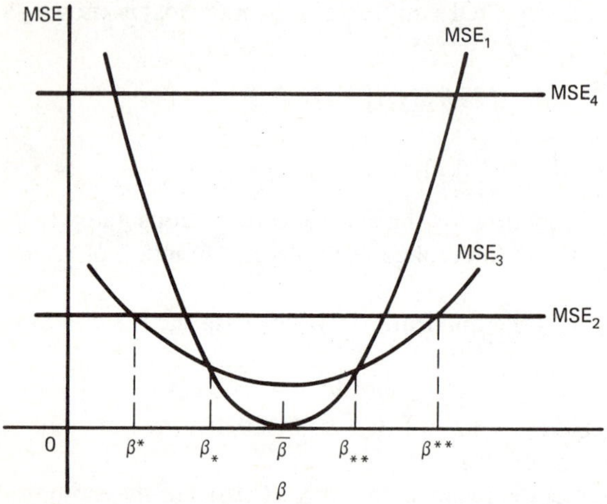

Figure 4.3 The mean square error functions of four alternative estimators for β.

unbiased, so its MSE is equal to its variance. The posterior mean derived from a natural conjugate prior is the estimator $\hat{\beta}(3)$, and it will be biased if $\beta \neq \bar{\beta}$. Its MSE is equal to its variance $T\sigma^2\bar{\sigma}^4_\beta/(T\bar{\sigma}^2_\beta + \sigma^2)^2$ plus the square of its bias $\sigma^4(\bar{\beta} - \beta)^2/(T\bar{\sigma}^2_\beta + \sigma^2)^2$. Finally, $\hat{\beta}(4)$ is a somewhat artificial estimator that will be biased if $\bar{\beta} \neq 0$.

The four MSEs are graphed in Figure 4.3. It is clear that the estimators $\hat{\beta}(1)$, $\hat{\beta}(2)$, and $\hat{\beta}(3)$ are each best for some part of the parameter space. If our prior information is very accurate ($\beta_* < \beta < \beta_{**}$), we are better off discarding the sample information and choosing $\hat{\beta}(1)$. On the other hand, if our prior information is too biased ($\beta < \beta^*$ or $\beta > \beta^{**}$), we are better off choosing the sample mean $\hat{\beta}(2)$ and discarding the prior information. The estimator $\hat{\beta}(3)$ is a compromise between these extremes. The other estimator, $\hat{\beta}(4)$, is not best under any circumstances because its risk function is always greater than that of $\hat{\beta}(2)$. Estimators with this property are clearly undesirable and are called inadmissible.

More generally, an estimator $\hat{\theta}_1$ is *inadmissible* if there exists another estimator $\hat{\theta}_2$ such that

$$\rho(\theta, \hat{\theta}_1) \geq \rho(\theta, \hat{\theta}_2) \qquad \text{for all } \theta$$

with the strict inequality holding for some θ. If such a $\hat{\theta}_2$ cannot be found, then $\hat{\theta}_1$ is *admissible.*

Let us return to the problem of finding an appropriate estimator. Because there is no estimator that minimizes MSE for all θ, an additional criterion must be introduced. One possibility is to restrict the class of estimators to those that are unbiased and to minimize MSE from within this class by choosing the minimum variance unbiased estimator. As noted in Chapter 3, for our example on estimating β from a normal distribution, $\hat{\beta}(2) = \sum y_t/T$ is the minimum variance unbiased estimator.

Another possibility is to average MSE (or, more generally, risk) over all values of θ in the parameter space, using a prior density $g(\theta)$ as a weighting function. We can then choose an estimator that minimizes *average risk*. Specifically, average risk is given by

$$\begin{aligned}\bar{\rho}(\hat{\theta}) &= E_\theta[\rho(\theta, \hat{\theta})] \\ &= \int \rho(\theta, \hat{\theta})g(\theta)\, d\theta \\ &= \iint c(\theta - \hat{\theta})^2 f(\mathbf{y}|\theta)g(\theta)\, d\mathbf{y}\, d\theta \qquad (4.3.7)\end{aligned}$$

where, in the last line, we have assumed a quadratic loss function so that the inner integral is MSE. The estimator $\hat{\theta}$ that minimizes (4.3.7) is known as the Bayes' estimator. Thus we have two Bayesian estimators: one, obtained by minimizing expected posterior loss, is given in (4.3.3); whereas the one just derived, although it uses a prior density on θ, was essentially obtained within the sampling theory framework. Provided that the double integral in (4.3.7) converges, we can show that the two estimators are the same.

Using the fact that $f(\mathbf{y}|\theta)g(\theta) = g(\theta|\mathbf{y})f(\mathbf{y})$ and ignoring the constant, (4.3.7) can be written as

$$\bar{\rho}(\hat{\theta}) = \iint (\theta - \hat{\theta})^2 g(\theta|\mathbf{y})f(\mathbf{y})\, d\mathbf{y}\, d\theta \qquad (4.3.8)$$

Interchanging the order of integration yields

$$\bar{\rho}(\hat{\theta}) = \int f(\mathbf{y})\left[\int (\theta - \hat{\theta})^2 g(\theta|\mathbf{y})\, d\theta\right] d\mathbf{y} \qquad (4.3.9)$$

and this function will be minimized when the integral within the square brackets is minimized. This integral is equal to expected posterior loss, and hence the two estimators are identical.

Under certain conditions the double integral in (4.3.7) does not converge, and hence an estimator that minimizes this function does not exist. In particular, this situation arises if $g(\theta)$ is an improper prior. Nevertheless, we may still be able to obtain an estimator that minimizes expected posterior loss. Indeed, the sample mean in our example minimizes expected posterior loss when the posterior p.d.f. is derived from a noninformative improper prior.

An important sampling theory property of Bayesian estimators is that, if $g(\theta)$ is proper, then the Bayesian estimator that minimizes (4.3.7) [and also (4.3.1)] is admissible; however, if $g(\theta)$ is improper, then the Bayesian estimator that minimizes (4.3.1) may not be admissible.

In this section we have shown how decision theory can be used to obtain point estimates in both the Bayesian and sampling theory approaches to inference. We indicated the circumstances under which the two approaches lead to the same point estimate, and, in so doing, we introduced the important concepts of expected posterior loss, risk, average risk, and admissibility. We showed that the mean of the posterior p.d.f. is the optimal Bayesian point estimate for a quadratic loss function and that the median is optimal for a linear loss function.

4.4 Bayesian Inference for the Mean and Standard Deviation of a Normal Distribution

In this section the assumption of known variance is relaxed and we outline Bayesian inference procedures for both the mean β and the standard deviation σ of a normal distribution. A joint informative prior p.d.f. for (β, σ) is given in Section 4.4.1, the corresponding joint posterior p.d.f. is derived in Section 4.4.2, marginal posterior p.d.f's for β and σ are considered in 4.4.3, and the use of a noninformative prior for (β, σ) is considered in Section 4.4.4.

4.4.1 An Informative Prior for the Mean and Standard Deviation

When both β and σ are unknown, a joint prior distribution for both parameters needs to be specified. The natural conjugate prior for this problem is known as a *normal-gamma prior*. When combined with a normal likelihood function, it yields a posterior distribution that is also of the normal-gamma type. A normal-gamma prior is such that the prior p.d.f. for β, conditional on σ, is a normal distribution, and the marginal prior p.d.f. for the reciprocal of the variance (the precision) is a gamma distribution. We will consider each of these components in turn.

When σ was known, the natural conjugate prior for β was $\beta \sim N(\bar{\beta}, \bar{\sigma}_\beta^2)$. Now that σ is unknown, the natural conjugate prior for β, *conditional on* σ, is a normal distribution. The dependence of this normal distribution on σ occurs through the prior variance $\bar{\sigma}_\beta^2$. In particular, it is convenient to write $\bar{\sigma}_\beta^2 = \sigma^2/\tau$ where τ is a prior parameter that controls the prior variance of β for a given σ^2. For a given σ^2, a high value for τ implies relatively precise prior information about β, and a low value implies relatively vague prior information about β. Thus, we specify $g(\beta|\sigma)$ such that

$$(\beta|\sigma) \sim N(\bar{\beta}, \sigma^2/\tau) \tag{4.4.1}$$

or alternatively,

$$g(\beta|\sigma) \propto \frac{1}{\sigma} \exp\left\{-\frac{\tau}{2\sigma^2}(\beta - \bar{\beta})^2\right\} \tag{4.4.2}$$

Because we are now concerned with inference about both β and σ, the term $(1/\sigma)$ appears in front of the exponent in (4.4.2) and cannot be absorbed into the proportionality constant. The remainder of the normalizing constant, $\sqrt{\tau/2\pi}$, has been absorbed into the proportionality constant.

To introduce the prior density for σ, we first recall the gamma distribution that was defined in Chapter 2. If θ is an unknown parameter with a gamma prior distribution, then its density function is of the form

$$g(\theta) \propto \theta^{\alpha-1} \exp\{-\theta/\gamma\} \tag{4.4.3}$$

where α and γ are positive prior parameters. If we set $\theta = 1/\sigma^2$, then θ is known as the precision parameter of the normal distribution. Furthermore, $g(\theta)$ is the natural conjugate prior for θ.

It is convenient to transform θ and the density function $g(\theta)$ in two ways. First, we reparameterize the density by letting

$$\alpha = \bar{v}/2 \quad \text{and} \quad \gamma = 2/\bar{v}\bar{s}^2$$

where $\bar{v}$ and $\bar{s}^2$ are two new parameters. Then, it is possible to show that [see Problem 4.10(a)]

$$z = \bar{v}\bar{s}^2\theta = \bar{v}\bar{s}^2/\sigma^2 \tag{4.4.4}$$

is a χ^2 random variable with $\bar{v}$ degrees of freedom and density function

$$g(z) \propto z^{\bar{v}/2-1} \exp\{-z/2\} \tag{4.4.5}$$

That is,

$$z = \frac{\bar{v}\bar{s}^2}{\sigma^2} \sim \chi^2_{(\bar{v})} \tag{4.4.6}$$

This transformation from θ to the random variable z, which has the more familiar χ^2 distribution will be useful when we are setting values for the prior parameters $\bar{v}$ and $\bar{s}^2$.

The second transformation is from z to the standard deviation σ. We make this transformation because we are more accustomed to working with the variance or the standard deviation than with the precision. Using the relationship between z and σ given in (4.4.4), the prior p.d.f. for σ can be derived as [see Problem 4.10(b)]

$$g(\sigma) \propto \frac{1}{\sigma^{\bar{\nu}+1}} \exp\left\{-\frac{\bar{\nu}\bar{s}^2}{2\sigma^2}\right\} \tag{4.4.7}$$

This density is often known as an *inverted-gamma* distribution or an inverted gamma-2 distribution. Its first and second moments around zero are

$$E[\sigma] = \frac{\sqrt{\bar{\nu}/2}\,\Gamma[(\bar{\nu}-1)/2]}{\Gamma(\bar{\nu}/2)}\bar{s} \quad \text{and} \quad E[\sigma^2] = \frac{\bar{\nu}\bar{s}^2}{\bar{\nu}-2} \tag{4.4.8}$$

and its mode is $[\bar{\nu}/(\bar{\nu}+1)]^{1/2}\bar{s}$. The function $\Gamma(.)$ is the gamma function that was introduced in Chapter 2. The normalizing constant that has been omitted from (4.4.7) is

$$k = \frac{2}{\Gamma(\bar{\nu}/2)}\left[\frac{\bar{\nu}\bar{s}^2}{2}\right]^{\bar{\nu}/2} \tag{4.4.9}$$

The joint prior p.d.f. for (β, σ) can now be written as

$$\begin{aligned} g(\beta, \sigma) &= g(\beta|\sigma)g(\sigma) \\ &\propto \frac{1}{\sigma}\exp\left\{-\frac{\tau}{2\sigma^2}(\beta-\bar{\beta})^2\right\}\frac{1}{\sigma^{\bar{\nu}+1}}\exp\left\{-\frac{\bar{\nu}\bar{s}^2}{2\sigma^2}\right\} \end{aligned} \tag{4.4.10}$$

To construct a prior p.d.f. of this type, we need to specify values for the prior parameters $\bar{\beta}$, τ, $\bar{\nu}$, and $\bar{s}^2$. This task is a harder one than specification of the prior when σ is known because it involves formulation of prior information about σ. It is reasonable to expect an investigator to be able to conceptualize his or her opinions about what are likely and unlikely values for β, but conceptualization about likely values of σ may be difficult. Nevertheless, using the LFC example that was introduced in Section 4.2, we illustrate how the parameters of the joint prior p.d.f. $g(\beta, \sigma)$ can be specified.

For the conditional prior p.d.f. $g(\beta|\sigma)$ we use the same prior information that was used in Section 4.2.1, but this time we condition it on $\sigma^2 = 4$. Thus, we have

$$P[5 < (\beta|\sigma^2 = 4) < 11] = 0.95 \tag{4.4.11}$$

Following the line of argument in Section 4.2.1, we can conclude

$$\bar{\beta} = 8 \quad \text{and} \quad \bar{\sigma}_{\beta}^2 = 2.3427 = \frac{\sigma^2}{\tau} = \frac{4}{\tau}$$

Thus, $\tau = 4/2.3427 = 1.7074$.

To illustrate how our prior information about β depends on σ^2, note that, for $\sigma^2 = 1$, our prior information is more precise

$$P[6.5 < (\beta|\sigma^2 = 1) < 9.5] = 0.95$$

and for $\sigma^2 = 9$ it is more vague

$$P[3.5 < (\beta|\sigma^2 = 9) < 12.5] = 0.95$$

One way of approaching specification of the prior p.d.f. $g(\sigma)$ is to consider the likely range of weekly receipts around the mean. Because 99.7% of all observations on the normal distribution lie within three standard deviations of the mean, the effective range of weekly receipts could be regarded as $\beta \pm 3\sigma$. Now suppose that we believe that there is a 1 in 20 chance (or 0.05 probability) that the range is less than $\beta \pm 2.55 = \beta \pm (3 \times 0.85)$. This belief can be expressed as

$$P[\sigma < 0.85] = 0.05 \tag{4.4.12}$$

Suppose also that we believe there is a 0.05 probability that the range is greater than $\beta \pm 12 = \beta \pm (3 \times 4)$. This belief is expressed as

$$P[\sigma > 4] = 0.05 \tag{4.4.13}$$

The probability statements in (4.4.12) and (4.4.13) can be used to find values for the parameters $\bar{v}$ and $\bar{s}^2$. Because probabilities associated with the inverted gamma distribution are not tabulated, we use the transformation $z = \bar{v}\bar{s}^2/\sigma^2$ given in (4.4.6) and tabulated values from the χ^2 distribution. We have

$$P[\sigma < 0.85] = P\left[\left(\frac{\bar{v}\bar{s}^2}{z}\right)^{1/2} < 0.85\right] = P\left[\frac{\bar{v}\bar{s}^2}{z} < 0.7225\right] = P\left[z > \frac{\bar{v}\bar{s}^2}{0.7225}\right]$$

$$P[\sigma > 4] = P\left[\left(\frac{\bar{v}\bar{s}^2}{z}\right)^{1/2} > 4\right] = P\left[\frac{\bar{v}\bar{s}^2}{z} > 16\right] = P\left[z < \frac{\bar{v}\bar{s}^2}{16}\right]$$

If we set $\bar{v} = 3$, then, from Table 3 at the end of the book,

$$P[\chi^2_{(3)} > 7.8147] = 0.05 \qquad \text{and} \qquad P[\chi^2_{(3)} < 0.3518] = 0.05$$

Since $z \sim \chi^2_{(\bar{v})}$, if $\bar{v} = 3$ is indeed a suitable value for $\bar{v}$, $\bar{s}^2$ should be such that it satisfies the two equations

$$\frac{3 \times \bar{s}^2}{0.7225} = 7.8147 \qquad \text{and} \qquad \frac{3 \times \bar{s}^2}{16} = 0.3518$$

Solving both these equations yields $\bar{s}^2 = 1.88$ (correct to two decimal places). If different values of $\bar{v}$ are tried on a trial and error basis, a single value of $\bar{s}^2$ that satisfies both probability statements cannot be found. Thus, $\bar{v} = 3$ and $\bar{s}^2 = 1.88$ are the prior parameter values that adequately reflect our prior information. It can be shown (see Problem 4.11) that the prior density $g(\sigma)$ with these parameter values has mode = 1.19, median = 1.54, and mean = 1.89.

We have obviously rigged this example so that the χ^2 table in the Appendix could be used to find values for the prior parameters. In a more general setting more extensive tables or an appropriate computer program would be necessary. See, for example, the SHAZAM instructions in the Computer Handbook.

Another way prior information is often formulated is from information provided by a previous sample. If, from a previous sample of size 4, we had a sample mean of $\hat{\beta} = 8$ and a sample variance of $\hat{\sigma}^2 = 1.88$, then, as we will see in Section 4.4.4, the values of the prior parameters would be $\bar{\beta} = 8$, $\bar{s}^2 = 1.88$, $\tau = 4$, and $\bar{v} = 3$.

Our complete prior information can now be summarized by substituting these values into the joint prior p.d.f. to yield

$$g(\beta, \sigma) \propto \frac{1}{\sigma} \exp\left\{-\frac{1.7074}{2\sigma^2}(\beta - 8)^2\right\} \frac{1}{\sigma^4} \exp\left\{-\frac{5.64}{2\sigma^2}\right\} \tag{4.4.14}$$

A discussion on the shapes of the graphs of the marginal priors $g(\sigma)$ and $g(\beta)$ will be postponed until after the posterior p.d.f.s have been derived.

4.4.2 Joint Posterior Density From an Informative Prior

The first step toward the joint posterior p.d.f. $g(\beta, \sigma|\mathbf{y})$ is to write the likelihood function in a convenient form. From (4.2.8) we can write

$$\begin{aligned}\sum_{t=1}^{T} (y_t - \beta)^2 &= T(\beta - \hat{\beta})^2 + \sum_{t=1}^{T} (y_t - \hat{\beta})^2 \\ &= T(\beta - \hat{\beta})^2 + v\hat{\sigma}^2 \end{aligned} \tag{4.4.15}$$

where $v = T - 1$ and $\hat{\sigma}^2 = (T-1)^{-1}\sum_{t=1}^{T}(y_t - \hat{\beta})^2$ is the sample variance. Then, the likelihood function can be written as

$$\begin{aligned} l(\beta, \sigma|\mathbf{y}) &\propto \frac{1}{\sigma^T} \exp\left\{-\frac{1}{2\sigma^2}\sum_{t=1}^{T}(y_t - \beta)^2\right\} \\ &\propto \frac{1}{\sigma^T} \exp\left\{-\frac{1}{2\sigma^2}[T(\beta - \hat{\beta})^2 + v\hat{\sigma}^2]\right\} \end{aligned} \tag{4.4.16}$$

In contrast to (4.2.9) where the variance was known, in (4.4.16) the second term in the exponent cannot be absorbed into the factor of proportionality.

The joint posterior p.d.f. is found by using Bayes' theorem to multiply (4.4.10) by (4.4.16). This step yields

$$g(\beta, \sigma|\mathbf{y}) \propto l(\beta, \sigma|\mathbf{y})g(\beta, \sigma)$$

$$\propto \frac{1}{\sigma^{T+\bar{v}+2}} \exp\left\{-\frac{1}{2\sigma^2}[T(\beta-\hat{\beta})^2 + v\hat{\sigma}^2 + \tau(\beta-\bar{\beta})^2 + \bar{v}\bar{s}^2]\right\} \tag{4.4.17}$$

To simplify this expression, we first note that (see Problem 4.13)

$$T(\beta-\hat{\beta})^2 + \tau(\beta-\bar{\beta})^2 = (\tau+T)(\beta-\bar{\bar{\beta}})^2 - (\tau+T)\bar{\bar{\beta}}^2 + \tau\bar{\beta}^2 + T\hat{\beta}^2 \tag{4.4.18}$$

where

$$\bar{\bar{\beta}} = \frac{\bar{\beta}\tau + \hat{\beta}T}{\tau + T} \tag{4.4.19}$$

Also note that

$$v\hat{\sigma}^2 + \bar{v}\bar{s}^2 = \sum_{t=1}^{T} y_t^2 - T\hat{\beta}^2 + \bar{v}\bar{s}^2$$

$$= \mathbf{y}'\mathbf{y} - T\hat{\beta}^2 + \bar{v}\bar{s}^2 \tag{4.4.20}$$

The term in square brackets in (4.4.17) is given by the sum of (4.4.18) and (4.4.20), which is

$$(\tau+T)(\beta-\bar{\bar{\beta}})^2 - (\tau+T)\bar{\bar{\beta}}^2 + \tau\bar{\beta}^2 + \mathbf{y}'\mathbf{y} + \bar{v}\bar{s}^2 = (\tau+T)(\beta-\bar{\bar{\beta}})^2 + \bar{\bar{v}}\bar{\bar{s}}^2 \tag{4.4.21}$$

where

$$\bar{\bar{v}}\bar{\bar{s}}^2 = \bar{v}\bar{s}^2 + \mathbf{y}'\mathbf{y} - (\tau+T)\bar{\bar{\beta}}^2 + \tau\bar{\beta}^2 \tag{4.4.22}$$

and $\bar{\bar{v}} = \bar{v} + T$. The reasons for these definitions of $\bar{\bar{v}}$ and $\bar{\bar{s}}^2$ will become apparent after substituting (4.4.21) into (4.4.17) and rearranging. This substitution and rearrangement yields

$$g(\beta, \sigma|\mathbf{y}) \propto \frac{1}{\sigma}\exp\left\{-\frac{(\tau+T)(\beta-\bar{\bar{\beta}})^2}{2\sigma^2}\right\}\cdot\frac{1}{\sigma^{\bar{\bar{v}}+1}}\exp\left\{-\frac{\bar{\bar{v}}\bar{\bar{s}}^2}{2\sigma^2}\right\}$$

$$\propto g(\beta|\sigma, \mathbf{y})g(\sigma|\mathbf{y}) \tag{4.4.23}$$

where

$$g(\beta|\sigma, \mathbf{y}) \propto \frac{1}{\sigma}\exp\left\{-\frac{(\tau+T)(\beta-\bar{\bar{\beta}})^2}{2\sigma^2}\right\} \tag{4.4.24}$$

and

$$g(\sigma|\mathbf{y}) \propto \frac{1}{\sigma^{\bar{\bar{v}}+1}}\exp\left\{-\frac{\bar{\bar{v}}\bar{\bar{s}}^2}{2\sigma^2}\right\} \tag{4.4.25}$$

A comparison of these posterior p.d.f.'s with the corresponding prior p.d.f.'s shows that the joint posterior p.d.f is of a normal-gamma type. The conditional posterior p.d.f. for β given σ, $g(\beta|\sigma, \mathbf{y})$, is a normal distribution with mean $\bar{\bar{\beta}}$ and variance $\sigma^2/(\tau + T)$, and the marginal posterior p.d.f. for σ, $g(\sigma|\mathbf{y})$, is an inverted-gamma p.d.f. with parameters $\bar{\bar{v}}$ and $\bar{\bar{s}}^2$.

As in the case when σ^2 was known, the posterior mean for β given in Equation 4.4.19 can be viewed as a weighted average of the prior mean and the sample mean with weights given by the respective precisions of each source of information. This interpretation is clear if we write

$$\bar{\bar{\beta}} = \frac{\bar{\beta}(\tau/\sigma^2) + \hat{\beta}(T/\sigma^2)}{(\tau/\sigma^2) + (T/\sigma^2)} \tag{4.4.26}$$

Furthermore, the posterior precision for β, given by $(\tau + T)/\sigma^2$, is equal to the sum of the prior precision τ/σ^2 and the precision of the sample information T/σ^2.

After observing the sample of 10 weeks given in Section 4.2.1, the values of the posterior parameters for the LFC example are

$$E[\beta|\mathbf{y}] = \bar{\bar{\beta}} = \frac{\bar{\beta}\tau + \hat{\beta}T}{\tau + T} = \frac{8 \times 1.7074 + 5.937 \times 10}{11.7074} = 6.238$$

$$\text{var}[\beta|\sigma, \mathbf{y}] = \frac{\sigma^2}{\tau + T} = \frac{\sigma^2}{11.7074}$$

$$\bar{\bar{v}} = T + \bar{v} = 13$$

$$\begin{aligned}\bar{\bar{v}}\bar{\bar{s}}^2 &= \bar{v}\bar{s}^2 + \mathbf{y}'\mathbf{y} - (\tau + T)\bar{\bar{\beta}}^2 + \tau\bar{\beta}^2 \\ &= 5.64 + 374.8375 - 11.7074 \times (6.238)^2 + 1.7074 \times 8^2 \\ &= 34.185\end{aligned}$$

$$\bar{\bar{s}}^2 = 34.185/13 = 2.63$$

The way in which the sample information has changed our prior information will be summarized in both a table and diagrams after we discuss how to obtain a marginal posterior p.d.f. for β.

4.4.3 Marginal Posterior Densities for the Mean and Standard Deviation

The joint posterior p.d.f. $g(\beta, \sigma|\mathbf{y})$ and the conditional posterior p.d.f. $g(\beta|\sigma, \mathbf{y})$ can be used for making joint inferences about (β, σ) and inferences about β conditional on σ, respectively. In practice, we are more likely to be interested in making unconditional inferences about β and/or σ. The relevant posterior p.d.f.'s on which to base unconditional inferences are the marginal posterior p.d.f.'s $g(\beta|\mathbf{y})$ and $g(\sigma|\mathbf{y})$.

The marginal posterior p.d.f. for σ has already been obtained in (4.4.25) by factoring the joint density as $g(\beta, \sigma|\mathbf{y}) = g(\beta|\sigma, \mathbf{y})g(\sigma|\mathbf{y})$ and recognizing $g(\sigma|\mathbf{y})$ as an inverted-gamma p.d.f. with parameters $\bar{\bar{\nu}}$ and $\bar{\bar{s}}^2$. When obtaining the marginal posterior p.d.f. for β, the parameter σ is called a *nuisance parameter* and it is eliminated by integrating it out of the joint density function. That is,

$$g(\beta|\mathbf{y}) = \int_0^\infty g(\beta, \sigma|\mathbf{y})\, d\sigma$$

$$= \int_0^\infty g(\beta|\sigma, \mathbf{y}) \cdot g(\sigma|\mathbf{y})\, d\sigma \tag{4.4.27}$$

The second equality emphasizes that $g(\beta|\mathbf{y})$ can be regarded as a weighted average of all the conditional densities $g(\beta|\sigma, \mathbf{y})$, with weights given by the marginal density $g(\sigma|\mathbf{y})$.

Thus, to obtain $g(\beta|\mathbf{y})$ we need

$$g(\beta|\mathbf{y}) = \int_0^\infty g(\beta, \sigma|\mathbf{y})\, d\sigma$$

$$\propto \int_0^\infty \frac{1}{\sigma^{\nu+2}} \exp\left\{-\frac{1}{2\sigma^2}[(\tau + T)(\beta - \bar{\bar{\beta}})^2 + \bar{\bar{\nu}}\bar{\bar{s}}^2]\right\} d\sigma \tag{4.4.28}$$

To solve this integral let $x = a/2\sigma^2$ where

$$a = (\tau + T)(\beta - \bar{\bar{\beta}})^2 + \bar{\bar{\nu}}\bar{\bar{s}}^2$$

Then,

$$dx = -a\sigma^{-3}\, d\sigma$$

$$d\sigma = -2^{-3/2}a^{1/2}x^{-3/2}\, dx$$

$$\sigma^{-(\bar{\bar{\nu}}+2)} = 2^{(\bar{\bar{\nu}}+2)/2}a^{-(\bar{\bar{\nu}}+2)/2}x^{(\bar{\bar{\nu}}+2)/2}$$

Using these three results, (4.4.28) can be written as

$$g(\beta|\mathbf{y}) \propto a^{-(\bar{\bar{\nu}}+2)/2} \int_0^\infty x^{(\bar{\bar{\nu}}+2)/2} e^{-x} a^{1/2} x^{-3/2}\, dx$$

$$= a^{-(\bar{\bar{\nu}}+1)/2} \int_0^\infty x^{(\bar{\bar{\nu}}-1)/2} e^{-x}\, dx$$

$$= a^{-(\bar{\bar{\nu}}+1)/2}\Gamma\left(\frac{\bar{\bar{\nu}}+1}{2}\right) \tag{4.4.29}$$

The term $\Gamma((\bar{\bar{v}}+1)/2)$ does not depend on β and so can be absorbed into the proportionality constant. Thus, the marginal posterior p.d.f. for β is given by

$$g(\beta|\mathbf{y}) \propto [\bar{\bar{v}}\bar{\bar{s}}^2 + (\tau + T)(\beta - \bar{\bar{\beta}})^2]^{-(\bar{\bar{v}}+1)/2}$$

$$\propto \left[1 + \frac{(\tau + T)(\beta - \bar{\bar{\beta}})^2}{\bar{\bar{v}}\bar{\bar{s}}^2}\right]^{-(\bar{\bar{v}}+1)/2} \tag{4.4.30}$$

To recognize the form of this distribution we need to digress for a moment to consider the density function for a random variable with the t-distribution. If x is a random variable that has the t-distribution with median μ, precision parameter h, and degrees of freedom parameter v, the kernel of its density function is given by

$$f(x) \propto \left[1 + \frac{h(x-\mu)^2}{v}\right]^{-(v+1)/2} \tag{4.4.31}$$

This distribution is symmetrical about μ, which, in addition to being the median, is also the mean (if $v > 1$) and the mode. When $v \leq 1$ the integral that defines the mean does not converge, so the mean does not exist. The variance of x exists for $v > 2$ and is given by $\text{var}[x] = v/h(v-2)$. The normalizing constant that has been omitted from (4.4.31) is

$$k = \frac{\Gamma[(v+1)/2]}{\Gamma(\frac{1}{2})\Gamma(v/2)}\left(\frac{h}{v}\right)^{1/2} \tag{4.4.32}$$

The importance of the t-distribution in the sampling theory approach to inference was demonstrated in Chapter 3. In that chapter a special case of the t-distribution was considered, namely, that case where $\mu = 0$ and $h = 1$. This special case is analogous to the standard normal distribution, which is a special case of the normal distribution where the mean is equal to 0 and the variance equal to 1.

A comparison of (4.4.31) with (4.4.30) shows that the marginal posterior p.d.f. for β is a t-distribution with mean $\bar{\bar{\beta}}$, precision $(\tau + T)/\bar{\bar{s}}^2$, and degrees of freedom $\bar{\bar{v}}$. Thus,

$$E[\beta|\mathbf{y}] = \bar{\bar{\beta}} \quad \text{and} \quad \text{var}[\beta|\mathbf{y}] = \frac{\bar{\bar{v}}\bar{\bar{s}}^2}{(\tau + T)(\bar{\bar{v}} - 2)}$$

This distribution summarizes all the information, both prior and sample, that an investigator has about β. The density function itself can be used to represent this information, or, it can be used to obtain point or interval estimates or to compare hypotheses.

A similar procedure could have been followed to derive the marginal prior p.d.f. $g(\beta)$. This p.d.f. will be a t-distribution with mean $\bar{\beta}$, precision $\tau/\bar{s}^2$, and degrees of freedom $\bar{v}$.

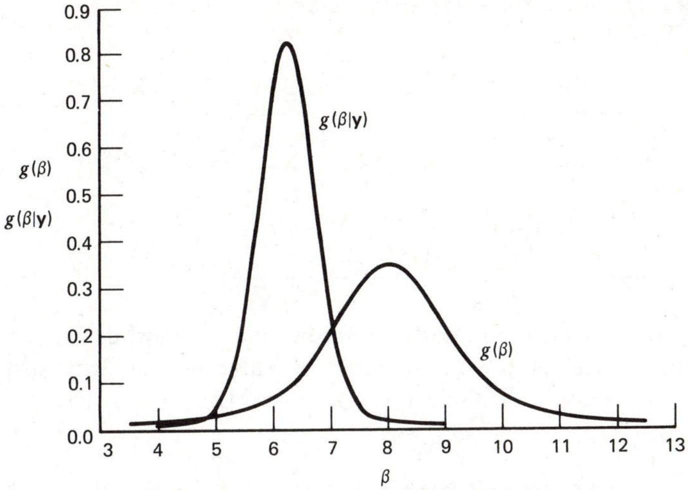

Figure 4.4 Prior and posterior t distributions for β.

The prior and posterior t-distributions for β in the LFC example are illustrated in Figure 4.4, while the inverted-gamma distributions for σ are illustrated in Figure 4.5. An examination of the posterior density for β relative to its prior indicates that the distribution has shifted to the left and it has a much lower variance. It appears that we were originally too optimistic about weekly receipts. As expected, our increased information about σ is reflected in a posterior p.d.f. $g(\sigma|\mathbf{y})$ that is sharper

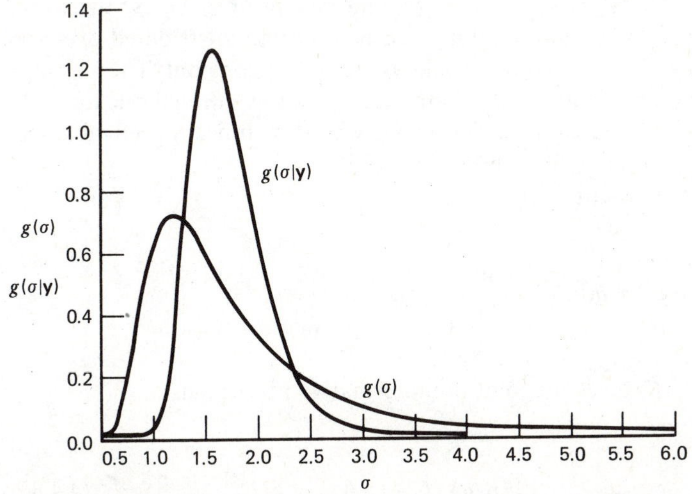

Figure 4.5 Prior and posterior inverted-gamma distributions for σ.

Table 4.1 Summary Statistics for Prior and Posterior Density Functions

	β		σ	
	Prior	Posterior	Prior	Posterior
Mean	8.0	6.24	1.89	1.72
Mode	8.0	6.24	1.19	1.56
Standard deviation	1.82	0.52	1.44	0.39

than the prior p.d.f. $g(\sigma)$. The prior and posterior means and standard deviations for β and σ and the modes for σ are compared in Table 4.1. Students are encouraged to verify the values in the table. (See Problem 4.12).

4.4.4 Inference for the Mean and Standard Deviation with a Noninformative Prior

If we have little or no prior information about β and σ, or we wish to present results in terms of a posterior p.d.f. that reflects sample information only, a noninformative prior for (β, σ) is required. To establish such a prior, we assume β and σ are a priori independent and find the joint noninformative prior p.d.f. from $g(\beta, \sigma) = g(\beta) \cdot g(\sigma)$ where $g(\beta)$ and $g(\sigma)$ are the marginal noninformative prior p.d.f.'s for β and σ, respectively. For $g(\beta)$ we assume, as we did when σ^2 was known, that β is uniformly distributed over the interval $-\infty < \beta < \infty$, and the prior p.d.f. is, therefore, $g(\beta) \propto$ constant. For $g(\sigma)$ we assume that $\ln \sigma$ is uniformly distributed over the interval $-\infty < \ln \sigma < \infty$, and the prior p.d.f. is $g(\ln \sigma) \propto$ constant. The assumption that *ln* σ rather than σ is uniformly distributed is a conventional one for scale parameters that lie between 0 and ∞. For details why this choice is preferable see, for example, Zellner (1971) or Box and Tiao (1973).

Transforming $g(\ln \sigma)$ to $g(\sigma)$ yields

$$g(\sigma) = g(\ln \sigma)\left|\frac{d \ln \sigma}{d\sigma}\right| = \text{constant} \cdot \frac{1}{\sigma} \propto \frac{1}{\sigma}$$

Multiplying $g(\sigma)$ by $g(\beta)$ gives the joint noninformative prior p.d.f.

$$g(\beta, \sigma) \propto \frac{1}{\sigma} \tag{4.4.33}$$

Using Bayes' theorem to multiply this prior by the likelihood function in (4.4.16) yields the joint posterior p.d.f.

$$\begin{aligned} g(\beta, \sigma|\mathbf{y}) &\propto g(\beta, \sigma)\cdot l(\beta, \sigma|\mathbf{y}) \\ &\propto \frac{1}{\sigma}\exp\left\{-\frac{(\beta-\hat{\beta})^2}{2\sigma^2/T}\right\}\cdot\frac{1}{\sigma^T}\exp\left\{-\frac{v\hat{\sigma}^2}{2\sigma^2}\right\} \\ &\propto g(\beta|\sigma, \mathbf{y})\cdot g(\sigma|\mathbf{y}) \end{aligned} \tag{4.4.34}$$

where the conditional posterior p.d.f. for β given σ is

$$g(\beta|\sigma, \mathbf{y}) \propto \frac{1}{\sigma}\exp\left\{-\frac{(\beta-\hat{\beta})^2}{2\sigma^2/T}\right\} \tag{4.4.35}$$

and the marginal posterior p.d.f. for σ is

$$g(\sigma|\mathbf{y}) \propto \frac{1}{\sigma^{v+1}}\exp\left\{-\frac{v\hat{\sigma}^2}{2\sigma^2}\right\} \tag{4.4.36}$$

where $v = T - 1$. Thus the joint posterior p.d.f. for (β, σ), derived from a noninformative prior, is of the normal-gamma form. The conditional p.d.f. $g(\beta|\sigma, \mathbf{y})$ is a normal distribution with mean $E[\beta|\sigma, \mathbf{y}] = \hat{\beta}$ and variance $\text{var}[\beta|\sigma, \mathbf{y}] = \sigma^2/T$. The marginal p.d.f. $g(\sigma|\mathbf{y})$ is an inverted-gamma density with parameters v and $\hat{\sigma}^2$.

These results are similar to those obtained using the sampling theory approach, a fact that should not be surprising given that they were derived from a noninformative prior. However, the interpretation is quite different. In both approaches we have $(\hat{\beta} - \beta) \sim N(0, \sigma^2/T)$ and $(v\hat{\sigma}^2/\sigma^2) \sim \chi^2_{(T-1)}$. However, in the sampling theory approach where $\hat{\beta}$ and $\hat{\sigma}^2$ are the random variables, these results imply that $\hat{\beta} \sim N(\beta, \sigma^2/T)$ and $\hat{\sigma}^2 \sim (\sigma^2/v)\chi^2_{(T-1)}$. In the Bayesian framework where the unknown parameters β and σ are the random variables, the results imply that $(\beta|\sigma) \sim N(\hat{\beta}, \sigma^2/T)$ and $\sigma \sim \sqrt{v\hat{\sigma}^2}(1/\sqrt{\chi^2_{(T-1)}})$. The random variable $\sqrt{v\hat{\sigma}^2}(1/\sqrt{\chi^2_{(T-1)}})$ is a constant multiplied by the inverse of the square root of a χ^2 random variable, and it has the inverted-gamma p.d.f. in (4.4.36).

These similarities between the two approaches do not hold for all statistical models. There are many models where the use of a noninformative prior leads to Bayesian results that are different from those from the sampling theory approach.

If we are interested in unconditional inference about β, the marginal posterior p.d.f. for β is required and it can be obtained by integrating σ out of the joint density along the same lines as were outlined in Section 4.4.3. This procedure yields

$$g(\beta|\mathbf{y}) \propto \left[1 + \frac{T(\beta-\hat{\beta})^2}{v\hat{\sigma}^2}\right]^{-(v+1)/2} \tag{4.4.37}$$

This p.d.f. is a t-distribution with mean $\hat{\beta}$, precision parameter $T/\hat{\sigma}^2$, and degrees of freedom v. Thus, the posterior mean and variance for β are

$$E[\beta|\mathbf{y}] = \hat{\beta} \qquad \text{and} \qquad \text{var}[\beta|\mathbf{y}] = \frac{v\hat{\sigma}^2}{T(v-2)}$$

Finding the marginal posterior p.d.f.'s for β and σ in the LFC example with a noninformative prior is left as an exercise. (See Problem 4.14).

If desired, the joint and marginal posterior p.d.f.'s for β and σ can be used to find point estimates, to find interval estimates, to derive predictive densities, and to compute posterior odds. Although the distributions are different, the principles to be followed are the same as those outlined for the model where σ^2 was known.

4.5 Summary and Guide to Further Reading

In this chapter we have outlined the Bayesian approach to inference with particular emphasis on inference for the mean and standard deviation of a normal distribution. The main features covered in the chapter are as follows.

1. The difference between the sampling theory and Bayesian approaches to inference were outlined.
2. An illustration of how to construct a normal informative prior density for the mean, when the standard deviation is known, was presented; and an illustration of a normal-gamma informative prior for the mean and standard deviation, when both are unknown, was also presented.
3. Normal and normal-gamma posterior densities were derived for the known and unknown standard deviation cases, respectively. These posterior densities were derived starting from both informative and noninformative priors.
4. Using inference about the mean when the standard deviation is known as an example, Bayesian procedures for point and interval estimation, hypothesis testing, and prediction were illustrated.
5. The relationship between estimators obtained using Bayesian decision theory and those obtained using decision theory within the sampling theory framework was explored.
6. Procedures for deriving marginal posterior densities from joint posterior densities were outlined.

Many statisticians strongly support the use of Bayesian rather than sampling theory techniques. They argue that, when using the sampling theory approach, researchers frequently use prior information in an ad hoc manner. For example, samples or models that lead to estimates that do not agree with a priori expectations are often discarded. Bayesians argue that it is preferable to incorporate such a priori information within a formal framework. Also, Bayesian procedures closely follow the objectives of researchers. Specifically, researchers are usually interested in how the sample information will modify their prior information, and this modification is precisely what the Bayes' theorem gives us. Another reason for supporting the Bayesian approach is its lack of dependence on the performance of estimators and tests in repeated and as yet unobserved samples. The justification for Bayesian estimators is based only on currently available information. Yet, if we are interested in performance in repeated samples, Bayesian estimators have the desirable property of admissibility. Bayesians also put forward a number of other reasons for using their techniques and, for details, we refer you to Zellner (1971), Box and Tiao (1973), and Berger (1985). We should also point out that many statisticians reject the Bayesian approach, mainly because it is based on the notion of subjective probability. Our stand is an intermediate one. We believe that the Bayesian approach is particularly useful for incorporating prior information and for use in decision theory and prediction problems, and that, conceptually, it does have many significant advantages over the sampling theory approach. However, it is unlikely to be ever regarded as a complete substitute for the sampling theory approach. We also believe that all students should be exposed to the Bayesian approach and that its study greatly enhances understanding of all statistical methodology.

4.6 Exercises

4.1 Prove the relationship given in (4.2.10).

4.2 Consider the hypotheses given in (4.2.27). Using the data and example given in conjunction with these hypotheses, show that, when a noninformative prior is used, the posterior odds ratio in favor of H_1 is 13.5.

4.3 Consider the following random sample of 20 observations from a normal distribution with unknown mean β and known variance $\sigma^2 = 2.89$.

5.27	4.29	1.72	5.36	7.52
7.30	6.00	8.18	4.35	3.09
5.33	5.32	5.89	5.35	4.20
6.21	8.15	5.10	4.25	6.14

Beginning with a noninformative prior for β,

(*a*) Derive the posterior p.d.f. for β. Give the mean and variance of this p.d.f.

(*b*) Find the predictive p.d.f. for a future value from the normal distribution.

(*c*) Consider the hypotheses $H_0: \beta \leq 6.074$ and $H_1: \beta > 6.074$. Find the posterior odds ratio in favor of H_0 relative to H_1. Using the sampling theory approach and a 5% significance level, test H_0 against H_1.

(*d*) Find a 95% HPD interval for β.

4.4 Repeat Problem 4.3 assuming that σ^2 is unknown and beginning with a noninformative prior for (β, σ).

4.5 Suppose that $y_1, y_2, \ldots, y_T$ is a random sample from a Poisson distribution with mean λ and that the prior distribution for λ is the gamma distribution

$$g(\lambda) \propto \lambda^{\alpha-1} e^{-\beta\lambda}$$

Find the posterior density for λ. What does this result tell you about the prior for λ?

4.6 Verify the MSEs of the estimators $\hat{\beta}(1)$, $\hat{\beta}(2)$, $\hat{\beta}(3)$, and $\hat{\beta}(4)$ given in Section 4.3.3.

4.7 (*a*) Suppose that a data-generating process is a normal process with unknown mean β and with known variance $\sigma^2 = 225$. A sample of size $T = 9$ is taken from this process, with the sample results 42, 56, 68, 56, 48, 36, 45, 71, and 64. If your prior judgments about β can be represented by a normal distribution with mean 50 and variance 14, what is your posterior distribution for β? From this distribution, find $P(\beta < 55)$ and $P(\beta \geq 55)$.

(*b*) The posterior odds in favor of $H_0: \beta \geq 55$ against the alternative $H_1: \beta < 55$ is given by $P(\beta \geq 55)/P(\beta < 55)$. What is the value of this ratio? Which hypothesis would you choose if

(*i*) The loss from choosing H_1 when H_0 is correct is equal to the loss from choosing H_0 when H_1 is correct?

(*ii*) The loss from choosing H_1 when H_0 is correct is twice as great as the loss from choosing H_0 when H_1 is correct?

(*c*) Suppose that you plan to take one more observation from the data-generating process.

(*i*) If $\beta = 55$, what is the probability that this observation will be greater than 60?

(*ii*) If you recognize that β is unknown, and, consequently, use the predictive density for the new observation, what is the probability that it will be greater than 60?

4.8 Derive conditions that must hold when an estimator $\hat{\theta}$ for a parameter θ minimizes expected posterior loss where the loss function is given by

(*a*) $\mu(\theta, \hat{\theta}) = 0 \quad \text{if } \theta - a < \hat{\theta} < \theta + a$

$\qquad = c \quad \text{if } \hat{\theta} > \theta + a \text{ or } \hat{\theta} < \theta - a$

where $c > 0$, $a > 0$ are constants.

(*b*) $\mu(\theta, \hat{\theta}) = 0 \quad \text{if } \theta - a < \hat{\theta} < \theta + a$

$\qquad = \hat{\theta} - (\theta + a) \quad \text{if } \hat{\theta} > \theta + a$

$\qquad = (\theta - a) - \hat{\theta} \quad \text{if } \hat{\theta} < \theta - a$

In each case interpret the estimator $\hat{\theta}$ on a diagram of the posterior density of θ.

4.9 Suppose that $(y_1, y_2, \ldots, y_T)$ is a random sample from a $N(\beta, \sigma^2)$ distribution.

(*a*) Find the marginal posterior density functions for β and σ when their priors are given by

$$g(\beta|\sigma) \propto \sigma^{-1} \exp\left\{-\frac{\tau}{2\sigma^2}(\beta - \bar{\beta})^2\right\}$$

and

$$g(\sigma) \propto \sigma^{-1}$$

where τ and $\bar{\beta}$ are prior parameters.

(*b*) Suppose that β and σ are a priori independent and that their marginal densities are

$$g(\beta) \propto \left[1 + \frac{1}{\mu}\left(\frac{\beta - \bar{\beta}}{\omega}\right)^2\right]^{-(\mu+1)/2}$$

and

$$g(\sigma) \propto \frac{1}{\sigma^{\bar{v}+1}} \exp\left\{-\frac{\bar{v}\bar{s}^2}{2\sigma^2}\right\}$$

where $\bar{\beta}$, ω, μ, $\bar{v}$, and $\bar{s}^2$ are prior parameters.

(*i*) What is the prior mean and variance for β?

(*ii*) Show that the marginal posterior density for β is proportional to the product of two "student" *t*-functions.

4.10 (*a*) Given that θ has the gamma p.d.f. given in (4.4.3), show that $z = \bar{\nu}\bar{s}^2\theta$ is a χ^2 random variable with $\bar{\nu}$ degrees of freedom and the p.d.f. given in (4.4.5).

(*b*) Use the p.d.f. in (4.4.5) to show that $\sigma = \sqrt{\bar{\nu}\bar{s}^2/z}$ has the inverted-gamma p.d.f. given in (4.4.7).

4.11 Show that the mode, median, and mean of the prior p.d.f. for σ given in Section 4.4.1 are given by 1.19, 1.54, and 1.89, respectively.

For this question and Problem 4.12, values of the gamma function need to be computed. These values can be calculated in the following way. When ν is even

$$\Gamma(\nu/2) = \left(\frac{\nu}{2} - 1\right)\left(\frac{\nu}{2} - 2\right)\cdots 3 \times 2 \times 1$$

When ν is odd

$$\Gamma(\nu/2) = \left(\frac{\nu}{2} - 1\right)\left(\frac{\nu}{2} - 2\right)\cdots \tfrac{3}{2} \times \tfrac{1}{2} \times \sqrt{\pi}$$

4.12 Verify the values given in Table 4.1.

4.13 Verify the expression given in (4.4.18).

4.14 Starting with a noninformative prior for (β, σ), derive marginal posterior p.d.f.'s for β and σ for the Louisiana Fried Chicken example.

4.7 References

Berger, J. O. (1985) *Statistical Decision Theory and Bayesian Analysis*, 2nd ed. New York: Springer-Verlag.

Box, G. E. P., and G. C. Tiao (1973) *Bayesian Inference in Statistical Analysis.* Reading, MA: Addison-Wesley.

Jones, J. M. (1977) *Introduction to Decision Theory.* Homewood, IL: Richard Irwin.

Leamer, E. E. (1978) *Specification Searches: Ad Hoc Inference with Nonexperimental Data.* New York: Wiley.

Spiegel, M. R. (1963) *Theory and Problems of Advanced Calculus.* New York: Schaum.

Zellner, A. (1971) *An Introduction to Bayesian Inference in Econometrics.* New York: Wiley.

PART 2

The General Linear Statistical Model

In the following three chapters, general linear sampling (statistical) models are specified, and the problem of estimating the corresponding unknown location vector and scale parameter is considered within both sampling theory and Bayesian contexts. The statistical model is developed first in summation notation and then specified in matrix-vector form. The results of sampling experiments are presented to demonstrate the repeated sampling nature of classical statistics and to demonstrate the statistical properties of the least squares estimation.

CHAPTER 5

Linear Statistical Models

5.1 Introduction

Given the definitions and basic concepts of statistics introduced in the preceding chapters, we now consider the problem of how to use a sample of data to learn about unknown location and scale parameters. In the simplest case, which was often discussed in the preceding chapters, the unknown parameters are the mean and variance of a distribution.

Two ways to generate sample information (observations) are to perform an experiment or to observe the results of an experiment. For example, one may design an experiment and generate the corresponding sample observations. Alternatively, one may observe outcomes, such as data on prices, incomes, and consumption, and view these as being the results of an experiment designed and carried out by society. Given the sample information from an experiment or contained in a set of passively generated data, the next step is to build a theoretical model that is thought to be consistent with the underlying sampling process and that identifies the corresponding unknown parameters of the sampling distribution thought to be relevant.

In this chapter we start with a simple linear-model world where the informational demands on the data involve only two or three unknown parameters. Understanding the simple linear models provides the foundation on which to build the more general statistical models that are covered in Sections 5.4 through 5.11 and the chapters ahead. To provide a transition from the summation notation, in this chapter we develop the results for the simple linear statistical model in both the summation and matrix-vector notations. Those who feel uncomfortable with the linear algebra form should refer to the early sections of Appendix A.

5.2 Linear Statistical Model 1

Consider a sample $\mathbf{y}$ of T observations that we assume have been drawn from a distribution that has a mean (location parameter) of β and a variance (scale parameter) of σ^2. Also assume that the T outcomes are independent from drawing to drawing. Thus, the random variable $y_t \sim (\beta, \sigma^2)$, and independence implies that the covariance $E[(y_t - \beta)(y_s - \beta)] = 0$ for $s \neq t$. In this context we can model each sample outcome y_t as composed of its mean β and an unobservable random component e_t. Consequently,

$$y_t = \beta + e_t \tag{5.2.1}$$

Since β is a parameter, and given the distributional assumptions on the random variable y_t, it follows that the random variable $y_t - \beta = e_t$ has mean $E[e_t] = 0$ and variance $E[e_t - E[e_t]]^2 = E[e_t^2] = \sigma^2$ for all $t = 1, 2, \ldots, T$. Furthermore, the e_t are independently and identically distributed random variables. Although the random variables y_t and e_t have different location parameters β and 0, their scale parameters are identical.

The T equations, one for each y_t, may be written as

$$\begin{aligned} y_1 &= \beta + e_1 \\ y_2 &= \beta + e_2 \\ &\vdots \\ y_T &= \beta + e_T \end{aligned} \tag{5.2.2}$$

If we represent the sample observations by the vector $\mathbf{y} = (y_1, y_2, \ldots, y_T)'$, we may write the model representing the set of equations as

$$\begin{bmatrix} y_1 \\ y_2 \\ \vdots \\ y_T \end{bmatrix} = \begin{bmatrix} 1 \\ 1 \\ \vdots \\ 1 \end{bmatrix} \beta + \begin{bmatrix} e_1 \\ e_2 \\ \vdots \\ e_T \end{bmatrix} = \begin{bmatrix} \beta \\ \beta \\ \vdots \\ \beta \end{bmatrix} + \begin{bmatrix} e_1 \\ e_2 \\ \vdots \\ e_T \end{bmatrix} \tag{5.2.3a}$$

Letting $\mathbf{x}$ represent a vector of ones and $\mathbf{e} = (e_1, e_2, \ldots, e_T)'$, we may write (5.2.3a) compactly as

$$\mathbf{y} = \mathbf{x}\beta + \mathbf{e} \tag{5.2.3b}$$

where, in a repeated-sampling context, $E[\mathbf{y}] = \mathbf{x}\beta$ and $E[\mathbf{e}] = \mathbf{0}$. This model was used as an example on a number of occasions in Chapter 3. It is considered here in a slightly different context as an introduction to linear statistical models that contain two or more location parameters.

In terms of the covariance, we have assumed that the random variables y_t are statistically independent and, equivalently, so are the e_t. Since $E[\mathbf{e}] = \mathbf{0}$, for the vector of random variables $\mathbf{e}$, the corresponding matrix of covariances may be represented by continued use of the expectation operator

$$E\{[\mathbf{e} - E[\mathbf{e}]][\mathbf{e} - E[\mathbf{e}]]'\} = E[\mathbf{ee}'] \tag{5.2.4a}$$

Thus,

$$E[\mathbf{ee}'] = E\left[\begin{bmatrix} e_1 \\ e_2 \\ \vdots \\ e_T \end{bmatrix}_{(T \times 1)} [e_1 \quad e_2 \quad \cdots \quad e_T]_{(1 \times T)}\right] \tag{5.2.4b}$$

or

$$E[\mathbf{ee}'] = \begin{bmatrix} E[e_1^2] & E[e_1 e_2] & \cdots & E[e_1 e_T] \\ E[e_2 e_1] & E[e_2^2] & \cdots & E[e_2 e_T] \\ \vdots & \vdots & \ddots & \vdots \\ E[e_T e_1] & E[e_T e_2] & \cdots & E[e_T^2] \end{bmatrix}_{(T \times T)} \tag{5.2.4c}$$

Since, by assumption, e_i and e_j are independent random variables, the covariance between e_i and e_j, for $i \neq j$, is 0. Thus, $E[e_i e_j] = 0$, for $i \neq j$, and we may write (5.2.4c) as

$$E[\mathbf{ee}'] = \begin{bmatrix} \sigma^2 & 0 & \cdots & 0 \\ 0 & \sigma^2 & \cdots & 0 \\ \vdots & \vdots & \ddots & \vdots \\ 0 & 0 & \cdots & \sigma^2 \end{bmatrix} \tag{5.2.4d}$$

$$= \sigma^2 \begin{bmatrix} 1 & 0 & \cdots & 0 \\ 0 & 1 & \cdots & 0 \\ \vdots & \vdots & \ddots & \vdots \\ 0 & 0 & \cdots & 1 \end{bmatrix} = \sigma^2 I_T \tag{5.2.4e}$$

In the last expression in (5.2.4e), I_T denotes a Tth order identity matrix and $\sigma^2 I_T$ is a scalar diagonal matrix.

Given these stochastic assumptions, let us interpret this result. Note that the variance of each e_i is defined as $E[e_i - E[e_i]]^2 = E[e_i^2]$ and, by assumption, each of these expectations is σ^2. These terms fall on the diagonal in (5.2.4c) and (5.2.4d). Also note that the covariance between e_i and e_j is defined as $E[e_i - E[e_i]][e_j - E[e_j]] = E[e_i e_j] = E[e_j e_i]$ and that these terms fall in the i, jth, and j, ith positions in (5.2.4c). As indicated, all these expectations are 0 because we have assumed that all of the e_i are statistically independent. Consequently, the matrix

$$E[(\mathbf{e} - E[\mathbf{e}])(\mathbf{e} - E[\mathbf{e}])'] \tag{5.2.5}$$

is said to be the covariance matrix of the vector $\mathbf{e}$ as it contains the variance of the ith element of $\mathbf{e}$, e_i, in the ith diagonal position and the covariance between e_i and e_j in the (i, j)th position. Since $E[e_i e_j] = E[e_j e_i]$, this square matrix is its own transpose and is thus said to be symmetric. Likewise, the random vector $\mathbf{y}$ has mean $E[\mathbf{y}] = E[\mathbf{x}\beta + \mathbf{e}] = \mathbf{x}\beta$ and covariance matrix $E[(\mathbf{y} - \mathbf{x}\beta)(\mathbf{y} - \mathbf{x}\beta)'] = E[\mathbf{ee}'] = \sigma^2 I_T$.

To summarize, if we have a random sample $y_1, \ldots, y_T$, each with probability density functions $f(y_t)$, mean β, and variance σ^2, we may write the linear statistical model that describes the imagined sampling process as

$$\mathbf{y} = \mathbf{x}\beta + \mathbf{e} \tag{5.2.3b}$$

where the $(T \times 1)$ observable random vector $\mathbf{y}$ has mean $E[\mathbf{y}] = \mathbf{x}\beta$ and covariance matrix $\sigma^2 I_T$ and the *un*observable random vector $\mathbf{e}$ has mean $E[\mathbf{e}] = \mathbf{0}$ and covariance matrix $\sigma^2 I_T$. In the next section we specify a more general linear statistical model that includes (5.2.3b) as a special case and consider how the sample of y_t values may be used to learn about the unknown location and scale parameters.

5.3 Linear Statistical Model 2

In the previous section, our concern was with the specification of a model that could be used to describe the data-generating process for a sample of data with a single location parameter β and the scale parameter σ^2. In this section we introduce additional information and recognize that economic variables are interrelated and that the value that one variable takes on may condition the mean outcome for another variable. Thus, for example, from economic theory we are led to visualize that price conditions the level of consumption of a particular commodity, the level of an input conditions the level of output, and the level of consumption is affected by the level of income.

To model this type of situation, let y_t be the outcome or response variable and x_{t2} be the known design, explanatory, instrument, or conditioning variable. Thus, y_t is a random variable and x_{t2} is fixed or nonstochastic. Consequently, we may model the observed random variable y_t as

$$y_t = E[y_t] + e_t = \beta_1 + x_{t2}\beta_2 + e_t \tag{5.3.1}$$

where β_1 reflects the level and β_2 reflects the slope of the relationship that is linear in terms of the parameters. The parameters β_1, β_2, and the random variable e_t are unobserved and unobservable. We continue to assume that the random variable e_t has the stochastic characteristics discussed in Section 5.2. Thus, e_t is an independently and identically distributed random variable with mean $E[e_t] = 0$, variance

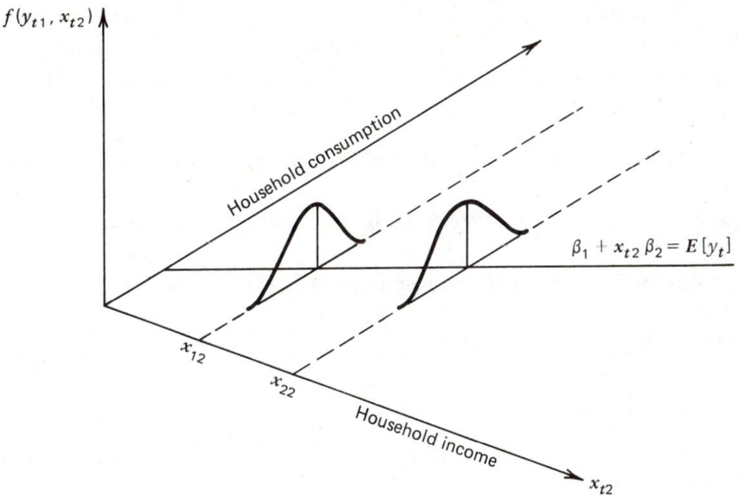

Figure 5.1 The p.d.f. for y_t for two levels of the design variable x_{t2}.

$E[(e_t)^2] = \sigma^2$, and covariance $E[(e_t e_s)] = 0$ for $t \neq s$. This implies that the random vector $\mathbf{e} \sim (\mathbf{0}, \sigma^2 I_T)$. For a given value of the design variable x_{t2}, the random variable y_t has mean $E[y_t] = \beta_1 + x_{t2}\beta_2$ and variance $E[(y_t - \beta_1 - x_{t2}\beta_2)^2] = E[e_t^2] = \sigma^2$.

If e_t and y_t are normally distributed random variables, then $f(y_t|x_{t2}) \sim N(\beta_1 + x_{t2}\beta_2, \sigma^2)$. Using household consumption and income as an example, this relationship is depicted graphically in Figure 5.1. A particular value of y, say y_1, consists of two parts; the first part is given by the line $\beta_1 + x_{t2}\beta_2$ at the point x_{12} whereas the second part, e_1, is given by a drawing from the distribution (p.d.f.) centered at $\beta_1 + x_{12}\beta_2$.

Given (5.3.1), we may write the statistical model for the sample $y_1, y_2, \ldots, y_T$ as

$$\begin{bmatrix} y_1 \\ y_2 \\ \vdots \\ y_T \end{bmatrix} = \begin{bmatrix} 1 \\ 1 \\ \vdots \\ 1 \end{bmatrix} \beta_1 + \begin{bmatrix} x_{12} \\ x_{22} \\ \vdots \\ x_{T2} \end{bmatrix} \beta_2 + \begin{bmatrix} e_1 \\ e_2 \\ \vdots \\ e_T \end{bmatrix} \tag{5.3.2}$$

or, compactly, as

$$\mathbf{y} = \mathbf{x}_1\beta_1 + \mathbf{x}_2\beta_2 + \mathbf{e} = (\mathbf{x}_1 \quad \mathbf{x}_2)\begin{pmatrix} \beta_1 \\ \beta_2 \end{pmatrix} + \mathbf{e} = X\boldsymbol{\beta} + \mathbf{e} \tag{5.3.3a}$$

where $\mathbf{x}_1$ is a $(T \times 1)$ vector of ones as in (5.2.3a) and $\mathbf{x}_2$ is a $(T \times 1)$ vector of values of x_{t2} the control variable; X is a $(T \times 2)$ known matrix, and $\boldsymbol{\beta}$ is a (2×1) vector of unknown location parameters. The random vector $\mathbf{y}$ has mean $E[\mathbf{y}] = X\boldsymbol{\beta}$ and covariance matrix

$$E[(\mathbf{y} - X\boldsymbol{\beta})(\mathbf{y} - X\boldsymbol{\beta})'] = E[\mathbf{e}\mathbf{e}'] = \sigma^2 I_T \tag{5.3.4}$$

Note, again, that $\mathbf{y}$ and X are observed and $\boldsymbol{\beta}$, σ^2, and $\mathbf{e}$ are unobserved and unobservable.

Given that the sample observations are generated in line with the statistical model,

$$\mathbf{y} = \mathbf{x}_1\beta_1 + \mathbf{x}_2\beta_2 + \mathbf{e} \tag{5.3.3a}$$

and

$$\mathbf{e} \sim (\mathbf{0}, \sigma^2 I_T) \tag{5.3.3b}$$

the question is how to make use of the sample information $\mathbf{y}$ to estimate the unknown location parameters β_1 and β_2 and the scale parameter σ^2.

5.3.1 Estimating the Location Parameters

Given a theoretical model for explaining how the sample data are generated, let us for the moment assume that the scale parameter σ^2 is known. The problem then is how best to use our sample information $\mathbf{y}$, in conjunction with the known vector $\mathbf{x}_2$, to estimate the unknowns (β_1 and β_2) that represent the unknown level and slope coefficients for the economic relationship that is under study.

How do we find a rule (estimator) that will specify how the sample data should be used to estimate $\boldsymbol{\beta}$? One way is to define an objective or criterion that we wish the rule to attain. One such criterion is called the least squares criterion. According to this criterion, given a sample of observed values of the random variables y_1, $y_2, \ldots, y_T$, to obtain an estimate $\mathbf{b}$ for the unknown parameter vector $\boldsymbol{\beta} = (\beta_1, \beta_2)'$, an estimator is chosen that minimizes the error sum of squares $\Sigma e_t^2 = \mathbf{e}'\mathbf{e}$ where e_t and $\mathbf{e}$ are defined in (5.3.2) and (5.3.3a) and, here and elsewhere in this chapter, $\Sigma = \sum_{t=1}^{T}$.

Formally, we can state this criterion as: Given the sample observations $\mathbf{y}$, find values for β_1 and β_2 that minimize

$$\begin{aligned} S &= \Sigma(y_t - x_{t1}\beta_1 - x_{t2}\beta_2)^2 \\ &= \mathbf{e}'\mathbf{e} = (\mathbf{y} - \mathbf{x}_1\beta_1 - \mathbf{x}_2\beta_2)'(\mathbf{y} - \mathbf{x}_1\beta_1 - \mathbf{x}_2\beta_2) \\ &= (\mathbf{y} - X\boldsymbol{\beta})'(\mathbf{y} - X\boldsymbol{\beta}) = \mathbf{y}'\mathbf{y} - 2\boldsymbol{\beta}'X'\mathbf{y} + \boldsymbol{\beta}'X'X\boldsymbol{\beta} \end{aligned} \tag{5.3.5}$$

The minimization of this quadratic form is a common problem in calculus. In this case we need to find the minimizing values b_1 and b_2 for β_1 and β_2 that make the partial derivatives vanish. For our problem, these derivatives are

$$\frac{\partial S}{\partial \beta_1} = -2\Sigma(y_t - x_{t1}\beta_1 - x_{t2}\beta_2) = -2(\Sigma y_t - T\beta_1 - \Sigma x_{t2}\beta_2)$$

$$= -2(\Sigma y_t) + 2(T \quad \Sigma x_{t2})\begin{pmatrix}\beta_1 \\ \beta_2\end{pmatrix} = -2\mathbf{x}_1'\mathbf{y} + 2\mathbf{x}_1'[\mathbf{x}_1 \quad \mathbf{x}_2]\boldsymbol{\beta} \qquad (5.3.6a)$$

$$\frac{\partial S}{\partial \beta_2} = -2[\Sigma x_{t2}(y_t - x_{t1}\beta_1 - x_{t2}\beta_2)]$$

$$= -2(\Sigma x_{t2}y_t - \Sigma x_{t1}x_{t2}\beta_1 - \Sigma x_{t2}^2\beta_2)$$

$$= -2(\Sigma x_{t2}y_t - \Sigma x_{t2}\beta_1 - \Sigma x_{t2}^2\beta_2)$$

$$= -2(\Sigma x_{t2}y_t) + 2(\Sigma x_{t1}x_{t2} \quad \Sigma x_{t2}^2)\begin{pmatrix}\beta_1 \\ \beta_2\end{pmatrix}$$

$$= -2\mathbf{x}_2'\mathbf{y} + 2\mathbf{x}_2'[\mathbf{x}_1 \quad \mathbf{x}_2]\boldsymbol{\beta} \qquad (5.3.6b)$$

Using rules of differentiation with respect to a vector, it is possible to write the derivatives in terms of the more compact matrix notation (see Section A.17 of the Linear Algebra Appendix). Specifically, making use of (5.3.5),

$$\frac{\partial(\mathbf{y} - X\boldsymbol{\beta})'(\mathbf{y} - X\boldsymbol{\beta})}{\partial\boldsymbol{\beta}} = \frac{\partial(\mathbf{y}'\mathbf{y} - 2\boldsymbol{\beta}'X'\mathbf{y} + \boldsymbol{\beta}'X'X\boldsymbol{\beta})}{\partial\boldsymbol{\beta}}$$

$$= -2X'\mathbf{y} + 2X'X\boldsymbol{\beta}$$

$$= -2\begin{bmatrix}\mathbf{x}_1'\mathbf{y} \\ \mathbf{x}_2'\mathbf{y}\end{bmatrix} + 2\begin{bmatrix}\mathbf{x}_1' \\ \mathbf{x}_2'\end{bmatrix}[\mathbf{x}_1 \quad \mathbf{x}_2]\boldsymbol{\beta}$$

$$= -2\begin{bmatrix}\mathbf{x}_1'\mathbf{y} \\ \mathbf{x}_2'\mathbf{y}\end{bmatrix} + 2\begin{bmatrix}\mathbf{x}_1'\mathbf{x}_1 & \mathbf{x}_1'\mathbf{x}_2 \\ \mathbf{x}_2'\mathbf{x}_1 & \mathbf{x}_2'\mathbf{x}_2\end{bmatrix}\boldsymbol{\beta}$$

$$= -2\begin{bmatrix}\Sigma y_t \\ \Sigma x_{t2}y_t\end{bmatrix} + 2\begin{bmatrix}T & \Sigma x_{t2} \\ \Sigma x_{t2} & \Sigma x_{t2}^2\end{bmatrix}\begin{bmatrix}\beta_1 \\ \beta_2\end{bmatrix} \qquad (5.3.7)$$

To find minimizing values b_1 and b_2, we set the derivatives [(5.3.6a) and (5.3.6b) or (5.3.7)] equal to zero; this yields

$$\begin{aligned} Tb_1 + \Sigma x_{t2}b_2 &= \Sigma y_t \\ \Sigma x_{t2}b_1 + \Sigma x_{t2}^2 b_2 &= \Sigma x_{t2}y_t \end{aligned} \qquad (5.3.8a)$$

In matrix-vector form (5.3.7), we have the following set of linear equations.

$$\begin{aligned} \mathbf{x}_1'\mathbf{x}_1 b_1 + \mathbf{x}_1'\mathbf{x}_2 b_2 &= \mathbf{x}_1'\mathbf{y} \\ \mathbf{x}_2'\mathbf{x}_1 b_1 + \mathbf{x}_2'\mathbf{x}_2 b_2 &= \mathbf{x}_2'\mathbf{y} \end{aligned} \tag{5.3.8b}$$

which may be written as

$$\begin{bmatrix} \mathbf{x}_1'\mathbf{x}_1 & \mathbf{x}_1'\mathbf{x}_2 \\ \mathbf{x}_2'\mathbf{x}_1 & \mathbf{x}_2'\mathbf{x}_2 \end{bmatrix} \begin{bmatrix} b_1 \\ b_2 \end{bmatrix} = \begin{bmatrix} \mathbf{x}_1'\mathbf{y} \\ \mathbf{x}_2'\mathbf{y} \end{bmatrix}$$

or

$$\begin{bmatrix} T & \Sigma x_{t2} \\ \Sigma x_{t2} & \Sigma x_{t2}^2 \end{bmatrix} \begin{bmatrix} b_1 \\ b_2 \end{bmatrix} = \begin{bmatrix} \Sigma y_t \\ \Sigma x_{t2} y_t \end{bmatrix}$$

or

$$X'X\mathbf{b} = X'\mathbf{y}$$

The specifications in (5.3.8a) and (5.3.8b) represent a system of linear-simultaneous equations that must be solved for b_1 and b_2. Following procedures outlined in Section A.8 of the Linear Algebra Appendix, and making use of the concept of the inverse of a matrix,

$$\begin{aligned} \mathbf{b} = \begin{bmatrix} b_1 \\ b_2 \end{bmatrix} &= (X'X)^{-1}X'\mathbf{y} = \begin{bmatrix} \mathbf{x}_1'\mathbf{x}_1 & \mathbf{x}_1'\mathbf{x}_2 \\ \mathbf{x}_2'\mathbf{x}_1 & \mathbf{x}_2'\mathbf{x}_2 \end{bmatrix}^{-1} \begin{bmatrix} \mathbf{x}_1'\mathbf{y} \\ \mathbf{x}_2'\mathbf{y} \end{bmatrix} \\ &= \begin{bmatrix} T & \Sigma x_{t2} \\ \Sigma x_{t2} & \Sigma x_{t2}^2 \end{bmatrix}^{-1} \begin{bmatrix} \Sigma y_t \\ \Sigma x_{t2} y_t \end{bmatrix} \\ &= \frac{1}{T(\Sigma x_{t2}^2) - (\Sigma x_{t2})^2} \begin{bmatrix} \Sigma x_{t2}^2 & -\Sigma x_{t2} \\ -\Sigma x_{t2} & T \end{bmatrix} \begin{bmatrix} \Sigma y_t \\ \Sigma x_{t2} y_t \end{bmatrix} \end{aligned} \tag{5.3.9}$$

where $T\Sigma x_{t2}^2 - (\Sigma x_{t2})^2 = T\Sigma(x_{t2} - \bar{x}_2)^2$ and $\bar{x}_2$ is the arithmetic mean of x_{t2}. Consequently,

$$\begin{aligned} b_1 &= \frac{(\Sigma x_{t2}^2 \Sigma y_t) - (\Sigma x_{t2} \Sigma x_{t2} y_t)}{T\Sigma(x_{t2} - \bar{x}_2)^2} \\ b_2 &= \frac{T(\Sigma x_{t2} y_t) - (\Sigma x_{t2})(\Sigma y_t)}{T\Sigma(x_{t2} - \bar{x}_2)^2} \end{aligned} \tag{5.3.10}$$

It is sometimes useful to simplify b_1 as $b_1 = \bar{y} - \bar{x}_2 b_2$ where $\bar{y}$ and $\bar{x}_2$ are the sample means for the observations on y and x_2, respectively. To summarize, **b**, the least squares estimator of the unknown parameters β_1 and β_2, results from solving the two simultaneous linear equations in (5.3.8). The resulting least squares estimator is

$$\mathbf{b} = (X'X)^{-1}X'\mathbf{y} \tag{5.3.11}$$

Note that the least squares estimator **b** is a linear function of the observations **y**.

5.3.2 Sampling Properties

Given a rule for using the sample data to estimate the unknown parameters β_1 and β_2, our next concern is with the sampling performance of the estimator. Since **b** is a linear function of the sample observations **y**, which is a random vector, the least squares estimator of the location vector **b** is also a random vector; that is, **b** is a vector of random variables. Consequently, if we make repeated use of the least squares estimator, the *estimate* of $\boldsymbol{\beta}$ will vary from sample to sample. Therefore, it seems reasonable to ask about the mean and sampling variability of this random vector.

In a repeated-sampling sense, we would like to know, even before we draw any samples, something about the sampling performance of the least squares estimator.

To learn about the mean vector for **b** or, on average, how the estimator **b** performs, we make use of the expectations operator E and investigate the $E[\mathbf{b}]$. Using (5.3.9),

$$\begin{aligned} E[\mathbf{b}] &= E[(X'X)^{-1}X'\mathbf{y}] = E[(X'X)^{-1}X'(X\boldsymbol{\beta} + \mathbf{e})] \\ &= E[(X'X)^{-1}X'X\boldsymbol{\beta} + (X'X)^{-1}X'\mathbf{e}] = E[I\boldsymbol{\beta}] + (X'X)^{-1}X'E(\mathbf{e}) \\ &= \boldsymbol{\beta} + (X'X)^{-1}X'\mathbf{0} = \boldsymbol{\beta} \end{aligned} \tag{5.3.12}$$

since by assumption $E[e_t] = 0$. Consequently, using the least squares estimator results in a linear rule for estimating β_1 and β_2 that is unbiased, that is, within a repeated-sampling context, on the *average*, the least squares rule is an unbiased rule, that is, on *average*, it hits the target β_1 and β_2. *This, of course, does not* mean that the estimates of β_1 and β_2 *from a sample of data* are unbiased. *What is unbiased is the rule or estimator and not the estimate that is related to a particular sample.* Thus, even before we draw a sample, we know that, if we use the least squares rule **b**, it will be an unbiased rule since $E[\mathbf{b} - \boldsymbol{\beta}] = \mathbf{0}$.

Having established that **b** is a random vector with mean $\boldsymbol{\beta}$, our next concern is with its sampling variability or precision. Consequently, we look at the *average* sampling variability of the estimator **b**. From (5.3.12), we know that

$$\mathbf{b} = \boldsymbol{\beta} + (X'X)^{-1}X'\mathbf{e} \tag{5.3.13a}$$

or, in other words, that

$$\mathbf{b} - \boldsymbol{\beta} = (X'X)^{-1}X'\mathbf{e} \tag{5.3.13b}$$

Since **b** is an unbiased rule, we may specify the covariance matrix for **b** as

$$E\{[\mathbf{b} - E(\mathbf{b})][\mathbf{b} - E(\mathbf{b})]'\} = E[(\mathbf{b} - \boldsymbol{\beta})(\mathbf{b} - \boldsymbol{\beta})'] \qquad (5.3.14a)$$

Making use of (5.3.13b), we express the covariance matrix $\Sigma_{\mathbf{b}}$ for the random vector **b** as

$$\Sigma_{\mathbf{b}} = E[(X'X)^{-1}X'\mathbf{ee}'X(X'X)^{-1}] = (X'X)^{-1}X'E[\mathbf{ee}']X(X'X)^{-1}$$

$$= \sigma^2(X'X)^{-1}X'IX(X'X)^{-1} = \sigma^2(X'X)^{-1} = \sigma^2\begin{bmatrix} T & \Sigma x_{t2} \\ \Sigma x_{t2} & \Sigma x_{t2}^2 \end{bmatrix}^{-1} \qquad (5.3.14b)$$

where use is made of the assumption that $E[\mathbf{ee}'] = \sigma^2 I_T$. Since $\mathbf{b} = (b_1, b_2)'$ is a two-dimensional random vector, the covariance $\Sigma_{\mathbf{b}}$ is the following (2×2) matrix.

$$\Sigma_{\mathbf{b}} = \begin{bmatrix} E[(b_1 - \beta_1)^2] & E[(b_1 - \beta_1)(b_2 - \beta_2)] \\ E[(b_1 - \beta_1)(b_2 - \beta_2)] & E[(b_2 - \beta_2)^2] \end{bmatrix}$$

$$= \begin{bmatrix} \operatorname{var}(b_1) & \operatorname{cov}(b_1, b_2) \\ \operatorname{cov}(b_1, b_2) & \operatorname{var}(b_2) \end{bmatrix} \qquad (5.3.14c)$$

Using the inverse of $X'X$ in (5.3.9), the variances and covariance of b_1 and b_2 are

$$\operatorname{var}(b_1) = \sigma^2\left[\frac{\Sigma x_{t2}^2}{T\Sigma(x_{t2} - \bar{x}_2)^2}\right] = \sigma^2 a_1 \qquad (5.3.15a)$$

$$\operatorname{var}(b_2) = \frac{\sigma^2}{\Sigma(x_{t2} - \bar{x}_2)^2} = \sigma^2 a_2 \qquad (5.3.15b)$$

$$\operatorname{cov}(b_1, b_2) = \sigma^2\left[\frac{-\bar{x}_2}{\Sigma(x_{t2} - \bar{x}_2)^2}\right] \qquad (5.3.15c)$$

Thus, we can specify in advance of the observations, the *average* precision of the least squares estimator **b**.

The sampling information that we have about the random variables b_1 and b_2 can be summarized as follows.

$$b_1 \sim (\beta_1, \sigma^2 a_1)$$

and

$$b_2 \sim (\beta_2, \sigma^2 a_2)$$

where a_1 and a_2 are defined in (5.3.15a) and (5.3.15b). One thing that is apparent from (5.3.15) is that the more dispersed the explanatory variable [i.e., the larger is $\Sigma(x_{t2} - \bar{x}_2)^2$], the greater the precision of b_1 and b_2. Also, because the number of terms in the summation $\Sigma(x_{t2} - \bar{x}_2)^2$ increases as sample size increases, an increase in sample size generally leads to an increase in precision. Finally, the smaller the error variance σ^2, which reflects the variability of y_t about its mean, the more precise are the estimators.

5.3.3 Prediction

One objective in obtaining estimates of the unknown parameters β_1 and β_2 is to be able to make informed predictions about the outcomes for the random variable y_t. If we can understand the relationship between y_t and x_{t2}, we can make predictions about the outcome for y_t for a given x_{t2}; this knowledge gives us the ability to exercise some control relative to the random variable y_t.

Given the least squares estimates of the parameters β_1 and β_2, we may form the following prediction equation

$$\hat{y}_0 = b_1 + x_{02} b_2 \tag{5.3.16a}$$

as a predictor for

$$y_0 = \beta_1 + x_{02}\beta_2 + e_0 \tag{5.3.16b}$$

The value y_0 is a future value of y_t for a given value of $x_{t2} = x_{02}$. The term e_0 is a future disturbance. The predictor $\hat{y}_0$ is called an unbiased predictor for y_0 if the mean of the prediction error $E[\hat{y}_0 - y_0] = E[\hat{e}_0]$ is 0. In this case unbiasedness is satisfied because

$$\begin{aligned} E[\hat{y}_0 - y_0] &= E[b_1 + x_{02}b_2 - \beta_1 - x_{02}\beta_2 - e_0] \\ &= E[b_1 - \beta_1] + x_{02}E[b_2 - \beta_2] - E[e_0] \\ &= 0 \end{aligned} \tag{5.3.16c}$$

Note that $\hat{y}_0$ can differ from y_0 because the estimates b_1 and b_2 will differ from their mean values β_1 and β_2 and because the future disturbance e_0 will differ from its implicit predictor, which is its mean value of 0.

The variance of the prediction error is given by

$$\begin{aligned} E[(\hat{y}_0 - y_0)^2] &= E[(b_1 - \beta_1)^2] + x_{02}^2 E[(b_2 - \beta_2)^2] + E[e_0^2] \\ &\quad + 2x_{02}E[(b_1 - \beta_1)(b_2 - \beta_2)] \\ &\quad - 2E[(b_1 - \beta_1)e_0] - 2E[(b_2 - \beta_2)e_0] \\ &= \operatorname{var}(b_1) + x_{02}^2 \operatorname{var}(b_2) + \operatorname{var}(e_0) \\ &\quad + 2x_{02}\operatorname{cov}(b_1, b_2) - 2\operatorname{cov}(b_1, e_0) - 2\operatorname{cov}(b_2, e_0) \end{aligned} \tag{5.3.17a}$$

Because b_1 and b_2 are based on past observations, and e_0 is a future disturbance, b_1 and b_2 will be independent of e_0, implying $\text{cov}(b_1, e_0) = \text{cov}(b_2, e_0) = 0$. Using this result and the result in (5.3.15), the expression (5.3.17a) reduces to

$$E[(\hat{y}_0 - y_0)^2] = \sigma^2 \left[1 + \frac{1}{T} + \frac{(x_{02} - \bar{x}_2)^2}{\Sigma(x_{t2} - \bar{x}_2)^2} \right] \tag{5.3.17b}$$

This result implies that, the farther x_{02} is from its mean $\bar{x}_2$, the larger the prediction error variance. To summarize, the least squares predictor $\hat{y}_0$, given by (5.3.16a), is an unbiased linear predictor of y_0, and the sampling variability of its prediction error is given by (5.3.17b). The prediction precision depends on the var e_0, the sample size, and the sampling variability of b_1 and b_2. Prediction outside the range of the x_{t2} used in estimation leads, from (5.3.17b), to large prediction or forecast sampling variance.

5.3.4 An Estimator of σ^2

Up to this point, we have assumed that σ^2 is known. For most real-world cases, for example, in estimating the parameters of consumption, demand, and production functions, the scale parameter σ^2 for the errors e_t is an unknown scalar. Unfortunately, the errors e_t are unobservable and, therefore, cannot be used to estimate σ^2. Given this situation, we must face the question of what information exists that can be used to obtain an estimate of the scale parameter σ^2. A natural estimate of the errors e_t is $\hat{e}_t = y_t - \hat{y}_t$, where $\hat{y}_t = b_1 + x_{t2}b_2$. Therefore, one alternative is to devise a rule to use this information. Recall that $E[e_t^2] = \sigma^2$ and, therefore, σ^2 is, in a repeated-sampling sense, the average value of e_t^2. Since e_t^2 is unobservable, substituting its observable counterpart $\hat{e}_t^2$ seems reasonable. Thus, we are led to the estimator,

$$\bar{s}^2 = \Sigma\hat{e}_t^2/T = \hat{\mathbf{e}}'\hat{\mathbf{e}}/T \tag{5.3.18}$$

which is the arithmetic average of the estimated squared residuals. This results in a scalar value that may be used as an estimator of σ^2. Later in this chapter we will propose another estimator for σ^2 that fulfills the condition (restriction) that the estimator chosen be unbiased.

This may be a good time to mention that there are often several competing rules (estimators) that specify how to use the sample information to estimate unknown parameters. How to choose an estimator from the relevant set of alternatives is a question that we will spend a good deal of time on in the coming chapters. As we will show in the next section, an unbiased estimator of σ^2 for this statistical model is $\hat{\sigma}^2 = \Sigma\hat{e}_t^2/(T-2) = \hat{\mathbf{e}}'\hat{\mathbf{e}}/(T-2)$.

5.3.5 A Measure of Success

In Chapter 2 we explored the relationship between random variables and, as a measure of association, defined a correlation coefficient. At this point, it might be interesting to pursue, under statistical model (5.3.1), the association between the random variables y_t and $\hat{y}_t = b_1 + x_{t2}b_2$. In using statistical model (5.3.1), we have introduced the "explanatory" variable x_{t2} in the hope of doing a better job of tracking the random variable y_t; better, that is, than using model (5.2.1) where the best estimator of y_t is the arithmetic mean $\bar{y} = \Sigma y_t/T$.

In terms of the y_t and $\hat{y}_t$ we may write

$$y_t = \bar{y} + (\hat{y}_t - \bar{y}) + y_t - \hat{y}_t$$

or

$$y_t - \bar{y} = (\hat{y}_t - \bar{y}) + (y_t - \hat{y}_t) \tag{5.3.19a}$$

where $y_t - \bar{y}$ is the deviation of y_t from the average $\bar{y}$, $y_t - \hat{y}_t = \hat{e}_t$ is the unexplained or error component, and $\hat{y}_t - \bar{y}$ is the explained component. Alternatively, it can be shown by using a little algebra that the sum of squared deviations of the y_t from $\bar{y}$ may be expressed as

$$\Sigma(y_t - \bar{y})^2 = \Sigma(\hat{y}_t - \bar{y})^2 + \Sigma(y_t - \hat{y}_t)^2 \tag{5.3.19b}$$

This tells us the total sum of squared deviations $\Sigma(y_t - \bar{y})^2$ is equal to the sum of the explained sum of squares $\Sigma(\hat{y}_t - \bar{y})^2$ and the sum of squares of error $\Sigma(y_t - \hat{y}_t)^2$. If we divide (5.3.19b) by the total sum of squares, we have

$$1 = \frac{\Sigma(\hat{y}_t - \bar{y})^2}{\Sigma(y_t - \bar{y})^2} + \frac{\Sigma(y_t - \hat{y}_t)^2}{\Sigma(y_t - \bar{y})^2}$$

or

$$\frac{\Sigma(\hat{y}_t - \bar{y})^2}{\Sigma(y_t - \bar{y})^2} = 1 - \frac{\Sigma(y_t - \hat{y}_t)^2}{\Sigma(y_t - \bar{y})^2} \tag{5.3.19c}$$

where $\Sigma(\hat{y}_t - \bar{y})^2/\Sigma(y_t - \bar{y})^2$ is a measure of the proportion of the total variation in y about its mean $\bar{y}$ that has been accounted for by using model (5.3.1) instead of model (5.2.1). The ratio

$$\frac{\Sigma(\hat{y}_t - \bar{y})^2}{\Sigma(y_t - \bar{y})^2} = R^2 \tag{5.3.19d}$$

is called the coefficient of determination and, of course, the closer R^2 is to one the better job we have done in tracking y_t with $\hat{y}_t = b_1 + x_{t2}b_2$ instead of using $\bar{y}$. A more complete discussion of this topic is given in Section 5.9.3.

5.3.6 An Example

To give this linear statistical model some operational content, consider the problem of estimating the parameters of a consumption function based on the data given in Table 5.1. Let us assume that the relationship between consumption, y_t, and income, x_{t2}, can be cast in the linear form

$$y_t = \beta_1 + x_{t2}\beta_2 + e_t \tag{5.3.20}$$

Hence, the following statistical model is appropriate

$$\mathbf{y} = \mathbf{x}_1\beta_1 + \mathbf{x}_2\beta_2 + \mathbf{e} = X\boldsymbol{\beta} + \mathbf{e} \tag{5.3.21}$$

where $\mathbf{x}_1$ is a vector of ones and $\mathbf{e}$ is a (20×1) real random vector with mean vector $\mathbf{0}$ and covariance $\sigma^2 I_{20}$.

Use of the least-squares rule (5.3.11) for this problem means that we must solve the following system of linear equations (5.3.8).

$$\begin{aligned} Tb_1 + \Sigma x_{t2} b_2 &= \Sigma y_t \\ \Sigma x_{t2} b_1 + \Sigma(x_{t2}^2) b_2 &= \Sigma x_{t2} y_t \end{aligned} \tag{5.3.22a}$$

or, in vector form,

$$\begin{aligned} \mathbf{x}_1'\mathbf{x}_1 b_1 + \mathbf{x}_1'\mathbf{x}_2 b_2 &= \mathbf{x}_1'\mathbf{y} \\ \mathbf{x}_2'\mathbf{x}_1 b_1 + \mathbf{x}_2'\mathbf{x}_2 b_2 &= \mathbf{x}_2'\mathbf{y} \end{aligned} \tag{5.3.22b}$$

This yields, for the data in Table 5.1, the simultaneous linear equations

$$\begin{bmatrix} 20 & 492.94 \\ 492.94 & 12{,}332.04 \end{bmatrix} \begin{bmatrix} b_1 \\ b_2 \end{bmatrix} = \begin{bmatrix} 434.94 \\ 10{,}870.53 \end{bmatrix} \tag{5.3.22c}$$

Solving this system of equations produces the least squares estimator

$$\begin{aligned} \mathbf{b} = (X'X)^{-1}X'\mathbf{y} &= \begin{bmatrix} 20 & 492.94 \\ 492.94 & 12{,}332.04 \end{bmatrix}^{-1} \begin{bmatrix} 434.94 \\ 10{,}870.53 \end{bmatrix} \\ &= \begin{bmatrix} 3.3777597 & -0.1350168 \\ -0.1350168 & 0.0054780 \end{bmatrix} \begin{bmatrix} 434.94 \\ 10{,}870.53 \end{bmatrix} = \begin{bmatrix} 1.4178 \\ 0.8248 \end{bmatrix} = \begin{bmatrix} b_1 \\ b_2 \end{bmatrix} \end{aligned} \tag{5.3.23}$$

The solution to (5.3.9) yields, by use of the least squares rule, estimates of β_1, the level intercept parameter, and β_2, the slope parameter. The value 0.8248 is an estimate for β_2, the marginal propensity to consume, and represents the estimated change in consumption for each unit change in income. It is, therefore, a parameter that has important economic policy implications.

Table 5.1 Aggregate Consumption and Income Data for 20 Time Periods

Time period	Consumption	Income
1	15.30	17.30
2	19.91	21.91
3	20.94	23.14
4	19.66	21.86
5	21.32	23.72
6	18.33	20.73
7	19.59	22.19
8	21.30	23.90
9	20.93	23.73
10	21.64	24.44
11	21.90	24.90
12	20.50	23.50
13	22.83	26.03
14	23.49	26.69
15	24.20	27.60
16	23.05	26.45
17	24.01	27.61
18	25.83	29.43
19	25.15	28.95
20	25.06	28.86

Given estimates (b_1, b_2) from a sample of data $\mathbf{y}$, the next question concerns the sampling variability or precision of this random vector. From (5.3.14) we know that the covariance matrix for $\mathbf{b}$ is

$$\Sigma_{\mathbf{b}} = \sigma^2(X'X)^{-1} = \sigma^2\begin{bmatrix} \mathbf{x}_1'\mathbf{x}_1 & \mathbf{x}_1'\mathbf{x}_2 \\ \mathbf{x}_2'\mathbf{x}_1 & \mathbf{x}_2'\mathbf{x}_2 \end{bmatrix}^{-1}$$

$$= \sigma^2\begin{bmatrix} T & \Sigma x_{t2} \\ \Sigma x_{t2} & \Sigma x_{t2}^2 \end{bmatrix}^{-1} = \sigma^2\begin{bmatrix} 20 & 492.94 \\ 492.94 & 12{,}332.04 \end{bmatrix}^{-1}$$

$$= \sigma^2\begin{bmatrix} 3.3778 & -0.1350 \\ -0.1350 & 0.0055 \end{bmatrix} \tag{5.3.24}$$

Consequently, the sampling variability of b_1 is $3.38\sigma^2$, and the sampling variability of the random variable b_2 is $0.0055\sigma^2$. At this point, we have no basis for saying anything about the magnitude of the unknown scale parameter σ^2. However, it appears that we have been able to estimate the slope parameter β_2 more precisely than the level or intercept parameter β_1.

If we use the unbiased estimator of the scale parameter given in Section 5.3.4, the estimate of σ^2 for the consumption income sample data is

$$\hat{\sigma}^2 = \frac{\Sigma \hat{e}_t^2}{T - 2} = \frac{0.99751}{18} = 0.055417 \tag{5.3.25}$$

Consequently, the estimated covariance matrix for the least squares rule $\mathbf{b}$ is

$$\hat{\Sigma}_{\mathbf{b}} = \hat{\sigma}^2(X'X)^{-1} = \hat{\sigma}^2\begin{bmatrix} T & \Sigma x_{t2} \\ \Sigma x_{t2} & \Sigma x_{t2}^2 \end{bmatrix}^{-1}$$

$$= 0.055417\begin{bmatrix} 3.3778 & -0.1350 \\ -0.1350 & 0.0055 \end{bmatrix} = \begin{bmatrix} 0.1871869 & -0.00748229 \\ -0.00748229 & 0.000303578 \end{bmatrix} \tag{5.3.26}$$

where the elements on the diagonal are estimates of the sampling variability of b_1 and b_2. As an example, the estimate of the variance for the marginal propensity to consume b_2 is $\widehat{\text{var}}(b_2) = 0.000303578$, and this empirical result *implies* a rather high degree of precision for the estimator of the unknown parameter β_2.

Given parameter estimates b_1 and b_2, we have [in line with (5.3.23)] the prediction equation

$$\hat{y}_t = 1.4178 + 0.8248x_{t2} \tag{5.3.27}$$

which indicates that, for each unit change in income x_2, on average there is a 0.8248 change in consumption y. Consequently, (5.3.27) can be used for a given level of income x_{02} to predict the level of consumption y_0. If we assume that income $x_{02} = 22$, the predicted mean consumption level is

$$\hat{y}_0 = 1.4178 + 0.8248(22) = 19.5637 \tag{5.3.28}$$

Conversely, $y_t - \hat{y}_t = \hat{e}_t$ provides an estimate of the unknown and unobservable e_t. Also, (5.3.17b) can be used to obtain an estimate of the sampling variability attached to the prediction error $\hat{e}_0$. The corresponding coefficient of determination is $R^2 = 0.992$. This result indicates a high degree of association between the random variables y_t and $\hat{y}_t$.

In this example we have used a simple linear statistical model (5.3.1) in conjunction with sample information (Table 5.1) and the least squares estimator (5.3.9) to estimate the unknown parameters of a consumption function and to make predictions about the average level of consumption, given a particular level of income. In addition, the covariance matrix (5.3.14) provided a basis for gauging the sampling precision of using the least squares estimator $\mathbf{b}$ to estimate the unknown parameters β_1 and β_2. Finally, (5.3.17b) provides a basis for estimating the sampling variability of the prediction error $\hat{e}_0$.

5.3.7 The Linear Form

In this chapter we have studied a situation in which one variable is thought to be a linear function of another variable. Our task has been, within the context of a simple linear statistical model, to use a sample of economic data to estimate the coefficients of that *linear* function. We should emphasize that the theoretical model (5.3.1) is an attempt to describe, within a stochastic context, how one variable is related to another and, as such, it is an attempt at economic model building. Specifying the algebraic form and the underlying stochastic assumptions converts an economic model into a statistical (econometric) model. It should be noted at this point that the statistical model studied in Sections 5.2 and 5.3 was *linear in the parameters but not necessarily linear in the variables.* As an example, in the consumption function problem, we could have used, instead of the form that is linear in the variables,

$$y_t = \beta_1 + x_{t2}\beta_2 + e_t \tag{5.3.29}$$

the alternative nonlinear in the explanatory variable functional forms,

$$y_t = \beta_1 + x_{t2}^2\beta_2 + e_t \tag{5.3.30}$$

or

$$y_t = \beta_1 + \left(\frac{1}{x_{t2}}\right)\beta_2 + e_t \tag{5.3.31}$$

In the consumption function problem, the use of (5.3.31) means that consumption y_t approaches β_1 as the level of income x_{t2} becomes very large. Forms (5.3.30) and (5.3.31), although linear in the parameters β_1 and β_2, are nonlinear in the variables. These three functional forms are three very different ways of modeling the data and lead to estimates of the unknown parameters that have very different economic implications.

There are also many models that could be specified that are nonlinear in the parameters. One possibility in this context, which is nonlinear in the parameters β_1 and β_2, is the statistical model,

$$y_t = \beta_1 x_{t2}^{\beta_2} \exp\{e_t\} \tag{5.3.32a}$$

One nice feature of this model is that it can be rewritten in a linear form—that is, it can be rewritten as the linear model,

$$\ln y_t = \ln \beta_1 + \beta_2 \ln x_{t2} + e_t \tag{5.3.32b}$$

where the nonlinear relationship between the variables is reduced to a relationship that is linear in the parameters. This gives the technique we have studied a very wide range of applications. For a more complete discussion of nonlinear relations and the transformation of variables, see Johnston (1984, pp. 60–74).

5.3.8 Exercises

Consider the problem of estimating a production function that expresses the relationship between the level of output of a commodity and the level of input of a factor and assume that you have the input-output data given in Table 5.2.

5.3.1 Assume that the data can be described by the statistical model, $\mathbf{y} = \mathbf{x}_1\beta_1 + \mathbf{x}_2\beta_2 + \mathbf{e}$, where the real random vector $\mathbf{e} \sim (\mathbf{0}, \sigma^2 I_T)$ and $x_{t1} = 1$. Set up the $X'X$ matrix and $X'\mathbf{y}$ vector corresponding to the data and determine the inverse of $X'X$. With these results, use the least-squares rule to estimate β_1 and β_2.

5.3.2 Give an economic interpretation to the estimated parameters.

5.3.3 Compute $\hat{\mathbf{e}} = \mathbf{y} - \hat{\mathbf{y}} = \mathbf{y} - \mathbf{x}_1 b_1 - \mathbf{x}_2 b_2$ and use the unbiased estimator to compute an estimate of the scale parameter, σ^2.

5.3.4 Given the estimate of σ^2 in Exercise 5.3.3 and $(X'X)^{-1}$ in Exercise 5.3.1, develop an estimate of the covariance matrix for b_1, b_2 and interpret the results.

5.3.5 Assume that the data can be described by the functional form $y_t = \beta_1 x_{t2}^{\beta_2} e_t$. Write the model in a linear form and use the least squares rule to estimate β_1 and β_2.

Table 5.2 A Sample of Input-Output Observations

Input x	Output y
1.00	0.58
2.00	1.10
3.00	1.20
4.00	1.30
5.00	1.95
6.00	2.55
7.00	2.60
8.00	2.90
9.00	3.45
10.00	3.50
11.00	3.60
12.00	4.10
13.00	4.35
14.00	4.40
15.00	4.50

5.3.6 Give an economic interpretation of the results from Exercise 5.3.5 and compare with the results of Exercise 5.3.1.

5.3.7 Use the results of Exercises 5.3.1 and 5.3.5 to plot the respective production functions. For each functional form, predict the output from eight units of input and estimate the corresponding prediction error.

5.3.8 With the linear-in-variables model of Exercise 5.3.1, the input levels in Table 5.2, and the estimated coefficients for β_1, β_2, and σ^2 that were obtained in Exercises 5.3.1 and 5.3.3, use the instructions in the Computer Handbook to develop 10 samples of the output data. Given the data, use the least squares rule to estimate β_1 and β_2 for each sample and discuss the reason for the alternative estimates.

5.3.9 For the 10 samples, obtain the means of b_1 and b_2 and compare the results with the true parameters β_1 and β_2.

5.3.10 Use the unbiased estimator to obtain an estimate of σ^2 for each sample. Compute the mean of the estimates of σ^2 and compare the result with the true scale parameter σ^2.

5.3.11 Compute an estimate of the covariance matrix for b_1 and b_2 for each sample. Obtain the average of the estimated covariance matrices and compare it with the true covariance matrix, $\Sigma_{\mathbf{b}}$.

5.3.12 Discuss within the context of this chapter the sampling theory approach to inference as it relates to evaluating estimator performance.

5.3.13 For the location and scale parameter statistical model given in (5.2.3b), (a) develop the least squares estimator for the location parameter β, (b) show that this is an unbiased rule, and (c) develop an estimator of the precision for the least squares estimator of β and interpret the result.

5.3.14 In the linear statistical model $\mathbf{y} = X\boldsymbol{\beta} + \mathbf{e} = \mathbf{x}_1\beta_1 + \mathbf{x}_2\beta_2 + \mathbf{e}$ where $\mathbf{e} \sim (\mathbf{0}, \sigma^2 I_T)$, $\mathbf{x}_1$ is a $(T \times 1)$ vector of 1s, $\mathbf{x}_2$ is the treatment variable,

$$\mathbf{b} = \begin{bmatrix} b_1 \\ b_2 \end{bmatrix} = (X'X)^{-1}X'\mathbf{y}$$

and $\bar{y}$ and $\bar{x}_2$ are the arithmetic means of $\mathbf{y}$ and $\mathbf{x}_2$.

(*a*) Show that $b_1 = \bar{y}_1 - b_2\bar{x}_2$ and

$$b_2 = \frac{(\mathbf{x}_2 - \bar{x}_2\mathbf{x}_1)'(\mathbf{y} - \bar{y}\mathbf{x}_1)}{(\mathbf{x}_2 - \bar{x}_2\mathbf{x}_1)'(\mathbf{x}_2 - \bar{x}_2\mathbf{x}_1)} = \frac{\Sigma[(x_{t2} - \bar{x}_2)(y_t - \bar{y})]}{\Sigma(x_{t2} - \bar{x}_2)^2}$$

(*b*) Show that

$$(\mathbf{y} - X\mathbf{b})'(\mathbf{y} - X\mathbf{b}) = (\mathbf{y} - \bar{y}\mathbf{x}_1)'(\mathbf{y} - \bar{y}\mathbf{x}_1) - \frac{[(\mathbf{x}_2 - \bar{x}_2\mathbf{x}_1)'(\mathbf{y} - \bar{y}_{x1})]^2}{(\mathbf{x}_2 - \bar{x}_2\mathbf{x}_1)'(\mathbf{x}_2 - \bar{x}_2\mathbf{x}_1)}$$

(*c*) If you could select any values for the treatment variable $\mathbf{x}_2$, how would you choose the treatment values in order to minimize the sampling variance of b_2?

(*d*) When $x_{t2} = x_{02}$, derive the variance of the prediction error (5.3.17b) and discuss its sampling theory interpretation.

(*e*) In terms of the squared deviations of $\mathbf{y}$ from its mean, show that (5.3.19b) holds.

5.4 The General Linear Statistical Model—Model 3

As we have noted before, in order to cope with the problems of estimation and inference in economics, the statistical model must be consistent with the sampling process by which the data are or could have been generated. Since most economic relations involve two or more economic variables in order to describe this multivariable sampling process, we must extend and reparameterize the simple linear statistical models discussed in the preceding sections of this chapter. It is to this task that we turn.

5.4.1 Specification of the Statistical Model

In the quest for a statistical model that will reflect the interrelationships among economic variables and also capture the nature of much economic data relating to economic processes and institutions, the remainder of this chapter and the next two chapters consider multivariable variants of the linear statistical models introduced in Sections 5.2 and 5.3.

To model the type of behavioral and technical relationships that form the conceptual foundations of economic theory, let us visualize a sample of data relating to such important economic variables as consumption, production, price, cost, GNP, or proportion of the work force that is unemployed and consider the underlying question of what variable or variables could have or actually determined the outcomes we have observed. For a specific problem, this would lead us to an economic model that describes how we believe the outcome data were determined. To be specific, let us assume that we have a sample of data relating to the per capita consumption of beef in which the observations are monthly and cover the time period 1979 through 1980. If these data are typical of many economic series, a cursory look at the data would show a good deal of variability in per capita beef consumption both within and between years. A conjecture as to the reason for this variability, recalling a bit of the microeconomic theory of consumer choice, might lead to the conclusion that it is probably a result of monthly variations in the price of beef, monthly variations in the price of competing products such as pork, and monthly changes in the level of per capita income. If we decide to ignore the many other economic variables that might condition the level of monthly per capita beef consumption and concentrate on this simple economic model or explanation, the next question concerns whether these variables actually condition the level of per capita beef consumption and, if each variable does have an impact on the level of beef consumption, how much effect does a change in the level of each explanatory variable have. For example, if the price of beef affects the level of per capita beef consumption and if the price of beef increases by 10 cents a pound, what is the magnitude of change in the consumption of beef?

One way to gain knowledge is to experiment. Consequently, in the face of limited or perhaps no information about the interrelationships among economic variables, knowledge can be gained by visualizing the observed data as the result of the outcome of experiments. In order to have a theoretical framework on which to couch the experimental design or the basis for modeling the data generation or sampling process visualized, we extend and reparameterize the linear statistical models that were developed in Sections 5.2 and 5.3. In the general case, additional ancillary, explanatory, or instrument variables take on different values that condition or affect the mean outcome for the sample observations $\mathbf{y}$. Consequently, if we think the outcome vector $\mathbf{y}$ is conditioned by K known instrument or control variables $\mathbf{x}_1, \mathbf{x}_2, \ldots, \mathbf{x}_K$ and that these variables are connected to the observed outcome variable $\mathbf{y}$ by an unknown $(K \times 1)$ parameter vector $\boldsymbol{\beta}$, then the earlier statistical models may be generalized and written in a parameterized form as

$$\begin{aligned} \mathbf{y} &= \mathbf{x}_1\beta_1 + \mathbf{x}_2\beta_2 + \cdots + \mathbf{x}_K\beta_K + \mathbf{e} \\ &= X\boldsymbol{\beta} + \mathbf{e} \end{aligned} \tag{5.4.1}$$

where X is a $(T \times K)$ matrix. The outcome vector $\mathbf{y}$ is therefore visualized as being composed of a systematic and a random component. The systematic part of $\mathbf{y}$ is specified to be a function linear in the parameters but not necessarily linear in the explanatory (predictor) variables $(\mathbf{x}_1, \mathbf{x}_2, \ldots, \mathbf{x}_K) = X$, which are nonstochastic, fixed, or controlled variables. As before, $\mathbf{y} - \mathbf{x}_1\beta_1 - \mathbf{x}_2\beta_2 - \cdots - \mathbf{x}_K\beta_K = \mathbf{e}$ is a random vector representing the unpredictable or uncontrollable errors associated with the outcome of the experiment. Since the sample observations $\mathbf{y}$ are a function of deterministic (signal) and random components, the T elements of $\mathbf{y}$ are observable random variables, and thus $\mathbf{y}$ is an observable random vector. The deterministic part is often called the signal, whereas the random component is often referred to as the noise.

In the controlled experiment or the experiment carried out by society, $\mathbf{y}$ is an observed random vector and $X = (\mathbf{x}_1, \mathbf{x}_2, \ldots, \mathbf{x}_K)$ is chosen and is thus nonstochastic and known. The random errors $\mathbf{e}$ are unobservable, however, because $X\boldsymbol{\beta}$ involves unknown and unobservable parameters. If we use the theoretical model shown in (5.4.1) to reflect the sampling process for the beef demand problem discussed earlier, then the statistical model would be

$$\mathbf{y} = \mathbf{x}_1\beta_1 + \mathbf{x}_2\beta_2 + \mathbf{x}_3\beta_3 + \mathbf{x}_4\beta_4 + \mathbf{e} \tag{5.4.2a}$$

where $\mathbf{y}$ is a $(T \times 1)$ vector of observations on the monthly per capita consumption of beef, $\mathbf{x}_2$ is a $(T \times 1)$ vector representing the monthly prices of beef, $\mathbf{x}_3$ is a $(T \times 1)$ vector representing the monthly prices of pork, $\mathbf{x}_4$ is a $(T \times 1)$ vector representing the monthly levels of income, and $\mathbf{x}_1$ is a $(T \times 1)$ vector of unit values, so that β_1 is the intercept or the unknown constant pertaining to the level of the regression hyperplane. The expression (5.4.2a) may be written compactly as

$$\mathbf{y} = X\boldsymbol{\beta} + \mathbf{e} \tag{5.4.2b}$$

where, if $K = 4$, X is a $(T \times 4)$ design matrix of known values of explanatory or treatment variables and $\boldsymbol{\beta}$ is a (4×1) column vector of unknown parameters.

5.4.1a The Error Vector

If, as in Sections 5.2 and 5.3, we assume that the uncontrollable and unpredictable $\mathbf{e}$ can be viewed as an unobservable real random vector with a mean vector of $\mathbf{0}$ and a covariance of $\sigma^2 I$, then $\mathbf{y}$ is an observable random vector with mean vector

$$\begin{aligned} E[\mathbf{y}] &= E[X\boldsymbol{\beta}] + E[\mathbf{e}] \\ &= X\boldsymbol{\beta} + \mathbf{0} = X\boldsymbol{\beta} \end{aligned} \tag{5.4.3a}$$

and covariance

$$E[(\mathbf{y} - E[\mathbf{y}])(\mathbf{y} - E[\mathbf{y}])'] = E[(\mathbf{y} - X\boldsymbol{\beta})(\mathbf{y} - X\boldsymbol{\beta})'] = E[\mathbf{e}\mathbf{e}'] = \sigma^2 I_T \tag{5.4.3b}$$

Thus each element of the observable random vector has a mean that depends on a particular row of X. However, the variances for different elements of $\mathbf{y}$ are assumed to be identical. In referring to the random vectors $\mathbf{e}$ and $\mathbf{y}$ we can say that in the statistical model they are assumed to be random vectors with mean vectors of zero and $X\boldsymbol{\beta}$, respectively, and covariance $\sigma^2 I$. The scale parameter σ^2 is, in general unknown. Note that at this point we have made no assumption about the form of the distribution for the random vectors $\mathbf{y}$ and $\mathbf{e}$.

5.4.1b The Sampling Process

Within an experimental context we may think of the treatment variables $\mathbf{x}_1$, $\mathbf{x}_2, \ldots, \mathbf{x}_K$ as taking on values described by a particular experimental design. If we denote the alternative values of the treatment variables by $x_{t1}, x_{t2}, \ldots, x_{tK}$, then the sample observations or observed random variables y_t, for $t = 1, 2, \ldots, T$, may be visualized as being randomly selected from the distribution with the p.d.f. $f(y_t|x_{t1}, x_{t2}, \ldots, x_{tK}, \boldsymbol{\beta}, \sigma^2)$. Therefore, we randomly select an observation y_1 from the distribution where the $x_{11}, x_{12}, \ldots, x_{1K}$ have been preselected and the sampling process is repeated until T observations are generated. That is,

$$\begin{aligned} y_1 &= x_{11}\beta_1 + x_{12}\beta_2 + \cdots + x_{1K}\beta_K + e_1 \\ y_2 &= x_{21}\beta_1 + x_{22}\beta_2 + \cdots + x_{2K}\beta_K + e_2 \\ &\vdots \\ y_T &= x_{T1}\beta_1 + x_{T2}\beta_2 + \cdots + x_{TK}\beta_K + e_T \end{aligned} \tag{5.4.4a}$$

Thus to obtain the T sample observations we repeat the process of randomly selecting an outcome from an observable random variable that has mean $x_{t1}\beta_1 + x_{t2}\beta_2 + \cdots + x_{tK}\beta_K$ and variance σ^2. Again we emphasize that the process is repeated with preselected values of the control or treatment variables until T sample observations have been drawn. For all statistical models discussed in this chapter it is assumed that the sample observations have been generated by the sampling process described herein.

Alternatively, suppose the location parameter vector $\boldsymbol{\beta}$ and the unknown scale parameter σ^2, corresponding to the variance of the random variable e_t, are known. How would we go about generating a sample of T observations for the random variable y_t that is consistent with the linear statistical model of (5.4.2) and (5.4.3)? Since the values of the treatment variables $x_{t1}, x_{t2}, \ldots, x_{tK}$ are preselected (known) and we have assumed the coefficients $\boldsymbol{\beta}$ are also known, the systematic part, $\mathbf{y}^s$, of (5.4.2a) is also known, that is, $\mathbf{y}^s = X\boldsymbol{\beta}$, and this is known for all T treatments. In addition, if the mean and variance of the random variable e_t are known and if we had a random number generator consistent with the parameters of this random variable, we could generate T drawings of the random variable and then add them to the T systematic values y_t^s, that is, the y_t would be determined as follows:

$$\begin{aligned} y_1 &= y_1^s + e_1 = \mathbf{x}_1'\boldsymbol{\beta} + e_1 \\ y_2 &= y_2^s + e_2 = \mathbf{x}_2'\boldsymbol{\beta} + e_2 \\ &\vdots \\ y_T &= y_T^s + e_T = \mathbf{x}_T'\boldsymbol{\beta} + e_T \end{aligned} \tag{5.4.4b}$$

where $\mathbf{x}_t'$ is the tth row of the X matrix. After the experimenter or the economic system has selected the values of the design matrix X that forms the basis for the experimental design, this is exactly the experimental process that we visualize as being followed to generate the $\mathbf{y}$ sample values for the economic variables we observe. The problem facing the econometrician is how, given X, to use the information in $\mathbf{y}$ to obtain an estimate of the unknowns $\boldsymbol{\beta}$ and σ^2.

5.4.1c The Statistical Model

Given the sampling process just described, we may for the T sample observations restate the statistical model written in compact form as

$$\mathbf{y} = X\boldsymbol{\beta} + \mathbf{e} \tag{5.4.5}$$

where

$$\mathbf{y} = \begin{bmatrix} y_1 \\ y_2 \\ \vdots \\ y_T \end{bmatrix} \tag{5.4.6}$$

is a $(T \times 1)$ vector of observed random variables and

$$X = \begin{bmatrix} x_{11} & x_{12} & \cdots & x_{1K} \\ x_{21} & x_{22} & \cdots & x_{2K} \\ \vdots & \vdots & \ddots & \vdots \\ x_{T1} & x_{T2} & \cdots & x_{TK} \end{bmatrix} \tag{5.4.7}$$

is a known $(T \times K)$ nonstochastic design matrix with independent column vectors. Independence means that no column $\mathbf{x}_i$ can be written as a linear combination of the other columns. Therefore, for example, we cannot write

$$\mathbf{x}_1 = c_2\mathbf{x}_2 + c_3\mathbf{x}_3 + \cdots c_K\mathbf{x}_K$$

where the c_i's are some set of constants. This implies that X has rank K and that the $(K \times K)$ matrix $X'X$ is nonsingular. The vector

$$\boldsymbol{\beta} = \begin{bmatrix} \beta_1 \\ \beta_2 \\ \vdots \\ \beta_K \end{bmatrix} \tag{5.4.8}$$

is a fixed $(K \times 1)$ vector of unknown parameters that we wish to estimate from the sample information $\mathbf{y}$;

$$\mathbf{e} = \begin{bmatrix} e_1 \\ e_2 \\ \vdots \\ e_T \end{bmatrix} \tag{5.4.9}$$

is a $(T \times 1)$ vector of unobservable random errors from an unknown distribution that has mean vector

$$E[\mathbf{e}] = \mathbf{0} \tag{5.4.10}$$

and covariance matrix

$$E[\mathbf{ee}'] = E\begin{bmatrix} e_1e_1 & e_1e_2 & \cdots & e_1e_T \\ e_2e_1 & e_2e_2 & \cdots & e_2e_T \\ \vdots & \vdots & \ddots & \vdots \\ e_Te_1 & e_Te_2 & \cdots & e_Te_T \end{bmatrix} = \begin{bmatrix} \sigma^2 & & & 0 \\ & \sigma^2 & & \\ & & \ddots & \\ 0 & & & \sigma^2 \end{bmatrix}_{(T \times T)} = \sigma^2 I_T \tag{5.4.11}$$

These properties imply that the random vector $\mathbf{e}$ has elements that are uncorrelated with one another and that they have identical means and variances. The scale parameter σ^2 is usually unknown, and I_T is a Tth order identity matrix. In summary, we are stating that the expected value of each e_t is 0, the e_t are uncorrelated, and the e_t have common and unknown variance σ^2. In later chapters these strong assumptions underlying the sampling process will be dropped. At this point what we want is an idealized, special case model to work with. The error variance σ^2 adds another unknown parameter that must be estimated from the sample information $\mathbf{y}$. Thus for the linear statistical model (5.4.5) there are $(K + 1)$ parameters $\boldsymbol{\beta}$ and σ^2, to be estimated from the data. In the statistical model $\boldsymbol{\beta}$, σ^2, and $\mathbf{e}$ are unknown and unobservable, whereas $\mathbf{y}$ is observed and X is known.

Finally, let us reemphasize that the $(T \times K)$ design matrix X is assumed to be composed of K fixed explanatory variables. In an experimental context these variables would be considered treatment or control variables and their design would be specified by the researcher. In economics the experiment is usually designed and carried out by society, and the researcher is a passive observer in the data-generation process. The assumption that X is a fixed matrix means that for all possible situations under repeated sampling, the matrix X would take on the same values. The observed random vector $\mathbf{y}$ would vary from sample to sample. Only one sample vector $\mathbf{y}$ is actually observed. In this situation, if both X and $\mathbf{y}$ are thought of as random, then the repetition of X implies that it has a singular distribution and thus takes on the same values in repeated samples. Alternatively, $\mathbf{y}$ may be thought of as a random vector with a distribution that is conditional on the matrix X.

5.4.2 An Example

To make clear the type of sampling model that will be analyzed in this chapter, let us return to the problem of determining the impact of various economic variables on the level of beef consumption. Using (5.4.4) and (5.4.5) as a basis for specifying the statistical model, we may write our theoretical sampling model as

$$\mathbf{y} = \mathbf{x}_1\beta_1 + \mathbf{x}_2\beta_2 + \mathbf{x}_3\beta_3 + \mathbf{x}_4\beta_4 + \mathbf{e} \tag{5.4.12}$$

where the sample observations $\mathbf{y}$ are the observed values of the monthly per capita consumption of beef for the years 1979 and 1980 and are denoted by the (24×1) outcome vector

$$\mathbf{y} = \begin{bmatrix} y_1 \\ y_2 \\ \vdots \\ y_{24} \end{bmatrix} \tag{5.4.13}$$

Also $\mathbf{x}_2$, the known monthly price of beef; $\mathbf{x}_3$, the monthly price of pork; and $\mathbf{x}_4$, the monthly per capita income may be denoted by the (24×1) vectors

$$\mathbf{x}_2 = \begin{bmatrix} x_{1,2} \\ x_{2,2} \\ \vdots \\ x_{24,2} \end{bmatrix}; \quad \mathbf{x}_3 = \begin{bmatrix} x_{1,3} \\ x_{2,3} \\ \vdots \\ x_{24,3} \end{bmatrix}; \quad \mathbf{x}_4 = \begin{bmatrix} x_{1,4} \\ x_{2,4} \\ \vdots \\ x_{24,4} \end{bmatrix} \tag{5.4.14a}$$

and the variable reflecting the intercept of the hyperplane is denoted by the (24×1) vector

$$\mathbf{x}_1 = \begin{bmatrix} x_{1,1} \\ x_{2,1} \\ \vdots \\ x_{24,1} \end{bmatrix} = \begin{bmatrix} 1 \\ 1 \\ \vdots \\ 1 \end{bmatrix} \tag{5.4.14b}$$

This of course is a vector of unit values, and in this as well as in future models it will occupy the first column of the X matrix. To close the statistical model, $\mathbf{e}$ is a (24×1) unobservable random vector that we assume has a mean vector zero and covariance $\sigma^2 I_{24}$; that is, $\mathbf{e} \sim (\mathbf{0}, \sigma^2 I_{24})$. Consequently, we may in terms of (5.4.4) write the statistical model as

$$\begin{aligned} y_1 &= \beta_1 + x_{1,2}\,\beta_2 + x_{1,3}\,\beta_3 + x_{1,4}\beta_4 + e_1 \\ y_2 &= \beta_1 + x_{2,2}\,\beta_2 + x_{2,3}\,\beta_3 + x_{2,4}\beta_4 + e_2 \\ \vdots\ & \quad\ \vdots \qquad \vdots \qquad\quad \vdots \qquad\quad \vdots \qquad \vdots \\ y_{24} &= \beta_1 + x_{24,2}\beta_2 + x_{24,3}\beta_3 + x_{24,4}\beta_4 + e_{24} \end{aligned} \tag{5.4.15}$$

or compactly as

$$\mathbf{y} = X\boldsymbol{\beta} + \mathbf{e} \tag{5.4.16}$$

where

$$X = \begin{bmatrix} 1 & x_{1,2} & x_{1,3} & x_{1,4} \\ 1 & x_{2,2} & x_{2,3} & x_{2,4} \\ \vdots & \vdots & \vdots & \vdots \\ 1 & x_{24,2} & x_{24,3} & x_{24,4} \end{bmatrix} \tag{5.4.14c}$$

is a (24×4) matrix of known values. Since we have made the stochastic assumptions concerning the unobserved error $\mathbf{e}$ in line with (5.4.10) and (5.4.11), we have specified for analysis purposes a traditional statistical model that is linear in the parameters and in this case also linear in terms of the variables X.

5.4.3 A Critique of the Model

At this point it may be useful to look carefully at the conceptual framework that we have used to model the generation of the sample observations. Being precise about the set of assumptions underlying the statistical model will help reformulate or extend the model when this specification is not consistent with the sampling process by which the outcome data were generated.

First, note again that we have specified a statistical model that is linear in the unknown parameters. In line with the discussion of Section 5.3.7, the thing to remember at this point is that when we speak of a linear statistical model we mean that the specification is linear in the unknown parameters but not necessarily linear in the treatment or explanatory variables.

Because actual relationships are not always linear in the variables, there is usually a question as to what is the correct algebraic or functional form for a particular economic relation. Economic theory offers little help in this regard, and there is always a chance that a researcher may use, for example, a functional form linear in natural units, when one linear in logs is appropriate. This choice of an incorrect functional form is one particular type of specification error.

In terms of the explanatory variables, we have assumed that the elements of the X matrix are fixed or nonstochastic in repeated samples. This may be appropriate for laboratory experiments, in which the experimenter has control over the explanatory variables and can repeatedly observe the outcome of the dependent variable with the same fixed value or some designed values of the explanatory variables. In many social science studies and particularly in economic research, the explanatory variables in one equation are often generated as the dependent variables of other equations that are stochastic in nature and thus they would have neither the same fixed values in repeated samples nor the values that the investigator desires. Thus in an uncontrolled environment the outcome dependent variable **y** is often conditioned by explanatory variables that are stochastic in nature.

Also, as the statistical model is specified, it is assumed that the X matrix contains the correct set of explanatory variables. In real-world situations we seldom, if ever, know the correct set of explanatory variables, and, consequently, certain relevant variables may be excluded or certain extraneous variables may be included.

In terms of the outcome variable or sample observations **y**, we have assumed that it is measured without error. Few economic relations are free of random shocks, and few economic variables are free of measurement errors. Therefore, the assumption of no measurement error may be at variance with reality for particular samples of economic data.

Another set of assumptions that may be questionable are the stochastic assumptions that **e** is a random vector with elements that are uncorrelated and that have identical means and variances. In many cases for economic data, one or both assumptions may be violated.

In terms of the unknown parameter vector $\boldsymbol{\beta}$, we have assumed that the elements of this vector are fixed and do not vary from one observational microunit to another or do not vary from one time period to another. In economics the systems we work with are seldom stationary, and therefore the data-generation process for many problems may not be consistent with this specification.

The foregoing comments emphasize the special characteristics of the traditional linear statistical model. They also emphasize that statistical models, just like economic models, are built on a system of assumptions that are a simplification of reality. Therefore, this benchmark statistical model may not be consistent with many data samples reflecting economic processes and institutions. That this model does not cover all situations should not be surprising. Indeed, given the range of possibilities for economic data generation, to find that this special case statistical model was robust for a wide range of economic models would have been surprising. The reason for looking critically at the statistical model we have specified is to make you aware of what has been assumed and to indicate in applied work the importance of striving to achieve consistency between the sampling process by which the data were generated and the statistical model that is used for analysis purposes. As we will see in the chapters ahead, model misspecification may have rather severe statistical consequences.

5.5 Point Estimation

In Section 5.4 we specified a linear statistical model that formed one basis for modeling the sampling process by which a sample of economic data was generated.

For the situation in which T sample values have been observed we wrote the linear model as the T equations

$$y_t = \beta_1 + x_{t2}\beta_2 + \cdots + x_{tK}\beta_K + e_t \tag{5.5.1}$$

for $t = 1, 2, \ldots, T$, or, compactly in vector and matrix form as

$$\mathbf{y} = X\boldsymbol{\beta} + \mathbf{e} \tag{5.5.2}$$

where under this specification

1. The y_t are observed random variables, or $\mathbf{y}$ is an observed vector of random variables.
2. The x_{tK} are observable nonrandom known variables or X is a $(T \times K)$ design matrix of known values with linearly independent columns.
3. The $\beta_1, \beta_2, \ldots, \beta_K$ are the unknown parameters, or $\boldsymbol{\beta}$ is an unknown K-dimensional parameter vector. Specifying the connection between the mean of the observed random vector $\mathbf{y}$ and the explanatory variables in the form $X\boldsymbol{\beta}$ means that we take the relationship to be a linear function of the unknown parameters. At this point the values of the unknown parameters are unconstrained.
4. The e_t are unobservable random variables that are assumed to have mean $E[e_t] = 0$, variance $E[e_t^2] = \sigma^2$, and covariance $E[e_t e_s] = 0$, for $t \neq s$. This implies that $\mathbf{e}$ is an unobservable random vector with a $(T \times 1)$ mean vector $E(\mathbf{e}) = \mathbf{0}$ and scalar diagonal variance-covariance matrix $E[\mathbf{ee}'] = \sigma^2 I_T$, where in general the scalar σ^2 is unknown. These stochastic assumptions imply that (a)

$$E[y_t] = \beta_1 + x_{t2}\beta_2 + \cdots + x_{tK}\beta_K + E[e_t]$$

or

$$E[\mathbf{y}] = X\boldsymbol{\beta} = \mathbf{x}_1\beta_1 + \mathbf{x}_2\beta_2 + \cdots + \mathbf{x}_K\beta_K$$

and thus the statistical sampling model is on the average correct; (b) the errors are specified as *homoskedastic*; that is, we specify identical variances for the random variables e_t and y_t over all T drawings; and (c) the sampling process for the random variables e_t or y_t is an uncorrelated one. The converse of the specifications (b) and (c) is a sampling process that is *heteroskedastic* ($E[e_t^2] \neq E[e_s^2]$) and autocorrelated ($E[e_t e_s] \neq 0$). Random error processes that have these more complicated characteristics will be discussed in Chapter 9.

Given this parameterized version of the statistical model, which at this point we assume to be correct, the next question revolves around how we should use the sample of data $\mathbf{y}$ in order to estimate, or learn about, the unknown $(K + 1)$

parameters $\boldsymbol{\beta}$ and σ^2. In considering this problem, let us first focus on the problem of estimating the unknown coefficient vector $\boldsymbol{\beta}$ and then turn to the unknown scalar σ^2.

5.5.1 Estimating the $\boldsymbol{\beta}$ Vector

If we have a sample of observations $\mathbf{y}$ that are viewed as observed random variables relating to a particular economic variable that has been generated in line with (5.5.2) and the corresponding sampling process, then the next problem is to select a criterion that will lead to a rule for using the sample data that will permit us to get an estimate of the unknown coefficient vector $\boldsymbol{\beta}$. Remember that an estimate of the true $\boldsymbol{\beta}$ is the best that is available because we only have a sample of data. If, in a repeated sampling sense, we generated many samples of data, that is, many T-dimensional $\mathbf{y}$ vectors in line with the sampling process discussed for (5.5.2), we would expect the elements of $\mathbf{y}$ to vary from sample to sample. Thus, if we chose a criterion that leads to a particular rule to use with each sample of data, the resulting estimate of the $\boldsymbol{\beta}$ vector, say $\mathbf{b}$ would vary from sample to sample. Furthermore, since $\mathbf{b}$ is some function of the sample data $\mathbf{y}$, which is a random vector, the estimator $\mathbf{b}$ will also be a random vector.

5.5.2 The Least Squares Criterion

Given this base, let us now consider the selection of a criterion that will imply a particular rule for using the data, or, in traditional econometric parlance, an estimator. If we return to the statistical model (5.4.1) or (5.4.2) it might seem natural to choose a way of using the data to obtain an estimate $\boldsymbol{\beta}$ so as to make the resulting equation errors $(\mathbf{y} - X\boldsymbol{\beta})$ as small as possible, or, in other words, to make the systematic part of $\mathbf{y}$ as perfect as possible. Large equation errors $(\mathbf{y} - X\boldsymbol{\beta})$ may imply limited information concerning $\mathbf{y}$. It seems plausible that we should use a rule that avoids especially large equation errors. One way to do this is to choose a squared error loss or quadratic loss criterion that severely penalizes large error values. For our model (5.4.1), this type of criterion may be stated: Choose a rule for estimating $\boldsymbol{\beta}$ that makes the quadratic form

$$S = (\mathbf{y} - X\boldsymbol{\beta})'(\mathbf{y} - X\boldsymbol{\beta}) \tag{5.5.3}$$

as small as possible, that is, a minimum. Under this objective we would use the least squares criterion, a criterion discussed earlier in Chapter 5.

If we use the algebra of vectors and matrices, discussed in Sections A.2 and A.3 of Appendix A and introduced earlier in Chapter 5, we may rewrite the error sum of squares (sum of squared errors) given in (5.5.3) as

$$(\mathbf{y} - X\boldsymbol{\beta})'(\mathbf{y} - X\boldsymbol{\beta}) = (\mathbf{y}' - \boldsymbol{\beta}'X')(\mathbf{y} - X\boldsymbol{\beta}) = \mathbf{y}'\mathbf{y} - \boldsymbol{\beta}'X'\mathbf{y} - \mathbf{y}'X\boldsymbol{\beta} + \boldsymbol{\beta}'X'X\boldsymbol{\beta}$$
$$= \mathbf{y}'\mathbf{y} - 2\boldsymbol{\beta}'X'\mathbf{y} + \boldsymbol{\beta}'X'X\boldsymbol{\beta} \qquad (5.5.4)$$

where we note $\boldsymbol{\beta}'X'\mathbf{y}$ and $\mathbf{y}'X\boldsymbol{\beta}$ are scalars and are thus equal to each other. In particular

$$\underset{(1\times T)(T\times 1)}{\mathbf{y}'\mathbf{y}} = \underset{(1\times T)}{[y_1 \quad y_2 \quad \cdots \quad y_T]} \begin{bmatrix} y_1 \\ y_2 \\ \vdots \\ y_T \end{bmatrix}_{(T\times 1)} = y_1^2 + y_2^2 + \cdots + y_T^2 = \text{scalar}$$

$$2\boldsymbol{\beta}'X'\mathbf{y} = 2\underset{(1\times K)}{[\beta_1 \quad \beta_2 \quad \cdots \quad \beta_K]} \begin{bmatrix} x_{11} & x_{21} & \cdots & x_{T1} \\ x_{12} & x_{22} & \cdots & x_{T2} \\ \vdots & \vdots & \ddots & \vdots \\ x_{1K} & x_{2K} & \cdots & x_{TK} \end{bmatrix} \begin{bmatrix} y_1 \\ y_2 \\ \vdots \\ y_T \end{bmatrix}$$

$$= 2[\beta_1 \quad \beta_2 \quad \cdots \quad \beta_K] \begin{bmatrix} \mathbf{x}_1'\mathbf{y} \\ \mathbf{x}_2'\mathbf{y} \\ \vdots \\ \mathbf{x}_K'\mathbf{y} \end{bmatrix}$$

$$= 2[\beta_1\mathbf{x}_1'\mathbf{y} + \beta_2\mathbf{x}_2'\mathbf{y} + \cdots + \beta_K\mathbf{x}_K'\mathbf{y}] = \text{scalar}$$

$$\boldsymbol{\beta}'X'X\boldsymbol{\beta} = \underset{(1\times K)}{[\beta_1 \quad \beta_2 \quad \cdots \quad \beta_K]} \underset{(K\times T)}{\begin{bmatrix} x_{11} & x_{21} & \cdots & x_{T1} \\ x_{12} & x_{22} & \cdots & x_{T2} \\ \vdots & \vdots & \ddots & \vdots \\ x_{1K} & x_{2K} & \cdots & x_{TK} \end{bmatrix}} \underset{(T\times K)}{\begin{bmatrix} x_{11} & x_{12} & \cdots & x_{1K} \\ x_{21} & x_{22} & \cdots & x_{2K} \\ \vdots & \vdots & \ddots & \vdots \\ x_{T1} & x_{T2} & \cdots & x_{TK} \end{bmatrix}} \underset{(K\times 1)}{\begin{bmatrix} \beta_1 \\ \beta_2 \\ \vdots \\ \beta_K \end{bmatrix}}$$

$$(5.5.5)$$

$$= [\beta_1 \quad \beta_2 \quad \cdots \quad \beta_K] \begin{bmatrix} \mathbf{x}_1' \\ \mathbf{x}_2' \\ \vdots \\ \mathbf{x}_K' \end{bmatrix} [\mathbf{x}_1 \quad \mathbf{x}_2 \quad \cdots \quad \mathbf{x}_K] \begin{bmatrix} \beta_1 \\ \beta_2 \\ \vdots \\ \beta_K \end{bmatrix}$$

$$= \underset{(1\times K)}{[\beta_1 \quad \beta_2 \quad \cdots \quad \beta_K]} \underset{(K\times K)}{\begin{bmatrix} \mathbf{x}_1'\mathbf{x}_1 & \mathbf{x}_1'\mathbf{x}_2 & \cdots & \mathbf{x}_1'\mathbf{x}_K \\ \mathbf{x}_2'\mathbf{x}_1 & \mathbf{x}_2'\mathbf{x}_2 & \cdots & \mathbf{x}_2'\mathbf{x}_K \\ \vdots & \vdots & \ddots & \vdots \\ \mathbf{x}_K'\mathbf{x}_1 & \mathbf{x}_K'\mathbf{x}_2 & \cdots & \mathbf{x}_K'\mathbf{x}_K \end{bmatrix}} \underset{(K\times 1)}{\begin{bmatrix} \beta_1 \\ \beta_2 \\ \vdots \\ \beta_K \end{bmatrix}} = \text{scalar}$$

where, for example, $\mathbf{x}_1'\mathbf{x}_1 = x_{11}^2 + x_{21}^2 + \cdots + x_{T1}^2$, $\mathbf{x}_1'\mathbf{x}_2 = x_{11}x_{12} + x_{21}x_{22} + \cdots + x_{T1}x_{T2}$, and the $(K \times K)$ matrix $X'X$ has elements that are the sums of squares and cross products for the fixed explanatory variables. Expression (5.5.5) is a quadratic form since each term involves β_i^2 or $\beta_j\beta_i$.

Note that $\mathbf{x}_i$ is used to denote the **i**th column of the matrix X. In equation (5.4.4b), $\mathbf{x}_t'$ was used to denote the **t**th row of the matrix X. Both definitions will be used at different times throughout the book.

The quadratic matrix $X'X$ is symmetric, which means it is a square matrix with corresponding elements above and below the diagonal. Consequently it equals its own transpose. In addition, we will assume the design matrix X is such that the $X'X$ matrix is positive definite and thus nonsingular. This means that for *any* nonnull vector $\mathbf{z}$, the scalar $\mathbf{z}'X'X\mathbf{z} > 0$. If we let the symmetric $(K \times K)$ matrix $X'X = A = [a_{ij}]$, then the quadratic form

$$\boldsymbol{\beta}'X'X\boldsymbol{\beta} = [\beta_1 \quad \beta_2 \quad \cdots \quad \beta_K]\begin{bmatrix} a_{11} & a_{12} & \cdots & a_{1K} \\ a_{21} & a_{22} & \cdots & a_{2K} \\ \vdots & \vdots & \ddots & \vdots \\ a_{K1} & a_{K2} & \cdots & a_{KK} \end{bmatrix}\begin{bmatrix} \beta_1 \\ \beta_2 \\ \vdots \\ \beta_K \end{bmatrix} \tag{5.5.6}$$

$$= \sum_i \sum_j a_{ij}\beta_i\beta_j = a_{11}\beta_1^2 + a_{22}\beta_2^2 + \cdots$$
$$+ a_{KK}\beta_K^2 + 2a_{12}\beta_1\beta_2 + 2a_{13}\beta_1\beta_3$$
$$+ \cdots + 2a_{(K-1)K}\beta_{K-1}\beta_K$$

For a review of these concepts, see Sections A.13 and A.14 of Appendix A.

5.5.3 Minimizing the Quadratic Form

With this formal statement of the least squares criterion for the general linear model (5.5.2), we next turn to the problem, given the design matrix X and the observed random variables or sample observations $\mathbf{y}$, of determining the coefficient vector $\mathbf{b}$ that minimizes the quadratic form

$$S = (\mathbf{y} - X\boldsymbol{\beta})'(\mathbf{y} - X\boldsymbol{\beta}) = \mathbf{y}'\mathbf{y} - 2\boldsymbol{\beta}'X'\mathbf{y} + \boldsymbol{\beta}'X'X\boldsymbol{\beta} \tag{5.5.7}$$

This is a standard, unconstrained minimization problem, so classical calculus procedures may be used to find the optimum $\mathbf{b}$. Following the rules for matrix and vector differentiation (Section A.17 of Appendix A), we know that if A is a $(K \times K)$ symmetric matrix and if $\mathbf{z}$ and $\mathbf{w}$ are $(K \times 1)$ vectors, then

$$\frac{\partial(\mathbf{z}'\mathbf{w})}{\partial \mathbf{z}} = \frac{\partial(z_1 w_1 + z_2 w_2 + \cdots + z_K w_K)}{\partial \mathbf{z}} = \begin{bmatrix} \dfrac{\partial(\mathbf{z}'\mathbf{w})}{\partial z_1} \\ \dfrac{\partial(\mathbf{z}'\mathbf{w})}{\partial z_2} \\ \vdots \\ \dfrac{\partial(\mathbf{z}'\mathbf{w})}{\partial z_K} \end{bmatrix} = \mathbf{w} \tag{5.5.8}$$

Furthermore

$$\frac{\partial(\mathbf{z}'A\mathbf{z})}{\partial \mathbf{z}} = 2A\mathbf{z} \tag{5.5.9}$$

a result suggested from writing out the quadratic expression in (5.5.6). Returning to the quadratic form (5.5.7), since $\mathbf{y}$ and X are given, only $\boldsymbol{\beta}$ is unknown. Although $\boldsymbol{\beta}$ is a parameter vector, for analysis purposes we now treat the elements of $\boldsymbol{\beta}$ as variables. From calculus we know that the minimum or maximum of a multivariate function occurs where all the first-order partial derivatives are equal to 0. Thus the first partial derivatives for (5.5.7) are

$$\begin{aligned}
\frac{\partial S}{\partial \beta_1} &= \frac{\partial(\mathbf{y}'\mathbf{y})}{\partial \beta_1} - \frac{\partial(2\boldsymbol{\beta}'X'\mathbf{y})}{\partial \beta_1} + \frac{\partial(\boldsymbol{\beta}'X'X\boldsymbol{\beta})}{\partial \beta_1} = -2\mathbf{x}_1'\mathbf{y} + 2\mathbf{x}_1'X\boldsymbol{\beta} \\
\frac{\partial S}{\partial \beta_2} &= \frac{\partial(\mathbf{y}'\mathbf{y})}{\partial \beta_2} - \frac{\partial(2\boldsymbol{\beta}'X'\mathbf{y})}{\partial \beta_2} + \frac{\partial(\boldsymbol{\beta}'X'X\boldsymbol{\beta})}{\partial \beta_2} = -2\mathbf{x}_2'\mathbf{y} + 2\mathbf{x}_2'X\boldsymbol{\beta} \\
&\vdots \\
\frac{\partial S}{\partial \beta_K} &= \frac{\partial(\mathbf{y}'\mathbf{y})}{\partial \beta_K} - \frac{\partial(2\boldsymbol{\beta}'X'\mathbf{y})}{\partial \beta_K} + \frac{\partial(\boldsymbol{\beta}'X'X\boldsymbol{\beta})}{\partial \beta_K} = -2\mathbf{x}_K'\mathbf{y} + 2\mathbf{x}_K'X\boldsymbol{\beta}
\end{aligned} \tag{5.5.10}$$

One nice result for us is that, in dealing with a quadratic function such as (5.5.7), linear first partial derivatives result. The minimum of (5.5.7) is obtained by setting the first partials in (5.5.10) to 0 and solving for the optimum parameter vector $\mathbf{b}$. We may therefore write the equations on the right side of (5.5.10) as

$$\begin{aligned}
-2\mathbf{x}_1'\mathbf{y} + 2\mathbf{x}_1'X\mathbf{b} &= 0 & & & 2\mathbf{x}_1'X\mathbf{b} &= 2\mathbf{x}_1'\mathbf{y} \\
-2\mathbf{x}_2'\mathbf{y} + 2\mathbf{x}_2'X\mathbf{b} &= 0 & \quad\text{or}\quad & & 2\mathbf{x}_2'X\mathbf{b} &= 2\mathbf{x}_2'\mathbf{y} \\
&\vdots & & & &\vdots \\
-2\mathbf{x}_K'\mathbf{y} + 2\mathbf{x}_K'X\mathbf{b} &= 0 & & & 2\mathbf{x}_K'X\mathbf{b} &= 2\mathbf{x}_K'\mathbf{y}
\end{aligned} \tag{5.5.11}$$

which yields the following system of linear equations

$$\begin{aligned}
\mathbf{x}_1'\mathbf{x}_1 b_1 + \mathbf{x}_1'\mathbf{x}_2 b_2 + \cdots + \mathbf{x}_1'\mathbf{x}_K b_K &= \mathbf{x}_1'\mathbf{y} \\
\mathbf{x}_2'\mathbf{x}_1 b_1 + \mathbf{x}_2'\mathbf{x}_2 b_2 + \cdots + \mathbf{x}_2'\mathbf{x}_K b_K &= \mathbf{x}_2'\mathbf{y} \\
\vdots \qquad\qquad \vdots \qquad\qquad\qquad \vdots \quad &\quad\ \vdots \\
\mathbf{x}_K'\mathbf{x}_1 b_1 + \mathbf{x}_K'\mathbf{x}_2 b_2 + \cdots + \mathbf{x}_K'\mathbf{x}_K b_K &= \mathbf{x}_K'\mathbf{y}
\end{aligned} \tag{5.5.12}$$

To obtain the vector that minimizes the quadratic form (5.5.7), a system of K linear equations must be solved simultaneously for the K unknowns $\mathbf{b}$. Alternatively, the system of linear equations (5.5.12) may be equivalently written in matrix and vector form as

$$\begin{bmatrix} \mathbf{x}_1'\mathbf{x}_1 & \mathbf{x}_1'\mathbf{x}_2 & \cdots & \mathbf{x}_1'\mathbf{x}_K \\ \mathbf{x}_2'\mathbf{x}_1 & \mathbf{x}_2'\mathbf{x}_2 & \cdots & \mathbf{x}_2'\mathbf{x}_K \\ \vdots & \vdots & \ddots & \vdots \\ \mathbf{x}_K'\mathbf{x}_1 & \mathbf{x}_K'\mathbf{x}_2 & \cdots & \mathbf{x}_K'\mathbf{x}_K \end{bmatrix} \begin{bmatrix} b_1 \\ b_2 \\ \vdots \\ b_K \end{bmatrix} = \begin{bmatrix} \mathbf{x}_1'\mathbf{y} \\ \mathbf{x}_2'\mathbf{y} \\ \vdots \\ \mathbf{x}_K'\mathbf{y} \end{bmatrix} \tag{5.5.13}$$

where the left-hand matrix is identical to the sum of squares and cross-product matrix given in (5.5.5). Consequently, in matrix and vector notation we may compactly write (5.5.13), the system of K linear equations and K unknowns, as

$$X'X\mathbf{b} = X'\mathbf{y} \tag{5.5.14}$$

The method that we use to solve for the unknown coefficients in (5.5.13) or (5.5.14), and the method used in most computer programs involves computing the inverse of the square symmetric $(K \times K)$ matrix $X'X$. For a review of the inverse operation and its use in solving a system of linear equations, see Sections A.7 and A.8 of Appendix A.

5.5.4 The Least Squares Rule

Let us return to the set of linear equations represented by (5.5.14), namely,

$$X'X\mathbf{b} = X'\mathbf{y} \tag{5.5.14}$$

Since the matrix X is of rank K, the square symmetric matrix $X'X$ is nonsingular, and the inverse for $X'X$ exists. Therefore, we may premultiply both sides of (5.5.14) by $(X'X)^{-1}$ to obtain

$$(X'X)^{-1}X'X\mathbf{b} = (X'X)^{-1}X'\mathbf{y} \tag{5.5.15a}$$

or

$$\mathbf{b} = (X'X)^{-1}X'\mathbf{y} \tag{5.5.15b}$$

This yields **b** as the unique solution for the estimate of the unknown coefficient vector **β** and the minimizing vector **b** is known as the least squares estimator. So, using the least squares criterion and given the sample of data **y**, we now have a rule, $\mathbf{b} = (X'X)^{-1}X'\mathbf{y}$, for how to use the sample observations to solve for an estimate of the unknown coefficient vector **β**. Note that since the design matrix X is known, the matrix $(X'X)^{-1}X' = A$ is a known $(K \times T)$ matrix, and thus $\mathbf{b} = A\mathbf{y}$ is a linear function of the observed random vector **y**. Consequently, **b** is also a random vector. The least squares criterion has led us to a linear rule for estimating the unknown coefficient vector **β**. Let us repeat, in the current context, that *linear* means that **b** is a linear function of the observed random vector **y**.

5.5.5 An Example

While the topics covered in this chapter are fresh in your mind let us analyze a real-world economic problem that makes use of (1) the theoretical sampling model (5.4.1), (2) sample observations from an experiment, and (3) the least squares rule for estimating the unknown coefficient vector. In the theory of the firm, the production function expresses the technical relationship between the level of an input or inputs and the level of an output. Using this construct, let us investigate the results of an experiment in broiler (poultry meat) production. The average weight of an experimental lot of broilers and their corresponding level of average feed consumption was tabulated over the time period in which they changed from baby chickens to mature broilers ready for market. If, at time t, we denote the average weight of the experimental group of broilers as the output y_t, the total feed consumed by the input x_t, and ignore for the moment the equation errors, the economic model for this process could be represented simply as

$$y_t = f(x_t) \tag{5.5.16}$$

Since we usually expect a factor to be converted into an output at a decreasing rate of productivity, that is, each additional unit of input brings about a smaller increment of output, then the production function might appear as in Figure 5.2.

If we believe that an input-output relationship that increases at a decreasing rate reflects the transformation rates in broiler production, then the following functional form could be used to represent the broiler input-output relationship

$$y_t = \beta_1 + x_t\beta_2 + x_t^2\beta_3 \tag{5.5.17}$$

where we would expect the sign of β_2 to be positive and β_3 to be negative. Because we have not taken account of all factors involved in the broiler production process,

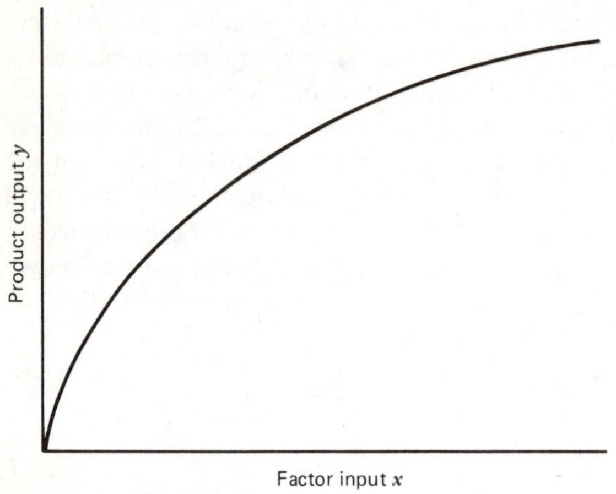

Figure 5.2 Hypothetical relationship between feed inputs x and broiler meat output y.

the specification should involve an equation error term, which would mean that (5.5.17) should be written for the tth observation as

$$y_t = \beta_1 + x_t\beta_2 + x_t^2\beta_3 + e_t \tag{5.5.18a}$$

If we take a sample period of 15 weeks and observe cumulative average feed inputs and the average broiler weights at the end of each week, the sampling model for the 15 sample observations may be expressed as

$$\begin{aligned} y_1 &= \beta_1 + x_{1,2}\beta_2 + x_{1,2}^2\beta_3 + e_1 \\ y_2 &= \beta_1 + x_{2,2}\beta_2 + x_{2,2}^2\beta_3 + e_2 \\ &\vdots \\ y_{15} &= \beta_1 + x_{15,2}\beta_2 + x_{15,2}^2\beta_3 + e_{15} \end{aligned} \tag{5.5.18b}$$

which can be written compactly as

$$\mathbf{y} = \mathbf{x}_1\beta_1 + \mathbf{x}_2\beta_2 + \mathbf{x}_3\beta_3 + \mathbf{e} = X\boldsymbol{\beta} + \mathbf{e} \tag{5.5.19}$$

where $\mathbf{y}$ is the observed average weight of the broilers at the end of each week, X is a (15×3) matrix of known values, $\mathbf{x}_1$ is a (15×1) vector of ones, $\mathbf{x}_2$ is a (15×1) vector reflecting the experimental cumulative level of average feed consumption, and $\mathbf{x}_3$ contains squares of the elements of $\mathbf{x}_2$. Note that the model specified in (5.5.19) is linear in the parameters β_1, β_2, and β_3, but not linear in the variables, since $x_{t3} = x_{t2}^2$.

Because of the design of the experiment, each sample weight observation could be represented as an independent random variable with a mean of $\mathbf{x}_t'\boldsymbol{\beta}$, where $\mathbf{x}_t'$ is the tth row of X, and a variance of σ^2 that is, $y_t \sim (\mathbf{x}_t'\boldsymbol{\beta}, \sigma^2)$. Thus the stochastic assumptions underlying our statistical model can be represented by specifying that $\mathbf{y}$ is a vector of random variables with mean vector $X\boldsymbol{\beta}$ and covariance $\sigma^2 I_{15}$. Consequently, $\mathbf{e}$ is a vector of random variables with mean vector zero and covariance $\sigma^2 I_{15}$.

By taking account of the production process for this particular output, we have attempted to specify a sampling model that is thought to be consistent with the experimental sampling process by which the sample observations (broiler meat outputs) were generated. We turn now to the problem of estimating the parameters of the production function (5.5.19).

The input-output data for the broiler experiment are given in Table 5.3. In the experiment, average broiler weights and average feed consumption were tabulated weekly over a period of 15 weeks.

Given these data and the statistical model (5.5.19) that describes the sampling process by which the data were generated, the next problem is to estimate from the sample of data the unknown response coefficients β_1, β_2, and β_3 and the scalar σ^2 for the statistical model

$$y_t = x_{1t}\beta_1 + x_{2t}\beta_2 + x_{2t}^2\beta_3 + \mathbf{e}_t$$

or

$$\mathbf{y} = X\boldsymbol{\beta} + \mathbf{e} = \mathbf{x}_1\beta_1 + \mathbf{x}_2\beta_2 + \mathbf{x}_3\beta_3 + \mathbf{e} \tag{5.5.20}$$

Table 5.3 Experimental Broiler Input-Output Data

End of Time Period	Average Weight of Broiler in Pounds	Average Cumulative Feed Inputs in Pounds
	$\mathbf{y}$	$\mathbf{x}_2$
1	0.58	1.00
2	1.10	2.00
3	1.20	3.00
4	1.30	4.00
5	1.95	5.00
6	2.55	6.00
7	2.60	7.00
8	2.90	8.00
9	3.45	9.00
10	3.50	10.00
11	3.60	11.00
12	4.10	12.00
13	4.35	13.00
14	4.40	14.00
15	4.50	15.00

where

$$
X = \begin{array}{c} \begin{array}{ccc} \mathbf{x}_1 & \mathbf{x}_2 & \mathbf{x}_3 = \mathbf{x}_2^2 \end{array} \\ \begin{bmatrix} 1 & 1.00 & 1.00 \\ 1 & 2.00 & 4.00 \\ 1 & 3.00 & 9.00 \\ 1 & 4.00 & 16.00 \\ 1 & 5.00 & 25.00 \\ 1 & 6.00 & 36.00 \\ 1 & 7.00 & 49.00 \\ 1 & 8.00 & 64.00 \\ 1 & 9.00 & 81.00 \\ 1 & 10.00 & 100.00 \\ 1 & 11.00 & 121.00 \\ 1 & 12.00 & 144.00 \\ 1 & 13.00 & 169.00 \\ 1 & 14.00 & 196.00 \\ 1 & 15.00 & 225.00 \end{bmatrix} \end{array} \quad \text{and} \quad \mathbf{y} = \begin{bmatrix} 0.58 \\ 1.10 \\ 1.20 \\ 1.30 \\ 1.95 \\ 2.55 \\ 2.60 \\ 2.90 \\ 3.45 \\ 3.50 \\ 3.60 \\ 4.10 \\ 4.35 \\ 4.40 \\ 4.50 \end{bmatrix} \tag{5.5.21}
$$

To estimate the unknown vector $\boldsymbol{\beta}$ we must solve the system of linear equations represented by (5.2.14), which for our problem is

$$
X'X\mathbf{b} = X'\mathbf{y} = \begin{bmatrix} \mathbf{x}_1'\mathbf{x}_1 & \mathbf{x}_1'\mathbf{x}_2 & \mathbf{x}_1'\mathbf{x}_3 \\ \mathbf{x}_2'\mathbf{x}_1 & \mathbf{x}_2'\mathbf{x}_2 & \mathbf{x}_2'\mathbf{x}_3 \\ \mathbf{x}_3'\mathbf{x}_1 & \mathbf{x}_3'\mathbf{x}_2 & \mathbf{x}_3'\mathbf{x}_3 \end{bmatrix} \begin{bmatrix} b_1 \\ b_2 \\ b_3 \end{bmatrix} = \begin{bmatrix} \mathbf{x}_1'\mathbf{y} \\ \mathbf{x}_2'\mathbf{y} \\ \mathbf{x}_3'\mathbf{y} \end{bmatrix} \tag{5.5.22a}
$$

Using the data in Table 5.3 and the matrix and vector representations of (5.5.21), we obtain

$$
\begin{bmatrix} 15.00 & 120.00 & 1240.00 \\ 120.00 & 124.00 & 14400.00 \\ 1240.00 & 14400.00 & 178312.00 \end{bmatrix} \begin{bmatrix} b_1 \\ b_2 \\ b_3 \end{bmatrix} = \begin{bmatrix} 42.08 \\ 418.53 \\ 4755.63 \end{bmatrix} \tag{5.5.22b}
$$

The inverse of the $X'X$ matrix is

$$
(X'X)^{-1} = \begin{bmatrix} 0.7934066 & -0.2043956 & 0.0109890 \\ -0.2043956 & 0.0656270 & -0.0038785 \\ 0.0109890 & -0.0038785 & 0.0002424 \end{bmatrix} \tag{5.5.23}
$$

and thus the sample estimate of the vector $\boldsymbol{\beta}$ is

$$\mathbf{b} = (X'X)^{-1}X'\mathbf{y} = \begin{bmatrix} 0.7934066 & -0.2043956 & 0.0109890 \\ -0.2043956 & 0.0656270 & -0.0038785 \\ 0.0109890 & -0.0038785 & 0.0002424 \end{bmatrix} \begin{bmatrix} 42.08 \\ 418.53 \\ 4755.63 \end{bmatrix}$$

$$= \begin{bmatrix} 0.10 \\ 0.42 \\ -0.008 \end{bmatrix} \quad (5.5.24)$$

and the estimated production function is

$$\hat{\mathbf{y}} = 0.10\mathbf{x}_1 + 0.42\mathbf{x}_2 - 0.008\mathbf{x}_3 \quad (5.5.25)$$

A graph of the estimated production function reflected by (5.5.25) is given in Figure 5.3. This empirical representation of the production function compares well with the theoretical model hypothesized in Figure 5.2.

As we hypothesized, the equation represented by (5.5.25) depicts a relationship between feed inputs and meat output that increases at a decreasing rate. We can represent the marginal productivity of the feed input by

$$\frac{\partial y}{\partial x_2} = \frac{\partial(\beta_1 + x_2\beta_2 + x_2^2\beta_3)}{\partial x_2} = \beta_2 + 2x_2\beta_3 = 0.42 - 0.016x_2 \quad (5.5.26)$$

which is a decreasing linear function. If we denote the price of broilers by p_b and the price of feed by p_f, then the optimum level of feed inputs or, alternatively, the

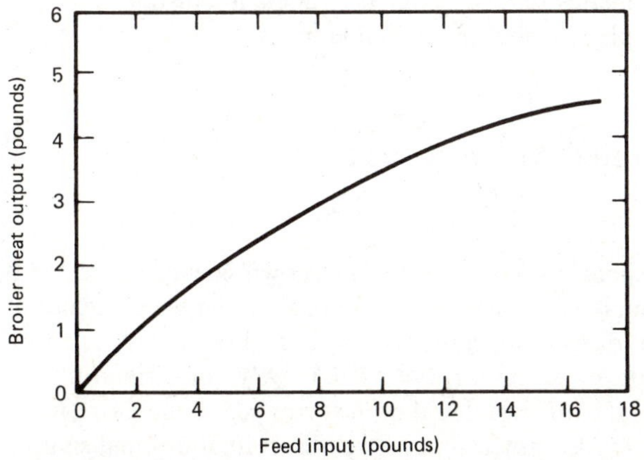

Figure 5.3 Transformation of feed into broiler meat with other inputs assumed to be constant.

optimum selling weight for the broiler is at the point

$$\frac{\partial y}{\partial x_2} = \frac{p_f}{p_b}$$

Thus if broilers are 30 cents a pound and feed is 6 cents a pound, the optimum level of feed input is 13.75 and the optimum selling weight is 4.37 pounds.

Let us emphasize again at this point that $\mathbf{y}$ in the problem represents a sample of data that for us are broiler weights taken over a 15-week period as the chickens were growing to maturity. If we conducted repeated experiments that produced repeated samples of broiler weights involving the same level of feed inputs, the $\mathbf{y}$ vector would undoubtedly vary from sample to sample. Since the estimate of the unknown coefficient vector $\mathbf{b} = (X'X)^{-1}X'\mathbf{y}$ is a function of $\mathbf{y}$, the estimates of $\boldsymbol{\beta}$ will vary from sample to sample. In other words, since the sample vector $\mathbf{y}$ is a random vector, the vector $\mathbf{b}$ is also random. Thus if $\mathbf{b}$ is a random vector it seems natural to ask, in a repeated sampling context what is its mean vector and what is its covariance (precision) matrix or sampling variability. These questions provide the basis for inference as we seek to generalize from the sample to a broader set of circumstances.

What we have obtained so far is a *point estimate* of the elements of the unknown coefficient (location) vector. Because the estimate depends on the particular sample of data observed, we do not know how close these results are to the true parameters. Recall from Chapter 2 that the sample space represents all outcomes that could have occurred for the particular experiment in which we are interested. On the other hand, the sample is that particular set of data that happened to turn up. The point estimates that we have obtained are based entirely on a particular set. At this juncture the point estimates represent our best guess about the unknown parameters based on the sample information available to us.

5.6 Sampling Properties of the Least Squares Rule

In the preceding section the point estimator of the unknown coefficient vector $\boldsymbol{\beta}$ was based on a particular sample of data. Let us now imagine that we make use of the same design matrix X and draw repeated samples of observable $\mathbf{y}$ random vectors. The least squares rule, or estimator, $\mathbf{b} = (X'X)^{-1}X'\mathbf{y}$, for estimating the vector $\boldsymbol{\beta}$, is a linear function of the observable random vector $\mathbf{y}$, and therefore, $\mathbf{b}$ is a vector of random variables. We also noted that as we observed additional sample vectors for $\mathbf{y}$ the estimate $\mathbf{b}$ for the $\boldsymbol{\beta}$ vector varied from sample to sample. Keeping this *repeated sampling process* in mind, let us look at the sampling characteristics for the random vector $\mathbf{b}$.

5.6.1 The Mean of the Least Squares Estimator

In investigating the mean vector for $\mathbf{b}$ we are asking the question, if we take repeated samples of the observable random $\mathbf{y}$ vector and for each observed random vector use the least squares rule to make an estimate of the $\boldsymbol{\beta}$ vector, what, on the average will be the result? If we make use of the notion of mathematical expectation, first introduced in Chapter 2, what we are really asking is what is the expected value of $\mathbf{b}$. This question was asked in Section 5.3.2 in connection with the linear model with one explantory variable and an X matrix with two columns. The results established in this earlier section are equally applicable for the extended model. For completeness, we repeat the derivations given earlier and reemphasize the relevant interpretations. Since

$$\mathbf{b} = (X'X)^{-1}X'\mathbf{y} \tag{5.6.1}$$

the expected value of $\mathbf{b}$ is

$$E[\mathbf{b}] = E[(X'X)^{-1}X'\mathbf{y}] \tag{5.6.2}$$

We have specified our sampling model as

$$\mathbf{y} = X\boldsymbol{\beta} + \mathbf{e}$$

and thus we may substitute for $\mathbf{y}$ in (5.6.2) and rewrite the equation as

$$\begin{aligned} E[\mathbf{b}] &= E[(X'X)^{-1}X'(X\boldsymbol{\beta} + \mathbf{e})] \\ &= E[(X'X)^{-1}X'X\boldsymbol{\beta} + (X'X)^{-1}X'\mathbf{e}] \\ &= E[\boldsymbol{\beta} + (X'X)^{-1}X'\mathbf{e}] \end{aligned} \tag{5.6.3a}$$

since $(X'X)^{-1}X'X = I_K$. Because the design matrix X is composed of known values, the $(X'X)^{-1}$ part of the right side of (5.6.3a) does not vary from sample to sample. Also, $\boldsymbol{\beta}$ is a parameter vector unaffected by the sampling process, and thus $E[\boldsymbol{\beta}] = \boldsymbol{\beta}$. These points and the fact that E is a linear operator, imply (5.6.3a) may be rewritten as

$$E[\mathbf{b}] = \boldsymbol{\beta} + (X'X)^{-1}X'E[\mathbf{e}] \tag{5.6.3b}$$

Hence the only random variables on the right side of (5.6.3b) belong to the random vector $\mathbf{e}$, which we have specified to have mean vector $E[\mathbf{e}] = \mathbf{0}$ and covariance matrix $\sigma^2 I_T$. Thus $(X'X)^{-1}X'E[\mathbf{e}] = \mathbf{0}$, a null vector, and therefore

$$E[\mathbf{b}] = \boldsymbol{\beta} \tag{5.6.4}$$

So, in a repeated sampling sense, if we make use of the least squares criterion [i.e., choose the coefficient vector that minimizes $S = (\mathbf{y} - X\boldsymbol{\beta})'(\mathbf{y} - X\boldsymbol{\beta})$ with the linear statistical model (5.5.2), then, *on the average*, the least squares rule $\mathbf{b} = (X'X)^{-1}X'\mathbf{y}$ yields the true population parameter $\boldsymbol{\beta}$. When this happens in the sampling theory approach to inference we say that the estimator or rule has the statistical property of being unbiased, that is,

$$E[\mathbf{b} - \boldsymbol{\beta}] = \mathbf{0} \tag{5.6.5}$$

Later on we will discuss the normative content of "being correct on the average." For now let us simply note that, even though we may be right on the average, some of the estimates from the various samples may miss the mark very badly. Therefore, in a sampling theory world, in which outcomes are evaluated in a repeated sampling framework, although using an unbiased rule such as $\mathbf{b}$ would lead us to the correct $\boldsymbol{\beta}$ if we could sample repeatedly, the particular estimate of $\boldsymbol{\beta}$ that we get from a single specific sample might depart from the true parameters in both sign and magnitude. If the estimate is used for decision purposes, erroneous decisions or actions may result. For example, in the broiler production function problem, the sample of broiler weights $\mathbf{y}$ may cause us to estimate $\boldsymbol{\beta}$ incorrectly and, thus, the marginal productivity of the feed input. In a decision context when the appropriate input and output prices are used, if the sample $\mathbf{y}$ is perverse, the estimated coefficients could lead to incorrect marketing weights for the broilers and thus to a loss in returns.

5.6.2 The Covariance Matrix

Because the estimated coefficient vector $\mathbf{b}$ may vary from sample, to sample or, in other words, is a vector of random variables with sampling distributions, it would be useful to have an estimate of the variability or precision of the point estimates and a basis for assessing variability or precision on the average.

The covariance matrix that expresses the sampling variability for the random vector $\mathbf{b}$ is defined as

$$E[(\mathbf{b} - E[\mathbf{b}])(\mathbf{b} - E[\mathbf{b}])'] \tag{5.6.6a}$$

Since from (5.6.4) we know that $E[\mathbf{b}] = \boldsymbol{\beta}$, we may write (5.6.6a) as

$$E[(\mathbf{b} - \boldsymbol{\beta})(\mathbf{b} - \boldsymbol{\beta})'] = E\left[\begin{bmatrix} b_1 - \beta_1 \\ b_2 - \beta_2 \\ \vdots \\ b_K - \beta_K \end{bmatrix}_{(K \times 1)} [b_1 - \beta_1, b_2 - \beta_2, \ldots, b_K - \beta_K]_{(1 \times K)}\right] \tag{5.6.6b}$$

which under the vector multiplication rule becomes

$$E[(\mathbf{b}-\boldsymbol{\beta})(\mathbf{b}-\boldsymbol{\beta})']$$

$$= E\begin{bmatrix} (b_1-\beta_1)^2 & (b_1-\beta_1)(b_2-\beta_2) & \cdots & (b_1-\beta_1)(b_K-\beta_K) \\ (b_2-\beta_2)(b_1-\beta_1) & (b_2-\beta_2)^2 & \cdots & (b_2-\beta_2)(b_K-\beta_K) \\ \vdots & \vdots & \ddots & \vdots \\ (b_K-\beta_K)(b_1-\beta_1) & (b_K-\beta_K)(b_2-\beta_2) & \cdots & (b_K-\beta_K)^2 \end{bmatrix}$$

The expectation of the $(K \times K)$ matrix is equal to the expectation of its individual elements, and thus (5.6.6b) becomes

$$E[(\mathbf{b}-\boldsymbol{\beta})(\mathbf{b}-\boldsymbol{\beta})']$$

$$= \begin{bmatrix} E[(b_1-\beta_1)^2] & E[(b_1-\beta_1)(b_2-\beta_2)] & \cdots & E[(b_1-\beta_1)(b_K-\beta_K)] \\ E[(b_2-\beta_2)(b_1-\beta_1)] & E[b_2-\beta_2]^2 & \cdots & E[b_2-\beta_2)(b_K-\beta_K] \\ \vdots & \vdots & \ddots & \vdots \\ E[(b_K-\beta_K)(b_1-\beta_1)] & E[(b_K-\beta_K)(b_2-\beta_2)] & \cdots & E[(b_K-\beta_K)^2] \end{bmatrix}$$

$$= \begin{bmatrix} \text{var}(b_1) & \text{cov}(b_1, b_2) & \cdots & \text{cov}(b_1, b_K) \\ \text{cov}(b_2, b_1) & \text{var}(b_2) & \cdots & \text{cov}(b_2, b_K) \\ \vdots & \vdots & \ddots & \vdots \\ \text{cov}(b_K, b_1) & \text{cov}(b_K, b_2) & \cdots & \text{var}(b_K) \end{bmatrix}$$

The elements on the diagonal of this $(K \times K)$ matrix are the variances of the individual elements of the **b** vector and the off-diagonal elements are the covariances.

From (5.6.3a) we can express **b** as

$$\mathbf{b} = \boldsymbol{\beta} + (X'X)^{-1}X'\mathbf{e} \tag{5.6.7}$$

and, if we replace **b** in (5.6.6a) with this expression, then we can write the covariance of **b** as

$$\begin{aligned} E[(\mathbf{b}-\boldsymbol{\beta})(\mathbf{b}-\boldsymbol{\beta})'] &= E[(\boldsymbol{\beta} + (X'X)^{-1}X'\mathbf{e} - \boldsymbol{\beta})(\boldsymbol{\beta} + (X'X)^{-1}X'\mathbf{e} - \boldsymbol{\beta})'] \\ &= E[(X'X)^{-1}X'\mathbf{e}\mathbf{e}'X(X'X)^{-1}] = (X'X)^{-1}X'E[\mathbf{e}\mathbf{e}']X(X'X)^{-1} \end{aligned} \tag{5.6.8a}$$

Since by assumption $E[\mathbf{e}\mathbf{e}'] = \sigma^2 I_T$, (5.6.8a) becomes

$$E[(\mathbf{b}-\boldsymbol{\beta})(\mathbf{b}-\boldsymbol{\beta})'] = \sigma^2(X'X)^{-1}X'X(X'X)^{-1} = \sigma^2(X'X)^{-1} \tag{5.6.8b}$$

The result in (5.6.8b) permits us to evaluate the average variability or precision matrix for the least squares estimator. Since X is known and therefore $(X'X)^{-1}$ is known, if we had an estimate of σ^2 we could develop an estimate of the covariance for **b** from a particular sample **y**. Furthermore, (5.6.8b) gives an expression for the average precision of **b** in repeated samples and thus provides a basis for comparing the sampling performance of the least squares estimator with other estimators that might be used to capture estimates of the unknown parameters from a sample of data. This is important because estimators or rules for using the sample data vary in terms of their sampling performance. Consequently, the on-the-average property, discussed in this section for the mean vector and covariance matrix for **b**, gives us a way, if we use the imaginary repeated sampling framework, to compare the sampling performance of alternative estimators over all data samples and over all possible values of the parameter space, even before the experiments are conducted or the data are collected.

5.7 Sampling Performance—The Gauss–Markov Result

So far we know that if we use the least squares criterion with the general linear model (5.5.2) that an estimator $\mathbf{b} = (X'X)^{-1}X'\mathbf{y}$ results, which

1. Is a linear function of the observable random vector **y**.
2. Is a random vector with a sampling distribution.
3. Is unbiased, and thus on the average correct.
4. Has a sampling precision or covariance matrix equal to $\sigma^2(X'X)^{-1}$.

Therefore, we can now make the statement that **b** is a K-dimensional random vector with a mean vector of $\boldsymbol{\beta}$ and a covariance matrix $\sigma^2(X'X)^{-1}$, that is, $\mathbf{b} \sim (\boldsymbol{\beta}, \sigma^2(X'X)^{-1})$. In addition, from the specification of the linear statistical model we also know that the random vector $\mathbf{y} \sim (X\boldsymbol{\beta}, \sigma^2 I_T)$ and the random vector $\mathbf{e} \sim (\mathbf{0}, \sigma^2 I_T)$.

Given the sampling process described by the linear statistical model, our task now is to compare the least squares estimator **b** with all other competing estimators. In order to make a comparison we restrict our analysis to the class of linear and unbiased estimators. Any estimator from this class can be written in the form

$$\bar{\boldsymbol{\beta}} = A\mathbf{y} \tag{5.7.1}$$

where A is a $(K \times T)$ matrix that does not depend on **y** or the unknown parameters. A particular member of the class is defined by specifying the matrix A. For example, the least squares estimator $\mathbf{b} = (X'X)^{-1}X'\mathbf{y}$ is the linear unbiased estimator given by $A = (X'X)^{-1}X'$. We are interested in finding the *best* linear unbiased estimator for $\boldsymbol{\beta}$. That is, we are interested in finding a matrix A that leads to an estimator $\bar{\boldsymbol{\beta}}$ that is best from within the whole class of linear unbiased estimators (the whole class of possible matrices represented by A). From the Gauss–Markov theorem, the proof of which is given later in this section, we will discover that the least squares estimator $\mathbf{b} = (X'X)^{-1}X'\mathbf{y}$ is in fact the best linear unbiased estimator. That is, there is no matrix A, other than $A = (X'X)^{-1}X'$, which will yield an estimator $\bar{\boldsymbol{\beta}}$ that is better than $\mathbf{b}$. However, before turning to this proof it is necessary to clarify what is meant by "best."

When we are comparing two unbiased estimators for a single parameter, the estimator with the lower variance is regarded as better. However, when we are considering estimators for a vector of parameters, we need to compare *covariance matrices.* For example, consider the covariance matrix for the least squares estimator, $\Sigma_{\mathbf{b}} = \sigma^2(X'X)^{-1}$ and the covariance matrix for any other linear unbiased estimator $\Sigma_{\bar{\boldsymbol{\beta}}}$. If $\mathbf{b}$ is to be better than $\bar{\boldsymbol{\beta}}$, then we need to describe the way in which the matrix $\Sigma_{\mathbf{b}}$ "is less than" the matrix $\Sigma_{\bar{\boldsymbol{\beta}}}$. The problem of how one matrix can be "less than" another is overcome by considering an estimator for any linear combination of the elements in the parameter vector $\boldsymbol{\beta}$.

If $\mathbf{a}' = (a_1, a_2, \ldots, a_K)$ is a $(1 \times K)$ vector of constants, then a linear combination of the elements in $\boldsymbol{\beta}$ is given by

$$\mathbf{a}'\boldsymbol{\beta} = a_1\beta_1 + a_2\beta_2 + \cdots + a_K\beta_K \tag{5.7.2}$$

The corresponding least squares estimator for this linear combination is, as we would suspect,

$$\mathbf{a}'\mathbf{b} = a_1b_1 + a_2b_2 + \cdots + a_Kb_K \tag{5.7.3}$$

In what follows, the elements in $\mathbf{a}$ can be any constants whatsoever. For example, if we are interested in just β_1, then we can define $\mathbf{a}$ as $\mathbf{a}' = (1, 0, \ldots, 0)$, so that $\mathbf{a}'\boldsymbol{\beta} = \beta_1$. As a second example, if we are interested in $\beta_1 + \beta_2$, then we can define $\mathbf{a}' = (1, 1, 0, \ldots, 0)$, yielding $\mathbf{a}'\boldsymbol{\beta} = \beta_1 + \beta_2$.

We are now in a position to define when an unbiased estimator $\mathbf{b}$ for a vector of parameters $\boldsymbol{\beta}$ is better than an alternative unbiased estimator $\bar{\boldsymbol{\beta}}$. We say that $\mathbf{b}$ is better than $\bar{\boldsymbol{\beta}}$ if

$$\text{var}(\mathbf{a}'\mathbf{b}) \le \text{var}(\mathbf{a}'\bar{\boldsymbol{\beta}}) \text{ for all } \mathbf{a} \tag{5.7.4}$$

Note that, by choosing $\mathbf{a}$ appropriately, (5.7.4) implies that $\text{var}(b_1) \le \text{var}(\bar{\beta}_1)$, $\text{var}(b_2) \le \text{var}(\bar{\beta}_2)$, $\text{var}(b_1 + b_2) \le \text{var}(\bar{\beta}_1 + \bar{\beta}_2)$, and so on. If $\Sigma_{\mathbf{b}}$ represents the covariance matrix for $\mathbf{b}$ and $\Sigma_{\bar{\boldsymbol{\beta}}}$ represents the covariance matrix for $\bar{\boldsymbol{\beta}}$, (5.7.4) can be rewritten as

$$\mathbf{a}'\Sigma_{\mathbf{b}}\mathbf{a} \le \mathbf{a}'\Sigma_{\bar{\boldsymbol{\beta}}}\mathbf{a} \tag{5.7.5}$$

or,

$$\mathbf{a}'(\Sigma_{\bar{\boldsymbol{\beta}}} - \Sigma_{\mathbf{b}})\mathbf{a} \ge 0 \tag{5.7.6}$$

If (5.7.6) holds for all **a**, then $\Sigma_{\bar{\boldsymbol{\beta}}} - \Sigma_{\mathbf{b}}$ is called a positive semidefinite (or nonnegative definite) matrix. See Section A.14 in Appendix A. Thus, we say that **b** is better than $\bar{\boldsymbol{\beta}}$ if the matrix $\Sigma_{\bar{\boldsymbol{\beta}}} - \Sigma_{\mathbf{b}}$ is positive semidefinite. This result implies that the variance of any linear combination of the elements in **b** is less than or equal to the variance of the same linear combination of the elements in $\bar{\boldsymbol{\beta}}$. See also Section 3.3.2.1.

In (5.7.1) $\bar{\boldsymbol{\beta}}$ represents the complete class of linear unbiased estimators. Thus, to prove that **b**, the least squares estimator, is the *best* linear unbiased estimator, we need to prove that $\Sigma_{\bar{\boldsymbol{\beta}}} - \Sigma_{\mathbf{b}}$ is a positive semidefinite matrix. We begin this proof by defining the $(K \times T)$ matrix C as $C = A - (X'X)^{-1}X'$ so that $\bar{\boldsymbol{\beta}}$ can be written as

$$\begin{aligned}\bar{\boldsymbol{\beta}} &= [(X'X)^{-1}X' + C]\mathbf{y} = [(X'X)^{-1}X' + C](X\boldsymbol{\beta} + \mathbf{e}) \\ &= \boldsymbol{\beta} + CX\boldsymbol{\beta} + (X'X)^{-1}X'\mathbf{e} + C\mathbf{e} \end{aligned} \tag{5.7.7}$$

In (5.7.7), $\bar{\boldsymbol{\beta}}$ represents the class of all linear estimators. If we are to restrict this class further to only the class of linear *unbiased* estimators, then certain restrictions need to be placed on the matrix C. To find these restrictions we take expectations of both sides of (5.7.7) to obtain

$$\begin{aligned} E[\bar{\boldsymbol{\beta}}] &= E[\boldsymbol{\beta} + CX\boldsymbol{\beta} + (X'X)^{-1}X'\mathbf{e} + C\mathbf{e}] \\ &= \boldsymbol{\beta} + CX\boldsymbol{\beta} + (X'X)^{-1}X'E[\mathbf{e}] + CE[\mathbf{e}] \\ &= \boldsymbol{\beta} + CX\boldsymbol{\beta} \end{aligned} \tag{5.7.8}$$

For unbiasedness we require $E[\bar{\boldsymbol{\beta}}] = \boldsymbol{\beta}$. Thus, we require $CX\boldsymbol{\beta} = \mathbf{0}$. Now, for $CX\boldsymbol{\beta} = \mathbf{0}$ to hold for all possible values of the parameter vector $\boldsymbol{\beta}$, we require $CX = \mathbf{0}$. Thus, $CX = \mathbf{0}$ is the restriction that must be placed on C in order for $\bar{\boldsymbol{\beta}}$ to represent the class of all linear *unbiased* estimators.

We are now in a position to compare covariance matrices. From (5.7.7), and using the requirement that $CX = \mathbf{0}$, we have

$$\bar{\boldsymbol{\beta}} - \boldsymbol{\beta} = (X'X)^{-1}X'\mathbf{e} + C\mathbf{e}$$

We can express the covariance matrix for $\bar{\boldsymbol{\beta}}$ as

$$\begin{aligned} \Sigma_{\bar{\boldsymbol{\beta}}} = E[(\bar{\boldsymbol{\beta}} - \boldsymbol{\beta})(\bar{\boldsymbol{\beta}} - \boldsymbol{\beta})'] &= E[((X'X)^{-1}X'\mathbf{e} + C\mathbf{e})((X'X)^{-1}X'\mathbf{e} + C\mathbf{e})'] \\ &= E[(X'X)^{-1}X'\mathbf{e}\mathbf{e}'X(X'X)^{-1} + (X'X)^{-1}X'\mathbf{e}\mathbf{e}'C' \\ &\quad + C\mathbf{e}\mathbf{e}'X(X'X)^{-1} + C\mathbf{e}\mathbf{e}'C'] \\ &= (X'X)^{-1}X'E[\mathbf{e}\mathbf{e}']X(X'X)^{-1} + (X'X)^{-1}X'E[\mathbf{e}\mathbf{e}']C' \\ &\quad + CE[\mathbf{e}\mathbf{e}']X(X'X)^{-1} + CE[\mathbf{e}\mathbf{e}']C' \end{aligned} \tag{5.7.9}$$

Since $E[\mathbf{e}\mathbf{e}'] = \sigma^2 I_T$, it follows that

$$\Sigma_{\bar{\boldsymbol{\beta}}} = \sigma^2(X'X)^{-1} + \sigma^2(X'X)^{-1}X'C' + \sigma^2 CX(X'X)^{-1} + \sigma^2 CC' \tag{5.7.10}$$

Since CX and thus $X'C'$ must be equal to null matrices for the property of unbiasedness to be fulfilled, the second and third terms on the right-side of (5.7.10) are null matrices and

$$\Sigma_{\bar{\boldsymbol{\beta}}} = \sigma^2(X'X)^{-1} + \sigma^2 CC'$$
$$= \Sigma_{\mathbf{b}} + \sigma^2 CC' \tag{5.7.11}$$

or

$$\Sigma_{\bar{\boldsymbol{\beta}}} - \Sigma_{\mathbf{b}} = \sigma^2 CC' \tag{5.7.12}$$

In Section A.3 of Appendix A it is shown that a matrix multiplied by its own transpose is always positive semidefinite. That is, CC' will always be positive semidefinite, irrespective of how the matrix C is defined. Because σ^2 is positive, $\sigma^2 CC'$ will also be positive semidefinite, and hence $\Sigma_{\bar{\boldsymbol{\beta}}} - \Sigma_{\mathbf{b}}$ will be positive semidefinite. This is the result we set out to prove.

Note that the two covariance matrices will only be equal when $C = 0$. However, when $C = 0$, the estimator $\bar{\boldsymbol{\beta}}$ reduces to the least squares estimator $\mathbf{b}$.

To summarize, the Gauss–Markov result in equation (5.7.12) implies that out of the class of linear unbiased estimators, the least squares estimator is best, where best implies minimum variance. Thus the least squares estimator is the *best linear unbiased estimator* (BLUE). This result also means that if we are content with the linear unbiased family of estimators for the unknown K-dimensional $\boldsymbol{\beta}$ coefficient vector in our basic linear statistical model, then we can use the least squares estimator with the assurance that no other estimator has a superior sampling performance, where the criterion for superiority is minimum variance or maximum sampling precision.

It is interesting to note that in developing an estimator for the unknown $\boldsymbol{\beta}$ vector we started with the criterion of minimizing the error sum of squares for the random equation errors $(\mathbf{y} - X\boldsymbol{\beta})$. This criterion in turn led to an estimator or rule for using the sample observations $\mathbf{y}$ to estimate $\boldsymbol{\beta}$ that satisfied the sampling criterion of being best linear unbiased. In the chapters to follow we will find that other criteria generate the same estimator.

5.8 Estimating the Scalar Parameter σ^2

Having obtained a point estimate of the unknown coefficient vector $\boldsymbol{\beta}$, we now turn to a basis for estimating σ^2, the variance of the elements of the random vectors $\mathbf{y}$ and $\mathbf{e}$. The quadratic form (5.5.3) that was used in obtaining a least squares estimator of $\boldsymbol{\beta}$ does not contain σ^2, and therefore does not provide a basis for its estimation.

From our stochastic assumptions regarding the error vector $\mathbf{e}$, we know that $E[\mathbf{e}'\mathbf{e}] = E[e_1^2] + E[e_2^2] + \cdots + E[e_T^2] = T\sigma^2$. Thus it would seem that if we had a sample of observations for the random error vector $\mathbf{y} - X\boldsymbol{\beta} = \mathbf{e}$, we could use this sample as a basis for estimating σ^2. Unfortunately, since $\boldsymbol{\beta}$ is unknown and unobservable, the random vector $\mathbf{e}$ is unobservable. If we are to estimate σ^2 on the basis of information that we have, this will involve the observed random $\mathbf{y}$ vector and its least squares counterpart $\hat{\mathbf{y}} = X\mathbf{b}$ that results from making use of the estimated coefficient vector $\mathbf{b}$. Thus if $\hat{\mathbf{y}} = X\mathbf{b}$, where $X\mathbf{b}$ is an estimator of $E[\mathbf{y}] = X\boldsymbol{\beta}$, then

$$\mathbf{y} - \hat{\mathbf{y}} = \hat{\mathbf{e}} \qquad \text{or} \qquad \mathbf{y} = X\mathbf{b} + \hat{\mathbf{e}} \tag{5.8.1}$$

and the vector $\hat{\mathbf{e}}$, frequently referred to as the vector of least squares residuals, provides a least squares sample analog of the vector of unobservable errors $\mathbf{e}$. Since

$$\hat{\mathbf{y}} = X\mathbf{b} = X(X'X)^{-1}X'\mathbf{y} \tag{5.8.2}$$

we may rewrite (5.8.1) as

$$\hat{\mathbf{e}} = \mathbf{y} - X\mathbf{b} = \mathbf{y} - X(X'X)^{-1}X'\mathbf{y} = (I_T - X(X'X)^{-1}X')\mathbf{y} \tag{5.8.3}$$

Furthermore, since $\mathbf{y} = X\boldsymbol{\beta} + \mathbf{e}$ we may write (5.8.3) as

$$\hat{\mathbf{e}} = (I_T - X(X'X)^{-1}X')(X\boldsymbol{\beta} + \mathbf{e}) = (I_T - X(X'X)^{-1}X')\mathbf{e} = M\mathbf{e} \tag{5.8.4}$$

which expresses $\hat{\mathbf{e}}$ as a linear function of the unobservable random errors. The matrix M is of dimension $(T \times T)$ and symmetric.

An interesting thing about the $(T \times T)$ symmetric matrix M is that

$$\begin{aligned} MM' &= MM = M^2 = M \\ &= [I_T - X(X'X)^{-1}X'][I_T - X(X'X)^{-1}X'] = [I_T - X(X'X)^{-1}X'] \end{aligned}$$

Matrices that satisfy this condition are called *idempotent* matrices (see Section A.12 of Appendix A). If we use the quadratic form $\hat{\mathbf{e}}'\hat{\mathbf{e}}$ instead of $\mathbf{e}'\mathbf{e}$ as a basis for estimating the scalar σ^2, then it can be written as

$$\begin{aligned} \hat{\mathbf{e}}'\hat{\mathbf{e}} &= \mathbf{e}'(I_T - X(X'X)^{-1}X')(I_T - X(X'X)^{-1}X')\mathbf{e} \\ &= \mathbf{e}'M'M\mathbf{e} = \mathbf{e}'M\mathbf{e} \\ &= \mathbf{e}'(I_T - X(X'X)^{-1}X')\mathbf{e} \end{aligned} \tag{5.8.5}$$

This yields a quadratic form in terms of the vector $\mathbf{e}$ and the matrix

$$M = (I_T - X(X'X)^{-1}X')$$

If we now investigate what would happen on the average if we made use of the quadratic form (5.8.5) as an estimator of σ^2, we need to evaluate

$$\begin{aligned} E[\hat{\mathbf{e}}'\hat{\mathbf{e}}] &= E[(\mathbf{y} - X\mathbf{b})'(\mathbf{y} - X\mathbf{b})] \\ &= E[\mathbf{e}'(I_T - X(X'X)^{-1}X')\mathbf{e}] \\ &= E[\mathbf{e}'M\mathbf{e}] \end{aligned} \tag{5.8.6a}$$

A simple way to evaluate the expectation of this quadratic form is to make use of the concept of the *trace* of a matrix, which is discussed in Section A.4 of Appendix A. Since $\mathbf{e}'M\mathbf{e}$ is a scalar, it is equal to its trace. Consequently,

$$E[\hat{\mathbf{e}}'\hat{\mathbf{e}}] = E[\text{tr}(\mathbf{e}'M\mathbf{e})] \tag{5.8.6b}$$

One property of the trace is that for the product of matrices AB and BA we have $\text{tr}(AB) = \text{tr}(BA)$. Here it is of course required that AB and BA exist. Also, for three matrices A, B, and C, the $\text{tr}(ABC) = \text{tr}(CAB) = \text{tr}(BCA)$. Because of this property, we can write (5.8.6b) as

$$E[\hat{\mathbf{e}}'\hat{\mathbf{e}}] = E[\text{tr}(\mathbf{e}'M\mathbf{e})] = E[\text{tr}(M\mathbf{e}\mathbf{e}')]$$

Because $\text{tr}(\cdot)$ and $E[\cdot]$ are both linear operators, it is possible to write $\text{tr}(E[z]) = E[\text{tr}(z)]$ for any argument z. Using this result, we have

$$\begin{aligned} E[\hat{\mathbf{e}}'\hat{\mathbf{e}}] &= \text{tr}\{ME[\mathbf{e}\mathbf{e}']\} = \text{tr}[M(\sigma^2 I_T)] = \sigma^2\text{tr}(M) \\ &= \sigma^2\text{tr}[I_T - X(X'X)^{-1}X'] \\ &= \sigma^2[\text{tr}(I_T) - \text{tr}(X(X'X)^{-1}X')] \\ &= \sigma^2[\text{tr}(I_T) - \text{tr}(X'X(X'X)^{-1})] \\ &= \sigma^2[\text{tr}(I_T) - \text{tr}(I_K)] \\ &= \sigma^2(T - K) \end{aligned} \tag{5.8.6c}$$

Consequently,

$$E\left[\frac{\hat{\mathbf{e}}'\hat{\mathbf{e}}}{T - K}\right] = \left(\frac{1}{T - K}\right)\sigma^2(T - K) = \sigma^2 \tag{5.8.6d}$$

Thus if we let $\hat{\mathbf{e}}'\hat{\mathbf{e}}/(T - K) = \hat{\sigma}^2$, then

$$\begin{aligned} \hat{\sigma}^2 &= \frac{(\mathbf{y} - X\mathbf{b})'(\mathbf{y} - X\mathbf{b})}{T - K} = \frac{\mathbf{y}'(I_T - X(X'X)^{-1}X')\mathbf{y}}{T - K} \\ &= \frac{\mathbf{y}'\mathbf{y} - \mathbf{b}'X'\mathbf{y}}{T - K} \end{aligned} \tag{5.8.6e}$$

which is a quadratic form in terms of the observable vector $\mathbf{y}$. The resulting quadratic estimator $\hat{\sigma}^2$ for the unknown scalar σ^2, will be an unbiased estimator, since

$$E\left[\frac{\hat{\mathbf{e}}'\hat{\mathbf{e}}}{T-K}\right] = E[\hat{\sigma}^2] = \sigma^2 \tag{5.8.6f}$$

Let us emphasize again that in developing this rule for using the data we have remained in the class of estimators for σ^2 that are both quadratic and unbiased. We now have estimators for both $\boldsymbol{\beta}$ and σ^2 that are based on particular ways to use the sample information. The least squares estimator $\mathbf{b}$ is a linear form in $\mathbf{y}$, and the unbiased estimator of the variance $\hat{\sigma}^2$ is a quadratic form in the observable random vector $\mathbf{y}$.

If we return to the broiler production function example and use the unbiased estimator of the error variance σ^2, then the sample estimate is

$$\hat{\sigma}^2 = \frac{(\mathbf{y} - \mathbf{x}_1 b_1 - \mathbf{x}_2 b_2 - \mathbf{x}_3 b_3)'(\mathbf{y} - \mathbf{x}_1 b_1 - \mathbf{x}_2 b_2 - \mathbf{x}_3 b_3)}{T-K}$$

$$= \frac{\mathbf{y}'\mathbf{y} - \mathbf{b}'X'\mathbf{y}}{T-K} = \frac{0.3405}{15-3} = 0.0284 \tag{5.8.7}$$

Finally, we should emphasize that $\hat{\sigma}^2$ is a random variable and that our estimate of σ^2 will vary from sample to sample. It has a sampling distribution with mean $E[\hat{\sigma}^2] = \sigma^2$. At this point the variance of the random variable $\hat{\sigma}^2$ remains to be evaluated.

5.8.1 Estimating the Covariance Matrix for b

Since (5.8.6e) provides an unbiased estimator of σ^2, we may use this rule with a sample of data to obtain an estimate of the variance-covariance matrix for the least squares rule $\mathbf{b}$. For the production function example the variance-covariance matrix is

$$\hat{\Sigma}_{\mathbf{b}} = \hat{\sigma}^2(X'X)^{-1} = 0.0284\begin{bmatrix} 0.79 & -0.20 & 0.011 \\ -0.20 & 0.066 & -0.004 \\ 0.011 & -0.004 & 0.0002 \end{bmatrix}$$

$$= \begin{bmatrix} 0.0225 & -0.0058 & 0.0003 \\ -0.0058 & 0.0019 & -0.0001 \\ 0.0003 & -0.0001 & 0.000007 \end{bmatrix} \tag{5.8.8}$$

The diagonal elements of (5.8.8) contain the estimated sampling variances for the elements of $\mathbf{b}$, and the off-diagonal elements contain the estimated covariances for these random variables.

It is interesting to think of another way in which to obtain an estimate of the covariance matrix $\sigma^2(X'X)^{-1}$. Perhaps an investigator could obtain, in a repeated sample context, 10 sets of sample observations on the $\mathbf{y}$ vector and then use each set of sample observations with the fixed design matrix X to obtain 10 sets of least squares estimates. The 10 estimates of the $\boldsymbol{\beta}$ vector might then be used to compute an estimate of the mean for each element of the $\boldsymbol{\beta}$ vector and to compute an estimate of their variances and covariances. In making use of (5.8.8) we make use of only one sample of data $\mathbf{y}$ (and in many cases this may be the only sample information available) to obtain a point estimate of the unknown covariance matrix.

5.9 Prediction and Degree of Explanation

Up to this point we have considered the question of how to use the sample information to obtain point estimates of $\boldsymbol{\beta}$ and σ^2 and then we have gone on to investigate the sampling properties of the estimators thereby generated. Now let us turn from the problem of parameter estimation and consider (1) the problem of predicting the values of the outcome variable $\mathbf{y}$ for different levels of the explanatory or treatment variables X, and (2) the degree to which we have succeeded in reducing the unexplained error variance of $\mathbf{y}$ by using the general model involving K parameters and explanatory variables rather than the single parameter model discussed in Section 5.2.

5.9.1 Prediction

The preceding sections have emphasized the problem of determining rules for estimating the unknown parameters for a particular parameterized linear statistical model and ascertaining the sampling performance of the rules. For many decision problems in economics, emphasis on parameter estimation is the correct focus. In some instances, however, the investigator's major concern is in predicting the values of the outcome variable $\mathbf{y}$, for various levels of the explanatory variables.

Within this context consider the linear statistical model $\mathbf{y} = X\boldsymbol{\beta} + \mathbf{e}$ and the problem of choosing a prediction function that will minimize the squared error of prediction (loss). For notational convenience let us denote the subsequent, future, or outside the sample values as $\mathbf{y}_0$ and the subsequent values of the explanatory variables as X_0, where $\mathbf{y}_0$ is a $(T_0 \times 1)$ vector and X_0 is a $(T_0 \times K)$ matrix of known values. The sampling model for the T_0 sample values is $\mathbf{y}_0 = X_0\boldsymbol{\beta} + \mathbf{e}_0$, where $\mathbf{e}_0$ is a $(T_0 \times 1)$ vector with mean vector $\mathbf{0}$ and covariance $\sigma^2 I_{T_0}$, and $\mathbf{e}_0$ is independent of $\mathbf{e}$. We therefore assume the sampling or data-generating process remains the same for $\mathbf{y}_0$ as it was for $\mathbf{y}$.

If we continue to let $\mathbf{b} = (X'X)^{-1}X'\mathbf{y}$ represent the least squares estimator, then

$$\hat{\mathbf{y}}_0 = X_0\mathbf{b} \tag{5.9.1}$$

is the least squares prediction function, where $X_0\mathbf{b}$ is the estimator of $X_0\boldsymbol{\beta}$. In this context the expected, or on the average in repeated samples prediction error, is

$$\begin{aligned} E[\hat{\mathbf{y}}_0 - \mathbf{y}_0] &= E[X_0\mathbf{b} - \mathbf{y}_0] = E[X_0\mathbf{b} - X_0\boldsymbol{\beta} - \mathbf{e}_0] \\ &= X_0E[\mathbf{b} - \boldsymbol{\beta}] - E[\mathbf{e}_0] = \mathbf{0} \end{aligned} \tag{5.9.2}$$

Thus the least squares prediction function, which is a linear function of the random vector $\mathbf{b}$ is, in a repeated sampling sense, unbiased.

Since $(\hat{\mathbf{y}}_0 - \mathbf{y}_0)$ is a random vector, the next question concerns its sampling variability. Thus we should consider the covariance matrix for the prediction error. It may be defined as

$$\begin{aligned} E[(\hat{\mathbf{y}}_0 - \mathbf{y}_0)(\hat{\mathbf{y}}_0 - \mathbf{y}_0)'] &= E[(X_0\mathbf{b} - X_0\boldsymbol{\beta} - \mathbf{e}_0)(X_0\mathbf{b} - X_0\boldsymbol{\beta} - \mathbf{e}_0)'] \\ &= E[(X_0(\mathbf{b} - \boldsymbol{\beta}) - \mathbf{e}_0)((\mathbf{b} - \boldsymbol{\beta})'X_0' - \mathbf{e}_0')] \\ &= X_0E[(\mathbf{b} - \boldsymbol{\beta})(\mathbf{b} - \boldsymbol{\beta})']X_0' + E[\mathbf{e}_0\mathbf{e}_0'] \\ &= \sigma^2[X_0(X'X)^{-1}X_0' + I_{T_0}] \end{aligned} \tag{5.9.3a}$$

which indicates the sampling error and thus sampling variability is composed of two parts: (1) the equation error $\mathbf{e}_0$, and (2) the error in estimating the unknown parameters $\boldsymbol{\beta}$. The covariance terms $X_0E[(\mathbf{b} - \boldsymbol{\beta})\mathbf{e}_0']$ and $E[\mathbf{e}_0(\mathbf{b} - \boldsymbol{\beta})']X_0$, which arise in the derivation of (5.9.3a), are 0 because $\mathbf{b}$, the least-squares estimator from past observations, and $\mathbf{e}_0$, the future disturbance vector, are uncorrelated. The function $X_0\mathbf{b}$ is a best linear unbiased predictor of $\mathbf{y}_0$, and this implies that the prediction error of any other linear unbiased predictor of $\mathbf{y}_0$ will be inferior in terms of its sampling variance. That is, any other linear unbiased predictor of $\mathbf{y}_0$ has a covariance matrix that exceeds (5.9.3a), the least squares covariance matrix, by a positive definite matrix, a result that follows from the Gauss–Markov theorem.

In some cases an investigator might be interested in the conditional mean forecasting problem, where $E[\mathbf{y}_0]$ rather than $\mathbf{y}_0$, is considered. Now $E[\mathbf{y}_0] = X_0\boldsymbol{\beta}$, and the least squares estimator of $X_0\boldsymbol{\beta}$ is $X_0\mathbf{b}$. This estimator has mean $X_0\boldsymbol{\beta}$ and is thus unbiased. The covariance matrix for the random vector $(X_0\mathbf{b} - X_0\boldsymbol{\beta}) = X_0(\mathbf{b} - \boldsymbol{\beta})$ is

$$\begin{aligned} E[X_0(\mathbf{b} - \boldsymbol{\beta})(\mathbf{b} - \boldsymbol{\beta})'X_0'] &= X_0E[(\mathbf{b} - \boldsymbol{\beta})(\mathbf{b} - \boldsymbol{\beta})']X_0' \\ &= \sigma^2X_0(X'X)^{-1}X_0' \end{aligned} \tag{5.9.4a}$$

In this case also, the least squares estimator of $X_0\boldsymbol{\beta}$ is best linear unbiased and any other linear unbiased estimator of $X_0\boldsymbol{\beta}$ has a covariance matrix that exceeds (5.9.4a) by a positive definite matrix. Note how the covariance depends on the sampling error of $\mathbf{b}$ and the choice of values X_0 for the treatment variables.

5.9.2 An Example

In the broiler production function example let us assume that we want to predict broiler meat output at the stage when 10 pounds of feed has been consumed. In this case, $\mathbf{x}_0' = [1 \quad 10 \quad 100]$ and the predicted value of $\hat{y}_0 = \mathbf{x}_0'\mathbf{b} = 0.10 + x_{02}0.421 - x_{02}^2 0.008 = 0.10 + (10)0.421 - (100)0.008 = 3.51$ pounds. The sampling variance of the forecast error is $E[(\hat{y}_0 - y_0)^2] = \sigma^2\mathbf{x}_0'(X'X)^{-1}\mathbf{x}_0 + \sigma^2$, and the estimate of the sampling variance is

$$\hat{\sigma}^2[1 \quad 10 \quad 100]\begin{bmatrix} 0.79 & -0.20 & 0.011 \\ -0.20 & 0.066 & -0.004 \\ 0.011 & -0.004 & 0.0003 \end{bmatrix}\begin{bmatrix} 1 \\ 10 \\ 100 \end{bmatrix} + \hat{\sigma}^2 = 0.0322 \tag{5.9.3b}$$

Alternatively, an estimate of the sampling variability of the estimator of $\mathbf{x}_0'\boldsymbol{\beta}$ is

$$\hat{\sigma}^2(\mathbf{x}_0'(X'X)^{-1}\mathbf{x}_0) = 0.0038 \tag{5.9.4b}$$

which is smaller than (5.9.3b) because it does not contain the equation error variance.

5.9.3 Degree of Explanation

In Section 5.2 we used a single parameter to represent the mean vector of the random vector $\mathbf{y}$. In this chapter we have hypothesized that the mean outcome for the $\mathbf{y}$ vector is conditioned by the values that other ancillary or explanatory variables take, that is, $E[\mathbf{y}] = X\boldsymbol{\beta}$. Because we have made use of $K - 1$ additional variables in the statistical model, one interesting question pertains to what proportion of the total variability of $\mathbf{y}$ is accounted for by taking into account all the K instrument or control variables in the design matrix X. As a basis for deriving this descriptive measure let us write our least squares prediction equation as

$$\mathbf{y} = X\mathbf{b} + \hat{\mathbf{e}} = \hat{\mathbf{y}} + \hat{\mathbf{e}} \tag{5.9.5}$$

where $\hat{\mathbf{y}}$ is the part explained by including the X variables and $\hat{\mathbf{e}}$ is an estimate of the vector of unexplained errors. One measure of variability is the sum of squares $\mathbf{y}'\mathbf{y}$, which in terms of (5.9.5) is

$$\mathbf{y}'\mathbf{y} = \mathbf{b}'X'X\mathbf{b} + \hat{\mathbf{e}}'\hat{\mathbf{e}} + 2\mathbf{b}'X'\hat{\mathbf{e}} \tag{5.9.6}$$

The last expression is zero, since $\hat{\mathbf{e}} = (I - X(X'X)^{-1}X')\mathbf{y}$ and

$$X'(I - X(X'X)^{-1}X') = 0$$

Therefore, the sum of squares for $\mathbf{y}$ may be partitioned into the two components, one accounted for by the explanatory variables and one unexplained

$$\begin{aligned} \mathbf{y}'\mathbf{y} &= \mathbf{b}'X'X\mathbf{b} + \hat{\mathbf{e}}'\hat{\mathbf{e}} \\ &= \hat{\mathbf{y}}'\hat{\mathbf{y}} + \hat{\mathbf{e}}'\hat{\mathbf{e}} \end{aligned} \tag{5.9.7}$$

It is conventional, however, to measure the variation in $\mathbf{y}$ about its mean $\bar{y}$ as

$$\sum_{t=1}^{T} (y_t - \bar{y})^2 = \mathbf{y}'\mathbf{y} - T\bar{y}^2$$

Then (5.9.7) can be rewritten, by subtracting $T\bar{y}^2$ from each side, as

$$\begin{aligned} \mathbf{y}'\mathbf{y} - T\bar{y}^2 &= (\hat{\mathbf{y}}'\hat{\mathbf{y}} - T\bar{y}^2) + \hat{\mathbf{e}}'\hat{\mathbf{e}} \\ &= (\hat{\mathbf{y}}'\hat{\mathbf{y}} - T\bar{\hat{y}}^2) + \hat{\mathbf{e}}'\hat{\mathbf{e}} \end{aligned} \tag{5.9.8}$$

The last step in (5.9.8) follows since, when the model contains an intercept term

$$\bar{\hat{y}} = \sum_{t=1}^{T} \frac{\hat{y}_t}{T} = \frac{\mathbf{x}_1'\hat{\mathbf{y}}}{T} = \frac{\mathbf{x}_1'X\mathbf{b}}{T} = \frac{\mathbf{x}_1'\mathbf{y}}{T} = \bar{y}$$

where use is made of the first row of (5.5.12). In (5.9.8) the term $\mathbf{y}'\mathbf{y} - T\bar{y}^2$ is called the (corrected) total sum of squares (SST), $(\hat{\mathbf{y}}'\hat{\mathbf{y}} - T\bar{\hat{y}}^2)$ is called the sum of squares due to regression (SSR) and represents the portion of the total sum of squares that is explained by the regression, and $\hat{\mathbf{e}}'\hat{\mathbf{e}}$ is the sum of squared errors (SSE) and is the portion of the variation in $\mathbf{y}$ about its mean that is not explained by the linear regression model. The term $\hat{\mathbf{e}}'\hat{\mathbf{e}}$ is also referred to as the residual sum of squares.

A frequently reported summary statistic is the *coefficient of determination*, denoted R^2, that expresses the sample proportion of the variability in $\mathbf{y}$ that is explained by the linear model. That is,

$$R^2 = \frac{\text{SSR}}{\text{SST}} = 1 - \frac{\text{SSE}}{\text{SST}} \tag{5.9.9}$$

It should be noted that alternative, but algebraically equivalent, forms of R^2 often appear. The alternative forms are based on the equivalent forms of SSR.

$$\begin{aligned} \text{SSR} &= \hat{\mathbf{y}}'\hat{\mathbf{y}} - T\bar{y}^2 = \mathbf{b}'X'X\mathbf{b} - T\bar{y}^2 \\ &= \mathbf{b}'X'\mathbf{y} - T\bar{y}^2 \end{aligned} \tag{5.9.10}$$

where the last equality comes from the fact that

$$\mathbf{b}'X'X\mathbf{b} = \mathbf{b}'X'\hat{\mathbf{y}} = \mathbf{b}'X'(\mathbf{y} + \hat{\mathbf{e}}) = \mathbf{b}'X'\mathbf{y} \tag{5.9.11}$$

since

$$X'\hat{\mathbf{e}} = X'(\mathbf{y} - X\mathbf{b}) = X'\mathbf{y} - X'X\mathbf{b} = 0 \tag{5.9.12}$$

For the broiler production function example

$$R^2 = \frac{\mathbf{b}'X'\mathbf{y} - T\bar{y}^2}{\mathbf{y}'\mathbf{y} - T\bar{y}^2} = \frac{(0.1005 \quad 0.4213 \quad -0.00805)\begin{bmatrix} 42.08 \\ 418.53 \\ 4755.63 \end{bmatrix} - 15(2.81)^2}{142.61 - 15(2.81)^2}$$

$$= 0.986$$

and thus the linearly parameterized model has been quite successful in explaining the original variability in the sample.

Two final interpretative notes should be made. First, a useful way to think about R^2 is that it is the square of the simple correlation coefficient between the $\mathbf{y}$ and $\hat{\mathbf{y}}$. That is

$$R^2 = \frac{[\sum_{t=1}^{T}(y_t - \bar{y})(\hat{y}_t - \bar{y})]^2}{\sum_{t=1}^{T}(y_t - \bar{y})^2 \sum_{t=1}^{T}(\hat{y}_t - \bar{y})^2}$$

Consequently, the R^2 can be thought of as a measure of linear association between y_t and $\hat{y}_t$ and, therefore, as a measure of goodness of fit. Second, R^2 may not be confined to the unit interval if the formulas used above are applied to situations involving other than the linear statistical model and the least squares estimator $\mathbf{b}$. In particular, R^2 can become negative if, for example, the formulas are applied to the simultaneous equations models described in Chapter 15. The reason for results of this type is that in other contexts $\bar{\hat{y}}$ is not necessarily equal to $\bar{y}$ and $X'\hat{\mathbf{e}}$ does not necessarily equal zero. Therefore, caution should always be taken when interpreting R^2 for other than the usual linear model with a column one ones in the design matrix.

The R^2 measure has a serious weakness when it is used as a basis for comparing the goodness of fit of alternative models. In particular, as variables are added to a model, the R^2 never decreases. In fact, the R^2 can be increased by increasing the number of variables in the model, K, to T. A measure of the explanatory ability of a model that deals with this deficiency is the adjusted R^2, which is denoted by $\bar{R}^2$, and is defined as

$$\bar{R}^2 = 1 - \frac{\hat{\mathbf{e}}'\hat{\mathbf{e}}/(T - K)}{(\mathbf{y}'\mathbf{y} - T\bar{y}^2)/(T - 1)}$$

$$= 1 - \left(\frac{T - 1}{T - K}\right)(1 - R^2)$$

where $\hat{\mathbf{e}}'\hat{\mathbf{e}}/(T - K)$ and $(\mathbf{y}'\mathbf{y} - T\bar{y}^2)/(T - 1)$ are unbiased estimators of the variances for $\mathbf{e}$ and $\mathbf{y}$, which means R^2 is adjusted for the unbiased components.

The adjusted $\bar{R}^2$ will decline if the addition of an extra variable produces too small a reduction in $(1 - R^2)$ to compensate for the increase in $(T - 1)/(T - K)$. It should be pointed out, however, even at this early stage, that the use of R^2 or $\bar{R}^2$ for model specification purposes can have serious statistical consequences, as we will learn in Chapter 20.

5.10 A Monte Carlo Experiment to Demonstrate the Sampling Performance of the Least Squares Estimator

In the preceding sections of this chapter we specified a general linear statistical model, and on the basis of this particular specification developed, within a sampling theory context, linear and quadratic rules that yielded estimates of the unknown parameters $\boldsymbol{\beta}$ and σ^2. Using analytical methods we found that these estimators satisfied certain statistical properties, such as unbiasedness and minimum variance. To aid in understanding both the restrictions and the inferential reach of the model and the sampling theory approach to inference, we make use of the following sampling model within the context of a Monte Carlo sampling experiment.

In a Monte Carlo or sampling study, the researcher specifies a theoretical statistical model that reflects the underlying sampling process, *generates* samples of data consistent with this process, develops estimates of the unknown parameters consistent with one or more rules, and analyzes the estimates to determine sampling characteristics. In the experiment we play the role of nature and assume that we know the true location and scale parameters, $\boldsymbol{\beta}$ and σ^2. Use is then made of a particular design matrix and random number generator to produce repeated samples of the vector $\mathbf{y}$.

5.10.1 The Sampling Experiment

Consider the sampling model

$$\mathbf{y} = X\boldsymbol{\beta} + \mathbf{e} = \mathbf{x}_1\beta_1 + \mathbf{x}_2\beta_2 + \mathbf{x}_3\beta_3 + \mathbf{e} = 10.0\mathbf{x}_1 + 0.40\mathbf{x}_2 + 0.60\mathbf{x}_3 + \mathbf{e} \quad (5.10.1)$$

where $\mathbf{y}$ is a (20×1) vector of observations, $\mathbf{e}$ is a (20×1) random vector with mean vector zero and covariance matrix $\sigma^2 I_{20} = 2I_{20}$, and X is the following

(20 × 3) design matrix.

$$
X = \begin{array}{c} \begin{matrix} \mathbf{x}_1 & \mathbf{x}_2 & \mathbf{x}_3 \end{matrix} \\ \begin{bmatrix}
1 & 0.693 & 0.693 \\
1 & 1.733 & 0.693 \\
1 & 0.693 & 1.386 \\
1 & 1.733 & 1.386 \\
1 & 0.693 & 1.792 \\
1 & 2.340 & 0.693 \\
1 & 1.733 & 1.792 \\
1 & 2.340 & 1.386 \\
1 & 2.340 & 1.792 \\
1 & 0.693 & 0.693 \\
1 & 0.693 & 1.386 \\
1 & 1.733 & 0.693 \\
1 & 1.733 & 1.386 \\
1 & 0.693 & 1.792 \\
1 & 2.340 & 0.693 \\
1 & 1.733 & 1.792 \\
1 & 2.340 & 1.386 \\
1 & 2.340 & 1.792 \\
1 & 1.733 & 1.386 \\
1 & 0.693 & 0.693
\end{bmatrix} \end{array} \tag{5.10.2}
$$

Using a random number generator for a uniform distribution where each value in the sample space can be observed with equal probability, with mean 0, a range of $\sqrt{24}$, and covariance $\sigma^2 I_{20} = 2I_{20}$, 500 samples $n = 1, 2, \ldots, 500$, of the $(T \times 1)$ vector $\mathbf{e}$, where $T = 20$, were generated. These random errors were then used in conjunction with the known location parameter vector $\boldsymbol{\beta} = (10.0, 0.4, 0.6)'$ and the (20 × 3) design matrix. First, the systematic portion $\mathbf{y}_s = X\boldsymbol{\beta}$ was calculated, and then, to produce $N = 500$ samples of size 20 of the observed (20 × 1) vector $\mathbf{y}$, the random errors were added, that is, $\mathbf{y}_s + \mathbf{e} = \mathbf{y}$. Therefore, the sampling model is constructed to reflect the following sampling process. We randomly select an observation y_1 from the distribution with p.d.f. $f(y; x_1 = x_{11}, x_2 = x_{12}, x_3 = x_{13})$, such that $y_1 = 10.0x_{11} + 0.4x_{12} + 0.6x_{13} + e_1$. Then we select a second observation y_2 at random from the distribution with p.d.f. $f(y;\ x_1 = x_{21},\ x_2 = x_{22},\ x_3 = x_{23})$, such that $y_2 = 10.0x_{21} + 0.4x_{22} + 0.6x_{23} + e_2$, and repeat this process until 20 values of y are drawn for each of the 500 samples.

5.10.2 The Sampling Results

Given the sample observations, least square estimates were obtained for the coefficient vector $\boldsymbol{\beta}$ for each of the 500 samples. To give an idea of the sampling variability of the estimates from sample to sample, point estimates of $\boldsymbol{\beta}$ and σ^2 for the first 10 samples are given in Table 5.4. The sampling variability in the estimated coefficient values is quite striking. For example, for all 500 samples, the sample estimates for $\beta_2 = 0.4$ vary over the range of -0.15 to 0.97 and the sample estimates of $\sigma^2 = 2.0$ vary over the range 1.79 to 2.93.

The average values of the estimates of β_i and σ^2 over the 500 samples, which is the empirical analogues of the expected values, are

$$\textstyle\sum_n b_{1n}/500 = 9.96, \sum_n b_{2n}/500 = 0.39, \sum_n b_{3n}/500 = 0.64, \text{ and } \sum_n \hat{\sigma}_n^2/500 = 1.99.$$

Thus, despite the sampling variability of the estimates reflected in Table 5.4 and in the empirical distributions given in the Computer Handbook, as expected, when all 500 samples are considered the averages of the estimates closely approximates the true parameter values.

The covariance matrix for $\mathbf{b}$ for this experiment is

$$\boldsymbol{\Sigma}_{\mathbf{b}} = \sigma^2(X'X)^{-1} = 2(X'X)^{-1} = \begin{bmatrix} 1.313 & -0.306 & -0.583 \\ -0.306 & 0.221 & -0.029 \\ -0.583 & -0.029 & 0.496 \end{bmatrix} \tag{5.10.3}$$

Table 5.4 Point Estimates for β_1, β_2, β_3, and σ^2 for 10 Samples of Size 20

Sample number	Point estimates of β_1	Point estimates of β_2	Point estimates of β_3	Point estimates of σ^2
1	9.46	0.80	0.39	1.79
2	10.09	0.24	0.34	1.94
3	9.97	0.97	-0.09	2.35
4	8.93	0.69	0.27	2.18
5	9.09	0.68	0.75	1.97
6	9.91	0.72	1.64	1.92
7	11.01	0.12	0.91	1.84
8	9.49	0.27	0.68	2.20
9	10.75	0.49	0.79	2.93
10	10.19	-0.15	0.84	2.11

The corresponding variances for b_1, b_2, and b_3 estimated from the 500 samples are

$$\widehat{\text{var}}\, b_1 = \frac{1}{500} \sum_n (b_{1n} - \bar{b}_1)^2 = 1.332$$

$$\widehat{\text{var}}\, b_2 = \frac{1}{500} \sum_n (b_{2n} - \bar{b}_2)^2 = 0.214$$

$$\widehat{\text{var}}\, b_3 = \frac{1}{500} \sum_n (b_{3n} - \bar{b}_3)^2 = 0.482$$

and in each case the empirical variances are consistent with the true variances on the diagonal of (5.10.3).

The empirical distributions (frequency counts of the number of estimated values b_i at each level) for each of the elements of the estimated $\boldsymbol{\beta}$ vector and σ^2, for 500 samples, are given in the Computer Handbook. In line with the central limit theorem noted in Chapter 3 and to be discussed in Chapter 6, the empirical frequency distribution for each of the estimates of β_i, approach normal distributions. Also, the empirical distribution for $\hat{\sigma}^2$ is consistent with the Lindeberg–Levy central limit theorem, which says that, under conditions normally fulfilled in practice, $\sqrt{T}(\hat{\sigma}^2 - \sigma^2) \rightarrow N(0, \mu_4 - \sigma^4)$, where μ_4 is the fourth moment for the independent and identically distributed random variables e_t.

For some empirical comparisons concerning the impact of increasing sample size, the Monte Carlo experiment was repeated with 250 samples of size 40. The resulting estimated average variances were var $b_1 = 0.69(1.33)$, var $b_2 = 0.11(0.21)$, and var $b_3 = 0.26(0.48)$. The numbers in parentheses are the corresponding averages of the estimated variances for samples of size 20.

5.11 Some Concluding Remarks

In this chapter we have considered the conventional general linear statistical model, and we have evaluated some of the statistical consequences of using certain rules or estimators in capturing the unknown parameters. In the next chapter we become more exact in specifying the model, and we specify that the random errors $\mathbf{e}$ are normally distributed and have a mean vector $\mathbf{0}$ and covariance $\sigma^2 I_T$. Under this distributional specification we consider the problems of point and interval estimation and hypothesis testing.

Let us note that the asymptotic results discussed in Chapter 3 hold for the general linear model and call attention again to the elegant result called the central limit theorem. For the statistical model analyzed in this chapter this result implies that the random vector $\mathbf{b}$ has a limiting multivariate normal distribution that has mean vector $\boldsymbol{\beta}$ and covariance $\sigma^2(X'X)^{-1}$. As we see in Chapter 6, the fact that $\mathbf{b}$ has an approximate normal distribution permits us to compute approximate probabilities concerning the vector $\mathbf{b}$ and thus to find approximate confidence intervals and to test specific hypotheses without knowing the particular distribution for $\mathbf{e}$ or $\mathbf{y}$.

5.12 Exercises

To illustrate the sampling theory results for the general linear statistical model, use the design matrix X presented in Section 5.10.1; assume that $\mathbf{e}$ is a uniform random vector with mean 0, a range of 1, and a covariance matrix of $\sigma^2 I = 0.08333I$; and assume the following linear statistical model.

$$\mathbf{y} = X\boldsymbol{\beta} + \mathbf{e} = 10.0\mathbf{x}_1 + 0.4\mathbf{x}_2 + 0.6\mathbf{x}_3 + \mathbf{e} \tag{5.12.1}$$

Following the instructions in the Computer Handbook for this Monte Carlo sampling experiment, generate 2000 values of the errors e_t and use these to obtain 100 samples of $\mathbf{y}$ of 20 observations each.

5.1 Use 10 of the 100 samples to obtain sample estimates of $\beta_1, \beta_2, \beta_3, \sigma^2$, and R^2.

5.2 Compute the estimated covariance matrix $\hat{\Sigma}_{\mathbf{b}}$ for each sample and compare with its true counterpart. Give an interpretation to and compare the diagonal elements of the estimated covariance matrices.

5.3 Compute the mean and variance for the 10 samples for each of the parameters estimated in Exercise 5.1 and compare these average values with the true parameters. Note any agreement or disagreement with the expected theoretical results.

5.4 Combine the 10 samples of 20 observations each into five samples of 40 observations each and repeat Exercises 5.1 and 5.2. Discuss the sampling implications of increasing sample size.

5.5 Repeat Exercises 5.1 and 5.4 for all 100 and 50 samples of data and analyze and contrast the results.

5.6 Construct empirical frequency distributions for the estimates obtained in Exercise 5.5 and compare and interpret the results.

5.7 Design and carry through a Monte Carlo sampling experiment for a statistical model of the type discussed in Section 5.10 and used in the preceding exercises. For example, choose a design matrix and the corresponding location vector; let the errors e_t be drawn from a uniform distribution with mean 0, a range of $2\sqrt{3}$, and a variance $\sigma^2 = 1$; and let T for each sample be 15 and the numbers of samples $N = 100$. Generate the 100 samples of $\mathbf{y}$, estimate the unknown parameters, and statistically evaluate the results. Using the 100 samples of $\mathbf{y}$ that you have generated, choose an incorrect functional form (e.g., one linear in logs) and evaluate the statistical implications of this model misspecification.

5.8 Suppose you are reading a journal article concerned with estimating the unknown parameters of a production function and the author has specified the statistical model as follows.

$$\mathbf{y} = \mathbf{x}_1\beta_1 + \mathbf{x}_2\beta_2 + \mathbf{x}_3\beta_3 + \mathbf{e}$$

where $\mathbf{y}$ is a $(T \times 1)$ vector of outputs from $M \leq T$ firms, $\mathbf{x}_1$ is a $(T \times 1)$ vector of ones, $\mathbf{x}_2$ is a $(T \times 1)$ vector of labor inputs, $\mathbf{x}_3$ is a $(T \times 1)$ vector of capital inputs, and $\mathbf{e}$ is a $(T \times 1)$ random vector with mean vector $\mathbf{0}$ and covariance $\sigma^2 I_T$. Describe the sampling scheme that the investigator has specified for generating the outputs $\mathbf{y}$ and indicate what the stochastic assumptions imply for the assumed characteristics of the firms in the sample.

5.9 Suppose that an investigator is using the statistical model $\mathbf{y} = X\boldsymbol{\beta} + \mathbf{e}$, where $\mathbf{e} \sim (\mathbf{0}, \sigma^2 I_T)$, $T = 13$, and $K = 3$ and the following system of linear equations results from minimizing the quadratic form $(\mathbf{y} - X\boldsymbol{\beta})'(\mathbf{y} - X\boldsymbol{\beta})$:

$$\begin{aligned} b_1 + 2b_2 + b_3 &= 3 \\ 2b_1 + 5b_2 + b_3 &= 9 \\ b_1 + b_2 + 6b_3 &= -8 \end{aligned}$$

(*a*) Set up the problem in matrix-vector form; solve, using the method outlined in Appendix A for the relevant inverse matrix; and find $\mathbf{b}$.

(*b*) If $\mathbf{y}'\mathbf{y} = 53$, find $\hat{\sigma}^2$.

(*c*) Find the variance-covariance matrix for $\mathbf{b}$ and interpret.

5.10 (*a*) Given the traditional linear statistical model $\mathbf{y} = X\boldsymbol{\beta} + \mathbf{e}$, where $\mathbf{e} \sim (\mathbf{0}, \sigma^2 I_T)$, let $\bar{\boldsymbol{\beta}} = C^*\mathbf{y}$ be a linear unbiased estimator of $\boldsymbol{\beta}$. Show that the linear unbiased estimator $\mathbf{b} = (X'X)^{-1}X'\mathbf{y}$ is superior in a minimum variance sense to $\bar{\boldsymbol{\beta}}$.

(*b*) Given the linear unbiased estimator $\bar{\boldsymbol{\beta}}$, find the C^* that leads to a minimum variance estimator subject to the unbiasedness constraint $C^*X = I_K$. How does this compare with the least squares estimator.

5.11 For the linear statistical model considered in this chapter, when estimating σ^2, consider the set of all quadratic estimators $\mathbf{y}'Q\mathbf{y}$, where Q is some symmetric $(T \times T)$ matrix. What condition needs to be imposed so that the estimator does not depend on the unknown parameter $\boldsymbol{\beta}$?

5.12 In terms of the coefficient of determination R^2, discuss the implications of using a statistical model that does not include an intercept term, that is $\beta_1 = 0$.

5.13 Assume a functional form that is linear in logs for the broiler example; estimate the unknown parameters and interpret and contrast the results with those obtained from the quadratic functional form used in the text. How would you make a choice between these two functional forms?

5.13 References and Guide to Further Reading

Discussions of point estimation for the linear statistical model discussed in this chapter can be found in many current textbooks. The books listed here represent a variety of treatments and levels of difficulty, and each in some way is unique. To ensure a breadth of understanding, one or more of these books along with those mentioned in the References for Chapters 2 and 3 should be read concurrently with this chapter.

Goldberger, A. A. (1964) *Econometric Theory.* New York: Wiley.

Graybill, F. A. (1983) *Introduction to Matrices with Applications in Statistics.* Belmont, Ca: Wadsworth.

Graybill, F. A. (1976) *Theory and Application of the Linear Model.* North Scituate, Ma: Duxbury Press.

Intriligator, M. (1977) *Econometric Models, Techniques and Applications.* Englewood Cliffs, NJ: Prentice-Hall.

Johnston, J. (1984) *Econometric Methods.* New York: McGraw-Hill.

Kmenta, J. (1986) *Elements of Econometrics.* New York: Macmillan.

Maddala, G. S. (1977) *Econometrics.* New York: McGraw-Hill.

Pindyck, R., and D. Rubinfeld. (1981) *Econometric Models and Economic Forecasts.* New York: McGraw-Hill.

Searle, S. S. (1982) *Matrix Algebra Useful for Statistics.* New York: Wiley.

Theil, H. (1971) *Principles of Econometrics.* New York: Wiley.

Wonnacott, T. H., and R. J. Wonnacott. (1980) *Regression: A Second Course in Statistics.* New York: Wiley.

CHAPTER 6

The Normal General Linear Statistical Model

In Chapter 5 we specified and analyzed the linear statistical model

$$\mathbf{y} = X\boldsymbol{\beta} + \mathbf{e} \tag{6.1.1}$$

where $\mathbf{y}$ is a $(T \times 1)$ vector of observed sample values, X is a $(T \times K)$ matrix of known values of the explanatory variables, $\boldsymbol{\beta}$ is a K-dimensional vector of unknown coefficients, and $\mathbf{e}$ is an unobservable $(T \times 1)$ vector of uncorrelated and identically distributed random variables with mean 0 and variance σ^2. That is, $\mathbf{e} \sim (\mathbf{0}, \sigma^2 I_T)$ and no assumption was made about the form of the distribution of $\mathbf{e}$. In this chapter we change the stochastic assumptions about the random vector $\mathbf{e}$ to the extent that we now also specify $\mathbf{e}$ to be a vector of *normally* distributed random variables with mean vector $\mathbf{0}$ and covariance $\sigma^2 I_T$, that is, $\mathbf{e} \sim N(\mathbf{0}, \sigma^2 I_T)$. If indeed the independently and identically distributed random errors e_t represent the combined effect of a large number of explanatory or control variables that have been excluded from the design matrix, then a good case can be made that the e_t will be approximately normally distributed. This additional assumption changes the statistical model by changing the amount of information used in specifying the statistical model.

The problem before us is to consider the normal version of the general linear model. As a first task, we develop a rule for using the sample observations, generated under a normal sampling process, that leads to point estimates of the unknown vector $\boldsymbol{\beta}$ and the scalar σ^2. Given these results, we investigate the sampling properties of these rules, and finally we consider the problem of inference related to interval estimation and hypothesis testing. The results of a Monte Carlo sampling experiment will be used to reflect the empirical counterparts of the concepts developed.

6.1 Maximum Likelihood Estimation

6.1.1 Analytical Representation of the Sample Information

In this chapter we assume the unobservable errors $\mathbf{e}$ to be a vector of normally distributed random variables with mean vector $\mathbf{0}$ and scalar identity covariance

$\sigma^2 I_T$. This implies for the model (6.1.1) that the sample vector $\mathbf{y}$ is a multivariate normally distributed random vector with mean vector $X\boldsymbol{\beta}$ and covariance $\sigma^2 I_T$, that is, $\mathbf{y} \sim N(X\boldsymbol{\beta}, \sigma^2 I_T)$. Thus in collecting our sample we visualize a process in which we randomly select an observation y_1 from a population with the distribution $N(\mathbf{x}_1'\boldsymbol{\beta}, \sigma^2)$, where the elements of $\mathbf{x}_1' = (x_{11}, x_{12}, \ldots, x_{1K})$ are specified, fixed numbers. Then we select a second observation y_2 from a population with the distribution $N(\mathbf{x}_2'\boldsymbol{\beta}, \sigma^2)$, where $\mathbf{x}_2' = (x_{21}, x_{22}, \ldots, x_{2K})$ and repeat the sampling process until T observations are drawn. Since we know the random observation vector $\mathbf{y}$ is distributed as a multivariate normal with mean vector $X\boldsymbol{\beta}$ and covariance $\sigma^2 I_T$, we can analytically express the density function for a particular sample observation as

$$f(y_t|\mathbf{x}_t, \boldsymbol{\beta}, \sigma^2) = (2\pi\sigma^2)^{-1/2} \exp\left[\frac{-(y_t - \mathbf{x}_t'\boldsymbol{\beta})^2}{2\sigma^2}\right] \tag{6.1.2}$$

Since the observations are assumed to be *independent* drawings, we can express the joint density function of the sample as

$$\begin{aligned} f(y_1, y_2, \ldots, y_T) &= f(y_1)f(y_2)\ldots f(y_T) \\ &= f(\mathbf{y}|X, \boldsymbol{\beta}, \sigma^2) = (2\pi\sigma^2)^{-T/2} \exp\left[-\frac{(\mathbf{y} - X\boldsymbol{\beta})'(\mathbf{y} - X\boldsymbol{\beta})}{2\sigma^2}\right] \end{aligned} \tag{6.1.3}$$

and this joint density function can be used to make probability statements about the complete vector $\mathbf{y}$. One problem, of course, in this parameterized formulation, is that $\boldsymbol{\beta}$ and σ^2 are unknown and unobserved.

6.1.2 The Criterion–The Likelihood Principle

As in Chapter 5, after we have specified the statistical model and the corresponding sampling process, the sample observations tell us nothing about the unknown parameters $\boldsymbol{\beta}$ and σ^2 unless we can agree on an estimation criterion. One criterion that was first proposed by Fisher about a half-century ago is that, after the sample observations have been collected, we should then choose those values of the unknown parameters, in this case $\boldsymbol{\beta}$ and σ^2, that would, under the multivariate normal specification, maximize the probability of obtaining the sample actually observed. This criterion, the likelihood principle, makes explicit the idea that only the observed y's should be relevant to conclusions or evidence about $\boldsymbol{\beta}$ and σ^2. The key concept in the likelihood principle is the likelihood function.

Because probability is a property of the sample, it is customary to use likelihood as a property of the unknown parameters. Once the sample is drawn, we can express the joint normal density function (6.1.3), which involves the unknown parameters $\boldsymbol{\beta}$ and σ^2, as the following likelihood function.

$$\ell(\boldsymbol{\beta}, \sigma^2 | \mathbf{y}, X) = (2\pi\sigma^2)^{-T/2} \exp\left[- \frac{(\mathbf{y} - X\boldsymbol{\beta})'(\mathbf{y} - X\boldsymbol{\beta})}{2\sigma^2} \right] \tag{6.1.4}$$

This function, which depends on the outcome of random variables, provides the framework, or basis, for pursuing the criterion of selecting the values of $\boldsymbol{\beta}$ and σ^2 that will maximize the likelihood function. The intuitive reason for calling it a likelihood function is that, given $\mathbf{y}$, a $\boldsymbol{\beta}$ for which (6.1.4) is large is more likely to be the true $\boldsymbol{\beta}$ than a $\boldsymbol{\beta}$ for which (6.1.4) is small; that is, $\mathbf{y}$ is a more plausible occurrence if (6.1.4) is large. In the likelihood principle we assume all the relevant experimental information is contained in the likelihood function based on the density of $\mathbf{y}$.

6.1.3 The Maximum Likelihood Estimator

The first step toward finding maximum likelihood estimators for $\boldsymbol{\beta}$ and σ^2 is to write the likelihood function (6.1.4) in the log form

$$\ln \ell(\boldsymbol{\beta}, \sigma^2 | \mathbf{y}, X) = -\frac{T}{2} \ln 2\pi - \frac{T}{2} \ln \sigma^2 - \frac{(\mathbf{y} - X\boldsymbol{\beta})'(\mathbf{y} - X\boldsymbol{\beta})}{2\sigma^2} \tag{6.1.5}$$

As pointed out in Chapter 3, the values for $\boldsymbol{\beta}$ and σ^2 that maximize ℓ are identical to those that maximize $\ln \ell$, and it is often more algebraically convenient to maximize $\ln \ell$.

6.1.3a Maximum Likelihood Estimator for $\boldsymbol{\beta}$

The maximum likelihood estimator for $\boldsymbol{\beta}$ that maximizes (6.1.5) can easily be found by noting some similarities between the log-likelihood function $\ln \ell$, and the least squares criterion function $(\mathbf{y} - X\boldsymbol{\beta})'(\mathbf{y} - X\boldsymbol{\beta})$ that was considered in Chapter 5. Since the last term in (6.1.5) is the only one that contains $\boldsymbol{\beta}$, maximizing $\ln \ell$ with respect to $\boldsymbol{\beta}$ is equivalent to maximizing

$$-\frac{(\mathbf{y} - X\boldsymbol{\beta})'(\mathbf{y} - X\boldsymbol{\beta})}{2\sigma^2} \tag{6.1.6}$$

with respect to $\boldsymbol{\beta}$. Furthermore, given the negative sign and the constant $2\sigma^2$, it is clear that maximizing (6.1.6) with respect to $\boldsymbol{\beta}$ is equivalent to minimizing

$$S = (\mathbf{y} - X\boldsymbol{\beta})'(\mathbf{y} - X\boldsymbol{\beta}) \tag{6.1.7}$$

with respect to $\boldsymbol{\beta}$. The function S is, however, simply the least squares criterion. Consequently, the least squares estimator $\mathbf{b} = (X'X)^{-1}X'\mathbf{y}$ that minimizes (6.1.7) is precisely the same as the maximum likelihood estimator for $\boldsymbol{\beta}$ that maximizes $\ln \ell$.

Throughout most of the book we will use the notation "$\sim$" above a parameter to denote the maximum likelihood estimator of that parameter. Thus, in this chapter, we will use the notation $\tilde{\boldsymbol{\beta}}$ to denote the maximum likelihood estimator for $\boldsymbol{\beta}$. We have just argued that this estimator is

$$\tilde{\boldsymbol{\beta}} = \mathbf{b} = (X'X)^{-1}X'\mathbf{y} \tag{6.1.8}$$

In the remainder of this chapter, $\tilde{\boldsymbol{\beta}}$ is identical to the least squares estimator $\mathbf{b}$. In subsequent chapters, where models with other stochastic assumptions are studied, the maximum likelihood estimator $\tilde{\boldsymbol{\beta}}$ is not necessarily identical to the least squares estimator.

Because, in the context of this chapter, the maximum likelihood estimator for $\boldsymbol{\beta}$ is identical to the least squares estimator $\mathbf{b}$, its sampling properties are the same. In particular, its mean and covariance matrix are

$$E[\tilde{\boldsymbol{\beta}}] = \boldsymbol{\beta} \qquad \text{and} \qquad E[(\tilde{\boldsymbol{\beta}} - \boldsymbol{\beta})(\tilde{\boldsymbol{\beta}} - \boldsymbol{\beta})'] = \sigma^2(X'X)^{-1} \tag{6.1.9}$$

and we know that it is the minimum variance estimator from within the class of all unbiased estimators that are linear functions of $\mathbf{y}$. As we will see later, because of the additional assumption that $\mathbf{y}$ is normally distributed, it is not necessary to consider only *linear* functions of $\mathbf{y}$; it is possible to show that $\tilde{\boldsymbol{\beta}} = (X'X)^{-1}X'\mathbf{y}$ is the minimum variance estimator from within the class of all unbiased estimators.

Because $\tilde{\boldsymbol{\beta}}$ is a linear function of $\mathbf{y}$, another consequence of the fact that $\mathbf{y}$ is a *normal* random vector is that $\tilde{\boldsymbol{\beta}}$, also, will be a normal random vector. Thus, for the maximum likelihood estimator for $\boldsymbol{\beta}$ we have the result

$$\tilde{\boldsymbol{\beta}} = (X'X)^{-1}X'\mathbf{y} \sim N[\boldsymbol{\beta}, \sigma^2(X'X)^{-1}] \tag{6.1.10}$$

This result will be used later for hypothesis testing and interval estimation.

6.1.3b Maximum Likelihood Estimator for σ^2

To derive the maximum likelihood estimator for σ^2 we need to use differential calculus, rather than by way of analogy with another criterion such as least squares. The first step is to take the partial derivative of the log-likelihood function in (6.1.5) with respect to σ^2. This procedure yields

$$\frac{\partial \ln \ell(\boldsymbol{\beta}, \sigma^2 | \mathbf{y}, X)}{\partial \sigma^2} = -\frac{T}{2\sigma^2} + \frac{1}{2\sigma^4}(\mathbf{y} - X\boldsymbol{\beta})'(\mathbf{y} - X\boldsymbol{\beta}) \tag{6.1.11}$$

To obtain the maximizing value we set this derivative equal to 0; that is,

$$-\frac{T}{2\tilde{\sigma}^2} + \frac{1}{2(\tilde{\sigma}^2)^2}(\mathbf{y} - X\tilde{\boldsymbol{\beta}})'(\mathbf{y} - X\tilde{\boldsymbol{\beta}}) = 0 \tag{6.1.12}$$

where $\tilde{\sigma}^2$ and $\tilde{\boldsymbol{\beta}}$ are the maximum likelihood estimators for σ^2 and $\boldsymbol{\beta}$, respectively. Solving (6.1.12) for $\tilde{\sigma}^2$ yields

$$\tilde{\sigma}^2 = \frac{(\mathbf{y} - X\tilde{\boldsymbol{\beta}})'(\mathbf{y} - X\tilde{\boldsymbol{\beta}})}{T} = \frac{\tilde{\mathbf{e}}'\tilde{\mathbf{e}}}{T} \tag{6.1.13}$$

where $\tilde{\mathbf{e}} = \mathbf{y} - X\tilde{\boldsymbol{\beta}} = \mathbf{y} - X\mathbf{b} = \hat{\mathbf{e}}$ is identical to the vector of least squares residuals.

Thus, the maximum likelihood rule yields an estimator for σ^2 that is a quadratic function of $\mathbf{y}$. Like other estimators, $\tilde{\sigma}^2$ will be a random variable, varying from sample to sample, so its sampling properties will be of interest. To find the mean of $\tilde{\sigma}^2$ we recall from (5.8.6c) that

$$E[\tilde{\mathbf{e}}'\tilde{\mathbf{e}}] = E[\mathbf{e}'(I - X(X'X)^{-1}X')\mathbf{e}] = \sigma^2(T - K) \tag{6.1.14}$$

Thus, the mean or expected value of $\tilde{\sigma}^2$ is

$$E[\tilde{\sigma}^2] = E\left[\frac{\tilde{\mathbf{e}}'\tilde{\mathbf{e}}}{T}\right] = \sigma^2\frac{(T - K)}{T} \tag{6.1.15}$$

Since we require $E[\hat{\sigma}^2] = \sigma^2$ for $\hat{\sigma}^2$ to be unbiased, it is clear that the maximum likelihood estimator $\tilde{\sigma}^2$ is biased. However, the bias does diminish as sample size T increases and K remains fixed.

Because $\tilde{\sigma}^2$ is a biased estimator, the more common estimator for σ^2 is the unbiased one given in Chapter 5, namely

$$\hat{\sigma}^2 = \frac{(\mathbf{y} - X\tilde{\boldsymbol{\beta}})'(\mathbf{y} - X\tilde{\boldsymbol{\beta}})}{T - K} \tag{6.1.16}$$

Note that $\hat{\sigma}^2 = [T/(T - K)]\tilde{\sigma}^2$, so only a simple adjustment is required to move from one estimator to the other.

Not only is the mean of $\hat{\sigma}^2$ (and of $\tilde{\sigma}^2$) of interest, but so too is the probability distribution. As we will see, the probability distribution for $\hat{\sigma}^2$ is useful for hypothesis testing and interval estimation. To examine this probability distribution we first examine the probability distribution for

$$\frac{(\mathbf{y} - X\tilde{\boldsymbol{\beta}})'(\mathbf{y} - X\tilde{\boldsymbol{\beta}})}{\sigma^2} = \frac{\tilde{\mathbf{e}}'\tilde{\mathbf{e}}}{\sigma^2} = \frac{\mathbf{e}'(I_T - X(X'X)^{-1}X')\mathbf{e}}{\sigma^2} = \frac{\mathbf{e}'M\mathbf{e}}{\sigma^2} \tag{6.1.17}$$

where $M = I_T - X(X'X)^{-1}X'$ is an idempotent matrix. The numerator in (6.1.17) is a quadratic form involving the normal random vector $\mathbf{e}$. Theorems on the distributions of quadratic forms in normal random vectors were given in Section 2.5.9 of Chapter 2. In particular, the result in (2.5.18), translated into the context of this chapter, says that, if $\mathbf{e} \sim N(\mathbf{0}, \sigma^2 I_T)$, and M is idempotent, then $\mathbf{e}'M\mathbf{e}/\sigma^2$ has a χ^2-distribution with degrees of freedom equal to the rank of M. From a result in Section A.12 of Appendix A, the rank of an idempotent matrix is equal to its trace. We know from Chapter 5 that

$$\begin{aligned} \text{tr}(M) &= \text{tr}[I_T - X(X'X)^{-1}X'] \\ &= \text{tr}(I_T) - \text{tr}[X'X(X'X)^{-1}] \\ &= T - \text{tr}(I_K) \\ &= T - K \end{aligned}$$

Thus, the rank of M is $T - K$. Collecting all these results we have

$$\frac{(T-K)\hat{\sigma}^2}{\sigma^2} = \frac{\tilde{\mathbf{e}}'\tilde{\mathbf{e}}}{\sigma^2} = \frac{\mathbf{e}'M\mathbf{e}}{\sigma^2} \sim \chi^2_{(T-K)} \tag{6.1.18}$$

This is an important result that is used later for inference. When we talk of the probability distribution of just $\hat{\sigma}^2$, we usually say $\hat{\sigma}^2 \sim [\sigma^2/(T-K)]\chi^2_{(T-K)}$. That is, $\hat{\sigma}^2$ is distributed as a constant multiplied by a $\chi^2_{(T-K)}$-distribution.

We can use the result in (6.1.18) to find the mean and variance of $\hat{\sigma}^2$. We know that the mean of a χ^2 random variable is equal to its degrees of freedom. Thus,

$$E\left[\frac{(T-K)\hat{\sigma}^2}{\sigma^2}\right] = T - K \tag{6.1.19a}$$

and, multiplying both sides by $\sigma^2/(T-K)$,

$$E[\hat{\sigma}^2] = \sigma^2 \tag{6.1.19b}$$

as was derived back in Chapter 5 without the normality assumption. For the variance we note that the variance of a χ^2 random variable is equal to twice its degrees of freedom. Thus,

$$\text{var}\left[\frac{(T-K)\hat{\sigma}^2}{\sigma^2}\right] = 2(T-K) \tag{6.1.20a}$$

or

$$\frac{(T-K)^2}{\sigma^4}\,\text{var}(\hat{\sigma}^2) = 2(T-K) \tag{6.1.20b}$$

and

$$\text{var}(\hat{\sigma}^2) = \frac{2\sigma^4}{T-K} \tag{6.1.20c}$$

The normality assumption has provided additional information, sufficient for us to derive this expression for the variance of $\hat{\sigma}^2$. In the context of Chapter 5, it is not possible to derive the variance of $\hat{\sigma}^2$ without further assumptions about the moments or the distribution of **e**.

6.1.3c Independence of $\hat{\sigma}^2$ and $\tilde{\beta}$

Another important result is that the random vector $\tilde{\boldsymbol{\beta}}$ is independent of the random variable $\hat{\sigma}^2$. Since $\hat{\sigma}^2 = \tilde{\mathbf{e}}'\tilde{\mathbf{e}}/(T - K)$, this will be true if $\tilde{\mathbf{e}}$ and $\tilde{\boldsymbol{\beta}}$ are independent. Since both $\tilde{\mathbf{e}}$ and $\tilde{\boldsymbol{\beta}}$ are normal random vectors, to show that they are independent it is sufficient to show that the matrix containing the covariances between the elements of $\tilde{\mathbf{e}}$ and the elements of $\tilde{\boldsymbol{\beta}}$ is 0. This matrix is

$$\begin{aligned} E[\tilde{\mathbf{e}}(\tilde{\boldsymbol{\beta}} - \boldsymbol{\beta})'] &= E[(I - X(X'X)^{-1}X')\mathbf{e}\mathbf{e}'X(X'X)^{-1}] \\ &= (I - X(X'X)^{-1}X')E[\mathbf{e}\mathbf{e}']X(X'X)^{-1} \\ &= \sigma^2[(I - X(X'X)^{-1}X')X(X'X)^{-1}] \\ &= 0 \end{aligned} \tag{6.1.21}$$

and so $\tilde{\boldsymbol{\beta}}$ and $\hat{\sigma}^2$ are independent. This result also follows directly from the last result in Section 2.5.9.

6.1.3d Sufficiency and Sampling Performance of $\tilde{\beta}$ and $\hat{\sigma}^2$

So far we have been able to summarize the information in the Tth order random vector **y** in terms of the $K + 1$ statistics $\tilde{\boldsymbol{\beta}}, \hat{\sigma}^2$. It would be nice to show that $\tilde{\boldsymbol{\beta}}$ and $\hat{\sigma}^2$ contain all the information about $\boldsymbol{\beta}$ and σ^2 that the sample information **y** contains. If so, then we can say that $\tilde{\boldsymbol{\beta}}$ and $\hat{\sigma}^2$ are sufficient statistics (see Section 3.3 of Chapter 3). To do this, it is necessary to show that $f(\mathbf{y}|X, \boldsymbol{\beta}, \sigma^2) = g(\tilde{\boldsymbol{\beta}}, \hat{\sigma}^2|\boldsymbol{\beta}, \sigma^2)$ where $g(\cdot)$ contains the observations **y** only in the form of $\tilde{\boldsymbol{\beta}}, \hat{\sigma}^2$. Since $(\mathbf{y} - X\boldsymbol{\beta}) = (\mathbf{y} - X\tilde{\boldsymbol{\beta}} + X\tilde{\boldsymbol{\beta}} - X\boldsymbol{\beta})$, this means

$$\begin{aligned} (\mathbf{y} - X\boldsymbol{\beta})'(\mathbf{y} - X\boldsymbol{\beta}) &= (\mathbf{y} - X\tilde{\boldsymbol{\beta}} + X\tilde{\boldsymbol{\beta}} - X\boldsymbol{\beta})'(\mathbf{y} - X\tilde{\boldsymbol{\beta}} + X\tilde{\boldsymbol{\beta}} - X\boldsymbol{\beta}) \\ &= (\mathbf{y} - X\tilde{\boldsymbol{\beta}})'(\mathbf{y} - X\tilde{\boldsymbol{\beta}}) + (\boldsymbol{\beta} - \tilde{\boldsymbol{\beta}})'X'X(\boldsymbol{\beta} - \tilde{\boldsymbol{\beta}}) \\ &= (T - K)\hat{\sigma}^2 + (\boldsymbol{\beta} - \tilde{\boldsymbol{\beta}})'X'X(\boldsymbol{\beta} - \tilde{\boldsymbol{\beta}}) \end{aligned} \tag{6.1.22}$$

Therefore,

$$\begin{aligned} f(\mathbf{y}|X, \boldsymbol{\beta}, \sigma^2) &= \frac{1}{(2\pi\sigma^2)^{T/2}} \exp\left[-(\mathbf{y} - X\boldsymbol{\beta})'(\mathbf{y} - X\boldsymbol{\beta})\frac{1}{2\sigma^2}\right] \\ &= \frac{1}{(2\pi\sigma^2)^{T/2}} \exp\left\{\frac{-1}{2\sigma^2}[(T - K)\hat{\sigma}^2 + (\boldsymbol{\beta} - \tilde{\boldsymbol{\beta}})'X'X(\boldsymbol{\beta} - \tilde{\boldsymbol{\beta}})]\right\} \\ &= g(\tilde{\boldsymbol{\beta}}, \hat{\sigma}^2|\boldsymbol{\beta}, \sigma^2) \end{aligned} \tag{6.1.23}$$

Consequently, we conclude that $\tilde{\boldsymbol{\beta}}, \hat{\sigma}^2$ are a set of sufficient statistics.

One advantage of finding a set of sufficient statistics is that, under usual conditions, if the sufficient statistics are unbiased estimators of some parameters of interest, then it follows immediately that the unbiased estimators are *best* unbiased estimators. In our case, because $\tilde{\boldsymbol{\beta}}$ and $\hat{\sigma}^2$ are sufficient statistics from the multivariate normal distribution, and because they are unbiased estimators for $\boldsymbol{\beta}$ and σ^2, respectively, it follows that they are minimum variance unbiased estimators. Note that this is a much stronger result than the one in Chapter 5 where we used the Gauss–Markov theorem to establish that, for the general linear statistical model *without the normality assumption*, the estimator $\mathbf{b} = (X'X)^{-1}X'\mathbf{y}$ is best out of the class of *linear* unbiased estimators. We also indicated that the quadratic estimator $\hat{\sigma}^2 = (\mathbf{y} - X\mathbf{b})'(\mathbf{y} - X\mathbf{b})/(T - K)$ is unbiased. Now, since the normality assumption permits the joint density function for the sample and hence the likelihood function to be analytically specified, it is possible to obtain the much stronger results that $\tilde{\boldsymbol{\beta}}$ and $\hat{\sigma}^2$ are minimum variance unbiased estimators from their respective classes of all unbiased estimators.

6.1.3e The Cramér–Rao Lower Bound and Sampling Performance of $\tilde{\boldsymbol{\beta}}$ and $\hat{\sigma}^2$

Another method for investigating whether or not $\tilde{\boldsymbol{\beta}}$ and $\hat{\sigma}^2$ are best unbiased estimators is to consider the lower bound that can be derived using the Cramér–Rao inequality and the resulting *information matrix*, which was first considered in Chapter 3 for the case of a normal distribution with unknown mean and variance. The Cramér–Rao inequality makes use of the fact that the square of a covariance is at most equal to the product of the corresponding variances. In stating this result for the normal linear statistical model, we will represent the $(K + 1)$ unknown parameters as $\boldsymbol{\gamma} = (\beta_1, \beta_2, \ldots, \beta_K, \sigma^2)'$ and remember that the likelihood function $\ell(\boldsymbol{\gamma}|\mathbf{y}, X)$, as a function of the random sample $\mathbf{y}$, is random, and therefore the derivatives of the likelihood function with respect to $\boldsymbol{\gamma}$ are random. If we assume that the likelihood function is twice differentiable, the information matrix for $\boldsymbol{\gamma}$ is defined as

$$I(\boldsymbol{\gamma}) = -E\left[\frac{\partial^2 \ln \ell(\boldsymbol{\gamma}|\mathbf{y}, X)}{\partial\boldsymbol{\gamma}\,\partial\boldsymbol{\gamma}'}\right] \tag{6.1.24a}$$

which is the negative of the expectation of the matrix of second-order derivatives.

The inverse of the information matrix provides a lower bound for the sampling precision for unbiased estimators of $\boldsymbol{\gamma}$. That is, $\Sigma_{\hat{\boldsymbol{\gamma}}} \geq I(\boldsymbol{\gamma})^{-1}$ in the sense that $\Sigma_{\hat{\boldsymbol{\gamma}}} - I(\boldsymbol{\gamma})^{-1}$ is positive semidefinite. For our statistical model the elements of the matrix (6.1.24a) are the second-order derivatives of the likelihood function (6.1.5). Carrying out this differentiation yields

$$I(\gamma) = -E\begin{bmatrix} -\frac{1}{\sigma^2}X'X & -\frac{1}{\sigma^4}(X'\mathbf{y} - X'X\boldsymbol{\beta}) \\ -\frac{1}{\sigma^4}(X'\mathbf{y} - X'X\boldsymbol{\beta})' & \frac{T}{2\sigma^4} - \frac{1}{\sigma^6}(\mathbf{y} - X\boldsymbol{\beta})'(\mathbf{y} - X\boldsymbol{\beta}) \end{bmatrix}$$

$$= \begin{bmatrix} \frac{1}{\sigma^2}X'X & 0 \\ 0 & \frac{T}{2\sigma^4} \end{bmatrix} \tag{6.1.24b}$$

and

$$I(\gamma)^{-1} = \begin{bmatrix} \sigma^2(X'X)^{-1} & \mathbf{0} \\ \mathbf{0}' & \frac{2\sigma^4}{T} \end{bmatrix} \tag{6.1.25a}$$

The covariance for the unbiased estimators $\tilde{\boldsymbol{\beta}}$ and $\hat{\sigma}^2$ is

$$\Sigma_{(\tilde{\boldsymbol{\beta}}, \hat{\sigma}^2)} = \begin{bmatrix} \sigma^2(X'X)^{-1} & \mathbf{0} \\ \mathbf{0}' & \frac{2\sigma^4}{T-K} \end{bmatrix} \tag{6.1.25b}$$

and this means that the Cramér–Rao lower bound is attained for the covariance of $\tilde{\boldsymbol{\beta}} = \mathbf{b}$ but not for the unbiased estimator $\hat{\sigma}^2$. As we mentioned when discussing sufficiency, this gives us a stronger result than the Gauss–Markov theorem because it means that the maximum likelihood estimator of $\boldsymbol{\beta}$ is best in a larger class of estimators that does not include the linear restriction. Also, although the variance of $\hat{\sigma}^2$ does not attain the lower bound, it can be shown by other methods that an unbiased estimator of σ^2 with variance lower than $2\sigma^4/(T-K)$ does not exist. This result implies that $\hat{\sigma}^2$ is best unbiased.

6.1.4 Summary Statement

For the linear statistical model $\mathbf{y} = X\boldsymbol{\beta} + \mathbf{e}$, where $\mathbf{e} \sim N(\mathbf{0}, \sigma^2 I_T)$

1. The maximum likelihood estimator for $\boldsymbol{\beta}$ is $\tilde{\boldsymbol{\beta}} = (X'X)^{-1}X'\mathbf{y}$.

2. The maximum likelihood estimator for σ^2 is $\tilde{\sigma}^2 = (\mathbf{y} - X\tilde{\boldsymbol{\beta}})'(\mathbf{y} - X\tilde{\boldsymbol{\beta}})/T$.

3. The maximum likelihood estimator $\tilde{\boldsymbol{\beta}}$ is a best unbiased estimator of $\boldsymbol{\beta}$.

4. The maximum likelihood estimator $\tilde{\sigma}^2$ is a biased estimator of σ^2.

5. $\tilde{\boldsymbol{\beta}}$ is a normal random vector with mean $\boldsymbol{\beta}$ and covariance $\sigma^2(X'X)^{-1}$.

6. $[T/(T-K)]\tilde{\sigma}^2 = (\mathbf{y} - X\tilde{\boldsymbol{\beta}})'(\mathbf{y} - X\tilde{\boldsymbol{\beta}})/(T-K) = \hat{\sigma}^2$ is a best unbiased estimator of σ^2.
7. The quadratic form

$$\frac{\tilde{\mathbf{e}}'\tilde{\mathbf{e}}}{\sigma^2} = \frac{\mathbf{e}'(I - X(X'X)^{-1}X')\mathbf{e}}{\sigma^2} = (T-K)\frac{\hat{\sigma}^2}{\sigma^2}$$

is distributed as a χ^2 random variable with $(T-K)$ degrees of freedom.
8. The linear form $\tilde{\boldsymbol{\beta}} = \mathbf{b}$ and the quadratic form $\hat{\sigma}^2$ are independent.

6.1.5 A Sampling Experiment

In order to emphasize the sampling theory basis of these analytical results, a Monte Carlo sampling experiment was performed based on the following statistical model and design matrix:

$$\mathbf{y} = X\boldsymbol{\beta} + \mathbf{e} = 10.0\mathbf{x}_1 + 0.4\mathbf{x}_2 + 0.6\mathbf{x}_3 + \mathbf{e} \qquad (6.1.26)$$

where $\mathbf{e}$ is a normal random vector with mean vector zero and variance $\sigma^2 = 0.0625$. The (20×3) design matrix, the random vector for the first sample $\mathbf{u}_1$, where $u_t \sim N(0, 1)$ and $\mathbf{e}_1 = \sqrt{0.0625}\,\mathbf{u}_1$, and the outcome vector for the first sample $\mathbf{y}_1$ are given in (6.1.27).

$\mathbf{y}_1$	$\mathbf{u}_1$	X: $\mathbf{x}_1$	$\mathbf{x}_2$	$\mathbf{x}_3$
10.7413	0.1930	1	0.693	0.693
10.9830	−0.5041	1	1.733	0.693
10.5292	−2.3183	1	0.693	1.386
11.5891	0.2572	1	1.733	1.386
11.7983	1.7837	1	0.693	1.792
11.7586	1.6270	1	2.340	0.693
11.9454	0.7078	1	1.733	1.792
12.3305	2.2516	1	2.340	1.386
11.8958	−0.4618	1	2.340	1.792
10.3561	−1.3475	1	0.693	0.693
11.1673	0.2338	1	0.693	1.386
11.1656	0.2262	1	1.733	0.693
11.6819	0.6286	1	1.733	1.386
11.4135	0.2443	1	0.693	1.792
11.2097	−0.5685	1	2.340	0.693
11.9817	0.8531	1	1.733	1.792
12.3243	2.2266	1	2.340	1.386
12.0298	0.0742	1	2.340	1.792
11.3930	−0.5271	1	1.733	1.386
10.8940	0.8041	1	0.693	0.693

(6.1.27)

By the use of the statistical model described by (6.1.26) and (6.1.27) and the sampling process described in Section 6.1.1, 500 **y** samples of size 20 were generated and one sample is displayed in (6.1.27). To give a note of realism, assume that (6.1.26) is a log linear production function, where x_2 is the log of capital, x_3 is the log of labor, and β_2 and β_3 are the elasticities of production in regard to capital and labor.

For this model, which uses the design matrix (6.1.27), the corresponding $(X'X)^{-1}$ matrix is

$$(X'X)^{-1} = \begin{bmatrix} 0.6566 & -0.1531 & -0.2917 \\ -0.1531 & 0.1105 & -0.0144 \\ -0.2917 & -0.0144 & 0.2482 \end{bmatrix} \tag{6.1.28}$$

6.1.5a The Sampling Results

Given the 500 samples of 20 observations each, maximum likelihood–least squares estimates were obtained for the coefficient vector $\boldsymbol{\beta} = (\beta_1, \beta_2, \beta_3)'$. To give an idea of the sampling variability of the estimates, point estimates of $\boldsymbol{\beta}$ are given for the first 10 samples, along with the unbiased estimate of the variance $\hat{\sigma}^2$, in Table 6.1. Note, for example, that the estimates of $\beta_3 = 0.60$, vary over the range of 0.337 to 0.771 and the estimates of $\sigma^2 = 0.0625$ vary over the range 0.036 to 0.114.

The empirical covariance matrix for $\tilde{\boldsymbol{\beta}}$ is

$$\hat{\Sigma}_{\tilde{\boldsymbol{\beta}}(500)} = \begin{bmatrix} 0.0417 & -0.0097 & -0.0185 \\ -0.0097 & 0.0070 & -0.0009 \\ -0.0185 & -0.0009 & 0.0158 \end{bmatrix} \tag{6.1.29}$$

Table 6.1 Point Estimates of $\beta_1, \beta_2, \beta_3$, and σ^2 for 10 Samples of Data

Sample Number	$\tilde{\beta}_1$	$\tilde{\beta}_2$	$\tilde{\beta}_3$	$\hat{\sigma}^2$
1	9.770	0.524	0.693	0.079
2	10.014	0.278	0.771	0.114
3	10.484	0.215	0.495	0.061
4	10.263	0.322	0.523	0.093
5	9.731	0.457	0.708	0.036
6	10.239	0.272	0.571	0.039
7	10.477	0.356	0.337	0.077
8	10.085	0.287	0.604	0.059
9	9.885	0.413	0.702	0.068
10	10.237	0.347	0.502	0.080

Thus the average of the outcomes for the variance of the estimates over 500 replications are very close to those for the true covariance matrix

$$\hat{\Sigma}_{\tilde{\beta}} = \begin{bmatrix} 0.0410 & -0.0096 & -0.0182 \\ -0.0096 & 0.0069 & -0.0009 \\ -0.0182 & -0.0009 & 0.0155 \end{bmatrix} \qquad (6.1.30)$$

Estimates of the variance for each $\tilde{\beta}_i$, for the first 10 samples, are given in Table 6.2.

The average values of the $b_i = \tilde{\beta}_i$ and $\hat{\sigma}^2$ over the 500 samples, along with the true parameters, are

$$\text{average } b_1 = 10.003\ (10.000)$$

$$\text{average } b_2 = 0.393\ (0.40)$$

$$\text{average } b_3 = 0.602\ (0.60)$$

$$\text{average } \hat{\sigma}^2 = 0.0635\ (0.0625)$$

Although on the average the estimates are on target, individual sample estimates sometimes badly miss the mark.

The empirical distribution for each of the b_i closely approaches its normal theoretical counterpart as the frequency graphs in Figures 6.1, 6.2, and 6.3 suggest. The empirical distribution for the ratio $(T - K)\hat{\sigma}^2/\sigma^2$, which is distributed as a $\chi^2_{(T-K)}$ random variable with mean $(T - K) = 17$ and variance $2(T - K)$ is presented in Figure 6.4. The mean for the 500 samples is 16.73, and this compares

Table 6.2 Estimated Variances for $\tilde{\beta}_1$, $\tilde{\beta}_2$, and $\tilde{\beta}_3$ for 10 Samples of Data

Sample Number	$(\sigma^2_{\tilde{\beta}_1} = 0.041)$ $\hat{\sigma}^2_{\tilde{\beta}_1}$	$(\sigma^2_{\tilde{\beta}_2} = 0.007)$ $\hat{\sigma}^2_{\tilde{\beta}_2}$	$(\sigma^2_{\tilde{\beta}_3} = 0.016)$ $\hat{\sigma}^2_{\tilde{\beta}_3}$
1	0.0522	0.0088	0.0020
2	0.0747	0.0126	0.0283
3	0.0400	0.0067	0.0151
4	0.0610	0.0103	0.0231
5	0.0239	0.0040	0.0090
6	0.0256	0.0043	0.0097
7	0.0505	0.0085	0.0191
8	0.0386	0.0065	0.0015
9	0.0447	0.0075	0.0017
10	0.0522	0.0088	0.0197

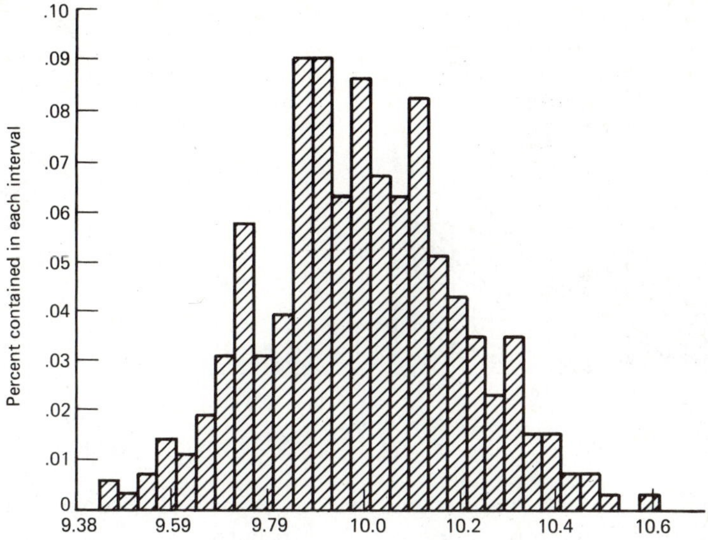

Figure 6.1 Empirical distribution of estimates of β_1.

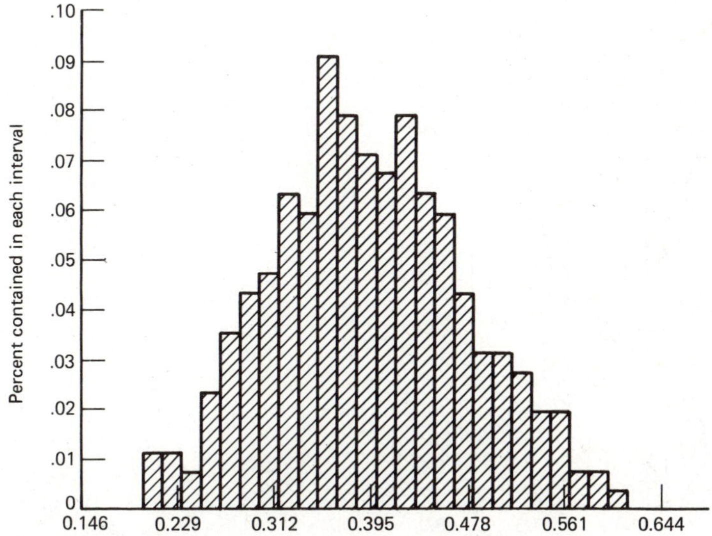

Figure 6.2 Empirical distribution of estimates of β_2.

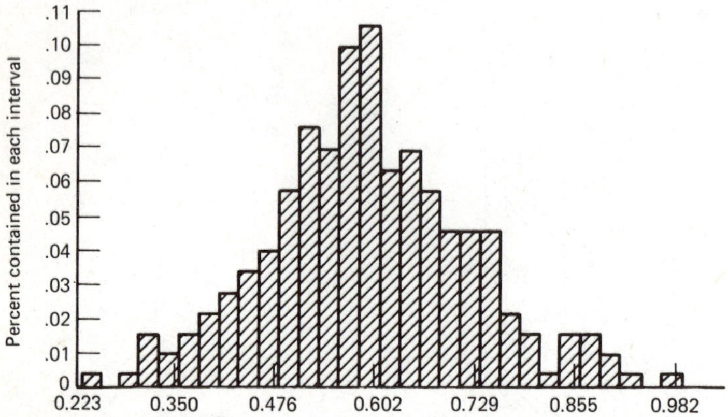

Figure 6.3 Empirical distribution of estimates of β_3.

closely to the mean of a χ^2 random variable with 17 degrees of freedom. The empirical distribution appears to be approximately distributed as a $\chi^2_{(17)}$ random variable.

In general, the Monte Carlo sampling results appear compatible with the analytical results obtained for the maximum likelihood estimator for the normal linear statistical model.

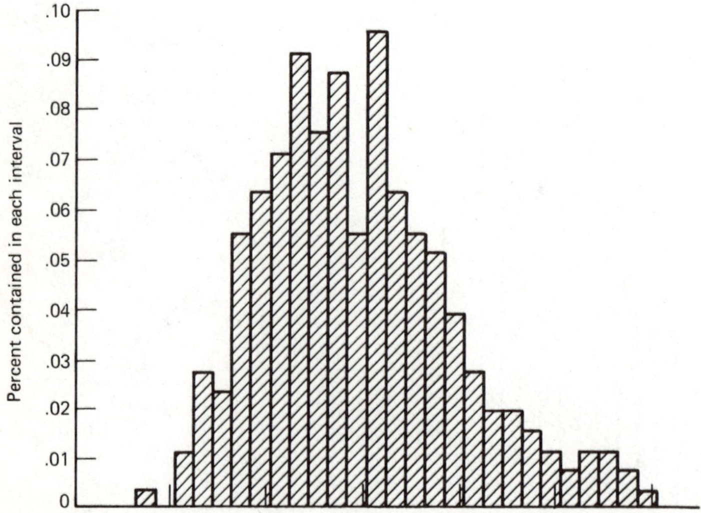

Figure 6.4 Empirical frequency distribution for the ratio $(T-K)\hat{\sigma}^2/\sigma^2 = (T-K)\hat{\sigma}^2/0.0625$.

6.2 Restricted Maximum Likelihood Estimation

In the previous section we made use of the likelihood principle in deriving estimators for the unknown location vector $\boldsymbol{\beta}$ and the scale parameter σ^2. In using this principle, we assumed that after the sample information was observed, all the relevant *experimental* information about $\boldsymbol{\beta}$ and σ^2 was contained in the likelihood function for the observed $\mathbf{y}$. At this point, it is important to note that the likelihood principle does not say that all information about $\boldsymbol{\beta}$ and σ^2 is contained in the likelihood function $\ell(\boldsymbol{\beta}, \sigma^2 | X; \mathbf{y})$, *only* that all the experimental information is.

In many econometric studies, other relevant information of a nonsample type may exist and may be available in a variety of forms. At this point, let us look at one of the simplest forms and assume that the investigator has exact information relative to a particular parameter or linear combination of parameters. For example, in estimating the log-linear production function $y_t = \beta_1 + \beta_2 x_{t2} + \beta_3 x_{t3}$, where x_{t2} is the logarithm of the capital input and x_{t3} is the logarithm of the labor input, information may be available that the firm is operating under the condition of constant returns to scale, that is, $\beta_2 + \beta_3 = 1$. Alternatively, in estimating a demand relation, information may be available from consumer theory on the homogeneity condition, or an estimate of, say, the income response coefficient may be available from previous empirical work.

In any event, if information of this type is available, it may be stated in the form of the following set of linear relations or linear equality restrictions:

$$R\boldsymbol{\beta} = \mathbf{r} \tag{6.2.1}$$

where $\mathbf{r}$ is a $(J \times 1)$ vector of known elements and R is a $(J \times K)$ known prior information design matrix of rank $J \leq K$ that expresses the structure of the information on the individual parameters β_i or some linear combination of the elements of the $\boldsymbol{\beta}$ vector. Information concerning the parameters, such as β_1 equal to some scalar k, the sum of the coefficients equal to unity, and β_2 equal to β_3, may be specified in the $R\boldsymbol{\beta} = \mathbf{r}$ format as

$$\begin{bmatrix} 1 & 0 & 0 & 0 & \cdots & 0 \\ 1 & 1 & 1 & 1 & \cdots & 1 \\ 0 & 1 & -1 & 0 & \cdots & 0 \end{bmatrix} \begin{bmatrix} \beta_1 \\ \beta_2 \\ \vdots \\ \beta_K \end{bmatrix} = \begin{bmatrix} k \\ 1 \\ 0 \end{bmatrix} \tag{6.2.2}$$

where $J = 3$. If the first J elements of the coefficient vector were specified to be equal to a particular J dimensional constant vector $\mathbf{r}$, this information could be specified as

$$[I_J \quad 0_{(K-J)}] \begin{bmatrix} \boldsymbol{\beta}_J \\ \boldsymbol{\beta}_{K-J} \end{bmatrix} = \mathbf{r} \tag{6.2.3}$$

where I_J is a Jth-order identity matrix and $\mathbf{r}$ is a $(J \times 1)$ known vector.

Given information in the form of (6.2.1), the question is how to combine it with the information contained in the sample observations $\mathbf{y}$. Because information on the individual parameters and combinations therefore is specified to be known with certainty, there is no sampling variability from sample to sample, and linear equality relations (6.2.1) may be taken as givens or restrictions in any sampling and estimation process. In the general linear statistical model considered in this chapter, using either the least-squares criterion or the likelihood principle resulted in the least squares estimator $\mathbf{b} = (X'X)^{-1}X'\mathbf{y}$, which has mean vector $\boldsymbol{\beta}$ and covariance $\Sigma_{\mathbf{b}} = \sigma^2(X'X)^{-1}$. Since the $X'X$ matrix is not assumed diagonal, restrictions on particular coefficients or their linear combinations reflected by (6.2.1) condition the values that other estimated coefficients may take on. If we use either the likelihood or the least squares criterion applied to both the sample information $\mathbf{y}$ and the nonsample information $R\boldsymbol{\beta} = \mathbf{r}$, we are faced with the problem of finding the vector $\mathbf{b}^*$ that minimizes the quadratic form

$$S = (\mathbf{y} - X\boldsymbol{\beta})'(\mathbf{y} - X\boldsymbol{\beta}) \tag{6.2.4}$$

subject to

$$R\boldsymbol{\beta} = \mathbf{r} \qquad \text{or} \qquad R\boldsymbol{\beta} - \mathbf{r} = \mathbf{0} \tag{6.2.1}$$

Since (6.2.1) appear as linear equality restrictions, classical Lagrangian procedures may be applied to yield the Lagrange function

$$\mathscr{L} = \mathbf{e}'\mathbf{e} + 2(\mathbf{r}' - \boldsymbol{\beta}'R')\boldsymbol{\lambda} \tag{6.2.5}$$

or

$$\begin{aligned}\mathscr{L} &= (\mathbf{y} - X\boldsymbol{\beta})'(\mathbf{y} - X\boldsymbol{\beta}) + 2(\mathbf{r}' - \boldsymbol{\beta}'R')\boldsymbol{\lambda} \\ &= \mathbf{y}'\mathbf{y} - 2\boldsymbol{\beta}'X'\mathbf{y} + \boldsymbol{\beta}'X'X\boldsymbol{\beta} + 2(\mathbf{r}' - \boldsymbol{\beta}'R')\boldsymbol{\lambda}\end{aligned}$$

where $\boldsymbol{\lambda}$ is the $(J \times 1)$ vector of Lagrange multipliers. The 2 in front of the last term appears to make life easier later on and does not affect the outcome, since $\mathbf{r}' - \boldsymbol{\beta}'R' = \mathbf{0}$ by assumption. To determine the optimum values, we set the partial derivatives of $\mathscr{L}$ with respect to $\boldsymbol{\beta}$ and $\boldsymbol{\lambda}$ equal to $\mathbf{0}$ to find a stationary point of the Lagrangian function.

$$(i) \quad \frac{\partial \mathscr{L}}{\partial \boldsymbol{\beta}} = -2X'\mathbf{y} + 2X'X\mathbf{b}^* - 2R'\boldsymbol{\lambda}^* = \mathbf{0} \tag{6.2.6a}$$

$$(ii) \quad \frac{\partial \mathscr{L}}{\partial \boldsymbol{\lambda}} = 2(\mathbf{r} - R\mathbf{b}^*) = \mathbf{0} \tag{6.2.6b}$$

From (6.2.6a) we get

$$X'X\mathbf{b}^* = X'\mathbf{y} + R'\boldsymbol{\lambda}^*$$

hence

$$(X'X)^{-1}(X'X)\mathbf{b}^* = (X'X)^{-1}(X'\mathbf{y} + R'\boldsymbol{\lambda}^*)$$

and thus

$$\mathbf{b}^* = \mathbf{b} + (X'X)^{-1}R'\boldsymbol{\lambda}^* \tag{6.2.7}$$

where $\mathbf{b}$ is the unrestricted least squares estimator.

From (6.2.7), multiplying by R, we get

$$R\mathbf{b}^* = R\mathbf{b} + R(X'X)^{-1}R'\boldsymbol{\lambda}^* = \mathbf{r} \tag{6.2.8}$$

Since $(X'X)^{-1}$ is positive definite, $R(X'X)^{-1}R'$ is a positive definite matrix with rank J, which is less than or equal to K, the rank of $(X'X)^{-1}$. Since $R(X'X)^{-1}R'$ is nonsingular, we may express (6.2.8) as

$$\boldsymbol{\lambda}^* = [R(X'X)^{-1}R']^{-1}(R\mathbf{b}^* - R\mathbf{b}) \tag{6.2.9}$$

or

$$\boldsymbol{\lambda}^* = [R(X'X)^{-1}R']^{-1}(\mathbf{r} - R\mathbf{b})$$

because from (6.2.6) the restricted minimization problem must satisfy the side condition $R\mathbf{b}^* = \mathbf{r}$. Using this value for the vector $\boldsymbol{\lambda}^*$, we get, from (6.2.7), the estimator

$$\mathbf{b}^* = \mathbf{b} + (X'X)^{-1}R'[R(X'X)^{-1}R']^{-1}(\mathbf{r} - R\mathbf{b}) \tag{6.2.10}$$

This rule, for using both the sample and nonsample data, is called the *restricted least squares* or *maximum likelihood estimator* and differs from the unrestricted least squares estimator $\mathbf{b}$ by a linear function of the vector $(\mathbf{r} - R\mathbf{b})$.

6.2.1 Mean and Covariance

Since $\mathbf{b}$ is a random vector, the rule implied by (6.2.10) means that $\mathbf{b}^*$ is also a random vector. The restricted least squares random vector has mean

$$\begin{aligned} E[\mathbf{b}^*] &= E\{\mathbf{b} + (X'X)^{-1}R'[R(X'X)^{-1}R']^{-1}(\mathbf{r} - R\mathbf{b})\} \\ &= E[\mathbf{b}] + (X'X)^{-1}R'[R(X'X)^{-1}R']^{-1}(\mathbf{r} - RE[\mathbf{b}]) \\ &= \boldsymbol{\beta} + (X'X)^{-1}R'[R(X'X)^{-1}R']^{-1}(\mathbf{r} - R\boldsymbol{\beta}) \\ &= \boldsymbol{\beta} + (X'X)^{-1}R'[R(X'X)^{-1}R']^{-1}\boldsymbol{\delta} \\ &= \boldsymbol{\beta} \end{aligned} \tag{6.2.11}$$

because our side condition, $\boldsymbol{\delta} = \mathbf{r} - R\boldsymbol{\beta} = \mathbf{0}$, is true by assumption. Therefore, $\mathbf{b}^*$ is unbiased if $\mathbf{r} - R\boldsymbol{\beta} = \boldsymbol{\delta} = \mathbf{0}$. That is, $\mathbf{b}^*$ is unbiased if the restrictions are correct. Before we calculate the variance-covariance matrix of $\mathbf{b}^*$ remember that

$$\mathbf{b} = (X'X)^{-1}X'\mathbf{y} = (X'X)^{-1}X'(X\boldsymbol{\beta} + \mathbf{e}) = \boldsymbol{\beta} + (X'X)^{-1}X'\mathbf{e} \tag{6.2.12}$$

Correspondingly, we get from (6.2.10)

$$\begin{aligned}\mathbf{b}^* - \boldsymbol{\beta} &= (X'X)^{-1}X'\mathbf{e} + (X'X)^{-1}R'[R(X'X)^{-1}R']^{-1}(\mathbf{r} - R\boldsymbol{\beta} - R(X'X)^{-1}X'\mathbf{e})\\ &= (X'X)^{-1}X'\mathbf{e} - (X'X)^{-1}R'[R(X'X)^{-1}R']^{-1}R(X'X)^{-1}X'\mathbf{e}\end{aligned} \tag{6.2.13}$$

which can be written as

$$\mathbf{b}^* - \boldsymbol{\beta} = M^*(X'X)^{-1}X'\mathbf{e} \tag{6.2.14}$$

since

$$\mathbf{r} - R\boldsymbol{\beta} = \mathbf{0}$$

and where

$$M^* = I - (X'X)^{-1}R'[R(X'X)^{-1}R']^{-1}R$$

Making use of (6.2.14), we can express the variance-covariance matrix for $\mathbf{b}^*$ as

$$\begin{aligned}\text{var } \mathbf{b}^* = \Sigma_{\mathbf{b}^*} &= E[(\mathbf{b}^* - E[\mathbf{b}^*])(\mathbf{b}^* - E[\mathbf{b}^*])'] = E[(\mathbf{b}^* - \boldsymbol{\beta})(\mathbf{b}^* - \boldsymbol{\beta})']\\ &= E[M^*(X'X)^{-1}X'\mathbf{e}\mathbf{e}'X(X'X)^{-1}M^{*\prime}]\\ &= M^*(X'X)^{-1}X'E[\mathbf{e}\mathbf{e}']X(X'X)^{-1}M^{*\prime}\\ &= \sigma^2 M^*(X'X)^{-1}M^{*\prime}\end{aligned} \tag{6.2.15}$$

since $E[\mathbf{e}\mathbf{e}'] = \sigma^2 I$. Furthermore, since

$$\begin{aligned}M^*(X'X)^{-1}M^* &= [I - (X'X)^{-1}R'[R(X'X)^{-1}R']^{-1}R](X'X)^{-1}\\ &\quad \times [I - (X'X)^{-1}R'[R(X'X)^{-1}R']^{-1}R]'\\ &= (X'X)^{-1} - 2(X'X)^{-1}R'[R(X'X)^{-1}R']^{-1}R(X'X)^{-1}\\ &\quad + (X'X)^{-1}R'[R(X'X)^{-1}R']^{-1}R(X'X)^{-1}R'\\ &\quad \times [R(X'X)^{-1}R']^{-1}R(X'X)^{-1}\\ &= (X'X)^{-1} - (X'X)^{-1}R'[R(X'X)^{-1}R']^{-1}R(X'X)^{-1}\\ &= \{I - (X'X)^{-1}R'[R(X'X)^{-1}R']^{-1}R\}(X'X)^{-1} = M^*(X'X)^{-1}\end{aligned} \tag{6.2.16}$$

where the term in braces is the idempotent matrix M^*, we can write the variance–covariance matrix $\Sigma_{\mathbf{b}^*}$ as

$$\Sigma_{\mathbf{b}^*} = \sigma^2 M^*(X'X)^{-1} = \sigma^2(X'X)^{-1} - \sigma^2(X'X)^{-1}R'[R(X'X)^{-1}R']^{-1}R(X'X)^{-1}$$
$$= \Sigma_{\mathbf{b}} - C \tag{6.2.17}$$

Thus

$$\Sigma_{\mathbf{b}} - \Sigma_{\mathbf{b}^*} = \sigma^2(X'X)^{-1}R'[R(X'X)^{-1}R']^{-1}R(X'X)^{-1} = C \tag{6.2.18}$$

where C is a positive semidefinite matrix. Consequently, the variance-covariance matrix for the restricted least squares estimator $\Sigma_{\mathbf{b}^*}$ has diagonal elements that are equal to or less than the corresponding elements of the unrestricted least squares estimator $\Sigma_{\mathbf{b}}$. The estimator $\mathbf{b}^*$ is best linear unbiased within the class of unbiased estimators that are linear functions of $\mathbf{y}$ and that also satisfy the constraints of (6.2.1). If we assume the sample information vector $\mathbf{y}$ is multivariate normal, then $\mathbf{b}^* \sim N(\boldsymbol{\beta}, \sigma^2 M^*(X'X)^{-1}M^{*\prime})$.

6.2.2 Consequences of Incorrect Restrictions

In applied work we are usually never completely sure that the nonsample information is correct. If the restrictions are inconsistent with the parameters of the sampling model that generated the data, that is, if the restrictions are incorrect and $\mathbf{r} - R\boldsymbol{\beta} = \boldsymbol{\delta} \neq \mathbf{0}$, then from (6.2.11) the restricted least squares estimator has mean

$$E[\mathbf{b}^*] = E[\mathbf{b} + (X'X)^{-1}R'[R(X'X)^{-1}R']^{-1}(\mathbf{r} - R\mathbf{b})]$$
$$= E[\mathbf{b} + (X'X)^{-1}X'\mathbf{e} + (X'X)^{-1}R'[R(X'X)^{-1}R']^{-1}$$
$$\times (\mathbf{r} - R\mathbf{b} - R(X'X)^{-1}X'\mathbf{e})]$$
$$= \boldsymbol{\beta} + (X'X)^{-1}R'[R(X'X)^{-1}R']^{-1}\boldsymbol{\delta} \tag{6.2.19}$$

which means that the restricted least squares estimator $\mathbf{b}^*$ is biased. However, its covariance matrix is in the fixed X case

$$\Sigma_{\mathbf{b}^*} = E[(\mathbf{b}^* - E[\mathbf{b}^*])(\mathbf{b}^* - E[\mathbf{b}^*])']$$
$$= E[\{\boldsymbol{\beta} + (X'X)^{-1}R'[R(X'X)^{-1}R']^{-1}\boldsymbol{\delta}$$
$$+ M^*(X'X)^{-1}X'\mathbf{e} - \boldsymbol{\beta} - (X'X)^{-1}R'[R(X'X)^{-1}R']^{-1}\boldsymbol{\delta}\}]$$
$$\times [\{\boldsymbol{\beta} + (X'X)^{-1}R'[R(X'X)^{-1}R']^{-1}\boldsymbol{\delta}$$
$$+ M^*(X'X)^{-1}X'\mathbf{e} - \boldsymbol{\beta} - (X'X)^{-1}R'[R(X'X)^{-1}R']^{-1}\boldsymbol{\delta}\}']$$
$$= \sigma^2(X'X)^{-1} - \sigma^2(X'X)^{-1}R'[R(X'X)^{-1}R']^{-1}R(X'X)^{-1} \tag{6.2.20}$$

which is the same as the covariance matrix for the unbiased restricted least squares estimator (6.2.17). Therefore, whether the restrictions are correct or incorrect or the restricted estimator is biased or unbiased, the restricted least squares estimator has a precision matrix that is superior to the least squares estimator that uses only sample information. Thus the restricted least-squares estimator **b*** has excellent precision relative to its least squares and maximum likelihood counterparts **b** and $\tilde{\boldsymbol{\beta}}$, but it may possibly result in a biased rule. Since we now have two estimators for the location vector $\boldsymbol{\beta}$, the question arises as to how to choose between **b** and **b***. This is one of the interesting questions discussed in Chapter 20.

6.2.3 An Example

To give an idea of the sampling performance of the restricted least squares estimator **b***, we make use of the Monte Carlo sampling experiment reported in Section 6.1.5. Assume we have the nonsample information

$$R\boldsymbol{\beta} = [0 \quad 1 \quad 1]\begin{bmatrix}\beta_1\\ \beta_2\\ \beta_3\end{bmatrix} = \beta_2 + \beta_3 = 1 \tag{6.2.21}$$

and that this information is used with the sample information for the 500 replications. To give an idea of the sampling performance of the restricted least squares estimator, 500 estimates of $\boldsymbol{\beta}$ and σ^2 were obtained. Of particular interest is the following covariance matrix $\Sigma_{\mathbf{b}^*}$ for the 500 replications.

$$\Sigma_{\mathbf{b}^*} = \begin{bmatrix} 0.0036 & -0.0015 & 0.0015\\ -0.0015 & 0.0052 & -0.0052\\ 0.0015 & -0.0052 & 0.0052\end{bmatrix} \tag{6.2.22}$$

Comparing this result with the unrestricted least squares covariance of Section 6.1.5a, we note how the use of the nonsample information (6.2.21) has increased the precision with which the unknown location vector $\boldsymbol{\beta}$ can be estimated.

The average of the 500 estimates for $\boldsymbol{\beta}$ are $\bar{b}_1^* = 9.993$, $\bar{b}_2^* = 0.3957$, and $\bar{b}_3^* = 0.6043$. Since the nonsample information (restriction) is correct, we expect the restricted estimator to be unbiased and the empirical results reflect that the average of the estimates for each β_k over the 500 samples is on target.

6.3 Interval Estimation

Given the maximum likelihood point estimates for $\boldsymbol{\beta}$ and σ^2, let us now face the problem that the estimates we obtain vary from sample to sample and, for some decision problems, interval estimates are important. Since the maximum likelihood estimator $\tilde{\boldsymbol{\beta}}$ is distributed as a normal random vector with mean $\boldsymbol{\beta}$ and covariance $\sigma^2(X'X)^{-1}$, the problem is now one of obtaining individual and joint confidence regions when the elements of the random vector $\tilde{\boldsymbol{\beta}}$ are not independent.

6.3.1. A Single Linear Combination of the β Vector

Given that $\boldsymbol{\beta} \sim N[\boldsymbol{\beta}, \sigma^2(X'X)^{-1}]$, within the context of Section 6.2 we know that under a general linear transformation $R\tilde{\boldsymbol{\beta}} \sim N[R\boldsymbol{\beta}, \sigma^2 R(X'X)^{-1}R']$ where R is a $(J \times K)$ known matrix. Let $R_1\tilde{\boldsymbol{\beta}}$ represent a *single* linear combination of $\tilde{\boldsymbol{\beta}}$, where R_1 is a $(1 \times K)$ *row* vector of known values. Consequently,

$$R_1\tilde{\boldsymbol{\beta}} \sim N[R_1\boldsymbol{\beta}, \sigma^2 R_1(X'X)^{-1}R_1'] \tag{6.3.1}$$

or, alternatively,

$$(R_1\tilde{\boldsymbol{\beta}} - R_1\boldsymbol{\beta}) \sim N[0, \sigma^2 R_1(X'X)^{-1}R_1'] \tag{6.3.2}$$

Since $R_1(X'X)^{-1}R_1'$ is a scalar, we know that

$$\frac{R_1(\tilde{\boldsymbol{\beta}} - \boldsymbol{\beta})}{\sigma\sqrt{R_1(X'X)^{-1}R_1'}} = z \tag{6.3.3}$$

is distributed as a standard normal variable, with mean zero and unit variance. As a result, if we know σ^2, and thus σ, we can pick an interval $[-z_{(\alpha/2)}, z_{(\alpha/2)}]$ and, since the standard normal random variable is tabled, make a probability statement about the interval containing the true parameter. In other words, if we represent the standard normal random variable by z and its density function by $f(z)$, then

$$\int_{-z_{(\alpha/2)}}^{z_{(\alpha/2)}} f(z)\,dz = 1 - \alpha \tag{6.3.4a}$$

where $-z_{(\alpha/2)}$ and $z_{(\alpha/2)}$ are the critical values associated with a certain probability or level of statistical significance α for the standard normal random variable. That is, for the critical values of the standard normal random variable $z_{(\alpha/2)}$,

$$\Pr[-z_{(\alpha/2)} \leq z \leq z_{(\alpha/2)}] = 1 - \alpha \tag{6.3.4b}$$

Hence we can write the interval estimate for $R_1\boldsymbol{\beta}$ as

$$\Pr\left[-z_{(\alpha/2)} \leq \frac{R_1\tilde{\boldsymbol{\beta}} - R_1\boldsymbol{\beta}}{\sigma\sqrt{R_1(X'X)^{-1}R_1'}} \leq z_{(\alpha/2)}\right] = 1 - \alpha \tag{6.3.4c}$$

If we set the significance level at $\alpha = .05$, we should attain, in a repeated sampling sense, the result that, on the average, the interval $[-z_{(\alpha/2)}, z_{(\alpha/2)}]$ would contain the statistic $(R_1\tilde{\boldsymbol{\beta}} - R_1\boldsymbol{\beta})/\sigma\sqrt{R_1(X'X)^{-1}R_1'}$, 95 percent of the time. That is, if we take repeated samples of data and estimate $R_1\boldsymbol{\beta}$ by $R_1\tilde{\boldsymbol{\beta}}$, on the average, 95 times out of 100 such an interval will contain $(R_1\tilde{\boldsymbol{\beta}} - R_1\boldsymbol{\beta})/\sigma\sqrt{R_1(X'X)^{-1}R_1'}$. If σ is known, we then have a basis for developing an interval estimate for $R_1\boldsymbol{\beta}$ because (6.3.4c) may be rewritten as

$$\Pr[R_1\tilde{\boldsymbol{\beta}} - z_{(\alpha/2)}\sigma\sqrt{R_1(X'X)^{-1}R_1'} \leq R_1\boldsymbol{\beta} \leq R_1\tilde{\boldsymbol{\beta}} + z_{(\alpha/2)}\sigma\sqrt{R_1(X'X)^{-1}R_1'}] = 1 - \alpha \qquad (6.3.4d)$$

One problem in using (6.3.4d) is that, in most experimental or applied situations, σ^2, and thus σ, is unknown. If we use an unbiased estimator of σ^2 we will have to consider the distribution of the random variable

$$\frac{R_1\tilde{\boldsymbol{\beta}} - R_1\boldsymbol{\beta}}{\hat{\sigma}\sqrt{R_1(X'X)^{-1}R_1'}} \qquad (6.3.5a)$$

Fortunately, this distribution was considered many years ago by W. S. Gossett, who called himself "student." He considered the problem of inference that arises when working with the ratio of a standard normal deviate to the square root of an independent χ^2 random variable divided by its degrees of freedom. Noting that $\tilde{\boldsymbol{\beta}}$ and σ^2 are independent, an example of such a ratio is

$$\frac{\dfrac{R_1\tilde{\boldsymbol{\beta}} - R_1\boldsymbol{\beta}}{\sigma\sqrt{R_1(X'X)^{-1}R_1'}}}{\left[\dfrac{(T-K)\hat{\sigma}^2}{\sigma^2(T-K)}\right]^{1/2}} = \frac{R_1\tilde{\boldsymbol{\beta}} - R_1\boldsymbol{\beta}}{\hat{\sigma}\sqrt{R_1(X'X)^{-1}R_1'}} = t_{(T-K)} \qquad (6.3.5b)$$

and, as discussed in Section 2.5.8, this random variable is distributed as a student t random variable with $(T - K)$ degrees of freedom. This random variable has been tabled for various degrees of freedom and significance (α) levels. Therefore, as in (6.3.4b), the t-distribution can be used to restate the random interval as

$$\Pr[-t_{(T-K,\alpha/2)} \leq t_{(T-K)} \leq t_{(T-K,\alpha/2)}] = 1 - \alpha \qquad (6.3.5c)$$

In other words

$$\Pr\left[-t_{(T-K,\alpha/2)} \leq \frac{R_1\tilde{\boldsymbol{\beta}} - R_1\boldsymbol{\beta}}{\hat{\sigma}\sqrt{R_1(X'X)^{-1}R_1'}} \leq t_{(T-K,\alpha/2)}\right] = 1 - \alpha \qquad (6.3.6a)$$

or

$$\Pr[R_1\tilde{\boldsymbol{\beta}} - t_{(T-K,\alpha/2)}\hat{\sigma}\sqrt{R_1(X'X)^{-1}R_1'} \leq R_1\boldsymbol{\beta} \leq R_1\tilde{\boldsymbol{\beta}} + t_{(T-K,\alpha/2)}\hat{\sigma}\sqrt{R_1(X'X)^{-1}R_1'}] = 1 - \alpha \qquad (6.3.6b)$$

which means that if we compute interval estimates for $R_1\boldsymbol{\beta}$ over repeated samples,

$(1 - \alpha)100$ percent of the time the interval estimates will contain the true linear combination $R_1\boldsymbol{\beta}$.

If we think of R_1 as a row vector with all zero elements except one element that is of unit value, that is, $R_1 = [0 \quad 0 \ldots 1 \ldots 0]$, then we can define the ratios of (6.3.5) for a single coefficient and use the result to specify the interval estimate for a particular coefficient. Therefore, (6.3.5) becomes for the kth coefficient

$$\frac{\tilde{\beta}_k - \beta_k}{\hat{\sigma}\sqrt{a^{kk}}} = t_{(T-K)} \tag{6.3.7a}$$

where a^{kk} is the kth diagonal element of the $(X'X)^{-1}$ matrix. Consequently, for a particular coefficient the interval estimate is

$$\Pr[\tilde{\beta}_k - t_{(T-K,\alpha/2)}\hat{\sigma}\sqrt{a^{kk}} \le \beta_k \le \tilde{\beta}_k + t_{(T-K,\alpha/2)}\hat{\sigma}\sqrt{a^{kk}}] = 1 - \alpha \tag{6.3.7b}$$

Because the end points of the inequality are functions of observable random variables, the intervals are random. The probability statement concerns the proportion of the time, $(1 - \alpha)$, that the inequalities are satisfied.

To give an idea of the sampling variability of the random intervals, Table 6.3 gives interval estimates for β_1 and β_2 for the first 10 samples of data from the Monte Carlo experiment. In developing the interval estimates the statistical level of significance $\alpha = .05$ was used.

Note that in sample 3 the interval estimates do not contain the true coefficients. In all other cases the intervals contain the true parameters. For the 500 samples, as

Table 6.3 Point and Interval Estimates for β_1 and β_2 for 10 Samples of Data

Sample	$\beta_1 = 10.00$			$\beta_2 = 0.40$		
Number	Point	Interval		Point	Interval	
1	9.770	10.25	9.29	0.524	0.72	0.33
2	10.014	10.59	9.44	0.278	0.51	0.04
3	10.484	10.91	10.06	0.215	0.39	0.04
4	10.263	10.78	9.74	0.322	0.54	0.11
5	9.731	10.06	9.41	0.457	0.59	0.32
6	10.239	10.58	9.90	0.272	0.41	0.13
7	10.477	10.95	10.00	0.356	0.55	0.16
8	10.035	10.50	9.67	0.287	0.46	0.12
9	9.885	10.33	9.44	0.413	0.60	0.23
10	10.237	10.72	9.75	0.347	0.54	0.15

suggested by theory, β_1 was contained in 92% of the intervals, β_2 was contained in 95% of the intervals, and β_3 was contained in 95% of the intervals.

6.3.2 Two or More Linear Combinations of the $\boldsymbol{\beta}$ Vector

Given interval estimates for individual or linear combinations of parameters, let us turn to the question of joint or simultaneous interval estimates. This situation would occur in applied work if a joint confidence interval for the income and price coefficients in a demand relation or the labor and capital coefficients in a production function were desired. As an expository exercise, let us consider the problem of using maximum likelihood estimates to obtain simultaneous confidence intervals for the case of two linear combinations of the parameters.

Suppose we are concerned with the two linear combinations $R_1\boldsymbol{\beta}$ and $R_2\boldsymbol{\beta}$ where R_1 and R_2 are $(1 \times K)$ row vectors. These two linear combinations can be written in matrix algebra notation as $R\boldsymbol{\beta}$, where

$$R = \begin{bmatrix} R_1 \\ R_2 \end{bmatrix}$$

is a $(2 \times K)$ matrix. From results on the multivariate normal distribution in Section 2.5.7 we can say that

$$R\tilde{\boldsymbol{\beta}} \sim N[R\boldsymbol{\beta}, \sigma^2 R(X'X)^{-1}R'] \tag{6.3.8}$$

That is, $R\tilde{\boldsymbol{\beta}}$ is a two-dimensional normal random vector with mean $R\boldsymbol{\beta}$ and covariance matrix $\sigma^2 R(X'X)^{-1}R'$.

Furthermore, it follows from the result in Section 2.5.9, that

$$\begin{aligned}(R\tilde{\boldsymbol{\beta}} - R\boldsymbol{\beta})'[\sigma^2 R(X'X)^{-1}R']^{-1}(R\tilde{\boldsymbol{\beta}} - R\boldsymbol{\beta}) \\ = \frac{(\tilde{\boldsymbol{\beta}} - \boldsymbol{\beta})'R'[R(X'X)^{-1}R']^{-1}R(\tilde{\boldsymbol{\beta}} - \boldsymbol{\beta})}{\sigma^2} \sim \chi^2_{(2)}\end{aligned} \tag{6.3.9}$$

This result could be used to obtain a joint confidence region for the two linear combinations contained in $R\boldsymbol{\beta}$, if σ^2 were known. Given that σ^2 is unknown, we use a result on the ratio of independent χ^2 random variables to form an F random variable that does not depend on σ^2. From (6.1.18) we know that $(T - K)\hat{\sigma}^2/\sigma^2$ is distributed as a $\chi^2_{(T-K)}$ random variable. Also, using the result in Section 6.1.3c, $(T - K)\hat{\sigma}^2/\sigma^2$ and the $\chi^2_{(2)}$ random variable in (6.3.9) are independent. It is also possible to derive the result in (6.3.9) and to show independence, using other results on the distribution and independence of quadratic forms. You are encouraged to deepen your understanding in this regard by attempting Exercise 6.15.

Since an F random variable is defined as the ratio of two independent χ^2 random variables divided by their degrees of freedom, we can form the following random variable

$$\lambda = \frac{(\tilde{\boldsymbol{\beta}} - \boldsymbol{\beta})'R'[R(X'X)^{-1}R']^{-1}R(\tilde{\boldsymbol{\beta}} - \boldsymbol{\beta})/2\sigma^2}{\dfrac{(T-K)\hat{\sigma}^2}{\sigma^2}\Big/(T-K)}$$

$$= \frac{(\tilde{\boldsymbol{\beta}} - \boldsymbol{\beta})'R'[R(X'X)^{-1}R']^{-1}R(\tilde{\boldsymbol{\beta}} - \boldsymbol{\beta})}{2\hat{\sigma}^2} \tag{6.3.10}$$

which follows an $F_{(2, T-K)}$-distribution. Since λ does not contain σ^2, it can be used to construct a $(1 - \alpha)$ percent confidence region for the two linear combinations of $\boldsymbol{\beta}$ contained in $R\boldsymbol{\beta}$. Working in this direction we have

$$\Pr[\lambda \leq F_{(2, T-K, \alpha)}] = 1 - \alpha \tag{6.3.11a}$$

or

$$\Pr\left\{\frac{1}{2\hat{\sigma}^2}[(\tilde{\boldsymbol{\beta}} - \boldsymbol{\beta})'R_1'R_1(\tilde{\boldsymbol{\beta}} - \boldsymbol{\beta})a_1^{11} + 2(\tilde{\boldsymbol{\beta}} - \boldsymbol{\beta})'R_1'R_2(\tilde{\boldsymbol{\beta}} - \boldsymbol{\beta})a_1^{12} + (\tilde{\boldsymbol{\beta}} - \boldsymbol{\beta})'R_2'R_2(\tilde{\boldsymbol{\beta}} - \boldsymbol{\beta})a_1^{22}] \leq F_{(2, T-K)}\right\} = 1 - \alpha \tag{6.3.11b}$$

where a^{ij} are the elements of $[R(X'X)^{-1}R']^{-1}$. The probability statement (6.3.11b) denotes a joint confidence interval in the form of an ellipse with $R\tilde{\boldsymbol{\beta}}$ as its center.

If R_1 and R_2 are the unit vectors $R_1 = (1\ 0 \ldots 0)$ and $R_2 = (0\ 1\ 0 \ldots 0)$ and we are considering joint confidence intervals for two individual coefficients, for example, β_1 and β_2, then (6.3.11b) becomes

$$\Pr\left\{\frac{1}{2\hat{\sigma}^2}[(\tilde{\beta}_1 - \beta_1)^2 a_1^{11} + 2(\tilde{\beta}_1 - \beta_1)(\tilde{\beta}_2 - \beta_2)a_1^{12} + (\tilde{\beta}_2 - \beta_2)^2 a_1^{22}] \leq F_{(2, T-K, \alpha)}\right\} = 1 - \alpha \tag{6.3.11c}$$

which is an ellipse with $\tilde{\beta}_1$ and $\tilde{\beta}_2$ as its center. A picture of the simultaneous confidence interval for the special case (6.3.11c) is given in Figure 6.5. In this case, when the general statistical model applies and the variances for $\tilde{\beta}_1$ and $\tilde{\beta}_2$ are quite different, if the rectangular joint confidence region that comes from simultaneously

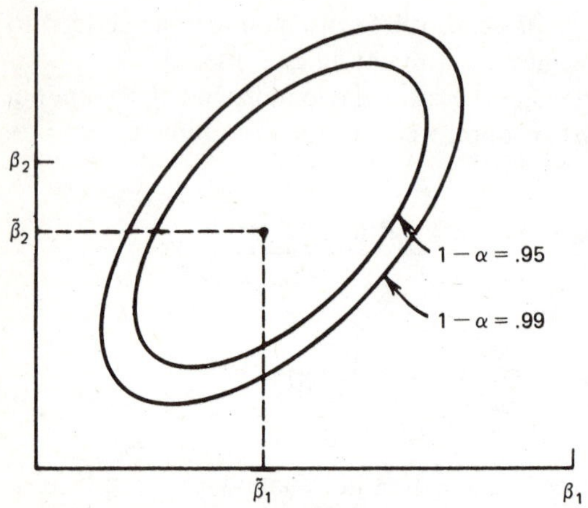

Figure 6.5 Joint confidence regions for β_1 and β_2.

using the individual confidence intervals was used, the difference in the inference between the rectangle (incorrect) and the ellipse (correct) could be quite striking.

6.3.2a An Example of Joint Confidence Intervals

To clarify the concept of simultaneous confidence intervals, let us use the results from the first sample of the Monte Carlo experiment discussed in Section 6.1.6 and develop joint confidence intervals for β_2 and β_3. Making use of (6.3.11c) and a level of significance of $\alpha = 0.05$, the expression (equation for the ellipse) for the joint confidence interval for β_2 and β_3 is

$$\frac{1}{0.159}[(0.52 - \beta_2)^2 9.1198 + 2(0.52 - \beta_2)(0.69 - \beta_3)0.5301$$
$$+ (0.69 - \beta_3)^2 4.0592] \leq 3.59 \qquad (6.3.11d)$$

A graph of the ellipse is given in Figure 6.6.

6.3.2b Joint Interval Estimation–Orthonormal Case

As a special case, consider the linear statistical model $y = Z\boldsymbol{\theta} + \mathbf{e}$, with the usual stochastic assumptions, where the design matrix Z is such that $Z'Z = I_K$. Consequently, the maximum likelihood estimator $\tilde{\boldsymbol{\theta}} \sim N(\boldsymbol{\theta}, \sigma^2 I_K)$.

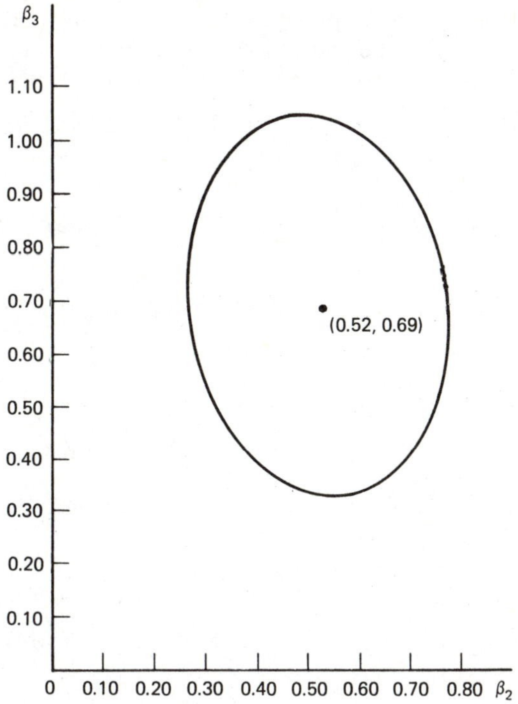

Figure 6.6 A graph of the simultaneous confidence interval for β_2 and β_3 for the first sample of the Monte Carlo experiment.

For this statistical model we know that $(\tilde{\theta}_1 - \theta_1)/\sigma$ and $(\tilde{\theta}_2 - \theta_2)/\sigma$ are independent standard normal random variables. Consequently, the random vector

$$\begin{bmatrix} \dfrac{\tilde{\theta}_1 - \theta_1}{\sigma} \\ \dfrac{\tilde{\theta}_2 - \theta_2}{\sigma} \end{bmatrix}$$

has a mean $\mathbf{0}$ vector and covariance $\sigma^2 I_2$. Therefore, the sum of squares

$$\begin{bmatrix} \dfrac{\tilde{\theta}_1 - \theta_1}{\sigma} \\ \dfrac{\tilde{\theta}_2 - \theta_2}{\sigma} \end{bmatrix}' \begin{bmatrix} \dfrac{\tilde{\theta}_1 - \theta_1}{\sigma} \\ \dfrac{\tilde{\theta}_2 - \theta_2}{\sigma} \end{bmatrix} = \left(\frac{\tilde{\theta}_1 - \theta_1}{\sigma}\right)^2 + \left(\frac{\tilde{\theta}_2 - \theta_2}{\sigma}\right)^2 \tag{6.3.12}$$

is distributed as a $\chi^2_{(2)}$ random variable. From the previous section we know that $(T - K)\hat{\sigma}^2/\sigma^2$ is distributed as a $\chi^2_{(T-K)}$ and that $\tilde{\boldsymbol{\theta}}$ and $\hat{\sigma}^2$ are independent random variables. If we define a new random variable that is a ratio of these two independent χ^2 random variables and divide each χ^2 random variable by its respective degrees of freedom, then the ratio

$$\frac{\dfrac{\dfrac{[\tilde{\theta}_1 - \theta_1, \tilde{\theta}_2 - \theta_2]I_2\begin{bmatrix}\tilde{\theta}_1 - \theta_1 \\ \tilde{\theta}_2 - \theta_2\end{bmatrix}}{\sigma^2}}{2}}{\dfrac{\dfrac{(T-K)\hat{\sigma}^2}{\sigma^2}}{(T-K)}} = \frac{(\tilde{\theta}_1 - \theta_1)^2 + (\tilde{\theta}_2 - \theta_2)^2}{2\hat{\sigma}^2} = F_{(2, T-K)} \tag{6.3.13}$$

is distributed as an F random variable with 2 and $(T - K)$ degrees of freedom, and noted by $F_{(2,T-K)}$.

Consequently, we may write the joint confidence region for θ_1 and θ_2 as

$$\Pr\left[\left\{\frac{1}{2\hat{\sigma}^2}((\tilde{\theta}_1 - \theta_1)^2 + (\tilde{\theta}_2 - \theta_2)^2)\right\} \leq F_{(2, T-K, \alpha)}\right] = 1 - \alpha \tag{6.3.14}$$

where

$$\int_0^{F(\cdot, \alpha)} f(F)\, dF = 1 - \alpha$$

and $f(F)$ is the density function for the F random variable.

In this case, where $\tilde{\theta}_1$ and $\tilde{\theta}_2$ are independent, the joint confidence expression for a given α level defines a circle with $(\tilde{\theta}_1, \tilde{\theta}_2)$ as the center. The estimated joint confidence interval from a particular sample of data might then appear as in Figure 6.7.

We should note at this point that individual confidence intervals for either β_1 or β_2 specify a range for either parameter that does not consider the value of the other parameter. It might be tempting to try to interpret these individual confidence intervals simultaneously. Then the rectangular region *abcd* in Figure 6.8 might be thought to define the joint confidence region.

The correct confidence region, which is a circle, is clearly different from that which results by using the individual intervals simultaneously. In the orthonormal case, where the variances of $\tilde{\theta}_1$ and $\tilde{\theta}_2$ are equal, the rectangular region approximates the correct joint confidence intervals. As we saw in the previous subsection, in the general (nonorthonormal) case where $\tilde{\beta}_1$ and $\tilde{\beta}_2$ have variances that are

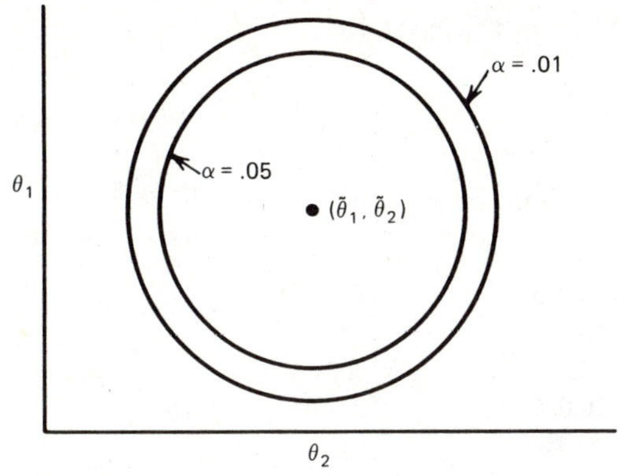

Figure 6.7 Joint confidence regions, orthonormal case.

different in size and are not independent, the joint confidence region becomes an ellipse, and the rectangular confidence region may badly miss the mark.

6.3.3 Interval Estimation of σ^2

Having developed individual and joint interval estimates for the parameters contained in the $\boldsymbol{\beta}$ vector, let us now turn to the other unknown parameter σ^2. We already know that the random variable $(T - K)\hat{\sigma}^2/\sigma^2$ is distributed as a χ^2 random variable with $(T - K)$ degrees of freedom. Therefore, given the lower and upper critical $\chi^2_{(\cdot)}$ values $c_1 = \chi^2_{(T-K, \alpha/2)}$ and $c_2 = \chi^2_{(T-K, 1-\alpha/2)}$, where α is the level of significance and

$$\int_{c_1}^{c_2} f(\chi^2_{(\cdot)})\, d\chi^2_{(\cdot)} = 1 - \alpha$$

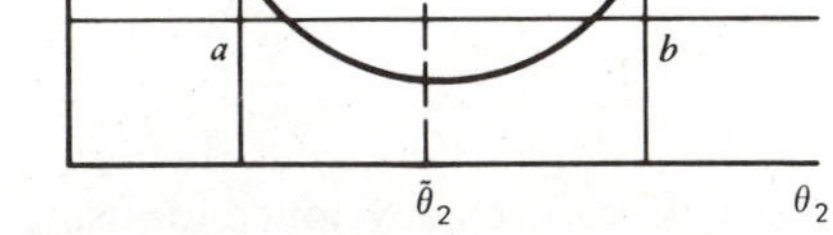

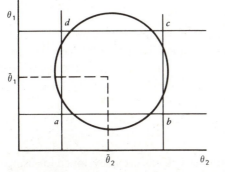

Figure 6.8 Correct and incorrect joint confidence regions.

Table 6.4 Interval Estimates for σ^2 from the First 10 Monte Carlo Samples, $\alpha = 0.05$, $T - K = 17$, $\chi^2_{(17, 0.025)} = 7.56$, and $\chi^2_{(17, 0.975)} = 30.19$

Sample Number	Point Estimate	Interval Estimate	
1	0.07953	0.04478	0.17874
2	0.1138	0.0641	0.2558
3	0.0609	0.0343	0.1369
4	0.0929	0.0523	0.2087
5	0.0363	0.0205	0.0817
6	0.0390	0.0220	0.0877
7	0.0768	0.0433	0.1726
8	0.0588	0.0331	0.1320
9	0.0680	0.0383	0.1529
10	0.07951	0.04477	0.17869

where $f(\chi^2)$ is the density function, we can make the statement

$$\Pr[\chi^2_{(T-K, \alpha/2)} \leq \chi^2_{(T-K)} \leq \chi^2_{(T-K, 1-\alpha/2)}] = 1 - \alpha \tag{6.3.15}$$

or

$$\Pr\left[c_1 \leq \frac{(T-K)\hat{\sigma}^2}{\sigma^2} \leq c_2\right] = 1 - \alpha$$

This implies that

$$\Pr\left[\frac{(T-K)\hat{\sigma}^2}{\chi^2_{(T-K, 1-\alpha/2)}} \leq \sigma^2 \leq \frac{(T-K)\hat{\sigma}^2}{\chi^2_{(T-K, \alpha/2)}}\right] = 1 - \alpha$$

which is the usual repeated sample basis for inference, since the end points within the brackets are random variables and will vary from sample to sample. Using Equation (6.3.15) and $\alpha = 0.05$, the interval estimates for σ^2 are given in Table 6.4 for the first ten samples of the Monte Carlo experiment. All intervals except that for the second sample contain the parameter value $\sigma^2 = 0.0625$. For the complete experiment, 96 percent of the 500 intervals contained the true parameter.

6.3.4 Prediction Interval Estimator

In the previous sections of this chapter the framework has been developed for using $\mathbf{x}_0'\tilde{\boldsymbol{\beta}}$ as a basis for predicting the average outcome for $\mathbf{x}_0'\boldsymbol{\beta}$, from a particular level of the treatment variables $\mathbf{x}_0'$. Unfortunately, from a prediction standpoint or for decision purposes what is desired is not the mean outcome for $\mathbf{x}_0$, but rather the outcome for y_0 from a *single or particular* $\mathbf{x}_0$. If within the context of our linear statistical model we view this outcome for y_0 as a random variable, then it might be useful to be able to determine in advance an interval for the random outcome y_0.

Since the random variable $y_0 \sim N(\mathbf{x}_0'\boldsymbol{\beta}, \sigma^2)$, if we had the good fortune of knowing $\boldsymbol{\beta}$ and σ^2, it would be possible to develop an interval that would contain y_0 with probability $(1-\alpha)$. However, since $\boldsymbol{\beta}$ and σ^2 are unknown, we must consider how to construct an interval of the form noted in Section 6.3.1. If we replace the unknown parameters by point estimates derived earlier in this chapter, then, in contrast to interval estimation for unknown parameters such as β_k or σ^2, this problem is concerned with using the predictor $\hat{y}_0 = \mathbf{x}_0'\tilde{\boldsymbol{\beta}}$ to construct a prediction interval for the random variable $y_0 = \mathbf{x}_0'\boldsymbol{\beta} + e_0$. Such an interval will predict with probability $(1-\alpha)$ in the sense that, after repeated sampling from the joint distribution for $(\mathbf{y}' \quad y_0)'$, $(1-\alpha)$ percent of the confidence intervals would contain the realized y_0's.

In developing the prediction interval we are concerned with the prediction error

$$\hat{y}_0 - y_0 = \mathbf{x}_0'\tilde{\boldsymbol{\beta}} - \mathbf{x}_0'\boldsymbol{\beta} - e_0 = \mathbf{x}_0'(\tilde{\boldsymbol{\beta}} - \boldsymbol{\beta}) - e_0 \tag{6.3.16}$$

which involves the equation error e_0 and the estimation error $\tilde{\boldsymbol{\beta}} - \boldsymbol{\beta}$. This normal random variable has a mean

$$E[\mathbf{x}_0'(\tilde{\boldsymbol{\beta}} - \boldsymbol{\beta}) - e_0] = 0 \tag{6.3.17}$$

and a variance

$$\begin{aligned} E\{[\mathbf{x}_0'(\tilde{\boldsymbol{\beta}} - \boldsymbol{\beta}) - e_0]^2\} &= E[\mathbf{x}_0'(\tilde{\boldsymbol{\beta}} - \boldsymbol{\beta})(\tilde{\boldsymbol{\beta}} - \boldsymbol{\beta})'\mathbf{x}_0 - 2\mathbf{x}_0'(\tilde{\boldsymbol{\beta}} - \boldsymbol{\beta})e_0 + e_0^2] \\ &= E[\mathbf{x}_0'(\tilde{\boldsymbol{\beta}} - \boldsymbol{\beta})(\tilde{\boldsymbol{\beta}} - \boldsymbol{\beta})'\mathbf{x}_0] - 2E[\mathbf{x}_0'(\tilde{\boldsymbol{\beta}} - \boldsymbol{\beta})e_0] + E[e_0^2] \\ &= \sigma^2\mathbf{x}_0'(X'X)^{-1}\mathbf{x}_0 + \sigma^2 \\ &= \sigma^2[\mathbf{x}_0'(X'X)^{-1}\mathbf{x}_0 + 1] \end{aligned} \tag{6.3.18}$$

where we have used the fact that $\tilde{\boldsymbol{\beta}}$ and e_0 are independent and thus

$$E[\mathbf{x}_0'(\tilde{\boldsymbol{\beta}} - \boldsymbol{\beta})e_0] = E[\mathbf{x}_0'(\tilde{\boldsymbol{\beta}} - \boldsymbol{\beta})]E[e_0] = 0$$

Consequently, the random variable

$$\frac{\mathbf{x}_0'\tilde{\boldsymbol{\beta}} - y_0}{\sigma\sqrt{(\mathbf{x}_0'(X'X)^{-1}\mathbf{x}_0 + 1)}} \tag{6.3.19}$$

is distributed as a standard normal random variable with a mean of 0 and a variance of 1. This means that the random variable

$$\frac{\dfrac{\mathbf{x}_0'\tilde{\boldsymbol{\beta}} - y_0}{\sigma\sqrt{(\mathbf{x}_0'(X'X)^{-1}\mathbf{x}_0 + 1)}}}{\sqrt{\dfrac{(T-K)\hat{\sigma}^2/\sigma^2}{T-K}}} = \frac{\mathbf{x}_0'\tilde{\boldsymbol{\beta}} - y_0}{\hat{\sigma}\sqrt{(\mathbf{x}_0'(X'X)^{-1}\mathbf{x}_0 + 1)}} \tag{6.3.20}$$

is distributed as a t random variable with $(T - K)$ degrees of freedom. As before, we may write

$$\Pr[-t_{(T-K,\alpha/2)} \le t_{(T-K)} \le t_{(T-K,\alpha/2)}] = 1 - \alpha$$

or

$$\Pr\left[-t_{(T-K,\alpha/2)} \le \frac{\mathbf{x}_0'\tilde{\boldsymbol{\beta}} - y_0}{\hat{\sigma}\sqrt{(\mathbf{x}_0'(X'X)^{-1}\mathbf{x}_0 + 1)}} \le t_{(T-K,\alpha/2)}\right] = 1 - \alpha$$

which can be rewritten as

$$\begin{aligned}\Pr[\mathbf{x}_0'\tilde{\boldsymbol{\beta}} - t_{(T-K,\alpha/2)}\hat{\sigma}\sqrt{(\mathbf{x}_0'(X'X)^{-1}\mathbf{x}_0 + 1)}\\ \le y_0 \le \mathbf{x}_0'\tilde{\boldsymbol{\beta}} + t_{(T-K,\alpha/2)}\hat{\sigma}\sqrt{(\mathbf{x}_0'(X'X)^{-1}\mathbf{x}_0 + 1)}] = 1 - \alpha\end{aligned} \tag{6.3.21}$$

We remark again that this interval is similar to the previously discussed confidence intervals involving a known parameter where only the limits are random. The difference here is that we are concerned with the unknown value of a random variable, and everything on the right side of (6.3.20) is random. In terms of interpretation, the prediction interval (6.3.21) predicts with probability $(1 - \alpha)$ that the value of the random variable is contained within it.

For the first sample from the Monte Carlo experiment, if we choose $\alpha = 0.05$, $\mathbf{x}_0 = [1 \quad 1 \quad 1]'$, the prediction interval may be written as

$$10.98 - (2.11)(0.28)\sqrt{0.097 + 1.0} \le y_0 \le 10.98 + (2.11)(0.28)\sqrt{0.097 + 1.0}$$

$$10.98 - 0.6188 \le y_0 \le 10.98 + 0.6188$$

$$10.36 \le y_0 \le 11.61.$$

6.4 Hypothesis Testing

Interval estimation or confidence intervals is a major problem in making statistical inferences from the data. Another problem area, related to the evaluation of confidence intervals, is that of hypothesis testing. Many decision problems require a basis for deciding whether or not a parameter or parameter vector is in a specified subspace ω of the parameter space Ω. For example, in developing the maximum likelihood point estimates for $\boldsymbol{\beta}$ and σ^2, we were concerned with the parameter space

$$\Omega = \{\boldsymbol{\beta}, \sigma^2; \boldsymbol{\beta} \in E_K, \sigma^2 > 0\} \tag{6.4.1}$$

where E_K is the K-dimensional Euclidean space, involving the space of K-dimensional vectors. Consequently, the elements of $\boldsymbol{\beta}$ are unrestricted and σ^2 is restricted to be positive.

Alternatively, we may have the conjecture or general linear hypothesis that the parameters of the $\boldsymbol{\beta}$ vector are contained in the subspace for which $R\boldsymbol{\beta} = \mathbf{r}$, where R is a $(J \times K)$ known hypothesis design matrix of rank $J \leq K$ and $\mathbf{r}$ is a $(J \times 1)$ known vector. R has the same characteristics as the matrix used in forming the system of linear restrictions in Section 6.2. In the context of traditional hypothesis testing, $H_0: R\boldsymbol{\beta} = \mathbf{r}$ is the null hypothesis. For example, in the two-dimensional space, if the hypothesis is $\beta_1 = \beta_2$, or $\beta_1 - \beta_2 = 0$, then in general notation,

$$R\boldsymbol{\beta} = \mathbf{r} \qquad \text{or} \qquad (1 \quad -1)\begin{pmatrix} \beta_1 \\ \beta_2 \end{pmatrix} = 0 \tag{6.4.2}$$

In the two-dimensional space this linear hypothesis may be depicted as

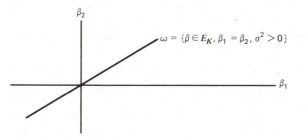

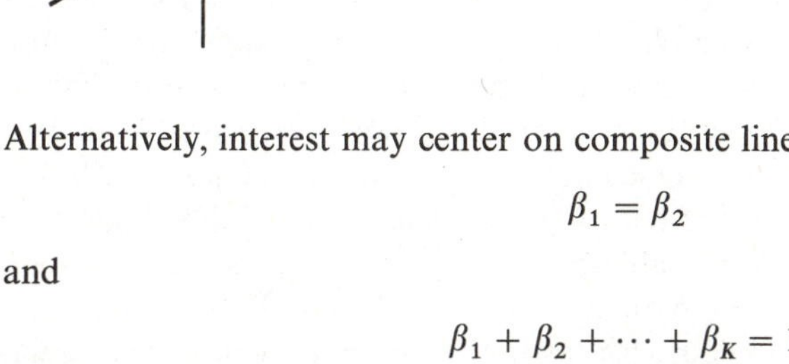

Alternatively, interest may center on composite linear hypotheses such as

$$\beta_1 = \beta_2$$

and

$$\beta_1 + \beta_2 + \cdots + \beta_K = 1$$

Within our framework for expressing the linear hypotheses $R\boldsymbol{\beta} = \mathbf{r}$ this can be written as

$$R\boldsymbol{\beta} = \begin{bmatrix} 1 & -1 & 0 & \cdots & 0 \\ 1 & 1 & 1 & \cdots & 1 \end{bmatrix} \boldsymbol{\beta} = \begin{bmatrix} 0 \\ 1 \end{bmatrix}$$

Another example might be the hypotheses

$$\beta_1 - 3\beta_3 = 6\beta_4$$

$$\frac{\beta_1}{\beta_2} = 4$$

The hypotheses may be expressed in our general linear framework as

$$\begin{bmatrix} 1 & 0 & -3 & -6 & 0 & \cdots & 0 \\ 1 & -4 & 0 & 0 & 0 & \cdots & 0 \end{bmatrix} \boldsymbol{\beta} = \begin{bmatrix} 0 \\ 0 \end{bmatrix}$$

One general linear hypothesis that is often used is the case where $R\boldsymbol{\beta} = I_K\boldsymbol{\beta} = \mathbf{r} = \boldsymbol{\beta}_0$. Under this specification, the K-dimensional parameter vector $\boldsymbol{\beta}$ is hypothesized to be equal to a known K-dimensional vector $\boldsymbol{\beta}_0$. In this case, the null hypothesis is $H_0:\boldsymbol{\beta} = \boldsymbol{\beta}_0$ and the alternative hypothesis is $H_1:\boldsymbol{\beta} \neq \boldsymbol{\beta}_0$.

Given the alternative representations of the parameter space, what is needed is a basis for testing whether the data are consistent with H_0 and a decision rule to use in determining whether to accept or reject H_0. Thus we need a test statistic and a basis for partitioning the sample space into acceptance and rejection regions. In developing a mechanism of this form two types of errors are possible. We can get a sample value of the test statistic that lies in the rejection region and reject H_0 when in fact it is true—a Type I error. Alternatively, we can get a value of the test statistic that falls in the acceptance region and accept H_0 when it is false—a Type II error.

Given this scenario, it usually is not possible to choose acceptance and rejection regions for a given sample size T to minimize both errors. Usually, a maximum acceptable Type I error α is chosen and then the critical rejection region that minimizes the probability of a Type II error is found.

One way of approaching the problem of finding a suitable test is to find a test statistic that has a known distribution when the null hypothesis $R\boldsymbol{\beta} = \mathbf{r}$ is true, and which has another distribution when H_0 is not true. Knowledge of the distribution of the statistic under H_0 permits the setting of acceptance and rejection regions such that the probability of a Type I error is fixed at some prespecified level. It is also desirable for tests that are constructed in this way to have high power. That is, it is desirable that the probability of rejecting H_0 when H_0 is false be high. One method for obtaining tests with desirable power characteristics is the likelihood ratio principle that was introduced in Section 3.5.3 of Chapter 3.

Our presentation of a test procedure for testing $H_0:R\boldsymbol{\beta} = \mathbf{r}$ against the alternative $H_1:R\boldsymbol{\beta} \neq \mathbf{r}$ will proceed as follows: We begin by suggesting a statistic that has a known distribution under H_0. Then, we outline how this same statistic can be obtained using the likelihood ratio principle, thus proving that it has desirable power characteristics. In the process of viewing the test statistic as a likelihood ratio test statistic we will discover that it has two additional representations that provide meaningful and useful interpretations.

To suggest a statistic that has a known distribution under H_0 we follow the same line of reasoning as was used to establish a joint confidence region for two linear combinations of the elements in $\boldsymbol{\beta}$ (see Section 6.3.2). Let us reiterate that argument for the more general case of a matrix R that is of dimension $(J \times K)$ rather than $(2 \times K)$. We have

$$R\tilde{\boldsymbol{\beta}} \sim N[R\boldsymbol{\beta}, \sigma^2 R(X'X)^{-1}R'] \tag{6.4.3}$$

Then, from Section 2.5.9,

$$Q_1 = \frac{(R\tilde{\boldsymbol{\beta}} - R\boldsymbol{\beta})'[R(X'X)^{-1}R']^{-1}(R\tilde{\boldsymbol{\beta}} - R\boldsymbol{\beta})}{\sigma^2} \sim \chi^2_{(J)} \tag{6.4.4}$$

To eliminate the unknown σ^2 we use the facts that

$$Q_2 = \frac{(T - K)\hat{\sigma}^2}{\sigma^2} \sim \chi^2_{(T-K)} \tag{6.4.5}$$

and that the expressions in (6.4.4) and (6.4.5) are independent. The ratio of Q_1 to Q_2, each divided by its degrees of freedom, forms an F-statistic. That is,

$$\begin{aligned}\lambda_1 &= \frac{Q_1/J}{Q_2/(T-K)} \\ &= \frac{(R\tilde{\boldsymbol{\beta}} - R\boldsymbol{\beta})'[R(X'X)^{-1}R']^{-1}(R\tilde{\boldsymbol{\beta}} - R\boldsymbol{\beta})}{J\hat{\sigma}^2} \sim F_{(J,\,T-K)}\end{aligned} \tag{6.4.6}$$

Now, when $H_0\colon R\boldsymbol{\beta} = \mathbf{r}$ is true, λ_1 becomes

$$\lambda = \frac{(R\tilde{\boldsymbol{\beta}} - \mathbf{r})'[R(X'X)^{-1}R']^{-1}(R\tilde{\boldsymbol{\beta}} - \mathbf{r})}{J\hat{\sigma}^2} \sim F_{(J,\,T-K)} \tag{6.4.7}$$

This expression does not depend on any unknown parameters and has a known distribution when H_0 is true. It thus can be used as a test statistic, where we reject H_0 when λ is greater than the appropriate critical value taken from tabulated values of the F-distribution with J and $(T - K)$ degrees of freedom. Note that $R\tilde{\boldsymbol{\beta}}$ can be regarded as the unrestricted estimator for $R\boldsymbol{\beta}$, and that, other things being equal, the further the unrestricted estimator $R\tilde{\boldsymbol{\beta}}$ is from the set of restricted values $\mathbf{r}$, the greater λ is likely to be, and the more likely it is that H_0 will be rejected.

We will now show that λ can be viewed as a likelihood ratio test statistic, and therefore, that it has some intuitive appeal and some desirable power characteristics.

6.4.1 The Likelihood Ratio Test Statistic

The likelihood ratio test statistic reflects the compatibility between a sample of data and the null hypothesis through a comparison of constrained and unconstrained likelihood functions. If we represent the general linear hypothesis about the unknown parameters as $R\boldsymbol{\beta} = \mathbf{r}$, where R is a $(J \times K)$ known hypothesis design matrix and $\mathbf{r}$ is $(J \times 1)$, the likelihood ratio is

$$\frac{\max \ell(\boldsymbol{\beta}, \sigma^2 | \mathbf{y}, X)}{\max \ell(\boldsymbol{\beta}, \sigma^2 | \mathbf{y}, X, R\boldsymbol{\beta} = \mathbf{r})} = \frac{\hat{\ell}(\Omega)}{\hat{\ell}(\omega)} = \lambda_0 \tag{6.4.8}$$

The numerator of (6.4.8) is the maximum of the unconstrained likelihood function, and the denominator is the maximum of the constrained likelihood function. If both likelihoods are maximized, one constrained and the other unconstrained, the value of the unconstrained will not be smaller than the value of the constrained, and hence the ratio $\lambda_0 \geq 1$. To see that this is a plausible test statistic, recall that we think of the likelihood function $\ell(\cdot)$ as a measure of how well $\boldsymbol{\beta}$ explains the given sample information $\mathbf{y}$. So if $\hat{\ell}(\Omega)$ is large compared to $\hat{\ell}(\omega)$, then the observed sample is best explained by some $\boldsymbol{\beta}$ in Ω and conversely. The critical question, and one that depends on the probability distribution of λ_0, is by how much should λ_0 exceed unity before some doubt is cast on the validity of the null hypothesis. You should note that in Chapter 3 $1/\lambda_0$ was referred to as the likelihood ratio, and H_0 was rejected if $1/\lambda_0$ was less than some critical value. In this section, because the inverse of the earlier statistic is employed, we reject H_0 when λ_0 is greater than some critical value. In this book we frequently use test statistics that reject H_0 for large values.

Returning to the likelihood ratio (6.4.8), $\ell(\boldsymbol{\beta}, \sigma^2 | \mathbf{y}, X)$ attains its maximum when $\boldsymbol{\beta} = \tilde{\boldsymbol{\beta}} = \mathbf{b}$, the unrestricted maximum likelihood estimator. Alternatively, $\ell(\boldsymbol{\beta}, \sigma^2 | \mathbf{y}, X, R\boldsymbol{\beta} = \mathbf{r})$ attains its maximum when $\boldsymbol{\beta} = \mathbf{b}^*$, the restricted maximum likelihood estimator that is consistent with the general linear hypothesis $R\boldsymbol{\beta} = \mathbf{r}$. Maximizing the likelihood functions results in finding estimators $\mathbf{b}$ and $\mathbf{b}^*$ that minimize the respective error sums of squares. After some algebra it is possible to show that rejecting H_0 when λ_0 is greater than a constant is equivalent to rejecting H_0 when

$$\lambda_0^* = \frac{(\mathbf{y} - X\mathbf{b}^*)'(\mathbf{y} - X\mathbf{b}^*)}{(\mathbf{y} - X\mathbf{b})'(\mathbf{y} - X\mathbf{b})} = \frac{\text{SSE}_\text{R}}{\text{SSE}_\text{U}} \tag{6.4.9}$$

is greater than a constant. Thus, questions concerning the compatibility of the data with the null hypothesis can be framed in terms of the compatibility of the unconstrained and constrained least squares estimators ($\mathbf{b}$ and $\mathbf{b}^*$), and their respective error sums of squares (SSE_U and SSE_R).

As it stands, the statistic λ_0^* is not very helpful because its distribution is not readily recognizable. However, we can apply a simple transformation to obtain a slightly modified statistic with a known distribution. This statistic is

$$\lambda = \frac{(\lambda_0^* - 1)(T - K)}{J}$$

$$= \frac{[(\mathbf{y} - X\mathbf{b}^*)'(\mathbf{y} - X\mathbf{b}^*) - (\mathbf{y} - X\mathbf{b})'(\mathbf{y} - X\mathbf{b})]/J}{(\mathbf{y} - X\mathbf{b})'(\mathbf{y} - X\mathbf{b})/(T - K)}$$

$$= \frac{\text{SSE}_\text{R} - \text{SSE}_\text{U}}{J\hat{\sigma}^2} \tag{6.4.10}$$

It can be shown that this statistic is identical to λ given in (6.4.7), and hence that it follows an F-distribution with $(J, T - K)$ degrees of freedom. Clearly, rejecting H_0 when λ_0^* is greater than some constant is equivalent to rejecting H_0 when λ is greater than another appropriately chosen constant. The interpretation that is placed on (6.4.10) is that when the constrained error sum of squares (SSE_R) is significantly greater than the unconstrained error sum of squares (SSE_U), there is some doubt about the validity of the constraints so they (the null hypothesis) are rejected.

If we choose a level of significance α to define the rejection region, and thus the critical value of $F_{(J, T-K, \alpha)}$, our rejection or acceptance decision hinges on whether the sample value of $F_{(J, T-K)}$ falls above (reject) or below (accept) the tabled critical value of F. For example, the rejection decision follows this line of reasoning: If $R\boldsymbol{\beta} = \mathbf{r}$ and λ follows an F-distribution, the sample F value that exceeds the relevant critical value of F would happen by chance, in a repeated sampling sense, α percent of the time. This signals that the probability of getting this F value, which is larger than the critical value, is quite small, and we therefore have grounds for rejecting the hypothesis. The acceptance decision follows if just the reverse is true. This means that we reject the hypothesis H_0: $R\boldsymbol{\beta} = \mathbf{r}$ if and only if $\lambda \geq F_{(J, T-K, \alpha)}$, where $F_{(J, T-K, \alpha)}$ is the upper (critical) probability for the central F random variable with J and $(T - K)$ degrees of freedom.

The remaining task is to prove the equivalence of the two expressions for λ given in (6.4.7) and (6.4.10). We will also derive a third expression that is intuitively appealing. Note that the denominators in the two expressions are identical, so our task is to prove that

$$\text{SSE}_\text{R} - \text{SSE}_\text{U} = \hat{\mathbf{e}}^{*\prime}\hat{\mathbf{e}}^* - \hat{\mathbf{e}}'\hat{\mathbf{e}} = (R\mathbf{b} - \mathbf{r})'[R(X'X)^{-1}R']^{-1}(R\mathbf{b} - \mathbf{r}) \tag{6.4.11}$$

where $\hat{\mathbf{e}} = \mathbf{y} - X\mathbf{b}$ is the vector of unconstrained least squares residuals and $\hat{\mathbf{e}}^* = \mathbf{y} - X\mathbf{b}^*$ is the vector of constrained least squares residuals. We have

$$\hat{\mathbf{e}}^* = \mathbf{y} - X\mathbf{b}^*$$

$$= \mathbf{y} - X[\mathbf{b} + (X'X)^{-1}R'[R(X'X)^{-1}R']^{-1}(\mathbf{r} - R\mathbf{b})]$$

$$= \hat{\mathbf{e}} - X(X'X)^{-1}R'[R(X'X)^{-1}R']^{-1}(\mathbf{r} - R\mathbf{b}) \tag{6.4.12}$$

Thus,

$$\begin{aligned}
\hat{\mathbf{e}}^{*\prime}\hat{\mathbf{e}}^{*} &= \hat{\mathbf{e}}'\hat{\mathbf{e}} + (\mathbf{r} - R\mathbf{b})'[R(X'X)^{-1}R']^{-1}R(X'X)^{-1}X'X \\
&\quad \times (X'X)^{-1}R'[R(X'X)^{-1}R']^{-1}(\mathbf{r} - R\mathbf{b}) \\
&\quad - \hat{\mathbf{e}}'X(X'X)^{-1}R'[R(X'X)^{-1}R']^{-1}(\mathbf{r} - R\mathbf{b}) \\
&\quad - (\mathbf{r} - R\mathbf{b})'[R(X'X)^{-1}R']^{-1}R(X'X)^{-1}X'\hat{\mathbf{e}} \\
&= \hat{\mathbf{e}}'\hat{\mathbf{e}} + (R\mathbf{b} - \mathbf{r})'[R(X'X)^{-1}R']^{-1}(R\mathbf{b} - \mathbf{r}) \qquad (6.4.13)
\end{aligned}$$

because $X'\hat{\mathbf{e}} = \mathbf{0}$. Moving $\hat{\mathbf{e}}'\hat{\mathbf{e}}$ to the left side of (6.4.13) proves the result.

To derive the third useful expression for the test statistic λ we begin with the constrained least squares estimator

$$\mathbf{b}^* = \mathbf{b} + (X'X)^{-1}R'[R(X'X)^{-1}R']^{-1}(\mathbf{r} - R\mathbf{b}) \qquad (6.4.14)$$

from which it follows that

$$X(\mathbf{b}^* - \mathbf{b}) = X(X'X)^{-1}R'[R(X'X)^{-1}R']^{-1}(\mathbf{r} - R\mathbf{b}) \qquad (6.4.15)$$

If both sides of (6.4.15) are multiplied by their respective transposes, we have

$$(\mathbf{b}^* - \mathbf{b})'X'X(\mathbf{b}^* - \mathbf{b}) = (\mathbf{r} - R\mathbf{b})'[R(X'X)^{-1}R']^{-1}(\mathbf{r} - R\mathbf{b}) \qquad (6.4.16)$$

The right side of this expression is the numerator for λ given in (6.4.7). Thus, the third expression for λ is

$$\lambda = \frac{(\mathbf{b}^* - \mathbf{b})'X'X(\mathbf{b}^* - \mathbf{b})}{J\hat{\sigma}^2} \qquad (6.4.17)$$

This expression is an appealing one because it shows that the greater the divergence between the unconstrained and constrained estimators ($\mathbf{b}$ and $\mathbf{b}^*$), the more likely it is that the null hypothesis will be rejected.

Finally, we note that the special case $R\boldsymbol{\beta} = I_K\boldsymbol{\beta} = \mathbf{r}$ is used in many textbooks and computer programs. In other words, each element of the K dimensional vector $\boldsymbol{\beta}$ is hypothesized to be equal to a known constant that is often 0. Therefore, the null hypothesis is $H_0\colon \boldsymbol{\beta} = \mathbf{r}$ and the alternative is $H_1\colon \boldsymbol{\beta} \neq \mathbf{r}$. This formulation leads, using the foregoing procedures, to the test statistic

$$\lambda = \frac{(\mathbf{b} - \mathbf{r})'X'X(\mathbf{b} - \mathbf{r})}{K\hat{\sigma}^2} \qquad (6.4.18)$$

which is distributed as a F random variable with K and $(T - K)$ degrees of freedom. The likelihood ratio test statistic for this case is discussed in great detail in the first edition of this book (Judge, et al. 1982, pp. 190–193).

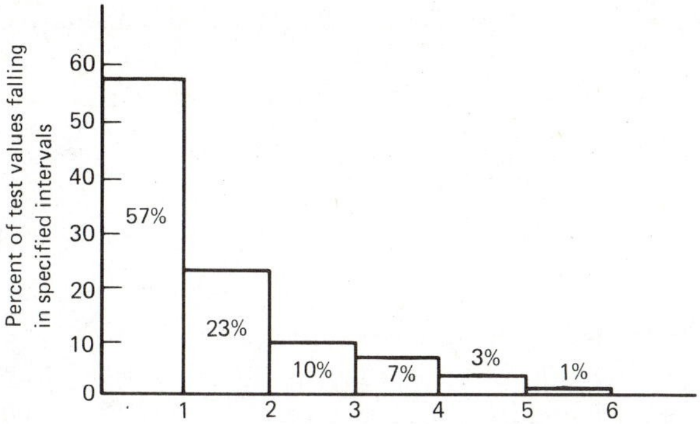

Figure 6.9 Empirical distribution of Monte Carlo sample test values.

6.4.1a Empirical Test Results

To give an idea of the variability of the sample $F_{(\cdot)}$ values we use the first 10 samples of the Monte Carlo experiment discussed in Section 6.1.5. In developing the test statistic the hypotheses that $\beta_2 = 0.40$ and $\beta_3 = 0.60$ were used. Since the hypotheses were true the resulting test values should be distributed as an F random variable with 2 and 17 degrees of freedom (see 6.4.7). For $\alpha = 0.05$ the critical $F_{(2,17)}$ value is 3.59. The values of the test statistic for the first 11 Monte Carlo samples are 1.17, 1.02, 3.10, 0.46, 1.15, 2.01, 2.04, 0.98, 0.33, 0.44, and 4.39. Out of this group of test values only one exceeds the critical F value. For the 500 samples 94% of the values of the test statistic were equal to or less than $F_{(2,17,\alpha=0.05)} = 3.59$.

The empirical distribution of the values of the test statistics for the 500 samples is given in Figure 6.9.

6.4.2 A Single Hypothesis

In many cases we are interested in testing a single hypothesis involving a particular coefficient or some linear combination of the coefficients. For example, we might have the hypothesis $\beta_1 = r_1$ or $\beta_1 + \beta_2 + \cdots + \beta_K = r_1$, where r_1 is any scalar, including 0. Within the general linear hypothesis framework under discussion these single hypotheses could be represented as

$$R_1\boldsymbol{\beta} = [1 \quad 0 \quad 0 \quad \cdots \quad 0]\boldsymbol{\beta} = \mathbf{r}_1 \tag{6.4.19}$$

and

$$R_1\boldsymbol{\beta} = [1 \quad 1 \quad \cdots \quad 1]\boldsymbol{\beta} = r_1 \tag{6.4.20}$$

where $\mathbf{R}_1$ is a row vector of dimension K. In this case the hypothesis design matrix R becomes a vector, and the test statistic (6.4.7) or (6.4.10) becomes, since $J = 1$,

$$\begin{aligned}\lambda &= \frac{(\mathbf{R}_1\mathbf{b} - r_1)[R_1(X'X)^{-1}R_1']^{-1}(\mathbf{R}_1\mathbf{b} - r_1)}{\hat{\sigma}^2} \sim F_{(1,\,T-K)} \\ &= \frac{(R_1\mathbf{b} - r_1)^2}{\hat{\sigma}^2[R_1(X'X)^{-1}\mathbf{R}_1']} \sim F_{(1,\,T-K)}\end{aligned} \tag{6.4.21}$$

where $\hat{\sigma}^2[R_1(X'X)^{-1}R_1']$ is a scalar and is an estimate of the variance of $R_1\mathbf{b} - r_1$. Consequently, we reject the single hypothesis if $\lambda \geq F_{(1,\,T-K,\alpha)}$. In the special case of the linear hypothesis (6.4.18), involving the single coefficient β_1 and $r_1 = 0$, the test statistic becomes

$$\frac{b_1^2}{\hat{\sigma}^2[R_1(X'X)^{-1}R_1']} \sim F_{(1,\,T-K)} \tag{6.4.22}$$

From distribution theory, we know that, for the single hypothesis special case,

$$F_{(1,\,T-K)} = t_{(T-K)}^2 \tag{6.4.23}$$

where $t_{(T-K)}$ is the student t random variable with $(T - K)$ degrees of freedom. Therefore, (6.4.21) becomes

$$\lambda = \frac{(R_1\mathbf{b} - r_1)^2}{\hat{\sigma}^2[R_1(X'X)^{-1}R_1']} \sim t_{(T-K)}^2 \tag{6.4.24}$$

where

$$\frac{(\mathbf{R}_1\mathbf{b} - r_1)}{\hat{\sigma}\sqrt{R_1(X'X)^{-1}R_1'}} \sim t_{(T-K)} \tag{6.4.25}$$

In this case we reject the hypothesis if the absolute value of (6.4.25) is greater than the critical value $t_{(T-K,\alpha/2)}$.

To see the close tie between hypothesis testing and interval estimation, note that we would accept the hypothesis if and only if $r_1 = \mathbf{R}_1\boldsymbol{\beta}$ is in the interval

$$[R_1\mathbf{b} - t_{(T-K,\alpha/2)}\hat{\sigma}\sqrt{R_1(X'X)^{-1}R_1'} \leq r_1 \leq R_1\mathbf{b} + t_{(T-K,\alpha/2)}\hat{\sigma}\sqrt{R_1(X'X)^{-1}R_1'}] \tag{6.4.26}$$

To give an idea of the sampling characteristics of the t-test statistic, the sample test values for the first 10 samples of the Monte Carlo experiment, discussed in Section 6.1.5, are given in Table 6.5. These t values are developed under the individual hypotheses $\beta_1 = 10.0$, $\beta_2 = 0.40$, and $\beta_3 = 0.60$.

Table 6.5 Values of the *t*-Statistic for 10 Monte Carlo Samples

Sample number	t-statistic $H_0{:}\beta_1 = 10.0$	$H_0{:}\beta_2 = 0.40$	$H_0{:}\beta_3 = 0.60$
1	1.01	1.31	0.66
2	0.05	1.09	1.02
3	2.42	−2.26	−0.85
4	1.07	−0.77	−0.51
5	−1.74	0.90	1.14
6	1.49	−1.95	−0.29
7	2.12	−0.48	−1.91
8	0.43	−1.40	0.03
9	−0.55	0.14	0.79
10	1.04	−0.57	−0.70

For the Monte Carlo experiment involving 500 samples and $\alpha = 0.05$, the following percentage of the test values exceeded the critical value $t_{(17)} = 2.11$.

$$8\% \text{ of } |t(b_1)| \geq t_{(17,0.025)} = 2.11$$

$$5\% \text{ of } |t(b_2)| \geq t_{(17,0.025)} = 2.11$$

$$5\% \text{ of } |t(b_3)| \geq t_{(17,0.025)} = 2.11$$

Under the $H_0{:}\ \beta_1 = 10.0$, $H_0{:}\ \beta_2 = 0.40$, and $H_0{:}\ \beta_3 = 0.60$, the empirical distributions of $t(b_1)$, $t(b_2)$, and $t(b_3)$ for the 500 samples are given in Figures 6.10, 6.11, and 6.12.

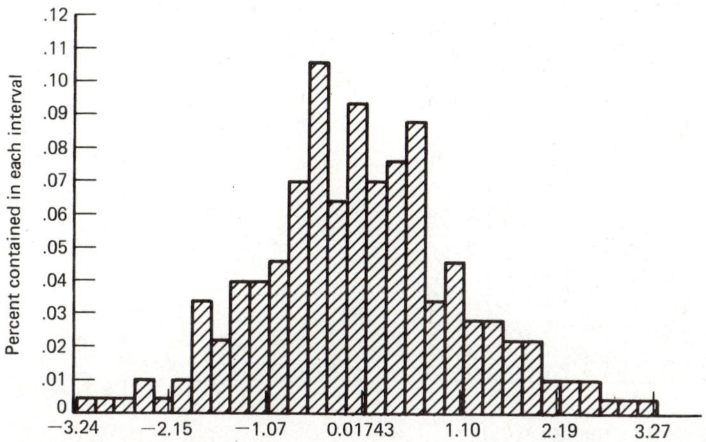

Figure 6.10 Empirical values for $t(b_1)$.

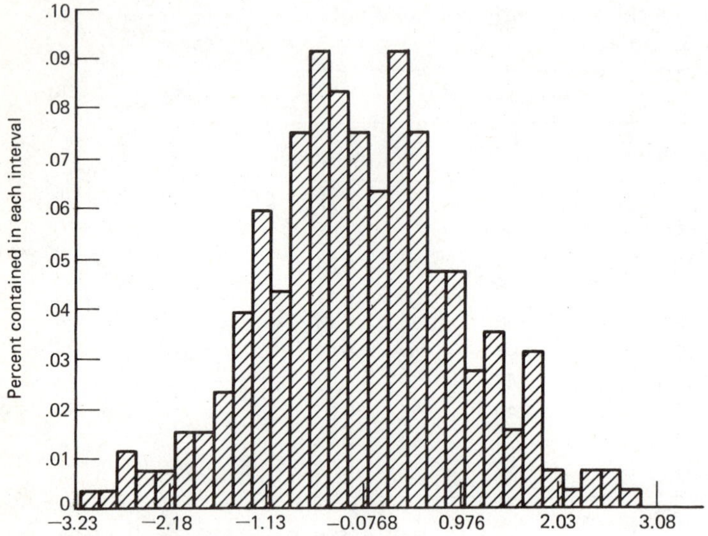

Figure 6.11 Empirical values for $t(b_2)$.

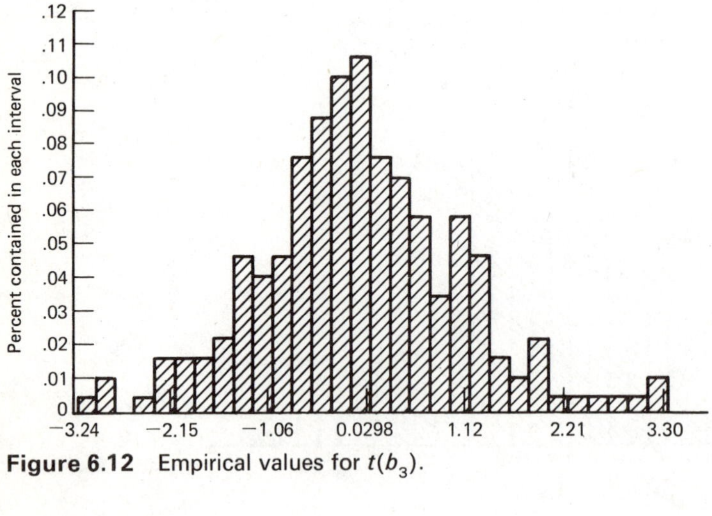

Figure 6.12 Empirical values for $t(b_3)$.

Note that each of the distributions take on the expected symmetrical shape about zero.

6.4.3 Testing a Hypothesis about σ^2

Consider now the hypothesis $H_0: \sigma^2 = \sigma_0^2$ versus the hypothesis $H_1: \sigma^2 \neq \sigma_0^2$. The framework for this testing mechanism follows from earlier results that showed that

$$\frac{(T-K)\hat{\sigma}^2}{\sigma^2} \sim \chi^2_{(T-K)} \qquad (6.4.27)$$

If we hypothesize that the scalar $\sigma^2 = \sigma_0^2$ and assume that the hypothesis is correct, the quadratic form is

$$(T-K)\frac{\hat{\sigma}^2}{\sigma_0^2} \sim \chi^2_{(T-K)} \qquad (6.4.28)$$

We therefore reject the hypothesis if the sample test value (6.4.28) is less than $\chi^2_{(T-K,\alpha/2)}$ or greater than $\chi^2_{(T-K,1-\alpha/2)}$ or, within an interval estimation context, if σ_0^2 falls outside the interval

$$\left[\frac{(T-K)\hat{\sigma}^2}{\chi^2_{(T-K,1-\alpha/2)}}, \frac{(T-K)\hat{\sigma}^2}{\chi^2_{(T-K,\alpha/2)}}\right] \qquad (6.4.29)$$

The empirical distribution of the quadratic form (6.4.28) for the 500 Monte Carlo samples given in Figure 6.4 conforms closely to the theoretical $\chi^2_{(17)}$ distribution.

As an example of hypothesis testing consider the estimate of σ^2 for the first sample, which is $\hat{\sigma}^2 = 0.0795$, and the hypothesis that $\sigma^2 = 0.0625$ is the true value. Then the empirical counterpart of (6.4.28) for this sample is

$$(T-K)\frac{\hat{\sigma}^2}{\sigma_0^2} = \frac{(17)(0.0795)}{0.0625} = 21.63 \qquad (6.4.30)$$

The critical values for $\chi^2_{(17)}$ for $\alpha = 0.05$ are 7.56 and 30.19, so in this case the null hypothesis would not be rejected.

6.5 Summary Statement

So far in this chapter we have extended the linear statistical model to include the assumption that the random vector **e** is normally distributed. Under this assumption we obtained, within the framework of point estimation, maximum likelihood estimators for the unknown parameter vector $\boldsymbol{\beta}$ and the scalar σ^2, and with a view to statistical inference, developed a basis for interval estimation and hypothesis testing. Some of the major results contained so far in the chapter are summarized here.

1. The maximum likelihood estimator of $\boldsymbol{\beta}$ is $\tilde{\boldsymbol{\beta}} = \mathbf{b} = (X'X)^{-1}X'\mathbf{y}$,
$$\tilde{\boldsymbol{\beta}} \sim N(\boldsymbol{\beta}, \sigma^2(X'X)^{-1}),$$
and $\tilde{\boldsymbol{\beta}}$ is a best unbiased estimator of $\boldsymbol{\beta}$.
2. The maximum likelihood estimator of σ^2 is $\tilde{\sigma}^2 = (\mathbf{y} - X\tilde{\boldsymbol{\beta}})'(\mathbf{y} - X\tilde{\boldsymbol{\beta}})/T$, and this is a biased estimator of σ^2.
3. The estimator $\hat{\sigma}^2 = (\mathbf{y} - X\tilde{\boldsymbol{\beta}})'(\mathbf{y} - X\tilde{\boldsymbol{\beta}})/(T - K)$ is best unbiased, and the random variable $(T - K)\hat{\sigma}^2/\sigma^2$ is distributed as a χ^2 random variable with $(T - K)$ degrees of freedom.
4. $\tilde{\boldsymbol{\beta}}$ and $\hat{\sigma}^2$ are independently distributed.
5. The ratio $(R_1\tilde{\boldsymbol{\beta}} - R_1\boldsymbol{\beta})/\hat{\sigma}\sqrt{R_1(X'X)^{-1}R_1'}$, where R_1 is a $(1 \times K)$ row vector, is distributed as a t random variable with $(T - K)$ degrees of freedom. This test statistic provides the framework for testing single hypotheses and making interval estimates for the unknown scalar $R_1\boldsymbol{\beta}$.
6. For the $(J \times K)$ matrix R of Rank J the random variable
$$\frac{(\tilde{\boldsymbol{\beta}} - \boldsymbol{\beta})'R'[R(X'X)^{-1}R']^{-1}R(\tilde{\boldsymbol{\beta}} - \boldsymbol{\beta})}{J\hat{\sigma}^2}$$
is distributed as an F with J and $(T - K)$ degrees of freedom. This test statistic provides the framework and basis for testing the general linear hypotheses $R\boldsymbol{\beta} = \mathbf{r}$ and for computing interval estimates for the unknown vector $R\boldsymbol{\beta}$.
7. The random variable $(T - K)\hat{\sigma}^2/\sigma^2 \sim \chi^2_{(T-K)}$ provides the distributional basis for making interval estimates for σ^2 and testing the hypothesis $\sigma^2 = \sigma_0^2$.

6.6 Asymptotic Properties of the Least Squares Estimator

Earlier in this chapter we noted that the least squares (LS) estimator of the parameter vector $\boldsymbol{\beta}$ was best linear unbiased if the errors were independently and identically distributed with 0 mean. In addition, if the errors were normally distributed, then the maximum likelihood-LS estimator of $\boldsymbol{\beta}$ was best unbiased and various test statistics were constructed as a basis for hypothesis tests and interval estimates for the unknown location vector.

In this section we are concerned with whether the LS estimator possesses the desirable asymptotic property of consistency and whether there is some basis for hypothesis tests and interval estimates when the errors are not normally distributed.

To examine these two questions we introduce the assumption

$$\lim_{T\to\infty}\left(\frac{X'X}{T}\right) = Q \tag{6.6.1}$$

where Q is a finite nonsingular matrix. This assumption implies that, as T increases, the elements of $X'X$ do not increase at a greater rate than T and that the explanatory variables are not linearly dependent in the limit. To aid appreciation of these two conditions let us consider examples where each is violated.

Consider the simple regression model with a linear time trend. That is,

$$y_t = \beta_1 + \beta_2 t + e_t \tag{6.6.2}$$

In this case,

$$X'X = \begin{bmatrix} T & \sum_{t=1}^{T} t \\ \sum_{t=1}^{T} t & \sum_{t=1}^{T} t^2 \end{bmatrix}$$

$$= \begin{bmatrix} T & T(T+1)/2 \\ T(T+1)/2 & T(T+1)(2T+1)/6 \end{bmatrix} \tag{6.6.3}$$

and

$$\lim_{T\to\infty}\left(\frac{X'X}{T}\right) = \begin{bmatrix} 1 & \infty \\ \infty & \infty \end{bmatrix} \tag{6.6.4}$$

which is clearly not finite. Thus, when our explanatory variables are trended, the assumption in (6.6.1) will not be satisfied. It can be shown, however, that the results to be presented in this section still hold under less restrictive assumptions about the matrix X. In particular, the lack of trend assumption is not a critical one. See Judge, et al. (1985, Section 5.3.5) for more details.

The assumption that Q is nonsingular is more critical. An example where it is violated is the linear model

$$y_t = \beta_1 + \beta_2 \lambda^t + e_t \tag{6.6.5}$$

where λ is known but such that $|\lambda| < 1$. In this case

$$X'X = \begin{bmatrix} T & \sum_{t=1}^{T} \lambda^t \\ \sum_{t=1}^{T} \lambda^t & \sum_{t=1}^{T} \lambda^{2t} \end{bmatrix}$$

$$= \begin{bmatrix} T & \dfrac{\lambda - \lambda^{T+1}}{1 - \lambda} \\ \dfrac{\lambda - \lambda^{T+1}}{1 - \lambda} & \dfrac{\lambda^2 - \lambda^{2(T+1)}}{1 - \lambda^2} \end{bmatrix} \tag{6.6.6}$$

and

$$\lim_{T \to \infty} \left(\frac{X'X}{T} \right) = \begin{bmatrix} 1 & 0 \\ 0 & 0 \end{bmatrix} \tag{6.6.7}$$

Thus, although $X'X$ is nonsingular for all finite T, $X'X/T$ is singular in the limit, (6.6.1) is violated, and the results to be presented in this section will not hold.

6.6.1 Consistency

We now consider some results that are useful for proving the consistency of the least squares estimator $\mathbf{b} = (X'X)^{-1}X'\mathbf{y}$ in the general linear model $\mathbf{y} = X\boldsymbol{\beta} + \mathbf{e}$. First, from (6.6.1) and the assumptions $E[\mathbf{e}] = \mathbf{0}$ and $E[\mathbf{ee}'] = \sigma^2 I$, it is possible to show that

$$\text{plim} \frac{X'\mathbf{e}}{T} = \mathbf{0} \tag{6.6.8}$$

The concept of "plim" refers to the "probability limit," and (6.6.8) implies that as $T \to \infty$ the probability distribution of $T^{-1}X'\mathbf{e}$ collapses to the single point 0. Refer back to Section 3.3.3 of Chapter 3 for further information.

A second useful result is *Slutsky's theorem*, which states that if $g(\cdot)$ is a continuous function and z_T is some random variable that depends on T, then

$$\text{plim } g(z_T) = g(\text{plim } z_T) \tag{6.6.9}$$

if plim z_T exists. This theorem extends to vectors and matrices in a natural way that should become apparent in the following proof of consistency of the least squares estimator. We have

$$\mathbf{b} = \boldsymbol{\beta} + \left(\frac{X'X}{T} \right)^{-1} \frac{X'\mathbf{e}}{T} \tag{6.6.10}$$

and

$$\begin{aligned}
\text{plim } \mathbf{b} &= \boldsymbol{\beta} + \text{plim}\left(\frac{X'X}{T}\right)^{-1} \frac{X'\mathbf{e}}{T} \\
&= \boldsymbol{\beta} + \text{plim}\left(\frac{X'X}{T}\right)^{-1} \text{plim } \frac{X'\mathbf{e}}{T} \qquad \text{from Slutsky's theorem} \\
&= \boldsymbol{\beta} + \left(\text{plim } \frac{X'X}{T}\right)^{-1} \text{plim } \frac{X'\mathbf{e}}{T} \qquad \text{also from Slutsky's theorem} \\
&= \boldsymbol{\beta} + Q^{-1}\mathbf{0} \quad \text{from (6.6.1) and (6.6.8)} \\
&= \boldsymbol{\beta}
\end{aligned} \tag{6.6.11}$$

In going from $(\text{plim } X'X/T)^{-1}$ to Q^{-1} we have used the result that when X is nonstochastic, $\text{plim } X'X/T = \lim X'X/T$. Note that if Q is singular then the second term in the proof of (6.6.11) would not necessarily disappear despite the fact that $\text{plim } X'\mathbf{e}/T = \mathbf{0}$.

It is also possible to prove that the least squares estimator is consistent by proving that its bias and variance go to 0 as $T \to \infty$. Since $\mathbf{b}$ is unbiased for all T, its bias will be $\mathbf{0}$ as $T \to \infty$. The variance can be shown to approach zero as follows.

$$\Sigma_{\mathbf{b}} = \frac{\sigma^2}{T}\left(\frac{X'X}{T}\right)^{-1} \tag{6.6.12}$$

$$\begin{aligned}
\lim_{T \to \infty} \Sigma_{\mathbf{b}} &= \lim \frac{\sigma^2}{T}\left(\lim \frac{X'X}{T}\right)^{-1} \\
&= 0\, Q^{-1} \\
&= 0
\end{aligned} \tag{6.6.13}$$

To prove consistency of the *least squares variance estimator* we need one further result known as *Khinchine's theorem.* This theorem states that the sample mean computed from a random sample of independent identically distributed observations will be a consistent estimator of the population mean. For our purposes we regard the squares of the errors, $e_1^2, e_2^2, \ldots, e_T^2$ as a random sample of independently, identically distributed "observations" with population mean $E[e_t^2] = \sigma^2$. The "sample mean" is given by

$$\frac{1}{T}\sum_{t=1}^{T} e_t^2 = \frac{\mathbf{e}'\mathbf{e}}{T} \tag{6.6.14}$$

and, from Khinchine's theorem

$$\text{plim } \frac{\mathbf{e}'\mathbf{e}}{T} = \sigma^2 \tag{6.6.15}$$

We are now in a position to prove consistency of the least squares variance estimator

$$
\begin{aligned}
\hat{\sigma}^2 &= \frac{\hat{\mathbf{e}}'\hat{\mathbf{e}}}{T-K} \\
&= \frac{1}{T-K}\mathbf{e}'(I - X(X'X)^{-1}X')\mathbf{e} \\
&= \left(\frac{T}{T-K}\right)\left(\frac{\mathbf{e}'\mathbf{e}}{T} - \frac{\mathbf{e}'X}{T}\left(\frac{X'X}{T}\right)^{-1}\frac{X'\mathbf{e}}{T}\right) \qquad (6.6.16)
\end{aligned}
$$

Using the results established so far in this section we have

$$
\begin{aligned}
\text{plim}\ \hat{\sigma}^2 &= \text{plim}\left(\frac{T}{T-K}\right)\left(\text{plim}\ \frac{\mathbf{e}'\mathbf{e}}{T} - \text{plim}\ \frac{\mathbf{e}'X}{T}\left(\text{plim}\ \frac{X'X}{T}\right)^{-1}\text{plim}\ \frac{X'\mathbf{e}}{T}\right) \\
&= 1(\sigma^2 - \mathbf{0}\cdot Q^{-1}\cdot\mathbf{0}) \\
&= \sigma^2 \qquad (6.6.17)
\end{aligned}
$$

Thus, $\hat{\sigma}^2$ is a consistent estimator for σ^2. If the errors are normally distributed, then it is possible to show that $\hat{\sigma}^2$ is a consistent estimator by showing that its bias and variance approach zero as $T \to \infty$. See Exercise 6.14.

6.6.2 Inference

Our next problem is to consider a basis for hypothesis tests and interval estimation for $\boldsymbol{\beta}$ when the errors are not normally distributed. We will simply sketch the necessary steps and results. For more details, you can consult Judge, et al. (1985, Chapter 5). We retain the assumption in (6.6.1).

1. From a central limit theorem it is possible to show that the limiting distribution of $T^{-1/2}X'\mathbf{e}$ is a multivariate normal with mean $\mathbf{0}$ and covariance matrix $\sigma^2 Q$. We write this result as

$$\frac{X'\mathbf{e}}{\sqrt{T}} \xrightarrow{d} N(\mathbf{0}, \sigma^2 Q) \qquad (6.6.18)$$

2. We can write

$$\sqrt{T}(\mathbf{b} - \boldsymbol{\beta}) = \left(\frac{X'X}{T}\right)^{-1}\frac{X'\mathbf{e}}{\sqrt{T}} \qquad (6.6.19)$$

Because $\lim (X'X/T)^{-1} = Q^{-1}$, the limiting distribution of (6.6.19) is identical to the limiting distribution of $Q^{-1}X'\mathbf{e}/\sqrt{T}$. The covariance matrix of the limiting distribution of $Q^{-1}X'\mathbf{e}/\sqrt{T}$ will be

$$\bar{V}\left(Q^{-1}\frac{X'\mathbf{e}}{\sqrt{T}}\right) = Q^{-1}\bar{V}\left(\frac{X'\mathbf{e}}{\sqrt{T}}\right)Q^{-1} = \sigma^2 Q^{-1}QQ^{-1} = \sigma^2 Q^{-1} \quad (6.6.20)$$

where we have used the notation $\bar{V}(\cdot)$ to denote the covariance matrix of the limiting distribution. Thus $\sqrt{T}(\mathbf{b} - \boldsymbol{\beta})$ has a limiting distribution that is multivariate normal with mean $\mathbf{0}$ and covariance matrix $\sigma^2 Q^{-1}$. We write this result as

$$\sqrt{T}(\mathbf{b} - \boldsymbol{\beta}) \xrightarrow{d} N(\mathbf{0}, \sigma^2 Q^{-1}) \quad (6.6.21)$$

3. The usual theorems about the distributions of particular functions of the left side of (6.6.21) also hold for limiting distributions. Thus, if R is a known $(J \times K)$ matrix of rank J, it can be shown that

$$\sqrt{T}(R\mathbf{b} - R\boldsymbol{\beta}) \xrightarrow{d} N(\mathbf{0}, \sigma^2 RQ^{-1}R') \quad (6.6.22)$$

and

$$\frac{T(R\mathbf{b} - R\boldsymbol{\beta})'(RQ^{-1}R')^{-1}(R\mathbf{b} - R\boldsymbol{\beta})}{\sigma^2} \xrightarrow{d} \chi^2_{(J)} \quad (6.6.23)$$

4. In (6.6.23) we can replace the unknown quantities Q and σ^2 by $(X'X/T)$ and $\hat{\sigma}^2$ without changing the limiting distribution. Thus, we have

$$\lambda^* = \frac{(R\mathbf{b} - R\boldsymbol{\beta})'[R(X'X)^{-1}R']^{-1}(R\mathbf{b} - R\boldsymbol{\beta})}{\hat{\sigma}^2} \xrightarrow{d} \chi^2_{(J)} \quad (6.6.24)$$

This statistic, in conjunction with the $\chi^2_{(J)}$-distribution, can be used to construct hypothesis tests or interval estimates for any linear combinations of $\boldsymbol{\beta}$ such as the special cases dealt with in Section 6.4. When $J = 1$ the result in (6.6.24) is equivalent to

$$\omega = \frac{R\mathbf{b} - R\boldsymbol{\beta}}{\hat{\sigma}\sqrt{R(X'X)^{-1}R'}} \xrightarrow{d} N(0, 1) \quad (6.6.25)$$

This result can be used to construct confidence intervals or hypothesis tests about a single element, β_i, in the vector $\boldsymbol{\beta}$ by defining R as

$$R = (0 \;\; \ldots \;\; 0 \;\; 1 \;\; 0 \;\; \ldots \;\; 0)$$

where 1 appears in the ith position.

5. The results in (6.6.24) and (6.6.25) differ slightly from those developed in Sections 6.3 and 6.4. First, the result for the statistic ω in (6.6.25) suggests that the normal distribution should be used as the basis for hypothesis tests and confidence intervals, whereas in Section 6.3.4 our results suggested the t-distribution should be employed. Thus, from a theoretical point of view, when the errors are not normally distributed our inferences should be based on a normal distribution rather than a t-distribution. From a practical standpoint, however, it is quite possible that the t-distribution is a better approximation in finite samples, and in large samples it makes no difference because the t-distribution converges to the standard normal.

An analogous situation exists with the statistic λ^* in (6.6.24) and the conventional F statistic developed in Section 6.4 and given by

$$\lambda_1 = \frac{\lambda^*}{J} = \frac{(R\mathbf{b} - R\boldsymbol{\beta})'[R(X'X)^{-1}R']^{-1}(R\mathbf{b} - R\boldsymbol{\beta})}{J\hat{\sigma}^2} \tag{6.6.26}$$

When $\mathbf{e}$ is normally distributed, $\lambda_1 \sim F_{(J,T-K)}$. However, when $\mathbf{e}$ is not normally distributed, the finite sample distribution of λ_1 is not known, so, theoretically, we should use λ^*, which approximately follows a $\chi^2_{(J)}$ distribution. In practice, the statistic λ_1, which will reject a true null hypothesis less frequently, may provide a better finite sample approximation. As $T \to \infty$, the choice between λ^* and λ_1 makes little difference because $JF_{(J,T-K)} \xrightarrow{d} \chi^2_{(J)}$.

In this section we have shown that the least squares estimator $\mathbf{b}$ and the least squares variance estimator $\hat{\sigma}^2$ each possess the desirable asymptotic property of consistency. Furthermore, we have shown that when the error vector $\mathbf{e}$ is not normally distributed, but still satisfies $E(\mathbf{e}) = \mathbf{0}$ and the error components of $\mathbf{e}$ are independent and identically distributed, and we make an assumption about the limiting behavior of the matrix $X'X$, then the inference procedures we developed in Section 6.4 will hold approximately for large samples.

6.7 Exercises

Consult the Computer Handbook for the sampling procedures to be used in generating samples of 20 observations based on the statistical model presented in Section 6.1.5.

6.7.1 Individual Exercises

6.1 Obtain five $\mathbf{y}$ samples of 20 observations each from the Monte Carlo experiment noted in Section 6.1.5 and use these data with the design matrix

(6.1.27) to compute maximum likelihood estimates of β_1, β_2, β_3, and σ^2 for each data sample. Also obtain estimates for the unbiased estimator $\hat{\sigma}^2$.

6.2 Compute the estimated covariance matrix for each sample and compare with the true covariance matrix

$$\Sigma_{\tilde{\boldsymbol{\beta}}} = \sigma^2(X'X)^{-1} = \begin{bmatrix} 0.0410 & -0.0096 & -0.0182 \\ -0.0096 & 0.0069 & -0.0009 \\ -0.0182 & -0.0009 & 0.0155 \end{bmatrix}$$

Give an interpretation to and compare the diagonal elements of each estimated covariance matrix.

6.3 Compute the mean and variance for each of the estimated parameters for the five samples from Exercise 6.1 and compare these averages with the true parameters.

6.4 Using a level of statistical significance of $\alpha = 0.05$, compute and compare interval estimates for β_1, β_2, β_3, and σ^2 for your five data samples.

6.5 Using a level of statistical significance of $\alpha = 0.05$ and your first data sample, test the hypothesis that

(*a*) $\beta_2 = 0$
(*b*) $\beta_3 = 1$
(*c*) $\beta_2 + \beta_3 = 1$
(*d*) $\sigma^2 = 0.05$

and interpret the results for each separate hypothesis.

6.6 For the design matrix (6.1.27), develop a P matrix such that $P'X'XP = I_3$ and $\mathbf{y} = XPP^{-1}\boldsymbol{\beta} + \mathbf{e} = Z\boldsymbol{\theta} + \mathbf{e}$. Using an $\alpha = 0.05$ and the first sample of data, develop joint confidence intervals for θ_2 and θ_3 and interpret.

6.7 Using an $\alpha = 0.05$ and the results from your first sample of data, develop a joint confidence interval for β_2 and β_3 and compare with the results of Exercise 6.6.

6.8 Using an $\alpha = 0.05$ and the results from your first sample of data, set up the general linear hypothesis and test the joint hypothesis that

(*a*) $\beta_1 = 0$, $\beta_2 = 0$, and $\beta_3 = 0$
(*b*) $\beta_1 = 5.0$ and $\beta_2 + \beta_3 = 1$ and interpret the results

6.9 Using the results from your first sample and values $x_2 = 2$ and $x_3 = 1.5$, compute the predicted value for y and develop the corresponding interval estimate for y using an $\alpha = 0.05$.

6.10 Show that the *likelihood* ratio test for the general normal linear statistical model leads to the following ratio of quadratic forms

$$\frac{(\mathbf{y} - X\mathbf{b}^*)'(\mathbf{y} - X\mathbf{b}^*)}{(\mathbf{y} - X\mathbf{b})'(\mathbf{y} - X\mathbf{b})}$$

6.11 Let Q be any $(J \times J)$ nonsingular matrix. Develop the test statistic for $H_0: QR\boldsymbol{\beta} = Q\mathbf{r}$ versus $H_1: QR\boldsymbol{\beta} \neq Q\mathbf{r}$ and compare to the hypothesis test for $R\boldsymbol{\beta} = \mathbf{r}$ that was developed in this chapter.

6.12 Assume that X is a $(T \times K)$ matrix with rank K and R is a $(J \times K)$ matrix with rank J. Show that $R(X'X)^{-1}R'$ is a positive definite matrix. Show that

$$X(X'X)^{-1}R'[R(X'X)^{-1}R']^{-1}R(X'X)^{-1}X'$$

has rank and trace equal to J.

6.13 What is a minimum mean squared error estimator for σ^2 and what is its variance and bias?

6.14 Assuming $\mathbf{e} \sim N(\mathbf{0}, \sigma^2 I)$, the ML estimator for σ^2 is given by

$$\tilde{\sigma}^2 = \frac{1}{T}(\mathbf{y} - X\mathbf{b})'(\mathbf{y} - X\mathbf{b})$$

(*a*) Show that

$$E(\tilde{\sigma}^2) - \sigma^2 = -\frac{K}{T}\sigma^2$$

(*b*) Show that

$$\text{Var}(\tilde{\sigma}^2) = \frac{2(T - K)\sigma^4}{T^2}$$

(*c*) Prove that $\tilde{\sigma}^2$ is a consistent estimator for σ^2.

6.15 (*a*) Show that

$$(\tilde{\boldsymbol{\beta}} - \boldsymbol{\beta})'R'[R(X'X)^{-1}R']^{-1}R(\tilde{\boldsymbol{\beta}} - \boldsymbol{\beta})$$
$$= \mathbf{e}'X(X'X)^{-1}R'[R(X'X)^{-1}R']^{-1}R(X'X)^{-1}X'\mathbf{e}$$

(*b*) Show that $X(X'X)^{-1}R'[R(X'X)^{-1}R']^{-1}R(X'X)^{-1}X'$ is an idempotent matrix of rank J where J is the row dimension and rank of R.

(*c*) Based on your results in (*a*) and (*b*), and given that $\mathbf{e} \sim N(\mathbf{0}, \sigma^2 I_T)$, what can you say about the distribution of

$$(\tilde{\boldsymbol{\beta}} - \boldsymbol{\beta})'R'[R(X'X)^{-1}R']^{-1}R(\tilde{\boldsymbol{\beta}} - \boldsymbol{\beta})/\sigma^2$$

(*d*) In Section 6.1.3b, it was shown that

$$\frac{(T-K)\hat{\sigma}^2}{\sigma^2} = \frac{\mathbf{e}'(I - X(X'X)^{-1}X')\mathbf{e}}{\sigma^2} \sim \chi^2_{(T-K)}$$

Show that

$$[I - X(X'X)^{-1}X']X(X'X)^{-1}R'[R(X'X)^{-1}R']^{-1}R(X'X)^{-1}X' = 0.$$

What is the significance of this result? See Sections 2.5.9 and 6.3.2.

6.7.2 Group or Class Exercises

6.16 Design and carry through a Monte Carlo experiment for a statistical model of the type used in section 6.1.5, using parameter values and a design matrix of your choice and the normal random errors corresponding to an appropriate random number generator discussed in the Computer Handbook. Compute the corresponding parameter point and interval estimates and test statistics and graph their empirical distributions. Compare the Monte Carlo results with their theoretical counterparts and conduct the tests necessary for inference purposes.

6.8 References and Guide to Further Reading

Discussions of point estimation for the linear statistical model discussed in this chapter can be found in many current textbooks. The books listed here represent a variety of treatments and levels of difficulty, and each in some way is unique. To ensure a breadth of understanding, one or more of these books, along with those mentioned in the references of Chapters 2 and 3, should be read concurrently with this chapter.

Goldberger, A. A. (1964) *Econometric Theory.* New York: Wiley.

Graybill, F. A. (1976) *Theory and Application of the Linear Model.* North Scituate, MA: Duxbury Press.

Intriligator, M. (1977). *Econometric Models, Techniques and Applications.* Englewood Cliffs, NJ: Prentice-Hall.

Johnston, J. (1972) *Econometric Methods.* New York: McGraw-Hill.

Judge, G. G., W. E. Griffiths, R. C. Hill, H. Lütkepohl, and T. C. Lee (1985) *The*

Theory and Practice of Econometrics, 2nd ed., New York: Wiley.

Kmenta, J. (1986) *Elements of Econometrics.* New York: Macmillan.

Maddala, G. S. (1977) *Econometrics.* New York: McGraw-Hill.

Theil, H. (1971) *Principles of Econometrics.* New York: Wiley.

Wonnacott, T. H., and R. J. Wonnacott (1980) *Regression: A Second Course in Statistics.* New York: Wiley.

CHAPTER 7

Bayesian Analysis of the Normal Linear Statistical Model

7.1 Introduction

The Bayesian approach to inference was introduced in Chapter 4 in the context of learning about the mean of a normal distribution. We now extend the analysis of Chapter 4 and examine the Bayesian approach to inference for the $(K \times 1)$ parameter vector $\boldsymbol{\beta}$ in the normal linear statistical model

$$\mathbf{y} = X\boldsymbol{\beta} + \mathbf{e} \tag{7.1.1}$$

where $\mathbf{y}$ is a $(T \times 1)$ vector of observations on a dependent variable, X is a $(T \times K)$ matrix of observations on K explanatory variables, and $\mathbf{e}$ is a $(T \times 1)$ unobservable disturbance vector that follows a multivariate normal distribution with mean vector $E[\mathbf{e}] = \mathbf{0}$ and covariance matrix $E[\mathbf{ee}'] = \sigma^2 I$. This model was studied from a sampling theory viewpoint in Chapters 5 and 6. In these chapters we were concerned with finding estimators that performed well in repeated samples and with using the sampling distribution of the estimators to construct confidence intervals or to test hypotheses about the unknown parameters $\boldsymbol{\beta}$ and σ^2. The techniques employed were dependent only on the sample observations; no framework existed for formally including any prior information that might be available on $\boldsymbol{\beta}$ and/or σ.

In the Bayesian analysis of this chapter, prior information on parameters is introduced using a prior p.d.f. For example, in the case where σ^2 is known, Bayesian analysis begins by assigning a prior p.d.f. $g(\boldsymbol{\beta})$ to the parameter vector $\boldsymbol{\beta}$. When sample observations become available, their contribution to our knowledge about $\boldsymbol{\beta}$ is expressed in terms of the likelihood function $\ell(\boldsymbol{\beta}|\mathbf{y})$; this likelihood function is used, via Bayes' theorem, to modify our prior knowledge, forming the posterior p.d.f. $g(\boldsymbol{\beta}|\mathbf{y})$. Specifically,

$$g(\boldsymbol{\beta}|\mathbf{y}) \propto \ell(\boldsymbol{\beta}|\mathbf{y})g(\boldsymbol{\beta}) \tag{7.1.2}$$

The posterior p.d.f. expresses our current state of knowledge (both prior and sample) about $\boldsymbol{\beta}$. Whereas the sampling theory approach to inference is concerned with how a rule or estimator will perform in a number of future hypothetical repeated samples, the Bayesian approach is concerned with using the current information (as expressed by the posterior p.d.f.) in the best possible way. The posterior p.d.f. can be used simply as an expression of our knowledge about a parameter, or it can be used to derive a point estimate, an interval estimate, a predictive p.d.f. for future observations, or a posterior odds ratio for two alternative hypotheses. The performance of point and interval estimates in repeated samples is not necessarily of paramount importance in the Bayesian approach, although many Bayesian point estimates do have good sampling theory properties.

Bayesian inference for the normal linear statistical model is introduced in Section 7.2, using a simple model with only one explanatory variable and no intercept term and with the assumption that σ^2 is known. In Section 7.3 the more general case with K explanatory variables is considered, but still with the assumption that σ^2 is known. The techniques are illustrated using a production function example in Section 7.4. Point estimation and the construction of posterior odds ratios are taken up in Sections 7.5 and 7.6, respectively. The consequences of relaxing the assumption of known σ^2 are treated in Section 7.7.

7.2 A Simple Model

To introduce Bayesian analysis of the normal linear statistical model, we begin with a simple linear model with one explanatory variable and no intercept term. An example of such a model is the long-run consumption function

$$y_t = \beta x_t + e_t \tag{7.2.1}$$

where x_t denotes "permanent" income in the tth time period, y_t denotes "permanent" consumption in the tth time period, and e_t is an independent normal random variable with 0 mean and known variance, $\sigma^2 = 2.25$. The assumption that σ^2 is known is a simplifying one that will be relaxed later in the chapter. We will abstract from possible difficulties associated with measuring permanent income and permanent consumption and assume that we have available the 15 observations in Table 7.1.

Table 7.1 A Sample of Observations on Consumption (y_t) and Income (x_t)

y_t	x_t	y_t	x_t	y_t	x_t
5.84	4.0	3.43	6.0	12.54	12.0
4.00	6.0	6.60	8.0	6.78	10.0
5.30	5.0	11.79	11.0	12.97	14.0
8.12	7.0	7.46	9.0	11.25	13.0
5.97	9.0	8.49	7.0	12.54	15.0

Our objective is to use the sample of observations in Table 7.1 to learn about, or to make inferences about, the marginal propensity to consume β. If we employed the sampling theory approach to inference outlined in Chapter 6, we would begin by computing the least squares estimate for β, namely

$$b = \frac{\sum_{t=1}^{T} x_t y_t}{\sum_{t=1}^{T} x_t^2} = \frac{1248.28}{1392} = 0.89675 \tag{7.2.2}$$

Furthermore, recalling that σ^2 is known, and that $b \sim N(\beta, \sigma^2/\sum_{t=1}^{T} x_t^2)$, the normal distribution can be used to construct the following 95% confidence interval for β,

$$b \pm 1.96(\sigma^2/\textstyle\sum_{t=1}^{T} x_t^2)^{1/2} = 0.89675 \pm 1.96 \times 1.5/\sqrt{1392}$$

or

$$(0.81795, 0.97555) \tag{7.2.3}$$

This method of presenting results, as a point and a confidence interval, is typical of the sampling theory approach to inference.

For a parameter such as the marginal propensity to consume the foregoing confidence interval is a fairly wide one, indicating that the sample has not provided us with very precise information. It would be advantageous if we could improve the precision of our information about β by including any prior information we might have. Furthermore, there would be very few economists who would not have at least some prior information about the marginal propensity to consume; given that this prior information is available, it seems foolhardy not to take advantage of it. In contrast to the sampling theory approach to inference, the Bayesian approach provides a formal framework for including such prior information.

The other main distinguishing feature of the Bayesian approach is the way in which information about a parameter is presented. As we already mentioned, in the sampling theory approach this information is usually presented in terms of point and interval estimates. Probability statements are made about future hypothetical estimates, not about what are likely and what are unlikely values for the parameter. In the Bayesian approach, information about a parameter is expressed in terms of the posterior p.d.f. The posterior p.d.f. is a direct statement of the (subjective) probability of the parameter taking on particular values.

These two features, the inclusion of prior information via a prior p.d.f. and the presentation of results in terms of a posterior p.d.f., will now be illustrated using the consumption function example.

7.2.1 Bayesian Inference with an Informative Prior

Suppose that our prior information about β is such that there is 0.9 probability that β lies between 0.75 and 0.95, there is a 50–50 chance that β is above (or below) 0.85, and that our prior views can be adequately expressed in terms of a normal distribution. The Bayesian approach begins by using this prior knowledge to construct a prior p.d.f. for β. In this case, the prior p.d.f. will be a normal distribution and, because there is a 50–50 chance that β is above or below 0.85, the mean of the normal prior p.d.f. will be $\bar{\beta} = 0.85$. Furthermore, we have that

$$P(0.75 < \beta < 0.95) = 0.9 \tag{7.2.4}$$

If the variance of the prior distribution for β is denoted by $\bar{\sigma}_\beta^2$, then, using properties of the normal distribution, we can write

$$P\left(-1.645 < \frac{\beta - \bar{\beta}}{\bar{\sigma}_\beta} < 1.645\right) = 0.9$$

or

$$P(\bar{\beta} - 1.645\bar{\sigma}_\beta < \beta < \bar{\beta} + 1.645\bar{\sigma}_\beta) = 0.9 \tag{7.2.5}$$

Because (7.2.4) and (7.2.5) are equivalent probability statements, it follows that

$$\bar{\beta} - 1.645\bar{\sigma}_\beta = 0.75 \quad \text{and} \quad \bar{\beta} + 1.645\bar{\sigma}_\beta = 0.95$$

Substituting $\bar{\beta} = 0.85$ and solving either of these equations for $\bar{\sigma}_\beta$ yields

$$1.645\bar{\sigma}_\beta = 0.1$$

or

$$\bar{\sigma}_\beta = 0.06079$$

Thus, our prior p.d.f. for β is given by

$$\beta \sim N[0.85, (0.06079)^2] \tag{7.2.6}$$

This p.d.f. will be denoted by $g(\beta)$.

It could be argued that the normal distribution, which has a range from $-\infty$ to ∞, is an inappropriate prior p.d.f. for the long-run marginal propensity to consume, which almost certainly could not be outside the range 0 to 1. However, in an introductory text such as this one it is necessary to use examples that turn out to be convenient. Also, even with the normally distributed prior that we have constructed, the probability that β lies outside the interval 0 to 1 is very small. Specifically, it can be shown that $P(\beta > 1) < 0.007$ and $P(\beta < 0) < 0.3 \times 10^{-16}$.

The next step in Bayesian analysis is to use Bayes' theorem to combine the prior information, which we have just formulated, with the likelihood function for a set of sample observations such as those in Table 7.1. Such a combination yields the posterior p.d.f. for β, $g(\beta|\mathbf{y})$, which summarizes all our information (prior and sample) about β. The vector $\mathbf{y} = (y_1, y_2, \ldots, y_T)'$ is used to denote the sample observations. In the context of our example where σ^2 is known and β is the only unknown parameter, Bayes' theorem can be written as

$$g(\beta|\mathbf{y}) \propto \ell(\beta|\mathbf{y})g(\beta) \tag{7.2.7}$$

where the likelihood function is given by

$$\ell(\beta|\mathbf{y}) \propto \exp\left\{-\sum_{t=1}^{T}(y_t - \beta x_t)^2/2\sigma^2\right\} \tag{7.2.8}$$

and the prior p.d.f. $g(\beta)$ is

$$g(\beta) \propto \exp\{-(\beta - \bar{\beta})^2/2\bar{\sigma}_\beta^2\} \tag{7.2.9}$$

In line with the conventions we adopted in Chapter 4, the constants of proportionality have been omitted from (7.2.8) and (7.2.9). Note that our prior information is such that $\bar{\beta} = 0.85$ and $\bar{\sigma}_\beta^2 = (0.06079)^2$, and we have assumed that the variance of the sample disturbance is given by $\sigma^2 = 2.25$.

Multiplying (7.2.8) and (7.2.9), and using the result in Exercise 7.1 to avoid some tedious algebra, yields the posterior p.d.f.

$$\begin{aligned} g(\beta|\mathbf{y}) &\propto \exp\left\{-\sum_{t=1}^{T}(y_t - \beta x_t)^2/2\sigma^2 - (\beta - \bar{\beta})^2/2\bar{\sigma}_\beta^2\right\} \\ &= \exp\left\{-\frac{1}{2}\left(\frac{\sum_{t=1}^{T} x_t^2}{\sigma^2} + \frac{1}{\bar{\sigma}_\beta^2}\right)\left(\beta - \frac{\sum_{t=1}^{T} x_t y_t/\sigma^2 + \bar{\beta}/\bar{\sigma}_\beta^2}{\sum_{t=1}^{T} x_t^2/\sigma^2 + 1/\bar{\sigma}_\beta^2}\right)^2 - k\right\} \end{aligned} \tag{7.2.10}$$

where k is a constant that does not depend on β and that, therefore, can be absorbed into the factor of proportionality. If we let

$$\begin{aligned} \bar{\bar{\beta}} &= \frac{\sum_{t=1}^{T} x_t y_t/\sigma^2 + \bar{\beta}/\bar{\sigma}_\beta^2}{\sum_{t=1}^{T} x_t^2/\sigma^2 + 1/\bar{\sigma}_\beta^2} \\ &= \frac{b\sum_{t=1}^{T} x_t^2/\sigma^2 + \bar{\beta}/\bar{\sigma}_\beta^2}{\sum_{t=1}^{T} x_t^2/\sigma^2 + 1/\bar{\sigma}_\beta^2} \\ &= \frac{h_s b + h_0\bar{\beta}}{h_s + h_0} \end{aligned} \tag{7.2.11}$$

where

$$b = \sum_{t=1}^{T} x_t y_t \Big/ \sum_{t=1}^{T} x_t^2, \qquad h_s = \sum_{t=1}^{T} x_t^2/\sigma^2 \quad \text{and} \quad h_0 = 1/\bar{\sigma}_\beta^2$$

and if

$$\bar{\bar{\sigma}}_\beta^2 = \frac{1}{\dfrac{\sum_{t=1}^{T} x_t^2}{\sigma^2} + \dfrac{1}{\bar{\sigma}_\beta^2}} = \frac{1}{h_s + h_0} = \frac{1}{h_1} \tag{7.2.12}$$

where $h_1 = h_s + h_0$, then the posterior p.d.f. in (7.2.10) can be written as

$$g(\beta|\mathbf{y}) \propto \exp\{-(\beta - \bar{\bar{\beta}})^2/2\bar{\bar{\sigma}}_\beta^2\} \tag{7.2.13}$$

The right side of this expression is the kernel of a normal p.d.f. with mean $\bar{\bar{\beta}}$ and variance $\bar{\bar{\sigma}}_\beta^2$. That is,

$$(\beta|\mathbf{y}) \sim N(\bar{\bar{\beta}}, \bar{\bar{\sigma}}_\beta^2) \tag{7.2.14}$$

Thus, we have shown that when we begin with a normal prior p.d.f. for β, and combine it with the likelihood function for β with known σ^2, the resulting posterior p.d.f. for β is also a normal p.d.f. In other words, $g(\beta)$ given in (7.2.9) is a natural conjugate prior for the likelihood function given in (7.2.8).

The quantities h_0, h_s and h_1 represent the precisions of the various sources of information about β. The precision of the prior information, $h_0 = 1/\bar{\sigma}_\beta^2$, is equal to the inverse of the variance of the prior p.d.f. for β. The precision of the sample information, $h_s = \sum_{t=1}^T x_t^2/\sigma^2$, is equal to the inverse of the variance of the posterior p.d.f. for β, which is obtained when a *noninformative* prior is used; this posterior p.d.f. reflects only sample information and will be considered in the next subsection. Alternatively, h_s can be viewed as the inverse of the variance of the sampling theory least squares estimator $b = \sum_{t=1}^T x_t y_t/\sum_{t=1}^T x_t^2$. The precision of the posterior information is equal to the sum of the prior and sample precisions, $h_1 = h_0 + h_s$, and is also equal to the reciprocal of the variance of the posterior p.d.f. for β, $h_1 = 1/\bar{\bar{\sigma}}_\beta^2$.

Given these definitions of precisions, it can be seen that $\bar{\bar{\beta}}$ (the posterior mean for β given in Equation 7.2.11) is a weighted average of the prior mean $\bar{\beta}$, and the least squares estimator b, with the weights being equal to the precisions of each source of information.

For our consumption function example we find that the various precisions are given by

$$h_0 = \frac{1}{(0.06079)^2} = 270.60 \qquad h_s = \frac{1392}{2.25} = 618.67$$

$$h_1 = h_0 + h_s = 889.27$$

and the posterior mean and variance are

$$\bar{\bar{\beta}} = \frac{618.67 \times 0.89675 + 270.6 \times 0.85}{889.27} = 0.88253$$

$$\bar{\bar{\sigma}}_\beta^2 = \frac{1}{h_1} = 0.001125 = (0.033534)^2$$

Thus, for our posterior p.d.f. we have

$$(\beta|\mathbf{y}) \sim N[0.88253, (0.033534)^2] \tag{7.2.15}$$

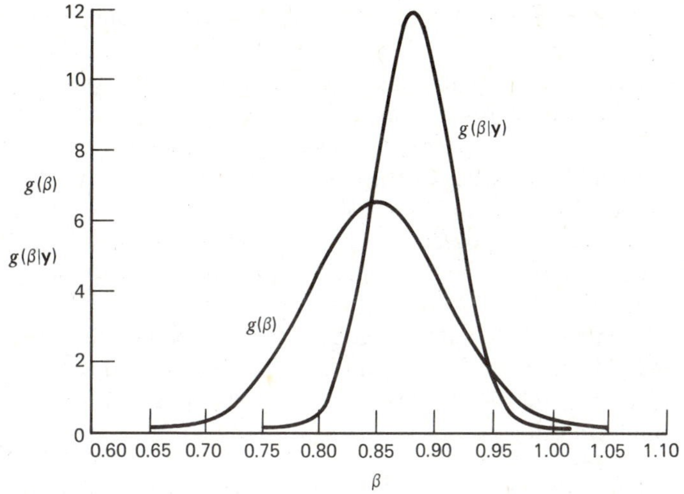

Figure 7.1 Prior and posterior p.d.f.'s for the marginal propensity to consume.

The prior and posterior p.d.f.'s for β are graphed in Figure 7.1. The sample information has moved the distribution to the right and made it much sharper, reflecting the fact that the mean has increased from 0.85 to 0.88 and the standard deviation has fallen from 0.0608 to 0.0335.

The presentation of the posterior p.d.f. for β, as in (7.2.15) or Figure 7.1, is an example of one of the conventional ways of presenting results from Bayesian inference. It is frequently not necessary to take an analysis any further. However, if desired, the posterior p.d.f. can be used for deriving and presenting further information such as a point estimate, a HPD interval, a posterior odds ratio for two alternative hypotheses about β, and a predictive p.d.f. for future values of the dependent variable. Methods for deriving such information were discussed in Chapter 4 in connection with inference for the mean of a normal distribution. These methods require little or no modification to be applied in the current context, so we will leave their application as a problem (Exercise 7.2).

7.2.2 Bayesian Inference with a Noninformative Prior

Although the inclusion of prior information is one of the main distinguishing features of the Bayesian approach to inference, it is possible, and indeed sometimes desirable, to follow the Bayesian approach without including substantial prior information. If prior knowledge about a parameter is vague or diffuse, or if it is advantageous to present results in terms of a posterior p.d.f. that is completely dominated by the sample information, then Bayesian analysis with a noninformative prior is suitable.

In this subsection we continue with the consumption function example $y_t = x_t\beta + e_t$, and we illustrate how to set up a noninformative prior p.d.f. for β and how to derive the corresponding posterior p.d.f. Because we hold strong prior views about what are likely and unlikely values for the marginal propensity to consume β, this example is not an ideal one to use to illustrate noninformative prior information. Nevertheless, we will proceed under the assumption that we are completely ignorant about β, even to the extent that β could lie anywhere in the range $-\infty$ to ∞.

To specify a noninformative prior p.d.f. we follow the convention that was introduced in Section 4.2.2, namely, that for parameters that can take values from $-\infty$ to ∞, a uniform prior p.d.f. is employed. In the context of our current example, we have the uniform prior

$$g(\beta) \propto \text{constant} \qquad -\infty < \beta < \infty \tag{7.2.16}$$

This p.d.f. is regarded as vague or noninformative because it implies that all finite intervals of equal length are equally likely to contain β. Also, as indicated in Section 4.2.2, it is termed an improper prior p.d.f. because it does not integrate to unity (or any other finite constant). This property is not regarded as undesirable, because we can still derive a proper posterior p.d.f. on which inferences can be based.

To derive the posterior p.d.f. that corresponds to the noninformative prior in (7.2.16) we use Bayes' theorem and obtain

$$\begin{aligned} g(\beta|\mathbf{y}) &\propto g(\beta)\ell(\beta|\mathbf{y}) \\ &\propto \text{constant} \times \exp\left\{-\sum_{t=1}^{T}(y_t - \beta x_t)^2/2\sigma^2\right\} \end{aligned} \tag{7.2.17}$$

Clearly, the posterior p.d.f. will be of the same form as the likelihood function. To rewrite (7.2.17) in a more convenient form, we will use the result

$$\sum_{t=1}^{T}(y_t - \beta x_t)^2 = \sum_{t=1}^{T} x_t^2(\beta - b)^2 + \sum_{t=1}^{T} y_t^2 - b^2\sum_{t=1}^{T} x_t^2 \tag{7.2.18}$$

where $b = \sum_{t=1}^{T} x_t y_t / \sum_{t=1}^{T} x_t^2$. You are encouraged to verify this result for yourself. Substituting (7.2.18) into (7.2.17) and rearranging yields

$$g(\beta|\mathbf{y}) \propto \exp\left\{-\left(\sum_{t=1}^{T} x_t^2/2\sigma^2\right)(\beta - b)^2\right\} \exp\left\{-\left(\sum_{t=1}^{T} y_t^2 - b^2\sum_{t=1}^{T} x_t^2\right)/2\sigma^2\right\} \tag{7.2.19}$$

The second term in this expression can be absorbed into the proportionality constant because it does not depend on β (and because we have assumed that σ^2 is known). Thus, as the final expression for the posterior p.d.f. for β, we have

$$g(\beta|\mathbf{y}) \propto \exp\left\{-\left(\sum_{t=1}^{T} x_t^2/2\sigma^2\right)(\beta - b)^2\right\} \tag{7.2.20}$$

This expression is the kernel of a normal p.d.f. with mean b and variance $\sigma^2/\sum_{t=1}^{T} x_t^2$. Hence, when a noninformative prior on β is used, and the variance σ^2 is known, the posterior p.d.f. for β is given by

$$(\beta|\mathbf{y}) \sim N\left[b, \sigma^2\bigg/\sum_{t=1}^{T} x_t^2\right] \tag{7.2.21}$$

Note that this result is similar to the sampling theory result, although the interpretation is quite different. The sampling theory result is that the least squares estimator $b \sim N(\beta, \sigma^2/\sum_{t=1}^{T} x_t^2)$; probability statements are made about possible values for b *before* a sample is taken. The Bayesian result in (7.2.21) makes it possible to make probability statements about possible values of β *after* a sample has been taken.

Applying the foregoing analysis to the available data on the consumption function example yields

$$(\beta|\mathbf{y}) \sim N[0.89675, (0.040204)^2] \tag{7.2.22}$$

A graph of this p.d.f. is presented in Figure 7.2, along with the informative prior, and the posterior p.d.f. derived from the informative prior. Including all three

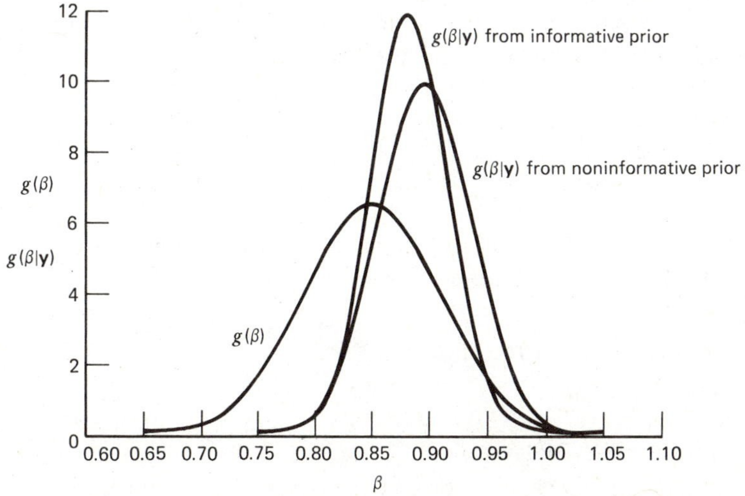

Figure 7.2 Prior and posterior p.d.f.'s for the marginal propensity to consume.

p.d.f.'s on the one graph clearly shows the contributions of the prior and sample information to the posterior p.d.f.

The statements made at the end of the previous subsection, concerning the presentation of results, are equally appropriate at this point. The results can be presented in terms of the complete posterior p.d.f., or use can be made of point estimates, HPD intervals, or posterior odds ratios.

7.3 Bayesian Inference for the General Linear Model with Known Disturbance Variance

The simple model that was analyzed in Section 7.2 is a good device for introducing Bayesian inference in the linear statistical model, but, because it only contains one explanatory variable and no intercept term, it is a very restrictive model. It is important to generalize the results of the previous section to the general linear statistical model with K explanatory variables, one of which may be an intercept term. Thus, in this section we are concerned with the model

$$\mathbf{y} = X\boldsymbol{\beta} + \mathbf{e} \tag{7.3.1}$$

where $\mathbf{y}$ is a $(T \times 1)$ vector of observations on a dependent variable, X is a $(T \times K)$ matrix of observations on K explanatory variables, $\boldsymbol{\beta}$ is a $(K \times 1)$ vector of unknown coefficients, and $\mathbf{e} \sim N(\mathbf{0}, \sigma^2 I)$, with σ^2 assumed known. We are interested in learning about the $(K \times 1)$ vector $\boldsymbol{\beta}$.

The learning process within a Bayesian framework involves specifying a prior p.d.f. for $\boldsymbol{\beta}$, collecting a sample of observations $\mathbf{y}$ that is represented by the likelihood function, and combining the prior and likelihood functions to form a posterior p.d.f. These steps are examined for a natural conjugate informative prior p.d.f. in Subsection 7.3.1 and for a noninformative prior p.d.f. in Subsection 7.3.2. An example is given in Section 7.4. As we will see, the main features that distinguish the analysis in these sections from that in the previous section are the use of multivariate posterior and prior p.d.f.'s for $\boldsymbol{\beta}$, and the fact that joint inferences about the elements in $\boldsymbol{\beta}$ may be relevant.

7.3.1 Posterior Distribution from an Informative Prior

The natural conjugate prior p.d.f. for $\boldsymbol{\beta}$, when σ^2 is known, is the multivariate normal p.d.f.

$$g(\boldsymbol{\beta}) \propto \exp\left\{-\tfrac{1}{2}(\boldsymbol{\beta} - \bar{\boldsymbol{\beta}})'\Sigma_{\boldsymbol{\beta}}(\boldsymbol{\beta} - \bar{\boldsymbol{\beta}})\right\} \tag{7.3.2}$$

where $\bar{\boldsymbol{\beta}}$ is the prior mean and $\bar{\Sigma}_{\boldsymbol{\beta}}$ is the prior covariance matrix for $\boldsymbol{\beta}$. To use this p.d.f. as an informative prior for $\boldsymbol{\beta}$ we need to assign values to $\bar{\boldsymbol{\beta}}$ and $\bar{\Sigma}_{\boldsymbol{\beta}}$, based on our prior knowledge. This task is considerably more difficult than specifying the parameters for a univariate prior p.d.f. because of the need to specify prior covariances in the matrix $\bar{\Sigma}_{\boldsymbol{\beta}}$. Nevertheless, methods do exist for using prior knowledge to specify such values, and one method will be illustrated in Section 7.4.

In (7.3.2) we have omitted the constant of proportionality, which is equal to $(2\pi)^{-K/2}|\bar{\Sigma}_{\boldsymbol{\beta}}|^{-1/2}$, leaving the kernel of the multivariate normal density. The kernel is sufficient to identify a p.d.f. as being of the multivariate normal form. The multivariate normal is, of course, only one of many distributions that might be appropriate for expressing prior information. Because it is a natural conjugate prior for the normal likelihood, the multivariate normal combines easily with the likelihood and is a good example for an introductory text.

Ignoring irrelevant constants, and using the fact that σ^2 is known, the likelihood function for $\boldsymbol{\beta}$, given a sample $\mathbf{y}' = (y_1, y_2, \ldots, y_T)$, is

$$\ell(\boldsymbol{\beta}|\mathbf{y}) \propto \exp\{-(\mathbf{y} - X\boldsymbol{\beta})'(\mathbf{y} - X\boldsymbol{\beta})/2\sigma^2\} \tag{7.3.3}$$

Before multiplying the prior $g(\boldsymbol{\beta})$ by the likelihood $\ell(\boldsymbol{\beta}|\mathbf{y})$, it is convenient to make some slight changes to $g(\boldsymbol{\beta})$. Let $A = \sigma^2\bar{\Sigma}_{\boldsymbol{\beta}}^{-1}$ so that $\bar{\Sigma}_{\boldsymbol{\beta}}^{-1} = A/\sigma^2$. Furthermore, define a symmetric matrix $A^{1/2}$ that has the property $A^{1/2}A^{1/2} = A$. Using results in A.11 of Appendix A, it can be shown that if A is a positive definite matrix (as it will be in this case), then a symmetric $A^{1/2}$ with the required property will always exist. We do not need to know how to compute $A^{1/2}$, this matrix is simply a convenient device for simplifying the required algebra.

Given these new definitions, the prior p.d.f. in (7.3.2) can be rewritten as

$$g(\boldsymbol{\beta}) \propto \exp\{-(A^{1/2}\bar{\boldsymbol{\beta}} - A^{1/2}\boldsymbol{\beta})'(A^{1/2}\bar{\boldsymbol{\beta}} - A^{1/2}\boldsymbol{\beta})/2\sigma^2\} \tag{7.3.4}$$

Using Bayes' theorem we now obtain

$$\begin{aligned}
g(\boldsymbol{\beta}|\mathbf{y}) &\propto g(\boldsymbol{\beta})\ell(\boldsymbol{\beta}|\mathbf{y}) \\
&\propto \exp\{-[(A^{1/2}\bar{\boldsymbol{\beta}} - A^{1/2}\boldsymbol{\beta})'(A^{1/2}\bar{\boldsymbol{\beta}} - A^{1/2}\boldsymbol{\beta}) + (\mathbf{y} - X\boldsymbol{\beta})'(\mathbf{y} - X\boldsymbol{\beta})]/2\sigma^2\} \\
&= \exp\left\{-\frac{1}{2\sigma^2}\left[\begin{pmatrix} A^{1/2}\bar{\boldsymbol{\beta}} - A^{1/2}\boldsymbol{\beta} \\ \mathbf{y} - X\boldsymbol{\beta} \end{pmatrix}'\begin{pmatrix} A^{1/2}\bar{\boldsymbol{\beta}} - A^{1/2}\boldsymbol{\beta} \\ \mathbf{y} - X\boldsymbol{\beta} \end{pmatrix}\right]\right\} \\
&= \exp\{-(\mathbf{w} - G\boldsymbol{\beta})'(\mathbf{w} - G\boldsymbol{\beta})/2\sigma^2\}
\end{aligned} \tag{7.3.5}$$

where

$$\mathbf{w} = \begin{pmatrix} A^{1/2}\bar{\boldsymbol{\beta}} \\ \mathbf{y} \end{pmatrix} \quad \text{and} \quad G = \begin{pmatrix} A^{1/2} \\ X \end{pmatrix}$$

The $[(K + T) \times 1]$ vector $\mathbf{w}$ and the $[(K + T) \times K]$ matrix G are also definitions of convenience; they will not be retained after simplification of the posterior p.d.f. in (7.3.5).

It is useful to introduce a result given in Exercise 7.3, namely

$$(\mathbf{w} - G\boldsymbol{\beta})'(\mathbf{w} - G\boldsymbol{\beta}) = (\boldsymbol{\beta} - \bar{\bar{\boldsymbol{\beta}}})'G'G(\boldsymbol{\beta} - \bar{\bar{\boldsymbol{\beta}}}) + (\mathbf{w} - G\bar{\bar{\boldsymbol{\beta}}})'(\mathbf{w} - G\bar{\bar{\boldsymbol{\beta}}}) \tag{7.3.6}$$

where

$$\begin{aligned}
\bar{\bar{\boldsymbol{\beta}}} &= (G'G)^{-1}G'\mathbf{w} \\
&= \left[(A^{1/2} \quad X')\begin{pmatrix} A^{1/2} \\ X \end{pmatrix}\right]^{-1}(A^{1/2} \quad X')\begin{pmatrix} A^{1/2}\bar{\boldsymbol{\beta}} \\ \mathbf{y} \end{pmatrix} \\
&= (A + X'X)^{-1}(A\bar{\boldsymbol{\beta}} + X'\mathbf{y}) \\
&= (A + X'X)^{-1}(A\bar{\boldsymbol{\beta}} + X'X\mathbf{b})
\end{aligned} \tag{7.3.7}$$

and $\mathbf{b} = (X'X)^{-1}X'\mathbf{y}$. The second term in (7.3.6) does not contain $\boldsymbol{\beta}$. Thus, when (7.3.6) is substituted into the exponent in (7.3.5), the second term can be absorbed into the proportionality constant yielding

$$\begin{aligned}
g(\boldsymbol{\beta}|\mathbf{y}) &\propto \exp\{-(\boldsymbol{\beta} - \bar{\bar{\boldsymbol{\beta}}})'G'G(\boldsymbol{\beta} - \bar{\bar{\boldsymbol{\beta}}})/2\sigma^2\} \\
&= \exp\{-(\boldsymbol{\beta} - \bar{\bar{\boldsymbol{\beta}}})'(A + X'X)(\boldsymbol{\beta} - \bar{\bar{\boldsymbol{\beta}}})/2\sigma^2\} \\
&= \exp\{-\tfrac{1}{2}(\boldsymbol{\beta} - \bar{\bar{\boldsymbol{\beta}}})'(\bar{\Sigma}_{\boldsymbol{\beta}}^{-1} + X'X/\sigma^2)(\boldsymbol{\beta} - \bar{\bar{\boldsymbol{\beta}}})\} \\
&= \exp\{-\tfrac{1}{2}(\boldsymbol{\beta} - \bar{\bar{\boldsymbol{\beta}}})'\bar{\bar{\Sigma}}_{\boldsymbol{\beta}}^{-1}(\boldsymbol{\beta} - \bar{\bar{\boldsymbol{\beta}}}\}
\end{aligned} \tag{7.3.8}$$

where

$$\bar{\bar{\Sigma}}_{\boldsymbol{\beta}}^{-1} = \bar{\Sigma}_{\boldsymbol{\beta}}^{-1} + X'X/\sigma^2 \tag{7.3.9}$$

and

$$\begin{aligned}
\bar{\bar{\boldsymbol{\beta}}} &= (A + X'X)^{-1}(A\bar{\boldsymbol{\beta}} + X'X\mathbf{b}) \\
&= [\bar{\Sigma}_{\boldsymbol{\beta}}^{-1} + X'X/\sigma^2]^{-1}[\bar{\Sigma}_{\boldsymbol{\beta}}^{-1}\bar{\boldsymbol{\beta}} + (X'X/\sigma^2)\mathbf{b}]
\end{aligned} \tag{7.3.10}$$

The kernel in (7.3.8) is recognizable as that of a multivariate normal distribution with mean $\bar{\bar{\boldsymbol{\beta}}}$ and covariance matrix $\bar{\bar{\Sigma}}_{\boldsymbol{\beta}}$. Thus, for the posterior p.d.f. for $\boldsymbol{\beta}$, we have

$$(\boldsymbol{\beta}|\mathbf{y}) \sim N(\bar{\bar{\boldsymbol{\beta}}}, \bar{\bar{\Sigma}}_{\boldsymbol{\beta}}) \tag{7.3.11}$$

To interpret the posterior mean and covariance matrix we generalize the precision concepts that were used in scalar form in Section 7.2. The precision matrix of the prior p.d.f. is $\bar{\Sigma}_{\boldsymbol{\beta}}^{-1}$, the inverse of the prior covariance matrix. The precision matrix for the sample information is $X'X/\sigma^2$, which can be viewed as the inverse of the covariance matrix of the posterior p.d.f. derived from a noninformative prior, (Section 7.3.2), or as the inverse of the covariance matrix of the sampling theory least squares estimator. The posterior precision matrix is, similarly, the inverse of the posterior covariance matrix, and, as indicated in (7.3.9), it is equal to the sum of the prior precision and the sampling precision. The expression for the posterior mean $\bar{\bar{\boldsymbol{\beta}}}$ given in (7.3.10) illustrates that the posterior mean is a matrix weighted average of the prior mean $\bar{\boldsymbol{\beta}}$ and the least squares estimator $\mathbf{b}$, with the weights given by the respective precision matrices.

The properties of matrix-weighted averages have been studied by Chamberlain and Leamer (1976) and Leamer (1978, 1982). One property is that, except under special and unlikely circumstances, it will not be true that $\bar{\bar{\boldsymbol{\beta}}}$ lies between $\mathbf{b}$ and $\bar{\boldsymbol{\beta}}$, in the sense that each element in $\bar{\bar{\boldsymbol{\beta}}}$ lies between the corresponding elements from the other two vectors. This result is in contrast to the case of a simple weighted average. A simple illustrative example is provided in Section 7.4.

Another point worth noting is that a natural conjugate prior is equivalent to assuming that we have information from some previous hypothetical sample. If this hypothetical sample information is combined with our current sample and the combined sample is used in conjunction with a noninformative prior, we would get results identical to those just presented.

The multivariate posterior p.d.f. in (7.3.8) is an expression of our knowledge about the complete vector $\boldsymbol{\beta}$. An example is given in Section 7.4 where a two-dimensional HPD region is computed. If we wish to express our knowledge about a single parameter from the vector $\boldsymbol{\beta}$, say β_1, then we need to derive the univariate marginal posterior p.d.f. for β_1. This task is an easy one because all marginal p.d.f.'s from a multivariate normal distribution are also normal distributions. In particular, $(\beta_1|\mathbf{y}) \sim N(\bar{\bar{\beta}}_1, c_{11})$ where $\bar{\bar{\beta}}_1$ is the first element of $\bar{\bar{\boldsymbol{\beta}}}$ and c_{11} is the first diagonal element of the matrix $\bar{\bar{\Sigma}}_{\boldsymbol{\beta}}$.

7.3.2 Posterior Distribution from a Noninformative Prior

To generalize the analysis in Section 7.2.2. to a model with K explanatory variables and a $(K \times 1)$ parameter vector $\boldsymbol{\beta}$, we begin by assigning a noninformative prior to $\boldsymbol{\beta}$, assuming that each element in $\boldsymbol{\beta}$ could lie in the interval $-\infty$ to ∞. The conventional noninformative prior for the kth element in $\boldsymbol{\beta}$ is $g(\beta_k) \propto$ constant. Since we are assuming ignorance about all the elements in $\boldsymbol{\beta}$, it seems reasonable to assume these elements are a priori independent, in which case the noninformative prior p.d.f. for the complete vector becomes

$$\begin{aligned} g(\boldsymbol{\beta}) &= g(\beta_1)g(\beta_2)\cdots g(\beta_K) \\ &\propto \text{constant} \end{aligned} \tag{7.3.12}$$

Using the result in (7.3.6), but in terms of notation relevant for this section, the likelihood function can be written as

$$\begin{aligned}\ell(\boldsymbol{\beta}|\mathbf{y}) &\propto \exp\{-(\mathbf{y}-X\boldsymbol{\beta})'(\mathbf{y}-X\boldsymbol{\beta})/2\sigma^2\} \\ &\propto \exp\{-[(\boldsymbol{\beta}-\mathbf{b})'X'X(\boldsymbol{\beta}-\mathbf{b}) + (\mathbf{y}-X\mathbf{b})'(\mathbf{y}-X\mathbf{b})]/2\sigma^2\} \\ &\propto \exp\{-(\boldsymbol{\beta}-\mathbf{b})'X'X(\boldsymbol{\beta}-\mathbf{b})/2\sigma^2\} \qquad (7.3.13)\end{aligned}$$

where $\mathbf{b} = (X'X)^{-1}X'\mathbf{y}$ is the least squares estimator. Since the prior p.d.f. is proportional to a constant, the posterior p.d.f. is identical to the likelihood, namely

$$g(\boldsymbol{\beta}|\mathbf{y}) \propto \exp\{-(\boldsymbol{\beta}-\mathbf{b})'X'X(\boldsymbol{\beta}-\mathbf{b})/2\sigma^2\} \qquad (7.3.14)$$

This p.d.f. is a multivariate normal with mean $\mathbf{b}$ and covariance matrix $\sigma^2(X'X)^{-1}$. Thus, for the posterior p.d.f. derived from a noninformative prior, with σ^2 known, we have

$$(\boldsymbol{\beta}|\mathbf{y}) \sim N[\mathbf{b}, \sigma^2(X'X)^{-1}] \qquad (7.3.15)$$

As we found in the simple introductory example in Section 7.2, this result is similar in form, but not in interpretation, to the sampling theory result. The sampling theory result is $\mathbf{b} \sim N[\boldsymbol{\beta}, \sigma^2(X'X)^{-1}]$ and is concerned with probability statements about future hypothetical values of $\mathbf{b}$. The Bayesian result is concerned with probability statements about $\boldsymbol{\beta}$, given our current state of knowledge; that is, given the observed sample information.

If we wish to make inferences about a single element in $\boldsymbol{\beta}$, or to summarize our knowledge about a single element in $\boldsymbol{\beta}$, then it is straightforward to extract a univariate marginal normal posterior p.d.f. from the joint posterior p.d.f. in (7.3.15).

7.4 An Example

In this section we use a Cobb–Douglas production function to illustrate how to specify a natural conjugate prior and how to derive the posterior p.d.f. from that natural conjugate prior. Consider the model

$$\mathbf{y} = \beta_1\mathbf{x}_1 + \beta_2\mathbf{x}_2 + \beta_3\mathbf{x}_3 + \mathbf{e} \qquad (7.4.1)$$

where $\mathbf{e} \sim N(\mathbf{0}, \sigma^2 I)$, the vectors $\mathbf{y}$, $\mathbf{x}_1$, $\mathbf{x}_2$, and $\mathbf{x}_3$ are observable, and we wish to estimate $\boldsymbol{\beta} = (\beta_1, \beta_2, \beta_3)'$. Our prior information will depend on the type of process represented by (7.4.1). Let us assume that it comes originally from the Cobb–Douglas production function

$$Q_t = \alpha L_t^{\beta_2} K_t^{\beta_3} \exp(e_t) \qquad (7.4.2)$$

where Q_t, L_t, and K_t represent output, labor, and capital, respectively, and $y_t = \ln Q_t$, $x_{t1} \equiv 1$, $x_{2t} = \ln L_t$, $x_{3t} = \ln K_t$, and $\beta_1 = \ln \alpha$. It is clear that if we take logarithms of (7.4.2) we obtain (7.4.1).

In terms of prior information about β_2 and β_3 we would expect, from economic theory, that $0 < \beta_2 < 1$ and $0 < \beta_3 < 1$. Strictly speaking, these constraints cannot be handled with a normal prior distribution where the range is $-\infty$ to $+\infty$. In practice, however, by appropriately setting the prior variances of β_2 and β_3, the probability of these parameters being outside the range 0 to 1 can be made very small.

We will assume that our prior information about β_2, β_3, and the returns to scale $\beta_2 + \beta_3$ is such that

$$E[\beta_2] = E[\beta_3] = 0.5 \qquad E[\beta_2 + \beta_3] = 1.0 \tag{7.4.3}$$

$$P(0.9 < \beta_2 + \beta_3 < 1.1) = 0.9 \tag{7.4.4}$$

$$P(0.2 < \beta_2 < 0.8) = P(0.2 < \beta_3 < 0.8) = 0.9 \tag{7.4.5}$$

Thus, we feel confident that the returns to scale $\beta_2 + \beta_3$ is close to unity, but we are rather uncertain about the relative contributions of β_2 and β_3. For β_1 we assume that our prior information is such that

$$E[\beta_1] = 5.0 \qquad \text{and} \qquad P(-10 < \beta_1 < 20) = 0.9 \tag{7.4.6}$$

and that our prior knowledge about β_1 is not affected by (is independent of) our prior knowledge concerning β_2 and β_3. In line with Section 7.3 we will assume that σ^2 is known and, in particular, that its value is $\sigma^2 = 0.09$. Furthermore, we will assume that our prior views about $\boldsymbol{\beta}$ can be adequately represented by a normal distribution.

We are now in a position to compute values for the prior mean $\bar{\boldsymbol{\beta}}$ and the prior covariance matrix $\Sigma_{\boldsymbol{\beta}}$. The prior mean can be written down immediately as

$$E[\boldsymbol{\beta}] = \bar{\boldsymbol{\beta}} = (5.0, 0.5, 0.5)' \tag{7.4.7}$$

To obtain the prior variance for β_2 (and that for β_3) we begin by noting that for a standard normal random variable z,

$$P(-1.645 < z < 1.645) = 0.9 \tag{7.4.8}$$

Using properties of the normal distribution we have

$$P\left(-1.645 < \frac{\beta_2 - 0.5}{\sqrt{\text{var}(\beta_2)}} < 1.645\right) = 0.9$$

from which we obtain

$$P(0.5 - 1.645\sqrt{\text{var}(\beta_2)} < \beta_2 < 0.5 + 1.645\sqrt{\text{var}(\beta_2)}) = 0.9 \tag{7.4.9}$$

Since (7.4.5) and (7.4.9) are identical probability statements we can write

$$0.5 - 1.645\sqrt{\text{var}(\beta_2)} = 0.2 \qquad \text{and} \qquad 0.5 + 1.645\sqrt{\text{var}(\beta_2)} = 0.8$$

Solving either of these equations yields

$$\text{var}(\beta_2) = (0.3/1.645)^2 = 0.03325912 \tag{7.4.10}$$

Following a similar procedure for β_3 and β_1 yields

$$\text{var}(\beta_3) = (0.3/1.645)^2 = 0.03325912 \tag{7.4.11}$$

$$\text{var}(\beta_1) = (15/1.645)^2 = 83.14779 \tag{7.4.12}$$

To establish the prior covariances we first note that

$$\text{cov}(\beta_1, \beta_2) = \text{cov}(\beta_1, \beta_3) = 0 \tag{7.4.13}$$

because β_1 is a priori independent of β_2 and β_3. For the covariance between β_2 and β_3 we begin by using the information in (7.4.3) and (7.4.4) to derive

$$\text{var}(\beta_2 + \beta_3) = (0.1/1.645)^2 = 0.00369546$$

Then,

$$\text{var}(\beta_2 + \beta_3) = \text{var}(\beta_2) + \text{var}(\beta_3) + 2\,\text{cov}(\beta_2, \beta_3)$$

or

$$0.00369546 = 2 \times 0.03325912 + 2\,\text{cov}(\beta_2, \beta_3)$$

Solving this equation yields

$$\text{cov}(\beta_2, \beta_3) = -0.03141139 \tag{7.4.14}$$

Collecting the terms in equations (7.4.10) to (7.4.14) gives the prior covariance matrix

$$\bar{\Sigma}_{\boldsymbol{\beta}} = \begin{bmatrix} 83.14779 & 0.0 & 0.0 \\ 0.0 & 0.03325912 & -0.03141139 \\ 0.0 & -0.03141139 & 0.03325912 \end{bmatrix} \tag{7.4.15}$$

This example of specification of a natural conjugate prior may have left you rather uneasy about the general problem of specifying an informative prior distribution. It is relatively easy to use percentiles of the normal distribution, as we have done, to specify a prior mean and variance for each of the elements in $\boldsymbol{\beta}$. It is difficult, however, even for the trained statistician, to conceptualize prior information in terms of the covariances of the elements in $\boldsymbol{\beta}$. In our example we were fortunate to be able to use an economically meaningful quantity, the returns to scale, to assess the covariance between β_2 and β_3. This would not have been quite so easy if there were more than two inputs or if our function was not a Cobb–Douglas production function. Such difficulties have led to research into the assessment or elicitation of prior density functions. Various approaches have been suggested, and we refer you to Dickey (1980), Kadane (1980), Kadane et al (1980), Winkler (1967, 1977, 1980), and Zellner (1972).

Returning to our example, we now assume we have available the sample of 20 observations listed in Table 7.2. If we were following a sampling theory approach we would compute a value for the least squares estimator and its covariance matrix. Carrying out these computations yields

$$\mathbf{b} = (X'X)^{-1}X'\mathbf{y} = (9.770, 0.524, 0.693)' \tag{7.4.16}$$

Table 7.2 A Sample of Observations on the Cobb–Douglas Production Function

y	x_1	x_2	x_3
10.74126	1	0.693	0.693
10.98296	1	1.733	0.693
10.52923	1	0.693	1.386
11.58911	1	1.733	1.386
11.79831	1	0.693	1.792
11.75854	1	2.340	0.693
11.94535	1	1.733	1.792
12.33049	1	2.340	1.386
11.89575	1	2.340	1.792
10.35612	1	0.693	0.693
11.16725	1	0.693	1.386
11.16556	1	1.733	0.693
11.68194	1	1.733	1.386
11.41347	1	0.693	1.792
11.20968	1	2.340	0.693
11.98168	1	1.733	1.792
12.32426	1	2.340	1.386
12.02976	1	2.340	1.792
11.39302	1	1.733	1.386
10.89403	1	0.693	0.693

and

$$\sigma^2(X'X)^{-1} = 0.09\begin{bmatrix} 0.65660 & -0.15312 & -0.29171 \\ -0.15312 & 0.11049 & -0.01443 \\ -0.29171 & -0.01443 & 0.24824 \end{bmatrix} \tag{7.4.17}$$

In the Bayesian approach we derive instead the posterior p.d.f. for $\boldsymbol{\beta}$. From Section 7.3 we know that this p.d.f. will be normal, and, for this particular sample of observations, its mean and covariance matrix will be

$$\begin{aligned} \bar{\bar{\boldsymbol{\beta}}} &= [\bar{\Sigma}_{\boldsymbol{\beta}}^{-1} + X'X/\sigma^2]^{-1}[\bar{\Sigma}_{\boldsymbol{\beta}}^{-1}\bar{\boldsymbol{\beta}} + (X'X/\sigma^2)\mathbf{b}] \\ &= (10.028, 0.476, 0.548)' \end{aligned} \tag{7.4.18}$$

and

$$\begin{aligned} \bar{\bar{\Sigma}}_{\boldsymbol{\beta}} &= [\bar{\Sigma}_{\boldsymbol{\beta}}^{-1} + X'X/\sigma^2]^{-1} \\ &= \begin{bmatrix} 0.011045 & -0.003196 & -0.001256 \\ -0.003196 & 0.006396 & -0.005315 \\ -0.001256 & -0.005315 & 0.007508 \end{bmatrix} \end{aligned} \tag{7.4.19}$$

These results can be used to describe our current state of knowledge about any single parameter, such as β_2, or any set of parameters, such as β_2 and β_3. The marginal posterior p.d.f. for β_2 is

$$(\beta_2|\mathbf{y}) \sim N(0.476, 0.006395)$$

This p.d.f., along with the prior p.d.f.,

$$\beta_2 \sim N(0.5, 0.033259)$$

are graphed in Figure 7.3. The influence of the sample information on the prior information is clear. It has led to a posterior p.d.f. that, relative to the prior, has much lower variance (indicating our knowledge is more precise) and the distribution has moved slightly to the left. Further illustration of the change in precision can be obtained by comparing HPD intervals from the prior and posterior p.d.f.'s. (We will call Bayesian interval estimates from both the prior and posterior p.d.f.'s "HPD intervals," despite the fact that it is more conventional to use HPD as an abbreviation for highest posterior density rather than highest prior density.) From the *prior* p.d.f. for β_2 the 90% HPD interval was (0.2, 0.8). The 90% HPD interval from the *posterior* p.d.f. for β_2 is (0.344, 0.608). (You are encouraged to verify that this latter interval is correct.)

As an example of presenting information about a set of parameters, we will find joint 95% HPD regions for β_2 and β_3 from both prior and posterior p.d.f.'s. Considering first the prior p.d.f., it follows, from a result in Chapter 2, that

$$Q_0 = \begin{pmatrix} \beta_2 - \bar{\beta}_2 \\ \beta_3 - \bar{\beta}_3 \end{pmatrix}' \begin{pmatrix} \operatorname{var}(\beta_2) & \operatorname{cov}(\beta_2, \beta_3) \\ \operatorname{cov}(\beta_2, \beta_3) & \operatorname{var}(\beta_3) \end{pmatrix}^{-1} \begin{pmatrix} \beta_2 - \bar{\beta}_2 \\ \beta_3 - \bar{\beta}_3 \end{pmatrix} \sim \chi^2_{(2)} \tag{7.4.20}$$

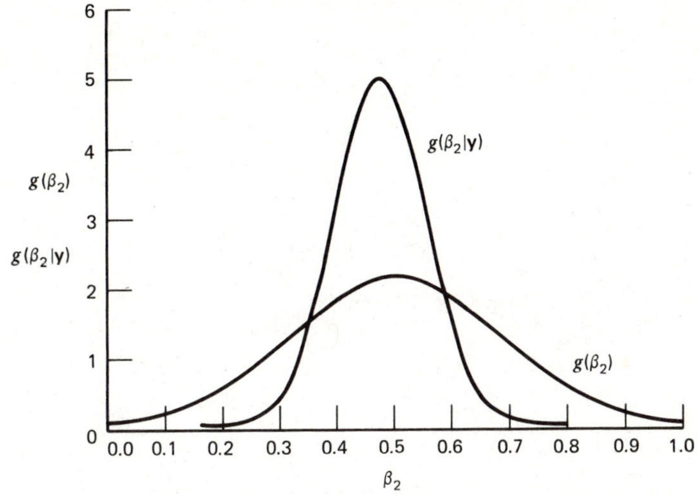

Figure 7.3 Prior and posterior p.d.f.'s for β_2 when σ is known.

Substituting in the values for the prior means, variances, and covariance given in (7.4.7) and (7.4.15), and taking the inverse, yields

$$\begin{aligned} Q_0 &= \begin{pmatrix} \beta_2 - 0.5 \\ \beta_3 - 0.5 \end{pmatrix}' \begin{pmatrix} 278.33 & 262.87 \\ 262.87 & 278.33 \end{pmatrix} \begin{pmatrix} \beta_2 - 0.5 \\ \beta_3 - 0.5 \end{pmatrix} \\ &= 278.33(\beta_2 - 0.5)^2 + 278.33(\beta_3 - 0.5)^2 + 525.74(\beta_2 - 0.5)(\beta_3 - 0.5) \end{aligned} \tag{7.4.21}$$

From tables of the $\chi^2_{(2)}$ distribution we find that

$$P(Q_0 \leq 5.99) = 0.95$$

Thus, the 95% HPD region from the prior p.d.f. is given by those values of β_2 and β_3 inside the ellipse

$$278.33(\beta_2 - 0.5)^2 + 278.33(\beta_3 - 0.5)^2 + 525.74(\beta_2 - 0.5)(\beta_3 - 0.5) = 5.99 \tag{7.4.22}$$

Following a similar procedure based on the posterior means, variances, and covariance given in (7.4.18) and (7.4.19) yields the 95% HPD region from the posterior p.d.f. You are encouraged to verify that this region will be those values of β_2 and β_3 inside the ellipse

$$380.23(\beta_2 - 0.476)^2 + 323.97(\beta_3 - 0.548)^2 + 538.61(\beta_2 - 0.476)(\beta_3 - 0.548) = 5.99 \tag{7.4.23}$$

The two ellipses are graphed in Figure 7.4.

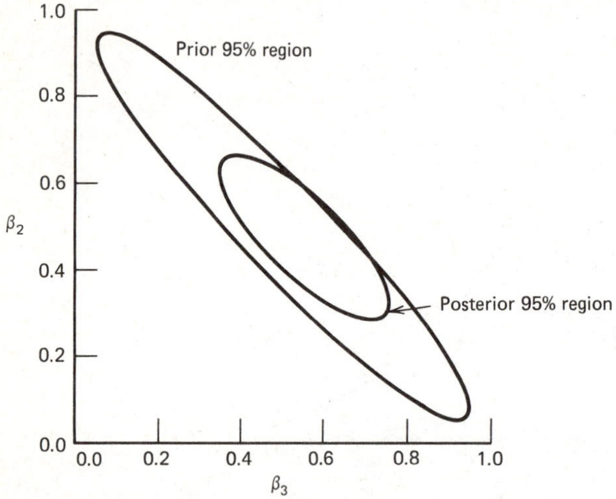

Figure 7.4 Prior and posterior 95% probability regions for β_2 and β_3 when σ is known.

The larger ellipse is the 95% region based on our prior information; it is centered around the line $\beta_2 + \beta_3 = 1$ (constant returns to scale), and it reflects the large degree of uncertainty about the relative contributions of β_2 and β_3 to the returns to scale. The 95% posterior region is represented by the smaller ellipse; it shows how the sample information has made our knowledge about β_2 and β_3 much more precise. It still tends to be centered around the line $\beta_2 + \beta_3 = 1$, although it has moved slightly to the northeast, intersecting the prior ellipse. The movement to the northeast is a reflection of the fact that the sum of the posterior means is slightly greater than unity, $\bar{\bar{\beta}}_2 + \bar{\bar{\beta}}_3 = 1.024$.

7.5 Point Estimation

7.5.1 The Posterior Mean as a Point Estimator

Details of point estimation within the Bayesian framework and the relationship between Bayesian and sampling theory estimates were outlined in Chapter 4. In that chapter we indicated how a Bayesian estimator can be obtained by first specifying a loss function that depends on the estimator and the unknown parameter value and then choosing that estimator that minimizes expected posterior loss. We found that, when the loss function is quadratic the mean of the posterior density function is the optimal point estimator and, when the loss function is linear, the posterior median is optimal. These were general results, and so they hold for the model and parameters under discussion in this chapter. However, it is instructive to consider a more general quadratic loss function that depends on the difference between a vector of parameters and its estimator.

Specifically, consider the loss function

$$L = (\boldsymbol{\beta} - \boldsymbol{\beta}^*)'B(\boldsymbol{\beta} - \boldsymbol{\beta}^*) \tag{7.5.1}$$

where B is a known positive definite matrix and $\boldsymbol{\beta}^*$ is an estimator for $\boldsymbol{\beta}$. The Bayesian point estimator is given by $\boldsymbol{\beta}^*$ that minimizes $E[L]$, where the expectation is taken with respect to $g(\boldsymbol{\beta}|\mathbf{y})$. If, in (7.5.1), we add and subtract $E[\boldsymbol{\beta}]$ and take expectations, we have

$$\begin{aligned} E[L] &= E[(\boldsymbol{\beta} - E[\boldsymbol{\beta}]) + (E[\boldsymbol{\beta}] - \boldsymbol{\beta}^*)]'B[(\boldsymbol{\beta} - E[\boldsymbol{\beta}]) + (E[\boldsymbol{\beta}] - \boldsymbol{\beta}^*)] \\ &= E[(\boldsymbol{\beta} - E[\boldsymbol{\beta}])'B(\boldsymbol{\beta} - E[\boldsymbol{\beta}])] + [(E[\boldsymbol{\beta}] - \boldsymbol{\beta}^*)'B(E[\boldsymbol{\beta}] - \boldsymbol{\beta}^*)] \end{aligned} \tag{7.5.2}$$

with the last equality occurring because $(E[\boldsymbol{\beta}] - \boldsymbol{\beta}^*)$ is nonstochastic (with respect to $\boldsymbol{\beta}$) and the cross-product terms are 0. Because the first term in (7.5.2) does not involve $\boldsymbol{\beta}^*$ and because B is positive definite, $E[L]$ will be a minimum when $\boldsymbol{\beta}^* = E[\boldsymbol{\beta}]$. Thus we have generalized the Chapter 4 result concerning a scalar parameter to the case involving a vector of parameters. The posterior mean minimizes expected posterior loss for the general quadratic loss function in (7.5.1).

In the context of the linear statistical model considered in Section 7.3 and 7.4, where we were interested in the parameter vector $\boldsymbol{\beta}$, and the disturbance variance σ^2 was assumed known, the posterior mean was

$$\begin{aligned} E[\boldsymbol{\beta}|\mathbf{y}] = \bar{\bar{\boldsymbol{\beta}}} &= [\bar{\Sigma}_{\boldsymbol{\beta}}^{-1} + X'X/\sigma^2]^{-1}[\bar{\Sigma}_{\boldsymbol{\beta}}^{-1}\bar{\boldsymbol{\beta}} + (X'X/\sigma^2)\mathbf{b}] \\ &= (A + X'X)^{-1}(A\bar{\boldsymbol{\beta}} + X'X\mathbf{b}) \end{aligned} \tag{7.5.3}$$

where $\bar{\Sigma}_{\boldsymbol{\beta}}^{-1} = A/\sigma^2$. This estimator is the optimal Bayesian one under quadratic loss.

Before discussing the sampling theory properties of this estimator, it is useful to compare it with a "stochastic restrictions" estimator that will be introduced in Chapter 20. In Section 20.2.2 it is shown that when stochastic nonsample information of the form $\mathbf{r} = R\boldsymbol{\beta} + \mathbf{v}$, where $\mathbf{v} \sim N(\mathbf{0}, \sigma^2\Omega)$, is available, the Aitken or generalized least squares estimator is

$$\hat{\boldsymbol{\beta}} = (X'X + R'\Omega^{-1}R)^{-1}(X'\mathbf{y} + R'\Omega^{-1}\mathbf{r}) \tag{7.5.4}$$

This estimator can be viewed within a Bayesian context where, instead of establishing a prior p.d.f. on $\boldsymbol{\beta}$, we use a prior of the form $R\boldsymbol{\beta} \sim N(R\bar{\boldsymbol{\beta}}, \sigma^2\Omega)$ on the set of linear combinations $R\boldsymbol{\beta}$. Using this prior, and setting $\mathbf{r} = R\bar{\boldsymbol{\beta}}$ leads to a posterior mean given by (7.5.4). For a discussion of the different interpretations implied by the Bayesian and stochastic restrictions approaches, see Swamy and Mehta (1983).

The sampling theory properties of Bayesian estimators are sometimes of interest, despite the fact that many Bayesian researchers would present their results in terms of posterior p.d.f.'s and not concern themselves with estimator performance in repeated samples. In connection with sampling theory properties, we noted in Chapter 4 that if a proper prior is used, a Bayesian estimator will always be admissible in the sense that its risk function will never exceed that of another estimator for all points in the parameter space. If an improper prior is employed, however, this result will not necessarily hold. In particular, it can be shown that $\mathbf{b} = (X'X)^{-1}X'\mathbf{y}$, the posterior mean obtained from a noninformative improper prior (and the least squares estimator), will be inadmissible if $K \geq 3$. The inadmissibility of the least squares estimator will be illustrated in Section 7.5.2 and mentioned again in Chapter 20. In the remainder of this section we compare its sampling theory properties with those of the posterior mean $\bar{\bar{\boldsymbol{\beta}}}$.

Although $\mathbf{b}$ is minimum variance unbiased, it is possible for $\bar{\bar{\boldsymbol{\beta}}}$ to be an improvement on two counts. First $\bar{\bar{\boldsymbol{\beta}}}$ may be biased but have a variance sufficiently lower than that of $\mathbf{b}$ to make its mean square error less than that of $\mathbf{b}$. Second, $\mathbf{b}$ is only minimum variance unbiased from within the class of estimators that are functions of the sample information $\mathbf{y}$. The estimator $\bar{\bar{\boldsymbol{\beta}}}$ depends on both sample and prior information. If MSE[ ] denotes the mean square error matrix, then

$$\begin{aligned}\text{MSE}[\mathbf{b}] &= \text{cov}[\mathbf{b}] + \text{bias}[\mathbf{b}] \cdot \text{bias}[\mathbf{b}]' \\ &= \sigma^2(X'X)^{-1}\end{aligned}$$

Also it can be shown that (see Exercise 7.4)

$$\text{bias}[\bar{\bar{\boldsymbol{\beta}}}] = E[\bar{\bar{\boldsymbol{\beta}}}] - \boldsymbol{\beta} = WA\boldsymbol{\delta} \tag{7.5.5}$$

where $W = (A + X'X)^{-1}$ and $\boldsymbol{\delta} = \bar{\boldsymbol{\beta}} - \boldsymbol{\beta}$, and that

$$\text{cov}[\bar{\bar{\boldsymbol{\beta}}}] = E[(\bar{\bar{\boldsymbol{\beta}}} - E[\bar{\bar{\boldsymbol{\beta}}}])(\bar{\bar{\boldsymbol{\beta}}} - E[\bar{\bar{\boldsymbol{\beta}}}])'] = \sigma^2 WX'XW' \tag{7.5.6}$$

Thus

$$\text{MSE}[\bar{\bar{\boldsymbol{\beta}}}] = \sigma^2 WX'XW' + WA\boldsymbol{\delta}\boldsymbol{\delta}'A'W' \tag{7.5.7}$$

and, using the mean square error criterion, we say that $\bar{\bar{\boldsymbol{\beta}}}$ is better than $\mathbf{b}$ if

$$C = \sigma^2(X'X)^{-1} - \sigma^2 WX'XW' - WA\boldsymbol{\delta}\boldsymbol{\delta}'A'W' \tag{7.5.8}$$

is a positive definite matrix.

The conditions for this result to hold have been studied in detail by Giles and Rayner (1979). We will simply note their general result and consider the case of unbiased prior information. Their general result is that C is positive definite if and only if

$$\lambda = \boldsymbol{\delta}'[\sigma^2(X'X)^{-1} + 2\sigma^2 A^{-1}]^{-1}\boldsymbol{\delta} \leq 1 \tag{7.5.9}$$

When $\boldsymbol{\beta} = \bar{\boldsymbol{\beta}}$, and consequently $\boldsymbol{\delta} = \mathbf{0}$, we say that our prior information is unbiased. Under these circumstances $\bar{\bar{\boldsymbol{\beta}}}$ is also unbiased and $\lambda = 0 < 1$, implying that $\bar{\bar{\boldsymbol{\beta}}}$ will always be better than $\mathbf{b}$. When $\boldsymbol{\delta} \neq \mathbf{0}$, whether or not (7.5.9) holds will depend on the magnitude of the prior bias relative to the precision of the sample and prior information.

Note that $\lambda \leq 1$ implies that the mean square error of any linear combination of the elements of $\bar{\bar{\boldsymbol{\beta}}}$, for example, $\boldsymbol{\eta}'\bar{\bar{\boldsymbol{\beta}}}$, will be less than the mean square error of the corresponding linear combination of elements of $\mathbf{b}$, $\boldsymbol{\eta}'\mathbf{b}$. However, when $\lambda > 1$, we may find that MSE$[\boldsymbol{\eta}'\bar{\bar{\boldsymbol{\beta}}}]$ is less than MSE$[\boldsymbol{\eta}'\mathbf{b}]$ for some choices of $\boldsymbol{\eta}$ but greater for others.

7.5.2 Empirical Bayes' Estimation

The empirical Bayes' estimator is a point estimator that possesses characteristics of both sampling theory and Bayesian estimators. In this section we follow Casella (1985) and introduce empirical Bayes' estimation using the problem of estimating K means.

Specifically, assume we have K normally distributed random variables, each of which has a different mean β_k, but the same known variance σ^2. Suppose also that we have n observations on each of the random variables. This set up is frequently referred to as a balanced one-way analysis of variance. If the jth observation on the kth random variable is given by y_{kj}, then this model can be written as

$$y_{kj} = \beta_k + e_{kj} \qquad k = 1, 2, \ldots, K$$
$$j = 1, 2, \ldots, n \tag{7.5.10}$$

where the e_{kj} are independent and identically distributed normal random variables with 0 mean and known variance σ^2. In terms of the notation of the previous sections in this chapter, and earlier chapters, (7.5.10) can be written as

$$\mathbf{y} = X\boldsymbol{\beta} + \mathbf{e} \tag{7.5.11}$$

where (1) $\mathbf{y} = (y_{11}, y_{12}, \ldots, y_{1n}, y_{21}, y_{22}, \ldots, y_{2n}, \ldots, y_{K1}, y_{K2}, \ldots, y_{Kn})'$ is a $(Kn \times 1)$ vector; (2) X is the following $(Kn \times K)$ matrix of dummy variables (see Chapters 10, 11)

$$X = \begin{bmatrix} \mathbf{j}_n & \mathbf{0} & \cdots & \mathbf{0} \\ \mathbf{0} & \mathbf{j}_n & \cdots & \mathbf{0} \\ \vdots & & & \vdots \\ \mathbf{0} & \mathbf{0} & \cdots & \mathbf{j}_n \end{bmatrix}$$

with $\mathbf{j}_n = (1, 1, \ldots, 1)'$ being an $(n \times 1)$ vector with all elements equal to unity; (3) the K unknown means that we wish to estimate are given by $\boldsymbol{\beta} = (\beta_1, \beta_2, \ldots, \beta_K)'$; and (4) $\mathbf{e} \sim N(\mathbf{0}, \sigma^2 I_{Kn})$.

The special structure of this model is such that $X'X = nI_K$, and $X'\mathbf{y}$ has the kth element given by $\sum_{j=1}^{n} y_{kj}$. The least squares estimator becomes the vector of sample means for each of the random variables, namely,

$$\mathbf{b} = (X'X)^{-1}X'\mathbf{y} = \frac{1}{n}X'\mathbf{y} = \frac{1}{n}\begin{bmatrix} \sum_{j=1}^{n} y_{1j} \\ \sum_{j=1}^{n} y_{2j} \\ \vdots \\ \sum_{j=1}^{n} y_{Kj} \end{bmatrix} = \begin{bmatrix} \bar{y}_1 \\ \bar{y}_2 \\ \vdots \\ \bar{y}_K \end{bmatrix} = \bar{\mathbf{y}} \qquad (7.5.12)$$

Its covariance matrix is given by $\sigma^2(X'X)^{-1} = (\sigma^2/n)I_K$. Thus, as the sampling theory estimator for $\boldsymbol{\beta}$, we have

$$\bar{\mathbf{y}} \sim N[\boldsymbol{\beta}, (\sigma^2/n)I_K] \qquad (7.5.13)$$

To derive a Bayesian estimator for $\boldsymbol{\beta}$ we begin by specifying a prior p.d.f. for each of the means. We will assume that each β_k is a priori independent, and that in each case β_k has a normal prior p.d.f. with mean μ and variance τ^2. That is,

$$\beta_k \sim N(\mu, \tau^2) \qquad (7.5.14)$$

In terms of our notation in Section 7.3, the prior mean vector is

$$\bar{\boldsymbol{\beta}} = (\mu, \mu, \ldots, \mu)' = \mu\mathbf{j}_K \qquad (7.5.15)$$

and the prior covariance matrix is

$$\bar{\Sigma}_{\boldsymbol{\beta}} = \tau^2 I_K. \qquad (7.5.16)$$

Assuming quadratic loss, the Bayesian point estimator is the posterior mean

$$\begin{aligned}\bar{\bar{\boldsymbol{\beta}}} &= [\bar{\Sigma}_{\boldsymbol{\beta}}^{-1} + X'X/\sigma^2]^{-1}[\bar{\Sigma}_{\boldsymbol{\beta}}^{-1}\bar{\boldsymbol{\beta}} + (X'X/\sigma^2)\mathbf{b}] \\ &= [(1/\tau^2)I_K + (n/\sigma^2)I_K]^{-1}[(1/\tau^2)\mu\mathbf{j}_K + (n/\sigma^2)\bar{\mathbf{y}}] \\ &= \frac{(1/\tau^2)\mu\mathbf{j}_K + (n/\sigma^2)\bar{\mathbf{y}}}{(1/\tau^2) + (n/\sigma^2)} \qquad (7.5.17)\end{aligned}$$

Thus, the Bayesian estimator of the kth mean β_k is a weighted average of the prior mean μ and the sample mean $\bar{y}_k$, with weights given by the precisions $(1/\tau^2)$ and (n/σ^2). It can be written as

$$\begin{aligned}\bar{\bar{\beta}}_k &= \frac{(1/\tau^2)\mu + (n/\sigma^2)\bar{y}_k}{(1/\tau^2) + (n/\sigma^2)} \\ &= \frac{\sigma^2/n}{(\sigma^2/n) + \tau^2}\mu + \frac{\tau^2}{(\sigma^2/n) + \tau^2}\bar{y}_k \qquad (7.5.18)\end{aligned}$$

You are encouraged to work through the algebra required to derive the second line in (7.5.18).

So far we have not introduced any new concepts; we have simply examined the nature of the least squares and Bayesian estimators for a special type of model. Where the empirical Bayes' estimator differs from the Bayesian estimator in (7.5.18) is in the treatment of the prior parameters μ and τ^2. The pure Bayesian estimator takes the values of μ and τ^2 as given, whereas the empirical Bayes' estimator uses estimates of μ and τ^2 obtained from the data. To estimate μ and τ^2 we consider the marginal distribution of the $\bar{y}_k$; that is, the distribution of $\bar{y}_k$ not conditional on β_k. Since $\bar{y}_k \sim N(\beta_k, \sigma^2/n)$ and $\beta_k \sim N(\mu, \tau^2)$, we can write

$$\bar{y}_k = \beta_k + \bar{e}_k \quad \text{and} \quad \beta_k = \mu + v_k \tag{7.5.19}$$

where $\bar{e}_k \sim N(0, \sigma^2/n)$, $v_k \sim N(0, \tau^2)$, and $\bar{e}_k$ and v_k are independent. From (7.5.19)

$$\bar{y}_k = \mu + (\bar{e}_k + v_k) \tag{7.5.20}$$

This expression indicates that the marginal (unconditional) distribution of $\bar{y}_k$ is

$$\bar{y}_k \sim N(\mu, \sigma^2/n + \tau^2) \tag{7.5.21}$$

Using this unconditional distribution we first note that, since $E(\bar{y}_k) = \mu$, a natural estimator for μ is the sample mean $\bar{\bar{y}} = \sum_{k=1}^{K} \bar{y}_k/K$.

Next we need to find an estimator for $[(\sigma^2/n)/(\sigma^2/n + \tau^2)]$, the weight attached to μ in the weighted average for the posterior mean in (7.5.18). Working in this direction we note that

$$\frac{\sum_{k=1}^{K} (\bar{y}_k - \bar{\bar{y}})^2}{\sigma^2/n + \tau^2} \sim \chi^2_{(K-1)} \tag{7.5.22}$$

Thus, the inverse of the quantity in (7.5.22) will be distributed as the reciprocal of a χ^2 random variable with $(K - 1)$ degrees of freedom. From a result in Exercise 7.5, the expectation of the reciprocal of a χ^2 random variable is the reciprocal of 2 less than its degrees of freedom. Hence, we can write

$$E\left[\frac{\sigma^2/n + \tau^2}{\sum_{k=1}^{K} (\bar{y}_k - \bar{\bar{y}})^2}\right] = \frac{1}{K - 3} \tag{7.5.23}$$

or, alternatively,

$$E\left[\frac{(K - 3)(\sigma^2/n)}{\sum_{k=1}^{K} (\bar{y}_k - \bar{\bar{y}})^2}\right] = \frac{\sigma^2/n}{\sigma^2/n + \tau^2} \tag{7.5.24}$$

The left side of this equation, with the expectation operator dropped, provides a natural estimator for the weight attached to μ in (7.5.18). Substituting this estimator, and $\bar{\bar{y}}$, into (7.5.18) gives the empirical Bayes' estimator

$$\bar{\bar{\beta}}_k^* = \left[\frac{(K - 3)(\sigma^2/n)}{\sum_{k=1}^{K} (\bar{y}_k - \bar{\bar{y}})^2}\right]\bar{\bar{y}} + \left[1 - \frac{(K - 3)(\sigma^2/n)}{\sum_{k=1}^{K} (\bar{y}_k - \bar{\bar{y}})^2}\right]\bar{y}_k \tag{7.5.25}$$

Thus, the empirical Bayes' estimator is a weighted average of the kth group mean $\bar{y}_k$ and the overall mean $\bar{y}$, with weights determined by the data. Furthermore, it is identical to the James–Stein estimator and has a similar form to "Bayesian pretest estimators." Details about these estimators can be found in Judge, et al. (1985, Chapters 3 and 4) and references therein.

The empirical Bayes' estimator has good sampling theory properties. Providing $K \geq 4$, it can be shown that $\bar{\bar{\boldsymbol{\beta}}}^* = (\bar{\bar{\beta}}_1^*, \bar{\bar{\beta}}_2^*, \ldots, \bar{\bar{\beta}}_K^*)'$ dominates the least squares estimator $\bar{\mathbf{y}}$ in the sense that the trace of its mean square error matrix is always less than or equal to the trace of the mean square error matrix for $\bar{\mathbf{y}}$. In Figure 7.5, tr[MSE]/K is graphed for the least squares estimator, the empirical Bayes' estimator, and the pure Bayesian estimator (posterior mean), for the parameter values $K = 5$, $\sigma^2/n = 1$, $\tau^2 = 1$, and $\mu = 0$. For the least squares estimator tr[MSE]/K is constant and equal to 1. The posterior mean is better than the other two estimators when $\boldsymbol{\beta}'\boldsymbol{\beta}$ is small and each β_k does not differ greatly from the prior mean μ. As the spread of the β_k around $\mu = 0$ increases, and $\boldsymbol{\beta}'\boldsymbol{\beta}$ becomes larger, the posterior mean becomes worse than the other two estimators. The empirical Bayes' estimator is not as good as the posterior mean for low values of $\boldsymbol{\beta}'\boldsymbol{\beta}$, but it is better than the least squares estimator and it has the advantage of never getting worse than least squares, even when $\boldsymbol{\beta}'\boldsymbol{\beta}$ is large.

Expressions for tr[MSE] for $\bar{\mathbf{y}}$ and $\bar{\bar{\boldsymbol{\beta}}}$ are left as an exercise. See Exercise 7.6. The expression for tr[MSE] for $\bar{\bar{\boldsymbol{\beta}}}^*$ involves the expectation of the reciprocal of a noncentral χ^2 random variable, and a series expansion is necessary to compute this expectation. See Efron and Morris (1973) and Judge and Bock (1978, p. 172) for details.

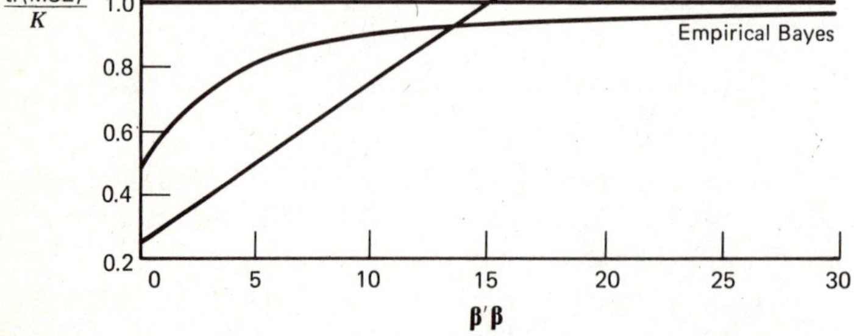

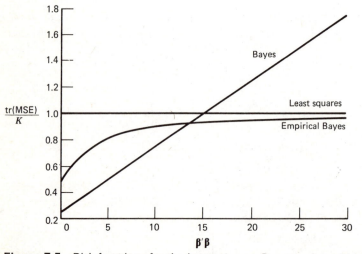

Figure 7.5 Risk functions for the least squares, Bayes and empirical Bayes' estimators.

7.6 Comparing Hypotheses and Posterior Odds

As was noted in Section 4.2.4, the Bayesian approach to hypothesis testing involves the comparison of hypotheses using a posterior odds ratio, rather than the rejection or acceptance of a null hypothesis based on whether or not the value of a statistic exceeds some critical value. The hypotheses considered in Section 4.2.4 were one-sided hypotheses of the form $H_0: \beta \leq c$ versus $H_1: \beta > c$. For hypotheses such as these the posterior odds ratio in favor of H_0 relative to H_1 is

$$K_{01} = \frac{P(H_0|\mathbf{y})}{P(H_1|\mathbf{y})} = \frac{P[\beta \leq c|\mathbf{y}]}{P[\beta > c|\mathbf{y}]} \tag{7.6.1}$$

Given a sample $\mathbf{y}$ and a posterior p.d.f. $g(\beta|\mathbf{y})$, it is relatively straightforward to compute the probabilities in (7.6.1) and hence the posterior odds ratio K_{01}.

Complications arise, however, if we wish to compare a point null hypothesis such as $H_0: \beta = c$ with an alternative $H_1: \beta \neq c$. It is not meaningful to compute $P(H_0|\mathbf{y}) = P(\beta = c|\mathbf{y})$ because c is just a single point from a continuous posterior p.d.f., and its associated probability will be 0. To overcome this problem, we assign positive prior probabilities $P(H_0)$ and $P(H_1)$ to each of the hypotheses, and then, based on sample information, we modify the prior probabilities to form the posterior probabilities $P(H_0|\mathbf{y})$ and $P(H_1|\mathbf{y})$, and the posterior odds ratio $P(H_0|\mathbf{y})/P(H_1|\mathbf{y})$. The assignment of a positive prior probability to the single point $H_0: \beta = c$ seems a reasonable way to proceed; the fact that the hypothesis $H_0: \beta = c$ is being considered implies that there must be some a priori belief that it is true.

The posterior probability of a hypothesis is calculated from the prior probability through the formula

$$P(H_i|\mathbf{y}) = \frac{P(H_i)f(\mathbf{y}|H_i)}{f(\mathbf{y})} \qquad i = 0, 1 \tag{7.6.2}$$

Using (7.6.2), the posterior odds ratio is given by

$$K_{01} = \frac{P(H_0|\mathbf{y})}{P(H_1|\mathbf{y})} = \frac{P(H_0)f(\mathbf{y}|H_0)}{P(H_1)f(\mathbf{y}|H_1)} \tag{7.6.3}$$

The p.d.f.'s $f(\mathbf{y}|H_0)$ and $f(\mathbf{y}|H_1)$ are marginal (unconditional) p.d.f.'s for the data $\mathbf{y}$; they are derived by averaging over (integrating out) the unknown parameters, where the weights attached to the unknown parameters are given by their prior p.d.f's. This process, and the computation of a posterior odds ratio, will be illustrated using the production function example introduced in Section 7.4.

The production function example was

$$y_t = \beta_1 + \beta_2 x_{2t} + \beta_3 x_{3t} + e_t \tag{7.6.4}$$

where y_t, x_{2t}, and x_{3t} are the logarithms of output, labor, and capital, respectively. The disturbances (e_t's) were independent normal random variables with 0 mean and known variance $\sigma^2 = 0.09$. The prior p.d.f. on $\boldsymbol{\beta} = (\beta_1, \beta_2, \beta_3)'$ was multivariate normal with mean $\bar{\boldsymbol{\beta}} = (5, 0.5, 0.5)'$ and the covariance matrix $\bar{\Sigma}_{\boldsymbol{\beta}}$ given in (7.4.15). The hypotheses that we will compare are

$$H_0: \beta_2 + \beta_3 = 1 \tag{7.6.5}$$

$$H_1: \beta_2 + \beta_3 \neq 1 \tag{7.6.6}$$

That is, we will consider the evidence in favor of constant returns to scale against the alternative of nonconstant returns to scale.

The first step is to obtain $f(\mathbf{y}|H_1)$, the marginal p.d.f. for the data when β_2 and β_3 are unrestricted. Working in this direction, we write the data generation process and the prior information in obvious matrix notation as

$$\mathbf{y} = X\boldsymbol{\beta} + \mathbf{e} \qquad \text{and} \qquad \boldsymbol{\beta} = \bar{\boldsymbol{\beta}} + \mathbf{v} \tag{7.6.7}$$

where $E[\mathbf{ee}'] = \sigma^2 I_T$ and $E[\mathbf{vv}'] = \bar{\Sigma}_{\boldsymbol{\beta}}$. From (7.6.7) we obtain

$$\mathbf{y} = X\bar{\boldsymbol{\beta}} + X\mathbf{v} + \mathbf{e} \tag{7.6.8}$$

where $E[(X\mathbf{v} + \mathbf{e})(X\mathbf{v} + \mathbf{e})'] = X\bar{\Sigma}_{\boldsymbol{\beta}}X' + \sigma^2 I_T$. Using the fact that the sum of two normally distributed random vectors also follows a normal distribution, the marginal (unconditional with respect to $\boldsymbol{\beta}$) distribution for $(\mathbf{y}|H_1)$ is

$$(\mathbf{y}|H_1) \sim N[X\bar{\boldsymbol{\beta}}, X\bar{\Sigma}_{\boldsymbol{\beta}}X' + \sigma^2 I_T] \tag{7.6.9}$$

Its p.d.f. is

$$f(\mathbf{y}|H_1) = (2\pi)^{-T/2}|X\bar{\Sigma}_{\boldsymbol{\beta}}X' + \sigma^2 I_T|^{-1/2}$$
$$\times \exp\{-\tfrac{1}{2}(\mathbf{y} - X\bar{\boldsymbol{\beta}})'(X\bar{\Sigma}_{\boldsymbol{\beta}}X' + \sigma^2 I_T)^{-1}(\mathbf{y} - X\bar{\boldsymbol{\beta}})\} \tag{7.6.10}$$

It is convenient to use the following results, which are left as a problem (Exercise 7.7). Define A such that $\bar{\Sigma}_{\boldsymbol{\beta}} = \sigma^2 A^{-1}$, then

$$|XA^{-1}X' + I_T| = \frac{|A + X'X|}{|A|} \tag{7.6.11}$$

and

$$(\mathbf{y} - X\bar{\boldsymbol{\beta}})'(XA^{-1}X' + I_T)^{-1}(\mathbf{y} - X\bar{\boldsymbol{\beta}}) = RSS_1 + Q_1 \tag{7.6.12}$$

where

$$RSS_1 = (\mathbf{y} - X\mathbf{b})'(\mathbf{y} - X\mathbf{b}) \tag{7.6.13}$$

$$Q_1 = (\mathbf{b} - \bar{\boldsymbol{\beta}})'[A^{-1} + (X'X)^{-1}]^{-1}(\mathbf{b} - \bar{\boldsymbol{\beta}}) \tag{7.6.14}$$

and

$$\mathbf{b} = (X'X)^{-1}X'\mathbf{y} \tag{7.6.15}$$

The ratio of determinants on the right side of (7.6.11) is the ratio of the determinant of the precision matrix for the posterior information to the determinant of the precision matrix for the prior information; RSS_1 is the residual sum of squares that is obtained when the least squares estimator $\mathbf{b}$ is used; and Q_1 is a measure of the compatibility of the prior and sample information. The further $\mathbf{b}$ deviates from $\bar{\boldsymbol{\beta}}$, the greater will be Q_1.

Replacing $\bar{\Sigma}_{\boldsymbol{\beta}}$ by $\sigma^2 A^{-1}$, and using the results in (7.6.11) and (7.6.12), we can write (7.6.10) as

$$\begin{aligned} f(\mathbf{y}|H_1) &= (2\pi)^{-T/2}\sigma^{-T}|XA^{-1}X' + I_T|^{-1/2} \\ &\quad \times \exp\left\{-\frac{1}{2\sigma^2}(\mathbf{y} - X\bar{\boldsymbol{\beta}})'(XA^{-1}X' + I_T)^{-1}(\mathbf{y} - X\bar{\boldsymbol{\beta}})\right\} \\ &= (2\pi)^{-T/2}\sigma^{-T}(|A|/|A + X'X|)^{1/2} \exp\left\{-\frac{1}{2\sigma^2}(RSS_1 + Q_1)\right\} \end{aligned} \tag{7.6.16}$$

The next task is to specify our prior information about $\boldsymbol{\beta}$ given H_0 is true and to use this prior information to find an expression for $f(\mathbf{y}|H_0)$. When $H_0\colon \beta_2 + \beta_3 = 1$ is true, the model in (7.6.4) can be rewritten as

$$y_t = \beta_1 + \beta_2 x_{2t} + (1 - \beta_2)x_{3t} + e_t$$

or

$$y_t - x_{3t} = \beta_1 + \beta_2(x_{2t} - x_{3t}) + e_t$$

or

$$q_t = \beta_1 + \beta_2 z_t + e_t \tag{7.6.17}$$

where $q_t = y_t - x_{3t}$ and $z_t = x_{2t} - x_{3t}$. Using obvious matrix notation, (7.6.17) becomes

$$\mathbf{q} = Z\boldsymbol{\gamma} + \mathbf{e} \tag{7.6.18}$$

where $\boldsymbol{\gamma} = (\beta_1, \beta_2)'$. We are now in a position to specify our prior information under H_0. As before, we assume $\mathbf{e} \sim N(\mathbf{0}, \sigma^2 I)$, with $\sigma^2 = 0.09$. For $\boldsymbol{\gamma}$ we take a subset of the prior information under H_1. Specifically, we assume that $\boldsymbol{\gamma} \sim N(\bar{\boldsymbol{\gamma}}, \bar{\Sigma}_{\boldsymbol{\gamma}})$ where

$$\bar{\boldsymbol{\gamma}} = (\bar{\beta}_1, \bar{\beta}_2)' = (5.0, 0.5)' \tag{7.6.19}$$

and

$$\bar{\Sigma}_{\boldsymbol{\gamma}} = \begin{bmatrix} \text{var}(\beta_1) & \text{cov}(\beta_1, \beta_2) \\ \text{cov}(\beta_1, \beta_2) & \text{var}(\beta_2) \end{bmatrix} = \begin{bmatrix} 83.15 & 0.0 \\ 0.0 & 0.03326 \end{bmatrix} \tag{7.6.20}$$

Following a similar procedure to that adopted under H_1, we let $\bar{\Sigma}_\gamma = \sigma^2 B^{-1}$, $\hat{\gamma} = (Z'Z)^{-1}Z'\mathbf{q}$,

$$RSS_0 = (\mathbf{q} - Z\hat{\gamma})'(\mathbf{q} - Z\hat{\gamma}) \tag{7.6.21}$$

and

$$Q_0 = (\hat{\gamma} - \bar{\gamma})'[B^{-1} + (Z'Z)^{-1}]^{-1}(\hat{\gamma} - \bar{\gamma}) \tag{7.6.22}$$

Then, it is possible to show that

$$f(\mathbf{y}|H_0) = (2\pi)^{-T/2}\sigma^{-T}(|B|/|B + Z'Z|)^{1/2} \exp\left\{-\frac{1}{2\sigma^2}(RSS_0 + Q_0)\right\} \tag{7.6.23}$$

Returning to the expression for posterior odds given in (7.6.3), we insert the results for $f(\mathbf{y}|H_0)$ and $f(\mathbf{y}|H_1)$ to obtain

$$K_{01} = \frac{P(H_0)(|B|/|B + Z'Z|)^{1/2}}{P(H_1)(|A|/|A + X'X|)^{1/2}} \exp\left\{-\frac{1}{2\sigma^2}(RSS_0 - RSS_1 + Q_0 - Q_1)\right\} \tag{7.6.24}$$

This result is our final expression for the posterior odds ratio. We can place the following interpretation on each of the terms.

1. The greater the prior odds $P(H_0)/P(H_1)$, the greater will be the posterior odds.
2. The term $|B|/|(B + Z'Z)|$ and its counterpart in the denominator are measures of the precision of the prior information on $\boldsymbol{\beta}$ relative to the precision of the posterior information. Other things equal, these terms mean that we will favor the hypothesis with more prior information.
3. Goodness-of-fit considerations are given by the residual sums of squares terms RSS_0 and RSS_1. The conventional sampling theory test statistic for testing a set of linear restrictions with known disturbance variance is the χ^2 statistic $(RSS_0 - RSS_1)/\sigma^2$. As expected, the greater the value of this statistic, the lower will be the posterior odds in favor of H_0.
4. The terms Q_0 and Q_1 are measures of the compatibility of the prior and sample information. The further $\mathbf{b}$ deviates from $\bar{\boldsymbol{\beta}}$, for example, the greater will be Q_1 and, other things equal, the greater will be the posterior odds in favor of H_0.

Thus, relative to the sampling theory approach, the posterior odds formulation introduces three additional, prior related, types of information.

We will now calculate the posterior odds in favor of constant returns to scale in the production function example. The values of the various quantities that need to be substituted into (7.6.24) are

$$\bar{\boldsymbol{\beta}} = \begin{bmatrix} 5.0 \\ 0.5 \\ 0.5 \end{bmatrix} \qquad A^{-1} = \begin{bmatrix} 923.9 & 0.0 & 0.0 \\ 0.0 & 0.3695 & -0.349 \\ 0.0 & -0.349 & 0.3695 \end{bmatrix}$$

$$\bar{\boldsymbol{\gamma}} = \begin{bmatrix} 5.0 \\ 0.5 \end{bmatrix} \qquad B^{-1} = \begin{bmatrix} 923.9 & 0.0 \\ 0.0 & 0.3695 \end{bmatrix}$$

$$\mathbf{b} = \begin{bmatrix} 9.770 \\ 0.524 \\ 0.693 \end{bmatrix} \qquad X'X = \begin{bmatrix} 20.00 & 31.022 & 25.305 \\ 31.022 & 57.238 & 39.781 \\ 25.305 & 39.781 & 36.076 \end{bmatrix}$$

$$\hat{\boldsymbol{\gamma}} = \begin{bmatrix} 10.062 \\ 0.461 \end{bmatrix} \qquad Z'Z = \begin{bmatrix} 20.000 & 5.717 \\ 5.717 & 13.754 \end{bmatrix}$$

$$RSS_0 = 1.49436 \qquad RSS_1 = 1.35199$$

$$\left[\frac{|B|}{|(B + Z'Z)|}\right]^{1/2} = 0.0031429 \qquad Q_0 = 0.031151$$

$$\left[\frac{|A|}{|(A + X'X)|}\right]^{1/2} = 0.0029926 \qquad Q_1 = 0.158432$$

Making these substitutions yields a posterior odds ratio of

$$K_{01} = \frac{P(H_0|\mathbf{y})}{P(H_1|\mathbf{y})} = \frac{P(H_0)}{P(H_1)} \times 1.05016 \times \exp\left\{-\frac{0.01509}{0.18}\right\}$$

$$= 0.966 \frac{P(H_0)}{P(H_1)} \tag{7.6.25}$$

with prior odds ratio of unity we have

$$K_{01} = 0.966 \tag{7.6.26}$$

The χ^2 statistic that would be calculated if the same test were performed within a sampling theory framework has the value

$$\chi^2_{(1)} = \frac{RSS_0 - RSS_1}{\sigma^2} = \frac{1.49436 - 1.35199}{0.09} = 1.58 \tag{7.6.27}$$

Because the posterior odds ratio is slightly less than unity, the Bayesian approach gives a small degree of support for the alternative hypothesis. On the other hand, using a 5% significance level and the sampling theory approach, we would not reject H_0 because 1.58 is less than the critical value $\chi^2_{(1)} = 3.84$. This difference in results can be explained in terms of the way in which each approach treats Type I and Type II errors.

The sampling theory approach treats Type I and Type II errors asymmetrically. For a given significance level the probability of a Type I error is held constant whatever the sample size, and the probability of a Type II error declines as T increases. This situation favors H_0 when T is small and favors H_1 when T is large. In contrast, the Bayesian approach treats both errors symmetrically and favors neither hypothesis as T increases. For the sampling theory effect to be achieved within the Bayesian framework, we would need to make the prior odds ratio a decreasing function of sample size. Similarly, for the Bayesian effect to be achieved within the sampling theory framework, the significance level would need to be a decreasing function of sample size. In our example the sample size is relatively small, and from the sampling theory viewpoint, the sample evidence is insufficient to reject H_0. The hypothesis H_0 is favored despite the fact that the small sample size means the probability of a Type II error could be quite large. The fact that the posterior odds ratio slightly favors H_1 is a reflection of the additional weight the Bayesian approach places on Type II errors when T is small.

The procedure that has been illustrated in this section does not have to be restricted to point hypotheses such as constant returns to scale. The same procedure can be applied to any two hypotheses (including nonnested hypotheses) that can be formulated in terms of $H_0\colon \mathbf{q} = Z\boldsymbol{\gamma} + \mathbf{e}$ and $H_1\colon \mathbf{y} = X\boldsymbol{\beta} + \mathbf{e}$. We assumed that σ^2 is known and the same under each hypothesis. The case where σ^2 is unknown and possibly different under each hypothesis is outlined in Judge, et al. (1985, p. 129); the same example, but for σ^2 unknown, is given in Judge, et al. (1982, p. 240).

As a final point, we note that it is usually necessary for the marginal p.d.f.'s $f(\mathbf{y}|H_0)$ and $f(\mathbf{y}|H_1)$ to be proper p.d.f.'s, and for their integrating constants to be included. Difficulties can arise if an attempt is made to use improper priors for $g(\boldsymbol{\gamma}|H_0)$ and $g(\boldsymbol{\beta}|H_1)$. However, for those parameters that have identical assumptions under each hypothesis, it is sometimes possible to specify an improper prior without adversely affecting the computation of the posterior odds ratio. For further details and references to the literature see Judge, et al. (1985, Chapter 4).

7.7 Bayesian Inference for the General Linear Model with Unknown Disturbance Variance

The assumption of known variance σ^2 is a convenient one for introducing Bayesian inference for the general linear model, but it is not a realistic one in practice. In practice, σ^2 is seldom known, so it is necessary to consider prior and posterior p.d.f.'s for σ, as well as the consequences of an unknown σ on the prior and posterior p.d.f.'s for $\boldsymbol{\beta}$. These questions are dealt with in this section. The specification of a joint informative prior p.d.f. is considered in Section 7.7.1; the corresponding joint posterior p.d.f. is derived in Section 7.7.2; marginal distributions and details of the multivariate t-distribution are considered in Section 7.7.3; the results corresponding to a noninformative joint prior p.d.f. for $\boldsymbol{\beta}$ and σ are summarized in Section 7.7.4.

7.7.1 A Joint Informative Prior for $\boldsymbol{\beta}$ and σ

In line with the earlier sections in this chapter, we consider the model

$$\mathbf{y} = X\boldsymbol{\beta} + \mathbf{e} \tag{7.7.1}$$

where $\mathbf{e} \sim N(\mathbf{0}, \sigma^2 I)$, but we now assume σ^2 is unknown. Consequently, it becomes necessary to specify a joint prior p.d.f. for both $\boldsymbol{\beta}$ and σ. The informative prior that we will consider is a multivariate normal-gamma prior that is a generalization of the prior considered in Section 4.4.1. This prior is a natural conjugate prior in the sense that, when it is combined with the likelihood function, it yields a posterior p.d.f. that also belongs to the normal-gamma family of distributions. The multivariate normal-gamma p.d.f. is such that the conditional p.d.f. for $\boldsymbol{\beta}$ given σ is a multivariate normal p.d.f., and the marginal p.d.f. for the precision (the reciprocal of the variance) is a gamma distribution. The p.d.f. for σ is known as an inverted-gamma p.d.f., or, as Raiffa and Schlaifer (1961) call it, an inverted gamma-2 distribution. We consider each of these components and an example.

When σ was known, the natural conjugate prior p.d.f. for $\boldsymbol{\beta}$ was $\boldsymbol{\beta} \sim N(\bar{\boldsymbol{\beta}}, \bar{\Sigma}_{\boldsymbol{\beta}})$. It did not explicitly depend on σ. For unknown σ the natural conjugate prior p.d.f. for $\boldsymbol{\beta}$, conditional on σ, is a multivariate normal. Thus, the way in which the normal prior p.d.f. for $\boldsymbol{\beta}$ depends on σ needs to be made explicit. This dependence is achieved by setting $\bar{\Sigma}_{\boldsymbol{\beta}} = \sigma^2 A^{-1}$. Instead of using our prior information on $\boldsymbol{\beta}$ to specify the matrix $\bar{\Sigma}_{\boldsymbol{\beta}}$, we express our prior information in terms of the matrix A. Alternatively, we specify $\bar{\Sigma}_{\boldsymbol{\beta}}$ for a given value of σ^2, and then derive A. For example, in the production function model of Section 7.4, when σ^2 was known to be 0.09, we had

$$\begin{aligned}\bar{\Sigma}_{\boldsymbol{\beta}} &= \begin{bmatrix} 83.14779 & 0.0 & 0.0 \\ 0.0 & 0.03325912 & -0.03141139 \\ 0.0 & -0.03141139 & 0.03325912 \end{bmatrix} \\ &= 0.09 \begin{bmatrix} 923.86 & 0.0 & 0.0 \\ 0.0 & 0.369546 & -0.349015 \\ 0.0 & -0.349015 & 0.369546 \end{bmatrix} \\ &= \sigma^2 A^{-1} \end{aligned} \tag{7.7.2}$$

If σ^2 is unknown, but we specify the foregoing matrix for $\bar{\Sigma}_{\boldsymbol{\beta}}$ conditional on $\sigma^2 = 0.09$, then A^{-1} can be derived as given in the second line of (7.7.2). If we wish to find $\bar{\Sigma}_{\boldsymbol{\beta}}$ conditional on another value of σ^2, then it is assumed that A^{-1} remains the same, but that $\bar{\Sigma}_{\boldsymbol{\beta}}$ changes in direct proportion to changes in σ^2. For example, if σ^2 was doubled to 0.18, then the elements in $\bar{\Sigma}_{\boldsymbol{\beta}}$, conditional on $\sigma^2 = 0.18$, would be double those in the first line of (7.7.2). We thus have $(\boldsymbol{\beta}|\sigma) \sim N[\bar{\boldsymbol{\beta}}, \sigma^2 A^{-1}]$ and the multivariate normal prior p.d.f. for $\boldsymbol{\beta}$ given σ can be written as

$$\begin{aligned} g(\boldsymbol{\beta}|\sigma) &= (2\pi)^{-K/2}\sigma^{-K}|A|^{1/2} \exp\{-(\boldsymbol{\beta} - \bar{\boldsymbol{\beta}})'A(\boldsymbol{\beta} - \bar{\boldsymbol{\beta}})/2\sigma^2\} \\ &\propto \sigma^{-K} \exp\{-(\boldsymbol{\beta} - \bar{\boldsymbol{\beta}})'A(\boldsymbol{\beta} - \bar{\boldsymbol{\beta}})/2\sigma^2\} \end{aligned} \tag{7.7.3}$$

The assignment of values to $\bar{\boldsymbol{\beta}}$ and A completely specifies this prior p.d.f. For our example we will use $\bar{\boldsymbol{\beta}} = (5.0, 0.5, 0.5)'$, as we did earlier, and the matrix A implied by the values for the elements of A^{-1} given in (7.7.2).

For the marginal prior p.d.f. for σ we use the inverted-gamma p.d.f. that was introduced in Section 4.4.1, namely

$$\begin{aligned} g(\sigma) &= \frac{2}{\Gamma(\bar{\nu}/2)}\left(\frac{\bar{\nu}\bar{s}^2}{2}\right)^{\bar{\nu}/2} \frac{1}{\sigma^{\bar{\nu}+1}} \exp\left\{-\frac{\bar{\nu}\bar{s}^2}{2\sigma^2}\right\} \\ &\propto \frac{1}{\sigma^{\bar{\nu}+1}} \exp\left\{-\frac{\bar{\nu}\bar{s}^2}{2\sigma^2}\right\}. \end{aligned} \tag{7.7.4}$$

Prior knowledge about σ, and properties of the χ^2-distribution, are used to assign values to the prior parameters $\bar{\nu}$ and $\bar{s}^2$. If we have no prior knowledge about σ, we can express our ignorance by setting $\bar{\nu} = 0$ and using the uninformative improper p.d.f. $g(\sigma) \propto 1/\sigma$.

To obtain a prior density for σ in the production function example, we will assume that our prior information is such that $P(\sigma < 0.3) = 0.5$ and $P(\sigma > 0.65) = 0.05$. Following the approach adopted in Section 4.4.1, this information can be used to obtain $\bar{\nu}$ and $\bar{s}$ by noting that $(\bar{\nu}\bar{s}^2/\sigma^2)$ has a $\chi^2_{(\bar{\nu})}$ distribution. Therefore, for some constant c, we can write

$$P(\sigma > c) = P\left(\frac{\bar{\nu}\bar{s}^2}{\sigma^2} < \frac{\bar{\nu}\bar{s}^2}{c^2}\right) = P\left(\chi^2_{(\bar{\nu})} < \frac{\bar{\nu}\bar{s}^2}{c^2}\right)$$

We require $\bar{\nu}$ and $\bar{s}$ such that

$$P\left(\chi^2_{(\bar{\nu})} > \frac{\bar{\nu}\bar{s}^2}{(0.3)^2}\right) = 0.5 \qquad \text{and} \qquad P\left(\chi^2_{(\bar{\nu})} < \frac{\bar{\nu}\bar{s}^2}{(0.65)^2}\right) = 0.05$$

From the tables for the χ^2-distribution function at the end of this book we find that

$$P(\chi^2_{(4)} > 3.36) = 0.5 \qquad \text{and} \qquad P(\chi^2_{(4)} < 0.711) = 0.05$$

Thus, if we take $\bar{\nu} = 4$, we have $4\bar{s}^2/(0.3)^2 = 3.36$ and $4\bar{s}^2/(0.65)^2 = 0.711$. A value for $\bar{s}^2$ that approximately satisfies both these equations is 0.0754, and we will regard this as adequate to represent our prior information. In summary, we will take as our prior density for σ an inverted-gamma density with parameters $\bar{\nu} = 4$ and $\bar{s}^2 = 0.0754$. This density has a median of 0.3 and, from (4.4.8), its mode and mean are given respectively by 0.2456 and 0.3441. After evaluation of the constants, it can be written as

$$g(\sigma) = 0.04548\sigma^{-5}e^{-(0.1508/\sigma^2)} \tag{7.7.5}$$

To obtain an expression for the joint normal-gamma prior p.d.f. for $(\boldsymbol{\beta}, \sigma)$, we combine (7.7.3) with (7.7.4), yielding

$$\begin{aligned} g(\boldsymbol{\beta}, \sigma) &= g(\boldsymbol{\beta}|\sigma)g(\sigma) \\ &\propto \sigma^{-K-\bar{\nu}-1} \exp\{-[\bar{\nu}\bar{s}^2 + (\boldsymbol{\beta} - \bar{\boldsymbol{\beta}})'A(\boldsymbol{\beta} - \bar{\boldsymbol{\beta}})]/2\sigma^2\} \end{aligned} \tag{7.7.6}$$

By integrating σ out of (7.7.6), it is possible to show that the marginal prior p.d.f. for $\boldsymbol{\beta}$ is in the form of a multivariate t-distribution. This process, and the nature of the multivariate t-distribution, will be discussed later in this section.

To prove that (7.7.6) is a natural conjugate prior, we must show that the posterior density function derived from it will also be of the normal-gamma form. It is the joint posterior p.d.f. to which we now turn.

7.7.2 Joint Posterior Density Function for $\boldsymbol{\beta}$ and σ

The likelihood function for $\boldsymbol{\beta}$ and σ given a sample of observations $\mathbf{y} = (y_1, y_2, \ldots, y_T)'$ and the model in (7.7.1) can be written as

$$\begin{aligned} \ell(\boldsymbol{\beta}, \sigma|\mathbf{y}) &= (2\pi)^{-T/2}\sigma^{-T} \exp\{-(\mathbf{y} - X\boldsymbol{\beta})'(\mathbf{y} - X\boldsymbol{\beta})/2\sigma^2\} \\ &\propto \sigma^{-T} \exp\{-(\mathbf{y} - X\boldsymbol{\beta})'(\mathbf{y} - X\boldsymbol{\beta})/2\sigma^2\} \end{aligned} \tag{7.7.7}$$

Using Bayes' theorem, the joint posterior p.d.f. for $\boldsymbol{\beta}$ and σ is obtained by multiplying the prior in (7.7.6) by the likelihood in (7.7.7).

$$\begin{aligned} g(\boldsymbol{\beta}, \sigma|\mathbf{y}) &\propto g(\boldsymbol{\beta}, \sigma)\ell(\boldsymbol{\beta}, \sigma|\mathbf{y}) \\ &\propto \sigma^{-T-K-\bar{\nu}-1} \exp\{-[\bar{\nu}\bar{s}^2 + (\boldsymbol{\beta} - \bar{\boldsymbol{\beta}})'A(\boldsymbol{\beta} - \bar{\boldsymbol{\beta}}) \\ &\qquad + (\mathbf{y} - X\boldsymbol{\beta})'(\mathbf{y} - X\boldsymbol{\beta})]/2\sigma^2\} \end{aligned} \tag{7.7.8}$$

To simplify this expression we use the same convenient devices that were introduced in Section 7.3.1. Specifically, let

$$\mathbf{w} = \begin{pmatrix} A^{1/2}\bar{\boldsymbol{\beta}} \\ \mathbf{y} \end{pmatrix} \quad \text{and} \quad G = \begin{pmatrix} A^{1/2} \\ X \end{pmatrix}$$

then, it follows that (7.7.8) can be written as

$$\begin{aligned} g(\boldsymbol{\beta}, \sigma|\mathbf{y}) &\propto \sigma^{-T-K-\bar{\nu}-1} \exp\{-[\bar{\nu}\bar{s}^2 + (\mathbf{w} - G\boldsymbol{\beta})'(\mathbf{w} - G\boldsymbol{\beta})]/2\sigma^2\} \\ &= \sigma^{-T-K-\bar{\nu}-1} \exp\{-[\bar{\nu}\bar{s}^2 + (\boldsymbol{\beta} - \bar{\bar{\boldsymbol{\beta}}})'G'G(\boldsymbol{\beta} - \bar{\bar{\boldsymbol{\beta}}}) \\ &\qquad + (\mathbf{w} - G\bar{\bar{\boldsymbol{\beta}}})'(\mathbf{w} - G\bar{\bar{\boldsymbol{\beta}}})]/2\sigma^2\} \\ &= \sigma^{-T-K-\bar{\nu}-1} \exp\{-[\bar{\bar{\nu}}\bar{\bar{s}}^2 \\ &\qquad + (\boldsymbol{\beta} - \bar{\bar{\boldsymbol{\beta}}})'(A + X'X)(\boldsymbol{\beta} - \bar{\bar{\boldsymbol{\beta}}})]/2\sigma^2\} \end{aligned} \tag{7.7.9}$$

where

$$\begin{aligned} \bar{\bar{\boldsymbol{\beta}}} &= (G'G)^{-1}G'\mathbf{w} \\ &= (A + X'X)^{-1}(A\bar{\boldsymbol{\beta}} + X'X\mathbf{b}) \end{aligned} \tag{7.7.10}$$

and

$$\begin{aligned} \bar{\bar{\nu}}\bar{\bar{s}}^2 &= \bar{\nu}\bar{s}^2 + (\mathbf{w} - G\bar{\bar{\boldsymbol{\beta}}})'(\mathbf{w} - G\bar{\bar{\boldsymbol{\beta}}}) \\ &= \bar{\nu}\bar{s}^2 + (\mathbf{y} - X\bar{\bar{\boldsymbol{\beta}}})'(\mathbf{y} - X\bar{\bar{\boldsymbol{\beta}}}) + (\bar{\boldsymbol{\beta}} - \bar{\bar{\boldsymbol{\beta}}})'A(\bar{\boldsymbol{\beta}} - \bar{\bar{\boldsymbol{\beta}}}) \\ &= \bar{\nu}\bar{s}^2 + \mathbf{y}'\mathbf{y} + \bar{\boldsymbol{\beta}}'A\bar{\boldsymbol{\beta}} - \bar{\bar{\boldsymbol{\beta}}}'(A + X'X)\bar{\bar{\boldsymbol{\beta}}} \end{aligned} \tag{7.7.11}$$

There are two major differences between (7.7.9) and the expression derived in (7.3.8) for the case when σ^2 was known. The first difference is that $\sigma^{-T-K-\bar{\nu}-1}$ is included in (7.7.9). When σ was known, powers of σ were absorbed into the proportionality constant. The second difference is that the term $-(\bar{\bar{\nu}}\bar{\bar{s}}^2/2\sigma^2)$ appears in the exponent in (7.7.9). The numerator of this term is made up of the prior parameter product $\bar{\nu}\bar{s}^2$, and the term $(\mathbf{w} - G\bar{\bar{\boldsymbol{\beta}}})'(\mathbf{w} - G\bar{\bar{\boldsymbol{\beta}}})$. This latter term also entered the analysis when σ^2 was known, but in that case it was absorbed into the proportionality constant.

In Equation 7.7.11 the product $\bar{\bar{\nu}}\bar{\bar{s}}^2$ is defined, but the separate parameters $\bar{\bar{\nu}}$ and $\bar{\bar{s}}^2$ are not. To give separate definitions for $\bar{\bar{\nu}}$ and $\bar{\bar{s}}^2$, and to show that the joint posterior density $g(\boldsymbol{\beta}, \sigma|\mathbf{y})$ is of the normal-gamma form, we rewrite (7.7.9) as

$$\begin{aligned} g(\boldsymbol{\beta}, \sigma|\mathbf{y}) &\propto \frac{1}{\sigma^K} \exp\left\{-\frac{1}{2\sigma^2}(\boldsymbol{\beta} - \bar{\bar{\boldsymbol{\beta}}})'(A + X'X)(\boldsymbol{\beta} - \bar{\bar{\boldsymbol{\beta}}})\right\} \cdot \frac{1}{\sigma^{\bar{\bar{\nu}}+1}} \exp\left\{-\frac{\bar{\bar{\nu}}\bar{\bar{s}}^2}{2\sigma^2}\right\} \\ &\propto g(\boldsymbol{\beta}|\sigma, \mathbf{y})g(\sigma|\mathbf{y}) \end{aligned} \tag{7.7.12}$$

where

$$\bar{\bar{\nu}} = T + \bar{\nu} \tag{7.7.13}$$

$$g(\boldsymbol{\beta}|\sigma, \mathbf{y}) \propto \frac{1}{\sigma^K} \exp\left\{-\frac{1}{2\sigma^2}(\boldsymbol{\beta} - \bar{\bar{\boldsymbol{\beta}}})'(A + X'X)(\boldsymbol{\beta} - \bar{\bar{\boldsymbol{\beta}}})\right\} \tag{7.7.14}$$

and

$$g(\sigma|\mathbf{y}) \propto \frac{1}{\sigma^{\bar{\bar{\nu}}+1}} \exp\left\{-\frac{\bar{\bar{\nu}}\bar{\bar{s}}^2}{2\sigma^2}\right\} \tag{7.7.15}$$

The posterior parameter $\bar{\bar{\nu}}$ is defined as $T + \bar{\nu}$, so as to make the marginal posterior density for σ an inverted-gamma p.d.f. with parameters $\bar{\bar{\nu}}$ and $\bar{\bar{s}}^2$. The parameter $\bar{\bar{s}}^2$ is obtained by dividing $\bar{\bar{\nu}}\bar{\bar{s}}^2$ in (7.7.11) by $\bar{\bar{\nu}}$. The conditional posterior p.d.f. for $\boldsymbol{\beta}$ given σ is a multivariate normal with mean $\bar{\bar{\boldsymbol{\beta}}}$ and covariance matrix $\sigma^2(A + X'X)^{-1}$.

Interpretations identical to those given when σ^2 was known can be placed on the posterior mean $\bar{\bar{\boldsymbol{\beta}}}$ and the posterior precision matrix

$$\bar{\bar{\Sigma}}_{\boldsymbol{\beta}}^{-1} = (A + X'X)/\sigma^2 = \bar{\Sigma}_{\boldsymbol{\beta}}^{-1} + X'X/\sigma^2$$

The posterior precision matrix is equal to the sum of the prior and sample precision matrices, and the posterior mean is a matrix-weighted average of the prior mean $\bar{\boldsymbol{\beta}}$ and the least squares estimator $\mathbf{b}$, with weights given by their respective precision matrices.

Before applying these concepts to the production function example, we will investigate how to obtain marginal posterior p.d.f.'s for the elements in $\boldsymbol{\beta}$.

7.7.3 Marginal Posterior Density Function for $\boldsymbol{\beta}$

The marginal posterior density function for σ was derived as the inverted-gamma p.d.f. given in (7.7.15), simply by factoring the joint posterior p.d.f. $g(\boldsymbol{\beta}, \sigma|\mathbf{y})$ into the conditional p.d.f. $g(\boldsymbol{\beta}|\sigma, \mathbf{y})$ and the marginal p.d.f. $g(\sigma|\mathbf{y})$. It is not as straightforward to obtain the marginal posterior p.d.f. $g(\boldsymbol{\beta}|\mathbf{y})$, which requires integration of σ out of the joint p.d.f. $g(\boldsymbol{\beta}, \sigma|\mathbf{y})$. The required integral is

$$\begin{aligned} g(\boldsymbol{\beta}|\mathbf{y}) &= \int_0^\infty g(\boldsymbol{\beta}, \sigma|\mathbf{y})\, d\sigma \\ &\propto \int_0^\infty \sigma^{-\bar{\bar{\nu}}-K-1} \exp\{-a/2\sigma^2\}\, d\sigma \end{aligned} \tag{7.7.16}$$

where

$$a = \bar{\bar{\nu}}\bar{\bar{s}}^2 + (\boldsymbol{\beta} - \bar{\bar{\boldsymbol{\beta}}})'(A + X'X)(\boldsymbol{\beta} - \bar{\bar{\boldsymbol{\beta}}}) \tag{7.7.17}$$

The integral in (7.7.16) is evaluated using properties of the gamma function along similar lines to the derivation given in Chapter 4, Equations 4.4.28 and 4.4.29. The result is

$$\begin{aligned} g(\boldsymbol{\beta}|\mathbf{y}) &\propto a^{-(\bar{\bar{\nu}}+K)/2} \\ &\propto [\bar{\bar{\nu}}\bar{\bar{s}}^2 + (\boldsymbol{\beta} - \bar{\bar{\boldsymbol{\beta}}})'(A + X'X)(\boldsymbol{\beta} - \bar{\bar{\boldsymbol{\beta}}})]^{-(\bar{\bar{\nu}}+K)/2} \\ &\propto \left[1 + \frac{1}{\bar{\bar{\nu}}}(\boldsymbol{\beta} - \bar{\bar{\boldsymbol{\beta}}})' \frac{(A + X'X)}{\bar{\bar{s}}^2}(\boldsymbol{\beta} - \bar{\bar{\boldsymbol{\beta}}})\right]^{-(\bar{\bar{\nu}}+K)/2} \end{aligned} \tag{7.7.18}$$

This marginal posterior p.d.f. for $\boldsymbol{\beta}$ is known as a multivariate t-distribution with mean $\bar{\bar{\boldsymbol{\beta}}}$, precision matrix $\bar{\bar{s}}^{-2}(A + X'X)$, covariance matrix $[\bar{\bar{\nu}}/(\bar{\bar{\nu}} - 2)]\bar{\bar{s}}^2(A + X'X)^{-1}$, and degrees of freedom parameter $\bar{\bar{\nu}}$. It is unlikely that you will have encountered this multivariate distribution before, so we will digress and consider some of its properties.

7.7.3a A Digression on the Multivariate *t*-Distribution

In this section we state, without proof, a number of results concerning the multivariate t-distribution. The random vector $\mathbf{x} = (x_1, x_2, \ldots, x_p)'$ has a multivariate t-distribution with mean vector $\boldsymbol{\mu} = (\mu_1, \mu_2, \ldots, \mu_p)'$, precision matrix H, and parameter ν, if its density function is given by

$$f(\mathbf{x}|\nu, \boldsymbol{\mu}, H) = \frac{\Gamma[(p+\nu)/2]|H|^{1/2}}{(\nu\pi)^{p/2}\Gamma(\nu/2)}\left[1 + \frac{1}{\nu}(\mathbf{x} - \boldsymbol{\mu})'H(\mathbf{x} - \boldsymbol{\mu})\right]^{-(p+\nu)/2} \tag{7.7.19}$$

The quantity outside the square brackets is a constant, so we can recognize the form of the multivariate t from the kernel, which is the term within the square brackets. Also, the mean and covariance matrix for $\mathbf{x}$ are given by

$$E[\mathbf{x}] = \boldsymbol{\mu} \quad \text{and} \quad \operatorname{cov}(\mathbf{x}) = \frac{\nu}{\nu - 2}H^{-1} \tag{7.7.20}$$

with the mean requiring $\nu > 1$ and the covariance $\nu > 2$.

Let $V = H^{-1}$ and partition $\mathbf{x}$, $\boldsymbol{\mu}$, H, and V conformably so that we have

$$\mathbf{x} = \begin{bmatrix}\mathbf{x}^{(1)}\\ \mathbf{x}^{(2)}\end{bmatrix}, \boldsymbol{\mu} = \begin{bmatrix}\boldsymbol{\mu}^{(1)}\\ \boldsymbol{\mu}^{(2)}\end{bmatrix}, H = \begin{bmatrix}H_{11} & H_{12}\\ H_{21} & H_{22}\end{bmatrix} \quad \text{and} \quad V = \begin{bmatrix}V_{11} & V_{12}\\ V_{21} & V_{22}\end{bmatrix} \tag{7.7.21}$$

Then the marginal distribution for $\mathbf{x}^{(1)}$ is multivariate t with

$$E[\mathbf{x}^{(1)}] = \boldsymbol{\mu}^{(1)} \quad \text{and} \quad \operatorname{cov}[\mathbf{x}^{(1)}] = \frac{\nu}{\nu - 2}V_{11} = \frac{\nu}{\nu - 2}(H_{11} - H_{12}H_{22}^{-1}H_{21})^{-1} \tag{7.7.22}$$

In particular, if $\mathbf{x}^{(1)}$ is a scalar random variable, say x_1, then it has a univariate t-distribution with mean μ_1, variance $(\nu/(\nu - 2))V_{11}$, and degrees of freedom parameter ν.

The conditional distribution of $(\mathbf{x}^{(1)}|\mathbf{x}^{(2)})$ is also multivariate t with

$$E[\mathbf{x}^{(1)}|\mathbf{x}^{(2)}] = \boldsymbol{\mu}^{(1)} + H_{11}^{-1}H_{12}(\mathbf{x}^{(2)} - \boldsymbol{\mu}^{(2)}) \tag{7.7.23}$$

$$\operatorname{cov}[\mathbf{x}^{(1)}|\mathbf{x}^{(2)}] = \frac{\nu + p_2}{p_2 + \nu - 2}\cdot\frac{\nu + (\mathbf{x}^{(2)} - \boldsymbol{\mu}^{(2)})'V_{22}^{-1}(\mathbf{x}^{(2)} - \boldsymbol{\mu}^{(2)})}{\nu + p_2}H_{11}^{-1} \tag{7.7.24}$$

and degrees of freedom parameter $\nu + p_2$, where p_2 is the dimension of $\mathbf{x}^{(2)}$.

Finally we note that the linear form $\mathbf{w} = L\mathbf{x}$ will also have a multivariate t-distribution with

$$E[\mathbf{w}] = L\boldsymbol{\mu} \quad \text{and} \quad \text{cov}[\mathbf{w}] = \frac{v}{v-2} LVL' \tag{7.7.25}$$

The relationship between the general expression for the multivariate t in (7.7.19) and the multivariate t posterior p.d.f. $g(\boldsymbol{\beta}|\mathbf{y})$ given in (7.7.18) should be clear. Equation (7.7.18) is obtained by setting $\mathbf{x} = \boldsymbol{\beta}$, $\boldsymbol{\mu} = \bar{\bar{\boldsymbol{\beta}}}$, $H = \bar{\bar{s}}^{-2}(A + X'X)$, $v = \bar{\bar{v}}$ and $p = K$.

7.7.3b Marginal Posterior Density for a Single Element of $\boldsymbol{\beta}$

If K, the dimension of $\boldsymbol{\beta}$, is greater than 2, the presentation of results in terms of the complete posterior p.d.f. for $\boldsymbol{\beta}$ becomes rather unwieldy. It is much easier to interpret results if they are presented in terms of single elements in $\boldsymbol{\beta}$, or joint HPD intervals for pairs of elements in $\boldsymbol{\beta}$. From the result in (7.7.22), it follows that a single element in $\boldsymbol{\beta}$, say β_1, has a posterior p.d.f. that is a univariate t-distribution with mean $\bar{\bar{\beta}}_1$, precision parameter $(\bar{\bar{s}}^2 a^{11})^{-1}$, variance $[\bar{\bar{v}}/(\bar{\bar{v}} - 2)]\bar{\bar{s}}^2 a^{11}$, and degrees of freedom $\bar{\bar{v}}$, where a^{11} is the first diagonal element of $(A + X'X)^{-1}$. The equation of this density function is given by

$$g(\beta_1|\mathbf{y}) = \frac{\Gamma[(\bar{\bar{v}}+1)/2]}{\Gamma(\frac{1}{2})\Gamma(\bar{\bar{v}}/2)(\bar{\bar{v}}\bar{\bar{s}}^2 a^{11})^{1/2}} \left[1 + \frac{(\beta_1 - \bar{\bar{\beta}}_1)^2}{\bar{\bar{v}}\bar{\bar{s}}^2 a^{11}}\right]^{-(v+1)/2} \tag{7.7.26}$$

Examples of a univariate posterior p.d.f. for a single element in $\boldsymbol{\beta}$, and an HPD interval for a pair of elements in $\boldsymbol{\beta}$, are given in the next subsection. We conclude this subsection by noting that the same analysis could have been applied to the joint prior p.d.f. $g(\boldsymbol{\beta}, \sigma)$. Specifically, it can be shown that integrating σ out of the normal-gamma prior leads to the following multivariate t, marginal prior p.d.f. for $\boldsymbol{\beta}$

$$g(\boldsymbol{\beta}) \propto \left[1 + \frac{1}{\bar{v}\bar{s}^2}(\boldsymbol{\beta} - \bar{\boldsymbol{\beta}})'A(\boldsymbol{\beta} - \bar{\boldsymbol{\beta}})\right]^{-(\bar{v}+K)/2} \tag{7.7.27}$$

This distribution has mean $\bar{\boldsymbol{\beta}}$, precision matrix $\bar{s}^{-2}A$, and covariance matrix $[\bar{v}/(\bar{v} - 2)]\bar{s}^2 A^{-1}$; the individual elements in $\boldsymbol{\beta}$ have corresponding univariate t priors.

7.7.3c The Production Function Example Revisited

We now return to the production function example that was considered in Section 7.4 and redo the analysis under the assumption that σ^2 is unknown. Values of the prior parameters that were derived earlier are $\bar{v} = 4$, $\bar{s}^2 = 0.0754$,

$$A^{-1} = \begin{bmatrix} 923.86 & 0.0 & 0.0 \\ 0.0 & 0.369546 & -0.349015 \\ 0.0 & -0.349015 & 0.369546 \end{bmatrix} \quad \text{and} \quad \bar{\boldsymbol{\beta}} = \begin{bmatrix} 5.0 \\ 0.5 \\ 0.5 \end{bmatrix}$$

The sample information derived from the data in Table 7.2 is

$$(X'X)^{-1} = \begin{bmatrix} 0.65660 & -0.15312 & -0.29171 \\ -0.15312 & 0.11049 & -0.01443 \\ -0.29171 & -0.01443 & 0.24824 \end{bmatrix} \qquad \mathbf{b} = \begin{bmatrix} 9.770 \\ 0.524 \\ 0.693 \end{bmatrix}.$$

$\mathbf{y}'\mathbf{y} = 2632.54$ and $\hat{\sigma}^2 = 0.07953$. Combining the prior information with the sample information gives as values for the posterior parameters

$$(A + X'X)^{-1} = \begin{bmatrix} 0.12272 & -0.03551 & -0.01395 \\ -0.03551 & 0.07107 & -0.05906 \\ -0.01395 & -0.05906 & 0.08343 \end{bmatrix} \qquad \bar{\bar{\boldsymbol{\beta}}} = \begin{bmatrix} 10.028 \\ 0.476 \\ 0.548 \end{bmatrix}$$

$\bar{\bar{s}}^2 = 0.0755$ and $\bar{\bar{v}} = 24$.

These four quantities $(A + X'X)^{-1}$, $\bar{\bar{\boldsymbol{\beta}}}$, $\bar{\bar{s}}^2$, and $\bar{\bar{v}}$, are sufficient to describe any joint, conditional, or marginal posterior density that might be of interest. As examples, in Figures 7.6 and 7.7 we have graphed the marginal posterior density functions for β_2 and σ, respectively. For comparative purposes the graphs of the corresponding prior density functions are also presented. In both cases, the improved precision of the posterior information relative to the prior information is clear. The prior p.d.f. for β_2 is very flat, suggesting β_2 could lie almost anywhere in the interval (0, 1); on the other hand, with the posterior p.d.f., the probability that β_2 lies outside the interval (0.3, 0.7) is very small. These intervals were obtained by casual examination of the graphs; more precise HPD intervals could, of course,

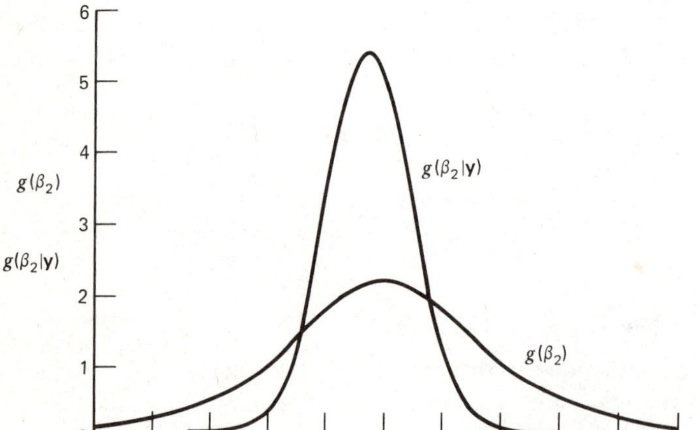

Figure 7.6 Prior and posterior p.d.f.'s for β_2 when σ is unknown.

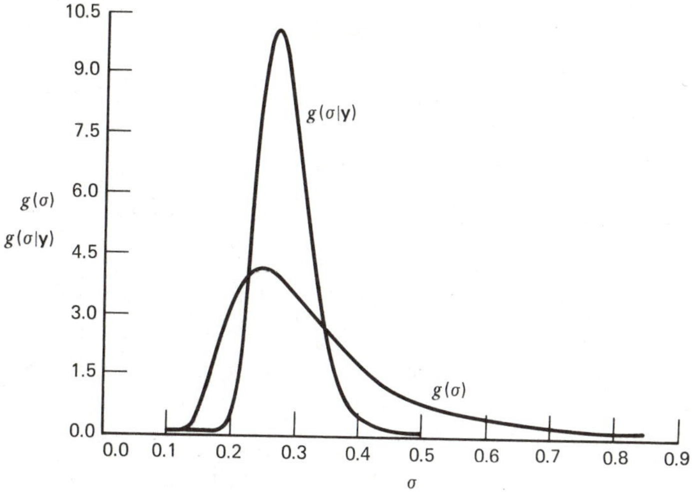

Figure 7.7 Prior and posterior p.d.f.'s for σ.

also be calculated. A similar casual examination of the prior and posterior p.d.f.'s for σ indicates that, before the sample information, σ could lie almost anywhere in the interval (0.15, 0.7); after including the sample information the interval narrows to approximately (0.2, 0.4). For the precise functional forms and normalizing constants of the p.d.f.'s, see Exercise 7.9.

It might also be of interest to find and compare prior and posterior probability regions for a pair of parameters. When σ^2 was known, such regions were derived by making use of the χ^2-distribution. As we will see, with an unknown σ^2 we make use of the F-distribution.

In (7.7.27) we indicated that the marginal prior p.d.f. for $\boldsymbol{\beta}$ was a multivariate t with mean $\bar{\boldsymbol{\beta}}$, precision matrix $\bar{s}^{-2}A$, and degrees of freedom parameter $\bar{\nu}$. Using a result in Zellner (1971, p. 385), it follows that the quadratic form

$$Q = \frac{(\boldsymbol{\beta} - \bar{\boldsymbol{\beta}})'A(\boldsymbol{\beta} - \bar{\boldsymbol{\beta}})}{K\bar{s}^2} \tag{7.7.28}$$

has an F-distribution with K and $\bar{\nu}$ degrees of freedom. We will consider a 95% HPD region for the parameters β_2 and β_3, and, therefore, we need not consider the complete vector that is specified in (7.7.28). Using results given on the multivariate t-distribution in Section 7.7.3a, and specific values from A^{-1}, the relevant result for β_2 and β_3 is

$$Q_0 = \frac{\begin{pmatrix} \beta_2 - \bar{\beta}_2 \\ \beta_3 - \bar{\beta}_3 \end{pmatrix}' \begin{pmatrix} 0.369546 & -0.349015 \\ -0.349015 & 0.369546 \end{pmatrix}^{-1} \begin{pmatrix} \beta_2 - \bar{\beta}_2 \\ \beta_3 - \bar{\beta}_3 \end{pmatrix}}{2\bar{s}^2} \sim F_{(2,4)} \tag{7.7.29}$$

Substituting values for $\bar{\beta}_2$, $\bar{\beta}_3$, and $\bar{s}^2$, and expanding, yields

$$Q_0 = 166.1(\beta_2 - 0.5)^2 + 166.1(\beta_3 - 0.5)^2 + 313.8(\beta_2 - 0.5)(\beta_3 - 0.5) \quad (7.7.30)$$

From tables of the $F_{(2,4)}$-distribution we find that

$$P(Q_0 \leq 6.94) = 0.95$$

Thus, the 95% HPD region from the prior p.d.f. is given by those values of β_2 and β_3 inside the ellipse

$$166.1(\beta_2 - 0.5)^2 + 166.1(\beta_3 - 0.5)^2 + 313.8(\beta_2 - 0.5)(\beta_3 - 0.5) = 6.94 \quad (7.7.31)$$

Following a similar procedure, but using the posterior information $\bar{\bar{\boldsymbol{\beta}}}$, $(A + X'X)^{-1}$, $\bar{\bar{v}}$ and $\bar{\bar{s}}^2$, and the $F_{(2,24)}$-distribution, it is possible to derive a 95% HPD region from the posterior p.d.f. You are encouraged to verify that this region consists of all values of β_2 and β_3 inside the ellipse

$$226.6(\beta_2 - 0.476)^2 + 193.1(\beta_3 - 0.548)^2 + 321(\beta_2 - 0.476)(\beta_3 - 0.548) = 3.40 \quad (7.7.32)$$

The two 95% HPD ellipses are graphed in Figure 7.8. It is interesting to compare these ellipses with those obtained in Figure 7.4 where σ was assumed to be known and equal to 0.3. In both cases the ellipses tend to be centered around the line

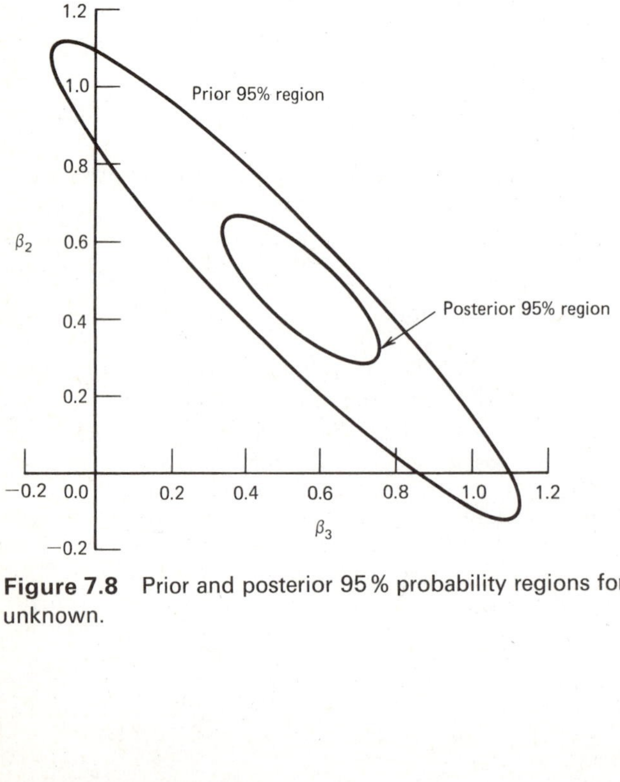

Figure 7.8 Prior and posterior 95% probability regions for β_2 and β_3 when σ is unknown.

$\beta_2 + \beta_3 = 1$. However, in Figure 7.8, where σ is unknown, the prior ellipse covers a much greater region than does the prior ellipse in Figure 7.4. Roughly speaking, the ellipses for σ unknown (Figure 7.8) can be regarded as unconditional ones, obtained by averaging all possible conditional ellipses for alternative values of σ; the marginal p.d.f.'s $g(\sigma)$ and $g(\sigma|\mathbf{y})$ are the weighting functions in the averaging process. The graphs in Figure 7.4 represent one set of conditional ellipses, those for $\sigma = 0.3$. In the prior case, relatively large values of σ are quite possible [as reflected by $g(\sigma)$], so the prior unconditional ellipse is quite large, reflecting the added uncertainty created by possibly large values of σ. After observation of the sample, the posterior p.d.f. $g(\sigma|\mathbf{y})$ suggests that large values of σ are no longer possible and that it is quite likely that σ lies below 0.3. Thus, the posterior conditional ellipse for $\sigma = 0.3$ (Figure 7.4) is of similar shape to the posterior unconditional ellipse (Figure 7.8).

7.7.4 Posterior Densities from a Noninformative Prior

The final case to be considered when σ is unknown is that where a noninformative prior is specified for $\boldsymbol{\beta}$ and σ. As has been mentioned in earlier sections where noninformative priors were considered, we adopt noninformative priors if there is no prior knowledge about the parameters or if we wish to present posterior results that are completely dominated by sample information. In this section we will simply present the major results without giving complete derivations. Interested students are encouraged to verify the results.

The conventional noninformative prior for $(\boldsymbol{\beta}, \sigma)$ is the improper p.d.f.

$$g(\boldsymbol{\beta}, \sigma) \propto \frac{1}{\sigma} \tag{7.7.33}$$

Using (7.3.13) the likelihood function can be written as

$$\ell(\boldsymbol{\beta}, \sigma|\mathbf{y}) \propto \sigma^{-T} \exp\{-[v\hat{\sigma}^2 + (\boldsymbol{\beta} - \mathbf{b})'X'X(\boldsymbol{\beta} - \mathbf{b})]/2\sigma^2\} \tag{7.7.34}$$

where $\mathbf{b} = (X'X)^{-1}X'\mathbf{y}$ is the least squares estimator, $v\hat{\sigma}^2 = (\mathbf{y} - X\mathbf{b})'(\mathbf{y} - X\mathbf{b})$ is the residual sum of squares from the least squares estimator, and $v = T - K$ is the number of degrees of freedom.

The joint posterior p.d.f. from the noninformative prior is, therefore,

$$\begin{aligned} g(\boldsymbol{\beta}, \sigma|\mathbf{y}) &\propto g(\boldsymbol{\beta}, \sigma)\ell(\boldsymbol{\beta}, \sigma|\mathbf{y}) \\ &\propto \sigma^{-(T+1)} \exp\{-[v\hat{\sigma}^2 + (\boldsymbol{\beta} - \mathbf{b})'X'X(\boldsymbol{\beta} - \mathbf{b})]/2\sigma^2\} \end{aligned} \tag{7.7.35}$$

By factoring the joint density as $g(\boldsymbol{\beta}, \sigma|\mathbf{y}) = g(\boldsymbol{\beta}|\sigma, \mathbf{y}) \cdot g(\sigma|\mathbf{y})$ it is possible to show that the marginal posterior p.d.f. for σ is the inverted-gamma density

$$g(\sigma|\mathbf{y}) \propto \frac{1}{\sigma^{v+1}} \exp\left\{-\frac{v\hat{\sigma}^2}{2\sigma^2}\right\} \tag{7.7.36}$$

Furthermore, integrating σ out of (7.7.35) shows that the marginal posterior p.d.f. for $\boldsymbol{\beta}$ is the multivariate t density

$$g(\boldsymbol{\beta}|\mathbf{y}) \propto \left[1 + \frac{1}{v\hat{\sigma}^2}(\boldsymbol{\beta} - \mathbf{b})'X'X(\boldsymbol{\beta} - \mathbf{b})\right]^{-(K+v)/2} \tag{7.7.37}$$

This density has mean vector $\mathbf{b}$, precision matrix $\hat{\sigma}^{-2}X'X$, covariance matrix $[v/(v-2)]\hat{\sigma}^2(X'X)^{-1}$, and degrees of freedom parameter v.

Both (7.7.36) and (7.7.37) can be obtained by setting $v = 0$ and $A = 0$ in the expressions for the marginal posterior p.d.f.'s that were derived from an informative prior in Section 7.7.3. Thus, (7.7.36) and (7.7.37) can be viewed as special cases of the posterior p.d.f.'s derived from an informative prior, and further analysis, such as the derivation of marginal posterior p.d.f.'s for single elements in $\boldsymbol{\beta}$ or the derivation of HPD intervals and regions, can proceed in a similar manner.

7.8 Summary and Guide to Further Reading

In this chapter we introduced the Bayesian approach to inference for the general linear statistical model. The main features covered were as follows.

1. A simple consumption function model with no intercept term and one slope coefficient was used to introduce prior and posterior p.d.f.'s and to illustrate the application of Bayes' theorem. This example was followed for both informative and noninformative priors, but under the assumption that σ^2 was known.
2. The simple model was extended to allow for a general K-dimensional parameter vector. Again, posterior p.d.f.'s were derived for informative and noninformative priors. A Cobb–Douglas production function was used as an illustrative example.
3. Point estimation was considered from a Bayesian and a sampling theory point of view. The posterior mean is the optimal Bayesian point estimator under quadratic loss; its sampling theory properties were compared with those of the least squares estimator and an empirical Bayes' estimator.

4. The posterior odds approach for comparing hypotheses, one of which is a point hypothesis, was described; the posterior odds ratio in favor of constant returns to scale was computed for the production function example.
5. The assumption of known σ^2 was relaxed and posterior p.d.f.'s for both $\boldsymbol{\beta}$ and σ were derived for both informative and noninformative prior p.d.f.'s. The production function example was again used as an illustration.

The material in this chapter and Chapter 4 can only be regarded as an introduction to Bayesian inference. For more details, and for a guide to the literature, we recommend the books by Zellner (1971), Box and Tiao (1973), Leamer (1978), Berger (1985), and Judge, et al. (1985, Chapter 4). Finally, we note that the Bayesian approach to inference is not universally accepted by statisticians, nor is its use as widespread as that of the sampling theory approach. Some reject the Bayesian approach because of its subjective probability foundations; others prefer the sampling theory approach because of difficulties associated with assessment of informative prior distributions and because computer software packages for Bayesian inferences are not as widespread as those for sampling theory inference. Nevertheless, Bayesian analysis seems to have grown in relative importance in recent years, and, in terms of the introduction of prior information and the natural assignment of probability statements to unknown parameters and hypotheses, the Bayesian approach has decided advantages. Certainly, no introductory econometrics text would be complete without some chapters on Bayesian inference.

7.9 Exercises

7.1 Show that

$$\sum (y_t - x_t\beta)^2/\sigma^2 + (\beta - \bar{\beta})^2/\bar{\sigma}_\beta^2 = \left(\frac{\sum x_t^2}{\sigma^2} + \frac{1}{\bar{\sigma}_\beta^2}\right)\left(\beta - \frac{\sum x_t y_t/\sigma^2 + \bar{\beta}/\bar{\sigma}_\beta^2}{\sum x_t^2/\sigma^2 + 1/\bar{\sigma}_\beta^2}\right)^2 + k$$

where k does not depend on β.

7.2 In Section 7.2.1 the posterior p.d.f. for β in the model $y_t = x_t\beta + e_t$ was found to be

$$(\beta|\mathbf{y}) \sim N[0.88253, (0.033534)^2]$$

Use the posterior p.d.f. to find

(*a*) The 90% HPD interval for β.

(*b*) The posterior odds in favor of $H_0: \beta < 0.9$ relative to the alternative $H_1: \beta \geq 0.9$.

(*c*) The predictive p.d.f. for y_{T+1} (a future value of y) given that $x_{T+1} = 15$.

7.3 Prove that

$$(\mathbf{w} - G\boldsymbol{\beta})'(\mathbf{w} - G\boldsymbol{\beta}) = (\boldsymbol{\beta} - \bar{\bar{\boldsymbol{\beta}}})'G'G(\boldsymbol{\beta} - \bar{\bar{\boldsymbol{\beta}}}) + (\mathbf{w} - G\bar{\bar{\boldsymbol{\beta}}})'(\mathbf{w} - G\bar{\bar{\boldsymbol{\beta}}})$$

where $\bar{\bar{\boldsymbol{\beta}}} = (G'G)^{-1}G'\mathbf{w}$.

7.4 Show that the estimator $\bar{\bar{\boldsymbol{\beta}}} = W(A\bar{\boldsymbol{\beta}} + X'\mathbf{y})$, where $W = (A + X'X)^{-1}$, has bias $E[\bar{\bar{\boldsymbol{\beta}}}] - \boldsymbol{\beta} = WA(\bar{\boldsymbol{\beta}} - \boldsymbol{\beta})$ and covariance matrix $\text{cov}(\bar{\bar{\boldsymbol{\beta}}}) = \sigma^2 WX'XW'$.

7.5 Prove that the expectation of the reciprocal of a χ^2 random variable is the reciprocal of two less than its degrees of freedom.

7.6 Show that, for the special model defined in Section 7.5.2 in connection with empirical Bayes' estimation,

(*a*) $\text{tr}[\text{MSE}(\mathbf{b})] = K\sigma^2/n$

(*b*) $\text{tr}[\text{MSE}(\bar{\bar{\boldsymbol{\beta}}})] = \dfrac{K\tau^4\sigma^2/n + (\sigma^4/n^2)(\boldsymbol{\beta} - \mu\mathbf{j}_K)'(\boldsymbol{\beta} - \mu\mathbf{j}_K)}{(\tau^2 + \sigma^2/n)^2}$

7.7 Prove that

(*a*) $|I + XA^{-1}X'| = |A + X'X|\cdot|A^{-1}|$

(*b*) $[A^{-1} + (X'X)^{-1}]^{-1} = X'X - X'X(A + X'X)^{-1}X'X$

(*c*) $(I + XA^{-1}X')^{-1} = I - X(A + X'X)^{-1}X'$

(*d*) $(\mathbf{y} - X\mathbf{b})'(\mathbf{y} - X\mathbf{b}) + (\mathbf{b} - \bar{\boldsymbol{\beta}})'[A^{-1} + (X'X)^{-1}]^{-1}(\mathbf{b} - \bar{\boldsymbol{\beta}})$
$(\mathbf{y} - X\bar{\boldsymbol{\beta}})'(I + XA^{-1}X')^{-1}(\mathbf{y} - X\bar{\boldsymbol{\beta}})$

7.8 Show that evaluation of the integral in (7.7.16) leads to the result in (7.7.18).

7.9 If β has a univariate t-distribution with mean $\bar{\beta}$, precision parameter h, and degrees of freedom v, its p.d.f. is given by

$$g(\beta) = \frac{\Gamma[(1 + v)/2]}{\Gamma(v/2)}\left(\frac{h}{v\pi}\right)^{1/2}\left[1 + \frac{h}{v}(\beta - \bar{\beta})^2\right]^{-(1+v)/2}$$

If σ has an inverted gamma-2 p.d.f. with parameters $\bar{v}$ and $\bar{s}^2$, its p.d.f. is given by

$$g(\sigma) = \frac{2}{\Gamma(\bar{v}/2)}\left(\frac{\bar{v}\bar{s}^2}{2}\right)^{\bar{v}/2}\frac{1}{\sigma^{\bar{v}+1}}\exp\left\{-\frac{\bar{v}\bar{s}^2}{2\sigma^2}\right\}$$

Use these results to show that the equations of the prior and posterior p.d.f's graphed in Figures 7.6 and 7.7 are given by

$$g(\beta_2) = 2.2465[1 + 8.9722(\beta_2 - 0.5)^2]^{-2.5}$$

$$g(\beta_2|\mathbf{y}) = 5.3902[1 + 7.7663(\beta_2 - 0.476)^2]^{-12.5}$$

$$g(\sigma) = 0.04548\sigma^{-5}e^{-0.1508/\sigma^2}$$

$$g(\sigma|\mathbf{y}) = (1.5325 \times 10^{-8})\sigma^{-25}e^{-0.906/\sigma^2}$$

7.10 Consider the consumption function example in Section 7.2, but assume that σ is unknown. Find the posterior p.d.f's for β and σ for each of the following prior p.d.f.'s.

(*a*) $(\beta|\sigma) \sim N[0.85, \sigma^2/608.861]$
$\sigma \sim$ inverted-gamma with $\bar{\nu} = 3, \bar{s}^2 = 2.5$

(*b*) $(\beta|\sigma) \sim N[0.85, \sigma^2/225]$
$g(\sigma) \propto \sigma^{-1}$

7.11 Use the posterior p.d.f. for β obtained in Exercise 7.10(b) to find

(*a*) The 90% HPD interval for β.

(*b*) The posterior odds in favor of $H_0: \beta < 0.9$ relative to the alternative $H_1: \beta \geq 0.9$.

(*c*) The predictive p.d.f. for y_{T+1} (a future value of y) given that $x_{T+1} = 15$.

7.12 Find the marginal posterior p.d.f.'s for β_2 and σ for the production function example when σ is unknown and noninformative priors on both $\boldsymbol{\beta}$ and σ are employed.

7.13 Consider the model $\mathbf{y} = X\boldsymbol{\beta} + \mathbf{e}$ where $\mathbf{e} \sim N(\mathbf{0}, \sigma^2 I)$, $\sigma^2 = 1$, and $\boldsymbol{\beta}$ is an unknown vector of parameters with prior density $g(\boldsymbol{\beta}) \propto$ constant. Find the posterior density function for $\boldsymbol{\beta}$. Find the posterior mean and covariance matrix for $\boldsymbol{\beta}$ when

$$\mathbf{y}' = (6, 2, 3, 0, -1, 4, -3, 1)$$

and

$$X' = \begin{pmatrix} 1 & 1 & 1 & 1 & 1 & 1 & 1 & 1 \\ 4 & 1 & 2 & 1 & 0 & 2 & -1 & 1 \end{pmatrix}$$

7.14 Repeat Exercise 7.13 under the assumption that σ is no longer known and instead has prior density $g(\sigma) \propto \sigma^{-1}$.

7.15 Consider the production function example in Section 7.4. Find the posterior mean and variance of the returns to scale parameter $\eta = \beta_2 + \beta_3$ when

(*a*) σ is known and equal to 0.3

(*b*) σ is unknown and the prior p.d.f. in (7.7.5) is employed

7.16 Consider the model

$$\mathbf{y} = \mathbf{x}_1\beta_1 + \mathbf{x}_2\beta_2 + \mathbf{e}$$

where $\mathbf{e} \sim N(\mathbf{0}, \sigma^2 I)$, $\sigma^2 = 1$, and you have the following prior distribution for $\boldsymbol{\beta}$

$$g(\boldsymbol{\beta}) \sim N\left[\begin{pmatrix} 1 \\ 1 \end{pmatrix}, \begin{pmatrix} 2 & 0 \\ 0 & 1 \end{pmatrix}\right]$$

Suppose, also, that you have the following sample information

$$T = 5 \qquad X'X = \begin{bmatrix} 5 & 5 \\ 5 & 15 \end{bmatrix} \qquad X'\mathbf{y} = \begin{bmatrix} 10 \\ 23 \end{bmatrix} \qquad \mathbf{y}'\mathbf{y} = 40.$$

(*a*) Find the least squares estimate for $\boldsymbol{\beta} = (\beta_1, \beta_2)'$.
(*b*) Find the mean of the posterior density for $\boldsymbol{\beta}$.
(*c*) Give an expression for the marginal posterior density for β_2.
(*d*) Assuming prior odds of unity, find the posterior odds in favor of $H_0: \beta_1 = \beta_2 = 0$.

7.17 Consider the general linear model $\mathbf{y} = X\boldsymbol{\beta} + \mathbf{e}$ where

$$\mathbf{e} \sim N(\mathbf{0}, \sigma^2 I)$$

Find the marginal posterior density functions for $\boldsymbol{\beta}$ and σ when their priors are given by

$$g(\boldsymbol{\beta}|\sigma) \propto \sigma^{-K} \exp\left\{-\frac{k}{2\sigma^2}(\boldsymbol{\beta} - \bar{\boldsymbol{\beta}})'X'X(\boldsymbol{\beta} - \bar{\boldsymbol{\beta}})\right\}$$

and

$$g(\sigma) \propto \frac{1}{\sigma}$$

where k and $\bar{\boldsymbol{\beta}}$ are prior parameters. What is the posterior mean for $\boldsymbol{\beta}$? What is its posterior variance?

7.18 The "ridge regression" estimator is given by

$$\boldsymbol{\beta}^* = (X'X + kI)^{-1}X'\mathbf{y}$$

Under what conditions on A and $\bar{\boldsymbol{\beta}}$ is $\boldsymbol{\beta}^*$ equal to the posterior mean $\bar{\bar{\boldsymbol{\beta}}}$ given in (7.3.7)? Do you think the implied prior distribution is likely to be an appropriate one for many economic examples?

7.19 Consider the model $\mathbf{y} = \mathbf{x}\beta + \mathbf{e}$ where $E[\mathbf{e}\mathbf{e}'] = \sigma^2 I$, β is a scalar,

$$\mathbf{y} = (0 \quad -1 \quad 1 \quad 2 \quad 5 \quad 1 \quad 1 \quad -2 \quad -2 \quad -6)'$$

and

$$\mathbf{x} = (0 \quad 1 \quad 2 \quad 3 \quad 4 \quad 0 \quad -1 \quad -2 \quad -3 \quad -4)'$$

Also, suppose that your prior information about β and σ can be summarized via the densities

$$(\beta|\sigma) \sim N(2, \sigma^2)$$

$$g(\sigma) \propto \sigma^{-3} \exp\{-1/\sigma^2\}$$

(*a*) What are the values of $\bar{\nu}$ and $\bar{s}^2$ in the prior density for σ?

(*b*) Write down the joint prior density $g(\beta, \sigma)$.

(*c*) What is the least squares estimate for β?

(*d*) What is the conditional posterior density $g(\beta|\sigma, \mathbf{y})$? Give its mean and variance.

(*e*) Give the marginal posterior densities for β and σ. Include the normalizing constants. What are $E[\beta|\mathbf{y}]$ and $\text{var}[\beta|\mathbf{y}]$?

(*f*) Assuming prior odds of unity, find the posterior odds in favor of $H_0: \beta = 1$ against the alternative, $H_1: \beta \neq 1$. [Assume $g(\sigma|H_0) = g(\sigma|H_1)$.]

(*g*) Under what conditions (on β and σ^2) will the MSE of the posterior mean be less than the MSE of the least squares estimator?

7.10 References

Berger, J. O. (1985) *Statistical Decision Theory and Bayesian Analysis*, 2nd ed. New York: Springer-Verlag.

Box, G. E. P., and G. C. Tiao (1973) *Bayesian Inference in Statistical Analysis.* Reading, MA: Addison-Wesley.

Casella, G. (1985) "An Introduction to Empirical Bayes Data Analysis." *The American Statistician*, 39, 83–87.

Chamberlain, G., and E. E. Leamer (1976) "Matrix Weighted Averages and Posterior Bounds." *Journal of the Royal Statistical Society*, Series B, 38, 73–84.

Dickey, J. M. (1980) "Beliefs about Beliefs, a Theory for Stochastic Assessments of Subjective Probabilities." In J. M. Bernardo et al. eds. *Bayesian Statistics*, Proceedings of the First International Meeting held in Valencia, Spain, May, 1979.

Efron, B., and C. Morris (1973) "Stein's Estimation Rule and its Competitors—An Empirical Bayes Approach." *Journal of the American Statistical Association*, 68, 117–130.

Giles, D. E. A., and A. C. Rayner (1979) "The Mean Squared Errors of the Maximum Likelihood and Natural-Conjugate Bayes Regression Estimators." *Journal of Econometrics*, 11, 319–334.

Judge, G. G., and M. E. Bock (1978) *The Statistical Implications of Pre-Test and Stein-Rule Estimators in Econometrics.* Amsterdam: North-Holland.

Judge, G. G., R. C. Hill, W. E. Griffiths, H. Lütkepohl, and T. C. Lee (1982) *Introduction to the Theory and Practice of Econometrics*, 1st ed. New York: Wiley.

Judge, G. G., W. E. Griffiths, R. C. Hill, H. Lütkepohl, and T. C. Lee (1985) *The Theory and Practice of Econometrics*, 2nd ed., New York: Wiley.

Kadane, J. B. (1980) "Predictive and Structural Methods for Eliciting Prior Distributions." In A. Zellner, ed. *Bayesian Analysis in Ecomometrics and Statistics: Essays in Honour of Harold Jeffreys.* Amsterdam: North-Holland.

Kadane, J. B., J. M. Dickey, R. L. Winkler, W. S. Smith, and S. C. Peters (1980) "Interactive Elicitation of Opinion for a Normal Linear Model." *Journal of the American Statistical Association*, 75, 845–854.

Leamer, E. E. (1978) *Specification Searches*, New York: Wiley.

Leamer, E. E. (1982). "Sets of Posterior Means with Bounded Variance Priors." *Econometrica*, 50, 725–736.

Raiffa, H., and R. Schlaifer (1961) *Applied Statistical Decision Theory*. Boston: Harvard University.

Swamy, P. A. V. B., and J. S. Mehta (1983) "Ridge Regression Estimation of the Rotterdam Model." *Journal of Econometrics*. 22, 365–390.

Winkler, R. L. (1967) "The Assessment of Prior Distributions in Bayesian Analysis." *Journal of the American Statistical Association*, 62, 776–800.

Winkler, R. L. (1977) "Prior Distributions and Model-Building in Regression Analysis." In A. Aykac and C. Brumat, eds. *New Developments in the Applications of Bayesian Methods*, Amsterdam: North-Holland.

Winkler, R. L. (1980) "Prior Information, Predictive Distributions, and Bayesian Model-Building," In A. Zellner, ed. *Bayesian Analysis in Econometrics and Statistics: Essays in Honor of Harold Jeffreys.* Amsterdam: North-Holland.

Zellner, A. (1971) *An Introduction to Bayesian Analysis in Econometrics*. New York: Wiley.

Zellner, A. (1972) "On Assessing Informative Prior Distributions for Regression Coefficients." Manuscript, H. G. B. Alexander Research Foundation, Graduate School of Business, University of Chicago.

PART 3

Generalizations of the Linear Statistical Model

In Part 3 we change the linear statistical model by relaxing the assumptions that (1) the covariance matrix for the error vector **e** is equal to a scalar multiplied by the identity matrix, (2) the parameters are constant for all observations, (3) the statistical model is linear in the parameters, and (4) the design matrix X is fixed and nonstochastic. First, instead of assuming that the covariance matrix for the error vector is $\sigma^2 I_T$, we extend the specification to $\sigma^2 \mathbf{\Psi}$, where $\mathbf{\Psi}$ is any positive definite symmetric matrix. The statistical consequences of this change in the statistical model are outlined, and alternative estimators to cope with this problem are developed and evaluated. Examples that fit into this framework include heteroskedasticity, autocorrelation, variable parameter models, sets of equations with contemporaneously correlated error terms, and the error components model for pooling time-series and cross-sectional data. Next, methods for estimating models that are nonlinear in the parameters are outlined and illustrated. Finally, a new design matrix in which the regressors are assumed to be stochastic is considered. A common feature of many of the classes of estimators considered in Part 3 is the need for the application of asymptotic theory. The concepts of consistency, probability limits, and asymptotic distributions are applied.

CHAPTER 8

General Linear Statistical Model with Nonscalar Identity Covariance Matrix

In Chapters 5 through 7, in specifying the linear statistical model $\mathbf{y} = X\boldsymbol{\beta} + \mathbf{e}$, we used the simplifying assumption that the elements of the random error vector $\mathbf{e}$ were uncorrelated and had an identical variance. That is, we assumed that $E[\mathbf{ee}'] = \sigma^2 I_T$. Although this assumption is consistent with many sampling processes by which data are generated in economics, it is also inappropriate in many cases.

For example, when using cross-section data to estimate a firm or household relationship it is likely that large disturbances (e_t's) will tend to be associated with large firms or high-income households, and small errors with small firms or low-income households. This situation, which implies that the e_t's have different variances, is known as *heteroskedasticity*. Another such example is the use of time-series data, in which case the impact of e_t on the dependent variable will not always be completely instantaneous, therefore implying that the e_t's are correlated. Finally, we can often write a number of equations on different firms or individuals as one single model in the form $\mathbf{y} = X\boldsymbol{\beta} + \mathbf{e}$. In this situation errors for different firms or individuals at the same point in time are likely to be correlated.

Therefore, the scalar identity covariance assumption concerning the error vector $\mathbf{e}$ has to some extent been a matter of convenience rather than a specification for all cases and at all times. The three circumstances just mentioned—heteroskedasticity, autocorrelation, and equation error-related sets of regression equations—are all violations of the scalar identity covariance matrix assumption, and we will deal with them in detail in Chapters 9 and 11. For the moment we consider the general case in which the covariance matrix for the error vector is

$$E[\mathbf{ee}'] = \boldsymbol{\Phi} = \sigma^2\boldsymbol{\Psi}$$

where $\boldsymbol{\Psi}$ is a known real positive definite symmetric matrix. Thus in the following section we assume that $\mathbf{e}$ is a real random vector with mean vector $\mathbf{0}$ and covariance $\sigma^2\boldsymbol{\Psi}$. In later sections we add the assumption that $\mathbf{e}$ is normally distributed and in Chapters 9 and 11 we consider the statistical implications of an unknown $\boldsymbol{\Psi}$.

You should recognize that the questions asked and the procedures we use for defining estimators and evaluating their sampling properties for this statistical model are, in general, the same as those used in Chapters 5 and 6. We first define a statistical model that describes the sampling process consistent with how we visualize the data as having been generated. Next, we must have some criterion that forms the basis for developing a rule that describes how to use the data to estimate the unknown parameters. Then, we evaluate within a sampling theory context the sampling properties of the rule and determine how "good" it is relative to other rules. If the normal error assumption is permissible, then maximum likelihood estimation is considered and inference as it relates to interval estimation and hypothesis testing is pursued. As we change statistical models in the chapters ahead, we will repeat again and again these questions and make use of the same evaluation procedures.

8.1 The Statistical Model and Estimators

In this section we investigate the problems of estimation and inference for the statistical model

$$\mathbf{y} = X\boldsymbol{\beta} + \mathbf{e} \tag{8.1.1}$$

where $\mathbf{y}$ is a $(T \times 1)$ vector of observations, X is a known $(T \times K)$ design matrix, $\boldsymbol{\beta}$ is a $(K \times 1)$ vector of unknown coefficients, and $\mathbf{e}$ is a $(T \times 1)$ random vector with mean vector $E[\mathbf{e}] = \mathbf{0}$ and covariance matrix $E[\mathbf{ee}'] = \boldsymbol{\Phi} = \sigma^2\boldsymbol{\Psi}$, where $\boldsymbol{\Psi}$ is a $(T \times T)$ known positive definite symmetric matrix and σ^2 is an unknown scalar. This error process differs from the classical-traditional uncorrelated-identical random process analyzed in Chapter 5 in that the variances of the random variables e_t are not all identical and/or there may be a nonzero covariance between e_t and e_τ if $t \neq \tau$.

It will sometimes be convenient, particularly when dealing with heteroskedasticity and sets of linear equations, to assume that $\sigma^2 = 1$. This assumption is equivalent to saying that the complete covariance matrix $\boldsymbol{\Phi}$ is known. When we write $\boldsymbol{\Phi} = \sigma^2\boldsymbol{\Psi}$ where $\boldsymbol{\Psi}$ is known and σ^2 is unknown, we are saying that it is not necessary to assume complete knowledge of the covariance matrix $\boldsymbol{\Phi}$; it is sufficient to assume knowledge of $\boldsymbol{\Psi}$, the matrix obtained after any unknown scale factor σ^2 has been factored out. Examples of this distinction will be provided in Chapter 9 when heteroskedasticity is being discussed.

8.1.1 The Least Squares Estimator of $\boldsymbol{\beta}$

We now face the question of how to best estimate the unknown parameters $\boldsymbol{\beta}$ and σ^2, based on the sample $\mathbf{y}$, which is a random vector with mean $E[\mathbf{y}] = E[X\boldsymbol{\beta} + \mathbf{e}] = X\boldsymbol{\beta}$ and covariance $E[(\mathbf{y} - X\boldsymbol{\beta})(\mathbf{y} - X\boldsymbol{\beta})'] = \boldsymbol{\Phi} = \sigma^2\boldsymbol{\Psi}$. Because the least squares rule developed when we analyzed the traditional model in Chapter 5 had good statistical properties for that statistical model, we might be led to use that rule for the statistical model (8.1.1). This rule would again lead to the estimator

$$\mathbf{b} = (X'X)^{-1}X'\mathbf{y} = (X'X)^{-1}X'[X\boldsymbol{\beta} + \mathbf{e}] = \boldsymbol{\beta} + (X'X)^{-1}X'\mathbf{e} \tag{8.1.2}$$

The random vector **b** has mean

$$E[\mathbf{b}] = E[\boldsymbol{\beta} + (X'X)^{-1}X'\mathbf{e}] = \boldsymbol{\beta} \tag{8.1.3}$$

and is thus unbiased. We seem to be on solid ground so far because we still have the unbiasedness property in our favor. Given an unbiased rule, the next question concerns the sampling precision of **b**. To investigate this property, we evaluate the covariance of **b**, which is

$$\begin{aligned} E[(\mathbf{b} - \boldsymbol{\beta})(\mathbf{b} - \boldsymbol{\beta})'] &= E[(\boldsymbol{\beta} + (X'X)^{-1}X'\mathbf{e} - \boldsymbol{\beta})(\boldsymbol{\beta} + (X'X)^{-1}X'\mathbf{e} - \boldsymbol{\beta})'] \\ &= E[(X'X)^{-1}X'\mathbf{e}\mathbf{e}'X(X'X)^{-1}] \\ &= (X'X)^{-1}X'\boldsymbol{\Phi}X(X'X)^{-1} \\ &= \sigma^2(X'X)^{-1}X'\boldsymbol{\Psi}X(X'X)^{-1} \end{aligned} \tag{8.1.4}$$

Since $\boldsymbol{\Psi} \neq I$ this covariance matrix is different from $\Sigma_{\mathbf{b}} = \sigma^2(X'X)^{-1}$, the covariance matrix developed for the least squares estimator in Chapter 5. Thus, although the least squares estimator applied *directly* to (8.1.1) is unbiased, there is some question about whether or not it still remains best. Note that $\sigma^2(X'X)^{-1}$ is no longer the correct formula for the covariance of **b** and that using standard computer regression routines would, on the average, produce incorrect estimated standard errors, in that the elements of $\sigma^2(X'X)^{-1}$ may understate or overstate the true variances and covariances.

8.1.2 The Generalized Least Squares Estimator

Let us investigate the possibility of developing a best linear unbiased estimator for $\boldsymbol{\beta}$ when the error process has the covariance matrix $E[\mathbf{e}\mathbf{e}'] = \sigma^2\boldsymbol{\Psi}$. The first step in this direction is to transform the statistical model $\mathbf{y} = X\boldsymbol{\beta} + \mathbf{e}$ by multiplying it by a $(T \times T)$ matrix P which has the property that $P\boldsymbol{\Psi}P' = I_T$. From Section A.11 of Appendix A we know that, since $\boldsymbol{\Psi}$ is positive definite, a matrix P with the property $P\boldsymbol{\Psi}P' = I_T$ always exists. Such a P may not be unique, but the important feature is its existence.

Using the matrix P to transform the model yields

$$P\mathbf{y} = PX\boldsymbol{\beta} + P\mathbf{e} \tag{8.1.5}$$

or

$$\mathbf{y}^* = X^*\boldsymbol{\beta} + \mathbf{e}^* \tag{8.1.6}$$

where $\mathbf{y}^* = P\mathbf{y}$, $X^* = PX$ and $\mathbf{e}^* = P\mathbf{e}$. The transformed error vector $\mathbf{e}^*$ has mean

$$E[\mathbf{e}^*] = E[P\mathbf{e}] = PE[\mathbf{e}] = \mathbf{0} \tag{8.1.7}$$

and covariance matrix

$$E[\mathbf{e}^*\mathbf{e}^{*\prime}] = E[P\mathbf{e}\mathbf{e}'P'] = PE[\mathbf{e}\mathbf{e}']P' = \sigma^2 P\mathbf{\Psi}P' = \sigma^2 I_T \tag{8.1.8}$$

Thus, the transformed error vector $\mathbf{e}^*$ has the same properties as were assumed for the original error vector in Chapters 5 through 7; its elements are uncorrelated and have identical variances.

The result in (8.1.8) also provides us with another interpretation for the scalar σ^2. It is viewed as the variance of the transformed error term. Instances when it is convenient to assume $\sigma^2 = 1$ are equivalent to instances where it is convenient to choose P such that the transformed error term has a variance of unity.

Since the transformed model in (8.1.6) satisfies the assumptions outlined in Chapter 5, we know that the least squares estimator

$$\hat{\boldsymbol{\beta}} = (X^{*\prime}X^*)^{-1}X^{*\prime}\mathbf{y}^* \tag{8.1.9}$$

is best linear unbiased. Writing this estimator in terms of the original observations, we have

$$\hat{\boldsymbol{\beta}} = (X'P'PX)^{-1}X'P'P\mathbf{y} \tag{8.1.10}$$

Furthermore, since $P\mathbf{\Psi}P' = I_T$, it follows that

$$\mathbf{\Psi} = P^{-1}P'^{-1}$$

and

$$\mathbf{\Psi}^{-1} = P'P \tag{8.1.11}$$

Thus, the least squares estimator applied to the transformed observations is given by

$$\hat{\boldsymbol{\beta}} = (X'\mathbf{\Psi}^{-1}X)^{-1}X'\mathbf{\Psi}^{-1}\mathbf{y} \tag{8.1.12}$$

This estimator is known as the *generalized least squares estimator*. It is the best linear unbiased estimator for $\boldsymbol{\beta}$ in the model $\mathbf{y} = X\boldsymbol{\beta} + \mathbf{e}$ when $E[\mathbf{e}] = \mathbf{0}$ and $E[\mathbf{e}\mathbf{e}'] = \sigma^2\mathbf{\Psi}$. We have proved that $\hat{\boldsymbol{\beta}} = (X'\mathbf{\Psi}^{-1}X)^{-1}X'\mathbf{\Psi}^{-1}\mathbf{y}$ is best linear unbiased by

1. Transforming the model so that the transformed error vector $\mathbf{e}^*$ has a covariance matrix given by $E[\mathbf{e}^*\mathbf{e}^{*\prime}] = \sigma^2 I_T$.

2. Using the Gauss–Markov theorem from Chapter 5 to assert that the least squares estimator $\hat{\boldsymbol{\beta}} = (X^{*\prime}X^*)^{-1}X^{*\prime}\mathbf{y}^*$ is best linear unbiased.

3. Showing that $\hat{\boldsymbol{\beta}} = (X^{*\prime}X^*)^{-1}X^{*\prime}\mathbf{y}^* = (X'\mathbf{\Psi}^{-1}X)^{-1}X'\mathbf{\Psi}^{-1}\mathbf{y}$.

Since $\hat{\boldsymbol{\beta}}$ is unbiased, its mean is

$$\begin{aligned} E[\hat{\boldsymbol{\beta}}] &= (X'\mathbf{\Psi}^{-1}X)^{-1}X'\mathbf{\Psi}^{-1}E[\mathbf{y}] \\ &= (X'\mathbf{\Psi}^{-1}X)^{-1}X'\mathbf{\Psi}^{-1}X\boldsymbol{\beta} \\ &= \boldsymbol{\beta} \end{aligned} \tag{8.1.13}$$

Using results from Chapter 5, its covariance matrix is

$$\Sigma_{\hat{\boldsymbol{\beta}}} = \sigma^2(X^{*\prime}X^*)^{-1} = \sigma^2(X'\boldsymbol{\Psi}^{-1}X)^{-1} \tag{8.1.14}$$

In general, this covariance matrix differs from the covariance matrix obtained by using the least squares rule directly with the original untransformed model; that is,

$$\sigma^2(X'\boldsymbol{\Psi}^{-1}X)^{-1} \neq \sigma^2(X'X)^{-1}X'\boldsymbol{\Psi}X(X'X)^{-1}$$

In fact, since the generalized least squares estimator is best linear unbiased, and hence is at least as good as the least squares estimator $\mathbf{b} = (X'X)^{-1}X'\mathbf{y}$, it follows that

$$\Sigma_{\mathbf{b}} - \Sigma_{\hat{\boldsymbol{\beta}}} = \sigma^2(X'X)^{-1}X'\boldsymbol{\Psi}X(X'X)^{-1} - \sigma^2(X'\boldsymbol{\Psi}^{-1}X)^{-1} = D \tag{8.1.15}$$

must be a positive semidefinite matrix. This result may be proved by showing that

$$\Sigma_{\mathbf{b}} - \Sigma_{\hat{\boldsymbol{\beta}}} = \sigma^2 A\boldsymbol{\Psi}A' \tag{8.1.16}$$

where

$$A = (X'X)^{-1}X' - (X'\boldsymbol{\Psi}^{-1}X)^{-1}X'\boldsymbol{\Psi}^{-1}$$

Finally, we note that the least squares criterion function in terms of the transformed observations is equivalent to a "weighted" least squares criterion function in terms of the original observations. That is, $\hat{\boldsymbol{\beta}}$ is that value of $\boldsymbol{\beta}$ that minimizes

$$\begin{aligned}(\mathbf{y}^* - X^*\boldsymbol{\beta})'(\mathbf{y}^* - X^*\boldsymbol{\beta}) &= (\mathbf{y} - X\boldsymbol{\beta})'P'P(\mathbf{y} - X\boldsymbol{\beta}) \\ &= (\mathbf{y} - X\boldsymbol{\beta})'\boldsymbol{\Psi}^{-1}(\mathbf{y} - X\boldsymbol{\beta})\end{aligned} \tag{8.1.17}$$

8.1.3 An Unbiased Estimator for σ^2

If we use the conventional least squares rule to estimate $\boldsymbol{\beta}$, that is, $\mathbf{b} = (X'X)^{-1}X'\mathbf{y}$, and also use the conventional quadratic estimator for σ^2, that is,

$$\hat{\sigma}^2 = \frac{(\mathbf{y} - X\mathbf{b})'(\mathbf{y} - X\mathbf{b})}{T - K}$$

then

$$\begin{aligned}E[\hat{\sigma}^2] &= E\left[\frac{\mathbf{y}'(I - X(X'X)^{-1}X')\mathbf{y}}{T-K}\right] \\ &= E\left[\frac{\mathbf{e}'(I - X(X'X)^{-1}X')\mathbf{e}}{T-K}\right] \\ &= \operatorname{tr} E\,\frac{[\mathbf{e}\mathbf{e}'(I - X(X'X)^{-1}X')]}{T-K} \\ &= \sigma^2\,\frac{\operatorname{tr} \boldsymbol{\Psi}(I - X(X'X)^{-1}X')}{T-K} \neq \sigma^2\end{aligned} \tag{8.1.18}$$

However, the variance estimator resulting from the generalized least squares estimator (8.1.10), namely, the random variable

$$\hat{\sigma}_g^2 = \frac{(\mathbf{y}^* - X^*\hat{\boldsymbol{\beta}})'(\mathbf{y}^* - X^*\hat{\boldsymbol{\beta}})}{T-K}$$

$$= \frac{(\mathbf{y} - X\hat{\boldsymbol{\beta}})'\Psi^{-1}(\mathbf{y} - X\hat{\boldsymbol{\beta}})}{T-K} \tag{8.1.19}$$

has a mean $E[\hat{\sigma}_g^2] = \sigma^2$ and is thus an unbiased estimator of σ^2.

8.1.4 Summary

If Ψ is known, the generalized least squares estimator $\hat{\boldsymbol{\beta}} = (X'\Psi^{-1}X)^{-1}X'\Psi^{-1}\mathbf{y}$ for the unknown coefficient vector $\boldsymbol{\beta}$ in statistical model (8.1.1) is best linear unbiased. The conventional least squares estimator $\mathbf{b} = (X'X)^{-1}X'\mathbf{y}$ applied to the statistical model (8.1.1) leads to a rule that is unbiased, but it has a sampling variability that is inferior to the generalized least squares estimator; that is, $\mathbf{b}$ is not a minimum variance unbiased estimator of $\boldsymbol{\beta}$.

Also, under the nonscalar identity covariance linear statistical model the conventional least squares estimator of σ^2, which is

$$\hat{\sigma}^2 = \frac{(\mathbf{y} - X\mathbf{b})'(\mathbf{y} - X\mathbf{b})}{T-K}$$

is a biased quadratic estimator of σ^2. The generalized least squares estimator $\hat{\sigma}_g^2 = (\mathbf{y} - X\hat{\boldsymbol{\beta}})'\Psi^{-1}(\mathbf{y} - X\hat{\boldsymbol{\beta}})/(T-K)$ is an unbiased estimator of σ^2.

8.1.5 A Sampling Experiment

To illustrate the analytical results in the previous sections, a Monte Carlo sampling experiment was performed using the model

$$\mathbf{y} = X\boldsymbol{\beta} + \mathbf{e} = 10.0\mathbf{x}_1 + 0.4\mathbf{x}_2 + 0.6\mathbf{x}_3 + \mathbf{e} \tag{8.1.20}$$

where $\mathbf{e}$ is a normal random vector with mean vector zero and covariance matrix

$$E[\mathbf{ee}'] = \sigma^2\Psi = \frac{\sigma^2}{1-\rho^2}\begin{bmatrix} 1 & \rho & \rho^2 & \cdots & \rho^{T-1} \\ \rho & 1 & \rho & \cdots & \rho^{T-2} \\ \rho^2 & \rho & 1 & \cdots & \rho^{T-3} \\ \vdots & \vdots & \vdots & \ddots & \vdots \\ \rho^{T-1} & \rho^{T-2} & \rho^{T-3} & \cdots & 1 \end{bmatrix} \tag{8.1.21}$$

with $\rho = 0.9$ and $\sigma^2 = 0.0625$. This covariance matrix arises when we have a model with first-order autoregressive errors. Such a model is discussed in depth in Chapter 9. At this time we will simply note that (8.1.21) is an obvious example of a general covariance matrix and that the transformed observations $\mathbf{y}^* = P\mathbf{y}$ and $X^* = PX$, which are such that $P'P = \mathbf{\Psi}^{-1}$, are given by

$$y_1^* = \sqrt{1-\rho^2}\,y_1 \qquad y_t^* = y_t - \rho y_{t-1}$$

and

$$x_{1k}^* = \sqrt{1-\rho^2}\,x_{1k} \qquad x_{tk}^* = x_{tk} - \rho x_{t-1,k} \qquad \begin{aligned} k &= 1, 2, 3, \\ t &= 2, 3, \ldots, T \end{aligned}$$

The details concerning why this is a suitable transformation are provided in Chapter 9.

The matrix of explanatory variables used is

$$X = \begin{bmatrix} \mathbf{x}_1 & \mathbf{x}_2 & \mathbf{x}_3 \\ 1 & 0.693 & 0.693 \\ 1 & 1.733 & 0.693 \\ 1 & 0.693 & 1.386 \\ 1 & 1.733 & 1.386 \\ 1 & 0.693 & 1.792 \\ 1 & 2.340 & 0.693 \\ 1 & 1.733 & 1.792 \\ 1 & 2.340 & 1.386 \\ 1 & 2.340 & 1.792 \\ 1 & 0.693 & 0.693 \\ 1 & 0.693 & 1.386 \\ 1 & 1.733 & 0.693 \\ 1 & 1.733 & 1.386 \\ 1 & 0.693 & 1.792 \\ 1 & 2.340 & 0.693 \\ 1 & 1.733 & 1.792 \\ 1 & 2.340 & 1.386 \\ 1 & 2.340 & 1.792 \\ 1 & 1.733 & 1.386 \\ 1 & 0.693 & 0.693 \end{bmatrix} \tag{8.1.22}$$

This provides sufficient information to calculate the true covariance matrices of the generalized least squares estimator $\hat{\boldsymbol{\beta}} = (X'\boldsymbol{\Psi}^{-1}X)^{-1}X'\boldsymbol{\Psi}^{-1}\mathbf{y}$ and the least squares estimator $\mathbf{b} = (X'X)^{-1}X'\mathbf{y}$ as well as the mean of the (biased) variance estimator $\hat{\sigma}^2 = (\mathbf{y} - X\mathbf{b})'(\mathbf{y} - X\mathbf{b})/(T - K)$. These calculations yield

$$\Sigma_{\hat{\boldsymbol{\beta}}} = \sigma^2(X'\boldsymbol{\Psi}^{-1}X)^{-1} = \begin{bmatrix} 0.18394 & -0.00750 & -0.01094 \\ -0.00750 & 0.00455 & 0.00231 \\ -0.01094 & 0.00231 & 0.00835 \end{bmatrix} \tag{8.1.23}$$

$$\Sigma_{\mathbf{b}} = \sigma^2(X'X)^{-1}X'\boldsymbol{\Psi}X(X'X)^{-1} = \begin{bmatrix} 0.23897 & -0.02687 & -0.02873 \\ -0.02687 & 0.01261 & 0.01004 \\ -0.02873 & 0.01004 & 0.01860 \end{bmatrix} \tag{8.1.24}$$

$$\begin{aligned} E[\hat{\sigma}^2] &= \frac{\sigma^2 \operatorname{tr}[\boldsymbol{\Psi}(I - X(X'X)^{-1}X')]}{T - K} \\ &= \left[\frac{\sigma^2}{T - K}\right]\{\operatorname{tr}(\boldsymbol{\Psi}) - \operatorname{tr}[X'\boldsymbol{\Psi}X(X'X)^{-1}]\} \\ &= 0.16049 \end{aligned} \tag{8.1.25}$$

Note that, as expected, the generalized least squares estimator is more efficient than the least squares estimator, and $\hat{\sigma}^2$ is biased. In this particular case $\hat{\sigma}^2$ is biased upward.

The model in (8.1.20), (8.1.21), and (8.1.22), was used to generate 500 samples of $\mathbf{y}$, each of size 20. To give an idea of the sampling variability of the estimates and to compare the least squares results with those obtained using generalized least squares, Table 8.1 presents $\hat{\beta}_3$, b_3, $\hat{\sigma}_g^2$, $\hat{\sigma}^2$, $\widehat{\operatorname{var}}(\hat{\beta}_3)$, and $\widehat{\operatorname{var}}(b_3)$ for 10 of the samples. The term $\widehat{\operatorname{var}}(\hat{\beta}_3)$ is given by the last diagonal element of $\hat{\sigma}_g^2(X'\boldsymbol{\Psi}^{-1}X)^{-1}$, and $\widehat{\operatorname{var}}(b_3)$ is given by the last diagonal element of $\hat{\sigma}^2(X'X)^{-1}$. The latter estimator is a biased estimator of $\operatorname{var}(b_3)$, which is given by the last diagonal element of $\sigma^2(X'X)^{-1}X'\boldsymbol{\Psi}X(X'X)^{-1}$. The fact that we have chosen the last element in $\boldsymbol{\beta}$ has no special significance; we are simply using it as an example.

On examining the first two columns of Table 8.1 we see that, as expected, b_3 is more variable than $\hat{\beta}_3$. The range of the $\hat{\beta}_3$'s is from 0.329 to 0.749 and that for the b_3's is from 0.293 to 0.753. Note that, although $\hat{\beta}_3$ is better than b_3 in terms of repeated samples, it is quite possible, in any one sample, for b_3 to be closer to the true parameter value 0.6; for example, see sample number 8. The averages over 500 samples are $\bar{\hat{\beta}}_3 = 0.596$ and $\bar{b}_3 = 0.596$.

The sampling variability of the variance estimates $\hat{\sigma}_g^2$ and $\hat{\sigma}^2$ is illustrated in columns 3 and 4 of Table 8.1, and it is clear, as the analytical results suggest, that $\hat{\sigma}^2$ is biased upward. The averages over 500 samples are $\overline{\hat{\sigma}_g^2} = 0.0635$ and $\overline{\hat{\sigma}^2} = 0.1568$, compared with the true means of 0.0625 and 0.1605, respectively.

Table 8.1 Generalized Least Squares and Least Squares Estimates for 10 Samples of Data

Sample Number	$\hat{\beta}_3$ ($\beta_3 = 0.6$)	b_3 ($\beta_3 = 0.6$)	$\hat{\sigma}_g^2$ ($\sigma^2 = 0.0625$)	$\hat{\sigma}^2$ ($E[\hat{\sigma}^2] = 0.1605$)	$\hat{\sigma}_{\hat{\beta}_3}^2$ ($\sigma_{\hat{\beta}_3}^2 = 0.0083$)	$\hat{\sigma}_{b_3}^2$ ($\sigma_{b_3}^2 = 0.0186$)
1	0.644	0.731	0.0850	0.1852	0.0114	0.0460
2	0.589	0.745	0.1100	0.2584	0.0146	0.0642
3	0.641	0.557	0.0686	0.2430	0.0092	0.0603
4	0.534	0.497	0.0927	0.3852	0.0124	0.0956
5	0.749	0.753	0.0267	0.0370	0.0036	0.0092
6	0.584	0.660	0.0459	0.0562	0.0061	0.0140
7	0.329	0.293	0.0597	0.1079	0.0080	0.0268
8	0.685	0.646	0.0615	0.2140	0.0082	0.0531
9	0.634	0.707	0.0708	0.1062	0.0095	0.0264
10	0.382	0.450	0.0606	0.0561	0.0081	0.0139

From the last two columns of the table, we see that the estimates of $\text{var}(\hat{\beta}_3)$ give us a reasonable indication of the true sampling variability in $\hat{\beta}_3[\text{var}(\hat{\beta}_3) = 0.0083]$, but that the same is not true for b_3. The true variance of b_3 is 0.0186. However, if we incorrectly use least squares procedures to estimate this variance, it appears, from the 10 samples in the table, that we will generally be overestimating it. In other words, our estimates are more reliable than we are led to believe. This is supported by comparing the averages from 500 samples, $\overline{\widehat{\text{var}}(\hat{\beta}_3)} = 0.0085$ and $\overline{\widehat{\text{var}}(b_3)} = 0.0389$, with the true values, $\text{var}(\hat{\beta}_3) = 0.0083$ and $\text{var}(b_3) = 0.0186$.

An idea of the accuracy (or inaccuracy) of the estimates calculated from a 500-sample Monte Carlo study can be obtained by comparing the estimated mean square-error matrices of $\hat{\boldsymbol{\beta}}$ and $\mathbf{b}$ with their true covariance matrices. For example, if $\mathbf{b}_{(i)}$ is the least squares estimate from the ith sample, the estimated mean square error matrix for $\mathbf{b}$ is

$$\frac{1}{500}\sum_{i=1}^{500}[\mathbf{b}_{(i)} - \boldsymbol{\beta}][\mathbf{b}_{(i)} - \boldsymbol{\beta}]'$$

Calculating these matrices for $\hat{\boldsymbol{\beta}}$ and $\mathbf{b}$ yields, respectively,

$$\begin{bmatrix} 0.184 & -0.007 & -0.013 \\ -0.007 & 0.004 & 0.002 \\ -0.013 & 0.002 & 0.009 \end{bmatrix} \quad \text{and} \quad \begin{bmatrix} 0.235 & -0.026 & -0.029 \\ -0.026 & 0.011 & 0.009 \\ -0.029 & 0.009 & 0.018 \end{bmatrix} \tag{8.1.26}$$

A comparison of these values with those given in (8.1.23) and (8.1.24) shows that in most cases the estimates are quite close to the true values.

8.2 The Normal Linear Statistical Model

In this section we add the assumption that the random vector $\mathbf{e}$ is normally distributed. Also, we retain the assumptions that $E[\mathbf{e}] = \mathbf{0}$ and $E[\mathbf{ee}'] = \sigma^2\boldsymbol{\Psi}$, where, again, $\boldsymbol{\Psi}$ is a known $(T \times T)$ symmetric positive definite matrix. In Chapter 6, when working with normal but uncorrelated and identically distributed errors, that is, $E[\mathbf{ee}'] = \sigma^2 I_T$, we were able to write the joint density function for the observations and the error vector as

$$\begin{aligned} f(\mathbf{y}|X, \boldsymbol{\beta}, \sigma^2) &= \frac{1}{(2\pi\sigma^2)^{T/2}} \exp\left[-\frac{(\mathbf{y} - X\boldsymbol{\beta})'(\mathbf{y} - X\boldsymbol{\beta})}{2\sigma^2}\right] \\ &= (2\pi\sigma^2)^{-T/2}|I_T|^{-1/2} \exp\left[-\frac{(\mathbf{y} - X\boldsymbol{\beta})' I_T (\mathbf{y} - X\boldsymbol{\beta})}{2\sigma^2}\right] \end{aligned} \tag{8.2.1}$$

The counterpart of this multivariate density function for the general covariance case may be analytically expressed as

$$f(\mathbf{y}|X, \boldsymbol{\beta}, \sigma^2) = (2\pi\sigma^2)^{-T/2} |\boldsymbol{\Psi}|^{-1/2} \exp\left[-\frac{(\mathbf{y} - X\boldsymbol{\beta})'\boldsymbol{\Psi}^{-1}(\mathbf{y} - X\boldsymbol{\beta})}{2\sigma^2} \right] \quad (8.2.2)$$

Thus when we use the maximum likelihood principle introduced in Chapters 3 and 6, we may write the likelihood function as

$$\ell(\boldsymbol{\beta}, \sigma^2 | \mathbf{y}, X) = (2\pi\sigma^2)^{-T/2} |\boldsymbol{\Psi}|^{-1/2} \exp\left[-\frac{(\mathbf{y} - X\boldsymbol{\beta})'\boldsymbol{\Psi}^{-1}(\mathbf{y} - X\boldsymbol{\beta})}{2\sigma^2} \right] \quad (8.2.3a)$$

and the log likelihood function as

$$\ln \ell(\boldsymbol{\beta}, \sigma^2 | \mathbf{y}, X) = -\frac{T}{2} \ln 2\pi - \frac{T}{2} \ln \sigma^2 - \frac{1}{2} \ln |\boldsymbol{\Psi}| - \frac{(\mathbf{y} - X\boldsymbol{\beta})'\boldsymbol{\Psi}^{-1}(\mathbf{y} - X\boldsymbol{\beta})}{2\sigma^2} \quad (8.2.3b)$$

To find $\tilde{\boldsymbol{\beta}}$ and $\tilde{\sigma}_g^2$ that maximize this likelihood function, we solve the normal equations

$$\left. \frac{\partial \ln \ell(\boldsymbol{\beta}, \sigma^2 | \mathbf{y}, X)}{\partial \boldsymbol{\beta}} \right|_{\tilde{\boldsymbol{\beta}}} = \frac{1}{\tilde{\sigma}_g^2} [X'\boldsymbol{\Psi}^{-1}\mathbf{y} - (X'\boldsymbol{\Psi}^{-1}X)\tilde{\boldsymbol{\beta}}] = \mathbf{0} \quad (8.2.4a)$$

$$\left. \frac{\partial \ln \ell(\boldsymbol{\beta}, \sigma^2 | \mathbf{y}, X)}{\partial \sigma^2} \right|_{\tilde{\boldsymbol{\beta}}, \tilde{\sigma}_g^2} = -\frac{T}{2\tilde{\sigma}_g^2} + \frac{1}{2\tilde{\sigma}_g^4} (\mathbf{y} - X\tilde{\boldsymbol{\beta}})'\boldsymbol{\Psi}^{-1}(\mathbf{y} - X\tilde{\boldsymbol{\beta}}) = 0 \quad (8.2.4b)$$

Consequently, the maximum likelihood estimators for the unknown parameters are

$$\tilde{\boldsymbol{\beta}} = (X'\boldsymbol{\Psi}^{-1}X)^{-1}X'\boldsymbol{\Psi}^{-1}\mathbf{y} \quad (8.2.5)$$

and

$$\tilde{\sigma}_g^2 = \frac{(\mathbf{y} - X\tilde{\boldsymbol{\beta}})'\boldsymbol{\Psi}^{-1}(\mathbf{y} - X\tilde{\boldsymbol{\beta}})}{T} \quad (8.2.6)$$

The maximum likelihood estimator $\tilde{\boldsymbol{\beta}}$ is the same as the generalized least squares estimator $\hat{\boldsymbol{\beta}}$, a result that is consistent with Chapters 5 and 6 for the traditional (scalar identity) linear statistical model. The maximum likelihood estimator of $\boldsymbol{\beta}$ is therefore best linear unbiased.

The maximum likelihood estimator $\tilde{\sigma}_g^2$ is a biased estimator of σ^2 and, of course, differs from the unbiased estimator

$$\hat{\sigma}_g^2 = \frac{(\mathbf{y} - X\hat{\boldsymbol{\beta}})'\boldsymbol{\Psi}^{-1}(\mathbf{y} - X\hat{\boldsymbol{\beta}})}{T - K}$$

in (8.1.19) by the factor $T/(T - K)$.

We should note that, as in Chapter 6, when the normality assumption is added we may make use of the Cramér–Rao inequality and information matrix; this result implies that (1) the estimator of σ^2 given in (8.1.19) becomes a best unbiased estimator of σ^2 and, (2) the maximum likelihood estimator $\tilde{\boldsymbol{\beta}}$ is a best unbiased estimator, that is, the restriction to linear estimators is no longer necessary.

8.3 Sampling Distributions of $\tilde{\boldsymbol{\beta}}$ and $\hat{\sigma}_g^2$

The maximum likelihood estimator $\tilde{\boldsymbol{\beta}} = (X'\boldsymbol{\Psi}^{-1}X)^{-1}X'\boldsymbol{\Psi}^{-1}\mathbf{y}$ is a linear function of the normally distributed random vector $\mathbf{y}$ and therefore $\tilde{\boldsymbol{\beta}}$ is a multivariate normal random vector with mean vector $\boldsymbol{\beta}$ and covariance $\sigma^2(X'\boldsymbol{\Psi}^{-1}X)^{-1}$. Consequently, $(\tilde{\boldsymbol{\beta}} - \boldsymbol{\beta})$ is a normal random vector with mean vector $\mathbf{0}$ and covariance $\sigma^2(X'\boldsymbol{\Psi}^{-1}X)^{-1}$. For an individual element $\tilde{\beta}_k$, for $k = 1, 2, \ldots, K$, the random variable

$$\frac{\tilde{\beta}_k - \beta_k}{\sigma\sqrt{c^{kk}}}$$

is a normally distributed random variable with mean 0 and variance 1, where c^{kk} is the (k, k) element of $(X'\boldsymbol{\Psi}^{-1}X)^{-1}$.

The distribution of the quadratic form $(T - K)\hat{\sigma}_g^2/\sigma^2$ can be investigated by following the same procedure as outlined in Section 6.1.3b of Chapter 6, but using instead the transformed observations $\mathbf{y}^* = P\mathbf{y}$ and $X^* = PX$. Specifically, we can write

$$\begin{aligned}\frac{(T - K)\hat{\sigma}_g^2}{\sigma^2} &= \frac{(\mathbf{y} - X\tilde{\boldsymbol{\beta}})'\boldsymbol{\Psi}^{-1}(\mathbf{y} - X\tilde{\boldsymbol{\beta}})}{\sigma^2}\\ &= \frac{(\mathbf{y}^* - X^*\tilde{\boldsymbol{\beta}})'(\mathbf{y}^* - X^*\tilde{\boldsymbol{\beta}})}{\sigma^2}\\ &= \frac{\hat{\mathbf{e}}^{*\prime}\hat{\mathbf{e}}^*}{\sigma^2}\\ &= \frac{\mathbf{e}^{*\prime}(I_T - X^*(X^{*\prime}X^*)^{-1}X^{*\prime})\mathbf{e}^*}{\sigma^2} \qquad (8.3.1)\end{aligned}$$

where $\hat{\mathbf{e}}^* = \mathbf{y}^* - X^*\tilde{\boldsymbol{\beta}}$. Because $\mathbf{e}^* = P\mathbf{e} \sim N(\mathbf{0}, \sigma^2 I_T)$, and because

$$[I_T - X^*(X^{*\prime}X^*)^{-1}X^{*\prime}]$$

is an idempotent matrix of rank $(T - K)$, it follows from Section 2.5.8 of Chapter 2, that

$$\frac{(T-K)\hat{\sigma}_g^2}{\sigma^2} \sim \chi^2_{(T-K)} \tag{8.3.2}$$

Also, since $\tilde{\boldsymbol{\beta}} - \boldsymbol{\beta} = (X^{*\prime}X^*)^{-1}X^{*\prime}\mathbf{e}^*$, and since the product of $[I_T - X^*(X^{*\prime}X^*)^{-1}X^{*\prime}]$ and $(X^{*\prime}X^*)^{-1}X^{*\prime}$ is equal to a null matrix, it follows that $\tilde{\boldsymbol{\beta}}$ and $\hat{\sigma}_g^2$ are independent.

8.4 Interval Estimators

Given the distributional results of the previous section, we may follow the format of Section 6.12 to develop interval estimates for $\boldsymbol{\beta}$ and σ^2.

First, in terms of the interval estimates for individual coefficients, if R_1 is a $(1 \times K)$ vector, then we know that the random variable $R_1\tilde{\boldsymbol{\beta}}$ is normally distributed with mean $R_1\boldsymbol{\beta}$ and variance $\sigma^2 R_1(X'\Psi^{-1}X)^{-1}R_1'$. Thus the random variable

$$\frac{R_1\tilde{\boldsymbol{\beta}} - R_1\boldsymbol{\beta}}{\sigma\sqrt{R_1(X'\Psi^{-1}X)^{-1}R_1'}} \sim N(0, 1)$$

and is a standardized normal random variable. Therefore, we know that

$$\Pr\left[-z_{(\alpha/2)} \leq \frac{R_1\tilde{\boldsymbol{\beta}} - R_1\boldsymbol{\beta}}{\sigma\sqrt{R_1(X'\Psi^{-1}X)^{-1}R_1'}} \leq z_{(\alpha/2)}\right] = 1 - \alpha \tag{8.4.1}$$

Alternatively, if σ^2 is unknown, we know from Chapter 6 that the random variable

$$\frac{R_1\tilde{\boldsymbol{\beta}} - R_1\boldsymbol{\beta}}{\hat{\sigma}_g\sqrt{R_1(X'\Psi^{-1}X)^{-1}R_1'}}$$

is distributed as a t random variable with $(T - K)$ degrees of freedom. The $t_{(T-K)}$ random variable would therefore replace the standard normal random variable in (8.4.1) when developing interval estimates.

A joint confidence region for $R\boldsymbol{\beta}$ where R is a $(J \times K)$ known matrix can also be established using results similar to those in Chapter 6. In this case we have $R\tilde{\boldsymbol{\beta}} \sim N[R\boldsymbol{\beta}, \sigma^2 R(X'\Psi^{-1}X)^{-1}R']$ and thus

$$\frac{(\tilde{\boldsymbol{\beta}} - \boldsymbol{\beta})'R'[R(X'\Psi^{-1}X)^{-1}R']^{-1}R(\tilde{\boldsymbol{\beta}} - \boldsymbol{\beta})}{\sigma^2} \sim \chi^2_{(J)} \tag{8.4.2}$$

Using this result, that $(T-K)\hat{\sigma}_g^2/\sigma^2 \sim \chi^2_{(T-K)}$, and that the two χ^2 random variables are independent, we have

$$\frac{(\tilde{\boldsymbol{\beta}}-\boldsymbol{\beta})'R'[R(X'\boldsymbol{\Psi}^{-1}X)^{-1}R']^{-1}R(\tilde{\boldsymbol{\beta}}-\boldsymbol{\beta})}{J\hat{\sigma}_g^2} \sim F_{(J,T-K)} \tag{8.4.3}$$

As in Section 6.3, (8.4.3) can be used to establish a joint confidence region for $R\boldsymbol{\beta}$.

In terms of an interval estimate for σ^2, since $(T-K)\hat{\sigma}_g^2/\sigma^2$ is distributed as a χ^2 random variable with $(T-K)$ degrees of freedom, we can state that, for suitable critical values c_1 and c_2,

$$\Pr\left[\chi^2_{(T-K,c_1)} \le \frac{(T-K)\hat{\sigma}_g^2}{\sigma^2} \le \chi^2_{(T-K,c_2)}\right] = 1-\alpha$$

and from this result we can construct a confidence interval for σ^2.

8.5 Hypothesis Testing

Tests concerning general linear hypotheses about $\boldsymbol{\beta}$, such as $R\boldsymbol{\beta} = \mathbf{r}$, where R is a $(J \times K)$ known matrix and $\mathbf{r}$ is a $(J \times 1)$ known vector, follow directly from the result given in (8.4.3).

Assuming H_0 to be true, $R\boldsymbol{\beta}$ in (8.4.3) can be replaced by $\mathbf{r}$, yielding the statistic

$$\lambda_1 = \frac{(R\tilde{\boldsymbol{\beta}}-\mathbf{r})'[R(X'\boldsymbol{\Psi}^{-1}X)^{-1}R']^{-1}(R\tilde{\boldsymbol{\beta}}-\mathbf{r})}{J\hat{\sigma}_g^2} \tag{8.5.1}$$

which is distributed as an F random variable with J and $(T-K)$ degrees of freedom, if the null hypothesis is true. Also, along the lines of Section 6.4.1, it can be shown that λ_1 results from the likelihood ratio principle.

Thus, the hypothesis-testing framework of Chapters 3 and 6 extends directly to the more general statistical model involving a general disturbance covariance matrix.

In terms of hypothesis-testing for σ^2 we know from Section 8.4 that $(T-K)\hat{\sigma}_g^2/\sigma^2$ is distributed as a χ^2 random variable with $(T-K)$ degrees of freedom. If we hypothesize that $\sigma^2 = \sigma_0^2$ and the hypothesis is correct, then

$$\frac{(T-K)\hat{\sigma}_g^2}{\sigma_0^2} \tag{8.5.2}$$

is distributed as a $\chi^2_{(T-K)}$ random variable. Consequently, as in Section 6.4, if a level of significance is selected, then (8.5.2) provides the basis for a hypothesis-testing mechanism.

As a final piece of information from our Monte Carlo experiment (Section 8.1.5), the empirical distributions for $\hat{\beta}_3$, b_3, and the two t statistics

$$t_1 = \frac{\hat{\beta}_3 - 0.6}{\hat{\sigma}_g\sqrt{c^{33}}} \qquad \text{and} \qquad t_2 = \frac{b_3 - 0.6}{\hat{\sigma}\sqrt{a^{33}}}$$

where c^{33} is the (3, 3)th element of $(X'\Psi^{-1}X)^{-1}$ and a^{33} is the (3, 3)th element of $(X'X)^{-1}$, are presented in the Computer Handbook. Note that t_1 will have a t-distribution but that, because of the reasons outlined in Section 8.6, t_2 will not have a t-distribution.

The empirical distribution of b_3 is more spread out than β_3, further illustrating that b_3 is relatively inefficient. A comparison of the empirical distributions for t_1 and t_2 indicates that t_2 is more closely centered around 0 than is t_1. This is likely to be a reflection of the earlier result that $\hat{\sigma}\sqrt{a^{33}}$ is, in most cases, an overestimate of the true variance of b_3. If we test the hypothesis $H_0\colon \beta_3 = 0.6$ against the alternative $H_1\colon \beta_3 \neq 0.6$ at the 5% significance level, our critical value is $|t| = 2.11$. In the Monte Carlo experiment, the percentage of rejections for this test was 6 for t_1 and 2 for t_2. This low percentage for t_2 is another consequence of the biased estimator for the variance of b_3.

8.6 The Consequences of Using Least Squares Procedures

As you might have gathered from the discussion so far, in applied work it is much easier to assume that $E[\mathbf{ee}'] = \sigma^2 I_T$ and use the least squares techniques of Chapters 5 and 6 than it is to assume that $E[\mathbf{ee}'] = \sigma^2\Psi$ and use the techniques of this and some of the following chapters. Thus it is relevant to ask what are the consequences of using least squares techniques when, in fact, $E[\mathbf{ee}'] = \sigma^2\Psi \neq \sigma^2 I_T$. We have already noted some of these.

1. The least squares estimator $\mathbf{b} = (X'X)^{-1}X'\mathbf{y}$ will be unbiased but will be inefficient relative to the generalized least squares estimator

$$\hat{\boldsymbol{\beta}} = (X'\Psi^{-1}X)^{-1}X'\Psi^{-1}\mathbf{y}$$

2. The covariance matrix of $\mathbf{b}$ will be $\sigma^2(X'X)^{-1}X'\Psi X(X'X)^{-1}$, not $\sigma^2(X'X)^{-1}$.
3. The estimator $\hat{\sigma}^2 = (\mathbf{y} - X\mathbf{b})'(\mathbf{y} - X\mathbf{b})/(T - K)$ will be a biased estimator of σ^2.

Another important consequence that we have not yet stressed is that the interval estimation and hypothesis-testing procedures of Chapter 6 will no longer be appropriate, largely because of the last two of the foregoing results. Together they imply that, for the covariance matrix of **b**, we will be incorrectly using $\hat{\sigma}^2(X'X)^{-1}$ to estimate $\sigma^2(X'X)^{-1}X'\Psi X(X'X)^{-1}$. This is a biased estimator, and it invalidates the interval estimates and tests.

Let us further investigate by considering the statistics used to construct a joint confidence interval for the elements of $R\boldsymbol{\beta}$, for the special case where $R = I_K$. In Chapter 6 we used the results

$$\mathbf{b} \sim N[\boldsymbol{\beta}, \sigma^2(X'X)^{-1}] \tag{8.6.1}$$

$$g_1 = \frac{(\mathbf{b}-\boldsymbol{\beta})'X'X(\mathbf{b}-\boldsymbol{\beta})}{\sigma^2} = \frac{\mathbf{e}'X(X'X)^{-1}X'\mathbf{e}}{\sigma^2} \sim \chi^2_{(K)} \tag{8.6.2}$$

$$g_2 = \frac{(T-K)\hat{\sigma}^2}{\sigma^2} = \frac{\mathbf{e}'(I - X(X'X)^{-1}X')\mathbf{e}}{\sigma^2} \sim \chi^2_{(T-K)} \tag{8.6.3}$$

and the quadratic forms in (8.6.2) and (8.6.3) are independent. Because, in Chapter 6, $E[\mathbf{ee}'] = \sigma^2 I_T$, the results in (8.6.2) and (8.6.3) could be proved by showing that $X(X'X)^{-1}X'$ and $I - X(X'X)^{-1}X'$ are idempotent. Independence follows because $X(X'X)^{-1}X'(I - X(X'X)^{-1}X') = 0$.

To investigate the distributions of the statistics in (8.6.2) and (8.6.3) under the assumption that $E[\mathbf{ee}'] = \sigma^2\Psi$, we need to rewrite the expressions in terms of the vector $\mathbf{e}^* = P\mathbf{e}$, which is such that $E[\mathbf{e}^*\mathbf{e}^{*\prime}] = \sigma^2 I_T$. Rewriting yields

$$g_1 = \frac{\mathbf{e}^{*\prime}P'^{-1}X(X'X)^{-1}X'P^{-1}\mathbf{e}^*}{\sigma^2} \tag{8.6.4}$$

and

$$g_2 = \frac{\mathbf{e}^{*\prime}P'^{-1}(I - X(X'X)^{-1}X')P^{-1}\mathbf{e}^*}{\sigma^2} \tag{8.6.5}$$

It is not difficult to show that $P'^{-1}X(X'X)^{-1}X'P^{-1}$ and

$$P'^{-1}(I - X(X'X)^{-1}X')P^{-1}$$

are not idempotent and that their product is not the null matrix. Thus g_1 and g_2 no longer have χ^2 distributions, and it appears that they are not even independent. Consequently, the ratio

$$\frac{g_1/K}{g_2/(T-K)}$$

will not have the F-distribution, and interval estimates and hypotheses tests based on it will be invalid. Instead, as outlined in Sections 8.4 and 8.5, we should base our interval estimates and hypotheses tests on the generalized least squares estimator.

8.7 Prediction

So far in this chapter, we have been concerned with using T past observations, $\mathbf{y}$ and X, to estimate and test hypotheses about the parameter vector $\boldsymbol{\beta}$ in the model

$$\mathbf{y} = X\boldsymbol{\beta} + \mathbf{e} \tag{8.7.1}$$

where $E[\mathbf{e}] = \mathbf{0}$ and $E[\mathbf{e}\mathbf{e}'] = \sigma^2\boldsymbol{\Psi}$. In this section, we turn to the problem of predicting T_0 future observations, which will be denoted by the $(T_0 \times 1)$ vector $\mathbf{y}_0$, and which will be assumed to be generated by the model,

$$\mathbf{y}_0 = X_0\boldsymbol{\beta} + \mathbf{e}_0 \tag{8.7.2}$$

In (8.7.2) the $(T_0 \times K)$ matrix X_0 is assumed to be known and the disturbance vector $\mathbf{e}_0$ is assumed to have the same properties (be drawn from the same distribution) as the past disturbance vector $\mathbf{e}$.

When we considered the prediction problem in Chapter 5 where the elements of $\mathbf{e}$ and $\mathbf{e}_0$ were assumed to be independently and identically distributed ($E[\mathbf{e}\mathbf{e}'] = \sigma^2 I_T$, $E[\mathbf{e}_0\mathbf{e}_0'] = \sigma^2 I_{T_0}$ and $E[\mathbf{e}\mathbf{e}_0'] = 0$), the best linear unbiased predictor for $\mathbf{y}_0$ was $\hat{\mathbf{y}}_0 = X_0\mathbf{b}$. In this case, if we consider the two components of $X_0\boldsymbol{\beta} + \mathbf{e}_0$ in turn, it is clear that $X_0\mathbf{b}$ is used as a predictor for $X_0\boldsymbol{\beta}$ and that the $\mathbf{0}$ vector is used as a predictor for $\mathbf{e}_0$. Using $\mathbf{0}$ to predict $\mathbf{e}_0$ is the best we can do because $E[\mathbf{e}_0] = \mathbf{0}$, and because our past observations $\mathbf{y}$ and X do not contain any information about the future disturbance vector. However, when we introduce the assumption of a more general disturbance covariance matrix, the situation changes. Under these circumstances, it is possible for the elements of the future disturbance vector $\mathbf{e}_0$ to be correlated with those of the past disturbance vector $\mathbf{e}$. Consequently, our past observations may contain some information about possible future disturbance values and it may be possible to improve on the $\mathbf{0}$ vector as our best predictor for $\mathbf{e}_0$.

To investigate this problem, we combine (8.7.1) and (8.7.2) and write the combined model as

$$\begin{bmatrix} \mathbf{y} \\ \mathbf{y}_0 \end{bmatrix} = \begin{bmatrix} X \\ X_0 \end{bmatrix}\boldsymbol{\beta} + \begin{bmatrix} \mathbf{e} \\ \mathbf{e}_0 \end{bmatrix} \tag{8.7.3}$$

where the combined covariance matrix for $(\mathbf{e}', \mathbf{e}_0')'$ is given by

$$E\left[\begin{pmatrix} \mathbf{e} \\ \mathbf{e}_0 \end{pmatrix}(\mathbf{e}' \quad \mathbf{e}_0')\right] = \sigma^2\begin{bmatrix} \boldsymbol{\Psi} & V \\ V' & \boldsymbol{\Psi}_0 \end{bmatrix} = \sigma^2 Q \tag{8.7.4}$$

The $(T_0 \times T_0)$ matrix $\sigma^2\boldsymbol{\Psi}_0$ is the covariance matrix of the future disturbance vector $\mathbf{e}_0$; the $(T \times T_0)$ matrix $\sigma^2 V$ contains the covariances between the elements of $\mathbf{e}$ and $\mathbf{e}_0$. In line with the earlier sections of this chapter, Ψ, Ψ_0, and V are assumed known.

It is convenient to introduce a transformation matrix P such that

$$PQP' = I_{T+T_0} \tag{8.7.5}$$

Earlier in this chapter, we indicated that a matrix P satisfying (8.7.5) always exists providing Q (or an equivalent matrix) is positive definite. It can also be shown that such a transformation matrix is not unique, and that one possible choice for P is a matrix that is lower triangular. See, for example, Graybill (1969, p. 189). For our purposes, it is convenient to define P as a lower triangular matrix so that (8.7.5) can be partitioned as

$$\begin{bmatrix} P_{11} & 0 \\ P_{21} & P_{22} \end{bmatrix}\begin{bmatrix} \Psi & V \\ V' & \Psi_0 \end{bmatrix}\begin{bmatrix} P'_{11} & P'_{21} \\ 0 & P'_{22} \end{bmatrix} = \begin{bmatrix} I_T & 0 \\ 0 & I_{T_0} \end{bmatrix}$$

or

$$\begin{bmatrix} P_{11}\Psi & P_{11}V \\ P_{21}\Psi + P_{22}V' & P_{21}V + P_{22}\Psi_0 \end{bmatrix}\begin{bmatrix} P'_{11} & P'_{21} \\ 0 & P'_{22} \end{bmatrix} = \begin{bmatrix} I_T & 0 \\ 0 & I_{T_0} \end{bmatrix} \tag{8.7.6}$$

There are three results from (8.7.6) that will later prove to be useful. The first is

$$P_{11}\Psi P'_{11} = I_T,$$

or

$$P'_{11}P_{11} = \Psi^{-1} \tag{8.7.7}$$

Thus, the $(T \times T)$ matrix P_{11} is equivalent to the matrix P that was used in Section 8.1 to transform the observations and to obtain the generalized least squares estimator.

For the second useful result, we use

$$P_{21}\Psi P'_{11} + P_{22}V'P'_{11} = 0$$

Postmultiplying both sides of this equation by P_{11} yields

$$P_{21}\Psi P'_{11}P_{11} + P_{22}V'P'_{11}P_{11} = 0$$

Using (8.7.7) and rearranging gives

$$P_{21} = -P_{22}V'\Psi^{-1}$$

or, noting that P_{22} will be nonsingular,

$$P_{22}^{-1}P_{21} = -V'\Psi^{-1} \tag{8.7.8}$$

To establish the third result, we use, from (8.7.6),

$$P_{21}\Psi P'_{21} + P_{22}V'P'_{21} + P_{21}VP'_{22} + P_{22}\Psi_0 P'_{22} = I_{T_0}$$

Premultiplying by P_{22}^{-1} and postmultiplying by $P_{22}'^{-1}$ yields

$$\begin{aligned} P_{22}^{-1}P_{22}'^{-1} &= P_{22}^{-1}P_{21}\mathbf{\Psi}P_{21}'P_{22}'^{-1} + V'P_{21}'P_{22}'^{-1} + P_{22}^{-1}P_{21}V + \mathbf{\Psi}_0 \\ &= V'\mathbf{\Psi}^{-1}\mathbf{\Psi}\mathbf{\Psi}^{-1}V - V'\mathbf{\Psi}^{-1}V - V'\mathbf{\Psi}^{-1}V + \mathbf{\Psi}_0 \\ &= \mathbf{\Psi}_0 - V'\mathbf{\Psi}^{-1}V \end{aligned} \tag{8.7.9}$$

Having established these preliminary results, we can now turn to the problem of finding the best linear unbiased predictor. Multiplying both sides of (8.7.3) by P yields the following transformed observations

$$\begin{bmatrix} \mathbf{y}^* \\ \mathbf{y}_0^* \end{bmatrix} = \begin{bmatrix} P_{11} & 0 \\ P_{21} & P_{22} \end{bmatrix} \begin{bmatrix} \mathbf{y} \\ \mathbf{y}_0 \end{bmatrix} = \begin{bmatrix} P_{11}\mathbf{y} \\ P_{21}\mathbf{y} + P_{22}\mathbf{y}_0 \end{bmatrix} \tag{8.7.10}$$

$$\begin{bmatrix} X^* \\ X_0^* \end{bmatrix} = \begin{bmatrix} P_{11}X \\ P_{21}X + P_{22}X_0 \end{bmatrix} \tag{8.7.11}$$

$$\begin{bmatrix} \mathbf{e}^* \\ \mathbf{e}_0^* \end{bmatrix} = \begin{bmatrix} P_{11}\mathbf{e} \\ P_{21}\mathbf{e} + P_{22}\mathbf{e}_0 \end{bmatrix} \tag{8.7.12}$$

The transformed model

$$\begin{bmatrix} \mathbf{y}^* \\ \mathbf{y}_0^* \end{bmatrix} = \begin{bmatrix} X^* \\ X_0^* \end{bmatrix}\boldsymbol{\beta} + \begin{bmatrix} \mathbf{e}^* \\ \mathbf{e}_0^* \end{bmatrix}, \qquad E\left[\begin{pmatrix} \mathbf{e}^* \\ \mathbf{e}_0^* \end{pmatrix}(\mathbf{e}^{*\prime} \quad \mathbf{e}_0^{*\prime})\right] = \sigma^2 I_{T+T_0} \tag{8.7.13}$$

satisfies the assumptions of the model in Section 5.9.1, and so we can immediately write down the best linear unbiased predictor for $\mathbf{y}_0^*$ as

$$\hat{\mathbf{y}}_0^* = X_0^*\hat{\boldsymbol{\beta}} \tag{8.7.14}$$

where $\hat{\boldsymbol{\beta}}$ is the generalized least squares estimator

$$\begin{aligned} \hat{\boldsymbol{\beta}} = (X^{*\prime}X^*)^{-1}X^{*\prime}\mathbf{y}^* &= (X'P_{11}'P_{11}X)^{-1}X'P_{11}'P_{11}\mathbf{y} \\ &= (X'\mathbf{\Psi}^{-1}X)^{-1}X'\mathbf{\Psi}^{-1}\mathbf{y} \end{aligned} \tag{8.7.15}$$

To transform (8.7.14) from the best linear unbiased predictor for $\mathbf{y}_0^*$ to the best linear unbiased predictor for $\mathbf{y}_0$, we note that, from (8.7.10),

$$\mathbf{y}_0 = P_{22}^{-1}\mathbf{y}_0^* - P_{22}^{-1}P_{21}\mathbf{y} \tag{8.7.16}$$

The best linear unbiased predictor for $\mathbf{y}_0$ is, therefore,

$$\begin{aligned} \hat{\mathbf{y}}_0 &= P_{22}^{-1}\hat{\mathbf{y}}_0^* - P_{22}^{-1}P_{21}\mathbf{y} \\ &= P_{22}^{-1}X_0^*\hat{\boldsymbol{\beta}} - P_{22}^{-1}P_{21}\mathbf{y} \\ &= (P_{22}^{-1}P_{21}X + X_0)\hat{\boldsymbol{\beta}} - P_{22}^{-1}P_{21}\mathbf{y} \\ &= X_0\hat{\boldsymbol{\beta}} - P_{22}^{-1}P_{21}(\mathbf{y} - X\hat{\boldsymbol{\beta}}) \\ &= X_0\hat{\boldsymbol{\beta}} + V'\mathbf{\Psi}^{-1}(\mathbf{y} - X\hat{\boldsymbol{\beta}}) \end{aligned} \tag{8.7.17}$$

The first component in (8.7.17), $X_0\hat{\boldsymbol{\beta}}$, can be viewed as the best linear unbiased estimator for $X_0\boldsymbol{\beta}$. The second component, $V'\boldsymbol{\Psi}^{-1}(\mathbf{y} - X\hat{\boldsymbol{\beta}})$, is the best linear unbiased predictor for $\mathbf{e}_0$; it consists of the generalized least squares residuals $\hat{\mathbf{e}} = \mathbf{y} - X\hat{\boldsymbol{\beta}}$, and a weighting factor $V'\boldsymbol{\Psi}^{-1}$, which depends on the correlation between past and future disturbances.

To derive the covariance matrix of the prediction error, we first note that

$$\hat{\mathbf{y}}_0 - \mathbf{y}_0 = P_{22}^{-1}(\hat{\mathbf{y}}_0^* - \mathbf{y}_0^*)$$

Consequently,

$$E[(\hat{\mathbf{y}}_0 - \mathbf{y}_0)(\hat{\mathbf{y}}_0 - \mathbf{y}_0)'] = P_{22}^{-1}E[(\hat{\mathbf{y}}_0^* - \mathbf{y}_0^*)(\hat{\mathbf{y}}_0^* - \mathbf{y}_0^*)']P_{22}'^{-1}$$

From the results in Section 5.9.1, the covariance matrix for the prediction error $(\hat{\mathbf{y}}_0^* - \mathbf{y}_0^*)$ is given by $\sigma^2[I + X_0^*(X^{*\prime}X^*)^{-1}X_0^{*\prime}]$. Thus, we have

$$\begin{aligned}
E[(\hat{\mathbf{y}}_0 &- \mathbf{y}_0)(\hat{\mathbf{y}}_0 - \mathbf{y}_0)'] \\
&= \sigma^2[P_{22}^{-1}P_{22}'^{-1} + P_{22}^{-1}X_0^*(X^{*\prime}X^*)^{-1}X_0^{*\prime}P_{22}'^{-1}] \\
&= \sigma^2[\boldsymbol{\Psi}_0 - V'\boldsymbol{\Psi}^{-1}V + (P_{22}^{-1}P_{21}X + X_0)(X^{*\prime}X^*)^{-1}(X'P_{21}'P_{22}'^{-1} + X_0')] \\
&= \sigma^2[\boldsymbol{\Psi}_0 - V'\boldsymbol{\Psi}^{-1}V + (X_0 - V'\boldsymbol{\Psi}^{-1}X)(X'\boldsymbol{\Psi}^{-1}X)^{-1}(X_0' - X'\boldsymbol{\Psi}^{-1}V)]
\end{aligned} \tag{8.7.18}$$

The second line uses results in (8.7.9) and (8.7.11), whereas the last line uses results in (8.7.7) and (8.7.8).

The two important results that we have established in this section are the best linear unbiased predictor in (8.7.17) and the covariance matrix of its prediction error in (8.7.18). Given any linear model with a general disturbance covariance structure where $\boldsymbol{\Psi}$, $\boldsymbol{\Psi}_0$, and V are known, equations (8.7.17) and (8.7.18) can be used to construct confidence intervals for predictions or to test whether a recently realized observation on the dependent variable could have been generated from the same model that generated the past observations. In practice, simplified and estimated versions of (8.7.17) and (8.7.18) are usually employed. Simplifications occur when specific structures are assumed for $\boldsymbol{\Psi}$ and V. For example, the first-order autoregressive error model to be studied in Section 9.3 and the error components model to be studied in Section 11.3 both lead to specific simplified versions of the equations. Estimated versions of (8.7.17) and (8.7.18) are usually used because, typically, $\boldsymbol{\Psi}$ and V will depend on one or more unknown parameters that need to be estimated. It is worthwhile pointing out that when $\boldsymbol{\Psi}$ and V are unknown and are replaced by estimates, the finite sample properties of the resulting predictor are no longer so readily established. Specifically, this predictor will no longer be best linear unbiased and (8.7.18) can only be regarded as an approximation to the covariance matrix of its prediction error.

8.8 Summary

In this chapter we have taken another step in generalizing the sampling model so that it will be compatible with a broader range of data-generation processes. Although the statistical model was more general than those considered in Chapters 2, 3, 5, and 6, we were able to transform the original model to a form that permitted the criteria and conclusions of Chapters 5 and 6 to be applied.

We recognize that Ψ is seldom known in practice. In future chapters we consider the statistical implications of using an estimated variance-covariance matrix. Alternative covariance structures will be discussed in Chapter 11, when disturbance-related sets of linear statistical models are considered, and in Chapter 9, when the problems of autocorrelated and heteroskedastic random errors are presented.

One item that we have failed to mention is goodness of fit when the disturbance covariance matrix is of the nonscalar identity type. For details on this topic as well as a more complete coverage of the other topics covered in this chapter refer to Chapters 8, 11, and 12 of the second edition of *The Theory and Practice of Econometrics.* Most econometric textbooks have sections on generalized least squares and related techniques for the general linear statistical model, with a nonscalar identity covariance matrix. For further reading we particularly recommend the other titles in the References for this chapter.

8.9 Exercises

8.9.1 Algebraic Exercises

8.1 Let $\boldsymbol{\beta}^* = A\mathbf{y}$ be any linear unbiased estimator for $\boldsymbol{\beta}$. Assuming that $E[\mathbf{ee}'] = \sigma^2\Psi$, show that the covariance matrix of $\boldsymbol{\beta}^*$ exceeds that of $\hat{\boldsymbol{\beta}} = (X'\Psi^{-1}X)^{-1}X'\Psi^{-1}\mathbf{y}$ by a positive semidefinite matrix.

8.2 Prove that $\hat{\sigma}_g^2$ is an unbiased estimator of σ^2.

8.3 Prove that

$$\frac{\mathbf{e}'X(X'\Psi X)^{-1}X'\mathbf{e}}{\sigma^2}$$

has a $\chi^2_{(K)}$ distribution.

8.4 Consider the model

$$y_t = \beta_1 + \beta_2 t + e_t \qquad t = 1, 2, 3, 4, 5$$

where $E[e_t] = 0$, $E[e_t^2] = \sigma^2 t^2$, and $E[e_t e_s] = 0$ for $t \neq s$. Let $\mathbf{e}' = (e_1, e_2, e_3, e_4, e_5)$, and $E[\mathbf{ee}'] = \sigma^2 \mathbf{\Psi}$.

(*a*) Specify $\mathbf{\Psi}$.
(*b*) Find $\mathbf{\Psi}^{-1}$.
(*c*) Find the covariance matrix of the least squares estimator for $\boldsymbol{\beta}' = (\beta_1, \beta_2)$.
(*d*) Find the covariance matrix of the generalized least squares estimator for $\boldsymbol{\beta}$.
(*e*) Find $E[\hat{\sigma}^2]$, where $\hat{\sigma}^2 = (\mathbf{y} - X\mathbf{b})'(\mathbf{y} - X\mathbf{b})/3$, and $\mathbf{b}$ is the least squares estimator.

8.9.2 Individual Numerical Exercises

The remaining problems are based on Monte Carlo experimental data that are discussed in the Computer Handbook. The data consists of 100 samples of **y**, each of size 20, and they were generated using the model

$$y_t = \beta_1 + \beta_2 x_{t2} + \beta_3 x_{t3} + e_t \tag{8.9.1}$$

where $e_t = \rho e_{t-1} + v_t$ and the v_t are independent normal random variables with 0 mean and variance $E[v_t^2] = \sigma_v^2$. The parameter values used were $\beta_1 = 10$, $\beta_2 = 1$, $\beta_3 = 1$, $\rho = 0.8$ and $\sigma_v^2 = 6.4$, and the design matrix was

$$X = \begin{bmatrix} 1.00 & 14.53 & 16.74 \\ 1.00 & 15.30 & 16.81 \\ 1.00 & 15.92 & 19.50 \\ 1.00 & 17.41 & 22.12 \\ 1.00 & 18.37 & 22.34 \\ 1.00 & 18.83 & 17.47 \\ 1.00 & 18.84 & 20.24 \\ 1.00 & 19.71 & 20.37 \\ 1.00 & 20.01 & 12.71 \\ 1.00 & 20.26 & 22.98 \\ 1.00 & 20.77 & 19.33 \\ 1.00 & 21.17 & 17.04 \\ 1.00 & 21.34 & 16.74 \\ 1.00 & 22.91 & 19.81 \\ 1.00 & 22.96 & 31.92 \\ 1.00 & 23.69 & 26.31 \\ 1.00 & 24.82 & 25.93 \\ 1.00 & 25.54 & 21.96 \\ 1.00 & 25.63 & 24.05 \\ 1.00 & 28.73 & 25.66 \end{bmatrix} \tag{8.9.2}$$

The structure of Ψ for this model is identical to that given in the sampling experiment in Section 8.1.5; however, the parameter values and design matrix are different. To carry out generalized least squares estimation, you should use the transformations specified in Section 8.1.5, but with the new observations and the new value of ρ.

8.5 Calculate the covariance matrices for the least squares estimator and the generalized least squares estimator and comment on the results.

8.6 Calculate the mean of the least squares error variance estimator

$$\hat{\sigma}^2 = \frac{(\mathbf{y} - X\mathbf{b})'(\mathbf{y} - X\mathbf{b})}{T - K}$$

8.7 Select five samples from the Monte Carlo data and for each sample compute values for the following estimators.

(*a*) The least squares estimator $\mathbf{b}$.

(*b*) The generalized least squares estimator $\hat{\boldsymbol{\beta}}$.

(*c*) The least squares error variance estimator $\hat{\sigma}^2$.

(*d*) The generalized least squares error variance estimator $\hat{\sigma}_g^2$.

Comment on the results.

8.8 In Exercise 8.7 your computer program is likely to have provided estimated covariance matrices for $\mathbf{b}$ and $\hat{\boldsymbol{\beta}}$. Using the element β_2 as an example, compare the various estimates of var(b_2) and var($\hat{\beta}_2$) with each other and with the relevant values from Exercise 8.5.

8.9 Use the results in Exercises 8.7 and 8.8 to calculate t values that would be used to test

(*a*) $H_0\colon \beta_2 = 0$ against $H_1\colon \beta_2 \neq 0$.

(*b*) $H_0\colon \beta_2 = 1$ against $H_1\colon \beta_2 \neq 1$.

Since we have two estimators and five samples, this involves, for each hypothesis, the calculation of 10 t values. Keeping in mind the validity or otherwise of each null hypothesis, comment on the results.

8.9.3 Individual or Group Exercises

8.10 Repeat Exercise 8.7 for all 100 samples and use the results to estimate the means of $\mathbf{b}$, $\hat{\boldsymbol{\beta}}$, $\hat{\sigma}^2$, and $\hat{\sigma}_g^2$ as well as the mean square error matrices of $\mathbf{b}$ and $\hat{\boldsymbol{\beta}}$. Are all these estimates reasonably close to their population counterparts?

8.11 Use all 100 samples to estimate the means of the variance estimators $\widehat{\text{var}}(b_2)$ and $\widehat{\text{var}}(\hat{\beta}_2)$. Comment on the results and their implications for testing hypotheses about β_2.

8.12 Repeat Exercise 8.9 for all 100 samples and calculate the proportion of Type I and Type II errors that are obtained when a 5% significance level is used. Comment.

8.13 Construct empirical distributions for b_2, $\hat{\beta}_2$, and the two t statistics used in Exercise 8.12 to test the null hypothesis $\beta_2 = 1.0$. Comment.

8.10 References

Dhrymes, P. J. (1978) *Introductory Econometrics.* New York: Springer-Verlag.

Graybill, F. A. (1969) *Introduction to Matrices with Applications in Statistics.* Belmont, CA: Wadsworth.

Intriligator, M. D. (1978) *Econometric Models, Techniques and Applications.* Englewood Cliffs, NJ: Prentice-Hall.

Judge, G. G., W. E. Griffiths, R. C. Hill, H. Lütkepohl, and T. C. Lee. (1985) *The Theory and Practice of Econometrics,* 2nd ed. New York: Wiley.

Schmidt, P. (1976) *Econometrics.* New York: Dekker.

Theil, H. (1971) *Principles of Econometrics.* New York: Wiley.

Wonnacott, R. J., and T. H. Wonnacott (1979) *Econometrics,* 2nd ed. New York: Wiley.

CHAPTER 9

General Linear Statistical Model with an Unknown Covariance Matrix

9.1 Background

In Chapter 8 we studied the general linear statistical model

$$\mathbf{y} = X\boldsymbol{\beta} + \mathbf{e} \tag{9.1.1}$$

where X is a $(T \times K)$ observable nonstochastic matrix, $\boldsymbol{\beta}$ is a $(K \times 1)$ vector of parameters to be estimated, $\mathbf{y}$ is a $(T \times 1)$ observable random vector, $\mathbf{e}$ is a $(T \times 1)$ unobservable random vector with properties

$$E[\mathbf{e}] = \mathbf{0} \quad \text{and} \quad E[\mathbf{e}\mathbf{e}'] = \boldsymbol{\Phi} = \sigma^2\boldsymbol{\Psi} \tag{9.1.2}$$

and $\boldsymbol{\Psi}$ is a known positive definite symmetric matrix. It was assumed that the scale parameter σ^2 was unknown, which, in conjunction with the known $\boldsymbol{\Psi}$, implies that the disturbance covariance matrix $\boldsymbol{\Phi}$ is known except for a factor of proportionality. We showed that under these conditions the generalized least squares estimator

$$\hat{\boldsymbol{\beta}} = (X'\boldsymbol{\Psi}^{-1}X)^{-1}X'\boldsymbol{\Psi}^{-1}\mathbf{y} \tag{9.1.3}$$

is best linear unbiased and has covariance matrix $\sigma^2(X'\boldsymbol{\Psi}^{-1}X)^{-1}$. Also we showed that the least squares estimator

$$\mathbf{b} = (X'X)^{-1}X'\mathbf{y} \tag{9.1.4}$$

is unbiased, but it is inefficient because its covariance matrix

$$\sigma^2(X'X)^{-1}X'\boldsymbol{\Psi}X(X'X)^{-1}$$

exceeds $\sigma^2(X'\boldsymbol{\Psi}^{-1}X)^{-1}$ in the sense that

$$\Delta = \sigma^2(X'X)^{-1}X'\boldsymbol{\Psi}X(X'X)^{-1} - \sigma^2(X'\boldsymbol{\Psi}^{-1}X)^{-1}$$

is a positive semidefinite matrix.

Thus if we assume that $E[\mathbf{e}\mathbf{e}'] = \sigma^2 I$ and use the least squares estimator $\mathbf{b}$, when in fact $E[\mathbf{e}\mathbf{e}'] = \sigma^2\boldsymbol{\Psi}$, we will not be obtaining the best out of the class of possible (linear) estimators. In addition, we are likely to obtain a biased estimator of the covariance matrix for $\mathbf{b}$, which, through hypothesis tests and interval estimation, could lead to misleading inferences about $\boldsymbol{\beta}$. The conventional estimator for the covariance matrix of $\mathbf{b}$ is $\hat{\sigma}^2(X'X)^{-1}$, where $\hat{\sigma}^2 = (\mathbf{y} - X\mathbf{b})'(\mathbf{y} - X\mathbf{b})/(T - K)$, and this is a biased estimator when $E[\mathbf{ee}'] = \sigma^2\mathbf{\Psi}$ because

$$E[\hat{\sigma}^2] = \frac{\sigma^2 \operatorname{tr}[\mathbf{\Psi}(I - X(X'X)^{-1}X')]}{\mathrm{T} - K} \neq \sigma^2 \tag{9.1.5}$$

and because

$$(X'X)^{-1} \neq (X'X)^{-1}X'\mathbf{\Psi}X(X'X)^{-1}$$

in general.

Given these results, the natural questions when approaching an applied problem are: How do we tell whether or not $\mathbf{\Psi} = I$ and, if $\mathbf{\Psi} \neq I$, how are the elements in $\mathbf{\Psi}$ determined? Before tackling these questions it is customary to make an assumption or specify a hypothesis about the structure of $\mathbf{\Psi}$. The procedures chosen for testing whether or not $\mathbf{\Psi} = I$ and for estimating the elements in $\mathbf{\Psi}$ will depend on that assumption. As we will see in this chapter, the type of assumptions that are reasonable will depend on the nature of the data and the economic environment in which they were generated. Given the sampling environment, the tests and estimators can be chosen accordingly.

In this chapter we examine tests and estimators first under the assumption that $\mathbf{\Psi}$ is a diagonal matrix (heteroskedasticity) and then under the assumption that $\mathbf{\Psi}$ is the covariance matrix corresponding to what is known as a first-order autoregressive error (autocorrelation). Whatever assumption is made about $\mathbf{\Psi}$, its elements will usually be unknown. Consequently, these elements cannot be determined; they can only be estimated. Replacing $\mathbf{\Psi}$ by an estimated matrix $\hat{\mathbf{\Psi}}$ in the expression for the generalized least squares estimator leads to what is known as an *estimated* or a *feasible* generalized least squares estimator. Before considering heteroskedasticity and autocorrelation in some detail, it is useful to consider the statistical properties of estimated generalized least squares estimators.

9.2 Estimated Generalized Least Squares

When $\mathbf{\Psi}$ is unknown, the generalized least squares estimator

$$\hat{\boldsymbol{\beta}} = (X'\mathbf{\Psi}^{-1}X)^{-1}X'\mathbf{\Psi}^{-1}\mathbf{y} \tag{9.2.1}$$

is no longer a feasible estimator. Instead, it is customary to replace $\mathbf{\Psi}$ with an estimated covariance matrix $\hat{\mathbf{\Psi}}$, which leads to the *estimated generalized least squares estimator* (or two-stage Aitken estimator) denoted by

$$\hat{\hat{\boldsymbol{\beta}}} = (X'\hat{\mathbf{\Psi}}^{-1}X)^{-1}X'\hat{\mathbf{\Psi}}^{-1}\mathbf{y} \tag{9.2.2}$$

The method for estimating $\mathbf{\Psi}$ depends on the assumptions made about its structure. In general, $\mathbf{\Psi}$ contains $[(T(T+1)/2)-1]$ different unknown parameters—the number of diagonal elements plus half the off-diagonal elements, less one, one being subtracted because the constant σ^2 has been factored out of $\mathbf{\Phi} = \sigma^2\mathbf{\Psi}$. This large number of unknown parameters cannot be satisfactorily estimated with only T observations, so, to restrict the number of unknown parameters in $\mathbf{\Psi}$, it is customary to make some further assumptions about the structure of this matrix. Specifically, it is usually assumed that the elements in $\mathbf{\Psi}$ are functions of a small number of unknown parameters, with this number remaining fixed as sample size T increases. Thus the problem of estimating $\mathbf{\Psi}$ reduces to one of estimating the smaller number of parameters. In later sections of this chapter the estimation methods, for two specific structures of $\mathbf{\Psi}$, heteroskedasticity and autocorrelation, will be considered. Further examples will be dealt with in Chapters 10 and 11.

At this point it is convenient to consider some general statistical properties of estimated generalized least squares estimators. These properties form the basis for hypothesis tests and interval estimates for $\boldsymbol{\beta}$. In Chapter 8 we discovered that the finite sample properties of the generalized least squares estimator $\hat{\boldsymbol{\beta}}$ could be readily derived from the properties of the least squares estimator $\mathbf{b}$. Unfortunately, evaluation of the finite sample properties of the estimated generalized least squares estimator

$$\hat{\hat{\boldsymbol{\beta}}} = (X'\hat{\mathbf{\Psi}}^{-1}X)^{-1}X'\hat{\mathbf{\Psi}}^{-1}\mathbf{y} = \boldsymbol{\beta} + (X'\hat{\mathbf{\Psi}}^{-1}X)^{-1}X'\hat{\mathbf{\Psi}}^{-1}\mathbf{e} \tag{9.2.3}$$

is a much more difficult problem. The difficulty arises because $\hat{\mathbf{\Psi}}$ and $\mathbf{e}$ are correlated. Any estimator for $\mathbf{\Psi}$ will usually depend on the sample observations and hence also on the disturbance vector $\mathbf{e}$. Thus, in contrast to (8.1.13), it is not possible to treat $\hat{\mathbf{\Psi}}^{-1}$ as fixed when taking the expectation of (9.2.3). Nevertheless, for most conventional estimators of $\mathbf{\Psi}$, it is possible to use alternative methods to prove that $\hat{\hat{\boldsymbol{\beta}}}$ is an unbiased estimator. See, for example, Magnus (1978) and Andrews (1986).

For the remaining properties of $\hat{\hat{\boldsymbol{\beta}}}$ we must resort to asymptotic approximations. Although $\hat{\hat{\boldsymbol{\beta}}}$ is unbiased, it is neither "best" nor "linear." It is not a linear function of $\mathbf{y}$ because $\hat{\mathbf{\Psi}}^{-1}$ will depend on $\mathbf{y}$; it is not minimum variance because in most cases it is not even possible to derive its finite sample covariance matrix. To investigate the asymptotic properties of $\hat{\hat{\boldsymbol{\beta}}}$ it is convenient to first investigate the asymptotic properties of the generalized least squares estimator $\hat{\boldsymbol{\beta}} = (X'\mathbf{\Psi}^{-1}X)^{-1}X'\mathbf{\Psi}^{-1}\mathbf{y}$, and then give sufficient conditions for the estimated generalized least squares and generalized least squares estimators to have the same limiting distribution. Consistency and asymptotic normality of $\hat{\boldsymbol{\beta}}$ are established by placing the same conditions on the transformed variables PX (where P is such that $P\mathbf{\Psi}P' = I$) as were placed on X in Section 6.6 of Chapter 6. Thus, we assume that the elements in PX are bounded and that

$$\lim_{T\to\infty}\left(\frac{X'\Psi^{-1}X}{T}\right) = V \tag{9.2.4}$$

is a finite nonsingular matrix. Along the lines of Section 6.6 it then follows that $\hat{\beta}$ and

$$\hat{\sigma}_g^2 = \frac{(\mathbf{y} - X\hat{\beta})'\Psi^{-1}(\mathbf{y} - X\hat{\beta})}{T - K} \tag{9.2.5}$$

are consistent estimators, and that

$$\sqrt{T}(\hat{\beta} - \beta) \xrightarrow{d} N(\mathbf{0}, \sigma^2 V^{-1}) \tag{9.2.6}$$

If $\hat{\hat{\beta}}$ is to be used for interval estimation and hypothesis tests about β, it is necessary to establish a result such as (9.2.6) for $\hat{\hat{\beta}}$. Working in this direction, it can be shown that $\hat{\hat{\beta}}$ and $\hat{\beta}$ will have the same limiting distribution if

$$\begin{aligned}
&\operatorname{plim}[\sqrt{T}(\hat{\hat{\beta}} - \beta) - \sqrt{T}(\hat{\beta} - \beta)] \\
&= \operatorname{plim}\left[\left(\frac{X'\hat{\Psi}^{-1}X}{T}\right)^{-1}\frac{X'\hat{\Psi}^{-1}\mathbf{e}}{\sqrt{T}} - \left(\frac{X'\Psi^{-1}X}{T}\right)^{-1}\frac{X'\Psi^{-1}\mathbf{e}}{\sqrt{T}}\right] \\
&= 0
\end{aligned} \tag{9.2.7}$$

Sufficient conditions for (9.2.7) to hold are that

$$\operatorname{plim}\left(\frac{X'\hat{\Psi}^{-1}X}{T}\right) = \operatorname{plim}\left(\frac{X'\Psi^{-1}X}{T}\right)$$

and

$$\operatorname{plim}\left(\frac{X'\hat{\Psi}^{-1}\mathbf{e}}{\sqrt{T}}\right) = \operatorname{plim}\left(\frac{X'\Psi^{-1}\mathbf{e}}{\sqrt{T}}\right)$$

or, equivalently

$$\operatorname{plim} T^{-1}X'(\hat{\Psi}^{-1} - \Psi^{-1})X = 0 \tag{9.2.8}$$

and

$$\operatorname{plim} T^{-1/2}X'(\hat{\Psi}^{-1} - \Psi^{-1})\mathbf{e} = \mathbf{0} \tag{9.2.9}$$

Thus, (9.2.8) and (9.2.9) are a common way of stating sufficient conditions for

$$\sqrt{T}(\hat{\hat{\beta}} - \beta) \xrightarrow{d} N(\mathbf{0}, \sigma^2 V^{-1}) \tag{9.2.10}$$

In practice, these conditions should be checked out for any specific structure of Ψ and the corresponding estimator $\hat{\Psi}$. However, most of the cases we study are such that (9.2.8) and (9.2.9) hold if the unknown parameters in Ψ are consistently estimated.

With the additional condition

$$\text{plim } T^{-1}\mathbf{e}'(\hat{\Psi}^{-1} - \Psi^{-1})\mathbf{e} = 0 \tag{9.2.11}$$

it is possible to show that

$$\hat{\hat{\sigma}}^2 = \frac{(\mathbf{y} - X\hat{\hat{\boldsymbol{\beta}}})'\hat{\Psi}^{-1}(\mathbf{y} - X\hat{\hat{\boldsymbol{\beta}}})}{T - K} \tag{9.2.12}$$

is a consistent estimator for σ^2.

We are now in a position to consider useful statistics for hypothesis testing and interval estimation. From (9.2.4) and (9.2.8) it follows that $(X'\hat{\Psi}^{-1}X)/T$ is a consistent estimator for V. Then, if interest centers on J linear combinations of the unknown coefficients, denoted by $R\boldsymbol{\beta}$ where R is $(J \times K)$ of rank J, the argument used to derive Equation 6.6.24 of Chapter 6 can be used to show that

$$\lambda_1 = \frac{(\hat{\hat{\boldsymbol{\beta}}} - \boldsymbol{\beta})'R'[R(X'\hat{\Psi}^{-1}X)^{-1}R']^{-1}R(\hat{\hat{\boldsymbol{\beta}}} - \boldsymbol{\beta})}{\hat{\hat{\sigma}}^2} \xrightarrow{d} \chi^2_{(J)} \tag{9.2.13}$$

This result can be used to test a hypothesis $R\boldsymbol{\beta} = \mathbf{r}$, or to construct confidence regions for $R\boldsymbol{\beta}$. A commonly used alternative is the statistic

$$\lambda_2 = \frac{\lambda_1}{J} = \frac{(\hat{\hat{\boldsymbol{\beta}}} - \boldsymbol{\beta})'R'[R(X'\hat{\Psi}^{-1}X)^{-1}R']^{-1}R(\hat{\hat{\boldsymbol{\beta}}} - \boldsymbol{\beta})}{J\hat{\hat{\sigma}}^2} \tag{9.2.14}$$

which is assumed to have an approximate $F_{(J,T-K)}$ distribution. This assumption is justified in the sense that $F_{(J,T-K)} \xrightarrow{d} \chi^2_{(J)}/J$. As $T \to \infty$, the choice between λ_1 and λ_2 makes little difference.

Although the theoretical justification for using λ_1 in conjunction with a critical value from the $\chi^2_{(J)}$-distribution is sounder than that for using λ_2 in conjunction with a critical value from the $F_{(J,T-K)}$-distribution, λ_2 seems to be more popular in applications. There are two likely reasons for this popularity. The first is that simulation studies have shown that, in many instances, the F-distribution will be a more accurate approximation in finite samples. The second reason is that when $H_0\colon R\boldsymbol{\beta} = \mathbf{r}$ is of interest, and $R\boldsymbol{\beta}$ in λ_2 is replaced by $\mathbf{r}$, yielding

$$\lambda_2^* = \frac{(R\hat{\hat{\boldsymbol{\beta}}} - \mathbf{r})'[R(X'\hat{\Psi}^{-1}X)^{-1}R']^{-1}(R\hat{\hat{\boldsymbol{\beta}}} - \mathbf{r})}{J\hat{\hat{\sigma}}^2} \tag{9.2.15}$$

λ_2^* is automatically computed by most standard software packages. The statistic λ_2^* is identical to the finite sample statistic given in Equation 8.5.1 of Chapter 8, except that the unknown covariance matrix $\mathbf{\Psi}$ has been replaced by $\hat{\mathbf{\Psi}}$. Its computation is automatic because if $\hat{P}$ is a matrix such that $\hat{P}'\hat{P} = \hat{\mathbf{\Psi}}^{-1}$, then usual least squares procedures applied to the transformed model

$$\hat{P}\mathbf{y} = \hat{P}X\boldsymbol{\beta} + \hat{P}\mathbf{e} \tag{9.2.16}$$

will yield both the estimated generalized least squares estimator $\hat{\hat{\boldsymbol{\beta}}}$ and a value for the statistic λ_2^* for any specified H_0: $R\boldsymbol{\beta} = \mathbf{r}$.

These results mean that, if $\mathbf{\Psi}$ is estimated, and least squares is applied to an appropriately transformed model, then the techniques outlined in Chapters 5 and 6 are justified asymptotically. The remainder of this chapter is concerned with two examples, heteroskedasticity and autocorrelation. For both these examples we will consider, among other things, the structure of $\mathbf{\Psi}$, how to estimate $\mathbf{\Psi}$, and how to obtain an appropriately transformed model.

9.3 Heteroskedasticity

9.3.1 Economic and Statistical Environment

For the general linear statistical model $\mathbf{y} = X\boldsymbol{\beta} + \mathbf{e}$, where $E[\mathbf{e}] = \mathbf{0}$ and $E[\mathbf{ee}'] = \sigma^2\mathbf{\Psi} = \mathbf{\Phi}$, *heteroskedasticity* exists when the diagonal elements of $\mathbf{\Psi}$ are not all identical. In this section we consider the circumstances under which this is likely to occur.

Assume that we have observations on a number of economic units at a given point in time or, in other words, cross-section data. For example, suppose that our economic unit is a firm and that we are interested in estimating an industry cost function. One way of attempting this is to collect data on costs and output for a sample (cross-section) of firms and use it to estimate a model, such as

$$y_t = \beta_1 + \beta_2 x_t + \beta_3 x_t^2 + e_t \tag{9.3.1}$$

where y_t is average cost for the tth firm and x_t is output for the tth firm. Such a function might be appropriate if we expect the average cost function to be U-shaped.

Alternatively, (9.3.1) might be a reasonable model for quantifying the relationship between food expenditure and income. In this case cross-section data would consist of data on a sample of households, and y_t and x_t would be food expenditure

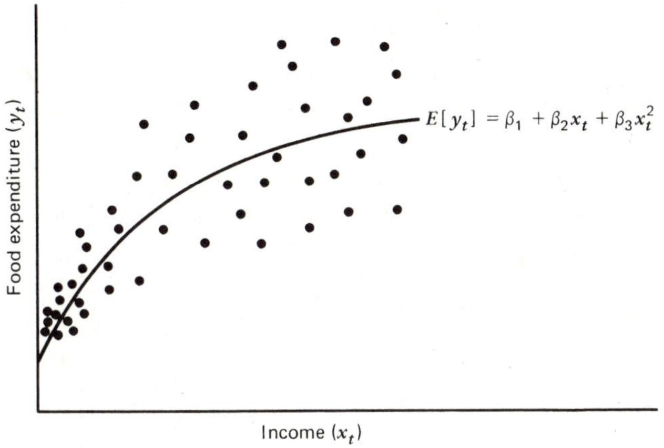

Figure 9.1 A hypothetical relationship between food expenditure and income.

and income, respectively, of the tth household. However, if (9.3.1) represented a cost function, we would expect $\beta_3 > 0$ and both the increasing and decreasing sections of the quadratic may be relevant. With the expenditure function we would expect $\beta_3 < 0$ and, as illustrated in Figure 9.1, the model would not be realistic if we did not confine our attention to the increasing section of the quadratic.

In both the foregoing examples it is reasonable to expect that when x is large individual observations on y are more likely to deviate farther from the mean function $E[y_t] = \beta_1 + \beta_2 x_t + \beta_3 x_t^2$ than when x_t is small. For example, we would expect food expenditure for all low-income households to be much the same in the sense that it would be almost totally explained by income. In high-income households, however, food expenditure is likely to depend on many other factors, so that part of expenditure that is not explained by income is more likely to vary considerably from household to household. In other words, the values of the errors e_t are more likely to be small for small x_t and large for large x_t. This result is depicted in Figure 9.1, where each dot represents a household observation on food expenditure and income, and the effect can be captured statistically by assuming that each e_t is drawn from a probability distribution with a different variance.

Thus we assume that

$$E[e_t] = 0 \qquad \text{and} \qquad E[e_t^2] = \sigma_t^2 \tag{9.3.2}$$

and a disturbance with these properties is called *heteroskedastic*. Conversely, if σ_t^2 is constant for all observations ($\sigma_t^2 = \sigma^2, t = 1, 2, \ldots, T$), the disturbance is *homoskedastic*. If, in addition, we assume that $E[e_t e_s] = 0$ for $t \neq s$, as will be the case if we have a random sample of firms or households, then the covariance matrix for the vector **e** can be written as

$$E[\mathbf{ee}'] = \mathbf{\Phi} = \begin{bmatrix} \sigma_1^2 & 0 & \cdots & 0 \\ 0 & \sigma_2^2 & \cdots & 0 \\ \vdots & \vdots & \ddots & \vdots \\ 0 & 0 & \cdots & \sigma_T^2 \end{bmatrix} \tag{9.3.3}$$

In this section we focus on inference for the general linear model when $\mathbf{\Phi}$ is a diagonal matrix like that in (9.3.3). We examine the generalized least squares estimator that can be used when the σ_t^2 are known, two examples of models where the σ_t^2 are unknown, and some methods for testing for heteroskedasticity.

9.3.2 Generalized Least Squares Estimation

Consider the model

$$\mathbf{y} = X\boldsymbol{\beta} + \mathbf{e} \tag{9.3.4}$$

where $E[\mathbf{e}] = \mathbf{0}$ and where (9.3.3) is written in shorthand notation as

$$E[\mathbf{ee}'] = \mathbf{\Phi} = \text{diag}(\sigma_1^2, \sigma_2^2, \ldots, \sigma_T^2) \tag{9.3.5}$$

If the σ_t^2, and hence $\mathbf{\Phi}$, are known, the generalized least squares estimator for $\boldsymbol{\beta}$ can be calculated, is best linear unbiased, and is given by

$$\hat{\boldsymbol{\beta}} = (X'\mathbf{\Phi}^{-1}X)^{-1}X'\mathbf{\Phi}^{-1}\mathbf{y} \tag{9.3.6}$$

In Chapter 8 we gave the generalized least squares estimator as

$$\hat{\boldsymbol{\beta}} = (X'\mathbf{\Psi}^{-1}X)^{-1}X'\mathbf{\Psi}^{-1}\mathbf{y} \tag{9.3.7}$$

where $\mathbf{\Phi} = \sigma^2\mathbf{\Psi}$, with σ^2 unknown and $\mathbf{\Psi}$ known. The two estimators are clearly the same because

$$(X'\mathbf{\Phi}^{-1}X)^{-1}X'\mathbf{\Phi}^{-1}\mathbf{y} = \left(\frac{X'\mathbf{\Psi}^{-1}X}{\sigma^2}\right)^{-1}\frac{X'\mathbf{\Psi}^{-1}\mathbf{y}}{\sigma^2} = (X'\mathbf{\Psi}^{-1}X)^{-1}X'\mathbf{\Psi}^{-1}\mathbf{y}$$

Throughout this section we sometimes use the formulation in (9.3.6) and sometimes use that in (9.3.7). In each instance the choice will depend on which is more convenient. You should keep in mind that they are the same. That is, multiplying the disturbance covariance matrix by a constant does not change the value of the generalized least squares estimator.

From the development in Chapter 8 we know that, if we can find a matrix P such that $P'P = \mathbf{\Phi}^{-1}$, (9.3.6) can be written as

$$\begin{aligned} \hat{\boldsymbol{\beta}} &= (X'P'PX)^{-1}X'P'P\mathbf{y} \\ &= (X^{*\prime}X^*)^{-1}X^{*\prime}\mathbf{y}^* \end{aligned} \tag{9.3.8}$$

where $X^* = PX$ and $\mathbf{y}^* = P\mathbf{y}$, so the generalized least squares estimator can be obtained by applying least squares to the transformed observations $\mathbf{y}^*$ and design matrix X^*. It is easy to verify that an appropriate P is

$$P = \operatorname{diag}(\sigma_1^{-1}, \sigma_2^{-1}, \ldots, \sigma_T^{-1}) \tag{9.3.9}$$

and that the transformed observations are therefore given by

$$\mathbf{y}^* = \begin{bmatrix} y_1^* \\ y_2^* \\ \vdots \\ y_T^* \end{bmatrix} = \begin{bmatrix} \sigma_1^{-1} & & & 0 \\ & \sigma_2^{-1} & & \\ & & \ddots & \\ 0 & & & \sigma_T^{-1} \end{bmatrix} \begin{bmatrix} y_1 \\ y_2 \\ \vdots \\ y_T \end{bmatrix} = \begin{bmatrix} y_1/\sigma_1 \\ y_2/\sigma_2 \\ \vdots \\ y_T/\sigma_T \end{bmatrix} \tag{9.3.10}$$

and

$$X^* = \begin{bmatrix} \mathbf{x}_1^{*\prime} \\ \mathbf{x}_2^{*\prime} \\ \vdots \\ \mathbf{x}_T^{*\prime} \end{bmatrix} = \begin{bmatrix} \sigma_1^{-1} & & & 0 \\ & \sigma_2^{-1} & & \\ & & \ddots & \\ 0 & & & \sigma_T^{-1} \end{bmatrix} \begin{bmatrix} \mathbf{x}_1' \\ \mathbf{x}_2' \\ \vdots \\ \mathbf{x}_T' \end{bmatrix} = \begin{bmatrix} \mathbf{x}_1'/\sigma_1 \\ \mathbf{x}_2'/\sigma_2 \\ \vdots \\ \mathbf{x}_T'/\sigma_T \end{bmatrix} \tag{9.3.11}$$

In (9.3.11) $\mathbf{x}_t^{*\prime}$ and $\mathbf{x}_t'$ are $(1 \times K)$ vectors containing, respectively, the transformed and untransformed tth observation on K explanatory variables. The tth observation for the whole model can be written as

$$\frac{y_t}{\sigma_t} = \frac{\mathbf{x}_t'}{\sigma_t}\boldsymbol{\beta} + \frac{e_t}{\sigma_t} \tag{9.3.12}$$

The variance of the transformed disturbance $e_t^* = e_t/\sigma_t$ is clearly a constant,

$$E[e_t^{*2}] = E\left[\left(\frac{e_t}{\sigma_t}\right)^2\right] = \frac{1}{\sigma_t^2} E[e_t^2] = \frac{\sigma_t^2}{\sigma_t^2} = 1 \tag{9.3.13}$$

and we can summarize with the following general result.

In a heteroskedastic error model the generalized least squares estimator is obtained by

(*i*) Dividing each observation (both dependent and explanatory variables) by the standard deviation of the error term for that observation, and

(*ii*) Applying the usual least squares procedures to the transformed observations.

This procedure is often known as *weighted least squares* because in the least squares criterion function each observation is weighted by the inverse of the standard deviation of the disturbance. In other words, the generalized least squares estimator is that $\boldsymbol{\beta}$ that minimizes

$$\sum_{t=1}^{T}\left(\frac{e_t}{\sigma_t}\right)^2 = (\mathbf{y} - X\boldsymbol{\beta})'\boldsymbol{\Phi}^{-1}(\mathbf{y} - X\boldsymbol{\beta}) \tag{9.3.14}$$

Observations with a relatively low σ_t are more reliable, are weighted more heavily, and hence play a greater role in the estimation process than those that are less reliable because they have a relatively high σ_t. This fact is more obvious when we write the generalized least squares estimator as

$$\hat{\boldsymbol{\beta}} = \left(\sum_{t=1}^{T}\sigma_t^{-2}\mathbf{x}_t\mathbf{x}_t'\right)^{-1}\sum_{t=1}^{T}\sigma_t^{-2}\mathbf{x}_t y_t \tag{9.3.15}$$

The validity of this expression as well as that in (9.3.14) is left as a problem (see Section 9.4.1, Exercise 9.4.1).

To calculate interval estimates or carry out hypothesis tests on the elements of $\boldsymbol{\beta}$, we need the covariance matrix for $\hat{\boldsymbol{\beta}}$, and, if our tests are to be exact rather than asymptotic, we also need to assume that $\mathbf{e}$ has a multivariate normal distribution. From the results of Chapter 8, and the foregoing discussion, the covariance matrix for $\hat{\boldsymbol{\beta}}$ is given by

$$\Sigma_{\hat{\boldsymbol{\beta}}} = (X^{*\prime}X^*)^{-1} = (X'\boldsymbol{\Phi}^{-1}X)^{-1} = \left(\sum_{t=1}^{T}\sigma_t^{-2}\mathbf{x}_t\mathbf{x}_t'\right)^{-1} \tag{9.3.16}$$

The way in which this matrix is used for interval estimation and hypothesis testing should be clear from Chapter 8.

9.3.2a An Example Where Variances are Known

In most heteroskedastic error models the different variances will be unknown, and the foregoing material is only useful in so far as it makes the procedures for unknown variances easier to describe. In some instances, however, it is reasonable to assume that the variance of each disturbance is, apart from a proportionality constant, a known function of some explanatory variable. For example, in Section 9.3.1 we considered the model

$$y_t = \beta_1 + \beta_2 x_t + \beta_3 x_t^2 + e_t \tag{9.3.17}$$

and indicated how this model could represent (for example) an industry cost function or an expenditure function. In the discussion of both these cases we suggested that the variance of e_t is likely to be directly related to x_t. If we were prepared to be more explicit and assume, for example, that

$$\sigma_t^2 = \sigma^2 x_t^2 \tag{9.3.18}$$

then we have a situation in which, apart from the constant σ^2, the variances are known. We could write

$$\mathbf{\Phi} = \sigma^2\mathbf{\Psi} = \sigma^2\begin{bmatrix} x_1^2 & & & 0 \\ & x_2^2 & & \\ & & \ddots & \\ 0 & & & x_T^2 \end{bmatrix}$$

and the generalized least squares estimator $\hat{\boldsymbol{\beta}} = (X'\mathbf{\Psi}^{-1}X)^{-1}X'\mathbf{\Psi}^{-1}\mathbf{y}$ could be found by applying least squares to the transformed model

$$\frac{y_t}{x_t} = \beta_1\left(\frac{1}{x_t}\right) + \beta_2 + \beta_3 x_t + \frac{e_t}{x_t} \tag{9.3.19}$$

Such a procedure may yield satisfactory estimates, but it would be legitimate to ask why we assume that $\sigma_t^2 = \sigma^2 x_t^2$, instead of, for instance, $\sigma_t^2 = \sigma^2|x_t|$ or $\sigma_t^2 = \sigma^2|x_t|^{1/2}$. A more general formulation would be to treat the power of the explanatory variable as an unknown parameter. For example, $\sigma_t^2 = \sigma^2 x_t^p$, where p is unknown. However, in this case the σ_t^2 will not be known, and generalized least squares cannot be used until p is estimated. This problem is considered in Section 9.3.4.

9.3.3 A Model With Two Unknown Variances

In the general heteroskedastic specification $\mathbf{\Phi} = \text{diag}(\sigma_1^2, \sigma_2^2, \ldots, \sigma_T^2)$, relaxing the assumption of known variances means that T unknown variances must be estimated with only T observations. It is unlikely that reasonable variance estimates could be obtained under such circumstances unless some further assumption is made that reduces the number of unknown parameters on which the variances depend. The simplest assumption, and one that often arises in practice, is that the sample can be partitioned into two subsets of observations, each subset corresponding to a different error variance. The error variance is assumed to be constant within each subset, so the complete model has only two unknown variances. It can be written as

$$\begin{bmatrix} \mathbf{y}_1 \\ \mathbf{y}_2 \end{bmatrix} = \begin{bmatrix} X_1 \\ X_2 \end{bmatrix}\boldsymbol{\beta} + \begin{bmatrix} \mathbf{e}_1 \\ \mathbf{e}_2 \end{bmatrix} \tag{9.3.20}$$

where $\mathbf{y}_i$ is $(T_i \times 1)$, X_i is $(T_i \times K)$, $\boldsymbol{\beta}$ is $(K \times 1)$, $\mathbf{e}_i$ is $(T_i \times 1)$, $\mathbf{y}' = (\mathbf{y}_1', \mathbf{y}_2')$, $X' = (X_1', X_2')$, $\mathbf{e}' = (\mathbf{e}_1', \mathbf{e}_2')$, and $T_1 + T_2 = T$. The error covariance matrix is given by

$$E[\mathbf{ee}'] = \mathbf{\Phi} = E\left[\begin{pmatrix} \mathbf{e}_1 \\ \mathbf{e}_2 \end{pmatrix}(\mathbf{e}_1' \quad \mathbf{e}_2')\right] = \begin{bmatrix} \sigma_1^2 I_{T_1} & 0 \\ 0 & \sigma_2^2 I_{T_2} \end{bmatrix} \tag{9.3.21}$$

A model such as (9.3.20) is likely to occur if there has been some kind of change during a sample period, and this change is likely to have caused a change in the error variance, but not in the coefficient vector. Alternatively, (9.3.20) could represent two equations for different households, firms, or geographic areas, where the coefficient vector is the same for each equation, but the variance is not.

The generalized least squares estimator for the model in (9.3.20) and (9.3.21) is given by (see Exercise 9.4.2 in Section 9.4.1)

$$\hat{\boldsymbol{\beta}} = (X'\boldsymbol{\Phi}^{-1}X)^{-1}X'\boldsymbol{\Phi}^{-1}\mathbf{y} = \left(\frac{X_1'X_1}{\sigma_1^2} + \frac{X_2'X_2}{\sigma_2^2}\right)^{-1}\left(\frac{X_1'\mathbf{y}_1}{\sigma_1^2} + \frac{X_2'\mathbf{y}_2}{\sigma_2^2}\right) \qquad (9.3.22)$$

To turn $\hat{\boldsymbol{\beta}}$ into a feasible (estimated) generalized least squares estimator, the variances σ_1^2 and σ_2^2 must be estimated. A number of possible estimators could be used (see, for example, Judge, et al, 1985, pp. 428–429), but the most convenient method is to use two least squares regressions, one on each of the subsets of observations. That is,

$$\hat{\sigma}_i^2 = \frac{(\mathbf{y}_i - X_i\mathbf{b}_i)'(\mathbf{y}_i - X_i\mathbf{b}_i)}{T_i - K} \qquad i = 1, 2 \qquad (9.3.23)$$

where $\mathbf{b}_i = (X_i'X_i)^{-1}X_i'\mathbf{y}_i$. This procedure will work providing $T_i > K$, and, as demonstrated in Section 5.8, it leads to unbiased estimators for σ_1^2 and σ_2^2. Substituting the estimators in (9.3.23) into (9.3.22) yields the estimated generalized least squares estimator for $\boldsymbol{\beta}$, namely

$$\hat{\hat{\boldsymbol{\beta}}} = (X'\hat{\boldsymbol{\Phi}}^{-1}X)^{-1}X'\hat{\boldsymbol{\Phi}}^{-1}\mathbf{y} = \left(\frac{X_1'X_1}{\hat{\sigma}_1^2} + \frac{X_2'X_2}{\hat{\sigma}_2^2}\right)^{-1}\left(\frac{X_1'\mathbf{y}_1}{\hat{\sigma}_1^2} + \frac{X_2'\mathbf{y}_2}{\hat{\sigma}_2^2}\right) \qquad (9.3.24)$$

Using the asymptotic results of Section 9.2, hypothesis tests and interval estimates can be formed by treating $\hat{\hat{\boldsymbol{\beta}}}$ as an approximate normal random vector with mean $\boldsymbol{\beta}$ and covariance matrix estimated by $(X'\hat{\boldsymbol{\Phi}}^{-1}X)^{-1}$.

In this particular special case, following Taylor (1978), it is also possible to derive some of the finite sample properties of $\hat{\hat{\boldsymbol{\beta}}}$. These properties are not sufficiently well developed to permit derivation of finite sample tests and confidence intervals for $\boldsymbol{\beta}$, but the finite sample covariance matrix has been derived, and it can be used in efficiency comparisons with other estimators. Of particular interest is a comparison between the least squares estimator, the estimated generalized least squares estimator, and a preliminary-test estimator. This last estimator will first be introduced, then we will give such a comparison. For a more complete discussion of pre-test estimation, see Section 20.3.1.

9.3.3a A Preliminary-Test Estimator

Before using the estimated generalized least squares estimator specified in (9.3.24), a researcher is likely to carry out a test to see if the two variances σ_1^2 and σ_2^2 are indeed different. If they appear to be identical, it may not be worth proceeding any further than the least squares estimator $\mathbf{b} = (X'X)^{-1}X'\mathbf{y}$.

It is straightforward to construct a suitable test for testing the null hypothesis

$$H_0: \sigma_1^2 = \sigma_2^2 \tag{9.3.25}$$

against either

$$H_1^A: \sigma_1^2 \neq \sigma_2^2 \quad \text{or} \quad H_1^B: \sigma_1^2 > \sigma_2^2 \tag{9.3.26}$$

From Equation 6.1.18 of Chapter 6, we know that the random variable

$$\frac{(T_i - K)\hat{\sigma}_i^2}{\sigma_i^2} \sim \chi^2_{(T_i - K)} \qquad i = 1, 2 \tag{9.3.27}$$

Furthermore, these two χ^2 statistics ($i = 1$ and $i = 2$) are independent because they were obtained from separate estimates from each of the subsets of observations $\mathbf{y}_1$ and $\mathbf{y}_2$, which are independently distributed random vectors. Thus, using the definition of an F random variable (Equation 2.5.15 of Chapter 2), it follows that

$$\frac{\hat{\sigma}_1^2}{\sigma_1^2} \bigg/ \frac{\hat{\sigma}_2^2}{\sigma_2^2} \sim F_{(T_1 - K,\, T_2 - K)} \tag{9.3.28}$$

Under the null hypothesis where $\sigma_1^2 = \sigma_2^2$,

$$\frac{\hat{\sigma}_1^2}{\hat{\sigma}_2^2} \sim F_{(T_1 - K, T_2 - K)} \tag{9.3.29}$$

The test is therefore carried out by computing $(\hat{\sigma}_1^2/\hat{\sigma}_2^2)$ and comparing this value with a critical value from the F-distribution. For H_1^A the null hypothesis will be rejected if $(\hat{\sigma}_1^2/\hat{\sigma}_2^2)$ is too big or too small; for H_1^B it will be rejected if $\hat{\sigma}_1^2/\hat{\sigma}_2^2$ is too big.

A typical researcher who is investigating whether or not heteroskedasticity is present is likely to choose the least squares estimator $\mathbf{b}$ if the null hypothesis is accepted, and the estimated generalized least squares estimator $\hat{\hat{\boldsymbol{\beta}}}$ if the null hypothesis is rejected. This procedure is actually equivalent to using a third estimator, say $\boldsymbol{\beta}^*$, which is known as a preliminary-test or "pretest" estimator. It is given by

$$\boldsymbol{\beta}^* = \begin{cases} \mathbf{b} & \text{if } H_0: \sigma_1^2 = \sigma_2^2 \text{ is accepted} \\ \hat{\hat{\boldsymbol{\beta}}} & \text{if } H_0: \sigma_1^2 = \sigma_2^2 \text{ is rejected} \end{cases} \tag{9.3.30}$$

The finite sample covariance matrix for $\boldsymbol{\beta}^*$ has been derived by Greenberg (1980). Thus, it is possible to compare the efficiencies of the least squares, estimated generalized least squares, and pretest estimators. See Greenberg (1980) and Mandy (1984).

In Figure 9.2 the performance of the various estimators is illustrated. Efficiency is measured by the trace of the finite sample covariance matrix. Two pretest estimators are considered, one where the alternative is $H_1^A: \sigma_1^2 \neq \sigma_2^2$, and one where

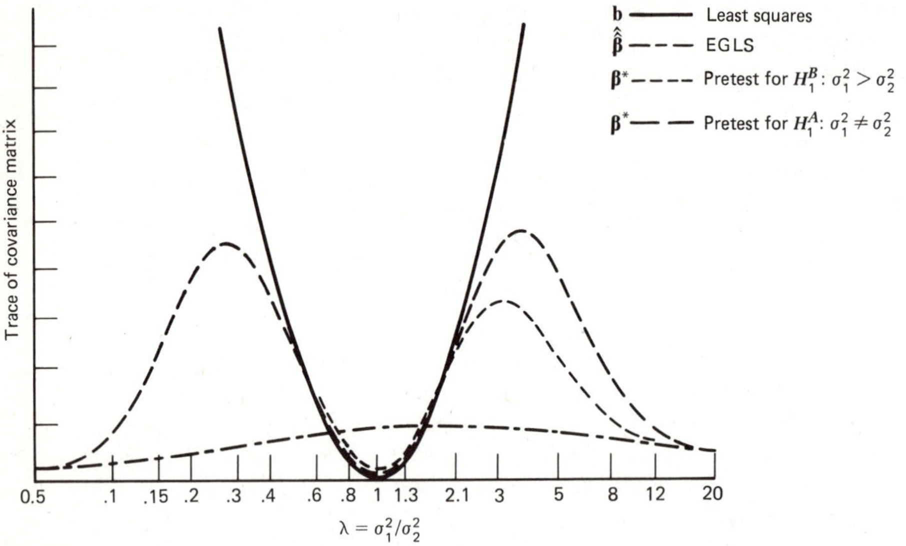

Figure 9.2 Efficiencies of pretest and conventional estimators, double log scale.

it is $H_1^B: \sigma_1^2 > \sigma_2^2$. The first comparison to consider is between the least squares and estimated generalized least squares (EGLS) estimators. When heteroskedasticity is mild ($\lambda = \sigma_1^2/\sigma_2^2$ is close to 1), least squares is better than EGLS, reflecting the fact that $\hat{\hat{\boldsymbol{\beta}}}$ depends on the estimated variances $\hat{\sigma}_1^2$ and $\hat{\sigma}_2^2$, which will exhibit sampling error. If $\hat{\sigma}_1^2$ and $\hat{\sigma}_2^2$ were known with certainty, the generalized least squares estimator would be used, and it would always be more efficient than least squares, except at the point $\lambda = \sigma_1^2/\sigma_2^2 = 1$, where it would be identical. When we move from $\hat{\boldsymbol{\beta}}$ to $\hat{\hat{\boldsymbol{\beta}}}$, and the variances σ_1^2 and σ_2^2 are not estimated exactly, there is a region in the parameter space for λ where least squares is best. However, the EGLS estimator becomes considerably better than least squares as the degree of heteroskedasticity increases ($\lambda = \sigma_1^2/\sigma_2^2$ becomes large or small).

The efficiencies of the pretest estimators reflect the fact that when the null hypothesis is correct or nearly correct, the least squares estimator is chosen most of the time, but, as the null hypothesis becomes increasingly implausible, the frequency with which the EGLS estimator is chosen increases. For large λ, the pretest estimator for $H_1^B: \sigma_1^2 > \sigma_2^2$ is more efficient than that for $H_1^A: \sigma_1^2 \neq \sigma_2^2$, reflecting the fact that the one-tailed test has a larger rejection region, and hence the EGLS estimator is chosen more often. For small λ, the pretest estimator for $H_1^B: \sigma_1^2 > \sigma_2^2$ becomes identical to least squares.

The general behaviour illustrated in Figure 9.2 is not specific to the heteroskedastic error model. There are many instances where a choice between two estimators is made dependent on a preliminary hypothesis test, and a pretest estimator is thereby generated. The variance of the pretest estimator typically lies between the variances of the other two estimators and is almost identical to one or the other under circumstances where the null hypothesis is accepted or rejected almost always.

9.3.4 A Model With Multiplicative Heteroskedasticity

In Section 9.3.2 it was suggested that heteroskedastic error models often arise because the error variance is related to some explanatory variable. The model $\sigma_t^2 = \sigma^2 x_t^p$ was suggested as a general variance specification that would be reasonable if just one explanatory variable is involved. In this case σ^2 and p are the only unknown parameters in the error covariance matrix, so this specification reduces the number of unknown variance parameters from T to 2. In this section we consider estimation of these variance parameters, and the estimated generalized least squares estimator that results, but we do so in the context of a more general model. Specifically, we assume that each σ_t^2 is an exponential function of S explanatory variables, and hence that the model is given by

$$y_t = \mathbf{x}_t'\boldsymbol{\beta} + e_t \tag{9.3.31}$$

$$E[e_t^2] = \sigma_t^2 = \exp[\mathbf{z}_t'\boldsymbol{\alpha}] \qquad t = 1, 2, \ldots, T \tag{9.3.32}$$

where $\mathbf{z}_t' = (z_{t1} z_{t2} \ldots z_{tS})$ is a $(1 \times S)$ vector containing the tth observation on S nonstochastic explanatory variables and $\boldsymbol{\alpha} = (\alpha_1 \alpha_2 \ldots \alpha_S)'$ is an $(S \times 1)$ vector of unknown coefficients. The first element in $\mathbf{z}_t$ will be taken as unity $(z_{t1} \equiv 1)$, and, in practice, the other z's could be identical to, or functions of, the x's.

This specification reduces the problem of estimating T σ_t^2's, to that of estimating the S dimensional vector $\boldsymbol{\alpha}$. The applied worker must now choose not only $\mathbf{x}_t$, the variables that explain changes in y_t, but also $\mathbf{z}_t$, the variables that explain changes in the variance of y_t. Fortunately, we will usually have a good idea of the relevant z's.

Because the function in (9.3.32) can be written as

$$\sigma_t^2 = \exp[\alpha_1] \cdot \exp[\alpha_2 z_{t2}] \ldots \exp[\alpha_S z_{tS}] \tag{9.3.33}$$

it is often referred to as *multiplicative heteroskedasticity*: the various components of the variance are related in a multiplicative fashion. Other functions have been studied (see Judge, et al., (1985), for details), but this one has some advantages (see

Harvey, 1976) and is popular in applied work. Note that if $S = 2$, $z_{t2} = \ln x_t$, $\alpha_1 = \ln \sigma^2$, and $\alpha_2 = p$, we have

$$\begin{aligned}\sigma_t^2 &= \exp[\mathbf{z}_t'\boldsymbol{\alpha}] = \exp[\alpha_1 + \alpha_2 z_{t2}] \\ &= \exp(\alpha_1)\exp(p \ln x_t) = \sigma^2 x_t^p \end{aligned} \tag{9.3.34}$$

which is the special case described as reasonable for one explanatory variable.

The relationship between the scale factor σ^2 and the parameter α_1 is worth emphasizing. The reparameterization $\sigma^2 = \exp(\alpha_1)$, or $\alpha_1 = \ln \sigma^2$, will later prove to be convenient. It means that the general expression in (9.3.32) can be written as

$$\begin{aligned}\sigma_t^2 &= \exp[\mathbf{z}_t'\boldsymbol{\alpha}] \\ &= \exp[\alpha_1 + \alpha_2 z_{t2} + \cdots + \alpha_S z_{tS}] \\ &= \sigma^2 \exp[\alpha_2 z_{t2} + \cdots + \alpha_S z_{tS}] \\ &= \sigma^2 \exp[\mathbf{z}_t^{*\prime}\boldsymbol{\alpha}^*] \end{aligned} \tag{9.3.35}$$

where $\mathbf{z}_t^{*\prime} = (z_{t2}, \ldots, z_{tS})$ and $\boldsymbol{\alpha}^* = (\alpha_2, \ldots, \alpha_S)'$. In matrix algebra notation this relationship becomes

$$\begin{aligned}\boldsymbol{\Phi} &= \begin{bmatrix} \exp(\mathbf{z}_1'\boldsymbol{\alpha}) & & & \\ & \exp(\mathbf{z}_2'\boldsymbol{\alpha}) & & \\ & & \ddots & \\ & & & \exp(\mathbf{z}_T'\boldsymbol{\alpha}) \end{bmatrix} \\ &= \sigma^2\boldsymbol{\Psi} = \sigma^2 \begin{bmatrix} \exp(\mathbf{z}_1^{*\prime}\boldsymbol{\alpha}^*) & & & \\ & \exp(\mathbf{z}_2^{*\prime}\boldsymbol{\alpha}^*) & & \\ & & \ddots & \\ & & & \exp(\mathbf{z}_T^{*\prime}\boldsymbol{\alpha}^*) \end{bmatrix} \end{aligned} \tag{9.3.36}$$

9.3.4a Estimating $\boldsymbol{\alpha}$

If we are able to obtain an estimator $\hat{\boldsymbol{\alpha}}$, it can be used to find estimates $\hat{\sigma}_t^2 = \exp[\mathbf{z}_t'\hat{\boldsymbol{\alpha}}]$, $t = 1, 2, \ldots, T$, which in turn can be used to obtain an estimated generalized least squares estimator for $\boldsymbol{\beta}$. Working in this direction, we first take logs of (9.3.32) to obtain

$$\ln \sigma_t^2 = \mathbf{z}_t'\boldsymbol{\alpha} \tag{9.3.37}$$

If the σ_t^2 were known, then this equation could be used to shed some light on $\boldsymbol{\alpha}$. Since they are not, we use instead the squares of the least squares residuals. These residuals are likely to be big when σ_t^2 is big, and small when σ_t^2 is small. The tth least squares residual is defined as

$$\hat{e}_t = y_t - \mathbf{x}_t'\mathbf{b} \tag{9.3.38}$$

where $\mathbf{b} = (X'X)^{-1}X'\mathbf{y}$. Adding $\ln \hat{e}_t^2$ to both sides of (9.3.37) yields

$$\ln \hat{e}_t^2 + \ln \sigma_t^2 = \mathbf{z}_t'\boldsymbol{\alpha} + \ln \hat{e}_t^2$$

or

$$\ln \hat{e}_t^2 = \mathbf{z}_t'\boldsymbol{\alpha} + v_t \tag{9.3.39}$$

where

$$v_t = \ln \hat{e}_t^2 - \ln \sigma_t^2 = \ln(\hat{e}_t^2/\sigma_t^2) \tag{9.3.40}$$

Equation 9.3.39 can be regarded as a regression model where $\ln \hat{e}_t^2$ is the tth observation on the dependent variable, $\mathbf{z}_t'$ is a $(1 \times S)$ vector containing the tth observation on S explanatory variables, v_t is the tth disturbance, and $\boldsymbol{\alpha}$ is an unknown vector of parameters to be estimated. In matrix notation it can be written as

$$\mathbf{q} = Z\boldsymbol{\alpha} + \mathbf{v} \tag{9.3.41}$$

where $Z = (\mathbf{z}_1\mathbf{z}_2 \ldots \mathbf{z}_T)'$, $\mathbf{q} = (\ln e_1^2 \ln \hat{e}_2^2 \ldots \ln \hat{e}_T^2)'$ and $\mathbf{v} = (v_1 v_2 \ldots v_T)'$. One way to estimate $\boldsymbol{\alpha}$ is to apply least squares to (9.3.41). This yields the estimator

$$\hat{\boldsymbol{\alpha}} = (Z'Z)^{-1}Z'\mathbf{q} = \left(\sum_{t=1}^{T} \mathbf{z}_t\mathbf{z}_t'\right)^{-1} \sum_{t=1}^{T} \mathbf{z}_t \ln \hat{e}_t^2 \tag{9.3.42}$$

However, do we have any grounds for using $\hat{\boldsymbol{\alpha}}$ as an estimator for $\boldsymbol{\alpha}$? What are its properties? Since $\hat{\boldsymbol{\alpha}} = \boldsymbol{\alpha} + (Z'Z)^{-1}Z'\mathbf{v}$, the properties of $\hat{\boldsymbol{\alpha}}$ will depend on those of $\mathbf{v}$. Unfortunately, the finite sample properties of the elements in $\mathbf{v}$ are complicated. They have nonzero means and are heteroskedastic and autocorrelated. To make some headway we must resort to asymptotic properties. In this regard, we first note that, under some assumptions about the limiting behavior of the explanatory variables, the tth least squares residual $\hat{e}_t$ will converge in distribution to its corresponding error e_t. To demonstrate this result, we assume that $\lim T^{-1}X'X = Q$ and $\lim T^{-1}X'\Psi X = V_0$ are both finite and nonsingular and consider the mean and variance of $\hat{e}_t - e_t$. Specifically, we have

$$E[\hat{e}_t - e_t] = -\mathbf{x}_t'(X'X)^{-1}X'E[\mathbf{e}] = 0$$

and

$$\begin{aligned} E[(\hat{e}_t - e_t)^2] &= \mathbf{x}_t'(X'X)^{-1}X'E[\mathbf{ee}']X(X'X)^{-1}\mathbf{x}_t \\ &= \sigma^2\mathbf{x}_t'(X'X)^{-1}X'\Psi X(X'X)^{-1}\mathbf{x}_t \\ &= \frac{\sigma^2}{T}\mathbf{x}_t'\left(\frac{X'X}{T}\right)^{-1}\frac{X'\Psi X}{T}\left(\frac{X'X}{T}\right)^{-1}\mathbf{x}_t \end{aligned}$$

Since $\mathbf{x}_t$ remains fixed as $T \to \infty$, we have that the bias and variance of $(\hat{e}_t - e_t)$ approach 0 as $T \to \infty$, and therefore that $\text{plim}(\hat{e}_t - e_t) = 0$. It then follows that $\hat{e}_t \xrightarrow{p} e_t$ and hence that $\hat{e}_t \xrightarrow{d} e_t$.

Given this result, it follows that $v_t = \ln(\hat{e}_t^2/\sigma_t^2)$ will converge in distribution to the random variable $\ln(e_t^2/\sigma_t^2)$. Also, if this random variable is denoted by v_t^* and if we assume that e_t is normally distributed, then (e_t^2/σ_t^2) has a $\chi^2_{(1)}$ distribution and v_t^* will be distributed as the log of a χ^2 random variable with 1 degree of freedom. Furthermore, the v_t^* will be uncorrelated. Using this information it is possible (Harvey, 1976) to show that

$$E[v_t^*] = -1.2704 \tag{9.3.43}$$

$$\text{var}(v_t^*) = E[(v_t^* - E[v_t^*])^2] = 4.9348 \tag{9.3.44}$$

and

$$\text{cov}(v_t^*, v_\tau^*) = 0 \qquad \text{for } t \neq \tau \tag{9.3.45}$$

Thus, in terms of its limiting distribution, the elements in the vector $\mathbf{v}$ satisfy the least squares assumptions of constant variance (homoskedasticity) and no autocorrelation, but the assumption of 0 mean is violated. In the conventional least squares regression model the consequences of having a disturbance with nonzero mean are not great, providing the model contains a constant term (or intercept coefficient). It can be shown (Section 9.4, Exercise 9.4.3) that the estimate of the intercept coefficient will be biased, but the estimates of the slope coefficients remain unbiased. In the context of our problem, where the limiting distribution of v_t has a mean of -1.2704, the consequence is that the intercept α_1 will not be consistently estimated, but the remaining elements in the estimator $\hat{\boldsymbol{\alpha}}$ will be consistent. That is,

$$\text{plim}\,\hat{\boldsymbol{\alpha}} = \begin{bmatrix} \alpha_1 - 1.2704 \\ \alpha_2 \\ \vdots \\ \alpha_S \end{bmatrix} = \boldsymbol{\alpha} - 1.2704\mathbf{d} \tag{9.3.46}$$

where $\mathbf{d} = (1 \quad 0 \quad \cdots \quad 0)'$. Furthermore, the covariance matrix of the limiting distribution of $\hat{\boldsymbol{\alpha}}$ will be given by $4.9348\Sigma_{zz}^{-1}$ where $\Sigma_{zz} = \lim T^{-1}Z'Z$ exists and is nonsingular; also,

$$\sqrt{T}(\hat{\boldsymbol{\alpha}} - \boldsymbol{\alpha} + 1.2704\mathbf{d}) \xrightarrow{d} N(\mathbf{0}, 4.9348\Sigma_{zz}^{-1}) \tag{9.3.47}$$

We can summarize all these results as follows. An estimate for $\boldsymbol{\alpha}$ can be found by regressing the log of the squared least squares residuals on Z. The finite sample properties of this estimator are unknown, but we know the mean and variance of its limiting distribution. The first element of the estimator, $\hat{\alpha}_1$, is inconsistent with an inconsistency of -1.2704, but the remaining elements $\hat{\alpha}_2, \hat{\alpha}_3, \ldots, \hat{\alpha}_S$ are all consistent estimators. The matrix $4.9348(Z'Z)^{-1}$ can be used to approximate the covariance matrix of $\hat{\boldsymbol{\alpha}}$. In Section 9.3.5 we will see how the result in (9.3.47) can be used to derive a test for heteroskedasticity.

9.3.4b The Estimated Generalized Least Squares Estimator

From the estimator for $\boldsymbol{\alpha}$ that has just been derived it is possible to estimate each of the variances, $\hat{\sigma}_t^2 = \exp\{\mathbf{z}_t'\hat{\boldsymbol{\alpha}}\}$ and form the estimated generalized least squares estimator

$$\hat{\hat{\boldsymbol{\beta}}} = (X'\hat{\boldsymbol{\Phi}}^{-1}X)^{-1}X'\hat{\boldsymbol{\Phi}}^{-1}\mathbf{y} = \left(\sum_{t=1}^{T}\hat{\sigma}_t^{-2}\mathbf{x}_t\mathbf{x}_t'\right)^{-1}\sum_{t=1}^{T}\hat{\sigma}_t^{-2}\mathbf{x}_t y_t$$

$$= \left(\sum_{t=1}^{T}\exp(-\mathbf{z}_t'\hat{\boldsymbol{\alpha}})\mathbf{x}_t\mathbf{x}_t'\right)^{-1}\sum_{t=1}^{T}\exp(-\mathbf{z}_t'\hat{\boldsymbol{\alpha}})\mathbf{x}_t y_t \tag{9.3.48}$$

Whether or not this is a reasonable procedure will depend on whether or not $\hat{\hat{\boldsymbol{\beta}}}$ has the favorable asymptotic properties outlined in Section 9.2. In this regard, one point that is likely to bother you is that $\hat{\alpha}_1$ is inconsistent. Fortunately, $\hat{\hat{\boldsymbol{\beta}}}$ does not depend on $\hat{\alpha}_1$, which can be factored out as a proportionality constant. Specifically, using (9.3.35), (9.3.36), and the corresponding estimated quantities, the estimated generalized least squares estimator can also be written as

$$\hat{\hat{\boldsymbol{\beta}}} = (X'\hat{\boldsymbol{\Psi}}^{-1}X)^{-1}X'\hat{\boldsymbol{\Psi}}^{-1}\mathbf{y}$$

$$= \left(\sum_{t=1}^{T}\exp(-\mathbf{z}_t^{*\prime}\hat{\boldsymbol{\alpha}}^*)\mathbf{x}_t\mathbf{x}_t'\right)^{-1}\sum_{t=1}^{T}\exp(-\mathbf{z}_t^{*\prime}\hat{\boldsymbol{\alpha}}^*)\mathbf{x}_t y_t \tag{9.3.49}$$

Since $\hat{\boldsymbol{\alpha}}^* = (\hat{\alpha}_2, \hat{\alpha}_3, \ldots, \hat{\alpha}_S)'$, the estimator $\hat{\hat{\boldsymbol{\beta}}}$ only depends on the consistently estimated elements of $\hat{\boldsymbol{\alpha}}$. The quantity $\exp(\hat{\alpha}_1)$ cancels just like the scale factor σ^2 cancels when we move from $(X'\boldsymbol{\Phi}^{-1}X)^{-1}X'\boldsymbol{\Phi}^{-1}\mathbf{y}$ to $(X'\boldsymbol{\Psi}^{-1}X)^{-1}X'\boldsymbol{\Psi}^{-1}\mathbf{y}$.

Following Section 9.2, $\hat{\hat{\boldsymbol{\beta}}}$ is approximately normally distributed with mean $\boldsymbol{\beta}$ and a covariance matrix that is consistently estimated by $\hat{\hat{\sigma}}^2(X'\hat{\boldsymbol{\Psi}}^{-1}X)^{-1}$, where $\hat{\hat{\sigma}}^2 = (\mathbf{y} - X\hat{\hat{\boldsymbol{\beta}}})'\hat{\boldsymbol{\Psi}}^{-1}(\mathbf{y} - X\hat{\hat{\boldsymbol{\beta}}})/(T-K)$. The usual hypothesis tests and interval estimates can be based on this result. The estimated generalized least squares estimator and a consistent estimate of its covariance matrix can be computed by dividing all observations by either $[\exp(\mathbf{z}_t^{*\prime}\hat{\boldsymbol{\alpha}}^*)]^{1/2}$ or $[\exp(\mathbf{z}_t'\hat{\boldsymbol{\alpha}})]^{1/2}$, and applying the usual least squares techniques. The fact that $[\exp(\mathbf{z}_t^{*\prime}\hat{\boldsymbol{\alpha}}^*)]^{1/2}$ and $[\exp(\mathbf{z}_t'\hat{\boldsymbol{\alpha}})]^{1/2}$ lead to the same estimated covariance matrix is left as a problem (Exercise 9.4.4 in Section 9.4).

9.3.5 Testing for Heteroskedasticity

An important question facing the applied worker is whether or not the procedures just described should be employed. If heteroskedasticity does not exist, then least squares will yield a best linear unbiased estimator of the coefficients as well as unbiased variance estimates, and it is not necessary to go through the additional estimation stages described in the previous section. However, if heteroskedasticity goes undetected, our least squares estimator will not be the best obtainable, and a biased variance estimator is likely to lead to misleading inferences. Consequently, it is of interest to test for heteroskedasticity; in this section we discuss three possible tests, but the results of Section 9.3.3a should be kept clearly in mind. The first is a natural test to use when, as an alternative hypothesis, we are considering the multiplicative heteroskedastic specification in Section 9.3.4. The second test, known as the Goldfeld–Quandt test, is suggested for circumstances in which, assuming that heteroskedasticity does exist, it is possible to order the observations according to increasing variance. Finally, for cases in which we assume that each variance may be a function of more than one explanatory variable but we do not necessarily wish to impose the multiplicative specification, we describe the Breusch–Pagan test.

9.3.5a Testing for Multiplicative Heteroskedasticity

In Section 9.3.4 we considered the model $y_t = \mathbf{x}_t'\boldsymbol{\beta} + e_t$, where

$$E[e_t^2] = \sigma_t^2 = \exp(\mathbf{z}_t'\boldsymbol{\alpha}) = \exp(\alpha_1)\cdot\exp(\mathbf{z}_t^{*\prime}\boldsymbol{\alpha}^*) = \sigma^2\cdot\exp(\mathbf{z}_t^{*\prime}\boldsymbol{\alpha}^*) \tag{9.3.50}$$

Treating this model as an alternative to one with homoskedastic errors is equivalent to testing the null hypothesis $H_0\colon \boldsymbol{\alpha}^* = \mathbf{0}$ against the alternative $H_1\colon \boldsymbol{\alpha}^* \neq \mathbf{0}$. For this test we can use the estimator $\hat{\boldsymbol{\alpha}} = (Z'Z)^{-1}Z'\mathbf{q}$, which was defined in (9.3.42), and the result in (9.3.47). Let D be the matrix $(Z'Z)^{-1}$ with its first row and first column deleted. Then, from (9.3.47),

$$\hat{\boldsymbol{\alpha}}^* \sim N[\boldsymbol{\alpha}^*, 4.9348D] \tag{9.3.51}$$

and

$$\frac{(\hat{\boldsymbol{\alpha}}^* - \boldsymbol{\alpha}^*)'D^{-1}(\hat{\boldsymbol{\alpha}}^* - \boldsymbol{\alpha}^*)}{4.9348} \sim \chi^2_{(S-1)} \tag{9.3.52}$$

hold approximately.

Under the null hypothesis $\boldsymbol{\alpha}^* = \mathbf{0}$ the statistic in (9.3.52) reduces to $\hat{\boldsymbol{\alpha}}^{*\prime}D^{-1}\hat{\boldsymbol{\alpha}}^*/4.9348$, so, to test for heteroskedasticity, we can calculate this quantity and compare it with the relevant significance point of the χ^2 distribution. For computational ease it is worth noting that the numerator $\hat{\boldsymbol{\alpha}}^{*\prime} D^{-1} \hat{\boldsymbol{\alpha}}^*$ is the regression (or explained) sum of squares obtained when estimating $\boldsymbol{\alpha}$ and that the test just described is asymptotically equivalent to the F test for testing that all coefficients, except the intercept, are 0. This is the F test whose value is routinely provided by most computer programs.

9.3.5b The Goldfeld–Quandt Test

The Goldfeld–Quandt test is a slight modification of the test based on the statistic $(\hat{\sigma}_1^2/\hat{\sigma}_2^2)$ given in (9.3.29). This statistic was derived under the assumption that, under H_1, the sample could be partitioned into two subsets of observations where the error variance is different for each subset, but is constant within a subset. The estimates $\hat{\sigma}_1^2$, $\hat{\sigma}_2^2$ were computed from separate regressions on each of the subsets.

For the Goldfeld–Quandt test the alternative hypothesis is

$$H_1: \sigma_1^2 \leq \sigma_2^2 \leq \cdots \leq \sigma_T^2 \tag{9.3.53}$$

That is, under H_1, the observations can be ordered according to increasing variances. This alternative is in contrast with that considered in Section 9.3.3a where there were only two different variances under the alternative hypothesis. The basis of the test is the same, however. If H_1 is true, then an estimated variance $\hat{\sigma}_2^2$ that is based on a separate regression on the last half of the observations is likely to be higher than an estimated variance $\hat{\sigma}_1^2$ that is based on a regression on the first half of the observations. The slight modification of the test statistic comes about through Goldfeld and Quandt's suggestion that the test could be made more powerful by omitting some of the central observations that contribute little toward making $\hat{\sigma}_2^2$ big or $\hat{\sigma}_1^2$ small. Also, the test is usually stated in terms of the residual sums of squares of each regression, S_2 and S_1 say, because $\hat{\sigma}_2^2$ and $\hat{\sigma}_1^2$ are not really estimators for two corresponding variances σ_2^2 and σ_1^2.

Thus, the steps for implementing the test are

1. Assuming H_1 is true, order the observations according to increasing error variance.
2. Omit r central observations.
3. Run two separate regressions, one using the first $(T - r)/2$ observations and the other using the last $(T - r)/2$ observations.
4. Compute the statistic $\lambda = S_2/S_1$ where S_1 and S_2 are the residual sums of squares from the first and second regressions, respectively. Under the null hypothesis of homoskedasticity, λ has an F-distribution with $[(T - r - 2K)/2, (T - r - 2K)/2]$ degrees of freedom.
5. Compare the computed value for λ with a relevant critical value from the F-distribution and accept or reject the null hypothesis accordingly.

The optimum choice of r is not obvious. Large values are likely to increase the power of the test through an increase in the value of the F statistic but decrease the power through a reduction in degrees of freedom. From experience, reasonably satisfactory values are $r = 4$ for $T = 30$ and $r = 10$ for $T = 60$. Also, it is not essential that the two regressions be based on the same number of observations. If the number of observations does differ, then the degrees of freedom and the test statistic must be changed accordingly.

The relevance of this test depends on our ability to order the observations according to increasing variance. If the variance is directly related to one of the explanatory variables or some exogenous variable that may not be included in the equation, such an ordering is possible, and the test is likely to prove useful. When the observations are not correctly ordered, the test will be of doubtful power. Finally, it is worth noting that, unlike the other tests described in this section, the Goldfeld-Quandt test is an exact test and does not rely on asymptotic properties.

9.3.5c The Breusch–Pagan Test

In some instances we may wish to entertain the alternative hypothesis that the variance is some function (but not necessarily multiplicative) of more than one explanatory variable. If this is the case, the test in Section 9.3.5a would be too restrictive, and, for the Goldfeld–Quandt test, it would not be possible to order the observations according to increasing variance. As an alternative, we can use the Breusch–Pagan test.

Assume that under H_1

$$\sigma_t^2 = h(\mathbf{z}_t'\boldsymbol{\alpha}) = h(\alpha_1 + \mathbf{z}_t^{*\prime}\boldsymbol{\alpha}^*) \tag{9.3.54}$$

where h is any function independent of t, $\mathbf{z}_t' = (1, \mathbf{z}_t^{*\prime}) = (1, z_{t2}, z_{t3}, \ldots, z_{tS})$ is a vector of observable explanatory variables, and $\boldsymbol{\alpha}' = (\alpha_1, \boldsymbol{\alpha}^{*\prime}) = (\alpha_1, \alpha_2, \ldots, \alpha_S)$ is a vector of unknown coefficients. This set of conditions clearly includes $\sigma_t^2 = \exp(\mathbf{z}_t'\boldsymbol{\alpha})$ as a special case. Under the null hypothesis $\boldsymbol{\alpha}^* = \mathbf{0}$ and the assumption that the e_t are normally distributed, it can be shown that one-half the difference between the total sum of squares and the residual sum of squares from the regression

$$\frac{\hat{e}_t^2}{\tilde{\sigma}^2} = \mathbf{z}_t'\boldsymbol{\alpha} + v_t \tag{9.3.55}$$

is distributed asymptotically as $\chi^2_{(S-1)}$. The $\hat{e}_t = y_t - \mathbf{x}_t'\mathbf{b}$ are the least squares residuals, and $\tilde{\sigma}^2 = \sum_{t=1}^{T} \hat{e}_t^2/T$.

This test is obviously very similar to that given in Section 9.3.5a. To see the difference, let SSR be the explained or regression sum of squares obtained by regressing $\hat{e}_t^2$ on $\mathbf{z}_t$. Then, the Breusch–Pagan test statistic is identical to SSR/$2\tilde{\sigma}^4$. In (9.3.52), when $\boldsymbol{\alpha}^* = \mathbf{0}$, the numerator is the regression sum of squares from the regression of $\ln \hat{e}_t^2$ on $\mathbf{z}_t$, and the denominator is 4.9348 instead of $2\tilde{\sigma}^4$. Both statistics depend on the assumption of normally distributed errors. A third test statistic that is asymptotically equivalent and that is still valid when the errors are not normally distributed is TR^2 where R^2 is the square of the multiple correlation coefficient in the regression of $\hat{e}_t^2$ on $\mathbf{z}_t$. For details, see Judge et al. (1985, p. 447).

A number of researchers have found that in finite samples the Breusch–Pagan test rejects the null hypothesis when it is true less frequently than indicated by the selected Type I error. Thus, the finite sample significance level may be less than that chosen on the basis of asymptotic theory.

9.3.6 Summary

In this section we have

1. Defined heteroskedasticity and indicated when it is likely to arise.
2. Given details of generalized least squares estimation when the variances are known.
3. Given details of estimated generalized least squares estimation when the variances are unknown and when (a) a two-variance sample partition exists and (b) multiplicative heteroskedasticity exists.
4. Described some tests for heteroskedasticity.

The material on estimated generalized least squares and multiplicative heteroskedasticity is based on Harvey (1976) and is only one of a large number of specifications that have been suggested in the literature. For details of other specifications, see Judge et al. (1985, Chapter 11). Furthermore, we have not reported all of Harvey's findings. Harvey examined maximum likelihood estimation of $\boldsymbol{\alpha}$ and $\boldsymbol{\beta}$, showed that the estimator $\hat{\boldsymbol{\alpha}}$ that we reported above is asymptotically inefficient, and suggested an alternative estimator. We have not given details of this estimator since we have already provided sufficient detail for the beginning student, and *since finding an asymptotically more efficient estimator for* $\boldsymbol{\alpha}$ *does not necessarily improve the already asymptotically efficient estimated generalized least squares estimator for* $\boldsymbol{\beta}$. See Chapter 12 for further details.

The section on testing for heteroskedasticity was based on Goldfeld and Quandt (1965, 1972) and Breusch and Pagan (1979). As with estimation, a large number of other tests have been suggested in the literature, and details of most of these are given in Judge et al. (1985, Chapter 11). We have chosen the two that we consider most useful in terms of performance and ease of computation.

9.3.7 An Example

In this section we illustrate the foregoing techniques with an example. The first three columns of Table 9.1 contain the observed (20×1) vectors $\mathbf{y}$, $\mathbf{x}_2$, and $\mathbf{x}_3$, which represent a sample from the model

$$y_t = \beta_1 + \beta_2 x_{t2} + \beta_3 x_{t3} + e_t \tag{9.3.56}$$

where the e_t are normally and independently distributed, with

$$E[e_t] = 0, \quad E[e_t^2] = \sigma_t^2, \quad \text{and} \quad \sigma_t^2 = \exp\{\alpha_1 + \alpha_2 x_{t2}\} \tag{9.3.57}$$

The observations $\mathbf{y}$ were generated using the parameter values $\boldsymbol{\beta} = (\beta_1, \beta_2, \beta_3)' = (10, 1, 1)'$ and $\boldsymbol{\alpha} = (\alpha_1, \alpha_2)' = (-3, 0.3)'$.

If this were a real-world problem we would not have all this information; we would only have the observations $\mathbf{y}$, $\mathbf{x}_2$, and $\mathbf{x}_3$ and perhaps some a priori knowledge that suggests that the model in (9.3.56) is reasonable. We may suspect that the disturbance is heteroskedastic and that the variance depends on x_{t2}, but this kind of knowledge will certainly not always exist.

Table 9.1 Data for Heteroskedasticity Example

$\mathbf{y}$	$\mathbf{x}_2$	$\mathbf{x}_3$	σ_t^2	$\hat{\mathbf{e}}$
41.65077	14.53	16.74	3.8923	1.96496
40.99370	15.30	16.81	4.9037	−0.03286
39.78592	15.92	19.50	5.9062	−4.94658
50.31161	17.41	22.12	9.2350	0.50699
56.97006	18.37	22.34	12.3172	5.36149
52.41802	18.83	17.47	14.1399	4.90674
51.74554	18.84	20.24	14.1824	1.45540
59.74142	19.71	20.37	18.4120	7.88565
46.64725	20.01	12.71	20.1459	−4.06485
46.96075	20.26	22.98	21.7149	−8.40564
51.27611	20.77	19.33	25.3049	−1.29215
49.41824	21.17	17.04	28.5313	−1.52658
51.52437	21.34	16.74	30.0241	0.59812
54.41408	22.91	19.81	48.0864	−2.16509
60.90809	22.96	31.92	48.8132	−7.83017
66.65003	23.69	26.31	60.7642	2.30136
81.31264	24.82	25.93	85.2851	15.47776
58.26339	25.54	21.96	105.8476	−4.80087
54.18337	25.63	24.05	108.7444	−11.11366
77.73936	28.73	25.66	275.6136	5.71998

For the purpose of this example, we will assume that we are in doubt about whether heteroskedasticity exists, but that, if it does exist, we have reason to believe (correctly) that the variances are directly related to x_{t2}. Given this state of knowledge it is convenient to order the observations according to the magnitude of x_{t2} and to begin by finding least squares estimates of the elements of $\boldsymbol{\beta}$.

These are

$$\mathbf{b} = (X'X)^{-1}X'\mathbf{y}$$

$$= \begin{bmatrix} 20.00 & 416.74 & 420.03 \\ 416.74 & 8946.93 & 8925.56 \\ 420.03 & 8925.56 & 9190.06 \end{bmatrix}^{-1} \begin{bmatrix} 1086.9 \\ 23255.6 \\ 23480.8 \end{bmatrix} = \begin{bmatrix} -0.991 \\ 1.651 \\ 0.997 \end{bmatrix} \tag{9.3.58}$$

If we incorrectly assumed that the disturbances are homoskedastic, we would estimate the covariance matrix of $\mathbf{b}$ using $\hat{\sigma}^2(X'X)^{-1}$, where

$$\hat{\sigma}^2 = (\mathbf{y} - X\mathbf{b})'(\mathbf{y} - X\mathbf{b})/17 = 42.787$$

This yields

$$\hat{\Sigma}_{\mathbf{b}} = \hat{\sigma}^2(X'X)^{-1} = \begin{bmatrix} 81.598 & -2.580 & -1.223 \\ -2.580 & 0.235 & -0.111 \\ -1.223 & -0.111 & 0.168 \end{bmatrix} \tag{9.3.59}$$

The square roots of the diagonal elements of this matrix are called the standard errors of the least squares estimates, and it is customary when reporting results to put these in parentheses below the estimated coefficients. Thus our results so far can be reported as

$$\begin{aligned} \mathbf{y} = \underset{(9.033)}{-0.991\mathbf{x}_1} + \underset{(0.485)}{1.651\mathbf{x}_2} + \underset{(0.410)}{0.997\mathbf{x}_3} + \hat{\mathbf{e}} \end{aligned} \tag{9.3.60}$$

Since the real covariance matrix for $\mathbf{b}$ is $\Sigma_{\mathbf{b}} = (X'X)^{-1}X'\Phi X(X'X)^{-1}$, where Φ is a diagonal matrix containing the elements $\sigma_1^2, \sigma_2^2, \ldots, \sigma_T^2$, the estimator $\hat{\Sigma}_{\mathbf{b}}$ is biased, and inferences based on the estimates in (9.3.60) could be misleading. To investigate this possibility, we have calculated the diagonal elements of $\mathbf{\Phi}$ (see the fourth column in Table 9.1), and these lead to the true covariance matrix

$$\Sigma_{\mathbf{b}} = (X'X)^{-1}X'\mathbf{\Phi}X(X'X)^{-1} = \begin{bmatrix} 136.160 & -6.188 & -0.926 \\ -6.188 & 0.431 & -0.100 \\ -0.926 & -0.100 & 0.144 \end{bmatrix} \tag{9.3.61}$$

In practice we can never calculate this matrix because $\mathbf{\Phi}$ is unknown. In this case, however, it is instructive to calculate the matrix because it gives an idea of the errors that might be involved. Comparing the diagonal elements of (9.3.59) with those of (9.3.61) indicates that in this particular sample ignoring heteroskedasticity leads us to underestimate the variances of b_1 and b_2; this is not true for b_3, where the variance estimate is slightly larger than its true value. Thus, if these results persisted in repeated samples (but it should be emphasized that they may not), it would mean that b_1 and b_2 are less reliable than indicated by their standard errors, and b_3 is more reliable.

Because it is best linear unbiased, the generalized least squares estimator $\hat{\boldsymbol{\beta}} = (X'\boldsymbol{\Phi}^{-1}X)^{-1}X'\boldsymbol{\Phi}^{-1}\mathbf{y}$ is more efficient than the least squares estimator. Its covariance matrix is given by

$$\Sigma_{\boldsymbol{\beta}} = (X'\boldsymbol{\Phi}^{-1}X)^{-1} = \begin{bmatrix} 38.978 & -1.156 & -0.939 \\ -1.156 & 0.128 & -0.058 \\ -0.939 & -0.058 & 0.103 \end{bmatrix} \tag{9.3.62}$$

and a comparison of the diagonal elements of this matrix with those in (9.3.61) gives an indication of the inefficiency of least squares. The results obtained using the generalized least squares estimator are

$$\underset{}{\mathbf{y}} = \underset{(6.243)}{0.937\mathbf{x}_1} + \underset{(0.358)}{1.629\mathbf{x}_2} + \underset{(0.321)}{0.926\mathbf{x}_3} + \hat{\mathbf{e}}_g \tag{9.3.63}$$

Note that the generalized least squares estimates for β_1 and β_2 are slightly closer to their respective real parameter values than the least squares estimates b_1 and b_2; but the same is not true for β_3. This result illustrates that although generalized least squares estimates will be better than least squares on average, in any one given sample there is no guarantee that the generalized least squares estimates will be closer to the real parameters than the least squares estimates.

Of course, in practice $\boldsymbol{\Phi}$ is unknown, and the results in (9.3.62) and (9.3.63) cannot be obtained. Consequently, we return now to the more realistic situation in which we have just obtained least squares estimates and we suspect that heteroskedasticity exists. The next step is to test for heteroskedasticity, and for this purpose we illustrate the Breusch–Pagan and Goldfeld–Quandt tests.

From Section 9.3.5c we carry out the Breusch–Pagan test by regressing $(\hat{e}_t^2/\tilde{\sigma}^2)$ on $\mathbf{z}_t'$, where $\hat{e}_t = y_t - \mathbf{x}_t'\mathbf{b}$, $\tilde{\sigma}^2 = \Sigma\hat{e}_t^2/T$, and $\mathbf{z}_t' = (1, x_{t2})$. This specification of $\mathbf{z}_t$ assumes that we suspect that the variances are related to x_{t2} but not to x_{t3}. The least squares residuals are given in the last column in Table 9.1, and, also, note that $\tilde{\sigma}^2 = [(T - K)/T]\hat{\sigma}^2 = 36.3692$. After carrying out the regression we find that the relevant statistic is given by

$$\begin{aligned} q &= \tfrac{1}{2}\,(\text{regression sum of squares}) \\ &= \tfrac{1}{2}\,(47.452 - 39.396) \\ &= 4.03 \end{aligned}$$

Under the null hypothesis of homoskedasticity q has an asymptotic $\chi^2_{(1)}$ distribution, and, at a 5% significance level, the critical value for this test is 3.84. Thus, at a 5% significance level, we would (correctly) conclude that heteroskedasticity exists.

For the Goldfeld–Quandt test we omit the four central observations and run two separate regressions, one on observations 1 to 8 and the other on observations 13 to 20. The residual sums of squares from these regressions are 54.158 and 472.90, respectively, and this result leads to an F statistic given by

$$F = \frac{S_2}{S_1} = \frac{472.90}{54.158} = 8.73$$

At a 5% significance level the critical value for $F_{(5,\ 5)}$ is 5.05, and so, using the Goldfeld–Quandt test, we again conclude that heteroskedasticity does exist.

Assuming that we wish to model the heteroskedasticity as $\sigma_t^2 = \exp(\alpha_1 + \alpha_2 x_{t2})$, the next step is to estimate α_1 and α_2 and use these estimates to obtain an estimated generalized least squares estimator. Employing the estimator discussed earlier in this chapter we have

$$\hat{\boldsymbol{\alpha}} = (Z'Z)^{-1}Z'\mathbf{q} = \begin{bmatrix} 20.00 & 416.74 \\ 416.74 & 8946.93 \end{bmatrix}^{-1} \begin{bmatrix} 39.42 \\ 917.68 \end{bmatrix} = \begin{bmatrix} -5.646 \\ 0.366 \end{bmatrix} \qquad (9.3.64)$$

Although it does not make any difference for the purpose of estimating $\boldsymbol{\beta}$, we may wish to adjust $\hat{\alpha}_1$ by its asymptotic bias. Because $\operatorname{plim} \hat{\alpha}_1 = \alpha_1 - 1.2704$, the estimator $\bar{\alpha}_1 = \hat{\alpha}_1 + 1.2704$ is consistent, and its value in this case is $\bar{\alpha}_1 = -4.376$, an estimate that is somewhat closer to the true parameter value of -3.

After calculating $\exp(\mathbf{z}_t^{*\prime}\hat{\boldsymbol{\alpha}}^*) = \exp(\hat{\alpha}_2 x_{t2})$, $t = 1, 2, \ldots, T$, and transforming $\mathbf{y}$, $\mathbf{x}_1$, $\mathbf{x}_2$, and $\mathbf{x}_3$, we obtain the estimated generalized least squares estimator

$$\begin{aligned} \hat{\hat{\boldsymbol{\beta}}} &= (X'\hat{\boldsymbol{\Psi}}^{-1}X)^{-1}X'\hat{\boldsymbol{\Psi}}^{-1}\mathbf{y} \\ &= \begin{bmatrix} 0.0209 & 0.3581 & 0.3934 \\ 0.3581 & 6.2705 & 6.7972 \\ 0.3924 & 6.7972 & 7.5365 \end{bmatrix}^{-1} \begin{bmatrix} 0.9660 \\ 16.8424 \\ 18.4123 \end{bmatrix} = \begin{bmatrix} 1.010 \\ 1.657 \\ 0.896 \end{bmatrix} \end{aligned} \qquad (9.3.65)$$

Its estimated covariance matrix is

$$\hat{\Sigma}_{\hat{\hat{\boldsymbol{\beta}}}} = \hat{\hat{\sigma}}^2(X'\hat{\boldsymbol{\Psi}}^{-1}X)^{-1} = \begin{bmatrix} 50.271 & -1.487 & -1.276 \\ -1.487 & 0.174 & -0.080 \\ -1.276 & -0.080 & 0.141 \end{bmatrix} \qquad (9.3.66)$$

where $\hat{\hat{\sigma}}^2 = (\mathbf{y} - X\hat{\hat{\boldsymbol{\beta}}})'\hat{\boldsymbol{\Psi}}^{-1}(\mathbf{y} - X\hat{\hat{\boldsymbol{\beta}}})/17$. Reporting the results in the usual way, we have

$$\underset{(7.090)}{\mathbf{y} = 1.010\mathbf{x}_1} + \underset{(0.417)}{1.657\mathbf{x}_2} + \underset{(0.375)}{0.896\mathbf{x}_3} + \hat{\mathbf{e}} \qquad (9.3.67)$$

The coefficient estimates in (9.3.67) are quite similar to the least squares and generalized least squares estimates. However, the standard errors in (9.3.67) appear to be a better reflection of the precision of the estimates than are the corresponding ones provided by least squares.

In this regard it is worth pointing out that we do not really know what sample size is large enough for the asymptotic properties of estimated generalized least squares to be a "good approximation" to the finite sample properties. It is quite possible that $T = 20$ is not large enough. The group exercises in the next section should shed some light on this.

As a final point, while checking the calculations in this example you should keep in mind that all intermediate results reported herein are rounded off. Where these intermediate results are used again for further calculations the numbers as stored in the computer, not their rounded-off versions, are used.

9.4 Exercises on Heteroskedasticity

9.4.1 Algebraic Exercises

9.4.1 For the set up considered in Section 9.3.2, prove that

$$(a)\ (\mathbf{y} - X\boldsymbol{\beta})'\boldsymbol{\Phi}^{-1}(\mathbf{y} - X\boldsymbol{\beta}) = \sum_{t=1}^{T} \left(\frac{e_t}{\sigma_t}\right)^2$$

$$(b)\ (X'\boldsymbol{\Phi}^{-1}X)^{-1}X'\boldsymbol{\Phi}^{-1}\mathbf{y} = \left(\sum_{t=1}^{T} \sigma_t^{-2}\mathbf{x}_t\mathbf{x}_t'\right)^{-1} \sum_{t=1}^{T} \sigma_t^{-2}\mathbf{x}_t y_t$$

9.4.2 For the set up in Section 9.3.3, prove that the generalized least squares estimator for $\boldsymbol{\beta}$ is given by

$$\hat{\boldsymbol{\beta}} = \left(\frac{X_1'X_1}{\sigma_1^2} + \frac{X_2'X_2}{\sigma_2^2}\right)^{-1}\left(\frac{X_1'\mathbf{y}_1}{\sigma_1^2} + \frac{X_2'\mathbf{y}_2}{\sigma_2^2}\right)$$

9.4.3 Consider the linear model

$$\mathbf{y} = X\boldsymbol{\beta} + \mathbf{e} = \mathbf{j}\beta_1 + X_s\boldsymbol{\beta}_s + \mathbf{e}$$

where $X = (\mathbf{j}, X_s)$, $\mathbf{j} = (1, 1, \ldots, 1)'$, $\boldsymbol{\beta}' = (\beta_1, \boldsymbol{\beta}_s')$,

$$E[\mathbf{e}] = \mu\mathbf{j} \quad \text{and} \quad E[(\mathbf{e} - \mu\mathbf{j})(\mathbf{e} - \mu\mathbf{j})'] = \sigma^2 I$$

Prove that the least squares estimator $\mathbf{b} = (X'X)^{-1}X'\mathbf{y}$ has mean

$$E[\mathbf{b}] = \begin{bmatrix} \beta_1 + \mu \\ \boldsymbol{\beta}_s \end{bmatrix}$$

and covariance matrix $\sigma^2(X'X)^{-1}$.

9.4.4 Prove that the following two estimated covariance matrices are identical.

1. $\hat{\hat{\sigma}}^2(X'\hat{\boldsymbol{\Psi}}^{-1}X)^{-1}$

where

$$\hat{\hat{\sigma}}^2 = (\mathbf{y} - X\hat{\hat{\boldsymbol{\beta}}})'\hat{\boldsymbol{\Psi}}^{-1}(\mathbf{y} - X\hat{\hat{\boldsymbol{\beta}}})/(T - K)$$

and

$$\hat{\boldsymbol{\Psi}} = \text{diag}[\exp(\mathbf{z}_1^{*\prime}\boldsymbol{\alpha}^*), \ldots, \exp(\mathbf{z}_T^{*\prime}\hat{\boldsymbol{\alpha}}^*)].$$

2. $\hat{\tau}^2(X'\hat{\boldsymbol{\Phi}}^{-1}X)^{-1}$

where

$$\hat{\tau}^2 = (\mathbf{y} - X\hat{\hat{\boldsymbol{\beta}}})'\hat{\boldsymbol{\Phi}}^{-1}(\mathbf{y} - X\hat{\hat{\boldsymbol{\beta}}})/(T - K)$$

and

$$\hat{\boldsymbol{\Phi}} = \text{diag}[\exp(\mathbf{z}_1'\hat{\boldsymbol{\alpha}}), \ldots, \exp(\mathbf{z}_T'\hat{\boldsymbol{\alpha}})].$$

See Section 9.3.4 for the meaning of the remaining notation.

9.4.5 Consider the model

$$y_t = \mathbf{x}_t'\boldsymbol{\beta} + e_t$$

where

$$E[e_t] = 0, \quad E[e_t e_s] = 0 \quad \text{for } t \neq s$$

and

$$E[e_t^2] = \sigma_t^2 = \exp\{\mathbf{z}_t'\boldsymbol{\alpha}\}.$$

Suppose that

$$\mathbf{y} = \begin{bmatrix} 4 \\ 8 \\ 6 \\ 2 \\ 9 \end{bmatrix} \quad X = \begin{bmatrix} 1 & 2 \\ 1 & 5 \\ 1 & 2 \\ 1 & 1 \\ 1 & 10 \end{bmatrix} \quad Z = \begin{bmatrix} 1 & 2 \\ 1 & 3 \\ 1 & 1 \\ 1 & 0 \\ 1 & 2 \end{bmatrix}$$

The notation is the same as that used in Section 9.3.

(*a*) Find values for the estimators $\mathbf{b}$, $\hat{\boldsymbol{\alpha}}$, and $\hat{\hat{\boldsymbol{\beta}}}$.

(*b*) Construct two 95% confidence intervals for β_2—an inappropriate one that uses the least squares results and an appropriate one that uses the generalized least squares results.

(*c*) Test the hypothesis $\alpha_2 = 0$.

9.4.6 Consider the model

$$y_t = x_t\beta + e_t \qquad t = 1, 2, \ldots, T$$

where x_t is a single explanatory variable, β is a scalar unknown parameter, and

$$E[e_t] = 0, \quad E[e_t^2] = \sigma_t^2, \quad E[e_t e_s] = 0 \quad t \neq s$$

(*a*) Under what assumptions about σ_t^2 is each of the following estimators best linear unbiased?

(i) $\hat{\beta} = \dfrac{\sum x_t y_t}{\sum x_t^2}$

(ii) $\hat{\beta} = \dfrac{\sum y_t}{\sum x_t}$

(iii) $\hat{\beta} = \dfrac{1}{T}\sum\left(\dfrac{y_t}{x_t}\right)$

(*b*) Let $\sigma_t^2 = \sigma^2 x_t^2$ and $\sum x_t^2 = T$. Show that

$$\frac{V(\hat{\beta})}{V(b)} = \frac{T}{\sum x_t^4}$$

where $V(\hat{\beta})$ is the variance of the generalized least squares estimator and $V(b)$ is the variance of the ordinary least squares estimator.

9.4.2 Individual Numerical Exercises

Suppose that you have available Monte Carlo experimental data (see the Computer Handbook) consisting of 100 samples of $\mathbf{y}$, each of size 20, generated using the model

$$y_t = \beta_1 + \beta_2 x_{t2} + \beta_3 x_{t3} + e_t \tag{9.4.1}$$

where the e_t are normally and independently distributed with

$$E[e_t] = 0,\ E[e_t^2] = \sigma_t^2,$$

and

$$\sigma_t^2 = \exp(\alpha_1 + \alpha_2 x_{t2}) \tag{9.4.2}$$

The parameter values are $\beta_1 = 10$, $\beta_2 = 1$, $\beta_3 = 1$, $\alpha_1 = -2$, and $\alpha_2 = 0.25$, and the design matrix, ordered according to the magnitude of x_{t2}, is

$$X = \begin{bmatrix} 1.00 & 14.53 & 16.74 \\ 1.00 & 15.30 & 16.81 \\ 1.00 & 15.92 & 19.50 \\ 1.00 & 17.41 & 22.12 \\ 1.00 & 18.37 & 22.34 \\ 1.00 & 18.83 & 17.47 \\ 1.00 & 18.84 & 20.24 \\ 1.00 & 19.71 & 20.37 \\ 1.00 & 20.01 & 12.71 \\ 1.00 & 20.26 & 22.98 \\ 1.00 & 20.77 & 19.33 \\ 1.00 & 21.17 & 17.04 \\ 1.00 & 21.34 & 16.74 \\ 1.00 & 22.91 & 19.81 \\ 1.00 & 22.96 & 31.92 \\ 1.00 & 23.69 & 26.31 \\ 1.00 & 24.82 & 25.93 \\ 1.00 & 25.54 & 21.96 \\ 1.00 & 25.63 & 24.05 \\ 1.00 & 28.73 & 25.66 \end{bmatrix} \tag{9.4.3}$$

9.4.7 Calculate the covariance matrices for

(*a*) The generalized least squares estimator

$$\hat{\boldsymbol{\beta}} = (X'\boldsymbol{\Phi}^{-1}X)^{-1}X'\boldsymbol{\Phi}^{-1}\mathbf{y}$$

(*b*) The least squares estimator

$$\mathbf{b} = (X'X)^{-1}X'\mathbf{y}$$

(*c*) The generalized least squares estimator that incorrectly assumes that $\sigma_t^2 = \sigma^2 x_{t2}^2$ and that we will denote by $\hat{\boldsymbol{\beta}}^*$. Note that the theoretical expression for the covariance matrix of $\hat{\boldsymbol{\beta}}^*$ was not given earlier in the chapter, so its derivation is the first step toward answering this equation.

Comment on the relative efficiency of the three estimators.

9.4.8 Select five samples from the Monte Carlo data. For each sample compute values for the following estimators.

(*a*) The least squares estimator **b**.

(*b*) The estimator

$$\hat{\boldsymbol{\alpha}} = \left(\sum_{t=1}^{T} \mathbf{z}_t \mathbf{z}_t'\right)^{-1} \sum_{t=1}^{T} \mathbf{z}_t \ln \hat{e}_t^2$$

where $\mathbf{z}_t = (1, x_{t2})'$ and $\hat{e}_t = y_t - \mathbf{x}_t'\mathbf{b}$.

(*c*) The estimated generalized least squares estimator for $\boldsymbol{\beta}$ that uses $\hat{\boldsymbol{\alpha}}$, call it $\hat{\hat{\boldsymbol{\beta}}}$.

(*d*) The generalized least squares estimator $\hat{\boldsymbol{\beta}}^*$ that incorrectly assumes that $\sigma_t^2 = \sigma^2 x_{t2}^2$.

Compare the various estimates with one another and with the true parameter values.

9.4.9 The computer program used in Exercise 9.4.8 to obtain values of the estimators $\mathbf{b}$, $\hat{\hat{\boldsymbol{\beta}}}$, and $\hat{\boldsymbol{\beta}}^*$ is also likely to yield estimates of the covariance matrices of these estimators. In all three cases, however, the variance estimates could be biased. Explain why. Also, taking the parameter β_3 as an example, compare the various estimates of $\widehat{\text{var}}(b_3)$, $\widehat{\text{var}}(\hat{\hat{\beta}}_3)$, and $\widehat{\text{var}}(\hat{\beta}_3^*)$ with the relevant answers in 9.4.7.

9.4.10 Use the results in Exercises 9.4.8 and 9.4.9 to calculate t values that would be used to test

(*a*) $H_0\colon \beta_3 = 0$ against $H_1\colon \beta_3 \neq 0$

(*b*) $H_0\colon \beta_3 = 1$ against $H_1\colon \beta_3 \neq 1$

Since we have three estimators and five samples, this involves, for each hypothesis, the calculation of 15 t values. Keeping in mind the validity or otherwise of each null hypothesis, comment on the results.

9.4.11 Using the same five samples that were used in Exercises 9.4.8 through 9.4.10, test for heteroskedasticity using

(*a*) The Breusch–Pagan test statistic.

(*b*) The Goldfeld–Quandt test with four central observations omitted.

9.4.3 Group Exercises

9.4.12 Repeat Exercise 9.4.8 for all 100 samples and use the results to estimate the mean and mean square error matrix for each estimator. For example, for **b**, estimates of its mean and mean square error matrix are given by

$$\frac{1}{100}\sum_{i=1}^{100}\mathbf{b}(i) \quad \text{and} \quad \frac{1}{100}\sum_{i=1}^{100}[(\mathbf{b}(i)-\boldsymbol{\beta})(\mathbf{b}(i)-\boldsymbol{\beta})']$$

where $\mathbf{b}(i)$ is the least squares estimator from the ith sample. Use these results and those of Exercise 9.4.7 to answer the following questions.

(*a*) Do any of the estimators appear to be biased?

(*b*) By comparing the estimated means and mean square errors of **b** and $\hat{\boldsymbol{\beta}}^*$ with the true ones, comment on the extent of the sampling error in the Monte Carlo experiment.

(*c*) With respect to $\hat{\boldsymbol{\alpha}}$ and $\hat{\hat{\boldsymbol{\beta}}}$, are the approximate covariance matrices, which are based on asymptotic results, good approximations of the finite sample covariance matrices?

(*d*) Does knowledge of the correct form of heteroskedasticity enable more efficient estimation of $\boldsymbol{\beta}$?

(*e*) Based on the estimated mean square error matrices, is the relative efficiency of **b**, $\hat{\hat{\boldsymbol{\beta}}}$, and $\hat{\boldsymbol{\beta}}^*$ what you would expect?

9.4.13 Use all 100 samples to estimate the means of the variance estimators $\text{var}(b_3)$, $\widehat{\text{var}}(\hat{\hat{\beta}}_3)$, and $\widehat{\text{var}}(\hat{\beta}_3^*)$ that were obtained in Exercise 9.4.9. Based on these results and those in Exercise 9.4.7, do you think that (a) ignoring heteroskedasticity or (b) assuming the wrong form of heteroskedasticity, can lead to misleading inferences about β_3?

9.4.14 Repeat Exercise 9.4.10 for all 100 samples and calculate the proportion of Type I and Type II errors that are obtained when (a) a 5% significance level is used and (b) a 10% significance level is used. Do these results support your conclusions in Exercise 9.4.13?

9.4.15 Repeat Exercise 9.4.11 for all 100 samples. Which test, the Breusch–Pagan test or the Goldfeld–Quandt test, appears to be more powerful?

9.5 Autocorrelation

9.5.1 Background and Model

In Section 9.3 we studied the general linear statistical model

$$\mathbf{y} = X\boldsymbol{\beta} + \mathbf{e} \tag{9.5.1}$$

where $\mathbf{y}$ is a $(T \times 1)$ observable random vector, X is a $(T \times K)$ nonstochastic matrix of explantory variables, $\boldsymbol{\beta}$ is a $(K \times 1)$ vector of parameters to be estimated, and $\mathbf{e}$ is a $(T \times 1)$ unobservable random vector with

$$E[\mathbf{e}] = \mathbf{0} \quad \text{and} \quad E[\mathbf{ee}'] = \boldsymbol{\Phi} \tag{9.5.2}$$

In addition, we assumed that $\boldsymbol{\Phi}$ is a diagonal matrix with not all of its diagonal elements equal. We defined this concept as heteroskedasticity and noted that it was one example of how the assumption $E[\mathbf{ee}'] = \sigma^2 I$ is likely to be violated, particularly when using cross-section data.

In this section we are concerned with another example of how the assumption $E[\mathbf{ee}'] = \sigma^2 I$ can be violated. In particular, we are interested in a situation where the sample observations $\mathbf{y}$ and the control variables X occur at different points in time and, consequently, are known as time-series observations. Such observations could be collected for a single economic unit, such as a firm or a household, or they could be aggregate quantities for a whole region or an economy. For example, time-series data on consumption, investment, and income, among other variables, are frequently used to estimate macroeconomic relationships, such as consumption and investment functions.

When the general linear model $\mathbf{y} = X\boldsymbol{\beta} + \mathbf{e}$ is used to describe the generation of data over time, it is common for the relationship to be dynamic in nature. When the effects of changes in economic variables are not instantaneous, this can be captured by specifying a model where (1) y_t depends on past values of itself, (2) X contains current and lagged values of some explanatory variables, and/or (3) the equation error e_t depends on the values of previous errors.

The first condition implies that X is stochastic and is studied under the heading Distributed Lag Models in Chapter 17. The second condition does not require any more assumptions than those made for least squares estimation in Chapters 5 and 6. However, if there are too many lagged variables, it can be advantageous to place restrictions on the coefficients; this aspect is considered in Chapters 17 and 20. The third condition is the one in which we are currently interested; it is known as *autocorrelation.* Its existence implies that the total effect of a random error is not instantaneous, but is also felt in future periods, and, after some reflection, it is clear that this is a reasonable assumption for many economic relationships.

There are many possible forms of autocorrelation, and each one leads to a different structure for the error covariance matrix (see Judge, et al., 1985, Chapter 8, for a review). The most popular form of autocorrelation and one that has proved to be useful in many applications is known as the *first-order autoregressive process.* We will consider this process here.

We write the tth observation on the general linear model as

$$y_t = \mathbf{x}_t'\boldsymbol{\beta} + e_t \tag{9.5.3}$$

where

$$e_t = \rho e_{t-1} + v_t \tag{9.5.4}$$

and, as before, $\mathbf{x}_t' = (x_{t1}, x_{t2}, \ldots, x_{tK})$ is a $(1 \times K)$ vector containing the tth observation on K nonstochastic explanatory variables and $\boldsymbol{\beta}$ is a $(K \times 1)$ vector of coefficients to be estimated. Through (9.5.4) it is assumed that the current disturbance e_t depends on the error in the previous period, e_{t-1}, and on another error, v_t, which is assumed to have 0 mean and constant variance and to be uncorrelated over time. That is,

$$E[v_t] = 0, \quad E[v_t^2] = \sigma_v^2, \quad \text{and} \quad E[v_t v_s] = 0 \qquad \text{for } t \neq s \tag{9.5.5}$$

These assumptions constitute the *general linear statistical model with first-order autoregressive disturbance.* The parameter ρ is unknown, and, along with $\boldsymbol{\beta}$, we may wish to estimate it.

The statistical properties of v_t given in (9.5.5) are identical to those assumed for e_t in Chapters 5 through 7. Thus, if $\mathbf{v}' = (v_1, v_2, \ldots, v_T)$, the properties can be written in matrix notation as

$$E[\mathbf{v}] = \mathbf{0} \quad \text{and} \quad E[\mathbf{v}\mathbf{v}'] = \sigma^2 I \tag{9.5.6}$$

For the purpose of estimating $\boldsymbol{\beta}$, however, we are interested in the statistical properties of e_t, and the mean and covariance matrix for $\mathbf{e} = (e_1, e_2, \ldots, e_T)'$.

To derive these quantities we assume that the process has been operating for a long period into the past and that $|\rho| < 1$. When the condition $|\rho| < 1$ is satisfied, the first-order autoregressive process is *stationary.* A stationary process is such that the mean, the variance, and the covariances of the e_t do not change over time. Under these circumstances it is possible to use recursive substitution or lag operator notation (see Exercise 9.6.1 and Section 16.2.4) to show that

$$\begin{aligned} e_t &= v_t + \rho v_{t-1} + \rho^2 v_{t-2} + \cdots \\ &= \sum_{i=0}^{\infty} \rho^i v_{t-i} \end{aligned} \tag{9.5.7}$$

This equation indicates that the error e_t can be expressed as the weighted sum of a time series of uncorrelated and identically distributed random errors v_t, v_{t-1},

$v_{t-2}, \ldots$, with the weights $1, \rho, \rho^2, \ldots$. These weights decline geometrically with time if $0 < \rho < 1$. This situation implies that the influence of factors that affect **y** and that have not been captured by the X matrix is not felt instantaneously, but is distributed over time. The term e_t consists of the influence of current events (v_t), the influence of events that occurred one period ago (ρv_{t-1}), the influence of events that occurred two periods ago ($\rho^2 v_{t-2}$), and so on. Alternatively, if (9.5.7) is extended into the future as

$$\begin{aligned} e_t &= v_t + \rho v_{t-1} + \rho^2 v_{t-2} + \cdots \\ e_{t+1} &= v_{t+1} + \rho v_t + \rho^2 v_{t-1} + \cdots \\ e_{t+2} &= v_{t+2} + \rho v_{t+1} + \rho^2 v_t + \cdots \\ &\vdots \end{aligned} \tag{9.5.8}$$

we see that, as we go farther into the future, the contribution of a given term, say, v_t, declines. If $0 < \rho < 1$, its contribution will always have the same sign, and if $-1 < \rho < 0$, its contribution will oscillate in sign. If $|\rho| \geq 1$, then, as we progress through time, the variance of e_t increases, eventually becoming infinite. The systematic part of y_t becomes dominated by the disturbance, and the model as it stands is difficult to analyze.

We turn now to the mean and covariance matrix for $\mathbf{e} = (e_1, e_2, \ldots, e_T)'$. From (9.5.7)

$$E[e_t] = \sum_{i=0}^{\infty} \rho^i E[v_{t-i}] = 0 \tag{9.5.9}$$

For the diagonal elements of $E[\mathbf{ee}'] = \mathbf{\Phi}$ we require $\text{var}(e_t)$. Because the process is stationary and the variance does not change over time, taking the variance of both sides of $e_t = \rho e_{t-1} + v_t$ yields

$$\text{var}(e_t) = \rho^2 \, \text{var}(e_{t-1}) + \text{var}(v_t) \tag{9.5.10}$$

or

$$\sigma_e^2 = \rho^2 \sigma_e^2 + \sigma_v^2 \tag{9.5.11}$$

Solving for σ_e^2 yields

$$\sigma_e^2 = \frac{\sigma_v^2}{1 - \rho^2} \tag{9.5.12}$$

The elements in $\mathbf{\Phi}$ adjacent to the diagonal are given by

$$\begin{aligned} E[e_t e_{t-1}] &= \rho E[e_{t-1}^2] + E[e_{t-1} v_t] \\ &= \rho \sigma_e^2 = \frac{\rho \sigma_v^2}{1 - \rho^2} \end{aligned} \tag{9.5.13}$$

The covariance between two errors two periods apart is

$$E[e_t e_{t-2}] = \rho E[e_{t-1} e_{t-2}] + E[e_{t-2} v_t]$$
$$= \rho^2 \sigma_e^2 = \frac{\rho^2 \sigma_v^2}{1 - \rho^2} \qquad (9.5.14)$$

Continuing with this process yields, for two errors s periods apart,

$$E[e_t e_{t-s}] = \rho^s \sigma_e^2 = \frac{\rho^s \sigma_v^2}{1 - \rho^2} \qquad (9.5.15)$$

To derive the correlation between two equation errors s periods apart we divide (9.5.15) by (9.5.12) and obtain

$$\frac{E[e_t e_{t-s}]}{\{E[e_t^2] E[e_{t-s}^2]\}^{1/2}} = \frac{\rho^s \sigma_v^2/(1 - \rho^2)}{\sigma_v^2/(1 - \rho^2)} = \rho^s \qquad (9.5.16)$$

Thus the greater the time interval between two disturbances, the smaller will be the correlation between them.

We are now in a position to write the covariance matrix for $\mathbf{e}$. From (9.5.12) to (9.5.15) it is given by

$$\mathbf{\Phi} = E[\mathbf{ee}'] = E \begin{bmatrix} e_1^2 & e_1 e_2 & \cdots & e_1 e_T \\ e_2 e_1 & e_2^2 & \cdots & e_2 e_T \\ \vdots & \vdots & \ddots & \vdots \\ e_T e_1 & e_T e_2 & \cdots & e_T^2 \end{bmatrix}$$

$$= \frac{\sigma_v^2}{1 - \rho^2} \begin{bmatrix} 1 & \rho & \rho^2 & \cdots & \rho^{T-1} \\ \rho & 1 & \rho & \cdots & \rho^{T-2} \\ \rho^2 & \rho & 1 & \cdots & \rho^{T-3} \\ \vdots & \vdots & \vdots & \ddots & \vdots \\ \rho^{T-1} & \rho^{T-2} & \rho^{T-3} & \cdots & 1 \end{bmatrix} \qquad (9.5.17)$$

In Chapter 8 we wrote $\mathbf{\Phi}$ as $\sigma^2 \mathbf{\Psi}$, where $\mathbf{\Psi}$ was known and σ^2 was unknown. It will be convenient in this section to treat the variance σ_v^2 as the scalar σ^2 and to write, therefore,

$$\mathbf{\Phi} = \sigma_v^2 \mathbf{\Psi} \qquad (9.5.18)$$

where

$$\mathbf{\Psi} = \frac{1}{1 - \rho^2} \begin{bmatrix} 1 & \rho & \cdots & \rho^{T-1} \\ \rho & 1 & \cdots & \rho^{T-2} \\ \vdots & \vdots & \ddots & \vdots \\ \rho^{T-1} & \rho^{T-2} & \cdots & 1 \end{bmatrix} \qquad (9.5.19)$$

Before turning to estimation, we briefly summarize the contents of this section. We have introduced the general linear statistical model $\mathbf{y} = X\boldsymbol{\beta} + \mathbf{e}$ with a first-order autoregressive error $e_t = \rho e_{t-1} + v_t$, and we have indicated that it is frequently a reasonable model when time-series data are being used. The nature of the model's disturbance term was described, and its properties were derived. In particular, we showed that the correlation between two errors s periods apart is given by ρ^s, which means that the error covariance matrix $E[\mathbf{ee}'] = \boldsymbol{\Phi}$ does not have zeros as the off-diagonal elements and hence that it cannot be written as $\sigma^2 I$. Consequently, it is an example of the general linear statistical model with a general covariance matrix. When ρ and hence $\boldsymbol{\Psi}$ is known, the results outlined in Chapter 8 are relevant. Furthermore, the properties of least squares reiterated in Section 9.1 hold, as do the results on estimated generalized least squares given in Section 9.2 for the case where $\boldsymbol{\Psi}$ is unknown. In the remainder of this section we specialize and extend these previous results for the definition of $\boldsymbol{\Psi}$ given in (9.5.19).

9.5.2 Estimation

In this section we are concerned with estimation of the $(K \times 1)$ parameter vector $\boldsymbol{\beta}$ in the model

$$\mathbf{y} = X\boldsymbol{\beta} + \mathbf{e} \tag{9.5.20}$$

where $\mathbf{y}$, X, and $\mathbf{e}$ have their earlier definitions, $\mathbf{e}$ has the properties

$$E[\mathbf{e}] = \mathbf{0}, \quad E[\mathbf{ee}'] = \boldsymbol{\Phi} = \sigma_v^2 \boldsymbol{\Psi} \tag{9.5.21}$$

$$\boldsymbol{\Psi} = \frac{1}{1-\rho^2} \begin{bmatrix} 1 & \rho & \cdots & \rho^{T-1} \\ \rho & 1 & \cdots & \rho^{T-2} \\ \vdots & \vdots & & \vdots \\ \rho^{T-1} & \rho^{T-2} & \cdots & 1 \end{bmatrix} \tag{9.5.22}$$

the tth element of $\mathbf{e}$ is given by

$$e_t = \rho e_{t-1} + v_t \tag{9.5.23}$$

and $\mathbf{v} = (v_1, v_2, \ldots, v_T)'$ has the properties

$$E[\mathbf{v}] = \mathbf{0}, \quad E[\mathbf{vv}'] = \sigma_v^2 I \tag{9.5.24}$$

The inefficiency of the least squares estimator $\mathbf{b} = (X'X)^{-1}X'\mathbf{y}$ and the bias of the least squares covariance matrix estimator $\hat{\sigma}^2(X'X)^{-1}$ have received a great deal of attention for this model. See Judge, et al. (1985, pp. 278–282) for a review of this research. The results depend heavily on the X matrix, so it is hard to generalize. For some X matrices $\mathbf{b}$ can be as efficient as generalized least squares, but for others, its relative efficiency can be extremely poor. Also, we cannot generalize about the direction of the bias when $\hat{\sigma}^2(X'X)^{-1}$ is used to estimate $\sigma^2(X'X)^{-1}X'\mathbf{\Psi}X(X'X)^{-1}$. However, if we have a model with one explanatory variable, this variable is positively autocorrelated, and ρ is positive, then it can be shown that the least squares variance estimator is biased downward and the bias can be substantial. If these circumstances hold and autocorrelation goes undetected, we are likely to overstate the reliability of our coefficient estimates.

Because the presence of autocorrelation will, in general, have adverse effects on least squares procedures, it is desirable to use alternative methods of estimation. We will first consider generalized least squares and then estimated generalized least squares. Two other alternatives, nonlinear least squares and maximum likelihood, will be considered in Chapter 12.

9.5.2a Generalized Least Squares Estimation

From Chapter 8 we know that when ρ is a *known* parameter, the generalized least squares estimator is best linear unbiased and it is given by

$$\hat{\boldsymbol{\beta}} = (X'\mathbf{\Psi}^{-1}X)^{-1}X'\mathbf{\Psi}^{-1}\mathbf{y} \tag{9.5.25}$$

Also, we can calculate $\hat{\boldsymbol{\beta}}$ using the following steps.

1. Find a matrix P such that $P'P = \mathbf{\Psi}^{-1}$.
2. Calculate the transformed observations $\mathbf{y}^* = P\mathbf{y}$ and $X^* = PX$.
3. Apply least squares to the transformed model

$$\mathbf{y}^* = X^*\boldsymbol{\beta} + \mathbf{e}^* \tag{9.5.26}$$

where $\mathbf{e}^* = P\mathbf{e}$, to obtain the generalized least squares estimator

$$\hat{\boldsymbol{\beta}} = (X^{*\prime}X^*)^{-1}X^{*\prime}\mathbf{y}^* \tag{9.5.27}$$

This estimator is identical to the one in (9.5.25). To find the transformation matrix P, we first need to specify the inverse of $\mathbf{\Psi}$. Using direct multiplication (Exercise 9.6.2), it can be shown that

$$\mathbf{\Psi}^{-1} = \begin{bmatrix} 1 & -\rho & 0 & \cdots & 0 & 0 \\ -\rho & 1+\rho^2 & -\rho & \cdots & 0 & 0 \\ 0 & -\rho & 1+\rho^2 & \cdots & 0 & 0 \\ \vdots & \vdots & \vdots & & \vdots & \vdots \\ 0 & 0 & 0 & \cdots & 1+\rho^2 & -\rho \\ 0 & 0 & 0 & \cdots & -\rho & 1 \end{bmatrix} \tag{9.5.28}$$

Then it is possible to show that the appropriate transformation matrix is

$$P = \begin{bmatrix} \sqrt{1-\rho^2} & 0 & 0 & \cdots & 0 & 0 \\ -\rho & 1 & 0 & \cdots & 0 & 0 \\ 0 & -\rho & 1 & \cdots & 0 & 0 \\ \vdots & \vdots & \vdots & & \vdots & \vdots \\ 0 & 0 & 0 & \cdots & 1 & 0 \\ 0 & 0 & 0 & \cdots & -\rho & 1 \end{bmatrix} \tag{9.5.29}$$

Applying this matrix to $\mathbf{y}$ and X leads to the following set of transformed observations.

$$\mathbf{y}^* = \begin{bmatrix} \sqrt{1-\rho^2}\, y_1 \\ y_2 - \rho y_1 \\ y_3 - \rho y_2 \\ \vdots \\ y_T - \rho y_{T-1} \end{bmatrix}$$

$$X^* = \begin{bmatrix} \sqrt{1-\rho^2} & \sqrt{1-\rho^2}\, x_{12} & \cdots & \sqrt{1-\rho^2}\, x_{1K} \\ 1-\rho & x_{22} - \rho x_{12} & \cdots & x_{2K} - \rho x_{1K} \\ 1-\rho & x_{32} - \rho x_{22} & \cdots & x_{3K} - \rho x_{2K} \\ \vdots & \vdots & \ddots & \vdots \\ 1-\rho & x_{T2} - \rho x_{T-1,2} & \cdots & x_{TK} - \rho x_{T-1,K} \end{bmatrix} \tag{9.5.30}$$

As listed in step 3, the generalized least squares estimator is obtained by applying the usual least squares procedures to these transformed observations. Note that the first observation is treated differently from the remainder. The transformed model for the first observation is given by

$$\sqrt{1-\rho^2}\, y_1 = \sqrt{1-\rho^2}\, \mathbf{x}_1'\boldsymbol{\beta} + e_1^* \tag{9.5.31}$$

where $e_1^* = \sqrt{1-\rho^2}\, e_1$, whereas for the others it is given by

$$y_t - \rho y_{t-1} = (\mathbf{x}_t - \rho \mathbf{x}_{t-1})'\boldsymbol{\beta} + v_t \tag{9.5.32}$$

where $v_t = e_t - \rho e_{t-1}$, $t = 2, 3, \ldots, T$.

It can be shown that e_1^* has 0 mean, the same variance as $v_1 = e_1 - \rho e_0$, and is uncorrelated with $v_2, \ldots, v_T$. Thus, as we would expect, the errors in (9.5.31) and (9.5.32) will be uncorrelated and homoskedastic, and the least squares estimator applied to those equations will be best linear unbiased.

The covariance matrix for $\hat{\boldsymbol{\beta}}$ is given by

$$\Sigma_{\hat{\boldsymbol{\beta}}} = \sigma_v^2(X^{*\prime}X^*)^{-1} = \sigma_v^2(X'\Psi^{-1}X)^{-1} \tag{9.5.33}$$

An estimate of this covariance matrix is given by $\hat{\sigma}_v^2(X'\Psi^{-1}X)^{-1}$, where

$$\hat{\sigma}_v^2 = \frac{(\mathbf{y}^* - X^*\hat{\boldsymbol{\beta}})'(\mathbf{y}^* - X^*\hat{\boldsymbol{\beta}})}{T - K}$$

$$= \frac{(\mathbf{y} - X\hat{\boldsymbol{\beta}})'\Psi^{-1}(\mathbf{y} - X\hat{\boldsymbol{\beta}})}{T - K} \tag{9.5.34}$$

If the unrealistic assumption of known ρ was in fact true, then $\hat{\boldsymbol{\beta}}$ and $\Sigma_{\hat{\boldsymbol{\beta}}} = \hat{\sigma}_v^2(X'\Psi^{-1}X)^{-1}$ could be used to construct interval estimates and hypothesis tests along the lines described in Chapter 8.

In early work (Cochrane and Orcutt, 1949) using the general linear model with first-order autoregressive errors it was common to drop the transformed first observation given in (9.5.31) and to estimate $\boldsymbol{\beta}$ from the remaining $(T - 1)$ transformed observations given by (9.5.32). This process is equivalent to (1) defining a $[(T - 1) \times T]$ transformation matrix P_0, which is equal to P with its first row deleted, (2) obtaining the transformed observations $\mathbf{y}_0^* = P_0\mathbf{y}$ and $X_0^* = P_0X$, and (3) calculating the least squares estimator

$$\hat{\boldsymbol{\beta}}_0 = (X_0^{*\prime}X_0^*)^{-1}X_0^{*\prime}\mathbf{y}_0^* \tag{9.5.35}$$

Because $P_0'P_0 \neq \Psi^{-1}$, this is only an approximate generalized least squares estimator, and it will not be as efficient as the estimator $\hat{\boldsymbol{\beta}}$, which uses all T observations. See Exercises 9.6.3 and 9.6.4 for further information.

9.5.2b Estimated Generalized Least Squares Estimation

In real-world problems ρ is not known, and the techniques described in the previous section cannot be employed. We can, however, obtain an estimator for ρ, say $\hat{\rho}$, and use this estimator in place of the actual parameter. The estimated ρ can be used to calculate the transformed observations in (9.5.30), and the application of least squares to the transformed observations yields the *estimated generalized least squares estimator*

$$\hat{\hat{\boldsymbol{\beta}}} = (X'\hat{P}'\hat{P}X)^{-1}X'\hat{P}'\hat{P}\mathbf{y} = (X'\hat{\Psi}^{-1}X)^{-1}X'\hat{\Psi}^{-1}\mathbf{y} \tag{9.5.36}$$

where $\hat{P}$ and $\hat{\Psi}^{-1}$ are, respectively, the matrices P and Ψ^{-1} (Equations 9.5.29 and 9.5.28) with ρ replaced by $\hat{\rho}$. Also, using obvious definitions, we can define an approximate estimated generalized least squares estimator as

$$\hat{\hat{\boldsymbol{\beta}}}_0 = (X'\hat{P}_0'\hat{P}_0X)^{-1}X'\hat{P}_0'\hat{P}_0\mathbf{y} \tag{9.5.37}$$

The first problem is to estimate ρ. For this purpose we note that if the disturbances (e_t's) were known, then ρ could be treated as a coefficient in the linear model

$$e_t = \rho e_{t-1} + v_t \qquad t = 2, 3, \ldots, T \tag{9.5.38}$$

This suggests that if we replace the e_t by the least squares residuals $\hat{e}_t = y_t - \mathbf{x}_t'\mathbf{b} = y_t - \mathbf{x}_t'(X'X)^{-1}X'\mathbf{y}$, we will have an operational model for estimating ρ. This model is

$$\hat{e}_t = \rho\hat{e}_{t-1} + \hat{v}_t \tag{9.5.39}$$

and the least squares estimator for ρ obtained from it is

$$\hat{\rho} = \frac{\sum_{t=2}^{T} \hat{e}_t\hat{e}_{t-1}}{\sum_{t=2}^{T} \hat{e}_{t-1}^2} \tag{9.5.40}$$

Under some assumptions about the limiting behavior of the explanatory variables it is possible to show that $\hat{\rho}$ is a consistent estimator for ρ.

When ρ is replaced by $\hat{\rho}$ and, correspondingly, the generalized least squares estimator $\hat{\boldsymbol{\beta}}$ is replaced by the estimated generalized least squares estimator $\hat{\hat{\boldsymbol{\beta}}}$, the best linear unbiased property is no longer retained. The finite sample properties of $\hat{\hat{\boldsymbol{\beta}}}$ are unknown at present, so we are forced to rely on its asymptotic properties and to hope that these are a reasonable approximation in finite samples.

Under the conditions in (9.2.8) through (9.2.11) we can show that $\hat{\hat{\boldsymbol{\beta}}}$ and $\hat{\boldsymbol{\beta}}$ have the same asymptotic distribution. In particular, $\sqrt{T}(\hat{\hat{\boldsymbol{\beta}}} - \boldsymbol{\beta})$ will be asymptotically normal with mean vector $\mathbf{0}$ and covariance matrix $\sigma_v^2 V^{-1} = \sigma_v^2 \lim[T(X'\boldsymbol{\Psi}^{-1}X)^{-1}]$. This information can be used to construct approximate confidence intervals and to carry out approximate hypothesis tests provided that the unknown matrix $\sigma_v^2 V^{-1}$ is replaced with a consistent estimator, such as $\hat{\hat{\sigma}}_v^2 T(X'\hat{\boldsymbol{\Psi}}^{-1}X)^{-1}$, where

$$\hat{\hat{\sigma}}_v^2 = \frac{(\mathbf{y} - X\hat{\hat{\boldsymbol{\beta}}})'\hat{\boldsymbol{\Psi}}^{-1}(\mathbf{y} - X\hat{\hat{\boldsymbol{\beta}}})}{T - K} \tag{9.5.41}$$

This variance estimator is the usual one obtained when a least squares computer package is applied to the transformed observations.

9.5.2c Other Estimators

A large number of alternative estimation procedures for the first-order autoregressive error model have appeared in the literature. All the suggested estimators for $\boldsymbol{\beta}$ are of the estimated generalized least squares type given in (9.5.36) or the approximate alternative which discards the first observation (9.5.37). Where the estimators differ is in the procedure for estimating ρ; different estimates for ρ will, of course, lead to different values for $\hat{\hat{\boldsymbol{\beta}}}$ and $\hat{\hat{\boldsymbol{\beta}}}_0$. A discussion of some of the alternative estimators follows; for a more complete review see Judge, et al. (1985, Chapter 8).

Historically, the first estimator suggested was by Cochrane and Orcutt (1949). Their procedure was an iterative one where the estimate for ρ given in (9.5.40) was first used to form the estimator $\hat{\hat{\boldsymbol{\beta}}}_0$ given in (9.5.37). Then, another set of residuals

$\tilde{\mathbf{e}} = \mathbf{y} - X\hat{\hat{\boldsymbol{\beta}}}_0$ was computed, these residuals are used to re-estimate ρ as in (9.5.40), $\boldsymbol{\beta}$ was re-estimated using (9.5.37), another set of residuals was obtained, and so on until convergence occurred. There have been a number of developments since the days of Cochrane and Orcutt, but the terms "Cochrane–Orcutt estimator" or "Cochrane–Orcutt procedure" are still common place. Unfortunately, the terms are often used in different ways by different authors. To some, the distinguishing feature of the Cochrane–Orcutt procedure was that it omitted the first transformed observation in the estimation of $\boldsymbol{\beta}$, a feature that has since been recognized as undesirable because of the resulting loss in efficiency. Thus, the term Cochrane–Orcutt estimator is often used to refer to estimators that drop the first observation. A distinction is sometimes made between the "two-step" Cochrane–Orcutt estimator, which is given by (9.5.37) and is based on the first estimate of ρ, and the "iterative" Cochrane–Orcutt estimator, which is the original iterative estimator described in Section 9.5.2b.

Other authors have treated the iterative nature of the Cochrane–Orcutt estimator as its distinguishing feature. Consequently, iterative procedures based on slight modifications of the original iterative procedure are also sometimes referred to as Cochrane–Orcutt procedures. In particular, the iterative procedure with the first transformed observation *included* is sometimes called the Cochrane–Orcutt procedure. An important reference that falls into this category is the SHAZAM manual and program (White, Haun and Horsman, 1987). The SHAZAM manual also refers to an iterative maximum likelihood procedure as a modified Cochrane–Orcutt procedure. Iterative Cochrane–Orcutt and maximum likelihood estimators are discussed in more detail in Chapter 12. The purpose of the foregoing discussion is to point out that the econometric profession has used the term "Cochrane–Orcutt estimator" ambiguously, and hence that caution should be exercised when reading the literature.

In finite samples all the preceding estimators tend to underestimate ρ and such underestimation can have serious consequences for finite sample confidence interval estimation when X contains some trended explanatory variables. See Griffiths and Beesley (1984) for the results of some Monte Carlo experiments that illustrate this fact. To try and alleviate the problem, some attempts have been made to adjust the estimator $\hat{\rho}$ given in (9.5.40). For the case where there is one explanatory variable, and $X\boldsymbol{\beta}$ is a polynomial of degree m in this explanatory variable, Beesley, Doran, and Griffiths (1987) have evaluated the adjusted estimator

$$\hat{\hat{\rho}} = \hat{\rho} + T^{-1}[(m + 1)(1 + \hat{\rho}) + 2\hat{\rho}] \qquad (9.5.42)$$

This estimator did lead to a considerable improvement in the accuracy of finite sample confidence interval estimation for $\boldsymbol{\beta}$, but for $T = 50$ and $\rho > 0.9$, there was still room for further improvement.

9.5.3 Testing for First-Order Autoregressive Errors

When using time-series data to estimate an economic relationship, it is difficult to know in advance whether the assumption of a first-order autoregressive error is reasonable, and, therefore, it is difficult to know a priori whether the estimation techniques described in the previous section should be employed. To establish whether or not autocorrelation is likely to exist, the null hypothesis $H_0: \rho = 0$ can be tested against the alternative $H_1: \rho \neq 0$ or a one-sided alternative. Rejection of H_0 suggests that the techniques in the previous section should be used, whereas acceptance of H_0 implies that the least squares techniques of Chapter 6 are adequate.

9.5.3a An Asymptotic Test

Under suitable assumptions it can be shown that $\hat{\rho}$ will be approximately normal with mean ρ and variance $(1 - \rho^2)/T$. Thus, the quantity

$$z = \frac{\hat{\rho} - \rho}{\sqrt{(1 - \rho^2)/T}} \tag{9.5.43}$$

will have an approximate standard normal distribution. If the null hypothesis is true, this statistic becomes

$$z = \sqrt{T}\hat{\rho} \tag{9.5.44}$$

and, consequently, at the 5% significance level, in a two-sided test, we reject H_0 if

$$|\sqrt{T}\hat{\rho}| \geq 1.96$$

9.5.3b The Durbin–Watson Test

The foregoing test provides a quick means for assessing the likelihood of autocorrelation, but because it is only an asymptotic test, it may not be an accurate guide in finite samples; furthermore it is not as powerful as the common finite sample alternative, the Durbin–Watson test. The Durbin–Watson test was developed by Durbin and Watson (1950, 1951, 1971) and is based on the statistic

$$d = \frac{\sum_{t=2}^{T} (\hat{e}_t - \hat{e}_{t-1})^2}{\sum_{t=1}^{T} \hat{e}_t^2} = \frac{\hat{\mathbf{e}}' A \hat{\mathbf{e}}}{\hat{\mathbf{e}}'\hat{\mathbf{e}}} \tag{9.5.45}$$

where $\hat{\mathbf{e}} = (\hat{e}_1, \hat{e}_2, \ldots, \hat{e}_T)' = \mathbf{y} - X\mathbf{b}$ is the vector of least squares residuals and

$$A = \begin{bmatrix} 1 & -1 & 0 & \cdots & 0 & 0 \\ -1 & 2 & -1 & \cdots & 0 & 0 \\ 0 & -1 & 2 & \cdots & 0 & 0 \\ \vdots & \vdots & \vdots & & \vdots & \vdots \\ 0 & 0 & 0 & \cdots & 2 & -1 \\ 0 & 0 & 0 & \cdots & -1 & 1 \end{bmatrix} \tag{9.5.46}$$

It can be shown that $0 < d < 4$; a value of d close to 0 indicates positive autocorrelation ($\rho > 0$), a value close to 4 indicates negative autocorrelation ($\rho < 0$), and a value around 2 suggests no autocorrelation ($\rho = 0$). To appreciate this relationship between d and the level of autocorrelation, it is useful to derive an approximate relationship between d and the estimated correlation coefficient $\hat{\rho}$. Expanding (9.5.45) yields

$$\begin{aligned} d &= \frac{\sum_{t=2}^{T} \hat{e}_t^2 + \sum_{t=2}^{T} \hat{e}_{t-1}^2 - 2\sum_{t=2}^{T} \hat{e}_t \hat{e}_{t-1}}{\hat{\mathbf{e}}'\hat{\mathbf{e}}} \\ &= \frac{\hat{\mathbf{e}}'\hat{\mathbf{e}} + \hat{\mathbf{e}}'\hat{\mathbf{e}} - 2\sum_{t=2}^{T} \hat{e}_t \hat{e}_{t-1} - \hat{e}_1^2 - \hat{e}_T^2}{\hat{\mathbf{e}}'\hat{\mathbf{e}}} \\ &= 2 - 2\gamma_1 \hat{\rho} - \gamma_2 \end{aligned} \tag{9.5.47}$$

where

$$\gamma_1 = \frac{\sum_{t=2}^{T} \hat{e}_{t-1}^2}{\hat{\mathbf{e}}'\hat{\mathbf{e}}} \quad \text{and} \quad \gamma_2 = \frac{\hat{e}_1^2 + \hat{e}_T^2}{\hat{\mathbf{e}}'\hat{\mathbf{e}}} \tag{9.5.48}$$

When T is large, $\gamma_1 \approx 1$ and $\gamma_2 \approx 0$, which leads to

$$d \approx 2 - 2\hat{\rho} \quad \text{or} \quad \hat{\rho} \approx 1 - \tfrac{1}{2}d \tag{9.5.49}$$

Sometimes, $1 - d/2$ is used as an alternative estimator for ρ.

The result in (9.5.49) suggests that when $\hat{\rho}$ is close to 0, indicating no autocorrelation, d will be close to 2. Also, as $\hat{\rho}$ approaches 1, indicating positive autocorrelation, d will approach 0; and as $\hat{\rho}$ approaches -1, d will approach 4. Therefore, if we were testing the null hypothesis $\rho = 0$ against the alternative $\rho > 0$, we would expect to reject the null hypothesis if $d < c$, where c is some critical value. Alternatively, if the alternative hypothesis were $\rho < 0$, we would expect to reject the null hypothesis if d were greater than some critical value. To establish the appropriate critical values, we require knowledge of the probability distribution of d under the assumption that $\rho = 0$. It is to this question that we now turn. We will assume that $\mathbf{e}$ is a normally distributed random vector.

From Chapter 6 we know that

$$\hat{\mathbf{e}} = [I - X(X'X)^{-1}X']\mathbf{e} = M\mathbf{e} \tag{9.5.50}$$

which implies that

$$d = \frac{\mathbf{e}'MAM\mathbf{e}}{\mathbf{e}'M\mathbf{e}} \tag{9.5.51}$$

and thus d can be expressed in terms of the ratio of two quadratic forms, both of which contain the disturbance vector $\mathbf{e}$. However, unlike the cases considered in Chapter 6, the numerator does not have a χ^2 distribution, and the numerator and denominator are not independent. Another expression for d that can be derived, and that is useful for numerically computing the probability distribution of d, is

$$d = \frac{\sum_{i=1}^{T-K} \theta_i z_i^2}{\sum_{i=1}^{T-K} z_i^2} \tag{9.5.52}$$

where $\theta_1, \theta_2, \ldots, \theta_{T-K}$ are the nonzero characteristic roots of MA, and the z_i are independent standard normal random variables. In (9.5.52) d is expressed as the ratio of a weighted sum of squares of $(T - K)$ standard normal random variables to the unweighted sum of squares of the same $(T - K)$ standard normal random variables. The probability distribution of this quantity can be derived numerically for given θ_i. See, for example, Imhof (1961). Once the probability distribution has been derived, appropriate critical values or critical regions for accepting or rejecting H_0 can be established.

A problem arises, however, because the θ_i depend on the matrix of explanatory variables X. For each possible X there will be a different set of θ_i, a different probability distribution for d, and hence different critical values for the test. Unlike more conventional tests based on normal, t-, χ^2-, or F-distributions, it is impossible to tabulate critical values that are relevant for all problems. There are a number of possible solutions to this dilemma. The easiest solution is to use a computer program such as SHAZAM (White 1978, White and Horsman 1986) that will compute the appropriate tail probability. If the computed value of the Durbin–Watson statistic is (say) $\bar{d}$, then SHAZAM will compute $F(\bar{d})$ where F is the distribution function of the Durbin–Watson statistic d under $H_0\colon \rho = 0$. In other words, SHAZAM finds $P[d \leq \bar{d} | H_0\colon \rho = 0]$. If the alternative hypothesis is $H_1\colon \rho > 0$, and a 5% significance level is being employed, then H_0 will be rejected when this probability is less than 0.05. If the 5% significance level is retained, but the alternative hypothesis is $H_1\colon \rho \neq 0$, then H_0 will be rejected if the probability is less than 0.025 or greater than 0.975.

At the time when Durbin and Watson first suggested their test, computing was not sufficiently advanced for the automatic computation of appropriate tail probabilities. As a partial solution, they considered two other statistics, d_L and d_U, which do not depend on X, and which always bound d, whatever the X matrix under consideration. They derived the probability distributions of d_L and d_U and tabulated critical values d_L^* and d_U^* for each of these statistics. For example, if the alternative hypothesis is $H_1: \rho > 0$, and a 5% significance level is employed, d_L^* and d_U^* would be such that

$$P[d_U < d_U^*] = 0.05 \quad \text{and} \quad P[d_L < d_L^*] = 0.05 \tag{9.5.53}$$

These critical values, which depend only on T and K, are given in Table 5 at the end of this book.

To see how the values d_L and d_U can help, let us assume that we are testing the null hypothesis $\rho = 0$ against the alternative $\rho > 0$ and that we wish to use a 5% significance level. Ideally, we would like to find a value d^* such that $P[d < d^*] = 0.05$. Then, if our calculated value for d is less than d^*, we would reject the null hypothesis; otherwise we would accept it. Unfortunately, as we have already seen, d^* depends on X, so it is impossible to tabulate d^* values that are suitable for all problems. However, assuming that we have tabulated values for d_L^* and d_U^*, we can take advantage of the relationship between d, d_L, and d_U to establish what is known as the bounds test. To describe the bounds test we first note that, because $d_L \le d \le d_U$, it is possible to show that

$$P[d < d_L^*] \le P[d < d^*] = 0.05 \le P[d < d_U^*] \tag{9.5.54}$$

This result, illustrated in Figure 9.3, means that if we find a calculated value of d, for example, $\bar{d}$, such that $\bar{d} < d_L^*$, then $\bar{d}$ will certainly be less than d^*, so we would reject the null hypothesis. On the other hand, if $\bar{d} > d_U^*$, then it must also be greater than d^*, in which case we would accept the null hypothesis. However, when $d_L^* < \bar{d} < d_U^*$, it is impossible, without obtaining information about d^*, to determine whether $\bar{d} < d^*$ or $\bar{d} > d^*$. In these circumstances, the bounds test is regarded as inconclusive.

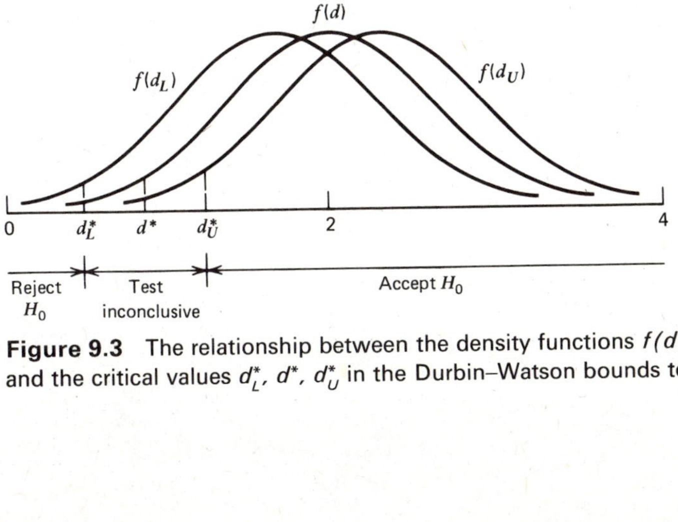

Figure 9.3 The relationship between the density functions $f(d_L)$, $f(d)$, and $f(d_U)$ and the critical values d_L^*, d^*, d_U^* in the Durbin–Watson bounds test.

As already indicated, the easiest solution to an inconclusive bounds test is to use a program (such as SHAZAM) that computes the tail probability associated with $\bar{d}$. If such software is not available, then an approximation suggested by Durbin and Watson (1971) can be used. In this approximation d^* is found from

$$d^* = a + bd_U^* \tag{9.5.55}$$

where a and b are chosen such that

$$E[d] = a + bE[d_U] \tag{9.5.56}$$

and

$$\text{var}[d] = b^2 \text{ var}[d_U] \tag{9.5.57}$$

To calculate a and b we need $E[d]$, $\text{var}[d]$, $E[d_U]$, and $\text{var}[d_U]$. Values for the latter two quantities, $E[d_U]$ and $\text{var}[d_U]$, for different values of T and K, are provided in Table 6 at the end of this book. The quantities $E[d]$ and $\text{var}[d]$ will depend on the X matrix of the problem under consideration and, consequently, need to be calculated for any problem where the $d^* = a + bd_U^*$ approximation is to be implemented. Fortunately, these calculations are not difficult, and it should be relatively straightforward to incorporate them into most least squares computer programs. It can be shown that

$$E[d] = \frac{P}{T - K} \tag{9.5.58}$$

and

$$\text{var}[d] = \frac{2}{(T - K)(T - K + 2)}(Q - PE[d]) \tag{9.5.59}$$

where

$$P = 2(T - 1) - \text{tr}[X'AX(X'X)^{-1}] \tag{9.5.60}$$

and

$$Q = 2(3T - 4) - 2\,\text{tr}[X'A^2X(X'X)^{-1}] + \text{tr}[\{X'AX(X'X)^{-1}\}^2] \tag{9.5.61}$$

If Δ is the first difference operator such that $\Delta x_{ti} = x_{t+1,i} - x_{ti}$, then the (i, j)th element of $X'AX$ is

$$\sum_{t=1}^{T-1} \Delta x_{ti} \Delta x_{tj}$$

whereas that for $X'A^2X$ is

$$\sum_{t=1}^{T-2} \Delta^2 x_{ti} \Delta^2 x_{tj} + (x_{2i} - x_{1i})(x_{2j} - x_{1j}) + (x_{Ti} - x_{T-1,i})(x_{Tj} - x_{T-1,j}).$$

To summarize, the easiest way to test for autocorrelation is to use a computer program that will compute $P[d < \bar{d} | H_0: \rho = 0]$. For testing the null hypothesis of no autocorrelation ($H_0: \rho = 0$) against the alternative of positive autocorrelation ($H_1: \rho > 0$), the null hypothesis is rejected if this probability is less than the chosen level of significance. If appropriate software is not available the steps are

1. Obtain the least squares estimator $\mathbf{b} = (X'X)^{-1}X'\mathbf{y}$ and the corresponding residuals $\hat{\mathbf{e}} = \mathbf{y} - X\mathbf{b}$.
2. Calculate the corresponding value of the Durbin–Watson statistic $\bar{d} = \hat{\mathbf{e}}'A\hat{\mathbf{e}}/\hat{\mathbf{e}}'\hat{\mathbf{e}}$.
3. Choose a significance level and find, from the tables, the critical values d_L^* and d_U^* that correspond to this significance level.
4. If $\bar{d} < d_L^*$, reject H_0; and if $\bar{d} > d_U^*$, accept H_0.
5. If $d_L^* < \bar{d} < d_U^*$, use tabulated values of $E[d_U]$ and $\text{var}[d_U]$ and computed values of $E[d]$ and $\text{var}[d]$ to find a and b such that (9.5.56) and (9.5.57) hold.
6. Calculate $d^* = a + bd_U^*$.
7. If $\bar{d} < d^*$, reject H_0; otherwise, accept H_0.

If the alternative hypothesis is one of negative autocorrelation ($H_1: \rho < 0$), steps 4 through 7 are replaced by

4*. If $\bar{d} > 4 - d_L$, reject H_0; and if $\bar{d} < 4 - d_U^*$, accept H_0.
5*. If $4 - d_U^* < \bar{d} < 4 - d_L^*$, calculate a and b as in step 5.
6*. Calculate $d^{**} = a + b(4 - d_L^*)$.
7*. If $\bar{d} > d^{**}$, reject H_0; otherwise, accept H_0.

As a final point we note that there are some circumstances, for example when X does not contain an intercept, when the power of the Durbin–Watson test can be very low (see Krämer, 1985).

9.5.3c An Example

The following sample data will be used to illustrate how to test for autocorrelation.

$$\mathbf{y}' = (4 \quad 7 \quad 7.5 \quad 4 \quad 2 \quad 3 \quad 5 \quad 4.5 \quad 7.5 \quad 5)$$

$$X' = \begin{bmatrix} 1 & 1 & 1 & 1 & 1 & 1 & 1 & 1 & 1 & 1 \\ 2 & 4 & 6 & 3 & 1 & 2 & 3 & 4 & 8 & 6 \end{bmatrix}$$

Considering first the asymptotic test outlined in Section 9.5.3a, we find that

$$z = \sqrt{T}\hat{\rho} = \sqrt{10} \times 0.4639 = 1.467 < 1.645$$

Thus, if a 5% significance level is used, and we are testing the null hypothesis $H_0: \rho = 0$ against the one-sided alternative $H_1: \rho > 0$, the null hypothesis of no autocorrelation cannot be rejected.

Turning to the Durbin–Watson test, we find that $\bar{d} = 1.037$ and that $P[d \leq 1.037 | \rho = 0] = 0.029$. Thus, in this case, since $0.029 < 0.05$, we reject the null hypothesis and conclude that positive autocorrelation does exist. The main reason for the two different test outcomes is likely to be the small sample size, $T = 10$. The asymptotic test is unlikely to be reliable; in particular, $\hat{\rho}$ is likely to be a serious underestimate of ρ.

If computation of $P[d \leq 1.037 | \rho = 0]$ is not possible, then the following procedure can be adopted. Using a 5% significance level, and noting that $T = 10$ and $K = 2$, we find (from Table 5 at the end of the book) that the critical values of the bounds test are

$$d_L^* = 0.879 \quad \text{and} \quad d_U^* = 1.320$$

Consequently, $d_L^* < \bar{d} < d_U^*$ and the bounds test is inconclusive.

To overcome this problem we will approximate the critical value d^* using (9.5.55) through (9.5.57). The first step in this direction is to calculate $E[d]$ and $\text{var}[d]$. Using the notation in (9.5.58) through (9.5.61) we have

$$(X'X)^{-1} = \frac{1}{429}\begin{bmatrix} 195 & -39 \\ -39 & 10 \end{bmatrix}$$

$$(\Delta X)' = \begin{bmatrix} 0 & 0 & 0 & 0 & 0 & 0 & 0 & 0 & 0 \\ 2 & 2 & -3 & -2 & 1 & 1 & 1 & 4 & -2 \end{bmatrix}$$

$$(\Delta^2 X)' = \begin{bmatrix} 0 & 0 & 0 & 0 & 0 & 0 & 0 & 0 \\ 0 & -5 & 1 & 3 & 0 & 0 & 3 & -6 \end{bmatrix}$$

$$X'AX = \begin{bmatrix} 0 & 0 \\ 0 & 44 \end{bmatrix} \qquad X'A^2X = \begin{bmatrix} 0 & 0 \\ 0 & 88 \end{bmatrix}$$

$$\text{tr}[X'AX(X'X)^{-1}] = 1.026541 \qquad \text{tr}[X'A^2X(X'X)^{-1}] = 2.051282$$

$$\text{tr}\{[X'AX(X'X)^{-1}]^2\} = 1.051940 \qquad P = 16.97436$$

and $Q = 48.94938$. Thus, we have $E[d] = 16.97436/8 = 2.12179$ and

$$\text{var}[d] = \tfrac{1}{80}(Q - PE[d]) = 0.32333$$

The next step is to calculate a and b from (9.5.56) and (9.5.57). Using the values for $E[d]$ and $\text{var}[d]$ that we have just calculated, and the values for $E[d_U]$ and $\text{var}[d_U]$ in Table 6 at the end of the book, these equations become

$$2.12179 = a + 2.238b$$

and

$$0.32333 = 0.29824b^2$$

Thus

$$b = (0.32333/0.29824)^{1/2} = 1.04121$$

$$a = 2.12179 - (2.238)(1.0412) = -0.2084$$

and the approximate critical value for the test is

$$d^* = a + bd_U^* = -0.2084 + (1.04121)(1.32) = 1.166$$

Comparing this value with our test statistic we find

$$\bar{d} = 1.037 < d^*$$

and so, in line with our earlier finding, we reject the null hypothesis in favor of the alternative of positive autocorrelation.

9.5.3d Durbin's *h* Statistic

One of the assumptions of this chapter is that the matrix X is nonstochastic. This assumption is relaxed in different ways in later chapters. Of interest to us in this section is a case in which X contains lagged values of the dependent variable. (See Section 17.4 for more details about this type of model.) Under these circumstances it has been shown that the Durbin–Watson statistic has reduced power and is biased toward 2. As an alternative, Durbin (1970) developed an asymptotic test that is based on the h statistic

$$h = \hat{\rho}\left(\frac{T}{1 - T\hat{V}(b_1)}\right)^{1/2} \tag{9.5.62}$$

where $\hat{\rho}$ is given in Equation 9.5.40 (and could be replaced by $1 - (1/2)d$) and $\hat{V}(b_1)$ is the least squares estimate of the variance of the coefficient of y_{t-1}. Under the null hypothesis of no autocorrelation, h is asymptotically normal with 0 mean and unit variance, and, for testing against the alternative of first-order autoregressive errors, it is valid even if X contains lags of y that are greater than 1.

It is clear that h cannot be calculated if $T\hat{V}(b_1) \geq 1$. For this case, Durbin suggests an asymptotically equivalent test, namely, regress the least squares residuals $\hat{e}_t$ on $\hat{e}_{t-1}$ and X, where X includes the relevant lagged y's, and test the significance of the coefficient of $\hat{e}_{t-1}$ using standard least squares procedures.

A number of Monte Carlo studies that evaluate the finite sample power and size of Durbin's h-test have appeared in the literature. Some of these studies indicate that the power can be quite low, and that the finite sample size of the test is often quite different from its asymptotic size. This test should therefore be used with caution, particularly in small samples.

9.5.4 A Pretest Estimator

When a choice between the least squares estimator **b** and the estimated generalized least squares estimator $\hat{\hat{\boldsymbol{\beta}}}$ is made on the basis of the outcome of the Durbin–Watson test, a preliminary-test estimator is generated. If an alternative hypothesis of positive or negative autocorrelation is entertained, it is given by

$$\hat{\boldsymbol{\beta}}^* = \begin{cases} \mathbf{b} & \text{if } d^* < d < d^{**} \\ \hat{\hat{\boldsymbol{\beta}}} & \text{if } d < d^* \text{ or } d > d^{**} \end{cases}$$

where d^* and d^{**} are the critical values for the Durbin–Watson test for the two-tailed alternative hypothesis $H_1: \rho \neq 0$. In Figure 9.4 the efficiencies of $\hat{\hat{\boldsymbol{\beta}}}$ and $\hat{\boldsymbol{\beta}}^*$, relative to that of **b**, are graphed for a typical problem.

When ρ is close to 0 the estimated generalized least squares estimator is worse than least squares, reflecting the fact that an estimated ρ leads to an estimator that is less efficient than an estimator that uses the true value of ρ. Note that, when $\rho = 0$, the least squares estimator "uses the true value of ρ." The pretest estimator is better than estimated generalized least squares when ρ is close to 0, but, because a null hypothesis of $\rho = 0$ will still be rejected 5% of the time (assuming a 5% significance level), it is not as good as least squares. As $|\rho|$ becomes larger, the pretest estimator becomes worse than estimated generalized least squares, reflecting the number of Type II errors. For large $|\rho|$ there are few Type II errors, and the pretest estimator becomes almost identical to the estimated generalized least squares estimator. As would be expected, both these estimators are considerably better than least squares when $|\rho|$ is large.

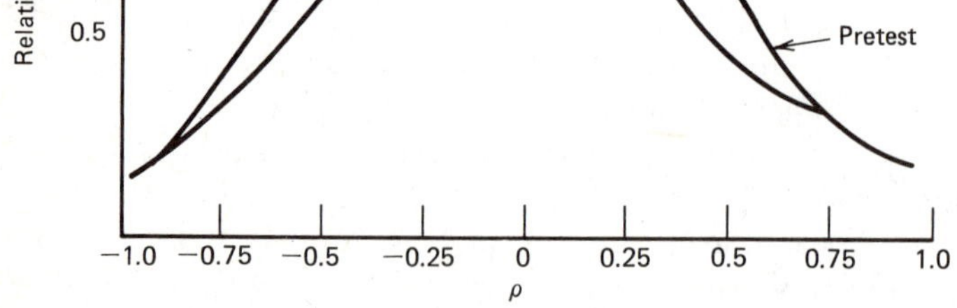

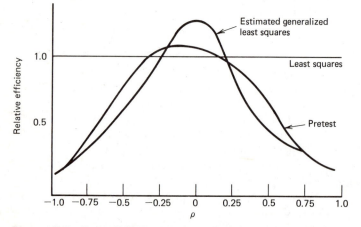

Figure 9.4 Trace (MSE) of each estimator relative to that of the least squares estimator.

9.5.5 Prediction Implications of Autocorrelated Errors

In Section 8.6 the problem of predicting T_0 future observations $\mathbf{y}_0$ generated by the model

$$\mathbf{y}_0 = X_0\boldsymbol{\beta} + \mathbf{e}_0 \tag{9.5.63}$$

was considered. It was assumed that $E[\mathbf{e}_0] = \mathbf{0}$, that $E[\mathbf{e}_0\mathbf{e}_0'] = \sigma^2\boldsymbol{\Psi}_0$, and that the process generating the future disturbances $\mathbf{e}_0$ was the same as that which generated the past disturbances $\mathbf{e}$ in the model $\mathbf{y} = X\boldsymbol{\beta} + \mathbf{e}$. The possibility of correlation between future and past disturbances was allowed for by defining $E[\mathbf{e}\mathbf{e}_0'] = \sigma^2 V$. It was shown that the best linear unbiased predictor for y_0 is given by

$$\hat{\mathbf{y}}_0 = X_0\hat{\boldsymbol{\beta}} + V'\boldsymbol{\Psi}^{-1}(\mathbf{y} - X\hat{\boldsymbol{\beta}}) \tag{9.5.64}$$

and that the covariance matrix of its prediction error is

$$\begin{aligned} E[(\hat{\mathbf{y}}_0 - \mathbf{y}_0)(\hat{\mathbf{y}}_0 - \mathbf{y}_0)'] = \sigma^2[&\boldsymbol{\Psi}_0 - V'\boldsymbol{\Psi}^{-1}V \\ &+ (X_0 - V'\boldsymbol{\Psi}^{-1}X)(X'\boldsymbol{\Psi}^{-1}X)^{-1}(X_0' - X'\boldsymbol{\Psi}^{-1}V)] \end{aligned} \tag{9.5.65}$$

In this section we are concerned with specializing these results to the first-order autoregressive error model. Thus, we assume that $\sigma^2 = \sigma_v^2$, that $\boldsymbol{\Psi}$ is defined by (9.5.19), and that $\boldsymbol{\Psi}_0$ has a structure similar to that of $\boldsymbol{\Psi}$. The matrix $\sigma_v^2 V'$ is given by

$$\begin{aligned} \sigma_v^2 V' = E[\mathbf{e}_0\mathbf{e}'] &= E\begin{bmatrix} e_{T+1} \\ e_{T+2} \\ \vdots \\ e_{T+T_0} \end{bmatrix}[e_1 \quad e_2 \quad \cdots \quad e_T] \\ &= E\begin{bmatrix} e_{T+1}e_1 & e_{T+1}e_2 & \cdots & e_{T+1}e_T \\ e_{T+2}e_1 & e_{T+2}e_2 & \cdots & e_{T+2}e_T \\ \vdots & \vdots & \ddots & \vdots \\ e_{T+T_0}e_1 & e_{T+T_0}e_2 & \cdots & e_{T+T_0}e_T \end{bmatrix} \\ &= \frac{\sigma_v^2}{1-\rho^2}\begin{bmatrix} \rho^T & \rho^{T-1} & \cdots & \rho \\ \rho^{T+1} & \rho^T & \cdots & \rho^2 \\ \vdots & \vdots & \ddots & \vdots \\ \rho^{T+T_0-1} & \rho^{T+T_0-2} & \cdots & \rho^{T_0} \end{bmatrix} \end{aligned} \tag{9.5.66}$$

Because the covariances in V are nonzero, it is possible to use information about the past disturbances $\mathbf{e}$ to help predict the future disturbances $\mathbf{e}_0$.

We will use an intuitive argument to derive the simplified version of (9.5.64), which results when $\mathbf{e}$ follows a first-order autoregressive error. The same result can be obtained by appropriate substitution for V and $\mathbf{\Psi}^{-1}$ in (9.5.64). See Exercise 9.6.5.

The vector $\mathbf{y}_0$ consists of two components, $X_0\boldsymbol{\beta}$ and $\mathbf{e}_0$. The best predictor (estimator) of $X_0\boldsymbol{\beta}$ is $X_0\hat{\boldsymbol{\beta}}$ where $\hat{\boldsymbol{\beta}} = (X'\mathbf{\Psi}^{-1}X)^{-1}X'\mathbf{\Psi}^{-1}\mathbf{y}$ is the generalized least squares estimator. To develop a predictor for $\mathbf{e}_0$, we first consider its first element, which is given by

$$e_{T+1} = \rho e_T + v_{T+1} \tag{9.5.67}$$

where v_{T+1} has 0 mean and is uncorrelated with $(v_1, v_2, \ldots, v_T)$. This situation suggests that if e_T were known, a reasonable predictor for e_{T+1} would be

$$\hat{e}_{T+1} = \rho e_T \tag{9.5.68}$$

Similarly,

$$e_{T+2} = \rho e_{T+1} + v_{T+2} = \rho^2 e_T + \rho v_{T+1} + v_{T+2} \tag{9.5.69}$$

which suggests that

$$\hat{e}_{T+2} = \rho^2 e_T \tag{9.5.70}$$

would be a reasonable predictor for e_{T+2}. If we continue this process and substitute $\hat{e}_T = y_T - \mathbf{x}'_T\hat{\boldsymbol{\beta}}$ for the unknown e_T, we have, as a predictor for $\mathbf{e}_0$,

$$\hat{\mathbf{e}}_0 = \begin{bmatrix} \rho \\ \rho^2 \\ \vdots \\ \rho^{T_0} \end{bmatrix} (y_T - \mathbf{x}'_T\hat{\boldsymbol{\beta}}) = \mathbf{w}(y_T - \mathbf{x}'_T\hat{\boldsymbol{\beta}}) \tag{9.5.71}$$

Combining this result with $X_0\hat{\boldsymbol{\beta}}$ yields

$$\hat{\mathbf{y}}_0 = X_0\hat{\boldsymbol{\beta}} + \mathbf{w}(y_T - \mathbf{x}'_T\hat{\boldsymbol{\beta}}) \tag{9.5.72}$$

The tth term in this predictor is

$$\hat{y}_{T+t} = \mathbf{x}'_{T+t}\hat{\boldsymbol{\beta}} + \rho^t(y_T - \mathbf{x}'_T\hat{\boldsymbol{\beta}}) \tag{9.5.73}$$

and thus, the contribution of the second term diminishes as we attempt to predict further into the future.

The proof that (9.5.72) is best linear unbiased, and derivation of the covariance matrix of the prediction error, is left as an exercise (Problem 9.6.5). These results depend on the assumption that Ψ and V are known. In the first-order autoregressive process this will be true if ρ is known. In practice, though, ρ will not be known and must be replaced by an estimate. Under these circumstances it is no longer guaranteed that $\mathbf{y}_0$ is best linear unbiased. Nevertheless, on intuitive grounds it would still seem to be a reasonable predictor to use. For some research into the asymptotic properties of predictors that are based on estimated covariance matrices see Baillie (1979).

9.5.6 An Example

In this section we illustrate estimation, testing, and prediction with an example. We will assume the first three columns of Table 9.2 are (20×1) vectors of time-series observations represented by $\mathbf{y}$, $\mathbf{x}_2$, and $\mathbf{x}_3$; and that they are related through the model

$$\mathbf{y} = \mathbf{x}_1\beta_1 + \mathbf{x}_2\beta_2 + \mathbf{x}_3\beta_3 + \mathbf{e} \tag{9.5.74}$$

Table 9.2 Data for Example Problem

$\mathbf{y}$	$\mathbf{x}_2$	$\mathbf{x}_3$	$\mathbf{y}^*$	$\mathbf{x}_1^*$	$\mathbf{x}_2^*$	$\mathbf{x}_3^*$
42.08376	14.53	16.74	35.36930	0.84045	12.21174	14.06913
41.48572	15.30	16.81	18.68101	0.45811	7.42636	7.73878
39.05569	15.92	19.50	16.57504	0.45811	7.62910	10.39085
45.08922	17.41	22.12	23.92538	0.45811	8.78313	11.55317
51.66982	18.37	22.34	27.23648	0.45811	8.93572	10.35342
51.18388	18.83	17.47	23.18458	0.45811	8.87550	5.36420
54.77771	18.84	20.24	27.04174	0.45811	8.63623	10.77320
60.33432	19.71	20.37	30.65089	0.45811	9.50082	9.40217
49.75518	20.01	12.71	17.06069	0.45811	9.32937	1.67173
55.45921	20.26	22.98	28.49743	0.45811	9.41681	16.09259
52.46684	20.77	19.33	22.41412	0.45811	9.79133	6.87740
50.67572	21.17	17.04	22.24452	0.45811	9.91497	6.56529
51.64282	21.34	16.74	24.18222	0.45811	9.86821	7.50621
56.18829	22.91	19.81	28.20363	0.45811	11.34609	10.73878
66.21643	22.96	31.92	35.76862	0.45811	10.54533	21.18518
63.22733	23.69	26.31	27.34539	0.45811	11.24823	9.01291
68.96477	24.82	25.93	34.70259	0.45811	11.98265	11.67291
64.25953	25.54	21.96	26.88829	0.45811	12.09032	7.90882
63.75415	25.63	24.05	28.93263	0.45811	11.79016	12.15012
69.68355	28.73	25.66	35.13589	0.45811	14.84139	12.62757

where $\mathbf{x}_1$ is a (20×1) vector of 1s, $E[\mathbf{e}] = \mathbf{0}$, and $E[\mathbf{ee}'] = \sigma_v^2\Psi$. For example, (9.5.74) could be a Cobb–Douglas production function where y_t, x_{t2}, and x_{t3} denote the logarithms of output, labor, and capital, respectively, in the tth time period.

We are unlikely to know the structure of the disturbance covariance matrix Ψ, so we begin by using least squares to estimate $\boldsymbol{\beta} = (\beta_1, \beta_2, \beta_3)'$. This yields

$$\mathbf{b} = (X'X)^{-1}X'\mathbf{y}$$

$$= \begin{bmatrix} 20.00 & 416.74 & 420.03 \\ 416.74 & 8946.93 & 8925.56 \\ 420.03 & 8925.56 & 9190.06 \end{bmatrix}^{-1} \begin{bmatrix} 1097.97 \\ 23465.33 \\ 23607.05 \end{bmatrix}$$

$$= \begin{bmatrix} 3.842 \\ 1.811 \\ 0.634 \end{bmatrix}$$

After calculating the residuals $\hat{\mathbf{e}} = \mathbf{y} - X\mathbf{b}$, we find, for the value of the Durbin–Watson statistic,

$$\bar{d} = \frac{\hat{\mathbf{e}}'A\hat{\mathbf{e}}}{\hat{\mathbf{e}}'\hat{\mathbf{e}}} = 0.9094$$

The 5% critical values for the bounds test when $T = 20$ and $K = 3$ are $d_L^* = 1.100$ and $d_U^* = 1.537$. Thus, $\bar{d} < d_L^*$, and the Durbin–Watson test suggests the existence of positively autocorrelated disturbances. Alternatively, using SHAZAM we find that $P[d < 0.9094 | \rho = 0] = 0.0011 < 0.05$, a strong indication of autocorrelation. The presence of autocorrelation means that we can find a more efficient estimator than $\mathbf{b}$, and that the covariance matrix

$$\hat{\sigma}^2(X'X)^{-1} = \begin{bmatrix} 19.91 & -0.299 & -0.630 \\ -0.299 & 0.041 & -0.027 \\ -0.630 & -0.027 & 0.057 \end{bmatrix}$$

where $\hat{\sigma}^2 = \hat{\mathbf{e}}'\hat{\mathbf{e}}/17 = 10.443$, is likely to be a biased estimator of the covariance matrix for $\mathbf{b}$.

We can attempt to overcome these problems by assuming $\sigma_v^2\Psi$ is the covariance matrix of a first-order autoregressive disturbance $e_t = \rho e_{t-1} + v_t$. Under this assumption we can estimate ρ and then obtain the estimated generalized least squares estimator $\hat{\hat{\boldsymbol{\beta}}} = (X'\hat{P}'\hat{P}X)^{-1}X'\hat{P}'\hat{P}\mathbf{y}$, where $\hat{P}$ is such that $\hat{P}'\hat{P} = \hat{\Psi}^{-1}$.

An estimate of ρ is given by

$$\hat{\rho} = \frac{\sum \hat{e}_t \hat{e}_{t-1}}{\sum \hat{e}_{t-1}^2} = 0.541889$$

This value is then used to obtain the transformed observations

$$\mathbf{y}^* = \hat{P}\mathbf{y} \qquad \mathbf{x}_1^* = \hat{P}\mathbf{x}_1 \qquad \mathbf{x}_2^* = \hat{P}\mathbf{x}_2 \qquad \text{and} \qquad \mathbf{x}_3^* = \hat{P}\mathbf{x}_3$$

which are given in the last four columns of Table 9.2. As an example of how these values are calculated, consider the first three transformed observations for $\mathbf{y}$.

$$y_1^* = (1 - \hat{\rho}^2)^{1/2} y_1 = (1 - 0.293644)^{1/2} 42.08376 = 35.3693$$

$$y_2^* = y_2 - \hat{\rho} y_1 = 41.48572 - (0.541889)(42.08376) = 18.6810$$

$$y_3^* = y_3 - \hat{\rho} y_2 = 39.05569 - (0.541889)(41.48572) = 16.5750$$

We are now in a position to estimate $\boldsymbol{\beta}$. The estimated generalized least squares estimator yields

$$\begin{aligned}
\hat{\hat{\boldsymbol{\beta}}} &= (X'\hat{P}'\hat{P}X)^{-1} X'\hat{P}'\hat{P}\mathbf{y} \\
&= (X^{*\prime}X^*)^{-1} X^{*\prime}\mathbf{y}^* \\
&= \begin{bmatrix} 4.694 & 98.199 & 98.676 \\ 98.199 & 2145.863 & 2118.945 \\ 98.676 & 2118.945 & 2399.470 \end{bmatrix}^{-1} \begin{bmatrix} 258.173 \\ 5595.601 \\ 5765.573 \end{bmatrix} \\
&= \begin{bmatrix} 4.050 \\ 1.672 \\ 0.759 \end{bmatrix}
\end{aligned}$$

The estimated covariance matrix for $\hat{\hat{\boldsymbol{\beta}}}$ is

$$\hat{\hat{\sigma}}_v^2 (X'\hat{P}'\hat{P}X)^{-1} = \begin{bmatrix} 37.568 & -1.513 & -0.209 \\ -1.513 & 0.087 & -0.015 \\ -0.209 & -0.015 & 0.024 \end{bmatrix}$$

where

$$\hat{\hat{\sigma}}_v^2 = (\mathbf{y}^* - X^*\hat{\hat{\boldsymbol{\beta}}})'(\mathbf{y}^* - X^*\hat{\hat{\boldsymbol{\beta}}})/17 = 7.159$$

A comparison of the estimated covariance matrices for $\hat{\hat{\boldsymbol{\beta}}}$ and $\mathbf{b}$ indicates that the estimated variances for b_1 and b_2 are likely to understate the true variances. It is much more difficult to conclude anything about the estimated variance for b_3; the inequality relationship

$$\widehat{\text{var}}(b_3) = 0.057 > 0.024 = \widehat{\text{var}}(\hat{\hat{\beta}}_3)$$

is that suggested by theory.

Since the estimator $\hat{\rho}$ is usually biased downward in finite samples, it is interesting to examine the results from an adjusted estimator for ρ. The estimator $\hat{\hat{\rho}}$ given in (9.5.42) was designed for a model with only one explanatory variable. Nevertheless, it may provide some improvement over $\hat{\rho}$. If we assume x_{t2} approximately follows a linear trend and set $m = 1$, an estimate for ρ from the adjusted estimator is

$$\begin{aligned}\hat{\hat{\rho}} &= \hat{\rho} + T^{-1}[(m + 1)(1 + \hat{\rho}) + 2\hat{\rho}] \\ &= 0.54189 + (20)^{-1}[2 \times 1.54189 + 2 \times 0.54189] \\ &= 0.75027\end{aligned}$$

The estimated generalized least squares estimate of $\boldsymbol{\beta}$ corresponding to $\hat{\hat{\rho}} = 0.75027$ and its estimated covariance matrix are given by

$$\hat{\hat{\boldsymbol{\beta}}} = (3.782, 1.662, 0.780).$$

$$\Sigma_{\hat{\hat{\boldsymbol{\beta}}}} = \begin{bmatrix} 71.556 & -2.968 & -0.219 \\ -2.968 & 0.152 & -0.011 \\ -0.219 & -0.011 & 0.021 \end{bmatrix}$$

This set of estimates is quite similar to that obtained for $\hat{\rho} = 0.54189$. However, the estimated variances for $\hat{\hat{\beta}}_1$ and $\hat{\hat{\beta}}_2$ have almost doubled. Since we do not have knowledge of the true underlying parameters, we cannot, of course, say which set of estimates is better. More light will be shed on this question in the exercises in Section 9.6. In the meantime this example illustrates that caution must be exercised when drawing inferences in small samples on the basis of asymptotic theory.

Finally, we predict a future value of y given $\mathbf{x}'_{T+1} = (1, 20, 20)$. We will use the estimates based on $\hat{\rho} = 0.54189$. The predictor that uses the estimated generalized least squares estimator, but ignores the fact that e_{T+1} will be correlated with the previous disturbance, is given by

$$y^*_{T+1} = \mathbf{x}'_{T+1}\hat{\hat{\boldsymbol{\beta}}} = (1, 20, 20)\begin{pmatrix} 4.050 \\ 1.672 \\ 0.759 \end{pmatrix} = 52.686$$

When we make use of the information that e_{T+1} is correlated with the disturbances in the sample period, we obtain the predictor

$$\begin{aligned}\hat{y}_{T+1} &= \mathbf{x}'_{T+1}\hat{\hat{\boldsymbol{\beta}}} + \hat{\rho}(y_T - \mathbf{x}'_T\hat{\hat{\boldsymbol{\beta}}}) \\ &= 52.686 + 0.54189(69.68355 - 71.58443) \\ &= 51.656\end{aligned}$$

9.5.7 Concluding Remarks

In this section we have examined the general linear statistical model with first-order autoregressive errors, and in connection with this model we have discussed:

1. The circumstances under which it is likely to be reasonable.
2. The consequences of using least squares.
3. Generalized and estimated generalized least squares estimation.
4. The Durbin–Watson and two other tests for autocorrelation.
5. A pretest estimator.
6. Best linear unbiased prediction.

It should be emphasized that many other possible error structures could be used in any attempt to model autocorrelated errors. Some possibilities are autoregressive errors of an order higher than 1, moving-average errors, and combined autoregressive moving-average errors. For details of these error processes, refer to Judge, et al. (1985, Chapter 8). Also, these processes are discussed in Chapter 16 of this book in connection with time-series analysis. One of the differences between Chapter 16 and the current section is that in this section the autocorrelated errors are unobservable; in Chapter 16 the variable that is assumed to follow a particular autocorrelation process is observable.

The only feasible estimator for $\boldsymbol{\beta}$ that was considered in this section was the estimated generalized least squares estimator. Other commonly used alternatives that will be discussed in Chapter 12 are the nonlinear and maximum likelihood estimators. All these estimators have the same asymptotic properties, so any choice between them must be made on the basis of Monte Carlo evidence on small sample properties and on computational convenience. Available Monte Carlo evidence on efficiency suggests the maximum likelihood estimator is best, so, if a suitable computer program is available, this estimator is recommended. However, in circumstances where only a standard least squares package is available, the estimated generalized least squares estimator is recommended.

For testing for autocorrelation, we have concentrated on the Durbin–Watson test. For a review of other tests, refer to Judge, et al. (1985, Chapter 8). Finally, we note that in applied work autocorrelation is often regarded as an indication of model misspecification, so, sometimes, rather than adjust the estimation procedure, the model is adjusted.

9.6 Problems on Autocorrelation

9.6.1 General Exercises

9.6.1 Given the AR(1) error process $e_t = \rho e_{t-1} + v_t$ where $|\rho| < 1$, use recursive substitution (or lag operator notion if it is familiar) to prove that

$$e_t = \sum_{i=0}^{\infty} \rho^i v_{t-i}$$

9.6.2 (*a*) Verify that $\Psi\Psi^{-1} = I$, where Ψ is given in (9.5.22) and Ψ^{-1} in (9.5.28).
(*b*) Verify that $P'P = \Psi^{-1}$, where P is given in (9.5.29).

9.6.3 (*a*) Find $P_0'P_0$, where P_0 is the $[(T-1) \times T]$ matrix obtained by deleting the first row of P in (9.5.29) and compare it with Ψ^{-1}, the matrix in (9.5.28).
(*b*) Show that the covariance matrix of the approximate generalized least squares estimator $\hat{\boldsymbol{\beta}}_0$ is $\sigma_v^2(X'P_0'P_0X)^{-1}$.

9.6.4 (*a*) Calculate the covariance matrices and compare the relative efficiency of the estimators $\mathbf{b}$, $\hat{\boldsymbol{\beta}}$, and $\hat{\boldsymbol{\beta}}_0$ in the model

$$y_t = \beta_1 + \beta_2 t + e_t \qquad t = 1, 2, \ldots, 10$$
$$e_t = 0.8e_{t-1} + v_t$$

where the v_t are independent and identically distributed random variables with 0 mean and unit variance. To reduce the computational load we note that

$$X'\Psi X = \begin{bmatrix} 150.8194 & 829.5064 \\ 8.29.5064 & 5020.2833 \end{bmatrix}$$

(*b*) For the example in part (a), calculate the first product moment around zero for

(*i*) The two transformed explanatory variables used for $\hat{\boldsymbol{\beta}}$ (the two columns in PX), and

(*ii*) The two transformed explanatory variables used for $\hat{\boldsymbol{\beta}}_0$ (the two columns in P_0X).

Give an intuitive reason why the approximate estimator $\hat{\boldsymbol{\beta}}_0$ is less efficient than $\hat{\boldsymbol{\beta}}$.

9.6.5 For the case where $\mathbf{e}$ follows a first-order autoregressive process show that

(*a*)
$$\hat{\mathbf{y}}_0 = X_0\hat{\boldsymbol{\beta}} + V'\Psi^{-1}(\mathbf{y} - X\hat{\boldsymbol{\beta}})$$
$$= X_0\hat{\boldsymbol{\beta}} + \mathbf{w}(y_T - \mathbf{x}_T'\hat{\boldsymbol{\beta}})$$

where $\mathbf{w}$, Ψ, and V have been defined in Section 9.5.5; and

(*b*) The covariance matrix of the prediction error can be written as

$$\sigma_v^2\left[X_0CX_0' + \Psi_0 - X_0C\mathbf{x}_T\mathbf{w}' - \mathbf{w}\mathbf{x}_T'CX_0' - \mathbf{w}\left(\frac{1}{1-\rho^2} - \mathbf{x}_T'C\mathbf{x}_T\right)\mathbf{w}'\right]$$

where $C = (X'\Psi^{-1}X)^{-1}$.

9.6.6 In the general linear model with normally distributed first-order autoregressive errors suppose that $\rho = 0.6$ and that we have the observations

$$\mathbf{y} = \begin{bmatrix} 4 \\ 8 \\ 6 \\ 2 \\ 9 \end{bmatrix} \qquad X = \begin{bmatrix} 1 & 2 \\ 1 & 5 \\ 1 & 2 \\ 1 & 1 \\ 1 & 10 \end{bmatrix}$$

(*a*) Find the transformed observations $\mathbf{y}^*$ and X^*.

(*b*) Find the generalized least squares estimates for $\boldsymbol{\beta} = (\beta_1, \beta_2)'$.

(*c*) Find $E[d]$ (assuming that $\rho = 0$), where d is the Durbin–Watson statistic.

9.6.7 Suppose that you have run a least squares regression where $T = 20$ and $K = 4$ and that you have found that

$$\hat{\rho} = \frac{\sum_{t=2}^{T}\hat{e}_t\hat{e}_{t-1}}{\sum_{t=2}^{T}\hat{e}_{t-1}^2} = 0.5$$

$\hat{\mathbf{e}}'\hat{\mathbf{e}} = 40$, $\hat{e}_1^2 = 1$, and $\hat{e}_T^2 = 4$.

(*a*) Use the asymptotic distribution of $\sqrt{T}(\hat{\rho} - \rho)$ to test for autocorrelation.

(*b*) Obtain the exact value of the Durbin–Watson statistic and use it to test for autocorrelation.

9.6.2 Individual Exercises Using Monte Carlo Data

For the remaining problems, use an appropriate computer program to generate 100 samples of $\mathbf{y}$, each of size 20, for the model

$$y_t = \beta_1 + \beta_2 x_{t2} + \beta_3 x_{t3} + e_t \tag{9.6.1}$$

where $e_t = \rho e_{t-1} + v_t$ and the v_t are independent normal random variables with 0 mean and variance $E[v_t^2] = \sigma_v^2$. Suggested parameter values are $\beta_1 = 10$, $\beta_2 = 1$, $\beta_3 = 1$, $\rho = 0.8$, and $\sigma_v^2 = 6.4$, and the same design matrix as was used in Section 9.4.2, namely,

$$X = \begin{bmatrix} 1.00 & 14.53 & 16.74 \\ 1.00 & 15.30 & 16.81 \\ 1.00 & 15.92 & 19.50 \\ 1.00 & 17.41 & 22.12 \\ 1.00 & 18.37 & 22.34 \\ 1.00 & 18.83 & 17.47 \\ 1.00 & 18.84 & 20.24 \\ 1.00 & 19.71 & 20.37 \\ 1.00 & 20.01 & 12.71 \\ 1.00 & 20.26 & 22.98 \\ 1.00 & 20.77 & 19.33 \\ 1.00 & 21.17 & 17.04 \\ 1.00 & 21.34 & 16.74 \\ 1.00 & 22.91 & 19.81 \\ 1.00 & 22.96 & 31.92 \\ 1.00 & 23.69 & 26.31 \\ 1.00 & 24.82 & 25.93 \\ 1.00 & 25.54 & 21.96 \\ 1.00 & 25.63 & 24.05 \\ 1.00 & 28.73 & 25.66 \end{bmatrix} \tag{9.6.2}$$

9.6.8 Calculate the covariance matrices for the following estimators

(*a*) The generalized least squares estimator

$$\hat{\boldsymbol{\beta}} = (X'\boldsymbol{\Psi}^{-1}X)^{-1}X'\boldsymbol{\Psi}^{-1}\mathbf{y}$$

(*b*) The least squares estimator

$$\mathbf{b} = (X'X)^{-1}X'\mathbf{y}$$

Comment on the relative efficiency of the two estimators.

9.6.9 Select five samples from the Monte Carlo data and, for each sample, compute the following estimators. (Estimates for the first sample using the random numbers given in the Computer Handbook are given in Section 9.5.6).

(*a*) The least squares estimator $\mathbf{b}$.

(*b*) The estimator $\hat{\rho}$.

(*c*) The estimated generalized least squares estimator for $\boldsymbol{\beta}$ that uses $\hat{\rho}$, call it $\hat{\hat{\boldsymbol{\beta}}}$.

Compare the various estimates with one another and with the true parameter values.

9.6.10 The computer program used in Exercise 9.6.9 to obtain values of the estimators $\mathbf{b}$ and $\hat{\hat{\boldsymbol{\beta}}}$ is also likely to yield estimates of the covariance matrices of these estimators. In both cases, however, the variance estimates could be biased. Explain why. Also, taking the parameter β_2 as an example, compare the various estimates of $\text{var}(b_2)$ and $\text{var}(\hat{\hat{\beta}}_2)$ with the relevant answers in Exercise 9.6.8.

9.6.11 Use the results in Exercises 9.6.9 and 9.6.10 to calculate t values that would be used to test

(*a*) $H_0\colon \beta_2 = 0$ against $H_1\colon \beta_2 \neq 0$.

(*b*) $H_0\colon \beta_2 = 1$ against $H_1\colon \beta_2 \neq 1$.

Since we have two estimators and five samples, this involves, for each hypothesis, the calculation of 10 t values. Keeping in mind the validity or otherwise of each null hypothesis, comment on the results.

9.6.12 Given that $\mathbf{x}'_{T+1} = (1 \quad 20 \quad 20)$, for each of the five samples calculate values for the following two predictors

(*a*) $y^*_{T+1} = \mathbf{x}'_{T+1}\hat{\hat{\boldsymbol{\beta}}}$.

(*b*) $\hat{y}_{T+1} = \mathbf{x}'_{T+1}\hat{\hat{\boldsymbol{\beta}}} + \hat{\rho}(y_T - \mathbf{x}'_T\hat{\hat{\boldsymbol{\beta}}})$.

9.6.13 Given the X matrix in (9.6.2), calculate the mean and variance of the Durbin–Watson statistic and use this information and the mean and variance of the Durbin–Watson upper bound (statistical Table 6) to find an approximate critical value for the Durbin–Watson test. Use a 5% significance level.

9.6.14 Using the same five samples that were used in Exercises 9.6.9 through 9.6.12, an alternative hypothesis of positive autocorrelation, and a 5% significance level, test for autocorrelation using

(*a*) The Durbin–Watson test (use the critical value obtained in Exercise 9.6.13 or a program that computes the tail probability).

(*b*) The asymptotic test described in Section 9.5.3a (use a critical value of 1.645).

9.6.3 Group Exercises Using Monte Carlo Data

9.6.15 Repeat Exercise 9.6.9 for all 100 samples and use the results to estimate the mean and mean square error matrix for each estimator. For example, for **b**, estimates of its mean and mean square error matrix are given, respectively, by

$$\frac{1}{100}\sum_{i=1}^{100}\mathbf{b}(i) \quad \text{and} \quad \frac{1}{100}\sum_{i=1}^{100}[(\mathbf{b}(i)-\boldsymbol{\beta})(\mathbf{b}(i)-\boldsymbol{\beta})']$$

where $\mathbf{b}(i)$ is the least squares estimator from the ith sample. Use these results and those of Exercise 9.6.8 to answer the following questions.

(*a*) Do any of the estimators appear to be biased?

(*b*) By comparing the estimated mean and mean square error of **b** with the true counterparts, comment on the extent of the sampling error in the Monte Carlo experiment.

(*c*) Is $\sigma^2(X'\Psi^{-1}X)^{-1}$ a good approximation of the finite sample mean square error matrix of $\hat{\hat{\boldsymbol{\beta}}}$?

9.6.16 Use all 100 samples to estimate the means of the variance estimators $\widehat{\text{var}}(b_2)$ and $\widehat{\text{var}}(\hat{\hat{\beta}}_2)$ that were obtained in Exercise 9.6.10. Comment on the results, particularly with respect to your answers to Exercise 9.6.8.

9.6.17 Repeat Exercise 9.6.11 for all 100 samples and calculate the proportion of Type I and Type II errors obtained when a 5% significance level is used. Comment.

9.6.18 Repeat Exercise 9.6.14 for all 100 samples. Is the Durbin–Watson test more powerful than the asymptotic test?

9.7 References

Andrews, D. W. K. (1986) "A Note on the Unbiasedness of Feasible GLS, Quasi-Maximum Likelihood, Robust, Adaptive, and Spectral Estimators of the Linear Model." *Econometrica*, 54, 687–698.

Baillie R. T. (1979) "The Asymptotic Mean Squared Error of Multistep Prediction from the Regression Model with Autoregressive Errors." *Journal of the American Statistical Association*, 74, 175–184.

Beesley, P. A., H. E. Doran, and W. E. Griffiths (1987) "Further Attempts at Improving the Finite Sample Accuracy of Interval Estimation in a Linear Model with First-Order Autoregressive Error and Trended Explanatory Variable."

Working Paper, Department of Econometrics, University of New England, Armidale, Australia.

Breusch, T. S., and A. R. Pagan (1979) "A Simple Test for Heteroscedasticity and Random Coefficient Variation." *Econometrica*, 47, 1287–1294.

Cochrane, D., and G. H. Orcutt (1949) "Application of Least Squares Regressions to Relationships Containing Autocorrelated Error Terms." *Journal of the American Statistical Association*, 44, 32–61.

Durbin, J. (1970) "Testing for Serial Correlation in Least-Squares Regression When Some of the Regressors Are Lagged Dependent Variables." *Econometrica*, 38, 410–421.

Durbin, J., and G. S. Watson (1950) "Testing for Serial Correlation in Least Squares Regression I." *Biometrika*, 37, 409–428.

Durbin, J., and G. S. Watson (1951) "Testing for Serial Correlation in Least Squares Regression II." *Biometrika*, 38, 159–178.

Durbin, J., and G. S. Watson (1971) "Testing for Serial Correlation in Least Squares Regression III." *Biometrika*, 58, 1–42.

Goldfeld, S. M., and R. E. Quandt (1965) "Some Tests for Homoscedasticity." *Journal of the American Statistical Association*, 60, 539–547.

Goldfeld, S. M., and R. E. Quandt (1972) *Nonlinear Methods in Econometrics.* Amsterdam: North-Holland.

Greenberg, E. (1980) "Finite Sample Moments of a Preliminary-Test Estimator in the Case of Possible Heteroscedasticity." *Econometrica*, 48, 1805–1813.

Griffiths, W. E., and P. A. Beesley (1984) "The Small-Sample Properties of Some Preliminary Test Estimators in a Linear Model with Autocorrelated Errors." *Journal of Econometrics*, 25, 49–61.

Harvey, A. C. (1976) "Estimating Regression Models with Multiplicative Heteroscedasticity." *Econometrica*, 44, 461–465.

Imhof, J. P. (1961) "Computing the Distribution of Quadratic Forms in Normal Variables." *Biometrika*, 48, 419–426.

Judge, G. G., W. E. Griffiths, R. C. Hill, H. Lütkepohl, and T. C. Lee (1985) *The Theory and Practice of Econometrics*, 2nd ed. New York: Wiley.

Krämer, W. (1985) "The Power of the Durbin-Watson Test for Regressions Without an Intercept." *Journal of Econometrics*, 28, 363–370.

Magnus, J. R. (1978) "Maximum Likelihood Estimation of the GLS Model with Unknown Parameters in the Disturbance Covariance Matrix." *Journal of Econometrics*, 7, 281–312.

Mandy, D. M. (1984) "The Moments of a Pre-Test Estimator Under Possible Heteroscedasticity." *Journal of Econometrics*, 25, 29–33.

Taylor, W. E. (1978) "The Heteroscedastic Linear Model: Exact Finite Sample Results." *Econometrica*, 46, 663–675.

White, K. J. (1978) "A General Computer Program for Econometric Methods —SHAZAM." *Econometrica*, 46, 239–240.

White, K. J., S. Haun and N. G. Horsman (1987). *SHAZAM, The Econometrics Computer Program Version 6.1: User's Reference Manual.* Vancouver: University of British Columbia.

9.A Appendix: Resampling Methods

Recently, a great deal of attention has been directed to a computer-intensive approach to statistical inference based on data resampling. These methods have been extensively discussed by Miller (1974), Efron (1979, 1982), Peters and Freedman (1984), Freedman and Peters (1984), and Wu (1986). Resampling methods are used when appropriate sampling results are not available and one wishes a nonparametric method of estimating measures of precision. By resampling the estimated errors after, say, a linear model has been fitted to the data, "pseudo sample data y^*" are generated that permits the model to be refitted. Monte Carlo empirical distributions involving the pseudo sample observations are used to approximate the unobservable sampling distributions and provide measures of sampling variability, confidence intervals, and, sometimes, bias.

These resampling methods have appeared under the interesting names of jackknife and bootstrap, and most of the theoretical work has been done for the independently and identically distributed (i.i.d.) errors case. The objective of this appendix is expository in nature; in order to present the basis for these procedures, both the i.i.d. case and a specification that takes into account the special characteristics of economic data will be considered.

As a basis for discussing these methods, consider first the traditional linear statistical model

$$\mathbf{y} = X\boldsymbol{\beta} + \mathbf{e} \tag{9.A.1}$$

with a nonrandom $(T \times K)$ design matrix of rank K. The random errors e_t are assumed to come from an unknown distribution with mean 0 and variance σ^2. The least squares estimator is $\mathbf{b} = (X'X)^{-1}X'\mathbf{y}$, and the least squares residuals are given by $\hat{\mathbf{e}} = \mathbf{y} - X\mathbf{b}$ or $\hat{e}_t = y_t - \mathbf{x}_t'\mathbf{b}$. Also $\mathbf{b} - \boldsymbol{\beta} = (X'X)^{-1}X'\mathbf{e}$. Our interest is on the sampling distribution of $\mathbf{b} - \boldsymbol{\beta}$.

9.A.1 The Bootstrap

First, consider the bootstrap. The basic idea is to approximate the distribution of $\mathbf{b} - \boldsymbol{\beta}$ by an empirical distribution derived from the data. To do this, many data sets are generated from $X\mathbf{b} + \hat{\mathbf{e}}$. Each data set is then used to compute $\mathbf{b}$ and obtain an empirical distribution that is used as an approximation of the distribution of $\mathbf{b} - \boldsymbol{\beta}$. To generate the data sets from the underlying model and sample, estimates of the unobservable errors, $\hat{e}_t = y_t - \mathbf{x}_t'\mathbf{b}$, are obtained by drawing T times *with replacement* from the normalized residuals $\{\hat{e}_t/(1 - KT^{-1})^{1/2}\}$. The resulting $\mathbf{e}^* = (e_1^*, e_2^*, \ldots, e_T^*)'$ are used to generate the pseudo data $\mathbf{y}^* = X\mathbf{b} + \mathbf{e}^*$. The unknown parameter vector $\boldsymbol{\beta}$ is then estimated by $\mathbf{b}^* = (X'X)^{-1}X'\mathbf{y}^*$ for each data set, and the empirical distribution of $\mathbf{b}^* - \mathbf{b}$ is used to approximate that of $\mathbf{b} - \boldsymbol{\beta}$. As Efron (1979) shows for this case, the bootstrap variance estimator $\Sigma_{\mathbf{b}^*} = \Sigma_{\mathbf{b}} = \sigma^2(X'X)^{-1}$ and $E[\mathbf{b}^*] = \mathbf{b}$. If, however, heteroskedasticity exists and thus $\Sigma_{\mathbf{e}} = \Lambda = \text{diag}(\sigma_1^2, \sigma_2^2, \ldots, \sigma_T^2)$, then $\Sigma_{\mathbf{b}^*}$ is, in general, biased and inconsistent since we are resampling as if the errors are i.i.d. when they are not. The true covariance of $\mathbf{b}$ is $\Sigma_{\mathbf{b}} = (X'X)^{-1}X'\Lambda X(X'X)^{-1}$.

9.A.2 The Jackknife

In the jackknife resampling procedure, estimates of the model are recomputed t times, each time dropping one of the observations; and the variability of the estimates is used as an estimate of the variability of the original estimator. In this context, if we let $\mathbf{b}^+ = \mathbf{b}_{(t)}$ be the estimate of $\boldsymbol{\beta}$ obtained by *recomputing* $\mathbf{b}$ with the tth pair $(y_t, \mathbf{x}_t')$ deleted from the sample, then

$$\mathbf{b}_{(t)} = \mathbf{b} - (X'X)^{-1}\mathbf{x}_t e_t^+ \tag{9.A.2}$$

where $\mathbf{x}_t$ denotes the tth row of X, $e_t^+ = \hat{e}_t/(1 - k_{tt})$ and k_{tt} is the tth diagonal element of the matrix $X(X'X)^{-1}X'$. The corresponding jackknife estimator of the covariance of $\mathbf{b}$ is

$$[(T-1)/T]\sum_{t=1}^{T}\left[\mathbf{b}_{(t)} - (1/T)\sum_{s=1}^{T}\mathbf{b}_{(s)}\right]\left[\mathbf{b}_{(t)} - (1/T)\sum_{s=1}^{T}\mathbf{b}_{(s)}\right]' \tag{9.A.3}$$

In order to reduce computations, it can be shown [MacKinnon and White (1985)] that (9.A.3) reduces to

$$[(T-1)/T](X'X)^{-1}[X'\Lambda^+X - (1/T)X'\mathbf{e}^+\mathbf{e}^{+\prime}X](X'X)^{-1} \tag{9.A.4}$$

where Λ^+ is a $(T \times T)$ diagonal matrix with diagonal elements e_t^{+2} and $\mathbf{e}^+$ is a vector of the e_t^+'s. This delete-one-jackknife is one alternative to White's (1980) heteroskedasticity-consistent covariance matrix estimator

$$(X'X)^{-1}X'\hat{\Lambda}X(X'X)^{-1} \tag{9.A.5}$$

where $\hat{\Lambda} = \text{diag}(\hat{e}_1^2, \hat{e}_2^2, \ldots, \hat{e}_T^2)$, or the Hinkley (1977) counterpart, which is (9.A.5) with a $T/(T-K)$ degrees-of-freedom correction.

9.A.3 An Example

To give the resampling procedures operational content, we use the sampling model described in Section 6.1.5 of Chapter 6. The normal linear model is

$$y_t = \mathbf{x}_t'\boldsymbol{\beta} + e_t = x_{1t}10 + x_{2t}0.4 + x_{3t}0.6 + e_t \tag{9.A.6}$$

where $e_t \sim N(0, 0.0625)$ and $t = 1, 2, \ldots, 20$. To make the example consistent with the inference problems discussed in this chapter, we augment the i.i.d. sampling model and consider the heteroskedastic case when $E[e_t^2] = \sigma_t^2 = 0.0625(1 + x_{2t}^2 + x_{3t}^2)$. In these examples, each of the experiments will be replicated 500 times.

First, for expository purposes, let us use the assumption of i.i.d. errors and compare the performance of the least squares, bootstrap, and jackknife estimators as a basis for obtaining measures of precision as reflected by the standard errors of $\mathbf{b}$; that is, the square roots of the diagonal elements of the covariance for $\mathbf{b}$. These resulting standard errors are

	b_1	b_2	b_3	
Least squares	0.2285	0.0937	0.1405	
Bootstrap	0.2298	0.0981	0.1402	(9.A.7)
Jackknife	0.2381	0.1208	0.1419	

As expected, the bootstrap and least squares results are very close to each other. In this example because of sampling errors, the estimators yield results that are close to but not completely on target to the true standard errors which are 0.2025, 0.0809, and 0.1246.

In the heteroskedastic case, when $\sigma_t^2 = 0.0625(1 + x_{2t}^2 + x_{3t}^2)$ and the precision matrix is $(X'X)^{-1}X'\Lambda X(X'X)^{-1}$, the results for the standard errors are

	b_1	b_2	b_3	
Least squares	0.5440	0.2232	0.3345	
Bootstrap	0.5474	0.2230	0.3317	
Jackknife	0.4881	0.2789	0.3258	(9.A.8)
White	0.4162	0.2385	0.2690	

In this example, when compared to the true standard errors (0.4133, 0.1925, and 0.2905), none of the estimators did very well. This was expected for the least squares and bootstrap where the inherent heteroskedasticity among the e_t is lost in the process of the i.i.d. sampling. The jackknife and White heteroskedastic-consistent estimators, although perhaps acceptable for the first and third standard errors, are inferior to the least squares and bootstrap results for the second. Let us emphasize that the objective of this appendix has been to introduce resampling schemes; because of the small sample size and number of replications, no statistical significance should be attached to these results. For a good discussion of the sampling results in the heteroskedastic case, refer to MacKinnon and White (1985).

If in the statistical model (9.A.1) the covariance of $\mathbf{e}$ is Σ and this must be estimated from the data by $\hat{\Sigma}$, then these resampling procedures may be applied within a generalized least squares context (Freedman and Peters, 1984). Since the conventional asymptotic covariance $(X'\hat{\Sigma}^{-1}X)^{-1}$ may not be a good approximation in finite samples because $\hat{\Sigma}$ is not a good estimate of Σ, these resampling procedures offer a viable alternative for inference.

9.A.4 References

Efron, B. (1979) "Bootstrap Methods: Another Look at the Jackknife." *Annals of Statistics*, 7, 1–26.

Efron, B. (1982) *The Jackknife, the Bootstrap and Other Resampling Plans.* Philadelphia: Siam Publishing.

Freedman, D., and S. C. Peters (1984) "Bootstrapping a Regression Equation: Some Empirical Results." *Journal of the American Statistical Association*, 79, 97–106.

Hinkley, D. V. (1977) "Jackknifing in Unbalanced Situations." *Technometrics*, 19, 285–292.

MacKinnon, J. G., and H. White (1985) "Some Heteroskedastic Consistent Covariance Estimators with Improved Finite Sample Properties." *Journal of Econometrics*, 29, 305–325.

Miller, R. G. (1979) "The Jackknife—A Review." *Biometrika*, 61, 1–15.

Peters, S. C., and D. Freedman (1984) "Some Notes on the Bootstrap in Regression Problems." *Journal of Business and Economic Statistics*, 2, 406–409.

White, H. (1980) "A Heteroskedasticity-Consistent Covariance Matrix and a Direct Test for Heteroskedasticity." *Econometrica*, 48, 817–838.

White, K., S. Haun and N. Horsman (1987) *SHAZAM; Users Reference Manual.* Version 6. Vancouver: University of British Columbia.

Wu, C. F. G. (1986) "Jackknife, Bootstrap and Other Resampling Methods in Regression Analysis." *Annals of Statistics*, 14, 1261–1295.

CHAPTER 10

Dummy Variables and Varying Parameter Models

10.1 Introduction

A basic assumption of the regression models studied in Chapters 5 through 7 is that the parameter vector $\boldsymbol{\beta}$ does not vary across sample observations. That is, the location vector $\boldsymbol{\beta}$ is the same for all observations in the sample. If the location parameters are not constant for all sample observations, the statistical model is changed and thus the usual least squares (LS) or generalized least squares (GLS) estimators lose their nice properties. In fact, if these rules are used, it is not clear *what* they are estimators of. In this chapter we explore various ways to combine sets of observations, for the purpose of estimation, when the assumption of constant parameters may be violated. Many of the topics discussed in this chapter can and do apply directly to problems associated with pooling time-series and cross-sectional data, but the primary discussion of that topic is contained in Chapter 11. In this chapter we focus on models with parameters that vary in some systematic and/or random way across partitions of the sample data, or even from observation to observation.

The first model we consider, in Section 10.2, incorporates dummy variables to capture discrete shifts in the parameters generating the data. We present an array of these models that reflects varying degrees of generality and flexibility. In Section 10.3 we use the dummy variable models to test for parameter changes. Section 10.4 contains a generalization of the switching regression model in which the parameters vary systematically in response to changes in some auxiliary explanatory variables. Consequently, an effort is made actually to model the parameter variation explicitly. Finally, in Section 10.5 we consider the Hildreth–Houck random coefficients model in which the parameter values are conceivably different for every single observation, but which have a well-defined probability structure. We conclude the chapter with a summary and a guide to the broad literature on random and varying parameter models.

10.2 Use of Dummy Variables in Estimation

There are many cases in which a sample can be divided into two or more partitions in which some or all of the location parameters may differ. Common situations include seasonality models, in which explanatory variables have different effects depending on the season of the year; models that allow behavioral differences in geographic regions; models that permit different response coefficients during unusual time periods, such as war years; models that allow for different behavioral parameters for individuals based on qualitative factors such as sex, race, level of educational attainment, and marital status.

To be specific, consider the linear statistical model

$$y_t = \beta_1 + x_{t2}\beta_2 + \cdots + x_{tK}\beta_K + e_t \qquad t = 1, \ldots, T \tag{10.2.1}$$

where the x's are nonstochastic and the $e_t \sim N(0, \sigma^2)$. Under the usual classical assumptions of Chapters 6 and 7, if the parameters β_k are fixed for all T observations, then the best linear unbiased estimator of the regression parameters is the least squares–maximum likelihood estimator. Suppose, however, we believe there is a difference in some of or all the regression parameters for a subset of the observations. To keep matters simple, but perfectly general, suppose the observations are ordered (under the assumptions of the classical linear statistical model the order of the observations does not matter) so that the parameter structure is different for observations $t = 1, \ldots, T_1$ (the first sample partition) and $t = T_1 + 1, T_1 + 2, \ldots, T$ (the second sample partition). We will first consider the case when only the intercept β_1 is thought to have different values in the two partitions (samples) and then consider the cases in which the other location (slope) parameters may differ.

10.2.1 Intercept is Allowed to Change

To allow for a change in the intercept parameter across the sample partition, we define a dummy variable

$$D_t = \begin{cases} 0 & \text{if } t = 1, \ldots, T_1 \\ 1 & \text{if } t = T_1 + 1, \ldots, T \end{cases} \tag{10.2.2}$$

Then we rewrite the statistical model as

$$y_t = \beta_1 + D_t\delta + x_{t2}\beta_2 + \cdots + x_{tK}\beta_K + e_t \qquad t = 1, \ldots, T \tag{10.2.3}$$

The effect of including the term $D_t \cdot \delta$ is to allow for a different regression intercept term in the two sample partitions. To see this, note that

$$E[y_t] = \begin{cases} \beta_1 + x_{t2}\beta_2 + \cdots + x_{tK}\beta_K & t = 1, \ldots, T_1 \\ (\beta_1 + \delta) + x_{t2}\beta_2 + \cdots + x_{tK}\beta_K & t = T_1 + 1, \ldots, T \end{cases} \tag{10.2.4}$$

Thus for the second sample partition the intercept is $(\beta_1 + \delta)$ rather than β_1. This is depicted in Figure 10.1 for the case where $K = 2$ and $\delta > 0$. The parameter δ represents the difference between the intercept values in the two sample partitions.

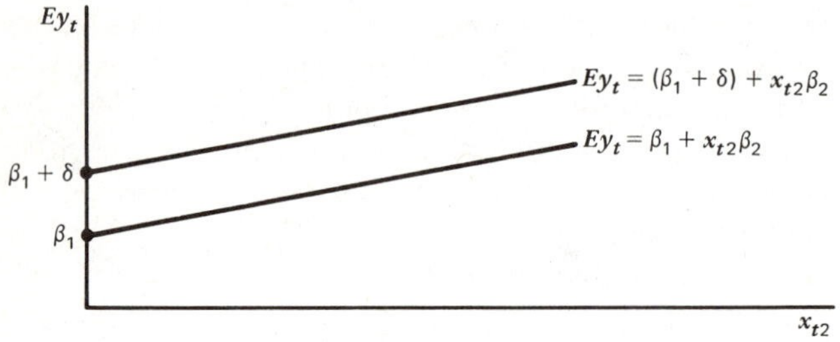

Figure 10.1 Effect of inclusion of an "Intercept Dummy Variable."

If all the usual regression assumptions hold for (10.2.3), the parameter δ, and all the others, can be estimated by LS.

A clearer understanding of how a dummy variable "works" can be gained by writing the model in a matrix form. Suppose the sample partition 1 contains T_1 observations and sample partition 2 contains T_2, so $T = T_1 + T_2$. Let $\mathbf{j}_T$ be a $(T \times 1)$ vector of ones, and for notational simplicity let $\mathbf{j}_1$ and $\mathbf{j}_2$ denote $(T_1 \times 1)$ and $(T_2 \times 1)$ vectors of ones. Then the regression model (10.2.3) can be written in partitioned form

$$\begin{bmatrix} \mathbf{y}_1 \\ \mathbf{y}_2 \end{bmatrix} = \begin{bmatrix} \mathbf{j}_1 & \mathbf{0} & X_1 \\ \mathbf{j}_2 & \mathbf{j}_2 & X_2 \end{bmatrix} \begin{bmatrix} \beta_1 \\ \delta \\ \boldsymbol{\beta}. \end{bmatrix} + \begin{bmatrix} \mathbf{e}_1 \\ \mathbf{e}_2 \end{bmatrix} \tag{10.2.5}$$

where $\mathbf{y}_1$ and $\mathbf{y}_2$ are $(T_1 \times 1)$ and $(T_2 \times 1)$ partitions containing observations on the dependent variable, X_1 and X_2 are $(T_1 \times (K-1))$ and $(T_2 \times (K-1))$ matrices of observations on the nonconstant explanatory variables, $\boldsymbol{\beta}.$ is the $(K-1) \times 1$ vector containing the slope parameters $\beta_2, \ldots, \beta_K$. Finally $\mathbf{e}_1$ and $\mathbf{e}_2$ are correspondingly partitioned vectors of random disturbances. Since it is extremely important that this partitioned matrix form be understood, we will write (10.2.5) in detail as

$$\begin{bmatrix} y_1 \\ y_2 \\ \vdots \\ y_{T_1} \\ \hline y_{T_1+1} \\ \vdots \\ y_T \end{bmatrix} = \begin{bmatrix} 1 & 0 & x_{12} & & x_{1K} \\ 1 & 0 & x_{22} & \cdots & x_{2K} \\ \vdots & \vdots & \vdots & & \vdots \\ 1 & 0 & x_{T_1,2} & & x_{T_1,K} \\ \hline 1 & 1 & x_{T_1+1,2} & & x_{T_1+1,K} \\ \vdots & \vdots & \vdots & \cdots & \vdots \\ 1 & 1 & x_{T2} & & x_{TK} \end{bmatrix} \begin{bmatrix} \beta_1 \\ \delta \\ \beta_2 \\ \vdots \\ \beta_K \end{bmatrix} + \begin{bmatrix} e_1 \\ e_2 \\ \vdots \\ e_{T_1} \\ \hline e_{T_1+1} \\ \vdots \\ e_T \end{bmatrix} \tag{10.2.6}$$

The first column of the "stacked" design matrix is a $(T \times 1)$ column of ones that is the variable associated with the basic or overall intercept parameter β_1. The second column contains the values of the dummy variable D_t associated with the increment in the intercept, δ, which is added to the overall intercept parameter for the observations in the second sample partition. It is extremely important to realize that, despite the partitioned nature of the matrices involved, both (10.2.5) and (10.2.6) can be written more simply as $\mathbf{y} = X\boldsymbol{\beta} + \mathbf{e}$ and that the parameter vector $\boldsymbol{\beta}$ can be estimated using the usual LS rule.

The question might well be asked why an intercept for the second partition was not estimated directly. The answer is, we could have. Let us define a second dummy variable as

$$C_t = 1 - D_t = \begin{cases} 1 & \text{if } t = 1, \ldots, T_1 \\ 0 & \text{if } t = T_1 + 1, \ldots, T \end{cases} \tag{10.2.7}$$

and rewrite (10.2.3) as

$$y_t = C_t \beta_{11} + D_t \beta_{21} + x_{t2}\beta_2 + \cdots + x_{tK}\beta_K + e_t \tag{10.2.8}$$

In the model (10.2.8), the regression functions for the two sample partitions are

$$E[y_t] = \begin{cases} \beta_{11} + x_{t2}\beta_2 + \cdots + x_{tK}\beta_K & \text{if } t = 1, \ldots, T_1 \\ \beta_{21} + x_{t2}\beta_2 + \cdots + x_{tK}\beta_K & \text{if } t = T_1 + 1, \ldots, T \end{cases} \tag{10.2.9}$$

Thus β_{11} is the intercept for the first sample partition [and equal to β_1 in (10.2.3)] and β_{21} is the intercept in the second partition [and equal to $\beta_1 + \delta$ in (10.2.3)].

Note that in (10.2.8) there is no "overall" intercept term. In matrix terms the reason for its omission is clear, as (10.2.8) is

$$\begin{bmatrix} \mathbf{y}_1 \\ \mathbf{y}_2 \end{bmatrix} = \begin{bmatrix} \mathbf{j}_1 & \mathbf{0} & X_1 \\ \mathbf{0} & \mathbf{j}_2 & X_2 \end{bmatrix} \begin{bmatrix} \beta_{11} \\ \beta_{21} \\ \boldsymbol{\beta}. \end{bmatrix} + \begin{bmatrix} \mathbf{e}_1 \\ \mathbf{e}_2 \end{bmatrix} \tag{10.2.10}$$

If we had included an overall intercept term in (10.2.8), then there would be a $(T \times 1)$ vector of ones in the design matrix, which would be *exactly* collinear with $D_t + C_t = 1$ so that least squares estimation would break down owing to failure of the rank condition for X. Specifically, unbiased and consistent estimators of the overall intercept, β_{11}, and β_{21} cannot be constructed if an overall intercept term is included since all those parameters are not identified. We will call (10.2.10) the "sets of equations" format and (10.2.5) the "dummy variable" format for the underlying structure.

To illustrate the use, and equivalence, of these two model formulations, consider the data in Table 10.1 labeled y_A, x_2, and x_3. Suppose the data relate to a model of capital investment by a U.S. firm. That is, imagine that y_A, x_2, and x_3 are measures of investment, lagged profit, and lagged capital stock, all in real dollars. The sample

Table 10.1 Artificial investment data

Year	y_A	y_B	y_C	x_2	x_3
1935	41.718	41.718	41.718	1170.6	97.8
1936	61.093	61.093	61.093	2015.8	104.4
1937	68.616	68.616	68.616	2803.3	118.0
1938	77.193	77.193	77.193	2039.7	156.2
1939	121.413	105.879	173.565	2256.2	172.6
1940	118.226	101.432	165.398	2132.2	186.6
1941	105.236	85.355	140.378	1834.1	220.9
1942	123.326	97.424	145.064	1588.0	287.8
1943	105.849	77.058	129.540	1749.4	319.9
1944	95.336	66.419	117.035	1687.2	321.3
1945	120.509	91.745	151.976	2007.7	319.6
1946	110.411	110.411	110.411	2208.3	346.0
1947	114.447	114.447	114.447	1656.7	456.4
1948	122.085	122.085	122.085	1604.4	543.4
1949	86.129	86.129	86.129	618.3	555.1
1950	143.956	143.956	143.956	1610.5	647.4
1951	167.543	167.543	167.543	1819.4	671.3
1952	162.048	162.048	162.048	2079.7	726.1
1953	175.922	175.922	175.922	2371.6	800.3
1954	214.173	214.173	214.173	2759.9	888.9

data contains the war years, which we take to be 1939–1945. The true regression function, used to generate the data, is

$$E[y_t] = -10.0 + 0.03x_{t2} + 0.15x_{t3} + 20D_t \tag{10.2.11}$$

where D_t is the dummy variable

$$D_t = \begin{cases} 1 & \text{if year} = 1939, \ldots, 1945 \\ 0 & \text{otherwise} \end{cases}$$

The observations on y_A were generated by adding a $N(0, \sigma^2 = 100)$ random disturbance to $E[y_t]$ in (10.2.11).

In Table 10.2 we report the results of various ordinary least squares (OLS) regressions.

In Table 10.2, Model 1 is the regression model with no dummy variable included, Model 2 includes the dummy variable D_t, and Model 3 is the set of equations equivalent. You will note that in Model 2 the estimated coefficient of D_t is $\hat{\delta} = 28.288$, which is, except for rounding, the difference between the estimated coefficients of C_t and D_t, $\hat{\delta} = \hat{\beta}_{21} - \hat{\beta}_{11} = 18.099 - (-10.190)$. Furthermore, the

Table 10.2 OLS Regression Results for Dependent Variable y_A (Standard Errors in Parentheses)

Model	1	2	3
Intercept	8.152	−10.190	—
	(16.68)	(11.72)	
D_t	—	28.288	18.099
		(5.95)	(11.26)
C_t	—	—	−10.190
			(11.72)
x_2	0.028	0.028	0.028
	(0.0080)	(0.0053)	(0.0053)
x_3	0.140	0.163	0.163
	(0.016)	(0.012)	(0.012)
$\hat{\sigma}^2$	303.52	133.58	133.58
		↑	↑
		Equation (10.2.3)	Equation (10.2.8)

estimated covariance matrix for Model 3 is reported in Table 10.3. From that we can compute

$$\begin{aligned}\operatorname{var}(\hat{\delta}) &= \operatorname{var}(\hat{\beta}_{21}) + \operatorname{var}(\hat{\beta}_{11}) - 2\operatorname{cov}(\hat{\beta}_{21}, \hat{\beta}_{11}) \\ &= 126.859 + 137.354 - 2(114.424) \\ &= 35.365\end{aligned}$$

the square root of which is 5.95, which is identical to the standard error of $\hat{\delta}$ in Model 2. In all respects but interpretation the model formulations are equivalent.

Table 10.3 Covariance Matrix of Parameter Estimates in Model 3

	D	C	x_2	x_3
D	126.8591	114.424	−0.0529091	−0.0290572
C	114.424	137.3539	−0.052448	−0.0578449
x_2	−0.0529091	−0.052448	0.00002845202	−0.0000036976
x_3	−0.0290572	−0.0578449	−0.0000036976	0.0001380281

10.2.2 The Intercept and Some Slope Parameters Change

We now will allow for the possibility that, in addition to a possible difference in the intercept parameter, some of, but not all, the slope parameters change as well. In order to treat the situation as generally as possible, we will divide the $(K-1)$ explanatory variables in (10.2.1) into two groups; those P variables with coefficients that are allowed to change and the remaining $Q = (K-1) - P$ with coefficients that are thought to be constant under this scenario. Then, the appropriately modified model is

$$\begin{aligned} y_t = \beta_1 + D_t\delta_1 + x_{t2}\beta_2 + x_{t2}D_t\delta_2 + \cdots + x_{t,P+1}\beta_{P+1} \\ + x_{t,P+1}D_t\delta_{P+1} + x_{t,P+2}\beta_{P+2} + \cdots + x_{tK}\beta_K + e_t \end{aligned} \qquad (10.2.12)$$

In addition to the intercept dummy variable D_t, there are P "interaction" variables $x_{tk} \cdot D_t$. The effect of these interaction variables on the regression function is

$$E[y_t] \begin{cases} = \beta_1 + x_{t2}\beta_2 + \cdots + x_{tK}\beta_K & \text{if } t = 1, \ldots, T_1 \\ = (\beta_1 + \delta_1) + x_{t2}(\beta_2 + \delta_2) + \cdots + x_{t,P+1}(\beta_{P+1} + \delta_{P+1}) & \\ \quad + x_{t,P+2}\beta_{P+2} + \cdots + x_{tK}\beta_K & \text{if } t = T_1 + 1, \ldots, T \end{cases} \qquad (10.2.13)$$

The parameters δ_i, $i = 2, \ldots, P + 1$, represent increments to the slope parameters for observations in the second sample partition. Consider a simple statistical model where $K = 2$ and the variable x_{t2} has a parameter that is allowed to change (so $P = K - 1 = 1$ and $Q = 0$). This effect is depicted in Figure 10.2.

To write this model in matrix terms, let X_{i1} be the $(T_i \times P)$ matrix of observations on the P-regressors in partition i whose coefficients are thought to change. Let X_{i2} be the $(T_i \times Q)$ matrix of observations on the Q-explanatory

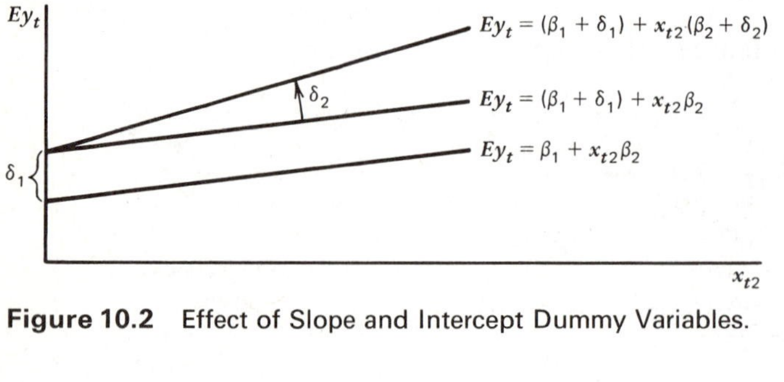

Figure 10.2 Effect of Slope and Intercept Dummy Variables.

variables with constant parameters. Denote the parameter partitions by $\boldsymbol{\beta}'_{.1} = (\beta_2, \ldots, \beta_{P+1})$, $\boldsymbol{\beta}'_{.2} = (\beta_{P+2}, \ldots, \beta_K)$ and $\boldsymbol{\delta}' = (\delta_2, \ldots, \delta_{P+1})$. Then

$$\begin{bmatrix} \mathbf{y}_1 \\ \mathbf{y}_2 \end{bmatrix} = \begin{bmatrix} \mathbf{j}_1 & 0 & X_{11} & 0 & X_{12} \\ \mathbf{j}_2 & \mathbf{j}_2 & X_{21} & X_{21} & X_{22} \end{bmatrix} \begin{bmatrix} \beta_1 \\ \delta_1 \\ \boldsymbol{\beta}_{.1} \\ \boldsymbol{\delta} \\ \boldsymbol{\beta}_{.2} \end{bmatrix} + \begin{bmatrix} \mathbf{e}_1 \\ \mathbf{e}_2 \end{bmatrix} \tag{10.2.14}$$

The model (10.2.14) is written in its "dummy variable" format. The equivalent sets of equations format is

$$\begin{bmatrix} \mathbf{y}_1 \\ \mathbf{y}_2 \end{bmatrix} = \begin{bmatrix} \mathbf{j}_1 & 0 & X_{11} & 0 & X_{12} \\ 0 & \mathbf{j}_2 & 0 & \mathrm{X}_{21} & \mathrm{X}_{22} \end{bmatrix} \begin{bmatrix} \beta_{11} \\ \beta_{21} \\ \boldsymbol{\beta}_{11} \\ \boldsymbol{\beta}_{21} \\ \boldsymbol{\beta}_{.2} \end{bmatrix} + \begin{bmatrix} \mathbf{e}_1 \\ \mathbf{e}_2 \end{bmatrix}$$

where β_{11} and β_{21} $(= \beta_1 + \delta_1)$ are separate intercept parameters for the two partitions, $\boldsymbol{\beta}_{11}$ $(= \boldsymbol{\beta}_{.1})$ and $\boldsymbol{\beta}_{21}$ $(= \boldsymbol{\beta}_{.1} + \boldsymbol{\delta})$ are separate slope parameters for the partitions. As in the case when only the intercept parameter was allowed to change, the two formulations are logically equivalent, the only difference being a matter of convenience to the user.

To illustrate these models, continue the example begun earlier. Using the same regressor values x_2 and x_3 from Table 10.2, the regression function is altered as

$$E[y_t] = -10.0 + 20D_t + 0.03x_{t2} + 0.15x_{t3} - 0.09x_{t3}D_t \tag{10.2.15}$$

Adding the same $N(0, \sigma^2 = 100)$ disturbances as before yields the variable labeled y_B in Table 10.1. Regression results are reported in Table 10.4. Model 1 is a model with no dummy variables present; Model 2 contains a slope and intercept dummy; and Model 3 is the equivalent sets of equations format. As with the earlier case, the estimated coefficient of the dummy variable D_t in Model 2 is exactly the difference between the coefficients in Model 3 of D_t (intercept in second partition) and C_t (intercept in first partition). Furthermore, the estimated coefficient of $x_{t3}D_t$ in Model 2 corresponds in Model 3 to the difference in the coefficient of x_3 in partition 1 (that of $x_{t3}C_t$) and the coefficient on x_3 in partition 2 (that of $x_{t3}D_t$). Using the covariance matrix of parameter estimates for Model 3 in Table 10.5, you may verify that the standard errors of coefficients on D_t and $x_{t3}D_t$ in Model 2 can be calculated from the results for Model 3.

Table 10.4 OLS Regression Results for Dependent Variable y_B

Model	1	2	3
Intercept	−8.883	−7.593	
	(12.95)	(10.20)	
D_t		71.427	63.834
		(17.88)	(20.61)
C_t			−7.593
			(10.199)
x_{t2}	0.029	0.025	0.025
	(0.0062)	(0.0047)	(0.0047)
x_{t3}	0.157	0.168	
	(0.013)	(0.010)	
$x_{t3} \cdot D_t$		−0.251	−0.084
		(0.064)	(0.063)
$x_{t3} \cdot C_t$			0.168
			(0.010)
$\hat{\sigma}^2$	182.99	100.12	100.12

10.2.3 The Intercept and All Slope Parameters are Allowed to Change

In the two previous cases not all the parameters were thought to be different across the sample partitions. In both cases some variables were restricted to have their parameters remain constant across the partitions. Now we will explore the consequences of letting all the parameters in the equation differ in the two sets of sample observations. The model modified to include a dummy variable on each regressor, including the intercept, is

$$y_t = \beta_1 + D_t\delta_1 + \sum_{k=2}^{K} (x_{tk}\beta_k + x_{tk}D_t\delta_k) + e_t \tag{10.2.16}$$

Table 10.5 Covariance of Estimates for Model 3 in Table 10.4

	D	C	x_2	x_3D	x_3C
D	424.7143	104.4823	−0.0578231	−1.15188	0.01199838
C	104.4823	104.0185	−0.0403445	−0.107518	−0.0414409
x_2	−0.0578231	−0.0403445	0.00002232765	0.00005950296	−0.000004633
x_3D	−1.15188	−0.107518	0.00005950296	0.003977939	−0.000012347
x_3C	0.01199838	−0.0414409	−0.000004633	−0.000012347	0.0001069228

In matrix form the dummy variable model is

$$\begin{bmatrix} \mathbf{y}_1 \\ \mathbf{y}_2 \end{bmatrix} = \begin{bmatrix} \mathbf{j}_1 & \mathbf{0} & X_{1.} & 0 \\ \mathbf{j}_2 & \mathbf{j}_2 & X_{2.} & X_{2.} \end{bmatrix} \begin{bmatrix} \beta_1 \\ \delta_1 \\ \boldsymbol{\beta}. \\ \boldsymbol{\delta} \end{bmatrix} + \begin{bmatrix} \mathbf{e}_1 \\ \mathbf{e}_2 \end{bmatrix} \tag{10.2.17}$$

where $X_{1.}$ and $X_{2.}$ are $(T_i \times (K-1))$ and contain the observations on the $(K-1)$ nonconstant regressors, $\boldsymbol{\beta}. = (\beta_2, \ldots, \beta_K)'$, and $\boldsymbol{\delta} = (\delta_2, \ldots, \delta_K)'$. The equivalent sets of equations format is

$$\begin{bmatrix} \mathbf{y}_1 \\ \mathbf{y}_2 \end{bmatrix} = \begin{bmatrix} \mathbf{j}_1 & \mathbf{0} & X_{1.} & 0 \\ \mathbf{0} & \mathbf{j}_2 & 0 & X_{2.} \end{bmatrix} \begin{bmatrix} \beta_{11} \\ \beta_{21} \\ \boldsymbol{\beta}_{1.} \\ \boldsymbol{\beta}_{2.} \end{bmatrix} + \begin{bmatrix} \mathbf{e}_1 \\ \mathbf{e}_2 \end{bmatrix} \tag{10.2.18}$$

where $\beta_{21}(= \beta_1 + \delta_1)$ is the intercept for partition 2 and $\boldsymbol{\beta}_{1.}$ and $\boldsymbol{\beta}_{2.}$ are separate sets of slope parameters for the partitions.

By reordering the parameters in (10.2.18) we obtain

$$\begin{bmatrix} \mathbf{y}_1 \\ \mathbf{y}_2 \end{bmatrix} = \begin{bmatrix} (\mathbf{j}_1 \;\; X_{1.}) & 0 \\ 0 & (\mathbf{j}_2 \;\; X_{2.}) \end{bmatrix} \begin{bmatrix} \beta_{11} \\ \boldsymbol{\beta}_{1.} \\ \beta_{21} \\ \boldsymbol{\beta}_{2.} \end{bmatrix} + \begin{bmatrix} \mathbf{e}_1 \\ \mathbf{e}_2 \end{bmatrix}$$

$$= \begin{bmatrix} X_1 & 0 \\ 0 & X_2 \end{bmatrix} \begin{bmatrix} \boldsymbol{\beta}_1 \\ \boldsymbol{\beta}_2 \end{bmatrix} + \begin{bmatrix} \mathbf{e}_1 \\ \mathbf{e}_2 \end{bmatrix} = X\boldsymbol{\beta} + \mathbf{e} \tag{10.2.19}$$

Applying LS to (10.2.19) yields estimators for the stacked parameter vector $\boldsymbol{\beta}$:

$$\mathbf{b} = \begin{bmatrix} \mathbf{b}_1 \\ \mathbf{b}_2 \end{bmatrix} = \begin{bmatrix} (X_1'X_1)^{-1}X_1'\mathbf{y}_1 \\ (X_2'X_2)^{-1}X_2'\mathbf{y}_2 \end{bmatrix}$$

which is simply the result of applying LS to each of the sample partitions separately. This "makes sense" as we have allowed completely different parametric structures across the two partitions. Several remarks are in order:

1. In the earlier cases where either just the intercept changed or the intercept and just some of the slope parameters we could *not* have obtained equivalent results by estimating two regressions. In both cases *some* parameters were restricted to be the same. To impose those restrictions, the data from the two sample partitions had to be appropriately ordered and the resulting parametric model estimated. Alternatively, the unrestricted model (10.2.19) could have been restricted using appropriately defined linear restrictions, $R\boldsymbol{\beta} = \mathbf{r}$, and restricted least squares applied (see Exercises 10.3 and 10.4). In either case only one model is estimated.

2. Estimating the model (10.2.19) is not *completely* the same as estimating separate regressions for the two sample partitions. Two completely separate regressions would produce two estimates of σ^2, which, to this point, we have assumed is identical across partitions. The estimator of the error variance from (10.2.19) is

$$\begin{aligned}\hat{\sigma}^2 = [&(\mathbf{y}_1 - X_1\mathbf{b}_1)'(\mathbf{y}_1 - X_1\mathbf{b}_1) \\ &+ (\mathbf{y}_2 - X_2\mathbf{b}_2)'(\mathbf{y}_2 - X_2\mathbf{b}_2)]/(T_1 + T_2 - 2K)\end{aligned} \qquad (10.2.20)$$

We see in the numerator that the sum of squared errors from (10.2.20) is the sum of squared errors from the two separate regressions. A "pooled" estimate of the error variance σ^2 can therefore be constructed easily. However, it is *not* either estimate provided on the two LS regression computer printouts, and, of course, the t-values and F and R^2 values are also not equivalent to those from (10.2.19).

3. It should be apparent that we can allow all the parameters to differ across the two sample partitions only if the rank condition holds for each separate sample partition and, in particular, only if $T_1 \geq K$ and $T_2 \geq K$. Otherwise, although we may think the parameters have changed, we cannot obtain unbiased estimators for all $2K$ of them. Actually this "problem" extends to the earlier situations as well. For example, suppose there is but one observation ($T_2 = 1$) that we believe has different structural parameters than the other $T_1 = (T - 1)$ observations. Then we could allow *at most* one parameter (either the intercept or one slope) to differ. If we allowed (or tried to allow) more than one parameter to change for that single observation, the resulting design matrix would fail the rank condition and LS estimates of the stacked model could not be obtained. See Exercise 10.5 for further exploration of this point. Surprisingly, it is still possible to *test* for change in greater than $\min(T_1, T_2)$ parameters. This result is discussed in Exercise 10.6.

10.2.4 Two or More Sets of Dummy Variables

Many times there are two or more sets of qualitative factors that might affect the regression constant term or condition the response of the dependent variable to changes in one or more independent variables. For example, in examining household consumption behavior, one may want to allow for qualitative factors such as sex or race of the head of household, level of educational attainment (i.e., high school, college), or geographic region. Qualitative factors may not only affect slopes and intercepts but they may interact as well. For example, the effect of the head of the household being female may differ by region of the country in which the household lives. For illustration purposes consider the geographic region as being either North or South. Then interactions may be accounted for by defining the dummy variables

$$F_t = \begin{cases} 1 & \text{if head of household is female} \\ 0 & \text{if male} \end{cases}$$

$$S_t = \begin{cases} 1 & \text{if household lives in a Southern state} \\ 0 & \text{if Northern} \end{cases}$$

If we consider the regression model

$$E[y_t] = \beta_1 + F_t\delta_1 + S_t\delta_2 + F_tS_t\delta_3 + x_t\beta_2 \tag{10.2.21}$$

the inclusion of each of the dummy variables and their product allows for a different regression intercept for each of the possibilities:

Category	**Intercept**	**(F_t, S_t)**
Male head-North	β_1	(0, 0)
Male head-South	$\beta_1 + \delta_2$	(0, 1)
Female head-North	$\beta_1 + \delta_1$	(1, 0)
Female head-South	$\beta_1 + \delta_1 + \delta_2 + \delta_3$	(1, 1)

The coefficients of the dummy variables then are increments to the intercept in the base-case (male head-North), δ_1 capturing the sex effect, δ_2 the regional effect, and δ_3 allowing for the possibility that being a female head of household in the South has an effect that is not simply the sum of the regional and sex effects. More will be said about this interpretation in Section 10.4 when we discuss systematically varying parameter models. See Exercise 10.7 for practice in interacting two or more dummy variables with continuous regressors.

10.2.5 Switching Regression Models

Models that use dummy variables imply the presence of identifiable parameter regimes that hold for well-defined subsets of the entire sample. In this section we consider similar models but with additional constraints. The models will be presented in the time-series framework because they are somewhat more natural in that setting. In addition, the sample will be split into only two subsets, although the generalization to more than two groups is straightforward.

Let the observations that fall into different parameter regimes be split into two groups of T_1 and T_2 observations, where $T_1 + T_2 = T$. These groups do not have to contain observations that are sequential in time, but they may, and it is convenient to think of them as if they do. The two regimes can be written as

$$y_t = \begin{cases} \mathbf{x}'_{t1}\boldsymbol{\beta}_1 + e_{t1} & \text{if } t \in \{T_1\} \\ \mathbf{x}'_{t2}\boldsymbol{\beta}_2 + e_{t2} & \text{if } t \in \{T_2\} \end{cases} \tag{10.2.22}$$

or, in matrix notation, as

$$\begin{bmatrix} \mathbf{y}_1 \\ \mathbf{y}_2 \end{bmatrix} = \begin{bmatrix} X_1 & 0 \\ 0 & X_2 \end{bmatrix} \begin{bmatrix} \boldsymbol{\beta}_1 \\ \boldsymbol{\beta}_2 \end{bmatrix} + \begin{bmatrix} \mathbf{e}_1 \\ \mathbf{e}_2 \end{bmatrix} = X\boldsymbol{\beta} + \mathbf{e} \tag{10.2.23}$$

Now let us stipulate that the pieces of the regression function in (10.2.22) must join at a point $T_1 \in \{1, T\}$. That is, at the point T_1,

$$E[y_{T_1}] = \mathbf{x}'_{T_1}\boldsymbol{\beta}_1 = \mathbf{x}'_{T_1}\boldsymbol{\beta}_2 \tag{10.2.24}$$

The condition (10.2.24) may be conveniently imposed by adding the constraint $\mathbf{x}'_{T_1}(\boldsymbol{\beta}_1 - \boldsymbol{\beta}_2) = 0$ to (10.2.23). The result is a piecewise (continuous) regression function.

Points like T_1, where the switch in the regression function takes place, are called "join" points because those are the points where the regression regimes are joined together. The models we have considered so far have assumed that the point, or points, of structural change are known. If this is not true, then the join points can be treated as parameters to be estimated. This problem is surveyed by Goldfeld and Quandt (1973). Given the model (10.2.23), if we assume that $e_{t1} \sim N(0, \sigma^2)$ and $e_{t2} \sim N(0, \sigma^2)$ and that no autocorrelation is present, the likelihood function, conditional on T_1, is

$$\mathscr{L}(\boldsymbol{\beta}_1, \boldsymbol{\beta}_2, \sigma^2 | T_1) = (2\pi)^{-T/2}(\sigma^2)^{-T/2}$$
$$\times \exp\left\{-\frac{1}{2\sigma^2}\left[\sum_{t=1}^{T_1} (y_t - \mathbf{x}'_t\boldsymbol{\beta}_1)^2 + \sum_{t=T_1+1}^{T} (y_t - \mathbf{x}'_t\boldsymbol{\beta}_2)^2\right]\right\} \tag{10.2.25}$$

An estimate of T_1 is chosen by searching over values of T_1 and choosing the value that maximizes the value of the likelihood function. A likelihood ratio test for the hypothesis of no structural change is performed by comparing the maximum value of the likelihood function (10.2.25) to the restricted likelihood function based on the assumption that a single regression function is appropriate for the entire sample.

An alternative test for structural shifts, when the join point is unknown, is suggested by Farley and Hinich (1970) and Farley, Hinich, and McGuire (1975). They approximate a discrete structural change at an unknown point by a continuous linear shift. That is, they assume the model $y_t = \mathbf{x}_t'\boldsymbol{\beta}_t + \mathbf{e}_t$ where $\boldsymbol{\beta}_t = \boldsymbol{\beta} + t\boldsymbol{\delta}$. Substituting for $\boldsymbol{\beta}_t$, the model becomes $y_t = \mathbf{x}_t'\boldsymbol{\beta} + t\mathbf{x}_t'\boldsymbol{\delta} + e_t$. A test for no structural change is then carried out by testing the joint hypothesis that $\boldsymbol{\delta} = \mathbf{0}$. Farley, Hinich, and McGuire (1975) note that this test is not very powerful unless the sample size or the structural shift is large.

10.2.6 Summary and Guide to Further Reading on Dummy Variables

In this section we have surveyed basic models using dummy variables to capture discrete shifts in the regression function. For more examples and general discussions of the use and interpretation of dummy variable models see Kmenta (1986, Chapter 11), Johnston (1984, Chapter 6), and Gujarati (1978, Chapter 13).

When designing dummy variable schemes, care must be taken regarding some important special cases or issues related to interpretation. In semilogarithmic regression models, for example, the interpretation of dummy variables is not straightforward. See Halvorsen and Palmquist (1980), Kennedy (1981), and Giles (1982).

In the context of switching regression models and piecewise regression models, there is a great amount of literature offering generalizations of what we have presented. See Judge, et al. (1985, pp. 798–806) for a survey. Bayesian procedures for handling structural change models are considered by Broemeling (1985, Chapter 7). A special case of switching regression regimes, and an important one, are those models designed to deal with seasonality. See Johnston (1984, Chapter 6), and Judge, et al. (1985, pp. 800–802). An interesting treatment of asymmetric structural change is offered by Houck (1977); it allows the effects of increases in variables to be different from the effects of decreases in those same variables, which might be the case when estimating short- or long-run supply functions, for example.

10.3 The Use of Dummy Variables to Test for a Change in the Location Vector

The dummy variable and sets of equations frameworks of Section 10.2 can be used in a straightforward way to test for the presence of changing parameter vectors. In Section 10.2 we stressed the equivalence of the dummy variable and sets of equations formats in estimation; they are likewise equivalent in the testing context.

To illustrate, we will consider the model in (10.2.16). The dependent variable y_C in Table 10.1 was generated using this structure and, in particular,

$$\begin{aligned} E[y_t] &= \beta_1 + \delta_1 D_t + \beta_2 x_{t2} + \delta_2 x_{t2} D_t + \beta_3 x_{t3} + \delta_3 x_{t3} D_t \\ &= -10.0 + 20D_t + 0.03x_{t2} + 0.03x_{t2} D_t + 0.15x_{t3} - 0.09x_{t3} D_t \end{aligned} \quad (10.3.1)$$

where the basic model is described in Section 10.2.1.

To test the hypothesis of no parameter change, we must test the joint hypothesis that $H_0: \delta_1 = \delta_2 = \delta_3 = 0$ against the alternative that at least one of the three hypotheses is not true. How we proceed to carry out and interpret the results of the test depends on the error process assumptions we are willing to make. If the random disturbances are independent and identically distributed normal random variables with zero mean and variance σ^2, we may use the F-test statistic developed in Chapter 6. For methods of carrying out the test under more general error process assumptions, see Exercises 10.10 through 10.12. A convenient form of the F-statistic in the current context is

$$u = \frac{(SSE_R - SSE_u)}{J\hat{\sigma}^2} \quad (10.3.2)$$

Table 10.6 OLS Estimates of Equation (10.3.1)

Model	Unrestricted	Restricted
Intercept	−8.221	24.278
	(10.66)	(31.19)
D_t	94.153	—
	(66.84)	
x_{t2}	0.0254	0.0321
	(0.0050)	(0.015)
$x_{t2}D_t$	0.0211	—
	(0.025)	
x_{t3}	0.167	0.108
	(0.011)	(0.030)
$x_{t3}D_t$	−0.274	
	(0.092)	
SSE	1488.57	18040.10
$\hat{\sigma}^2$	106.33	1061.18

$$u = \frac{SSE_R - SSE_u}{J\hat{\sigma}^2} = \frac{18040.10 - 1488.57}{3(106.33)} = 51.89$$

$F_{(3,14,\alpha=0.01)} = 5.56$

where SSE_R is the sum of squared errors from the model "restricted" by the null hypothesis, $\delta_1 = \delta_2 = \delta_3 = 0$; SSE_u is the sum of squared errors from the unrestricted model, (10.3.1), J is the number of hypotheses, and $\hat{\sigma}^2 = SSE_u/(T - 2K)$ is the unbiased estimator of the error variance in the unrestricted model. If the hypothesis is true, this test statistic has an F-distribution with J and $(T - 2K)$ degrees of freedom. To carry out the test, we estimate the restricted and unrestricted forms of the model and report the results in Table 10.6.

On the basis of the empirical results, we reject the hypothesis that there has been no structural change. It is interesting to note that if we tested the individual hypotheses $H_0: \delta_i = 0$ using the standard t-test ($t_{(0.01,14)} = 2.977, t_{(0.05.14)} = 2.145$) that only δ_3 appears significantly different from 0 at the $\alpha = 0.05$ level. There are two factors at work here. First, joint and individual hypotheses tests are not equivalent. Second, it must be remembered that only seven observations are being used to estimate the three coefficients of the dummy variables. Thus, although there is evidence that the regression functions for the two sample partitions are different, the individual parameters are not very precisely estimated for the smaller sample partition. For further exposition of testing for changing parameter structures see Fisher (1970) and Johnston (1984, pp. 207–223).

10.4 Systematically Varying Parameter Models

In Section 10.2 we presented dummy variable and switching regression models that permitted discrete changes in some of or all the regression parameters, including the intercept. We now present generalizations of such models that are not only useful in and of themselves but that also provide a general framework for most varying and random parameter models. To introduce the idea, we return to the model in (10.2.1) *but* we add an observation subscript (t) to the intercept parameter, so that

$$y_t = \beta_{1t} + x_{t2}\beta_2 + \cdots + x_{tK}\beta_K + e_t \qquad t = 1, \ldots, T \tag{10.4.1}$$

In this model the slopes of the regression function remain constant over the sample *but* the intercept may shift for each and every observation. How we model the shifting intercept determines how it will be interpreted and how the model should be estimated. For the present we will assume that β_{1t} varies *systematically* in a way that can be completely explained by exogenous factors. The case when β_{1t} varies *randomly* is considered in the following section. Let the parameter β_{1t} then be "modeled" as

$$\beta_{1t} = \delta_1 + z_t\delta_2 \tag{10.4.2}$$

where δ_1 and δ_2 are parameters and z_t is an exogenous explanatory variable designed to explain the variations in the intercept β_{1t}. The relation (10.4.2) is introduced into (10.4.1) by substitution, yielding

$$y_t = \delta_1 + z_t\delta_2 + x_{t2}\beta_2 + \cdots + x_{tK}\beta_K + e_t \tag{10.4.3}$$

The parameters δ_1 and δ_2 represent additional regression parameters to estimate in this context. If z_t is a dummy variable, then we have the dummy variable model (10.2.3). Clearly (10.4.2) could contain additional explanatory variables, which would add additional terms to the regression model, but that is all.

In addition to allowing the intercept to vary systematically, one could also impose such structures on other regression parameters that are thought to vary across the sample. For example, if we allow β_2 to vary as

$$\beta_{2t} = \gamma_1 + w_t\gamma_2 \tag{10.4.4}$$

then the regression model that incorporates (10.4.2) and (10.4.4) is

$$y_t = \delta_1 + z_t\delta_2 + x_{t2}\gamma_1 + x_{t2}w_t\gamma_2 + x_{t3}\beta_3 + \cdots + x_{tK}\beta_K + e_t \tag{10.4.5}$$

Note that modeling a slope parameter as exhibiting systematic variation creates an interaction term in the regression model. The parameters of the auxiliary relations (10.4.2) and (10.4.4), sometimes called "hyperparameters," are estimated along with the remaining parameters. It is useful to note once again that if w_t and z_t are dummy variables we have generated a model like that in Section 10.2.2. This process may be extended to more of the parameters β_k in the basic model or even to the hyperparameters themselves.

In the context of systematic parameter variation it is clear how one would test for the absence of systematic parameter variation. In (10.4.5) we test the hypotheses that the parameters δ_2 and/or γ_2 are zero. This is straightforward as long as one *knows* how to structure the models of systematic parameter variation, like (10.4.2) and (10.4.4). In the absence of such information there is temptation to consider broadly defined surrogate variables. In time-series models one might use auxiliary relations that are polynomials in calendar time to capture effects of unknown, time-related effects on structural parameters. As always, however, the temptation to engage in mechanical curve-fitting exercises is to be avoided.

10.5 Hildreth–Houck Random Coefficient Models

In this section we extend the results of the previous section to allow the possibility that coefficients may vary systematically and/or *randomly*. As illustrated in (10.4.3) and (10.4.5) the effect of introducing *systematic* parameter variation is to introduce interaction terms between explanatory variables whose parameters (or hyperparameters) are fixed over the sample period. Thus the essential character of the regression framework is not altered. The effect of assuming *random* parameter variation is somewhat different.

Following Hildreth and Houck (1968), consider the linear model, after any systematic parameter variation has been substituted in,

$$y_t = \beta_{t1} + \beta_{t2}x_{t2} + \cdots + \beta_{tK}x_{tK} \qquad t = 1, \ldots, T \tag{10.5.1}$$

This representation differs from the usual model in two respects: first, there is no error term; second, each of the unknown parameters has a time (observation) subscript, which implies that for each observation all the coefficients may change. In this section we assume that each parameter is a random variable. If this assumption can conveniently be represented as

$$\beta_{tk} = \bar{\beta}_k + u_{tk} \qquad k = 1, \ldots, K \tag{10.5.2}$$

where $\bar{\beta}_k$ is nonstochastic and regarded as a mean response coefficient and u_{tk} is a random disturbance with $E[u_{tk}] = 0$, $\text{var}(u_{tk}) = \alpha_k^2$, and

$$\text{cov}(u_{tk}, u_{sl}) = \begin{cases} 0 & t \neq s \\ \alpha_{kl} & t = s \end{cases} \tag{10.5.3}$$

the model (10.5.1) becomes

$$\begin{aligned} y_t &= \bar{\beta}_1 + u_{t1} + \sum_{k=2}^{K} (\bar{\beta}_k + u_{tk})x_{tk} \\ &= \bar{\beta}_1 + \sum_{k=2}^{K} (\bar{\beta}_k + u_{tk})x_{tk} + u_{t1} \end{aligned} \tag{10.5.4}$$

Thus the random component u_{t1} acts as the equation's error term. If (10.5.1) had an additive disturbance, its variance could not be estimated separately from that of u_{t1}.

We are interested in estimating the mean response vector $\bar{\boldsymbol{\beta}} = (\bar{\beta}_1, \ldots, \bar{\beta}_K)'$ and the covariance matrix of the disturbance vector $\mathbf{v}_t = (u_{t1}, \ldots, u_{tK})'$, which is $E(\mathbf{v}_t\mathbf{v}_t') = \Sigma$. Let $\mathbf{x}_t' = (1, x_{t2}, x_{t3}, \ldots, x_{tK})$. Then we may rewrite (10.5.4) as

$$y_t = \mathbf{x}_t'(\bar{\boldsymbol{\beta}} + \mathbf{v}_t) = \mathbf{x}_t'\bar{\boldsymbol{\beta}} + \mathbf{x}_t'\mathbf{v}_t = \mathbf{x}_t'\bar{\boldsymbol{\beta}} + e_t \tag{10.5.5}$$

which looks just like the usual linear model except that the error term e_t is heteroskedastic, with variance $\sigma_t^2 = \mathbf{x}_t'\Sigma\mathbf{x}_t$. If Σ is known, the generalized least squares estimator for $\bar{\boldsymbol{\beta}}$ is BLUE and is given by

$$\hat{\bar{\boldsymbol{\beta}}} = (X'\boldsymbol{\Phi}^{-1}X)^{-1}X'\boldsymbol{\Phi}^{-1}\mathbf{y} \tag{10.5.6}$$

where $\mathbf{\Phi}$ is a diagonal matrix with elements $\sigma_1^2, \sigma_2^2, \ldots, \sigma_T^2$ and $\hat{\bar{\boldsymbol{\beta}}}$ has covariance matrix $(X'\mathbf{\Phi}^{-1}X)^{-1}$. Given that we have a best linear unbiased estimator for the mean of the random coefficients, given by (10.5.6), the question of estimation of the actual coefficient values $\boldsymbol{\beta}_t$ in any particular time period arises. Actually, since $\boldsymbol{\beta}_t$ is random, it is better to say that we *predict* the values of the random vector $\boldsymbol{\beta}_t$. Since $\hat{\boldsymbol{\beta}}_t = \bar{\boldsymbol{\beta}} + \mathbf{v}_t$, to obtain an improved predictor for $\boldsymbol{\beta}_t$ we can add to the estimator of $\bar{\boldsymbol{\beta}}$, given in (10.5.6), a prediction of $\mathbf{v}_t$. Griffiths (1972) has shown that an appropriate predictor of $\mathbf{v}_t$ is

$$\Sigma\mathbf{x}_t(\mathbf{x}_t'\Sigma\mathbf{x}_t)^{-1}(y_t - \mathbf{x}_t'\hat{\bar{\boldsymbol{\beta}}})$$

Combining these results, the best linear unbiased predictor of $\boldsymbol{\beta}_t$ is

$$\hat{\boldsymbol{\beta}}_t = \hat{\bar{\boldsymbol{\beta}}} + \Sigma\mathbf{x}_t(\mathbf{x}_t'\,\Sigma\mathbf{x}_t)^{-1}(y_t - \mathbf{x}_t'\hat{\bar{\boldsymbol{\beta}}})$$

where $\mathbf{x}_t' = (1, x_{t2}, x_{t3}, \ldots, x_{tK})$ is the tth row of X.

To make $\hat{\bar{\boldsymbol{\beta}}}$ and $\hat{\boldsymbol{\beta}}_t$ operational, Σ must be estimated. For this purpose let $N = K(K+1)/2$ and write the variance of $\mathbf{x}_t'\mathbf{v}_t$ as

$$\text{var}(\mathbf{x}_t'\mathbf{v}_t) = \mathbf{x}_t'\Sigma\mathbf{x}_t = \mathbf{z}_t'\boldsymbol{\alpha} \tag{10.5.7}$$

where $\boldsymbol{\alpha}$ is an $(N \times 1)$ vector containing the distinct elements of Σ, and $\mathbf{z}_t' = (1, z_{t2}, \ldots, z_{tN})$ is found by calculating $\mathbf{x}_t' \otimes \mathbf{x}_t'$ and combining identical elements. For example, if $K = 3$, then $\boldsymbol{\alpha}' = (\alpha_1^2, \alpha_{12}, \alpha_{13}, \alpha_2^2, \alpha_{23}, \alpha_3^2)$ and $\mathbf{z}_t' = (1, 2x_{t2}, 2x_{t3}, x_{t2}^2, 2x_{t2}x_{t3}, x_{t3}^2)$. An unbiased estimator for $\hat{\boldsymbol{\alpha}}$ is

$$\hat{\boldsymbol{\alpha}} = (F'F)^{-1}F'\dot{\hat{\mathbf{e}}}$$

where $\dot{\hat{\mathbf{e}}}$ is the vector $\dot{\hat{\mathbf{e}}} = (\hat{e}_1^2, \hat{e}_2^2, \ldots, \hat{e}_T^2)'$ and the $\hat{e}_t$ are the least squares residuals $y_t - \mathbf{x}_t'(X'X)^{-1}X'\mathbf{y}$ and $F = \dot{M}Z$, where $\dot{M}$ contains the squares of the elements of $M = I - X(X'X)^{-1}X'$ and Z is the $(T \times N)$ matrix whose tth row is $\mathbf{z}_t'$. Unfortunately, this estimator for $\boldsymbol{\alpha}$ may not produce estimates that obey the restrictions that the elements of $\boldsymbol{\alpha}$ are the elements of a covariance matrix and that Σ is positive semidefinite. (See Chapter 19 of Judge, et al., 1985, and the references cited there for more on this problem.)

Finally, in addition to estimation, the applied worker is likely to be interested in testing for randomness in the coefficients. As is clear from (10.5.7), the type of randomness discussed here leads to a heteroskedastic model of the type discussed in Chapter 9, so for testing purposes, the tests discussed in Chapter 9 are appropriate. In particular, the Breusch–Pagan test is likely to be satisfactory.

10.6 Summary and Guide to Further Reading

In this chapter we have reviewed models that incorporate the possibility that structural parameters are not constant over all sample observations. Making an incorrect assumption about the constancy of the regression function means not only that usual estimation procedures may be inappropriate, but also that the interpretation of the regression parameters is incorrect. The dummy variable and switching regression models allow for the possibility of one or more discrete shifts in the parameter regimes. Systematically varying and random coefficient models allow the parameters to change on an observation by observation basis. In each case the effort is to make the regression function flexible enough to accommodate the true data generation process and yet be as parsimonious as possible with respect to the number of parameters that must be estimated. Further attention is paid to these issues in Chapter 11, which is devoted to the use of time-series and cross-section data. When combining different types of data, allowance is made for differences in the behavioural parameters of cross-sectional units.

There is a vast literature on models that incorporate varying and random parameters. The models we have presented in this chapter are standard ones, but many more schemes of modeling parameter variation exist. For a review of the literature and more references see Judge, et al. (1985, Chapter 19). One entire class of models treated there that is not treated here are time-series models in which a dynamic structure is placed on the parameters, which may or may not be stationary. Other surveys of the literature that are useful include Chow (1983), Raj and Ullah (1981), and Nicholls and Pagan (1985).

10.7 Exercises

10.1 Use the artificial investment data in Table 10.1 on the variables labeled y_A, x_2, and x_3 to estimate the model (10.2.3). Your results should agree with those in column 2 of Table 10.2. Use these parameter estimates and estimated covariance matrix to estimate the parameter β_{21} (the coefficient of D_t) in model (10.2.8) *and* its standard error. Your results should agree with those in column 3 of Table 10.2.

10.2 Use the artificial investment data in Table 10.1 on the variables labeled y_B, x_2, and x_3 to estimate the dummy variable model reported in column 2 of Table 10.4. Use these estimated coefficients and their covariance matrix to obtain the estimated coefficient and standard error of D_t in the "sets of equations" model in column 3 of Table 10.4.

10.3 The variable y_A in Table 10.1 was generated using (10.2.11) as the true regression function. Write the data for that model in the sets of equations framework (10.2.18) and estimate the resulting model using restricted least squares, the restriction being $\boldsymbol{\beta}_{1.} = \boldsymbol{\beta}_{2.}$ or

$$R\boldsymbol{\beta} = [\mathbf{0} \quad \mathbf{0} \quad I_2 - I_2]\boldsymbol{\beta} = \mathbf{0}$$

Compare these results to those in column 3 of Table 10.2.

10.4 The variable y_B in Table 10.1 was generated using (10.2.15) as the true regression function. Write the data for that model in the unrestricted form (10.2.19) and estimate the model subject to the restriction that the coefficients on x_2 in the two sample partitions are equal. Compare the resulting parameter estimates to column 3 of Table 10.4.

10.5 Consider the regression model $y_t = \beta_1 + x_{t2}\beta_2 + x_{t3}\beta_3 + e_t$, $t = 1, \ldots, T$. Suppose that for observations $t = 1$ and 2 the location parameters β_1, β_2, and β_3 are thought to be different from the other $(T - 2)$ observations. Write out the dummy variable or sets of equations model for this situation and discuss the resulting difficulties for estimation.

10.6 In Exercise 10.5, the problems for estimation of too few observations in a sample partition to carry out unrestricted estimation was noted. Interestingly, it is nonetheless possible to test for changes in the parameters. Let the sample partitions contain $T_1 < K$ and $T_2 > K$ observations. Let $\hat{\mathbf{e}}_2 = \mathbf{y}_2 - X_2\mathbf{b}_2$ be the vector of LS residuals from the regression fit to the second partition. Then the appropriate test statistic for the hypothesis of no structural change is

$$u = \frac{(SSE_R - \hat{\mathbf{e}}_2'\hat{\mathbf{e}}_2)/T_1}{\hat{\mathbf{e}}_2'\hat{\mathbf{e}}_2/(T_2 - K)}$$

which has an $F_{(T_1, T_2 - K)}$ distribution if the hypothesis is true. See Fisher (1970) for the proof of this result. Apply this test to the data on the variables y_C, x_2, and x_3 in Table 10.1 assuming that the war *only* affected observations in years 1943 and 1944.

10.7 (*a*) In (10.2.21) dummy variables were allowed to interact. Using the dummy variables F_t and S_t defined there, write down the model in which the qualitative factors of sex and geographic location have no effect on the intercept but *do* affect the slope of the regression function. Draw a sketch of the resulting regression functions, assuming a separate nonzero effect for sex, geographic region, and their interaction. Label them carefully.

(*b*) Revise (10.2.21) so that the geographic regions are North, South, East, and West. You will need to define some additional dummy variables.

10.8 Using the artificial investment data on y_c, x_2, and x_3 in Table 10.1, estimate the piecewise continuous regression model represented by (10.2.23) and (10.2.24). Assume that there is a single structural break at year $T_1 = 1945$.

10.9 Extend the results of Exercise 10.8 and the piecewise continuous model to allow for two structural breaks, one at year 1939 and one at year 1945. Estimate and evaluate the resulting model.

10.10 Consider the dependent variable y_C in Table 10.1, which was generated using the structure in (10.3.1). Suppose we wish to allow the error variance to differ in the two sample partitions. In that case the "usual" F statistic (10.3.2) and its equivalents are inappropriate as a basis for testing for a parametric change. An asymptotic alternative is to "correct" for the heteroskedasticity that may be present and apply an F or χ^2 test to the transformed data. Carry out a test for no change in the parameter values while allowing for the error-variance in partition 1 (σ_1^2) to be different from that in the second partition (σ_2^2).

10.11 Repeat Exercise 10.10 assuming that the heteroskedasticity in the sample is of the form $\sigma_t^2 = \sigma^2 x_{t2}$ (not related to any possible parameter shifts). What are the consequences of this (incorrect) assumption?

10.12 Using the data on y_C, x_2, and x_3 in Table 10.1, carry out the test for no change in the parameter values across the sample partitions under the assumption that the errors follow a first-order autocorrelation process. What are the consequences of this (incorrect) assumption?

10.8 References

Broemeling, L. (1985) *Bayesian Analysis of Linear Models.* New York: Dekker.

Chow, G. (1983) "Random and Changing Coefficient Models." In Z. Griliches and M. Intriligator, (eds.). *Handbook of Econometrics*, Chapter 21. Amsterdam: North-Holland.

Farley, J., and M. Hinich (1970) "Testing for a Shifting Slope Coefficient in a Linear Model." *Journal of the American Statistical Association*, 65, 1320–1329.

Farley, J., M. Hinich, and T. McGuire (1975) "Some Comparisons of Tests for a Shift in the Slopes of a Multivariate Linear Time Series Model." *Journal of Econometrics*, 3, 297–318.

Fisher, F. (1970) "Tests on Equality Between Sets of Coefficients in Two Linear Regressions: An Expository Note." *Econometrica*, 28, 361–366.

Giles, D. (1982) "The Interpretation of Dummy Variables in Semilogarithmic Equations." *Economics Letters*, 10, 77–79.

Goldfeld, S., and R. Quandt (1973) "The Estimation of Structural Shifts by Switching Regressions." *Annals of Economic and Social Measurement*, 2, 475–485.

Griffiths, W. E. (1972) "Estimation of Actual Response Coefficients in the Hildreth–Houck Random Coefficients Model." *Journal of the American Statistical Association*, 67, 633–635.

Gujarati, D. (1978) *Basic Econometrics*. New York: McGraw-Hill.

Halvorsen, R., and R. Palmquist (1980) "The Interpretation of Dummy Variables in Semilogarithmic Equations." *American Economic Review*, 70, 474–475.

Hildreth, C., and J. Houck (1968) "Some Estimators for a Linear Model with Random Coefficients." *Journal of the American Statistical Association*, 63, 584–595.

Houck, J. (1977) "An Approach to Specifying and Estimating Nonreversible Functions," *American Journal of Agricultural Economics*, 51, 570–572.

Johnston, J. (1984) *Econometric Methods*, 3rd ed. New York: McGraw-Hill.

Judge, G. G., W. E. Griffiths, R. C. Hill, H. Lütkepohl, T. C. Lee (1985) *The Theory and Practice of Econometrics*, 2nd ed. New York: Wiley.

Kennedy, P. (1981) "Estimation with Correctly Interpreted Dummy Variables in Semilogarithmic Equations." *American Economic Review*, 71, 801.

Kmenta, J. (1986) *Elements of Econometrics*, 2nd ed. New York: Macmillan.

Nicholls, D., and A. Pagan (1985) "Varying Coefficient Regression." In E. Hannan, P. Krishnaiah, and M. Rao, (eds.). *Handbook of Statistics*, Vol. 5, Chapter 16. Amsterdam: Elsevier.

Raj, B., and A. Ullah (1981) *Econometrics, A Varying Coefficients Approach*. London: Croom-Helm.

CHAPTER 11

Sets of Linear Statistical Models

11.1 Introduction

In most of the earlier chapters we concentrated on estimation and hypothesis testing for the parameter vector $\boldsymbol{\beta}$ in the single equation model $\mathbf{y} = X\boldsymbol{\beta} + \mathbf{e}$. Different estimation methods and tests were considered, depending on what further assumptions were made about the disturbance covariance matrix $E[\mathbf{ee}'] = \sigma^2\boldsymbol{\Psi}$. In this Chapter we turn to a situation where there is more than one equation to estimate. For example, interest might center on demand equations for a number of commodities, investment functions for a number of firms, or consumption functions for subsets of the population. Suppose that time-series data suitable for estimation of a number of demand equations are available. The disturbances in these different equations at a given time are likely to reflect some common unmeasurable or omitted factors, and hence could be correlated. The same is also likely to be true when time-series observations are used to estimate different investment functions for different firms, different consumption functions for different subsets of the population, or many other examples. With investment functions for a number of firms, the general state of the economy (a variable often not explicitly included) is likely to have similar effects on the disturbances of the different functions. In the study of agricultural supply response, the effect of weather in a given year is likely to have related effects on the disturbances for different crops. Correlation between disturbances from different equations at a given time is known as *contemporaneous correlation.* It is distinct from "autocorrelation," which, as we saw in a previous chapter, refers to correlation over time for the disturbances in a single equation. When contemporaneous correlation exists, it may be more efficient to estimate all equations jointly, rather than to estimate each one separately using least squares. The appropriate joint estimation technique is often known as seemingly unrelated regressions estimation; it is considered in detail in Section 11.2. Although seemingly unrelated regressions are usually described in the context of estimating a number of equations using time-series data, they can be equally relevant for cross-sectional data. If cross-sectional household data were used to estimate expenditure functions for a number of commodities, then it is quite likely that some unmeasurable characteristics of a given household could have similar effects on the disturbances of all the expenditure functions.

In many instances the use of seemingly unrelated regressions can be regarded as one method for pooling time-series and cross-sectional data. For example, if time-series data on a number of firms are used to estimate an investment function for each firm, we are, in effect, pooling the cross-section of firms with the time-series data on each firm. The distinguishing features of seemingly unrelated regressions as a method for pooling time-series and cross-sectional data are contemporaneous correlation in the disturbances and the assumption that each cross-sectional unit has a different coefficient vector. Other pooling methods make alternative assumptions about the disturbance terms and about how the coefficients change over cross-sections or time. One method that is more restrictive than seemingly unrelated regressions because it does not entertain the possibility of contemporaneous correlation, and because it assumes all cross-sectional units have identical coefficient vectors except for the intercept term, is the dummy variable or covariance model. In this model differences over cross-sectional units are assumed to be reflected in the intercept term; the cross-sectional units provide natural partitions for which dummy variables can be defined. This model is discussed in Section 11.4. A third pooling method, known as the error components model, is outlined in Section 11.5. In this model all cross-sectional units are assumed to have the same coefficient vector, but the disturbance term is a composite one made up of a unit-specific random element and another element that is random over both time and cross-sections. The question of choosing between alternative models is addressed in Section 11.6.

11.2 Seemingly Unrelated Regression Equations

As a vehicle for introducing contemporaneous correlation and the conditions under which it is possible to improve on separate least squares estimation of a number of equations, let us consider the following set of three log-linear demand equations:

$$\begin{aligned}
\ln q_{1t} &= \beta_{10} + \beta_{11} \ln p_{1t} + \beta_{14} \ln y_t + e_{1t} \\
\ln q_{2t} &= \beta_{20} + \beta_{22} \ln p_{2t} + \beta_{24} \ln y_t + e_{2t} \\
\ln q_{3t} &= \beta_{30} + \beta_{33} \ln p_{3t} + \beta_{34} \ln y_t + e_{3t}
\end{aligned} \tag{11.2.1}$$

It is assumed that quantity demanded of the ith commodity q_i depends on own price p_i and income y. It would be more realistic to include other prices in each equation; and, indeed, in Exercise 11.3.7 we include p_1, p_2, and p_3 in all equations. For the moment, the specification in (11.2.1) is more convenient. The subscripts on the β's reflect the fact that $\ln p_2$ and $\ln p_3$ have been omitted from the first equation ($\beta_{12} = \beta_{13} = 0$), $\ln p_1$ and $\ln p_3$ have been omitted from the second equation ($\beta_{21} = \beta_{23} = 0$), and $\ln p_1$ and $\ln p_2$ have been omitted from the third equation ($\beta_{31} = \beta_{32} = 0$).

The three demand equations can be written in the usual matrix algebra notation as

$$\begin{aligned} \mathbf{y}_1 &= X_1\boldsymbol{\beta}_1 + \mathbf{e}_1 \\ \mathbf{y}_2 &= X_2\boldsymbol{\beta}_2 + \mathbf{e}_2 \\ \mathbf{y}_3 &= X_3\boldsymbol{\beta}_3 + \mathbf{e}_3 \end{aligned} \tag{11.2.2}$$

where

$$\mathbf{y}_i = \begin{bmatrix} \ln q_{i1} \\ \ln q_{i2} \\ \vdots \\ \ln q_{iT} \end{bmatrix} \qquad X_i = \begin{bmatrix} 1 & \ln p_{i1} & \ln y_1 \\ 1 & \ln p_{i2} & \ln y_2 \\ \vdots & \vdots & \vdots \\ 1 & \ln p_{iT} & \ln y_T \end{bmatrix} \tag{11.2.3}$$

$$i = 1, 2, 3$$

$$\boldsymbol{\beta}_1 = \begin{bmatrix} \beta_{10} \\ \beta_{11} \\ \beta_{14} \end{bmatrix} \qquad \boldsymbol{\beta}_2 = \begin{bmatrix} \beta_{20} \\ \beta_{22} \\ \beta_{24} \end{bmatrix} \qquad \boldsymbol{\beta}_3 = \begin{bmatrix} \beta_{30} \\ \beta_{33} \\ \beta_{34} \end{bmatrix} \tag{11.2.4}$$

and

$$\mathbf{e}_i = \begin{bmatrix} e_{i1} \\ e_{i2} \\ \vdots \\ e_{iT} \end{bmatrix} \qquad i = 1, 2, 3 \tag{11.2.5}$$

Thus, y_1 and X_1 contain all T observations on the dependent and explanatory variables in the demand equation for commodity 1, $\mathbf{y}_2$ and X_2 contain all T observations on the dependent and explanatory variables in the demand equation for commodity 2, and $\mathbf{y}_3$ and X_3 contain all T observations on the dependent and explanatory variables in the demand equation for commodity 3. Similarly, $\boldsymbol{\beta}_1$, $\boldsymbol{\beta}_2$, and $\boldsymbol{\beta}_3$ are the (3×1) coefficient vectors for each of the equations and $\mathbf{e}_1$, $\mathbf{e}_2$, and $\mathbf{e}_3$ are the $(T \times 1)$ disturbance vectors for each of the equations.

The assumptions we will employ are

1. All disturbances have a zero mean,

$$E[e_{it}] = 0 \qquad i = 1, 2, 3; \quad t = 1, 2, \ldots, T \tag{11.2.6}$$

2. In a given equation the disturbance variance is constant over time, but each equation can have a different variance,

$$\left.\begin{aligned} \text{var}(e_{1t}) &= E[e_{1t}^2] = \sigma_1^2 = \sigma_{11} \\ \text{var}(e_{2t}) &= E[e_{2t}^2] = \sigma_2^2 = \sigma_{22} \\ \text{var}(e_{3t}) &= E[e_{3t}^2] = \sigma_3^2 = \sigma_{33} \end{aligned}\right\} \quad t = 1, 2, \ldots, T \qquad (11.2.7)$$

The notation σ_{ii} is just an alternative way of writing σ_i^2.

3. Two disturbances in different equations but corresponding to the same time period are correlated (contemporaneous correlation),

$$\text{covar}(e_{it}e_{jt}) = E[e_{it}e_{jt}] = \sigma_{ij} \qquad i, j = 1, 2, 3 \qquad (11.2.8)$$

4. Disturbances in different time periods, whether they are in the same equation or not, are uncorrelated (autocorrelation does not exist),

$$\text{covar}(e_{it}e_{js}) = E[e_{it}e_{js}] = 0 \qquad \text{for } t \neq s \text{ and } i, j = 1, 2, 3 \qquad (11.2.9)$$

In matrix notation these assumptions can be written compactly as

$$E[\mathbf{e}_i] = \mathbf{0} \quad \text{and} \quad E[\mathbf{e}_i\mathbf{e}_j'] = \sigma_{ij}I \qquad i, j = 1, 2, 3 \qquad (11.2.10)$$

Because $E[\mathbf{e}_1\mathbf{e}_1'] = \sigma_{11}I$, least squares applied to the first equation is the best linear unbiased estimator in the sense that it is the best estimator that is a linear unbiased function of $\mathbf{y}_1$. However, because of the existence of contemporaneous correlation, it is possible to obtain a better linear unbiased estimator that is a function of $\mathbf{y}_1$, $\mathbf{y}_2$, and $\mathbf{y}_3$. A similar result holds for the second and third equations. To illustrate how the improvement occurs, we write the three equations in (11.2.2) as the following "super model"

$$\underset{(3T \times 1)}{\begin{bmatrix} \mathbf{y}_1 \\ \mathbf{y}_2 \\ \mathbf{y}_3 \end{bmatrix}} = \underset{(3T \times 9)}{\begin{bmatrix} X_1 & 0 & 0 \\ 0 & X_2 & 0 \\ 0 & 0 & X_3 \end{bmatrix}} \underset{(9 \times 1)}{\begin{bmatrix} \boldsymbol{\beta}_1 \\ \boldsymbol{\beta}_2 \\ \boldsymbol{\beta}_3 \end{bmatrix}} + \underset{(3T \times 1)}{\begin{bmatrix} \mathbf{e}_1 \\ \mathbf{e}_2 \\ \mathbf{e}_3 \end{bmatrix}} \qquad (11.2.11)$$

The matrix dimensions appear underneath each matrix; in the $(3T \times 9)$ matrix, "0" refers to a $(T \times 3)$ matrix of zeros.

Using obvious notation we can rewrite (11.2.11) as

$$\mathbf{y} = X\boldsymbol{\beta} + \mathbf{e} \qquad (11.2.12)$$

Thus we can write the three-equation "supermodel" in the framework of a single equation linear model with special definitions for $\mathbf{y}$, X, $\boldsymbol{\beta}$, and $\mathbf{e}$.

The natural question that now arises is whether $\boldsymbol{\beta}$, the vector containing the coefficients from all three equations, can be satisfactorily estimated by applying least squares, or some other technique, to (11.2.12). The first point to note is that it can be shown that least squares applied to the system in (11.2.12) is identical to applying least squares separately to each of the three equations (see Exercise 11.3.1). Thus, there is no benefit to be gained from applying least squares to the whole system.

To investigate whether generalized least squares is worthwhile, we consider the covariance matrix of the joint disturbance vector **e**. This matrix is given by

$$
\begin{aligned}
\mathbf{\Phi} = E[\mathbf{ee}'] &= E\left[\begin{pmatrix} \mathbf{e}_1 \\ \mathbf{e}_2 \\ \mathbf{e}_3 \end{pmatrix} (\mathbf{e}_1' \quad \mathbf{e}_2' \quad \mathbf{e}_3')\right] \\
&= \begin{bmatrix} E\mathbf{e}_1\mathbf{e}_1' & E\mathbf{e}_1\mathbf{e}_2' & E\mathbf{e}_1\mathbf{e}_3' \\ E\mathbf{e}_2\mathbf{e}_1' & E\mathbf{e}_2\mathbf{e}_2' & E\mathbf{e}_2\mathbf{e}_3' \\ E\mathbf{e}_3\mathbf{e}_1' & E\mathbf{e}_3\mathbf{e}_2' & E\mathbf{e}_3\mathbf{e}_3' \end{bmatrix} \\
&= \begin{bmatrix} \sigma_{11}I & \sigma_{12}I & \sigma_{13}I \\ \sigma_{12}I & \sigma_{22}I & \sigma_{23}I \\ \sigma_{13}I & \sigma_{23}I & \sigma_{33}I \end{bmatrix} \\
&= \begin{bmatrix} \sigma_{11} & \sigma_{12} & \sigma_{13} \\ \sigma_{12} & \sigma_{22} & \sigma_{23} \\ \sigma_{13} & \sigma_{23} & \sigma_{33} \end{bmatrix} \otimes I_T \\
&= \Sigma \otimes I_T \qquad (11.2.13)
\end{aligned}
$$

The disturbance covariance matrix $\mathbf{\Phi}$ is of dimension $(3T \times 3T)$ with each $(T \times T)$ submatrix being equal to a scalar multiplied by a T-dimensional identity matrix. Kronecker product notation can be used to write the matrix in the convenient form $\Sigma \otimes I_T$. See Section A.15 of Appendix A. An important point to note is that $\mathbf{\Phi}$ cannot be written as a scalar multiplied by a $3T$-dimensional identity matrix. Thus, from results in Chapter 8, it follows that the generalized least squares estimator

$$
\begin{aligned}
\hat{\boldsymbol{\beta}} &= (X'\mathbf{\Phi}^{-1}X)^{-1}X'\mathbf{\Phi}^{-1}\mathbf{y} \\
&= [X'(\Sigma^{-1} \otimes I)X]^{-1}X'(\Sigma^{-1} \otimes I)\mathbf{y} \qquad (11.2.14)
\end{aligned}
$$

is the best linear unbiased estimator for $\boldsymbol{\beta}$. It has lower variance than the least squares estimator for $\boldsymbol{\beta}$ because it takes into account the contemporaneous correlation between the disturbances in different equations. Because a gain in efficiency can be achieved by combining a number of equations that, at first glance, seem unrelated, Zellner (1962) has given the equations the title of "seemingly unrelated regression equations."

There are two conditions under which least squares is identical to generalized least squares and under which, therefore, there is nothing to be gained by treating the equations as a system. The first is when all contemporaneous correlations are zero. In our example, this condition is

$$\sigma_{12} = \sigma_{13} = \sigma_{23} = 0 \tag{11.2.15}$$

This result is an intuitively reasonable one since it is the existence of these correlations that makes the equations related. The proof that (11.2.15) implies $\mathbf{b} = (X'X)^{-1}X'\mathbf{y} = \hat{\boldsymbol{\beta}} = (X'\boldsymbol{\Phi}^{-1}X)^{-1}X'\boldsymbol{\Phi}^{-1}\mathbf{y}$ is left as a problem (Exercise 11.3.2). The second condition is not so obvious. However, it can be shown that least squares and generalized least squares will yield identical results if the explanatory variables in each equation are identical. In terms of the current example, this condition is

$$X_1 = X_2 = X_3 \tag{11.2.16}$$

Since X_1 contains $\ln p_1$, X_2 contains $\ln p_2$, and X_3 contains $\ln p_3$, this condition clearly does not hold. However, if each equation contained the prices of all three commodities (the cross elasticities were not 0), then (11.2.16) would hold, with each X_i being given by

$$X_i = \begin{bmatrix} 1 & \ln p_{11} & \ln p_{21} & \ln p_{31} & \ln y_1 \\ 1 & \ln p_{12} & \ln p_{22} & \ln p_{32} & \ln y_2 \\ \vdots & \vdots & \vdots & \vdots & \vdots \\ 1 & \ln p_{1T} & \ln p_{2T} & \ln p_{3T} & \ln y_T \end{bmatrix} \tag{11.2.17}$$

Under these conditions least squares and generalized least squares yield identical results. A proof of this proposition is given in Section 11.2.2.

In Sections 11.2.1 and 11.2.2 we summarize the foregoing results for a general model consisting of M seemingly unrelated regression equations. The question of estimating the unknown covariance matrix Σ is taken up in Section 11.2.3.

11.2.1 General Model Specification

In a general specification of M seemingly unrelated regression equations the ith equation is given by

$$\mathbf{y}_i = X_i\boldsymbol{\beta}_i + \mathbf{e}_i \qquad i = 1, 2, \ldots, M \tag{11.2.18}$$

where $\mathbf{y}_i$ and $\mathbf{e}_i$ are of dimension $(T \times 1)$, X_i is $(T \times K_i)$, and $\boldsymbol{\beta}_i$ is $(K_i \times 1)$. Note that each equation does not have to have the same number of explanatory variables. Combining all equations into one big model yields

$$\begin{bmatrix} \mathbf{y}_1 \\ \mathbf{y}_2 \\ \vdots \\ \mathbf{y}_M \end{bmatrix} = \begin{bmatrix} X_1 & & & \\ & X_2 & & \\ & & \ddots & \\ & & & X_M \end{bmatrix} \begin{bmatrix} \boldsymbol{\beta}_1 \\ \boldsymbol{\beta}_2 \\ \vdots \\ \boldsymbol{\beta}_M \end{bmatrix} + \begin{bmatrix} \mathbf{e}_1 \\ \mathbf{e}_2 \\ \vdots \\ \mathbf{e}_M \end{bmatrix} \tag{11.2.19}$$

or alternatively,

$$\mathbf{y} = X\boldsymbol{\beta} + \mathbf{e} \tag{11.2.20}$$

where the definitions of $\mathbf{y}$, X, $\boldsymbol{\beta}$, and $\mathbf{e}$ are obvious from (11.2.19) and where their dimensions are, respectively, $(MT + 1)$, $(MT \times K)$, $(K \times 1)$, and $(MT \times 1)$, with $K = \sum_{i=1}^{M} K_i$. Thus the specification (11.2.20) has precisely the form of the linear statistical model considered in earlier chapters.

Given that e_{it} is the error for the ith equation in the tth time period, the assumption of contemporaneous disturbance correlation, but no correlation over time, implies that $E[e_{it}e_{js}] = \sigma_{ij}$ if $t = s$, but 0 if $t \neq s$. Alternatively, $E[\mathbf{e}_i\mathbf{e}_j'] = \sigma_{ij}I_T$, and the covariance matrix for the complete error vector can be written as

$$\boldsymbol{\Phi} = E[\mathbf{ee}'] = \begin{bmatrix} \sigma_{11}I_T & \sigma_{12}I_T & \cdots & \sigma_{1M}I_T \\ \sigma_{21}I_T & \sigma_{22}I_T & \cdots & \sigma_{2M}I_T \\ \vdots & \vdots & & \vdots \\ \sigma_{M1}I_T & \sigma_{M2}I_T & \cdots & \sigma_{MM}I_T \end{bmatrix} = \Sigma \otimes I_T \tag{11.2.21}$$

where

$$\Sigma = \begin{bmatrix} \sigma_{11} & \sigma_{12} & \cdots & \sigma_{1M} \\ \sigma_{21} & \sigma_{22} & \cdots & \sigma_{2M} \\ \vdots & \vdots & & \vdots \\ \sigma_{M1} & \sigma_{M2} & \cdots & \sigma_{MM} \end{bmatrix} \tag{11.2.22}$$

The matrix Σ is, of course, symmetric, so that $\sigma_{ij} = \sigma_{ji}$. We will also assume that it is nonsingular and hence positive definite.

In most applications $\mathbf{y}_i$ and X_i, for $i = 1, 2, \ldots, M$, will contain observations on variables for T different time periods, and the subscript i corresponds to a particular economic or geographic unit, such as a household, a firm, or a state. Thus, as mentioned in the introduction to this chapter, the joint model in (11.2.20) can be regarded as one way in which time-series and cross-sectional data can be combined. Other models for combining time-series and cross-sectional data are outlined in Sections 11.4 and 11.5. These models differ depending on the assumptions made about the coefficient and error vectors in each equation.

11.2.2 Estimation with Known Covariance Matrix

When the system (11.2.19) is viewed as the single equation (11.2.20) we can estimate $\boldsymbol{\beta}$ and hence all the $\boldsymbol{\beta}_i$ by the generalized least squares procedures that were discussed in Chapter 8. Thus, using the results of Chapter 8, the generalized least squares estimator

$$\hat{\boldsymbol{\beta}} = (X'\boldsymbol{\Phi}^{-1}X)^{-1}X'\boldsymbol{\Phi}^{-1}\mathbf{y} = [X'(\Sigma^{-1} \otimes I)X]^{-1}X'(\Sigma^{-1} \otimes I)\mathbf{y} \quad (11.2.23)$$

is best linear unbiased. Written in detail, $\hat{\boldsymbol{\beta}}$ becomes

$$\hat{\boldsymbol{\beta}} = \begin{bmatrix} \hat{\boldsymbol{\beta}}_1 \\ \hat{\boldsymbol{\beta}}_2 \\ \vdots \\ \hat{\boldsymbol{\beta}}_M \end{bmatrix} = \begin{bmatrix} \sigma^{11}X_1'X_1 & \sigma^{12}X_1'X_2 & \cdots & \sigma^{1M}X_1'X_M \\ \sigma^{12}X_2'X_1 & \sigma^{22}X_2'X_2 & \cdots & \sigma^{2M}X_2'X_M \\ \vdots & \vdots & & \vdots \\ \sigma^{1M}X_M'X_1 & \sigma^{2M}X_M'X_2 & \cdots & \sigma^{MM}X_M'X_M \end{bmatrix}^{-1} \begin{bmatrix} \sum_{i=1}^{M} \sigma^{1i}X_1'\mathbf{y}_i \\ \sum_{i=1}^{M} \sigma^{2i}X_2'\mathbf{y}_i \\ \vdots \\ \sum_{i=1}^{M} \sigma^{Mi}X_M'\mathbf{y}_i \end{bmatrix} \quad (11.2.24)$$

where σ^{ij} is the (i,j)th element of Σ^{-1}. The covariance matrix for $\hat{\boldsymbol{\beta}}$ is given by $(X'\boldsymbol{\Phi}^{-1}X)^{-1} = [X'(\Sigma^{-1} \otimes I)X]^{-1}$.

If interest centers on one equation, for example, the ith, and only estimators that are a function of $\mathbf{y}_i$ are considered, then the least squares estimator $\mathbf{b}_i = (X_i'X_i)^{-1}X_i'\mathbf{y}_i$ is the minimum variance, linear unbiased estimator. As noted in the preceding paragraph, however, we can improve on this estimator by considering a wider class, namely linear unbiased estimators, that are a function of $\mathbf{y}$. Within this class $\hat{\boldsymbol{\beta}}_i$, the ith vector component of $\hat{\boldsymbol{\beta}}$, is better than $\mathbf{b}_i$ because it allows for the correlation between $\mathbf{e}_i$ and error vectors of the other equations and because it uses information on explanatory variables that are included in the system but excluded from the i th equation. In general, the efficiency gain tends to be higher when the errors among different equations are highly correlated.

There are two cases for the statistical model system (11.2.20) when $\mathbf{b} = \hat{\boldsymbol{\beta}}$ and thus there is no gain in efficiency. One case occurs when Σ is a diagonal matrix, that is, $\sigma_{ij} = 0$ for all $i \neq j$. This situation implies, of course, that there is in fact no correlation between the random errors of different equations.

The second case occurs when the explanatory variables are identical for all equations. That is,

$$X_1 = X_2 = \cdots = X_M = \bar{X} \quad (11.2.25)$$

Under these circumstances $X = I_M \otimes \bar{X}$, and, using rules for the algebra of Kronecker products (Section A.15), we can write

$$\begin{aligned}
\hat{\boldsymbol{\beta}} &= [X'(\Sigma^{-1} \otimes I_T)X]^{-1}X'(\Sigma^{-1} \otimes I_T)\mathbf{y} \\
&= [(I_M \otimes \bar{X}')(\Sigma^{-1} \otimes I_T)(I_M \otimes \bar{X})]^{-1}(I_M \otimes \bar{X}')(\Sigma^{-1} \otimes I_T)\mathbf{y} \\
&= [\Sigma^{-1} \otimes \bar{X}'\bar{X}]^{-1}(\Sigma^{-1} \otimes \bar{X}')\mathbf{y} \\
&= [\Sigma \otimes (\bar{X}'\bar{X})^{-1}](\Sigma^{-1} \otimes \bar{X}')\mathbf{y} \\
&= [I_M \otimes (\bar{X}'\bar{X})^{-1}\bar{X}']\mathbf{y} \\
&= [(I_M \otimes \bar{X})'(I_M \otimes \bar{X})]^{-1}(I_M \otimes \bar{X})'\mathbf{y} \\
&= (X'X)^{-1}X'\mathbf{y} = \mathbf{b}
\end{aligned} \tag{11.2.26}$$

To verify the step in this proof that uses $[I_M \otimes (\bar{X}'\bar{X})^{-1}\bar{X}'] = (X'X)^{-1}X'$, you should consult the definition of X in (11.2.20) and write out in full the components of $(X'X)^{-1}X'$.

Thus, we have shown that use of the generalized least squares estimator $\hat{\boldsymbol{\beta}}$ does not lead to a gain in efficiency when each equation contains the same explanatory variables. In general, any gain in efficiency tends to be higher when the explanatory variables in the different equations are not highly correlated.

11.2.3 Estimation with Unknown Covariance Matrix

In practice the variances and covariances (σ_{ij}'s) are unknown and must be estimated, with their estimates being used in (11.2.23) to form an estimated generalized least squares estimator. To estimate the σ_{ij} we first estimate each equation by least squares $\mathbf{b}_i = (X_i'X_i)^{-1}X_i'\mathbf{y}_i$ and obtain the least squares residuals $\hat{\mathbf{e}}_i = \mathbf{y}_i - X_i\mathbf{b}_i$. Consistent estimates of the variances and covariances are then given by

$$\hat{\sigma}_{ij} = \frac{1}{T}\hat{\mathbf{e}}_i'\hat{\mathbf{e}}_j = \frac{1}{T}\sum_{t=1}^{T}\hat{e}_{it}\hat{e}_{jt} \tag{11.2.27}$$

Because T is used as the divisor in (11.2.27), the $\hat{\sigma}_{ij}$ will be biased in finite samples. Unlike in the single equation model, there is no completely satisfactory "degrees of freedom correction" that will lead to unbiased variance and covariance estimators for all models. The difficulty is that different equations can have different numbers of regressors and that a divisor that is satisfactory for estimating a variance for one equation is unlikely to be satisfactory for estimating a covariance where two equations are involved. One alternative to using T is to use $T - (K/M)$ where (K/M) is the average number of coefficients per equation. This divisor has the advantage of being constant for the whole system, and it leads to unbiased variance estimates when each equation has the same number of coefficients. The asymptotic properties of the estimated generalized least squares estimator for $\boldsymbol{\beta}$ remain the same irrespective of which (consistent) divisor is used.

If we define $\hat{\Sigma}$ as the matrix Σ with the unknown σ_{ij} replaced by the estimates $\hat{\sigma}_{ij}$, then the corresponding estimated generalized least squares estimator for $\boldsymbol{\beta}$ can be written as

$$\hat{\hat{\boldsymbol{\beta}}} = [X'(\hat{\Sigma}^{-1} \otimes I)X]^{-1}X'(\hat{\Sigma}^{-1} \otimes I)\mathbf{y} \tag{11.2.28}$$

This estimator is the one that is generally used in practice and that is often referred to as Zellner's *seemingly unrelated regression* (*SUR*) *estimator.*

Another estimator for $\boldsymbol{\beta}$ is defined by using (11.2.27) and (11.2.28) in an iterative procedure. A new set of variance estimates can be obtained from

$$\hat{\hat{\sigma}}_{ij} = T^{-1}(\mathbf{y}_i - X_i\hat{\hat{\boldsymbol{\beta}}}_i)'(\mathbf{y}_j - X_j\hat{\hat{\boldsymbol{\beta}}}_j) \tag{11.2.29}$$

where $\hat{\hat{\boldsymbol{\beta}}}' = (\hat{\hat{\boldsymbol{\beta}}}'_1, \hat{\hat{\boldsymbol{\beta}}}'_2, \ldots, \hat{\hat{\boldsymbol{\beta}}}'_M)$. These estimates can be used to form a new estimator for $\boldsymbol{\beta}$, and so on, until convergence. When the random errors follow a multivariate normal distribution this estimator will be the maximum likelihood estimator.

Under appropriate conditions, both estimators, the one based on a single estimate of the disturbance covariance matrix, and the iterative estimator, will have the same limiting distribution. This distribution is approximately normal with mean $\boldsymbol{\beta}$ and a covariance matrix that is consistently estimated by $[X'(\hat{\Sigma}^{-1} \otimes I)X]^{-1}$. Thus, $\hat{\hat{\boldsymbol{\beta}}}$ and the iterative estimator for $\boldsymbol{\beta}$ will be asymptotically more efficient than the least squares estimator. In finite samples, however, there will be a region in the parameter space for Σ where least squares is more efficient than the other estimators. When the contemporaneous correlations are small, the generalized least squares estimator will only be slightly more efficient than the least squares estimator. With the estimated generalized least squares estimator, there is a loss in finite sample efficiency because Σ is replaced by the uncertain estimator $\hat{\Sigma}$. If the contemporaneous correlations are small, this loss in efficiency could be sufficiently great to make least squares better than estimated generalized least squares. The extreme case is when Σ is diagonal. In this case least squares is best. The estimator $\hat{\hat{\boldsymbol{\beta}}}$ can only be as good (in finite samples) if $\hat{\Sigma}$ is diagonal, an extremely unlikely event. If the explanatory variables are identical for each equation, then Σ and $\hat{\Sigma}$ play no role because $\mathbf{b} = \hat{\boldsymbol{\beta}} = \hat{\hat{\boldsymbol{\beta}}}$. When the estimators are numerically equal they are obviously equally efficient.

11.2.4 An Example and Monte Carlo Experiment

As an example, consider the data in Table 11.1, where $\mathbf{x}_{12}$ and $\mathbf{x}_{22}$ are the market values and $\mathbf{x}_{13}$ and $\mathbf{x}_{23}$ are the capital stocks of General Electric and Westinghouse, respectively, for the period 1934 through 1953, as tabulated in Theil (1971). The dependent variables $\mathbf{y}_1$ and $\mathbf{y}_2$ may be regarded as investment figures for the two companies. They are actually artificially generated.

Using least squares estimation for each equation of the system

$$\begin{aligned} \mathbf{y}_1 &= \mathbf{x}_{11}\beta_{11} + \mathbf{x}_{12}\beta_{12} + \mathbf{x}_{13}\beta_{13} + \mathbf{e}_1 \\ \mathbf{y}_2 &= \mathbf{x}_{21}\beta_{21} + \mathbf{x}_{22}\beta_{22} + \mathbf{x}_{23}\beta_{23} + \mathbf{e}_2 \end{aligned} \tag{11.2.30}$$

where $\mathbf{x}_{11} = \mathbf{x}_{21}$ are (20×1) vectors of ones, we obtained the following estimates:

$$\mathbf{b}_1 = \begin{bmatrix} 5.279 \\ 0.024 \\ 0.156 \end{bmatrix}, \mathbf{b}_2 = \begin{bmatrix} -0.571 \\ 0.062 \\ 0.072 \end{bmatrix}, \hat{\Sigma} = \begin{bmatrix} 859.93 & 305.96 \\ 305.96 & 186.15 \end{bmatrix} \tag{11.2.31}$$

Table 11.1 Data for Example Model

$\mathbf{y}_1$	$\mathbf{x}_{12}$	$\mathbf{x}_{13}$	$\mathbf{y}_2$	$\mathbf{x}_{22}$	$\mathbf{x}_{23}$
40.05292	1170.6	97.8	2.52813	191.5	1.8
54.64859	2015.8	104.4	24.91888	516.0	0.8
40.31206	2803.3	118.0	29.34270	729.0	7.4
84.21099	2039.7	156.2	27.61823	560.4	18.1
127.57240	2256.2	172.6	60.35945	519.9	23.5
124.87970	2132.2	186.6	50.61588	628.5	26.5
96.55514	1834.1	220.9	30.70955	537.1	36.2
131.16010	1588.0	287.8	60.69605	561.2	60.8
77.02764	1749.4	319.9	30.00972	617.2	84.4
46.96689	1687.2	321.3	42.50750	626.7	91.2
100.65970	2007.7	319.6	58.61146	737.2	92.4
115.74670	2208.3	346.0	46.96287	760.5	86.0
114.58260	1656.7	456.4	57.87651	581.4	111.1
119.87620	1604.4	543.4	43.22093	662.3	130.6
105.56990	1431.8	618.3	22.87143	583.8	141.8
148.42660	1610.5	647.4	52.94754	635.2	136.7
194.36220	1819.4	671.3	71.23030	723.8	129.7
158.20370	2079.7	726.1	61.72550	864.1	145.5
163.09300	2371.6	800.3	85.13053	1193.5	174.8
227.56340	2759.9	888.9	88.27518	1188.9	213.5

The divisor $T - (K/M)$ was used to obtain $\hat{\Sigma}$. Substituting $\hat{\Sigma}$ into (11.2.28) gives an estimated generalized least squares or seemingly unrelated regression estimate

$$\hat{\hat{\boldsymbol{\beta}}}' = (2.564, 0.024, 0.160, -3.266, 0.065, 0.080)$$

We know that the estimated generalized least squares estimator $\hat{\hat{\boldsymbol{\beta}}}$ is asymptotically superior, or at least not inferior, to the least squares estimator $\mathbf{b}$. However, as we discussed earlier, such is not necessarily the case in small samples. It is interesting, therefore, to investigate the small sample properties of $\mathbf{b}$ and $\hat{\hat{\boldsymbol{\beta}}}$ in a Monte Carlo experiment. Vectors $\mathbf{y}_1$ and $\mathbf{y}_2$, each of size 20 were generated 250 times using the model

$$\begin{aligned} \mathbf{y}_1 &= -28\mathbf{x}_{11} + 0.04\mathbf{x}_{12} + 0.14\mathbf{x}_{13} + \mathbf{e}_1 \\ \mathbf{y}_2 &= -1.3\mathbf{x}_{21} + 0.06\mathbf{x}_{22} + 0.06\mathbf{x}_{23} + \mathbf{e}_2 \end{aligned} \tag{11.2.32}$$

where the regressors are as in (11.2.30) and the $\mathbf{e}_1$, $\mathbf{e}_2$ are normal random vectors with mean zero and joint variance-covariance matrix

$$E\left[\begin{pmatrix}\mathbf{e}_1\\ \mathbf{e}_2\end{pmatrix}(\mathbf{e}_1' \quad \mathbf{e}_2')\right] = \boldsymbol{\Phi} = \Sigma \otimes I_{20} = \begin{bmatrix} 660 & 175 \\ 175 & 90 \end{bmatrix} \otimes I_{20} \tag{11.2.33}$$

Methods for generating multivariate normal random variables are given in the Appendix to this chapter. The first of the 250 generated samples is that given in Table 11.1.

The average values of both the least squares and seemingly unrelated regression estimates together with their standard deviations are presented in Table 11.2. Although we have used samples of only 20 observations, the seemingly unrelated regression estimates have a slightly smaller sampling variance than their least squares counterparts with the exception of β_{13}. This result is also reflected in the frequency distributions in Figure 11.1.

Table 11.2 Means and Standard Deviations of Least Squares and Seemingly Unrelated Estimates from 250 Samples

	Least Squares	SUR
β_{11}	−27.369 (29.505)	−27.455 (28.064)
β_{12}	0.039 (0.0142)	0.039 (0.0135)
β_{13}	0.141 (0.0226)	0.142 (0.0231)
β_{21}	−1.614 (7.8950)	−1.546 (7.3595)
β_{22}	0.060 (0.0155)	0.060 (0.0146)
β_{22}	0.062 (0.0495)	0.063 (0.0489)

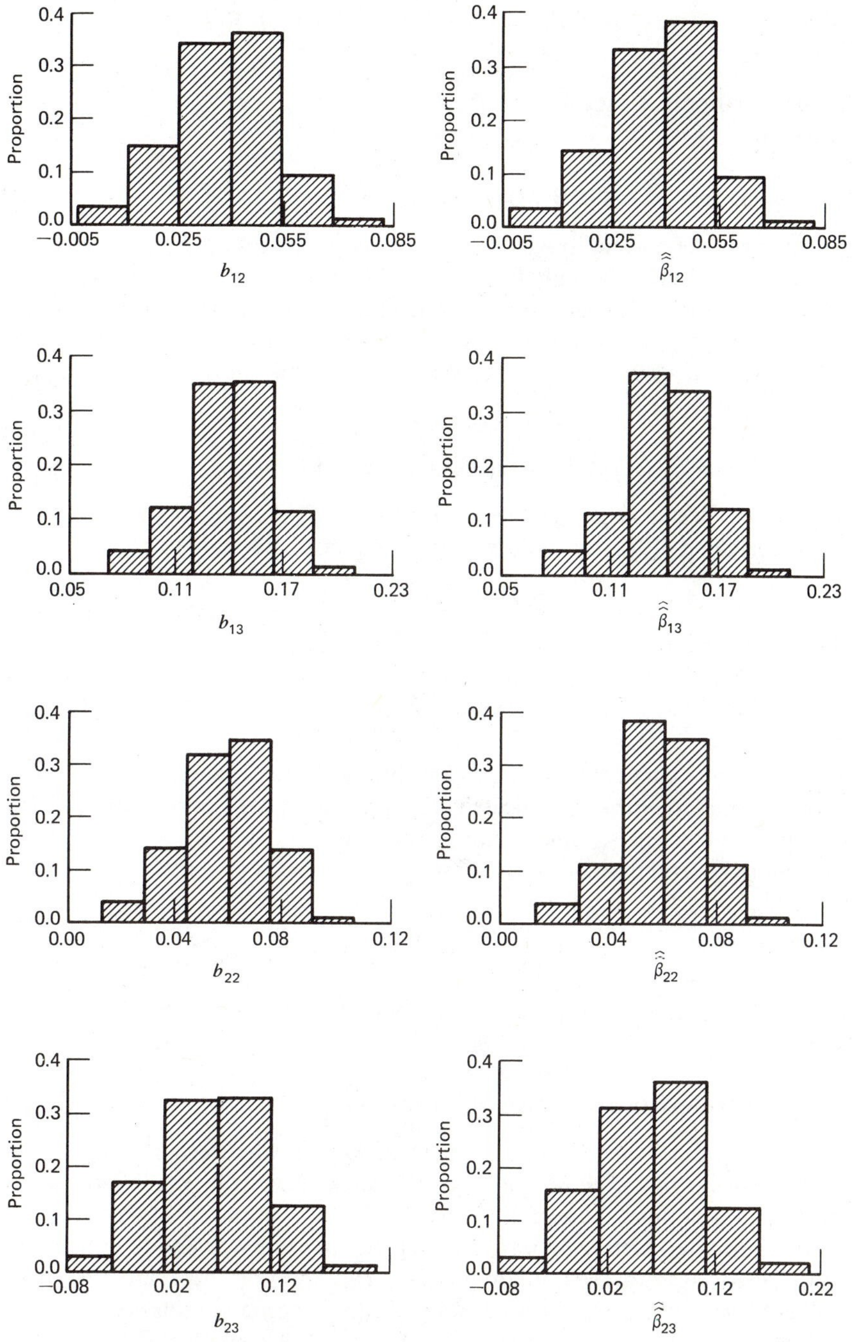

Figure 11.1 Empirical distributions of least squares and seemingly unrelated regression estimates.

11.2.5 Hypothesis Testing and Restricted Estimation

11.2.5a Testing for Contemporaneous Correlation

If contemporaneous correlation does not exist, least squares applied separately to each equation is fully efficient and there is no need to employ the seemingly unrelated regression estimator. Thus, it is useful to test whether the contemporaneous covariances are 0. In the context of the three-equation demand system used to introduce equation systems, the null and alternative hypotheses for this test are

$$H_0 \colon \sigma_{12} = \sigma_{13} = \sigma_{23} = 0$$

$$H_1 \colon \text{at least one covariance is nonzero}$$

An appropriate test statistic is the Lagrange multiplier statistic, suggested by Breusch and Pagan (1980). In the three equation case, this statistic is given by

$$\lambda = T(r_{21}^2 + r_{31}^2 + r_{32}^2) \qquad (11.2.34)$$

where r_{ij}^2 is the squared correlation

$$r_{ij}^2 = \frac{\hat{\sigma}_{ij}^2}{\hat{\sigma}_{ii}\hat{\sigma}_{jj}}. \qquad (11.2.35)$$

Under H_0, λ has an asymptotic χ^2-distribution with 3 degrees of freedom. Therefore, the null hypothesis is rejected if λ is greater than the critical value from a $\chi^2_{(3)}$-distribution for a prespecified significance level.

In the more general case of M equations, the statistic is given by

$$\lambda = T \sum_{i=2}^{M} \sum_{j=1}^{i-1} r_{ij}^2 \qquad (11.2.36)$$

Under H_0, λ has an asymptotic χ^2 distribution with $M(M-1)/2$ degrees of freedom.

11.2.5b Linear Restrictions on the Coefficients

Consider a set of linear restrictions of the form $R\boldsymbol{\beta} = \mathbf{r}$, where R and $\mathbf{r}$ are known matrices of dimensions $(J \times K)$ and $(J \times 1)$, respectively. It is possible to extend the analysis in Sections 6.2 and 6.4 of Chapter 6, and Section 8.5 of Chapter 8, to construct a restricted seemingly unrelated regression estimator and to construct a test statistic for testing the null hypothesis $H_0 \colon R\boldsymbol{\beta} = \mathbf{r}$. There are two main differences between the earlier procedures and those adopted in this section. First, the restricted estimator and the relevant test statistic will now depend on Σ, which, because it is unknown, needs to be replaced by the estimator $\hat{\Sigma}$. This replacement means that estimator properties and test statistics are based on asymptotic rather than finite sample distributions. Secondly, it is now possible to test and impose restrictions that relate the coefficients in one equation with the coefficients in other equations. This possibility is of particular interest in economics. For example, if the coefficient vectors for each equation are all equal, $\boldsymbol{\beta}_1 = \boldsymbol{\beta}_2 = \cdots = \boldsymbol{\beta}_M$, the use of data aggregated over microunits does not lead to aggregation bias (Zellner, 1962). Also, some aspects of economic theory, such as the Slutsky conditions in demand analysis, often suggest symmetric and other linear relationships between coefficients in different equations.

The restricted generalized least squares estimator is obtained by minimizing

$$(\mathbf{y} - X\boldsymbol{\beta})'(\Sigma^{-1} \otimes I)(\mathbf{y} - X\boldsymbol{\beta}) \tag{11.2.37}$$

subject to the linear restrictions $R\boldsymbol{\beta} = \mathbf{r}$. It is given by

$$\hat{\boldsymbol{\beta}}^* = \hat{\boldsymbol{\beta}} + CR'(RCR')^{-1}(\mathbf{r} - R\hat{\boldsymbol{\beta}}) \tag{11.2.38}$$

where

$$C = [X'(\Sigma^{-1} \otimes I)X]^{-1} \tag{11.2.39}$$

and

$$\hat{\boldsymbol{\beta}} = CX'(\Sigma^{-1} \otimes I)\mathbf{y} \tag{11.2.40}$$

When Σ is replaced by the estimator $\hat{\Sigma}$ defined in (11.2.27), we get the restricted seemingly unrelated regression estimator

$$\hat{\hat{\boldsymbol{\beta}}}^* = \hat{\hat{\boldsymbol{\beta}}} + \hat{C}R'(R\hat{C}R')^{-1}(\mathbf{r} - R\hat{\hat{\boldsymbol{\beta}}}) \tag{11.2.41}$$

where

$$\hat{C} = [X'(\hat{\Sigma}^{-1} \otimes I)X]^{-1} \tag{11.2.42}$$

and

$$\hat{\hat{\boldsymbol{\beta}}} = \hat{C}X'(\hat{\Sigma}^{-1} \otimes I)\mathbf{y} \tag{11.2.43}$$

Under the usual assumptions about the limiting behavior of X, and assuming the restrictions $R\boldsymbol{\beta} = \mathbf{r}$ are true, in large samples the distribution of $\hat{\hat{\boldsymbol{\beta}}}^*$ can be approximated by a normal distribution with mean $\boldsymbol{\beta}$ and a covariance matrix that is consistently estimated by $\hat{C} - \hat{C}R'(R\hat{C}R')^{-1}R\hat{C}$. This result is a natural extension of that given in (6.2.17) of Chapter 6.

Turning to the question of testing $H_0\colon R\boldsymbol{\beta} = \mathbf{r}$ against the alternative $H_1\colon R\boldsymbol{\beta} \neq \mathbf{r}$, we note that, when H_0 is true,

$$R\hat{\boldsymbol{\beta}} \sim N(\mathbf{r}, RCR') \tag{11.2.44}$$

Thus,

$$g = (R\hat{\boldsymbol{\beta}} - \mathbf{r})'(RCR')^{-1}(R\hat{\boldsymbol{\beta}} - \mathbf{r}) \sim \chi^2_{(J)} \tag{11.2.45}$$

This result is a finite sample one (providing the errors are normally distributed), but it is not operational because it depends on the unknown covariance matrix Σ. When Σ is replaced by $\hat{\Sigma}$, we have

$$\hat{g} = (R\hat{\hat{\boldsymbol{\beta}}} - \mathbf{r})'(R\hat{C}R')^{-1}(R\hat{\hat{\boldsymbol{\beta}}} - \mathbf{r}) \xrightarrow{d} \chi^2_{(J)} \tag{11.2.46}$$

Since (11.2.46) only holds when H_0 is true, we reject H_0 if a calculated value for $\hat{g}$ exceeds the appropriate critical value from a $\chi^2_{(J)}$-distribution.

Another way of developing a test statistic for testing $H_0: R\boldsymbol{\beta} = \mathbf{r}$ against $H_1: R\boldsymbol{\beta} \neq \mathbf{r}$ is to begin with an extended version of the single-equation F test that was described in Sections 6.4 and 8.5. Using similar arguments, and assuming the errors are normally distributed, it can be shown that

$$\lambda_F = \frac{g/J}{(\mathbf{y} - X\hat{\boldsymbol{\beta}})'(\Sigma^{-1} \otimes I)(\mathbf{y} - X\hat{\boldsymbol{\beta}})/(MT - K)} \sim F_{(J, MT-K)} \tag{11.2.47a}$$

To make this statistic operational, we need to replace Σ by $\hat{\Sigma}$, g by $\hat{g}$, and $\hat{\boldsymbol{\beta}}$ by $\hat{\hat{\boldsymbol{\beta}}}$. Then, there are two results that need to be considered. First, the operational statistic that results will only have an approximate $F_{(J,MT-K)}$ distribution. Secondly, it can be shown that the denominator in (11.2.47a) converges in probability to one and hence can be omitted, leaving

$$\hat{\lambda}_F = \frac{\hat{g}}{J} \tag{11.2.47b}$$

as a new operational statistics that has an approximate $F_{(J,MT-K)}$ distribution. Since $J\hat{\lambda}_F = \hat{g} \xrightarrow{d} \chi^2_{(J)}$, and since $JF_{(J,MT-K)} \xrightarrow{d} \chi^2_{(J)}$, the statistics $\hat{g}$ and $\hat{\lambda}_F$ are, in this sense, asymptotically equivalent. In finite samples, use of the F statistic $\hat{\lambda}_F$ rather than the χ^2 statistic $\hat{g}$ will lead to rejection of the null hypothesis in a smaller number of cases. This "more cautious" approach has been recommended by Theil (1971, pp. 402–403); subsequent Monte Carlo studies [see Woodland (1986) and references and discussion therein] have suggested that such caution is justified. Additional caution can be exercised by employing a degrees of freedom correction in the estimation of Σ. If the divisor $T - (K/M)$ is used in place of T, $\hat{g}$ and $\hat{\lambda}_F$ will be smaller and the null hypothesis will be rejected less frequently. For further discussion see Woodland (1986).

Both $\hat{g}$ and $\hat{\lambda}_F$ can be written in terms of restricted and unrestricted residual sums of squares. Such a formulation could be convenient if a computer program that automatically computes $\hat{g}$ or $\hat{\lambda}_F$ is not available. The relationship is (see Exercise 11.3.4)

$$\begin{aligned}\hat{g} &= (R\hat{\hat{\boldsymbol{\beta}}} - \mathbf{r})'(R\hat{C}R')^{-1}(R\hat{\hat{\boldsymbol{\beta}}} - \mathbf{r}) \\ &= (\mathbf{y} - X\hat{\hat{\boldsymbol{\beta}}}^*)'(\hat{\Sigma}^{-1} \otimes I)(\mathbf{y} - X\hat{\hat{\boldsymbol{\beta}}}^*) - (\mathbf{y} - X\hat{\hat{\boldsymbol{\beta}}})(\hat{\Sigma}^{-1} \otimes I)(\mathbf{y} - X\hat{\hat{\boldsymbol{\beta}}})\end{aligned} \tag{11.2.48}$$

where $\hat{\hat{\boldsymbol{\beta}}}^*$ is the restricted seemingly unrelated regression estimator defined in (11.2.41). Writing $\hat{g}$ in this way indicates how the test can be viewed as one that examines whether the imposition of restrictions has led to a significant increase in the residual sum of squares.

In addition, rather than use the expression in (11.2.41), it is often easier to obtain the restricted estimator $\hat{\hat{\boldsymbol{\beta}}}^*$ by rewriting the model (11.2.19) to incorporate the restrictions. For example, if $K_1 = K_2 = \cdots = K_M = k$, and we wish to impose the restrictions $\boldsymbol{\beta}_1 = \boldsymbol{\beta}_2 = \cdots = \boldsymbol{\beta}_M$, (11.2.19) can be written as

$$\begin{bmatrix} \mathbf{y}_1 \\ \mathbf{y}_2 \\ \vdots \\ \mathbf{y}_M \end{bmatrix} = \begin{bmatrix} X_1 \\ X_2 \\ \vdots \\ X_M \end{bmatrix} \boldsymbol{\beta}_1 + \begin{bmatrix} \mathbf{e}_1 \\ \mathbf{e}_2 \\ \vdots \\ \mathbf{e}_M \end{bmatrix} \tag{11.2.49}$$

or, equivalently, as

$$\mathbf{y} = X^*\boldsymbol{\beta}_1 + \mathbf{e} \tag{11.2.50}$$

where X^* is of order $(MT \times k)$. The M vector components of $\hat{\hat{\boldsymbol{\beta}}}^*$ will all be the same, and one of them can be obtained by applying estimated generalized least squares to (11.2.50). This yields

$$\hat{\hat{\boldsymbol{\beta}}}_1^* = [X^{*\prime}(\hat{\Sigma}^{-1} \otimes I)X^*]^{-1}X^{*\prime}(\hat{\Sigma}^{-1} \otimes I)\mathbf{y} \tag{11.2.51}$$

and the restricted residual sum of squares can be written as

$$(\mathbf{y} - X\hat{\hat{\boldsymbol{\beta}}}^*)'(\hat{\Sigma}^{-1} \otimes I)(\mathbf{y} - X\hat{\hat{\boldsymbol{\beta}}}^*) = (\mathbf{y} - X^*\hat{\hat{\boldsymbol{\beta}}}_1^*)'(\hat{\Sigma}^{-1} \otimes I)(\mathbf{y} - X^*\hat{\hat{\boldsymbol{\beta}}}_1^*) \tag{11.2.52}$$

A natural question that arises when considering computation of either of the restricted estimator formulations $\hat{\hat{\boldsymbol{\beta}}}^*$ or $\hat{\hat{\boldsymbol{\beta}}}_1^*$, is whether Σ should be estimated from unrestricted least squares residuals [as suggested in (11.2.27)] or from restricted least squares residuals. That is, should we use $\hat{\mathbf{e}} = [I - X(X'X)^{-1}X']\mathbf{y}$ or $\mathbf{e}^* = [I - X^*(X^{*\prime}X^*)^{-1}X^{*\prime}]\mathbf{y}$? Since we are interested in the probability distribution of $\hat{g}$ (or of $\hat{\lambda}_F$) when the null hypothesis $R\boldsymbol{\beta} = \mathbf{r}$ is true, it could be argued that it is more logical to base $\hat{g}$ (or $\hat{\lambda}_F$) on an estimate of Σ that assumes the null hypothesis is true. However, there is no easy way of resolving the question. Only asymptotic results are available and, asymptotically, it makes no difference which estimator for Σ is used. When an iterative procedure is used to estimate $\boldsymbol{\beta}$ and Σ, the choice between the two estimators for Σ boils down to a choice between the Wald and Lagrange multiplier test statistics. For details of these statistics, and some interesting reformulations, see Judge, et al. (1985, pp. 472–476).

11.2.6 A Further Example

Let us reconsider the three demand equations outlined in (11.2.1), namely,

$$\ln q_{it} = \beta_{i0} + \beta_{ii} \ln p_{it} + \beta_{i4} \ln y_t + e_{it} \qquad i = 1, 2, 3 \qquad (11.2.53)$$

Thirty observations on prices, quantities, and income are given in Table 11.3. These data were used to estimate each equation using least squares, the seemingly unrelated regression (SUR) estimator, and the restricted seemingly unrelated

Table 11.3 Data for Demand Model

p_1	p_2	p_3	y	q_1	q_2	q_3
10.763	4.474	6.629	487.648	11.632	13.194	45.770
13.033	10.836	13.774	364.877	12.029	2.181	13.393
9.244	5.856	4.063	541.037	8.916	5.586	104.819
4.605	14.010	3.868	760.343	33.908	5.231	137.269
13.045	11.417	14.922	421.746	4.361	10.930	15.914
7.706	8.755	14.318	578.214	17.594	11.854	23.667
7.405	7.317	4.794	561.734	18.842	17.045	62.057
7.519	6.360	3.768	301.470	11.637	2.682	52.262
8.764	4.188	8.089	379.636	7.645	13.008	31.916
13.511	1.996	2.708	478.855	7.881	19.623	123.026
4.943	7.268	12.901	433.741	9.614	6.534	26.255
8.360	5.839	11.115	525.702	9.067	9.397	35.540
5.721	5.160	11.220	513.067	14.070	13.188	32.487
7.225	9.145	5.810	408.666	15.474	3.340	45.838
6.617	5.034	5.516	192.061	3.041	4.716	26.867
14.219	5.926	3.707	462.621	14.096	17.141	43.325
6.769	8.187	10.125	312.659	4.118	4.695	24.330
7.769	7.193	2.471	400.848	10.489	7.639	107.017
9.804	13.315	8.976	392.215	6.231	9.089	23.407
11.063	6.874	12.883	377.724	6.458	10.346	18.254
6.535	15.533	4.115	343.552	8.736	3.901	54.895
11.063	4.477	4.962	301.599	5.158	4.350	45.360
4.016	9.231	6.294	294.112	16.618	7.371	25.318
4.759	5.907	8.298	365.032	11.342	6.507	32.852
5.483	7.077	9.638	256.125	2.903	3.770	22.154
7.890	9.942	7.122	184.798	3.138	1.360	20.575
8.460	7.043	4.157	359.084	15.315	6.497	44.205
6.195	4.142	10.040	629.378	22.240	10.963	44.443
6.743	3.369	15.459	306.527	10.012	10.140	13.251
11.977	4.806	6.172	347.488	3.982	8.637	41.845

regression estimator under the restriction that the price elasticities for all commodities are equal ($\beta_{11} = \beta_{22} = \beta_{33}$). Tests for contemporaneous correlation and for the validity of the restrictions $\beta_{11} = \beta_{22} = \beta_{33}$ were also carried out.

Considering first the test for contemporaneous correlation outlined in Section 11.2.5a, we obtain, from the least squares residuals

$$r_{12}^2 = \frac{\hat{\sigma}_{12}^2}{\hat{\sigma}_{11}\hat{\sigma}_{22}} = \frac{(-0.019135)^2}{0.13978 \times 0.18276} = 0.0143$$

$$r_{13}^2 = \frac{\hat{\sigma}_{13}^2}{\hat{\sigma}_{11}\hat{\sigma}_{33}} = \frac{(-0.040329)^2}{0.13978 \times 0.031437} = 0.3701$$

$$r_{23}^2 = \frac{\hat{\sigma}_{23}^2}{\hat{\sigma}_{22}\hat{\sigma}_{33}} = \frac{(-0.037133)^2}{0.18276 \times 0.031437} = 0.2400$$

Then,

$$\lambda = 30(0.0143 + 0.3701 + 0.24) = 18.73$$

The 5% critical value from the χ^2-distribution with 3 degrees of freedom is 7.81. Hence we reject the null hypothesis and conclude that contemporaneous correlation does exist. (From the sample correlations it appears that $\sigma_{23} \neq 0$ and $\sigma_{13} \neq 0$ but that σ_{12} might very well be 0.)

The linear restrictions $\beta_{11} = \beta_{22} = \beta_{33}$ can be written alternatively as $\beta_{11} - \beta_{22} = 0$ and $\beta_{11} - \beta_{33} = 0$. Writing these restrictions in the format $R\boldsymbol{\beta} = \mathbf{r}$ yields

$$\begin{bmatrix} 0 & 1 & 0 & 0 & -1 & 0 & 0 & 0 & 0 \\ 0 & 1 & 0 & 0 & 0 & 0 & 0 & -1 & 0 \end{bmatrix} \begin{bmatrix} \beta_{10} \\ \beta_{11} \\ \beta_{14} \\ \beta_{20} \\ \beta_{22} \\ \beta_{24} \\ \beta_{30} \\ \beta_{33} \\ \beta_{34} \end{bmatrix} = \begin{bmatrix} 0 \\ 0 \end{bmatrix}$$

Using the divisor $T - (K/M)$ to estimate Σ, the calculated value of the F-statistic used to test $H_0: R\boldsymbol{\beta} = \mathbf{r}$ against the alternative $H_1: R\boldsymbol{\beta} \neq \mathbf{r}$ (see Equation 11.2.47b) is $\hat{\lambda}_F = 0.569$. The 5% critical value from an F-distribution with (2,81) degrees of freedom is approximately 3.13. Since $0.569 < 3.13$, we accept the null hypothesis.

Four sets of estimates are tabulated in Table 11.4, with the standard errors of the estimates appearing in parentheses below those estimates. Each set of estimates is plausible, with the direct price elasticities all being negative and all income elasticities being positive.

Table 11.4 Demand Equation Estimates

Parameter	Least Squares	SUR	Restricted SUR (Using $\hat{\mathbf{e}}$)	Restricted SUR (Using $\mathbf{e}^*$)
β_{10}	−5.17	−4.57	−4.44	−4.50
	(1.42)	(1.39)	(1.37)	(1.38)
β_{11}	−0.566	−0.909	−0.985	−0.953
	(0.215)	(0.137)	(0.034)	(0.045)
β_{14}	1.434	1.452	1.456	1.455
	(0.229)	(0.228)	(0.228)	(0.230)
β_{20}	−3.64	−3.19	−2.94	−3.00
	(1.61)	(1.58)	(1.56)	(1.56)
β_{22}	−0.648	−0.865	−0.985	−0.953
	(0.188)	(0.132)	(0.034)	(0.045)
β_{24}	1.144	1.137	1.133	1.134
	(0.261)	(0.261)	(0.261)	(0.260)
β_{30}	0.274	0.352	0.321	0.249
	(0.663)	(0.652)	(0.652)	(0.733)
β_{33}	−0.964	−0.999	−0.985	−0.953
	(0.065)	(0.036)	(0.034)	(0.045)
β_{34}	0.871	0.869	0.870	0.871
	(0.108)	(0.108)	(0.108)	(0.122)

Two sets of restricted SUR estimates are presented: those where Σ has been estimated from unrestricted least squares residuals ($\hat{\mathbf{e}}$), and those where Σ has been estimated from restricted least squares residuals ($\mathbf{e}^*$). The divisor $T - (K/M)$ was used in both cases. The unrestricted SUR estimates are more efficient than least squares, and the restricted SUR estimates are more efficient than the unrestricted SUR estimates. The standard errors give some indication of these efficiency differences, but caution must be exercised because the standard errors are only estimates of the square roots of the true variances.

11.2.7 Sets of Equations with Unequal Numbers of Observations

11.2.7a Theoretical Consequences

So far we have studied a set of equations where the number of observations on each equation was the same. This may not always be the case, however. If we were investigating investment functions for a number of firms, for example, it would not be surprising to find that the available data on different firms correspond to different time periods. Thus, in this section we allow for the possibility that the available number of observations is different for different equations, and we investigate the implications for the estimation results in Sections 11.2.2 and 11.2.3.

There are two main consequences of the situation outlined here. First, the generalized least squares estimator of the vector containing the coefficients from all the equations can still be obtained in a straightforward manner, but it does not reduce to the same expression obtained when the numbers of observations are equal. Second, the choice of an estimator for the disturbance covariance becomes a problem. Following Schmidt (1977), we illustrate these facts with a system of two seemingly unrelated regression equations

$$\begin{bmatrix} \mathbf{y}_1 \\ \mathbf{y}_2 \end{bmatrix} = \begin{bmatrix} X_1 & 0 \\ 0 & X_2 \end{bmatrix} \begin{bmatrix} \boldsymbol{\beta}_1 \\ \boldsymbol{\beta}_2 \end{bmatrix} + \begin{bmatrix} \mathbf{e}_1 \\ \mathbf{e}_2 \end{bmatrix} \tag{11.2.54}$$

where there are T observations on the first equation and $(T + N)$ observations on the second equation. When (11.2.54) is written as

$$\mathbf{y} = X\boldsymbol{\beta} + \mathbf{e} \tag{11.2.55}$$

this implies that $\mathbf{y}$ and $\mathbf{e}$ are of dimension $(2T + N)$, X is $[(2T + N) \times (K_1 + K_2)]$, and $\boldsymbol{\beta}$ is $[(K_1 + K_2) \times 1]$. In line with the earlier assumptions it will be assumed that the vectors $(e_{1t} \quad e_{2t})'$ are independently and identically distributed with 0 mean and covariance matrix

$$\Sigma = \begin{bmatrix} \sigma_{11} & \sigma_{12} \\ \sigma_{12} & \sigma_{22} \end{bmatrix} \tag{11.2.56}$$

This, in turn, implies that

$$E[\mathbf{ee}'] = \boldsymbol{\Phi} = \begin{bmatrix} \sigma_{11}I_T & \sigma_{12}I_T & 0 \\ \sigma_{12}I_T & \sigma_{22}I_T & 0 \\ 0 & 0 & \sigma_{22}I_N \end{bmatrix} \neq \Sigma \otimes I_T \tag{11.2.57}$$

and the generalized least squares estimator

$$\hat{\boldsymbol{\beta}} = (X'\boldsymbol{\Phi}^{-1}X)^{-1}X'\boldsymbol{\Phi}^{-1}\mathbf{y} \neq [X'(\Sigma^{-1} \otimes I)X]^{-1}X'(\Sigma^{-1} \otimes I)\mathbf{y} \tag{11.2.58}$$

Thus, although the generalized least squares estimator is readily attainable, it does not reduce to the expression given in (11.2.23). To obtain the corresponding expression we can partition X_2 and $\mathbf{y}_2$ as

$$X_2 = \begin{bmatrix} X_2^* \\ X_2^0 \end{bmatrix} \quad \text{and} \quad \mathbf{y}_2 = \begin{bmatrix} \mathbf{y}_2^* \\ \mathbf{y}_2^0 \end{bmatrix}$$

where $\mathbf{y}_2^*$ contains T observations, $\mathbf{y}_2^0$ contains N observations, and X_2^* and X_2^0 are the corresponding sets of regressors. In this case $\hat{\boldsymbol{\beta}}$ can be written as

$$\hat{\boldsymbol{\beta}} = \begin{bmatrix} \hat{\boldsymbol{\beta}}_1 \\ \hat{\boldsymbol{\beta}}_2 \end{bmatrix} = \begin{bmatrix} \sigma^{11} X_1' X_1 & \sigma^{12} X_1' X_2^* \\ \sigma^{12} X_2^{*\prime} X_1 & \sigma^{22} X_2^{*\prime} X_2^* + \dfrac{1}{\sigma_{22}} X_2^{0\prime} X_2^0 \end{bmatrix}^{-1}$$
$$\times \begin{bmatrix} \sigma^{11} X_1' \mathbf{y}_1 + \sigma^{12} X_1' \mathbf{y}_2^* \\ \sigma^{12} X_2^{*\prime} \mathbf{y}_1 + \sigma^{22} X_2^{*\prime} \mathbf{y}_2^* + \dfrac{1}{\sigma_{22}} X_2^{0\prime} \mathbf{y}_2^0 \end{bmatrix} \tag{11.2.59}$$

where σ^{ij} is the (i, j)th element of Σ^{-1}. If the additional N observations $(X_2^0, \mathbf{y}_2^0)$ are ignored, the estimator is identical to (11.2.23).

Because the covariance matrix Σ is usually unknown, we need an estimate for this matrix in order to compute an estimated generalized least squares estimate $\hat{\hat{\boldsymbol{\beta}}}$ of $\boldsymbol{\beta}$. From (11.2.27) the following variance and covariance estimates are suggested.

$$\hat{\sigma}_{11} = \frac{(\mathbf{y}_1 - X_1\mathbf{b}_1)'(\mathbf{y}_1 - X_1\mathbf{b}_1)}{T}$$
$$\hat{\sigma}_{12} = \hat{\sigma}_{21} = \frac{(\mathbf{y}_1 - X_1\mathbf{b}_1)'(\mathbf{y}_2^* - X_2^*\mathbf{b}_2)}{T} \tag{11.2.60}$$
$$\hat{\sigma}_{22} = \frac{(\mathbf{y}_2 - X_2\mathbf{b}_2)'(\mathbf{y}_2 - X_2\mathbf{b}_2)}{T + N}$$

where $\mathbf{b}_1$ and $\mathbf{b}_2$ are the least squares estimates of the first and second equations, respectively. Unfortunately, the resulting estimate

$$\hat{\Sigma} = \begin{bmatrix} \hat{\sigma}_{11} & \hat{\sigma}_{12} \\ \hat{\sigma}_{21} & \hat{\sigma}_{22} \end{bmatrix} \tag{11.2.61}$$

may not be positive definite. To avoid this problem, we could ignore the N observations $(X_2^0, \mathbf{y}_2^0)$ and use the estimator $\hat{\Sigma}$ derived in Section 11.2.3. Asymptotically, this estimator is equivalent to (11.2.61). Other possibilities for estimating the covariance matrix Σ are discussed in Judge, et al. (1985, pp. 480–483).

11.2.7b An Example

As an example, we again use the data in Table 11.1 and delete the last five observations of the first equation. Such a situation could arise in practice if the considered companies recorded the data for different time periods. Clearly, in this example $T = 15$ and $N = 5$.

The least squares estimates for the second equation are as in (11.2.31), and

$$\mathbf{b}_1' = (28.463, 0.017, 0.114)$$

The covariance estimate computed acording to (11.2.60) is

$$\hat{\Sigma} = \begin{bmatrix} 756.41 & 282.10 \\ 282.10 & 158.22 \end{bmatrix}$$

Using these variance and covariance estimates in (11.2.59), we get as an estimated generalized least squares estimate,

$$\hat{\hat{\boldsymbol{\beta}}}' = (27.05, 0.013, 0.149, 0.197, 0.057, 0.108)$$

11.2.8 Model Extensions

In Section 11.1 we mentioned that the sets-of-linear-equations model can usually be regarded as one possible model for pooling time-series and cross-sectional data. Given this nature of the data, there are a number of possible extensions that could be made. We saw, in Chapter 9, that the assumption of heteroskedasticity is often a reasonable one when cross-sectional data are being used, and the assumption of autocorrelation is often a reasonable one when time-series data are being used. Because the diagonal elements of the covariance matrix Σ are not necessarily identical, the assumptions of the seemingly unrelated regression model already allow for heteroskedasticity across cross-sectional units. Indeed, the existence of contemporaneous correlation means that allowance is also made for nonzero covariances between the disturbances for different cross-sectional units. However, no allowance for autocorrelation over time has yet been made. A simple way to introduce autocorrelation is to assume that the disturbance in each equation follows the first-order autoregressive process discussed in Section 9.5. One could assume that the autocorrelation coefficient ρ is the same for all equations, or, more realistically, that each equation has a different first-order autoregressive process described by ρ_i, say. When the disturbance in a given equation depends not only on past disturbance values for that equation but also on past values of the disturbances in other equations, the first-order autoregressive process can be generalized to a *vector autoregressive process*. Estimation of these alternative models is discussed in Judge, et al. (1985, pp. 483–493). Some special cases where the coefficient vector is the same for all equations (see Equation 11.2.49) are considered by Kmenta (1986, pp. 618–625). He develops estimators for both Σ diagonal and Σ not diagonal and under the assumption that the errors for each cross-sectional unit follow a first-order autoregressive process.

In a practical setting it is quite likely that extensions such as these will result in a more realistic model. However, it should also be kept in mind that more general models bring with them more parameters to estimate. The greater the number of parameters, the greater the number of observations likely to be needed to obtain reliable estimates. In particular, a reasonable number of time-series observations is needed to estimate an autocorrelation coefficient for each cross-sectional unit. It would be pointless to use one of Kmenta's models if only 10 observations (say) were available on each cross-sectional unit. For further reading on seemingly unrelated regressions, Srivastava and Giles (1987) should be consulted.

11.3 Problems on Seemingly Unrelated Regressions

11.3.1 General Exercises

11.3.1 Prove that application of least squares separately to each of the equations in (11.2.2) yields the same results as application of least squares to the "super model" in (11.2.12).

11.3.2 For the model given in (11.2.11) and (11.2.12), and the definition of Σ given in (11.2.13), prove that $\sigma_{12} = \sigma_{13} = \sigma_{23} = 0$ implies that

$$\mathbf{b} = (X'X)^{-1}X'\mathbf{y} = \hat{\boldsymbol{\beta}} = [X'(\Sigma^{-1} \otimes I)X]^{-1}X'(\Sigma^{-1} \otimes I)\mathbf{y}$$

11.3.3 Show that $\hat{\sigma}_{ij}$ in (11.2.27) is a consistent estimator for σ_{ij} under the assumptions

$$\operatorname{plim} \frac{X_i'\mathbf{e}_j}{T} = \mathbf{0} \qquad \text{for } i, j = 1, 2, \ldots, M$$

and

$$\operatorname{plim} \frac{X_i'X_j}{T} = \lim \frac{X_i'X_j}{T}$$

is finite and nonsingular for $i, j = 1, 2, \ldots, M$.

11.3.4 Prove the result in (11.2.48).

11.3.5 Prove that

$$(\mathbf{y} - X\hat{\hat{\boldsymbol{\beta}}})'(\hat{\Sigma}^{-1} \otimes I)(\mathbf{y} - X\hat{\hat{\boldsymbol{\beta}}}) = \operatorname{tr}[S\hat{\Sigma}^{-1}]$$

where S is an $(M \times M)$ matrix with (i, j)th element equal to $(\mathbf{y}_i - X_i\hat{\hat{\boldsymbol{\beta}}}_i)'(\mathbf{y}_j - X_j\hat{\hat{\boldsymbol{\beta}}}_j)$. If $\hat{\Sigma}$ is based on the residuals of the estimated generalized least squares estimator $\hat{\hat{\boldsymbol{\beta}}}$, rather than the residuals of the least squares estimator $\mathbf{b}$, to what does the foregoing expression simplify?

11.3.6 Consider the following model.

$$\mathbf{y}_1 = \mathbf{x}_1\beta_{11} + \mathbf{x}_2\beta_{12} + \mathbf{e}_1$$
$$\mathbf{y}_2 = \mathbf{x}_3\beta_{21} + \mathbf{x}_4\beta_{22} + \mathbf{e}_2$$

where the covariance matrix for $\mathbf{e} = (\mathbf{e}_1', \mathbf{e}_2')'$ is $\Sigma \otimes I$ with

$$\Sigma = \begin{bmatrix} \sigma^2 & \sigma^2 \\ \sigma^2 & 2\sigma^2 \end{bmatrix}$$

Suppose that data on the dependent and explanatory variables yields

$\mathbf{y}_1'\mathbf{y}_1 = 3000$	$\mathbf{y}_1'\mathbf{y}_2 = 500$	$\mathbf{y}_1'\mathbf{x}_1 = -200$	$\mathbf{y}_1'\mathbf{x}_2 = 400$
$\mathbf{y}_1'\mathbf{x}_3 = 200$	$\mathbf{y}_1'\mathbf{x}_4 = 100$	$\mathbf{y}_2'\mathbf{y}_2 = 1000$	$\mathbf{y}_2'\mathbf{x}_1 = 150$
$\mathbf{y}_2'\mathbf{x}_2 = -200$	$\mathbf{y}_2'\mathbf{x}_3 = 30$	$\mathbf{y}_2'\mathbf{x}_4 = -20$	$\mathbf{x}_1'\mathbf{x}_1 = 100$
$\mathbf{x}_1'\mathbf{x}_2 = 0$	$\mathbf{x}_1'\mathbf{x}_3 = 0$	$\mathbf{x}_1'\mathbf{x}_4 = 0$	$\mathbf{x}_2'\mathbf{x}_2 = 300$
$\mathbf{x}_2'\mathbf{x}_3 = 0$	$\mathbf{x}_2'\mathbf{x}_4 = 0$	$\mathbf{x}_3'\mathbf{x}_3 = 20$	$\mathbf{x}_3'\mathbf{x}_4 = 10$
$\mathbf{x}_4'\mathbf{x}_4 = 10$			

(*a*) Find the best linear unbiased estimates of β_{11}, β_{12}, β_{21}, and β_{22}.
(*b*) Repeat part (*a*) under the restrictions $\beta_{11} = \beta_{21}$ and $\beta_{12} = \beta_{22}$.
(*c*) Test the restrictions imposed in (*b*), given that $T = 15$.

11.3.7 Consider the three-equation demand system

$$\ln q_{it} = \beta_{i0} + \beta_{i1} \ln p_{1t} + \beta_{i2} \ln p_{2t} + \beta_{i3} \ln p_{3t} + \beta_{i4} \ln y_t + e_{it}$$
$$i = 1, 2, 3$$

and the data given in Table 11.3. Demand theory suggests that the coefficients satisfy the following constraints:

Engel condition: $w_1\beta_{14} + w_2\beta_{24} + w_3\beta_{34} = 1$

Homogeneity conditions: $\beta_{i1} + \beta_{i2} + \beta_{i3} + \beta_{i4} = 0 \qquad i = 1, 2, 3$

Symmetry conditions: $\dfrac{\beta_{ij}}{w_j} + \beta_{i4} = \dfrac{\beta_{ji}}{w_i} + \beta_{j4} \qquad i, j = 1, 2, 3\ (i \neq j)$

where $w_i = p_i q_i / y$ $(i = 1, 2, 3)$ is the budget share for the ith commodity. Using the sample means for the budget shares, namely

$$\bar{w}_i = T^{-1} \sum_{t=1}^{T} (p_{it} q_{it} / y_t),$$

(*a*) Write the 7 constraints in the form $R\boldsymbol{\beta} = \mathbf{r}$.
(*b*) Estimate the three equations using both least squares and the restricted seemingly unrelated regression estimator.

(*c*) Test for contemporaneous correlation.

(*d*) Test the validity of the demand theory constraints:

(*i*) All at once.

(*ii*) Each group separately.

11.3.2 Exercises Using Monte Carlo Data

Generate 100 samples each of size 20 from the model in (11.2.32) and (11.2.33).

11.3.8 Use five samples of the data to estimate the model using

(*a*) Least squares.

(*b*) Generalized least squares.

(*c*) Estimated generalized least squares.

Compare the various estimates.

11.3.9 Calculate the covariance matrices for the estimators in (*a*) and (*b*) of Exercise 11.3.8.

11.3.10 Using all 100 sets of the estimates obtained in Problem 11.3.8, calculate the mean and variance of each parameter estimate and comment on the results.

11.4 Pooling Time-Series and Cross-Sectional Data Using Dummy Variables

A simple framework that is often used for pooling time-series and cross-sectional data is that provided by dummy variables. In Chapter 10 we saw how dummy variables provide a convenient means of allowing for differences in coefficients that might occur for different samples or for different sample partitions. With pooled time-series and cross-sectional data the different cross-sectional units provide natural sample partitions for which different coefficients or different structures may exist. In this section we are concerned with a model where differences in cross-sectional units can be adequately captured by specifying a different intercept coefficient for each cross-sectional unit. Differences in intercepts are modeled using dummy variables. The model can be viewed as a special case of the seemingly unrelated regression model of Section 11.2, where $\Sigma = \sigma^2 I$ and where the coefficients for all equations are identical, except for the intercepts. Other models are discussed in Sections 11.5 and 11.6.

Assuming we have $i = 1, 2, \ldots, N$ cross-sectional observations, and $t = 1, 2, \ldots, T$ time-series observations, the (i, t)th observation on the dummy variable model with which we are concerned can be written as

$$y_{it} = \beta_{1i} + \sum_{k=2}^{K} \beta_k x_{kit} + e_{it} \tag{11.4.1}$$

where β_{1i} represents the intercept coefficient for the ith cross-sectional unit (or *individual*), the β_k represent the slope coefficients that are common to all individuals, y_{it} is the dependent variable, the x_{kit} are the explanatory variables, and the e_{it} are independent and identically distributed random variables with $E[e_{it}] = 0$ and $E[e_{it}^2] = \sigma_e^2$.

This model is often known as a dummy variable model because it is possible (and convenient) to write it as

$$y_{it} = \sum_{j=1}^{N} \beta_{1j} D_{jt} + \sum_{k=2}^{K} \beta_k x_{kit} + e_{it} \tag{11.4.2}$$

where the D_{jt} are known as dummy variables and take values equal to 0 or 1. Specifically,

$$D_{jt} = \begin{cases} 1 & \text{if } j = i \\ 0 & \text{if } j \neq i \end{cases}$$

Thus there is a dummy variable corresponding to each individual, and the dummy variable that corresponds to individual j will take the value unity for observations on individual j but will be 0 for observations on other individuals.

If we let $\mathbf{j}_T = (1 \quad 1 \quad \cdots \quad 1)'$ be a $(T \times 1)$ vector of onces, then, for the ith individual, (11.4.2) can be written in matrix notation as

$$\mathbf{y}_i = \beta_{1i}\mathbf{j}_T + X_{si}\boldsymbol{\beta}_s + \mathbf{e}_i \qquad i = 1, 2, \ldots, N \tag{11.4.3}$$

where

$$\mathbf{y}_i = \begin{bmatrix} y_{i1} \\ y_{i2} \\ \vdots \\ y_{iT} \end{bmatrix} \qquad X_{si} = \begin{bmatrix} x_{2i1} & x_{3i1} & \cdots & x_{Ki1} \\ x_{2i2} & x_{3i2} & \cdots & x_{Ki2} \\ \vdots & \vdots & \ddots & \vdots \\ x_{2iT} & x_{3iT} & \cdots & x_{KiT} \end{bmatrix} \qquad \mathbf{e}_i = \begin{bmatrix} e_{i1} \\ e_{i2} \\ \vdots \\ e_{iT} \end{bmatrix}$$

and $\boldsymbol{\beta}_s = (\beta_2 \quad \beta_3 \quad \cdots \quad \beta_K)'$. If we let $K' = K - 1$, then it can be noted that $\boldsymbol{\beta}_s$ is a $(K' \times 1)$ vector of slope coefficients and X_{si} is a $(T \times K')$ matrix of observations on the explanatory variables (excluding the constant term) for the ith individual.

The complete set of NT observations can be written as

$$\begin{bmatrix} \mathbf{y}_1 \\ \mathbf{y}_2 \\ \vdots \\ \mathbf{y}_N \end{bmatrix} = \begin{bmatrix} \mathbf{j}_T & \mathbf{0} & \cdots & \mathbf{0} & X_{s1} \\ \mathbf{0} & \mathbf{j}_T & \cdots & \mathbf{0} & X_{s2} \\ \vdots & \vdots & \ddots & \vdots & \vdots \\ \mathbf{0} & \mathbf{0} & \cdots & \mathbf{j}_T & X_{sN} \end{bmatrix} \begin{bmatrix} \beta_{11} \\ \beta_{12} \\ \vdots \\ \beta_{1N} \\ \boldsymbol{\beta}_s \end{bmatrix} + \begin{bmatrix} \mathbf{e}_1 \\ \mathbf{e}_2 \\ \vdots \\ \mathbf{e}_N \end{bmatrix} \tag{11.4.4}$$

which, using Kronecker product notation, is equivalent to

$$\mathbf{y} = [I_N \otimes \mathbf{j}_T \quad X_s]\begin{pmatrix} \boldsymbol{\beta}_1 \\ \boldsymbol{\beta}_s \end{pmatrix} + \mathbf{e} \tag{11.4.5}$$

where $\mathbf{y}' = (\mathbf{y}'_1, \mathbf{y}'_2, \ldots, \mathbf{y}'_N)$, $X'_s = (X'_{s1}, X'_{s2}, \ldots, X'_{sN})$, $\mathbf{e}' = (\mathbf{e}'_1, \mathbf{e}'_2, \ldots, \mathbf{e}'_N)$, $\boldsymbol{\beta}'_1 = (\beta_{11}, \beta_{12}, \ldots, \beta_{1N})$, and $I_N \otimes \mathbf{j}_T$ is the $(NT \times N)$ matrix of dummy variables

$$I_N \otimes \mathbf{j}_T = \begin{bmatrix} \mathbf{j}_T & \mathbf{0} & \cdots & \mathbf{0} \\ \mathbf{0} & \mathbf{j}_T & \cdots & \mathbf{0} \\ \vdots & \vdots & \ddots & \vdots \\ \mathbf{0} & \mathbf{0} & \cdots & \mathbf{j}_T \end{bmatrix} \tag{11.4.6}$$

At this point it is worth emphasizing that, in (11.4.5) the complete $[NT \times (N + K')]$ matrix of explanatory variables

$$[I_N \otimes \mathbf{j}_T \quad X_s]$$

does not contain a constant term.

11.4.1 Parameter Estimation

Of primary interest in (11.4.5) is the estimation of $\boldsymbol{\beta}_1$ and $\boldsymbol{\beta}_s$. The vector $\boldsymbol{\beta}_1$ contains the N intercept terms, one for each individual, whereas $\boldsymbol{\beta}_s$ is the vector of slope coefficients, which are assumed to be the same for all individuals. Theoretically, this estimation problem does not pose any difficulties. The disturbance vector $\mathbf{e}$ has mean $\mathbf{0}$ and covariance matrix $\sigma_e^2 I_{NT}$, and $[I_N \otimes \mathbf{j}_T \quad X_s]$ is a known nonstochastic matrix of rank $(N + K')$. Therefore, the Gauss–Markov theorem of Chapter 6 is relevant, and the least squares estimator

$$\begin{bmatrix} \mathbf{b}_1 \\ \mathbf{b}_s \end{bmatrix} = \begin{bmatrix} TI_N & (I_N \otimes \mathbf{j}_T)'X_s \\ X'_s(I_N \otimes \mathbf{j}_T) & X'_sX_s \end{bmatrix}^{-1} \begin{bmatrix} (I_N \otimes \mathbf{j}_T)'\mathbf{y} \\ X'_s\mathbf{y} \end{bmatrix} \tag{11.4.7}$$

is best linear unbiased, with mean $(\boldsymbol{\beta}'_1, \boldsymbol{\beta}'_s)'$ and covariance matrix

$$\Sigma_{(\mathbf{b}'_1, \mathbf{b}'_s)} = \sigma_e^2 \begin{bmatrix} TI_N & (I_N \otimes \mathbf{j}_T)'X_s \\ X'_s(I_N \otimes \mathbf{j}_T) & X'_sX_s \end{bmatrix}^{-1} \tag{11.4.8}$$

In both (11.4.7) and (11.4.8) the term TI_N arises because

$$(I_N \otimes \mathbf{j}_T)'(I_N \otimes \mathbf{j}_T) = I_N \otimes \mathbf{j}_T'\mathbf{j}_T = I_N \otimes T = TI_N$$

However, although there are no theoretical problems involved in obtaining $(\mathbf{b}_1' \quad \mathbf{b}_s')$, there could be some numerical problems. The matrix inversion in (11.4.7) is of order $(N + K')$, so if there are many cross-sectional units (N is large), this inversion may be unreliable. Under these circumstances it is advisable to calculate $\mathbf{b}_1$ and $\mathbf{b}_s$ using an alternative expression, derived by taking the *partitioned inverse*, which is discussed in Appendix A.7. The alternative expressions for $\mathbf{b}_1$ and $\mathbf{b}_s$ are (see Exercise 11.7.2)

$$\begin{aligned}\mathbf{b}_s &= (X_s'(I_N \otimes D_T)X_s)^{-1}X_s'(I_N \otimes D_T)\mathbf{y} \\ &= \left(\sum_{i=1}^{N} X_{si}'D_T X_{si}\right)^{-1} \sum_{i=1}^{N} X_{si}'D_T\mathbf{y}_i \end{aligned} \tag{11.4.9}$$

and

$$b_{1i} = \bar{y}_{i.} - \bar{\mathbf{x}}_{i.}'\mathbf{b}_s \qquad i = 1, 2, \ldots, N \tag{11.4.10}$$

where

$$D_T = I_T - \frac{\mathbf{j}_T\mathbf{j}_T'}{T}$$

$$\bar{y}_{i.} = \frac{1}{T}\sum_{t=1}^{T} y_{it} \qquad \bar{\mathbf{x}}_{i.}' = (\bar{x}_{2i.}, \bar{x}_{3i.}, \ldots, \bar{x}_{Ki.}) \tag{11.4.11}$$

and

$$\bar{x}_{ki.} = \frac{1}{T}\sum_{t=1}^{T} x_{kit} \qquad k = 2, 3, \ldots, K$$

In (11.4.9) the matrix inversion is only of order K' and the estimates of the intercepts b_{1i}, $i = 1, 2, \ldots, N$ are straightforward to obtain using (11.4.10).

Let us investigate the nature of the estimator in (11.4.9). It is possible to show that (see Exercise 11.7.1) D_T is idempotent, which implies that $I_N \otimes D_T$ is also idempotent. It is then possible to write

$$\begin{aligned}\mathbf{b}_s &= (X_s'(I_N \otimes D_T)'(I_N \otimes D_T)X_s)^{-1}X_s'(I_N \otimes D_T)'(I_N \otimes D_T)\mathbf{y} \\ &= (Z'Z)^{-1}Z'\mathbf{w} \end{aligned} \tag{11.4.12}$$

where $Z = (I_N \otimes D_T)X_s$ and $\mathbf{w} = (I_N \otimes D_T)\mathbf{y}$ are, respectively, transformed observations on the explanatory variables and transformed observations on the dependent variable. These transformed observations are given by

$$Z = \begin{bmatrix} D_T X_{s1} \\ D_T X_{s2} \\ \vdots \\ D_T X_{sN} \end{bmatrix} \quad \text{and} \quad \mathbf{w} = \begin{bmatrix} D_T \mathbf{y}_1 \\ D_T \mathbf{y}_2 \\ \vdots \\ D_T \mathbf{y}_N \end{bmatrix} \tag{11.4.13}$$

where

$$D_T X_{si} = \begin{bmatrix} x_{2i1} - \bar{x}_{2i.} & \cdots & x_{Ki1} - \bar{x}_{Ki.} \\ x_{2i2} - \bar{x}_{2i.} & \cdots & x_{Ki2} - \bar{x}_{Ki.} \\ \vdots & \ddots & \vdots \\ x_{2iT} - \bar{x}_{2i.} & \cdots & x_{KiT} - \bar{x}_{Ki.} \end{bmatrix} \tag{11.4.14}$$

and

$$D_T \mathbf{y}_i = \begin{bmatrix} y_{i1} - \bar{y}_{i.} \\ y_{i2} - \bar{y}_{i.} \\ \vdots \\ y_{iT} - \bar{y}_{i.} \end{bmatrix} \qquad i = 1, 2, \ldots, N \tag{11.4.15}$$

Thus the matrix D_T, when used to transform the observations on the ith individual (X_{si} and $\mathbf{y}_i$), has the effect of expressing each variable in terms of its deviation from the mean for the ith individual. You are encouraged to verify this fact (Equations 11.4.14 and 11.4.15).

This result implies that, to obtain the least squares estimator of the slope coefficients in the dummy variable model, we can express each variable in terms of deviations from the individual means and run a least squares regression without the constant term. Also, to see that this is an intuitively reasonable procedure, we can average (11.4.1) over time and subtract the result from (11.4.1). This yields

$$y_{it} - \bar{y}_{i.} = \sum_{k=2}^{K} \beta_k(x_{kit} - \bar{x}_{ki.}) + e_{it} - \bar{e}_{i.} \tag{11.4.16}$$

where the definition of $\bar{e}_{i.}$ is obvious, and the estimator $\mathbf{b}_s$ can be viewed as least squares applied to this equation.

To summarize, if we wish to estimate $\boldsymbol{\beta}_1$ and $\boldsymbol{\beta}_s$ in the dummy variable model in (11.4.5) and if N is small, we can set up the variables as illustrated in (11.4.4) and apply least squares. Alternatively, if N is large, we can proceed in two stages: the slope coefficients $\boldsymbol{\beta}_s$ can be estimated by setting up the variables as shown in (11.4.14) and (11.4.15) and applying least squares; the intercept terms $\boldsymbol{\beta}_1$ can then be estimated by application of (11.4.10).

11.4.2 Variance Estimation

It is worthwhile to give a word of warning concerning estimation of σ_e^2. Both estimation techniques just described lead to the same residual vector. That is, it is possible to show that

$$\hat{\mathbf{e}} = \mathbf{y} - [I_N \otimes \mathbf{j}_T \quad X_s]\begin{bmatrix} \mathbf{b}_1 \\ \mathbf{b}_s \end{bmatrix} = (I_N \otimes D_T)\mathbf{y} - (I_N \otimes D_T)X_s\mathbf{b}_s \tag{11.4.17}$$

Then, from Chapter 6, an unbiased estimator of σ_e^2 is given by

$$\hat{\sigma}_e^2 = \frac{\hat{\mathbf{e}}'\hat{\mathbf{e}}}{NT - (N + K')} \tag{11.4.18}$$

and this will be the estimate provided by most computer programs if $\boldsymbol{\beta}_1$ and $\boldsymbol{\beta}_s$ are estimated simultaneously. However, if we use the second estimation technique, where $\mathbf{b}_s$ is obtained as a first step, the variance estimator is likely to be

$$\overset{*}{\sigma}{}_e^2 = \frac{\hat{\mathbf{e}}'\hat{\mathbf{e}}}{NT - K'} \tag{11.4.19}$$

and this will be a biased estimator for σ_e^2. Consequently, under these circumstances it is advisable to "correct" $\overset{*}{\sigma}{}_e^2$ by multiplying by $[(NT - K')/(NT - N - K')]$. The standard errors of the coefficients also need to be adjusted correspondingly.

11.4.3 An Alternative Parameterization

Many computer programs automatically insert a constant term, which often leads novice dummy-variable users to include both a constant term and a dummy variable for each individual. If this happens, part of the matrix of explanatory variables will be of the form

$$[\mathbf{j}_{NT} \quad I_N \otimes \mathbf{j}_T] = \begin{bmatrix} \mathbf{j}_T & \mathbf{j}_T & \mathbf{0} & \cdots & \mathbf{0} \\ \mathbf{j}_T & \mathbf{0} & \mathbf{j}_T & \cdots & \mathbf{0} \\ \vdots & \vdots & \vdots & \ddots & \vdots \\ \mathbf{j}_T & \mathbf{0} & \mathbf{0} & \cdots & \mathbf{j}_T \end{bmatrix} \tag{11.4.20}$$

In this matrix the first column (the constant term) is equal to the sum of the next N columns (the dummy variables). Consequently, the columns are linearly dependent or, in other words, the matrix of explanatory variables is not of full rank. This means that the equivalent of the $X'X$ matrix will be singular and that it is impossible to obtain unique estimates of the coefficients.

This problem is a consequence of introducing too many parameters. Before introducing the constant term we already had an intercept for each of the N

individuals; no additional information can be obtained by introducing the constant.

Because of this problem it is often convenient to reparameterize the model so that it includes a constant. We can do this by simply omitting one of the dummy variables. Let us omit the first dummy variable. Then the matrix in (11.4.20) becomes

$$\left[\mathbf{j}_{NT} \quad \begin{pmatrix}\mathbf{0}'_{N-1}\\ I_{N-1}\end{pmatrix} \otimes \mathbf{j}_T\right] = \begin{bmatrix}\mathbf{j}_T & \mathbf{0} & \cdots & \mathbf{0}\\ \mathbf{j}_T & \mathbf{j}_T & \cdots & \mathbf{0}\\ \vdots & \vdots & & \vdots\\ \mathbf{j}_T & \mathbf{0} & \cdots & \mathbf{j}_T\end{bmatrix} \tag{11.4.21}$$

What effect does this have on our parameter estimates? To investigate this question we rewrite our model (Equation 11.4.2) as

$$\begin{aligned} y_{it} &= \beta_{11}D_{1t} + \sum_{j=2}^{N}\beta_{1j}D_{jt} + \sum_{k=2}^{K}\beta_k x_{kit} + e_{it} \\ &= \delta_1 D_{1t} + \sum_{j=2}^{N}(\delta_1 + \delta_j)D_{jt} + \sum_{k=2}^{K}\beta_k x_{kit} + e_{it} \\ &= \delta_1\sum_{j=1}^{N}D_{jt} + \sum_{j=2}^{N}\delta_j D_{jt} + \sum_{k=2}^{K}\beta_k x_{kit} + e_{it} \\ &= \delta_1 + \sum_{j=2}^{N}\delta_j D_{jt} + \sum_{k=2}^{K}\beta_k x_{kit} + e_{it} \end{aligned} \tag{11.4.22}$$

The second line in (11.4.22) is obtained by defining $\delta_1 = \beta_{11}$ as the intercept for individual 1 and $\delta_j = \beta_{1j} - \beta_{11}$, $j = 2, 3, \ldots, N$ as the difference between the intercept for the jth individual and that for individual 1. The third line in (11.4.22) uses straightforward algebra, and the last line uses the result that $\sum_{j=1}^{N} D_{jt} = 1$. Also, the final line is in a form that uses (11.4.21) as part of the matrix of explanatory variables. Thus the reparameterized model can be written as

$$\mathbf{y} = \left[\mathbf{j}_{NT} \quad \begin{pmatrix}\mathbf{0}'_{N-1}\\ I_{N-1}\end{pmatrix} \otimes \mathbf{j}_T \quad X_s\right]\begin{bmatrix}\boldsymbol{\delta}\\ \boldsymbol{\beta}_s\end{bmatrix} + \mathbf{e} \tag{11.4.23}$$

where $\boldsymbol{\delta}' = (\delta_1, \delta_2, \ldots, \delta_N)$. Least squares can be applied to this model to obtain estimates $\mathbf{d}$ and $\mathbf{b}_s$, and the only difference between these estimates and those obtained from the previous model is that, with the exception of the first element d_1, $\mathbf{d}$ is a vector of estimates of the differences between the $(N - 1)$ intercepts β_{12}, $\beta_{13}, \ldots, \beta_{1N}$ and the intercept for the first individual, β_{11}. If we choose to use (11.4.23) instead of (11.4.5), estimates of the intercepts can be obtained from

$$b_{1j} = d_j + d_1 \qquad j = 2, 3, \ldots, N \tag{11.4.24}$$

and they will be identical to those in the vector $\mathbf{b}_1$ obtained from the original model.

To summarize, it may be more convenient to reformulate the model so that it includes a constant term. This can be achieved by dropping one of the dummy variables, and, when this is done, the new coefficients will have a different interpretation. However, estimates of corresponding coefficients will be identical.

11.4.4 Testing the Dummy Variable Coefficients

A question frequently asked is: Is there evidence to suggest that different individuals have different intercepts, or would the model be adequate if we simply assumed that all the intercepts are identical? If they are all the same and the other assumptions of the model continue to hold, then there is no basis for differentiating the time-series cross-sectional nature of the data, and, for estimation purposes, the data can be treated as one sample of NT observations.

The question can be framed in terms of the hypotheses

$$H_0\colon \beta_{11} = \beta_{12} = \cdots = \beta_{1N}$$

$$H_1\colon \text{the } \beta_{1j} \text{ are not all equal}$$

or, using the reparameterized model, in terms of the hypotheses

$$H_0\colon \delta_2 = \delta_3 = \cdots = \delta_N = 0$$

$$H_1\colon \text{the } \delta_j \text{ are not all zero}$$

Both null hypotheses represent a set of linear restrictions on coefficients, so they could be formulated in terms of the $R\boldsymbol{\beta} = \mathbf{r}$ framework of Chapter 6. In that chapter we mentioned that when testing a set of linear restrictions, one way to calculate the relevant F statistic is to write it in terms of restricted and unrestricted residual sums of squares. In the context of our hypotheses the F statistic is given by

$$F = \frac{(\bar{\mathbf{e}}'\bar{\mathbf{e}} - \hat{\mathbf{e}}'\hat{\mathbf{e}})/(N-1)}{\hat{\mathbf{e}}'\hat{\mathbf{e}}/(NT - N - K')} \tag{11.4.25}$$

where

1. $\bar{\mathbf{e}}'\bar{\mathbf{e}}$ is the residual sum of squares from the restricted model

$$y_{it} = \beta_{11} + \sum_{k=2}^{K} \beta_k x_{kit} + e_{it} \tag{11.4.26}$$

2. $\hat{\mathbf{e}}'\hat{\mathbf{e}}$ is the residual sum of squares from the unrestricted model

$$y_{it} = \beta_{11} + \sum_{j=2}^{N} \delta_j D_{jt} + \sum_{k=2}^{K} \beta_k x_{kit} + e_{it} \tag{11.4.27}$$

3. $(N - 1)$ is the number of linear restrictions
4. $(NT - N - K')$ is the number of degrees of freedom in the unrestricted model.

Under the null hypothesis the statistic in (11.4.25) has the F distribution with $[(N - 1), (NT - N - K')]$ degrees of freedom, and the test is implemented in the usual way.

In applied work it is often tempting to make a judgment about whether some dummy variables should be excluded by examining the t values associated with individual coefficients. Such a practice should not be encouraged. It does provide some information, but, if dummy variables are dropped when t tests are insignificant, two different parameterizations of the same problem can lead to different dummy variables being omitted. For this reason, the joint test in (11.4.25) is preferred.

11.4.5 An Example

Suppose that, for a given industry, we have 10 years ($T = 10$) of data on total cost (y) and output (x) for a sample of four firms ($N = 4$). Also suppose that we wish to estimate the total cost function for each firm and that these functions can be written as

$$y_{it} = \beta_{1i} + \beta_2 x_{it} + e_{it}, \qquad \begin{aligned} i &= 1, 2, 3, 4 \\ t &= 1, 2, \ldots, 10 \end{aligned}$$

where the e_{it} are independent identically distributed random variables with 0 mean and variance σ_e^2. The hypothetical data on these four firms is given in Table 11.5.

When the notation of the previous sections is related to this example, the $(K' \times 1)$ vector $\boldsymbol{\beta}_s$ becomes the scalar, β_2, $\boldsymbol{\beta}_1' = (\beta_{11}, \beta_{12}, \beta_{13}, \beta_{14})$, and the $(NT \times K')$ matrix X_s is simply an $(NT \times 1)$ vector that we will call $\mathbf{x} = (\mathbf{x}_1', \mathbf{x}_2', \mathbf{x}_3', \mathbf{x}_4')'$. Since $N = 4$, this problem is not large, and $\boldsymbol{\beta}_1$ and β_2 could easily be estimated simultaneously by setting up

$$[I_4 \otimes \mathbf{j}_{10} \quad \mathbf{x}]$$

as the matrix of explanatory variables. However, it is instructive to consider the approach based on deviations from firm means, so we will proceed in this direction.

Table 11.5 Data on Cost (y) and Output (x) for Four Firms

Time Period	Cost				Output			
	$i = 1$	$i = 2$	$i = 3$	$i = 4$	$i = 1$	$i = 2$	$i = 3$	$i = 4$
1	43.72	51.03	43.90	64.29	38.46	32.52	32.86	41.86
2	45.86	27.75	23.77	42.16	35.32	18.71	18.52	28.33
3	4.74	35.72	28.60	61.99	3.78	27.01	22.93	34.21
4	40.58	35.85	27.71	34.26	35.34	18.66	25.02	15.69
5	25.86	43.28	40.38	47.67	20.83	25.58	35.13	29.70
6	36.05	48.52	36.43	45.14	36.72	39.19	27.29	23.03
7	50.94	64.18	19.31	35.31	41.67	47.70	16.99	14.80
8	42.48	38.34	16.55	35.43	30.71	27.01	12.56	21.53
9	25.60	45.39	30.97	54.33	23.70	33.57	26.76	32.86
10	49.81	43.69	46.60	59.23	39.53	27.32	41.42	42.25

For the means we have

$$\bar{y}_{1.} = 36.564 \qquad \bar{y}_{2.} = 43.375 \qquad \bar{y}_{3.} = 31.422 \qquad \bar{y}_{4.} = 47.981$$

$$\bar{x}_{1.} = 30.606 \qquad \bar{x}_{2.} = 29.727 \qquad \bar{x}_{3.} = 25.948 \qquad \bar{x}_{4.} = 28.426$$

and the observations in terms of deviations from the firm means, $(I_4 \otimes D_{10})\mathbf{y}$ and $(I_4 \otimes D_{10})\mathbf{x}$, are given in Table 11.6.

Then, using the estimator in (11.4.9) and (11.4.12), the estimate of the slope coefficient is

$$\begin{aligned} b_2 &= [\mathbf{x}'(I_4 \otimes D_{10})\mathbf{x}]^{-1}\mathbf{x}'(I_4 \otimes D_{10})\mathbf{y} \\ &= (3474.836)^{-1} \cdot 3888.442 \\ &= 1.119029 \end{aligned}$$

and the estimates of the four intercepts are (from Equation 11.4.10)

$$\begin{aligned} b_{11} &= 36.564 - (30.606)(1.119029) = 2.315 \\ b_{12} &= 43.375 - (29.727)(1.119029) = 10.110 \\ b_{13} &= 31.422 - (25.948)(1.119029) = 2.385 \\ b_{14} &= 47.981 - (28.426)(1.119029) = 16.171 \end{aligned}$$

The estimate of the variance of the disturbance term is

$$\hat{\sigma}_e^2 = \frac{\hat{\mathbf{e}}'\hat{\mathbf{e}}}{NT - N - K'} = \frac{491.47896}{35} = 14.042256$$

Table 11.6 Data on Cost and Output in Terms of Deviations from Firm Means

Time	Cost				Output			
Period	$i = 1$	$i = 2$	$i = 3$	$i = 4$	$i = 1$	$i = 2$	$i = 3$	$i = 4$
1	7.156	7.655	12.478	16.309	7.854	2.793	6.912	13.434
2	9.296	−15.625	−7.652	−5.821	4.714	−11.017	−7.428	−0.096
3	−31.824	−7.655	−2.822	14.009	−26.826	−2.717	−3.018	5.784
4	4.016	−7.525	−3.712	−13.721	4.734	−11.067	−0.928	−12.736
5	−10.704	−0.095	8.958	−0.311	−9.776	−4.147	9.182	1.274
6	−0.514	5.145	5.008	−2.841	6.114	9.463	1.342	−5.396
7	14.376	20.805	−12.112	−12.671	11.064	17.973	−8.958	−13.626
8	5.916	−5.035	−14.872	−12.551	0.104	−2.717	−13.388	−6.896
9	−10.964	2.015	−0.452	6.349	−6.906	3.843	0.812	4.434
10	13.246	0.315	15.178	11.249	8.924	−2.407	15.472	13.824

and this leads to a standard error for b_2, given by

$$[\hat{\sigma}_e^2(\mathbf{x}'(I_4 \otimes D_{10})\mathbf{x})^{-1}]^{1/2} = [14.042256 \cdot (3474.836)^{-1}]^{1/2} = 0.06357$$

The four estimated cost functions can now be summarized using one equation with dummy variables, given by

$$y_{it} = 2.315D_{1t} + 10.110D_{2t} + 2.385D_{3t} + 16.171D_{4t} + \underset{(0.064)}{1.119}x_{it} + \hat{e}_{it}$$

We have not provided the standard errors of the coefficients of the dummy variables because, as mentioned in Section 11.4.4, it is usually more meaningful to test them as a group.

With this in mind, we will test the null hypothesis

$$H_0\colon \beta_{11} = \beta_{12} = \beta_{13} = \beta_{14}$$

against the alternative that the β_{1i} are not all equal. To do this we first use the data in Table 11.5 to estimate the restricted model

$$y_{it} = \beta_{11} + \beta_2 x_{it} + e_{it}$$

and obtain

$$y_{it} = 7.385 + 1.132x_{it} + \bar{e}_{it}$$

The residual sum of squares from this estimated equation is

$$\bar{\mathbf{e}}'\bar{\mathbf{e}} = 1838.98022$$

and this leads to the following F statistic (see Equation 11.4.25)

$$F = \frac{(1838.98022 - 491.47896)/3}{491.47896/35} = 31.99$$

For (3, 35) degrees of freedom and a 5 percent significance level, the critical F value is $2.87 < 31.99$, so we reject the null hypothesis and conclude that the intercepts of the four firms' cost functions are not all the same.

11.5 Pooling Time-Series and Cross-Sectional Data Using Error Components

In this section we again consider the model

$$y_{it} = \beta_{1i} + \sum_{k=2}^{K} \beta_k x_{kit} + e_{it} \tag{11.5.1}$$

but instead of assuming that the β_{1i} are fixed coefficients, we assume that they are independent random variables with a mean $\bar{\beta}_1$ and variance σ_μ^2. We will say more about these alternative assumptions in Section 11.6. For the moment we simply note that, if the β_{1i} are random, it is necessary to view the N individuals as a random sample from some larger population, and it is the population parameters $(\bar{\beta}_1, \beta_2, \ldots, \beta_K)$ that we wish to learn about.

We can write

$$\beta_{1i} = \bar{\beta}_1 + \mu_i \tag{11.5.2}$$

where $E[\mu_i] = 0$, $E[\mu_i^2] = \sigma_\mu^2$, and $E[\mu_i \mu_j] = 0$ for $i \neq j$; and we will also assume that the μ_i are uncorrelated with the e_{jt}. That is, $E[\mu_i e_{jt}] = 0$. Equation 11.5.1 now becomes

$$y_{it} = \bar{\beta}_1 + \sum_{k=2}^{K} \beta_k x_{kit} + \mu_i + e_{it} \tag{11.5.3}$$

which, when written in matrix notation for the ith individual, is

$$\mathbf{y}_i = X_i \boldsymbol{\beta} + \mu_i \mathbf{j}_T + \mathbf{e}_i \tag{11.5.4}$$

where $\mathbf{y}_i$, $\mathbf{j}_T$, and $\mathbf{e}_i$ were defined in the previous section (Equation 11.4.3), $X_i = (\mathbf{j}_T \; X_{si})$ is a $(T \times K)$ matrix of observations on the explanatory variables (including the constant term) for the ith individual, and $\boldsymbol{\beta}' = (\bar{\beta}_1, \beta_2, \ldots, \beta_K)$. In (11.5.4) the term $(\mu_i \mathbf{j}_T + \mathbf{e}_i)$ can be regarded as a composite disturbance vector that has mean $\mathbf{0}$ and covariance matrix

$$\begin{aligned} V &= E[(\mu_i \mathbf{j}_T + \mathbf{e}_i)(\mu_i \mathbf{j}_T + \mathbf{e}_i)'] \\ &= E[\mu_i^2]\mathbf{j}_T\mathbf{j}_T' + \mathbf{j}_T E[\mu_i \mathbf{e}_i'] + E[\mu_i \mathbf{e}_i]\mathbf{j}_T' + E[\mathbf{e}_i \mathbf{e}_i'] \\ &= \sigma_\mu^2 \mathbf{j}_T \mathbf{j}_T' + \sigma_e^2 I_T \\ &= \begin{bmatrix} \sigma_\mu^2 + \sigma_e^2 & \sigma_\mu^2 & \cdots & \sigma_\mu^2 \\ \sigma_\mu^2 & \sigma_\mu^2 + \sigma_e^2 & \cdots & \sigma_\mu^2 \\ \vdots & \vdots & \ddots & \vdots \\ \sigma_\mu^2 & \sigma_\mu^2 & \cdots & \sigma_\mu^2 + \sigma_e^2 \end{bmatrix} \end{aligned} \tag{11.5.5}$$

The structure of this covariance matrix is such that, for a given individual, the correlation between any two disturbances in different time periods is the same. Thus in contrast to a first-order autoregressive model, the correlation is constant and does not decline as the disturbances become farther apart in time. Another feature of this matrix is that V does not depend on i, which implies that, not only is the correlation constant over time, it is identical for all individuals.

The complete set of NT observations can be written as

$$\begin{bmatrix} \mathbf{y}_1 \\ \mathbf{y}_2 \\ \vdots \\ \mathbf{y}_N \end{bmatrix} = \begin{bmatrix} X_1 \\ X_2 \\ \vdots \\ X_N \end{bmatrix} \boldsymbol{\beta} + \begin{bmatrix} \mu_1 \mathbf{j}_T \\ \mu_2 \mathbf{j}_T \\ \vdots \\ \mu_N \mathbf{j}_T \end{bmatrix} + \begin{bmatrix} \mathbf{e}_1 \\ \mathbf{e}_2 \\ \vdots \\ \mathbf{e}_N \end{bmatrix} \tag{11.5.6}$$

or, using obvious definitions, it can be written more compactly as

$$\mathbf{y} = X\boldsymbol{\beta} + \boldsymbol{\mu} \otimes \mathbf{j}_T + \mathbf{e} \tag{11.5.7}$$

To find the covariance matrix of the composite disturbance in (11.5.7) we note that $E[\boldsymbol{\mu}\boldsymbol{\mu}'] = \sigma_\mu^2 I_N$, $E[\mathbf{e}\mathbf{e}'] = \sigma_e^2 I_{NT}$, and $E[(\boldsymbol{\mu} \otimes \mathbf{j}_T)\mathbf{e}'] = 0$. Then we have

$$\begin{aligned} \boldsymbol{\Phi} &= E[(\boldsymbol{\mu} \otimes \mathbf{j}_T + \mathbf{e})(\boldsymbol{\mu} \otimes \mathbf{j}_T + \mathbf{e})'] \\ &= \sigma_\mu^2 I_N \otimes \mathbf{j}_T \mathbf{j}'_T + \sigma_e^2 I_{NT} \\ &= I_N \otimes [\sigma_\mu^2 \mathbf{j}_T \mathbf{j}'_T + \sigma_e^2 I_T] \\ &= I_N \otimes V \end{aligned} \tag{11.5.8}$$

Thus the covariance matrix for the complete $(NT \times 1)$ disturbance vector is block diagonal with each block given by (11.5.5). The block diagonal property arises because the disturbance vectors corresponding to different individuals are uncorrelated. That is,

$$E[(\mu_i \mathbf{j}_T + \mathbf{e}_i)(\mu_j \mathbf{j}_T + \mathbf{e}_j)'] = 0 \qquad \text{for } i \neq j$$

So far in this section we have been describing the assumptions and features of the error components model and, in particular, the structure of its disturbance covariance matrix. We now turn to the problem of estimating $\boldsymbol{\beta}$.

11.5.1 Generalized Least Squares Estimation

It is clear from the foregoing discussion that the covariance matrix for the error components model is not of the scalar-identity type, and, consequently, the model and estimation framework examined in Chapter 8 is relevant. Thus if σ_μ^2 and σ_e^2 (and, consequently, V and $\boldsymbol{\Phi}$) are known, then for estimation of $\boldsymbol{\beta}$ the generalized least squares estimator

$$\hat{\boldsymbol{\beta}} = (X'\boldsymbol{\Phi}^{-1}X)^{-1}X'\boldsymbol{\Phi}^{-1}\mathbf{y} \tag{11.5.9}$$

is best linear unbiased. The easiest way to obtain the generalized least squares estimator is to first find transformed observations $\mathbf{y}^* = P\mathbf{y}$ and $X^* = PX$, where P

is such that $P'P = c\Phi^{-1}$ and c is any scalar. Then, as we have noted in a number of earlier chapters, least squares is applied to the transformed observations to yield

$$\hat{\boldsymbol{\beta}} = (X^{*\prime}X^*)^{-1}X^{*\prime}\mathbf{y}^* = (X'P'PX)^{-1}X'P'P\mathbf{y} = (X'\boldsymbol{\Phi}^{-1}X)^{-1}X'\boldsymbol{\Phi}^{-1}\mathbf{y} \quad (11.5.10)$$

We begin the search for a suitable transformation matrix by noting that

$$\boldsymbol{\Phi}^{-1} = (I_N \otimes V)^{-1} = I_N \otimes V^{-1} \quad (11.5.11)$$

and that (see Exercise 11.7.4)

$$V^{-1} = \frac{\mathbf{j}_T\mathbf{j}_T'}{T\sigma_1^2} + \frac{D_T}{\sigma_e^2} \quad (11.5.12)$$

where $\sigma_1^2 = T\sigma_\mu^2 + \sigma_e^2$ and $D_T = I_T - \mathbf{j}_T\mathbf{j}_T'/T$.
Also, if we define a matrix P_* as

$$P_* = I_T - \alpha\frac{\mathbf{j}_T\mathbf{j}_T'}{T} \quad (11.5.13)$$

where

$$\alpha = 1 - \frac{\sigma_e}{\sigma_1} \quad (11.5.14)$$

then it can be shown that (Exercise 11.7.5) $P_*'P_* = \sigma_e^2 V^{-1}$, which implies that the complete transformation matrix is

$$P = I_N \otimes P_* \quad (11.5.15)$$

because

$$P'P = (I_N \otimes P_*)'(I_N \otimes P_*) = I_N \otimes P_*'P_* = I_N \otimes \sigma_e^2 V^{-1} = \sigma_e^2(I_N \otimes V^{-1})$$
$$= \sigma_e^2\boldsymbol{\Phi}^{-1}$$

The next question to investigate is the nature of the transformed observations $\mathbf{y}^*$ and X^*. They are given by

$$\mathbf{y}^* = P\mathbf{y} = (I_N \otimes P_*)\mathbf{y} = \begin{bmatrix} P_*\mathbf{y}_1 \\ P_*\mathbf{y}_2 \\ \vdots \\ P_*\mathbf{y}_N \end{bmatrix}$$

and

$$X^* = PX = (I_N \otimes P_*)X = \begin{bmatrix} P_*X_1 \\ P_*X_2 \\ \vdots \\ P_*X_N \end{bmatrix} \quad (11.5.16)$$

Examining the ith vector component of $\mathbf{y}^*$, we have

$$P_* \mathbf{y}_i = \left(I_T - \frac{\alpha \mathbf{j}_T \mathbf{j}_T'}{T} \right) \mathbf{y}_i = \mathbf{y}_i - \alpha \bar{y}_{i.} \mathbf{j}_T \tag{11.5.17}$$

and, similarly, the corresponding component of X^* is

$$P_* X_i = [(1-\alpha)\mathbf{j}_T \quad \mathbf{x}_{2i} - \alpha \bar{x}_{2i.} \mathbf{j}_T \quad \cdots \quad \mathbf{x}_{Ki} - \alpha \bar{x}_{Ki.} \mathbf{j}_T] \tag{11.5.18}$$

where $\mathbf{x}_{ki} = (x_{ki1}, x_{ki2}, \ldots, x_{kiT})'$. Typical elements of (11.5.17) and (11.5.18) are

$$y_{it}^* = y_{it} - \alpha \bar{y}_{i.} \qquad \text{and} \qquad x_{kit}^* = x_{kit} - \alpha \bar{x}_{ki.}$$

Thus the transformed observations are obtained by

1. Calculating the individual means for each variable

$$\bar{y}_{i.} = \frac{\mathbf{j}_T' \mathbf{y}_i}{T} \qquad \text{and} \qquad \bar{x}_{ki.} = \frac{\mathbf{j}_T' \mathbf{x}_{ki}}{T} \qquad k = 2, 3, \ldots, K; i = 1, 2, \ldots, N$$

2. Expressing the original observations in terms of deviations from a fraction (α) of their individual means. For the constant term this amounts to replacing a column of ones with a column containing the constant $(1 - \alpha)$.

The generalized least squares estimator $\hat{\boldsymbol{\beta}} = (X'\boldsymbol{\Phi}^{-1}X)^{-1}X'\boldsymbol{\Phi}^{-1}\mathbf{y}$ is obtained by applying least squares to the equation

$$y_{it} - \alpha \bar{y}_{i.} = (1-\alpha)\bar{\beta}_1 + \sum_{k=2}^{K} (x_{kit} - \alpha \bar{x}_{ki.})\beta_k + e_{it} \tag{11.5.19}$$

This can be contrasted with the dummy variable estimator of the slope coefficients, $\mathbf{b}_s$, which is obtained by applying least squares to (see Equation 11.4.16)

$$y_{it} - \bar{y}_{i.} = \sum_{k=2}^{K} (x_{kit} - \bar{x}_{ki.})\beta_k + e_{it} - \bar{e}_{i.} \tag{11.5.20}$$

In fact, if we define $\hat{\boldsymbol{\beta}}_s$ as the generalized least squares estimator of the slope coefficients, obtained by appropriately partitioning $\hat{\boldsymbol{\beta}}$, then it can be shown that $\hat{\boldsymbol{\beta}}_s$ is a matrix weighted average of the dummy variable estimator $\mathbf{b}_s$ and the estimator for $\boldsymbol{\beta}_s$ obtained by carrying out a regression on the individual means. This latter estimator is also encountered in the next section, and we will denote it by $\boldsymbol{\beta}_s^*$. Because it only uses variation between individuals it is often known as the *between estimator*. The generalized least squares estimator can be viewed as an efficient combination of $\boldsymbol{\beta}_s^*$ and the dummy variable estimator $\mathbf{b}_s$, which uses variation within individuals. For more details, see Judge, et al. (1985, p. 523) and references therein.

11.5.2 Estimation of Variance Components

In practice, the generalized least squares estimator $\hat{\boldsymbol{\beta}}$ cannot be used because the variance components σ_μ^2 and σ_e^2 are unknown. Following the practice established in many of the earlier chapters, however, it is possible to replace σ_μ^2 and σ_e^2 with estimates $\hat{\sigma}_\mu^2$ and $\hat{\sigma}_e^2$. When this is done the covariance matrix $\boldsymbol{\Phi}$ is replaced with its estimate $\hat{\boldsymbol{\Phi}}$, and the resulting estimator for $\boldsymbol{\beta}$ is an estimated generalized least squares estimator

$$\hat{\hat{\boldsymbol{\beta}}} = (X'\hat{\boldsymbol{\Phi}}^{-1}X)^{-1}X'\hat{\boldsymbol{\Phi}}^{-1}\mathbf{y} \tag{11.5.21}$$

This estimator is most easily obtained by following the transformation procedure in the previous section, with $\alpha = 1 - \sigma_e/\sigma_1$ replaced by $\hat{\alpha} = 1 - \hat{\sigma}_e/\hat{\sigma}_1$. For conventional estimators of σ_μ^2 and σ_e^2, and under appropriate assumptions about the limiting behavior of X, it can be shown that both $\hat{\boldsymbol{\beta}}$ and $\hat{\hat{\boldsymbol{\beta}}}$ have the same limiting distribution as N or $T \to \infty$.

A large number of alternative estimators for σ_μ^2 and σ_e^2 have been suggested in the literature (Judge, et al., 1985, p. 525); the pair outlined in the following have been chosen because they are unbiased and because they have a certain amount of intuitive appeal.

To estimate σ_e^2 we can use the residuals from the dummy variable estimator. Specifically, an unbiased estimator for σ_e^2 is given by

$$\hat{\sigma}_e^2 = \frac{\hat{\mathbf{e}}'\hat{\mathbf{e}}}{NT - N - K'} \tag{11.5.22}$$

where

$$\hat{\mathbf{e}} = (I_N \otimes D_T)\mathbf{y} - (I_N \otimes D_T)X_s\mathbf{b}_s \tag{11.5.23}$$

The proof that $\hat{\sigma}_e^2$ is unbiased is left as a problem (Exercise 11.7.6).

The next step is to estimate $\sigma_1^2 = T\sigma_\mu^2 + \sigma_e^2$. This is achieved by using the residuals from a regression on the individual means. If we average the original model (Equation 11.5.3) over time we obtain

$$\bar{y}_{i.} = \bar{\beta}_1 + \sum_{k=2}^{K} \beta_k \bar{x}_{ki.} + \mu_i + \bar{e}_{i.} \qquad i = 1, 2, \ldots, N \tag{11.5.24}$$

and the variance of the disturbance term in this equation is

$$\operatorname{var}(\mu_i + \bar{e}_{i.}) = \sigma_\mu^2 + \frac{\sigma_e^2}{T} = \frac{\sigma_1^2}{T} \tag{11.5.25}$$

Also, $(\mu_i + \bar{e}_{i.})$ is uncorrelated with $(\mu_j + \bar{e}_{j.})$ when $i \neq j$. These results imply that the usual least squares estimator obtained from (11.5.24) will be an unbiased estimator of σ_1^2/T. Specifically, (11.5.24) can be written in matrix notation as

$$\bar{\mathbf{y}} = \bar{X}\boldsymbol{\beta} + \mathbf{v} \tag{11.5.26}$$

where $\bar{\mathbf{y}}$ is of dimension $(N \times 1)$ with typical element $\bar{y}_{i.}$, $\bar{X}$ is of dimension $(N \times K)$ with typical element $\bar{x}_{ki.}$, and $\mathbf{v}$ is of dimension $(N \times 1)$ with typical element $\mu_i + \bar{e}_i$. The least squares estimator for $\boldsymbol{\beta}$, from (11.5.26), is

$$\boldsymbol{\beta}^* = (\bar{X}'\bar{X})^{-1}\bar{X}'\mathbf{y} \tag{11.5.27}$$

and the unbiased estimator of σ_1^2/T is

$$\frac{\hat{\sigma}_1^2}{T} = \frac{\mathbf{v}^{*\prime}\mathbf{v}^*}{N - K} \tag{11.5.28}$$

where

$$\mathbf{v}^* = \bar{\mathbf{y}} - \bar{X}\boldsymbol{\beta}^* \tag{11.5.29}$$

An unbiased estimator for σ_μ^2 can then be obtained from

$$\hat{\sigma}_\mu^2 = \frac{\hat{\sigma}_1^2 - \hat{\sigma}_e^2}{T} \tag{11.5.30}$$

A disadvantage of the estimator in (11.5.30) is that it can lead to negative variance estimates. In the event that this occurs, the researcher should rethink the model formulation rather than proceed with the estimated generalized least squares estimator for $\boldsymbol{\beta}$.

In many of the presentations in the literature (e.g., Judge, et al., 1985, p. 523) the between estimator $\boldsymbol{\beta}^*$ is based on NT rather than on N observations because each of the N means is *repeated* T times. This practice will not change the estimator $\boldsymbol{\beta}^*$, but it will make the residual sum of squares T times larger. Consequently, in this case we would be estimating σ_1^2, not σ_1^2/T.

We are now in a position to summarize the estimated generalized least squares procedure.

1. Calculate the dummy variable estimator, either in terms of the dummy variables and original observations or in terms of the observations expressed as deviations from the individual means. The latter estimator is

$$\mathbf{b}_s = [X_s'(I_N \otimes D_T)X_s]^{-1}X_s'(I_N \otimes D_T)\mathbf{y}$$

2. Use the residuals from step 1 to calculate

$$\hat{\sigma}_e^2 = \frac{\hat{\mathbf{e}}'\hat{\mathbf{e}}}{NT - N - K'}$$

3. Estimate $\boldsymbol{\beta}$ using the observations on the individual means

$$\boldsymbol{\beta}^* = (\bar{X}'\bar{X})^{-1}\bar{X}'\bar{\mathbf{y}}$$

4. Use the residuals from step 3 to calculate

$$\frac{\hat{\sigma}_1^2}{T} = \frac{\mathbf{v}^{*\prime}\mathbf{v}^*}{N-K}$$

5. Check to see that $\hat{\sigma}_\mu^2 = (\hat{\sigma}_1^2 - \hat{\sigma}_e^2)/T$ is positive.
6. Calculate $\hat{\alpha} = 1 - \hat{\sigma}_e/\hat{\sigma}_1$.
7. Find the transformed observations

$$y_{it}^* = y_{it} - \hat{\alpha}\bar{y}_{i.} \qquad \text{and} \qquad x_{kit}^* = x_{kit} - \hat{\alpha}\bar{x}_{ki.}$$

8. Find $\hat{\hat{\boldsymbol{\beta}}}$ by running a least squares regression on the transformed observations.

11.5.3 Prediction of Random Components

In addition to the estimation of $\boldsymbol{\beta}$, we may be interested in predicting the μ_i's, because this prediction describes how the behavior of different individuals varies as well as provides a basis for more efficient prediction of future observations on a given individual. Using the framework of Section 8.7 (see Exercise 11.7.7) it is possible to show that the best linear unbiased predictor for μ_i is

$$\hat{\mu}_i = \left(\frac{\sigma_\mu^2}{\sigma_1^2}\right)\mathbf{j}_T'(\mathbf{y}_i - X_i\hat{\boldsymbol{\beta}}) \tag{11.5.31}$$

and it can be viewed as a proportion of the generalized least squares residual allocation to $\hat{\mu}_i$, the precise proportion depending on the relative variances σ_μ^2 and σ_e^2. It is best linear unbiased in the sense that $E[\hat{\mu}_i - \mu_i] = 0$ and $E[(\hat{\mu}_i - \mu_i)^2]$ is smaller than the prediction error variance of any other predictor that is unbiased and a linear function of $\mathbf{y}$. The expectation is taken with respect to repeated sampling over both time and individuals.

The variance components will, in practice, be unknown, but they can be replaced by the estimates suggested in Section 11.5.2. Replacement yields an intuitively reasonable predictor, but the best linear unbiased property is no longer guaranteed.

11.5.4 Testing the Specification

If $\mu_i = 0$ or, equivalently, $\sigma_\mu^2 = 0$, the individual components do not exist and the least squares estimator is best linear unbiased. To test this hypothesis we could, as mentioned in Section 11.4.4, use the dummy variable estimator and the F test based on the restricted and unrestricted residual sums of squares. An alternative, which requires only the restricted residuals, is a test based on the Lagrange multiplier statistic (Breusch and Pagan, 1980). Under the null hypothesis $\sigma_\mu^2 = 0$, Breusch and Pagan show that

$$\lambda = \frac{NT}{2(T-1)}\left[\frac{\bar{\mathbf{e}}'(I_N \otimes \mathbf{j}_T\mathbf{j}_T')\bar{\mathbf{e}}}{\bar{\mathbf{e}}'\bar{\mathbf{e}}} - 1\right]^2 \qquad (11.5.32)$$

is asymptotically distributed as $\chi^2_{(1)}$, where $\bar{\mathbf{e}}$ is the vector of least squares residuals obtained by regressing $\mathbf{y}$ on X. For computational purposes it is worth noting that

$$\bar{\mathbf{e}}'(I_N \otimes \mathbf{j}_T\mathbf{j}_T')\bar{\mathbf{e}} = \sum_{i=1}^{N}\left(\sum_{t=1}^{T}\bar{e}_{it}\right)^2 \qquad (11.5.33)$$

11.5.5 The Example Continued

We now return to the example in Section 11.4.5 where we were estimating the cost functions for four firms. However, instead of assuming that the intercepts are fixed coefficients, we will assume that they are independent random variables with mean $\bar{\beta}_1$ and variance σ_μ^2. Thus we have

$$y_{it} = \bar{\beta}_1 + \beta_2 x_{it} + \mu_i + e_{it}$$

where $i = 1, 2, 3, 4$ and $t = 1, 2, \ldots, 10$. We will first find the estimated generalized least squares estimator for $\boldsymbol{\beta}' = (\bar{\beta}_1\ \beta_2)$ by following the steps summarized at the end of Section 11.5.2.

We have already calculated $\hat{\sigma}_e^2 = 14.042256$. To estimate σ_1^2 we carry out a regression on the four firm means and obtain

$$\bar{y}_{i\cdot} = -2.763 + 1.485\bar{x}_{i\cdot} + v_i^*$$

Then

$$\frac{\hat{\sigma}_1^2}{T} = \frac{\mathbf{v}^{*\prime}\mathbf{v}^*}{N-K} = \frac{133.1507557}{2} = 66.5754$$

and $\hat{\sigma}_1^2 = 665.754$. Checking $\hat{\sigma}_\mu^2$ to see if it is nonnegative, we have

$$\hat{\sigma}_\mu^2 = \frac{\hat{\sigma}_1^2 - \hat{\sigma}_e^2}{10} = 65.17$$

The factor used to transform the observations is

$$\hat{\alpha} = 1 - \frac{\hat{\sigma}_e}{\hat{\sigma}_1} = 0.854768$$

After transforming the observations and applying least squares we have, for the estimated generalized least squares estimates, $\hat{\hat{\beta}}_1 = 7.737534$ and $\hat{\hat{\beta}}_2 = 1.119303$, or

$$\hat{y}_{it} = 7.738 + \underset{(0.063)}{1.119}x_{it}$$

Note that $\hat{\hat{\beta}}_2$ is close to the dummy variable estimator of the slope coefficient $b_2 = 1.119029$. The likely reason for this is the fact that $\hat{\sigma}_1^2$ is large relative to $\hat{\sigma}_e^2$, making $\hat{\alpha}$ close to unity.

Also worth noting is the fact that, in an example such as this in which N is only 4, the estimate of σ_μ^2 is unlikely to be reliable. In fact, in terms of the small sample properties of estimators for $\boldsymbol{\beta}_s$, rather than using an unreliable estimate of σ_μ^2 in an estimated generalized least squares estimator, we are likely to be better off simply using the dummy variable estimator. This, of course, would not be true if the true variances were known.

For predicting the random components μ_1, μ_2, μ_3, and μ_4 we can use the predictor in (11.5.31) with $(\sigma_\mu^2/\sigma_1^2)$ replaced by $(\hat{\sigma}_\mu^2/\hat{\sigma}_1^2)$. This yields

$$\hat{\mu}_1 = \frac{65.17}{665.754}(-54.31) = -5.32$$

$$\hat{\mu}_2 = (0.0979)(23.64) = 2.31$$

$$\hat{\mu}_3 = (0.0979)(-53.59) = -5.25$$

$$\hat{\mu}_4 = (0.0979)(84.26) = 8.25$$

When these answers are compared with the corresponding estimates obtained from the dummy variable estimator they prove to be quite similar. Specifically, we could define a dummy variable estimator of the μ_i as

$$\tilde{\mu}_i = b_{1i} - \frac{1}{4}\sum_{j=1}^{4} b_{1j}, \qquad i = 1, 2, 3, 4$$

and this yields $\tilde{\mu}_1 = -5.43$, $\tilde{\mu}_2 = 2.36$, $\tilde{\mu}_3 = -5.36$, and $\tilde{\mu}_4 = 8.43$.

Finally, let us calculate the value of the Lagrange multiplier test statistic given in (11.5.32). To this end we have $\bar{\mathbf{e}}'(I_N \otimes \mathbf{j}_T\mathbf{j}_T')\bar{\mathbf{e}} = 13470$, $\bar{\mathbf{e}}'\bar{\mathbf{e}} = 1839$, and

$$\lambda = \frac{40}{18}\left[\frac{13470}{1839} - 1\right]^2 = 88.9$$

At the 5 percent significance level the critical value for this test is $\chi^2_{(1)} = 3.84$, so we clearly reject the null hypothesis that $\sigma_\mu^2 = 0$.

11.6 Choice of Model for Pooling

11.6.1 Dummy Variables versus Error Components

Both the dummy variable model (Section 11.4) and the error components model (Section 11.5) can be written as

$$\begin{aligned} \mathbf{y}_i &= X_i\boldsymbol{\beta} + \mu_i\mathbf{j}_T + \mathbf{e}_i \\ &= \mathbf{j}_T\bar{\beta}_1 + X_{si}\boldsymbol{\beta}_s + \mu_i\mathbf{j}_T + \mathbf{e}_i \end{aligned} \tag{11.6.1}$$

In the dummy variable model the μ_i are treated as fixed parameters that need to be estimated, whereas in the error components model the μ_i are treated as a sample of random drawings from a population, and they become part of the model's disturbance term. Least squares (or the "dummy variable estimator") is best linear unbiased for the dummy variable model, and generalized least squares is best linear unbiased for the error components model. We will frame the discussion in terms of the respective estimators for the slope coefficients, $\mathbf{b}_s$ in the case of the dummy variable model and $\hat{\boldsymbol{\beta}}_s$ (or $\hat{\hat{\boldsymbol{\beta}}}_s$) for the error components model.

A number of issues need to be considered when making a choice between fixed or random μ_i (and hence between $\mathbf{b}_s$ and $\hat{\boldsymbol{\beta}}_s$). The first consideration is the relative sizes of N and T. As $T \to \infty$ for fixed N, $\mathbf{b}_s$ and $\hat{\boldsymbol{\beta}}_s$ become identical. Under these circumstances the dummy variable estimator $\mathbf{b}_s$ is consistent and asymptotically efficient, even when the assumptions of the error components model hold. Thus, for large T and small N, there is likely to be little difference between the two estimators, and the natural choice is the one that is computationally easier, namely $\mathbf{b}_s$. When N is large and T is small, the two estimators can differ significantly, and other issues become important. In this case $\mathbf{b}_s$ is still consistent under the assumptions of the error components model, but it is no longer asymptotically efficient, so the question concerning whether the μ_i should be treated as fixed or random needs to be addressed.

One way of viewing the distinction between fixed and random components is as a distinction between conditional and unconditional inference. When the μ_i are fixed, our inference is conditional on the individuals (or cross-sectional units) in the sample. Conditional inference is likely to be appropriate if the individuals on which we have data cannot be regarded as a random sample from some larger population, or if we are particularly interested in those individuals in the sample. If the individuals in the sample can be regarded as a random sample from some larger population, and we are interested in inferences about the population, then unconditional inference that is implicit in the errors components approach is appropriate.

A further consideration is whether the μ_i are likely to be correlated with the X_i. Mundlak (1978) argues that in most applications there is likely to be some relationship between the unmeasurable individual attributes (the μ_i) and the measurable time-varying attributes (the X_i). If such correlation does exist, the estimator $\hat{\boldsymbol{\beta}}_s$ will be biased, but the dummy variable estimator $\mathbf{b}_s$ is not. Thus, conditional inference could be more appropriate if an investigator suspects that μ_i and X_i are correlated. Alternatively, Hausman and Taylor (1981) use knowledge about which vectors in X_i are correlated with the μ_i to develop an efficient instrumental variables estimator. For further information, and an excellent discussion of these issues see Hsiao (1986, pp. 41–52).

As we have mentioned, if N is large and T is small, and the assumptions of the error components model hold, $\hat{\boldsymbol{\beta}}_s$ will be more efficient than $\mathbf{b}_s$. A relevant question is: How large should N be for the estimated generalized least squares estimator $\hat{\hat{\boldsymbol{\beta}}}_s$ to be more efficient than $\mathbf{b}_s$ in finite samples? Taylor (1980) shows that, even in moderately sized samples $[T \geq 3,\ N - K \geq 9;\ T \geq 2,\ N - K \geq 10]$, $\hat{\hat{\boldsymbol{\beta}}}_s$ will be better.

Because both $\mathbf{b}_s$ and $\hat{\boldsymbol{\beta}}_s$ are consistent estimators when the assumptions of the error components model hold, but only $\mathbf{b}_s$ is consistent if, for example, μ_i and X_i are correlated, a test of the appropriateness of the assumptions can be based on whether or not the difference $\mathbf{b}_s - \hat{\boldsymbol{\beta}}_s$ is significant. Hausman (1978) shows that

$$m = (\mathbf{b}_s - \hat{\boldsymbol{\beta}}_s)'(M_1 - M_0)^{-1}(\mathbf{b}_s - \hat{\boldsymbol{\beta}}_s) \tag{11.6.2}$$

has an asymptotic $\chi^2_{(K')}$ distribution, where $M_1 = \sigma_e^2[X'_s(I_N \otimes D_T)X_s]^{-1}$ is the covariance matrix for the dummy variable estimator $\mathbf{b}_s$ and M_0 is the covariance matrix for the generalized least squares estimator of the slope coefficients $\hat{\boldsymbol{\beta}}_s$. That is, M_0 is the matrix $(X'\boldsymbol{\Phi}^{-1}X)^{-1}$ with its first row and column deleted. The unknown variances in $\hat{\boldsymbol{\beta}}_s$, M_0, and M_1 can be replaced by $\hat{\sigma}_\mu^2$ and $\hat{\sigma}_e^2$ without affecting the asymptotic distribution of m. If the null hypothesis is true, then, asymptotically, $\mathbf{b}_s$ and $\hat{\boldsymbol{\beta}}_s$ differ only through sampling error. However, if μ_i and X_i are correlated, $\hat{\boldsymbol{\beta}}_s$ and $\mathbf{b}_s$ could differ widely, and it is hoped that this will be reflected in the test. Rejection of the null hypothesis suggests that the error components model is not appropriate and that we are likely to be better off using $\mathbf{b}_s$ and regarding the inference as conditional on the μ_i in the sample, or using an estimator that explicitly considers the correlation. Further information on testing is provided by Hausman and Taylor (1981).

11.6.2 Other Models for Pooling Data

The pooling models discussed in this chapter are only a few of the alternatives that are available. Other possibilities make alternative assumptions about the way in which the coefficients change and about the error structure. The seemingly unrelated regression model can be viewed as a model where all individuals have different coefficient vectors and where these coefficient vectors are regarded as fixed. If the individuals represent a random sample from some larger population, then it might be more appropriate to view the different coefficient vectors as random drawings from a particular probability distribution. This assumption leads to a class of random coefficient models popularized by Swamy (1970).

One possible extension of the dummy variable and error components models is to allow not only for individual-specific effects, but also for time-specific effects. These different effects could be captured by just the intercept term, or they may be applied to all slope coefficients as well. An example of the latter type of model is that studied by Hsiao (1974). Dynamic models, including models with coefficients that evolve over time, have also been suggested in the literature. For a review and summary of the many possible models, refer to Judge, et al. (1985, Chapter 13) and Hsiao (1986).

11.7 Problems on Dummy Variables and Error Components

11.7.1 Algebraic Exercises

11.7.1 Prove that $D_T = I_T - \mathbf{j}_T\mathbf{j}_T'/T$ is an idempotent matrix.

11.7.2 Use results on the partitioned inverse of a matrix to show that (11.4.7) is equivalent to (11.4.9) and (11.4.10).

11.7.3 Prove that the result in (11.4.17) is correct.

11.7.4 Show that the inverse of $V = \sigma_\mu^2 \mathbf{j}_T\mathbf{j}_T' + \sigma_e^2 I_T$ is

$$V^{-1} = \frac{\mathbf{j}_T\mathbf{j}_T'}{T\sigma_1^2} + \frac{D_T}{\sigma_e^2}$$

where $\sigma_1^2 = T\sigma_\mu^2 + \sigma_e^2$ and $D_T = I_T - \mathbf{j}_T\mathbf{j}_T'/T$.

11.7.5 Show that $P_*'P_* = \sigma_e^2 V^{-1}$, where V^{-1} is given in Exercise 11.7.4,

$$P_* = I_T - \alpha \mathbf{j}_T\mathbf{j}_T'/T$$

and $\alpha = 1 - \sigma_e/\sigma_1$.

11.7.6 Let $A = I_N \otimes D_T$. Show that (Equation 11.5.23)

(*a*) $\hat{\mathbf{e}} = A\mathbf{y} - AX_s\mathbf{b}_s = (A - AX_s(X_s'AX_s)^{-1}X_s'A)\mathbf{e}$.

(*b*) A has rank $N(T-1)$.

(*c*) $A - AX_s(X_s'AX_s)^{-1}X_s'A$ is idempotent of rank $N(T-1) - K'$.
(*d*) $\hat{\sigma}_e^2$ in (11.5.22) is an unbiased estimator.

11.7.7 In Chapter 8 (Equation 8.7.17) we showed that a general expression for a best linear unbiased predictor is

$$\hat{\mathbf{y}}_0 = X_0\hat{\boldsymbol{\beta}} + V'\boldsymbol{\Psi}^{-1}(\mathbf{y} - X\hat{\boldsymbol{\beta}})$$

For the context of the error components model let $\mathbf{y}_0' = \boldsymbol{\mu}' = (\mu_1, \mu_2, \ldots, \mu_N)$, $X_0 = 0$, $V = E[(\boldsymbol{\mu} \otimes \mathbf{j}_T + \mathbf{e})\boldsymbol{\mu}']$, and $\boldsymbol{\Psi} = \boldsymbol{\Phi}$.

Use this information to show that the best linear unbiased predictor for $\boldsymbol{\mu}$ is given by (11.5.31).

11.7.2 Individual Numerical Exercises

For the remaining problems, generate Monte Carlo data consisting of 50 samples from an error components model with individual effects, namely

$$y_{it} = \bar{\beta}_1 + \beta_2 x_{it} + \mu_i + e_{it'}, \quad \begin{matrix} i = 1, 2, 3, 4 \\ t = 1, 2, \ldots, 10 \end{matrix} \tag{11.7.1}$$

where $\bar{\beta}_1 = 10$ and $\beta_2 = 1$, the μ_i are i.i.d. $N(0, 14)$, and the e_{it} are i.i.d. $N(0, 16)$. The values of the explanatory variable, for the four individuals, are

$$\mathbf{x}_1 = \begin{bmatrix} 38.46 \\ 35.32 \\ 3.78 \\ 35.34 \\ 20.83 \\ 36.72 \\ 41.67 \\ 30.71 \\ 23.70 \\ 39.53 \end{bmatrix}, \quad \mathbf{x}_2 = \begin{bmatrix} 32.52 \\ 18.71 \\ 27.01 \\ 18.66 \\ 25.58 \\ 39.19 \\ 47.70 \\ 27.01 \\ 33.57 \\ 27.32 \end{bmatrix}, \quad \mathbf{x}_3 = \begin{bmatrix} 32.86 \\ 18.52 \\ 22.93 \\ 25.02 \\ 35.13 \\ 27.29 \\ 16.99 \\ 12.56 \\ 26.75 \\ 41.42 \end{bmatrix}, \quad \mathbf{x}_4 = \begin{bmatrix} 41.86 \\ 28.33 \\ 34.21 \\ 15.69 \\ 29.70 \\ 23.03 \\ 14.80 \\ 21.53 \\ 32.86 \\ 42.25 \end{bmatrix}$$

11.7.8 For the model in (11.7.1) calculate the variance of the following estimators for β_2.
(*a*) The least squares estimator $\tilde{b}_2$.
(*b*) The generalized least squares estimator $\hat{\beta}_2$.
(*c*) The dummy variable estimator b_2.
Comment on the relative efficiencies.

11.7.9 Select five samples from the Monte Carlo data and for each sample compute values for the estimators $\hat{\sigma}_1^2$, $\hat{\sigma}_e^2$, and $\hat{\sigma}_\mu^2$. If $\hat{\sigma}_\mu^2 < 0$, set $\hat{\sigma}_\mu^2 = 0$ and $\hat{\sigma}_1^2 = \hat{\sigma}_e^2$. Comment on the values.

11.7.10 For the same five samples compute values for the estimators $\tilde{b}_2$, b_2, and $\hat{\hat{\beta}}_2$, where $\hat{\hat{\beta}}_2$ is the estimated generalized least squares estimator for β_2 that uses the variance estimates obtained in Exercise 11.7.9. Note that b_2 may already have been calculated in Exercise 11.7.9. Compare the estimates with each other and with the true parameter values.

11.7.11 For each of the five samples, test the null hypothesis $\mu_1 = \mu_2 = \mu_3 = \mu_4 = 0$ by using

(*a*) The F test in (11.4.25).

(*b*) The statistic λ in (11.5.32)

In both cases use a 5 percent significance level.

11.7.12 For the same five samples compute estimates for μ_1, μ_2, μ_3, and μ_4 by using

(*a*) The predictor in (11.5.31) with σ_μ^2 and σ_e^2 replaced by $\hat{\sigma}_\mu^2$ and $\hat{\sigma}_e^2$.

(*b*) The dummy variable estimator, that is,

$$\tilde{\mu}_i = b_{1i} - \frac{1}{4}\sum_{j=1}^{4} b_{1j} \qquad i = 1, 2, 3, 4$$

Comment on the values.

11.7.3 Group Exercises

11.7.13 Use all 50 samples to estimate the mean square errors (MSEs) of the estimators $\tilde{b}_2$, b_2, and $\hat{\hat{\beta}}_2$ given in Exercise 11.7.10. With respect to the answers in Exercise 11.7.8, are the MSE estimates of $\tilde{b}_2$ and b_2 accurate? Comment on, and suggest reasons for, the relative efficiencies of $\tilde{b}_2$, b_2, and $\hat{\hat{\beta}}_2$.

11.7.14 Repeat Exercise 11.7.11 for all 50 samples. Which test appears to be more powerful?

11.8 References

Breusch, T. S., and A. R. Pagan (1980) "The LaGrange Multiplier Test and Its Applications to Model Specification in Econometrics," *Review of Economic Studies*, 47, 239–254.

Hausman, J. A. (1978) "Specification Tests in Econometrics." *Econometrica*, 46, 1251–1272.

Hausman, J. A., and W. E. Taylor (1981) "Panel Data and Unobservable Individual Effects." *Econometrica*, 49, 1377–1398.

Hsiao, C. (1974) "Statistical Inference for a Model with Both Random Cross Sectional and Time Effects." *International Economic Review*, 15, 12–30.

Hsiao, C. (1986) *Analysis of Panel Data*. Cambridge, Eng: Cambridge University Press.

Judge, G. G., W. E. Griffiths, R. C. Hill, H. Lütkepohl, and T. C. Lee (1985) *The Theory and Practice of Econometrics*, 2nd ed., New York: Wiley.

Kmenta, J. (1986) *Elements of Econometrics*, 2nd ed., New York: Macmillan.

Mundlak, Y. (1978) "On the Pooling of Time Series and Cross Section Data." *Econometrica*, 46, 69–85.

Schmidt, P. (1977) "Estimation of Seemingly Unrelated Regressions with Unequal Numbers of Observations." *Journal of Econometrics*, 5, 365–377.

Srivastava, V. K. and D. E. A. Giles (1987) *Seemingly Unrelated Regression Models: Estimation and Inference*. New York: Dekker.

Swamy, P. A. V. B. (1970) "Efficient Inference in a Random Coefficient Regression Model." *Econometrica*, 38, 311–323.

Taylor, W. E. (1980) "Small Sample Considerations in Estimation from Panel Data." *Journal of Econometrics*, 13, 203–223.

Theil, H. (1971) *Principles of Econometrics*. New York: Wiley.

Woodland, A. D. (1986) "An Aspect of the Wald Test for Linear Restrictions in the Seemingly Unrelated Regressions Model." *Economics Letters*, 20, 165–169.

Zellner, A. (1962) "An Efficient Method of Estimating Seemingly Unrelated Regressions and Tests of Aggregation Bias." *Journal of the American Statistical Association*, 57, 348–368.

11.A Appendix: Bivariate (Multivariate) Normal Random Variables

Bivariate normal random variables may be generated by the following procedures: Let Σ be the covariance matrix, C be the corresponding matrix of characteristic vectors, and D be the diagonal matrix of characteristic roots. Then $C\Sigma C' = D$ and $D^{-1/2}C\Sigma C'D^{-1/2} = D^{-1/2}DD^{-1/2} = I$ and $\Sigma = C'D^{1/2}D^{1/2}C$.

As an example, assume that the covariance matrix is

$$\Sigma = \begin{bmatrix} 1 & 1 \\ 1 & 2 \end{bmatrix}$$

with the corresponding matrix of characteristic vectors

$$C = \begin{bmatrix} 0.5257 & 0.8506 \\ 0.8506 & -0.5257 \end{bmatrix}$$

and the diagonal matrix of characteristic roots 2.6180 and 0.3820. Let

$$D^{1/2} = \begin{bmatrix} \sqrt{2.6180} & 0 \\ 0 & \sqrt{0.3820} \end{bmatrix} = \begin{bmatrix} 1.6180 & 0 \\ 0 & 0.6180 \end{bmatrix}$$

Thus

$$C'D^{1/2} = \begin{bmatrix} 0.8506 & 0.5257 \\ 1.3763 & -0.3249 \end{bmatrix}$$

Given the foregoing matrix, each pair of generated independent standard normal random variates, e_1 and e_2 are used with $C'D^{1/2}$ to obtain bivariate normal variates e_1^* and e_2^*.

$$\begin{bmatrix} 0.8506 & 0.5257 \\ 1.3763 & -0.3249 \end{bmatrix} \begin{bmatrix} e_1 \\ e_2 \end{bmatrix} = \begin{bmatrix} e_1^* \\ e_2^* \end{bmatrix}$$

The bivariate normal random variates e_1^* and e_2^* have mean

$$E\begin{bmatrix} e_1^* \\ e_2^* \end{bmatrix} = \begin{bmatrix} 0 \\ 0 \end{bmatrix}$$

and covariance matrix

$$E\begin{bmatrix} e_1^* \\ e_2^* \end{bmatrix}[e_1^* \quad e_2^*] = C'D^{1/2}\left(E\begin{bmatrix} e_1 \\ e_2 \end{bmatrix}[e_1 \quad e_2]\right)D^{1/2}C$$

$$= \begin{bmatrix} 0.8506 & 0.5257 \\ 1.3763 & -0.3249 \end{bmatrix} \begin{bmatrix} 1 & 0 \\ 0 & 1 \end{bmatrix} \begin{bmatrix} 0.8506 & 1.3763 \\ 0.5257 & -0.3249 \end{bmatrix}$$

$$= \begin{bmatrix} 1 & 1 \\ 1 & 2 \end{bmatrix} = \Sigma$$

Alternatively, if a computer package such as SHAZAM is available, the Cholesky matrix decomposition method may be used to obtain a nonsingular triangular matrix P such that $PP' = \Sigma$ or

$$P\left(E\begin{bmatrix} e_1 \\ e_2 \end{bmatrix}[e_1 \quad e_2]\right)P' = \Sigma$$

Consequently,

$$P\begin{bmatrix} e_1 \\ e_2 \end{bmatrix} = \begin{bmatrix} e_1^* \\ e_2^* \end{bmatrix}$$

For example, if

$$\Sigma = \begin{bmatrix} 3 & 2 \\ 2 & 8 \end{bmatrix}$$

this yields a Cholesky matrix

$$P = \begin{bmatrix} 1.732051 & 0 \\ 1.154701 & 2.581989 \end{bmatrix}$$

and

$$P\left(E\begin{bmatrix} e_1 \\ e_2 \end{bmatrix}[e_1 \quad e_2] \right)P' = \begin{bmatrix} 1.732051 & 0 \\ 1.154701 & 2.581989 \end{bmatrix}\begin{bmatrix} 1 & 0 \\ 0 & 1 \end{bmatrix}\begin{bmatrix} 1.732051 & 1.154701 \\ 0 & 2.581989 \end{bmatrix}$$

$$= \begin{bmatrix} 3 & 2 \\ 2 & 8 \end{bmatrix} = \Sigma$$

In a Monte Carlo sampling study, using the transformation matrix, these procedures are repeated for each of T pairs of random variables for each of the N samples.

CHAPTER 12

Nonlinear Least Squares and Nonlinear Maximum Likelihood Estimation

12.1 Introduction

Nonlinearities enter economic models in various forms. As we have seen in Chapters 5 and 6, if only the variables enter nonlinearly, the model can still be handled in the linear model framework. Furthermore, if the nonlinearity is in the parameters or in the variables and the parameters, it is sometimes possible to find a transformation to convert the considered model into a linear specification. Generally, however, this is not possible, and therefore we discuss a model of the general form

$$y_t = f(\mathbf{x}_t, \boldsymbol{\beta}) + e_t \tag{12.1.1}$$

in this chapter. In (12.1.1) $\mathbf{x}_t$ is an $(N \times 1)$ vector of independent variables, $\boldsymbol{\beta}$ is a $(K \times 1)$ parameter vector, y_t is the dependent variable whose mean is a function of $\mathbf{x}_t$ and $\boldsymbol{\beta}$, and e_t is a random error.

One example is the Cobb–Douglas production function

$$Q_t = \alpha L_t^{\beta_1} K_t^{\beta_2} + e_t \tag{12.1.2}$$

where Q_t is the output from a section of the economy, L_t is the labor input, and K_t is the capital input, all in period t. The parameters are α, β_1, and β_2. The latter two are the elasticities of Q_t with respect to L_t and K_t. Defining $y_t = Q_t$, $\mathbf{x}_t' = (L_t\ K_t)$, $\boldsymbol{\beta}' = (\alpha\ \beta_1\ \beta_2)$, and $f(\mathbf{x}_t, \boldsymbol{\beta}) = \alpha L_1^{\beta_1} K_t^{\beta_2}$, the Cobb–Douglas production function (12.1.2) has exactly the form (12.1.1). Note that, unlike linear specifications, the number of parameters, K, and the number of independent variables, N, do not necessarily coincide in nonlinear models.

Another example is a consumption function

$$C_t = \beta_1 + \beta_2 Y_t^{\beta_3} + e_t \tag{12.1.3}$$

which could arise if there is uncertainty as to the way the consumption expenditures C_t depend on the income Y_t. Why should the form

$$C_t = \beta_1 + \beta_2 Y_t + e_t$$

be a priori more plausible than

$$C_t = \beta_1 + \beta_2 Y_t^{1/2} + e_t$$

or a model with some other exponent of Y_t? To let the data answer this question, the consumption function could be set up as in (12.1.3).

It is not unusual that parameters entering in a nonlinear way in a regression model simply reflect our uncertainty as to what model adequately represents the relationship between two or more variables. To give another example, it may not be clear whether there is a linear relationship between a dependent variable y and an independent variable x or the logarithm of x. This uncertainty can be accounted for by using a Box–Cox transformation of x, that is,

$$y_t = \beta_1 + \beta_2\left(\frac{x_t^\lambda - 1}{\lambda}\right) + e_t \tag{12.1.4}$$

If $\lambda = 1$, we have a model

$$y_t = \alpha + \beta_2 x_t + e_t \tag{12.1.5}$$

where $\alpha = \beta_1 - \beta_2$. On the other hand, if $\lambda \to 0$ the model approaches the logarithmic specification

$$y_t = \beta_1 + \beta_2 \ln x_t + e_t \tag{12.1.6}$$

Specifying $\mathbf{x}_t' = (1\ x_t)$, $\boldsymbol{\beta}' = (\beta_1\ \beta_2\ \lambda)$, and $f(\mathbf{x}_t, \boldsymbol{\beta}) = \beta_1 + \beta_2(x_t^\lambda - 1)/\lambda$ the model (12.1.4) has precisely the form (12.1.1). Models of this kind, which cannot be transformed into a linear model, are sometimes called *intrinsically nonlinear* models.

If the error term is attached to the Cobb–Douglas production function in a multiplicative way, that is, if we specify

$$Q_t = \alpha L_t^{\beta_1} K_t^{\beta_2} e^{u_t} \tag{12.1.7}$$

the model is not intrinsically nonlinear because it can be linearized by taking logarithms:

$$\ln Q_t = \ln \alpha + \beta_1 \ln L_t + \beta_2 \ln K_t + u_t \tag{12.1.8}$$

We will discuss parameter estimation for intrinsically nonlinear models like (12.1.1) in Section 12.2. Just as in the case of linear models, estimation is based on minimizing or maximizing an objective function. We consider two types of objective functions: (1) the sum of squared errors and (2) the likelihood function. Under the standard assumptions for a linear-model the minimization or maximization can be carried out by simply solving a set of linear normal equations. However, the normal equations for a nonlinear model are, in general, nonlinear in the parameters, and to solve them can be a rather difficult task. For nonlinear least squares we will describe the Gauss–Newton and Newton–Raphson algorithms. For maximum likelihood estimation the Newton–Raphson algorithm, the method of scoring, and an algorithm usually attributed to Berndt, Hall, Hall, and Hausman (1974) will be described.

Maximum likelihood estimation of the linear model $\mathbf{y} = X\boldsymbol{\beta} + \mathbf{e}$ where $E[\mathbf{ee}'] = \sigma^2\boldsymbol{\Psi} \neq \sigma^2 I$ can be viewed as a nonlinear estimation problem. In Section 12.3 this question is examined for the multiplicative heteroskedastic error and first-order autoregressive error models discussed earlier in Chapter 9. Further nonlinear models, nonlinear seemingly unrelated regressions, and the Box–Cox transformation are considered in Sections 12.4 and 12.5, respectively.

12.2 Principles of Nonlinear Least Squares

To introduce nonlinear least squares estimation, let us consider the simple single parameter model

$$\begin{aligned} y_t &= f(\mathbf{x}_t, \beta) + e_t \\ &= \beta x_{t1} + \beta^2 x_{t2} + e_t \end{aligned} \tag{12.2.1}$$

where the e_t are independent and identically distributed random variables with mean 0 and variance σ^2. The nonlinear least squares estimate for β is defined as that value of β that minimizes the residual sum of squares

$$\begin{aligned} S(\beta) = \sum_{t=1}^{T} e_t^2 &= \sum_{t=1}^{T} [y_t - f(\mathbf{x}_t, \beta)]^2 \\ &= \sum_{t=1}^{T} (y_t - \beta x_{t1} - \beta^2 x_{t2})^2 \end{aligned} \tag{12.2.2}$$

The first-order condition or normal equation for the minimum of this function is given by

$$\begin{aligned} \frac{dS}{d\beta} &= 2 \sum_{t=1}^{T} [y_t - f(\mathbf{x}_t, \beta)]\left(-\frac{df(\mathbf{x}_t, \beta)}{d\beta}\right) \\ &= 2 \sum_{t=1}^{T} (y_t - \beta x_{t1} - \beta^2 x_{t2})(-x_{t1} - 2\beta x_{t2}) = 0 \end{aligned} \tag{12.2.3}$$

Rearranging (12.2.3) yields,

$$2\beta^3 \sum_{t=1}^{T} x_{t2}^2 + 3\beta^2 \sum_{t=1}^{T} x_{t1}x_{t2} + \beta\left(\sum_{t=1}^{T} x_{t1}^2 - 2\sum_{t=1}^{T} x_{t2}y_t\right) - \sum_{t=1}^{T} x_{t1}y_t = 0 \tag{12.2.4}$$

This equation is a cubic equation in β and will, therefore, yield three possible solutions. The nonlinear least squares estimate b is that solution which yields the smallest value for the residual sum of squares $S(\beta)$. The smallest value for $S(\beta)$ is known as the global minimum. Other minima (local minima) or maxima can exist.

As an example of the sum of squares function in (12.2.2), let us consider the data in Table 12.1 and the corresponding graph of $S(\beta)$ given in Figure 12.1. It is clear from this graph that the global minimum is reached at approximately $b = 1.2$. This value is, therefore, the nonlinear least squares estimate. Other approximate solutions to (12.2.4) are $\beta = -2$ (a local minimum) and $\beta = -1$ (a maximum).

With the linear function $y_t = x_t\beta + e_t$ the first-order condition for a minimum residual sum of squares is given by

$$b \sum_{t=1}^{T} x_t^2 = \sum_{t=1}^{T} x_t y_t \tag{12.2.5}$$

Solving this equation for b is straightforward, yielding $b = \sum x_t y_t / \sum x_t^2$. In a nonlinear least squares regression problem it is this step that is no longer

Table 12.1 Data for Single-Parameter Example

y	x_1	x_2
3.284	0.286	0.645
3.149	0.973	0.585
2.877	0.384	0.310
−0.467	0.276	0.058
1.211	0.973	0.455
1.389	0.543	0.779
1.145	0.957	0.259
2.321	0.948	0.202
0.998	0.543	0.028
0.379	0.797	0.099
1.106	0.936	0.142
0.428	0.889	0.296
0.011	0.006	0.175
1.179	0.828	0.180
1.858	0.399	0.842
0.388	0.617	0.039
0.651	0.939	0.103
0.593	0.784	0.620
0.046	0.072	0.158
1.152	0.889	0.704

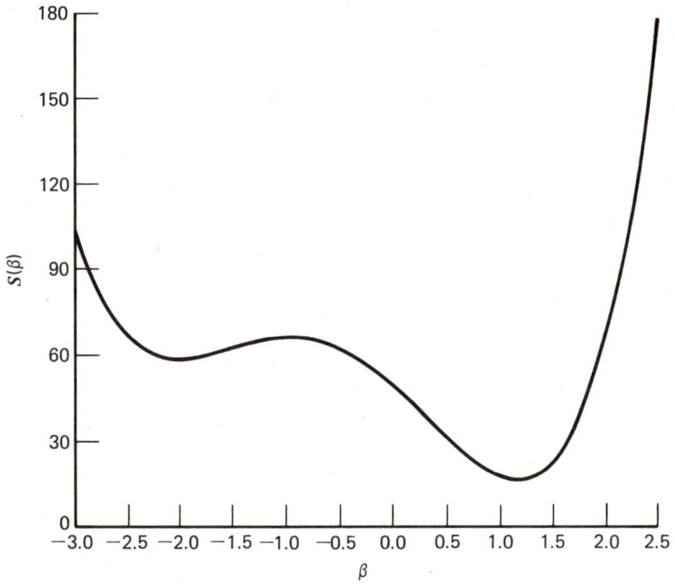

Figure 12.1 Residual sum of squares function for single-parameter example.

straightforward. Solving (12.2.4) for β is computationally a much more difficult task. In general, it is not possible to use the first-order conditions for a minimum to derive an analytical expression for the nonlinear least squares estimator. Instead, numerical methods must be used to obtain estimates.

In the context of Figure 12.1, we need to consider methods for locating the point given approximately by $b = 1.2$. A number of alternative computational algorithms are available. In the next section we introduce the Gauss–Newton algorithm and discuss the properties of the nonlinear least squares estimator in terms of the single-parameter model considered so far.

12.2.1 Nonlinear Least Squares Estimation for a Single Parameter

Consider again the single-parameter model

$$y_t = f(\mathbf{x}_t, \beta) + e_t \tag{12.2.6}$$

with corresponding residual sum of squares function

$$S(\beta) = \sum_{t=1}^{T} [y_t - f(\mathbf{x}_t, \beta)]^2 \tag{12.2.7}$$

and first-order condition for a minimum

$$\frac{dS}{d\beta} = -2 \sum_{t=1}^{T} [y_t - f(\mathbf{x}_t, \beta)]\left(- \frac{df(\mathbf{x}_t, \beta)}{d\beta}\right) = 0 \tag{12.2.8}$$

The problem is to find a value of β that satisfies the equation in (12.2.8) and that also leads to the global minimum of (12.2.7).

One way of approaching this problem is to replace $f(\mathbf{x}_t, \beta)$ by a first order (linear) Taylor series approximation. If we begin with some point β_1, then the first-order approximation of $f(\mathbf{x}_t, \beta)$ around the point β_1 is given by

$$f(\mathbf{x}_t, \beta) \simeq f(\mathbf{x}_t, \beta_1) + \left.\frac{df(\mathbf{x}_t, \beta)}{d\beta}\right|_{\beta_1} (\beta - \beta_1) \tag{12.2.9}$$

To gain some feel for this approximation, (12.2.9) can be rewritten as

$$\left.\frac{df(\mathbf{x}_t, \beta)}{d\beta}\right|_{\beta_1} \simeq \frac{f(\mathbf{x}_t, \beta) - f(\mathbf{x}_t, \beta_1)}{\beta - \beta_1} \tag{12.2.10}$$

The left side of this expression is the slope of the tangent to the curve $f(\mathbf{x}_t, \beta)$ at the point β_1. In Figure 12.2 this slope is represented by the ratio CB/BA. The ratio on the right side of (12.2.10) is an approximation to the slope and, in Figure 12.2, this approximation is given by DB/BA. Alternatively, the right side of (12.2.10) can be viewed as the slope of the straight line joining D and A, and this slope is being used to approximate the slope of CA.

It is convenient to introduce some less cumbersome notation for the derivative of $f(\mathbf{x}_t, \beta)$ with respect to β, evaluated at β_1. Thus, we will let $z_t(\beta) = df(\mathbf{x}_t, \beta)/d\beta$, and

$$z_t(\beta_1) = \left.\frac{df(\mathbf{x}_t, \beta)}{d\beta}\right|_{\beta_1} \tag{12.2.11}$$

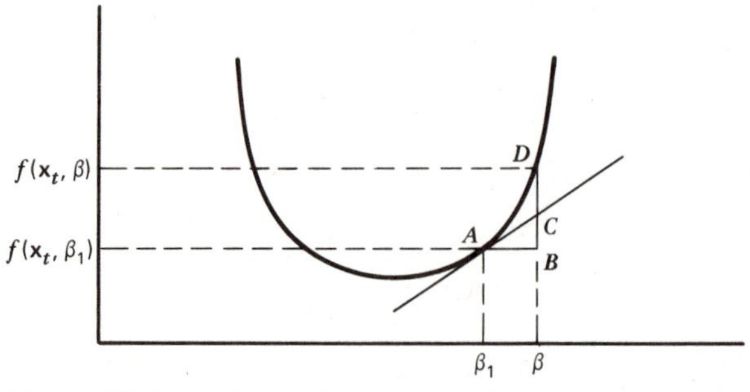

Figure 12.2 A first-order Taylor series approximation.

Using this notation, and substituting the Taylor series approximation in (12.2.9) into the residual sum of squares function in (12.2.7) yields

$$\begin{aligned} S(\beta) &= \sum_{t=1}^{T} [y_t - f(\mathbf{x}_t, \beta_1) - z_t(\beta_1)(\beta - \beta_1)]^2 \\ &= \sum_{t=1}^{T} [\bar{y}_t(\beta_1) - z_t(\beta_1)\cdot\beta]^2 \end{aligned} \tag{12.2.12}$$

where

$$\bar{y}_t(\beta_1) = y_t - f(\mathbf{x}_t, \beta_1) + z_t(\beta_1)\cdot\beta_1 \tag{12.2.13}$$

Note that, for a given value of β_1, both $\bar{y}_t(\beta_1)$ and $z_t(\beta_1)$ are observable. Thus, the residual sum of squares in (12.2.12) can be viewed as that which needs to be minimized to find a least squares estimate for β from the *linear* model

$$\bar{y}_t(\beta_1) = z_t(\beta_1)\cdot\beta + e_t \tag{12.2.14}$$

Malinvaud (1980) refers to (12.2.14) as the *linear pseudomodel*. The least squares estimate from this model is given by

$$\begin{aligned} \beta_2 &= \frac{\sum_{t=1}^{T} \bar{y}_t(\beta_1)\cdot z_t(\beta_1)}{\sum_{t=1}^{T} z_t(\beta_1)^2} \\ &= [\mathbf{z}(\beta_1)'\mathbf{z}(\beta_1)]^{-1}\mathbf{z}(\beta_1)'\bar{\mathbf{y}}(\beta_1) \end{aligned} \tag{12.2.15}$$

where

$$\mathbf{z}(\beta_1) = \begin{bmatrix} z_1(\beta_1) \\ z_2(\beta_1) \\ \vdots \\ z_T(\beta_1) \end{bmatrix} \quad \text{and} \quad \bar{\mathbf{y}}(\beta_1) = \begin{bmatrix} \bar{y}_1(\beta_1) \\ \bar{y}_2(\beta_1) \\ \vdots \\ \bar{y}_T(\beta_1) \end{bmatrix}$$

Thus, we have shown that if we begin with some initial value or guess for β, called β_1, and if we approximate the function $f(\mathbf{x}_t, \beta)$ by a first-order Taylor series around β_1, then a second value or estimate for β, called β_2, can be found by applying least squares to a new linear model, known as the linear pseudomodel. This process can be repeated, using β_2 to construct the linear pseudomodel

$$\bar{\mathbf{y}}(\beta_2) = \mathbf{z}(\beta_2)\cdot\beta + \mathbf{e} \tag{12.2.16}$$

which yields the least squares estimate

$$\beta_3 = [\mathbf{z}(\beta_2)'\mathbf{z}(\beta_2)]^{-1}\mathbf{z}(\beta_2)'\bar{\mathbf{y}}(\beta_2) \tag{12.2.17}$$

Continuing the process leads to a sequence of estimates $\beta_1, \beta_2, \beta_3, \beta_4, \beta_5, \ldots$. The obvious question at this point is where does such a procedure lead us? To shed some light on this question, we write the $(n+1)$th estimate as a function of the nth estimate as follows

$$\begin{aligned}\beta_{n+1} &= [\mathbf{z}(\beta_n)'\mathbf{z}(\beta_n)]^{-1}\mathbf{z}(\beta_n)'\bar{\mathbf{y}}(\beta_n)\\ &= [\mathbf{z}(\beta_n)'\mathbf{z}(\beta_n)]^{-1}\mathbf{z}(\beta_n)'[\mathbf{y} - \mathbf{f}(X, \beta_n) + \mathbf{z}(\beta_n)\cdot\beta_n]\\ &= \beta_n + [\mathbf{z}(\beta_n)'\mathbf{z}(\beta_n)]^{-1}\mathbf{z}(\beta_n)'[\mathbf{y} - \mathbf{f}(X, \beta_n)] \qquad (12.2.18)\end{aligned}$$

where $\mathbf{f}(X, \beta) = [f(\mathbf{x}_1, \beta), f(\mathbf{x}_2, \beta), \ldots, f(\mathbf{x}_T, \beta)]'$

Also, the first-order condition for a minimum given in (12.2.8) can be written in matrix algebra notation as

$$\mathbf{z}(\beta)'[\mathbf{y} - \mathbf{f}(X, \beta)] = 0 \qquad (12.2.19)$$

If two successive estimates are equal, $\beta_{n+1} = \beta_n$, it follows from (12.2.18) that $\mathbf{z}(\beta_n)'[\mathbf{y} - \mathbf{f}(X, \beta_n)] = 0$ and, therefore, that β_n satisfies the necessary condition for a minimum.

Thus, if we begin with some initial value β_1, and repeatedly apply the formula in (12.2.18) until convergence occurs, we will have reached a point that is a solution to the first-order condition in (12.2.19). The remaining question is whether this point is a global or a local minimum, or even a maximum. The usual way of locating the global minimum, or at least making the probability of locating the global minimum high, is to carry out the process for a number of different starting values (β_1's). If different starting values lead to different minima, the minimum with the lowest residual sum of squares is the one that corresponds to the nonlinear least squares estimate. To see why the process heads in the direction of a minimum rather than a maximum, note that the derivative of the residual sum of squares function (Equation 12.2.8) can be written as

$$\frac{dS}{d\beta} = -2\mathbf{z}(\beta)'[\mathbf{y} - \mathbf{f}(X, \beta)] \qquad (12.2.20)$$

and, therefore, (12.2.18) can be rewritten as

$$\beta_{n+1} = \beta_n - \frac{1}{2}[\mathbf{z}(\beta_n)'\mathbf{z}(\beta_n)]^{-1}\left.\frac{dS}{d\beta}\right|_{\beta_n} \qquad (12.2.21)$$

Now consider Figure 12.3. At the point β_1, the slope of the tangent $dS/d\beta$ is positive. Furthermore, since $\mathbf{z}(\beta)'\mathbf{z}(\beta)$ represents a sum of squares, $[\mathbf{z}(\beta)'\mathbf{z}(\beta)]^{-1}$ will always be positive. Thus, the second value of β defined by (12.2.21) will be less than the first; the change in β has been in the direction of the minimum. Similarly, if we begin at β_1^* where $dS/d\beta$ is negative, the change in β will be positive, again in the direction of a minimum, although in this case it is a local minimum.

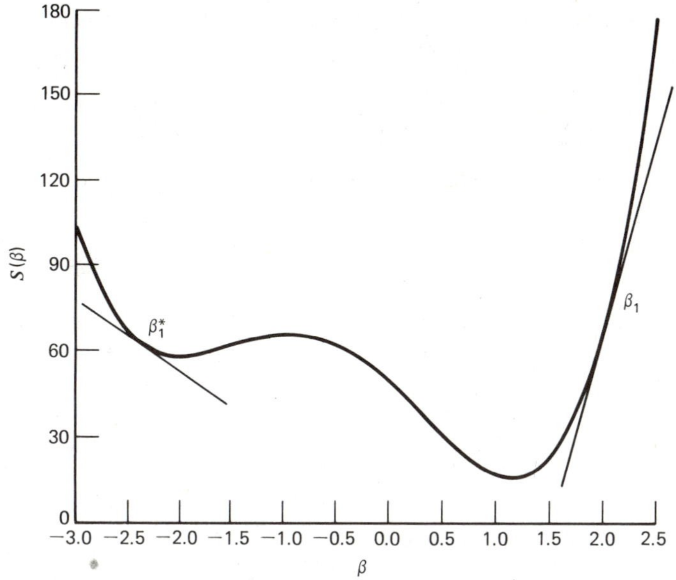

Figure 12.3 Two possible directions for the Gauss–Newton algorithm.

It is possible that changes such as these could always overshoot the minimum, or at least take a very long time to reach the minimum. To guard against this possibility, the algorithm in (12.2.21) is usually made a little more sophisticated by introducing a variable step length t_n. This change leads to an algorithm defined by

$$\begin{aligned}\beta_{n+1} &= \beta_n - t_n[\mathbf{z}(\beta_n)'\mathbf{z}(\beta_n)]^{-1} \left.\frac{dS}{d\beta}\right|_{\beta_n} \\ &= \beta_n + 2t_n[\mathbf{z}(\beta_n)'\mathbf{z}(\beta_n)]^{-1}\mathbf{z}(\beta_n)'[\mathbf{y} - \mathbf{f}(X, \beta_n)] \qquad (12.2.22)\end{aligned}$$

Different computer packages use different trial and error procedures for obtaining a "good" step length t_n at each iteration.

To summarize, one way of finding a nonlinear least squares estimate for β in the model $y_t = f(\mathbf{x}_t, \beta) + e_t$ is to use the *Gauss–Newton algorithm* defined by (12.2.18) or (12.2.22). This procedure may not work in the sense that it may not converge, or it may lead to a local minimum. To guard against these possibilities, a number of alternative starting values for β_1 should be tried. We turn now to the properties of the nonlinear least squares estimator.

12.2.1a Properties

Since the nonlinear least squares estimate b is in general a complicated nonlinear function of $\mathbf{y}$, it is impossible to establish its finite sample properties for the wide array of nonlinear models that may exist. In particular, the properties of best linear unbiased do not carry over from the linear model. It is possible, however, to consider asymptotic properties. Under appropriate conditions, which will be discussed later in terms of a more general nonlinear model with K parameters, it is possible to show that the nonlinear least squares estimator b is consistent, and that $\sqrt{T}(b - \beta)$ has a limiting normal distribution with mean 0 and variance $\sigma^2[\lim \mathbf{z}(\beta)'\mathbf{z}(\beta)/T]^{-1}$. Thus, for inference purposes we can treat b as having an approximate normal distribution with mean β and variance $\sigma^2[\mathbf{z}(\beta)'\mathbf{z}(\beta)]^{-1}$. The variance is consistently estimated by

$$\widehat{\operatorname{var}}(b) = \hat{\sigma}^2[\mathbf{z}(b)'\mathbf{z}(b)]^{-1} \tag{12.2.23}$$

where

$$\hat{\sigma}^2 = \frac{S(b)}{T - 1} \tag{12.2.24}$$

Conventional interval estimation and hypothesis-testing procedures can be carried out in the usual (linear) way, except that $X'X$ is replaced by $\mathbf{z}(b)'\mathbf{z}(b)$.

12.2.1b The Example Continued

We return now to the example introduced at the beginning of this section, namely

$$y_t = f(\mathbf{x}_t, \beta) + e_t = \beta x_{t1} + \beta^2 x_{t2} + e_t \tag{12.2.25}$$

For this model we have

$$z_t(\beta) = \frac{df(\mathbf{x}_t, \beta)}{d\beta} = x_{t1} + 2\beta x_{t2} \tag{12.2.26}$$

$$\mathbf{z}(\beta)'\mathbf{z}(\beta) = \sum_{t=1}^{T} (x_{t1} + 2\beta x_{t2})^2 \tag{12.2.27}$$

and

$$\mathbf{z}(\beta)'[\mathbf{y} - \mathbf{f}(X, \beta)] = \sum_{t=1}^{T} (x_{t1} + 2\beta x_{t2})(y_t - \beta x_{t1} - \beta^2 x_{t2}) \tag{12.2.28}$$

The Gauss–Newton algorithm defined in (12.2.18) is given by

$$\beta_{n+1} = \beta_n + \frac{\sum_{t=1}^{T}(x_{t1} + 2\beta_n x_{t2})(y_t - \beta_n x_{t1} - \beta_n^2 x_{t2})}{\sum_{t=1}^{T}(x_{t1} + 2\beta_n x_{t2})^2} \tag{12.2.29}$$

The iterations defined by (12.2.29) were carried out using the data in Table 12.1 and four different starting values. The results are given in Table 12.2. Note that, in the

Table 12.2 Iterations of the Gauss–Newton Algorithm

$\beta_1 = 4$			$\beta_1 = -0.9$		
n	β_n	$S(\beta_n)$	n	β_n	$S(\beta_n)$
1	4.000000	1226.89912	1	−0.900000	65.84007
2	2.032239	72.36060	2	−0.689307	64.49820
3	1.308562	17.45425	3	0.322688	37.47599
4	1.169699	16.31152	4	1.367249	18.61578
5	1.161445	16.30797	5	1.175455	16.31798
6	1.161213	16.30797	6	1.161625	16.30798
7	1.161207	16.30797	7	1.161218	16.30797
8	1.161207	16.30797	8	1.161207	16.30797
			9	1.161207	16.30797

$\beta_1 = -3$			$\beta_1 = -1.05$		
n	β_n	$S(\beta_n)$	n	β_n	$S(\beta_n)$
1	−3.000000	102.93069	1	−1.050000	65.85713
2	−2.323290	61.14292	2	−1.196026	65.23206
3	−2.112326	58.70033	3	−1.509215	62.44607
4	−2.052903	58.53688	4	−1.831210	59.31742
5	−2.036150	58.52450	5	−1.969877	58.60475
6	−2.031391	58.52352	6	−2.012307	58.53044
7	−2.030035	58.52344	7	−2.024579	58.52401
8	−2.029649	58.52343	8	−2.028091	58.52348
9	−2.029538	58.52343	9	−2.029094	58.52343
10	−2.029507	58.52343	10	−2.029380	58.52343
11	−2.029498	58.52343	11	−2.029462	58.52343
12	−2.029495	58.52343	12	−2.029485	58.52343
13	−2.029495	58.52343	13	−2.029492	58.52343
			14	−2.029494	58.52343
			15	−2.029494	58.52343

first two cases, the global minimum was reached, but in the last two cases the iterative process stopped at the local minimum.

The least squares estimate for β is given by $b = 1.1612$. An estimate of the disturbance variance is given by

$$\hat{\sigma}^2 = \frac{S(b)}{T-1} = \frac{16.30797}{19} = 0.85831$$

and an estimate of the variance of b is given by

$$\widehat{\text{var}}(b) = \hat{\sigma}^2[\mathbf{z}(b)'\mathbf{z}(b)]^{-1} = 0.85831(50.27135) = 0.017074$$

An approximate 95% confidence interval for β is

$$1.1612 \pm 1.96(0.017074)^{1/2}$$

or

$$(0.9051, 1.4173)$$

12.2.2 Nonlinear Least Squares Estimation of More Than One Parameter

In this section the procedures outlined in Section 12.2.1 are generalized for a nonlinear model

$$y_t = f(\mathbf{x}_t, \boldsymbol{\beta}) + e_t \tag{12.2.30}$$

which is dependent on a $(K \times 1)$ unknown parameter vector $\boldsymbol{\beta}$. Using matrix algebra notation that is compatible with that used in Section 12.2.1, (12.2.30) can be rewritten as

$$\mathbf{y} = \mathbf{f}(X, \boldsymbol{\beta}) + \mathbf{e} \tag{12.2.31}$$

It is assumed that $E[\mathbf{e}] = \mathbf{0}$ and $E[\mathbf{ee}'] = \sigma^2 I$. The nonlinear least squares estimate of the vector $\boldsymbol{\beta}$ is that value of $\boldsymbol{\beta}$ which minimizes the residual sum of squares

$$S(\boldsymbol{\beta}) = \mathbf{e}'\mathbf{e} = [\mathbf{y} - \mathbf{f}(X, \boldsymbol{\beta})]'[\mathbf{y} - \mathbf{f}(X, \boldsymbol{\beta})] \tag{12.2.32}$$

In this case there are K first-order conditions for a minimum, defined by setting the K-dimensional vector of derivatives $\partial S/\partial \boldsymbol{\beta}$ equal to the $\mathbf{0}$ vector. These first-order conditions are given by

$$\frac{\partial S}{\partial \boldsymbol{\beta}} = -2\frac{\partial \mathbf{f}(X, \boldsymbol{\beta})'}{\partial \boldsymbol{\beta}}[\mathbf{y} - \mathbf{f}(X, \boldsymbol{\beta})] = \mathbf{0} \tag{12.2.33}$$

where $\partial \mathbf{f}(X, \boldsymbol{\beta})'/\partial \boldsymbol{\beta}$ is a $(K \times T)$ matrix of derivatives with the (k, t)th element given by $\partial f(\mathbf{x}_t, \boldsymbol{\beta})/\partial \beta_k$. In line with the notation in the previous section we will use $Z(\boldsymbol{\beta})$ to denote the transpose of the matrix $\partial \mathbf{f}(X, \boldsymbol{\beta})'/\partial \boldsymbol{\beta}$. That is,

$$Z(\boldsymbol{\beta}) = \frac{\partial \mathbf{f}(X, \boldsymbol{\beta})}{\partial \boldsymbol{\beta}'} = \begin{bmatrix} \dfrac{\partial f(\mathbf{x}_1, \boldsymbol{\beta})}{\partial \beta_1} & \cdots & \dfrac{\partial f(\mathbf{x}_1, \boldsymbol{\beta})}{\partial \beta_K} \\ \vdots & \ddots & \vdots \\ \dfrac{\partial f(\mathbf{x}_T, \boldsymbol{\beta})}{\partial \beta_1} & \cdots & \dfrac{\partial f(\mathbf{x}_T, \boldsymbol{\beta})}{\partial \beta_K} \end{bmatrix} \tag{12.2.34}$$

When this matrix of derivatives is evaluated at a particular value for $\boldsymbol{\beta}$, say $\boldsymbol{\beta}_1$, it will be written as $Z(\boldsymbol{\beta}_1)$. Using (12.2.34), the first-order conditions for a minimum can be written as

$$Z(\boldsymbol{\beta})'[\mathbf{y} - \mathbf{f}(X, \boldsymbol{\beta})] = \mathbf{0} \tag{12.2.35}$$

To indicate how the Gauss–Newton algorithm can be used to find a solution to (12.2.35), we begin, as before, by approximating $\mathbf{f}(X, \boldsymbol{\beta})$ with a first-order Taylor series expansion around an initial point $\boldsymbol{\beta}_1$. The approximation for the tth observation is given by

$$f(\mathbf{x}_t, \boldsymbol{\beta}) \simeq f(\mathbf{x}_t, \boldsymbol{\beta}_1) + \left[\left.\frac{\partial f(\mathbf{x}_t, \boldsymbol{\beta})}{\partial \beta_1}\right|_{\boldsymbol{\beta}_1} \cdots \left.\frac{\partial f(\mathbf{x}_t, \boldsymbol{\beta})}{\partial \beta_K}\right|_{\boldsymbol{\beta}_1} \right] (\boldsymbol{\beta} - \boldsymbol{\beta}_1) \tag{12.2.36}$$

and including all T observations yields

$$\mathbf{f}(X, \boldsymbol{\beta}) \simeq \mathbf{f}(X, \boldsymbol{\beta}_1) + Z(\boldsymbol{\beta}_1)(\boldsymbol{\beta} - \boldsymbol{\beta}_1) \tag{12.2.37}$$

Substituting (12.2.37) into (12.2.31) yields

$$\mathbf{y} \simeq \mathbf{f}(X, \boldsymbol{\beta}_1) + Z(\boldsymbol{\beta}_1)(\boldsymbol{\beta} - \boldsymbol{\beta}_1) + \mathbf{e} \tag{12.2.38}$$

from which we can construct the linear pseudomodel

$$\bar{\mathbf{y}}(\boldsymbol{\beta}_1) = Z(\boldsymbol{\beta}_1)\boldsymbol{\beta} + \mathbf{e} \tag{12.2.39}$$

where

$$\bar{\mathbf{y}}(\boldsymbol{\beta}_1) = \mathbf{y} - \mathbf{f}(X, \boldsymbol{\beta}_1) + Z(\boldsymbol{\beta}_1)\boldsymbol{\beta}_1 \tag{12.2.40}$$

The least squares estimate from the linear model in (12.2.39) provides a second-round estimate for $\boldsymbol{\beta}$, namely,

$$\begin{aligned} \boldsymbol{\beta}_2 &= [Z(\boldsymbol{\beta}_1)'Z(\boldsymbol{\beta}_1)]^{-1}Z(\boldsymbol{\beta}_1)'\bar{\mathbf{y}}(\boldsymbol{\beta}_1) \\ &= \boldsymbol{\beta}_1 + [Z(\boldsymbol{\beta}_1)'Z(\boldsymbol{\beta}_1)]^{-1}Z(\boldsymbol{\beta}_1)'[\mathbf{y} - \mathbf{f}(X, \boldsymbol{\beta}_1)] \end{aligned} \tag{12.2.41}$$

Continuing this process, the nth iteration of the Gauss–Newton algorithm is given by

$$\boldsymbol{\beta}_{n+1} = \boldsymbol{\beta}_n + [Z(\boldsymbol{\beta}_n)'Z(\boldsymbol{\beta}_n)]^{-1}Z(\boldsymbol{\beta}_n)'[\mathbf{y} - \mathbf{f}(X, \boldsymbol{\beta}_n)] \tag{12.2.42}$$

When the process has converged $\boldsymbol{\beta}_{n+1} = \boldsymbol{\beta}_n$, so, from (12.2.42), it follows that the first-order conditions for a minimum $Z(\boldsymbol{\beta}_n)'[\mathbf{y} - \mathbf{f}(X, \boldsymbol{\beta}_n)] = \mathbf{0}$ must be satisfied. In these circumstances the point $\boldsymbol{\beta}_n$ could correspond to a local minimum or the global minimum. It will not correspond to a maximum because the positive definiteness of $[Z(\boldsymbol{\beta}_n)'Z(\boldsymbol{\beta}_n)]^{-1}$ ensures that the change $\boldsymbol{\beta}_{n+1} - \boldsymbol{\beta}_n$ will always be in the right direction. Although one can never be sure the global minimum has been found, the chances of missing the global minimum can be reduced by trying a number of different initial values for $\boldsymbol{\beta}_1$. Most standard computer packages also include a variable step length in the algorithm as we suggested in (12.2.22).

Under appropriate conditions the least squares estimate **b** will be approximately normally distributed with mean $\boldsymbol{\beta}$ and a covariance matrix that is consistently estimated by

$$\hat{\Sigma}_{\mathbf{b}} = \hat{\sigma}^2[Z(\mathbf{b})'Z(\mathbf{b})]^{-1} \tag{12.2.43a}$$

where

$$\hat{\sigma}^2 = \frac{S(\mathbf{b})}{T - K} \tag{12.2.43b}$$

This information can be used to form hypothesis tests and interval estimates in the usual way.

A set of sufficient conditions that is required for the asymptotic theory relating to **b** to be valid needs to be framed in terms of

1. The sequence of independent variables $\mathbf{x}_t$.
2. The function $f(\mathbf{x}_t, \boldsymbol{\beta})$.
3. The errors **e**.

To begin with the last-named, we have assumed that the e_t are independently, identically distributed with 0 mean and variance σ^2. These assumptions are sufficient if appropriately combined with conditions for the $\mathbf{x}_t$ and $f(\mathbf{x}_t, \boldsymbol{\beta})$.

With respect to $f(\mathbf{x}_t, \boldsymbol{\beta})$, note that we have used the differentiability of $f(\mathbf{x}_t, \boldsymbol{\beta})$, with respect to $\boldsymbol{\beta}$, in the foregoing derivations. To establish the asymptotic normality, it is convenient to assume that $f(\mathbf{x}_t, \boldsymbol{\beta})$ is continuous in both arguments and at least twice continuously differentiable with respect to $\boldsymbol{\beta}$.

Also, we have used the invertibility of $[Z(\mathbf{b})'Z(\mathbf{b})]$. In fact, as long as we are only concerned with the asymptotic behavior of the model it suffices to require

$$\frac{1}{T}[Z(\boldsymbol{\beta})'Z(\boldsymbol{\beta})] \tag{12.2.44}$$

to be nonsingular in the limit for $T \rightarrow \infty$. Although this may not be easy to verify in practice, because it depends on the sequence of independent variables $\mathbf{x}_t$, $t = 1, 2, \ldots, T$, it is sometimes obviously violated. This problem is similar to multicollinearity in linear models. The conditions for the sequence $\mathbf{x}_t$, $t = 1, 2, \ldots, T$ are such that it is bounded and well behaved in a certain sense as T approaches infinity. Since these properties may be difficult to establish for data that are not controlled by the investigator, they will not be spelled out here. Different sets of sufficient conditions to guarantee the consistency and asymptotic normality of nonlinear least squares estimators are given in the literature (see Jennrich, 1969; Malinvaud, 1980; and Fuller, 1976).

It is not quite satisfactory to know only the asymptotic properties of our estimators because we often do not know what sample size is sufficiently large for these asymptotic properties to hold approximately. If a large sample is not available, it is difficult to feel safe about the properties of the least squares estimators. However, given the current state of the art, there is not much hope for deriving generally valid small sample properties for nonlinear models because there are too many different possible nonlinear specifications.

12.2.3 Estimation of the Cobb–Douglas and CES Production Functions

In this section we illustrate nonlinear least squares estimation procedures with two examples: a Cobb–Douglas production function with an additive disturbance, and a constant elasticity of substitution (CES) production function. The same set of data is used to estimate both functions; it is given in Table 12.3.

12.2.3a The Cobb–Douglas Production Function

The Cobb–Douglas production function with additive disturbance term relating output (Q_t) to two inputs labor (L_t) and capital (K_t) is given by

$$Q_t = \beta_1 L_t^{\beta_2} K_t^{\beta_3} + e_t \tag{12.2.45}$$

It is assumed that the e_t are independent and identically distributed random variables with mean 0 and variance σ^2. This formulation is identical to that given in (12.1.2). It cannot be converted into an intrinsically linear model by taking logs because the disturbance enters in an additive rather than a multiplicative way.

To implement the Gauss–Newton algorithm, the $(T \times 3)$ matrix of first derivatives $Z(\boldsymbol{\beta}) = \partial \mathbf{f}(X, \boldsymbol{\beta})/\partial \boldsymbol{\beta}'$ is required, where the tth element of $\mathbf{f}(X, \boldsymbol{\beta})$ is given by

$$f(\mathbf{x}_t, \boldsymbol{\beta}) = \beta_1 L_t^{\beta_2} K_t^{\beta_3} \tag{12.2.46}$$

$\mathbf{x}_t' = (L_t, K_t)$ and $\boldsymbol{\beta}' = (\beta_1\ \beta_2, \beta_3)$. The tth row of $Z(\boldsymbol{\beta})$ is given by

$$\begin{aligned}\frac{\partial f(\mathbf{x}_t, \boldsymbol{\beta})}{\partial \boldsymbol{\beta}'} &= \left[\frac{\partial f(\mathbf{x}_t, \boldsymbol{\beta})}{\partial \beta_1}, \frac{\partial f(\mathbf{x}_t, \boldsymbol{\beta})}{\partial \beta_2}, \frac{\partial f(\mathbf{x}_t, \boldsymbol{\beta})}{\partial \beta_3}\right] \\ &= \left[L_t^{\beta_2} K_t^{\beta_3}, (\ln L_t)\beta_1 L_t^{\beta_2} K_t^{\beta_3}, (\ln K_t)\beta_1 L_t^{\beta_2} K_t^{\beta_3}\right]\end{aligned} \tag{12.2.47}$$

Table 12.3 Data for Production Function Examples

L_t	K_t	Q_t
0.228	0.802	0.256918
0.258	0.249	0.183599
0.821	0.771	1.212883
0.767	0.511	0.522568
0.495	0.758	0.847894
0.487	0.425	0.763379
0.678	0.452	0.623130
0.748	0.817	1.031485
0.727	0.845	0.569498
0.695	0.958	0.882497
0.458	0.084	0.108827
0.981	0.021	0.026437
0.002	0.295	0.003750
0.429	0.277	0.461626
0.231	0.546	0.268474
0.664	0.129	0.186747
0.631	0.017	0.020671
0.059	0.906	0.100159
0.811	0.223	0.252334
0.758	0.145	0.103312
0.050	0.161	0.078945
0.823	0.006	0.005799
0.483	0.836	0.723250
0.682	0.521	0.776468
0.116	0.930	0.216536
0.440	0.495	0.541182
0.456	0.185	0.316320
0.342	0.092	0.123811
0.358	0.485	0.386354
0.162	0.934	0.279431

Using the shorthand notation f_t^* to denote

$$f_t^* = f(\mathbf{x}_t, \boldsymbol{\beta})/\beta_1 = K_t^{\beta_2} L_t^{\beta_3} \tag{12.2.48}$$

(12.2.47) becomes

$$\frac{\partial f(\mathbf{x}_t, \boldsymbol{\beta})}{\partial \boldsymbol{\beta}'} = (f_t^*, \beta_1 f_t^* \ln L_t, \beta_1 f_t^* \ln K_t) \tag{12.2.49}$$

and the (3 × 3) matrix $Z(\boldsymbol{\beta})'Z(\boldsymbol{\beta})$ can be written as

$$Z(\boldsymbol{\beta})'Z(\boldsymbol{\beta}) = \begin{bmatrix} \sum_{t=1}^{T} f_t^{*2} & \beta_1 \sum_{t=1}^{T} f_t^{*2} \ln L_t & \beta_1 \sum_{t=1}^{T} f_t^{*2} \ln K_t \\ \beta_1 \sum_{t=1}^{T} f_t^{*2} \ln L_t & \beta_1^2 \sum_{t=1}^{T} f_t^{*2} (\ln L_t)^2 & \beta_1^2 \sum_{t=1}^{T} f_t^{*2} (\ln L_t)(\ln K_t) \\ \beta_1 \sum_{t=1}^{T} f_t^{*2} \ln K_t & \beta_1^2 \sum_{t=1}^{T} f_t^{*2} (\ln L_t)(\ln K_t) & \beta_1^2 \sum_{t=1}^{T} f_t^{*2} (\ln K_t)^2 \end{bmatrix} \tag{12.2.50}$$

The final ingredient for the Gauss–Newton algorithm is the (3 × 1) vector $Z(\boldsymbol{\beta})'[\mathbf{y} - \mathbf{f}(X, \boldsymbol{\beta})]$, which is given by

$$Z(\boldsymbol{\beta})'[\mathbf{y} - \mathbf{f}(X, \boldsymbol{\beta})] = \begin{bmatrix} \sum_{t=1}^{T} f_t^*(y_t - \beta_1 f_t^*) \\ \beta_1 \sum_{t=1}^{T} f_t^* \ln L_t(y_t - \beta_1 f_t^*) \\ \beta_1 \sum_{t=1}^{T} f_t^* \ln K_t(y_t - \beta_1 f_t^*) \end{bmatrix} \tag{12.2.51}$$

Assuming that we can locate a *global* minimum, the nonlinear least squares estimate for $\boldsymbol{\beta}$ is found by beginning with an initial value $\boldsymbol{\beta}_1$ and continually reapplying (12.2.42), or a modification of (12.2.42) that allows for a variable step length, until convergence occurs. The expressions given in (12.2.50) and (12.2.51) are used in this algorithm.

Using the data in Table 12.3 we get the following nonlinear least squares estimates and corresponding standard errors.

$$\mathbf{b} = \begin{pmatrix} 1.330 \\ 0.723 \\ 0.687 \end{pmatrix} \qquad \text{s.e.}(\mathbf{b}) = \begin{pmatrix} 0.129 \\ 0.132 \\ 0.115 \end{pmatrix} \tag{12.2.52}$$

The vector s.e.(**b**) is given by the square roots of the diagonal elements of $\hat{\sigma}^2[Z(\mathbf{b})'Z(\mathbf{b})]^{-1}$, where

$$\hat{\sigma}^2 = \frac{0.549618}{30} = 0.01832$$

Some words of warning are in order for students who try to reproduce the results in (12.2.52) using the program to which they have access. First, the minimizing vector **b** should be the same (or at least very very close) irrespective of what computer program is used. The same is not true for the vector of standard errors, however. As we will see in the next two sections, different computer packages often use different algorithms for finding the least squares estimate. Furthermore, the covariance matrix estimator $\hat{\sigma}^2[Z(\mathbf{b})'Z(\mathbf{b})]^{-1}$ typically arises only when the Gauss–Newton algorithm is used. Other algorithms lead naturally to other alternative estimators for the covariance matrix. Also, some programs compute the derivative matrix $Z(\boldsymbol{\beta})$ using analytical derivatives such as those we have specified in (12.2.47); others compute the derivatives numerically. All these factors mean that there is going to be some variation in standard errors across different computer packages. The extent of the variation will depend on the model and data. It is impossible to generalize about the likely extent, or about which standard errors are likely to be best. The results in (12.2.52) were obtained using the Gauss–Newton algorithm and the covariance matrix estimator $\hat{\sigma}^2[Z(\mathbf{b})'Z(\mathbf{b})]^{-1}$, but numerical rather than analytical derivatives were employed.

12.2.3b The CES Production Function

The constant elasticity of substitution (CES) production function that we will estimate is assumed to be given by

$$\ln Q_t = \beta_1 + \beta_4 \ln[\beta_2 L_t^{\beta_3} + (1 - \beta_2)K_t^{\beta_3}] + e_t \qquad (12.2.53)$$

where the e_t are again assumed to be independently and identically distributed with 0 mean and variance σ^2. The $(T \times 4)$ matrix of derivatives $Z(\boldsymbol{\beta})$ has tth row given by

$$\frac{\partial f(\mathbf{x}_t, \boldsymbol{\beta})}{\partial \boldsymbol{\beta}'} = \begin{bmatrix} 1 \\[1ex] \dfrac{\beta_4(L_t^{\beta_3} - K_t^{\beta_3})}{\beta_2 L_t^{\beta_3} + (1 - \beta_2)K_t^{\beta_3}} \\[2ex] \dfrac{\beta_4[\ln(L_t)\beta_2 L_t^{\beta_3} + \ln(K_t)(1 - \beta_2)K_t^{\beta_3}]}{\beta_2 L_t^{\beta_3} + (1 - \beta_2)K_t^{\beta_3}} \\[2ex] \ln[\beta_2 L_t^{\beta_3} + (1 - \beta_2)K_t^{\beta_3}] \end{bmatrix}' \qquad (12.2.54)$$

where $\mathbf{x}_t' = (L_t, K_t)$ and $\boldsymbol{\beta}' = (\beta_1, \beta_2, \beta_3, \beta_4)$. This result can be used to form the matrix $Z(\boldsymbol{\beta})'Z(\boldsymbol{\beta})$ and the vector $Z(\boldsymbol{\beta})'[\mathbf{y} - \mathbf{f}(X, \boldsymbol{\beta})]$, following similar procedures to those adopted for the Cobb–Douglas example.

The nonlinear least squares estimates that correspond to the data in Table 12.3 are given by

$$\mathbf{b} = \begin{pmatrix} 0.124 \\ 0.337 \\ -3.011 \\ -0.336 \end{pmatrix} \qquad \text{s.e.}(\mathbf{b}) = \begin{pmatrix} 0.078 \\ 0.136 \\ 2.232 \\ 0.272 \end{pmatrix} \tag{12.2.55}$$

The vector s.e.($\mathbf{b}$) is found from the square roots of the diagonal elements of the matrix $\hat{\sigma}^2[Z(\mathbf{b})'Z(\mathbf{b})]^{-1}$, where $\hat{\sigma}^2 = 1.76104/30 = 0.0587$, and where $Z(\mathbf{b})'Z(\mathbf{b})$ was computed using numerical rather than analytical derivatives.

12.2.4 The Newton–Raphson Algorithm

12.2.4a The Single-Parameter Case

To introduce the Newton–Raphson algorithm we return to a model with just one parameter. That is

$$\mathbf{y} = \mathbf{f}(X, \boldsymbol{\beta}) + \mathbf{e} \tag{12.2.56}$$

where $E[\mathbf{e}] = \mathbf{0}$ and $E[\mathbf{ee}'] = \sigma^2 I$. The problem is to find that value of β that minimizes

$$\begin{aligned} S(\beta) &= [\mathbf{y} - \mathbf{f}(X, \beta)]'[\mathbf{y} - \mathbf{f}(X, \beta)] \\ &= \sum_{t=1}^{T} [y_t - f(\mathbf{x}_t, \beta)]^2 \end{aligned} \tag{12.2.57}$$

When considering the Gauss–Newton algorithm, we began by replacing $f(\mathbf{x}_t, \beta)$ with a first-order Taylor series approximation around an initial point β_1. With the Newton–Raphson algorithm we begin by replacing $S(\beta)$ with a second-order Taylor series approximation, namely

$$S(\beta) \simeq S(\beta_1) + \left.\frac{dS}{d\beta}\right|_{\beta_1} (\beta - \beta_1) + \frac{1}{2}\left.\frac{d^2S}{d\beta^2}\right|_{\beta_1} (\beta - \beta_1)^2 \tag{12.2.58}$$

Before proceeding with this approximation, let us use a diagram to gain some intuitive feel for how it works. Solving for the first derivative evaluated at β_1, (12.2.58) can be rewritten as

$$\left.\frac{dS}{d\beta}\right|_{\beta_1} \simeq \frac{S(\beta) - S(\beta_1)}{\beta - \beta_1} - \frac{1}{2}\left.\frac{d^2S}{d\beta^2}\right|_{\beta_1} (\beta - \beta_1) \tag{12.2.59}$$

Now consider Figure 12.4, which is similar to Figure 12.2 except that this time we are concerned with the function $S(\beta)$, not $f(\mathbf{x}_t, \beta)$. Equation (12.2.59) states that we

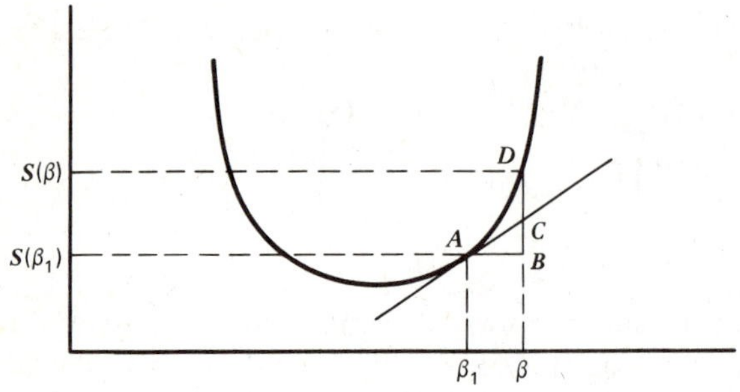

Figure 12.4 A second-order Taylor series approximation.

are approximating the slope of the tangent CA by the slope of the line joining D and A, less the amount $\frac{1}{2}(d^2S/d\beta^2)|_{\beta_1}(\beta - \beta_1)$. As would be expected, the magnitude of the last term that is subtracted from DA depends on how far β is from β_1, and on the rate at which the slope of the function $S(\beta)$ is changing. If $S(\beta)$ is a quadratic function, then (12.2.58) and (12.2.59) are exact relationships.

Returning to the minimization problem, our task is to find that value of β which minimizes (12.2.58), given that we begin with some known initial value β_1. Differentiating (12.2.58) with respect to β, and using the notation

$$h(\beta_1) = \left.\frac{d^2S}{d\beta^2}\right|_{\beta_1} \tag{12.2.60}$$

yields

$$\frac{dS}{d\beta} \simeq \left.\frac{dS}{d\beta}\right|_{\beta_1} + h(\beta_1)\cdot(\beta - \beta_1) \tag{12.2.61}$$

Setting this derivative equal to 0 and solving for β leads to a second value for β, say β_2, which is given by

$$\beta_2 = \beta_1 - h(\beta_1)^{-1}\left.\frac{dS}{d\beta}\right|_{\beta_1} \tag{12.2.62}$$

If $S(\beta)$ is quadratic, then β_2 will be exactly the least squares estimate. In the usual nonlinear case $S(\beta)$ will not be quadratic, and β_2 will not be the minimizing value because (12.2.61) is only an approximation. Continuing the procedure leads to the $(n + 1)$th value for β being given by

$$\beta_{n+1} = \beta_n - h(\beta_n)^{-1}\left.\frac{dS}{d\beta}\right|_{\beta_n} \tag{12.2.63}$$

If the process converges in the sense that $\beta_{n+1} = \beta_n$, then it must be true that $dS/d\beta|_{\beta_n} = 0$, the necessary condition for a minimum (or a maximum). The same two questions that arose in connection with the Gauss–Newton algorithm are also relevant here. How do we know whether repeated application of (12.2.63) will lead us toward a minimum, and, if a minimum is reached, how do we know whether the attained minimum is local or global?

The algorithm will lead in the right direction (toward a minimum) from the point β_1 if the second derivative $h(\beta_1)$ is positive. Since $h(\beta_1)$ will always be positive in a neighborhood of a minimum, we will go in the right direction if β_1 is sufficiently close to the minimizing value. It is possible to overstep, however. To guard against overstepping too far, a variable step length t_n can be introduced, which means we use the algorithm

$$\beta_{n+1} = \beta_n - t_n h(\beta_n)^{-1} \left.\frac{dS}{d\beta}\right|_{\beta_n} \tag{12.2.64}$$

At each iteration t_n is found such that $S(\beta_{n+1}) < S(\beta_n)$. If we begin at a point β_1 that is close to a maximum in the sense that $h(\beta_1)$ is negative, then (12.2.63) will lead us in the wrong direction, toward a maximum. To establish whether a particular minimum is local or global, a number of different starting values need to be tried.

Before turning to an example to illustrate these characteristics of the Newton–Raphson algorithm, it is instructive to investigate the relationship between the Gauss–Newton and Newton–Raphson algorithms. The Gauss–Newton algorithm was defined in (12.2.21) by

$$\beta_{n+1} = \beta_n - \frac{1}{2}[\mathbf{z}(\beta_n)'\mathbf{z}(\beta_n)]^{-1} \left.\frac{dS}{d\beta}\right|_{\beta_n} \tag{12.2.65}$$

Comparing this equation with (12.2.63), we see that both algorithms are of the form

$$\beta_{n+1} = \beta_n - p_n \left.\frac{dS}{d\beta}\right|_{\beta_n} \tag{12.2.66}$$

where

$$p_n = \begin{cases} \frac{1}{2}[\mathbf{z}(\beta_n)'\mathbf{z}(\beta_n)]^{-1} & \text{for the Gauss–Newton} \\ h(\beta_n)^{-1} & \text{for the Newton–Raphson} \end{cases}$$

Recalling the definitions of $\mathbf{z}(\beta)$ and $h(\beta)$, we have

$$\mathbf{z}(\beta)'\mathbf{z}(\beta) = \sum_{t=1}^{T} \left(\frac{df(\mathbf{x}_t, \beta)}{d\beta}\right)^2 \tag{12.2.67}$$

and

$$
\begin{aligned}
h(\beta) = \frac{d^2S}{d\beta^2} &= \frac{d^2}{d\beta^2}\left[\sum_{t=1}^{T} [y_t - f(\mathbf{x}_t, \beta)]^2\right] \\
&= \frac{d}{d\beta}\left[-2\sum_{t=1}^{T} [y_t - f(\mathbf{x}_t, \beta)] \frac{df(\mathbf{x}_t, \beta)}{d\beta}\right] \\
&= 2\sum_{t=1}^{T}\left[\left(\frac{df(\mathbf{x}_t, \beta)}{d\beta}\right)^2 - [y_t - f(\mathbf{x}_t, \beta)]\frac{d^2f(\mathbf{x}_t, \beta)}{d\beta^2}\right] \\
&= 2\mathbf{z}(\beta)'\mathbf{z}(\beta) - 2\sum_{t=1}^{T} [y_t - f(\mathbf{x}_t, \beta)]\frac{d^2f(\mathbf{x}_t, \beta)}{d\beta^2}
\end{aligned} \tag{12.2.68}
$$

Thus, the two algorithms are identical, except for the second term in the last line of (12.2.68). Note that since $E[y_t] = f(\mathbf{x}_t, \beta)$, this term has an expectation of 0. That is,

$$
E[\tfrac{1}{2}h(\beta)] = E\left[\frac{1}{2}\frac{d^2S}{d\beta^2}\right] = \mathbf{z}(\beta)'\mathbf{z}(\beta) \tag{12.2.69}
$$

Also, the existence of the second term in (12.2.68) means that $d^2S/d\beta^2$ can sometimes be negative, and hence the algorithm can head in the wrong direction. Finally, the result in (12.2.69) suggests that $2\hat{\sigma}^2 h(b)^{-1}$ might be a satisfactory alternative to $\hat{\sigma}^2[\mathbf{z}(b)'\mathbf{z}(b)]^{-1}$ as an estimator for the variance of b. Since $h(b)^{-1}$ is automatically computed as part of the Newton–Raphson algorithm, the estimator $2\hat{\sigma}^2 h(b)^{-1}$ is frequently used in conjunction with this algorithm. You should be careful not to confuse this result with that associated with maximization of the log-likelihood function via the Newton–Raphson algorithm. This question will be addressed in Section 12.2.5.

12.2.4b An Example

Returning to the example investigated in Section 12.2.1b, our problem is to use the Newton–Raphson algorithm to find that value of β that minimizes

$$
S(\beta) = \sum_{t=1}^{T} (y_t - \beta x_{t1} - \beta^2 x_{t2})^2 \tag{12.2.70}
$$

Working in this direction, we have

$$
\frac{dS}{d\beta} = -2\sum_{t=1}^{T} (y_t - \beta x_{t1} - \beta^2 x_{t2})(x_{t1} + 2\beta x_{t2}) \tag{12.2.71}
$$

and

$$h(\beta) = \frac{d^2 S}{d\beta^2} = 2 \sum_{t=1}^{T} [(x_{t1} + 2\beta x_{t2})^2 - (y_t - \beta x_{t1} - \beta^2 x_{t2})2x_{t2}] \quad (12.2.72)$$

Note that, as demonstrated in (12.2.68),

$$E\left[\frac{d^2 S}{d\beta^2}\right] = 2 \sum_{t=1}^{T} (x_{t1} + 2\beta x_{t2})^2 = 2\mathbf{z}(\beta)'\mathbf{z}(\beta) \quad (12.2.73)$$

The nth iteration of the Newton–Raphson process, (12.2.63), can now be written as

$$\beta_{n+1} = \beta_n + \frac{\sum_{t=1}^{T} (y_t - \beta_n x_{t1} - \beta_n^2 x_{t2})(x_{t1} + 2\beta_n x_{t2})}{\sum_{t=1}^{T} [(x_{t1} + 2\beta_n x_{t2})^2 - (y_t - \beta_n x_{t1} - \beta_n^2 x_{t2})2x_{t2}]} \quad (12.2.74)$$

A comparison of the iterations of the Newton–Raphson algorithm with those of the Gauss–Newton algorithm, for four different starting values (cases 1, 2, 3 and 4), are given in Table 12.4. The data used are those given in Table 12.1. In case 1, where the starting value of $\beta_1 = 1.0$ is relatively close to the global minimum, both algorithms converge to the global minimum in a small number of iterations. In case 2 the starting value of $\beta_1 = -2.0$ leads both algorithms to converge to the local minimum. With a starting value of $\beta_1 = 0.1$ (case 3), the Gauss–Newton algorithm converges to the global minimum; the Newton–Raphson algorithm at first heads toward the maximum, but overshoots, and then converges to the local minimum. In case 4, with a starting value of $\beta_1 = -0.9$, the Gauss–Newton algorithm converges to the global minimum, but the Newton–Raphson algorithm converges to the maximum (see Fig. 12.1). In general the Newton–Raphson algorithm is more efficient in the sense that it converges faster than the Gauss–Newton algorithm. However, the Gauss–Newton algorithm is more reliable because it has a higher probability of locating the global minimum. The estimate of the variance of b obtained using the Newton–Raphson algorithm is

$$\widehat{\text{var}}(b) = \hat{\sigma}^2[2h(b)^{-1}] = 0.85831 \times (48.957016)^{-1} = 0.017532$$

This value is slightly larger than $\hat{\sigma}^2[\mathbf{z}(b)'\mathbf{z}(b)]^{-1} = 0.017074$, which is the estimate provided by the Gauss–Newton algorithm.

12.2.4c The General *K* Parameter Case

For the nonlinear model

$$\mathbf{y} = \mathbf{f}(X, \boldsymbol{\beta}) + \mathbf{e} \quad (12.2.75)$$

Table 12.4 A Comparison of the Gauss-Newton and Newton-Raphson Algorithms

	Gauss-Newton			Newton-Raphson		
	n	β_n	$S(\beta_n)$	n	β_n	$S(\beta_n)$
Case 1	1	1.000000	17.47588	1	1.000000	17.47588
	2	1.163311	16.30819	2	1.186307	16.33922
	3	1.161263	16.30797	3	1.161684	16.30798
	4	1.161208	16.30797	4	1.161207	16.30797
	5	1.161207	16.30797	5	1.161207	16.30797
	6	1.161207	16.30797			
Case 2	1	−2.000000	58.54386	1	−2.000000	58.54386
	2	−2.021041	58.52514	2	−2.030665	58.52346
	3	−2.027080	58.52357	3	−2.029496	58.52343
	4	−2.028806	58.52344	4	−2.029494	58.52343
	5	−2.029298	58.52343	5	−2.029494	58.52343
	6	−2.029438	58.52343			
	7	−2.029478	58.52343			
	8	−2.029490	58.52343			
	9	−2.029493	58.52343			
	10	−2.029494	58.52343			
Case 3	1	0.100000	45.52900	1	0.100000	45.52900
	2	1.516732	23.69876	2	−2.096638	58.63819
	3	1.195398	16.36623	3	−2.034503	58.52404
	4	1.162362	16.30804	4	−2.029526	58.52343
	5	1.161237	16.30797	5	−2.029494	58.52343
	6	1.161207	16.30797	6	−2.029494	58.52343
	7	1.161207	16.30797			
Case 4	1	−0.900000	65.84007	1	−0.900000	65.84007
	2	−0.689307	64.49820	2	−0.975283	65.93952
	3	0.322688	37.47599	3	−0.977619	65.93961
	4	1.367249	18.61578	4	−0.977621	65.93961
	5	1.175455	16.31798	5	−0.977621	65.93961
	6	1.161625	16.30798			
	7	1.161218	16.30797			
	8	1.161207	16.30797			
	9	1.161207	16.30797			

where $\boldsymbol{\beta}$ is a K-dimensional vector of unknown parameters, $E[\mathbf{e}] = \mathbf{0}$ and $E[\mathbf{ee}'] = \sigma^2 I$, the nth iteration of the Newton–Raphson algorithm designed to find that value of $\boldsymbol{\beta}$ that minimizes $S(\boldsymbol{\beta}) = \mathbf{e}'\mathbf{e}$ is given by

$$\boldsymbol{\beta}_{n+1} = \boldsymbol{\beta}_n - H_n^{-1} \left.\frac{\partial S}{\partial \boldsymbol{\beta}}\right|_{\boldsymbol{\beta}_n} \tag{12.2.76}$$

where

$$\left.\frac{\partial S}{\partial \boldsymbol{\beta}}\right|_{\boldsymbol{\beta}_n} = \left.\left(\frac{\partial S}{\partial \beta_1}, \frac{\partial S}{\partial \beta_2}, \ldots, \frac{\partial S}{\partial \beta_K}\right)'\right|_{\boldsymbol{\beta}_n} \tag{12.2.77}$$

is the gradient vector evaluated at $\boldsymbol{\beta}_n$, and H_n is the $(K \times K)$ Hessian matrix evaluated at $\boldsymbol{\beta}_n$. That is,

$$H_n = \left.\frac{\partial^2 S}{\partial \boldsymbol{\beta} \partial \boldsymbol{\beta}'}\right|_{\boldsymbol{\beta}_n} = \left.\begin{bmatrix} \dfrac{\partial^2 S}{\partial \beta_1^2} & \cdots & \dfrac{\partial^2 S}{\partial \beta_1 \partial \beta_K} \\ \vdots & \ddots & \vdots \\ \dfrac{\partial^2 S}{\partial \beta_K \partial \beta_1} & \cdots & \dfrac{\partial^2 S}{\partial \beta_K^2} \end{bmatrix}\right|_{\boldsymbol{\beta}_n} \tag{12.2.78}$$

Equation 12.2.76 can be derived by finding the minimizing value for $\boldsymbol{\beta}$ after $S(\boldsymbol{\beta})$ has been approximated by a K-dimensional second-order Taylor series approximation around a predetermined value $\boldsymbol{\beta}_n$.

The characteristics of the algorithm discussed in conjunction with the single-parameter case also hold for the more general case. In particular, if H_n is positive definite, then the change $\boldsymbol{\beta}_{n+1} - \boldsymbol{\beta}_n$ will be in the right direction (toward a minimum). If $\boldsymbol{\beta}_n$ is not sufficiently close to a minimum, H_n may not be positive definite and the algorithm may head in the wrong direction. Also, if a minimum is reached, it could be a local rather than the global minimum. An estimate of the covariance matrix of the minimizing vector $\mathbf{b}$ is frequently taken as

$$\hat{\Sigma}_{\mathbf{b}} = 2\hat{\sigma}^2 \left.\left[\frac{\partial^2 S}{\partial \boldsymbol{\beta} \partial \boldsymbol{\beta}'}\right]^{-1}\right|_{\mathbf{b}} \tag{12.2.79}$$

where $\hat{\sigma}^2 = S(\mathbf{b})/(T - K)$. This estimator is justified because $E[\frac{1}{2}\partial^2 S/\partial \boldsymbol{\beta} \partial \boldsymbol{\beta}'] = Z(\boldsymbol{\beta})'Z(\boldsymbol{\beta})$ and because $\sigma^2[Z(\boldsymbol{\beta})'Z(\boldsymbol{\beta})]^{-1}$ has been established as the asymptotic covariance matrix for $\mathbf{b}$.

The Gauss–Newton and Newton–Raphson algorithms are just two of a very large number of possible algorithms. Most have the general form

$$\boldsymbol{\beta}_{n+1} = \boldsymbol{\beta}_n - t_n P_n \gamma_n \tag{12.2.80}$$

where $\gamma_n = \partial S/\partial \boldsymbol{\beta}|_{\boldsymbol{\beta}_n}$ is the gradient vector, P_n is (desirably) a positive definite matrix known as the direction matrix, and t_n is a positive number known as the step length. Most algorithms include some procedure for determining an "optimum" step length at each iteration; the feature that differentiates alternative algorithms is the definition of P_n. Ignoring the step length, which is usually variable at each iteration, we have seen that the Gauss–Newton algorithm is defined by $P_n = [Z(\boldsymbol{\beta}_n)'Z(\boldsymbol{\beta}_n)]^{-1}$ and that the Newton–Raphson algorithm is defined by $P_n = [\partial^2 S/\partial\boldsymbol{\beta}\partial\boldsymbol{\beta}']^{-1}|_{\boldsymbol{\beta}_n}$. A description of other algorithms and their direction matrices can be found in Judge, et al. (1985, Appendix B). Some of these are considered in the next subsection in the context of maximum likelihood estimation.

12.2.5 Maximum Likelihood Estimation

It is useful to consider maximum likelihood estimation of the model

$$\mathbf{y} = \mathbf{f}(X, \boldsymbol{\beta}) + \mathbf{e} \tag{12.2.81}$$

where $\mathbf{e} \sim N(\mathbf{0}, \sigma^2 I)$, and to contrast this procedure with the nonlinear least squares procedures considered so far and with maximum likelihood estimation of a more general class of models that is considered in Section 12.3. The likelihood function for the model in (12.2.81) is given by

$$\begin{aligned} \ell(\boldsymbol{\beta}, \sigma^2 | \mathbf{y}, X) &= \frac{1}{(2\pi\sigma^2)^{T/2}} \exp\left\{ -\frac{[\mathbf{y} - \mathbf{f}(X, \boldsymbol{\beta})]'[\mathbf{y} - \mathbf{f}(X, \boldsymbol{\beta})]}{2\sigma^2} \right\} \\ &= \frac{1}{(2\pi\sigma^2)^{T/2}} \exp\left\{ -\frac{S(\boldsymbol{\beta})}{2\sigma^2} \right\} \end{aligned} \tag{12.2.82}$$

and the log-likelihood by

$$\begin{aligned} L(\boldsymbol{\beta}, \sigma^2 | \mathbf{y}, X) &= \ln \ell(\boldsymbol{\beta}, \sigma^2 | \mathbf{y}, X) \\ &= -\frac{T}{2} \ln 2\pi - \frac{T}{2} \ln \sigma^2 - \frac{S(\boldsymbol{\beta})}{2\sigma^2} \end{aligned} \tag{12.2.83}$$

It is not, in general, possible to find an analytical expression for the maximum likelihood estimators $\tilde{\boldsymbol{\beta}}$ that is a value of $\boldsymbol{\beta}$ such that $\partial L/\partial\boldsymbol{\beta} = \mathbf{0}$. It is possible, however, to find an expression for the maximum likelihood estimator $\tilde{\sigma}^2$ as a function of $\boldsymbol{\beta}$. Differentiating (12.2.83) with respect to σ^2, setting this derivative equal to 0, and solving for σ^2, yields the estimator

$$\tilde{\sigma}^2 = \frac{S(\boldsymbol{\beta})}{T} \tag{12.2.84}$$

It is now possible to write the log-likelihood function just in terms of $\boldsymbol{\beta}$, or, in other words, to obtain the concentrated log-likelihood function, concentrated in terms of $\boldsymbol{\beta}$. This function is obtained by replacing σ^2 by $\tilde{\sigma}^2$ and is given by

$$\begin{aligned} L^*(\boldsymbol{\beta}|\mathbf{y}, X) &= -\frac{T}{2}\ln 2\pi - \frac{T}{2}\ln\frac{S(\boldsymbol{\beta})}{T} - \frac{T}{2} \\ &= \text{constant} - \frac{T}{2}\ln S(\boldsymbol{\beta}) \qquad (12.2.85) \end{aligned}$$

It is clear from this equation that the maximum likelihood estimator $\tilde{\boldsymbol{\beta}}$, which globally maximizes $L^*(\boldsymbol{\beta}|\mathbf{y}, X)$ is identical to the nonlinear least squares estimator $\mathbf{b}$, which globally minimizes $S(\boldsymbol{\beta})$. This conclusion could also have been drawn from (12.2.83), but (12.2.85) does make the relationship more evident, and it serves to introduce the useful concept of a concentrated log-likelihood function.

The equivalence of the maximum likelihood and nonlinear least squares estimators for $\boldsymbol{\beta}$ is not a general result that holds for all nonlinear models. It holds for all models that can be expressed in the form $\mathbf{y} = \mathbf{f}(X, \boldsymbol{\beta}) + \mathbf{e}$, where $\mathbf{e} \sim N(\mathbf{0}, \sigma^2 I)$. However, as we will see in Section 12.3, there is a broader class of models where the two estimators are not necessarily identical.

12.2.5a Properties

Let $\boldsymbol{\theta}' = (\boldsymbol{\beta}', \sigma^2)$, and let the maximum likelihood estimator for $\boldsymbol{\theta}'$ be denoted by $\tilde{\boldsymbol{\theta}}' = (\tilde{\boldsymbol{\beta}}', \tilde{\sigma}^2)$. Under appropriate regularity conditions

$$\sqrt{T}(\tilde{\boldsymbol{\theta}} - \boldsymbol{\theta}) \xrightarrow{d} N[\mathbf{0}, \lim[I(\boldsymbol{\theta})/T]^{-1}] \qquad (12.2.86)$$

where $I(\boldsymbol{\theta})$ is the information matrix (see Exercise 12.1)

$$\begin{aligned} I(\boldsymbol{\theta}) &= -E\left[\frac{\partial^2 L}{\partial\boldsymbol{\theta}\partial\boldsymbol{\theta}'}\right] = -E\begin{bmatrix} \dfrac{\partial^2 L}{\partial\boldsymbol{\beta}\partial\boldsymbol{\beta}'} & \dfrac{\partial^2 L}{\partial\boldsymbol{\beta}\partial\sigma^2} \\ \dfrac{\partial^2 L}{\partial\sigma^2\partial\boldsymbol{\beta}'} & \dfrac{\partial^2 L}{\partial(\sigma^2)^2} \end{bmatrix} \\ &= \begin{bmatrix} \sigma^{-2}[Z(\boldsymbol{\beta})'Z(\boldsymbol{\beta})] & \mathbf{0} \\ \mathbf{0}' & T/2\sigma^4 \end{bmatrix} \qquad (12.2.87) \end{aligned}$$

Thus, in the sense of the limiting distribution given in (12.2.86), the asymptotic covariance matrix for $\tilde{\boldsymbol{\beta}}$ is $\sigma^2[Z(\boldsymbol{\beta})'Z(\boldsymbol{\beta})]^{-1}$, a result that has already been given for the nonlinear least squares estimator.

12.2.5b Alternative Algorithms and Covariance Matrix Estimators

Three algorithms are commonly used to obtain maximum likelihood estimates: the Newton–Raphson, the method of scoring, and an algorithm usually attributed to Berndt, Hall, Hall and Hausman (1974). We will briefly consider each of these algorithms, with the last one being referred to as the BHHH algorithm.

Because the information matrix (12.2.87) is block diagonal, and because an estimate for σ^2 can readily be obtained from (12.2.84) once $\boldsymbol{\beta}$ has been estimated, it is sufficient to consider each of the algorithms in terms of $\boldsymbol{\beta}$ alone. Ignoring a possible variable step length, a general expression for all three algorithms is

$$\boldsymbol{\beta}_{n+1} = \boldsymbol{\beta}_n - P_n \left.\frac{\partial L}{\partial \boldsymbol{\beta}}\right|_{\boldsymbol{\beta}_n} \tag{12.2.88}$$

With the Newton–Raphson algorithm $P_n = [\partial^2 L/\partial\boldsymbol{\beta}\partial\boldsymbol{\beta}']^{-1}|_{\boldsymbol{\beta}_n}$ and (12.2.88) becomes

$$\begin{aligned}
\boldsymbol{\beta}_{n+1} &= \boldsymbol{\beta}_n - \left.\left[\frac{\partial^2 L}{\partial\boldsymbol{\beta}\partial\boldsymbol{\beta}'}\right]^{-1}\right|_{\boldsymbol{\beta}_n} \cdot \left.\frac{\partial L}{\partial \boldsymbol{\beta}}\right|_{\boldsymbol{\beta}_n} \\
&= \boldsymbol{\beta}_n - \left.\left[\frac{-1}{2\sigma^2}\frac{\partial^2 S}{\partial\boldsymbol{\beta}\partial\boldsymbol{\beta}'}\right]^{-1}\right|_{\boldsymbol{\beta}_n} \cdot \left.\left[\frac{-1}{2\sigma^2}\frac{\partial S}{\partial \boldsymbol{\beta}}\right]\right|_{\boldsymbol{\beta}_n} \\
&= \boldsymbol{\beta}_n - \left.\left[\frac{\partial^2 S}{\partial\boldsymbol{\beta}\partial\boldsymbol{\beta}'}\right]^{-1}\right|_{\boldsymbol{\beta}_n} \cdot \left.\frac{\partial S}{\partial \boldsymbol{\beta}}\right|_{\boldsymbol{\beta}_n}
\end{aligned} \tag{12.2.89}$$

which is precisely the nonlinear least squares algorithm specified in (12.2.76). In this case an estimate of the asymptotic covariance matrix for $\tilde{\boldsymbol{\beta}}$ can be found from

$$\hat{\Sigma}_{\tilde{\boldsymbol{\beta}}} = -\left.\left[\frac{\partial^2 L}{\partial\boldsymbol{\beta}\partial\boldsymbol{\beta}'}\right]^{-1}\right|_{\tilde{\boldsymbol{\beta}},\tilde{\sigma}^2} = 2\tilde{\sigma}^2\left.\left[\frac{\partial^2 S}{\partial\boldsymbol{\beta}\partial\boldsymbol{\beta}'}\right]^{-1}\right|_{\tilde{\boldsymbol{\beta}}} \tag{12.2.90}$$

Whereas the Newton–Raphson algorithm uses the inverse of the Hessian matrix of the log-likelihood function, the method of scoring uses the inverse of the expectation of the Hessian, or, in other words, the negative of the inverse of the information matrix; that is, $P_n = [E[\partial^2 L/\partial\boldsymbol{\beta}\partial\boldsymbol{\beta}']]^{-1}|_{\boldsymbol{\beta}_n}$. In this case we have

$$\begin{aligned}
\boldsymbol{\beta}_{n+1} &= \boldsymbol{\beta}_n - \left.\left[E\frac{\partial^2 L}{\partial\boldsymbol{\beta}\partial\boldsymbol{\beta}'}\right]^{-1}\right|_{\boldsymbol{\beta}_n} \cdot \left.\frac{\partial L}{\partial \boldsymbol{\beta}}\right|_{\boldsymbol{\beta}_n} \\
&= \boldsymbol{\beta}_n - \left[\frac{-1}{\sigma^2} Z(\boldsymbol{\beta}_n)'Z(\boldsymbol{\beta}_n)\right]^{-1} \cdot \left.\left[\frac{-1}{2\sigma^2}\frac{\partial S}{\partial \boldsymbol{\beta}}\right]\right|_{\boldsymbol{\beta}_n} \\
&= \boldsymbol{\beta}_n - \tfrac{1}{2}[Z(\boldsymbol{\beta}_n)'Z(\boldsymbol{\beta}_n)]^{-1} \cdot \left.\frac{\partial S}{\partial \boldsymbol{\beta}}\right|_{\boldsymbol{\beta}_n}
\end{aligned} \tag{12.2.91}$$

which is precisely the Gauss–Newton algorithm considered in (12.2.42). An estimate of the asymptotic covariance matrix for $\tilde{\boldsymbol{\beta}}$ is given by

$$\hat{\Sigma}_{\tilde{\boldsymbol{\beta}}} = -\left[E\frac{\partial^2 L}{\partial\boldsymbol{\beta}\partial\boldsymbol{\beta}'}\right]^{-1}\Bigg|_{\tilde{\boldsymbol{\beta}},\tilde{\sigma}^2} = \tilde{\sigma}^2[Z(\tilde{\boldsymbol{\beta}})'Z(\tilde{\boldsymbol{\beta}})]^{-1} \qquad (12.2.92)$$

To consider the BHHH algorithm, we need the log-likelihood for a single observation, namely

$$\begin{aligned} L_t &= L(\boldsymbol{\beta}, \sigma^2 \mid y_t, \mathbf{x}_t) \\ &= -\frac{1}{2}\ln 2\pi - \frac{1}{2}\ln \sigma^2 - \frac{[y_t - f(\mathbf{x}_t, \boldsymbol{\beta})]^2}{2\sigma^2} \end{aligned} \qquad (12.2.93)$$

With this algorithm P_n is defined as

$$\dot{P}_n = -\left[\sum_{t=1}^{T}\left(\frac{\partial L_t}{\partial\boldsymbol{\beta}}\right)\left(\frac{\partial L_t}{\partial\boldsymbol{\beta}'}\right)\right]^{-1}\Bigg|_{\boldsymbol{\beta}_n,\sigma_n^2} \qquad (12.2.94)$$

It will soon become evident why evaluation at σ_n^2 as well as $\boldsymbol{\beta}_n$ is required in this case. Now

$$\frac{\partial L_t}{\partial\boldsymbol{\beta}} = \frac{[y_t - f(\mathbf{x}_t, \boldsymbol{\beta})]}{\sigma^2}\frac{\partial f(\mathbf{x}_t, \boldsymbol{\beta})}{\partial\boldsymbol{\beta}} \qquad (12.2.95)$$

and hence this algorithm is given by

$$\begin{aligned} \boldsymbol{\beta}_{n+1} &= \boldsymbol{\beta}_n + \left[\sum_{t=1}^{T}\left(\frac{\partial L_t}{\partial\boldsymbol{\beta}}\right)\left(\frac{\partial L_t}{\partial\boldsymbol{\beta}'}\right)\right]^{-1}\Bigg|_{\boldsymbol{\beta}_n,\sigma_n^2}\cdot\frac{\partial L}{\partial\boldsymbol{\beta}}\Bigg|_{\boldsymbol{\beta}_n} \\ &= \boldsymbol{\beta}_n + \left[\sum_{t=1}^{T}\frac{[y_t - f(\mathbf{x}_t, \boldsymbol{\beta})]^2}{\sigma^4}\frac{\partial f(\mathbf{x}_t, \boldsymbol{\beta})}{\partial\boldsymbol{\beta}}\frac{\partial f(\mathbf{x}_t, \boldsymbol{\beta})}{\partial\boldsymbol{\beta}'}\right]^{-1}\Bigg|_{\boldsymbol{\beta}_n,\sigma_n^2}\cdot\left[\frac{-1}{2\sigma^2}\frac{\partial S}{\partial\boldsymbol{\beta}}\right]\Bigg|_{\boldsymbol{\beta}_n} \\ &= \boldsymbol{\beta}_n - \frac{1}{2}\sigma_n^2\left[\sum_{t=1}^{T}[y_t - f(\mathbf{x}_t, \boldsymbol{\beta}_n)]^2\frac{\partial f(\mathbf{x}_t, \boldsymbol{\beta})}{\partial\boldsymbol{\beta}}\cdot\frac{\partial f(\mathbf{x}_t, \boldsymbol{\beta})}{\partial\boldsymbol{\beta}'}\Bigg|_{\boldsymbol{\beta}_n}\right]^{-1}\cdot\frac{\partial S}{\partial\boldsymbol{\beta}}\Bigg|_{\boldsymbol{\beta}_n} \end{aligned}$$

(12.2.96)

This algorithm is not identical to any considered so far. However, it should be noted that

$$E\left[\sum_{t=1}^{T}\left(\frac{\partial L_t}{\partial\boldsymbol{\beta}}\right)\left(\frac{\partial L_t}{\partial\boldsymbol{\beta}'}\right)\right] = \frac{1}{\sigma^2}\sum_{t=1}^{T}\left(\frac{\partial f(\mathbf{x}_t, \boldsymbol{\beta})}{\partial\boldsymbol{\beta}}\frac{\partial f(\mathbf{x}_t, \boldsymbol{\beta})}{\partial\boldsymbol{\beta}'}\right) = \frac{1}{\sigma^2}Z(\boldsymbol{\beta})'Z(\boldsymbol{\beta}) \qquad (12.2.97)$$

Thus, replacing $\sum(\partial L_t/\partial\boldsymbol{\beta})(\partial L_t/\partial\boldsymbol{\beta}')$ by its expectation gives an algorithm identical to the Gauss–Newton and the method of scoring.

When the BHHH algorithm is used, a natural estimator for the asymptotic covariance matrix for $\tilde{\boldsymbol{\beta}}$ is

$$\hat{\Sigma}_{\tilde{\boldsymbol{\beta}}} = \left[\sum_{t=1}^{T}\left(\frac{\partial L_t}{\partial \boldsymbol{\beta}}\right)\left(\frac{\partial L_t}{\partial \boldsymbol{\beta}'}\right)\right]^{-1}\Bigg|_{\tilde{\boldsymbol{\beta}}, \tilde{\sigma}^2}$$

$$= \tilde{\sigma}^4\left[\sum_{t=1}^{T}[y_t - f(\mathbf{x}_t, \tilde{\boldsymbol{\beta}})]^2 \frac{\partial f(\mathbf{x}_t, \boldsymbol{\beta})}{\partial \boldsymbol{\beta}} \cdot \frac{\partial f(\mathbf{x}_t, \boldsymbol{\beta})}{\partial \boldsymbol{\beta}'}\Bigg|_{\tilde{\boldsymbol{\beta}}}\right]^{-1} \qquad (12.2.98)$$

Since the BHHH algorithm has not simplified to one of the special cases considered earlier, it is useful to illustrate it with the simple one-parameter model $y_t = \beta x_{t1} + \beta^2 x_{t2} + e_t$. You are encouraged to verify that, for this model, (12.2.96) becomes

$$\beta_{n+1} = \beta_n + \sigma_n^2 \frac{\sum_{t=1}^{T}[(y_t - \beta_n x_{t1} - \beta_n^2 x_{t2})(x_{t1} + 2\beta_n x_{t2})]}{\sum_{t=1}^{T}[(y_t - \beta_n x_{t1} - \beta_n^2 x_{t2})^2(x_{t1} + 2\beta_n x_{t2})^2]} \qquad (12.2.99)$$

and that (12.2.98) becomes

$$\widehat{\text{var}}(\tilde{\beta}) = \frac{\tilde{\sigma}^4}{\sum_{t=1}^{T}[(y_t - \tilde{\beta}x_{t1} - \tilde{\beta}^2 x_{t2})^2(x_{t1} + 2\tilde{\beta}x_{t2})^2]} \qquad (12.2.100)$$

Let us conclude this section with a summary of the three algorithms. All three algorithms can be written as

$$\boldsymbol{\beta}_{n+1} = \boldsymbol{\beta}_n - P_n \frac{\partial L}{\partial \boldsymbol{\beta}}\Bigg|_{\boldsymbol{\beta}_n} \qquad (12.2.101)$$

where

$$P_n = \begin{cases} \left[\dfrac{\partial^2 L}{\partial \boldsymbol{\beta}\partial \boldsymbol{\beta}'}\right]^{-1}\Bigg|_{\boldsymbol{\beta}_n} & \text{for the Newton–Raphson algorithm} \\ \left[E\dfrac{\partial^2 L}{\partial \boldsymbol{\beta}\partial \boldsymbol{\beta}'}\right]^{-1}\Bigg|_{\boldsymbol{\beta}_n} & \text{for the method of scoring} \\ -\left[\sum_{t=1}^{T}\left(\dfrac{\partial L_t}{\partial \boldsymbol{\beta}}\right)\left(\dfrac{\partial L_t}{\partial \boldsymbol{\beta}'}\right)\right]^{-1}\Bigg|_{\boldsymbol{\beta}_n, \sigma_n^2} & \text{for the BHHH algorithm} \end{cases} \qquad (12.2.102)$$

Furthermore, in each case $(-P_n)$ evaluated at $\tilde{\boldsymbol{\beta}}$ can serve as an estimator for the asymptotic covariance matrix for $\tilde{\boldsymbol{\beta}}$. What needs to be emphasized at this point is that the algorithms defined by (12.2.101), and the covariance matrix estimators given by $[-P_n|_{\tilde{\boldsymbol{\beta}}}]$, hold for the likelihood function for any model that satisfies the usual regularity conditions and that is a function of some vector of parameters $\boldsymbol{\beta}$. However, the simplifications given by the last equalities in (12.2.89), (12.2.90), (12.2.91), (12.2.92), (12.2.96), and (12.2.98) pertain only to the model $\mathbf{y} = \mathbf{f}(X, \boldsymbol{\beta}) + \mathbf{e}$, where $\mathbf{e} \sim N(\mathbf{0}, \sigma^2 I)$. Thus relationships such as that between the Gauss–Newton algorithm for nonlinear least squares and the method of scoring for maximum likelihood will not hold in general.

12.3 Estimation of Linear Models with General Covariance Matrix

12.3.1 General Considerations

In Chapter 9 we considered the linear model

$$\mathbf{y} = X\boldsymbol{\beta} + \mathbf{e} \tag{12.3.1}$$

where $\mathbf{y}$ is a $(T \times 1)$ vector of observations on a dependent variable, X is a $(T \times K)$ matrix of observations on K explanatory variables, $\boldsymbol{\beta}$ is a $(K \times 1)$ vector of parameters that we wish to estimate, and $\mathbf{e}$ is a random disturbance vector such that

$$E[\mathbf{e}] = \mathbf{0} \qquad \text{and} \qquad E[\mathbf{ee}'] = \sigma^2\boldsymbol{\Psi} \tag{12.3.2}$$

The $(T \times T)$ matrix $\boldsymbol{\Psi}$ was assumed to depend on a fixed number (say H) of unknown parameters that, in this section, we will denote by the $(H \times 1)$ parameter vector $\boldsymbol{\theta}$. The dimension of $\boldsymbol{\theta}$, and the precise way in which $\boldsymbol{\Psi}$ depends on $\boldsymbol{\theta}$, depends on what further assumptions are made about the data-generating process in (12.3.1). Two examples of possible structures for $\boldsymbol{\Psi}$ were considered in Chapter 9; that relating to a first-order autoregressive disturbance, and that which arises when $\mathbf{e}$ is heteroskedastic. Other structures were dealt with in Chapter 11. In all these cases the estimators for $\boldsymbol{\beta}$ that were considered were estimated generalized least squares or two-step Aitken estimators. They involved estimating $\boldsymbol{\theta}$ from least squares residuals, and then using this estimate in a generalized least squares estimator. Specifically, if we use the notation $\boldsymbol{\Psi}(\boldsymbol{\theta})$ to emphasize the dependence of $\boldsymbol{\Psi}$ on $\boldsymbol{\theta}$, and if $\hat{\boldsymbol{\theta}}$ is the estimate of $\boldsymbol{\theta}$ derived from least squares residuals, then the estimated generalized least squares estimator for $\boldsymbol{\beta}$ is given by

$$\hat{\hat{\boldsymbol{\beta}}} = [X'\boldsymbol{\Psi}(\hat{\boldsymbol{\theta}})^{-1}X]^{-1}X'\boldsymbol{\Psi}(\hat{\boldsymbol{\theta}})^{-1}\mathbf{y} \tag{12.3.3}$$

In this section we are again interested in the model defined by (12.3.1) and (12.3.2), but we wish to consider some alternatives to estimated generalized least squares estimation. In particular, we will examine nonlinear least squares, maximum likelihood, and Bayesian procedures. In the remainder of this section we consider some general aspects of each of these estimation procedures. Autocorrelation and heteroskedasticity are dealt with in Sections 12.3.2 and 12.3.3, respectively; some general approaches to hypothesis testing are considered in Section 12.3.4.

12.3.1a Nonlinear Least Squares Estimation

The generalized least squares estimator $\hat{\boldsymbol{\beta}} = [X'\boldsymbol{\Psi}(\boldsymbol{\theta})^{-1}X]^{-1}X'\boldsymbol{\Psi}(\boldsymbol{\theta})^{-1}\mathbf{y}$ is that value of $\boldsymbol{\beta}$ that minimizes $(\mathbf{y} - X\boldsymbol{\beta})'\boldsymbol{\Psi}(\boldsymbol{\theta})^{-1}(\mathbf{y} - X\boldsymbol{\beta})$. Also, for a given estimator $\hat{\boldsymbol{\theta}}$, usually obtained from least squares residuals, the estimated generalized least squares estimator $\hat{\hat{\boldsymbol{\beta}}} = [X'\boldsymbol{\Psi}(\hat{\boldsymbol{\theta}})^{-1}X]^{-1}X'\boldsymbol{\Psi}(\hat{\boldsymbol{\theta}})^{-1}\mathbf{y}$ is that value of $\boldsymbol{\beta}$ that minimizes $(\mathbf{y} - X\boldsymbol{\beta})'\boldsymbol{\Psi}(\hat{\boldsymbol{\theta}})^{-1}(\mathbf{y} - X\boldsymbol{\beta})$. The nonlinear least squares estimator for $(\boldsymbol{\beta}, \boldsymbol{\theta})$ is given by those values of $\boldsymbol{\beta}$ *and* $\boldsymbol{\theta}$ that simultaneously minimize

$$S(\boldsymbol{\beta}, \boldsymbol{\theta}) = (\mathbf{y} - X\boldsymbol{\beta})'\boldsymbol{\Psi}(\boldsymbol{\theta})^{-1}(\mathbf{y} - X\boldsymbol{\beta}) \tag{12.3.4}$$

To relate this problem to the framework introduced in Section 12.2, we begin by defining a matrix P to be such that $P'P = \boldsymbol{\Psi}(\boldsymbol{\theta})^{-1}$. Such a matrix will, of course, be a function of $\boldsymbol{\theta}$, but we will simply write P rather than $P(\boldsymbol{\theta})$ so as not to overly complicate the notation. Substituting $P'P$ into (12.3.4), we obtain

$$\begin{aligned} S(\boldsymbol{\beta}, \boldsymbol{\theta}) &= (\mathbf{y} - X\boldsymbol{\beta})'P'P(\mathbf{y} - X\boldsymbol{\beta}) \\ &= (P\mathbf{y} - PX\boldsymbol{\beta})'(P\mathbf{y} - PX\boldsymbol{\beta}) \\ &= (\mathbf{y}^* - X^*\boldsymbol{\beta})'(\mathbf{y}^* - X^*\boldsymbol{\beta}) \\ &= \mathbf{e}^{*\prime}\mathbf{e}^* \end{aligned} \tag{12.3.5}$$

where $\mathbf{y}^* = P\mathbf{y}$, $X^* = PX$, and $\mathbf{e}^* = P\mathbf{e}$. Note that both $\mathbf{y}^*$ and X^* will be functions of $\boldsymbol{\theta}$, and that $\mathbf{e}^*$ has the properties $E[\mathbf{e}^*] = \mathbf{0}$ and $E[\mathbf{e}^*\mathbf{e}^{*\prime}] = \sigma^2 I$. We are therefore concerned with nonlinear least squares estimation of $\boldsymbol{\beta}$ and $\boldsymbol{\theta}$ in the model

$$\mathbf{y}^* = X^*\boldsymbol{\beta} + \mathbf{e}^* \tag{12.3.6}$$

A general way of writing (12.3.6) is

$$\mathbf{f}(\mathbf{y}, X, \boldsymbol{\beta}, \boldsymbol{\theta}) = \mathbf{e}^* \tag{12.3.7}$$

The dependence of $\mathbf{y}^*$ and X^* on $\boldsymbol{\theta}$ means that $\boldsymbol{\beta}$ and $\boldsymbol{\theta}$ enter (12.3.6) in a nonlinear way. Also, it prevents us from writing (12.3.7) in the form $\mathbf{y} = \mathbf{f}(X, \boldsymbol{\beta}, \boldsymbol{\theta}) + \mathbf{e}^*$, which is more in line with the model considered in Section 12.2. Despite these differences, the principles of nonlinear least squares estimation outlined in Section 12.2 still hold. The Gauss–Newton and Newton–Raphson algorithms can still be applied to (12.3.7), but the alternative definition of the function $\mathbf{f}$ should be kept in mind at all times.

Because the estimator for $\boldsymbol{\beta}$ that minimizes (12.3.4) for a given $\boldsymbol{\theta}$ is the familiar generalized least squares estimator

$$\hat{\boldsymbol{\beta}}(\boldsymbol{\theta}) = [X'\boldsymbol{\Psi}(\boldsymbol{\theta})^{-1}X]^{-1}X'\boldsymbol{\Psi}(\boldsymbol{\theta})^{-1}\mathbf{y} \tag{12.3.8}$$

it is possible, and sometimes useful, to concentrate on the sum of squares function so that it is only a function of $\boldsymbol{\theta}$. This concentrated sum of squares function is

$$S^*(\boldsymbol{\theta}) = [\mathbf{y} - X\hat{\boldsymbol{\beta}}(\boldsymbol{\theta})]'\boldsymbol{\Psi}(\boldsymbol{\theta})^{-1}[\mathbf{y} - X\hat{\boldsymbol{\beta}}(\boldsymbol{\theta})] \tag{12.3.9}$$

One way of approaching nonlinear least squares estimation is to find that value of $\boldsymbol{\theta}$ that minimizes (12.3.9) and to then substitute that value into (12.3.8).

12.3.1b Maximum Likelihood Estimation

If, in addition to the model specification in (12.3.1) and (12.3.2), we assume that $\mathbf{e}$ and hence $\mathbf{y}$ are both normally distributed, the log-likelihood function for $(\boldsymbol{\beta}, \boldsymbol{\theta}, \sigma^2)$ can be written as (see Section 8.2 of Chapter 8)

$$\begin{aligned} L(\boldsymbol{\beta}, \boldsymbol{\theta}, \sigma^2 | \mathbf{y}, X) = & -\frac{T}{2}\ln(2\pi) - \frac{T}{2}\ln\sigma^2 - \frac{1}{2}\ln|\boldsymbol{\Psi}(\boldsymbol{\theta})| \\ & - \frac{1}{2\sigma^2}(\mathbf{y} - X\boldsymbol{\beta})'\boldsymbol{\Psi}(\boldsymbol{\theta})^{-1}(\mathbf{y} - X\boldsymbol{\beta}) \end{aligned} \tag{12.3.10}$$

From (8.2.5) and (8.2.6), maximization of L with respect to $\boldsymbol{\beta}$ and σ^2, conditional on $\boldsymbol{\theta}$, yields

$$\tilde{\boldsymbol{\beta}}(\boldsymbol{\theta}) = [X'\boldsymbol{\Psi}(\boldsymbol{\theta})^{-1}X]^{-1}X'\boldsymbol{\Psi}(\boldsymbol{\theta})^{-1}\mathbf{y} \tag{12.3.11}$$

and

$$\tilde{\sigma}^2(\boldsymbol{\theta}) = \frac{[\mathbf{y} - X\tilde{\boldsymbol{\beta}}(\boldsymbol{\theta})]'\boldsymbol{\Psi}(\boldsymbol{\theta})^{-1}[\mathbf{y} - X\tilde{\boldsymbol{\beta}}(\boldsymbol{\theta})]}{T} \tag{12.3.12}$$

Substituting (12.3.11) and (12.3.12) back into (12.3.10) and ignoring constants yields the concentrated log-likelihood function

$$L(\boldsymbol{\theta}) = -T\ln\{[\mathbf{y} - X\tilde{\boldsymbol{\beta}}(\boldsymbol{\theta})]'\boldsymbol{\Psi}(\boldsymbol{\theta})^{-1}[\mathbf{y} - X\tilde{\boldsymbol{\beta}}(\boldsymbol{\theta})]\} - \ln|\boldsymbol{\Psi}(\boldsymbol{\theta})| \tag{12.3.13}$$

The maximum likelihood estimator for $\boldsymbol{\theta}$, say $\tilde{\boldsymbol{\theta}}$, is that value of $\boldsymbol{\theta}$ for which $L(\boldsymbol{\theta})$ is a maximum, or, equivalently, that value of $\boldsymbol{\theta}$ for which

$$S(\boldsymbol{\theta}) = |\boldsymbol{\Psi}(\boldsymbol{\theta})|^{1/T}[\mathbf{y} - X\tilde{\boldsymbol{\beta}}(\boldsymbol{\theta})]'\boldsymbol{\Psi}(\boldsymbol{\theta})^{-1}[\mathbf{y} - X\tilde{\boldsymbol{\beta}}(\boldsymbol{\theta})] \tag{12.3.14}$$

is a minimum. Derivation of (12.3.13) and a proof that maximizing $L(\boldsymbol{\theta})$ is equivalent to minimizing $S(\boldsymbol{\theta})$, are left as problems (see Exercise 12.2). If we define $\tilde{\boldsymbol{\Psi}} = \boldsymbol{\Psi}(\tilde{\boldsymbol{\theta}})$, then the maximum likelihood estimators for $\boldsymbol{\beta}$ and σ^2 (not conditional on $\boldsymbol{\theta}$) are given by

$$\tilde{\boldsymbol{\beta}} = \tilde{\boldsymbol{\beta}}(\tilde{\boldsymbol{\theta}}) = (X'\tilde{\boldsymbol{\Psi}}^{-1}X)^{-1}X'\tilde{\boldsymbol{\Psi}}^{-1}\mathbf{y} \tag{12.3.15}$$

and

$$\tilde{\sigma}^2 = \tilde{\sigma}^2(\tilde{\boldsymbol{\theta}}) = \frac{(\mathbf{y} - X\tilde{\boldsymbol{\beta}})'\tilde{\Psi}^{-1}(\mathbf{y} - X\tilde{\boldsymbol{\beta}})}{T} \tag{12.3.16}$$

A comparison of $S(\boldsymbol{\theta})$ in (12.3.14) with $S^*(\boldsymbol{\theta})$ in (12.3.9) indicates that any difference between maximum likelihood and nonlinear least squares estimates can be attributed to the term $|\Psi(\boldsymbol{\theta})|^{1/T}$. If this term was equal to 1, the two estimators would be identical. Also, if $|\Psi(\boldsymbol{\theta})|$ does not depend on T, then as $T \to \infty$, $|\Psi(\boldsymbol{\theta})|^{1/T} \to 1$, and so, for large sample size, there should be little difference between the two estimators.

Let $\boldsymbol{\gamma}' = (\boldsymbol{\beta}', \sigma^2, \boldsymbol{\theta}')$ and $\tilde{\boldsymbol{\gamma}}' = (\tilde{\boldsymbol{\beta}}', \sigma^2, \tilde{\boldsymbol{\theta}}')$. Under appropriate regularity conditions,

$$\sqrt{T}(\tilde{\boldsymbol{\gamma}} - \boldsymbol{\gamma}) \xrightarrow{d} N\left[\mathbf{0}, \lim\left(\frac{I(\boldsymbol{\gamma})}{T}\right)^{-1}\right] \tag{12.3.17}$$

where $I(\boldsymbol{\gamma})$ is the information matrix $-E[\partial^2 L/\partial\boldsymbol{\gamma}\partial\boldsymbol{\gamma}']$. A general expression for $I(\boldsymbol{\gamma})$ is given by Judge, et al. (1985, p. 182). We will consider some special cases in the next two sections. Maximum likelihood estimators can be found using a number of algorithms, including those discussed in Section 12.2.5. Also, any of the covariance matrix estimators (estimators for $[I(\boldsymbol{\gamma})]^{-1}$) discussed in that section can be employed.

12.3.1c Bayesian Estimation

For Bayesian estimation of the model in (12.3.1) and (12.3.2) we retain the assumption of normally distributed disturbances and begin by specifying a prior density function for $(\boldsymbol{\beta}', \sigma, \boldsymbol{\theta}')$. The case we will consider is a noninformative prior for $\boldsymbol{\beta}$ and σ of the form $g(\boldsymbol{\beta}, \sigma) \propto \sigma^{-1}$, and an unspecified but independent prior on $\boldsymbol{\theta}$, namely $g(\boldsymbol{\theta})$. The prior $g(\boldsymbol{\beta}, \sigma) \propto \sigma^{-1}$ was used in conjunction with the general linear model with independent, identically distributed normal random errors in Section 7.7.4. The general prior $g(\boldsymbol{\theta})$ will be made more specific when we consider autocorrelation and heteroskedasticity. Thus we have, for the joint prior p.d.f.,

$$g(\boldsymbol{\beta}, \sigma, \boldsymbol{\theta}) = g(\boldsymbol{\beta})g(\sigma)g(\boldsymbol{\theta}) \propto \frac{g(\boldsymbol{\theta})}{\sigma} \tag{12.3.18}$$

The likelihood function for the model can be written as

$$\begin{aligned} \ell(\boldsymbol{\beta}, \sigma, \boldsymbol{\theta} | \mathbf{y}) &\propto \sigma^{-T}|\Psi|^{-1/2} \exp\left\{-\frac{1}{2\sigma^2}(\mathbf{y} - X\boldsymbol{\beta})'\Psi^{-1}(\mathbf{y} - X\boldsymbol{\beta})\right\} \\ &= \sigma^{-T}|\Psi|^{-1/2} \exp\left\{-\frac{1}{2\sigma^2}[\nu\hat{\sigma}^2 + (\boldsymbol{\beta} - \hat{\boldsymbol{\beta}})'X'\Psi^{-1}X(\boldsymbol{\beta} - \hat{\boldsymbol{\beta}})]\right\} \end{aligned} \tag{12.3.19}$$

where

$$\hat{\boldsymbol{\beta}} = (X'\boldsymbol{\Psi}^{-1}X)^{-1}X'\boldsymbol{\Psi}^{-1}\mathbf{y}$$

is the generalized least squares estimator for $\boldsymbol{\beta}$,

$$v\hat{\sigma}^2 = (\mathbf{y} - X\hat{\boldsymbol{\beta}})'\boldsymbol{\Psi}^{-1}(\mathbf{y} - X\hat{\boldsymbol{\beta}})$$

is the weighted residual sum of squares from the generalized least squares estimator, and

$$v = T - K$$

is the number of degrees of freedom.

The last line in (12.3.19) is derived along similar lines to the derivation of (7.7.34), the only difference being that $\mathbf{y}$ and X are replaced by their transformed counterparts $\mathbf{y}^* = P\mathbf{y}$ and $X^* = PX$, where P is such that $P'P = \boldsymbol{\Psi}^{-1}$. Note that $\hat{\boldsymbol{\beta}}$, $\hat{\sigma}^2$, and $\boldsymbol{\Psi}$ are all functions of $\boldsymbol{\theta}$.

Using Bayes' theorem to combine the prior density in (12.3.18) with the likelihood function in (12.3.19) yields the joint posterior p.d.f.

$$g(\boldsymbol{\beta}, \sigma, \boldsymbol{\theta}|\mathbf{y}) \propto g(\boldsymbol{\theta})\sigma^{-(T+1)}|\boldsymbol{\Psi}|^{-1/2} \exp\left\{-\frac{1}{2\sigma^2}[v\hat{\sigma}^2 + (\boldsymbol{\beta} - \hat{\boldsymbol{\beta}})'X'\boldsymbol{\Psi}^{-1}X(\boldsymbol{\beta} - \hat{\boldsymbol{\beta}})]\right\} \tag{12.3.20}$$

To summarize our information about any of the elements in $\boldsymbol{\beta}$, about σ, or about any of the elements in $\boldsymbol{\theta}$, it is customary to obtain relevant marginal posterior density functions by integrating the unwanted parameters out of the joint posterior in (12.3.20). If we attempt to head in this direction, we find that it is possible to integrate out $\boldsymbol{\beta}$ and σ and to obtain any of the posteriors $g(\boldsymbol{\beta}, \boldsymbol{\theta}|\mathbf{y})$, $g(\sigma, \boldsymbol{\theta}|\mathbf{y})$ and $g(\boldsymbol{\theta}|\mathbf{y})$. However, it is not generally possible to analytically integrate out $\boldsymbol{\theta}$ to obtain expressions for $g(\boldsymbol{\beta}|\mathbf{y})$ or $g(\sigma|\mathbf{y})$. In these cases numerical integration needs to be used.

To integrate out σ from (12.3.20) we use properties of the gamma function as outlined in Section 4.4.3 of Chapter 4. The result is

$$\begin{aligned} g(\boldsymbol{\beta}, \boldsymbol{\theta}|\mathbf{y}) &= \int_0^\infty g(\boldsymbol{\beta}, \sigma, \boldsymbol{\theta}|\mathbf{y})\, d\sigma \\ &\propto g(\boldsymbol{\theta})|\boldsymbol{\Psi}|^{-1/2}[v\hat{\sigma}^2 + (\boldsymbol{\beta} - \hat{\boldsymbol{\beta}})'X'\boldsymbol{\Psi}^{-1}X(\boldsymbol{\beta} - \hat{\boldsymbol{\beta}})]^{-T/2} \\ &= g(\boldsymbol{\theta})|\boldsymbol{\Psi}|^{-1/2}(v\hat{\sigma}^2)^{-T/2}\left[1 + \frac{(\boldsymbol{\beta} - \hat{\boldsymbol{\beta}})'X'\boldsymbol{\Psi}^{-1}X(\boldsymbol{\beta} - \hat{\boldsymbol{\beta}})}{v\hat{\sigma}^2}\right]^{-(v+K)/2} \end{aligned} \tag{12.3.21}$$

To integrate $\boldsymbol{\beta}$ out of (12.3.21), properties of the multivariate t-distribution (see Section 7.7.3a) are used. The result is

$$g(\boldsymbol{\theta}|\mathbf{y}) \propto g(\boldsymbol{\theta})|\Psi|^{-1/2}(v\hat{\sigma}^2)^{-v/2}|X'\Psi^{-1}X|^{-1/2} \tag{12.3.22}$$

This density function is not a commonly recognized one that can be analyzed analytically. To obtain its normalizing constant, its moments, or posterior probabilities about $\boldsymbol{\theta}$, numerical methods need to be employed. Finally, if interest centers on one of the elements in $\boldsymbol{\beta}$, say β_k, then it is convenient to obtain information about β_k by numerically analyzing $g(\beta_k, \boldsymbol{\theta}|\mathbf{y})$. This posterior p.d.f. is obtained by integrating the remaining $(K-1)$ elements in $\boldsymbol{\beta}$ out of (12.3.21). Again, properties of the multivariate-t density need to be used, and the result is

$$g(\beta_k, \boldsymbol{\theta}|\mathbf{y}) \propto g(\boldsymbol{\theta})|\Psi|^{-1/2}(v\hat{\sigma}^2)^{-(v+1)/2}|X'\Psi^{-1}X|^{-1/2}c_{kk}^{-1/2} \cdot\left[1 + \frac{(\beta_k - \hat{\beta}_k)^2}{c_{kk}v\hat{\sigma}^2}\right]^{-(v+1)/2} \tag{12.3.23}$$

where c_{kk} is the kth diagonal element of $(X'\Psi^{-1}X)^{-1}$. An example of how $g(\boldsymbol{\theta}|\mathbf{y})$ and $g(\beta_k, \boldsymbol{\theta}|\mathbf{y})$ can be analyzed numerically is given in the next section.

12.3.2 First-Order Autoregressive Errors

In this section we return to the model studied in Section 9.5, namely, the AR(1) error model whose tth observation is defined by

$$y_t = \mathbf{x}_t'\boldsymbol{\beta} + e_t \tag{12.3.24}$$

$$e_t = \rho e_{t-1} + v_t \tag{12.3.25}$$

where the v_t, $t = 1, 2, \ldots, T$ are independent and identically distributed random variables with 0 mean and constant variance σ_v^2. We will consider nonlinear least squares, maximum likelihood, and Bayesian estimation of $\boldsymbol{\beta}$ and ρ. You should review Sections 9.5.1 and 9.5.2 to ensure that you are familiar with the basic characteristics of the model that will not be repeated here.

12.3.2a Nonlinear Least Squares Estimation

To obtain nonlinear least squares estimates for $\boldsymbol{\beta}$ and ρ, we begin by writing (12.3.5) in the context of the AR(1) error model; that is,

$$\begin{aligned} S(\boldsymbol{\beta}, \rho) &= (\mathbf{y} - X\boldsymbol{\beta})'\Psi(\rho)^{-1}(\mathbf{y} - X\boldsymbol{\beta}) \\ &= \mathbf{e}^{*\prime}\mathbf{e}^{*} \\ &= (1-\rho^2)(y_1 - \mathbf{x}_1'\boldsymbol{\beta})^2 + \sum_{t=2}^{T} [y_t - \rho y_{t-1} - (\mathbf{x}_t - \rho\mathbf{x}_{t-1})'\boldsymbol{\beta}]^2 \end{aligned} \tag{12.3.26}$$

where

$$e_1^* = (1 - \rho^2)^{1/2}(y_1 - \mathbf{x}_1'\boldsymbol{\beta})$$

and

$$e_t^* = (y_t - \rho y_{t-1}) - (\mathbf{x}_t - \rho \mathbf{x}_{t-1})'\boldsymbol{\beta} \qquad t = 2, 3, \ldots, T$$

See (9.5.31) and (9.5.32). Nonlinear least squares estimates for $\boldsymbol{\beta}$ and ρ are those values that jointly minimize (12.3.26).

The most common algorithm used for minimizing (12.3.26) is a modification of one proposed by Cochrane and Orcutt (1949). Cochrane and Orcutt ignored the first term in (12.3.26), or, in other words, discarded the first transformed observation, and hence considered minimization of

$$\sum_{t=2}^{T} e_t^{*2} = \sum_{t=2}^{T} v_t^2 = \sum_{t=2}^{T} [y_t - \rho y_{t-1} - (\mathbf{x}_t - \rho \mathbf{x}_{t-1})'\boldsymbol{\beta}]^2 \qquad (12.3.27)$$

This problem can be viewed as finding nonlinear least squares estimates for $\boldsymbol{\beta}$ and ρ from the model

$$y_t = \rho y_{t-1} + \mathbf{x}_t'\boldsymbol{\beta} - \mathbf{x}_{t-1}'\boldsymbol{\beta}\rho + v_t \qquad t = 2, 3, \ldots, T \qquad (12.3.28)$$

where the nonlinearity arises because of the term $\mathbf{x}_{t-1}'\boldsymbol{\beta}\rho$. The Cochrane-Orcutt algorithm consisted of the following steps:

1. Find the least squares estimator $\mathbf{b} = (X'X)^{-1}X'\mathbf{y}$.

2. Set $\boldsymbol{\beta}$ at $\mathbf{b}$ and use least squares to estimate ρ from the model

$$y_t - \mathbf{x}_t'\mathbf{b} = \rho(y_{t-1} - \mathbf{x}_{t-1}'\mathbf{b}) + \text{error} \qquad (12.3.29)$$

(This yields the estimator $\hat{\rho}$ defined in Equation 9.5.40).

3. Fix ρ at $\hat{\rho}$ and use least squares to estimate $\boldsymbol{\beta}$ from the model

$$y_t - \hat{\rho} y_{t-1} = (\mathbf{x}_t - \hat{\rho}\mathbf{x}_{t-1})'\boldsymbol{\beta} + \text{error} \qquad (12.3.30)$$

4. Return to step 2 and (12.3.29) to re-estimate ρ, but with $\mathbf{b}$ replaced by the new estimate for $\boldsymbol{\beta}$.

5. Re-estimate $\boldsymbol{\beta}$ from (12.3.30), and continue until convergence.

Although there is no difference asymptotically, this procedure can be considerably less efficient in finite samples than one that retains the initial transformed observation. Thus, modifications to the Cochrane-Orcutt procedure that minimize the complete sum-of-squares function in (12.3.26) have been suggested, and these modifications are preferred.

As with most nonlinear least squares algorithms, a modified Cochrane-Orcutt procedure can converge to either a local or the global minimum. Another alternative that is computationally more expensive, but that is more likely to yield the global minimum, is to evaluate the concentrated sum-of-squares function in (12.3.9) for a large number of values of ρ in the interval $(-1, +1)$, and to pick that

ρ for which $S^*(\rho)$ is a minimum. This search procedure is usually carried out in two steps. In the first step, the neighborhood of the minimum is located by taking values of ρ at fairly wide intervals, for example, 0.05; in the second step the values of ρ are restricted to this neighborhood and taken at increments sufficiently small to achieve the desired degree of accuracy.

The asymptotic properties of the nonlinear least squares estimator for $(\boldsymbol{\beta}, \rho)$ are identical to those of the maximum likelihood estimator to which we now turn.

12.3.2b Maximum Likelihood Estimation

Under the assumption of normally distributed error terms, the maximum likelihood estimators for $\boldsymbol{\beta}$ and ρ are those values that minimize

$$\begin{aligned} S_L(\boldsymbol{\beta}, \rho) &= |\boldsymbol{\Psi}|^{1/T}(\mathbf{y} - X\boldsymbol{\beta})'\boldsymbol{\Psi}^{-1}(\mathbf{y} - X\boldsymbol{\beta}) \\ &= |\boldsymbol{\Psi}|^{1/T}\mathbf{e}^{*\prime}\mathbf{e}^* \end{aligned} \tag{12.3.31}$$

This expression is similar to that derived in (12.3.14), the difference being that, in (12.3.31), only σ_v^2 (not both $\boldsymbol{\beta}$ and σ_v^2) has been concentrated out. Replacing $\tilde{\boldsymbol{\beta}}$ by $\boldsymbol{\beta}$ in the derivation of (12.3.14) makes no essential difference.

Evaluating $|\boldsymbol{\Psi}|^{1/T}$ yields

$$|\boldsymbol{\Psi}|^{1/T} = |\boldsymbol{\Psi}^{-1}|^{-1/T} = |P|^{-2/T} = [(1 - \rho^2)^{1/2}]^{-2/T} = (1 - \rho^2)^{-1/T} \tag{12.3.32}$$

Thus, $S_L(\boldsymbol{\beta}, \rho)$ becomes

$$S_L(\boldsymbol{\beta}, \rho) = (1 - \rho^2)^{-1/T}\mathbf{e}^{*\prime}\mathbf{e}^* \tag{12.3.33}$$

Except for the term $(1 - \rho^2)^{-1/T}$, maximum likelihood and nonlinear least squares estimators for $\boldsymbol{\beta}$ and ρ are identical. The contribution of this term is greatest when T is small and $|\rho|$ is close to 1; if T is large and $|\rho|$ not too close to 1, its effect will be negligible.

If we define $\mathbf{e}^{**} = \mathbf{e}^*/(1 - \rho^2)^{1/2T}$, then any nonlinear least squares algorithm designed to minimize $\mathbf{e}^{*\prime}\mathbf{e}^*$ can be converted to a maximum likelihood algorithm by minimizing $\mathbf{e}^{**\prime}\mathbf{e}^{**}$. Specific algorithms that have appeared in the literature are those of Hildreth and Dent (1974) and Beach and MacKinnon (1978).

Turning to the asymptotic covariance matrix for the maximum likelihood and nonlinear least squares estimators, it can be shown that

$$\lim_{T\to\infty}\left(\frac{I(\boldsymbol{\beta}', \rho, \sigma_v^2)}{T}\right) = \begin{bmatrix} \lim \dfrac{X'\boldsymbol{\Psi}^{-1}X}{T\sigma_v^2} & \mathbf{0} & \mathbf{0} \\ \mathbf{0}' & \dfrac{1}{1-\rho^2} & 0 \\ \mathbf{0}' & 0 & \dfrac{1}{2\sigma_v^4} \end{bmatrix} \tag{12.3.34}$$

where $I(\boldsymbol{\beta}', \rho, \sigma_v^2)$ is the information matrix. Thus, approximate covariance and variance estimators are given by

$$\hat{\Sigma}_{\tilde{\boldsymbol{\beta}}} = \tilde{\sigma}_v^2(X'\tilde{\Psi}^{-1}X)^{-1} \tag{12.3.35}$$

$$\widehat{\text{var}}(\tilde{\rho}) = \frac{1 - \tilde{\rho}^2}{T} \tag{12.3.36}$$

and

$$\widehat{\text{var}}(\tilde{\sigma}_v^2) = \frac{2\tilde{\sigma}_v^4}{T} \tag{12.3.37}$$

The result in (12.3.36) was the basis for the asymptotic test statistic given in (9.5.43).

The example considered in Section 9.5.6, namely,

$$\mathbf{y} = \mathbf{x}_1\beta_1 + \mathbf{x}_2\beta_2 + \mathbf{x}_3\beta_3 + \mathbf{e} \tag{12.3.38}$$

was re-estimated using the same set of data (Table 9.2), but employing the nonlinear least squares and maximum likelihood estimators. The different estimates, and their asymptotic standard errors, are presented in Table 12.5, along with the estimated generalized least squares estimates obtained in Section 9.5.6. In this particular case there is little difference between the three sets of estimates; this outcome is not general, however. There can be substantial differences between the three estimation techniques. Monte Carlo evidence on finite sample properties suggests that ρ will usually be underestimated (in all three cases) and that the maximum likelihood estimator is usually better than the other two in terms of mean square error.

12.3.2c Bayesian Estimation

To make the general Bayesian results in Section 12.3.1c specific to the AR(1) error model we need to specify a prior $g(\rho)$, give an expression for $|\Psi|$, and recognize that

Table 12.5 Alternative Estimates of AR(1) Error Model

	β_1	β_2	β_3	ρ	σ_v^2
NLS: estimates	4.059	1.666	0.756	0.584	7.138
asy. s.e.	(6.461)	(0.308)	(0.154)	(0.182)	(2.257)
ML: estimates	4.055	1.670	0.762	0.559	6.074
asy. s.e.	(5.768)	(0.277)	(0.143)	(0.185)	(1.921)
EGLS: estimates	4.050	1.672	0.759	0.542	7.159
asy. s.e.	(6.129)	(0.295)	(0.156)	(0.188)	(2.264)

ρ replaces $\boldsymbol{\theta}$ in the expression for $v\hat{\sigma}^2$ and $\hat{\boldsymbol{\beta}}$. The prior we will employ is the uniform one

$$g(\rho) = \frac{1}{2} \qquad |\rho| < 1 \tag{12.3.39}$$

which treats all values of ρ between -1 and 1 as equally likely. In (12.3.32) we showed that $|\boldsymbol{\Psi}| = (1 - \rho^2)^{-1}$ and hence that

$$|\boldsymbol{\Psi}|^{-1/2} = (1 - \rho^2)^{1/2} \tag{12.3.40}$$

Thus, when we relate the expressions given in Section 12.3.1c for the various posterior p.d.f.'s to the AR(1) error model, the term $g(\boldsymbol{\theta})$ becomes absorbed into the proportionality constant and $|\boldsymbol{\Psi}|^{-1/2}$ becomes $(1 - \rho^2)^{1/2}$.

As an example of Bayesian analysis we will consider the model and data considered first in Section 9.5.6 and again in the previous section. The posterior p.d.f. for ρ, obtained by suitably modifying (12.3.22) in light of (12.3.40), is given by

$$g(\rho|\mathbf{y}) \propto (1 - \rho^2)^{1/2}(v\hat{\sigma}^2)^{-v/2}|X'\boldsymbol{\Psi}^{-1}X|^{-1/2} \tag{12.3.41}$$

The normalizing constant for this p.d.f. is given by numerically evaluating the integral in square brackets in (12.3.42) and then obtaining its reciprocal,

$$k = \left[\int_{-1}^{1} (1 - \rho^2)^{1/2}(v\hat{\sigma}^2)^{-v/2}|X'\boldsymbol{\Psi}^{-1}X|^{-1/2}d\rho\right]^{-1} \tag{12.3.42}$$

Once this constant has been obtained, the p.d.f. $g(\rho|\mathbf{y})$, which summarizes all our information about ρ, can be graphed (see Fig. 12.5). Other quantities of interest

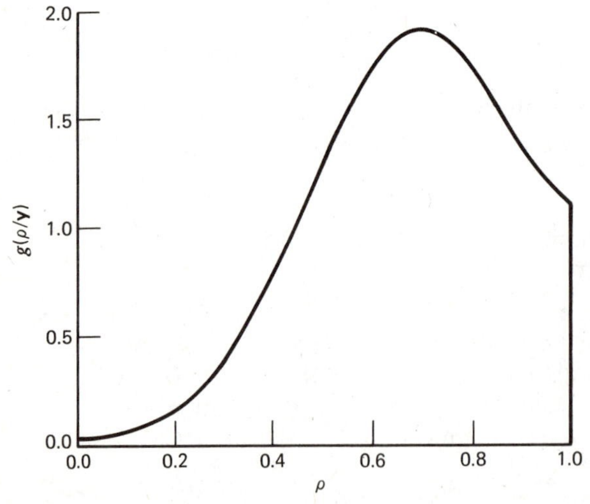

Figure 12.5 Posterior p.d.f. for ρ.

such as the posterior mean and variance of ρ, and the probability that ρ lies in some given interval, can also be obtained numerically. For example, the posterior mean is given by numerically evaluating

$$E[\rho|\mathbf{y}] = \int_{-1}^{1} \rho\, g(\rho|\mathbf{y})\, d\rho$$

$$= k\int_{-1}^{1} \rho(1-\rho^2)^{1/2}(v\hat{\sigma}^2)^{-v/2}|X'\mathbf{\Psi}^{-1}X|^{-1/2} d\rho \tag{12.3.43}$$

Using the data for the example problem, we find that

$$E[\rho|\mathbf{y}] = 0.667 \qquad \text{s.e. } [\rho|\mathbf{y}] = 0.194$$

and

$$P[(0.4 < \rho < 1.0)|\mathbf{y}] = 0.90$$

The point estimate of ρ, taken as the posterior mean, is somewhat higher than the sampling theory estimates given in Table 12.5. The high posterior probability that ρ lies between 0.4 and 1 strongly suggests that autocorrelation exists ($\rho \neq 0$).

To illustrate Bayesian inference about one of the elements in $\boldsymbol{\beta}$, we will use β_2. The joint posterior p.d.f. for β_2 and ρ, obtained by suitably modifying (12.3.23), is given by

$$g(\beta_2, \rho|\mathbf{y}) \propto (1-\rho^2)^{1/2}(v\hat{\sigma}^2)^{-(v+1)/2}|X'\mathbf{\Psi}^{-1}X|^{-1/2}c_{22}^{-1/2}\cdot\left[1 + \frac{(\beta_2 - \hat{\beta}_2)^2}{c_{22}v\hat{\sigma}^2}\right]^{-(v+1)/2} \tag{12.3.44}$$

To obtain the normalizing constant for this p.d.f., and to plot the marginal posterior p.d.f. $g(\beta_2|\mathbf{y})$, bivariate numerical integration is required. Carrying out this integration yields the p.d.f. $g(\beta_2|\mathbf{y})$, which is given in Figure 12.6. The mean and variance of this p.d.f. can, however, be obtained via univariate numerical integration. For example, the posterior mean for β_2 is given by

$$E[\beta_2|\mathbf{y}] = \int_{-1}^{1}\int_{-\infty}^{\infty} \beta_2 g(\beta_2, \rho|\mathbf{y})\, d\beta_2\, d\rho$$

$$= \int_{-1}^{1}\int_{-\infty}^{\infty} \beta_2 g(\beta_2|\rho, \mathbf{y}) g(\rho|\mathbf{y}) d\beta_2\, d\rho$$

$$= \int_{-1}^{1}\left[\int_{-\infty}^{\infty} \beta_2 g(\beta_2|\rho, \mathbf{y})\, d\beta_2\right] g(\rho|\mathbf{y})\, d\rho$$

$$= \int_{-1}^{1} \hat{\beta}_2 g(\rho|\mathbf{y})\, d\rho \tag{12.3.45}$$

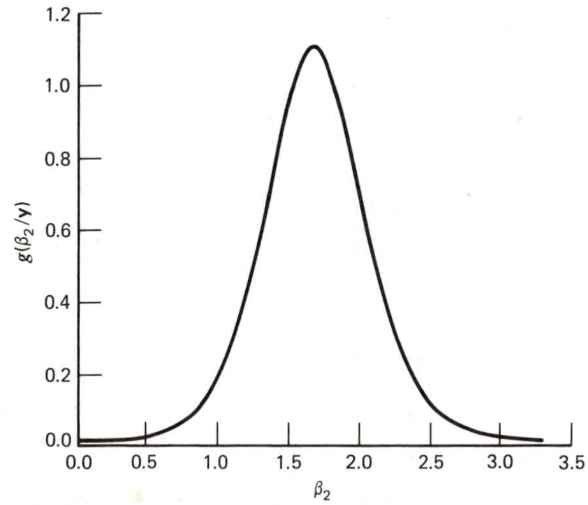

Figure 12.6 Marginal posterior p.d.f. for β_2.

Since the conditional posterior p.d.f. $g(\beta_2|\rho, \mathbf{y})$ is a univariate t-distribution with mean equal to the generalized least squares estimator $\hat{\beta}_2$, the integral in square brackets in (12.3.45) can simply be replaced by $\hat{\beta}_2$. Furthermore, the final result in (12.3.45) has a nice interpretation. It indicates that the Bayesian point estimator for β_2 (with quadratic loss) is a weighted average of all generalized least squares estimators for β_2 with weights given by the marginal posterior p.d.f. for ρ. Since all values of ρ and their associated posterior probabilities are used in the calculation of $E[\beta_2|\mathbf{y}]$, it is a much more satisfying estimator than the estimated generalized least squares, nonlinear least squares, and maximum likelihood estimators that are all just based on one point estimate of ρ. The posterior mean and standard deviation for β_2 in the example are given by

$$E[\beta_2|\mathbf{y}] = 1.691 \qquad \text{and} \qquad \text{s.e. } [\beta_2|\mathbf{y}] = 0.409$$

12.3.3 A Heteroskedastic Error Model

In this section we return to the multiplicative heteroskedastic error model that was studied in Section 9.3.4. It can be written as

$$y_t = \mathbf{x}_t'\boldsymbol{\beta} + e_t \tag{12.3.46}$$

where the e_t are independently distributed with mean $E[e_t] = 0$ and variance

$$E[e_t^2] = \sigma_t^2 = \exp\{\mathbf{z}_t'\boldsymbol{\alpha}\} = \sigma^2 \exp\{\mathbf{z}_t^{*\prime}\boldsymbol{\alpha}^*\} \tag{12.3.47}$$

where $\mathbf{z}_t' = (z_{t1}, \mathbf{z}_t^{*\prime}) = (1, \mathbf{z}_t^{*\prime})$ is a $(1 \times S)$ vector of variables on which the variance of e_t depends, and $\boldsymbol{\alpha}' = (\alpha_1, \boldsymbol{\alpha}^{*\prime}) = (\ln \sigma^2, \boldsymbol{\alpha}^{*\prime})$ is a $(1 \times S)$ vector of unknown coefficients. Our problem is to estimate $\boldsymbol{\beta}$ and $\boldsymbol{\alpha}$, with, usually, more interest centering on $\boldsymbol{\beta}$.

In Chapter 9 a two-step estimated generalized least squares estimator for $\boldsymbol{\beta}$ was considered; least squares residuals were used to estimate $\boldsymbol{\alpha}$, and the resulting estimator was used to form the estimated generalized least squares estimator $\hat{\hat{\boldsymbol{\beta}}} = (X'\hat{\boldsymbol{\Psi}}^{-1}X)^{-1}X'\hat{\boldsymbol{\Psi}}^{-1}\mathbf{y}$. For the relationship between $\boldsymbol{\Psi}$, $\boldsymbol{\alpha}$, and $\boldsymbol{\alpha}^*$, see (9.3.36). The nonlinear least squares, maximum likelihood, and Bayesian methods for estimation, which are the concern of this chapter, can also be applied to the multiplicative heteroskedastic error model. In this section we concentrate on maximum likelihood estimation, using results obtained by Harvey (1976); nonlinear and Bayesian estimation can proceed along the lines described in Section 12.3.1. See Surekha and Griffiths (1984) for an example of Bayesian estimation.

Let $E[\mathbf{ee}'] = \boldsymbol{\Phi}$ where $\boldsymbol{\Phi}$ is a diagonal matrix with tth diagonal element equal to $\sigma_t^2 = \exp\{\mathbf{z}_t'\boldsymbol{\alpha}\}$. Assuming $\mathbf{e}$ follows a multivariate normal distribution, the log-likelihood function for $(\boldsymbol{\beta}', \boldsymbol{\alpha}')$ can be written as

$$\begin{aligned} L(\boldsymbol{\beta}, \boldsymbol{\alpha} | \mathbf{y}, X, Z) &= -\frac{T}{2}\ln 2\pi - \frac{1}{2}\ln|\boldsymbol{\Phi}| - \frac{1}{2}(\mathbf{y} - X\boldsymbol{\beta})'\boldsymbol{\Phi}^{-1}(\mathbf{y} - X\boldsymbol{\beta}) \\ &= -\frac{T}{2}\ln 2\pi - \frac{1}{2}\sum_{t=1}^{T} \mathbf{z}_t'\boldsymbol{\alpha} - \frac{1}{2}\sum_{t=1}^{T} \exp\{-\mathbf{z}_t'\boldsymbol{\alpha}\}(y_t - \mathbf{x}_t'\boldsymbol{\beta})^2 \end{aligned} \tag{12.3.48}$$

A convenient algorithm for maximizing this likelihood function is the method of scoring. To set up this algorithm we need the information matrix, which can be derived (see Exercise 12.5) as

$$I(\boldsymbol{\beta}', \boldsymbol{\alpha}') = -E\begin{bmatrix} \dfrac{\partial^2 L}{\partial\boldsymbol{\beta}\partial\boldsymbol{\beta}'} & \dfrac{\partial^2 L}{\partial\boldsymbol{\beta}\partial\boldsymbol{\alpha}'} \\ \dfrac{\partial^2 L}{\partial\boldsymbol{\alpha}\partial\boldsymbol{\beta}'} & \dfrac{\partial^2 L}{\partial\boldsymbol{\alpha}\partial\boldsymbol{\alpha}'} \end{bmatrix} = \begin{bmatrix} X'\boldsymbol{\Phi}^{-1}X & 0 \\ 0 & \frac{1}{2}Z'Z \end{bmatrix} \tag{12.3.49}$$

where Z is the $(T \times S)$ matrix containing the vectors $\mathbf{z}_t'$, $t = 1, 2, \ldots, T$.

Before proceeding to the iterative process defined by the method of scoring, it is convenient to use (12.3.49) to examine the asymptotic covariance matrices for the maximum likelihood estimators $\tilde{\boldsymbol{\beta}}$ and $\tilde{\boldsymbol{\alpha}}$. We see that

$$\Sigma_{\tilde{\boldsymbol{\beta}}} = (X'\boldsymbol{\Phi}^{-1}X)^{-1} \quad \text{and} \quad \Sigma_{\tilde{\boldsymbol{\alpha}}} = 2(Z'Z)^{-1} \tag{12.3.50}$$

In Chapter 9 we found that the estimated generalized least squares estimator for $\boldsymbol{\beta}$ has an asymptotic covariance matrix equal to $(X'\boldsymbol{\Phi}^{-1}X)^{-1}$, and that the estimator for $\boldsymbol{\alpha}$ based on least squares residuals has an asymptotic covariance matrix of $4.9348(Z'Z)^{-1}$. Comparing these results with those in (12.3.50) indicates that the estimated generalized least squares estimator for $\boldsymbol{\beta}$ is asymptotically efficient, but that the estimator for $\boldsymbol{\alpha}$ that is based on least squares residuals is inefficient relative to its maximum likelihood counterpart.

Because the information matrix is block diagonal, the iterations for the method of scoring for $\boldsymbol{\beta}$ and $\boldsymbol{\alpha}$ can be considered separately. For $\boldsymbol{\beta}$ we have

$$\begin{aligned}
\boldsymbol{\beta}_{n+1} &= \boldsymbol{\beta}_n - \left[E \frac{\partial^2 L}{\partial \boldsymbol{\beta} \partial \boldsymbol{\beta}'}\bigg|_{\boldsymbol{\beta}_n, \boldsymbol{\alpha}_n} \right]^{-1} \frac{\partial L}{\partial \boldsymbol{\beta}}\bigg|_{\boldsymbol{\beta}_n, \boldsymbol{\alpha}_n} \\
&= \boldsymbol{\beta}_n + (X'\boldsymbol{\Phi}^{-1}X)^{-1}\big|_{\boldsymbol{\alpha}_n} X'\boldsymbol{\Phi}^{-1}(\mathbf{y} - X\boldsymbol{\beta}_n)\Big|_{\boldsymbol{\alpha}_n} \\
&= \boldsymbol{\beta}_n + \left[\sum_{t=1}^{T} \exp\{-\mathbf{z}_t'\boldsymbol{\alpha}_n\}\mathbf{x}_t\mathbf{x}_t' \right]^{-1} \sum_{t=1}^{T} \mathbf{x}_t \exp\{-\mathbf{z}_t'\boldsymbol{\alpha}_n\}(y_t - \mathbf{x}_t'\boldsymbol{\beta}_n)
\end{aligned} \tag{12.3.51}$$

and for $\boldsymbol{\alpha}$,

$$\begin{aligned}
\boldsymbol{\alpha}_{n+1} &= \boldsymbol{\alpha}_n - \left[E \frac{\partial^2 L}{\partial \boldsymbol{\alpha} \partial \boldsymbol{\alpha}'}\bigg|_{\boldsymbol{\beta}_n, \boldsymbol{\alpha}_n} \right]^{-1} \frac{\partial L}{\partial \boldsymbol{\alpha}}\bigg|_{\boldsymbol{\beta}_n, \boldsymbol{\alpha}_n} \\
&= \boldsymbol{\alpha}_n + \left[\sum_{t=1}^{T} \mathbf{z}_t\mathbf{z}_t' \right]^{-1} \sum_{t=1}^{T} \mathbf{z}_t[\exp\{-\mathbf{z}_t'\boldsymbol{\alpha}_n\}(y_t - \mathbf{x}_t'\boldsymbol{\beta}_n)^2 - 1]
\end{aligned} \tag{12.3.52}$$

Providing a global maximum has been reached, maximum likelihood estimates $\tilde{\boldsymbol{\beta}}$ and $\tilde{\boldsymbol{\alpha}}$ are found by repeated application of (12.3.51) and (12.3.52), after beginning with two starting vectors $\boldsymbol{\beta}_1$ and $\boldsymbol{\alpha}_1$.

As an example, (12.3.51) and (12.3.52) were applied to the set of data in Table 9.1, using $\hat{\hat{\boldsymbol{\beta}}}' = (1.010, 1.657, 0.896)$ and $\bar{\boldsymbol{\alpha}}' = (-4.376, 0.366)$ as starting values. The estimator $\hat{\hat{\boldsymbol{\beta}}}$ is the estimated generalized least squares one given in (9.3.65). The estimator $\bar{\boldsymbol{\alpha}}$ is given by $\hat{\boldsymbol{\alpha}}$ in (9.3.64), with the first element adjusted so as to yield a consistent estimator. The resulting iterations are given in Table 12.6, with the final set of estimates given by

$$\tilde{\boldsymbol{\beta}}' = (0.910, 1.603, 0.951) \qquad \tilde{\boldsymbol{\alpha}}' = (-1.195, 0.217)$$

The maximum likelihood estimate for $\boldsymbol{\beta}$ is similar to that obtained using estimated generalized least squares, but the estimate for $\boldsymbol{\alpha}$ has changed considerably.

Table 12.6 Iterations of the Method of Scoring

Iteration	β_1	β_2	β_3	α_1	α_2
1	1.01000	1.65700	0.89600	−4.37600	0.36600
2	1.01098	1.65695	0.89603	−1.19312	0.22393
3	0.91555	1.60448	0.94958	−1.23884	0.21995
4	0.91231	1.60355	0.95063	−1.20386	0.21776
5	0.91032	1.60305	0.95120	−1.19637	0.21740
6	0.90998	1.60297	0.95129	−1.19504	0.21734
7	0.90992	1.60296	0.95131	−1.19481	0.21733
8	0.90991	1.60295	0.95131	−1.19477	0.21732
9	0.90991	1.60295	0.95131	−1.19477	0.21732

12.3.4 Wald, Lagrange Multiplier, and Likelihood Ratio Tests

In Chapter 6 where we considered the general linear model $\mathbf{y} = X\boldsymbol{\beta} + \mathbf{e}$ with an error covariance matrix given by a scalar multiplied by the identity matrix, $E[\mathbf{ee}'] = \sigma^2 I$, an exact finite sample test statistic for testing linear hypotheses of the form $R\boldsymbol{\beta} = \mathbf{r}$ was derived. When we move to more general models such as

$$\mathbf{y} = X\boldsymbol{\beta} + \mathbf{e} \qquad E[\mathbf{e}] = \mathbf{0} \qquad E[\mathbf{ee}'] = \sigma^2\boldsymbol{\Psi}(\boldsymbol{\theta}) \tag{12.3.53}$$

where $\boldsymbol{\theta}$ is unknown, or when we are concerned with nonlinear functions of $\boldsymbol{\beta}$, only asymptotic properties of estimators and test statistics are generally available; also, for any given hypothesis, it is usually possible to construct a number of alternative test statistics, all of which have similar asymptotic properties. Associated with maximum likelihood estimation there are three principles—the Wald, the Lagrange multiplier, and the likelihood ratio principles—all of which can be used to construct a test statistic for testing a particular hypothesis. The resulting three statistics are generally different, but have similar asymptotic properties. They were described in Chapter 3 (Section 3.5.4) for the special case of a "simple" hypothesis of the form $H_0\colon \boldsymbol{\theta} = \boldsymbol{\theta}_0$, where $\boldsymbol{\theta}$ is any vector of parameters and $\boldsymbol{\theta}_0$ is a prespecified value for that vector.

In this section we describe the three test statistics within a more general framework where hypotheses about possible nonlinear functions of parameters are being tested. We do so in the context of the model (12.3.53), assuming that this model and restricted versions of it are estimated by maximum likelihood. However, the same general principles can be applied to other models estimated by maximum likelihood; also, in some cases estimators other than maximum likelihood can be used, providing they have the same properties as the maximum likelihood estimator.

Following Section 12.3.1b, let $\boldsymbol{\gamma}' = (\boldsymbol{\beta}', \sigma^2, \boldsymbol{\theta}')$ and let us consider the Wald, Lagrange multiplier, and likelihood ratio tests for testing

$$H_0: \mathbf{g}(\boldsymbol{\gamma}) = \mathbf{0} \tag{12.3.54}$$

against the alternative

$$H_1: \mathbf{g}(\boldsymbol{\gamma}) \neq \mathbf{0} \tag{12.3.55}$$

where $\mathbf{g}$ is a J-dimensional vector function. That is, we are testing J possibly nonlinear restrictions on the $(K + 1 + H)$ parameter vector $\boldsymbol{\gamma}$.

To introduce the Wald test, we recall, from (12.3.17), that

$$\sqrt{T}(\tilde{\boldsymbol{\gamma}} - \boldsymbol{\gamma}) \xrightarrow{d} N\left[\mathbf{0}, \lim\left(\frac{I(\boldsymbol{\gamma})}{T}\right)^{-1}\right] \tag{12.3.56}$$

where $\tilde{\boldsymbol{\gamma}}$ is the unrestricted (under H_1) maximum likelihood estimator for $\boldsymbol{\gamma}$ and $I(\boldsymbol{\gamma})$ is the information matrix. Then, using a result from asymptotic theory [see, for example, Judge, et al. (1985, p. 160)], it is possible to show that

$$\sqrt{T}[\mathbf{g}(\tilde{\boldsymbol{\gamma}}) - \mathbf{g}(\boldsymbol{\gamma})] \xrightarrow{d} N[\mathbf{0}, \lim\, TF'I(\boldsymbol{\gamma})^{-1}F] \tag{12.3.57}$$

where F is the $[(K + 1 + H) \times J]$ matrix of partial derivatives

$$F = \frac{\partial \mathbf{g}(\boldsymbol{\gamma})'}{\partial \boldsymbol{\gamma}} \tag{12.3.58}$$

Then, assuming $H_0: \mathbf{g}(\boldsymbol{\gamma}) = \mathbf{0}$ is true, it follows that

$$\lambda_W = \mathbf{g}(\tilde{\boldsymbol{\gamma}})'[\tilde{F}'I(\tilde{\boldsymbol{\gamma}})^{-1}\tilde{F}]^{-1}\mathbf{g}(\tilde{\boldsymbol{\gamma}}) \xrightarrow{d} \chi^2_{(J)} \tag{12.3.59}$$

where $\tilde{F}$ is the matrix F evaluated at $\boldsymbol{\gamma} = \tilde{\boldsymbol{\gamma}}$, and $I(\tilde{\boldsymbol{\gamma}})$ is a consistent estimator for $I(\boldsymbol{\gamma})$ based on $\tilde{\boldsymbol{\gamma}}$. As discussed in Sections 3.5.4 and 12.2.5, this consistent estimator could be $I(\boldsymbol{\gamma})$ itself evaluated at $\tilde{\boldsymbol{\gamma}}$, or it could be the negative of the Hessian of the log-likelihood function or the corresponding matrix in the BHHH algorithm. The statistic λ_W, used in conjunction with a critical value from the $\chi^2_{(J)}$-distribution is known as the Wald test.

To give some feel for $\mathbf{g}(\boldsymbol{\gamma})$ and F when a nonlinear restriction is involved, consider the following equation from the partial adjustment model that will be studied in Chapter 17

$$\begin{aligned} y_t &= \alpha_0\delta + \alpha_1\delta x_t + (1 - \delta)y_{t-1} + \delta e_t \\ &= \beta_1 + \beta_2 x_t + \beta_3 y_{t-1} + e_t^* \end{aligned} \tag{12.3.60}$$

Let us assume that y_0 is known and fixed and that the e_t^* are i.i.d. $N(0, \sigma^2)$. Assuming that y_0 is nonstochastic has the effect of making the maximum likelihood estimator for $\boldsymbol{\beta}' = (\beta_1, \beta_2, \beta_3)$ equal to the least squares estimator $\mathbf{b}' = (b_1, b_2, b_3)$. We have not yet given explicit consideration to models that contain a lagged value of the dependent variable. However, under appropriate additional assumptions, it can be shown that a consistent estimator of the information matrix is given by

$$I(\tilde{\boldsymbol{\gamma}}) = \begin{bmatrix} \dfrac{X'X}{\tilde{\sigma}^2} & \mathbf{0} \\ \mathbf{0}' & \dfrac{T}{2\tilde{\sigma}^4} \end{bmatrix} \tag{12.3.61}$$

where $\tilde{\boldsymbol{\gamma}}' = (\tilde{\boldsymbol{\beta}}', \tilde{\sigma}^2)$, and the three columns in X are a column of ones, a column of the x_t's, and a column containing lagged values of the dependent variable.

Let us consider the hypothesis

$$H_0\colon \alpha_1 = \frac{\beta_2}{1 - \beta_3} = 1 \tag{12.3.62}$$

In terms of the general hypothesis $\mathbf{g}(\boldsymbol{\gamma}) = \mathbf{0}$ given in (12.3.54), in this case $\mathbf{g}$ is only one-dimensional and we have

$$H_0\colon g(\boldsymbol{\gamma}) = \frac{\beta_2}{1 - \beta_3} - 1 = 0 \tag{12.3.63}$$

The matrix F becomes a vector, say $\mathbf{f}$, whose transpose is given by

$$\begin{aligned} \mathbf{f}' &= \left(\frac{\partial g}{\partial \beta_1}, \frac{\partial g}{\partial \beta_2}, \frac{\partial g}{\partial \beta_3}, \frac{\partial g}{\partial \sigma^2}\right) \\ &= [0, (1 - \beta_3)^{-1}, \beta_2(1 - \beta_3)^{-2}, 0] \end{aligned} \tag{12.3.64}$$

Also, we have

$$g(\tilde{\boldsymbol{\gamma}}) = \frac{b_2}{1 - b_3} - 1 = \hat{\alpha}_1 - 1 \tag{12.3.65}$$

Thus, the Wald statistic for testing (12.3.62) can be written as

$$\begin{aligned} \lambda_W &= [g(\tilde{\boldsymbol{\gamma}})]^2[\tilde{\mathbf{f}}' I(\tilde{\boldsymbol{\gamma}})^{-1}\tilde{\mathbf{f}}]^{-1} \\ &= \frac{(\hat{\alpha}_1 - 1)^2}{s_{\hat{\alpha}_1}^2} \xrightarrow{d} \chi^2_{(1)} \end{aligned} \tag{12.3.66}$$

where

$$
\begin{aligned}
s_{\tilde{\alpha}_1}^2 &= \tilde{\mathbf{f}}' I(\tilde{\boldsymbol{\gamma}})^{-1} \tilde{\mathbf{f}} \\
&= \tilde{\sigma}^2 [0, (1 - b_3)^{-1}, b_2(1 - b_3)^{-2}](X'X)^{-1} \begin{bmatrix} 0 \\ (1 - b_3)^{-1} \\ b_2(1 - b_3)^{-2} \end{bmatrix} \\
&= \tilde{\sigma}^2 [(1 - b_3)^{-2} a^{22} + b_2^2 (1 - b_3)^{-4} a^{33} + 2b_2(1 - b_3)^{-3} a^{23}] \qquad (12.3.67)
\end{aligned}
$$

and a^{ij} is the (i, j)th element of $(X'X)^{-1}$. The term $s_{\tilde{\alpha}_1}^2$ can be viewed as the asymptotic variance for the nonlinear function $\hat{\alpha}_1 = b_2/(1 - b_3)$. Also, it should be noted that because the hypothesis does not involve σ^2, $\partial g/\partial \sigma^2 = 0$, and because the information matrix is block diagonal, we could have considered the problem completely in terms of $\boldsymbol{\beta}$, and the corresponding part of the information matrix, $X'X/\sigma^2$.

Turning to the Lagrange multiplier and likelihood ratio test statistics for testing the nonlinear hypotheses $H_0: \mathbf{g}(\boldsymbol{\gamma}) = \mathbf{0}$, these statistics have the same general form as that given in Chapter 3. Specifically, the Lagrange multiplier test statistic is

$$\lambda_{LM} = \mathbf{S}(\tilde{\boldsymbol{\gamma}}_0)' I(\tilde{\boldsymbol{\gamma}}_0)^{-1} \mathbf{S}(\tilde{\boldsymbol{\gamma}}_0) \qquad (12.3.68)$$

where $\tilde{\boldsymbol{\gamma}}_0$ is the restricted maximum likelihood estimator obtained under the assumption that H_0 is true,

$$\mathbf{S}(\boldsymbol{\gamma}) = \partial L/\partial \boldsymbol{\gamma}$$

is the $[(K + 1 + H) \times 1]$ vector of first derivatives of the log-likelihood function with respect to $\boldsymbol{\gamma}$, and

$$\mathbf{S}(\tilde{\boldsymbol{\gamma}}_0)$$

is equal to $\mathbf{S}(\boldsymbol{\gamma})$ evaluated at $\boldsymbol{\gamma} = \tilde{\boldsymbol{\gamma}}_0$. Note that $\mathbf{S}(\tilde{\boldsymbol{\gamma}}) = \mathbf{0}$ because this is the first-order condition for the unrestricted maximum likelihood estimator $\tilde{\boldsymbol{\gamma}}$. Note, also, that for the Lagrange multiplier test the information matrix is evaluated at the restricted estimator $\tilde{\boldsymbol{\gamma}}_0$. The Lagrange multiplier test can be viewed as a test of whether $\mathbf{S}(\tilde{\boldsymbol{\gamma}}_0)$ is significantly different from $\mathbf{0}$. Under H_0, $\lambda_{LM} \xrightarrow{d} \chi^2_{(J)}$, the null hypothesis being rejected if λ_{LM} is too large.

The test is called the "Lagrange multiplier" test because it can also be written in terms of the Lagrange multiplier associated with restricted maximum likelihood estimation. The Lagrangian function for restricted maximum likelihood estimation can be written as

$$\phi(\boldsymbol{\gamma}, \boldsymbol{\eta}) = L(\boldsymbol{\gamma}) + \boldsymbol{\eta}' \mathbf{g}(\boldsymbol{\gamma}) \qquad (12.3.69)$$

where $\boldsymbol{\eta}$ is a J-dimensional vector of Lagrange multipliers. Differentiating $\phi(\boldsymbol{\gamma}, \boldsymbol{\eta})$ with respect to $\boldsymbol{\gamma}$ and setting this derivative to $\mathbf{0}$ yields part of the first-order conditions for the restricted maximum likelihood estimator $\tilde{\boldsymbol{\gamma}}_0$, namely

$$\mathbf{S}(\tilde{\boldsymbol{\gamma}}_0) + \tilde{F}_0 \boldsymbol{\eta}_0 = \mathbf{0} \tag{12.3.70}$$

where $\tilde{F}_0$ is the matrix $F = \partial \mathbf{g}'/\partial \boldsymbol{\gamma}$ evaluated at $\boldsymbol{\gamma}_0$, and $\boldsymbol{\eta}_0$ is the optimal solution for $\boldsymbol{\eta}$. Using (12.3.70), (12.3.68) can be written as

$$\lambda_{LM} = \boldsymbol{\eta}_0' \tilde{F}_0' I(\tilde{\boldsymbol{\gamma}}_0)^{-1} \tilde{F}_0 \boldsymbol{\eta}_0 \tag{12.3.71}$$

The likelihood ratio test is a test of whether the restricted and unrestricted maximized likelihood functions are significantly different. The statistic is given by

$$\lambda_{LR} = 2[L(\tilde{\boldsymbol{\gamma}}) - L(\tilde{\boldsymbol{\gamma}}_0)] \tag{12.3.72}$$

Under H_0, $\lambda_{LR} \xrightarrow{d} \chi^2_{(J)}$.

We will consider two examples of the three test statistics—the first is for testing a set of linear restrictions of the form $R\boldsymbol{\beta} = \mathbf{r}$; the second is for testing for heteroskedasticity in the multiplicative heteroskedastic error model.

12.3.4a Testing the Linear Restrictions $R\boldsymbol{\beta} = \mathbf{r}$

In this section we are concerned with testing $H_0: R\boldsymbol{\beta} = \mathbf{r}$ against the alternative $H_1: R\boldsymbol{\beta} \neq \mathbf{r}$ within the framework of Section 12.3.1b where the log-likelihood function was given by

$$L(\boldsymbol{\beta}, \sigma^2, \boldsymbol{\theta}) = -\frac{T}{2}\ln 2\pi - \frac{T}{2}\ln \sigma^2 - \frac{1}{2}\ln|\boldsymbol{\Psi}(\boldsymbol{\theta})| - \frac{1}{2\sigma^2}(\mathbf{y} - X\boldsymbol{\beta})'\boldsymbol{\Psi}(\boldsymbol{\theta})^{-1}(\mathbf{y} - X\boldsymbol{\beta}) \tag{12.3.73}$$

and, in general terms, the information matrix can be shown to be equal to

$$I(\boldsymbol{\beta}, \sigma^2, \boldsymbol{\theta}) = \begin{bmatrix} \dfrac{X'\boldsymbol{\Psi}(\boldsymbol{\theta})^{-1}X}{\sigma^2} & \mathbf{0} & 0 \\ \mathbf{0}' & -E\left(\dfrac{\partial^2 L}{\partial \sigma^4}\right) & -E\left(\dfrac{\partial^2 L}{\partial \sigma^2 \partial \boldsymbol{\theta}'}\right) \\ 0 & -E\left(\dfrac{\partial^2 L}{\partial \boldsymbol{\theta} \partial \sigma^2}\right) & -E\left(\dfrac{\partial^2 L}{\partial \boldsymbol{\theta} \partial \boldsymbol{\theta}'}\right) \end{bmatrix} \tag{12.3.74}$$

In terms of the general hypothesis $\mathbf{g}(\boldsymbol{\gamma}) = \mathbf{0}$, we have

$$H_0: \mathbf{g}(\boldsymbol{\gamma}) = \mathbf{r} - R\boldsymbol{\beta} = \mathbf{0} \tag{12.3.75}$$

Also, because $\mathbf{g}$ involves only $\boldsymbol{\beta}$, and because $I(\boldsymbol{\beta}, \sigma^2, \boldsymbol{\theta})$ is block diagonal with respect to $\boldsymbol{\beta}$ and $(\sigma^2, \boldsymbol{\theta})$, it is possible to ignore the lower diagonal block of $I(\boldsymbol{\beta}, \sigma^2, \boldsymbol{\theta})$ when constructing each of the test statistics.

When σ^2 and $\boldsymbol{\Psi}(\boldsymbol{\theta})$ are known, it can be shown (you are encouraged to verify this fact) that the three statistics are identical and can be written as

$$\lambda_W = \lambda_{LM} = \lambda_{LR} = \frac{(R\hat{\boldsymbol{\beta}} - \mathbf{r})'[R(X'\boldsymbol{\Psi}(\boldsymbol{\theta})^{-1}X)^{-1}R']^{-1}(R\hat{\boldsymbol{\beta}} - \mathbf{r})}{\sigma^2} \qquad (12.3.76)$$

where $\hat{\boldsymbol{\beta}} = (X'\boldsymbol{\Psi}^{-1}X)^{-1}X'\boldsymbol{\Psi}^{-1}\mathbf{y}$ is the unrestricted maximum likelihood estimator for $\boldsymbol{\beta}$ for known $\boldsymbol{\Psi}$. Because the three statistics are identical, they obviously have the same $\chi^2_{(J)}$-distribution—in this case an *exact* finite sample distribution—where J is the number of linearly independent rows in R.

When σ^2 and $\boldsymbol{\Psi}(\boldsymbol{\theta})$ are unknown, one way of approaching the problem is to find estimators for σ^2 and $\boldsymbol{\theta}$ and to substitute these for the corresponding true parameters in (12.3.76). With an appropriate choice of estimators the resulting statistic will have an asymptotic $\chi^2_{(J)}$-distribution and could therefore provide the basis for an approximate test. Two possible estimators for σ^2 and $\boldsymbol{\theta}$ are the unrestricted maximum likelihood estimators and the maximum likelihood estimators obtained under the assumption that H_0: $R\boldsymbol{\beta} = \mathbf{r}$ is correct. Let us denote these estimators by $(\tilde{\sigma}^2, \tilde{\boldsymbol{\theta}})$ and $(\tilde{\sigma}_0^2, \tilde{\boldsymbol{\theta}}_0)$, respectively. As an example of $(\tilde{\sigma}_0^2, \tilde{\boldsymbol{\theta}}_0)$, if imposition of $R\boldsymbol{\beta} = \mathbf{r}$ was equivalent to dropping an explanatory variable, then $(\tilde{\sigma}_0^2, \tilde{\boldsymbol{\theta}}_0)$ would be those estimators obtained by maximizing the likelihood function with the explanatory variable omitted. We will also need some notation for the various possible estimators for $\boldsymbol{\beta}$. Let

$$\tilde{\boldsymbol{\beta}} = [X'\boldsymbol{\Psi}(\tilde{\boldsymbol{\theta}})^{-1}X]^{-1}X'\boldsymbol{\Psi}(\tilde{\boldsymbol{\theta}})^{-1}\mathbf{y}$$

be the unrestricted maximum likelihood estimator for $\boldsymbol{\beta}$; let

$$\tilde{\boldsymbol{\beta}}_0 = [X'\boldsymbol{\Psi}(\tilde{\boldsymbol{\theta}}_0)^{-1}X]^{-1}X'\boldsymbol{\Psi}(\tilde{\boldsymbol{\theta}}_0)^{-1}\mathbf{y}$$

be the unrestricted maximum likelihood estimator for $\boldsymbol{\beta}$ conditional on the restricted estimator $\tilde{\boldsymbol{\theta}}_0$; and let

$$\tilde{\boldsymbol{\beta}}_0^* = \tilde{\boldsymbol{\beta}}_0 + (X'\boldsymbol{\Psi}(\tilde{\boldsymbol{\theta}}_0)^{-1}X)^{-1}R'[R(X'\boldsymbol{\Psi}(\tilde{\boldsymbol{\theta}}_0)^{-1}X)^{-1}R']^{-1}(\mathbf{r} - R\tilde{\boldsymbol{\beta}}_0)$$

be the restricted maximum likelihood estimator for $\boldsymbol{\beta}$.

The Wald test statistic is given by (12.3.76) with $(\hat{\boldsymbol{\beta}}, \sigma^2, \boldsymbol{\theta})$ replaced by $(\tilde{\boldsymbol{\beta}}, \tilde{\sigma}^2, \tilde{\boldsymbol{\theta}})$; the Lagrange multiplier test statistic is given by (12.3.76) with $(\hat{\boldsymbol{\beta}}, \sigma^2, \boldsymbol{\theta})$ replaced by $(\tilde{\boldsymbol{\beta}}_0, \tilde{\sigma}_0^2, \tilde{\boldsymbol{\theta}}_0)$; however, the likelihood ratio statistic can no longer be written in a form similar to (12.3.76). Let us consider a formal derivation of these results.

For the Wald statistic we have, from (12.3.75)

$$F' = \frac{\partial \mathbf{g}}{\partial \boldsymbol{\gamma}'} = (-R, \mathbf{0}, 0) \qquad (12.3.77)$$

and, using (12.3.74),

$$F'I(\boldsymbol{\gamma})^{-1}F = \sigma^2 R(X'\boldsymbol{\Psi}(\boldsymbol{\theta})^{-1}X)^{-1}R' \tag{12.3.78}$$

which leads to a Wald statistic of

$$\lambda_W = (R\tilde{\boldsymbol{\beta}} - \mathbf{r})'[R(X'\boldsymbol{\Psi}(\tilde{\boldsymbol{\theta}})^{-1}X)^{-1}R']^{-1}(R\tilde{\boldsymbol{\beta}} - \mathbf{r})/\tilde{\sigma}^2 \tag{12.3.79}$$

For the Lagrange multiplier statistic, it is convenient to use the formulation in (12.3.71). Differentiating the Lagrangian function in (12.3.69) with respect to $\boldsymbol{\beta}$ yields

$$\begin{aligned}\frac{\partial \phi}{\partial \boldsymbol{\beta}} &= \frac{\partial L}{\partial \boldsymbol{\beta}} + \frac{\partial \mathbf{g}'}{\partial \boldsymbol{\beta}} \boldsymbol{\eta} \\ &= \frac{1}{\sigma^2} X'\boldsymbol{\Psi}(\boldsymbol{\theta})^{-1}(\mathbf{y} - X\boldsymbol{\beta}) - R'\boldsymbol{\eta}\end{aligned} \tag{12.3.80}$$

Setting this derivative equal to $\mathbf{0}$ yields the restricted maximum likelihood estimators, so we have

$$R'\boldsymbol{\eta}_0 = \frac{1}{\tilde{\sigma}_0^2}[X'\boldsymbol{\Psi}(\tilde{\boldsymbol{\theta}}_0)^{-1}\mathbf{y} - X'\boldsymbol{\Psi}(\tilde{\boldsymbol{\theta}}_0)^{-1}X\tilde{\boldsymbol{\beta}}_0^*] \tag{12.3.81}$$

Premultiplying both sides of this equation first by $R(X'\boldsymbol{\Psi}(\tilde{\boldsymbol{\theta}}_0)^{-1}X)^{-1}$ and then by $[R(X'\boldsymbol{\Psi}(\tilde{\boldsymbol{\theta}}_0)^{-1}X)^{-1}R']^{-1}$ yields

$$\begin{aligned}\boldsymbol{\eta}_0 &= \frac{1}{\tilde{\sigma}_0^2}[R(X'\boldsymbol{\Psi}(\tilde{\boldsymbol{\theta}}_0)^{-1}X)^{-1}R']^{-1}[R\tilde{\boldsymbol{\beta}}_0 - R\tilde{\boldsymbol{\beta}}_0^*] \\ &= \frac{1}{\tilde{\sigma}_0^2}[R(X'\boldsymbol{\Psi}(\tilde{\boldsymbol{\theta}}_0)^{-1}X)^{-1}R']^{-1}[R\tilde{\boldsymbol{\beta}}_0 - \mathbf{r}]\end{aligned} \tag{12.3.82}$$

Substituting (12.3.82) and (12.3.78) into (12.3.71) gives the final result

$$\lambda_{LM} = (R\tilde{\boldsymbol{\beta}}_0 - \mathbf{r})'[R(X'\boldsymbol{\Psi}(\tilde{\boldsymbol{\theta}}_0)^{-1}X)^{-1}R']^{-1}(R\tilde{\boldsymbol{\beta}}_0 - \mathbf{r})/\tilde{\sigma}_0^2 \tag{12.3.83}$$

For the likelihood ratio test statistic we note that

$$L(\tilde{\boldsymbol{\beta}}, \tilde{\sigma}^2, \tilde{\boldsymbol{\theta}}) = -\frac{T}{2}\ln 2\pi - \frac{T}{2}\ln \tilde{\sigma}^2 - \frac{1}{2}\ln|\boldsymbol{\Psi}(\tilde{\boldsymbol{\theta}})| - \frac{T}{2} \tag{12.3.84}$$

and

$$L(\tilde{\boldsymbol{\beta}}_0^*, \tilde{\sigma}_0^2, \tilde{\boldsymbol{\theta}}_0) = -\frac{T}{2}\ln 2\pi - \frac{T}{2}\ln \tilde{\sigma}_0^2 - \frac{1}{2}\ln|\boldsymbol{\Psi}(\tilde{\boldsymbol{\theta}}_0)| - \frac{T}{2} \tag{12.3.85}$$

Subtracting (12.3.85) from (12.3.84) and multiplying the result by 2 gives the likelihood ratio test statistic

$$\lambda_{LR} = 2\left[\frac{T}{2}\ln \tilde{\sigma}_0^2 + \frac{1}{2}\ln|\boldsymbol{\Psi}(\tilde{\boldsymbol{\theta}}_0)| - \frac{T}{2}\ln \tilde{\sigma}^2 - \frac{1}{2}\ln|\boldsymbol{\Psi}(\tilde{\boldsymbol{\theta}})|\right]$$

$$= T\ln\left(\frac{\tilde{\sigma}_0^2|\boldsymbol{\Psi}(\tilde{\boldsymbol{\theta}}_0)|^{1/T}}{\tilde{\sigma}^2|\boldsymbol{\Psi}(\tilde{\boldsymbol{\theta}})|^{1/T}}\right) \tag{12.3.86}$$

Since all three statistics have the same asymptotic distribution, and their finite sample distributions are not generally known, there is no a priori reason to prefer one test over another. However, some finite sample results are available. Using results on inequalities related to logarithms (Savin, 1976; Berndt and Savin, 1977) or from the properties of conditional and unconditional maximized likelihood functions (Breusch, 1979), it is possible to show that

$$\lambda_W \geq \lambda_{LR} \geq \lambda_{LM} \tag{12.3.87}$$

These inequalities imply that, although the three tests are asymptotically equivalent, their finite sample distributions will not be the same. In particular, rejection of H_0 can be favored by selecting λ_W a priori, whereas acceptance of H_0 can be favored by selecting λ_{LM} a priori. Furthermore, the finite sample sizes of the tests will differ. If, for example, a (large sample) 5% significance level is employed and the LR test correctly states the probability of a Type I error as 0.05, then the probability of a Type I error will be less than 0.05 for the LM test, and greater than 0.05 for the Wald test. This source of conflict has led to some preliminary research into "correcting" the tests so that their sizes are comparable in finite samples. See, for example, Evans and Savin (1982) and Rothenberg (1984).

Finally, we note that there is a fourth test statistic that, in a particular sense, is asymptotically equivalent to the Wald test and that is frequently used to test the hypothesis $R\boldsymbol{\beta} = \mathbf{r}$. This statistic is the "estimated generalized least squares" version of the conventional F-statistic that was considered in Chapter 6. For details, see (9.2.15).

12.3.4b. Testing for Multiplicative Heteroskedasticity

As a second example of the Wald, Lagrange multiplier, and likelihood ratio tests, in this section we consider the problem of testing for heteroskedasticity when the alternative hypothesis is the multiplicative heteroskedastic error model that has been studied in Sections 9.3.4 and 12.3.3. The log-likelihood function for this model is

$$L(\boldsymbol{\beta}, \boldsymbol{\alpha}) = -\frac{T}{2}\ln 2\pi - \frac{1}{2}\sum_{t=1}^{T}\mathbf{z}_t'\boldsymbol{\alpha} - \frac{1}{2}\sum_{t=1}^{T}\exp\{-\mathbf{z}_t'\boldsymbol{\alpha}\}(y_t - \mathbf{x}_t'\boldsymbol{\beta})^2 \tag{12.3.88}$$

or, alternatively,

$$L(\boldsymbol{\beta}, \sigma^2, \boldsymbol{\alpha}^*) = -\frac{T}{2}\ln 2\pi - \frac{T}{2}\ln \sigma^2 - \frac{1}{2}\sum_{t=1}^{T} \mathbf{z}_t^{*\prime}\boldsymbol{\alpha}^*$$

$$- \frac{1}{2\sigma^2}\sum_{t=1}^{T} \exp\{-\mathbf{z}_t^{*\prime}\boldsymbol{\alpha}^*\}(y_t - \mathbf{x}_t'\boldsymbol{\beta})^2 \tag{12.3.89}$$

You should consult Sections 9.3.4 and 12.3.3 for the notational definitions. In the context of the current notation, we have $\boldsymbol{\gamma}' = (\boldsymbol{\beta}', \sigma^2, \boldsymbol{\alpha}^{*\prime})$ and the null hypothesis of homoskedastic errors is

$$H_0: \mathbf{g}(\boldsymbol{\gamma}) = \boldsymbol{\alpha}^* = \mathbf{0} \tag{12.3.90}$$

which is to be tested against the alternative

$$H_1: \mathbf{g}(\boldsymbol{\gamma}) = \boldsymbol{\alpha}^* \neq \mathbf{0} \tag{12.3.91}$$

Considering first the Wald test, we note that there are $S - 1$ restrictions [$\boldsymbol{\alpha}^*$ is of dimension $(S - 1)$], and $\partial\mathbf{g}/\partial\boldsymbol{\gamma}'$ is a $[(S - 1) \times (K + S)]$ matrix equal to

$$F' = \frac{\partial \mathbf{g}}{\partial \boldsymbol{\gamma}'} = (0, \mathbf{0}, I_{S-1}) \tag{12.3.92}$$

Using this result and the information matrix in (12.3.49), the Wald statistic in (12.3.59) becomes

$$\lambda_W = \tilde{\boldsymbol{\alpha}}^{*\prime}\left[2(\mathbf{0} \quad I_{S-1})(Z'Z)^{-1}\begin{pmatrix}\mathbf{0}'\\ I_{S-1}\end{pmatrix}\right]^{-1}\tilde{\boldsymbol{\alpha}}^*$$

$$= \frac{\tilde{\boldsymbol{\alpha}}^{*\prime}D^{-1}\tilde{\boldsymbol{\alpha}}^*}{2} \tag{12.3.93}$$

where D is the matrix $(Z'Z)^{-1}$ with its first row and first column deleted. Note that this is the same statistic as given in (9.3.52) except that 2 appears in the denominator instead of 4.9348, reflecting the fact that the maximum likelihood estimator $\tilde{\boldsymbol{\alpha}}^*$ is more efficient than the two-step estimator $\hat{\boldsymbol{\alpha}}^*$.

Using the example and results in Section 12.3.3, we have

$$\lambda_W = (0.21732)^2 \times (0.00379774)^{-1}/2 = 6.218$$

At the 5% level of significance the null hypothesis is rejected because 6.218 is greater than the 5% critical value of $\chi^2_{(1)} = 3.84$.

Turning to the Lagrange multiplier test, we have

$$\frac{\partial L}{\partial \boldsymbol{\alpha}} = -\frac{1}{2}\sum_{t=1}^{T} \mathbf{z}_t + \frac{1}{2}\sum_{t=1}^{T} \mathbf{z}_t \exp\{-\mathbf{z}_t'\boldsymbol{\alpha}\}(y_t - \mathbf{x}_t'\boldsymbol{\beta})^2 \tag{12.3.94}$$

The restricted maximum likelihood estimator obtained under the assumption that H_0 is true is given by

$$\tilde{\boldsymbol{\gamma}}_0' = (\mathbf{b}', \tilde{\sigma}_0^2, \mathbf{0}') \tag{12.3.95}$$

where $\mathbf{b} = (X'X)^{-1}X'\mathbf{y}$ is the least squares estimator and $\tilde{\sigma}_0^2 = (\mathbf{y} - X\mathbf{b})'(\mathbf{y} - X\mathbf{b})/T$ is the usual maximum likelihood estimator of the variance. Using (12.3.95) we can obtain the following expression for the general term $S(\tilde{\boldsymbol{\gamma}}_0)$

$$S(\tilde{\boldsymbol{\gamma}}_0) = \begin{bmatrix} \left.\dfrac{\partial L}{\partial \boldsymbol{\beta}}\right|_{\tilde{\boldsymbol{\gamma}}_0} \\ \left.\dfrac{\partial L}{\partial \boldsymbol{\alpha}}\right|_{\tilde{\boldsymbol{\gamma}}_0} \end{bmatrix} = \begin{bmatrix} \mathbf{0} \\ -\dfrac{1}{2}\sum_{t=1}^{T} \mathbf{z}_t + \dfrac{1}{2\tilde{\sigma}_0^2}\sum_{t=1}^{T} \mathbf{z}_t \hat{e}_t^2 \end{bmatrix} \tag{12.3.96}$$

where $\hat{e}_t = y_t - \mathbf{x}_t'\mathbf{b}$ is the tth least squares residual. The first K components of $S(\tilde{\boldsymbol{\gamma}}_0)$ are 0 because, when the constraint does not involve $\boldsymbol{\beta}$, the first-order condition from differentiating the Lagrangian function in (12.3.69) is

$$\frac{\partial \phi}{\partial \boldsymbol{\beta}} = \frac{\partial L}{\partial \boldsymbol{\beta}} = \mathbf{0} \tag{12.3.97}$$

The other components we will rewrite as

$$\left.\frac{\partial L}{\partial \boldsymbol{\alpha}}\right|_{\tilde{\boldsymbol{\gamma}}_0} = \frac{1}{2\tilde{\sigma}_0^2}\sum_{t=1}^{T} \mathbf{z}_t(\hat{e}_t^2 - \tilde{\sigma}_0^2) = \frac{1}{2\tilde{\sigma}_0^2}\sum_{t=1}^{T} \mathbf{z}_t q_t = \frac{1}{2\tilde{\sigma}_0^2} Z'\mathbf{q} \tag{12.3.98}$$

where $\mathbf{q}$ is a T-dimensional vector with tth element equal to $\hat{e}_t^2 - \tilde{\sigma}_0^2$. Using (12.3.96), (12.3.98), and the information matrix given in (12.3.49), the Lagrange multiplier statistic given in (12.3.68) can be written as

$$\lambda_{LM} = \frac{\mathbf{q}'Z(Z'Z)^{-1}Z'\mathbf{q}}{2\tilde{\sigma}_0^4} \tag{12.3.99}$$

This statistic is precisely the Breusch–Pagan test statistic that was given in Section 9.3.5c. It can be shown to be equal to one-half the regression sum of squares in the regression of $(\hat{e}_t^2/\tilde{\sigma}_0^2)$ on $\mathbf{z}_t$ (see Exercise 12.6). We have developed the Lagrange multiplier statistic in the context of an alternative hypothesis of multiplicative heteroskedasticity. However, as indicated in Section 9.3.5c, it is equally valid for any heteroskedastic alternative that is of the form $\sigma_t^2 = h(\mathbf{z}_t'\boldsymbol{\alpha}) = h(\alpha_1 + \mathbf{z}_t^{*\prime}\boldsymbol{\alpha}^*)$ where h is any function independent of t. When evaluated at $\boldsymbol{\alpha}^* = \mathbf{0}$, $\partial L/\partial \boldsymbol{\alpha}$ and the information matrix do not depend on the precise form of heteroskedasticity.

The example value for λ_{LM} has already been computed in Section 9.3.7. Specifically, we found that $\lambda_{LM} = 4.028$. Thus, since $4.028 > 3.84$, the Lagrange multiplier test also leads us to reject H_0 at the 5% significance level.

Finally, we derive an expression for the likelihood ratio test. We have

$$L(\tilde{\gamma}) = L(\tilde{\boldsymbol{\beta}}, \tilde{\boldsymbol{\alpha}}) = -\frac{T}{2}\ln 2\pi - \frac{1}{2}\sum_{t=1}^{T} \mathbf{z}_t'\tilde{\boldsymbol{\alpha}} - \frac{T}{2} \tag{12.3.100}$$

$$L(\tilde{\gamma}_0) = L(\mathbf{b}, \tilde{\sigma}_0^2, \mathbf{0}) = -\frac{T}{2}\ln 2\pi - \frac{T}{2}\ln \tilde{\sigma}_0^2 - \frac{T}{2} \tag{12.3.101}$$

from which we obtain

$$\lambda_{LR} = T \ln \tilde{\sigma}_0^2 - \sum_{t=1}^{T} \mathbf{z}_t'\tilde{\boldsymbol{\alpha}} \tag{12.3.102}$$

With the estimates from the example problem we obtain

$$\lambda_{LR} = 71.87442 - 66.67054 = 5.204$$

a value that leads to the same decision as was reached using the other two test statistics.

12.4 Nonlinear Seemingly Unrelated Regression Equations

In Chapter 11 we considered estimation of sets of linear equations under the title of seemingly unrelated regressions. We noted that it is frequently reasonable to assume the existence of contemporaneous correlation between the disturbances in different equations and that allowing for this correlation in the estimation process can lead to more efficient estimates. The same line of reasoning is equally valid for sets of nonlinear equations. In this section we extend the nonlinear single-equation analysis outlined earlier in this chapter to the case of more than one nonlinear equation, with the possible existence of contemporaneous correlation between errors in different equations.

Extending the notation used in Section 12.2, M nonlinear equations can be written as

$$\begin{aligned} \mathbf{y}_1 &= \mathbf{f}_1(X, \boldsymbol{\beta}) + \mathbf{e}_1 \\ \mathbf{y}_2 &= \mathbf{f}_2(X, \boldsymbol{\beta}) + \mathbf{e}_2 \\ &\vdots \\ \mathbf{y}_M &= \mathbf{f}_M(X, \boldsymbol{\beta}) + \mathbf{e}_M \end{aligned} \tag{12.4.1}$$

Letting $\mathbf{e}' = (\mathbf{e}_1', \mathbf{e}_2', \ldots, \mathbf{e}_M')$, it is assumed that $E[\mathbf{e}\mathbf{e}'] = \Sigma \otimes I_T$, where Σ is an $(M \times M)$ covariance matrix whose (i, j)th element is given by σ_{ij}, where $E[\mathbf{e}_i\mathbf{e}_j'] = \sigma_{ij}I_T$. The same matrix X and the same coefficient vector $\boldsymbol{\beta}$ appear in all equations to allow for the possibility that some explanatory variables, and some coefficients, could be common to more than one equation. Each equation can, of course, be a different nonlinear function of X and $\boldsymbol{\beta}$. We will consider two estimation procedures—a two-step estimation procedure and a maximum likelihood estimation procedure under the assumption that the errors are normally distributed.

12.4.1 Two-Step Estimation

When Σ is known, a nonlinear least squares estimator for $\boldsymbol{\beta}$, which is more efficient than that obtained by applying nonlinear least squares separately to each equation, can be found by minimizing the weighted sum of squares function

$$\mathbf{e}'(\Sigma^{-1} \otimes I_T)\mathbf{e} \tag{12.4.2}$$

Since Σ is typically unknown, one way of proceeding is to estimate Σ using residuals from separate application of nonlinear least squares to each equation, and to then, in a second step, find that value of $\boldsymbol{\beta}$ that minimizes (12.4.2), but with Σ replaced by an estimate $\hat{\Sigma}$. We can summarize this procedure as follows

1. Find estimates $\mathbf{b}_1, \mathbf{b}_2, \ldots, \mathbf{b}_M$ that minimize $\mathbf{e}_1'\mathbf{e}_1, \mathbf{e}_2'\mathbf{e}_2, \ldots, \mathbf{e}_M'\mathbf{e}_M$, respectively.
2. Compute each vector of residuals as $\hat{\mathbf{e}}_i = \mathbf{y}_i - \mathbf{f}_i(X, \mathbf{b}_i)$, $i = 1, 2, \ldots, M$.
3. Find estimates $\hat{\sigma}_{ij} = \hat{\mathbf{e}}_i'\hat{\mathbf{e}}_j/T$ and construct the corresponding matrix $\hat{\Sigma}$.
4. Find that value of $\boldsymbol{\beta}$ that minimizes $\mathbf{e}'(\hat{\Sigma}^{-1} \otimes I)\mathbf{e}$.

It can be shown, see for example Gallant (1975), that this estimator is consistent and asymptotically efficient when the errors are normally distributed. An estimate of the asymptotic covariance matrix for the two-step estimator, $\hat{\boldsymbol{\beta}}$ say, is given by

$$\hat{\Sigma}_{\hat{\boldsymbol{\beta}}} = \left[\frac{\partial \mathbf{e}'}{\partial \boldsymbol{\beta}}(\hat{\Sigma}^{-1} \otimes I_T)\frac{\partial \mathbf{e}}{\partial \boldsymbol{\beta}'}\right]^{-1}\Bigg|_{\hat{\boldsymbol{\beta}}} \tag{12.4.3}$$

Given that $\boldsymbol{\beta}$ is of dimension $(K \times 1)$, $\partial \mathbf{e}'/\partial \boldsymbol{\beta}$ is a $(K \times MT)$ matrix given by

$$\frac{\partial \mathbf{e}'}{\partial \boldsymbol{\beta}} = \left[\frac{\partial \mathbf{f}_1'}{\partial \boldsymbol{\beta}}, \frac{\partial \mathbf{f}_2'}{\partial \boldsymbol{\beta}}, \ldots, \frac{\partial \mathbf{f}_M'}{\partial \boldsymbol{\beta}}\right] \tag{12.4.4}$$

If each equation contains a different set of parameters, $\partial \mathbf{e}'/\partial \boldsymbol{\beta}$ is a block diagonal matrix. The joint two-step estimation procedure will not be more efficient than separate application of nonlinear least squares to each equation if either of two conditions holds. The first condition is that Σ is diagonal (there are no nonzero contemporaneous correlations); the second condition is that each function $\mathbf{f}_i(X, \boldsymbol{\beta}_i)$ is the same and dependent on the same set of explanatory variables, but a different coefficient vector $\boldsymbol{\beta}_i$ appears in each equation.

12.4.2 Maximum Likelihood Estimation

With the additional assumption that the errors are normally distributed, the log-likelihood function for $\boldsymbol{\beta}$ and Σ can be written as

$$\begin{aligned} L(\boldsymbol{\beta}, \Sigma) &= -\frac{TM}{2} \ln 2\pi - \frac{1}{2} \ln|\Sigma \otimes I_T| - \frac{1}{2} \mathbf{e}'(\Sigma^{-1} \otimes \mathbf{I}_T)\mathbf{e} \\ &= -\frac{TM}{2} \ln 2\pi - \frac{T}{2} \ln|\Sigma| - \frac{1}{2} \operatorname{tr}[S\Sigma^{-1}] \end{aligned} \tag{12.4.5}$$

where S is an $(M \times M)$ matrix with (i, j)th element equal to $\mathbf{e}_i'\mathbf{e}_j = [\mathbf{y}_i - \mathbf{f}_i(X, \boldsymbol{\beta})]'[\mathbf{y}_j - \mathbf{f}_j(X, \boldsymbol{\beta})]$. The derivation of the second line in (12.4.5) is left as a problem (Exercise 12.7).

Nonlinear maximization of (12.4.5) with respect to all the elements in $\boldsymbol{\beta}$ and Σ could be a daunting task, particularly if M is moderately large. Fortunately, it is possible to obtain an analytical expression for the maximum likelihood estimator for Σ as a function of $\boldsymbol{\beta}$ and to therefore concentrate the likelihood function so that it is a function of $\boldsymbol{\beta}$ alone. In this regard it is more convenient to differentiate $L(\boldsymbol{\beta}, \Sigma)$ with respect to Σ^{-1} rather than Σ, and some special rules of differentiation are required. It can be shown [see, for example, Dhrymes (1978, pp. 531–535)] that

$$\frac{\partial \ln|\Sigma^{-1}|}{\partial \Sigma^{-1}} = \Sigma \qquad \text{and} \qquad \frac{\partial \operatorname{tr}[S\Sigma^{-1}]}{\partial \Sigma^{-1}} = S \tag{12.4.6}$$

Noting that $-(T/2) \ln|\Sigma| = (T/2) \ln|\Sigma^{-1}|$, and using the results in (12.4.6), we have

$$\frac{\partial L}{\partial \Sigma^{-1}} = \frac{T}{2} \Sigma - \frac{1}{2} S \tag{12.4.7}$$

Setting this derivative equal to 0 and solving for Σ yields the estimator

$$\hat{\Sigma} = \frac{S}{T} \tag{12.4.8}$$

Note that S is a function of $\boldsymbol{\beta}$. Substituting (12.4.8) into (12.4.5) leads to the concentrated log-likelihood function

$$L^*(\boldsymbol{\beta}) = \text{constant} - \frac{T}{2} \ln|S| \tag{12.4.9}$$

Thus, the maximum likelihood estimator $\tilde{\boldsymbol{\beta}}$, is that value of $\boldsymbol{\beta}$ that minimizes

$$|S| = \left| \begin{bmatrix} \mathbf{e}_1'\mathbf{e}_1 & \cdots & \mathbf{e}_1'\mathbf{e}_M \\ \vdots & \ddots & \vdots \\ \mathbf{e}_M'\mathbf{e}_1 & \cdots & \mathbf{e}_M'\mathbf{e}_M \end{bmatrix} \right| \tag{12.4.10}$$

The maximum likelihood estimator for Σ is S/T, evaluated at $\tilde{\boldsymbol{\beta}}$. The asymptotic properties of $\tilde{\boldsymbol{\beta}}$ are the same as those of the two-step estimator $\hat{\boldsymbol{\beta}}$; in particular, the covariance matrix given in (12.4.3), but evaluated at $(\tilde{\boldsymbol{\beta}}, \tilde{\Sigma})$, is appropriate.

The foregoing treatment is similar to that provided by Harvey (1981, pp. 67–73, 98–99, 131–138) for a set of linear seemingly unrelated regression equations.

12.4.3 An Example: A Linear Expenditure System

Suppose that income y is totally expended on three commodities q_1, q_2, and q_3 whose prices are p_1, p_2, and p_3, respectively. It can be shown [see, for example, Powell (1974)] that if a consumer has a utility function of the form

$$U(q_1, q_2, q_3) = \sum_{i=1}^{3} \beta_i \ln(q_i - \gamma_i) \tag{12.4.11}$$

then the demand system corresponding to this utility function is given by the linear expenditure system

$$p_i q_i = p_i \gamma_i + \beta_i (y - p_1 \gamma_1 - p_2 \gamma_2 - p_3 \gamma_3) \qquad i = 1, 2, 3 \tag{12.4.12}$$

In this equation, expenditure on the ith commodity $p_i q_i$ is equal to subsistence expenditure $p_i \gamma_i$ plus a proportion β_i of what is known as supernumerary income $(y - p_1\gamma_1 - p_2\gamma_2 - p_3\gamma_3)$. It is called a *linear* expenditure system because expenditure is a linear function of income and prices; it is clearly not linear in the parameters $(\beta_1, \beta_2, \beta_3, \gamma_1, \gamma_2, \gamma_3)$. The $\gamma_i \geq 0$ represent subsistence quantities $(q_i > \gamma_i)$, and the β_i $(0 < \beta_i < 1)$ reflect the relative contribution of each commodity to utility after subsistence has been met.

Econometrically, the problem is to estimate the β_i and the γ_i, given a sample of data on prices, quantities, and income. Rewriting (12.4.12) to accommodate a sample $t = 1, 2, \ldots, T$ yields the following nonlinear statistical system

$$\begin{aligned}
p_{1t} q_{1t} &= p_{1t}\gamma_1 + \beta_1(y_t - p_{1t}\gamma_1 - p_{2t}\gamma_2 - p_{3t}\gamma_3) + e_{1t} \\
p_{2t} q_{2t} &= p_{2t}\gamma_2 + \beta_2(y_t - p_{1t}\gamma_1 - p_{2t}\gamma_2 - p_{3t}\gamma_3) + e_{2t} \\
p_{3t} q_{3t} &= p_{3t}\gamma_3 + \beta_3(y_t - p_{1t}\gamma_1 - p_{2t}\gamma_2 - p_{3t}\gamma_3) + e_{3t}
\end{aligned} \tag{12.4.13}$$

Given that $E[\mathbf{e}_t \mathbf{e}_t'] = \Sigma$, where $\mathbf{e}_t' = (e_{1t}, e_{2t}, e_{3t})$, and where Σ is not diagonal, this system can be viewed as a set of nonlinear seemingly unrelated regression equations. There is an added complication, however. Because $\sum_{i=1}^{3} p_{it} q_{it} = y_t$ (the sum of the dependent variables is equal to one of the explanatory variables for all t), it can be shown that $e_{1t} + e_{2t} + e_{3t} = 0$ and hence that Σ is singular, leading to a breakdown in both estimation procedures. The problem is overcome by estimating only two of the three equations, say the first two, and using the constraint $\sum_{i=1}^{3} \beta_i = 1$ to obtain an estimate of the remaining coefficient β_3. See Barten (1969).

The first two equations were estimated using the data in Table 11.3 and the maximum likelihood estimation procedure. The nature of the model provides some guide as to what might be good starting values for an iterative algorithm. Since the constraint min $q_{it} > \gamma_i$ should be satisfied, min q_{it} seems a reasonable starting value for γ_i. Also, the average budget shares, $T^{-1} \sum_{t=1}^{T} (p_{it} q_{it}/y_t)$, are likely to be good starting values for the β_i. Following these suggestions with our data led to the following starting values:

$$\gamma_1^0 = 2.903 \qquad \gamma_2^0 = 1.360 \qquad \gamma_3^0 = 13.251$$

$$\beta_1^0 = 0.20267 \qquad \beta_2^0 = 0.13429$$

The maximum likelihood estimates and their standard errors that were obtained are

$$\begin{array}{lll} \tilde{\gamma}_1 = \underset{(1.735)}{3.070} & \tilde{\gamma}_2 = \underset{(1.295)}{3.695} & \tilde{\gamma}_3 = \underset{(5.314)}{7.486} \\[2ex] \tilde{\beta}_1 = \underset{(0.037)}{0.205} & \tilde{\beta}_2 = \underset{(0.027)}{0.095} & \end{array}$$

The maximum likelihood estimate for β_3 is given by

$$\tilde{\beta}_3 = 1 - 0.205 - 0.095 = 0.700$$

The estimate for γ_3 does not satisfy our a priori constraints, but the remaining estimates are feasible.

12.5 Functional Form—The Box–Cox Transformation

A problem frequently faced by a researcher wishing to investigate the relationship between a dependent variable y and some explanatory variables $x_2, x_3, \ldots, x_K$ is the specification of the functional relationship between the variables. For example, two alternatives that are commonly considered are a linear relationship

$$y_t = \beta_1 + \beta_2 x_{t2} + \beta_3 x_{t3} + \cdots + \beta_K x_{tK} + e_t \tag{12.5.1}$$

and a log-linear relationship

$$\ln y_t = \alpha_1 + \alpha_2 \ln x_{t2} + \alpha_3 \ln x_{t3} + \cdots + \alpha_k \ln x_{tK} + e_t \tag{12.5.2}$$

Although economists usually have strong a priori information about what variables to include in a particular relationship, they usually have little information about its precise functional form.

The Box–Cox transformation, first introduced by Box and Cox (1964), has been popularized in economics by Zarembka (1968, 1974) as a device for letting the data determine what functional form is most appropriate. By applying a transformation to some of or all the variables in a relationship, a family of functions is created, with one particular member of this family being defined by specifying a particular value (or values) of the transformation parameter(s). The linear and log-linear functions in (12.5.1) and (12.5.2) are two members of the family. The functional form "determined by the data" is that functional form defined by the estimated value(s) of the transformation parameter(s).

To make these ideas specific, consider the following transformation of a variable z.

$$z^{(\lambda)} = \begin{cases} \dfrac{z^\lambda - 1}{\lambda} & \lambda \neq 0 \\ \ln z & \lambda = 0 \end{cases} \tag{12.5.3}$$

When $\lambda = 1$, $z^{(\lambda)} = z - 1$; when $\lambda = -1$, $z^{(\lambda)} = -z^{-1} + 1$; and when $\lambda = 0$, $z^{(\lambda)} = \ln z$ because $\lim_{\lambda \to 0} [(z^\lambda - 1)/\lambda] = \ln z$ from L'Hospital's rule. Application of this transformation to all the variables in a particular relationship yields the model

$$y_t^{(\lambda)} = \beta_1 + \beta_2 x_{t2}^{(\lambda)} + \cdots + \beta_K x_{tK}^{(\lambda)} + e_t \tag{12.5.4}$$

When $\lambda = 0$ this model is identical to the log-linear one in (12.5.2). For $\lambda = 1$, we have

$$y_t - 1 = \beta_1 + \beta_2(x_{t2} - 1) + \cdots + \beta_K(x_{tK} - 1) + e_t$$

or

$$\begin{aligned} y_t &= (\beta_1 - \beta_2 - \cdots - \beta_K + 1) + \beta_2 x_{t2} + \cdots + \beta_K x_{tK} + e_t \\ &= \beta_1^* + \beta_2 x_{t2} + \cdots + \beta_K x_{tK} + e_t \end{aligned} \tag{12.5.5}$$

This model is equivalent to the linear one given in (12.5.1). Other values of λ define other models, and, from an econometric standpoint, the idea is to estimate λ along with $\boldsymbol{\beta}' = (\beta_1, \beta_2, \ldots, \beta_K)$, and to therefore estimate the functional form.

An even more flexible family of functions is defined if we specify a different transformation parameter for each variable and hence attempt to estimate the function

$$y_t^{(\lambda_1)} = \beta_1 + \beta_2 x_{t2}^{(\lambda_2)} + \beta_3 x_{t3}^{(\lambda_3)} + \cdots + \beta_K x_{tK}^{(\lambda_K)} + e_t \tag{12.5.6}$$

This family could include, for example, some variables entering linearly ($\lambda_k = 1$), some entering in terms of logarithms ($\lambda_k = 0$), and some entering as reciprocals ($\lambda_k = -1$). This added flexibility does not come without some cost, however. Without a large number of observations it can be difficult to reliably estimate all the parameters in this model.

12.5.1 Maximum Likelihood Estimation

For estimating the parameters in (12.5.4) or (12.5.6) it has been standard practice to assume the errors (e_t's) are normally distributed and to apply maximum likelihood procedures. One difficulty with this approach [see the references in Fomby, Hill, and Johnson (1984, p. 425)] is that the normality assumption is incompatible with the transformation. As we will see, the log-likelihood function involves terms of the form $\ln y_t$ that are undefined for negative y_t, and yet, if the e_t are normally distributed, the possibility of negative y_t exists. Alternatively, the transformation approach implies the distribution of e_t is truncated, a characteristic not possessed by the normal distribution. To proceed pragmatically with maximum likelihood estimation we need to assume that the truncation effects are negligible and that the e_t are approximately independent, identically distributed normal random variables with 0 mean and variance σ^2.

Under this assumption, the joint density function for $\mathbf{e} = (e_1, e_2, \ldots, e_T)'$ is given by

$$f(\mathbf{e}) = (2\pi\sigma^2)^{-T/2} \exp\left\{ -\frac{\mathbf{e}'\mathbf{e}}{2\sigma^2} \right\} \tag{12.5.7}$$

Beginning first with the case where all variables are transformed using the same transformation parameter (Equation 12.5.4), the joint density function for $\mathbf{y} = (y_1, y_2, \ldots, y_T)'$ is given by

$$f(\mathbf{y}) = (2\pi\sigma^2)^{-T/2} \exp\left\{ -\frac{(\mathbf{y}^{(\lambda)} - X^{(\lambda)}\boldsymbol{\beta})'(\mathbf{y}^{(\lambda)} - X^{(\lambda)}\boldsymbol{\beta})}{2\sigma^2} \right\} \cdot \text{abs}\left(\left| \frac{\partial \mathbf{e}'}{\partial \mathbf{y}} \right| \right) \tag{12.5.8}$$

The determinant $|\partial \mathbf{e}'/\partial \mathbf{y}|$ is the Jacobian of the transformation from $\mathbf{e}$ to $\mathbf{y}$ (see Section 2.3.8). The notation $\mathbf{y}^{(\lambda)}$ and $X^{(\lambda)}$ is used to denote the collection of all T-transformed observations on the dependent and explanatory variables, respectively. That is, $\mathbf{y}^{(\lambda)} = (y_1^{(\lambda)}, \ldots, y_T^{(\lambda)})'$ and $X^{(\lambda)} = (\mathbf{j}, \mathbf{x}_2^{(\lambda)}, \ldots, \mathbf{x}_K^{(\lambda)})$ where $\mathbf{j}$ is a T-dimensional vector of ones, and a typical explanatory variable vector is $\mathbf{x}_k^{(\lambda)} = (x_{1k}^{(\lambda)}, \ldots, x_{Tk}^{(\lambda)})'$. It can be shown that (see Exercise 12.8)

$$\left| \frac{\partial \mathbf{e}'}{\partial \mathbf{y}} \right| = \prod_{t=1}^{T} y_t^{\lambda - 1} \tag{12.5.9}$$

Using this result, and (12.5.8), the log of the likelihood function is

$$L(\boldsymbol{\beta}, \sigma^2, \lambda|\mathbf{y}, X) = -\frac{T}{2}\ln 2\pi - \frac{T}{2}\ln \sigma^2 - \frac{1}{2\sigma^2}(\mathbf{y}^{(\lambda)} - X^{(\lambda)}\boldsymbol{\beta})'(\mathbf{y}^{(\lambda)} - X^{(\lambda)}\boldsymbol{\beta}) + (\lambda - 1)\sum_{t=1}^{T} \ln y_t \tag{12.5.10}$$

Differentiating this function with respect to $\boldsymbol{\beta}$ and σ^2, and setting the derivatives equal to 0 yields

$$\hat{\boldsymbol{\beta}}(\lambda) = (X^{(\lambda)\prime}X^{(\lambda)})^{-1}X^{(\lambda)\prime}\mathbf{y}^{(\lambda)} \tag{12.5.11}$$

and

$$\hat{\sigma}^2(\lambda) = \frac{[\mathbf{y}^{(\lambda)} - X^{(\lambda)}\hat{\boldsymbol{\beta}}(\lambda)]'[\mathbf{y}^{(\lambda)} - X^{(\lambda)}\hat{\boldsymbol{\beta}}(\lambda)]}{T} \tag{12.5.12}$$

Thus, for known λ, the maximum likelihood estimators are found by applying conventional formulas to the transformed observations. For unknown λ, we need to find the maximizing value $\tilde{\lambda}$, from which the maximum likelihood estimators for $\boldsymbol{\beta}$ and σ^2 are given by $\tilde{\boldsymbol{\beta}} = \hat{\boldsymbol{\beta}}(\tilde{\lambda})$ and $\tilde{\sigma}^2 = \hat{\sigma}^2(\tilde{\lambda})$, respectively.

To find $\tilde{\lambda}$, we substitute (12.5.11) and (12.5.12) into (12.5.10), yielding the concentrated log-likelihood function

$$L^*(\lambda) = \text{constant} - \frac{T}{2}\ln \hat{\sigma}^2(\lambda) + (\lambda - 1)\sum_{t=1}^{T} \ln y_t \tag{12.5.13}$$

Thus, estimation usually proceeds by first numerically finding that value of λ that maximizes (12.5.13), either by grid search or by an iterative algorithm, and then using the estimate $\tilde{\lambda}$ in the expressions in (12.5.11) and (12.5.12). Letting $\boldsymbol{\theta}' = (\boldsymbol{\beta}', \sigma^2, \lambda)$, an estimate of the asymptotic covariance matrix for $\tilde{\boldsymbol{\theta}}' = (\tilde{\boldsymbol{\beta}}', \tilde{\sigma}^2, \tilde{\lambda})$ is given by the inverse of the information matrix $I(\boldsymbol{\theta})$ evaluated at $\tilde{\boldsymbol{\theta}}$, or, alternatively, by the inverse of the negative of the Hessian of the log-likelihood, evaluated at $\tilde{\boldsymbol{\theta}}$. This latter estimator is given by

$$\left[-\frac{\partial^2 L}{\partial\boldsymbol{\theta}\partial\boldsymbol{\theta}'}\right]^{-1}\Bigg|_{\boldsymbol{\theta}=\tilde{\boldsymbol{\theta}}} \tag{12.5.14}$$

and expressions for its various components can be found in Fomby, Hill, and Johnson (1984, pp. 428–429).

If λ is known, then an estimate of the covariance matrix $\hat{\boldsymbol{\beta}}(\lambda)$ is given by

$$\hat{\sigma}^2(\lambda)(X^{(\lambda)\prime}X^{(\lambda)})^{-1} \tag{12.5.15}$$

Standard errors computed from (12.5.15) with λ replaced by $\tilde{\lambda}$ can be regarded as *conditional* standard errors, conditional on $\lambda = \tilde{\lambda}$. These standard errors will be lower than the unconditional ones provided by (12.5.14) and will therefore overstate the reliability of the estimator for $\boldsymbol{\beta}$.

12.5.1a Maximum Likelihood Estimation by Nonlinear Least Squares

If only σ^2 is concentrated out of the log-likelihood function, it is straightforward to show that the concentrated log-likelihood function is

$$L^*(\boldsymbol{\beta}, \lambda) = C_1 - \frac{T}{2}\ln\left[\frac{(\mathbf{y}^{(\lambda)} - X^{(\lambda)}\boldsymbol{\beta})'(\mathbf{y}^{(\lambda)} - X^{(\lambda)}\boldsymbol{\beta})}{T}\right] + (\lambda - 1)\sum_{t=1}^{T}\ln y_t \quad (12.5.16)$$

where C_1 is a constant. Letting C_2 be a new constant, it can be shown (see Exercise 12.9) that (12.5.16) is equal to

$$L^*(\boldsymbol{\beta}, \lambda) = C_2 - \frac{T}{2}\ln\left[\frac{(\mathbf{y}^{(\lambda)} - X^{(\lambda)}\boldsymbol{\beta})'(\mathbf{y}^{(\lambda)} - X^{(\lambda)}\boldsymbol{\beta})}{\bar{y}_G^{2\lambda}}\right] \quad (12.5.17)$$

where $\bar{y}_G = (y_1 \cdot y_2 \cdots y_T)^{1/T}$ is the geometric mean of the y_t. Finding those values for $(\boldsymbol{\beta}, \lambda)$ that maximize (12.5.17) is equivalent to finding those values that minimize $\mathbf{e}^{*\prime}\mathbf{e}^*$ where

$$\mathbf{e}^* = (\mathbf{y}^{(\lambda)} - X^{(\lambda)}\boldsymbol{\beta})/\bar{y}_G^{\lambda} \quad (12.5.18)$$

Thus, it is possible to write the maximization problem within a general nonlinear least squares framework, a framework that is particularly useful if suitable software is available.

12.5.1b Estimation with Different Transformation Parameters

If we turn now to the specification in (12.5.6), where each variable is subject to a different transformation, the log-likelihood function can be written as

$$L(\boldsymbol{\beta}, \sigma^2, \lambda_1, \boldsymbol{\lambda}) = -\frac{T}{2}\ln 2\pi - \frac{T}{2}\ln\sigma^2 - \frac{1}{2\sigma^2}(\mathbf{y}^{(\lambda_1)} - X^{(\boldsymbol{\lambda})}\boldsymbol{\beta})'(\mathbf{y}^{(\lambda_1)} - X^{(\boldsymbol{\lambda})}\boldsymbol{\beta})$$
$$+ (\lambda_1 - 1)\sum_{t=1}^{T}\ln y_t \quad (12.5.19)$$

where $\boldsymbol{\lambda}' = (\lambda_2, \lambda_3, \ldots, \lambda_K)$ and $X^{(\boldsymbol{\lambda})} = (\mathbf{j}, \mathbf{x}_2^{(\lambda_2)}, \ldots, \mathbf{x}_K^{(\lambda_K)})$. The same steps just outlined can be applied to this function, the difference being that, in this case, we have to deal with an additional $(K - 1)$ parameters that cannot be concentrated out.

12.5.2 An Example

The data in Table 12.7 were generated using the model

$$y_t = \beta_1^* + \beta_2 x_{t2} + \beta_3 x_{t3} + e_t \qquad (12.5.20)$$

where $\beta_1^* = 2$, $\beta_2 = \beta_3 = 1$ and the e_t are i.i.d. $N(0, \sigma^2)$ with $\sigma^2 = 2.25$. In terms of the more general Box–Cox formulation, (12.5.20) can be viewed as

$$y_t^{(\lambda_1)} = \beta_1 + \beta_2 x_{t2}^{(\lambda_2)} + \beta_3 x_{t3}^{(\lambda_3)} + e_t \qquad (12.5.21)$$

where $\beta_1 = \beta_1^* + \beta_2 + \beta_3 - 1 = 3$, $\beta_2 = \beta_3 = 1$, and $\lambda_1 = \lambda_2 = \lambda_3 = 1$. Equation 12.5.21 was estimated using maximum likelihood, first assuming $\lambda_1 = \lambda_2 = \lambda_3 = \lambda$, and then allowing for the possibility of different λ. The results are presented in Table 12.8.

The conditional standard errors for the $\tilde{\beta}_k$ are computed using $\hat{\sigma}^2(\tilde{\lambda})(X^{(\tilde{\lambda})\prime} X^{(\tilde{\lambda})})^{-1}$ as indicated in (12.5.15); the conditional standard errors for $\tilde{\sigma}^2$ were taken as $[2\hat{\sigma}^4(\tilde{\lambda})/T]^{1/2}$. The unconditional standard errors were derived from the BHHH estimate of the asymptotic covariance matrix as presented in (12.2.102), namely

$$\left[\sum_{t=1}^{T} \left(\frac{\partial L_t}{\partial \boldsymbol{\theta}}\right)\left(\frac{\partial L_t}{\partial \boldsymbol{\theta}'}\right)\right]^{-1} \qquad (12.5.22)$$

evaluated at $\tilde{\boldsymbol{\theta}}' = (\tilde{\boldsymbol{\beta}}', \tilde{\lambda}_1, \tilde{\lambda}_2, \tilde{\lambda}_3, \tilde{\sigma}^2)$ or $\tilde{\boldsymbol{\theta}}' = (\tilde{\boldsymbol{\beta}}', \tilde{\lambda}, \tilde{\sigma}^2)$. The derivatives in (12.5.22) were evaluated numerically.

The first set of estimates, obtained under the assumption that $\lambda_1 = \lambda_2 = \lambda_3$, is reasonable, although the estimate for λ is rather low, leading to a 95% confidence interval (0.607, 0.951) that does not contain the true value $\lambda = 1$. The estimates $\tilde{\beta}_2$ and $\tilde{\beta}_3$ are also somewhat lower than their true values of $\beta_2 = \beta_3 = 1$, but the corresponding 95% confidence intervals do contain the true values. The unconditional standard errors are only slightly larger than their conditional counterparts.

The estimates obtained under the assumption of different λ_k are extremely bad. Although a sample of size 40 would be regarded as moderately large for a number of other types of models, it is clearly not a sufficiently large sample for this very demanding model. An intuitive way of viewing the difficulty, taking x_2 as an example, is that there are two parameters β_2 and λ_2, both of which govern the effect of x_2 on y (or on $y^{(\lambda_1)}$). There could be a wide range of alternative values of β_2, λ_2 that lead to a similar effect of x_2 on y. For example, a high β_2 and a low λ_2 could have an effect similar to that from a low β_2 and a high λ_2. This possibility seems to be borne out by the ridiculous estimates of $\tilde{\beta}_2 = 25.846$ and $\tilde{\lambda}_2 = -1.536$, and the corresponding high unconditional standard errors of 73.34 and 2.30, respectively. Note that we have still been able to estimate λ_1 and σ^2 fairly accurately, but where the effect of a β_k can easily be confused with that from a λ_k, reliable estimation is

Table 12.7 Data for Box–Cox Transformation Example

x_2	x_3	y
5.381719	3.336064	11.007283
3.009112	5.232138	9.485100
4.375199	3.546423	6.444172
5.472562	5.590764	13.449126
4.701641	2.124140	11.501331
4.047996	3.869655	12.358151
5.855000	4.078571	12.995271
4.820906	3.933097	14.131402
2.453591	5.121045	8.881935
2.453289	3.521771	5.953811
2.512200	2.927539	7.790439
3.462947	4.706172	10.508419
3.816963	3.639600	10.399463
2.723284	4.589414	9.679147
4.203508	2.221079	7.571837
3.493063	5.657767	12.430480
4.294265	3.375917	13.010082
3.345298	5.094239	10.550837
5.096056	3.493393	9.798799
3.257751	2.634803	9.098704
5.331691	5.716792	10.804783
4.800605	5.066528	11.588434
3.941124	3.141868	9.877543
5.720727	2.194553	8.041930
4.536456	2.789461	13.275866
3.084652	4.212297	9.501099
4.508164	5.634752	10.303916
5.632088	4.536204	14.217142
4.889667	4.324151	9.392368
4.028880	3.201167	11.797746
3.825508	5.426684	13.318442
5.364851	4.563735	10.909186
4.445447	3.734707	13.380104
3.971793	4.092285	8.883878
5.899375	3.708031	7.875557
5.514231	3.824409	11.768390
4.328222	2.222048	9.822120
2.191853	5.540067	10.199920
5.982851	4.974421	14.951822
3.787909	4.886206	10.578265

Table 12.8 Parameter Estimates and Standard Errors for Box–Cox Model

		Same λ assumed			Different λ's assumed		
			Standard errors			Standard errors	
	True values	Parameter estimates	Conditional	Unconditional	Parameter estimates	Conditional	Unconditional
β_1	3	3.380	0.901	1.128	−8.471	4.413	26.127
β_2	1	0.746	0.230	0.278	25.846	7.202	73.338
β_3	1	0.574	0.227	0.278	1.610	0.581	5.264
λ	1	0.779		0.088			
λ_1	1				0.969		0.089
λ_2	1				−1.536		2.298
λ_3	1				0.391		2.513
σ^2	2.25	1.240	0.277	0.392	2.876	0.643	0.910

difficult. Also, conditional standard errors are a very misleading guide to reliability. Clearly, extreme caution must be exercised when attempting to estimate a model of this type, and no attempt should be made without a very large sample size.

12.6 Summary and Guide to Further Readings

This chapter has covered a vast array of models, estimators, and associated tests. We began by considering nonlinear least squares estimation of a model that is nonlinear in the parameters. The Gauss-Newton and Newton-Raphson algorithms were introduced within the framework of a simple one-parameter model and then generalized for the case of K unknown parameters. The Cobb-Douglas and CES production functions were used as examples. Maximum likelihood estimation and its associated algorithms and covariance matrix estimators were introduced and related to nonlinear least squares estimation. For more details and extensions of this material we recommend Amemiya (1983), Bard (1974), Burguete, Gallant, and Souza (1982), Gallant and Holly (1980), Gallant (1987), Goldfeld and Quandt (1972), and Harvey (1981, Chapters 3, 4).

The general linear model with a general unknown error covariance matrix can be viewed within the framework of nonlinear least squares and maximum likelihood. Bayesian estimation is also possible. The general aspects of these approaches were covered and then illustrated using a first-order autoregressive error model and a model with multiplicative heteroskedasticity. Further information on these topics and additional references can be found in Beach and MacKinnon (1978), Fomby and Guilkey (1978), Griffiths and Dao (1980), Harvey (1976, 1981), Judge, et al. (1985, Chapters 4, 5, 8, and 11), Magnus (1978), Spitzer (1979), and Zellner (1971). The Wald, Lagrange multiplier, and likelihood ratio tests were introduced in the context of the general linear model with general unknown covariance matrix, but they have much wider applicability. Some useful references on this topic that have not already been mentioned are Breusch and Pagan (1979, 1980), Engle (1984), Godfrey (1978), Gourieroux, Holly, and Monfort (1982), and Ruud (1984).

Nonlinear least squares estimation of a single equation can be extended to sets of nonlinear equations with contemporaneously correlated disturbances. Both two-step and maximum likelihood estimation were considered, and the linear expenditure system derived from a Klein-Rubin utility function was used as an example. For more details of nonlinear least squares estimation of systems see Gallant (1975, 1987), Barnett (1976), and Burguete, Gallant, and Souza (1982). Finally, we considered maximum likelihood estimation of the flexible functional form model provided by the Box-Cox transformation. Good reviews of the state of the art in flexible functional form analysis have been provided by Spitzer (1978, 1982a, 1982b, 1984).

Thirty years ago most of the techniques discussed in this chapter would have been regarded as out of the question or at least extremely difficult to implement because of their computational demands. There was a tendency to employ simpler estimators that could easily be computed even although those estimators may have been second best in terms of their finite sample properties. Indeed, there was no easy way of knowing whether a computationally more demanding estimator would have better statistical properties. Today, most of the estimators discussed in this chapter can be automatically computed by many standard software packages. Furthermore, there is a growing body of evidence that suggests that nonlinear maximum likelihood estimators frequently have better finite sample properties than do the computationally more simple alternatives. The type of material covered in this chapter is, therefore, becoming increasingly important as we continue to search for improved methods of inference.

12.7 Exercises

12.7.1 Individual Exercises

12.1 Derive the information matrix given in (12.2.87).

12.2 (*a*) Fill in the steps required to derive the concentrated log-likelihood function $L(\boldsymbol{\theta})$ in (12.3.13) from (12.3.10), (12.3.11), and (12.3.12).

(*b*) Show that the value of $\boldsymbol{\theta}$ that minimizes $S(\boldsymbol{\theta})$ in (12.3.14) is the same as that value which maximizes $L(\boldsymbol{\theta})$ in (12.3.13).

12.3 Perform the necessary integration to obtain $g(\boldsymbol{\beta}, \boldsymbol{\theta}|\mathbf{y})$, $g(\boldsymbol{\theta}|\mathbf{y})$, and $g(\beta_k, \boldsymbol{\theta}|\mathbf{y})$, which are given in (12.3.21), (12.3.22), and (12.3.23).

12.4 Prove the result in (12.3.34).

12.5 Derive the information matrix given in (12.3.49).

12.6 Prove that the Lagrange multiplier statistic in (12.3.99) is equal to one-half the regression sum of squares in the regression of $(\hat{e}_t^2/\tilde{\sigma}_0^2)$ on z_t.

12.7 (*a*) Prove that $\ln|\Sigma \otimes I_T| = T \ln|\Sigma|$.

(*b*) Let $\mathbf{e}' = (\mathbf{e}_1', \mathbf{e}_2', \ldots, \mathbf{e}_M')$ be a MT-dimensional row vector with each component, $\mathbf{e}_i$, of dimension T. Show that $\mathbf{e}'(\Sigma^{-1} \otimes I_T)\mathbf{e} = \text{tr}[S\Sigma^{-1}]$ where Σ is $(M \times M)$ and S is $(M \times M)$ with (i, j)th element equal to $\mathbf{e}_i'\mathbf{e}_j$.

12.8 In the context of the Box-Cox transformed model—Equation 12.5.8—show that

$$\left|\frac{\partial \mathbf{e}'}{\partial \mathbf{y}}\right| = \prod_{t=1}^{T} y_t^{\lambda-1}$$

12.9 Show that the two concentrated log-likelihood functions in (12.5.16) and (12.5.17) are equal.

12.10 (*a*) For the error components model studied in Section 11.5, specify the log-likelihood function for $\boldsymbol{\beta}$, σ_e^2 and $\lambda = \sigma_u^2/\sigma_e^2$ under the assumption that both error components μ_i and e_{it} are normally distributed.

(*b*) Using the first-order conditions for maximization of the log-likelihood function, derive three equations that could be solved iteratively for the maximum likelihood estimates $\tilde{\boldsymbol{\beta}}$, $\tilde{\sigma}_e^2$, and $\tilde{\lambda}$.

(*c*) Derive Wald, Lagrange multiplier, and likelihood ratio test statistics for testing the hypothesis $H_0\colon \lambda = 0$ against the alternative $H_1\colon \lambda > 0$.

12.11 Use the same set of random numbers that were used to derive the observations in Table 12.7, and the same vectors $\mathbf{x}_2$ and $\mathbf{x}_3$ that are in that table, to generate some observations $\mathbf{y}$ according to the model

$$\ln y_t = \beta_1 + \beta_2 \ln x_{t2} + \beta_3 \ln x_{t3} + e_t$$

where $\beta_1 = \beta_2 = \beta_3 = 1$ and $e_t \sim N(0, \sigma^2)$ with $\sigma^2 = 0.25$.
Estimate the models in (12.5.4) and (12.5.6) and comment on the results.

12.7.2 Monte Carlo Based Exercises

Most of the results in this chapter are only valid for large sample sizes. In econometrics, however, we typically work with small or moderate samples. Therefore, the small-sample and asymptotic distribution of the estimators or test statistics may differ substantially in practice. Also, the values of asymptotically equivalent test statistics will usually differ in small samples. You are invited to explore the small-sample properties of some of the estimators and test statistics by solving the following exercises.

The model under consideration is assumed to be

$$y_t = f(\mathbf{x}_t, \boldsymbol{\beta}) + e_t \qquad t = 1, 2, \ldots, 3 \tag{12.7.1}$$

where $f(\mathbf{x}_t, \boldsymbol{\beta}) = \beta_0 + \beta_1(x_{t1}^{\beta_2} + \beta_3 x_{t2})$ and the e_t are independently, normally distributed errors with mean 0 and variance $\sigma^2 = 1$. The true parameter values are $\beta_0 = 5$, $\beta_1 = \beta_2 = 2$, and $\beta_3 = 0.5$; and $x_{t1} = L_t$, and $x_{t2} = K_t$, $t = 1, 2, \ldots, 30$. The values for L_t and K_t are given in Table 12.3. We give the gradient and Hessian matrix of $f(\mathbf{x}_t, \boldsymbol{\beta})$ and thus provide all necessary derivatives for constructing the gradient and Hessian of the sum of squared errors objective function.

$$\left.\frac{\partial f}{\partial \boldsymbol{\beta}}\right|_{\boldsymbol{\beta}} = \begin{bmatrix} 1 \\ x_{t1}^{\beta_2} + \beta_3 x_{t2} \\ \beta_1 \ln(x_{t1}) x_{t1}^{\beta_2} \\ \beta_1 x_{t2} \end{bmatrix} \tag{12.7.2}$$

$$\left.\frac{\partial^2 f}{\partial \boldsymbol{\beta} \partial \boldsymbol{\beta}'}\right|_{\boldsymbol{\beta}} = \begin{bmatrix} 0 & 0 & 0 & 0 \\ \cdot & 0 & \ln(x_{t1}) x_{t1}^{\beta_2} & x_{t2} \\ \cdot & \cdot & \beta_1 [\ln(x_{t1})]^2 x_{t1}^{\beta_2} & 0 \\ \cdot & \cdot & \cdot & 0 \end{bmatrix} \tag{12.7.3}$$

12.7.2a Individual Numerical Exercises

12.12 Generate a sample of 30 values of y for the model (12.7.1) and compute nonlinear least squares estimates for $\boldsymbol{\beta}$ and σ^2. Apply different starting values for the numerical optimization algorithm of your choice. Compute also the approximate covariance matrix of $\mathbf{b}$.

12.13 Choose a significance level α and construct confidence intervals for the estimates.

12.14 Compute (nonlinear) least squares estimates that satisfy
(*a*) $b_1 = b_2$
(*b*) $b_1 = 1/b_3$
(*c*) $b_1 = b_2$ and $b_1 = 1/b_3$

12.15 Use the test statistics λ_W, λ_{LM}, and λ_{LR} to test the following null hypotheses.
(*a*) $H_0\colon \beta_1 = \beta_2$.
(*b*) $H_0\colon \beta_1 = 1/\beta_3$.
(*c*) $H_0\colon \beta_1 = \beta_2$ and $\beta_1 = 1/\beta_3$.
Compare the values of the test statistics and interpret.

12.7.2b Joint or Class Exercises

12.16 Compute the average values of the estimates of $\boldsymbol{\beta}$ and σ^2 from 100 samples and compare with the true values.

12.17 Construct empirical frequency distributions for $\mathbf{b}$ and $\hat{\sigma}^2$ and interpret.

12.18 Use the Kolmogorov–Smirnov D statistic or some other appropriate statistic to test the agreement between the empirical and theoretical asymptotic distributions.

12.19 Use the computed test statistics for the tests in Exercise 12.15 from 100 samples to perform a small-sample comparison of the asymptotically equivalent tests.

It is hoped that this Monte Carlo experiment will contribute to the understanding of the problems related to nonlinear models. But it should be kept in mind that we are dealing here with a very special case that should not lead to generalizations. Although an investigation of the small-sample properties of estimators for other nonlinear models could be performed in a similar way, the wide variety of possible specifications hinders the derivation of general results by Monte Carlo experiments of this type.

12.8 References

Amemiya, T. (1983) "Nonlinear Regression Models." In Z. Griliches and M. D. Intriligator (eds.) *Handbook of Econometrics.* Amsterdam, North-Holland, pp. 333–390.

Bard, Y. (1974) *Nonlinear Parameter Estimation.* New York, Academic Press.

Barnett, A. (1976). "Maximum Likelihood and Iterated Aitken Estimation of Nonlinear Systems of Equations." *Journal of the American Statistical Association*, 71, 354–360.

Barten, A. P. (1969) "Maximum Likelihood Estimation of a Complete Demand System." *European Economic Review*, 1, 7–73.

Beach, C. M., and J. G. MacKinnon (1978). "A Maximum Likelihood Procedure for Regression with Autocorrelated Errors." *Econometrica*, 46, 51–58.

Berndt, E. K., B. H. Hall, R. Hall, and J. A. Hausman (1974). "Estimation and Inference in Non-linear Structural Models." *Annals of Economic and Social Measurement*, 3, 653–665.

Berndt, E. R., and N. E. Savin (1977) "Conflict among Criteria for Testing Hypotheses in the Multivariate Regression Model." *Econometrica*, 45, 1263–1278.

Box, G. E. P., and D. R. Cox (1964) "An Analysis of Transformations." *Journal of the Royal Statistical Society, Series B*, 26, 211–243.

Breusch, T. S. (1979) "Conflict among Criteria for Testing Hypotheses: Extension and Comment" *Econometrica*, 47, 203–208.

Breusch, T. S., and A. R. Pagan (1979) "A Simple Test for Heteroscedasticity and Random Coefficient Variation." *Econometrica*, 47, 1287–1294.

Breusch, T. S., and A. R. Pagan (1980) "The Lagrange Multiplier Test and Its Applications to Model Specification in Econometrics." *Review of Economic Studies*, 47, 239–254.

Burguete, J. F., A. R. Gallant, and G. Souza (1982) "On the Unification of the Asymptotic Theory of Nonlinear Econometric Models." *Econometric Reviews*, 1, 151–190.

Cochrane, D., and G. H. Orcutt (1949) "Application of Least Squares Regressions to Relationships Containing Autocorrelated Error Terms." *Journal of the American Statistical Association*, 44, 32–61.

Dhrymes, P. J. (1978) *Introductory Econometrics.* New York, Springer-Verlag.

Engle, R. F. (1984) "Wald, Likelihood Ratio, and Lagrange Multiplier Tests in Econometrics." In Z. Griliches and M. Intriligator (eds.) *Handbook of Econometrics*, Vol. 2, Amsterdam, North-Holland, pp. 776–826.

Evans, G. B. A. and N. E. Savin (1982) "Conflict among the Criteria Revisited: The W, LR and LM Tests." *Econometrica*, 50, 737–748.

Fomby, T. B., R. C. Hill, and S. R. Johnson (1984) *Advanced Econometric Methods.* New York, Springer-Verlag.

Fomby, T. B., and D. K. Guilkey (1978) "On Choosing the Optimal Level of Significance for the Durbin-Watson Test and the Bayesian Alternative." *Journal of Econometrics*, 8, 203–214.

Fuller, W. A. (1976) *Introduction to Statistical Time Series.* New York, Wiley.

Gallant, A. R. (1975) "Seemingly Unrelated Nonlinear Regressions." *Journal of Econometrics*, 3, 35–50.

Gallant, A. R. (1987) *Nonlinear Statistical Models*, New York, Wiley.

Gallant, A. R., and A. Holly (1980) "Statistical Inference in an Implicit, Nonlinear, Simultaneous Equation Model in the Context of Maximum Likelihood Estimation." *Econometrica*, 48, 697–720.

Godfrey, L. G. (1978) "Testing for Multiplicative Heteroskedasticity." *Journal of Econometrics*, 8, 227–236.

Goldfeld, S. M. and R. E. Quandt (1972) *Nonlinear Methods in Econometrics.* Amsterdam, North-Holland.

Gourieroux, C., A. Holly, and A. Monfort (1982) "Likelihood Ratio Test, Wald Test, and Kuhn-Tucker Test in Linear Models with Inequality Constraints on the Regression Parameters." *Econometrica*, 50, 63–80.

Griffiths, W. E. and D. Dao (1980) "A Note on a Bayesian Estimator in an Autocorrelated Error Model." *Journal of Econometrics*, 12, 390-392.

Harvey, A. C. (1976) "Estimating Regression Models with Multiplicative Heteroscedasticity." *Econometrica*, 44, 461–465.

Harvey, A. C. (1981) *The Econometric Analysis of Time Series*, Halsted, New York.

Hildreth, C. and W. Dent (1974) "An Adjusted Maximum Likelihood Estimator" in W. Sellekaert, ed., *Econometrics and Economic Theory: Essays in Honor of Jan Tinbergen*, Macmillan, London, 3-25.

Jennrich, R. I. (1969) "Asymptotic Properties of Non-Linear Least Squares Estimators." *The Annals of Statistics*, 2, 633–643.

Judge, G. G., W. E. Griffiths, R. C. Hill, H. Lütkepohl and T. C. Lee (1985) *The Theory and Practice of Econometrics*, 2nd edition, Wiley, New York.

Magnus, J. (1978) "Maximum Likelihood Estimation of the GLS Model with Unknown Parameters in the Disturbance Covariance Matrix." *Journal of Econometrics*, 7, 281–312.

Malinvaud, E. (1980) *Statistical Methods of Econometrics*, 3rd ed., North-Holland, Amsterdam.

Powell, A. A. (1974) *Empirical Analytics of Demand Systems*, Heath, Lexington, MA.

Rothenberg, T. J. (1984) "Hypothesis Testing in Linear Models When the Error Covariance Matrix is Nonscalar." *Econometrica*, 52, 827–842.

Ruud, P. A. (1984) "Tests of Specification in Econometrics." *Econometric Reviews*, 3, 211–276.

Savin, N. E. (1976) "Conflict Among Testing Procedures in a Linear Regression Model with Autoregressive Disturbances." *Econometrica*, 44, 1303–1315.

Spitzer, J. J. (1978) "A Monte Carlo Investigation of the Box–Cox Transformation in Small Samples." *Journal of the American Statistical Association*, 73, 488–495.

Spitzer, J. J. (1979) "Small-Sample Properties of Nonlinear Least Squares and Maximum Likelihood Estimators in the Context of Autocorrelated Errors." *Journal of the American Statistical Association*, 74, 41–47.

Spitzer, J. J. (1982a) "A Primer on Box–Cox Estimation." *Review of Economics and Statistics*, 64, 307–313.

Spitzer, J. J. (1982b) "A Fast and Efficient Algorithm for the Estimation of Parameters in Models with the Box-and-Cox Transformation." *Journal of the American Statistical Association*, 77, 760–766.

Spitzer, J. J. (1984) "Variance Estimates in Models with the Box–Cox Transformation: Implications for Estimation and Hypothesis Testing." *The Review of Economics and Statistics*, 66, 645–652.

Sureka, K. and W. E. Griffiths (1984) "A Monte Carlo Comparison of Some Bayesian and Sampling Theory Estimates in Two Heteroscedastic Error Models." *Communications in Statistics* B, 13, 85–105.

Zarembka, P. (1968) "Functional Form in the Demand for Money." *Journal of the American Statistical Association*, 63, 502–511.

Zarembka, P. (1974) "Transformation of Variables in Econometrics." In P. Zarembka (ed.) *Frontiers in Econometrics*, New York, Academic Press.

Zellner, A. (1971) *An Introduction to Bayesian Inference in Econometrics.* New York, Wiley.

CHAPTER 13

Stochastic Regressors

In the previous chapters, the regressors, or explanatory variables, are assumed to be fixed or nonstochastic in repeated samples. This may be appropriate for laboratory experiments, in which the experimenter has control over the explanatory variables and can repeatedly observe the outcome of the dependent variable with the same fixed values or some designated values of the explanatory variables. In the social sciences and particularly in economics, the right-hand side explanatory variables in one equation are often generated as the outcome variables of other equations that are stochastic in nature. Thus they neither have the same fixed values in repeated samples nor do they have values that conform to the investigator's desired experimental design. Thus, under a nonexperimental or uncontrolled environment, the left-hand side dependent variable is often under the influence of explanatory variables that are stochastic in nature. In this situation we may question whether the least squares procedures developed in previous chapters are still applicable and, if not, what alternative estimation procedures are available.

In particular, we consider the linear statistical model

$$\mathbf{y} = Z\boldsymbol{\beta} + \mathbf{e} \tag{13.1}$$

where $\mathbf{y}$ is a $(T \times 1)$ vector of observations, $\boldsymbol{\beta}$ is a $(K \times 1)$ vector of unknown parameters, the $(T \times K)$ regressor matrix Z is stochastic, and $\mathbf{e}$ is a $(T \times 1)$ vector of random errors with the properties $E[\mathbf{e}] = \mathbf{0}$, and $E[\mathbf{ee}'] = \sigma^2 I_T$. We denote the stochastic regressor matrix as Z rather than the usual X to emphasize the difference between stochastic and fixed regressors. The basic problem of the stochastic regressors is that the least squares estimator $\mathbf{b} = (Z'Z)^{-1}Z'\mathbf{y}$ may not be unbiased because when taking the expectation of the random vector $\mathbf{b}$,

$$E[\mathbf{b}] = \boldsymbol{\beta} + E[(Z'Z)^{-1}Z'\mathbf{e}] \tag{13.2}$$

the $E[(Z'Z)^{-1}Z'\mathbf{e}]$ may not vanish. It may not vanish because $E[(Z'Z)^{-1}Z'\mathbf{e}]$ cannot be expressed as $(Z'Z)^{-1}Z'E[\mathbf{e}]$ as in the case of fixed regressors, nor, due to the stochastic nature of Z and $\mathbf{e}$, can it be expressed as $E[(Z'Z)^{-1}Z']E[\mathbf{e}]$ unless Z and $\mathbf{e}$ can be assumed to be independent.

In the following sections, we investigate the statistical consequences of alternative specifications relative to the stochastic regressor matrix Z and the stochastic error vector $\mathbf{e}$. We first consider the case where the regressors are stochastic but independent of the equation errors. Second, we consider the case where the regressors and the equation errors are not perfectly independent, in the sense that they are only independent of the contemporaneous (and sometimes succeeding) equation errors. Finally, we consider the case in which the regressors are not independent of the equation errors. The instrumental variable method is introduced as a way of dealing with general stochastic regressor models, such as the case of errors in variables.

13.1 Independent Stochastic Regressor Model

In this section, we consider a variant of the linear statistical model

$$\mathbf{y} = Z\boldsymbol{\beta} + \mathbf{e} \tag{13.1.1}$$

where the $(T \times K)$ regressor matrix Z is stochastic, but distributed independently of the $(T \times 1)$ random error vector $\mathbf{e}$. The independence of $\mathbf{e}$ and Z implies that

$$E[\mathbf{e}|Z] = E[\mathbf{e}] = \mathbf{0} \tag{13.1.2}$$

and

$$E[\mathbf{e}\mathbf{e}'|Z] = E[\mathbf{e}\mathbf{e}'] = \sigma^2 I_T \tag{13.1.3}$$

Thus, the assumption of the stochastic regressors being independent of the equation errors implies that the conditional distribution of the equation errors has the classical properties of $\mathbf{0}$ mean and homoskedastic variance.

Given the foregoing assumptions, we consider in the independent stochastic regressor model applying the least squares rule

$$\mathbf{b} = (Z'Z)^{-1}Z'\mathbf{y} \tag{13.1.4}$$

The least square estimator for the independent stochastic regressor model is still unbiased since

$$\begin{aligned} E[\mathbf{b}] &= \boldsymbol{\beta} + E[(Z'Z)^{-1}Z'\mathbf{e}] \\ &= \boldsymbol{\beta} + E[(Z'Z)^{-1}Z']E[\mathbf{e}] \\ &= \boldsymbol{\beta} \end{aligned} \tag{13.1.5}$$

where we make use of the fact that Z and $\mathbf{e}$ are independent and the expectation of the product of two independent random variables is equal to the product of the two expectations. In other words, if two random variables x and y are independent, then $E[xy] = E[x]E[y]$. However, the variance of the least squares estimator involves an expectation of the cross product matrix of the stochastic regressors

$$
\begin{aligned}
E[(\mathbf{b} - \boldsymbol{\beta})(\mathbf{b} - \boldsymbol{\beta})'] &= E[(Z'Z)^{-1}Z'\mathbf{e}\mathbf{e}'Z(Z'Z)^{-1}] \\
&= E[E[(Z'Z)^{-1}Z'\mathbf{e}\mathbf{e}'Z(Z'Z)^{-1}]|Z] \\
&= E[(Z'Z)^{-1}Z'\sigma^2 IZ(Z'Z)^{-1}] \\
&= \sigma^2 E[(Z'Z)^{-1}] \qquad (13.1.6)
\end{aligned}
$$

In evaluating (13.1.6), the following rule of mathematical expectation is used: If x and y are two random variables, then the expectation of x is related to the expectation of the conditional expectation of x, given y, as $E[x] = E_y[E[x|y]]$. (This rule can be derived from the fact that the *joint p.d.f.* of x and y can be expressed as the product of the *conditional p.d.f.* of y given x and the *marginal p.d.f.* of x. For mathematical expectation, see Section 2.4.) The scale parameter σ^2 can be estimated by

$$
\begin{aligned}
\hat{\sigma}^2 &= \hat{\mathbf{e}}'\hat{\mathbf{e}}/(T - K) \\
&= (\mathbf{y} - Z\mathbf{b})'(\mathbf{y} - Z\mathbf{b})/(T - K) \qquad (13.1.7)
\end{aligned}
$$

which is an unbiased estimator since

$$
\begin{aligned}
E[\hat{\sigma}^2] &= E[E[\hat{\sigma}^2|Z]] = E[E[(T-K)^{-1}\hat{\mathbf{e}}'\hat{\mathbf{e}}|Z]] \\
&= E[(T-K)^{-1}E[\hat{\mathbf{e}}'\hat{\mathbf{e}}|Z]] = E[(T-K)^{-1}(T-K)\sigma^2] \\
&= \sigma^2 \qquad (13.1.8)
\end{aligned}
$$

The variance-covariance matrix of the least squares estimator $\mathbf{b}$ can be estimated by $\hat{\sigma}^2(Z'Z)^{-1}$, which is also unbiased since

$$
\begin{aligned}
E[\hat{\sigma}^2(Z'Z)^{-1}] &= E[E[\hat{\sigma}^2(Z'Z)^{-1}|Z]] \\
&= E[\sigma^2(Z'Z)^{-1}] \\
&= \sigma^2 E(Z'Z)^{-1} \qquad (13.1.9)
\end{aligned}
$$

From this discussion we conclude that if the stochastic regressor matrix Z is independent of the equation error $\mathbf{e}$, the estimators $\mathbf{b}$, $\hat{\sigma}^2$, and $\hat{\sigma}^2(Z'Z)^{-1}$ are unbiased. In comparison with the fixed regressor model, the variance-covariance matrix of the estimator, $\mathbf{b}$ is $\sigma^2 E[(Z'Z)^{-1}]$ instead of $\sigma^2(Z'Z)^{-1}$. Also, the least squares estimator $\mathbf{b} = (Z'Z)^{-1}Z'\mathbf{y}$ is now a stochastic function of $\mathbf{y}$, not a linear estimator, and strictly speaking, not the BLUE of $\boldsymbol{\beta}$. However, if we consider the variance of the estimator as being conditional on a given Z, then the estimator is efficient.

It also can be shown that the least squares estimator $\mathbf{b}$ is still the maximum likelihood estimator of $\boldsymbol{\beta}$ if the equation errors are normally distributed and the distribution of Z does not involve the parameters $\boldsymbol{\beta}$ and σ^2. This results because the *p.d.f.* of **e** is identical to the *conditional p.d.f.* of **e** given Z, which, in turn, is equal to the *conditional p.d.f.* of **y** given Z.

In summary, if the stochastic regressor matrix Z is independent of the random equation error vector **e**, then the least squares estimator **b**, which is identical to the maximum likelihood estimator, is unbiased. The estimator of the variance of the equation error, $\hat{\sigma}^2 = \hat{\mathbf{e}}'\hat{\mathbf{e}}/(T - K)$ is an unbiased estimator of σ^2, whereas $\tilde{\sigma}^2 = \hat{\mathbf{e}}'\hat{\mathbf{e}}/T$ is a biased estimator of σ^2. The independence of the equation error and the stochastic regressors ensures that these estimators have the classical properties conditional for any matrix values of Z, and classical interval estimation and test procedures remain valid.

13.2 Partially Independent Stochastic Regressors

There are stochastic regressor models for which the equation error cannot be assumed fully independent of the stochastic regressors. An example is the partial adjustment model,

$$y_t = \beta x_t + \lambda y_{t-1} + e_t \tag{13.2.1}$$

which is often used in a model for the demand for a durable good. In this model y_t is a stock variable and the nonstochastic variable x_t is income; one of the explanatory variables is the lagged value of the dependent variable, which is stochastic. Although e_t can be assumed to be independent of the lagged value y_{t-1}, e_t cannot be assumed independent of y_t and its future values $y_{t+1}, y_{t+2} \ldots$.

The problem we confront when estimating the parameters of the regression equation (13.2.1) is that the explanatory variable y_{t-1} is determined by

$$y_{t-1} = \beta x_{t-1} + \lambda y_{t-2} + e_{t-1} \tag{13.2.2}$$

Consequently y_{t-1} is dependent on e_{t-1}. Also, y_{t-1} is in part determined by y_{t-2}, which in turn depends on e_{t-2}. Indeed, by backward substitution of (13.2.2) in (13.2.1), the following equation results.

$$\begin{aligned} y_t &= \beta x_t + \lambda(\beta x_{t-1} + \lambda y_{t-2} + e_{t-1}) + e_t \\ &= \beta x_t + \lambda\beta x_{t-1} + \lambda^2 y_{t-2} + \lambda e_{t-1} + e_t \end{aligned} \tag{13.2.3}$$

Applying the procedure n times, we find the variable y_t is dependent on all the current and past errors $e_t, e_{t-1}, e_{t-2}, \ldots$. The only tenable assumption in this case is that y_{t-1} may be independent of the current error e_t and the succeeding disturbances $e_{t+1}, e_{t+2}, \ldots, e_T$.

Since the explanatory variable y_{t-1} is not independent of all the error terms, one of the assumptions underlying the traditional linear statistical model is violated. Unfortunately, the finite sampling properties of the foregoing and many other estimators to be presented in the following chapters have not yet been derived. In many cases, however, it is possible to say something about the sampling distribution as the sample size increases. This has led statisticians and econometricians to use asymptotic properties of their estimators as a basis for estimator comparison and performance evaluation.

13.2.1 Some Asymptotic Results

It is possible to establish some asymptotic properties for the least squares estimator for the *general* stochastic regressor model

$$\mathbf{y} = Z\boldsymbol{\beta} + \mathbf{e} \tag{13.2.4}$$

where Z contains both the lagged values of y and the nonstochastic regressors $\mathbf{x}_t$, and has tth row given by

$$\mathbf{z}_t' = (y_{t-1}\ y_{t-2} \cdots y_{t-p}\ \mathbf{x}_t') \tag{13.2.5}$$

When $\mathbf{e}$ and Z are partially independent, we assume that e_t has mean 0 and variance σ^2. In addition, it is assumed that

$$\text{plim}\ \mathbf{e}'\mathbf{e}/T = \sigma^2 \tag{13.2.6}$$

and Z is such that

$$\text{plim}\ Z'Z/T = \Sigma_{zz} \tag{13.2.7}$$

is nonsingular and

$$\text{plim}\ Z'\mathbf{e}/T = \mathbf{0} \tag{13.2.8}$$

With these assumptions, it can be shown that the least squares estimator is consistent

$$\begin{aligned}
\text{plim}\ \mathbf{b} &= \text{plim}(Z'Z)^{-1}Z'\mathbf{y} \\
&= \boldsymbol{\beta} + \text{plim}(Z'Z/T)^{-1}(Z'\mathbf{e}/T) \\
&= \boldsymbol{\beta} + \text{plim}(Z'Z/T)^{-1}\ \text{plim}(Z'\mathbf{e}/T) \\
&= \boldsymbol{\beta} + \Sigma_{zz}^{-1} \cdot \mathbf{0} \\
&= \boldsymbol{\beta}
\end{aligned} \tag{13.2.9}$$

where Slutsky's theorem (see Sections 3.3.3 and 6.6) is used to evaluate the probability limit of the components of the probability limit of a product. Note that this derivation of the consistency of the least squares estimator parallels that of the least squares estimator in the standard regression model with fixed regressors in Chapter 6.

Both estimators $\tilde{\sigma}^2$ and $\hat{\sigma}^2$ of σ^2 can be shown to be consistent estimators since

$$\begin{aligned}
\text{plim}\, \tilde{\sigma}^2 &= \text{plim}\, \hat{\mathbf{e}}'\hat{\mathbf{e}}/T \\
&= \text{plim}(\mathbf{e}'\mathbf{e}/T) \\
&\quad - \text{plim}(\mathbf{e}'Z/T)\text{plim}(Z'Z/T)^{-1}\, \text{plim}(Z'\mathbf{e}/T) \\
&= \sigma^2 - \mathbf{0}\cdot\Sigma_{zz}^{-1}\cdot\mathbf{0} = \sigma^2
\end{aligned} \tag{13.2.10}$$

where $\hat{\mathbf{e}}'\hat{\mathbf{e}} = \mathbf{e}'\mathbf{e} - \mathbf{e}'Z(Z'Z)^{-1}Z'\mathbf{e}$ is used. Similarly,

$$\begin{aligned}
\text{plim}\, \hat{\sigma}^2 &= \text{plim}(T-K)^{-1}\hat{\mathbf{e}}'\hat{\mathbf{e}} \\
&= \text{plim}[T(T-K)^{-1}](\tilde{\sigma}^2) \\
&= \text{plim}[T(T-K)^{-1}]\text{plim}(\tilde{\sigma}^2) \\
&= \sigma^2
\end{aligned} \tag{13.2.11}$$

To determine the large sample properties of the least squares estimator $\mathbf{b} = (Z'Z)^{-1}Z'\mathbf{y}$, we need to determine the limiting distribution of

$$\sqrt{T}(\mathbf{b} - \boldsymbol{\beta}) = (Z'Z/T)^{-1}(Z'\mathbf{e}/\sqrt{T}) \tag{13.2.12}$$

It can be shown that

$$\sqrt{T}(\mathbf{b} - \boldsymbol{\beta}) \xrightarrow{d} N(\mathbf{0}, \sigma^2\Sigma_{zz}^{-1}) \tag{13.2.13}$$

Therefore, for large sample sizes, the covariance of the least squares estimator is $\sigma^2 T^{-1}\Sigma_{\psi\psi}^{-1} = \sigma^2\text{plim}(Z'Z/T)^{-1}/T$. If we use $Z'Z/T$ as an estimator for Σ_{zz}, the scale factor, T, cancels and the covariance estimator becomes $\hat{\sigma}^2(Z'Z)^{-1}$.

Consequently, when the regressor matrix Z is stochastic but contemporaneously independent of or uncorrelated with $\mathbf{e}$ so that $\text{plim}(Z'\mathbf{e}/T) = \mathbf{0}$ and $\text{plim}(Z'Z/T)$ is nonsingular, the classical results of the least squares estimation established in Chapters 6 and 8 hold asymptotically.

13.3 General Stochastic Regressor Models

For an autoregressive linear regression model of the type $y_t = \beta x_t + \lambda y_{t-1} + e_t$, in some cases e_t cannot be assumed to be contemporaneously independent of y_{t-1}. An example is the case when the errors of the model (13.2.1) are autocorrelated.

Another example is the case when the model (13.2.1) is derived from a geometric-distributed lag specification (see Chapter 17).

First, consider the case of autocorrelated equation errors. The simplest form of an autoregressive model of order 1, denoted by AR(1), with an autocorrelated equation error is

$$y_t = \beta y_{t-1} + e_t \tag{13.3.1}$$

$$e_t = \rho e_{t-1} + v_t \tag{13.3.2}$$

where v_t is assumed to have $E[v_t] = 0$, $E[v_t^2] = \sigma_v^2$, and $E[v_t v_s] = 0$ for $t \neq s$, and ρ and β are parameters to be estimated. In this model, as shown in Section 9.3,

$$E[e_t] = 0 \tag{13.3.3}$$

and

$$E[e_t^2] = \sigma_v^2/(1 - \rho^2) \tag{13.3.4}$$

Whereas v_t can be assumed to be independent of y_{t-1}, the equation error e_t and the stochastic regressor y_{t-1} cannot be assumed independent because both are functions of e_{t-1}. In particular,

$$\begin{aligned} E[e_t y_{t-1}] &= E[(\rho e_{t-1} + v_t) y_{t-1}] \\ &= \rho E[e_{t-1} y_{t-1}] + E[v_t y_{t-1}] \\ &= \cdots \\ &= [\sigma_v^2 \rho/(1 - \rho^2)] \sum_{t=0}^{\infty} \rho^i \beta^i \\ &\neq 0 \end{aligned} \tag{13.3.5}$$

Since e_t and y_{t-1} are not independent, the classical least squares procedure is not appropriate.

13.3.1 Instrumental Variable Estimation

As explained in the previous section, the inconsistency of the least squares estimator $\mathbf{b}$ results from the term $\text{plim}(Z'\mathbf{e}/T)$ being nonzero. It would be helpful, therefore, to understand the role played by the term $Z'\mathbf{e}$ in least squares estimation.

Consider a general stochastic linear regression model

$$\mathbf{y} = Z\boldsymbol{\beta} + \mathbf{e} \tag{13.3.6}$$

where Z contains observations of stochastic regressors. Assume there exists a $(T \times K)$ matrix X that is uncorrelated with $\mathbf{e}$ and highly correlated with Z so that

$$\text{plim } X'\mathbf{e}/T = \mathbf{0} \tag{13.3.7}$$

and

$$\text{plim } X'Z/T = \Sigma_{xz} \tag{13.3.8}$$

exists and is nonsingular. Furthermore, assume

$$\text{plim } X'\mathbf{y}/T = \Sigma_{xy} \tag{13.3.9}$$

also exists, so that we may use X' to premultiply the original equation, (13.3.6), to obtain

$$X'\mathbf{y} = X'Z\boldsymbol{\beta} + X'\mathbf{e} \tag{13.3.10}$$

Dividing both sides of (13.3.10) by T, taking the probability limit, and solving for $\boldsymbol{\beta}$, we have

$$\boldsymbol{\beta} = \Sigma_{xz}^{-1} \Sigma_{xy} \tag{13.3.11}$$

Substituting the sample moments $X'Z/T$ and $X'\mathbf{y}/T$ for the population moments Σ_{xz} and Σ_{xy}, we obtain the estimator

$$\mathbf{b}_{iv} = (X'Z)^{-1}X'\mathbf{y} \tag{13.3.12}$$

which is called the *instrumental variable estimator*. The foregoing method is called the *instrumental variable method*, and the variables $x_1, x_2, \ldots, x_K$ that generate the $(T \times K)$ matrix X are called *instrumental variables.*

The instrumental variable estimator $\mathbf{b}_{iv}$ is consistent because

$$\begin{aligned} \text{plim } \mathbf{b}_{iv} &= \text{plim}[(X'Z)^{-1}X'\mathbf{y}] \\ &= \text{plim}[(X'Z)^{-1}X'(Z\boldsymbol{\beta} + \mathbf{e})] \\ &= \text{plim}[\boldsymbol{\beta} + (X'Z)^{-1}X'\mathbf{e}] \\ &= \boldsymbol{\beta} + \text{plim}(X'Z/T)^{-1} \text{ plim}(X'\mathbf{e}/T) \\ &= \boldsymbol{\beta} + \Sigma_{xz}^{-1} \cdot \mathbf{0} \\ &= \boldsymbol{\beta} \end{aligned} \tag{13.3.13}$$

It is clearly crucial that X be uncorrelated with $\mathbf{e}$ but correlated with the explanatory variables Z so that the second-order moment matrix Σ_{xz} exists and is nonsingular. Without proof we state that if the asymptotic distribution of $X'\mathbf{e}/T^{1/2}$ is $N[\mathbf{0}, \sigma^2 \text{ plim}(X'X/T)]$, then we have, asymptotically,

$$\sqrt{T}(\mathbf{b}_{iv} - \boldsymbol{\beta}) \xrightarrow{d} N[\mathbf{0}, \sigma^2 \text{ plim}(X'Z/T)^{-1}(X'X/T)(Z'X/T)^{-1}] \tag{13.3.14}$$

Therefore, for large size samples, $\mathbf{b}_{iv}$ has a covariance matrix

$$T^{-1}\sigma^2\Sigma_{xz}^{-1}\Sigma_{xx}\Sigma_{zx}^{-1} \tag{13.3.15}$$

which can be consistently estimated by substituting the sample moments $X'Z/T$ and $X'X/T$ for Σ_{xz} and Σ_{xx} and $\hat{\sigma}^2$ for σ^2 to obtain $\hat{\sigma}^2(X'Z)^{-1}(X'X)(Z'X)^{-1}$. However, the variance of $\mathbf{b}_{iv}$ is not necessarily a minimum asymptotic variance since there may be many sets of instrumental variables that fulfill the requirement of being uncorrelated with the stochastic term and correlated with the stochastic regressors. The more correlated the instruments are with the stochastic regressors Z, the smaller is the asymptotic covariance matrix (see Dhrymes, 1974, pp. 296–297). Nevertheless, in a world of biased alternatives the instrumental variable estimator provides at least a consistent estimator.

Of course, a crucial problem related to instrumental variable estimation is the choice of the instruments. In subsequent chapters some models will be discussed where instrumental variables can be found. In fact, in the context of the standard regression model $\mathbf{y} = X\boldsymbol{\beta} + \mathbf{e}$ where the matrix of fixed regressors X is uncorrelated with the error vector $\mathbf{e}$, the regressors themselves may be chosen as instruments. In that case,

$$\mathbf{b}_{iv} = \mathbf{b} = (X'X)^{-1}X'\mathbf{y} \tag{13.3.16}$$

Hence the least squares estimator may also be interpreted as an instrumental variable estimator.

Generally the choice of the instruments will be more difficult and an instrumental variable estimator can be improved by choosing an appropriate set of instrumental variables. It is generally understood that if more information is incorporated in the estimation, the resulting estimator should be more efficient in the sense of reducing its asymptotic variance. Thus, if several sets of instrumental variables are available, a linear combination of these sets of variables can sometimes be used to form a new set of instrumental variables in order to improve the asymptotic estimator efficiency. In some cases, alternative estimation procedures are available that result in consistent estimators. An example is given in Section 17.4.

In addition to using instrumental variable estimation to obtain consistent estimators, there are other methods to obtain consistent estimators. One example is using a nonlinear method [Klein (1958)] to obtain consistent estimators. (See also Chapter 12 for other nonlinear estimations.) However, not very many stochastic regressor models can be estimated by a special technique such as that of Klein. In general, a consistent estimator can be obtained by using instrumental variable estimation.

13.3.2 A Numerical Example

Consider estimation of a consumption function

$$\mathbf{y} = \alpha \mathbf{z}_1 + \beta \mathbf{z}_2^* + \mathbf{u} \tag{13.3.17}$$

where $\mathbf{y}$ is a $(T \times 1)$ vector of consumptions, $\mathbf{z}_1$ is a $(T \times 1)$ vector of ones and $\mathbf{z}_2^*$ is a $(T \times 1)$ vector of true unobservable income. The observable income is a $(T \times 1)$ vector $\mathbf{z}_2$ but with $(T \times 1)$ vector of errors $\mathbf{v}$, or

$$\mathbf{z}_2 = \mathbf{z}_2^* + \mathbf{v} \tag{13.3.18}$$

Substitution of (13.3.18) in (13.3.17) gives a regression equation

$$\begin{aligned} \mathbf{y} &= \alpha \mathbf{z}_1 + \beta \mathbf{z}_2 + (\mathbf{u} - \beta \mathbf{v}) \\ &= \alpha \mathbf{z}_1 + \beta \mathbf{z}_2 + \mathbf{e} \end{aligned} \tag{13.3.19}$$

where $\mathbf{e} = \mathbf{u} - \beta \mathbf{v}$ and $\mathbf{z}_2$ is stochastic and cannot be assumed independent of $\mathbf{e}$, which includes $\mathbf{v}$. A direct application of least squares to (13.3.19) would yield parameter estimators that are not only biased but also inconsistent. Suppose that the true income $\mathbf{z}_2^*$ can be explained by investment $\mathbf{x}_2$, which is also a $(T \times 1)$ vector, or

$$\mathbf{z}_2^* = \pi_1 \mathbf{x}_1 + \pi_2 \mathbf{x}_2 \tag{13.3.20}$$

where $\mathbf{x}_1$ is a $(T \times 1)$ vector of ones. Substituting (13.3.20) in (13.3.18) gives

$$\mathbf{z}_2 = \pi_1 \mathbf{x}_1 + \pi_2 \mathbf{x}_2 + \mathbf{v} \tag{13.3.21}$$

This equation shows that investment explains income, therefore investment should be highly correlated with income, yet it can be assumed independent of the equation error $\mathbf{e}$. This suggests that investment can serve as an instrumental variable. The hypothetical data for the variables $\mathbf{x}_2$, $\mathbf{y}$, and $\mathbf{z}_2$ are given in Table 13.1

Using $\mathbf{x}_2$ as an instrumental variable vector for $\mathbf{z}_2$, the instrumental variable matrix X for estimating the simple consumption function is a (20×2) matrix of observations with the first column all 1's, that is $\mathbf{x}_1$, and the second column $\mathbf{x}_2$, and the Z matrix is also a (20×2) matrix of observations with first column all 1's and the second column $\mathbf{z}_2$. The cross moment matrices $X'Z$ and $X'\mathbf{y}$ are respectively

$$X'Z = \begin{bmatrix} 20 & 492.7800 \\ 58 & 1461.1740 \end{bmatrix}, \quad X'\mathbf{y} = \begin{bmatrix} 434.94 \\ 1286.7060 \end{bmatrix} \tag{13.3.22}$$

Table 13.1 Hypothetical Data for x_2, y, and z_2

Observation	x_2	y	z_2
1	2.0	15.30	17.30
2	2.0	19.91	21.91
3	2.2	20.94	22.96
4	2.2	19.66	21.86
5	2.4	21.32	23.72
6	2.4	18.33	20.73
7	2.6	19.59	22.19
8	2.6	21.30	23.90
9	2.8	20.93	23.73
10	2.8	21.64	24.44
11	3.0	21.90	24.90
12	3.0	20.50	23.50
13	3.2	22.83	26.05
14	3.2	23.49	26.69
15	3.4	24.20	27.60
16	3.4	23.05	26.45
17	3.6	24.01	27.61
18	3.6	25.83	29.43
19	3.8	25.15	28.95
20	3.8	25.06	28.86

The inverse matrix of $X'Z$ is

$$(X'Z)^{-1} = \begin{bmatrix} 2.27511 & -0.76728 \\ -0.09031 & 0.03114 \end{bmatrix} \tag{13.3.23}$$

Thus the instrumental variable estimates are

$$\begin{bmatrix} a_{iv} \\ b_{iv} \end{bmatrix} = (X'Z)^{-1}X'\mathbf{y} = \begin{bmatrix} 2.2734 \\ 0.7904 \end{bmatrix} \tag{13.3.24}$$

The sum of the squared residuals is 1.3435, which yields $\tilde{\sigma}^2 = 0.0672$ and $\hat{\sigma}^2 = 0.0746$. The asymptotic covariance matrix for a_{iv} and b_{iv} is estimated by

$$\tilde{\sigma}^2(X'Z)^{-1}X'X(Z'X)^{-1} = \begin{bmatrix} 0.2644 & -0.0106 \\ -0.0106 & 0.0004 \end{bmatrix} \tag{13.3.25}$$

The estimated asymptotic standard errors of a_{iv} and b_{iv} are respectively 0.5142 and 0.0207. The ratios of the parameter estimates and the asymptotic strandard errors are 4.4214 and 38.1167, respectively, for a_{iv} and b_{iv}. Thus, if these numbers are used as approximate t-values, both coefficients are significant at the 1% level.

13.4 Measurement Errors

The problem of stochastic regressors also arises when some explanatory variables cannot be measured accurately or simply cannot be directly observed or measured at all. The problems of unobservable and erroneously observed variables are becoming more important as researchers explore new areas of empirical research. The models constructed for many areas of scientific inquiry include theoretical or abstract variables, for which the measures are known to be imperfect or the scales of measurement do not exist at all. Examples of such variables are utility, ability, achievement, ambition, and political attitudes. No one has yet observed or measured ability, but it is often used in explaining an individual's earning or status attainment. For example, observable measures of an individual's success, such as income and occupational standing, may depend on schooling and an unobservable ability variable. In another model, permanent change in the earnings of individuals during any time period may be modeled as the sum of an unobserved initial human capital level and the previously accumulated permanent change in earnings.

Unobserved variables may be the result of measurement error in the observed magnitudes. An example is Friedman's (1957) permanent income hypothesis. In his consumption function model, permanent consumption c_p is proportional to permanent income y_p, that is, $c_p = by_p$. The actual observable measured income of any period for any individual or economy consists of the sum of permanent and transitory components y_p, y_T, that is, $y = y_p + y_T$. Also, actual measured consumption is viewed as consisting of a basic permanent component plus a random transitory component, that is, $c = c_p + c_T$. Another example is the adaptive expectations model, in which the quantity supplied may depend on the unobservable expected price, and the expectations are revised in proportion to the error associated with the previous level of expectations. Also, in the partial adjustment model, current values of the independent variables determine the unobservable desired value of the dependent variable, but only some fixed fraction of the desired adjustment is accomplished in one period. Thus the errors in variables problems are not only inseparable from the problem of unobservable variables, but are also related to the distributed lag models to be discussed in Chapter 17.

In some cases in empirical analysis the variables we measure are not really what we want to measure. For example, observed test scores may be used as a proxy for years of education; consequently, the proxy variables may be subject to large random measurement errors. Even for the observable variables the data may be subject to a variety of errors. Errors may be introduced by the wording of the survey questionnaires. Words such as weak or strong may imply different things to different respondents. Griliches (1974) notes that these errors arise because (1) in economics the data producers and data analyzers are separate, (2) there is fuzziness about what it is we would like to observe, and (3) the phenomena that we are trying to measure are complex.

13.4.1 Statistical Consequences of Errors in Variables

One way to conceptualize the errors in variables problem is to treat the true, or theoretically desired, measure as one variable and the actual observations as another variable. The difference between the two may then be defined as a stochastic error variable. In the bivariate case, let us assume that $\mathbf{z}$ and $\mathbf{y}$ are $(T \times 1)$ vectors of the observed or measured values of the true unobservable variables $\mathbf{z}^*$ and $\mathbf{y}^*$, respectively. Thus

$$\mathbf{z} = \mathbf{z}^* + \mathbf{u} \tag{13.4.1}$$

$$\mathbf{y} = \mathbf{y}^* + \mathbf{v} \tag{13.4.2}$$

where $\mathbf{u}$ and $\mathbf{v}$ denote $(T \times 1)$ error vectors. These random vectors are often assumed to have mean vectors

$$E[\mathbf{u}] = \mathbf{0} \tag{13.4.3}$$

$$E[\mathbf{v}] = \mathbf{0} \tag{13.4.4}$$

and constant variances for $\mathbf{u}$ and $\mathbf{v}$, respectively

$$E[\mathbf{u}\mathbf{u}'] = \sigma_u^2 I \tag{13.4.5}$$

and

$$E[\mathbf{v}\mathbf{v}'] = \sigma_v^2 I \tag{13.4.6}$$

Furthermore, they are assumed to be uncorrelated, that is

$$E[\mathbf{u}\mathbf{v}'] = 0 \tag{13.4.7}$$

and independent of the true values $\mathbf{z}^*$ and $\mathbf{y}^*$.

The unobservable variable or measurement error problem emerges when a researcher specifies that $\mathbf{y}^*$ is a function of $\mathbf{z}^*$ and we would like to measure the parameters of such a function. The exact linear relation may be specified as

$$\mathbf{y}^* = \mathbf{z}^*\beta \tag{13.4.8}$$

where β is the scalar parameter to be estimated and the variables $\mathbf{y}^*$ and $\mathbf{z}^*$ are assumed to be the deviations from their means. Since $\mathbf{y}^*$ and $\mathbf{z}^*$ are unobservable, what can be observed are $\mathbf{z}$ and $\mathbf{y}$. We must therefore transform the model (13.4.8) into one that involves observable variables. Thus the substitution of (13.4.1) and (13.4.2) into (13.4.8) yields

$$\mathbf{y} = \mathbf{z}\beta + \mathbf{e} \tag{13.4.9}$$

where

$$\mathbf{e} = \mathbf{v} - \mathbf{u}\beta \tag{13.4.10}$$

The statistical model (13.4.9) contains observable variables, but the stochastic term $\mathbf{e}$ involves errors in both $\mathbf{y}$ and $\mathbf{z}$. The stochastic error vector $\mathbf{e}$ has mean $\mathbf{0}$.

$$E[\mathbf{e}] = E[\mathbf{v}] - \beta E[\mathbf{u}] = \mathbf{0} \tag{13.4.11}$$

covariance matrix

$$\begin{aligned} E[\mathbf{e}\mathbf{e}'] &= E[\mathbf{v}\mathbf{v}'] + \beta^2 E[\mathbf{u}\mathbf{u}'] \\ &= \sigma_{\mathbf{v}}^2 I + \beta^2 \sigma_{\mathbf{u}}^2 I \end{aligned} \tag{13.4.12}$$

and thus fulfills the basic classical least squares requirements. The independence requirement between the stochastic term $\mathbf{e}$ and the explanatory variable $\mathbf{z}$ is violated, however, because the covariance between $\mathbf{z}$ and $\mathbf{e}$ is

$$\begin{aligned} E[(\mathbf{z} - E[\mathbf{z}])(\mathbf{e} - E[\mathbf{e}])'] &= E[\mathbf{u}(\mathbf{v} - \beta\mathbf{u})'] \\ &= -\beta E[\mathbf{u}\mathbf{u}'] \\ &= -\beta\sigma_{\mathbf{u}}^2 I \end{aligned} \tag{13.4.13}$$

Because of the dependency between $\mathbf{e}$ and $\mathbf{z}$ the classical least squares estimator is not unbiased, and the bias can be shown as follows. The least squares estimator is

$$b = (\mathbf{z}'\mathbf{z})^{-1}\mathbf{z}'\mathbf{y} \tag{13.4.14}$$

Substitution of (13.4.9) into (13.4.14) results in

$$b = \beta + (\mathbf{z}'\mathbf{z})^{-1}\mathbf{z}'\mathbf{e} \tag{13.4.15}$$

with expectation

$$E[b] = \beta + E[(\mathbf{z}'\mathbf{z})^{-1}\mathbf{z}'\mathbf{e}] \tag{13.4.16}$$

Because $\mathbf{z}$ is not independent of $\mathbf{e}$ the last term does not vanish, and thus b is biased. Even for large samples, the probability limit of b does not converge to β because

$$\begin{aligned} \operatorname{plim} b &= \beta + \operatorname{plim} T(\mathbf{z}'\mathbf{z})^{-1}\mathbf{z}'\mathbf{e}/T \\ &= \beta + \sigma_{\mathbf{z}}^{-2}(-\beta\sigma_{\mathbf{u}}^2) \\ &= \beta - \beta\sigma_{\mathbf{u}}^2/\sigma_{\mathbf{z}}^2 \end{aligned} \tag{13.4.17}$$

where plim $T(\mathbf{z}'\mathbf{z})^{-1} = \sigma_{\mathbf{z}}^{-2}$ is assumed to exist. From (13.4.1),

$$\sigma_{\mathbf{z}}^2 = \sigma_{\mathbf{z}^*}^2 + \sigma_{\mathbf{u}}^2 \tag{13.4.18}$$

because $\mathbf{z}^*$ and $\mathbf{u}$ are assumed to be independent. Therefore, the asymptotic bias in (13.4.17) may be expressed as

$$\operatorname{plim}(b - \beta) = -\beta\sigma_{\mathbf{u}}^2/(\sigma_{\mathbf{z}^*}^2 + \sigma_{\mathbf{u}}^2) \tag{13.4.19}$$

which is in direct proportion to β and will be small only if $\sigma_{\mathbf{z}^*}^2$ is relatively much larger than $\sigma_{\mathbf{u}}^2$.

The foregoing exposition extends readily to a general case of many variables, with some variables not subject to errors. For this treatment refer to Chapter 17 of Judge, et al. (1985).

13.4.2 Additional Equations for Nuisance Parameters

In estimation in the presence of measurement errors one may seek a consistent estimator via the maximum likelihood method. Unfortunately, unobservable variables and errors in variables not only cause problems in the classical least squares method, but they also cause problems when the maximum likelihood method is applied. The failure of the maximum likelihood method will not be shown here, but in this case it is the result of insufficient information. In other words, the model is not identified. Additional a priori information regarding the parameters is required. One form of additional information may be reflected by an equation relating observable variables to the unobservable variable and that contains nuisance parameters. The use of this kind of information will result in the instrumental variable estimation described in Section 13.3.1. To demonstrate the incorporation of an equation containing this additional information, consider the following model

$$\mathbf{y} = \mathbf{z}_1\alpha + \mathbf{z}^*\beta + \mathbf{v} \tag{13.4.20}$$

$$\mathbf{z} = \mathbf{z}^* + \mathbf{u} \tag{13.4.21}$$

$$\mathbf{z}^* = \mathbf{x}_1\pi_1 + \mathbf{x}_2\pi_2 + \cdots + \mathbf{x}_K\pi_K \tag{13.4.22}$$

where $\mathbf{x}_1$ is a $(T \times 1)$ column vector of ones and the π's are additional unknown parameters and $\mathbf{x}_2, \ldots, \mathbf{x}_K$ are ancillary variables that contain information about $\mathbf{z}^*$.

In this formulation the number of parameters in the model is no longer dependent on the sample size, and the T unknown incidental parameters $\mathbf{z}^*$ are now replaced by the K-dimensional unknown coefficient vector $\boldsymbol{\pi}$. The model was first considered by Zellner (1970) and Goldberger (1972) as a system of simultaneous equations. Indeed, substitution of (13.4.22) into (13.4.20) and (13.4.21) results in a two-equation model.

$$\mathbf{y} = \mathbf{z}_1\alpha + \mathbf{x}_1\beta\pi_1 + \mathbf{x}_2\beta\pi_2 + \cdots + \mathbf{x}_K\beta\pi_K + \mathbf{v} \tag{13.4.23}$$

$$\mathbf{z} = \mathbf{x}_1\pi_1 + \mathbf{x}_2\pi_2 + \cdots + \mathbf{x}_K\pi_K + \mathbf{u} \tag{13.4.24}$$

or, more compactly,

$$\mathbf{y} = X\boldsymbol{\pi}_z\beta + \mathbf{v} \tag{13.4.25}$$

$$\mathbf{z} = X\boldsymbol{\pi}_z + \mathbf{u} \tag{13.4.26}$$

where all the variables are assumed to have zero means so that the intercepts α and π_1 may be eliminated for simplicity, $X = (\mathbf{x}_2\mathbf{x}_3\cdots\mathbf{x}_K)$ is a $[T \times (K-1)]$ matrix, $\boldsymbol{\pi}_z = (\pi_2\pi_3\cdots\pi_K)'$ is a $[(K-1) \times 1]$ vector of parameters, and β is a scalar parameter.

To estimate β in (13.4.25) we must know $X\boldsymbol{\pi}_z$. Although X is a matrix of known variables, $\boldsymbol{\pi}_z$ is unknown. However, $\boldsymbol{\pi}_z$ can be estimated from (13.4.26). Thus a two-stage least squares procedure is suggested. In the first stage $\mathbf{z}$ is regressed on X to obtain

$$\hat{\boldsymbol{\pi}}_z = (X'X)^{-1}X'\mathbf{z} \tag{13.4.27}$$

In the second stage $\mathbf{y}$ is regressed on $\hat{\mathbf{z}}\ (= X\hat{\boldsymbol{\pi}}_z)$ to obtain one of the two-stage least squares estimators denoted by $\tilde{\beta}_{(\infty)}$ as

$$\tilde{\beta}_{(\infty)} = [\mathbf{z}'X(X'X)^{-1}X'\mathbf{z}]^{-1}\mathbf{z}'X(X'X)^{-1}X'\mathbf{y} \tag{13.4.28}$$

The use of infinity in $\tilde{\beta}_{(\infty)}$ is related to the variance ratio $\lambda = \sigma_v^2/\sigma_u^2$ and will become apparent in what follows. On the other hand, if we define

$$\boldsymbol{\pi}_y = \boldsymbol{\pi}_z\beta \tag{13.4.29}$$

we can rearrange (13.4.25) and (13.4.26) as

$$\mathbf{y} = X\boldsymbol{\pi}_y + \mathbf{v} \tag{13.4.30}$$

$$\mathbf{z} = X\boldsymbol{\pi}_y/\beta + \mathbf{u} \tag{13.4.31}$$

In this case, the two-stage least squares procedure is reversed. In the first stage $\mathbf{y}$ is regressed on X to obtain

$$\hat{\boldsymbol{\pi}}_y = (X'X)^{-1}X'\mathbf{y} \tag{13.4.32}$$

and in the second stage, $\mathbf{z}$ is regressed on $\hat{\mathbf{y}}\ (= X\hat{\boldsymbol{\pi}}_y)$ to obtain

$$\widehat{\left(\frac{1}{\beta}\right)} = [\mathbf{y}'X(X'X)^{-1}X'\mathbf{y}]^{-1}\mathbf{y}'X(X'X)^{-1}X'\mathbf{z} \tag{13.4.33}$$

We take the reciprocal of (13.4.33) as the basis for the estimator

$$\tilde{\beta}_{(0)} = [\mathbf{y}'X(X'X)^{-1}X'\mathbf{z}]^{-1}\mathbf{y}'X(X'X)^{-1}X'\mathbf{y} \tag{13.4.34}$$

Thus there are two two-stage least squares estimators, $\tilde{\beta}_{(\infty)}$ and $\tilde{\beta}_{(0)}$. One may be interpreted as a regression of $\mathbf{y}$ on $\mathbf{z}$ using $\hat{\mathbf{z}}$ as an instrumental variable, and the other may be interpreted as a regression of $\mathbf{y}$ on $\mathbf{z}$ using $\hat{\mathbf{y}}$ as an instrumental variable. Both two-stage least squares estimators are consistent. However, these estimators are not efficient, because in the process of estimating $\boldsymbol{\pi}_z$, information contained in $\mathbf{y}$ is not used, and in estimating $\boldsymbol{\pi}_y$, information contained in $\mathbf{z}$ is not used.

To improve the efficiency of the estimator for β, Zellner (1970) minimizes the following weighted sum of squares

$$S = (\mathbf{z} - X\boldsymbol{\pi}_z)'(\mathbf{z} - X\boldsymbol{\pi}_z)/\sigma_{\mathbf{u}}^2 + (\mathbf{y} - X\boldsymbol{\pi}_y)'(\mathbf{y} - X\boldsymbol{\pi}_y)/\sigma_{\mathbf{v}}^2 \tag{13.4.35}$$

In this weighted sum of squares, information contained in both $\mathbf{z}$ and $\mathbf{y}$ are used, and the resulting estimator should be more efficient. Minimization of (13.4.35) yields the following generalized least squares estimator (see Zellner, 1970) for $\boldsymbol{\pi}_z$

$$\tilde{\boldsymbol{\pi}}_z = [\hat{\boldsymbol{\pi}}_z + (\beta^2/\lambda)(\hat{\boldsymbol{\pi}}_y/\beta)]/(1 + \beta^2/\lambda) \tag{13.4.36a}$$

and the estimator for β

$$\tilde{\beta}_{(\lambda)} = [\hat{\mathbf{y}}'\hat{\mathbf{y}} - \lambda\hat{\mathbf{z}}'\hat{\mathbf{z}} + \sqrt{(\lambda\hat{\mathbf{z}}'\hat{\mathbf{z}} - \hat{\mathbf{y}}'\hat{\mathbf{y}})^2 + 4\lambda(\hat{\mathbf{z}}'\hat{\mathbf{y}})^2}]/(2\hat{\mathbf{z}}'\hat{\mathbf{y}}) \tag{13.4.36b}$$

where $\lambda = \sigma_v^2/\sigma_u^2$ may be estimated as

$$\hat{\lambda} = S_{yy}/S_{zz} \tag{13.4.37}$$

with

$$S_{\mathbf{yy}} = T^{-1}(\mathbf{y} - X\hat{\boldsymbol{\pi}}_y)'(\mathbf{y} - X\hat{\boldsymbol{\pi}}_y) \tag{13.4.38}$$

$$S_{\mathbf{zz}} = T^{-1}(\mathbf{z} - X\hat{\boldsymbol{\pi}}_z)'(\mathbf{z} - X\hat{\boldsymbol{\pi}}_z) \tag{13.4.39}$$

Zellner (1970) noted that $|\tilde{\beta}_{(\infty)}| \le |\tilde{\beta}_{(\lambda)}| \le |\tilde{\beta}_{(0)}|$.

Noting that the weighted sum of squares (13.4.35) is only a part of a log-likelihood function, Goldberger (1972) suggests that $\boldsymbol{\pi}_z$, $\boldsymbol{\pi}_y$, σ_u^2, and σ_v^2 be estimated jointly from the likelihood function. The parameter β may be estimated from (13.4.29) after $\boldsymbol{\pi}_z$ and $\boldsymbol{\pi}_y$ are estimated. To show the symmetry, Goldberger writes the model in the reduced form as

$$\mathbf{y} = X\boldsymbol{\pi}_y + \mathbf{v} \tag{13.4.40}$$

$$\mathbf{z} = X\boldsymbol{\pi}_z + \mathbf{u} \tag{13.4.41}$$

where $(\mathbf{u}' \ \mathbf{v}')'$ is normally distributed with mean $\mathbf{0}$ and variance

$$E\left[\begin{bmatrix}\mathbf{u}\\ \mathbf{v}\end{bmatrix}\begin{bmatrix}\mathbf{u}\\ \mathbf{v}\end{bmatrix}'\right] = \begin{bmatrix}\sigma_{\mathbf{u}}^2 I_T & 0\\ 0 & \sigma_{\mathbf{v}}^2 I_T\end{bmatrix} = \Omega \tag{13.4.42}$$

The joint *p.d.f.* for $\mathbf{u}$ and $\mathbf{v}$ is

$$\begin{aligned} f(\mathbf{u}, \mathbf{v}) = (2\pi)^{-T}|\Omega|^{-1/2} \exp[&-(\mathbf{y} - X\boldsymbol{\pi}_{\mathbf{y}})'(y - X\boldsymbol{\pi}_{\mathbf{y}})/(2\sigma_{\mathbf{v}}^2) \\ &-(\mathbf{z} - X\boldsymbol{\pi}_{\mathbf{z}})'(\mathbf{z} - X\boldsymbol{\pi}_{\mathbf{z}})/(2\sigma_{\mathbf{u}}^2)] \end{aligned} \tag{13.4.43}$$

which, when viewed as a function of the parameters $\boldsymbol{\pi}_z$, $\boldsymbol{\pi}_y$, σ_u^2, and σ_v^2, given $\mathbf{y}$ and $\mathbf{z}$, is the likelihood function. The log-likelihood is

$$\begin{aligned} \ln \ell(\boldsymbol{\pi}_{\mathbf{z}}, \boldsymbol{\pi}_{\mathbf{y}}, \sigma_{\mathbf{u}}^2, \sigma_{\mathbf{v}}^2 | \mathbf{y}, \mathbf{z}) = &-T\ln(2\pi) - \ln|\Omega|/2 \\ &-(\mathbf{y} - X\boldsymbol{\pi}_{\mathbf{y}})'(\mathbf{y} - X\boldsymbol{\pi}_{\mathbf{y}})/(2\sigma_{\mathbf{v}}^2) \\ &-(\mathbf{z} - X\boldsymbol{\pi}_{\mathbf{z}})'(\mathbf{z} - X\boldsymbol{\pi}_{\mathbf{z}})/(2\sigma_{\mathbf{u}}^2) \end{aligned} \tag{13.4.44}$$

Note that the last two terms of (13.4.44) contain the weighted sum of squares (13.4.35). If Ω is known, then maximizing (13.4.44) is equivalent to minimizing (13.4.35). If Ω is unknown, (13.4.44) or $\ell(\cdot)$ is maximized by taking the derivatives of $\ln \ell(\cdot)$ with respect to σ_u^2 and σ_v^2, setting them to 0, and solving for σ_u^2 and $\tilde{\sigma}_v^2$ to obtain the ML estimators $\tilde{\sigma}_u^2$ and $\tilde{\sigma}_v^2$. Then $\tilde{\sigma}_u^2$ and $\tilde{\sigma}_v^2$ are inserted back into (13.4.44) to obtain the concentrated likelihood function, which in turn is maximized with respect to $\boldsymbol{\pi}_z$ and $\boldsymbol{\pi}_y$. Since the first step produces

$$\tilde{\sigma}_{\mathbf{v}}^2 = T^{-1}(\mathbf{y} - X\tilde{\boldsymbol{\pi}}_{\mathbf{y}})'(\mathbf{y} - X\tilde{\boldsymbol{\pi}}_{\mathbf{y}}) \tag{13.4.45}$$

$$\tilde{\sigma}_{\mathbf{u}}^2 = T^{-1}(\mathbf{z} - X\tilde{\boldsymbol{\pi}}_{\mathbf{z}})'(\mathbf{z} - X\tilde{\boldsymbol{\pi}}_{\mathbf{z}}) \tag{13.4.46}$$

Goldberger suggests an iterative procedure to obtain $\tilde{\sigma}_u^2$, $\tilde{\sigma}_v^2$, $\tilde{\boldsymbol{\pi}}_z$, and $\tilde{\boldsymbol{\pi}}_y$. The generalized least squares estimators $\hat{\boldsymbol{\pi}}_z$ and $\hat{\boldsymbol{\pi}}_y$, as proposed by Zellner, are used as initial estimates in order to compute (13.4.45) and (13.4.46), or, equivalently, (13.4.38) and (13.4.39), then (13.4.37) and hence the new generalized least squares estimator (13.4.36b). Then, (13.4.44) is maximized, given $\tilde{\sigma}_{\mathbf{u}}^2$ and $\tilde{\sigma}_{\mathbf{v}}^2$, to obtain $\tilde{\boldsymbol{\pi}}_{\mathbf{z}}$ and $\tilde{\boldsymbol{\pi}}_{\mathbf{y}}$. The procedure is repeated until the estimates converge. On each round of the iteration, an explicit solution for β can be computed from (13.4.36b). As noted by Goldberger (1972), finite-sample-distribution considerations do not provide a basis for preferring the maximum likelihood estimation, or, equivalently, the iterative procedure described, to the initial Zellner estimates.

The system in (13.4.25) and (13.4.26) can be expanded to include an intercept term and other observable independent variables. For the intercept case Zellner (1971) shows that the same steps can be performed to obtain values for $\hat{\boldsymbol{\pi}}_{\mathbf{z}}$ (and $\hat{\beta}$), that will then be used to obtain the intercept $\hat{\alpha}$ as

$$\hat{\alpha} = (\mathbf{x}_1'\mathbf{x}_1)^{-1}\mathbf{x}_1'(\mathbf{y} - X\hat{\boldsymbol{\pi}}_{\mathbf{y}}) \tag{13.4.47}$$

where $\mathbf{x}_1$ is a $(T \times 1)$ column vector of one's. Equation (13.4.47) simply confirms that the regression equation passes through the means of all the variables in this case. The following numerical example demonstrates the estimation procedures described in this section.

13.4.3 A Numerical Example

To better understand the estimation procedures described in the previous section, a hypothetical model is constructed and the particular values for the parameters are assigned, a data set is created, and then the parameters are estimated by the three procedures described by Zellner. The model considered is

$$y_t = \alpha + \beta z_t^* + v_t \tag{13.4.48}$$

$$z_t = z_t^* + u_t \tag{13.4.49}$$

$$z_t^* = \pi_1 + \pi_2 x_{t2} + \pi_3 x_{t3} \tag{13.4.50}$$

and the hypothetical structure is constructed as follows.

$$y_t = 10 + 0.8 z_t^* + v_t \tag{13.4.51}$$

$$z_t = z_t^* + u_t \tag{13.4.52}$$

$$z_t^* = 2 + 3x_{t2} + 5x_{t3} \tag{13.4.53}$$

where u_t is assumed from $N(0, 0.2)$ and v_t is assumed from $N(0, 0.5)$. The values of x_{ti}, $(t = 1, 2, \ldots, 15; i = 2, 3)$ are assigned and u_t and v_t are generated by a computer in order to generate z_t^*, z_t, and y_t. The resulting data set is given in Table 13.2.

According to the procedures described in Section 13.4.2, the following steps are used to calculate $\tilde{\beta}_{(\infty)}$.

1. Regress $\mathbf{z}$ on $\mathbf{x}_i$ for $i = 2, 3$ (with intercept) to obtain $\hat{\mathbf{z}}$. The following regression results are obtained:

$$\begin{aligned} \hat{z}_t = \; & 17.241 \;\; + 0.82650 x_{t2} + 2.4458 x_{t3} \\ & (10.368) \quad\;\; (1.4912) \qquad (1.7471) \end{aligned} \tag{13.4.54}$$

where the numbers in the parentheses are standard errors of estimates. The explained sum of squared deviations from the mean of z_t is calculated as 23.19736, and the residual sum of squares or TS_{zz} is calculated as 3.304005 for future reference.

Table 13.2 A Hypothetical Data Set

Observation	$\mathbf{x}_2$	$\mathbf{x}_3$	u	v	z*	z	y
1.00	1.10	5.00	0.09	0.60	30.30	30.39	34.84
2.00	1.50	4.70	−0.23	1.57	30.00	29.77	35.57
3.00	1.70	4.60	−1.04	0.05	30.10	29.06	34.13
4.00	1.80	4.40	0.12	−0.37	29.40	29.52	33.15
5.00	2.00	4.20	0.80	0.57	29.00	29.80	33.77
6.00	2.30	4.00	0.73	−1.06	28.90	29.63	32.06
7.00	2.40	3.70	0.32	−0.13	27.70	28.02	32.03
8.00	2.70	3.60	1.01	0.37	28.10	29.11	32.85
9.00	3.00	3.50	−0.21	−0.88	28.50	28.29	31.92
10.00	3.10	3.20	−0.60	1.86	27.30	26.70	33.70
11.00	3.40	3.00	0.10	0.10	27.20	27.30	31.86
12.00	3.60	2.90	0.10	−0.87	27.30	27.40	30.97
13.00	3.90	2.60	0.28	0.97	26.70	26.98	32.33
14.00	4.00	2.50	0.11	−0.86	26.50	26.61	30.34
15.00	4.50	2.20	−0.25	1.21	26.50	26.25	32.41

2. Regress **y** on $\hat{\mathbf{z}}$ (with intercept) to obtain the parameter estimates a and b. The following results are obtained.

$$\begin{aligned}\hat{y}_t = {} & \underset{(5.6193)}{9.0970} + \underset{(0.1982)}{0.836784}\hat{z}_t\end{aligned} \tag{13.4.55}$$

where the numbers in the parentheses are standard errors of estimates. Therefore $\tilde{\beta}_{(\infty)} = 0.836784$.

In order to calculate $\tilde{\beta}_{(0)}$, the model is rewritten in the following form:

$$y_t = (\alpha + \beta\pi_1) + x_{t2}(\pi_2\beta) + x_{t3}(\pi_3\beta) + v_t \tag{13.4.56}$$

$$z_t = (-\alpha/\beta) + (\alpha + \pi_1\beta + x_{t2}\pi_2\beta + x_{t3}\pi_3\beta)(1/\beta) + u_t \tag{13.4.57}$$

In estimation, the following two steps are used.

1. Regress **y** on $\mathbf{x}_i$ for $i = 2, 3$ (with intercept) in order to calculate $\hat{\mathbf{y}}$. The following results are obtained.

$$\hat{y}_t = \underset{(13.1390)}{21.007} + \underset{(1.8898)}{1.0555}x_{t2} + \underset{(2.2142)}{2.4687}x_{t3} \tag{13.4.58}$$

The explained sum of squared deviations from the mean of y_t is also calculated as 16.25937, and the residual sum of squares or TS_{yy} is calculated as 11.83246 for future reference.

2. Regress $\mathbf{z}_2$ on $\hat{\mathbf{y}}$ (with intercept) to obtain the following regression results.

$$\begin{aligned}\hat{z}_t &= -10.832 + 1.1938\hat{y}_t \\ &\quad\ (4.1169) \qquad (0.1255)\end{aligned} \tag{13.4.59}$$

where the numbers in the parentheses are standard errors of estimates. Since the intercept -10.832 is actually $-\alpha/\beta$, and the slope 1.1938 is actually $1/\beta$, α and β can be derived as $\hat{\beta} = 1/1.1938 = 0.8377$ and $\hat{\alpha} = -(-10.832)/1.1938 = 9.0736$. Thus $\tilde{\beta}_{(0)} = 0.8377$.

For the third estimator $\tilde{\beta}_{(\lambda)}$, the cross product of z_{t2} and y_t is also calculated as

$$TS_{zy} = 19.41 \tag{13.4.60}$$

together with $TS_{zz} = 3.3040$ and $TS_{yy} = 11.8325$ as previously calculated. The variance ratio is then calculated as

$$\hat{\lambda} = S_{yy}/S_{zz} = TS_{yy}/TS_{zz} = 11.8325/3.3040 = 3.581248 \tag{13.4.61}$$

Using the values of $\hat{\lambda}$, $\hat{\mathbf{y}}'\hat{\mathbf{y}}$, $\hat{\mathbf{z}}'\hat{\mathbf{z}}$, and $\hat{\mathbf{y}}'\hat{\mathbf{z}}$ in (13.4.36b), we find the third estimate to be

$$\tilde{\beta}_{(\lambda)} = 0.8369214 \tag{13.4.62}$$

These results confirm Zellner's conclusion that $|\tilde{\beta}_{(\infty)}| \leq |\tilde{\beta}_{(\lambda)}| \leq |\tilde{\beta}_{(0)}|$, since $0.8368 \leq 0.8369 \leq 0.8377$. The estimate 0.8369 obtained from minimizing the weighted sum of squares can be used as an initial value for the maximum likelihood estimation, which must be solved iteratively. Given $\hat{\boldsymbol{\pi}}_y(\hat{\lambda}$ and $\hat{\beta})$, the intercept can be estimated by (13.4.47) as $\hat{\alpha} = 9.1133$.

13.5 Concluding Remarks

Whether or not the least squares estimators of the regression parameters will be unbiased, consistent, or inconsistent depends on whether the stochastic regressors are independent of, partially dependent on, or contemporaneously dependent on the disturbances. Since the assumption of independent stochastic regressors is sometimes hard to justify and thus the least squares estimator is not unbiased, we seek alternative estimating procedures that will give consistent estimators. The anatomy of the least squares method suggests that the instrumental variable method produces consistent estimators provided that the instrumental variables are uncorrelated with the error disturbances but correlated with the stochastic regressors. An instrumental variable estimator may not be efficient, but in the absence of other alternatives it at least provides a consistent estimator. There may be many variables that can be used as instrumental variables. Among the instrumental variable estimators, the one that makes use of the linear combination of all possible instrumental variables is believed to be more efficient than other instrumental variables estimators, since more information is incorporated. One problem is that we may not be able to identify all possible instrumental variables. Even if we can identify many instrumental variables, the auxiliary regression in creating a combined instrument will suffer a loss of degrees of freedom or run short of observations. For references for instrumental variables see Bowden and Turkington (1984).

The problem of stochastic regressors also arises when some explanatory variables cannot be measured accurately or simply cannot be directly observed or measured at all. The econometric problem of errors in variables is due mainly to insufficient information in estimating the parameters. Thus, if there is additional a priori knowledge about the parameters, it should be incorporated in estimating the parameters. If we have extraneous information in the form of additional equations for unobservable variables, we can use the auxiliary regression to obtain a combined instrumental variable to be used in the second-stage estimation. The resulting estimator will be consistent. However, the two-stage estimation procedure is not unique in that it depends on which variable is used as a dependent variable in the first-stage estimation. The procedure of minimizing the weighted sum of squares provides reasonable initial consistent estimates for the full-fledged maximum likelihood estimation. Suggest readings for errors in the variables are Aigner and Goldberger (1977), Aigner, Hsaio, Kapteyr and Wansbeek (1984), Fuller (1987) and Zellner (1971).

13.6 Exercises

13.6.1 Algebraic Exercises

13.1 Consider the model $\mathbf{y} = Z\boldsymbol{\beta} + \mathbf{e}$, where $\mathbf{y}$ is $(T \times 1)$, Z is $(T \times K)$ and stochastic, $\boldsymbol{\beta}$ is $(K \times 1)$, and $\mathbf{e}$ is $(T \times 1)$. Let X be a $(T \times J)$ matrix of instruments. If $K \leq J$, show that the use of the instrument $\hat{Z} = X(X'X)^{-1}X'Z$ results in the instrumental variable estimator

$$\tilde{\boldsymbol{\beta}} = (Z'X(X'X)^{-1}X'Z)^{-1}Z'X(X'X)^{-1}X'\mathbf{y}$$

13.2 Given the information in Exercise 13.1, show that if X has the same dimension and rank as Z, that is, $(T \times K)$, the instrumental variable estimator given in Exercise 13.1 is identical to

$$\tilde{\boldsymbol{\beta}} = (X'Z)^{-1}X'\mathbf{y}$$

13.6.2 Individual Numerical Exercises

Suppose that we observe **c** and **y** as listed in Table 13.3, and we want to estimate the consumption function

$$\mathbf{c} = \alpha\mathbf{j} + \beta\mathbf{y} + \mathbf{e}$$

in which both c, consumption , and y, income, are subject to errors of measurement

$$\mathbf{c} = \mathbf{c}^* + \mathbf{v}$$

$$\mathbf{y} = \mathbf{y}^* + \mathbf{u}$$

where $\mathbf{c}^*$ and $\mathbf{y}^*$ are true but unobservable permanent consumption and income, respectively, **j** is a vector of ones and the assumptions regarding **u** and **v** are described in (13.4.3) through (13.4.7). Therefore, **e** has mean $E[\mathbf{e}] = \mathbf{0}$ and variance $E[\mathbf{ee}'] = \sigma_v^2 I + \beta^2\sigma_u^2 I$. The following exercises use the data in Table 13.3.

Table 13.3 Hypothetical Data for i, g, c, and y

Observation	i	g	c	y
1	1.5	0.5	15.30	17.30
2	1.4	0.6	19.91	21.91
3	1.5	0.7	20.94	22.96
4	1.4	0.8	19.66	21.86
5	1.5	0.9	21.32	23.72
6	1.4	1.0	18.33	20.73
7	1.6	1.0	19.59	22.19
8	1.5	1.1	21.30	23.90
9	1.6	1.2	20.93	23.73
10	1.6	1.2	21.64	24.44
11	1.7	1.3	21.90	24.90
12	1.6	1.4	20.50	23.50
13	1.8	1.4	22.83	26.05
14	1.7	1.5	23.49	26.69
15	1.9	1.5	24.20	27.60
16	1.8	1.6	23.05	26.45
17	2.0	1.6	24.01	27.61
18	1.9	1.7	25.83	29.43
19	2.0	1.8	25.15	28.95
20	2.0	1.8	25.06	28.86

Suppose that $\mathbf{y} = \mathbf{c} + \mathbf{i} + \mathbf{g}$, where $\mathbf{g}$ is a vector of government expenditure. Thus, $\mathbf{i}$ and $\mathbf{g}$ are highly correlated with $\mathbf{y}$ and can be assumed independent of $\mathbf{e}$.

13.3 Using $\mathbf{i}$ as an instrumental variable, estimate the marginal propensity to consume β and the autonomous consumption α.

13.4 Using $\mathbf{g}$ as an instrumental variable, estimate the marginal propensity to consume and the autonomous consumption.

13.5 Using data given in Table 13.3, regress $\mathbf{y}$ on $\mathbf{i}$ and $\mathbf{g}$ (including a vector of 1's) in order to calculate $\hat{\mathbf{y}}$ as a forecast vector of $\mathbf{y}$, that is,

$$\hat{\mathbf{y}} = \hat{\pi}_1\mathbf{j} + \hat{\pi}_2\mathbf{i} + \hat{\pi}_3\mathbf{g}$$

where $\hat{\pi}_i$, $i = 1, 2, 3$ are least squares estimators. Using $\hat{\mathbf{y}}$, which is a linear combination of $\mathbf{i}$ and $\mathbf{g}$ as an instrumental variable, estimate the marginal propensity to consume and the autonomous consumption.

13.6 Given the hypothetical equations (13.4.51) through (13.4.53) with the assumptions that u_t is from $N(0, 0.2)$ and v_t is from $N(0, 0.5)$, one sample of 15 observations is generated from given values of $\mathbf{x}_2$ and $\mathbf{x}_3$, and the results are listed in Table 13.4.

Table 13.4

Observation	$\mathbf{x}_2$	$\mathbf{x}_3$	$\mathbf{u}$	$\mathbf{v}$	$\mathbf{z}^*$	$\mathbf{z}$	$\mathbf{y}$
1.00	1.10	5.00	−0.51	0.47	30.30	29.79	34.71
2.00	1.50	4.70	0.22	0.04	30.00	30.22	34.04
3.00	1.70	4.60	0.09	−0.31	30.10	30.19	33.77
4.00	1.80	4.40	0.43	−2.04	29.40	29.83	31.48
5.00	2.00	4.20	0.79	0.48	29.00	29.79	33.68
6.00	2.30	4.00	−0.14	−0.44	28.90	28.76	32.68
7.00	2.40	3.70	−0.16	0.79	27.70	27.54	32.95
8.00	2.70	3.60	0.29	0.63	28.10	28.39	33.11
9.00	3.00	3.50	−0.13	−0.16	28.50	28.37	32.64
10.00	3.10	3.20	−0.07	0.49	27.30	27.23	32.33
11.00	3.40	3.00	0.03	−0.22	27.20	27.23	31.54
12.00	3.60	2.90	0.58	0.51	27.30	27.88	32.35
13.00	3.90	2.60	−0.60	1.30	26.70	26.10	32.66
14.00	4.00	2.50	−0.43	0.00	26.50	26.07	31.20
15.00	4.50	2.20	−0.23	−1.26	26.50	26.27	29.94

Suppose that only $\mathbf{x}_2$, $\mathbf{x}_3$, $\mathbf{z}$, and $\mathbf{y}$ in Table 13.4 are observed, estimate the coefficients of the following model.

$$y_t = \alpha + \beta z_t^* + v_t$$

$$z_t = z_t^* + u_t$$

$$z_t^* = \pi_1 + \pi_2 x_{t2} + \pi_3 x_{t3}$$

using Zellner's three procedures described in Section 13.4.2.

13.7 References

Aigner, D. J., and A. S. Goldberger (eds.) (1977) *Latent Variables in Socioeconomic Models.* Amsterdam: North-Holland.

Aigner, D. J., C. Hsiao, A. Kapteyn, and T. Wansbeek (1984) "Latent Variables Models in Econometrics." In Z. Griliches and M. Intriligator, (eds.) *Handbook of Econometrics.* Amsterdam: North-Holland, pp. 1321–1393.

Bowden, R. J., and D. A. Turkington (1984) *Instrumental Variables.* New York, Cambridge University Press.

Dhrymes, P. J. (1974) *Econometrics: Statistical Foundations and Applications.* New York: Springer-Verlag.

Friedman, M. A. (1957) *A Theory of the Consumption Function.* Princeton, N.J., Princeton University Press.

Fuller, W. A. (1987) *Measurement Error Models.* New York, Wiley.

Goldberger, A. S. (1972) "Maximum-Likelihood Estimation of Regression Containing Unobservable Independent Variables." *International Economic Review,* 13, 1–15.

Griliches, Z. (1974) "Errors in Variables and Other Unobservables." *Econometrica,* 42, 971–998.

Judge, G. G., W. E. Griffiths, R. C. Hill, H. Lütkepohl, and T. C. Lee (1985) *The Theory and Practice of Econometrics* 2nd ed. New York, Wiley.

Klein, L. (1958) "The Estimation of Distributed Lags." *Econometrica,* 26, 553–565.

Zellner, A. (1970) "Estimation of Regression Relationships Containing Unobservable Independent Variables. *International Economic Review,* 11, 441–454.

Zellner, A. (1971) *An Introduction to Bayesian Inference in Econometrics.* New York: Wiley.

PART 4

Simultaneous Linear Statistical Models

In Part 4 we recognize the simultaneous nature of the economic data-generation process and specify a statistical model that is consistent with this type of sampling mechanism. Emphasis is directed to the problem of least squares bias, the identification of an equation within a system of equations, and the possibilities for estimation and inference with this instantaneous-feedback linear statistical model.

CHAPTER 14

An Introduction to Simultaneous Linear Statistical Models

14.1 Introduction

In each of the preceding chapters we have stressed the importance of understanding the sampling process by which the data were generated and then adapting the statistical models and estimators to the peculiarities of the data and the objectives of the research. We have recognized that economic variables are in reality random or stochastic variables whose properties can be described by probability distributions. We have further indicated the stochastic nature of the observed data and their relationships to stochastic nonobservable variables in the form of random errors in the variables or random errors in the equation. We have also noted that economic data are often passively generated in that the observed values come as a result of the existing economic structure and thus there are limited possibilities for controlling some of the important economic variables and isolating relations and capturing the corresponding relevant parameters.

Most conceptual frameworks for understanding economic processes and institutions recognize that there is a feedback between economic variables and that in economics everything depends on everything else. This idea translates into the realization that economic data that are a product of the existing economic system must then be described as a system of simultaneous relations among the random economic variables and that these relations involve current, future, and past (lagged) values of some of the variables. This scenario led Marschak (1950) to comment that "economic data are generated by systems of relations that are in general stochastic, dynamic and simultaneous." He further noted that, although these properties of the data give rise to many unsolved problems in statistical inference, they constitute the basic ingredients underlying economic theory, and quantitative knowledge of them is needed for economic practice.

Previous chapters have emphasized the stochastic nature of economic variables. Chapters 16, 17, and 18 will focus on the dynamic nature of economic variables. In this chapter we are concerned with the simultaneous and interdependent nature of economic variables and what this implies in terms of a statistical model and the basis for parameter estimation and inference.

Up to this point we have lived in the simple world of one-way causality. In a sense we have been saying that all outcomes have causes and they existed before the event. In modern parlance the state of a system determines its later state. That is, we have assumed that the explanatory variables in the design matrix have an impact on the outcome values of the left-hand random vector **y** but that there is no feedback in the other direction. For example, in a time context we have taken the view that the past leads inexorably to the present and the possibility that the future could influence the present was not considered.

Although this simple type of theoretical model is appropriate for describing the data-generation process for many economic relations, it is inconsistent with the data-generation process for many others. For example, in a partial equilibrium setting for a single commodity we visualize price, quantity demanded, and quantity supplied being determined simultaneously. Thus it is inappropriate to posit that price causes consumption or consumption causes prices. The values that these variables actually take (the observables) are determined jointly and interdependently. We may express this instantaneous feedback mechanism within an equilibrium setting as the following set of simultaneous equations:

$$\mathbf{y}^d = \mathbf{x}_1\alpha_1 + \mathbf{p}\beta_1 + \mathbf{e}_1 \tag{14.1.1a}$$

$$\mathbf{y}^s = \mathbf{x}_1\alpha_2 + \mathbf{p}\beta_2 + \mathbf{e}_2 \tag{14.1.1b}$$

$$\mathbf{y}^s = \mathbf{y}^d \tag{14.1.1c}$$

where $\mathbf{y}^d$ is a vector of observed values of the quantity demanded, $\mathbf{y}^s$ is a $(T \times 1)$ vector of observed values of the quantity supplied, $\mathbf{p}$ is a $(T \times 1)$ vector of prices, and $\mathbf{x}_1$ is a $(T \times 1)$ vector of unit values. Also, $\mathbf{e}_1$ and $\mathbf{e}_2$ are vectors of unobservable random variables, and when their stochastic properties are specified, (14.1.1a) to (14.1.1c) become a statistical model that expresses the simultaneous mechanism operating to jointly determine the price and quantity variables. In the model, (14.1.1a) is a demand relation, (14.1.1b) is a supply relation, and (14.1.1c) is the equilibrium condition that closes the system. The message here is that a system of simultaneous equations is needed to describe the underlying sampling process consistent with the generation of the observables.

Another simple feedback system that reflects the interdependent nature of aggregate economic variables is the following simple Keynesian model that describes the data-generation process for aggregate consumption **c** and aggregate income **y** for T periods of time.

$$\mathbf{c} = \mathbf{x}_1\alpha + \mathbf{y}\beta + \mathbf{e} \tag{14.1.2a}$$

$$\mathbf{y} = \mathbf{c} + \mathbf{i} \tag{14.1.2b}$$

where **i** is aggregate investment, which is assumed to be determined outside the system, and **e** is a vector of unobservable random variables. The relation (14.1.2a) is recognized as a consumption function, and β is the marginal propensity to consume. The two equations recognize and describe the interdependent nature of the outcomes for **c** and **y**, and when the stochastic properties of **e** are specified we have a statistical model expressing the simultaneous nature of the sampling process.

Although each of the models (14.1.1) and (14.1.2) contains a measure of realism in that it expresses the simultaneous nature of economic variable determination, each is a simplified version of the data-generation process for many real-world situations. Seldom can we look at a market in isolation as in (14.1.1), so we must consider the prices of other commodities and the feedback mechanism operating to determine the outcomes for the corresponding prices and quantities. Alternatively, in (14.1.2) it is probably unrealistic to assume that investment is determined outside the system, and thus the model would need to be expanded to reflect the interdependent nature of **c**, **y**, and **i**.

Given these notions, let us turn to the problem of specifying a general linear statistical model that takes into account the simultaneous-instantaneous feedback nature of economic variable determination.

14.2 Specification of the Sampling Model

To introduce the idea of simultaneity we must pay special attention to how economic variables are classified. Basically, each equation in the model may contain the following types of variables:

Endogenous, or jointly determined variables, have outcome values determined through the joint interaction with other variables within the system. Examples, within the context of a partial or general equilibrium system, are such variables as price, consumption, production, and income.

Exogenous variables are variables that affect the outcome of the endogenous variables, but whose values are determined outside the system. Exogenous variables thus are assumed to condition the outcome values of the endogenous variables but are not reciprocally affected because no feedback relation is assumed. Examples in this category are weather-related variables, such as rainfall and temperature, and the world price of a commodity for a country model that involves only a minor part of the production or consumption of the commodity. Another example is the investment variable in (14.1.2).

Lagged endogenous variables may be placed in the same category as the exogenous variables since for the current period the observed values are predetermined. The exogenous variables and lagged endogenous variables that may involve any length of lag are called *predetermined variables.* For statistical purposes the relevant distinction is between jointly dependent variables and predetermined variables.

The final classification of variables involves the nonobservable random errors, or, as they were called in the early simultaneous equation literature, random shocks or disturbances. We have already talked about the various specifications for these unobservable random variables in the previous chapters.

An economic model organizes the information available about the system under study and postulates the interrelationships among the observables. Consequently, in the formulation of the model one is concerned with such things as (1) classification of the economic variables, (2) the variables that enter an equation, (3) any possible lags involved, (4) nonsample information about a single parameter or combinations of parameters, and (5) how many equations there should be and how the system should be closed or made complete. The equations of the system are called *structural equations*, and the corresponding parameters are called *structural parameters*. The system of equations is *complete* if there are as many equations as there are endogenous variables.

The statistical model consistent with this sampling process also involves the algebraic form for each of the equations in the simultaneous system and the stochastic assumptions underlying the random error variables. For example, as in Chapter 11, the error variables may be specified as multivariate normal with zero mean vector and known or unknown covariance matrix.

In general, a system of simultaneous equations may include (1) behavioral equations, (2) technical equations, (3) institutional equations and accounting identities or definitional equations, and (4) equilibrium conditions. The behavioral equations seek to describe the responses of economic agents and as such may involve such economic relations as demand functions and consumption functions that describe consumer behavior and supply functions that describe producer behavior. The technical equations involve relations such as production functions, which depict the relationship between the input of factors and the output of a product. Examples of institutional equations are the tax rules and regulations that are determined and administered by the government. The accounting identities or definitional equations reflect economic relations, such as income equals consumption plus investment and government expenditure, or personal disposable income is equal to GNP minus tax. Equilibrium conditions specify, for example, the conditions under which prices and quantities are to be determined in a market. In a competitive market such as (14.1.1) an equilibrium price is obtained if the quantity demanded equals the quantity supplied.

Note that the institutional equations, accounting identities or definitional equations, and equilibrium conditions are deterministic and contain neither a stochastic term nor unknown parameters that need to be estimated. However, they provide the important feedback relations for the jointly determined variables. The behavioral equations and technical equations specify possible relationships among the endogenous and predetermined variables and contain stochastic disturbance terms as well as unknown parameters that are to be estimated. Let us note again that these equations express the basic structural relationships among economic variables for the phenomena that are being modeled and as such are called *structural equations.*

14.2.1 The Statistical Model

With these definitions and concepts, let us specify a statistical model that is consistent with the simultaneous-instantaneous feedback nature of many economic systems. In the model let us represent the T observations on the M endogenous variables by the $(T \times 1)$ vectors $\mathbf{y}_1, \mathbf{y}_2, \ldots, \mathbf{y}_M$; the K exogenous and predetermined variables by the $(T \times 1)$ vectors $\mathbf{x}_1, \mathbf{x}_2, \ldots, \mathbf{x}_K$, and the M random error variables by the $(T \times 1)$ vectors $\mathbf{e}_1, \mathbf{e}_2, \ldots, \mathbf{e}_M$. A general linear statistical model reflecting the M equations that represent the relationships among the jointly determined endogenous variables, the exogenous and predetermined variables, and the random errors, may be stated as

$$\begin{aligned}
\mathbf{y}_1\gamma_{11} + \mathbf{y}_2\gamma_{21} + \cdots + \mathbf{y}_M\gamma_{M1} + \mathbf{x}_1\beta_{11} + \mathbf{x}_2\beta_{21} + \cdots + \mathbf{x}_K\beta_{K1} + \mathbf{e}_1 &= \mathbf{0} \\
\mathbf{y}_1\gamma_{12} + \mathbf{y}_2\gamma_{22} + \cdots + \mathbf{y}_M\gamma_{M2} + \mathbf{x}_1\beta_{12} + \mathbf{x}_2\beta_{22} + \cdots + \mathbf{x}_K\beta_{K2} + \mathbf{e}_2 &= \mathbf{0} \\
\vdots \qquad\qquad\qquad\qquad & \vdots \\
\mathbf{y}_1\gamma_{1M} + \mathbf{y}_2\gamma_{2M} + \cdots + \mathbf{y}_M\gamma_{MM} + \mathbf{x}_1\beta_{1M} + \mathbf{x}_2\beta_{2M} + \cdots + \mathbf{x}_K\beta_{KM} + \mathbf{e}_M &= \mathbf{0}
\end{aligned} \tag{14.2.1}$$

where the γ's and the β's are the structural parameters of the system that are unknown and are thus to be estimated from the data. The stochastic assumptions for the unobservable random error vectors $\mathbf{e}_1, \mathbf{e}_2, \ldots, \mathbf{e}_M$ are the same as those for the set of regression equations analyzed in Chapter 11. That is, we assume that the structural disturbances are generated by a stationary multivariate process with

$$E[\mathbf{e}_i] = \mathbf{0} \qquad \text{for} \qquad i = 1, 2, \ldots, M \tag{14.2.2}$$

and

$$E[\mathbf{e}_i\mathbf{e}_i'] = \sigma_{ii}I_T = \sigma_i^2 I_T \qquad \text{for} \qquad i = 1, 2, \ldots, M \tag{14.2.3}$$

and

$$E[\mathbf{e}_i\mathbf{e}_j'] = \sigma_{ij}I_T \qquad \text{for} \qquad i \neq j \qquad \text{and} \qquad i, j = 1, 2, \ldots, M \tag{14.2.4}$$

or, compactly, as

$$E[\mathbf{e}_i\mathbf{e}_j'] = \sigma_{ij}I_T \qquad \text{for} \qquad i, j = 1, 2, \ldots, M \tag{14.2.5}$$

which, as in Chapter 11, implies that if $\mathbf{e}' = (\mathbf{e}_1', \mathbf{e}_2', \ldots, \mathbf{e}_M')$ then

$$E[\mathbf{e}\mathbf{e}'] = E\left[\begin{bmatrix}\mathbf{e}_1\\ \mathbf{e}_2\\ \vdots\\ \mathbf{e}_M\end{bmatrix}\begin{bmatrix}\mathbf{e}_1\\ \mathbf{e}_2\\ \vdots\\ \mathbf{e}_M\end{bmatrix}'\right] = \begin{bmatrix}\sigma_{11}I & \sigma_{12}I & \cdots & \sigma_{1M}I\\ \sigma_{21}I & \sigma_{22}I & \cdots & \sigma_{2M}I\\ \vdots & \vdots & \ddots & \vdots\\ \sigma_{M1}I & \sigma_{M2}I & \cdots & \sigma_{MM}I\end{bmatrix} = \Sigma \otimes I_T \quad (14.2.6)$$

The unknown contemporaneous covariance matrix Σ is an $(M \times M)$ symmetric and positive semidefinite matrix. It may be of less than full rank because some of the equations may appear in the form of identities with null error vectors. In estimation, the identities are substituted for so that the resulting system may be assumed to have an error covariance that is nonsingular. In matrix notation the linear statistical model may be written compactly as

$$Y\Gamma + XB + \mathbf{E} = 0 \quad (14.2.7)$$

where 0 is a $(T \times M)$ matrix of zeros,

$$Y = \begin{bmatrix}y_{11} & y_{12} & \cdots & y_{1M}\\ y_{21} & y_{22} & \cdots & y_{2M}\\ \vdots & \vdots & \ddots & \vdots\\ y_{T1} & y_{T2} & \cdots & y_{TM}\end{bmatrix}_{(T\times M)} = (\mathbf{y}_1 \quad \mathbf{y}_2 \quad \ldots \quad \mathbf{y}_M) \quad (14.2.8)$$

and

$$X = \begin{bmatrix}x_{11} & x_{12} & \cdots & x_{1K}\\ x_{21} & x_{22} & \cdots & x_{2K}\\ \vdots & \vdots & \ddots & \vdots\\ x_{T1} & x_{T2} & \cdots & x_{TK}\end{bmatrix}_{(T\times K)} = (\mathbf{x}_1 \quad \mathbf{x}_2 \quad \ldots \quad \mathbf{x}_K) \quad (14.2.9)$$

are the sample values taken by the jointly dependent and the predetermined variables, respectively, and

$$\mathbf{E} = \begin{bmatrix}e_{11} & e_{12} & \cdots & e_{1M}\\ e_{21} & e_{22} & \cdots & e_{2M}\\ \vdots & \vdots & \ddots & \vdots\\ e_{T1} & e_{T2} & \cdots & e_{TM}\end{bmatrix}_{(T\times M)} = (\mathbf{e}_1 \quad \mathbf{e}_2 \quad \ldots \quad \mathbf{e}_M) \quad (14.2.10)$$

is the matrix $\mathbf{E}$ of unobservable values taken by the random error vectors. The matrix

$$\Gamma = \begin{bmatrix}\gamma_{11} & \gamma_{12} & \cdots & \gamma_{1M}\\ \gamma_{21} & \gamma_{22} & \cdots & \gamma_{2M}\\ \vdots & \vdots & \ddots & \vdots\\ \gamma_{M1} & \gamma_{M2} & \cdots & \gamma_{MM}\end{bmatrix}_{(M\times M)} = (\boldsymbol{\Gamma}_1 \quad \boldsymbol{\Gamma}_2 \quad \ldots \quad \boldsymbol{\Gamma}_M) \quad (14.2.11)$$

is the $(M \times M)$ matrix of coefficients of the current endogenous variables, where each column refers to the coefficients for a particular equation in (14.2.1).

$$B = \begin{bmatrix} \beta_{11} & \beta_{12} & \cdots & \beta_{1M} \\ \beta_{21} & \beta_{22} & \cdots & \beta_{2M} \\ \vdots & \vdots & \ddots & \vdots \\ \beta_{K1} & \beta_{K2} & \cdots & \beta_{KM} \end{bmatrix}_{(K \times M)} = (\mathbf{B}_1 \quad \mathbf{B}_2 \quad \ldots \quad \mathbf{B}_M) \tag{14.2.12}$$

is a $(K \times M)$ matrix of unknown coefficients of the exogenous-predetermined variables, and each column contains the coefficients of a particular equation in (14.2.1). It is important to note that Y and $\mathbf{E}$ are of the same order, Γ is a square matrix of order M, and B is of order $(K \times M)$, where, in general, K may or may not be equal to M.

For the system to be complete Γ must be of order M, and if it is, in addition, nonsingular, then we may write the stochastic system represented by (14.2.7) in the following equivalent form.

$$Y\Gamma + XB + \mathbf{E} = 0$$

$$Y\Gamma\Gamma^{-1} + XB\Gamma^{-1} + \mathbf{E}\Gamma^{-1} = 0$$

$$Y + XB\Gamma^{-1} + \mathbf{E}\Gamma^{-1} = 0$$

$$Y = -XB\Gamma^{-1} - \mathbf{E}\Gamma^{-1} \tag{14.2.13a}$$

or

$$Y = X\Pi + V \tag{14.2.13b}$$

where

$$\Pi = -B\Gamma^{-1} = \begin{bmatrix} \pi_{11} & \pi_{12} & \cdots & \pi_{1M} \\ \pi_{21} & \pi_{22} & \cdots & \pi_{2M} \\ \vdots & \vdots & \ddots & \vdots \\ \pi_{K1} & \pi_{K2} & \cdots & \pi_{KM} \end{bmatrix} = (\boldsymbol{\pi}_1 \quad \boldsymbol{\pi}_2 \quad \ldots \quad \boldsymbol{\pi}_M) \tag{14.2.14}$$

is a $(K \times M)$ matrix of coefficients and $V = -\mathbf{E}\Gamma^{-1}$ is a $(T \times M)$ matrix

$$V = \begin{bmatrix} v_{11} & v_{12} & \cdots & v_{1M} \\ v_{21} & v_{22} & \cdots & v_{2M} \\ \vdots & \vdots & \ddots & \vdots \\ v_{T1} & v_{T2} & \cdots & v_{TM} \end{bmatrix} = (\mathbf{v}_1 \quad \mathbf{v}_2 \quad \ldots \quad \mathbf{v}_M) \tag{14.2.15}$$

The M equations in (14.2.13) are called *reduced form equations* in the literature, $\Pi = -B\Gamma^{-1}$ is called the matrix of *reduced form parameters*, and V is the matrix of *reduced form disturbances*. What this reparameterization does is to transform the system so that it is possible to express each endogenous variable as a linear function of all the exogenous and predetermined variables in the system.

The system of reduced form equations (14.2.13b) may, as discussed in Chapter 11, be rewritten in the form of a set of regression equations, that is,

$$\begin{bmatrix} \mathbf{y}_1 \\ \mathbf{y}_2 \\ \vdots \\ \mathbf{y}_M \end{bmatrix} = \begin{bmatrix} X & & & \\ & X & & \\ & & \ddots & \\ & & & X \end{bmatrix} \begin{bmatrix} \boldsymbol{\pi}_1 \\ \boldsymbol{\pi}_2 \\ \vdots \\ \boldsymbol{\pi}_M \end{bmatrix} + \begin{bmatrix} \mathbf{v}_1 \\ \mathbf{v}_2 \\ \vdots \\ \mathbf{v}_M \end{bmatrix} \tag{14.2.16}$$

or

$$\mathbf{y} = (I \otimes X)\boldsymbol{\pi} + \mathbf{v}$$

where the matrices (14.2.8), (14.2.9), and (14.2.14) in (14.2.15) have been rewritten in stacked form as in the seemingly unrelated regression model.

14.2.2 Some Asymptotic Specifications

In terms of the linear simultaneous statistical model (14.2.7) we have assumed that the errors in the different equations are stationary and temporally uncorrelated. With the asymptotic theory developed in Chapter 3 under general conditions this implies that

$$\operatorname{plim} T^{-1}\mathbf{E}'\mathbf{E} = \Sigma \tag{14.2.17a}$$

and means that the sample error covariance matrix converges in probability to a finite population covariance matrix. Hence we assume the normal random vector

$$\mathbf{e} = \begin{bmatrix} \mathbf{e}_1 \\ \mathbf{e}_2 \\ \vdots \\ \mathbf{e}_M \end{bmatrix} \sim N(\mathbf{0}, \Sigma \otimes I_T) \tag{14.2.17b}$$

Correspondingly, for the reduced form model (14.2.13b),

$$\operatorname{plim} T^{-1}V'V = \operatorname{plim} T^{-1}(\Gamma^{-1})'\mathbf{E}'\mathbf{E}\Gamma^{-1} = (\Gamma^{-1})'\Sigma\Gamma^{-1} = \Omega \tag{14.2.18a}$$

and, hence, the random vector

$$\mathbf{v} = \begin{bmatrix} \mathbf{v}_1 \\ \mathbf{v}_2 \\ \vdots \\ \mathbf{v}_M \end{bmatrix} \sim N(\mathbf{0}, (\Gamma^{-1})'\Sigma\Gamma^{-1} \otimes I_T) \qquad \text{or} \qquad N(\mathbf{0}, \Omega \otimes I_T) \qquad (14.2.18b)$$

It is customary to assume that the elements of X are generated by a stochastic process with nonsingular contemporaneous covariance matrix

$$\operatorname{plim} T^{-1}X'X = \Sigma_{xx} \qquad (14.2.19)$$

which means that the sample cross moment matrix of X converges in probability to a finite population moment matrix. It is also customary to assume that the generating process for X is contemporaneously uncorrelated with $\mathbf{E}$ and V, and thus

$$\operatorname{plim} T^{-1}X'\mathbf{E} = 0 \qquad (14.2.20a)$$

and

$$\begin{aligned} \operatorname{plim} T^{-1}X'V &= -\operatorname{plim}(T^{-1}X'\mathbf{E})\Gamma^{-1} \\ &= 0\Gamma^{-1} \\ &= 0 \end{aligned} \qquad (14.2.20b)$$

This implies that the sample cross moment matrix converges in probability to a null matrix. We now have two equivalent statistical models, (14.2.7) and (14.2.13b), which may be used to express the sampling process by which economic data are generated. Given the theoretical sampling model, let us now face the following questions: (1) What are the statistical implications of estimating the parameters of the structural equations in (14.2.7) by least squares? (2) How can we efficiently estimate the reduced form parameters in (14.2.13b)? and (3) When is it possible to go directly from estimates of the reduced form to estimates of the structural parameters?

Before turning to these questions, consider the following simple simultaneous equation linear statistical model.

$$\begin{aligned} \mathbf{y}_1 + \gamma_{21}\mathbf{y}_2 + \beta_{21}\mathbf{x}_2 + \mathbf{e}_1 &= \mathbf{0} \\ \mathbf{y}_2 + \gamma_{12}\mathbf{y}_1 + \beta_{12}\mathbf{x}_1 + \beta_{32}\mathbf{x}_3 + \mathbf{e}_2 &= \mathbf{0} \end{aligned} \qquad (14.2.21)$$

where the $\mathbf{y}_i$ are vectors of observations on endogenous variables and the $\mathbf{x}_i$ are vectors of observations on nonrandom exogenous variables. The random vectors $\mathbf{e}_1$ and $\mathbf{e}_2$ have the properties

$$E\begin{bmatrix} \mathbf{e}_1 \\ \mathbf{e}_2 \end{bmatrix} = 0 \qquad E\begin{bmatrix} \mathbf{e}_1 \\ \mathbf{e}_2 \end{bmatrix}[\mathbf{e}_1' \quad \mathbf{e}_2'] = \Sigma \otimes I_T$$

where

$$\Sigma = \begin{bmatrix} 5 & 1 \\ 1 & 1 \end{bmatrix}$$

Also, let $X = (\mathbf{x}_1 \quad \mathbf{x}_2 \quad \mathbf{x}_3)$, where the lim $T^{-1}X'X$ is known to be

$$\lim T^{-1}X'X = \begin{bmatrix} 1 & 1 & 0 \\ 1 & 2 & 0 \\ 0 & 0 & 1 \end{bmatrix}$$

and the true values of the parameters are

$$\gamma_{21} = 1 \qquad \gamma_{12} = 2 \qquad \beta_{21} = 2 \qquad \beta_{12} = 3 \qquad \beta_{32} = 1$$

The matrices Γ and B for the model when it is written in the form $Y\Gamma + XB + \mathbf{E} = 0$, may be written as

$$[\mathbf{y}_1 \quad \mathbf{y}_2]\underbrace{\begin{bmatrix} -1 & 2 \\ 1 & -1 \end{bmatrix}}_{\Gamma} + [\mathbf{x}_1 \quad \mathbf{x}_2 \quad \mathbf{x}_3]\underbrace{\begin{bmatrix} 0 & 3 \\ 2 & 0 \\ 0 & 1 \end{bmatrix}}_{B} + [\mathbf{e}_1 \quad \mathbf{e}_2] = 0$$

The corresponding reduced-form equations $Y = -XB\Gamma^{-1} - E\Gamma^{-1}$ are

$$[\mathbf{y}_1 \quad \mathbf{y}_2] = -[\mathbf{x}_1 \quad \mathbf{x}_2 \quad \mathbf{x}_3]\begin{bmatrix} 0 & 3 \\ 2 & 0 \\ 0 & 1 \end{bmatrix}\begin{bmatrix} -1 & 2 \\ 1 & -1 \end{bmatrix}^{-1} - [\mathbf{e}_1 \quad \mathbf{e}_2]\begin{bmatrix} -1 & 2 \\ 1 & -1 \end{bmatrix}^{-1} \tag{14.2.22}$$

The inverse of Γ is

$$\begin{bmatrix} -1 & 2 \\ 1 & -1 \end{bmatrix}^{-1} = \begin{bmatrix} 1 & 2 \\ 1 & 1 \end{bmatrix}$$

so these two reduced-form equations become

$$\mathbf{y}_1 = -3\mathbf{x}_1 - 2\mathbf{x}_2 - \mathbf{x}_3 - \mathbf{e}_1 - \mathbf{e}_2$$

$$\mathbf{y}_2 = -3\mathbf{x}_1 - 4\mathbf{x}_2 - \mathbf{x}_3 - 2\mathbf{e}_1 - \mathbf{e}_2$$

or

$$[\mathbf{y}_1 \quad \mathbf{y}_2] = -[\mathbf{x}_1 \quad \mathbf{x}_2 \quad \mathbf{x}_3]\begin{bmatrix} 3 & 3 \\ 2 & 4 \\ 1 & 1 \end{bmatrix} - [\mathbf{e}_1 \quad \mathbf{e}_2]\begin{bmatrix} 1 & 2 \\ 1 & 1 \end{bmatrix}$$

Numerically, for the first equation, where Γ_2^{-1} denotes the second column of Γ^{-1}, the relevant plim's are as follows.

$$(i)\ \text{plim}\,\frac{\mathbf{y}_2'\mathbf{y}_2}{T} = \boldsymbol{\pi}_2'\ \text{plim}\ X'XT^{-1}\boldsymbol{\pi}_2 + (\Gamma_2^{-1})'\Sigma\Gamma_2^{-1}$$

$$= (3\quad 4\quad 1)\lim\frac{X'X}{T}\begin{pmatrix}3\\4\\1\end{pmatrix} + (2\quad 1)\ \text{plim}\,\frac{E'E}{T}\begin{pmatrix}2\\1\end{pmatrix}$$

$$= (3\quad 4\quad 1)\begin{pmatrix}1 & 1 & 0\\1 & 2 & 0\\0 & 0 & 1\end{pmatrix}\begin{pmatrix}3\\4\\1\end{pmatrix} + (2\quad 1)\begin{pmatrix}5 & 1\\1 & 1\end{pmatrix}\begin{pmatrix}2\\1\end{pmatrix}$$

$$= 66 + 25 = 91 \tag{14.2.23}$$

$$(ii)\ \text{plim}\,\frac{\mathbf{x}_2'\mathbf{y}_2}{T} = -3\lim\frac{\mathbf{x}_2'\mathbf{x}_1}{T} - 4\lim\frac{\mathbf{x}_2'\mathbf{x}_2}{T} - \lim\frac{\mathbf{x}_2'\mathbf{x}_3}{T}$$

$$= -3\times 1 - 4\times 2 - 0 = -11 \tag{14.2.24}$$

$$(iii)\ \text{plim}\,\frac{\mathbf{y}_2'\mathbf{e}_1}{T} = -2\ \text{plim}\,\frac{\mathbf{e}_1'\mathbf{e}_1}{T} - \text{plim}\,\frac{\mathbf{e}_2'\mathbf{e}_1}{T}$$

$$= -2\times 5 - 1 = -11 \tag{14.2.25}$$

14.3 Least Squares Bias

Although the econometricians of the 1930s were aware that the statistical model used was not in many cases compatible with the sampling process by which the data were generated, they had no alternative other than to apply the least squares or maximum likelihood rule to each individual structural relation. From a sampling theory point of view they faced the following problem: Consider the ith equation of the system of equations (14.2.1). Although in (14.2.1) all the variables in the system appear in each equation, in practice usually only a few of the total number of endogenous and exogenous variables appear in each equation. Multiplication of each equation in (14.2.1) by a constant leaves the correctness of the equation unaffected. Consequently, we may arbitrarily set the value of one coefficient to be -1, and this is said to be a normalization rule. Therefore, if we normalize on the ith endogenous variable $\mathbf{y}_i$, that is, if we set the coefficient $\gamma_{ii} = -1$, we may write this equation as

$$Y\mathbf{\Gamma}_i + X\mathbf{B}_i + \mathbf{e}_i = \mathbf{0}$$

$$\mathbf{y}_i = Y_i\boldsymbol{\gamma}_i + Y_i^*\boldsymbol{\gamma}_i^* + X_i\boldsymbol{\beta}_i + X_i^*\boldsymbol{\beta}_i^* + \mathbf{e}_i$$

$$\mathbf{y}_i = Y_i\boldsymbol{\gamma}_i + X_i\boldsymbol{\beta}_i + \mathbf{e}_i$$

$$= (Y_i \quad X_i)\begin{pmatrix}\boldsymbol{\gamma}_i \\ \boldsymbol{\beta}_i\end{pmatrix} + \mathbf{e}_i \tag{14.3.1}$$

or, compactly, as

$$\mathbf{y}_i = Z_i\boldsymbol{\delta}_i + \mathbf{e}_i \tag{24.3.2}$$

where

$$\mathbf{\Gamma}_i = \begin{bmatrix} -1 \\ \boldsymbol{\gamma}_i \\ \boldsymbol{\gamma}_i^* \end{bmatrix} = \begin{bmatrix} -1 \\ \boldsymbol{\gamma}_i \\ \mathbf{0} \end{bmatrix} \qquad \mathbf{B}_i = \begin{bmatrix} \boldsymbol{\beta}_i \\ \boldsymbol{\beta}_i^* \end{bmatrix} = \begin{bmatrix} \boldsymbol{\beta}_i \\ \mathbf{0} \end{bmatrix}$$

$Y = [\mathbf{y}_i \quad Y_i \quad Y_i^*]$. $X = [X_i \quad X_i^*]$; $M = m_i + m_i^*$, $K = k_i + k_i^*$, Y_i^* are those m_i^* endogenous variables that appear in the ith equation with zero coefficients, that is, they do not appear in the ith equation; X_i^* are those k_i^* exogenous and predetermined variables that appear in the ith equation with zero coefficients; $\mathbf{y}_i$, Y_i, and X_i are those endogenous and exogenous variables that appear in the ith equation with nonzero coefficients. Consequently, $\mathbf{y}_i$ is a $(T \times 1)$ vector, Y_i is a $[T \times (m_i - 1)]$ matrix, $\boldsymbol{\gamma}_i$ is a $[(m_i - 1) \times 1]$ vector, X_i is a $(T \times k_i)$ matrix, $\boldsymbol{\beta}_i$ is a $(k_i \times 1)$ vector, $\mathbf{e}_i$ is an unobservable $(T \times 1)$ random vector with mean vector zero and covariance $\sigma_i^2 I_T$, where $Z_i = (Y_i \quad X_i)$, and

$$\boldsymbol{\delta}_i = \begin{pmatrix}\boldsymbol{\gamma}_i \\ \boldsymbol{\beta}_i\end{pmatrix}$$

Under this specification (14.3.2) the least squares estimator of $\boldsymbol{\delta}_i$ is

$$\hat{\boldsymbol{\delta}}_i = (Z_i'Z_i)^{-1}Z_i'\mathbf{y}_i \tag{14.3.3}$$

The mean of the random vector $\hat{\boldsymbol{\delta}}_i$ is

$$E[\hat{\boldsymbol{\delta}}_i] = E[(Z_i'Z_i)^{-1}Z_i'(Z_i\boldsymbol{\delta}_i + \mathbf{e}_i)]$$

$$= \boldsymbol{\delta}_i + E[(Z_i'Z_i)^{-1}Z_i'\mathbf{e}_i] \tag{14.3.4}$$

The last term in (14.3.4) does not vanish because Z_i contains endogenous variables that are jointly determined with $\mathbf{y}_i$ and are thus not independent of $\mathbf{e}_i$. Consequently, the estimator $\hat{\boldsymbol{\delta}}_i$ is biased, and

$$E[\hat{\boldsymbol{\delta}}_i] \neq \boldsymbol{\delta}_i \tag{14.3.5}$$

Furthermore, as the sample size increases, $\hat{\boldsymbol{\delta}}_i$ does not converge to $\boldsymbol{\delta}_i$ in probability, since

$$\begin{aligned} \text{plim } \hat{\boldsymbol{\delta}}_i &= \boldsymbol{\delta}_i + \text{plim } T[Z_i'Z_i]^{-1} \text{ plim } T^{-1}Z_i'\mathbf{e}_i \\ &\neq \boldsymbol{\delta}_i \end{aligned} \tag{14.3.6}$$

where plim $T^{-1}Z_i'\mathbf{e}_i$ does not converge to a zero vector because $Z_i = (Y_i \quad X_i)$ contains Y_i that is not independent of the error vector $\mathbf{e}_i$. Therefore, the least squares estimator applied directly to a structural equation containing two or more endogenous variables will be inconsistent, and if the statistical properties of unbiasedness and consistency for the structural parameters are considered important, then use of the least squares rule has serious statistical consequences.

To illustrate this point, consider the simultaneous equation statistical model (14.2.21) and let $Z_1 = [\mathbf{y}_2 \quad \mathbf{x}_2]$ and $\boldsymbol{\delta}_1 = [\gamma_{21} \quad \beta_{21}]'$. Under this notation and using the plims developed in (14.2.23), (14.2.24), and (14.2.25), the plim $\hat{\boldsymbol{\delta}}_1$ is

$$\begin{aligned} \text{plim } \hat{\boldsymbol{\delta}}_1 &= \boldsymbol{\delta}_1 + \text{plim}(Z_1'Z_1)^{-1}Z_1'\mathbf{e}_1 \\ &= \boldsymbol{\delta}_1 + \text{plim}\begin{bmatrix} T^{-1}\mathbf{y}_2'\mathbf{y}_2 & T^{-1}\mathbf{y}_2'\mathbf{x}_2 \\ T^{-1}\mathbf{x}_2'\mathbf{y}_2 & T^{-1}\mathbf{x}_2'\mathbf{x}_2 \end{bmatrix}^{-1} \text{plim}\begin{bmatrix} T^{-1}\mathbf{y}_2'\mathbf{e}_1 \\ T^{-1}\mathbf{x}_2'\mathbf{e}_1 \end{bmatrix} \\ &= \begin{bmatrix} 1 \\ 2 \end{bmatrix} + \begin{bmatrix} 91 & -11 \\ -11 & 2 \end{bmatrix}^{-1}\begin{bmatrix} -11 \\ 0 \end{bmatrix} \\ &= \begin{bmatrix} 1 \\ 2 \end{bmatrix} + \frac{1}{61}\begin{bmatrix} 2 & 11 \\ 11 & 91 \end{bmatrix}\begin{bmatrix} -11 \\ 0 \end{bmatrix} \\ &= \begin{bmatrix} 1 \\ 2 \end{bmatrix} - \frac{1}{61}\begin{bmatrix} 22 \\ 121 \end{bmatrix} \\ &= \frac{1}{61}\begin{bmatrix} 39 \\ 1 \end{bmatrix} = \begin{bmatrix} 0.6393 \\ 0.0164 \end{bmatrix} \end{aligned} \tag{14.3.7}$$

Because plim $(\hat{\boldsymbol{\delta}}_1 - \boldsymbol{\delta}_1) = -\frac{1}{61}(22 \quad 121)' \neq \mathbf{0}$, the least squares estimator is inconsistent.

The simple Keynesian model (14.1.2) is a good illustration of the bias that may arise when the least squares rule is applied directly to a structural equation. Following Haavelmo (1943), we depict in Figure 14.1 the system when observations for three time periods are involved.

$$\begin{aligned} \mathbf{c} &= \mathbf{x}_1\alpha + \mathbf{y}\beta + \mathbf{e} \\ \mathbf{y} &= \mathbf{c} + \mathbf{i} \end{aligned} \tag{14.3.8}$$

where $\mathbf{x}_1$, $\mathbf{c}$, $\mathbf{y}$, $\mathbf{i}$, and $\mathbf{e}$ are (3×1) vectors.

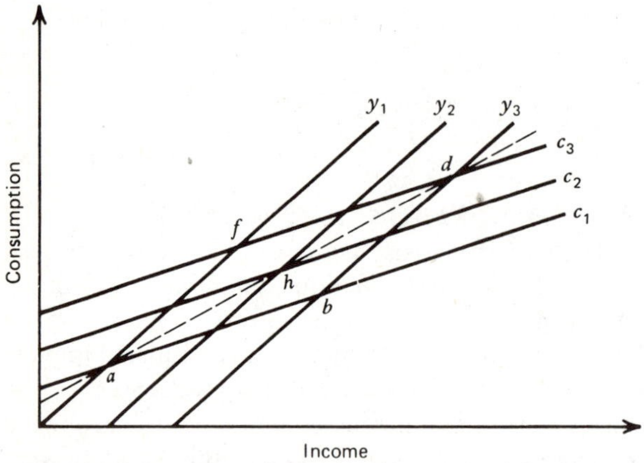

Figure 14.1 Hypothetical representation of a simple Keynesian model.

Let c_1, c_2, and c_3 represent three levels of the consumption function and let y_1, y_2, and y_3 represent three levels of the income relations ($y_i - i_i = c_i$), for three levels of investment. The outcome data that would result from the equilibrium values of the system would be contained within the parallelogram *a*, *b*, *f*, *d*. The relation that will result (estimates of α and β) when a least squares line is passed through the equilibrium points *a*, *h*, and *d*, for example, will overstate the magnitude of β and understate α. The smaller the fluctuation in investment, the more the parallelogram is tilted in a counterclockwise direction and the more we would tend incorrectly to estimate β, the marginal propensity to consume. From a policy standpoint, this would mean that we would also overstate the multiplier $1/(1 - \beta)$, and therefore the economic policy prescriptions would in general be too timid.

Since it is not possible to obtain consistent estimators of the structural parameters using the least squares rule, which by now has become a versatile old friend, let us turn our attention to the reduced-form equations and parameters and evaluate the possibility of estimating the unknown reduced-form parameters.

14.4 Estimation of the Reduced-Form Parameters

The system of reduced-form equations was developed in (14.2.13a) and (14.2.13b) and reformulated in the format of a set of regression equations in (14.2.16). If we choose the *i*th equation in (14.2.16)

$$\mathbf{y}_i = X\boldsymbol{\pi}_i + \mathbf{v}_i \tag{14.4.1}$$

then the least squares estimator for $\boldsymbol{\pi}_i$ is

$$\hat{\boldsymbol{\pi}}_i = (X'X)^{-1}X'\mathbf{y}_i \tag{14.4.2}$$

This estimator is consistent since

$$\begin{aligned} \text{plim } \hat{\boldsymbol{\pi}}_i &= \boldsymbol{\pi}_i + \text{plim } T(X'X)^{-1} \text{ plim } T^{-1}X'\mathbf{v}_i \\ &= \boldsymbol{\pi}_i \end{aligned} \tag{14.4.3}$$

where plim $T^{-1}X'\mathbf{v}_i = \mathbf{0}$ from (14.2.20b). The estimator will be unbiased if X contains no stochastic variables, such as the lagged value of a jointly dependent variable.

If we look at the system of reduced-form equations within the context of the seemingly unrelated regression format (14.2.16) and recognize that the X matrix for every reduced-form equation is the same, then we may write (14.2.16) as

$$\mathbf{y} = (I \otimes X)\boldsymbol{\pi} + \mathbf{v} \tag{14.4.4}$$

where $\otimes$ denotes the Kronecker product defined in Chapter 11 and in Section A.15 of Appendix A. The covariance matrix for the statistical model (14.2.16) may be written as $E[\mathbf{v}\mathbf{v}'] = \Omega \otimes I_T$. The generalized least squares estimator of Chapters 8, 9, and 11 applied to (14.2.16) or (14.4.4) is therefore

$$\begin{aligned} \hat{\boldsymbol{\pi}} &= [(I \otimes X)'(\Omega \otimes I)^{-1}(I \otimes X)]^{-1}(I \otimes X)'(\Omega \otimes I)^{-1}\mathbf{y} \\ &= [I \otimes (X'X)^{-1}X']\mathbf{y} \end{aligned} \tag{14.4.5}$$

which, as discussed in Section 11.1, is then identical to the least squares rule applied to each equation separately.

The covariance of the random vector $\hat{\boldsymbol{\pi}}$ is

$$\begin{aligned} E[(\hat{\boldsymbol{\pi}} - \boldsymbol{\pi})(\hat{\boldsymbol{\pi}} - \boldsymbol{\pi})'] &= E[(I \otimes X')(\Omega^{-1} \otimes I)(I \otimes X)]^{-1} \\ &= \Omega \otimes E(X'X)^{-1} \end{aligned} \tag{14.4.6}$$

The $(M \times M)$ unknown covariance matrix Ω may be consistently estimated by $\hat{\Omega}$ whose elements are

$$\hat{\omega}_{ij} = \frac{\hat{\mathbf{v}}_i'\hat{\mathbf{v}}_j}{T - K} \qquad \text{for} \qquad i, j = 1, 2, \ldots, M \tag{14.4.7}$$

where

$$\hat{\mathbf{v}}_i = \mathbf{y}_i - X\hat{\boldsymbol{\pi}}_i \tag{14.4.8}$$

In some special cases, if prior knowledge about some elements of the $\boldsymbol{\pi}$ vector is available, for example, zero coefficient restrictions or linear combinations of parameters within or across equations, the set of equations (14.2.16) may yield more efficient estimates of π than that resulting from M separate regressions.

14.5 The Problem of Going from the Reduced-Form Parameters to the Structural Parameters

We know from (14.2.13) that as we transformed the statistical model to the reduced form specification the following relationships evolved:

$$\Pi = -B\Gamma^{-1} \tag{14.5.1a}$$

or

$$\Pi\Gamma = -B \tag{14.5.1b}$$

and

$$\Omega = (\Gamma^{-1})'\Sigma\Gamma^{-1} \tag{14.5.2}$$

Since the reduced form parameters can be estimated consistently by using the least squares rule, it seems natural to try to estimate the structural parameters Γ, B, and Σ from $\hat{\Pi}$ and $\hat{\Omega}$. This procedure is known as indirect least squares (ILS), since we estimate the reduced-form parameters by the least squares rule and then use these estimates in conjunction with (14.5.1) and (14.5.2) to obtain estimates of the structural parameters. The indirect least squares estimator at least has the sampling property of consistency.

One problem with this method is that the indirect least squares procedure is not always successful in providing unique estimates of the structural parameters. This result occurs because the relations in (14.5.1) and (14.5.2) sometimes provide insufficient information for obtaining estimates of the structural parameters. There are M^2 parameters in Γ, MK parameters in B, and $M(M + 1)/2$ parameters in the symmetric covariance matrix Σ, or a total of $M(3M + 2K + 1)/2$ parameters to be estimated. To obtain unique estimates of the unknown parameters Γ, B, and Σ, we need as many relations as the number of unknowns. However, there are only MK relations in (14.5.1) and $M(M + 1)/2$ relations in (14.5.2), or a total of $M(M + 2K + 1)/2$ relations. Therefore, we need M^2 a priori restrictions on the parameters for uniqueness.

In many cases (except recursive systems, or any other model that implies restrictions on the elements of Σ), the derivation of estimates of Σ poses little problem if estimates of Γ can be derived from (14.5.1). Consequently, Σ may be estimated by

$$\hat{\Sigma} = \hat{\Gamma}'\hat{\Omega}\hat{\Gamma} \tag{14.5.3}$$

The problem remaining, then, is to derive estimates of the Γ and B matrices.

14.5.1 Types of Prior Information—Restrictions

In any real-world situation several types of prior information may exist regarding individual or linear combinations of the elements of Γ, B, and Σ. Some possibilities are:

1. Normalization.
2. Zero restrictions on the elements of Γ and B, that is, some endogenous, and exogenous and predetermined variables do not appear in each of the equations.
3. Restrictions among parameters within each structural equation.
4. Restrictions among parameters across structural equations.
5. Restrictions on some of the elements of Σ.

Each structural equation can be normalized so that $\gamma_{ii} = -1$ for $i = 1, 2, \ldots, M$, and therefore after normalization the parameters are unique relative to this constant of proportionality. A second type of restriction is that the parameters within a structural equation may have a certain relationship. For example, the accelerator principle in an investment function

$$i_t = a + b_1(y_t - y_{t-1}) + e_t$$

where i_t is investment and y_t is income, implies for the relation

$$i_t = a + b_1 y_t + b_2 y_{t-1} + e_t$$

that $b_2 = -b_1$. As an example of a third type of prior information, under constant returns to scale a Cobb–Douglas production function specification implies that the sum of the elasticities of production (which are the input coefficients for an algebraic form linear in logs) is unity. Restrictions on structural parameters across structural equations may include prior knowledge that two structural equations have the same coefficient for a certain variable or that the marginal propensity to consume of one consumer group is some fraction of that of another group. As an example of the last type of prior knowledge that involves the elements of Σ, consider the following recursive two-equation system:

$$-\mathbf{y}_1 + \beta_{11}\mathbf{x}_1 + \mathbf{e}_1 = \mathbf{0} \tag{14.5.4}$$

$$\gamma_{12}\mathbf{y}_1 - \mathbf{y}_2 + \beta_{12}\mathbf{x}_1 + \mathbf{e}_2 = \mathbf{0} \tag{14.5.5}$$

where γ_{11} and γ_{22} are normalized to be -1. In this system $\mathbf{e}_1$ and $\mathbf{x}_1$ affect $\mathbf{y}_1$, which in turn, together with $\mathbf{x}_1$ and $\mathbf{e}_2$, affect $\mathbf{y}_2$. In this type of mechanism the least squares rule would be appropriate if it can be assumed that $\mathbf{e}_1$ and $\mathbf{e}_2$ are uncorrelated, so that the covariance matrix involving $\mathbf{e}_1$ and $\mathbf{e}_2$ can be specified as

$$\begin{pmatrix} \sigma_{11}I_T & 0 \\ 0 & \sigma_{22}I_T \end{pmatrix} \tag{14.5.6}$$

The least squares rule is obviously appropriate for (14.5.4) since $\mathbf{x}_1$ is uncorrelated with $\mathbf{e}_1$. The least squares rule is also appropriate for (14.5.5) because $\mathbf{y}_1$ is only affected by $\mathbf{e}_1$ and uncorrelated with $\mathbf{e}_2$ if $\mathbf{e}_2$ is assumed uncorrelated with $\mathbf{e}_1$. Thus for the recursive system in which the Γ matrix is triangular, for example,

$$\Gamma = \begin{pmatrix} -1 & \gamma_{12} \\ 0 & -1 \end{pmatrix} \tag{14.5.7}$$

researchers often assume a diagonal covariance matrix Σ, which implies zero restrictions on the off-diagonal elements of Σ. Alternatively, if we can justify that the variance of a disturbance term is a k multiple of the variance of another disturbance term, for example, $\sigma_{ii} = k\sigma_{jj}$, then this restriction can serve as another form of prior information.

All the aforementioned a priori restrictions, when available, can be used with (14.5.1) and (14.5.2) to derive the parameter estimates $\hat{\Gamma}$ and $\hat{B}$. If enough restrictions are used, it will be possible to obtain a unique estimate for each of the unknown elements in Γ, B, and Σ.

As explained earlier, M^2 restrictions are needed to derive unique estimates for all the structural parameters. Since there are M normalizations, one for each equation, we need $M(M-1)$ other restrictions. If there is no information regarding the elements of Σ or regarding restrictions on parameters across structural equations, then $M-1$ restrictions are sufficient for each equation. Therefore, $M-1$ zero (exclusion) restrictions in each of M equations would enable us to derive the structural parameter estimates provided that the system of relations in (14.5.1) and (14.5.2), and the M^2 restrictions, are consistent and not linearly dependent. This rule will be considered in more detail in Section 14.6.

14.5.2 Indirect Least Squares: An Example

As an indication of the possibilities for estimation by indirect least squares and how prior information conditions the use of this procedure, consider the following statistical model involving four endogenous variables, four exogenous and/or predetermined variables, and four equations:

$$\begin{aligned}
&\mathbf{y}_1\gamma_{11} + \mathbf{y}_2\gamma_{21} + \mathbf{y}_4\gamma_{41} + \mathbf{x}_1\beta_{11} + \mathbf{x}_4\beta_{41} + \mathbf{e}_1 = \mathbf{0}\\
&\mathbf{y}_1\gamma_{12} + \mathbf{y}_2\gamma_{22} + \mathbf{x}_1\beta_{12} + \mathbf{x}_2\beta_{22} + \mathbf{e}_2 = \mathbf{0}\\
&\mathbf{y}_1\gamma_{13} + \mathbf{y}_2\gamma_{23} + \mathbf{y}_3\gamma_{33} + \mathbf{y}_4\gamma_{43} + \mathbf{x}_1\beta_{13} + \mathbf{x}_4\beta_{43} + \mathbf{e}_3 = \mathbf{0}\\
&\mathbf{y}_4\gamma_{44} + \mathbf{x}_1\beta_{14} + \mathbf{x}_2\beta_{24} + \mathbf{x}_3\beta_{34} + \mathbf{x}_4\beta_{44} + \mathbf{e}_4 = \mathbf{0}
\end{aligned} \tag{14.5.8}$$

or, in compact matrix notation

$$Y\Gamma + XB + \mathbf{E} = 0 \tag{14.5.9}$$

where

$$\Gamma = \begin{bmatrix} \gamma_{11} & \gamma_{12} & \gamma_{13} & 0 \\ \gamma_{21} & \gamma_{22} & \gamma_{23} & 0 \\ 0 & 0 & \gamma_{33} & 0 \\ \gamma_{41} & 0 & \gamma_{43} & \gamma_{44} \end{bmatrix} \tag{14.5.10}$$

$$B = \begin{bmatrix} \beta_{11} & \beta_{12} & \beta_{13} & \beta_{14} \\ 0 & \beta_{22} & 0 & \beta_{24} \\ 0 & 0 & 0 & \beta_{34} \\ \beta_{41} & 0 & \beta_{43} & \beta_{44} \end{bmatrix} \tag{14.5.11}$$

The zero elements in Γ and B indicate that the respective endogenous and exogenous variables appear in these equations with zero coefficients or restrictions.

The reduced-form counterpart of (14.5.8) is

$$Y = -XB\Gamma^{-1} - \mathbf{E}\Gamma^{-1} \tag{14.5.12}$$

$$Y = X\Pi + V$$

where

$$-B\Gamma^{-1} = \Pi = \begin{bmatrix} \pi_{11} & \pi_{12} & \pi_{13} & \pi_{14} \\ \pi_{21} & \pi_{22} & \pi_{23} & \pi_{24} \\ \pi_{31} & \pi_{32} & \pi_{33} & \pi_{34} \\ \pi_{41} & \pi_{42} & \pi_{43} & \pi_{44} \end{bmatrix} \tag{14.5.13}$$

is the (4×4) matrix of reduced-form coefficients. Suppose for the moment that we know the true reduced form parameters Π, then we may express (14.5.13) as $\Pi = -B\Gamma^{-1}$ or $\Pi\Gamma = -B$, and

$$\begin{bmatrix} \pi_{11} & \pi_{12} & \pi_{13} & \pi_{14} \\ \pi_{21} & \pi_{22} & \pi_{23} & \pi_{24} \\ \pi_{31} & \pi_{32} & \pi_{33} & \pi_{34} \\ \pi_{41} & \pi_{42} & \pi_{43} & \pi_{44} \end{bmatrix} \begin{bmatrix} \gamma_{11} & \gamma_{12} & \gamma_{13} & 0 \\ \gamma_{21} & \gamma_{22} & \gamma_{23} & 0 \\ 0 & 0 & \gamma_{33} & 0 \\ \gamma_{41} & 0 & \gamma_{43} & \gamma_{44} \end{bmatrix} = - \begin{bmatrix} \beta_{11} & \beta_{12} & \beta_{13} & \beta_{14} \\ 0 & \beta_{22} & 0 & \beta_{24} \\ 0 & 0 & 0 & \beta_{34} \\ \beta_{41} & 0 & \beta_{43} & \beta_{44} \end{bmatrix} \tag{14.5.14}$$

Given this system of equations, let us examine the possibility of estimating the unknown parameters in the first structural equation of (14.5.8), that is, the parameters γ_{11}, γ_{21}, γ_{41}, β_{11}, and β_{41}. Based on (14.5.14) the relationships involving these five parameters are

$$\begin{aligned} \pi_{11}\gamma_{11} + \pi_{12}\gamma_{21} + \pi_{14}\gamma_{41} &= -\beta_{11} \\ \pi_{21}\gamma_{11} + \pi_{22}\gamma_{21} + \pi_{24}\gamma_{41} &= 0 \\ \pi_{31}\gamma_{11} + \pi_{32}\gamma_{21} + \pi_{34}\gamma_{41} &= 0 \\ \pi_{41}\gamma_{11} + \pi_{42}\gamma_{21} + \pi_{44}\gamma_{41} &= -\beta_{41} \end{aligned} \tag{14.5.15}$$

Normalizing $\gamma_{11} = -1$ we can write the middle two equations of (14.5.15) as

$$\begin{aligned} \pi_{22}\gamma_{21} + \pi_{24}\gamma_{41} &= \pi_{21} \\ \pi_{32}\gamma_{21} + \pi_{34}\gamma_{41} &= \pi_{31} \end{aligned} \tag{14.5.16a}$$

or

$$\begin{bmatrix} \pi_{22} & \pi_{24} \\ \pi_{32} & \pi_{34} \end{bmatrix} \begin{bmatrix} \gamma_{21} \\ \gamma_{41} \end{bmatrix} = \begin{bmatrix} \pi_{21} \\ \pi_{31} \end{bmatrix} \tag{14.5.16b}$$

Since we have assumed that we know the π's in (14.5.16), we can solve for γ_{21} and γ_{41} if the (2×2) matrix in (14.5.16b) is nonsingular, that is, if the determinant

$$\begin{vmatrix} \pi_{22} & \pi_{24} \\ \pi_{32} & \pi_{34} \end{vmatrix} \neq 0 \tag{14.5.17}$$

After γ_{21} and γ_{41} are obtained, they can be used in the first and the fourth equations of (14.5.15) to obtain β_{11} and β_{41}. Thus in the first equation the restrictions are such that we can go directly from knowledge of the reduced-form parameters to the structural parameters. Consequently, we can obtain unique indirect least squares estimates of the structural parameters from least squares estimates of the reduced form parameters as long as (14.5.17) is true. Note in this case that the number of unknown parameters of the endogenous variables, namely γ_{21} and γ_{41}, is just exactly equal to the number of exogenous and/or predetermined variables appearing in the first equation with zero coefficients (restrictions). Also note that the number of zero restrictions, three, is exactly equal to the number of other equations in the system.

Now let us examine the possibility of solving for the parameters of the second structural equation when we know the reduced-form parameters. The set of relations involving the parameters of the second structural equation is (from the second columns of Γ and B)

$$\begin{aligned} \pi_{11}\gamma_{12} + \pi_{12}\gamma_{22} &= -\beta_{12} \\ \pi_{21}\gamma_{12} + \pi_{22}\gamma_{22} &= -\beta_{22} \\ \pi_{31}\gamma_{12} + \pi_{32}\gamma_{22} &= 0 \\ \pi_{41}\gamma_{12} + \pi_{42}\gamma_{22} &= 0 \end{aligned} \tag{14.5.18a}$$

Adding the normalization rule $\gamma_{22} = -1$ the system of equations (14.5.18a) becomes

$$\begin{aligned} \pi_{11}\gamma_{12} - \pi_{12} &= -\beta_{12} \\ \pi_{21}\gamma_{12} - \pi_{22} &= -\beta_{22} \\ \pi_{31}\gamma_{12} - \pi_{32} &= 0 \\ \pi_{41}\gamma_{12} - \pi_{42} &= 0 \end{aligned} \tag{14.5.18b}$$

We have four relations and three unknowns, γ_{12}, β_{12}, and β_{22}. There are more relations in (14.5.18b) than unknowns. One alternative might be to pick any set of three out of four relations to solve for the three unknowns. Note, however, a consequence of having an "extra" relation. The last two equations in (14.5.18b) imply that $\gamma_{12} = \pi_{32}/\pi_{31} = \pi_{42}/\pi_{41}$. Thus γ_{12} is equal to both ratios, and the true reduced-form parameters are such that the implied restriction $\pi_{32}\pi_{41} = \pi_{31}\pi_{42}$ holds true. Unfortunately, *estimates* of the reduced-form coefficients will in general not obey the restrictions, and thus two different indirect least squares estimates of γ_{12} are obtained. Both estimates can be shown to be consistent, but there is a question about their efficiency since not all the information in (14.5.18b) is used. Note here that the number of unknown coefficients of the endogenous variables is one fewer than the number of exogenous and/or predetermined variables appearing in the equation with zero coefficients. Also note that the number of zero restrictions, four, is more than the number of other equations in the system.

Let us now examine the parameters of the third structural equation. From (14.5.14) the set of linear equations is

$$\begin{aligned}
\pi_{11}\gamma_{13} + \pi_{12}\gamma_{23} + \pi_{13}\gamma_{33} + \pi_{14}\gamma_{43} &= -\beta_{13} \\
\pi_{21}\gamma_{13} + \pi_{22}\gamma_{23} + \pi_{23}\gamma_{33} + \pi_{24}\gamma_{43} &= 0 \\
\pi_{31}\gamma_{13} + \pi_{32}\gamma_{23} + \pi_{33}\gamma_{33} + \pi_{34}\gamma_{43} &= 0 \\
\pi_{41}\gamma_{13} + \pi_{42}\gamma_{23} + \pi_{43}\gamma_{33} + \pi_{44}\gamma_{43} &= -\beta_{43}
\end{aligned} \tag{14.5.19}$$

Again, we normalize the third diagonal element of Γ, which means that

$$\gamma_{33} = -1$$

When $\gamma_{33} = -1$ is substituted into (14.5.19), there will be five unknown parameters to be solved from the four relations. Unfortunately, the solution cannot be unique, and unless there is additional information concerning the structural parameters there will be an infinite number of arbitrary solutions. Indirect least squares estimation of the third equation is thus not possible. Note that for the third structural equation there are three unknown coefficients of the endogenous variables and only two exogenous and/or predetermined variables that appear in the equation with zero coefficients. Also note that the number of zero restrictions, two, is less than the number of other equations in the system.

Finally, for the fourth structural equation in (14.5.8), if we normalize on the coefficient of $\mathbf{y}_4$ and set $\gamma_{44} = -1$, the following set of equations results from (14.5.14):

$$\begin{aligned}
\pi_{14} &= \beta_{14} \\
\pi_{24} &= \beta_{24} \\
\pi_{34} &= \beta_{34} \\
\pi_{44} &= \beta_{44}
\end{aligned} \tag{14.5.20}$$

In this case we have four equations and four unknowns, and, in fact, the structural parameters of the exogenous and/or predetermined variables are equal to the reduced form parameters π_{14}, π_{24}, π_{34}, and π_{44}. This result seems reasonable because in this case the fourth equation contains only one endogenous variable. Consequently, in this special case, the least squares rule can be applied directly to the structural equation to estimate the unknown structural parameters and is equivalent to indirect least squares. Note that for the fourth equation the number of zero restrictions, three, is exactly equal to the number of other equations.

In applying the indirect least squares procedure to each equation of model (14.5.8) we have achieved different results. In the case of the first equation we were able to achieve unique estimates of the structural parameters. In the second equation we obtained several alternative possible estimates. In the third equation an infinite number of arbitrary estimates resulted for the unknown parameters. No unique estimates of the structural parameters exist when different sets of structural equations have the same reduced-form equations. The data generated from such systems are identical, and we call these alternative models *observationally equivalent*. In the fourth equation the coefficients of the structural equation may be estimated directly by using the least squares rule.

It would be nice if we could look at each equation in the model and tell by an inventory of the zero and nonzero coefficients whether or not the structural coefficients could be uniquely determined by applying the indirect least squares procedure. In Section 14.6 we will see if we can devise such an identification rule.

14.5.3 An Empirical Example

Consider the following simple Keynesian model.

$$\mathbf{c} = \alpha\mathbf{1} + \beta\mathbf{y} + \mathbf{e} \tag{14.5.21}$$

$$\mathbf{y} = \mathbf{c} + \mathbf{i} \tag{14.5.22}$$

and the corresponding reduced form equations

$$\mathbf{c} = \frac{\alpha}{1-\beta}\mathbf{1} + \frac{\beta}{1-\beta}\mathbf{i} + \frac{1}{1-\beta}\mathbf{e} \tag{14.5.23}$$

$$\mathbf{y} = \frac{\alpha}{1-\beta}\mathbf{1} + \frac{1}{1-\beta}\mathbf{i} + \frac{1}{1-\beta}\mathbf{e} \tag{14.5.24}$$

where **c**, **y**, and **i** are consumption, income, and investment, respectively and **1** is a vector of ones. The data for **c**, **y**, and **i** are given in Table 14.1 in Section 14.9.2. Using these data, the empirical reduced forms are

$$\mathbf{c} = 9.6071\ \mathbf{1} + 4.2455\ \mathbf{i} \tag{14.5.25}$$

$$\mathbf{y} = 9.0671\ \mathbf{1} + 5.2455\ \mathbf{i} \tag{14.5.26}$$

Using (14.5.23) and (14.5.25), we have

$$\frac{\hat{\alpha}}{1-\hat{\beta}} = 9.6071 \qquad \text{and} \qquad \frac{\hat{\beta}}{1-\hat{\beta}} = 4.2455$$

Solving for $\hat{\alpha}$ and $\hat{\beta}$ yields

$$\hat{\alpha} = 1.8320 \qquad \hat{\beta} = 0.8093$$

Solving for $\hat{\alpha}$ and $\hat{\beta}$ from (14.5.24) and (14.5.26) yields identical results.

14.6 Identifying an Equation within a System of Equations

In line with (14.3.1) let us write the ith equation from a system of M equations as

$$Y\boldsymbol{\Gamma}_i + X\mathbf{B}_i + \mathbf{e}_i = \mathbf{0} \tag{14.6.1}$$

where $\boldsymbol{\Gamma}_i$ is an $(M \times 1)$ vector of unknown structural coefficients of the jointly determined (endogenous) variables, $\mathbf{B}_i$ is a $(K \times 1)$ vector of unknown structural coefficients of the exogenous and lagged endogenous variables, and $\mathbf{e}_i$ is an unobserved random vector. In terms of the complete system of equations from (14.2.14) we can write

$$\Pi\Gamma = -B \tag{14.6.2a}$$

or

$$\Pi\Gamma + B = [\Pi \quad I_K]\begin{bmatrix}\Gamma \\ B\end{bmatrix} = 0 \tag{14.6.2b}$$

Since $\boldsymbol{\Gamma}_i$ and $\mathbf{B}_i$ are the ith columns of Γ and B, respectively, then (14.6.2) implies that for the ith equation

$$[\Pi \quad I_K]\begin{bmatrix}\boldsymbol{\Gamma}_i \\ \mathbf{B}_i\end{bmatrix} = \mathbf{0} \tag{14.6.3}$$

Since the matrix $[\Pi \quad I_K]$ has rank K, Equation 14.6.3 represents a system of K equations in $M + K$ variables. Because there are more unknowns than equations, M additional pieces of information are required to be able to solve for, or *identify*, the unknown parameters $\boldsymbol{\Gamma}_i$ and $\mathbf{B}_i$ in terms of the information contained in the elements of Π.

In this section we develop rules that can be used to determine whether an equation in a system of equations is identified. The rules are based on the assumption that linear homogeneous restrictions on the structural parameters, plus a normalization rule, are used to identify an equation. Consequently, the identifying restrictions can be written as

$$R_i\begin{bmatrix}\boldsymbol{\Gamma}_i \\ \mathbf{B}_i\end{bmatrix} = R_i\boldsymbol{\Delta}_i = \mathbf{0} \tag{14.6.4}$$

where R_i is a known $[J \times (M + K)]$ matrix of rank $J(<M + K)$. If a row of R_i has but a single nonzero element, which is unity, then the restriction is called an *exclusion* restriction because it implies that a specific parameter is zero, and, therefore the corresponding variable does not appear in the ith equation. These are by far the most common type of restrictions used to identify a structural equation.

Identification rules for the ith structural equation are based on (14.6.3) and (14.6.4). Equation 14.6.3 provides K pieces of information about the $M + K$ parameters of the ith structural equation. Equation 14.6.4 must then provide $M - 1$ new pieces of information. The combination of (14.6.3), (14.6.4), and the normalization rule then provides enough information so that the $(M + K)$ structural parameters of the ith equation may be solved for in terms of the reduced-form parameters Π, thus implying that the parameters of the ith equation are identified.

Let us combine (14.6.3) and (14.6.4) as

$$\begin{bmatrix} (\Pi \vdots I_K) \\ R_i \end{bmatrix} \mathbf{\Delta}_i = \mathbf{0} \tag{14.6.5}$$

Remembering that in addition to (14.6.5) we will impose a normalization rule, the theory of linear equations tells us that the rank of

$$\begin{bmatrix} (\Pi \vdots I_K) \\ R_i \end{bmatrix} \tag{14.6.6}$$

must be $M + K - 1$ for us to be able to solve for or identify $\mathbf{\Delta}_i$ in terms of Π. If this condition is satisfied, we are guaranteed that the information provided by (14.6.4) is independent of (14.6.3).

Unfortunately, checking the rank of (14.6.6) may not be an easy task since the parameters Π are complicated functions of the structural parameters, and we may be hard pressed to understand relations between them. Fortunately, there is a rank condition that is much easier to use. If we let

$$\Delta = \begin{bmatrix} \Gamma \\ B \end{bmatrix}$$

then it can be shown that the rank of (14.6.6) is $M + K - 1$ if and only if the rank of $(R_i\Delta)$ is $M - 1$.

14.6.1 Rank Condition for Identification

A necessary and sufficient condition for the identification of the ith equation using a priori restrictions

$$R_i\mathbf{\Delta}_i = \mathbf{0}$$

is that

$$\text{rank}(R_i\Delta) = M - 1$$

Since $R_i\Delta$ has M columns and the ith column, $R_i\boldsymbol{\Delta}_i$, has elements zero, for $R_i\Delta$ to have rank $M-1$ the number of rows must be at least $M-1$, and thus R_i must have rank at least equal to $M-1$. In other words, a necessary condition for the identification of the ith equation using the a priori restrictions

$$R_i\boldsymbol{\Delta}_i = \mathbf{0}$$

is that $J \geq M-1$, where J is the number of restrictions. This result is often called the order condition for identification.

The order condition is not sufficient for identification. A significant case where the order condition holds but the rank condition fails is when the coefficients of another equation satisfy the restrictions on the ith equation, that is,

$$R_i\boldsymbol{\Delta}_j = \mathbf{0} \qquad i \neq j$$

This result implies that two columns of $R_i\Delta$ are zero, so that its rank is less than or equal to $M-2$. This situation occurs when all the variables that are excluded from the ith structural equation are also excluded from another equation. Thus the rank condition requires that the excluded variables of the ith equation appear in each of the remaining $M-1$ equations such that no other equation or linear combination of equations can obey the restrictions.

We are now in a position to summarize the identification possibilities.

1. The ith equation is not identified if rank $(R_i\Delta) < M-1$. Underidentification certainly occurs when rank $(R_i) < M-1$. In this case it is not possible to solve for the structural parameters of the ith equation in terms of the reduced form parameters, and neither indirect least squares nor any other estimation technique will provide consistent estimators for the parameters of the ith equation.
2. The ith equation is just or exactly identified if rank $(R_i\Delta) = M-1$ and rank $(R_i) = M-1$. In this case the structural parameters can be expressed in terms of the reduced-form parameters in a unique way. The indirect least squares estimator is consistent and efficient.
3. The ith equation is overidentified if rank $(R_i\Delta) = M-1$ and rank $(R_i) > M-1$. In this case there are many ways in which the structural parameters can be expressed in terms of the reduced-form parameters. The indirect least squares estimator is consistent but is inefficient relative to other estimators.

As examples for the use of these rules let us reconsider the system of equations (14.5.8). For the first equation,

$$R_1 = \begin{bmatrix} 0 & 0 & 1 & 0 & 0 & 0 & 0 & 0 \\ 0 & 0 & 0 & 0 & 0 & 1 & 0 & 0 \\ 0 & 0 & 0 & 0 & 0 & 0 & 1 & 0 \end{bmatrix}$$

since $\mathbf{y}_3$, $\mathbf{x}_2$, and $\mathbf{x}_3$ are omitted. We see that the order condition for identification is satisfied because the number of rows of R_1 (exclusion restrictions) is three $(= M - 1)$. To check the rank condition, we form $R_1\Delta$ as

$$R_1\Delta = \begin{bmatrix} 0 & 0 & \gamma_{33} & 0 \\ 0 & \beta_{22} & 0 & \beta_{24} \\ 0 & 0 & 0 & \beta_{34} \end{bmatrix}$$

The rank of $R_1\Delta$ is 3 unless any one of γ_{33}, β_{22}, and β_{34} is zero. If, for example, $\beta_{34} = 0$, it would imply that $\mathbf{x}_3$ was omitted from all equations, and therefore, cannot be counted as an excluded exogenous variable for the identification of the first equation. If $\beta_{22} = 0$, then the excluded variables of the first equation, including $\mathbf{x}_2$, do not appear in the second equation. If we assume that γ_{33}, β_{22}, and β_{34} are nonzero, then $R_1\Delta$ has rank 3, and the first equation is exactly identified.

For the second equation, $\mathbf{y}_3$, $\mathbf{y}_4$, $\mathbf{x}_3$, and $\mathbf{x}_4$ are excluded. The restriction matrix R_2 has four rows, and thus the order condition is satisfied. Furthermore, $R_2\Delta$ is

$$R_2\Delta = \begin{bmatrix} 0 & 0 & \gamma_{33} & 0 \\ \gamma_{41} & 0 & \gamma_{43} & \gamma_{44} \\ 0 & 0 & 0 & \beta_{34} \\ \beta_{41} & 0 & \beta_{43} & \beta_{44} \end{bmatrix}$$

which has rank at most 3, even though it is of dimension (4×4), since the second column is zero. If the true parameter values γ's and β's are such that the matrix $R_2\Delta$ has rank 3, the second equation is overidentified.

The third equation is not identified by the order condition because there are only two excluded variables, and thus R_3 only has two $(< M - 1)$ rows. The fourth equation is exactly identified, which you may confirm.

In summary, the order and rank conditions for identification can be interpreted as follows. A necessary condition for exact or just identification is that there should be exactly $M - 1$ excluded variables in a structural equation to differentiate it from the other $M - 1$ equations. The sufficient rank condition is that each of the $M - 1$ excluded variables of the ith structural equation should appear in a particular equation to differentiate the ith structural equation from this particular equation, and, in addition, no linear combination of the other $M - 1$ equations can produce the ith structural equation.

The following practical rules are useful when examining an econometric model.

1. An equation that contains one endogenous variable and all predetermined variables in the system is just identified.
2. An equation that contains all the variables in the system is not identified.
3. If none of the excluded variables of the ith equation appears in the jth equation, the ith equation is not identified.

4. If two equations contain the same set of variables, both equations are not identified.
5. If the same excluded variables of the ith equation are also excluded from the jth equation, the ith equation fails the rank condition and is not identified.
6. If any excluded variable of the ith equation does not appear in any linear combination of the other $M - 1$ equations, the ith equation is not identified. (For an example, see Theil, 1971, p. 449.)

To summarize, the sample information contained in the endogenous variables Y may be used in conjunction with the least squares estimator to provide a consistent basis for estimating the unknown Π matrix of reduced-form coefficients. The resulting estimates of the reduced-form coefficient matrix Π contain all the information in the sample. However, unless additional information is provided, the structural parameters for the ith equation cannot be expressed in terms of the reduced-form parameters. The identification problem involves whether or not, in conjunction with the normalization rule, enough exclusion restrictions (information) exists to permit the structural parameters of the ith equation to be consistently estimated. In the cases of exact and overidentification this is possible, and the indirect least squares estimator is a consistent estimator since the structural estimators are continuous functions of the reduced-form estimators. When an equation is overidentified, however, the indirect least squares estimator is not efficient, and this situation motivates the discussion of alternative estimation techniques in Chapter 15.

14.7 Some Examples of Model Formulation, Identification, and Estimation

So far we have developed rules for determining whether an equation from a system of equations contains enough information (restrictions) to be identified and for its structural parameters to be consistently estimated. To make these concepts more operational and to provide an intuitive basis for the identification rules, let us consider a range of quasi-real-world econometric models that describe a variety of data-generation processes.

Suppose that we have a sample of observed values on price and quantity of a certain commodity, such as sugar, and that our objective is to estimate the parameters a and b of the relation

$$\mathbf{y}_1 = \mathbf{y}_2 a + \mathbf{x}_1 b + \mathbf{e}_1 \tag{14.7.1}$$

where $\mathbf{y}_1$ is a $(T \times 1)$ vector of observed values on the consumption of sugar, $\mathbf{y}_2$ is a $(T \times 1)$ vector of observed values on the price of sugar, $\mathbf{x}_1$ is a $(T \times 1)$ vector of ones, and $\mathbf{e}_1$ is a $(T \times 1)$ normally distributed random vector with mean zero and covariance $\sigma_{11}I_T$. Suppose that we proceed as in Chapter 6 and use the least squares rule to estimate a and b. Are we estimating a demand function, a supply function, or possibly neither? How do we interpret these results?

Suppose that the true relations that formed the basis for generating the data are

$$\begin{aligned} \text{Demand: } \mathbf{y}_1 &= \mathbf{y}_2\gamma_{21} + \mathbf{x}_1\beta_{11} + \mathbf{e}_1 \\ \text{Supply: } \mathbf{y}_1 &= \mathbf{y}_2\gamma_{22} + \mathbf{x}_1\beta_{12} + \mathbf{x}_2\beta_{22} + \mathbf{e}_2 \end{aligned} \tag{14.7.2}$$

where $\mathbf{x}_2$ is rainfall. If there is only a minor random disturbance in the demand relation, then a graph of the demand and supply relations and the corresponding equilibrium points might look as in Figure 14.2, since variations in rainfall would cause the supply relation to be unstable. The intersections of the demand and supply relations in Figure 14.2 trace out the equilibrium values, and it appears that the shifts in the supply function caused by the weather factor result in observed sample values associated with the demand function.

The observed equilibrium values indicated in Figure 14.2 could be used as a basis for estimating the unknown parameters of the demand relation by the least squares rule despite the fact that even in this case the least squares estimator is biased and inconsistent. That we may be able to estimate the parameters of the demand relation is also confirmed by the order condition, since the number of excluded variables from the demand relation is $M - 1 = 2 - 1 = 1$.

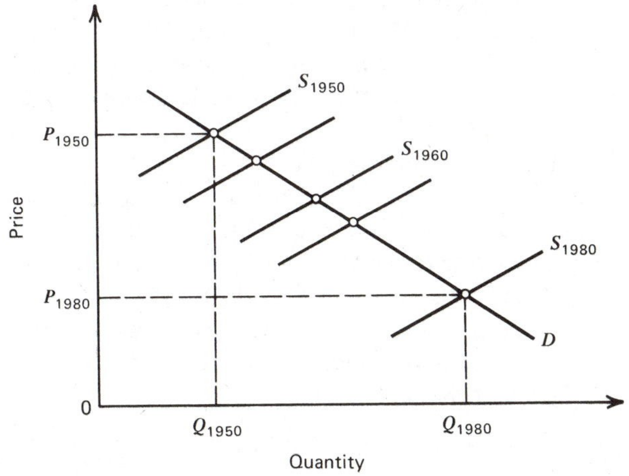

Figure 14.2 Stable demand and shifting supply.

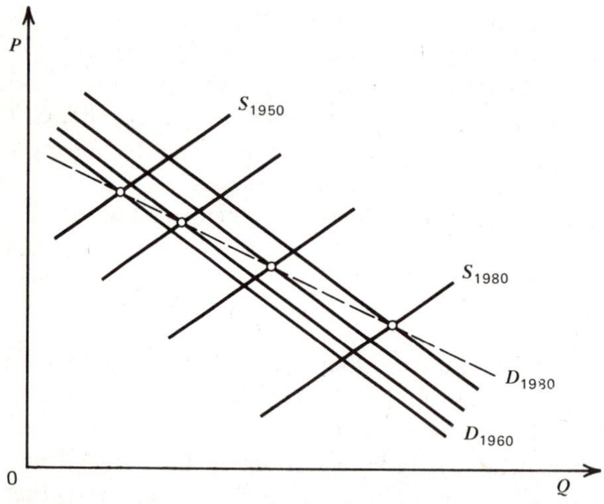

Figure 14.3 Stochastic demand and shifting supply.

More realistically, if the demand relation was subject to stochastic variation reflected by $\mathbf{e}_1$, it would not be perfectly stable and might generate a set of price-quantity equilibrium points such as shown in Figure 14.3.

If we apply the usual least squares rule to the demand function in the model (14.7.2), the least squares estimator will be biased, as can be seen from Figure 14.3, since the equilibrium price–quantity values represent the intersections of different demand and supply functions. Obviously, the information contained in the weather variable $\mathbf{x}_2$, should be used in the estimation process, in order to obtain a consistent estimator. Otherwise, even though there may be a perfect fit to these points with the usual least squares rule, the estimated equation will not be the demand function and will in fact be a hybrid of the demand and supply functions. A possible way to obtain a consistent estimator in this case is to use indirect least squares.

If our interest in (14.7.1) had centered on estimating the parameters of the supply relation, this would not have been possible either by the least squares estimator applied directly to the supply relation or by the indirect least squares estimator. We would have been alerted to this fact because the order condition fails. The number of excluded variables is $0 < M - 1$, thus the supply relation is not identified.

Alternatively, suppose we argue that the supply function for sugar is quite stable during the observation period, but the demand function for sugar shifts upward because of increases in income. The hypothesized model is

$$\begin{aligned} \text{Demand: } \mathbf{y}_1 &= \mathbf{y}_2\gamma_{21} + \mathbf{x}_1\beta_{11} + \mathbf{x}_3\beta_{31} + \mathbf{e}_1 \\ \text{Supply: } \mathbf{y}_1 &= \mathbf{y}_2\gamma_{22} + \mathbf{x}_1\beta_{12} + \mathbf{e}_2 \end{aligned} \tag{14.7.3}$$

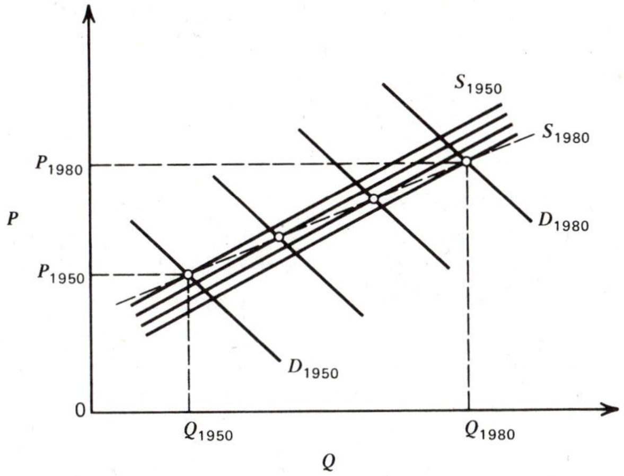

Figure 14.4 Stochastic but stable supply and shifting demand.

where $\mathbf{x}_3$ denotes income. In this case the supply function is just identified, whereas the demand function is not identified. A plot of the data would reveal that the equilibrium points resemble a supply function more than a demand function, as shown in Figure 14.4. In this case the indirect least squares rule applied to the relation in (14.7.1) would have yielded a price coefficient γ_{22} that was positive.

Suppose that the supply of sugar is also affected by the wage rate, and the true relations are

$$\begin{aligned} &\text{Demand: } \mathbf{y}_1 = \mathbf{y}_2\gamma_{21} + \mathbf{x}_1\beta_{11} + \mathbf{e}_1 \\ &\text{Supply: } \mathbf{y}_1 = \mathbf{y}_2\gamma_{22} + \mathbf{x}_1\beta_{12} + \mathbf{x}_2\beta_{22} + \mathbf{x}_4\beta_{42} + \mathbf{e}_2 \end{aligned} \tag{14.7.4}$$

where $\mathbf{x}_4$ is the wage rate, which is an exogenous variable. In this case, although the scatter points of observations are similar to those shown in Figure 14.3, shifts in the supply function are caused both by rainfall and by the wage rate. The demand relation is overidentified, since $J = 2 > M - 1 = 1$. Thus there are two exogenous variables that can be used to obtain consistent estimators. One possibility is to use only one or the other of the exogenous variables. The choice of either exogenous variable would yield a consistent estimator through indirect least squares, but neither is necessarily efficient because other estimates can be constructed that use all the information contained in $\mathbf{x}_2$ and $\mathbf{x}_4$. These procedures will be discussed in Chapter 15.

Finally, if the true data-generating process is represented by the following equations

$$\begin{aligned} \text{Demand: } \mathbf{y}_1 &= \mathbf{y}_2\gamma_{21} + \mathbf{x}_1\beta_{11} + \mathbf{x}_3\beta_{31} + \mathbf{e}_1 \\ \text{Supply: } \mathbf{y}_1 &= \mathbf{y}_2\gamma_{22} + \mathbf{x}_1\beta_{12} + \mathbf{x}_2\beta_{22} + \mathbf{e}_2 \end{aligned} \tag{14.7.5}$$

then relation (14.7.1) is a misspecified model. However, estimation of (14.7.5) is possible because by the counting rule both equations are just identified by the exogenous variables rainfall and income. All the parameters can be estimated uniquely and consistently by using the indirect least squares estimator. Since in this case all the information is used, the direct estimates of the reduced-form parameters by least squares are the same as the derived reduced-form parameters from the structural parameters, that is, $\hat{\Pi} = -\hat{B}\hat{\Gamma}^{-1}$.

These examples should indicate the important role of statistical model formulation in quantitative ventures and reflect to some extent the statistical implications of working with false models.

14.8 Summary and Guide to Further Reading

In estimating the parameters of a system of simultaneous equations, several problems arise. First, the direct application of the least squares rule to a structural equation, may result in an estimator that is biased. Further, the ordinary least squares estimator will not converge to the true parameter even when the sample size is increased. In searching for a consistent estimator, one possibility is to use the indirect least squares rule, which uses the estimates of the reduced form parameters as a basis for estimating the structural parameters. Unfortunately, although the indirect least squares rule is simple, it may not work in general because there may not be unique estimates for the structural parameters. This raises the identification question. The counting rule (necessary condition) for an equation within a system of M equations to be just identified is that there should be exactly $M - 1$ variables not appearing in the equation in order to differentiate the equation from the remaining $M - 1$ equations. The rank condition requires that the excluded variables of the ith equation appear in the remaining $M - 1$ equations in such a way that no other equation or linear combination of equations can obey the restrictions.

The method of indirect least squares does not work when there are more than $K + 1$ variables in the equation, where K is the number of exogenous and/or predetermined variables in the system. When there are fewer than $K + 1$ variables in the equation, the method of indirect least squares suggests alternative consistent estimates, and each estimate uses part of the information contained in the variables not appearing in the equation. In this case the alternative estimates are not efficient. In the next chapter we will continue the search for consistent and efficient estimators for the parameters of overidentified equations.

For early discussions of inference relative to a system of simultaneous equations, Haavelmo (1943) and Marshack (1950) provide a useful introduction. In terms of the identification problem, Fisher (1966) is a good source. Several books that cover the topics discussed in Chapters 14 and 15 in a rather complete fashion are Fomby, Hill, and Johnson (1984, pp. 439–471); Judge, et al. (1985, pp. 563–590); Schmidt (1976); and Theil (1971); pp. 429–539). Econometric models and the uses of econometric models are discussed in Intriligator (1978, Chapter 12 through 16) and Pindyck and Rubinfeld (1981, Chapters 12 through 14).

14.9 Exercises

14.9.1 Algebraic Exercises

14.9.1 Consider the following macroeconomic model

$$\mathbf{c} = a_1\mathbf{1} + a_2\mathbf{y} + \mathbf{e}_1$$

$$\mathbf{i} = b_1\mathbf{1} + b_2(\mathbf{y} - \mathbf{y}_{-1}) + \mathbf{e}_2$$

$$\mathbf{y} = \mathbf{c} + \mathbf{i} + \mathbf{g}$$

where $\mathbf{c}$ is consumption, $\mathbf{i}$ is investment, $\mathbf{y}$ is income, $\mathbf{y}_{-1}$ is lagged income, $\mathbf{g}$ is government expenditure, and $\mathbf{1}$ is a vector of ones.

(*a*) Classify the structural equations.

(*b*) Classify the variables.

(*c*) Solve for the reduced form equations.

14.9.2 Consider the model described in Exercise 14.9.1. Determine the identification of the consumption function and of the investment function.

14.9.3 Determine the order and rank conditions of identification of the equations in the following model:

$$\mathbf{y}_1 = \mathbf{y}_2\gamma_{21} + \mathbf{y}_3\gamma_{31} + \mathbf{x}_1\beta_{11} + \mathbf{e}_1$$

$$\mathbf{y}_2 = \mathbf{y}_1\gamma_{12} + \mathbf{x}_1\beta_{12} + \mathbf{x}_2\beta_{22} + \mathbf{x}_3\beta_{32} + \mathbf{x}_4\beta_{42} + \mathbf{e}_2$$

$$\mathbf{y}_3 = \mathbf{y}_1\gamma_{13} + \mathbf{y}_2\gamma_{23} + \mathbf{x}_1\beta_{13} + \mathbf{x}_5\beta_{53} + \mathbf{e}_3$$

14.9.4 Consider the simple Keynesian model

$$\mathbf{c} = \beta\mathbf{y} + \mathbf{e}$$

$$\mathbf{y} = \mathbf{c} + \mathbf{i}$$

where **c** is consumption, **y** is income and **i** is investment. Assume that each vector is $(T \times 1)$ and $E[\mathbf{e}] = \mathbf{0}$, and $E[\mathbf{ee}'] = \sigma^2 I_T$.

(*a*) Derive the reduced-form equations.

(*b*) Examine the reduced-form disturbances by finding their means and variances.

(*c*) Find the estimator of the reduced-form parameter for income.

(*d*) Obtain the indirect least squares estimator for β from the result of (*c*).

(*e*) Show that the result of (*d*) is the same as an instrumental variable estimator, the instrumental variable being investment (Chapter 13).

(*f*) Find the estimator of the reduced-form parameter for consumption.

(*g*) Obtain the indirect least squares estimator for β from the result of (*f*).

(*h*) Show that the result in (*g*) is the same as the result in (*d*).

(*i*) Determine the direction of the bias for the least squares estimator of β.

14.9.2 Individual Numerical Exercises

The remaining problems are based on data from Monte Carlo sampling experiments, using the following simple Keynesian model.

$$\mathbf{c} = \alpha\mathbf{1} + \beta\mathbf{y} + \mathbf{e} \qquad (14.9.1a)$$

$$\mathbf{y} = \mathbf{c} + \mathbf{i} \qquad (14.9.1b)$$

where **c**, **y**, and **i** are consumption, income, and investment, respectively, **e** is assumed normal with $E[\mathbf{e}] = \mathbf{0}$ and $E[\mathbf{ee}'] = \sigma^2 I = 0.2^2 I$. The parameter values used were $\alpha = 2$ and $\beta = 0.8$. The reduced-form equations are

$$\mathbf{c} = \frac{\alpha}{1-\beta}\mathbf{1} + \frac{\beta}{1-\beta}\mathbf{i} + \frac{1}{1-\beta}\mathbf{e} \qquad (14.9.2a)$$

$$\mathbf{y} = \frac{\alpha}{1-\beta}\mathbf{1} + \frac{1}{1-\beta}\mathbf{i} + \frac{1}{1-\beta}\mathbf{e} \qquad (14.9.2b)$$

The reduced form disturbances for both **c** and **y** are

$$\mathbf{v}_1 = \mathbf{v}_2 = \frac{1}{1-\beta}\mathbf{e} = \frac{1}{1-0.8}\mathbf{e} = 5\mathbf{e}$$

Thus, the reduced-form disturbances $\mathbf{v}_1$ and $\mathbf{v}_2$ are distributed as $N(\mathbf{0}, \mathrm{I})$. Given a series of 20 hypothetical values for **i** (the first column of Table 14.1) and the normal random disturbance (the last column of Table 14.1), the data for **c** and **y** are generated through the reduced-form equations (14.9.2). One of the samples is given in Table 14.1. In the real-world situation, only **i**, **c**, and **y** are observed. The values of the reduced-form disturbances are unobservable, and the true values of α and β are not known.

14.9.5 Using the data in Table 14.1, estimate the reduced-form equations for (14.9.2a) and (14.9.2b).

14.9.6 Using the data in Table 14.1, calculate the indirect least squares (ILS) estimates for α and β from (14.9.2a) and also from (14.9.2b). Are the ILS estimates obtained from both reduced-form equations identical?

Table 14.1 A Sample of Hypothetical Data for the Simple Keynesian Model

i	c	y	$\mathbf{v}_1 = \mathbf{v}_2$
2.0	18.19	20.19	0.193
2.0	17.50	19.50	−0.504
2.2	16.48	18.68	−2.318
2.2	19.06	21.26	0.257
2.4	21.38	23.78	1.784
2.4	21.23	23.63	1.627
2.6	21.11	23.71	0.708
2.6	22.65	25.25	2.252
2.8	20.74	23.54	−0.462
2.8	19.85	22.65	−1.348
3.0	22.23	25.23	0.234
3.0	22.23	25.23	0.226
3.2	23.43	26.63	0.629
3.2	23.04	26.24	0.244
3.4	23.03	26.43	−0.569
3.4	24.45	27.85	0.853
3.6	26.63	30.23	2.227
3.6	24.47	28.07	0.074
3.8	25.67	28.47	−0.527
3.8	26.00	29.80	0.804

14.9.7 Using the values of investment in Table 14.1 as an instrumental variable, calculate the instrumental variable estimator for α and β. Are the results the same as those from Exercise 14.9.6?

14.9.8 Using the data in Table 14.1, calculate the OLS estimates for α and β. Compare your results with the results of ILS estimates in Problem 14.9.6. Is the OLS estimate of the marginal propensity to consume β consistent with Exercise 14.9.4?

14.9.3 Numerical Group Exercises

14.9.9 Using the procedures presented in the Computer Handbook, generate 100 samples of **c** and **y** and calculate the OLS estimates for α and β. Can you find any estimate of β that is not biased upward? Compute the mean of the 100 estimates of α and β. Examine the degree of the empirical bias.

14.9.10 Calculate the ILS estimates for α and β for the 100 samples. Compute the mean of 100 estimates of α and β. Examine the degree of bias in these small sample sizes of 20 observations. Compare the bias of the ILS estimates with the bias of the OLS estimates.

14.9.11 Combine a pair of samples to make a sample of 40 observations. Compute the ILS estimates of α and β for the corresponding 50 samples. Calculate the mean and examine the bias of the parameter estimates. Are the empirical biases reduced from the results of 100 samples of size 20?

14.10 References

Fisher, F. M. (1966) *The Identification Problem in Econometrics.* New York: McGraw-Hill.

Fomby, T., C. Hill, and S. Johnson (1984) *Advanced Econometric Methods.* New York: Springer-Verlag.

Haavelmo, T. (1943) "The Statistical Implications of a System of Simultaneous Equations." *Econometrica,* 11:1–12.

Intriligator, M. (1978) *Econometric Models, Techniques and Applications.* Engelwood Cliffs, N.J.: Prentice-Hall.

Judge, G., W. Griffiths, C. Hill, H. Lütkepohl, and T. Lee (1985). *The Theory and Practice of Econometrics.* New York: Wiley.

Marshack, J. (1950) "Statistical Inference in Economics." In W. C. Hood and T. C. Koopmans (ed.) *Studies in Econometric Method.* New York: Wiley, pp. 1–26.
Pindyck, R., and D. Rubinfeld (1981) *Econometric Models and Economic Forecasts.* New York: McGraw–Hill.
Schmidt, P. (1976) *Econometrics.* New York: Dekker.
Theil, H. (1971). *Principles of Econometrics.* New York: Wiley.

CHAPTER 15

Estimation and Inference for Simultaneous Equation Statistical Models

In Chapter 14 we noted that the econometrician often works with nonexperimental, passively generated data, where little or no control is exercised by the investigator over the observed values of many of the economic variables. To cope with this we introduced a statistical model that took into account the simultaneous and interdependent nature of economic data-generation schemes. The implication of such a statistical model is that the classical least squares rule is no longer consistent because of the lack of statistical independence between the random variables representing the equation errors and those right-hand side economic variables whose values are determined within the system of equations.

The indirect least squares method provides consistent estimators for the reduced-form parameters, but the unique derivation of the parameters of a structural equation from the reduced-form parameters is possible only when the structural equation is just identified. Unfortunately, if we actually try to model the underlying data-generation process, not all structural equations are of the just identified form. Consequently, specifying models that we believe are consistent with the way in which the economic data were generated leads in many cases to structural equations that are overidentified. In this case the problem is how to make use of all the information contained in the model when carrying out estimation and inference relative to the unknown parameters of the structural equations. Given the importance of this problem for econometric practice, this chapter is devoted to a discussion of solution procedures that have been suggested over the last four decades.

In the following sections we begin by reviewing the indirect least squares method in order to isolate the estimation problem. In addition to the indirect least squares estimator, an instrumental variable estimator is demonstrated for estimating the unknown parameters of a just identified equation in a system of equations. This approach provides an insight as to how to handle the problem of estimating the unknown parameters of an overidentified equation in a system of equations. Within this context, the two-stage least squares estimator is derived and alternative ways of arriving at the same rule are noted and discussed. When the objective is joint estimation of the parameters for all the structural equations in the system, the seemingly unrelated regression technique permits us to use the information contained in the covariances among structural equation errors to construct a three-stage least squares estimator.

When it is possible to specify the probability distribution for the structural equation errors, maximum likelihood procedures may be applied. This approach leads to full information and limited information maximum likelihood estimators. The asymptotic and small-sample properties of alternative estimators are discussed, and their sampling performances are compared. Finally, the possible uses of an estimated system of simultaneous equations are discussed within the context of equilibrium analysis, forecasting, and simulation.

15.1 The Problem of Estimating the Parameters of an Overidentified Equation

As discussed in Chapter 14, the problem of estimating the parameters of an overidentified equation by the indirect least squares procedure is that too many prior restrictions must be imposed on the parameters. Although only part of this information may be used to derive consistent parameter estimators, these estimators are in general inefficient because some information is left unused. A procedure that uses all the sample and non sample information is therefore required if we are to achieve an asymptotically efficient estimator.

15.1.1 The Indirect Least Squares Approach

To understand the problem clearly and to point out the direction of the remedy, let us again examine the indirect least squares method. Following the notation defined in Chapter 14, we write the ith equation, where $i = 1, 2, \ldots, M$, as

$$Y\boldsymbol{\Gamma}_i + X\mathbf{B}_i + \mathbf{e}_i = \mathbf{0}$$

or

$$\begin{aligned}
\mathbf{y}_i &= Y_i\boldsymbol{\gamma}_i + Y_i^*\boldsymbol{\gamma}_i^* + X_i\boldsymbol{\beta}_i + X_i^*\boldsymbol{\beta}_i^* + \mathbf{e}_i \\
&= Y_i\boldsymbol{\gamma}_i + X_i\boldsymbol{\beta}_i + \mathbf{e}_i \\
&= (Y_i \quad X_i)\begin{pmatrix}\boldsymbol{\gamma}_i \\ \boldsymbol{\beta}_i\end{pmatrix} + \mathbf{e}_i \\
&= Z_i\boldsymbol{\delta}_i + \mathbf{e}_i
\end{aligned} \tag{15.1.1}$$

where

$$\boldsymbol{\Gamma}_i = \begin{bmatrix} -1 \\ \boldsymbol{\gamma}_i \\ \boldsymbol{\gamma}_i^* \end{bmatrix} = \begin{bmatrix} -1 \\ \boldsymbol{\gamma}_i \\ \mathbf{0} \end{bmatrix} \qquad \mathbf{B}_i = \begin{bmatrix} \boldsymbol{\beta}_i \\ \boldsymbol{\beta}_i^* \end{bmatrix} = \begin{bmatrix} \boldsymbol{\beta}_i \\ \mathbf{0} \end{bmatrix}$$

$Y = [\mathbf{y}_i \quad Y_i \quad Y_i^*]$, $X = [X_i \quad X_i^*]$, $M = m_i + m_i^*$, $K = k_i + k_i^*$, Y_i^* are those m_i^* endogeneous variables that appear in the ith equation with zero coefficients, X_i^* are those k_i^* exogeneous and predetermined variables that appear in the ith equation with zero coefficients, and $\mathbf{y}_i$, Y_i, and X_i are those jointly dependent and predetermined variables that appear in the ith equation with nonzero coefficients. Consequently, $\mathbf{y}_i$ is a $(T \times 1)$ vector, Y_i is a $[T \times (m_i - 1)]$ matrix, $\boldsymbol{\gamma}_i$ is an $[(m_i - 1) \times 1]$ vector, X_i is a $(T \times k_i)$ matrix, $\boldsymbol{\beta}_i$ is a $(k_i \times 1)$ vector, $\mathbf{e}_i$ is a $(T \times 1)$ vector, $Z_i = (Y_i \quad X_i)$, and

$$\boldsymbol{\delta}_i = \begin{pmatrix} \boldsymbol{\gamma}_i \\ \boldsymbol{\beta}_i \end{pmatrix}$$

From (14.5.1b) the set of relations that involves the structural coefficients and the reduced-form coefficients for the ith equation is

$$\Pi\boldsymbol{\Gamma}_i = -\mathbf{B}_i \qquad \text{or} \qquad \Pi\begin{bmatrix} -1 \\ \boldsymbol{\gamma}_i \\ \mathbf{0} \end{bmatrix} = \begin{bmatrix} -\boldsymbol{\beta}_i \\ \mathbf{0} \end{bmatrix} \tag{15.1.2}$$

where $\boldsymbol{\Gamma}_i$ and $\mathbf{B}_i$ are the ith columns of Γ and B, respectively. The reduced form parameters may be consistently estimated by $\hat{\Pi} = (X'X)^{-1}X'Y$. Therefore, using (15.1.2), we can write

$$(X'X)^{-1}X'(\mathbf{y}_i \quad Y_i \quad Y_i^*)\begin{bmatrix} -1 \\ \hat{\boldsymbol{\gamma}}_i \\ \mathbf{0} \end{bmatrix} = \begin{bmatrix} -\hat{\boldsymbol{\beta}}_i \\ \mathbf{0} \end{bmatrix} \tag{15.1.3}$$

where $\hat{\boldsymbol{\gamma}}_i$ and $\hat{\boldsymbol{\beta}}_i$ are the corresponding estimates of the structural parameters of Y_i and X_i. Multiplying both sides of (15.1.3) by $(X'X)$, we have

$$-X'\mathbf{y}_i + X'Y_i\hat{\boldsymbol{\gamma}}_i = -X'X\begin{bmatrix} \hat{\boldsymbol{\beta}}_i \\ \mathbf{0} \end{bmatrix} \tag{15.1.4}$$

Rearranging, we have

$$\begin{aligned} X'\mathbf{y}_i &= X'Y_i\hat{\boldsymbol{\gamma}}_i + X'X\begin{bmatrix} \hat{\boldsymbol{\beta}}_i \\ \mathbf{0} \end{bmatrix} \\ &= X'Y_i\hat{\boldsymbol{\gamma}}_i + X'X_i\hat{\boldsymbol{\beta}}_i \\ &= X'(Y_i \quad X_i)\begin{bmatrix} \hat{\boldsymbol{\gamma}}_i \\ \hat{\boldsymbol{\beta}}_i \end{bmatrix} \\ &= X'Z_i\hat{\boldsymbol{\delta}}_i \end{aligned} \tag{15.1.5}$$

Note that in (15.1.5) X' is of order $(K \times T)$, $Z_i = [Y_i \quad X_i]$ is of order $[T \times (m_i - 1 + k_i)]$, and

$$\hat{\boldsymbol{\delta}}_i = \begin{bmatrix} \hat{\boldsymbol{\gamma}}_i \\ \hat{\boldsymbol{\beta}}_i \end{bmatrix}$$

is of order $[(m_i - 1 + k_i) \times 1]$. Thus $X'Z_i$ is of order $[K \times (m_i - 1 + k_i)]$. If the ith equation is just identified, which requires that $K = m_i - 1 + k_i$, then $X'Z_i$ is a square matrix. Consequently, the indirect least squares estimator may be obtained as

$$\hat{\boldsymbol{\delta}}_{i(\mathrm{ILS})} = (X'Z_i)^{-1}X'\mathbf{y}_i \tag{15.1.6}$$

provided that $X'Z_i$ has full rank of $K = m_i - 1 + k_i$, which implies that the inverse of $X'Z_i$ exists. Thus the indirect least squares method only works when $X'Z_i$ is square and nonsingular.

If the ith equation is underidentified, then $K < m_i - 1 + k_i$ and the rank of $X'Z_i$ cannot exceed K. Thus, $X'Z_i$ is not square, and the indirect least squares method does not work.

If the ith equation is overidentified, $K > m_i - 1 + k_i$, there are more relations in (15.1.5) than the number of unknown parameters. Although any subset of $(m_i - 1 + k_i)$ relations from K relations in (15.1.5) may be used to obtain a consistent estimator, the estimator is not efficient because information that is contained in the excluded exogenous variables is discarded.

A careful examination of (15.1.5) reveals that (15.1.5) may be obtained by premultiplying the structural equation (15.1.1) by $T^{-1}X'$ and replacing $\boldsymbol{\delta}_i$ by $\hat{\boldsymbol{\delta}}_i$ and the transformed error vector $T^{-1}X'\mathbf{e}_i$ by its limiting null vector. Therefore, for just identified equations, $\hat{\boldsymbol{\delta}}_i$ is also the instrumental variable estimator that was discussed in Chapter 13. The set of instrumental variables in this case is the set of predetermined variables X. For an overidentified equation, the K instrumental variables in X must be transformed into a smaller set of $m_i - 1 + k_i$ variables in order to obtain a unique estimate of the unknown parameters. If the error vector $X'\mathbf{e}_i$ noted previously is retained, this leads to the following generalized least squares approach.

15.1.2 The Generalized Least Squares Approach

Let us return to the statistical model for the ith equation

$$\mathbf{y}_i = Y_i\boldsymbol{\gamma}_i + X_i\boldsymbol{\beta}_i + \mathbf{e}_i = Z_i\boldsymbol{\delta}_i + \mathbf{e}_i \tag{15.1.1}$$

and consider the transformed statistical model

$$\begin{aligned} X'\mathbf{y}_i &= X'Y_i\boldsymbol{\gamma}_i + X'X_i\boldsymbol{\beta}_i + X'\mathbf{e}_i \\ &= X'Z_i\boldsymbol{\delta}_i + X'\mathbf{e}_i \end{aligned} \tag{15.1.7}$$

where X is the $(T \times K)$ matrix of observations on all the exogenous and lagged endogenous variables in the entire system of structural equations and $Z_i = [Y_i \quad X_i]$. This transformation means that the new set of explanatory variables, when divided by T, that is, $X'Y_i/T$ and $X'X_i/T$, are sample cross-product moments, and thus as the sample size increases they may have in probability a nonstochastic limit. If the nonstochastic limits are assumed to exist, then in large samples $X'Z_i$ may be considered uncorrelated with the error term $X'\mathbf{e}_i$, and if we were to employ the generalized least squares rule for this model, we would obtain a consistent estimator of the unknown coefficient vectors $\boldsymbol{\gamma}_i$ and $\boldsymbol{\beta}_i$.

Before we apply the generalized least squares to the transformed model (15.1.7), we note that there are other alternative transformations. For example, Basmann (1957) considered a model that is obtained by premultiplying (15.1.1) by an idempotent matrix $X(X'X)^{-1}X'$ instead of X'. The merit of the transformation by an idempotent matrix is that the new design matrix will be asymptotically uncorrelated with the new equation errors, and the least squares estimation yields an estimator that possesses the statistical property of consistency. Although, in the following, we use the generalized least squares procedure on the model (15.1.7), you can work on the model that is premultiplied by $X(X'X)^{-1}X'$ and show that the same result can be obtained with ordinary least squares.

15.1.2a A Generalized Least Squares Estimator

In search of a consistent estimator, let us look first at the error vector $X'\mathbf{e}_i$. The mean of the random vector $E[X'\mathbf{e}_i]$ equals a zero vector even if X contains lagged endogenous variables that are contemporaneously uncorrelated with $\mathbf{e}_i$. However, since we assume that the errors $\mathbf{e}_i$ in the system are normally and independently distributed, the error vector $X'\mathbf{e}_i$ has a nonscalar identity covariance matrix. Thus it would seem, based on the results of Chapter 8, that the Aitken (GLS) estimator should be applied if we are to attain an estimator that is best within a large sample context.

To determine this estimator we need to know

$$\operatorname{var}(X'\mathbf{e}_i) = E[X'\mathbf{e}_i\mathbf{e}_i'X] = \sigma_{ii}E[X'X] \tag{15.1.8}$$

This matrix is not known, but because our primary interest at this point is with the asymptotic properties of the estimators it seems reasonable to substitute $\sigma_{ii}X'X$ for (15.1.8), if $\operatorname{plim} X'X/T = \lim_{T\to\infty} E[X'X/T]$, which we will assume.

Given $\sigma_{ii}X'X$, we may apply the generalized least squares rule of Chapter 8 to (15.1.7) to obtain the GLS estimator

$$\begin{aligned}\tilde{\boldsymbol{\delta}}_i &= [(X'Z_i)'(\sigma_{ii}X'X)^{-1}(X'Z_i)]^{-1}(X'Z_i)'(\sigma_{ii}X'X)^{-1}X'\mathbf{y}_i \\ &= [Z_i'X(X'X)^{-1}X'Z_i]^{-1}Z_i'X(X'X)^{-1}X'\mathbf{y}_i\end{aligned} \tag{15.1.9}$$

provided that the matrix $Z_i'X(X'X)^{-1}X'Z_i$ has an inverse. Since this matrix has dimension $m_i - 1 + k_i$, in order for it to have an inverse, the rank of X, which is K, must be equal to or greater than $m_i - 1 + k_i$, the rank of Z_i, because the rank $Z_i'X \leq \min\{\text{rank } Z_i, \text{rank } X\}$. Therefore, $m_i - 1 + k_i \leq K$ or, subtracting k_i from both sides,

$$m_i - 1 \leq k_i^* \tag{15.1.10}$$

where k_i^* is the number of exogenous and predetermined variables not in the ith structural equation. The inequality (15.1.10), is, as developed in Chapter 14, the necessary condition for identifying an equation in a system of equations. Therefore, for the estimator $\tilde{\boldsymbol{\delta}}_i$ to be viable, the structural equation must be either just identified or overidentified; with the latter, (15.1.10) holds as a strict inequality.

If the structural equation is just identified, $X'Z_i$ is a square matrix of order K, and the estimator $\tilde{\boldsymbol{\delta}}_i$ reduces to the indirect least squares estimator (15.1.6), that is,

$$\begin{aligned} \tilde{\boldsymbol{\delta}}_i &= [Z_i'X(X'X)^{-1}X'Z_i]^{-1}Z_i'X(X'X)^{-1}X'\mathbf{y}_i \\ &= (X'Z_i)^{-1}X'X(Z_i'X)^{-1}Z_i'X(X'X)^{-1}X'\mathbf{y}_i \\ &= (X'Z_i)^{-1}X'\mathbf{y}_i = \hat{\boldsymbol{\delta}}_i \end{aligned} \tag{15.1.11}$$

The generalized least squares estimator can be viewed as an instrumental variables estimator. The set of instrumental variables is $X(X'X)^{-1}X'Z_i$, a matrix of order $[T \times (m_i - 1 + k_i)]$.

15.1.2b Sampling Properties

To investigate the sampling properties of the generalized least squares estimator (15.1.9) and the estimators to follow, we assume that the ith equation is identified, that X contains only exogenous variables, and that

1.
$$\operatorname*{plim}_{T\to\infty} \frac{X'X}{T} = \lim_{T\to\infty} \frac{X'X}{T} = \Sigma_{xx}$$

exists where Σ_{xx} is nonsingular,

2.
$$E[\mathbf{e}_i\mathbf{e}_j'] = \sigma_{ij}I$$

and that the elements of X and $\mathbf{e}_i$ are independent, which implies,

3.
$$E[X'\mathbf{e}_i] = \mathbf{0}$$

The same results can also be established when X contains lagged endogenous variables providing some additional conditions, which guarantee the stability of the system, hold.

To show the consistency of

$$\begin{aligned}\tilde{\boldsymbol{\delta}}_i &= [Z_i'X(X'X)^{-1}X'Z_i]^{-1}Z_i'X(X'X)^{-1}X'\mathbf{y}_i \\ &= \boldsymbol{\delta}_i + [Z_i'X(X'X)^{-1}X'Z_i]^{-1}Z_i'X(X'X)^{-1}X'\mathbf{e}_i \qquad (15.1.9)\end{aligned}$$

we take probability limits to obtain

$$\begin{aligned}\text{plim } \tilde{\boldsymbol{\delta}}_i = \boldsymbol{\delta}_i &+ [(\text{plim } T^{-1}Z_i'X)(\text{plim } T(X'X)^{-1})(\text{plim } T^{-1}X'Z_i)]^{-1} \\ &\cdot (\text{plim } T^{-1}Z_i'X)(\text{plim } T(X'X)^{-1})(\text{plim } T^{-1}X'\mathbf{e}_i) \qquad (15.1.12)\end{aligned}$$

Since we have assumed that $\text{plim } T^{-1}X'X = \Sigma_{xx}$, this implies that $\text{plim } T(X'X)^{-1} = \Sigma_{xx}^{-1}$. We still need to evaluate $\text{plim } T^{-1}Z_i'X$ and $\text{plim } T^{-1}X'\mathbf{e}_i$. We have $\text{plim } T^{-1}X'\mathbf{e}_i = \mathbf{0}$ because

$$\lim E[X'\mathbf{e}_i] = \lim \mathbf{0} = \mathbf{0}$$

and

$$\lim \text{var}\left(\frac{X'\mathbf{e}_i}{T}\right) = \lim \frac{\sigma_{ii}}{T}\left(\frac{X'X}{T}\right) = \mathbf{0}$$

Also,

$$\begin{aligned}\text{plim } T^{-1}X'Z_i &= \text{plim } T^{-1}X'(Y_i \quad X_i) \\ &= (\text{plim } T^{-1}X'Y_i \quad \text{plim } T^{-1}X'X_i) \\ &= \left(\Sigma_{xx}\Pi_i \quad \Sigma_{xx}\begin{bmatrix} I_{k_i} \\ 0 \end{bmatrix}\right)\end{aligned}$$

which means that $\text{plim } T^{-1}X'Z_i$ has a finite limit. If we denote the finite limit of the cross-moment matrix $T^{-1}X'Z_i$ as Σ_{xz_i}, or

$$\text{plim } T^{-1}X'Z_i = \Sigma_{xz_i}$$

and its transpose as

$$\text{plim } T^{-1}Z_i'X = \Sigma_{z_ix}$$

then we can evaluate (15.1.12) as

$$\begin{aligned}\text{plim } \tilde{\boldsymbol{\delta}}_i &= \boldsymbol{\delta}_i + (\Sigma_{z_ix}\Sigma_{xx}^{-1}\Sigma_{xz_i})^{-1}\Sigma_{z_ix}\Sigma_{xx}^{-1} \cdot \mathbf{0} \\ &= \boldsymbol{\delta}_i \qquad (15.1.12)\end{aligned}$$

Identification of the ith equation is sufficient to ensure that Σ_{z_ix} is of rank $(m_i - 1 + k_i)$ and, hence, that $\Sigma_{z_ix}\Sigma_{xx}^{-1}\Sigma_{xz_i}$ is nonsingular. Thus we have shown that $\tilde{\boldsymbol{\delta}}_i$ is a consistent estimator for the structural parameters $\boldsymbol{\gamma}_i$ and $\boldsymbol{\beta}_i$.

Turning to the asymptotic distribution for $\tilde{\boldsymbol{\delta}}_i$, we first note that if $\mathbf{e}_i$ is normally distributed, then $T^{-1/2}X'\mathbf{e}_i$ will also be normally distributed (in finite samples and asymptotically) with mean zero and covariance matrix

$$E\left[\frac{X'\mathbf{e}_i\mathbf{e}_i'X}{T}\right] = \sigma_{ii}E\left[\frac{X'X}{T}\right]$$

Consequently, we can show that $X'\mathbf{e}_i/\sqrt{T}$ converges in distribution to a normal random vector with mean vector zero and covariance $\sigma_{ii}\Sigma_{xx}$.

Also, because

$$\text{plim}\left[\left(\frac{Z_i'X}{T}\right)\left(\frac{X'X}{T}\right)^{-1}\left(\frac{X'Z_i}{T}\right)\right]^{-1}\left(\frac{Z_i'X}{T}\right)\left(\frac{X'X}{T}\right)^{-1} = (\Sigma_{z_ix}\Sigma_{xx}^{-1}\Sigma_{xz_i})^{-1}\Sigma_{z_ix}\Sigma_{xx}^{-1}$$

it follows that

$$\sqrt{T}(\tilde{\boldsymbol{\delta}}_i - \boldsymbol{\delta}_i) = \left[\left(\frac{Z_i'X}{T}\right)\left(\frac{X'X}{T}\right)^{-1}\left(\frac{X'Z_i}{T}\right)\right]^{-1}\left(\frac{Z_i'X}{T}\right)\left(\frac{X'X}{T}\right)^{-1}\left(\frac{X'\mathbf{e}_i}{\sqrt{T}}\right) \tag{15.1.13}$$

converges in distribution to a normal random vector with mean zero and covariance matrix Q where

$$\begin{aligned} Q &= (\Sigma_{z_ix}\Sigma_{xx}^{-1}\Sigma_{xz_i})^{-1}\Sigma_{z_ix}\Sigma_{xx}^{-1}\sigma_{ii}\Sigma_{xx}\Sigma_{xx}^{-1}\Sigma_{xz_i}(\Sigma_{z_ix}\Sigma_{xx}^{-1}\Sigma_{xz_i})^{-1} \\ &= \sigma_{ii}(\Sigma_{z_ix}\Sigma_{xx}^{-1}\Sigma_{xz_i})^{-1} \end{aligned}$$

Therefore, the estimator $\tilde{\boldsymbol{\delta}}_i$ is consistent; that is,

$$\text{plim}\ \tilde{\boldsymbol{\delta}}_i = \boldsymbol{\delta}_i$$

and in large samples its covariance matrix can be approximated by

$$\Sigma_{\tilde{\boldsymbol{\delta}}_i} = \sigma_{ii}[Z_i'X(X'X)^{-1}X'Z_i]^{-1} \tag{15.1.14}$$

The covariance matrix $\Sigma_{\tilde{\boldsymbol{\delta}}_i}$ can be estimated by

$$\hat{\Sigma}_{\tilde{\boldsymbol{\delta}}_i} = \hat{\sigma}_{ii}[Z_i'X(X'X)^{-1}X'Z_i]^{-1} \tag{15.1.15}$$

with

$$\hat{\sigma}_{ii} = \frac{(\mathbf{y}_i - Z_i\tilde{\boldsymbol{\delta}}_i)'(\mathbf{y}_i - Z_i\tilde{\boldsymbol{\delta}}_i)}{\tau_i} \tag{15.1.16}$$

where both $\tau_i = T$ and $\tau_i = T - m_i + 1 - k_i$ make $\hat{\sigma}_{ii}$ a consistent estimator of σ_{ii}. If Z_i contains only nonstochastic exogenous variables, the choice $\tau_i = T - m_i + 1 - k_i$ provides an unbiased estimate of the residual variance.

In reference to the simple two equation simultaneous statistical model (14.2.21) in Section (14.2.1), we have

$$\operatorname{plim} \frac{X'Z_1}{T} = \operatorname{plim} \begin{bmatrix} T^{-1}\mathbf{x}_1'\mathbf{y}_2 & T^{-1}\mathbf{x}_1'\mathbf{x}_2 \\ T^{-1}\mathbf{x}_2'\mathbf{y}_2 & T^{-1}\mathbf{x}_2'\mathbf{x}_2 \\ T^{-1}\mathbf{x}_3'\mathbf{y}_2 & T^{-1}\mathbf{x}_3'\mathbf{x}_2 \end{bmatrix}$$

$$= \begin{bmatrix} -7 & 1 \\ -11 & 2 \\ -1 & 0 \end{bmatrix}$$

$$\operatorname{plim} T^{-1}[Z_1'X(X'X)^{-1}X'Z_1]$$

$$= \begin{bmatrix} -7 & -11 & -1 \\ 1 & 2 & 0 \end{bmatrix} \begin{bmatrix} 2 & -1 & 0 \\ -1 & 1 & 0 \\ 0 & 0 & 1 \end{bmatrix} \begin{bmatrix} -7 & 1 \\ -11 & 2 \\ -1 & 0 \end{bmatrix}$$

$$= \begin{bmatrix} -3 & -4 & -1 \\ 0 & 1 & 0 \end{bmatrix} \begin{bmatrix} -7 & 1 \\ -11 & 2 \\ -1 & 0 \end{bmatrix} = \begin{bmatrix} 66 & -11 \\ -11 & 2 \end{bmatrix}$$

$$\operatorname{plim} T[Z_1'X(X'X)^{-1}X'Z_1]^{-1} = \begin{bmatrix} 66 & -11 \\ -11 & 2 \end{bmatrix}^{-1} = \tfrac{1}{11}\begin{bmatrix} 2 & 11 \\ 11 & 66 \end{bmatrix}$$

The covariance matrix of the limiting distribution of $\sqrt{T}(\tilde{\boldsymbol{\delta}}_1 - \boldsymbol{\delta}_1)$ is

$$\sigma_{11} \operatorname{plim} T[Z_1'X(X'X)^{-1}X'Z_1]^{-1} = \begin{bmatrix} \frac{10}{11} & 5 \\ 5 & 30 \end{bmatrix}$$

15.1.2c A Two-stage Least Squares Estimator

The generalized least squares estimator $\tilde{\boldsymbol{\delta}}_i$ can be expressed in many forms, and each has its own interpretation in the literature. One well-known specification is the so-called two-stage least squares rule developed by Theil. To derive the corresponding two-stage least squares estimator let us write $\tilde{\boldsymbol{\delta}}_i$ as

$$\begin{aligned} \tilde{\boldsymbol{\delta}}_i &= [Z_i'X(X'X)^{-1}X'Z_i]^{-1}Z_i'X(X'X)^{-1}X'\mathbf{y}_i \\ &= [(Y_i \;\; X_i)'X(X'X)^{-1}X'(Y_i \;\; X_i)]^{-1}(Y_i \;\; X_i)'X(X'X)^{-1}X'\mathbf{y}_i \\ &= \begin{bmatrix} Y_i'X(X'X)^{-1}X'Y_i & Y_i'X(X'X)^{-1}X'X_i \\ X_i'X(X'X)^{-1}X'Y_i & X_i'X(X'X)^{-1}X'X_i \end{bmatrix}^{-1} \begin{bmatrix} Y_i'X(X'X)^{-1}X'\mathbf{y}_i \\ X_i'X(X'X)^{-1}X'\mathbf{y}_i \end{bmatrix} \end{aligned} \quad (15.1.17)$$

From Chapter 14, the reduced form (14.2.13b) is

$$Y = X\Pi + V$$

Let us partition according to the ith equation as

$$[\mathbf{y}_i \quad Y_i \quad Y_i^*] = X[\pi_i \quad \Pi_i \quad \Pi_i^*] + [\mathbf{v}_i \quad V_i \quad V_i^*]$$

where $\mathbf{y}_i$ is the $(T \times 1)$ vector of the ith jointly dependent variable, Y_i contains the other jointly dependent variables appearing in the ith equation, Y_i^* is the $(T \times m_i^*)$ matrix of the jointly dependent variables that do not appear in the ith equation, and $[\boldsymbol{\pi}_i \quad \Pi_i \quad \Pi_i^*]$ is the matrix of reduced-form coefficients partitioned accordingly. The least squares estimator of Π_i is $\hat{\Pi}_i = (X'X)^{-1}X'Y_i$, and thus

$$X(X'X)^{-1}X'Y_i = X\hat{\Pi}_i = \hat{Y}_i = Y_i - \hat{V}_i \tag{15.1.18}$$

where $\hat{Y}_i$ is the $[T \times (m_i - 1)]$ matrix of estimated values of Y_i. Thus, using the fact that $(X'X)^{-1}X'X = I$ and (15.1.18), (15.1.17) may be written as

$$\tilde{\boldsymbol{\delta}}_i = \begin{bmatrix} Y_i'X(X'X)^{-1}X'X(X'X)^{-1}X'Y_i & Y_i'X(X'X)^{-1}X'X_i \\ X_i'X(X'X)^{-1}X'Y_i & X_i'X(X'X)^{-1}X'X_i \end{bmatrix}^{-1}$$
$$\times \begin{bmatrix} Y_i'X(X'X)^{-1}X'\mathbf{y}_i \\ X_i'X(X'X)^{-1}X'\mathbf{y}_i \end{bmatrix}$$
$$= \begin{bmatrix} \hat{Y}_i'\hat{Y}_i & \hat{Y}_i'X_i \\ X_i'\hat{Y}_i & X_i'X_i \end{bmatrix}^{-1} \begin{bmatrix} \hat{Y}_i'\mathbf{y}_i \\ X_i'\mathbf{y}_i \end{bmatrix} \tag{15.1.19}$$

Thus if we let $\hat{Z}_i = [\hat{Y}_i \quad X_i]$, then the two-stage least squares estimator may be specified as

$$\tilde{\boldsymbol{\delta}}_i = [\hat{Z}_i'\hat{Z}_i]^{-1}\hat{Z}_i'\mathbf{y}_i \tag{15.1.20}$$

This estimator is also obtained if the least squares rule is applied to the following statistical model.

$$\mathbf{y}_i = [\hat{Y}_i \quad X_i]\boldsymbol{\delta}_i + \bar{\mathbf{e}}_i \tag{15.1.21}$$

In this context the two-stage least squares (2SLS) estimator is developed as follows.

Stage 1. Estimate the reduced form parameters Π_i by $\hat{\Pi}_i = (X'X)^{-1}X'Y_i$ and use these estimates to predict the sample values of $\hat{Y}_i$ where $\hat{Y}_i = X(X'X)^{-1}X'Y_i = X\hat{\Pi}_i$.

Stage 2. Based on the statistical model (15.1.21), use the least squares rule to obtain estimates of the structural parameters $\boldsymbol{\delta}_i$.

Estimates for all structural parameters in the system may be obtained by repeating this procedure for each structural equation.

15.2 The Search for an Asymptotically Efficient Estimator

Although we now have a consistent estimator for the unknown parameters in each just or overidentified structural equation, the question arises whether there is an asymptotically more efficient estimator. In using the generalized least squares or 2SLS estimator we estimate the structural parameters of each equation separately. Although the estimator for each equation makes use of information for all the exogenous and predetermined variables in the whole system, this estimator ignores information concerning the Y_i^*, which are the endogenous variables that appear in the system but not in the ith equation. It also ignores information that may be available concerning the error covariances $E[\mathbf{e}_i\mathbf{e}_j'] = \sigma_{ij}I$ for $i \neq j$. Zellner and Theil (1962) considered this situation and came up with the idea of using the seemingly unrelated regression model of Chapter 11 as a basis for incorporating this information. We now turn to an exposition of this idea.

15.2.1 The Three-stage Least Squares (3SLS) Estimator

In search of a more efficient estimator, Zellner and Theil, within the context of (15.1.7), wrote the whole system of M structural equations as

$$\begin{bmatrix} X'\mathbf{y}_1 \\ X'\mathbf{y}_2 \\ \vdots \\ X'\mathbf{y}_M \end{bmatrix} = \begin{bmatrix} X'Z_1 & & & \\ & X'Z_2 & & \\ & & \ddots & \\ & & & X'Z_M \end{bmatrix} \begin{bmatrix} \boldsymbol{\delta}_1 \\ \boldsymbol{\delta}_2 \\ \vdots \\ \boldsymbol{\delta}_M \end{bmatrix} + \begin{bmatrix} X'\mathbf{e}_1 \\ X'\mathbf{e}_2 \\ \vdots \\ X'\mathbf{e}_M \end{bmatrix} \tag{15.2.1}$$

or, compactly, using the Kronecker product notation developed in Section A.15 of Appendix A and used in Chapter 11, as

$$(I \otimes X')\mathbf{y} = (I \otimes X')Z\boldsymbol{\delta} + (I \otimes X')\mathbf{e} \tag{15.2.2}$$

where

$$Z = \begin{bmatrix} Z_1 & & & \\ & Z_2 & & \\ & & \ddots & \\ & & & Z_M \end{bmatrix}$$

is a $[TM \times \sum_{i=1}^{M} (m_i - 1 + k_i)]$ matrix,

$$\mathbf{y} = \begin{bmatrix} \mathbf{y}_1 \\ \mathbf{y}_2 \\ \vdots \\ \mathbf{y}_M \end{bmatrix}$$

is a $(TM \times 1)$ vector,

$$\boldsymbol{\delta} = \begin{bmatrix} \boldsymbol{\delta}_1 \\ \boldsymbol{\delta}_2 \\ \vdots \\ \boldsymbol{\delta}_M \end{bmatrix}$$

is a $[\sum_{i=1}^{M} (m_i - 1 + k_i) \times 1]$ vector, and

$$\mathbf{e} = \begin{bmatrix} \mathbf{e}_1 \\ \mathbf{e}_2 \\ \vdots \\ \mathbf{e}_M \end{bmatrix}$$

is a $(TM \times 1)$ vector. Since X is assumed exogenous and independent of $\mathbf{e}$, the covariance matrix of $(I \otimes X')\mathbf{e}$ is given by

$$\begin{aligned} E[(I \otimes X')\mathbf{ee}'(I \otimes X)] &= E[(I \otimes X')E[\mathbf{ee}'|X](I \otimes X)] \\ &= E[(I \otimes X')(\Sigma \otimes I)(I \otimes X)] \\ &= \Sigma \otimes E[X'X] \end{aligned} \tag{15.2.3}$$

where Σ is an unknown $(M \times M)$ matrix. Assuming that $(X'X/T)$ converges to a nonstochastic limit, $T^{-1}X'X$ will be a consistent estimator for $T^{-1}E[X'X]$, and we are able to replace (15.2.3) by $\Sigma \otimes X'X$.

Under this scenario the generalized least squares rule applied to (15.2.1) yields

$$\begin{aligned} \boldsymbol{\delta}^* &= \{Z'(I \otimes X')'[\Sigma^{-1} \otimes (X'X)^{-1}](I \otimes X')Z\}^{-1} \\ &\quad \times Z'(I \otimes X')'[\Sigma^{-1} \otimes (X'X)^{-1}](I \otimes X')\mathbf{y} \\ &= \{Z'[\Sigma^{-1} \otimes X(X'X)^{-1}X']Z\}^{-1}Z'[\Sigma^{-1} \otimes X(X'X)^{-1}X']\mathbf{y} \end{aligned} \tag{15.2.4}$$

Alternatively, since $X'X$ is a positive definite matrix we can, as in Chapter 8 and Section A.1 of Appendix A, make use of a P matrix such that $PX'XP' = I_K$ and rewrite (15.2.1) as

$$\begin{bmatrix} PX'\mathbf{y}_1 \\ PX'\mathbf{y}_2 \\ \vdots \\ PX'\mathbf{y}_M \end{bmatrix} = \begin{bmatrix} PX'Z_1 & & & \\ & PX'Z_2 & & \\ & & \ddots & \\ & & & PX'Z_M \end{bmatrix} \begin{bmatrix} \boldsymbol{\delta}_1 \\ \boldsymbol{\delta}_2 \\ \vdots \\ \boldsymbol{\delta}_M \end{bmatrix} + \begin{bmatrix} PX'\mathbf{e}_1 \\ PX'\mathbf{e}_2 \\ \vdots \\ PX'\mathbf{e}_M \end{bmatrix} \tag{15.2.5}$$

or, compactly, as

$$(I \otimes PX')\mathbf{y} = (I \otimes PX')Z\boldsymbol{\delta} + (I \otimes PX')\mathbf{e} \tag{15.2.6}$$

where the covariance of $(I \otimes PX')\mathbf{e}$ is $\Sigma \otimes I_K$.

If we rewrite (15.2.6) as

$$\mathscr{y} = W\boldsymbol{\delta} + \mathbf{w}^* \tag{15.2.7}$$

where $\mathscr{y} = (I \otimes PX')\mathbf{y}$, $W = (I \otimes PX')Z$, and $\mathbf{w}^* = (I \otimes PX')\mathbf{e}$, then the generalized least squares (seemingly unrelated) rule applied to (15.2.7) is

$$\begin{aligned}\boldsymbol{\delta}^* &= [W'(\Sigma^{-1} \otimes I)W]^{-1}W'(\Sigma^{-1} \otimes I)\mathscr{y} \\ &= \{Z'[\Sigma^{-1} \otimes X(X'X)^{-1}X']Z\}^{-1}Z'[\Sigma^{-1} \otimes X(X'X)^{-1}X']\mathbf{y}\end{aligned} \tag{15.2.8}$$

With either (15.2.4) or (15.2.8) use of the rule depends on the unknown elements of the covariance matrix Σ. To construct an operational version of $\boldsymbol{\delta}^*$, we may obtain a consistent estimator $\hat{\Sigma}$ of Σ by using elements $\hat{\sigma}_{ij}$ computed as follows:

$$\hat{\sigma}_{ij} = \frac{(\mathbf{y}_i - Z_i\tilde{\boldsymbol{\delta}}_i)'(\mathbf{y}_j - Z_j\tilde{\boldsymbol{\delta}}_j)}{\tau} \tag{15.2.9}$$

Where $\tilde{\boldsymbol{\delta}}$ is the GLS (two-stage least-squares estimator) in (15.1.11) and τ may be calculated as

$$\tau_1 = T \tag{15.2.10}$$

or

$$\tau_2 = \frac{(MT - p)}{M} \tag{15.2.11a}$$

where

$$p = \sum_{i=1}^{M} [(m_i - 1) + k_i]$$

is the number of estimated parameters in the model and m_i and k_i are the number of jointly dependent and predetermined variables in the ith equation. If there are J cross-equation restrictions in the model, then the proper division for τ is

$$\tau_3 = \frac{[MT - (p - J)]}{M} \tag{15.2.11b}$$

Thus, the operational estimator is

$$\hat{\boldsymbol{\delta}}^* = \{Z'[\hat{\Sigma}^{-1} \otimes X(X'X)^{-1}X']Z\}^{-1}Z'[\hat{\Sigma}^{-1} \otimes X(X'X)^{-1}X']\mathbf{y} \tag{15.2.12}$$

where $\hat{\Sigma}$ has elements $\hat{\sigma}_{ij}$.

We can summarize the estimation procedure as follows.

Stage 1. Obtain the M estimates $\tilde{\boldsymbol{\delta}}_i$, $i = 1, 2, \ldots, M$ in order to form the residual covariance matrix $\hat{\Sigma}$ whose elements are defined as (15.2.9). In other words, compute the estimate $\hat{\Sigma}$ by using 2SLS residuals.

Stage 2. Use $\hat{\Sigma}$ in (15.2.8) to obtain the three-stage least squares estimator $\hat{\boldsymbol{\delta}}^*$.

15.2.2 Sampling Properties

To show that the 3SLS estimator

$$\begin{aligned}\hat{\boldsymbol{\delta}}^* &= \{Z'[\hat{\Sigma}^{-1} \otimes X(X'X)^{-1}X']Z\}^{-1}Z'[\hat{\Sigma}^{-1} \otimes X(X'X)^{-1}X']\mathbf{y} \\ &= \boldsymbol{\delta} + \{Z'[\hat{\Sigma}^{-1} \otimes X(X'X)^{-1}X']Z\}^{-1}Z'[\hat{\Sigma}^{-1} \otimes X(X'X)^{-1}X']\mathbf{e} \quad (15.2.12)\end{aligned}$$

is consistent, assume each of the M structural equations is identified and take the probability limit to obtain

$$\begin{aligned}\text{plim } \hat{\boldsymbol{\delta}}^* &= \boldsymbol{\delta} + \text{plim}\{Z'[\hat{\Sigma}^{-1} \otimes X(X'X)^{-1}X']Z\}^{-1}Z'[\hat{\Sigma}^{-1} \otimes X(X'X)^{-1}X']\mathbf{e} \\ &= \boldsymbol{\delta} + \text{plim}\{Z'(I \otimes X')'[\hat{\Sigma}^{-1} \otimes (X'X)^{-1}](I \otimes X')Z\}^{-1} \\ &\quad \cdot Z'(I \otimes X')'[\hat{\Sigma}^{-1} \otimes (X'X)^{-1}](I \otimes X')\mathbf{e} \\ &= \boldsymbol{\delta} + \{[\text{plim } T^{-1}Z'(I \otimes X')'][\text{plim}(\hat{\Sigma}^{-1} \otimes T(X'X)^{-1})] \\ &\quad \cdot [\text{plim } T^{-1}(I \otimes X')Z]\}^{-1} \\ &\quad \cdot [\text{plim } T^{-1}Z'(I \otimes X')'][\text{plim}(\hat{\Sigma}^{-1} \otimes T(X'X)^{-1})][\text{plim } T^{-1}(I \otimes X')\mathbf{e}]\end{aligned} \quad (15.2.13)$$

Since we have assumed that plim $T^{-1}(X'X) = \Sigma_{xx}$, this implies that plim$(\hat{\Sigma}^{-1} \otimes T(X'X)^{-1}) = \Sigma^{-1} \otimes \Sigma_{xx}^{-1}$. Thus to evaluate (15.2.13) we need to evaluate plim $T^{-1}Z'(I \otimes X')'$ or its transpose, plim $T^{-1}(I \otimes X')Z$ and plim $T^{-1}(I \otimes X')\mathbf{e}$. Working in this direction we have plim $T^{-1}(I \otimes X')\mathbf{e} = \mathbf{0}$, because

$$\text{plim } T^{-1}(I \otimes X')\mathbf{e} = \begin{bmatrix} \text{plim } T^{-1}X'\mathbf{e}_1 \\ \text{plim } T^{-1}X'\mathbf{e}_2 \\ \vdots \\ \text{plim } T^{-1}X'\mathbf{e}_M \end{bmatrix} = \begin{bmatrix} \mathbf{0} \\ \mathbf{0} \\ \vdots \\ \mathbf{0} \end{bmatrix} = \mathbf{0}$$

Also from Section 15.1.2b

$$\begin{aligned}\text{plim } T^{-1}(I \otimes X')Z &= \begin{bmatrix} \text{plim } T^{-1}X'Z_1 & & & \\ & \text{plim } T^{-1}X'Z_2 & & \\ & & \ddots & \\ & & & \text{plim } T^{-1}X'Z_M \end{bmatrix} \\ &= \begin{bmatrix} \Sigma_{xz_1} & & & \\ & \Sigma_{xz_2} & & \\ & & \ddots & \\ & & & \Sigma_{xz_M} \end{bmatrix} = \Sigma_{xz}\end{aligned}$$

If we denote the transpose of Σ_{xz} by

$$\text{plim } T^{-1}Z'(I \otimes X')' = \Sigma_{zx}$$

we can evaluate (15.2.13) as

$$\begin{aligned}\text{plim } \hat{\boldsymbol{\delta}}^* &= \boldsymbol{\delta} + [\Sigma_{zx}(\Sigma^{-1} \otimes \Sigma_{xx}^{-1})\Sigma_{xz}]^{-1}\Sigma_{zx}(\Sigma^{-1} \otimes \Sigma_{xx}^{-1}) \cdot \mathbf{0} \\ &= \boldsymbol{\delta} \qquad (15.2.13)\end{aligned}$$

Consequently, if we add the assumption that each of the M structural equations is identified, it follows that the 3SLS estimator $\hat{\boldsymbol{\delta}}^*$ is a consistent estimator.

To establish its asymptotic distribution, we follow an argument similar to that used for the GLS-2SLS estimator. Specifically,

$$\begin{aligned}\sqrt{T}(\hat{\boldsymbol{\delta}}^* - \boldsymbol{\delta}) &= [T^{-1}Z'(I \otimes X')'(\hat{\Sigma}^{-1} \otimes T(X'X)^{-1})T^{-1}(I \otimes X')Z]^{-1} \\ &\quad \cdot T^{-1}Z'(I \otimes X')'(\hat{\Sigma}^{-1} \otimes T(X'X)^{-1})T^{-1/2}(I \otimes X')\mathbf{e} \qquad (15.2.14)\end{aligned}$$

and, if $\mathbf{e} \sim N(\mathbf{0}, \Sigma \otimes I)$, this implies (in finite samples and asymptotically) that $T^{-1/2}(I \otimes X')\mathbf{e}$ has a normal distribution with mean zero and covariance matrix

$$\begin{aligned}T^{-1}(I \otimes X')(\Sigma \otimes I)(I \otimes X')' &= T^{-1}(\Sigma \otimes X'X) \\ &= (\Sigma \otimes T^{-1}X'X) \qquad (15.2.15)\end{aligned}$$

Thus the limiting distribution of $T^{-1/2}(I \otimes X')\mathbf{e}$ is normal with mean zero and covariance matrix $\Sigma \otimes \Sigma_{xx}$. Then, along the lines of the 2SLS estimator, it follows that $\sqrt{T}(\hat{\boldsymbol{\delta}}^* - \boldsymbol{\delta})$ has a limiting normal distribution with mean zero and covariance matrix,

$$[\Sigma_{zx}(\Sigma^{-1} \otimes \Sigma_{xx}^{-1})\Sigma_{xz}]^{-1}. \qquad (15.2.16)$$

Because $T[Z'(\hat{\Sigma}^{-1} \otimes X(X'X)^{-1}X')Z]^{-1}$ is a consistent estimator for $[\Sigma_{zx}(\Sigma^{-1} \otimes \Sigma_{xx}^{-1})\Sigma_{xz}]^{-1}$, we can use

$$\hat{\Sigma}_{\hat{\delta}^*} = [Z'(\hat{\Sigma}^{-1} \otimes X(X'X)^{-1}X')Z]^{-1} \qquad (15.2.17)$$

as an estimator for the approximate covariance matrix of $\hat{\boldsymbol{\delta}}^*$, where $\hat{\Sigma}$ has elements $\hat{\sigma}_{ij}$ given in (15.2.9).

15.2.3 Estimator Comparisons

We will now show that the three-stage least squares estimator $\hat{\boldsymbol{\delta}}^*$ is asymptotically more efficient than the two-stage least squares estimator $\tilde{\boldsymbol{\delta}}_i$ applied to all the M structural equations. The asymptotic superiority will be reflected by the fact that the difference between the covariance matrices of the limiting distributions of $\sqrt{T}(\hat{\boldsymbol{\delta}}^* - \boldsymbol{\delta})$ and that of $\sqrt{T}(\tilde{\tilde{\boldsymbol{\delta}}} - \boldsymbol{\delta})$, where $\tilde{\tilde{\boldsymbol{\delta}}} = (\tilde{\tilde{\boldsymbol{\delta}}}'_1, \tilde{\tilde{\boldsymbol{\delta}}}'_2, \ldots, \tilde{\tilde{\boldsymbol{\delta}}}'_M)'$, is a positive semidefinite matrix. The relative inefficiency of the 2SLS estimator arises because it ignores the information contained in the off-diagonal elements of Σ.

For comparison purpose the GLS-2SLS estimator $\tilde{\tilde{\boldsymbol{\delta}}}$ for the parameter vector $\boldsymbol{\delta}$ of the whole system (15.2.1) is

$$\tilde{\tilde{\boldsymbol{\delta}}} = \begin{bmatrix} \tilde{\tilde{\boldsymbol{\delta}}}_1 \\ \tilde{\tilde{\boldsymbol{\delta}}}_2 \\ \vdots \\ \tilde{\tilde{\boldsymbol{\delta}}}_M \end{bmatrix} = \begin{bmatrix} Z'_1X(X'X)^{-1}X'Z_1 & & & \\ & Z'_2X(X'X)^{-1}X'Z_2 & & \\ & & \ddots & \\ & & & Z'_MX(X'X)^{-1}X'Z_M \end{bmatrix}^{-1}$$

$$\times \begin{bmatrix} Z'_1X(X'X)^{-1}X'\mathbf{y}_1 \\ Z'_2X(X'X)^{-1}X'\mathbf{y}_2 \\ \vdots \\ Z'_MX(X'X)^{-1}X'\mathbf{y}_M \end{bmatrix}$$

$$= [Z'(I \otimes X(X'X)^{-1}X')Z]^{-1}Z'(I \otimes X(X'X)^{-1}X')\mathbf{y} \tag{15.2.18}$$

The covariance matrix of the limiting distribution of $\tilde{\tilde{\boldsymbol{\delta}}}$ is

$$Q_1 = [\Sigma_{zx}(I \otimes \Sigma_{xx}^{-1})\Sigma_{xz}]^{-1}[\Sigma_{zx}(\Sigma \otimes \Sigma_{xx}^{-1})\Sigma_{xz}]\,[\Sigma_{zx}(I \otimes \Sigma_{xx}^{-1})\Sigma_{xz}]^{-1} \tag{15.2.19}$$

The covariance matrix of the limiting distribution of $\hat{\boldsymbol{\delta}}^*$ is

$$Q_2 = [\Sigma_{zx}(\Sigma^{-1} \otimes \Sigma_{xx}^{-1})\Sigma_{xz}]^{-1} \tag{15.2.20}$$

Given the covariance matrices of the limiting distributions of $\tilde{\tilde{\boldsymbol{\delta}}}$ and $\hat{\boldsymbol{\delta}}^*$, it is possible to show that

$$Q_1 - Q_2 = A(\Sigma \otimes \Sigma_{xx})A' \tag{15.2.21}$$

where

$$\begin{aligned} A = {} & [\Sigma_{zx}(I \otimes \Sigma_{xx}^{-1})\Sigma_{xz}]^{-1}\Sigma_{zx}(I \otimes \Sigma_{xx}^{-1}) \\ & - [\Sigma_{zx}(\Sigma^{-1} \otimes \Sigma_{xx}^{-1})\Sigma_{xz}]^{-1}\Sigma_{zx}(\Sigma^{-1} \otimes \Sigma_{xx}^{-1}) \end{aligned} \tag{15.2.22}$$

Since $(\Sigma \otimes \Sigma_{xx})$ is a positive definite matrix, this means that $A(\Sigma \otimes \Sigma_{xx})A'$ is a nonnegative definite matrix. Consequently, the asymptotic gain in efficiency of $\sqrt{T}(\hat{\boldsymbol{\delta}}^* - \boldsymbol{\delta})$ relative to $\sqrt{T}(\tilde{\tilde{\boldsymbol{\delta}}} - \boldsymbol{\delta})$ is established unless (*i*) the errors in the individual structural equations are uncorrelated and thus Σ is diagonal or (*ii*) each equation in the system of equations is just identified.

15.2.4 Limited and Full Information Maximum Likelihood Methods

Thus far, for estimation purposes, we have not taken into account the information concerning the assumption that the equation errors are jointly normally distributed. If we do this and write the system of equations as

$$\begin{bmatrix} \mathbf{y}_1 \\ \mathbf{y}_1 \\ \vdots \\ \mathbf{y}_M \end{bmatrix} = \begin{bmatrix} Z_1 & & & \\ & Z_2 & & \\ & & \ddots & \\ & & & Z_M \end{bmatrix} \begin{bmatrix} \boldsymbol{\delta}_1 \\ \boldsymbol{\delta}_2 \\ \vdots \\ \boldsymbol{\delta}_M \end{bmatrix} + \begin{bmatrix} \mathbf{e}_1 \\ \mathbf{e}_2 \\ \vdots \\ \mathbf{e}_M \end{bmatrix} \tag{15.2.23}$$

or

$$\mathbf{y} = Z\boldsymbol{\delta} + \mathbf{e} \tag{15.2.24}$$

where now we specify that $\mathbf{e}$ is a normal random vector with mean vector zero and covariance $\Sigma \otimes I_T$, then the joint probability density function of $\mathbf{e}$ is

$$g(\mathbf{e}) = (2\pi)^{-MT/2}|\Sigma \otimes I_T|^{-1/2} \exp[-\tfrac{1}{2}\mathbf{e}'(\Sigma \otimes I_T)^{-1}\mathbf{e}] \tag{15.2.25}$$

To transform the p.d.f. of $\mathbf{e}$, $g(\mathbf{e})$, into the p.d.f. of $\mathbf{y}$, say $f(\mathbf{y})$, we use a Jacobian transformation. Since the structural equations are linear, the Jacobian turns out to be nothing but the Tth power of the determinant of the Γ matrix. The transformation yields the joint p.d.f. for $\mathbf{y}$ as

$$f(\mathbf{y}) = (2\pi)^{-MT/2}|\Sigma \otimes I_T|^{-1/2}|\Gamma|^T \exp[-\tfrac{1}{2}(\mathbf{y} - Z\boldsymbol{\delta})'(\Sigma^{-1} \otimes I_T)(\mathbf{y} - Z\boldsymbol{\delta})] \tag{15.2.26}$$

When viewed as a function of the parameters in $\boldsymbol{\delta}$ and Σ, given observations $\mathbf{y}$ and Z the expression (15.2.26) is the likelihood function. Maximizing this function is equivalent to maximizing the following log-likelihood function.

$$\begin{aligned} \ln \ell(\boldsymbol{\delta}, \Sigma|\mathbf{y}, Z) = & -\frac{MT}{2}\ln(2\pi) + \frac{T}{2}\ln|\Sigma|^{-1} + T\ln|\Gamma| \\ & - \tfrac{1}{2}(\mathbf{y} - Z\boldsymbol{\delta})'(\Sigma^{-1} \otimes I_T)(\mathbf{y} - Z\boldsymbol{\delta}) \end{aligned} \tag{15.2.27}$$

where $|\Sigma \otimes I_T|^{-1/2} = |\Sigma|^{-T/2} = |\Sigma^{-1}|^{T/2}$ has been used.

The so-called full information maximum likelihood (FIML) estimation involves maximizing the log likelihood function (15.2.27) subject to any restrictions on the parameters Γ, B, and Σ of the type described in Section 14.5.1. Zero restrictions on Γ and B already appear in $\boldsymbol{\delta}$, since the vector $\boldsymbol{\delta}$ only consists of the structural coefficients that are nonzero. If the only restrictions are zero restrictions on Γ and B, then all we need to do is to maximize (15.2.27) with respect to the elements of $\boldsymbol{\delta}$ and Σ. This involves nonlinear functions in the elements of $\boldsymbol{\delta}$ when taking derivatives. Numerical nonlinear maximization techniques of the type discussed in Chapter 12 are often used in solving the problem. If no constraints are available for Σ, the resulting FIML estimator for $\boldsymbol{\delta}$ has the same asymptotic distribution as the 3SLS estimator $\hat{\boldsymbol{\delta}}^*$.

When the system is large, maximizing the nonlinear likelihood function with respect to $\boldsymbol{\delta}$ may pose computational difficulties. As an alternative, a single-equation method is available for estimating the unknown parameters of each structural equation or a proper subset of the system. For example, to estimate the unknown structural parameters for the ith equation

$$\mathbf{y}_i = Z_i\boldsymbol{\delta}_i + \mathbf{e}_i \tag{15.2.28}$$

where, as defined earlier, $Z_i = (Y_i \quad X_i)$, we may, in line with (15.2.26), write the joint p.d.f. for $\mathbf{y}_i$ and Y_i, the endogenous variables in the ith equation, as

$$f(\mathbf{y}_i, Y_i) = (2\pi)^{-m_iT/2}|\Sigma_* \otimes I_T|^{-1/2}|\Gamma_*|^T \times \exp[-\tfrac{1}{2}(\mathbf{y}_* - Z_*\boldsymbol{\delta}_*)'(\Sigma_*^{-1} \otimes I_T)(\mathbf{y}_* - Z_*\boldsymbol{\delta}_*)] \tag{15.2.29}$$

where Σ_* is an $(m_i \times m_i)$ submatrix of Σ, $\mathbf{y}_*$ is a subvector of $\mathbf{y}$, which includes $\mathbf{y}_1$, $\mathbf{y}_2, \ldots, \mathbf{y}_{m_i}$, Z_* is a submatrix of Z, involving $Z_1, Z_2, \ldots, Z_{m_i}$, and $\boldsymbol{\delta}_*$ is a subvector of $\boldsymbol{\delta}$, involving $\boldsymbol{\delta}_1, \boldsymbol{\delta}_2, \ldots, \boldsymbol{\delta}_{m_i}$. The log-likelihood function is

$$\ln \ell(\boldsymbol{\delta}_*, \Sigma_* | \mathbf{y}_*, X) = -\frac{Tm_i}{2}\ln(2\pi) - \frac{T}{2}\ln|\Sigma_*| + T\ln|\Gamma_*| - \tfrac{1}{2}(\mathbf{y}_* - Z_*\boldsymbol{\delta}_*)'(\Sigma_*^{-1} \otimes I_T)(\mathbf{y}_* - Z_*\boldsymbol{\delta}_*) \tag{15.2.30}$$

When (15.2.30) is maximized with respect to the elements of Σ_* and $\boldsymbol{\delta}_i$ that are contained in $\boldsymbol{\delta}_*$, subject to the identification restriction of the ith structural equation that

$$[\Pi \quad I_K]\begin{bmatrix}\boldsymbol{\Gamma}_i \\ \mathbf{B}_i\end{bmatrix} = \mathbf{0}$$

the resultant estimator is known as the limited information maximum likelihood (LIML) estimator.

Alternatively, if we write the reduced-form equations for the ith structural equation in the seemingly unrelated regression form of (14.4.4),

$$\mathbf{y}_* = (I \otimes X)\boldsymbol{\pi}_* + \mathbf{v}_* \tag{15.2.31}$$

where $\mathbf{y}_*$, $\boldsymbol{\pi}_*$, and $\mathbf{v}_*$ are the first m_i blocks of $\mathbf{y}$, $\boldsymbol{\pi}$, and $\mathbf{v}$, respectively. The likelihood function based on $\mathbf{v}_*$ is

$$\ell(\boldsymbol{\pi}_* | X, \mathbf{y}_*) = (2\pi)^{-m_iT/2}|\Omega_* \otimes I_T|^{-1/2} \times \exp\{-\tfrac{1}{2}(\mathbf{y}_* - (I \otimes X)\boldsymbol{\pi}_*)'(\Omega_*^{-1} \otimes I_T)(\mathbf{y}_* - (I \otimes X)\boldsymbol{\pi}_*)\} \tag{15.2.32}$$

where Ω_* is an $(m_i \times m_i)$ submatrix of the reduced-form covariance matrix Ω relating to $\mathbf{v}_*$. After the Jacobian transformation the log-likelihood function in terms of γ_i and $\boldsymbol{\beta}_i$ is the same as (15.2.30). In general, the LIML estimator is asymptotically less efficient than the FIML or 3SLS estimator, since it does not use all the information that is available in the system.

Pagan (1979) shows that the LIML estimates can be computed by using the seemingly unrelated regression technique, if we write the structural equation to be estimated as

$$\mathbf{y}_i = Z_i\boldsymbol{\delta}_i + \mathbf{e}_i \tag{15.2.33}$$

together with the reduced-form equation for Y_i in a vector form

$$\mathbf{y}_R = (I_{m_i-1} \otimes X)\boldsymbol{\pi}_R + \mathbf{v}_R \tag{15.2.34}$$

where $Z_i = (Y_i \quad X_i)$, $\mathbf{y}_R = \text{vec}(Y_i)$, $\boldsymbol{\pi}_R = \text{vec}(\Pi_i)$, and $\mathbf{v}_R = \text{vec}(V_i)$. This form results because the restrictions imposed on the reduced form of $\mathbf{y}_i$ and $\mathbf{y}_R$ are exactly the LIML restrictions. The seemingly unrelated regression is

$$\begin{bmatrix} \mathbf{y}_i \\ \mathbf{y}_R \end{bmatrix} = \begin{bmatrix} Z_i & 0 \\ 0 & I_{m_i-1} \otimes X \end{bmatrix} \begin{bmatrix} \boldsymbol{\delta}_i \\ \boldsymbol{\pi}_R \end{bmatrix} + \begin{bmatrix} \mathbf{e}_i \\ \mathbf{v}_R \end{bmatrix} \tag{15.2.35}$$

If the covariance matrix between the elements of $\mathbf{e}_i$ and the columns of $\mathbf{v}_i$ is

$$\begin{bmatrix} \sigma_i^2 & \boldsymbol{\phi}' \\ \boldsymbol{\phi} & \Omega^* \end{bmatrix} \otimes I_T \tag{15.2.36}$$

the estimator is

$$\begin{bmatrix} \hat{\boldsymbol{\delta}}_{i(\text{LIML})} \\ \hat{\boldsymbol{\pi}}_{R(\text{LIML})} \end{bmatrix} = \begin{bmatrix} Z_i'(a \otimes I)Z_i & Z_i'(\mathbf{b}' \otimes X) \\ (\mathbf{b} \otimes X')Z_i & C \otimes X'X \end{bmatrix}^{-1} \begin{bmatrix} Z_i'(a \otimes I) & Z_i'(\mathbf{b}' \otimes X) \\ \mathbf{b} \otimes X' & C \otimes X' \end{bmatrix} \begin{bmatrix} \mathbf{y}_i \\ \mathbf{y}_R \end{bmatrix} \tag{15.2.37}$$

where

$$\begin{bmatrix} \sigma_i^2 & \boldsymbol{\phi}' \\ \boldsymbol{\phi} & \Omega^* \end{bmatrix}^{-1} = \begin{bmatrix} a & \mathbf{b}' \\ \mathbf{b} & C \end{bmatrix}$$

By partitioned inversion, the result for the LIML estimator of $\boldsymbol{\delta}_i$ is

$$\hat{\boldsymbol{\delta}}_{i(\text{LIML})} = \sigma_i^2 QZ_i'M\mathbf{y}_i + aQZ_i'\bar{M}\mathbf{y}_i + QZ_i'(\mathbf{b}' \otimes \bar{M})\mathbf{y}_R \tag{15.2.38}$$

where $Q^{-1} = \sigma_i^{-2}Z_i'MZ_i + aZ_i'\bar{M}Z_i$, $M = X(X'X)^{-1}X'$ and $\bar{M} = I - M$. Let $\hat{Z}_i = (\hat{Y}_i \quad X_i)$ and $\hat{W}_i = Z_i - \hat{Z}_i$, then Q^{-1} can be simplified to $Q^{-1} = \sigma_i^{-2}\hat{Z}_i'\hat{Z}_i + a\hat{W}_i'\hat{W}_i$, and the following relation results

$$\begin{aligned} \hat{\boldsymbol{\delta}}_{i(\text{LIML})} = \tilde{\boldsymbol{\delta}}_{i(\text{2SLS})} - (\hat{Z}_i'\hat{Z}_i)^{-1}F(\hat{Z}_i'\hat{Z}_i)^{-1}\hat{Z}_i'\mathbf{y}_i + aQ\hat{Z}_i'M\mathbf{y}_i \\ + Q\hat{Z}_i'(\mathbf{b}' \otimes \bar{M})\mathbf{y}_R \end{aligned} \tag{15.2.39}$$

where $F = \hat{W}_i'(k_i I + \hat{W}_i(\hat{Z}_i'\hat{Z}_i)^{-1}\hat{W}_i')^{-1}\hat{W}_i$, $k_i = \sigma_i^{-2}a$, and $\tilde{\boldsymbol{\delta}}_{i(2SLS)} = (\hat{Z}_i'\hat{Z}_i)^{-1}\hat{Z}_i'\mathbf{y}_i$. Equation (15.2.39) establishes a relation between LIML and 2SLS.

15.3 Asymptotic and Finite Sampling Properties of the Alternative Estimators

In previous sections we have discussed alternative estimators based on the indirect least squares method, the generalized least squares procedure, the seemingly unrelated regression technique, and the maximum likelihood method. To perform tests of parameter significance we need to know something about the distribution of the various estimators or at least the asymptotic distributions. The asymptotic distributions for the 2SLS and 3SLS estimators are known to be normal. However, the small sample properties are not known, and, indeed, the mean of the 2SLS estimator may not exist in small samples.

For large sample properties, the asymptotic efficiencies of various estimators vary, since each estimator incorporates a different amount of information. The indirect least squares estimator achieves asymptotic efficiency when the considered structural equation is just identified. For overidentified equations the K relations in (15.1.5) derived from the indirect least squares approach exceeds the number of unknown parameters $(m_i - 1 + k_i)$ that are to be estimated. If the generalized least squares method is employed to fit the K relations in (15.1.5) for the $m_i - 1 + k_i$ parameters, with the error term $X'\mathbf{e}_i$ added as shown in the transformed model (15.1.7), we get the 2SLS estimator. The 3SLS estimator takes account of the fact that the structural equations may be disturbance related and makes use of the covariance matrix of the disturbances among the equations within the framework of the seemingly unrelated regression model. Therefore, the 3SLS estimator is asymptotically more efficient than the 2SLS estimator. The asymptotic covariance matrix of the 3SLS estimator is identical with that of the FIML estimator. Since the large sample covariance matrix of the maximum likelihood estimator is equal to the Cramér–Rao bound, the 3SLS estimator has the same property and is thus asymptotically efficient. In terms of computational ease, the 3SLS method is simpler than the FIML method, because the latter results in nonlinear equations in unknown parameters that must be solved. When prior information on the disturbance covariance matrix Σ is available, this can be used with FIML when obtaining maximum likelihood estimates of $\boldsymbol{\delta}$ and Σ.

For small sample properties it has been argued that, despite their inconsistency, classical least squares estimators retain a minimum variance property, and the covariance matrices of the classical least squares estimators may be less than those of the 2SLS estimators. Analytical work on the small-sample properties of structural parameter estimation procedures started around 1970. The past two decades have seen many new achievements, although, because of the analytical complexities involved in carrying through the necessary derivations, results are only available for certain special cases. However, considerable results from sampling experiments are available in the literature. These so-called Monte Carlo experiments are often performed by setting up a structural model with specified values of the structural coefficient matrices Γ, B, and Σ. The values of the predetermined variables are also specified, and the values of the jointly dependent variables are generated through the reduced-form equations in conjunction with the reduced-form disturbances. The disturbances are generated by a random-number generator of a digital computer that is consistent with a prespecified probability distribution. Many samples of different sizes are generated and used to estimate the structural parameters with different estimators. The resultant distributions of the sample estimates are summarized and compared. Although results vary among the experiments, in general, the asymptotic theory seems to provide a good guide to the small sample estimator performance.

15.4 An Example

In this section we illustrate the GLS-2SLS and the 3SLS estimators with an example. For comparison purposes the ordinary least squares and indirect least squares results are also shown. Table 15.1 contains the observed vectors $\mathbf{x}_1, \mathbf{x}_2, \mathbf{x}_3, \mathbf{x}_4, \mathbf{x}_5, \mathbf{y}_1, \mathbf{y}_2$, and $\mathbf{y}_3$, which represent a sample of data generated from the model

$$\begin{aligned}
\mathbf{y}_1 &= \mathbf{y}_2\gamma_{21} + \mathbf{y}_3\gamma_{31} + \mathbf{x}_1\beta_{11} + \mathbf{e}_1 \\
\mathbf{y}_2 &= \mathbf{y}_1\gamma_{12} + \mathbf{x}_1\beta_{12} + \mathbf{x}_2\beta_{22} + \mathbf{x}_3\beta_{32} + \mathbf{x}_4\beta_{42} + \mathbf{e}_2 \qquad (15.4.1a) \\
\mathbf{y}_3 &= \mathbf{y}_2\gamma_{23} + \mathbf{x}_1\beta_{13} + \mathbf{x}_2\beta_{23} + \mathbf{x}_5\beta_{53} + \mathbf{e}_3
\end{aligned}$$

or, in matrix form,

$$Y\Gamma + XB + \mathbf{E} = 0 \qquad (15.4.1b)$$

where the $\mathbf{e}_i$ are normally distributed with $E[\mathbf{e}_i] = \mathbf{0}$ and

$$E\left[\begin{bmatrix}\mathbf{e}_1\\ \mathbf{e}_2\\ \mathbf{e}_3\end{bmatrix}\begin{bmatrix}\mathbf{e}_1\\ \mathbf{e}_2\\ \mathbf{e}_3\end{bmatrix}'\right] = \Sigma \otimes I_T \qquad (15.4.2)$$

Table 15.1 Observations *X* and *Y*

x_1	x_2	x_3	x_4	x_5	y_1	y_2	y_3
1	3.06	1.34	8.48	28	359.27	102.96	578.49
1	3.19	1.44	9.16	35	415.76	114.38	650.86
1	3.30	1.54	9.90	37	435.11	118.23	684.87
1	3.40	1.71	11.02	36	440.17	120.45	680.47
1	3.48	1.89	11.64	29	410.66	116.25	642.19
1	3.60	1.99	12.73	47	530.33	140.27	787.41
1	3.68	2.22	13.88	50	557.15	143.84	818.06
1	3.72	2.43	14.50	35	472.80	128.20	712.16
1	3.92	2.43	15.47	33	471.76	126.65	722.23
1	4.15	2.31	16.61	40	538.30	141.05	811.44
1	4.35	2.39	17.40	38	547.76	143.71	816.36
1	4.37	2.63	18.83	37	539.00	142.37	807.78
1	4.59	2.69	20.62	56	677.60	173.13	983.53
1	5.23	3.35	23.76	88	943.85	223.21	1292.99
1	6.04	5.81	26.52	62	893.42	198.64	1179.64
1	6.36	6.38	27.45	51	871.00	191.89	1134.78
1	7.04	6.14	30.28	29	793.93	181.27	1053.16
1	7.81	6.14	25.40	22	850.36	180.56	1085.91
1	8.09	6.19	28.84	38	967.42	208.24	1246.99
1	9.24	6.69	34.36	41	1102.61	235.43	1401.94

The hypothetical structural coefficient matrices are

$$\Gamma = \begin{bmatrix} -1 & 0.2 & 0 \\ -10 & -1 & 2 \\ 2.5 & 0 & -1 \end{bmatrix} \tag{15.4.3}$$

$$B = \begin{bmatrix} -60 & 40 & -10 \\ 0 & -4 & 80 \\ 0 & -6 & 0 \\ 0 & 1.5 & 0 \\ 0 & 0 & 5 \end{bmatrix} \tag{15.4.4}$$

and the covariance matrix is

$$\Sigma = \begin{bmatrix} 227.55 & 8.91 & -56.89 \\ 8.91 & 0.66 & -1.88 \\ -56.89 & -1.88 & 15.76 \end{bmatrix} \tag{15.4.5}$$

The reduced-form coefficient matrix for the hypothetical model is

$$\Pi = -B\Gamma^{-1} = \begin{bmatrix} -142.50 & 11.50 & 13.00 \\ 110.00 & 18.00 & 116.00 \\ 15.00 & -3.00 & -6.00 \\ -3.75 & 0.75 & 1.50 \\ 6.25 & 1.25 & 7.50 \end{bmatrix} \tag{15.4.6}$$

In a real-world problem, Γ, B, Σ, and Π would be unknown. Only the observations in Table 15.1 would be available along with perhaps some a priori knowledge suggesting that the model in (15.4.1) is a reasonable one.

Now we turn to the problem of estimating the unknown parameters of Γ, B, and Σ, given the data in Table 15.1. Note that the model consists of three structural equations with three jointly dependent variables and five predetermined variables. Under the order condition, in a system of three equations, for an equation to be just identified the number of zero coefficients must be exactly equal to two. The first equation has four zero coefficients and is overidentified; the second equation has two zero coefficients and is just identified, the third equation has three zero coefficients and is overidentified. All three equations fulfill the sufficient rank condition as shown in the following. For the first equation the matrix

$$R_1\Delta = \begin{bmatrix} 0 & \beta_{22} & \beta_{23} \\ 0 & \beta_{32} & 0 \\ 0 & \beta_{42} & 0 \\ 0 & 0 & \beta_{53} \end{bmatrix} \tag{15.4.7}$$

has rank 2 ($= M - 1$). For the second equation the matrix

$$R_2\Delta = \begin{bmatrix} \gamma_{31} & 0 & \gamma_{33} \\ 0 & 0 & \beta_{53} \end{bmatrix} \tag{15.4.8}$$

has rank 2 ($= M - 1$). Finally, for the third equation the matrix

$$R_3\Delta = \begin{bmatrix} \gamma_{11} & \gamma_{12} & 0 \\ 0 & \beta_{32} & 0 \\ 0 & \beta_{42} & 0 \end{bmatrix} \tag{15.4.9}$$

also has rank 2 ($= M - 1$).

Using the data in Table 15.1, the cross-moment matrix (with respect to the origin), is shown in Table 15.2. Since the cross-moment matrix is symmetric, the

Table 15.2 A Matrix of Cross Moments with Respect to the Origin

$$\begin{bmatrix} X'X & X'Y \\ Y'X & Y'Y \end{bmatrix} =$$

	x_1	x_2	x_3	x_4	x_5	y_1	y_2	y_3
x_1	20							
x_2	99	552						
x_3	68	400	303					
x_4	377	2,120	1,554	8,269				
x_5	832	4,127	2,865	16,223	38,726			
y_1	12,818	70,554	51,030	273,480	560,170	9,183,700		
y_2	3,131	16,653	11,849	64,475	136,020	2,174,100	519,670	
y_3	18,091	96,985	69,266	375,430	786,650	12,651,000	3,016,900	17,525,000

upper triangular elements are omitted. Based on Table 15.2, the reduced-form coefficient matrix is estimated directly as

$$\hat{\Pi} = \begin{bmatrix} -137.84 & 12.54 & 10.67 \\ 108.54 & 17.41 & 117.77 \\ 14.05 & -3.32 & -7.91 \\ -3.21 & 1.01 & 1.56 \\ 6.17 & 1.21 & 7.47 \end{bmatrix} \tag{15.4.10}$$

which is obtained by inverting the (5×5) $X'X$ matrix in Table 15.2 and multiplying it by the $X'Y$ matrix in Table 15.2.

For comparison purposes, the estimates of Γ and B obtained from applying least squares directly to each of the structural equations are

$$\hat{\Gamma}_{(\text{OLS})} = \begin{bmatrix} -1 & 0.20 & 0 \\ -6.03 & -1 & 1.38 \\ 1.87 & 0 & -1 \end{bmatrix} \tag{15.4.11}$$

$$\hat{B}_{(\text{OLS})} = \begin{bmatrix} -107.27 & 39.53 & -1.34 \\ 0 & -3.87 & 90.97 \\ 0 & -6.07 & 0 \\ 0 & 1.64 & 0 \\ 0 & 0 & 5.80 \end{bmatrix} \tag{15.4.12}$$

Since the second equation is just identified, the indirect least squares estimates of the second structural equation parameters are calculated as follows.

$$\begin{bmatrix} \hat{\boldsymbol{\gamma}}_2 \\ \hat{\boldsymbol{\beta}}_2 \end{bmatrix} = (X'Z_2)^{-1}X'\mathbf{y}_2$$

or

$$\begin{bmatrix} \hat{\gamma}_{12} \\ \hat{\beta}_{12} \\ \hat{\beta}_{22} \\ \hat{\beta}_{32} \\ \hat{\beta}_{42} \end{bmatrix}_{(\text{ILS})} = \begin{bmatrix} 12{,}818 & 20 & 99 & 68 & 377 \\ 70{,}554 & 99 & 552 & 400 & 2{,}120 \\ 51{,}030 & 68 & 400 & 303 & 1{,}554 \\ 273{,}479 & 377 & 2{,}120 & 1{,}554 & 8{,}269 \\ 560{,}173 & 832 & 4{,}127 & 2{,}865 & 16{,}223 \end{bmatrix}^{-1} \begin{bmatrix} 3{,}131 \\ 16{,}653 \\ 11{,}849 \\ 64{,}475 \\ 136{,}025 \end{bmatrix} \tag{15.4.13}$$

$$= \begin{bmatrix} 0.1959 \\ 39.5511 \\ -3.8587 \\ -6.0693 \\ 1.6445 \end{bmatrix}$$

For the overidentified equations, the matrix $X'Z_i$ is not a square matrix and cannot be inverted, and thus the indirect least squares estimator cannot be used. The GLS-2SLS formula,

$$\tilde{\boldsymbol{\delta}}_i = (Z_i'X(X'X)^{-1}X'Z_i)^{-1}Z_i'X(X'X)^{-1}X'\mathbf{y}_i$$

is used to compute the parameter estimates for all the structural equations. For the first equation, the GLS-2SLS estimates are

$$\begin{bmatrix} \tilde{\gamma}_{21} \\ \tilde{\gamma}_{31} \\ \tilde{\beta}_{11} \end{bmatrix}_{(2SLS)} = \begin{bmatrix} 519{,}646 & 3{,}016{,}953 & 3{,}131 \\ 3{,}016{,}953 & 17{,}525{,}230 & 18{,}091 \\ 3{,}131 & 18{,}091 & 20 \end{bmatrix}^{-1} \begin{bmatrix} 2{,}174{,}091 \\ 12{,}650{,}710 \\ 12{,}818 \end{bmatrix} = \begin{bmatrix} -9.4047 \\ 2.4090 \\ -65.9709 \end{bmatrix} \tag{15.4.14}$$

For the second equation, which is just identified, the 2SLS estimates can also be computed. They are

$$\begin{bmatrix} \tilde{\gamma}_{12} \\ \tilde{\beta}_{12} \\ \tilde{\beta}_{22} \\ \tilde{\beta}_{32} \\ \tilde{\beta}_{42} \end{bmatrix}_{(2SLS)} = \begin{bmatrix} 9{,}183{,}599 & 12{,}818 & 70{,}554 & 1{,}029 & 273{,}479 \\ 12{,}818 & 20 & 99 & 68 & 377 \\ 70{,}544 & 99 & 552 & 400 & 2{,}120 \\ 51{,}030 & 68 & 400 & 303 & 1{,}554 \\ 273{,}479 & 377 & 2{,}120 & 1{,}554 & 8{,}269 \end{bmatrix}^{-1} \begin{bmatrix} 2{,}174{,}091 \\ 3{,}131 \\ 16{,}653 \\ 11{,}849 \\ 64{,}475 \end{bmatrix} = \begin{bmatrix} 0.1959 \\ 39.5511 \\ -3.8587 \\ -6.0693 \\ 1.6445 \end{bmatrix} \tag{15.4.15}$$

The results are identical to the indirect least-squares estimates presented earlier. For the third equation, the GLS-2SLS estimates are

$$\begin{bmatrix} \tilde{\gamma}_{23} \\ \tilde{\beta}_{13} \\ \tilde{\beta}_{23} \\ \tilde{\beta}_{53} \end{bmatrix}_{(2SLS)} = \begin{bmatrix} 519{,}646 & 3{,}131 & 16{,}653 & 136{,}025 \\ 3{,}131 & 20 & 99 & 832 \\ 16{,}653 & 99 & 552 & 4{,}126 \\ 136{,}025 & 832 & 4{,}127 & 38{,}726 \end{bmatrix}^{-1} \begin{bmatrix} 3{,}016{,}953 \\ 18{,}091 \\ 96{,}985 \\ 786{,}645 \end{bmatrix} = \begin{bmatrix} 1.9383 \\ -8.7672 \\ 80.9009 \\ 5.0718 \end{bmatrix} \tag{15.4.16}$$

To summarize, the GLS-2SLS estimates of the three structural equations are given in the following with corresponding estimated standard errors in parentheses below the estimates.

$$\begin{aligned}
y_1 &= \underset{(28.51)}{-65.97}x_1 - \underset{(1.96)}{9.40}y_2 + \underset{(0.31)}{2.41}y_3 + \hat{e}_1 \\
y_2 &= \underset{(1.05)}{39.55}x_1 + \underset{(0.004)}{0.20}y_1 - \underset{(0.52)}{3.86}x_2 - \underset{(0.48)}{6.07}x_3 + \underset{(0.14)}{1.64}x_4 + \hat{e}_2 \\
y_3 &= \underset{(8.12)}{-8.77}x_1 + \underset{(0.53)}{1.94}y_2 + \underset{(9.53)}{80.90}x_2 + \underset{(0.69)}{5.07}x_5 + \hat{e}_3
\end{aligned} \tag{15.4.17}$$

For the 3SLS estimator, the following formula is used:

$$\hat{\boldsymbol{\delta}}^* = [Z'(\hat{\Sigma}^{-1} \otimes X(X'X)^{-1}X')Z]^{-1}Z'(\hat{\Sigma}^{-1} \otimes X(X'X)^{-1}X')\mathbf{y}$$

The covariance matrix Σ is estimated by using (15.2.9) and option (15.2.10) as

$$\hat{\Sigma} = \begin{bmatrix} 257.55 & 11.11 & -60.05 \\ 11.11 & 0.87 & -2.14 \\ -60.05 & -2.14 & 16.72 \end{bmatrix} \tag{15.4.18}$$

The estimates for Γ and B, obtained by using the 3SLS estimator, are

$$\Gamma^*_{(3SLS)} = \begin{bmatrix} -1 & 0.20 & 0 \\ -9.64 & -1 & 2.22 \\ 2.45 & 0 & -1 \end{bmatrix} \tag{15.4.19}$$

and

$$B^*_{(3SLS)} = \begin{bmatrix} -63.19 & 39.21 & -11.85 \\ 0 & -3.75 & 75.90 \\ 0 & -6.14 & 0 \\ 0 & 1.54 & 0 \\ 0 & 0 & 4.67 \end{bmatrix} \tag{15.4.20}$$

To summarize, estimates of the unknown structural parameters and their corresponding standard errors in the three structural equations using the 3SLS rule are as follows:

$$\begin{aligned}
y_1 &= \underset{(25.75)}{-63.19}x_1 - \underset{(1.75)}{9.64}y_2 + \underset{(0.28)}{2.45}y_3 + \hat{e}_1 \\
y_2 &= \underset{(0.77)}{39.21}x_1 + \underset{(0.002)}{0.20}y_1 - \underset{(0.32)}{3.75}x_2 - \underset{(0.30)}{6.14}x_3 + \underset{(0.10)}{1.54}x_4 + \hat{e}_2 \\
y_3 &= \underset{(6.27)}{-11.85}x_1 + \underset{(0.34)}{2.22}y_2 + \underset{(6.29)}{75.90}x_2 + \underset{(0.41)}{4.67}x_5 + \hat{e}_3
\end{aligned} \tag{15.4.21}$$

Note that the estimated standard errors for the 3SLS estimates are smaller than those of the GLS-2SLS estimates given earlier. The derived reduced form parameter matrices for the OLS, 2SLS, and 3SLS estimates are as follows.

$$\hat{\Pi}_{(\mathrm{OLS})} = -\hat{B}\hat{\Gamma}^{-1} = \begin{bmatrix} -146.82 & 10.74 & 13.49 \\ 109.50 & 17.61 & 115.30 \\ 12.48 & -3.62 & -5.00 \\ -3.37 & 0.98 & 1.35 \\ 6.47 & 1.27 & 7.55 \end{bmatrix} \tag{15.4.22}$$

$$\tilde{\Pi}_{(\mathrm{2SLS})} = -\tilde{B}\tilde{\Gamma}^{-1} = \begin{bmatrix} -142.33 & 11.66 & 13.84 \\ 110.57 & 17.81 & 115.41 \\ 14.91 & -3.15 & -6.10 \\ -4.04 & 0.85 & 1.65 \\ 6.34 & 1.24 & 7.48 \end{bmatrix} \tag{15.4.23}$$

and

$$\hat{\Pi}^*_{(\mathrm{3SLS})} = -\hat{B}^*\hat{\Gamma}^{*-1} = \begin{bmatrix} -139.93 & 11.37 & 13.42 \\ 109.73 & 18.08 & 116.10 \\ 14.05 & -3.34 & -7.44 \\ -3.53 & 0.84 & 1.87 \\ 6.22 & 1.24 & 7.42 \end{bmatrix} \tag{15.4.24}$$

If one compares the foregoing three matrices with the original hypothetical reduced form parameter matrix given earlier, one will find that the 2SLS-derived reduced-form matrix is overall closest to the hypothetical Π matrix and the derived reduced-form matrix of the OLS has the largest deviation from the hypothetical matrix. *Note that this result is only from one sample and should not be considered as conclusive as to the sampling performance of the various estimators.* If many experiments are performed, the average result should support the theoretical properties that the 3SLS estimator is asymptotically most efficient and, as sample size increases, converges to the true parameter matrix faster than the 2SLS estimator. To demonstrate asymptotic properties, the experiments should consider different sample sizes.

15.5 On Using the Results of Econometric Models for Forecasting and Decision Purposes

One of the objectives of positive economics is to describe how economic data are generated. This type of knowledge is desired because, if the processes underlying the attained values of economic variables are understood, then we will be in a position to predict and/or exercise some control over the future outcomes of the variables. In this section we discuss how the results of econometric models may be used for forecasting and other purposes.

Suppose that we have formulated an econometric model as a system of simultaneous equations, collected the relevant data, and estimated the unknown parameters of the structural equations with one of the methods described in the previous sections. How do we make use of the econometric model? Some basic analysis might include the testing of economic hypotheses, analysis of equilibrium involving the methods of comparative statics, economic forecasting, simulation of alternative economic policies, and optimal control of the system.

To illustrate some of the possible uses of a system of simultaneous equations, consider the reduced form

$$\mathbf{y}_t' = \mathbf{x}_t'\Pi + \mathbf{v}_t' \tag{15.5.1a}$$

or

$$\mathbf{y}_t = \Pi'\mathbf{x}_t + \mathbf{v}_t \tag{15.5.1b}$$

where $\mathbf{y}_t'$, $\mathbf{x}_t'$, and $\mathbf{v}_t'$ are the tth rows of Y, X, and V, respectively. For instance, for the example model (15.4.1) we get

$$\begin{bmatrix} y_{1t} \\ y_{2t} \\ y_{3t} \end{bmatrix} = \begin{bmatrix} -142.50 & 110.00 & 15.00 & -3.75 & 6.25 \\ 11.50 & 18.00 & -3.00 & 0.75 & 1.25 \\ 13.00 & 116.00 & -6.00 & 1.50 & 7.50 \end{bmatrix} \begin{bmatrix} x_{1t} \\ x_{2t} \\ x_{3t} \\ x_{4t} \\ x_{5t} \end{bmatrix} + \begin{bmatrix} v_{1t} \\ v_{2t} \\ v_{3t} \end{bmatrix} \tag{15.5.1c}$$

In this form, the impact of variations in the exogenous variables $x_1, \ldots, x_5$ on the endogenous variables can be analyzed. For instance, a unit increase in x_5 will, on average, lead to an increase of 6.25 units in y_1, 1.25 units in y_2, and 7.50 units in y_3.

Of course, usually we will not be in the fortunate situation of knowing the true data-generation process. In that case, we would use an estimated Π matrix to determine the average response of the endogenous variables to changes in the exogenous variables. Using the 2SLS estimates from (15.4.23), the estimated average responses of y_1, y_2, and y_3 are 6.34, 1.24, and 7.48, respectively. If estimated parameters are used, the sampling variability should be taken into account in interpreting the results.

The reduced form (15.5.1) can also be used for prediction. If all the predetermined variables are exogenous as in the example (15.4.1), the optimal forecasts of the endogenous variables given a particular set of values for the exogenous variables, $\mathbf{x}_{t+h}$ say, are

$$\hat{\mathbf{y}}_{t+h} = \Pi'\mathbf{x}_{t+h} \tag{15.5.1d}$$

For instance, for the example model, if

$$\mathbf{x}'_{t+h} = (1, 8, 6, 23, 40) \tag{15.5.1e}$$

then

$$\hat{\mathbf{y}}_{t+h} = \begin{bmatrix} 991.25 \\ 204.75 \\ 1239.50 \end{bmatrix} \tag{15.5.1f}$$

The forecast error vector is $\mathbf{y}_{t+h} - \hat{\mathbf{y}}_{t+h} = \hat{\mathbf{v}}_{t+h}$ and hence the corresponding forecast error variance-covariance matrix is $\Omega = E[\mathbf{v}_t\mathbf{v}'_t]$. Again, we have not taken into account that Π will usually be estimated. This will lead to an increase in the forecast error variance-covariance. If use is made of 3SLS estimates, the corresponding $\hat{\mathbf{y}}_{t+h}$ is

$$\hat{\mathbf{y}}_{t+h} = \begin{bmatrix} 989.76 \\ 204.80 \\ 1237.33 \end{bmatrix} \tag{15.5.1g}$$

The exact expression of the forecast error covariance matrix for this case follows from results by Schmidt (1976, Chapter 5).

Often the vector of predetermined variables will involve lagged endogenous variables in addition to exogenous variables. In that case, the model is dynamic. A dynamic model permits us to trace how changes in the exogenous variables condition the time path of the endogenous variables over a period of time. For example, what is the new equilibrium of the system? How long does it take to get there?

Let us assume that only endogenous variables with one lag are present. If $\mathbf{x}'_t$ is partitioned into

$$\mathbf{x}'_t = (\mathbf{y}'_{t-1}\,\mathbf{z}'_t)$$

and Π is partitioned into

$$\Pi = \begin{pmatrix} F' \\ G' \end{pmatrix}$$

where the order of F' is $(M \times M)$, G' is $[(K - M) \times M]$, $\mathbf{x}_t'$ is $(1 \times K)$, $\mathbf{y}_{t-1}'$ is a $(1 \times M)$ vector of lagged endogenous variables, and $\mathbf{z}_t'$ contains the remaining $K - M$ exogenous variables and is $[1 \times (K - M)]$, then the reduced form becomes

$$\mathbf{y}_t' = (\mathbf{y}_{t-1}' \quad \mathbf{z}_t')\begin{pmatrix} F' \\ G' \end{pmatrix} + \mathbf{v}_t' \tag{15.5.2a}$$

or

$$\mathbf{y}_t = F\mathbf{y}_{t-1} + G\mathbf{z}_t + \mathbf{v}_t \tag{15.5.2b}$$

If we solve the difference equation (15.5.2b) for $\mathbf{y}_t$ by lagging one period and substituting, the first substitution results in

$$\begin{aligned} \mathbf{y}_t &= F(F\mathbf{y}_{t-2} + G\mathbf{z}_{t-1} + \mathbf{v}_{t-1}) + G\mathbf{z}_t + \mathbf{v}_t \\ &= F^2\mathbf{y}_{t-2} + FG\mathbf{z}_{t-1} + G\mathbf{z}_t + F\mathbf{v}_{t-1} + \mathbf{v}_t \end{aligned} \tag{15.5.3}$$

Substituting the lagged variable n times, we have

$$\begin{aligned} \mathbf{y}_t = F^{n+1}\mathbf{y}_{t-(n+1)} &+ F^nG\mathbf{z}_{t-n} + F^{n-1}G\mathbf{z}_{t-(n-1)} + \cdots + G\mathbf{z}_t \\ &+ F^n\mathbf{v}_{t-n} + F^{n-1}\mathbf{v}_{t-(n-1)} + \cdots + F\mathbf{v}_{t-1} + \mathbf{v}_t \end{aligned} \tag{15.5.4}$$

The effect of a change in $\mathbf{y}_{t-(n+1)}$ on $\mathbf{y}_t$ is F^{n+1}. If the system is stable, the effect of changes in $\mathbf{y}_{t-(n+1)}$ on $\mathbf{y}_t$ should diminish as n approaches infinity, that is,

$$\lim_{n\to\infty} F^{n+1} = 0$$

Assuming that the system is stable, we have the following *final form*

$$\mathbf{y}_t = \sum_{i=0}^{\infty} F^iG\mathbf{z}_{t-i} + \sum_{i=0}^{\infty} F^i\mathbf{v}_{t-i} \tag{15.5.5}$$

The effect of a change in $\mathbf{z}_{t-n}$ on $\mathbf{y}_t$ is F^nG, which is often called a *delayed-n multiplier* matrix. When $n = 0$ the multiplier effect G is current and is called an *impact multiplier* matrix.

As an example, consider the following estimated two-equation equilibrium model

$$\text{Supply:}\ q_t = 2 + 3p_t + 0.8q_{t-1} + 0.1w_t \tag{15.5.6a}$$

$$\text{Demand:}\ q_t = 10 - 2p_t - 0.3p_{t-1} + 0.5y_t \tag{15.5.6b}$$

where q is quantity, p is price, w is wage rate, and y is income. The endogenous variables are quantity and price, or, more precisely, the jointly dependent variables are q_t and p_t and the predetermined variables are q_{t-1}, p_{t-1}, w_t, and y_t. The reduced form equations are

$$q_t = 6.8 + 0.32q_{t-1} - 0.18p_{t-1} + 0.04w_t + 0.3y_t \tag{15.5.7a}$$

$$p_t = 1.6 - 0.16q_{t-1} - 0.06p_{t-1} - 0.02w_t + 0.1y_t \tag{15.5.7b}$$

The matrix F is

$$F = \begin{bmatrix} 0.32 & -0.18 \\ -0.16 & -0.06 \end{bmatrix} \tag{15.5.8}$$

Since this matrix has characteristic roots 0.2183 and 0.1617, which are smaller than 1 in absolute value, F^n approaches zero as $n \to \infty$. Thus the system in this example is stable. The effect of a change in p_{t-1} on q_t is -0.18, and the effect on p_t is -0.06. The effect of a change in w_t on q_t is 0.04 and on p_t is -0.02, and the effect of a change in y_t on q_t is 0.3 and on p_t is 0.1. The effect of a change in w_{t-1} and y_{t-1} on q_t and p_t may be calculated as

$$FG = \begin{bmatrix} 0.32 & -0.18 \\ -0.16 & -0.06 \end{bmatrix} \begin{bmatrix} 6.8 & 0.04 & 0.3 \\ 1.6 & -0.02 & 0.1 \end{bmatrix} = \begin{bmatrix} 1.888 & 0.0164 & 0.0780 \\ -1.184 & -0.0052 & -0.0540 \end{bmatrix} \tag{15.5.9}$$

Therefore the effects of change in w_{t-1} on q_t and p_t are 0.0164 and -0.0052, respectively, and the effects of a change in y_{t-1} on q_t and p_t are, respectively, 0.0780 and -0.0540. The delayed-n multipliers can be calculated, in general, as F^nG. Consequently, the impact of wage or income changes on future values of the endogenous variables p_t and q_t can be forecast, and we can also develop alternative scenarios for evaluating the effects of assumed changes in wages or income. In the foregoing discussion we have assumed that the estimated coefficients are correct. In reality, the coefficients would be estimated, and thus the predicted outcomes for q_t and p_t are random variables. More discussion of forecasting and interpreting dynamic models is contained in Chapter 18.

15.6 Summary

When we deal with a statistical model consistent with a system of simultaneous equations in which many variables are interdependent, the classical least squares rule is biased and does not converge to the true parameters even in large-size samples. The indirect least squares procedure is a viable approach in the case of just identified equations, since for the ILS estimator $\hat{\boldsymbol{\delta}}_i = (X'Z_i)^{-1}X'\mathbf{y}_i$, which can also be interpreted as an instrumental variable estimator, the $X'Z_i$ matrix is square and nonsingular. The necessary condition for $X'Z_i$ to be a square matrix is that $K = m_i + k_i - 1$, which is also the necessary condition for just identification. The necessary and sufficient condition for the square matrix $X'Z_i$ to be nonsingular is that $X'Z_i$ has rank $m_i + k_i - 1$.

In real-world situations, structural equations are often overidentified. To use all the information that is available to the researcher, a generalized least squares procedure may be used to estimate the structural parameters. This results in the 2SLS estimator, which, when all structural equations are specified in the seemingly unrelated regression form $\mathbf{y} = Z\boldsymbol{\delta} + \mathbf{e}$, has the form

$$\tilde{\boldsymbol{\delta}} = [Z'(I \otimes X(X'X)^{-1}X')Z]^{-1}Z'[I \otimes X(X'X)^{-1}X']\mathbf{y}$$

If the covariance matrix of the disturbances for all structural equations is considered, we obtain the 3SLS estimator

$$\hat{\boldsymbol{\delta}}^* = [Z'(\hat{\Sigma}^{-1} \otimes X(X'X)^{-1}X')Z]^{-1}Z'[\hat{\Sigma}^{-1} \otimes X(X'X)^{-1}X']\mathbf{y}$$

The ILS, 2SLS, and 3SLS estimators can be viewed as instrumental variable estimators, where the instrumental variables are, respectively, X [or $(I \otimes X)$ for all equations], $(I \otimes X(X'X)^{-1}X')Z$, and $(\hat{\Sigma}^{-1} \otimes X(X'X)^{-1}X')Z$. Note that the increasing amount of information contained in the instrumental variables corresponds to the improved efficiency of the 3SLS estimator. The 3SLS estimator has the same asymptotic properties as the full information maximum likelihood (FIML) estimator, whereas the 2SLS estimator has the same asymptotic properties as the limited information maximum likelihood (LIML) estimator. The 3SLS is favored over the FIML from the standpoint of computational ease, but FIML is more appropriate than the 3SLS if prior restrictions on Σ exist. The 3SLS estimator is asymptotically more efficient than the 2SLS estimator if the equation disturbances are correlated. The 3SLS estimator gains no efficiency over the 2SLS estimator if Σ is diagonal or all structural equations are just identified. In these cases the 3SLS estimator reduces to the 2SLS estimator, which is equal to the ILS estimator in the latter case.

The analytical investigation of small-sample properties of structural parameter estimators is of recent vintage. Most of the results are confined to limited information instrumental variable estimators and to a special case with two included endogenous variables. Some significant achievements in a general case include asymptotic expansions, proof of theorems on existence of moments, and expressions for the exact and approximate distributions of estimators. These results have been used to compare the relative merits of asymptotically equivalent estimators such as 2SLS and LIML. One of the implications of the recent findings [Mariano (1980)] is that in an econometric model with a high degree of overidentification and low degrees of freedom, the ordinary and two-stage least squares estimators will show similar patterns in their statistical behavior, whereas the LIML estimator is substantially different. Although we have made some progress from the analytical investigation of small-sample properties, many problems remain to be solved. Monte Carlo studies provide another route, and econometricians have used these to augment the analytical approach in learning about small sample properties of simultaneous equation estimators.

15.7 Exercises

15.7.1 Algebraic Exercises

15.7.1 Show that the 2SLS estimator is identical to the instrumental variable estimator that uses the calculated values $\hat{Y}_i$ and X_i as instrumental variables.

15.7.2 Show that the 2SLS estimator is also an instrumental variable estimator with instrumental variables $X(X'X)^{-1}X'Z_i$.

15.7.3 Show that if a structural equation is just identified, the 2SLS estimator reduces to the ILS estimator.

15.7.4 Show that the 3SLS estimator is an instrumental variable estimator with instrumental variables $[\hat{\Sigma}^{-1} \otimes X(X'X)^{-1}X']Z$.

15.7.5 Show that when all structural equations are just identified, the 3SLS estimator gains no efficiency over the 2SLS estimator, and the 3SLS estimator reduces to the 2SLS estimator.

15.7.6 Show that the 2SLS estimator of the marginal propensity to consume in the simple Keynesian model (14.9.1) is identical to the instrumental variable estimator with investment as the instrumental variable.

15.7.2 Individual Numerical Exercises

The remaining problems are based on Monte Carlo experimental data that you may generate using the instructions in the Computer Handbook. These data consist of 100 samples of $\mathbf{y}_1$, $\mathbf{y}_2$, and $\mathbf{y}_3$, each of size 20, and they were generated from the model described in Section 15.4. The fixed values of the predetermined variables X are given in Table 15.1. Using one or two of the 100 samples:

15.7.7 Estimate the reduced-form parameter matrix $\hat{\Pi} = (X'X)^{-1}X'Y$.

15.7.8 Compute the calculated values of Y as $\hat{Y} = X(X'X)^{-1}X'Y$.

15.7.9 Using $\hat{Z}_i = (\hat{Y}_i \quad X_i)$ as instrumental variables, estimate the parameters of the three structural equations that are described in Section 15.4.

15.7.10 Using the indirect least squares method, estimate the parameters of the second equation, which is just identified.

$$\mathbf{y}_2 = \mathbf{y}_1\gamma_{12} + \mathbf{x}_1\beta_{12} + \mathbf{x}_2\beta_{22} + \mathbf{x}_3\beta_{32} + \mathbf{x}_4\beta_{42} + \mathbf{e}_2$$

15.7.11 Using the 2SLS formula $\tilde{\boldsymbol{\delta}}_i = [Z_i'X(X'X)^{-1}X'Z_i]^{-1}Z_i'X(X'X)^{-1}X'\mathbf{y}_i$, estimate the parameters in each of the three structural equations.

15.7.12 Using the 3SLS formula

$$\hat{\boldsymbol{\delta}}^* = [Z'(\hat{\Sigma}^{-1} \otimes X(X'X)^{-1}X')Z]^{-1}Z'[\hat{\Sigma}^{-1} \otimes X(X'X)^{-1}X']\mathbf{y}$$

estimate the parameters of the first and the third structural equations jointly.

15.7.13 Using the 3SLS method, estimate all the parameters of the three structural equations jointly, and compare the results with results of Exercise 15.7.12.

13.7.3 Group Exercises

15.7.14 Repeat Exercises 15.7.11 and 15.7.12 for 100 samples and use the results to calculate the mean and variance of each parameter estimate. Construct empirical frequency distributions for each parameter estimate from the 100 samples.

15.7.15 Repeat Exercise 15.7.13 for all 100 samples and use the results to calculate the mean and variance of each parameter estimate. Construct empirical frequency distributions for each parameter estimate from the 100 samples.

15.7.16 Using the results of Exercises 15.7.14 and 15.7.15, compute the mean squared error for the 2SLS and 3SLS estimates. Which method has a smaller mean squared error?

15.7.17 Exclude $\mathbf{x}_2$ from equations two and three of the model presented in (15.4.1a). Repeat Exercise 15.7.13 for all 100 samples and compute the empirical bias and mean squared errors for the estimates for the misspecified model.

15.8 References

Over the last 50 years, a vast literature has evolved that is concerned in one way or another with the simultaneous equation statistical model. The following listings represent an introduction to some of the old and new pieces of this literature.

Basmann, R. L. (1957) "A General Classical Method of Linear Estimation of Coefficients in a Structural Equation." *Econometrica*, 25:77–83.

Dhrymes, P. (1974) *Econometrics.* New York, Springer-Verlag.

Fomby, T. B., R. C. Hill, and S. R. Johnson (1984) *Advanced Econometric Methods.* New York, Springer-Verlag.

Hood, W. C., and T. J. Koopmans (eds.) (1953) *Studies in Econometric Methods.* New York, Wiley.

Judge, G. G., W. E. Griffiths, R. C. Hill, H. Lütkepohl, and T. C. Lee (1985) *The Theory and Practice of Econometrics.*, 2nd. ed. New York, Wiley.

Mariano, R. S. (1980) "Analytical Small-Sample Distribution Theory in Econometrics: The Simultaneous-Equations Case." Discussion paper 8026, *CORE*, Louvain-LaNeuve, Belgium.

Pagan, A. (1979) "Some consequences of viewing LIML as an Iterated Aitken Estimator," *Economics Letters*, 3: 369–372.

Schmidt P. (1976) *Econometrics.* New York, Dekker.

Theil, H. (1971) *Principles of Econometrics.* New York, Wiley.

Zellner, A., and H. Theil (1962) "Three Stage Least Squares: Simultaneous Estimation of Simultaneous Equations." *Econometrica*, 30:54–78.

PART 5

Time-Series and Distributed Lag Models

In this part of the book, we examine the special problems of model specification and inference that arise when using time-series data. First we consider modeling the generation process of a single time-series variable and we discuss forecasting in the univariate time-series context. Then we consider distributed lag models with one endogenous and one exogenous time-series variable. In these models the dynamic nature of many economic relationships is explicitly recognized by incorporating lags of the endogenous and/or exogenous variables in the model. In the final chapter of this part models are considered for sets of time-series variables that may all be endogenous. We discuss the specification and estimation of such models and explain how they can be used for prediction and analysis purposes.

CHAPTER 16

Time-Series Analysis and Forecasting

16.1 Introduction

One objective of analyzing economic data is to predict the future values of certain variables. One approach to obtaining forecasts is to set up an econometric model, estimate its parameters from the available data, and then use this model to predict future values of the variables of interest. This approach was followed in previous chapters of this book. An alternative approach that has proved quite successful, especially for short-term forecasting, is to use only the past values of a particular variable to predict its future values. This method does not necessarily use economic knowledge we may have about the process that has generated the values for the particular variable under investigation. In this approach, it is assumed that the data are generated by a stochastic process and a model for that process is chosen and estimated using statistical tools.

Intuitively, it may seem that, by not using knowledge about the economic structure, we neglect information and thus make inefficient use of the data. This would in fact be true if the observed data were generated by precisely the models economists have provided to explain economic phenomena. Unfortunately, our information about the underlying sampling mechanism is generally incomplete, and thus economic and econometric models are at best rough approximations to reality. Therefore it should not be surprising that time-series models that use only the information from a set of observations on a single variable have in some instances provided forecasts that are superior to predictions from a large-scale econometric model.

The purpose of this chapter is (1) to discuss some possible ways of constructing a model for a stochastic process that may have generated an observed set of data, (2) to estimate the parameters of such a model, and (3) to use the obtained model to forecast future values of the considered variable. In Section 16.2 a mathematical model for a stochastic process and some of its properties are discussed. In Sections 16.3 through 16.5 particular stochastic processes are considered, and the manner in which they are fitted to a given set of data is described. A systematic summary of the model-building process is given in Section 16.6, followed by a discussion of how to use a model of a stochastic process for prediction in Section 16.7. In Section 16.8 attention is drawn to some limitations of the time-series modeling approach presented in this chapter, and we see how the time-series approach relates to the econometric approach investigated in earlier chapters. For the reader with a special interest in time-series, some guidelines for further study are provided in Section 16.9.

16.2 A Mathematical Model for Time-Series and Its Characteristics

16.2.1 Stochastic Processes

We call a sample $y_1, y_2, \ldots, y_T$, where the index denotes time points or intervals, a time-series. Time series of different sorts have been encountered in the previous chapters. For instance, the observations for the dependent and independent variables of the linear regression models discussed in some of the previous chapters may be time-series. We suppose that the observations are realizations of random variables $\mathscr{y}_1, \mathscr{y}_2, \ldots, \mathscr{y}_T$, respectively, and moreover we assume that these random variables are only a part of an infinite sequence of random variables, say $\mathscr{y}_{t_0}$, $\mathscr{y}_{t_0+1}, \ldots, \mathscr{y}_1, \mathscr{y}_2, \ldots$, where t_0 may be $-\infty$. This sequence is called a *stochastic process*. More precisely, this is a *discrete* stochastic process, because the time index t assumes only integer values. Note that we differentiate here between a random variable and its observed value. The former is denoted by a script letter, the latter by the usual italic. It is often convenient to denote the stochastic process simply by $\mathscr{y}_t$. In the following it will be clear from the context whether $\mathscr{y}_t$ denotes a single random variable or a stochastic process. It is not essential which time point is called 0 or 1, but for convenience these numbers are usually placed at the beginning of the sample period.

We have seen examples of stochastic processes, that is, of sequences of random variables in earlier chapters of the book. For instance, the errors of the linear statistical model discussed in Chapters 5 and 6 were assumed to be a sequence $\mathscr{e}_t$ of independent or uncorrelated identically distributed random variables with zero mean. If the sample consists of time series data, then it makes sense to view the finite sequence $\mathscr{e}_1, \mathscr{e}_2, \ldots, \mathscr{e}_T$ of error terms of a statistical model as a subsequence of an infinite sequence $\mathscr{e}_t$, $t = 0, \pm 1, \pm 2, \ldots$. Such a sequence of uncorrelated random variables with zero mean and identical finite variances is often called *white noise* by time-series analysts. If the $\mathscr{e}_t$ are normally distributed, they are called a *Gaussian white-noise* process.

Another example of a stochastic process was encountered in Section 9.5, where the errors of a linear statistical model were assumed to be generated by a process of the form

$$\mathscr{y}_t = \rho \mathscr{y}_{t-1} + \mathscr{e}_t \tag{16.2.1}$$

where ρ is a number between -1 and 1 and $\mathscr{e}_t$ is white noise, that is, $E[\mathscr{e}_t] = 0$, $\text{var}(\mathscr{e}_t) = \sigma_e^2 < \infty$ for all t, and $\text{cov}(\mathscr{e}_t, \mathscr{e}_s) = 0$ for $s \neq t$. Assuming that the process

y_t has been started at $t_0 = -\infty$ and all the y_t have bounded means and variances, it can be shown that $E[y_t] = 0$ and all the variances are identical, say σ_y^2. A process like that of (16.2.1) is called an autoregressive process of order one. It is important to note that in this case each random variable y_t depends on its predecessors in time.

We have mentioned in the introductory section that forecasting is one main objective of building time-series models. Therefore, it is important that the present and past of a time series allow us to draw conclusions for the future. If all members of a stochastic process are independent, knowledge of past values will not be helpful in predicting the future, which is then independent of the past. For this reason, the covariance as a measure of the linear dependence between the members of a series plays an important role in describing its characteristics. We will now turn to a discussion of the autocovariance function and the autocorrelation function of a stochastic process.

16.2.2 The Autocovariance and Autocorrelation Functions

The autocovariance function is an important tool in describing the stochastic structure of a time series because it gives us an idea of how the members of a time-series depend on one another. Recall that the covariance between two random variables x and y is defined to be $E[(x - E[x])(y - E[y])]$. Consequently, the covariance between two elements y_t and y_{t+k} of a stochastic process y_t is

$$\operatorname{cov}(y_t, y_{t+k}) = E[(y_t - E[y_t])(y_{t+k} - E[y_{t+k}])] \tag{16.2.2}$$

This is called *autocovariance* because it measures the linear dependence between members of a single stochastic process. For example, for a white-noise process the autocovariances are equal to 0 for all $k \neq 0$ by definition.

As another example, consider the autoregressive process (16.2.1). Since $E[y_t] = 0$, we get

$$\begin{aligned} \operatorname{cov}(y_t, y_{t+1}) &= E[y_t y_{t+1}] = E[y_t(\rho y_t + e_{t+1})] \\ &= \rho E[y_t^2] + E[y_t e_{t+1}] = \rho\sigma_y^2 \end{aligned} \tag{16.2.3}$$

where σ_y^2 is the variance of the y_t (see Section 9.5). The last equation follows since y_t is uncorrelated with e_{t+1}. More generally, we get, for nonnegative k,

$$\begin{aligned} \operatorname{cov}(y_t, y_{t+k}) &= E[y_t y_{t+k}] = E[y_t(\rho y_{t+k-1} + e_{t+k})] \\ &= \rho E[y_t y_{t+k-1}] + E[y_t e_{t+k}] = \rho E[y_t y_{t+k-1}] \\ &= \rho E[y_t(\rho y_{t+k-2} + e_{t+k-1})] = \rho^2 E[y_t y_{t+k-2}] \\ &= \cdots = \rho^k E[y_t y_t] = \rho^k \sigma_y^2 \end{aligned} \tag{16.2.4}$$

Note that the covariance of y_t and y_{t+k} does not depend on the time point t, but only on the distance the two random variables are apart in time, that is, on k, since σ_y^2 is time invariant. This enables us to abbreviate $\mathrm{cov}(y_t, y_{t+k})$ by γ_k, where, of course, $\gamma_0 = \sigma_y^2$. For the autoregressive process y_t, we have, consequently,

$$\gamma_k = \rho^k \sigma_y^2 \qquad \text{for } k = 0, 1, 2, \ldots \tag{16.2.5}$$

Clearly, since

$$\mathrm{cov}(y_t, y_{t+k}) = \mathrm{cov}(y_{t-k}, y_t) = \mathrm{cov}(y_t, y_{t-k})$$

we get

$$\gamma_k = \gamma_{-k} \tag{16.2.6}$$

Thus we have a sequence γ_k, $k = 0, \pm 1, \pm 2, \ldots$ of autocovariances of a stochastic process. This sequence is called an *autocovariance function* of the process y_t. From (16.2.6) it follows that it is only necessary to report the γ_k for nonnegative k.

The autocovariance function depends essentially on the unit of measurement of the random variables. For instance, it makes a difference whether the average quarterly wages in the United States are given in dollars (y_t) or cents (z_t). In this case,

$$E[z_t z_{t+k}] = E[(100y_t)(100y_{t+k})] = 10{,}000E[y_t y_{t+k}]$$

This is sometimes inconvenient, and therefore the autocovariances are normalized by dividing each γ_k by the variance $\gamma_0 = \sigma_y^2$ of the process to obtain the *autocorrelation function*

$$\rho_k = \frac{\gamma_k}{\gamma_0} \qquad k = 0, \pm 1, \pm 2, \ldots \tag{16.2.7}$$

For the autoregressive process (16.2.1) we get,

$$\rho_k = \frac{\rho^k \sigma_y^2}{\sigma_y^2} = \rho^k \qquad k = 1, 2, \ldots \tag{16.2.8}$$

Clearly, it is not necessary to report the ρ_k for $k \leq 0$ because $\rho_k = \rho_{-k}$ and $\rho_0 = 1$.

16.2.3 Stationary Stochastic Processes

Unfortunately, not all stochastic processes have the property that the covariance between two members depends only on their distance in time. We will call stochastic processes that do have this property and, moreover, have a constant mean and a finite variance *stationary processes.*

More formally, a stochastic process y_t is stationary, if

i. $E[y_t] = \mu$ for all t.
ii. $\text{var}(y_t) < \infty$ for all t.
iii. $\text{cov}(y_t, y_{t+k}) = E[(y_t - \mu)(y_{t+k} - \mu)] = \gamma_k$ for all t and k.

It is worth noting that for $k = 0$ condition (*iii*) implies of course that $\text{var}(y_t)$ is time invariant.

Clearly, a white-noise process is stationary, and so is an autoregressive process of the type (16.2.1). It is important that $|\rho| < 1$, because otherwise the variance of this process may not be finite, whereby condition (*ii*) for stationarity is violated.

Stationarity is an important property as it guarantees that there are no fundamental changes in the structure of the process that would render prediction difficult or impossible. We note that some authors define stationarity in a slightly different way.

16.2.4 The Lag Operator

In the following it is sometimes convenient to use the *lag operator* L to simplify notation. We define

$$Ly_t = y_{t-1} \tag{16.2.9}$$

where y_t and y_{t-1} are elements of a stochastic process. If we apply L twice, we get

$$L^2 y_t = L(Ly_t) = Ly_{t-1} = y_{t-2}$$

More generally,

$$L^n y_t = y_{t-n} \tag{16.2.10}$$

for any positive integer n. It is sometimes advantageous to use the definition

$$L^0 y_t = y_t \tag{16.2.11}$$

To illustrate the use of the lag operator, consider the process (16.2.1), which can be written as

$$y_t = \rho L y_t + e_t$$

or

$$(1 - \rho L) y_t = e_t$$

If y_t *and* x_t are stochastic processes such that

$$y_t = a + b x_t$$

where a and b are constants, then

$$L(a + bx_t) = Ly_t = y_{t-1} = a + bx_{t-1} = a + bLx_t$$

In the following sections we will sometimes deal with polynomials in the lag operator, such as

$$\alpha_p(L) = 1 + \alpha_1 L + \cdots + \alpha_p L^p \tag{16.2.12}$$

This notation enables us to write the term

$$y_t + \alpha_1 y_{t-1} + \cdots + \alpha_p y_{t-p}$$

compactly as

$$\alpha_p(L)y_t$$

More generally, we may use infinite polynomials or power series in the lag operator, such as

$$\phi_\infty(L) = 1 + \phi_1 L + \phi_2 L^2 + \cdots$$

If we have two operators $\phi_p(L)$ and $\psi_q(L)$ such that

$$\phi_p(L)\psi_q(L) = 1$$

where p and/or q may be infinity, then we call $\psi_q(L)$ the inverse of $\phi_p(L)$ and write

$$\psi_q(L) = \phi_p(L)^{-1}$$

For example, if

$$\phi_1(L) = 1 - \phi L$$

with $|\phi| < 1$, then

$$\phi_1(L)^{-1} = 1 + \phi L + \phi^2 L^2 + \cdots$$

since

$$\begin{aligned}\phi_1(L)\phi_1(L)^{-1} &= (1 - \phi L)(1 + \phi L + \phi^2 L^2 + \cdots)\\ &= 1 + \phi L + \phi^2 L^2 + \cdots - \phi L - \phi^2 L^2 - \phi^3 L^3 - \cdots = 1\end{aligned}$$

16.3 Autoregressive Processes

In the previous section we have stressed the importance of the dependence of a member y_t of a stochastic process on its past if forecasting is the objective of the analysis. This enables us to use the knowledge we have gathered in the past in the form of sample observations to predict future values of a variable. A simple example of a process for which such a dependence exists is the autoregressive (AR) process $y_t = \rho y_{t-1} + e_t$.

Usually the generating process of a time-series $y_1, y_2, \ldots, y_T$ will be unknown, and even if we had reasons to assume that this process is stationary, it can, of course, have a structure that is more complicated than the given simple autoregressive (AR) process. For instance, y_t may depend in a linear way not only on y_{t-1} but also on y_{t-2}, and so on. More generally, the process may have the form

$$y_t = \theta_1 y_{t-1} + \cdots + \theta_p y_{t-p} + e_t \tag{16.3.1}$$

where e_t is white noise, that is, $E[e_t] = 0$ for all t and $E[e_t e_s] = 0$ for $s \neq t$. In lag operator notation this can be written as

$$(1 - \theta_1 L - \theta_2 L^2 - \cdots - \theta_p L^p) y_t = e_t$$

A stochastic process of this form is called an autoregressive process of order p, which is abbreviated AR(p) process or simply AR(p). Assuming that the process is started in the infinite past and all y_t have bounded means and variances, it can be shown that such a process is stationary if all roots z_0 of the polynomial

$$\theta_p(z) = 1 - \theta_1 z - \theta_2 z^2 - \cdots - \theta_p z^p$$

have a modulus $|z_0| > 1$, where the modulus of a complex number $z = z_1 + iz_2$ is defined to be

$$|z| = \sqrt{z_1^2 + z_2^2} \tag{16.3.2}$$

For the AR(1) process $y_t = \rho y_{t-1} + e_t$ this comes down to requiring that $|\rho| < 1$ since the only solution of $1 - \rho z = 0$ is $z = 1/\rho$ and $|z| = |1/\rho| > 1$ is equivalent to $|\rho| < 1$. From Section 16.2 we know that if this condition is fulfilled, the autocorrelation function of the considered AR(1) process is given by

$$\rho_k = \rho^k \qquad \text{for} \quad k = 0, 1, 2, \ldots$$

Without going into the details, we mention that the autocorrelation function ρ_k of a stationary AR(p) tapers off as k increases. Some possible patterns of autocorrelations of AR(2) processes are given in Figure 16.1.

16.3.1 Estimation of Autoregressive Processes

Assuming that our sample $y_1, y_2, \ldots, y_T$ is indeed generated by an AR process, we need to find its order p and the values of the parameters $\theta_1, \theta_2, \ldots, \theta_p$ to describe this process. If we know the order p, (16.3.1) suggests how to find values of θ_1, $\theta_2, \ldots, \theta_p$, since this equation has precisely the form of a linear statistical model.

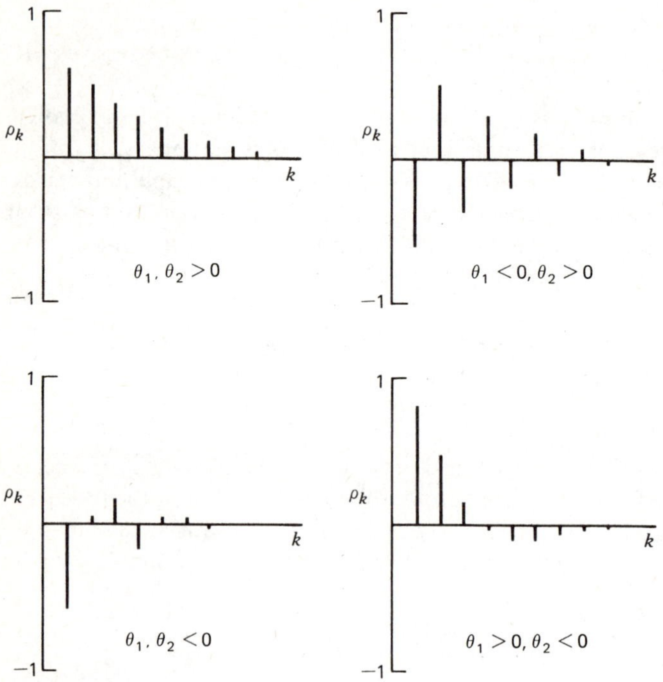

Figure 16.1 Some possible patterns of autocorrelation functions of AR(2) processes $[\mathscr{y}_t = \theta_1 \mathscr{y}_{t-1} + \theta_2 \mathscr{y}_{t-2} + \mathscr{e}_t]$.

Note, however, that the regressors $\mathscr{y}_{t-1}, \ldots, \mathscr{y}_{t-p}$ are stochastic variables. If the $\mathscr{e}_t$ are Gaussian white noise, an individual $\mathscr{e}_t$ represents a random shock, which is added to the system at time t and is independent of random variables at previous time points. Hence the regressors in a particular equation are independent of the error term. Thus, as we have seen in Chapter 13, we may estimate $\boldsymbol{\theta}_p = (\theta_1, \ldots, \theta_p)'$ by the least squares (LS) method.

Replacing the random variables by their observed values we get

$$\begin{aligned} y_{p+1} &= \theta_1 y_p + \cdots + \theta_p y_1 + e_{p+1} \\ y_{p+2} &= \theta_1 y_{p+1} + \cdots + \theta_p y_2 + e_{p+2} \\ &\vdots \\ y_T &= \theta_1 y_{T-1} + \cdots + \theta_p y_{T-p} + e_T \end{aligned}$$

or, in matrix notation,

$$\mathbf{y}_p = X_p \boldsymbol{\theta}_p + \mathbf{e} \tag{16.3.3}$$

where $\mathbf{y}_p = (y_{p+1}, \ldots, y_T)'$, $\mathbf{e} = (e_{p+1}, \ldots, e_T)'$, and

$$X_p = \begin{bmatrix} y_p & y_{p-1} & \cdots & y_1 \\ y_{p+1} & y_p & \cdots & y_2 \\ \vdots & \vdots & \ddots & \vdots \\ y_{T-1} & y_{T-2} & \cdots & y_{T-p} \end{bmatrix}$$

If the e_t and thus the y_t are normally distributed, the LS estimator of $\boldsymbol{\theta}_p$, with corresponding estimate

$$\hat{\boldsymbol{\theta}}_p = (X_p'X_p)^{-1}X_p'\mathbf{y}_p \tag{16.3.4}$$

is consistent and asymptotically normally distributed. That is,

$$\sqrt{T}(\hat{\boldsymbol{\theta}}_p - \boldsymbol{\theta}_p) \xrightarrow{d} N(\mathbf{0}, \Sigma_{\hat{\boldsymbol{\theta}}_p}) \tag{16.3.5}$$

where $\hat{\boldsymbol{\theta}}_p$ now denotes the LS estimator. The variance-covariance matrix $\Sigma_{\hat{\boldsymbol{\theta}}_p}$ is

$$\Sigma_{\hat{\boldsymbol{\theta}}_p} = \sigma_e^2 \begin{bmatrix} \gamma_0 & \gamma_1 & \gamma_2 & \cdots & \gamma_{p-1} \\ \gamma_1 & \gamma_0 & \gamma_1 & \cdots & \gamma_{p-2} \\ \vdots & \vdots & \vdots & & \vdots \\ \gamma_{p-1} & \gamma_{p-2} & \gamma_{p-3} & \cdots & \gamma_0 \end{bmatrix}^{-1}$$

where, as before, $\gamma_k = E[y_t y_{t+k}]$. The variance-covariance matrix can be consistently estimated by

$$\Sigma_{\hat{\boldsymbol{\theta}}_p} = \hat{\sigma}_e^2(X_p'X_p/T)^{-1} \tag{16.3.6}$$

where

$$\hat{\sigma}_e^2 = \frac{(\mathbf{y}_p - X_p\hat{\boldsymbol{\theta}}_p)'(\mathbf{y}_p - X_p\hat{\boldsymbol{\theta}}_p)}{T - 2p} \tag{16.3.7}$$

is the LS estimate of the variance σ_e^2 of the white-noise process e_t. Note that we use $T - 2p$ rather than $T - p$ in the denominator of (16.3.7), since we treat $y_1, \ldots, y_p$ as presample values *and* estimate p parameters.

Thus far we have implicitly assumed that the sample mean is zero, and thus it is reasonable to assume that the mean of the generating process is zero. If the mean of the data is not zero, then we can either subtract the sample mean from all observations prior to the analysis or we can use an intercept in the regression model, that is, we use

$$X_p^i = \begin{bmatrix} 1 & y_p & \cdots & y_1 \\ 1 & y_{p+1} & \cdots & y_2 \\ \vdots & \vdots & & \vdots \\ 1 & y_{T-1} & \cdots & y_{T-p} \end{bmatrix}$$

as the regression matrix and $\boldsymbol{\theta}_p' = (\nu, \theta_1, \ldots, \theta_p)'$ is the parameter vector. Note that ν is not the mean μ of the process y_t. Rather,

$$\mu = \frac{\nu}{1 - \theta_1 - \cdots - \theta_p} \tag{16.3.8}$$

Thus, two possible estimates of the process mean μ are

$$\bar{y} = \frac{1}{T} \sum_{t=1}^{T} y_t \tag{16.3.9}$$

and

$$\hat{\mu} = \frac{\hat{\nu}}{1 - \hat{\theta}_1 - \cdots - \hat{\theta}_p} \tag{16.3.10}$$

where the $\hat{\nu}, \hat{\theta}_1, \ldots, \hat{\theta}_p$ are the LS estimates. Under general conditions (e.g., if the y_t are normally distributed) the corresponding estimators are consistent and have identical asymptotic normal distributions. For instance,

$$\sqrt{T}\,(\hat{\mu} - \mu) \xrightarrow{d} N[0, \sigma_e^2(1 - \theta_1 - \cdots - \theta_p)^{-2}] \tag{16.3.11}$$

Furthermore, the estimators $\hat{\mu}$ and $\bar{y}$ are asymptotically independent of the estimators $\hat{\theta}_1, \ldots, \hat{\theta}_p$. This property is one reason why the estimation of $\boldsymbol{\theta}_p$ is often discussed in terms of zero mean processes. In practice, the sample mean may be subtracted from the data prior to estimating the other parameters. In this case the asymptotic distribution theory is not affected.

So far we have assumed that the AR order p is known. In practice, this is not the case. In some instances it may be possible to specify an upper bound for p, though. Of course the foregoing results remain valid if p is replaced by such an upper bound. If the upper bound is greater than the actual order p, we are estimating unnecessarily many parameters. Using a model with too many parameters for prediction may lead to inefficient forecasts (see Sections 16.7 and 20.4). Therefore it is desirable to specify the AR order adequately. We will now present one method for doing so.

16.3.2 Partial Autocorrelations

One way to identify the order of an adequate AR process for a given set of data is to estimate processes of increasing order k and test the significance of θ_k. This coefficient is called the kth *partial autocorrelation coefficient* and will be denoted by

θ_{kk} in the following since it is the kth coefficient of an AR process of order k. It measures the correlation between y_t and y_{t-k} not accounted for by an AR($k-1$). The sequence θ_{kk}, $k = 1, 2, \ldots$, of partial autocorrelations will be called the *partial autocorrelation function.* As a model for the data-generating process we choose an AR(p) such that

$$\theta_{kk}\begin{cases} \neq 0 & \text{for } k = p \\ = 0 & \text{for } k > p \end{cases}$$

To test the significance of θ_{kk} we need to know the distribution of its estimator. The corresponding estimate $\hat{\theta}_{kk}$ is obtained as the last coordinate of

$$\hat{\boldsymbol{\theta}}_k = (X_k' X_k)^{-1} X_k' \mathbf{y}_k$$

where we assume that the sample mean is zero or is subtracted from the data. It can be shown that for large sample size, if the order of the AR is in fact p, the estimated partial autocorrelations $\hat{\theta}_{kk}$ are approximately normally distributed with mean zero and variance $1/T$ for $k > p$, where T is, as usual, the sample size. Consequently, to check the significance of the $\hat{\theta}_{kk}$ approximate 95% confidence intervals,

$$\left(\hat{\theta}_{kk} - \frac{2}{\sqrt{T}}, \hat{\theta}_{kk} + \frac{2}{\sqrt{T}}\right) \tag{16.3.12}$$

can be used. Equivalently, it suffices to check whether the estimate $\hat{\theta}_{kk}$ falls within the two standard error bounds $\pm 2/\sqrt{T}$. Estimates of partial autocorrelation coefficients are shown in Table 16.2 and Figure 16.3 for the set of data given in Table 16.1 and plotted in Figure 16.2. Only $\hat{\theta}_{11}$ and $\hat{\theta}_{22}$ are outside the approximate two standard error bounds, and therefore we pick an AR(2) as a model for the data-generation process. The estimation results are

$$\hat{\boldsymbol{\theta}} = \begin{bmatrix} 0.45 \\ 0.30 \end{bmatrix} \qquad \hat{\sigma}_e^2 = 0.89$$

In fact, the data were artificially generated by the process

$$y_t = 0.5y_{t-1} + 0.3y_{t-2} + e_t$$

where normal random numbers with mean 0 and variance 1 are used as realizations of the e_t.

In practice, the situation will not always be as clear-cut as in this example. Therefore a number of other procedures and criteria for choosing the AR order have been proposed. Obviously, choosing the AR order comes down to selecting

Table 16.1 An Artificially Generated Sample, $y_t = 0.5y_{t-1} + 0.3y_{t-2} + e_t$

t	y_t	t	y_t	t	y_t	t	y_t
1	−1.245203	26	−2.155142	51	−1.701559	76	−0.448346
2	−2.229019	27	−1.205098	52	−0.557646	77	−1.407836
3	−0.102889	28	−1.125508	53	−0.935374	78	−1.416262
4	−2.504927	29	0.745601	54	−1.590731	79	−2.654282
5	−1.295782	30	0.745816	55	−1.392477	80	−1.568367
6	0.287210	31	1.652314	56	−0.702117	81	−1.182442
7	−0.000095	32	1.170398	57	−1.279344	82	0.377995
8	0.908003	33	1.748881	58	−1.310539	83	−1.028879
9	0.946282	34	0.915977	59	−1.206204	84	−1.402405
10	−0.775019	35	1.988901	60	0.213225	85	−0.865423
11	−0.868487	36	−0.225835	61	−0.614470	86	0.314383
12	1.500287	37	1.772048	62	0.430978	87	−0.569566
13	−1.351182	38	0.256119	63	1.281028	88	0.834981
14	−1.408163	39	2.398788	64	1.625546	89	1.322164
15	−1.945642	40	0.846766	65	2.695052	90	1.643056
16	−2.029809	41	0.736914	66	1.794567	91	1.302254
17	−1.642363	42	0.219055	67	1.082367	92	1.794244
18	−0.742933	43	1.099941	68	2.351032	93	2.026379
19	−0.519426	44	−0.906636	69	1.586859	94	0.345364
20	0.308898	45	0.620321	70	2.131216	95	−0.614447
21	−0.109768	46	0.079424	71	0.253485	96	0.979466
22	−0.720097	47	0.323415	72	−0.510527	97	2.082886
23	−1.523058	48	0.146697	73	−0.909131	98	2.011572
24	−1.481303	49	−1.114253	74	−1.097981	99	0.422207
25	−2.070795	50	−0.437410	75	−1.305027	100	1.239364

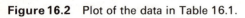

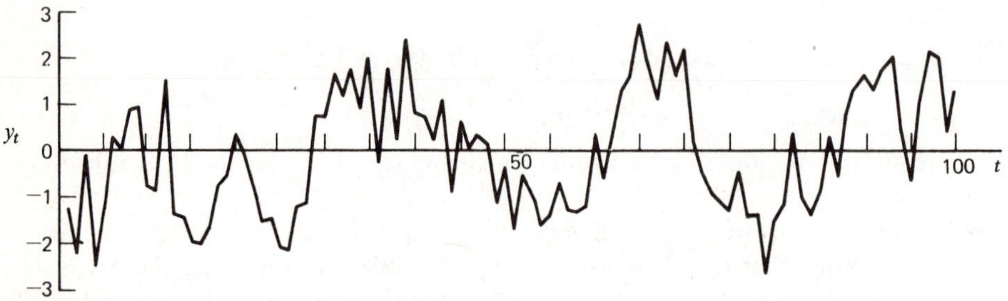

Figure 16.2 Plot of the data in Table 16.1.

Table 16.2 Sample Partial Autocorrelations of the Data in Table 16.1

k	1	2	3	4	5	6	7	8	9	10	11	12
$\hat{\theta}_{kk}$	0.66	0.30	−0.10	0.02	−0.16	0.02	−0.17	0.04	−0.07	−0.09	−0.02	−0.12

the number of variables in the regression model (16.3.3). Consequently, criteria for regressor choice (see Section 20.4) are relevant in the present context. For further discussion and references on this topic see Judge, et al. (1985, Chapter 7).

As a further example consider the data in Table 16.3, which are plotted in Figure 16.4. The estimated partial autocorrelations shown in Figure 16.5 taper off fairly slowly and even at high lags ($k = 12$ and 14) some exceed the approximate two standard error bounds in absolute value. Thus a rather high-order AR process would be required for an adequate representation of the data-generating process. Since the use of unnecessarily many parameters in the model for the data-generation process may result in forecast inefficiencies, the question arises whether a more parsimonious representation of this process can be found. In the next section we will discuss a class of processes that have infinite AR representations although they involve only finitely many parameters.

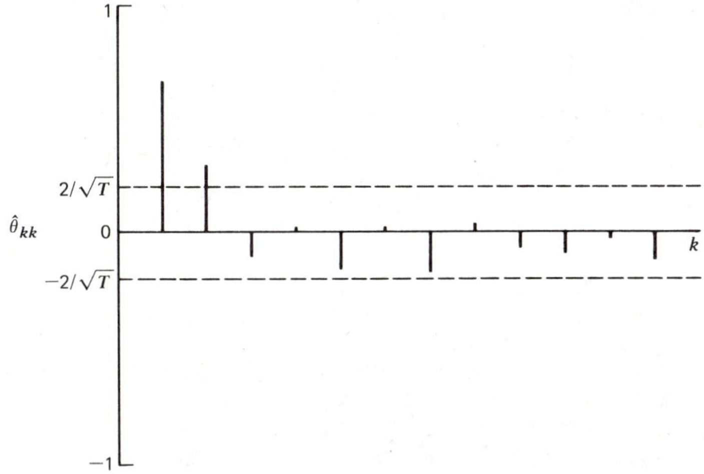

Figure 16.3 Estimated partial autocorrelations from Table 16.2.

Table 16.3 An Artificially Generated Sample, $y_t = e_t - 0.9e_{t-1}$

t	e_t	y_t	t	e_t	y_t
0	−0.487966				
1	0.157991	0.597160	42	−1.469131	−1.204321
2	0.567434	0.425242	43	0.790797	2.113015
3	−0.723142	−1.233832	44	−1.993653	−2.705370
4	0.952748	1.603576	45	−0.462137	1.332151
5	0.057963	−0.799510	46	0.776619	1.192542
6	0.750528	0.698362	47	0.021268	−0.677689
7	0.316484	−0.358992	48	0.006177	−0.012964
8	0.365814	0.080979	49	−1.573466	−1.579025
9	−1.079845	−1.409078	50	−0.012268	1.403852
10	−1.585600	−0.613740	51	0.953040	0.964081
11	1.171374	2.598415	52	−0.181376	−1.039112
12	−1.051963	−2.106200	53	−0.173663	−0.010425
13	−0.808789	0.137978	54	−0.168581	−0.012284
14	0.152331	0.880240	55	0.607456	0.759179
15	−0.019082	−0.156180	56	−0.091555	−0.638266
16	−1.187778	−1.170604	57	0.633747	0.716147
17	1.924980	2.993980	58	1.939169	1.368797
18	0.269352	−1.463130	59	−1.023926	−2.769179
19	0.115139	−0.127277	60	1.592862	2.514395
20	−0.517847	−0.621472	61	−1.737387	−3.170962
21	1.901253	2.367315	62	−0.110799	1.452849
22	0.244306	−1.466823	63	0.952289	1.052008
23	−0.732768	−0.952643	64	0.030768	−0.826292
24	−0.569184	0.090307	65	1.222983	1.195292
25	−0.808411	−0.296145	66	−1.992339	−3.093024
26	−0.087538	0.640032	67	−0.140704	1.652401
27	0.645137	0.723921	68	−0.068656	0.057977
28	−0.232471	−0.813094	69	1.478267	1.540058
29	−2.459868	−2.250645	70	−0.567206	−1.897647
30	1.178305	3.392187	71	0.777948	1.288433
31	−0.098060	−1.158535	72	0.326539	−0.373614
32	0.610345	0.698599	73	−0.604472	−0.898357
33	0.586847	0.037536	74	−0.368405	0.175619
34	−0.920892	−1.449054	75	0.625551	0.957116
35	1.143375	1.972178	76	−0.677268	−1.240264
36	0.584488	−0.444550	77	0.957143	1.566684
37	−1.660507	−2.186546	78	−0.264008	−1.125436
38	−0.179259	1.315197	79	1.643304	1.880911
39	0.579026	0.740359	80	−1.886489	−3.365463
40	−0.865261	−1.386384	81	−0.284194	1.413646
41	−0.294233	0.484501	82	0.202708	0.458482

Table 16.3 (*continued*)

t	e_t	y_t	t	e_t	y_t
83	−0.024008	−0.206445	92	0.947234	−0.349327
84	1.947531	1.969138	93	1.065889	0.213379
85	−0.652707	−2.405484	94	−0.058633	−1.017933
86	−0.242288	0.345148	95	−1.747454	−1.694684
87	0.539331	0.757390	96	−0.800252	0.772456
88	0.543913	0.058515	97	0.252943	0.973171
89	2.346873	1.857352	98	−0.885931	−1.113580
90	−0.817690	−2.929876	99	−1.691304	−0.893966
91	1.440623	2.176544	100	0.076985	1.599158

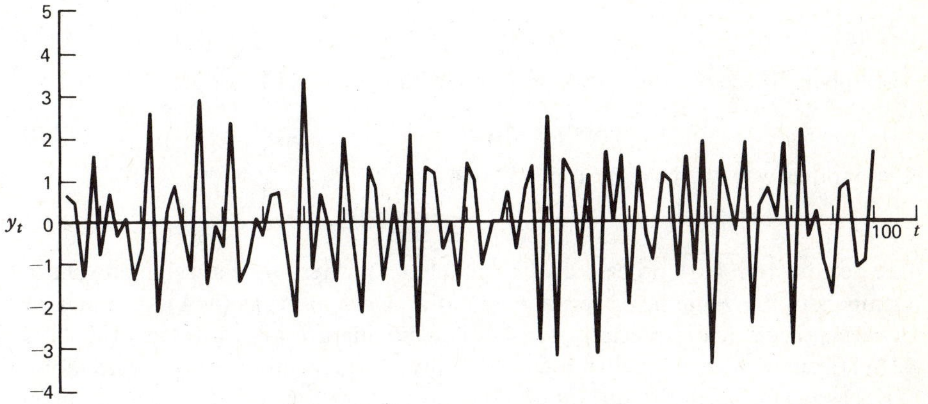

Figure 16.4 Plot of the sample in Table 16.3.

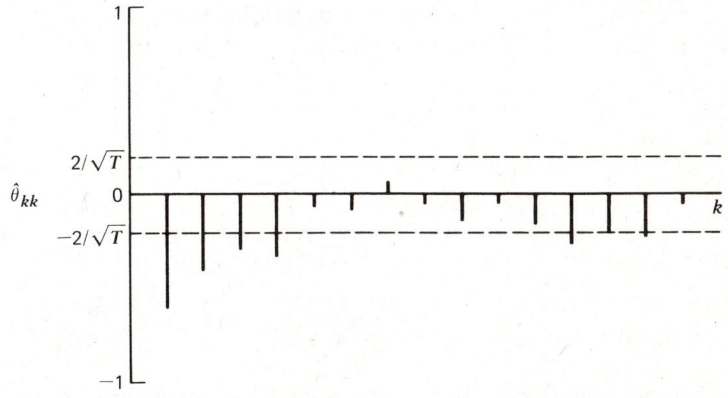

Figure 16.5 Sample partial autocorrelations of y_t in Table 16.3.

16.4 Moving Average Processes

In the previous section we encountered a process that cannot be represented well by a low-order AR process. In searching for a parsimonious representation, let us assume that the considered process has, in fact, an infinite AR representation of the form

$$y_t = -\alpha y_{t-1} - \alpha^2 y_{t-2} - \alpha^3 y_{t-3} - \cdots + e_t \tag{16.4.1}$$

or, using the lag operator,

$$(1 + \alpha L + \alpha^2 L^2 + \cdots)y_t = e_t \tag{16.4.2}$$

where e_t is again white noise and $|\alpha| < 1$.

Assuming that (16.4.1) holds for all integers t, we have in particular

$$y_{t-1} = -\alpha y_{t-2} - \alpha^2 y_{t-3} - \cdots + e_{t-1}$$

Multiplying this equation by α and subtracting from (16.4.1) we get

$$y_t = e_t - \alpha e_{t-1} = (1 - \alpha L)e_t \tag{16.4.3}$$

Put another way, we have multiplied (16.4.2) by

$$(1 + \alpha L + \alpha^2 L^2 + \cdots)^{-1} = 1 - \alpha L$$

(see Section 16.2.4). A process like that in (16.4.3), where y_t is a weighted sum of members of the white-noise series, is called a *moving average* (MA), or a *moving average process.* More precisely, (16.4.3) is a moving average of order 1 [in short MA(1)], since the weighted sum consists only of the members of the white-noise series associated with the current and the most recent time point. In our example, instead of approximating the process (16.4.1) by a high-order AR process, we can simply represent it as MA(1).

It can be shown that any stationary AR process can be written as an MA process. However, the process may have a much more complicated structure than that given in (16.4.3); that is, the order of the MA can be higher than 1 and may in fact be infinite. An MA process of order q, MA(q), has the form

$$\begin{aligned} y_t &= e_t + \alpha_1 e_{t-1} + \cdots + \alpha_q e_{t-q} \\ &= (1 + \alpha_1 L + \cdots + \alpha_q L^q)e_t = \alpha_q(L)e_t \end{aligned} \tag{16.4.4}$$

Such a process can be written as an infinite AR process if all roots of the polynomial

$$\alpha_q(z) = 1 + \alpha_1 z + \alpha_2 z^2 + \cdots + \alpha_q z^q$$

have modulus greater than 1, that is, the roots are outside the complex unit circle.

An MA process that meets this condition is called *invertible*. Without special notice we will henceforth assume that all MA processes are invertible.

16.4.1 Determining the Order of a Moving Average

Given a sample $y_1, y_2, \ldots, y_T$, how can we determine an adequate MA order of the generating process? To answer this question let us look at some characteristics of MA's. For expository purposes consider the MA(1) given in (16.4.3). The mean is

$$E[y_t] = E[e_t] - \alpha E[e_{t-1}] = 0$$

and the variance is

$$\begin{aligned} \operatorname{var}(y_t) &= E[(e_t - \alpha e_{t-1})^2] \\ &= E[e_t^2] - 2\alpha E[e_t e_{t-1}] + \alpha^2 E[e_{t-1}^2] \\ &= \sigma_e^2 + \alpha^2\sigma_e^2 = (1+\alpha^2)\sigma_e^2 \end{aligned} \tag{16.4.5}$$

where σ_e^2 is the variance of the e_t. The covariances of the process y_t are

$$\begin{aligned} \operatorname{cov}(y_t, y_{t+k}) &= E[y_t y_{t+k}] = E[(e_t - \alpha e_{t-1})(e_{t+k} - \alpha e_{t+k-1})] \\ &= E[e_t e_{t+k}] - \alpha E[e_{t-1}e_{t+k}] - \alpha E[e_t e_{t+k-1}] + \alpha^2 E[e_{t-1}e_{t+k-1}] \\ &= \begin{cases} \sigma_e^2 + \alpha^2\sigma_e^2 & \text{if } k = 0 \\ -\alpha\sigma_e^2 & \text{if } k = \pm 1 \\ 0 & \text{otherwise} \end{cases} \end{aligned} \tag{16.4.6}$$

This shows that (16.4.3) is stationary, and we can denote $\operatorname{cov}(y_t, y_{t+k})$ by γ_k because it does not depend on t, but only on k.

More generally, the autocovariances of the MA(q) given in (16.4.4) are

$$\gamma_k = \begin{cases} \sigma_e^2 \sum_{i=0}^{q-k} \alpha_i\alpha_{i+k} & \text{for } k = 0, 1, \ldots, q \\ 0 & \text{for } k > q \end{cases} \tag{16.4.7}$$

where $\alpha_0 = 1$. Consequently, the autocorrelations are

$$\rho_k = \begin{cases} \dfrac{\sum_{i=0}^{q-k} \alpha_i\alpha_{i+k}}{\sum_{i=0}^{q} \alpha_i^2} & \text{for } k = 0, 1, \ldots, q \\ 0 & \text{for } k > q \end{cases} \tag{16.4.8}$$

Thus the order of an MA corresponds to the maximum k for which ρ_k is nonzero. To determine whether a particular ρ_k is nonzero, we can use the available data to compute an estimate of this autocorrelation coefficient and then perform a significance test.

Given a time series $y_1, y_2, \ldots, y_T$, a commonly used estimate for ρ_k is

$$r_k = \frac{c_k}{c_0} \tag{16.4.9}$$

where

$$c_k = \frac{1}{T} \sum_{t=1}^{T-k} (y_t - \bar{y})(y_{t+k} - \bar{y}) \qquad \text{for } k = 0, 1, 2, \ldots, N_1 \tag{16.4.10}$$

and

$$\bar{y} = \frac{1}{T} \sum_{t=1}^{T} y_t$$

In (16.4.10), N_1 is a number that is small relative to T. Another possible estimator for ρ_k is

$$\bar{r}_k = \frac{\bar{c}_k}{c_0} \tag{16.4.11}$$

where

$$\bar{c}_k = \frac{1}{T-k} \sum_{t=1}^{T-k} (y_t - \bar{y})(y_{t+k} - \bar{y}) \qquad \text{for } k = 0, 1, 2, \ldots, N_2 < T \tag{16.4.12}$$

The estimator c_k and $\bar{c}_k$, and hence r_k and $\bar{r}_k$, are asymptotically equivalent.

The significance of the autocorrelations is often tested by checking whether the r_k or $\bar{r}_k$ are inside a region $\pm 2/\sqrt{T}$. The reasoning for this test is as follows. Suppose that the sample $y_1, y_2, \ldots, y_T$ consists of independent drawings from identical populations. Then for large T, independent of the sample mean, the r_k and $\bar{r}_k$ are approximately normally distributed with mean zero and variance $1/T$ under weak conditions. Thus for sufficiently large sample size T, if zero does not fall within the approximate 95% confidence interval

$$\left(r_k - \frac{2}{\sqrt{T}}, r_k + \frac{2}{\sqrt{T}}\right) \qquad \text{or} \qquad \left(\bar{r}_k - \frac{2}{\sqrt{T}}, \bar{r}_k + \frac{2}{\sqrt{T}}\right)$$

the null hypothesis $\rho_k = 0$ can be rejected at the 5% level. Apparently, this can be checked by determining whether r_k or $\bar{r}_k$ is between the approximate two standard error bounds $\pm 2/\sqrt{T}$.

It is perhaps worth noting that this procedure may be quite misleading if the sample size is not large since the small sample mean and variance of r_k may differ substantially from their asymptotic counterparts. For instance, if the y_t are normally distributed and come from a Gaussian white-noise process, it can be shown that

$$E[r_k] = -\frac{T-k}{T(T-1)} \tag{16.4.13}$$

and

$$\operatorname{var}(r_k) = \frac{T^4 - (k+3)T^3 + 3kT^2 + 2k(k+1)T - 4k^2}{(T+1)T^2(T-1)^2} \tag{16.4.14}$$

(Dufour and Roy, 1985). Thus we get, for example, for $k = 1$ and $T = 20$,

$$E[r_1] = -\frac{1}{20} = -0.05 \qquad \text{and} \qquad \operatorname{var}(r_1) = 0.043$$

whereas the corresponding approximations from the asymptotic theory are zero for the mean and 0.05 for the variance.

Moreover, for these results to hold it is assumed that the y_t are actually generated by a white-noise process. If the data generation process is not white noise, $1/T$ may even be a poor approximation to the variances of the $r_k(\bar{r}_k)$ if T is large. For instance, if $\rho_k \neq 0$ for $k \leq q$ and $\rho_k = 0$ for $k > q$, then the variance of $r_k(\bar{r}_k)$ is, according to Bartlett's formula, approximately

$$\frac{1 + 2(\rho_1^2 + \rho_2^2 + \cdots + \rho_q^2)}{T}$$

for $k > q$ (see Box and Jenkins, 1976). Keeping this in mind, we can use the $\pm 2/\sqrt{T}$ bounds to roughly check the significance of the sample autocorrelations. We should, however, look for regularities even if the sample autocorrelations are inside the $\pm 2/\sqrt{T}$ limits.

For the time-series in Table 16.3 the estimated autocorrelations are shown in Figure 16.6. Based on the foregoing considerations we identify an MA(1) as the generating process for these data.

16.4.2 Estimating the Parameters of a Moving Average

Given a sample $\mathbf{y} = (y_1, y_2, \ldots, y_T)'$, we assume in the following that the sample mean is zero. If the original sample does not meet this condition, the sample mean $\bar{y}$

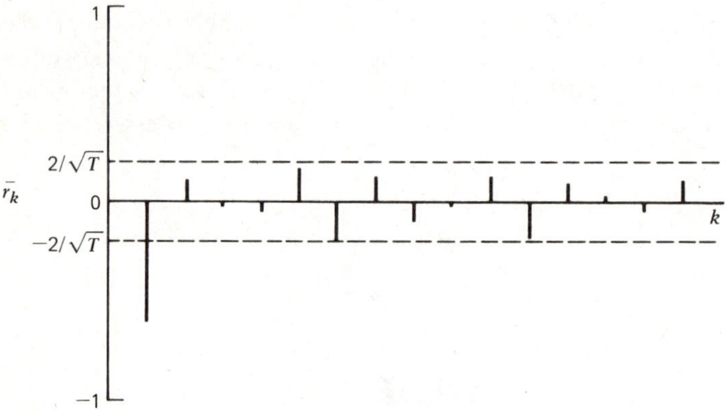

Figure 16.6 Sample autocorrelations of the y_t in Table 16.3.

should be subtracted from the original observations. Assuming that the data-generating process is an invertible MA(q) with normally distributed e_t, the parameters may be estimated using the maximum likelihood (ML) method. The likelihood function is

$$\ell(\boldsymbol{\alpha}, \sigma_e^2 | \mathbf{y}) = \frac{1}{(2\pi\sigma_e^2)^{T/2}} (\det \Sigma_{\mathbf{y}})^{-1/2} \exp(-\mathbf{y}'\Sigma_{\mathbf{y}}^{-1}\mathbf{y}/2\sigma_e^2) \qquad (16.4.15)$$

where $\boldsymbol{\alpha} = (\alpha_1, \ldots, \alpha_q)'$ and $\Sigma_{\mathbf{y}} = E[\mathbf{y}\mathbf{y}']$ is the covariance matrix of $\mathbf{y} = (y_1, \ldots, y_T)'$. Maximizing (16.4.15) gives ML estimators $\tilde{\boldsymbol{\alpha}}$ and $\tilde{\sigma}_e^2$. In contrast to, say Chapter 6, in general no closed-form expression of the estimator $\tilde{\boldsymbol{\alpha}}$ is available
where $\boldsymbol{\alpha} = (\alpha_1, \ldots, \alpha_q)'$ and $\Sigma_{\mathbf{y}} = E[\mathbf{y}\mathbf{y}']$ is the covariance matrix of $\mathbf{y} = (y_1, \ldots, y_T)'$. Maximizing (16.4.15) gives ML estimators $\tilde{\boldsymbol{\alpha}}$ and $\tilde{\sigma}_e^2$. In contrast to,
Furthermore $\tilde{\boldsymbol{\alpha}}$ is asymptotically independent of $\tilde{\sigma}_e^2$. For $\tilde{\boldsymbol{\alpha}}$ we have

$$\sqrt{T}(\tilde{\boldsymbol{\alpha}} - \boldsymbol{\alpha}) \xrightarrow{d} N(\mathbf{0}, \Sigma_{\tilde{\boldsymbol{\alpha}}}) \qquad (16.4.16)$$

where

$$\Sigma_{\tilde{\boldsymbol{\alpha}}} = \begin{bmatrix} \phi_0 & \phi_1 & \phi_2 & \cdots & \phi_{q-1} \\ \phi_1 & \phi_0 & \phi_1 & \cdots & \phi_{q-2} \\ \vdots & \vdots & \vdots & & \vdots \\ \phi_{q-1} & \phi_{q-2} & \phi_{q-3} & \cdots & \phi_0 \end{bmatrix}^{-1} \qquad (16.4.17)$$

Here $\phi_k = \sum_{i=0}^{\infty} \theta_i \theta_{i+k}$ and the θ_i are the coefficients of

$$\alpha_q(L)^{-1} = (1 + \alpha_1 L + \cdots + \alpha_q L^q)^{-1} = \sum_{i=0}^{\infty} \theta_i L^i$$

The actual computation of the parameter estimates is in general a complicated nonlinear optimization problem for which computer programs are available. To alleviate the computational burden, some simple procedures have been suggested and some of these are asymptotically equivalent to ML estimation. One such method is based on minimizing the sum of squared errors

$$S(\boldsymbol{\alpha}) = \sum_{t=1}^{T} e_t^2 = \sum_{t=1}^{T} (y_t - \alpha_1 e_{t-1} - \cdots - \alpha_q e_{t-q})^2 \tag{16.4.18}$$

Since the quantities e_t are unobserved they have to be replaced by the observed $y_1, \ldots, y_T$. To demonstrate this let us consider for expository purposes the MA(1)

$$y_t = e_t - \alpha e_{t-1} \tag{16.4.19}$$

with $|\alpha| < 1$. We have seen that it can be written as an infinite AR

$$y_t + \alpha y_{t-1} + \alpha^2 y_{t-2} + \cdots = e_t \tag{16.4.20}$$

Note that this transformation is possible because (16.4.19) is invertible and this is a reason for requiring the invertibility of MA processes. Instead of (16.4.18), we minimize

$$S(\alpha) = \sum_{t=1}^{T} (y_t + \alpha y_{t-1} + \alpha^2 y_{t-2} + \cdots + \alpha^{t-1} y_1)^2 \tag{16.4.21}$$

This expression differs from (16.4.18) because we have substituted

$$y_t + \alpha y_{t-1} + \alpha^2 y_{t-2} + \cdots + \alpha^{t-1} y_1$$

for e_t, and not the infinite sum

$$y_t + \alpha y_{t-1} + \alpha^2 y_{t-2} + \cdots + \alpha^{t-1} y_1 + \alpha^t y_0 + \alpha^{t+1} y_{-1} + \cdots$$

For $T \to \infty$ this is of no consequence, because $|\alpha| < 1$ so that $\alpha^t \to 0$ for $t \to \infty$ and hence the asymptotic properties of the obtained estimators are not affected.

The minimization of (16.4.21) is a nonlinear least squares problem. For the simple case with only one parameter known to be between -1 and 1, a grid search would be a possible strategy to find the minimum of $S(\alpha)$. If the number of parameters exceeds two, a numerical minimization algorithm is usually preferable.

For the example data in Table 16.3 we have identified an MA(1) as the generating process. Minimizing $S(\alpha)$ in (16.4.21), we get as an estimate for α

$$\hat{\alpha} = 0.96 \qquad \text{and} \qquad \hat{\sigma}_e^2 = \frac{S(\hat{\alpha})}{T-1} = 0.99 \qquad \text{or} \qquad \tilde{\sigma}_e^2 = \frac{S(\hat{\alpha})}{T} = 0.98$$

In fact, the data are generated realizations of the process

$$y_t = e_t - 0.9 e_{t-1} = (1 - 0.9L) e_t$$

where normal random numbers with mean 0 and variance 1 are used as values of the e_t. Thus, using (16.4.17) and (16.4.20), the variance of the asymptotic distribution of $\sqrt{T}\,(\hat{\alpha} - \alpha)$ is

$$\phi_0^{-1} = \left(\sum_{i=0}^{\infty} \alpha^{2i}\right)^{-1} = \left(\frac{1}{1-\alpha^2}\right)^{-1} = 1 - \alpha^2$$

Hence, in large samples the variance of the estimator $\hat{\alpha}$ is approximately $(1 - \alpha^2)/T = 0.19/T$. In practice the data-generation process is usually unknown. In that case the variance of $\hat{\alpha}$ may be estimated as $(1 - \hat{\alpha}^2)/T$.

It is perhaps worth emphasizing that in small samples the estimator obtained by minimizing (16.4.21) is not identical to the ML estimator. There is some Monte Carlo evidence that exact ML estimators are preferable in many small-sample situations.

Although the asymptotic efficiency of the estimator discussed in the foregoing rests on the assumption that the white-noise process e_t is normally distributed, it can be shown that consistency and asymptotic normality of the estimators can be derived under less restrictive conditions (see Fuller, 1976).

16.5 ARIMA Models

In Sections 16.3 and 16.4 we discussed two important classes of stochastic processes, the AR and MA processes. We indicated that AR processes have an MA representation and vice versa under certain conditions. It is the task of the investigator to identify a *parsimonious* representation of the generating process of a given data set. If the autocorrelations ρ_k have a cutoff point, that is, if they are 0 for all k greater than some small number and the partial autocorrelations θ_{kk} taper off for growing k, an MA representation is suggested. On the other hand, if the autocorrelations taper off and the partial autocorrelations have a cutoff point, an AR representation of the considered process is favored. There are cases, however, where neither sequence has a cutoff point or where the autocorrelations do not die out at all and taper off very slowly.

In the first case the considered process can often be represented parsimoniously in a form involving an AR and an MA component, such as

$$y_t = \theta y_{t-1} + e_t + \alpha e_{t-1} \tag{16.5.1}$$

or, equivalently,

$$(1 - \theta L)y_t = (1 + \alpha L)e_t$$

This process is called an *autoregressive moving-average process* of order (1, 1) or ARMA(1, 1). More generally, the process

$$y_t = \theta_1 y_{t-1} + \theta_2 y_{t-2} + \cdots + \theta_p y_{t-p} + e_t + \alpha_1 e_{t-1} + \cdots + \alpha_q e_{t-q} \tag{16.5.2}$$

or

$$(1 - \theta_1 L - \theta_2 L^2 - \cdots - \theta_p L^p)y_t = (1 + \alpha_1 L + \alpha_2 L^2 + \cdots + \alpha_q L^q)e_t$$

is called an ARMA(p, q) process or, briefly, ARMA(p, q).

In practice it can be difficult to identify adequate orders p and q. One possibility for determining these orders is to use the estimated autocorrelations and partial autocorrelations. In Figure 16.7 we give some possible patterns of autocorrelations and partial autocorrelations of ARMA(1, 1) processes.

If the autocorrelations die out very slowly, the process may be nonstationary. Suppose that we start a process

$$y_t = y_{t-1} + x_t \tag{16.5.3}$$

where x_t is a stationary process with mean $\mu \neq 0$, at time $t = 0$, with $y_0 = 0$ (see Figure 16.8). In this case

$$y_t = (y_{t-2} + x_{t-1}) + x_t = y_{t-3} + x_{t-2} + x_{t-1} + x_t$$
$$= \cdots = x_1 + x_2 + \cdots + x_t$$

and hence $E[y_t] = t\mu$. Thus the mean follows a linear trend, and, consequently, the series is not stationary because stationarity requires a constant mean. The estimated autocorrelations of such a process are depicted in Figure 16.9.

To remove the trend we can simply difference y_t and consider

$$x_t = y_t - y_{t-1} = (1 - L)y_t$$

which is stationary. Because it appears that differencing is a useful tool to convert nonstationary real-life processes to stationary processes, this data transformation has received considerable attention in the recent time-series literature. If x_t in (16.5.3) is an ARMA(p, q) process, then y_t is called an *autoregressive-integrated moving-average process*, denoted by ARIMA(p, 1, q). If $x_t = (1 - L)^d y_t$ is an ARMA(p, q) process, then y_t is an ARIMA(p, d, q) process, where d is a positive integer. A time-series that is stationary after d times differencing is sometimes said to be *homogeneous nonstationary of degree d.*

Once we have identified an ARIMA process to be an adequate representation of the data-generation process we need to estimate the parameters. If $q \neq 0$, this results in a nonlinear optimization problem and we suggest using available computer software for this purpose.

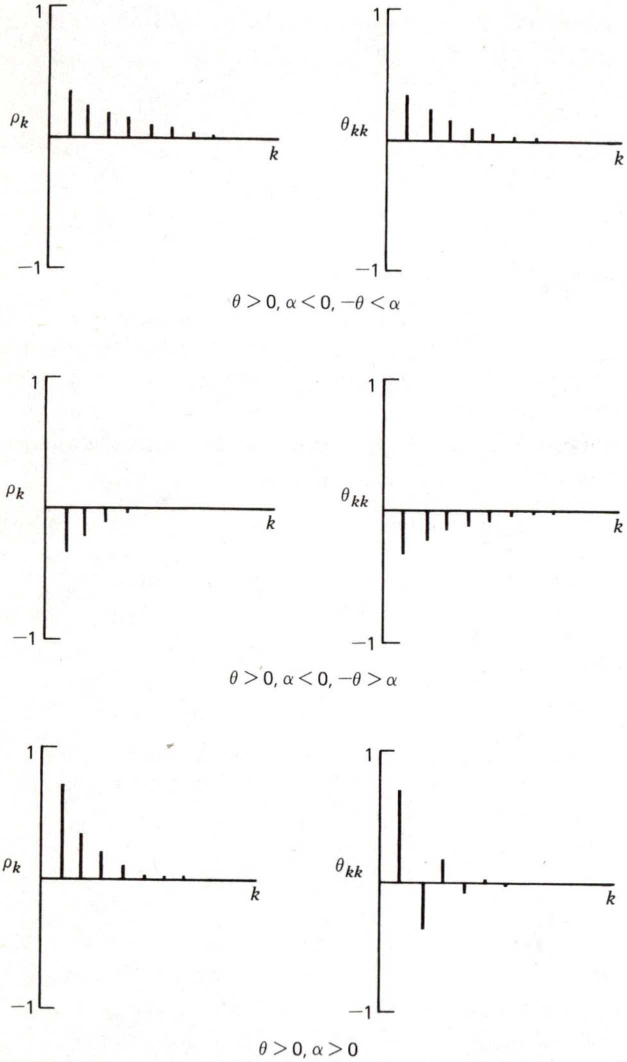

Figure 16.7 Some possible patterns of autocorrelations and partial autocorrelations of ARMA(1, 1) processes $[(1 - \theta L)y_t = (1 + \alpha L)e_t]$.

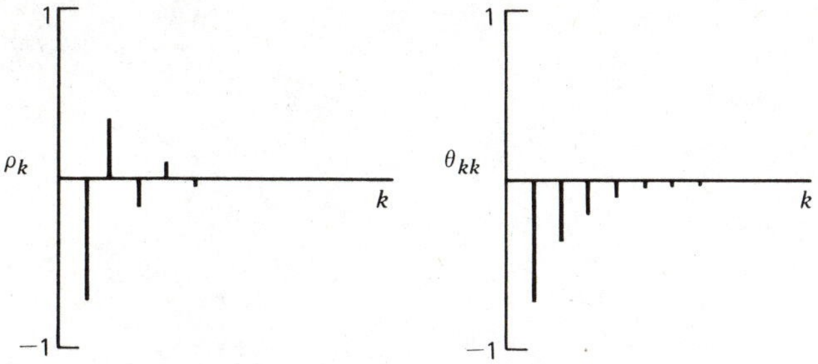

$\theta < 0, \alpha < 0$

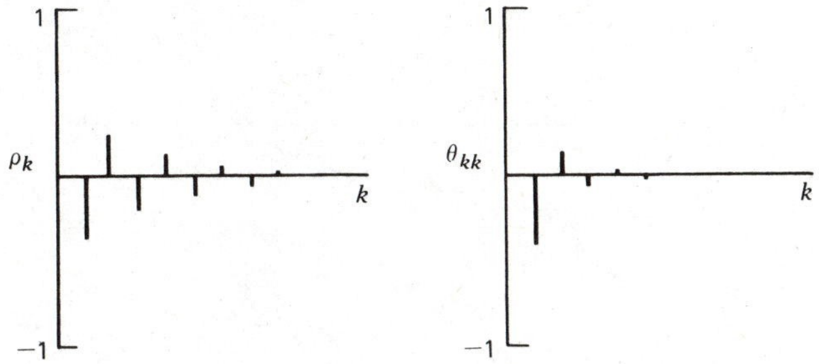

$\theta < 0, \alpha > 0, -\theta > \alpha$

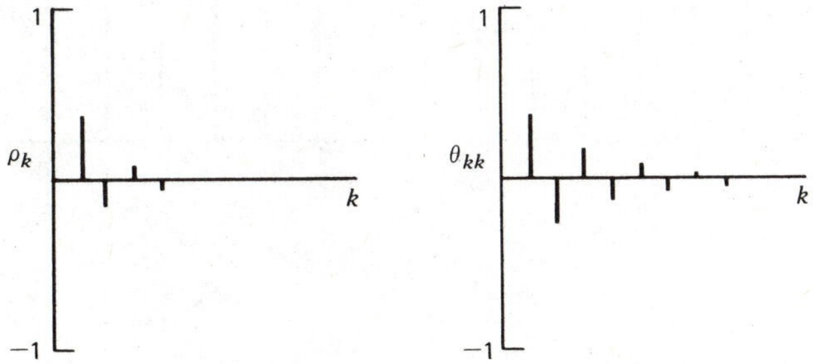

$\theta < 0, \alpha > 0, -\theta < \alpha$

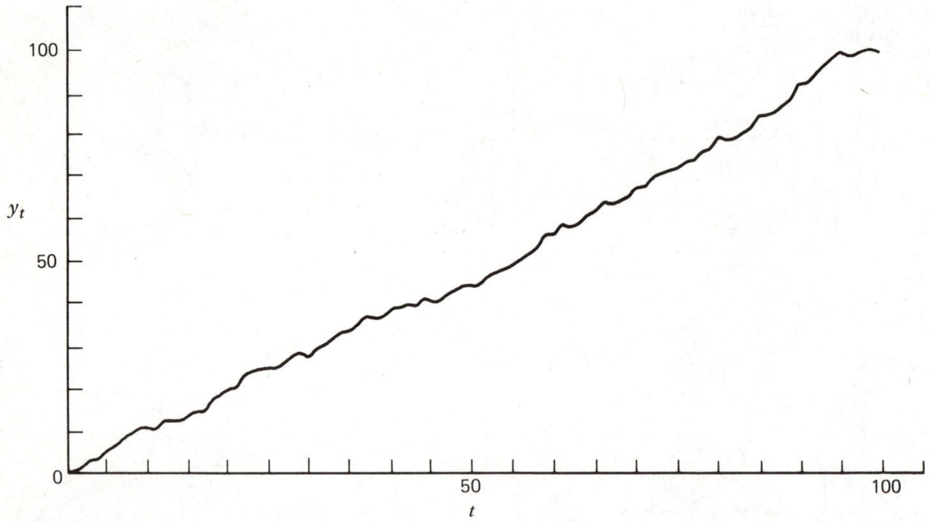

Figure 16.8 Plot of an artificially generated sample of $y_t = y_{t-1} + x_t$, where $x_t = 1 + e_t$.

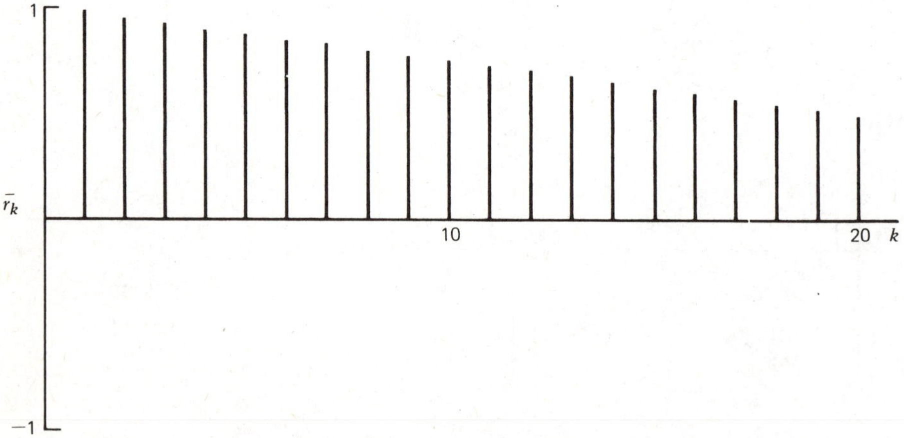

Figure 16.9 Sample autocorrelations of the data in Figure 16.8.

In the previous sections we have outlined some basics of what is known as the Box–Jenkins approach to time-series model building. In the next section we will give a systematic presentation of this approach and analyze a set of real-life data.

16.6 The Box–Jenkins Approach

The Box–Jenkins approach to time-series model building is a method of finding, for a given set of data, an ARIMA model that adequately represents the data-generating process. The method is customarily partitioned into three stages: identification, estimation, and diagnostic checking. We will give a brief exposition of each stage in the following and illustrate the single steps by analyzing the yearly price of corn in the United States, as coded by Quenouille (1957), which is given in Table 16.4. The series is plotted in Figure 16.10.

Table 16.4 Price of Corn in the United States

t	y_t	t	y_t	t	y_t	t	y_t
1867	944	1888	571	1909	790	1929	903
1868	841	1889	490	1910	712	1930	777
1869	911	1890	747	1911	831	1931	507
1870	768	1891	651	1912	742	1932	500
1871	718	1892	645	1913	847	1933	716
1872	634	1893	609	1914	850	1934	911
1873	735	1894	705	1915	830	1935	816
1874	858	1895	453	1916	1056	1936	1019
1875	673	1896	382	1917	1163	1937	714
1876	609	1897	466	1918	1182	1938	687
1877	604	1898	506	1919	1180	1939	754
1878	457	1899	525	1920	805	1940	791
1879	612	1900	595	1921	714	1941	876
1880	642	1901	829	1922	865	1942	962
1881	849	1902	654	1923	911	1943	1050
1882	733	1903	673	1924	1027	1944	1037
1883	672	1904	691	1925	846	1945	1104
1884	594	1905	660	1926	869	1946	1193
1885	559	1906	643	1927	928	1947	1334
1886	604	1907	754	1928	924	1948	1114
1887	678	1908	813				

Source: Quenouille (1957, Table 8.1a)

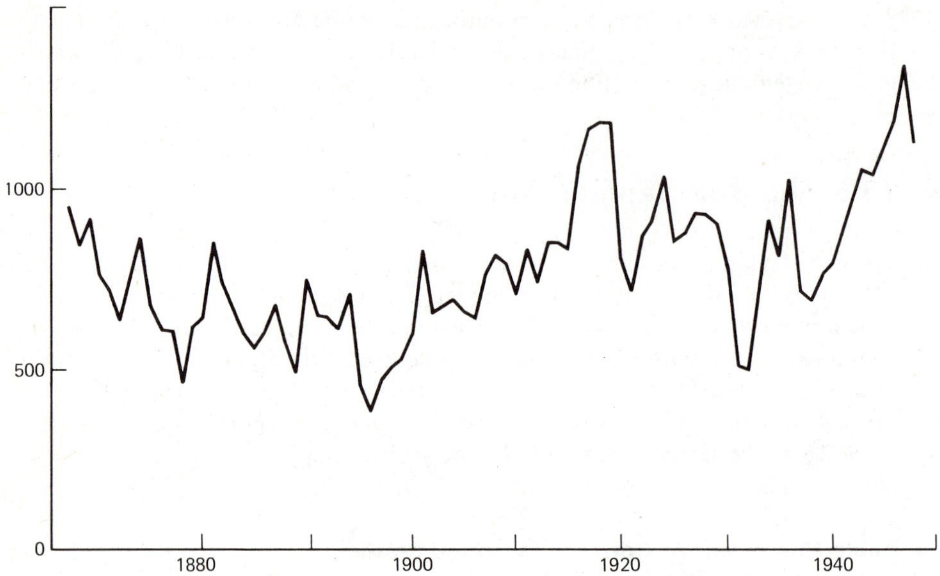

Figure 16.10 Plot of the corn price data in Table 16.4.

16.6.1 Identification

At the identification stage a tentative ARIMA model is specified for the data-generating process on the basis of the estimated autocorrelations and partial autocorrelations. Let us summarize the relevant knowledge gathered in the previous sections.

1. If the autocorrelations taper off slowly or do not die out, nonstationarity is indicated and differencing (usually not more than once or twice) is suggested until stationarity is obtained. Then an ARMA model is identified for the differenced series.
2. For an MA(q) process the autocorrelations $\rho_k = 0$ for $k > q$ and the partial autocorrelations taper off. To determine a cutoff point of the autocorrelation function the sample autocorrelations are used.
3. For an AR(p) the partial autocorrelations $\theta_{kk} = 0$ for $k > p$ and the autocorrelations taper off. A cutoff point of the partial autocorrelation function may be determined by comparing the estimates with $\pm 2/\sqrt{T}$, since $1/\sqrt{T}$ is the approximate standard deviation of the estimators $\hat{\theta}_{kk}$ for $k > p$.
4. If neither the autocorrelations nor the partial autocorrelations have a cutoff point, an ARMA model may be adequate. The AR and the MA degree have to

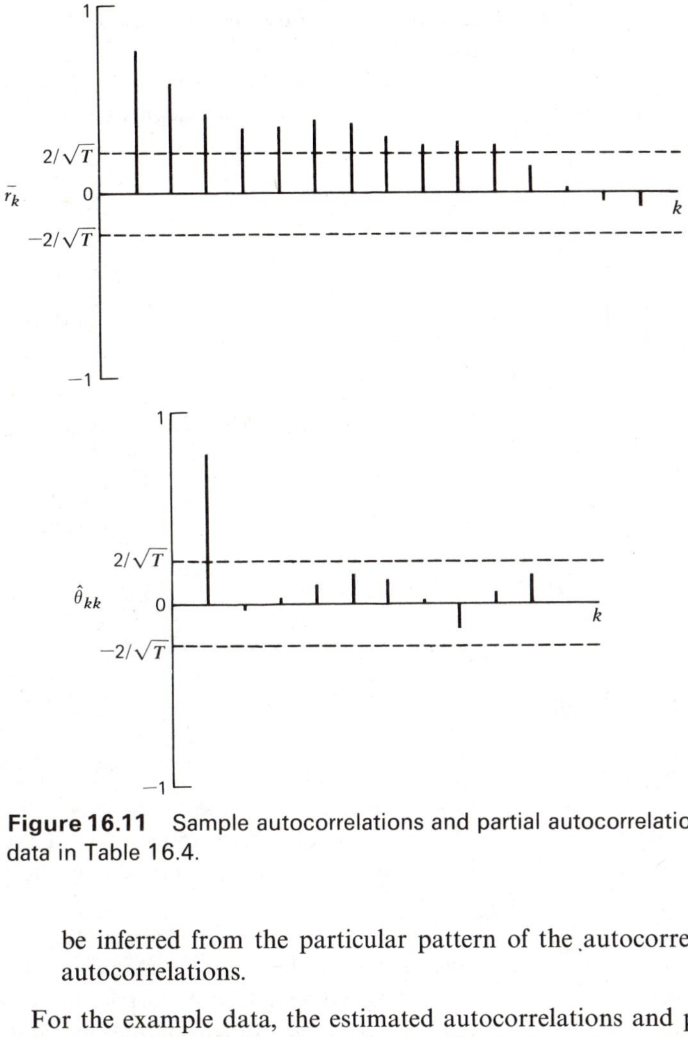

Figure 16.11 Sample autocorrelations and partial autocorrelations of the corn price data in Table 16.4.

be inferred from the particular pattern of the autocorrelations and partial autocorrelations.

For the example data, the estimated autocorrelations and partial autocorrelations are depicted in Figure 16.11. On the basis of these estimates an AR(1) is identified as a tentative model.

16.6.2 Estimation

The parameters of pure AR processes can be estimated by using regression methods as described in Section 16.3.1. If MA terms are involved, the minimization of the sum of squared errors or the maximization of the likelihood function requires nonlinear optimization methods. Using appropriate computer software can minimize the labor input in this part of the model-building cycle.

For the corn price data we have identified an AR(1) as a tentative model. Since the plot of the data in Figure 16.10 suggests a nonzero sample mean we use

$$y_t = \nu + \rho y_{t-1} + e_t \qquad t = 1868, \ldots, 1948 \tag{16.6.1}$$

as the estimation equation. The least squares estimates are

$$\begin{bmatrix} \hat{\nu} \\ \\ \hat{\rho} \end{bmatrix} = \begin{bmatrix} 155 \\ (56) \\ 0.80 \\ (0.07) \end{bmatrix} \qquad \hat{\sigma}_e^2 = 1.46 \times 10^4 \tag{16.6.2}$$

where the numbers in parentheses are approximate standard errors. As an estimate for the mean μ, we get from (16.3.10)

$$\hat{\mu} = \frac{\hat{\nu}}{1 - \hat{\rho}} = 775 \tag{16.6.3}$$

Using (16.3.11), an estimate of the asymptotic standard deviation of $\hat{\mu}$ is seen to be

$$\sqrt{\hat{\sigma}_e^2(1 - \hat{\rho})^{-2}/T} = \sqrt{1.46 \times 10^4(1 - 0.8)^{-2}/81} = 67.1$$

16.6.3 Diagnostic Checking

As the third step in the model-building cycle some checks on the model adequacy are suggested. Possibilities are (1) to do a residual analysis and (2) to overfit the specified model. For instance, if an ARMA(p, q) is identified and estimated, we could also estimate an ARMA($p + 1, q$) and an ARMA($p, q + 1$) model and test the significance of the extra parameters.

A residual analysis is usually based on the fact that the residuals of an adequate model should be approximately white noise. A plot of the residuals can be a useful tool in checking for outliers. Moreover, the estimated residual autocorrelations are usually examined. Recall that for a white-noise series the autocorrelations are zero. Therefore the significance of the residual autocorrelations is often checked by comparing with approximate two standard error bounds $\pm 2/\sqrt{T}$, where T is the sample size used in computing the estimates. Note, however, that the residuals from an ARMA model have actually a distribution that differs from white noise (see Box and Pierce, 1970). If the first residual autocorrelations are close to the critical bounds, this is a reason for concern about the adequacy of the model. For the model used in the example, the estimated residual autocorrelations are shown in Figure 16.12 and do not give rise to questioning the AR(1) model.

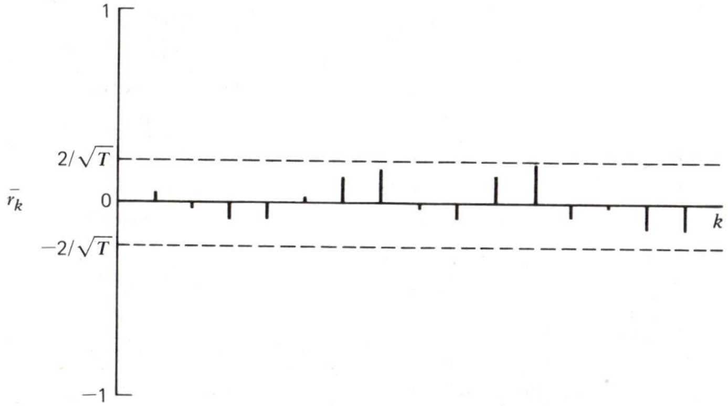

Figure 16.12 Estimated residual autocorrelations of the AR(1) model for the corn price data.

To check the overall acceptability of the residual autocorrelations the *portmanteau test statistic*

$$Q = T(T+2) \sum_{k=1}^{K} \frac{1}{T-k} r_k^2 \tag{16.6.4}$$

is often used (see Ljung and Box, 1978). Here the r_k are the autocorrelations of the estimation residuals and K is some prespecified number. Values of Q for different K may be computed in a residual analysis. For an ARMA(p, q) process the statistic Q is approximately χ^2-distributed with $K - p - q$ degrees of freedom if the ARMA orders are specified correctly. Experience suggests that a test based on the portmanteau statistic is not very powerful in small samples. If a model is rejected at the checking stage, the model-building cycle has to be repeated, starting with a new identification.

In working Exercise 16.1 you will soon find that identifying an adequate model for the generation process of a particular time-series by looking at the autocorrelations and partial autocorrelations may be difficult. Therefore, a number of alternative procedures and criteria have been developed to aid in selecting adequate time-series models. Further details and references for these procedures are given in Judge, et al. (1985, Section 7.5) and de Gooijer, et al. (1985).

16.7 Forecasting

In different situations different forecasting methods are appropriate. Suppose that we know the calendar sales of a department store over the last 3 years and we are asked to stock the store for the next winter. With so little information, a subjective prediction may be all that is possible, whereas if the figures of the last 25 years are available, it may be possible to build a time-series model and estimate its parameters. Whether or not to suffer the pains of using a time-series model for prediction may depend on the punishment for being wrong. To formalize, a cost function is set up that depends somehow on the error in predicting the future demand for calendars. In many cases the cost depends only on the size of the error, not on the direction of the deviation from the actual value. Therefore, a popular cost function is the expected squared forecasting error.

To put this in the framework of a time-series model, the objective is to predict the value of the random variable y_{T+h} on the basis of the information gathered up to time T. Let us denote the h-step ahead forecast at time T by $y_{T,h}$. Note that the forecast is a random variable that is a function of the random variables y_T, $y_{T-1}, \ldots$. Any particular forecast value computed on the basis of realizations of these random variables is regarded as a realization of $y_{T,h}$. From the foregoing discussion it follows that the minimization of the conditional expected quadratic forecasting error (forecast MSE), given the information up to time T,

$$E_T[y_{T+h} - y_{T,h}]^2 = E[(y_{T+h} - y_{T,h})^2 | y_T, y_{T-1}, \ldots] \tag{16.7.1}$$

is a meaningful objective. Here E_T denotes the conditional expectation given information up to period T. It can be shown that the conditional expectation of y_{T+h} given $y_T, y_{T-1}, \ldots$ is the optimal forecast that minimizes (16.7.1). In other words,

$$y_{T,h} = E_T[y_{T+h}] = E[y_{T+h} | y_T, y_{T-1}, \ldots] \tag{16.7.2}$$

This result permits one to determine the optimal forecasts of a variable generated by an ARMA process.

Consider the ARMA(p, q) process

$$\begin{aligned} y_t = \nu + \theta_1 y_{t-1} + \cdots + \theta_p y_{t-p} + e_t \\ + \alpha_1 e_{t-1} + \cdots + \alpha_q e_{t-q} \end{aligned} \tag{16.7.3}$$

where ν is a constant and suppose that this process is stationary so that it has an MA representation

$$y_t = \mu + e_t + \phi_1 e_{t-1} + \cdots = \mu + \sum_{i=0}^{\infty} \phi_i e_{t-i} \tag{16.7.4}$$

The coefficients of this representation can be computed using the relations

$$\mu = \nu/(1 - \theta_1 - \cdots - \theta_p)$$

$$\phi_1 = \alpha_1 + \theta_1$$

$$\vdots$$

$$\phi_n = \begin{cases} \alpha_n + \sum_{i=1}^{\min(n,p)} \theta_i \phi_{n-i} & \text{for } n = 1, 2, \ldots, q \\ \sum_{i=1}^{\min(n,p)} \theta_i \phi_{n-i} & \text{for } n > q \end{cases} \tag{16.7.5}$$

We also assume that (16.7.3) is invertible and has an AR representation

$$\begin{aligned} y_t &= \gamma + \eta_1 y_{t-1} + \eta_2 y_{t-2} + \cdots + e_t \\ &= \gamma + \sum_{i=1}^{\infty} \eta_i y_{t-i} + e_t \end{aligned} \tag{16.7.6}$$

where

$$\gamma = \nu/(1 + \alpha_1 + \cdots + \alpha_q)$$

and the η_i can be obtained by recursions similar to (16.7.5). We do not give the explicit expressions here since they are not needed in the following. The AR and MA representations show that for this process the information in $\{y_T, y_{T-1}, \ldots\}$ can equivalently be represented as $\{e_T, e_{T-1}, \ldots\}$ since each e_t can be computed from past and present y_s, $s \leq t$, and each y_t can be obtained from past and present e_s, $s \leq t$.

Assuming in addition that e_t and e_s are independent and not only uncorrelated for $s \neq t$, we can now determine the conditional expectation $E_T[y_{T+h}]$. For instance, for $h = 1$,

$$\begin{aligned} y_{T,1} = E_T[y_{T+1}] &= \nu + \theta_1 E_T[y_T] + \cdots + \theta_p E_T[y_{T+1-p}] \\ &\quad + E_T[e_{T+1}] + \alpha_1 E_T[e_T] + \cdots + \alpha_q E_T[e_{T+1-q}] \\ &= \nu + \theta_1 y_T + \cdots + \theta_p y_{T+1-p} + \alpha_1 e_T + \cdots + \alpha_q e_{T+1-q} \end{aligned}$$

where $E_T[y_t] = y_t$, $E_T[e_t] = e_t$ for $t \leq T$ has been used and $E_T[e_t] = E[e_t] = 0$ for $t > T$ follows from the independence assumption for the white-noise process.

For an arbitrary positive integer h we get

$$y_{T,h} = \nu + \theta_1 y_{T,h-1} + \cdots + \theta_p y_{T,h-p} + \alpha_h e_T + \cdots + \alpha_q e_{T+h-q} \tag{16.7.7}$$

if $h \leq q$ and

$$y_{T,h} = \nu + \theta_1 y_{T,h-1} + \cdots + \theta_p y_{T,h-p} \tag{16.7.8}$$

if $h > q$. Here $y_{T,j} = y_{T+j}$ for $j \leq 0$. With these formulas, forecasts can be computed recursively. Alternatively, the optimal predictor can be determined using the AR or MA representation of y_t.

$$\begin{aligned} y_{T,h} &= \gamma + \sum_{i=1}^{\infty} \eta_i y_{T,h-i} \\ &= \mu + \sum_{i=h}^{\infty} \phi_i e_{T+h-i} \end{aligned} \tag{16.7.9}$$

From the latter formula the forecast error is easy to obtain.

$$\begin{aligned} y_{T+h} - y_{T,h} &= \mu + \sum_{i=0}^{\infty} \phi_i e_{T+h-i} - \left(\mu + \sum_{i=h}^{\infty} \phi_i e_{T+h-i}\right) \\ &= \sum_{i=0}^{h-1} \phi_i e_{T+h-i} \end{aligned} \tag{16.7.10}$$

The forecast is unbiased since the expected error is zero,

$$E[y_{T+h} - y_{T,h}] = \sum_{i=0}^{h-1} \phi_i E[e_{T+h-i}] = 0$$

Furthermore the forecast MSE or variance is

$$\begin{aligned} \sigma_h^2 &= E_T[y_{T+h} - y_{T,h}]^2 = E[y_{T+h} - y_{T,h}]^2 \\ &= E\left[\sum_{i=0}^{h-1} \phi_i e_{T+h-i}\right]^2 = \sum_{i=0}^{h-1} \sum_{j=0}^{h-1} \phi_i \phi_j E[e_{T+h-i} e_{T+h-j}] \\ &= \sigma_e^2 \sum_{i=0}^{h-1} \phi_i^2 \end{aligned} \tag{16.7.11}$$

To illustrate these formulas we consider the ARMA(1, 1) process

$$y_t = \nu + \theta y_{t-1} + e_t + \alpha e_{t-1}$$

For this process

$$\begin{aligned} y_{T,1} &= \nu + \theta y_T + \alpha e_T \\ y_{T,2} &= \nu + \theta y_{T,1} \\ y_{T,3} &= \nu + \theta y_{T,2} \end{aligned}$$

The recursions in (16.7.5) imply the following coefficients of the MA representation of the present process.

$$\phi_1 = \alpha + \theta$$

$$\phi_2 = \theta\phi_1 = \alpha\theta + \theta^2$$

Thus, the forecast MSEs can be obtained from (16.7.11).

$$\sigma_1^2 = \sigma_e^2$$

$$\sigma_2^2 = \sigma_e^2[1 + (\alpha + \theta)^2]$$

$$\sigma_3^2 = \sigma_e^2[1 + (\alpha + \theta)^2 + (\alpha\theta + \theta^2)^2]$$

In practice, to compute forecast values, realizations of the y_t and/or e_t are needed. For expository purposes, consider the MA(1) $y_t = e_t - 0.9e_{t-1}$ that generated the time series in Table 16.3, where the values $e_0, \ldots, e_{100}$, that were actually used in computing the sample values $y_1, \ldots, y_{100}$, are also given. As a one-step-ahead forecast value we get

$$y_{100,1} = -0.9e_{100} = -0.069$$

and for $h > 1$,

$$y_{100,2} = y_{100,3} = y_{100,4} = \cdots = 0$$

The forecast MSEs are, according to (16.7.11),

$$\sigma_1^2 = \sigma_e^2 = 1.0 \qquad \sigma_2^2 = \sigma_3^2 = \cdots = (1 + \alpha_1^2)\sigma_e^2 = 1 + (-0.9)^2 = 1.81$$

Usually only realizations of the y_t will be available in practice. These realizations can be used to determine approximately the required e_t values with the infinite AR representation. For the MA(1) example process we get the AR representation

$$y_t = -\sum_{i=1}^{\infty} 0.9^i y_{t-i} + e_t$$

It is typical for stationary processes that the AR coefficients η_i die out rapidly for increasing i. Therefore we can use the infinite AR representation to determine the e_t even if only a finite number of observations y_t is available. Using the data from Table 16.3 we get

$$e_{100} \approx y_{100} + \sum_{i=1}^{99} 0.9^i y_{100-i}$$

since $0.9^{100} = 0.27 \times 10^{-4}$ and thus the $\eta_i = -0.9^i$ are very small for $i \geq 100$. For short time-series the approximation may be less precise.

So far, in this section, we have considered point forecasts, that is, for a given time series (realization of the data generation process) a single number is computed as h-step-ahead forecast value. Sometimes an interval is desired that will include the value of the variable of interest with a preassigned probability. To obtain an interval forecast, a distributional assumption for the process y_t is required. Assuming that the process is normally distributed, that is, e_t is a Gaussian white-noise process, the forecast error as a weighted sum of normal variates [see (16.7.10)] is then also normally distributed with mean zero and variance σ_h^2. Hence,

$$\frac{y_{T+h} - y_{T,h}}{\sigma_h} \sim N(0, 1) \tag{16.7.12}$$

From this result it follows that

$$\Pr(y_{T,h} - z_{(\alpha/2)}\sigma_h \leq y_{T+h} \leq y_{T,h} + z_{(\alpha/2)}\sigma_h) = 1 - \alpha$$

where $z_{(\alpha/2)}$ denotes the $(1 - (\alpha/2))100$ percentage point of the standard normal distribution. Thus, a $(1 - \alpha)100\%$ confidence interval is

$$y_{T,h} \pm z_{(\alpha/2)}\sigma_h \tag{16.7.13}$$

For the MA(1) example process the e_t in Table 16.3 are indeed pseudonormal random numbers with mean 0 and variance $\sigma_e^2 = 1$ so that (16.7.13) may be used to obtain $(1 - \alpha)100\%$ forecast intervals. For this example

$$y_{100,1} \pm z_{(\alpha/2)}\sigma_1 = -0.069 \pm z_{(\alpha/2)}$$

$$y_{100,h} \pm z_{(\alpha/2)}\sigma_h = \pm z_{(\alpha/2)}\sqrt{1.81} \qquad \text{for } h = 2, 3, \ldots$$

As another example, consider the corn price series in Table 16.4. In Section 16.6.2 the following estimated model for the data-generating process has been obtained [see (16.6.2)]:

$$y_t = 155 + 0.8y_{t-1} + e_t \qquad \hat{\sigma}_e^2 = 1.46 \times 10^4 \tag{16.7.14}$$

and the last value of the series is $y_{1948} = 1114$. Using these figures we get a one-step-ahead forecast value

$$\hat{y}_{1948,1} = 155 + 0.8 \cdot 1114 = 1046.2$$

and an estimate for the forecast MSE is

$$\hat{\sigma}_1^2 = \hat{\sigma}_e^2 = 1.46 \times 10^4$$

The forecast and its MSE are furnished with a caret to indicate that we have only obtained estimates of the desired quantities, since the actual data-generation process is unknown. Note that the AR(1) model is specified by a subjective assessment of the autocorrelations and partial autocorrelations and it is not necessarily the true generation process of the corn price data. Furthermore, the parameters of the model are unknown and have been estimated from the data.

If the data-generating process is assumed to be Gaussian (normally distributed) approximate $(1-\alpha)100\%$ forecast intervals can be determined. For instance, a 95% forecast interval for the coded corn price for 1949 is

$$\hat{y}_{1948,1} \pm z_{0.025}\hat{\sigma}_1 = 1046.2 \pm 1.96\sqrt{1.46 \times 10^4} = 1046.2 \pm 236.8$$

In order to compute the forecast MSE σ_h^2 for $h > 1$, the coefficients of the MA representation

$$y_t = \mu + \sum_{i=0}^{\infty} \phi_i e_{t-i} = 775 + \sum_{i=0}^{\infty} 0.8^i e_{t-i}$$

of (16.7.14) are needed. These have been used in setting up forecast intervals for $h = 2, 3, 4, 5$. The estimated point forecasts, forecast MSEs, and 95% forecast intervals are given in Table 16.5.

Of course, if estimated rather than known processes are used for prediction, this will have consequences for the forecast MSE. Although it is generally difficult to give an exact evaluation of the forecast MSE for estimated processes, it is possible to determine an approximation that takes into account the sampling variability from estimating the process parameters. Denoting by $\hat{y}_{T,h}$ the h-step forecast of an ARMA(p, q) process with estimated coefficients, the forecast error is

$$\begin{aligned} y_{T+h} - \hat{y}_{T,h} &= y_{T+h} - y_{T,h} + y_{T,h} - \hat{y}_{T,h} \\ &= (e_{T+h} + \phi_1 e_{T+h-1} + \cdots + \phi_{h-1} e_{T+1}) + (y_{T,h} - \hat{y}_{T,h}) \qquad (16.7.15) \end{aligned}$$

Table 16.5 Forecasting Results for the U.S. Corn Price Data

Point forecasts	Estimated mean square forecasting error	Approximate 95% forecast intervals
$\hat{y}_{1948,1} = 1046$	$\hat{\sigma}_1^2 = 1.46 \times 10^4$	(809, 1283)
$\hat{y}_{1948,2} = 992$	$\hat{\sigma}_2^2 = 2.39 \times 10^4$	(689, 1295)
$\hat{y}_{1948,3} = 949$	$\hat{\sigma}_3^2 = 2.99 \times 10^4$	(610, 1288)
$\hat{y}_{1948,4} = 914$	$\hat{\sigma}_4^2 = 3.38 \times 10^4$	(554, 1274)
$\hat{y}_{1948,5} = 886$	$\hat{\sigma}_5^2 = 3.62 \times 10^4$	(516, 1259)

Assuming that only data up to period T have been used for estimation, the term $(y_{T,h} - \hat{y}_{T,h})$ involves only variables up to period T and is consequently independent of $(y_{T+h} - y_{T,h})$, which involves only shocks e_t after period T. Therefore the MSE

$$\hat{\sigma}_h^2 = E[y_{T+h} - \hat{y}_{T,h}]^2 = \sigma_h^2 + E[y_{T,h} - \hat{y}_{T,h}]^2 \tag{16.7.16}$$

If the ARMA coefficients are estimated by ML, it can be shown that the term $E[y_{T,h} - \hat{y}_{T,h}]^2$ vanishes asymptotically as the sample size goes to infinity. Thus, for large samples, approximating $\hat{\sigma}_h^2$ by σ_h^2 is justified.

On the other hand, it can also be shown that

$$\sqrt{T}\,(y_{T,h} - \hat{y}_{T,h}) \xrightarrow{d} N(0, \omega_h^2) \tag{16.7.17}$$

where ω_h^2 is a positive constant that depends on the process y_t and the forecast horizon h. Thus, ω_h^2/T may be a better approximation of $E(y_{T,h} - \hat{y}_{T,h})^2$ than zero. This leads to an approximation

$$\hat{\sigma}_h^2 \approx \sigma_h^2 + \frac{1}{T}\,\omega_h^2 \tag{16.7.18}$$

To get an idea about the size of ω_h^2 we mention that for a zero mean AR(p) process $\omega_1^2 = \sigma_e^2 p$. Thus, (16.7.18) becomes for $h = 1$,

$$\hat{\sigma}_1^2 \approx \sigma_1^2 + \frac{p}{T}\,\sigma_e^2 = \sigma_e^2\left(1 + \frac{p}{T}\right) \tag{16.7.19}$$

In other words, if estimated rather than known parameters are used, the one-step forecast MSE is approximately inflated by a term $(1 + p/T)$. This result shows that choosing too high an order for an AR model leads to inefficient forecasts. For instance, if only an upper bound P for the AR order p is known then using an estimated AR(P) model for prediction results in an approximate MSE of $\sigma_e^2(1 + P/T)$. Provided $p < P$, this is greater than the approximate one-step forecast MSE $\sigma_e^2(1 + p/T)$ for an estimated AR(p).

So far we have restricted the discussion to forecasting stationary processes. For nonstationary ARIMA processes, that is, processes that have an ARMA representation after differencing a sufficient number of times, we can proceed as follows. Suppose that y_t is an ARIMA process such that $x_t = y_t - y_{t-1}$ is an ARMA process. Then

$$\begin{aligned} y_{T+h} &= x_{T+h} + y_{T+h-1} = x_{T+h} + x_{T+h-1} + y_{T+h-2} \\ &= \cdots = x_{T+h} + x_{T+h-1} + \cdots + x_{T+1} + y_T \end{aligned}$$

Thus the h-step-ahead forecast of y_{T+h} at time T can be computed as

$$y_{T,h} = x_{T,h} + x_{T,h-1} + \cdots + x_{T,1} + y_T$$

where the $x_{T,k}$, $k = 1, 2, \ldots, h$ are obtained as described in the foregoing. A similar formula can be derived if the difference operator has to be applied more than once to obtain a stationary ARMA process.

16.8 Limitations of ARIMA Models and Their Relationship to Econometric Models

It is now time to talk about the limitations of the approach presented in the previous sections. The given examples certainly do not cover the full range of possible time series. Some rather different looking plots of time series data are given in Figures 16.13 and 16.14.

The numbers of unemployed persons in West Germany in Figure 16.13 exhibit a distinct seasonal pattern. That is, the number of unemployed persons depends to some extent on the particular month for which it is recorded. This is a typical phenomenon for economic time series. The models we have presented in the previous sections are not designed to handle seasonality. Also, the seasonality should not be removed prior to a Box–Jenkins analysis by some sort of seasonal adjustment method because seasonal adjustment may distort the stochastic structure substantially. Therefore, Box and Jenkins suggest constructing seasonal ARIMA models (Box and Jenkins, 1976).

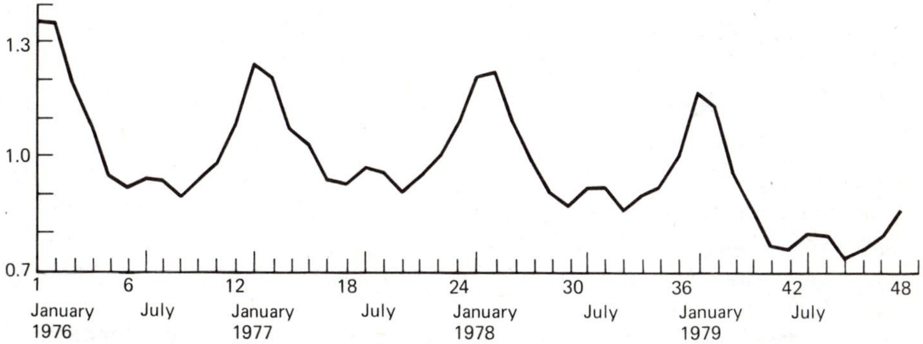

Figure 16.13 Millions of unemployed persons in West Germany. (*Source:* Statistisches Bundesamt of West Germany.)

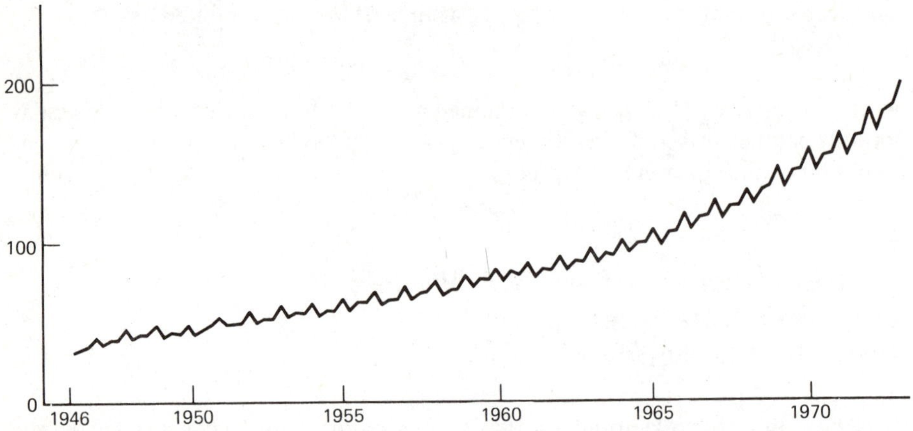

Figure 16.14 U.S. quarterly personal consumption expenditures in billions of U.S. dollars. (*Source:* U.S. Department of Commerce, Bureau of Economic Analysis.)

The U.S. personal consumption expenditures plotted in Figure 16.14 not only show a seasonal pattern but also show an upward trend. Such a trend may not be tractable by differencing. Rather, a logarithmic transformation prior to the differencing may be necessary. On the other hand, this trend may be caused by the economic growth and the implied increase in income. Thus there may be systematic components that could be beneficially used if they could be made explicit by economic theory.

This reasoning takes us back to econometric models. Suppose that we can write the process y_t as a sum of two components

$$y_t = s_t + v_t \tag{16.8.1}$$

where s_t is the systematic part and v_t is the random part; then we have exactly the form of the statistical model considered in earlier chapters where, for example,

$$s_t = \beta_1 x_{1t} + \cdots + \beta_K x_{Kt}$$

and v_t is the error term. As we have seen in Chapters 8 and 9, to increase the efficiency of an estimator for the parameter vector $\boldsymbol{\beta}$, the error process should be specified correctly. This means that if its true structure is unknown but we have reason to believe that this true structure is a stationary stochastic process, an ARMA model should be constructed for this term.

To be more specific, suppose that we are facing the linear statistical model

$$y_t = \mathbf{x}_t'\boldsymbol{\beta} + e_t \tag{16.8.2}$$

where $\mathbf{x}_t' = (x_{1t}, \ldots, x_{Kt})$, $\boldsymbol{\beta} = (\beta_1, \beta_2, \ldots, \beta_K)'$, and the y_t are time-series data. Then the random errors also form a time-series. One way to proceed in this case is to estimate the parameters in (16.8.2) by the least squares method in a first step, and in a second step build a time-series model for the residuals and use this model to improve the estimator of the parameter vector $\boldsymbol{\beta}$. This procedure is demonstrated in some detail in Chapter 9 for an AR(1) error process.

In many time-series texts the systematic part is split into a trend and a seasonal component. These components are sometimes removed by prefiltering the data (e.g., by applying seasonal adjustment procedures), and then the stochastic structure of what is left is investigated. Unfortunately, prefiltering methods have the disadvantage that they may not completely remove the trend and seasonal part or distort the stochastic component. In the next section we discuss some possible extensions of the material covered in this chapter and mention some literature for those with a broader interest in time-series analysis.

16.9 A Guide to Further Reading

In this chapter we have discussed some topics concerning the analysis of univariate time series. We have given some useful models for describing a stochastic process, and we have considered how such models can be fitted to a given set of data and how they can be used for prediction. We have tried to keep the discussion on an introductory level. As a consequence, many problems are omitted and not all topics are treated in sufficient detail to satisfy the reader with a special interest in the analysis of time series. We therefore recommend the following books for further studying.

A standard reference for ARIMA and seasonal ARIMA modeling is the book by Box and Jenkins (1976). Elementary expositions of their approach are also given by Pankratz (1983), Vandaele (1983), and Pindyck and Rubinfeld (1981). Granger and Newbold (1977) and Granger (1980) are especially concerned with the forecasting aspect of time-series analysis and discuss some forecasting methods that we have not gone into in this chapter. The latter also holds for the fairly elementary book by Chatfield (1975), which provides a solid introduction to many problems in the time-series area. Other introductory texts are Kendall (1973) and, with special emphasis on economic time series, Nerlove, Grether, and Carvalho (1979). A more mathematical treatment is given by Fuller (1976) and Anderson (1971), and, for the advanced reader, Priestley (1981), Hannan (1970), and Brillinger (1975) can be recommended. In the last-named references much more literature can be found to extend this incomplete list.

The following are important problems that we have omitted in this chapter. It was pointed out that the objective of building time-series models is not only to specify some adequate model for a given set of data but also to find a model with as few parameters as possible. Since there are many possible parameterizations besides AR, MA, and ARIMA models, it is reasonable to suspect that in some cases these models can be improved on in terms of parsimony. In this respect nonlinear models, especially bilinear models, have been investigated. Nonlinear models also have an advantage over linear specifications in that they may provide better forecasts, that is, predictions with lower expected quadratic forecasting error. Of course, if we leave the class of linear models, there is no reason to stick to linear forecasting formulas, and nonlinear forecasts may well be superior to their linear counterparts if the considered time series is not normally distributed.

Another problem of fundamental importance is the possible time dependence of the stochastic structure of economic data. We have discussed a certain form of a time-dependent mean, but if other types of changes of the characteristics of the random variables that build a stochastic process occur during the sample or forecasting period, the analysis may become extremely difficult. For references on these and some other topics in the time series area see Judge, et al. (1985, Chapter 7).

An important part of time-series analysis that we have completely ignored in this chapter is the *frequency domain analysis*, which uses the fact that many random variables can be decomposed into a finite or infinite sum of sine and cosine terms. Although this approach has been used in econometrics, the time-domain approach is often easier to interpret if economic variables are considered. For an introductory discussion of and references to frequency domain techniques see Judge, et al. (1985, Section 7.6).

Throughout this chapter we have been concerned with analyzing time-series for only a single variable. However, many economic variables are related to one another, and it seems plausible that such relationships can be used to improve our forecasts. Thus in the next chapters we will investigate time-series models relating two or more variables.

16.10 Exercises

16.1 Generate 100 realizations of each of the following processes by using standard normal random numbers for e_t.

$$(1 - 0.8L)y_t = e_t \tag{16.10.1}$$

$$(1 + 0.5L)y_t = (1 - 0.5L)e_t \tag{16.10.2}$$

$$(1 - 0.5L)y_t = (1 - 0.5L)e_t \tag{16.10.3}$$

$$(1 + 0.8L)y_t = (1 + 0.4L)e_t \tag{16.10.4}$$

$$(1 + 0.4L)y_t = (1 + 0.8L)e_t \tag{16.10.5}$$

$$(1 - L)y_t = (1 - 0.4L)e_t \tag{16.10.6}$$

$$(1 - 1.2L + 0.5L^2)y_t = e_t \tag{16.10.7}$$

$$y_t = (1 - 0.5L)e_t \tag{16.10.8}$$

$$y_t = (1 + 0.5L + 0.4L^2)e_t \tag{16.10.9}$$

$$y_t = (1 - 1.2L + 0.5L^2)e_t \tag{16.10.10}$$

Compute $\bar{r}_k$ and $\hat{\theta}_{kk}$ for $k = 1, \ldots, 15$ for each process and make up diagrams with these estimates. Mix the diagrams and try to identify the corresponding process for each.

16.2 Give the theoretical autocovariance and autocorrelation functions for the MA processes (16.10.8) through (16.10.10). Be sure and use the knowledge that $\sigma_e^2 = 1$.

16.3 Estimate the parameters of the MA(1) process (16.10.8) from the generated data. Use the approximate ML method outlined in Section 16.4.2.

16.4 Estimate the parameters of the AR processes (16.10.1) and (16.10.7) by least squares using the generated data.

16.5 Compute the point forecasts $y_{100,1}$, $y_{100,2}$, and $y_{100,3}$ of the AR(1) process (16.10.1). Compare these with the estimated point forecasts $\hat{y}_{100,1}$, $\hat{y}_{100,2}$, $\hat{y}_{100,3}$. Also compute $\sigma_1^2, \sigma_2^2, \sigma_3^2$, and $\hat{\sigma}_1^2, \hat{\sigma}_2^2, \hat{\sigma}_3^2$, the theoretical and estimated expected quadratic forecasting errors, respectively. Give interval forecasts based on true and estimated parameters.

16.6 Give the first five coefficients of the MA representation of the ARMA processes (16.10.2) through (16.10.4).

16.7 Plot the U.S. unemployment data given in Table 16.6 and compute the sample mean $\bar{y}$. Create a new data set by subtracting $\bar{y}$ from all observations (henceforth referred to as demeaned data). Estimate the autocorrelations and partial autocorrelations of the generating process of the demeaned data. Identify a tentative model and estimate its parameters. Check the residual autocorrelations and perform a portmanteau test and forecast the unemployment rate for the 12 quarters following the sample period.

Table 16.6 Seasonally Adjusted Quarterly U.S. Unemployment Rate

1948	I	3.73	1956	I	4.03	1965	I	4.90
	II	3.67		II	4.20		II	4.67
	III	3.77		III	4.13		III	4.37
	IV	3.83		IV	4.13		IV	4.10
1949	I	4.67	1957	I	3.93	1966	I	3.87
	II	5.87		II	4.10		II	3.80
	III	6.70		III	4.23		III	3.77
	IV	6.97		IV	4.93		IV	3.70
1950	I	6.40	1958	I	6.30	1967	I	3.77
	II	5.57		II	7.37		II	3.83
	III	4.63		III	7.33		III	3.83
	IV	4.23		IV	6.37		IV	3.93
1951	I	3.50	1959	I	5.83	1968	I	3.73
	II	3.10		II	5.10		II	3.57
	III	3.17		III	5.27		III	3.53
	IV	3.37		IV	5.60		IV	3.43
1952	I	3.07	1960	I	5.13	1969	I	3.37
	II	2.97		II	5.23		II	3.43
	III	3.23		III	5.53		III	3.60
	IV	2.83		IV	6.27		IV	3.60
1953	I	2.70	1961	I	6.80	1970	I	4.17
	II	2.57		II	7.00		II	4.80
	III	2.73		III	6.77		III	5.17
	IV	3.70		IV	6.20		IV	5.87
1954	I	5.27	1962	I	5.63	1971	I	5.93
	II	5.80		II	5.53		II	5.97
	III	5.97		III	5.57		III	5.97
	IV	5.33		IV	5.53		IV	5.97
1955	I	4.73	1963	I	5.77	1972	I	5.83
	II	4.40		II	5.73		II	5.77
	III	4.10		III	5.50		III	5.53
	IV	4.23		IV	5.57		IV	5.30
			1964	I	5.47			
				II	5.20			
				III	5.00			
				IV	5.00			

Source: *Business Statistics*, 1971 Biennial Edition, *Survey of Current Business*, January 1972 and January 1973. The quarterly data are averages of monthly data.

16.11 References

Anderson, T. W. (1971) *The Statistical Analysis of Time Series.* New York, Wiley.

Box, G. E. P., and G. M. Jenkins (1976) *Time Series Analysis: Forecasting and Control,* Rev. ed. San Francisco, Holden-Day.

Box, G. E. P., and D. A. Pierce (1970) "Distribution of Residual Autocorrelations in Autoregressive-Integrated Moving Average Time Series Models." *Journal of the American Statistical Association,* 65: 1509–1526.

Brillinger, D. R. (1975) *Time Series: Data Analysis and Theory.* New York, Holt, Rinehart Winston.

Chatfield, C. (1975) *The Analysis of Time Series: Theory and Practice.* London, Chapman and Hall.

Dufour, J.-M., and R. Roy (1985) "Some Robust Exact Results on Sample Autocorrelations and Tests of Randomness." *Journal of Econometrics,* 29, 257–273.

Fuller, W. A. (1976) *Introduction to Statistical Time Series.* New York, Wiley.

Gooijer, J. G. de, B. Abraham, A. Gould, and L. Robinson (1985) "Methods for Determining the Order of an Autoregressive-Moving Average Process: A Survey." *International Statistical Review,* 53, 301–329.

Granger, C. W. J. (1980) *Forecasting in Business and Economics.* New York, Academic Press.

Granger, C. W. J., and P. Newbold (1977) *Forecasting Economic Time Series.* New York, Academic Press.

Hannan, E. J. (1970) *Multiple Time Series.* New York, Wiley.

Judge, G. G., W. E. Griffiths, R. C. Hill, H. Lütkepohl, and T.-C. Lee (1985) *The Theory and Practice of Econometrics,* 2nd ed. New York, Wiley.

Kendall, M. (1973) *Time-Series.* London, Griffin.

Ljung, G. M., and G. E. P. Box (1978) "On a Measure of Lack of Fit in Time Series Models." *Biometrika,* 65, 297–303.

Nerlove, M., D. M. Grether, and J. L. Carvalho (1979), *Analysis of Economic Time Series: A Synthesis.* New York, Academic Press.

Pankratz, A. (1983) *Forecasting With Univariate Box-Jenkins Models: Concepts and Cases.* New York, Wiley.

Pindyck, R. S., and D. L. Rubinfeld (1981) *Econometric Models and Economic Forecasts,* 2nd ed. New York, McGraw-Hill.

Priestley, M. B. (1981) *Spectral Analysis and Time Series.* London, Academic Press.

Quenouille, M. H. (1957) *The Analysis of Multiple Time-Series.* London, Griffin.

Vandaele, W. (1983) *Applied Time Series and Box-Jenkins Models.* New York, Academic Press.

CHAPTER 17

Distributed Lags

17.1 Introduction

In many situations there is an obvious time lag between a decision made by some economic agent and the completion of the corresponding action. For instance, if a company decides to carry out an investment project, some time will elapse before it is completed. Taken together, all capital x_t appropriated at a time t by all firms of a particular region will induce payments y to be made in periods $t + 1, t + 2$, and so on. In other words, the capital expenditures y_t of period t depend on the capital appropriations of earlier time periods, $x_{t-1}, x_{t-2}, \ldots$.

There are also many examples of lags in consumer behavior. A higher income may cause a family to seek a new apartment but not until the present lease expires. If a person is promoted to a higher salary bracket, he or she may also move from the Chevrolet to the Mercedes class, but may want to wait for the new model. Also, a higher income may cause the household to graduate to a larger size of refrigerator, but if the present one is new, it will probably not be replaced at once. Thus, because of habit persistence and lags in consumer behavior, current consumption (y_t) is often hypothesized as a function of current and "lagged" income ($x_t, x_{t-1}, x_{t-2}, \ldots$).

A more general hypothesis is that the effect of a change in an independent variable is not felt all at once at a single point in time, but the impact is distributed over a number of future points in time. That is, the dependent variable y_t depends on lagged values of the independent variable. The length of the lag may sometimes be known a priori, but usually it is unknown and in some cases it is assumed to be infinite. The structure of the lag effect may take on a variety of shapes. For example, it may decline gradually or have a very small impact immediately following the cause, and rise fast, reaching its peak impact after a short interval and then tapering off slowly. These lagged effects arise from habit persistence, institutional or technological constraints, and/or expectational effects that link anticipations with experience. Thus in order to describe or model how economic data are generated, time lags must often be included in the behavioral and technical relations of an economic model.

Generally, if we only consider one dependent and one explanatory variable we get a model of the form

$$y_t = \alpha + \beta_0 x_t + \beta_1 x_{t-1} + \cdots + e_t = \alpha + \sum_{i=0}^{\infty} \beta_i x_{t-i} + e_t \qquad (17.1.1)$$

This model, involving two time series, will be treated in this chapter. In the present form, the interpretation of the parameters is straightforward. If the independent or exogenous variable x is increased by one unit in period t, the expected effect on the dependent variable will be β_0 in period t, β_1 in period $t + 1$, β_2 in period $t + 2$, and so on, provided, of course, that everything else is held constant. The total effect or *long-run effect* over all future periods will be $\sum_{i=0}^{\infty} \beta_i$.

There is one obvious problem with the specification (17.1.1). Without further assumptions, as it stands it contains an infinite number of parameters that cannot be estimated from a finite set of observations. The two basic approaches to limit the number of parameters are

1. To assume that $\beta_i = 0$ for i greater than some finite number N, and
2. To assume that the β_i can be written as a function of a finite number of parameters for all i.

For instance, if the *lag weights* β_i are assumed to decline geometrically with growing i, the specification $\beta_i = \alpha_1 \lambda^i$, where $0 < \lambda < 1$, has to be used (see Fig. 17.1).

The models obtained in the first approach are called *finite distributed lag models* because the lagged effect of a change in the independent variable is distributed over a finite number of time periods. Problems related to the estimation of these models

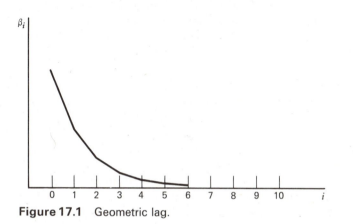

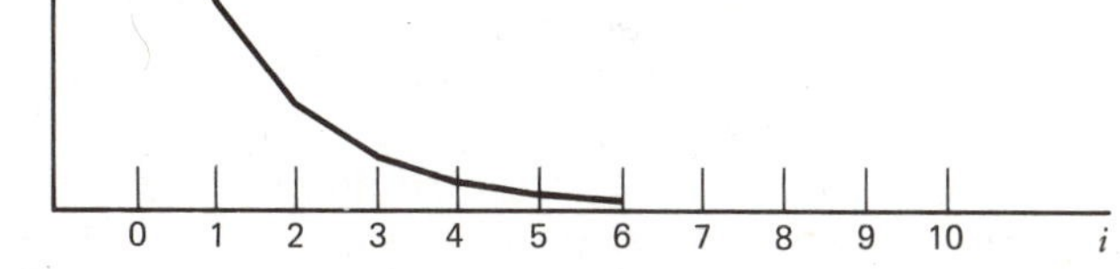

Figure 17.1 Geometric lag.

are treated in Sections 17.2 and 17.3 whereas *infinite distributed lag models* as assumed in the second approach will be considered in Section 17.4. A summary and concluding remarks are provided in the fifth section of this chapter.

17.2 Unrestricted Finite Distributed Lags

17.2.1 Estimation When the Lag Length is Known

In order to estimate the finite distributed lag model

$$y_t = \alpha + \beta_0 x_t + \cdots + \beta_N x_{t-N} + e_t \tag{17.2.1}$$

where N is a known, fixed number called the *lag length*, we use our standard vector and matrix notation

$$\mathbf{y} = X\boldsymbol{\beta} + \mathbf{e} \tag{17.2.2}$$

where, in this case,

$$\mathbf{y} = \begin{bmatrix} y_1 \\ y_2 \\ \vdots \\ y_T \end{bmatrix} \quad X = \begin{bmatrix} 1 & x_1 & x_0 & \cdots & x_{-N+1} \\ 1 & x_2 & x_1 & \cdots & x_{-N+2} \\ \vdots & \vdots & \vdots & & \vdots \\ 1 & x_T & x_{T-1} & \cdots & x_{T-N} \end{bmatrix} \quad \boldsymbol{\beta} = \begin{bmatrix} \alpha \\ \beta_0 \\ \vdots \\ \beta_N \end{bmatrix} \quad \mathbf{e} = \begin{bmatrix} e_1 \\ e_2 \\ \vdots \\ e_T \end{bmatrix}$$

Note that the X matrix involves presample values $x_{-N+1}, x_{-N+2}, \ldots, x_0$ for the x variable. It is assumed that these N observations are available in addition to the values $x_1, \ldots, x_T$. If $\mathbf{e}$ satisfies the standard assumptions, that is, $\mathbf{e} \sim (\mathbf{0}, \sigma^2 I)$, and the x_t are regarded as fixed, nonstochastic numbers, then based on the sample information $\mathbf{y}$ the LS (least squares) estimator $\mathbf{b} = (X'X)^{-1}X'\mathbf{y}$ is the best linear unbiased estimator of $\boldsymbol{\beta}$ (see Chapter 5).

There are some problems with this estimator in its present context. First, in practice the lag length N is rarely known. If the lag length N is replaced by some upper bound M and $M > N$, then the LS estimator of $\boldsymbol{\beta}_M = (\alpha, \beta_0, \beta_1, \ldots, \beta_M)'$ is inefficient since it ignores the restrictions $\beta_{N+1} = \beta_{N+2} = \cdots = \beta_M = 0$. This problem will be considered in the next section, where procedures for determining the lag length are discussed.

A second difficulty is that some columns of X may be nearly linearly dependent. This is the typical multicollinearity situation considered in Chapter 21. If the lag length N is short, 3 or 4, for example, this may not be a serious problem. In practice, however, a lag length around $N = 10$ is not unusual, and if x_t is a variable that does not change much or moves fairly regularly, there may be serious multicollinearity if the sample size is small. Multicollinearity implies that at least some of the parameters will not be estimated with much precision if the LS estimator is used. Different ways to cope with this problem in a finite distributed lag context have been suggested. One possibility is treated in Section 17.3.

17.2.2 Determining the Lag Length

If the true lag length N is unknown but an upper bound M is known, we have essentially the problem of choosing the correct set of regressors for a regression model. This problem is discussed in Section 20.4. In the present situation there is, however, one simplifying fact that makes it worthwhile to consider the special problem of choosing the lag length separately. In the present case the regressors x_t, $x_{t-1}, \ldots$ have a natural ordering. Therefore it is possible to set up the sequence of hypotheses

$$
\begin{array}{lll}
H_0^1\colon N = M - 1, \text{ that is, } \beta_M = 0 & \text{versus} & H_a^1\colon N = M, \text{ that is, } \beta_M \neq 0 \\
H_0^2\colon N = M - 2, \text{ that is, } \beta_{M-1} = 0 & \text{versus} & H_a^2\colon N = M - 1, \text{ that is,} \\
 & & \quad \beta_{M-1} \neq 0 \,|\, H_0^1 \\
\quad\vdots & & \quad\vdots \\
H_0^i\colon N = M - i, \text{ that is, } \beta_{M-i+1} = 0 & \text{versus} & H_a^i\colon N = M - i + 1, \text{ that is,} \\
 & & \quad \beta_{M-i+1} \neq 0 \\
 & & \quad |H_0^1, H_0^2, \ldots, H_0^{i-1} \\
\quad\vdots & & \quad\vdots
\end{array}
\tag{17.2.3}
$$

Here each null hypothesis is tested conditional on the previous ones being true. Thus, if H_0^1 is not rejected, it is assumed in the second test that it is true ($\beta_M = 0$). Similarly, if H_0^2 is not rejected, H_0^1 and H_0^2 are assumed to be true ($\beta_M = \beta_{M-1} = 0$) in the third test, and so on. In other words, the null hypotheses are tested sequentially starting with H_0^1 and the testing sequence terminates if the null hypothesis is rejected for the first time.

Assuming that the disturbances are normally distributed, $\mathbf{e} \sim N(\mathbf{0}, \sigma^2 I)$, F-tests or t-tests can be used in this sequential procedure. To write down the test statistics formally, we define

$$
\boldsymbol{\beta}_n = \begin{bmatrix} \alpha \\ \beta_0 \\ \vdots \\ \beta_n \end{bmatrix}, \qquad X_n = \begin{bmatrix} 1 & x_1 & x_0 & \cdots & x_{-n+1} \\ 1 & x_2 & x_1 & \cdots & x_{-n+2} \\ \vdots & \vdots & \vdots & & \vdots \\ 1 & x_T & x_{T-1} & \cdots & x_{T-n} \end{bmatrix}, \tag{17.2.4}
$$

and

$$\hat{\sigma}_n^2 = \frac{\text{SSE}_n}{T - n - 2} \tag{17.2.5}$$

where $\text{SSE}_n = (\mathbf{y} - X_n\mathbf{b}_n)'(\mathbf{y} - X_n\mathbf{b}_n)$ is the sum of squared errors for a model with lag length n and

$$\mathbf{b}_n = (X_n'X_n)^{-1}X_n'\mathbf{y} \tag{17.2.6}$$

Using this notation, the likelihood ratio statistic for testing the ith null hypothesis H_0^i can be written as

$$\lambda_i = \frac{\text{SSE}_{M-i} - \text{SSE}_{M-i+1}}{\hat{\sigma}_{M-i+1}^2} \tag{17.2.7}$$

From Chapter 6 we know that this statistic has an F-distribution with 1 and $T - M + i - 3$ degrees of freedom, if $H_0^1, H_0^2, \ldots, H_0^i$ are true. Note that $M - i + 3$ is just the number of parameters in a model with lag length $M - i + 1$ since there is an intercept and a zero-order lag in the model. Instead of using an F-test, a simple t-test for significance of the last coefficient β_{M-i+1} in the model

$$\mathbf{y} = X_{M-i+1}\boldsymbol{\beta}_{M-i+1} + \mathbf{e}$$

can be performed.

If this procedure is used, the choice of the order N depends on the significance levels used in the individual tests that are usually chosen to control the Type I error, that is, the probability of rejecting the null hypothesis although it is correct. In a sequential testing procedure of the foregoing type, however, the overall probability of rejecting H_0^i is not the individual significance level chosen for the ith test of the sequence (for $i > 1$). For instance, the probability of rejecting H_0^2 when it is true is the probability of rejecting H_0^1 or H_0^2. If $H_0^1, \ldots, H_0^i$ are true, the statistics $\lambda_1, \ldots, \lambda_i$ will have the corresponding F-distributions and λ_i can be shown to be independent of $\lambda_1, \ldots, \lambda_{i-1}$ for $i > 1$. Using the basic probability rule $\Pr(A$ or $B) = \Pr(A) + \Pr(B) - \Pr(A) \cdot \Pr(B)$ for independent events A and B, the overall Type I error of the ith test in the sequence is

$$\begin{aligned}
\varepsilon_i &= \Pr\{\lambda_i > F_{(1, T-M-3+i, \gamma_i)} \text{ or} \ldots \text{or } \lambda_1 > F_{(1, T-M-2, \gamma_1)}\} \\
&= \Pr\{\lambda_i > F_{(1, T-M-3+i, \gamma_i)}\} \\
&\quad + \Pr\{\lambda_{i-1} > F_{(1, T-M-4+i, \gamma_{i-1})} \text{ or} \ldots \text{or } \lambda_1 > F_{(1, T-M-2, \gamma_1)}\} \\
&\quad - \Pr\{\lambda_i > F_{(1, T-M-3+i, \gamma_i)}\} \\
&\quad \cdot \Pr\{\lambda_{i-1} > F_{(1, T-M-4+i, \gamma_{i-1})} \text{ or} \ldots \text{or } \lambda_1 > F_{(1, T-M-2, \gamma_1)}\} \\
&= \gamma_i + \varepsilon_{i-1} - \gamma_i\varepsilon_{i-1} = \gamma_i(1 - \varepsilon_{i-1}) + \varepsilon_{i-1} \qquad i = 1, 2, \ldots
\end{aligned} \tag{17.2.8}$$

where γ_i is the significance level of the ith individual test and $\varepsilon_0 = 0$. All probabilities are of course evaluated conditional on $H_0^1, \ldots, H_0^i$ being true. From (17.2.8) it follows that if we would use the same significance level for each individual test in the sequence, the Type I error will grow quite rapidly. For instance, if we choose $\gamma_k = 0.01$ for all k, we get $\varepsilon_1 = 0.01$, $\varepsilon_2 = 0.0199$, $\varepsilon_3 = 0.029701$, and so on. In practice, if the maximum lag length M is large, it may be a useful strategy to choose very small individual significance levels for the first tests in order to limit the overall probability of choosing too long a lag when this is unnecessary. In other words, the overall Type I error should be kept within a reasonable range even if a number of tests have to be carried out until the procedure terminates.

To illustrate the procedure outlined in the foregoing, we use the data on capital appropriations and expenditures given in Table 17.1. Similar data sets for these variables were used in many studies, including Almon's (1965) pioneering article on finite distributed lags. Our data set consists of quarterly data for the period 1953.I to 1974.IV, and hence we have 88 observations in the original sample. Assuming an upper bound for the lag length of $M = 10$, we use the first 10 observations as presample values and thus the remaining sample has size $T = 78$. The resulting sums of squared errors and LS variances $\hat{\sigma}_n^2$, $n = 0, 1, \ldots, 10$, are given in Table 17.2. The corresponding values of the F statistics are

$$\lambda_1 = \frac{\text{SSE}_9 - \text{SSE}_{10}}{\hat{\sigma}_{10}^2} = 1.033 \qquad (H_0^1\colon N = 9)$$

$$\lambda_2 = \frac{\text{SSE}_8 - \text{SSE}_9}{\hat{\sigma}_9^2} = 1.455 \qquad (H_0^2\colon N = 8)$$

$$\lambda_3 = \frac{\text{SSE}_7 - \text{SSE}_8}{\hat{\sigma}_8^2} = 4.287 \qquad (H_0^3\colon N = 7)$$

Using an individual significance level of $\gamma_3 = 0.05$ and noting that the critical value from the $F_{(1,68)}$ distribution is about 4 ($F_{(1,68,0.05)} = 4$) we can now terminate the testing procedure since $H_0^3\colon N = 7$ is rejected. The values λ_1 and λ_2 are smaller than the critical values from their respective F-distributions at any reasonable significance levels. Thus we choose a lag length of $\hat{N} = M - 2 = 8$. Note that in the testing procedure the sample size T is held constant ($T = 78$). In order to use the available sample information efficiently, it is advisable to re-estimate the chosen model using only $\hat{N}$ observations as presample values. With an effective sample size of $T = 80$ the following estimates are obtained.

$$\begin{aligned} y_t = {} & \underset{(56.5)}{32.4} + \underset{(0.03)}{0.04}\, x_t + \underset{(0.07)}{0.07}\, x_{t-1} + \underset{(0.09)}{0.18}\, x_{t-2} + \underset{(0.09)}{0.19}\, x_{t-3} \\ & + \underset{(0.09)}{0.17}\, x_{t-4} + \underset{(0.09)}{0.05}\, x_{t-5} + \underset{(0.10)}{0.05}\, x_{t-6} + \underset{(0.10)}{0.06}\, x_{t-7} + \underset{(0.06)}{0.13}\, x_{t-8} + \hat{e}_t \end{aligned} \tag{17.2.9}$$

Table 17.1 Seasonally Adjusted Quarterly Capital Appropriations (x) and Expenditures (y) in U.S. Manufacturing, 1953.I to 1974.IV in Millions of Current Dollars

t	y_t	x_t	t	y_t	x_t	t	y_t	x_t
1	2072	1767	31	2721	2271	61	5543	5952
2	2077	2061	32	2640	2711	62	5526	5723
3	2078	2289	33	2513	2394	63	5750	6351
4	2043	2047	34	2448	2457	64	5761	6636
5	2062	1856	35	2429	2720	65	5943	6799
6	2067	1842	36	2516	2703	66	6212	7753
7	1964	1866	37	2534	2992	67	6631	7595
8	1981	2279	38	2494	2516	68	6828	7436
9	1914	2688	39	2596	2817	69	6645	6679
10	1991	3264	40	2572	3153	70	6703	6475
11	2129	3896	41	2601	2756	71	6659	6319
12	2309	4014	42	2548	3269	72	6337	5860
13	2614	4041	43	2840	3657	73	6165	5705
14	2896	3710	44	2937	3941	74	5875	5521
15	3058	3383	45	3136	4123	75	5798	5920
16	3309	3431	46	3299	4656	76	5921	5937
17	3446	3613	47	3514	4906	77	5772	6570
18	3466	3205	48	3815	4344	78	5874	7087
19	3435	2426	49	4040	5080	79	5872	7206
20	3183	2330	50	4274	5539	80	6159	8431
21	2697	1954	51	4565	5583	81	6583	9718
22	2338	1936	52	4838	6147	82	6961	10921
23	2140	2201	53	5222	6545	83	7449	11672
24	2012	2233	54	5406	6770	84	8093	12199
25	2071	2690	55	5705	5955	85	9013	12865
26	2192	2940	56	5871	6015	86	9752	14985
27	2240	3127	57	5953	6029	87	10704	16378
28	2421	3131	58	5868	5975	88	11597	12680
29	2639	2872	59	5573	5894			
30	2733	2515	60	5672	5951			

Source: Conference Board.

Here the numbers in parentheses are the standard errors of the lag weight estimators conditional on $\hat{N} = 8$ being the "true" lag length.

One of the problems with the procedure described in the foregoing is that the distribution of the final estimates is only known if the chosen lag length $\hat{N}$ is assumed to be greater than or equal to the true lag length N. As noted earlier $\mathbf{b}_{\hat{N}}$ is inefficient if $\hat{N} > N$ and $\mathbf{b}_{\hat{N}}$ will be biased if $\hat{N} < N$. Furthermore, for proper

Table 17.2 Estimation Results for Capital Appropriations and Expenditures Data

Lag length n	Sum of squared errors SSE_n	LS variance estimate $\hat{\sigma}_n^2$	AIC(n)	SC(n)
0	46 113 030	606 750	13.290	13.290
1	27 622 060	368 294	12.803	12.833
2	15 288 790	206 605	12.237	12.298
3	8 415 885	115 286	11.666	11.756
4	5 282 236	73 364	11.226	11.347
5	3 860 799	54 377	10.938	11.089
6	3 036 641	43 381	10.723	10.905
7	2 617 053	37 928	10.600	10.812
8	2 461 847	36 204	10.565	10.807
9	2 409 515	35 963	10.569	10.841
10	2 372 389	35 945	10.579	10.881

inference it is desirable to know the unconditional distribution (not conditional on $\hat{N}$) of the *pretest estimator* $\mathbf{b}_{\hat{N}}$. That is, in evaluating the distribution of $\mathbf{b}_{\hat{N}}$ it should be taken into account that $\hat{N}$ is chosen in a sequential testing procedure. Unfortunately the unconditional distribution is in general not known (see Section 20.3.1).

A number of other procedures for choosing $\hat{N}$ have been proposed that are, however, subject to similar criticisms as the procedure discussed in the foregoing. For instance, it has been proposed to test the sequence of hypotheses

H_0^1: $N = M - 1$, that is, $\beta_M = 0$ versus H_a^1: $N = M$, that is, $\beta_M \neq 0$

H_0^2: $N = M - 2$, that is, $\beta_{M-1} = \beta_M = 0$ versus H_a^2: $N > M - 2$, that is, β_{M-1} or $\beta_M \neq 0$

$\vdots$

H_0^i: $N = M - i$, that is, $\beta_{M+1-i} = \cdots = \beta_M = 0$ versus H_a^i: $N > M - i$, that is, β_{M+1-i} or $\cdots$ or $\beta_M \neq 0$

$\vdots$

where each null hypothesis is tested against the full model with maximum lag length M. Again, likelihood ratio F-statistics can be used in this procedure. Such a sequence of tests has some undesirable properties in addition to those of the procedure in (17.2.3). One of them is that the statistics used in the sequence of tests will not be independent so that the Type I error of the testing sequence is difficult to determine. The procedure therefore cannot be recommended.

Another possibility of choosing the lag length would be to optimize some kind of objective function. For instance, one could choose $\hat{N}$ such that the adjusted $R^2(\bar{R}^2)$ is maximized. Following Chapter 5, the $\bar{R}^2$ measure for the present case is defined as

$$\bar{R}_n^2 = 1 - \frac{\hat{\sigma}_n^2}{\text{SST}/(T-1)} \tag{17.2.10}$$

where SST is the total sum of squares $\sum_{t=1}^{T}(y_t - \bar{y})^2$. Of course, $\bar{R}_n^2$ reaches its maximum when $\hat{\sigma}_n^2$ assumes a minimum. The first M (upper bound for the lag length) observations are again treated as presample values in computing the $\hat{\sigma}_n^2$. For these data the minimum is reached for $n = 10$ (see Table 17.2). Thus, based on this criterion, $\hat{N} = 10$ would be chosen as lag the length. Again, little is known about the unconditional distribution of the lag weight estimates when such an ad hoc criterion is used.

Other criteria that may be used for determining the lag length are summarized in Section 20.4 and in Judge, et al. (1985, Chapter 9). For instance, Akaike's AIC criterion,

$$\text{AIC}(n) = \ln \tilde{\sigma}_n^2 + \frac{2n}{T} \tag{17.2.11}$$

or Schwarz's SC criterion,

$$\text{SC}(n) = \ln \tilde{\sigma}_n^2 + \frac{n \ln T}{T} \tag{17.2.12}$$

may be used for model choice. Here $\tilde{\sigma}_n^2$ is the ML estimator of the residual variance obtained from a model with lag length n, that is, $\tilde{\sigma}_n^2 = \text{SSE}_n/T$. For both criteria the lag length estimate $\hat{N}$ is chosen so as to minimize the criterion used. For the example data the values of the two criteria are also given in Table 17.2. Both criteria assume the minimum for $n = 8$ so that $\hat{N} = 8$ is chosen as lag length. For a general critique of procedures for selecting the set of regressors, refer to Section 20.4.

As noted earlier, one problem in estimating the lag coefficients β_i is that there may be an almost linear dependence between the columns of the X matrix. In such a case, LS estimators of individual coefficients may be very imprecise. For the data used in the example, this problem is reflected in the relatively large standard errors of some of the estimates [see (17.2.9)]. In the context of choosing the lag length this problem is severe since it may cause the tests to have little power against the alternatives. In other words, in the testing procedures for selecting the lag length a null hypothesis H_0^i may not be rejected simply because there is insufficient sample information in favor of the alternative and not because H_0^i is true. Thus, the lag length may in fact be longer than is indicated by the testing procedures. One possible cure for the multicollinearity problem is discussed in the following section.

17.3 Finite Polynomial Lags

17.3.1 Estimation When the Lag Length and Polynomial Degree are Known

One possible method of reducing the effect of multicollinearity in this context that has been quite popular was proposed by Almon (1965). If the lag distribution has a smooth shape, the lag coefficients will fall on a smooth curve. Since polynomials are smooth functions, Almon suggests using polynomials to reduce the parameter space. For a finite number of points, $n + 1$, say, a polynomial of order not greater than n can be found that passes through these points (see Fig. 17.2*a*). The polynomial degree may be substantially lower than n if the points lie approximately on a smooth curve (see Fig. 17.2*b*). Since Almon pioneered this approach, polynomial lags are often called *Almon lags.*

To clarify this approach, suppose that we have only four lag weights $\beta_0, \beta_1, \beta_2,$ and β_3. Then there is a polynomial $P(n) = \alpha_0 + n\alpha_1 + n^2\alpha_2 + n^3\alpha_3$ such that

$$\begin{aligned}\beta_0 &= \alpha_0 + 0\alpha_1 + 0^2\alpha_2 + 0^3\alpha_3\\ \beta_1 &= \alpha_0 + 1\alpha_1 + 1^2\alpha_2 + 1^3\alpha_3\\ \beta_2 &= \alpha_0 + 2\alpha_1 + 2^2\alpha_2 + 2^3\alpha_3\\ \beta_4 &= \alpha_0 + 3\alpha_1 + 3^2\alpha_2 + 3^3\alpha_3\end{aligned}$$

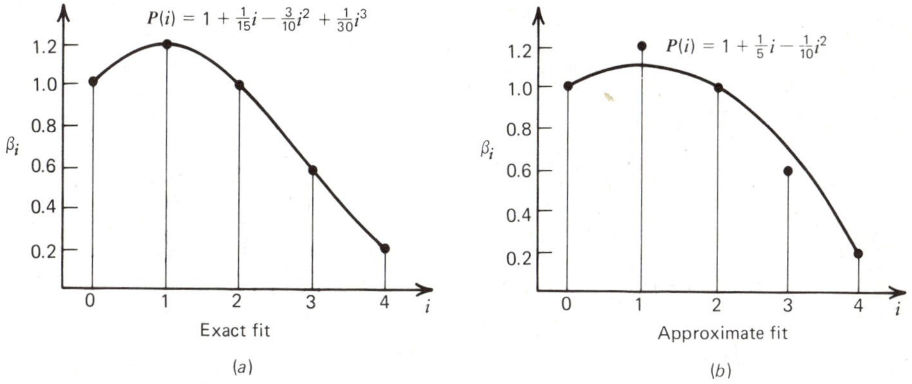

Figure 17.2 Polynomial lag weights.

or, in matrix notation,

$$\begin{bmatrix}\beta_0\\ \beta_1\\ \beta_2\\ \beta_3\end{bmatrix} = \begin{bmatrix}1 & 0 & 0 & 0 & \alpha_0\\ 1 & 1 & 1 & 1 & \alpha_1\\ 1 & 2 & 4 & 8 & \alpha_2\\ 1 & 3 & 9 & 27 & \alpha_3\end{bmatrix}$$

or

$$\boldsymbol{\beta} = W\boldsymbol{\alpha}$$

where $\boldsymbol{\beta}$, W, and $\boldsymbol{\alpha}$ have the obvious definitions. Here the number of polynomial coefficients equals the number of lag weights, and thus no constraints are imposed on the β_i by requiring this relationship to hold. Clearly, for any vector $\boldsymbol{\beta}$ there is a vector $\boldsymbol{\alpha}$ such that $\boldsymbol{\beta} = W\boldsymbol{\alpha}$ is fulfilled. Since W is nonsingular, $\boldsymbol{\alpha} = W^{-1}\boldsymbol{\beta}$.

To reduce the degree of the polynomial by 1 means to restrict α_3 to be zero so that

$$\begin{bmatrix}\beta_0\\ \beta_1\\ \beta_2\\ \beta_3\end{bmatrix} = \begin{bmatrix}1 & 0 & 0\\ 1 & 1 & 1\\ 1 & 2 & 4\\ 1 & 3 & 9\end{bmatrix}\begin{bmatrix}\alpha_0\\ \alpha_1\\ \alpha_2\end{bmatrix}$$

Similarly, the β_i falling on a polynomial of degree 1 means that

$$\begin{bmatrix}\beta_0\\ \beta_1\\ \beta_2\\ \beta_3\end{bmatrix} = \begin{bmatrix}1 & 0\\ 1 & 1\\ 1 & 2\\ 1 & 3\end{bmatrix}\begin{bmatrix}\alpha_0\\ \alpha_1\end{bmatrix}$$

More generally, if the lag weights $\beta_0, \beta_1, \ldots, \beta_N$ fall on a polynomial of order Q, that is,

$$\beta_i = P(i) = \alpha_0 + \alpha_1 i + \cdots + \alpha_Q i^Q \qquad i = 0, 1, \ldots, N$$

this system of equations can be written as

$$\begin{bmatrix}\beta_0\\ \beta_1\\ \vdots\\ \beta_N\end{bmatrix} = \begin{bmatrix}1 & 0 & 0 & \cdots & 0\\ 1 & 1 & 1 & \cdots & 1\\ 1 & 2 & 2^2 & \cdots & 2^Q\\ \vdots & \vdots & \vdots & \ddots & \vdots\\ 1 & N & N^2 & \cdots & N^Q\end{bmatrix}\begin{bmatrix}\alpha_0\\ \alpha_1\\ \vdots\\ \alpha_Q\end{bmatrix} \tag{17.3.1}$$

or, more compactly,

$$\boldsymbol{\beta} = H_Q\boldsymbol{\alpha}_Q \tag{17.3.2}$$

Since $\boldsymbol{\alpha}_Q$ involves only $Q + 1$ coefficients, we have reduced the parameter space from $N + 1$ to $Q + 1$ dimensions. In other words, we have imposed $N - Q$ restrictions on the β_i by restricting them to lie on a polynomial of degree Q. Note that the intercept term is deleted here to simplify the exposition.

Given the relationship (17.3.2) the linear model $\mathbf{y} = X\boldsymbol{\beta} + \mathbf{e}$ becomes

$$\mathbf{y} = XH_Q\boldsymbol{\alpha}_Q + \mathbf{e} = Z\boldsymbol{\alpha}_Q + \mathbf{e} \tag{17.3.3}$$

where $Z = XH_Q$. Using this model, the LS estimator for $\boldsymbol{\alpha}_Q$ is $\hat{\boldsymbol{\alpha}}_Q = (Z'Z)^{-1}Z'\mathbf{y}$ and the RLS (restricted least squares) estimator for $\boldsymbol{\beta}$ is

$$\hat{\boldsymbol{\beta}} = H_Q\hat{\boldsymbol{\alpha}}_Q = H_Q(Z'Z)^{-1}Z'\mathbf{y} \tag{17.3.4}$$

Thus, if we assume the model is correctly specified and $\mathbf{e} \sim (\mathbf{0}, \sigma^2 I)$

$$\hat{\boldsymbol{\alpha}}_Q \sim [\boldsymbol{\alpha}_Q, \sigma^2(Z'Z)^{-1}] \tag{17.3.5}$$

and hence $E[\hat{\boldsymbol{\beta}}] = E[H_Q\hat{\boldsymbol{\alpha}}_Q] = H_QE[\hat{\boldsymbol{\alpha}}_Q] = H_Q\boldsymbol{\alpha}_Q = \boldsymbol{\beta}$. Moreover,

$$\begin{aligned} E[(\hat{\boldsymbol{\beta}} - \boldsymbol{\beta})(\hat{\boldsymbol{\beta}} - \boldsymbol{\beta})'] &= E[(H_Q\hat{\boldsymbol{\alpha}}_Q - H_Q\boldsymbol{\alpha}_Q)(H_Q\hat{\boldsymbol{\alpha}}_Q - H_Q\boldsymbol{\alpha}_Q)'] \\ &= H_QE[(\hat{\boldsymbol{\alpha}}_Q - \boldsymbol{\alpha}_Q)(\hat{\boldsymbol{\alpha}}_Q - \boldsymbol{\alpha}_Q)']H'_Q \\ &= \sigma^2 H_Q(Z'Z)^{-1}H'_Q \end{aligned}$$

and thus

$$\hat{\boldsymbol{\beta}} \sim (\boldsymbol{\beta}, \sigma^2 H_Q(Z'Z)^{-1}H'_Q) \tag{17.3.6}$$

Consequently, if we know the true polynomial degree Q and the true lag length N, the estimation of the polynomial lag is straightforward. The more difficult part of a distributed lag analysis is to determine the correct polynomial degree and/or lag length. In the following we will discuss a possible procedure for specifying the polynomial degree under the assumption that the lag length has been determined previously.

17.3.2 Determining the Polynomial Degree

From the previous discussion it is obvious that choosing the polynomial degree Q comes down to choosing the dimension of the $\boldsymbol{\alpha}$ vector. This problem is similar to choosing the lag length as discussed in Section 17.2. For a fixed, known lag length N we can therefore use a sequential testing procedure to determine the polynomial degree Q. Starting with $Q = N$, the polynomial degree is sequentially reduced, and the implied parameter restrictions are tested using a likelihood ratio or t-test statistic. The polynomial degree corresponding to the last null hypothesis that cannot be rejected is taken as being an adequate choice. The null hypotheses to be tested sequentially are

$$
\begin{aligned}
&H_0^1\colon Q = N - 1, \\
&H_0^2\colon Q = N - 2, \text{ given } H_0^1 \\
&\quad\vdots \qquad\qquad\quad \vdots \\
&H_0^i\colon Q = N - i, \text{ given } H_0^1, \ldots, H_0^{i-1} \\
&\quad\vdots \qquad\qquad\quad \vdots
\end{aligned}
\tag{17.3.7}
$$

As in (17.2.3), each hypothesis is tested conditionally on the previous one being true. An appropriate test statistic for testing H_0^i is

$$\lambda_i = \frac{\text{SSE}_{N,N-i} - \text{SSE}_{N,N-i+1}}{\hat{\sigma}^2_{N,N-i+1}} \tag{17.3.8}$$

where

$$\text{SSE}_{N,Q} = (\mathbf{y} - Z\hat{\boldsymbol{\alpha}}_Q)'(\mathbf{y} - Z\hat{\boldsymbol{\alpha}}_Q) \tag{17.3.9}$$

is the sum of squared errors for a model with lag length N and polynomial degree Q, and

$$\hat{\sigma}^2_{N,Q} = \frac{\text{SSE}_{N,Q}}{T - Q - 1} \tag{17.3.10}$$

If $H_0^1, \ldots, H_0^i$ are true, the statistic λ_i has a central F-distribution with 1 and $T - N + i - 2$ degrees of freedom. The procedure is equivalent to using a t-test for the last coefficient of $\boldsymbol{\alpha}_{N-i+1}$ in testing H_0^i.

For the example data on capital appropriations (x) and expenditures (y) the values taken by the test statistics λ_i using a lag length of $N = 8$ are given in Table 17.3. Since H_0^6 is rejected using a level of significance $\gamma_6 = 0.05$ for the sixth individual test, we choose $\hat{Q} = N - 5 = 3$ as the polynomial degree. The unconstrained lags (estimated without intercept) and the polynomial lag weights for $\hat{Q} = 3$ are given in Figure 17.3. Concerning this example see also Exercises 17.9 and 17.10.

The sequential testing procedure described in the foregoing involves the same problems as the procedure for determining the lag length. In particular, the overall Type I error of the procedure is different from the Type I errors of the individual tests. This problem is aggravated if the lag length has also been determined by a

Table 17.3 Values of Test Statistics for Selecting the Polynomial Degree (Model without Intercept) $F_{(1,\cdot,0.05)} \simeq 4$, $F_{(1,\cdot,0.01)} \simeq 7$

i	H_0^i	λ_i
1	$Q = 7$	0.064
2	$Q = 6$	0.012
3	$Q = 5$	0.006
4	$Q = 4$	0.728
5	$Q = 3$	1.541
6	$Q = 2$	5.472
7	$Q = 1$	9.275
8	$Q = 0$	1.128

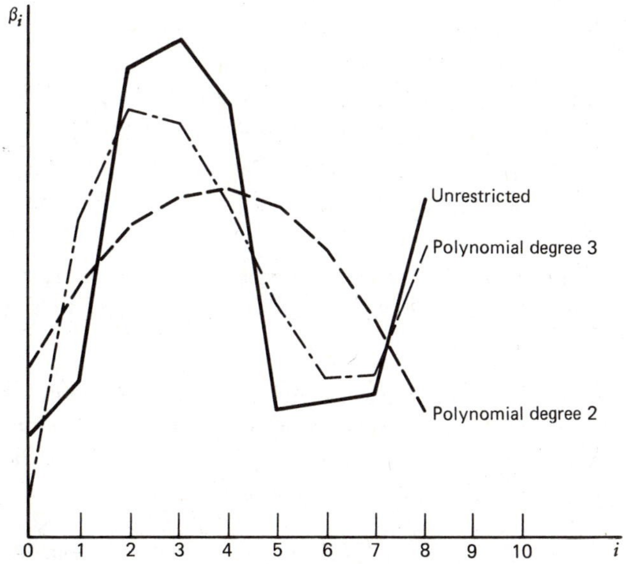

Figure 17.3 Lag weights for capital appropriations and expenditures data.

sequential testing procedure. In this case, the determination of lag length and polynomial degree has to be viewed as one procedure and the overall Type I error of that procedure is of interest. In general, this Type I error is unknown. Also, it should be kept in mind that the distribution of the resulting estimators of the lag coefficients is known conditionally on the lag length and polynomial degree being known. If these quantities are chosen by a statistical procedure, the resulting coefficient estimators are pretest estimators with generally unknown distributions. More details on choosing polynomial degree and lag length are given in Judge, *et al.* (1985, Chapter 9). Some problems related to the use of polynomial lags are summarized in the following.

17.3.3 Problems Related to the Use of Polynomial Lags

Since in practice the polynomial degree and lag length are rarely known in advance, it is useful to know the consequences of misspecifying these quantities. There are a number of studies on this topic [Judge, *et al.* (1985, Chapter 9)]. The main conclusions are

1. If the assumed polynomial degree is correct, but the assumed lag length is greater than the true lag length, the polynomial distributed lag estimator will generally be biased. It will definitely be biased if the difference between the assumed and true lag length is greater than the degree of the approximating polynomial.
2. If the assumed polynomial degree is correct, then understating the true lag length usually leads to bias in the polynomial distributed lag estimator.
3. If the assumed lag length is correct, but the assumed polynomial is of an order higher than the true polynomial, the polynomial distributed lag estimator is unbiased but inefficient.
4. If the assumed lag length is correct, but the assumed polynomial is of lower order than the true polynomial, then the polynomial distributed lag estimator is always biased.

In addition, it should be kept in mind that the testing procedures presented in the foregoing for determining the polynomial degree and lag length rely on assumptions that may not be satisfied in practice. We have assumed that the model errors e_t are identically, independently, normally distributed. Of course, it is possible that the errors of a dynamic model such as (17.2.1) are autocorrelated or heteroskedastic. A misspecified error process puts additional limits on the reliability of tests for the polynomial degree and the lag length.

17.4 Infinite Distributed Lags

Truncating the infinite distributed lag relationship (17.1.1) after a finite number of lags is reasonable because in practice the lag weights are not distinguishable from zero at high lags. Doing so, however, requires the determination of an adequate truncation point, which can cause problems of the type discussed in the previous section. Furthermore, a parameterization of the lag weights that leads to an infinite lag may require fewer parameters than a finite lag model. Moreover, it is sometimes theoretically more appealing to consider a model that allows explicitly for lags of infinite length if such a model is derived from theoretical considerations. Two behavioral hypotheses that lead to infinite distributed lag models will be presented in Section 17.4.1. In Section 17.4.2 the estimation of a special infinite distributed lag model is considered and some other infinite lag models are briefly described in Section 17.4.3.

17.4.1 Two Dynamic Economic Models

17.4.1a Adaptive Expectations

Assume that the supply of a commodity y that is related to the expected market price x^* can be modeled in the following way:

$$y_t = \alpha_0 + \alpha_1 x_t^* + e_t \tag{17.4.1}$$

where α_0 and α_1 are constant parameters and e_t is a random component. Furthermore, assume the expectations are revised in proportion to the difference between the expected and actual price in the previous period. In other words, the revision is proportional to the error in predicting the price in the previous period:

$$x_t^* - x_{t-1}^* = \lambda(x_{t-1} - x_{t-1}^*) \tag{17.4.2}$$

where $0 < \lambda < 1$ and x_{t-1} is the actual price in period $t - 1$. This situation may arise if the time to produce a commodity is long, as is the case for many agricultural goods.

To replace the unobservable x_t^* in (17.4.1) by an observable variable we solve (17.4.2) for x_{t-1}. This can be done conveniently by using the lag operator L, which was introduced in Section 16.2.4 and is defined by $Lx_t^* = x_{t-1}^*$. Thus we may write (17.4.2) as

$$\lambda x_{t-1} = x_t^* - (1 - \lambda)x_{t-1}^* = [1 - (1 - \lambda)L]x_t^* \tag{17.4.3}$$

It was also shown in Section 16.2.4 that the inverse of the operator $[1 - (1 - \lambda)L]$ is

$$[1 - (1 - \lambda)L]^{-1} = 1 + (1 - \lambda)L + (1 - \lambda)^2L^2 + \cdots \tag{17.4.4}$$

In other words,

$$[1 + (1 - \lambda)L + (1 - \lambda)^2L^2 + \cdots][1 - (1 - \lambda)L] = 1 \tag{17.4.5}$$

Hence premultiplying (17.4.3) by (17.4.4) gives

$$\begin{aligned} x_t^* &= [1 + (1 - \lambda)L + (1 - \lambda)^2L^2 + \cdots]\lambda x_{t-1} \\ &= \lambda x_{t-1} + \lambda(1 - \lambda)x_{t-2} + \lambda(1 - \lambda)^2 x_{t-3} + \cdots \end{aligned} \tag{17.4.6}$$

Substituting this in (17.4.1) results in

$$y_t = \alpha_0 + \alpha_1\lambda[x_{t-1} + (1 - \lambda)x_{t-2} + (1 - \lambda)^2 x_{t-3} + \cdots] + e_t \tag{17.4.7}$$

This is a special form of (17.1.1), with $\beta_0 = 0$, $\beta_1 = \alpha_1\lambda$, $\beta_2 = \alpha_1\lambda(1 - \lambda)$, $\beta_3 = \alpha_1\lambda(1 - \lambda)^2, \ldots$. Such a model is often called a *geometric lag* model since the lag weights decline geometrically (see Fig. 17.1).

17.4.1b Partial Adjustment

The partial adjustment hypothesis also leads to an infinite distributed lag model. The basic idea is that the current value of the independent variable determines the "desired" value of the dependent variable.

$$y_t^* = \alpha_0 + \alpha_1 x_t + v_t \tag{17.4.8}$$

but only some fixed fraction (γ) of the desired adjustment is accomplished in one period.

$$y_t - y_{t-1} = \gamma(y_t^* - y_{t-1}) \tag{17.4.9}$$

where $0 < \gamma < 1$ is the *coefficient of adjustment*. For instance, the desired investment of a firm may depend on the demand for its products. Because of institutional constraints, only a gradual adjustment to the desired level may be possible. Combining (17.4.8) and (17.4.9) gives

$$y_t = \alpha_0\gamma + \alpha_1\gamma x_t + (1 - \gamma)y_{t-1} + \gamma v_t \tag{17.4.10}$$

or

$$\begin{aligned} y_t &= \alpha_0 + \frac{\alpha_1\gamma}{1 - (1 - \gamma)L} x_t + \frac{\gamma}{1 - (1 - \gamma)L} v_t \\ &= \alpha_0 + \alpha_1\gamma x_t + \alpha_1\gamma(1 - \gamma)x_{t-1} + \alpha_1\gamma(1 - \gamma)^2 x_{t-2} + \cdots + u_t \end{aligned} \tag{17.4.11}$$

Again we have a geometric lag model. Estimation of this type of model will be discussed in the following.

17.4.2 Estimation of the Geometric Lag Model

17.4.2a Least Squares Estimation

Let us consider the geometric lag model in the form (17.4.10) or

$$y_t = \gamma_0 + \gamma_1 x_t + \lambda y_{t-1} + e_t \tag{17.4.12}$$

The parameters $\boldsymbol{\gamma} = (\gamma_0, \gamma_1, \lambda)'$ may be estimated by the least squares (LS) method if the e_t satisfy the standard conditions, that is, $\mathbf{e} = (e_2, \ldots, e_T)' \sim (\mathbf{0}, \sigma^2 I)$. However, we have a stochastic regressor situation with the lagged dependent variable being a regressor. Therefore, in line with results presented in Chapter 13, the LS estimator

$$\hat{\boldsymbol{\gamma}} = \begin{bmatrix} \hat{\gamma}_0 \\ \hat{\gamma}_1 \\ \hat{\lambda} \end{bmatrix} = (X'X)^{-1}X'\mathbf{y} \tag{17.4.13}$$

where

$$\mathbf{y} = \begin{bmatrix} y_2 \\ y_3 \\ \vdots \\ y_T \end{bmatrix} \quad \text{and} \quad X = \begin{bmatrix} 1 & x_2 & y_1 \\ 1 & x_3 & y_2 \\ \vdots & \vdots & \vdots \\ 1 & x_T & y_{T-1} \end{bmatrix}$$

is not best linear unbiased. It is consistent, though, and consistent estimators of the original parameters α_0, α_1 and γ in (17.4.10) can be obtained from $\hat{\boldsymbol{\gamma}}$ by noting that $\gamma_0 = \alpha_0\gamma$, $\gamma_1 = \alpha_1\gamma$, and $\lambda = 1 - \gamma$. Consequently,

$$\gamma = 1 - \lambda, \quad \alpha_0 = \frac{\gamma_0}{1-\lambda}, \quad \text{and} \quad \alpha_1 = \frac{\gamma_1}{1-\lambda}$$

Consistent estimators of these parameters are obtained by replacing γ_0, γ_1 and λ by their LS estimators.

Recall from Chapters 6 and 13 that the consistency of the LS estimator $\hat{\boldsymbol{\gamma}} = (X'X)^{-1}X'\mathbf{y} = \boldsymbol{\gamma} + (X'X)^{-1}X'\mathbf{e}$ follows by writing

$$\begin{aligned} \text{plim}\, \hat{\boldsymbol{\gamma}} &= \boldsymbol{\gamma} + \text{plim}\, [(X'X)^{-1}X'\mathbf{e}] \\ &= \boldsymbol{\gamma} + \text{plim}\left(\frac{X'X}{T}\right)^{-1} \text{plim}\left(\frac{X'\mathbf{e}}{T}\right) \end{aligned} \tag{17.4.14}$$

and assuming that plim $(X'X/T)$ is a nonsingular matrix, whereas plim $(X'\mathbf{e}/T)$ is zero. To understand the latter condition for the present case, note that

$$\frac{X'\mathbf{e}}{T} = \begin{bmatrix} \frac{1}{T}\sum_{t=2}^{T} e_t \\ \frac{1}{T}\sum_{t=2}^{T} x_t e_t \\ \frac{1}{T}\sum_{t=2}^{T} y_{t-1} e_t \end{bmatrix} \tag{17.4.15}$$

The probability limit of the first component,

$$\text{plim}\, \frac{1}{T}\sum_{t=2}^{T} e_t$$

is zero since the sample mean is a consistent estimator for $E[e_t] = 0$. Moreover, under general assumptions, the second component of (17.4.15) is a consistent estimator of $E[x_t e_t]$, which is zero since the exogenous variables x_t are assumed to be independent of the error terms e_t. In fact, at this stage the x_t may be assumed to be nonstochastic. Thus,

$$\text{plim}\, \frac{1}{T}\sum_{t=2}^{T} x_t e_t = 0$$

Finally, $\sum y_{t-1}e_t/T$ is a consistent estimator of $E[y_{t-1}e_t]$ and thus,

$$\text{plim}\, \frac{1}{T}\sum_{t=2}^{T} y_{t-1} e_t = 0$$

if y_{t-1} and e_t are uncorrelated. Hence, this latter condition is crucial for $\hat{\gamma}$ to be a consistent estimator of γ.

If e_t is correlated with e_{t-1}, the regressor y_{t-1} will be correlated with the disturbance e_t, and thus $\hat{\gamma}$ will be inconsistent. Consequently, if e_t is for example an autoregressive process or a moving average process, $\hat{\gamma}$ will be inconsistent. Note that y_{t-1} is correlated with e_{t-1} as this term is the disturbance of the equation

$$y_{t-1} = \gamma_0 + \gamma_1 x_{t-1} + \lambda y_{t-2} + e_{t-1}$$

Therefore, if e_t is correlated with e_{t-1}, e_t will also be correlated with y_{t-1}. If a geometric lag model of the form (17.4.7) with uncorrelated disturbances e_t is given, transforming it to the form (17.4.12) results in autocorrelated disturbances. Also, in the model (17.4.8), the errors may be autocorrelated, in which case autocorrelated disturbances will also be present in (17.4.12). In such situations alternatives to LS estimation are required.

17.4.2b Instrumental Variable Estimation

In Chapter 13 one possible method of coping with the estimation problem if errors and regressors are correlated was proposed. It was suggested that an instrumental variable estimator, which is consistent although not necessarily efficient, be used.

In our case the model is

$$\mathbf{y} = X\boldsymbol{\gamma} + \mathbf{e} \tag{17.4.16}$$

with $\mathbf{y}$, X, $\boldsymbol{\gamma}$, and $\mathbf{e}$ as in Section 17.4.2a. The instrumental variable estimator for this model is

$$\hat{\boldsymbol{\gamma}}_{iv} = (Z'X)^{-1}Z'\mathbf{y} \tag{17.4.17}$$

where Z is a $[(T-1) \times 3]$ matrix of instrumental variables that must satisfy the following conditions:

1. Z has to be correlated with X such that plim $T^{-1}Z'X = \Sigma_{zx}$ exists and is nonsingular.
2. Z should be uncorrelated with the error vector $\mathbf{e}$ in the sense that plim $T^{-1}Z'\mathbf{e} = \mathbf{0}$.

Since y_{t-1} depends on x_{t-1}, these two variables should be correlated. Also, x_{t-1} is assumed to be uncorrelated with the residuals. Thus x_{t-1} qualifies as an instrument for y_{t-1}, and the matrix

$$Z = \begin{bmatrix} 1 & x_2 & x_1 \\ 1 & x_3 & x_2 \\ \vdots & \vdots & \vdots \\ 1 & x_T & x_{T-1} \end{bmatrix} \tag{17.4.18}$$

fulfills the two desired requirements.

To illustrate the difference between instrumental variable and LS estimation we have generated 100 samples of size 100 using the model

$$y_t = x_t + 0.5y_{t-1} + u_t - 0.5u_{t-1} \tag{17.4.19}$$

where the u_t are artificially generated $N(0, 1)$ random numbers and the $x_1, x_2, \ldots, x_{100}$ are also $N(0, 1)$ random numbers. Note that there is no intercept in the model (i.e., $\gamma_0 = 0$), $\gamma_1 = 1.0$, and $\lambda = 0.5$. We have used the first 20, the first 50, and all 100 observations in each sample to compute instrumental variable and LS estimates. The resulting frequency distributions are given in Figures 17.4 and 17.5, respectively. For both estimation methods and both parameters the estimator variability decreases with increasing sample size. However, most of the LS estimates for λ fall in the interval (0.2, 0.4), which indicates that the LS estimator is inconsistent. To see why the results of this sampling experiment do not suggest

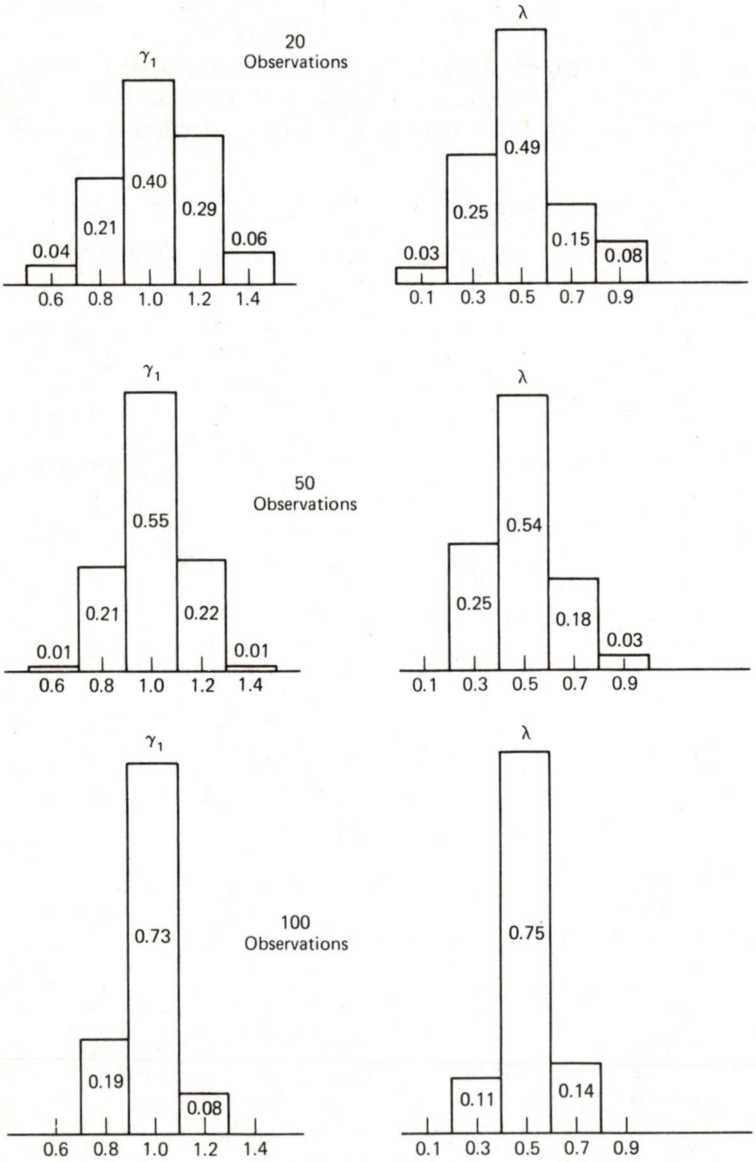

Figure 17.4 Frequency distributions for instrumental variable estimators.

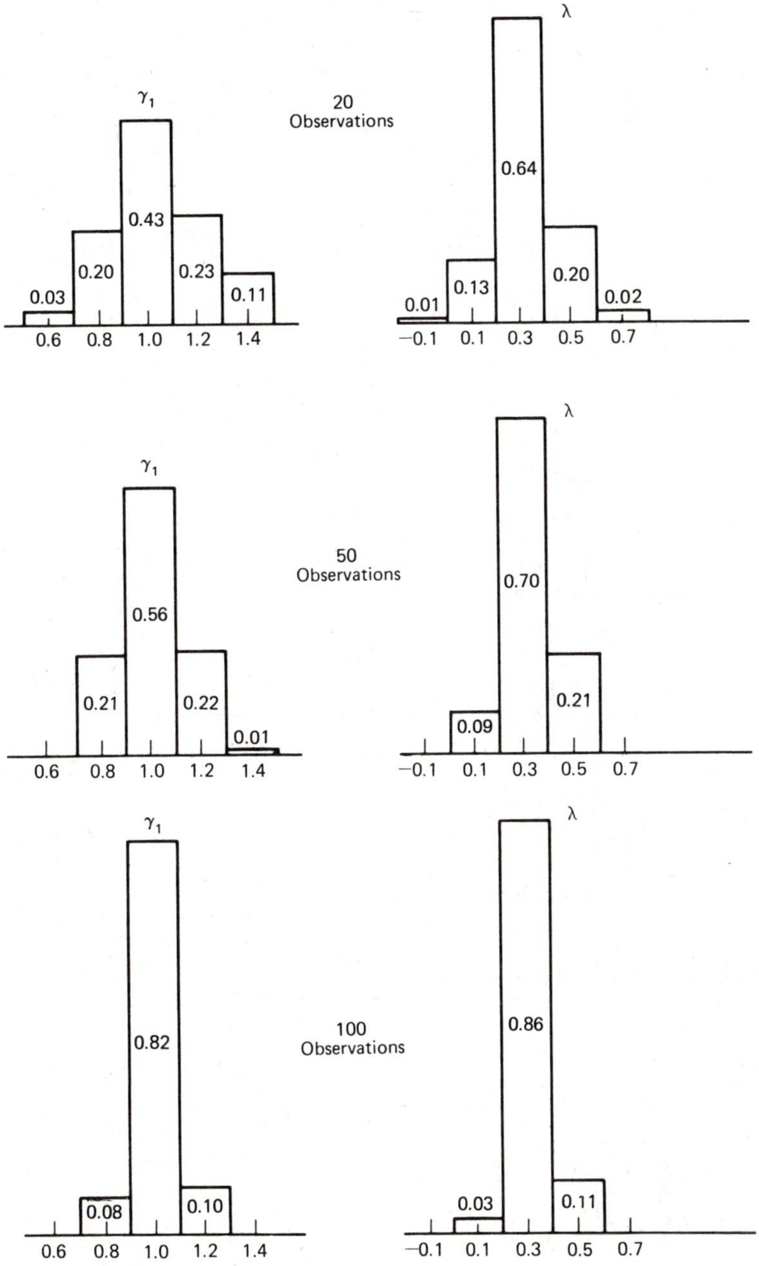

Figure 17.5 Frequency distributions for least squares estimators.

Table 17.4 Some Estimates of the Parameters of a Geometric Lag Model ($\gamma_1 = 1$, $\lambda = 0.5$)

Number of Data Set	Observations Used	LS Estimates		Instrumental Variable Estimates		ML Estimates	
		γ_1	λ	γ_1	λ	γ_1	λ
1	20	0.95	0.15	0.94	0.25	0.83	0.20
	50	0.85	0.36	0.82	0.65	0.88	0.50
	100	0.92	0.32	0.88	0.62	0.93	0.50
2	20	1.06	0.30	0.99	0.43	1.08	0.30
	50	1.20	0.18	1.20	0.29	1.24	0.40
	100	1.15	0.25	1.12	0.42	1.09	0.50
3	20	0.96	0.36	0.85	0.68	1.17	0.50
	50	0.97	0.28	0.95	0.44	1.01	0.50
	100	0.96	0.21	0.90	0.44	0.96	0.40
4	20	1.06	0.45	1.06	0.47	1.07	0.60
	50	0.93	0.27	0.98	0.63	1.01	0.60
	100	0.94	0.28	0.91	0.67	0.93	0.60
5	20	0.87	0.52	0.93	0.76	1.05	0.90
	50	0.86	0.30	0.98	0.50	0.86	0.70
	100	1.02	0.35	1.01	0.49	1.02	0.50

inconsistency of the LS estimator for γ_1, see Exercise 17.11. The estimation results obtained for five samples are given in Table 17.4.

17.4.2c Maximum Likelihood Estimation

The instrumental variable estimator does not require any specific assumption regarding the distribution of the error terms e_t. If such information exists, it is plausible that the instrumental variables estimator that neglects this information may be improved on in terms of asymptotic efficiency. If in the model

$$y_t = \alpha_0 + \gamma_1 x_t + \gamma_1 \lambda x_{t-1} + \gamma_1 \lambda^2 x_{t-2} + \cdots + e_t \tag{17.4.20}$$

the error terms $\mathbf{e} = (e_1, \ldots, e_T)'$ are $N(\mathbf{0}, \sigma^2 I)$ distributed, the maximum likelihood estimator can be used.

We note that (17.4.20) can be written as

$$y_t = \alpha_0 + \gamma_1 x_t + \gamma_1 \lambda x_{t-1} + \cdots + \gamma_1 \lambda^{t-1} x_1 + \eta \lambda^t + e_t \tag{17.4.21}$$

where

$$\eta = \gamma_1 x_0 + \gamma_1 \lambda x_{-1} + \gamma_1 \lambda^2 x_{-2} + \cdots \tag{17.4.22}$$

Since η does not depend on t, it can be treated as a further parameter in the model. Under the assumption that the e_t are independently, identically, normally distributed, the ML estimator is equivalent to the nonlinear LS estimator (see Chapter 12) that minimizes the sum of squared errors

$$\begin{aligned} S(\alpha_0, \gamma_1, \lambda, \eta) &= \sum_{t=1}^{T} e_t^2 \\ &= \sum_{t=1}^{T} [y_t - (\alpha_0 + \gamma_1 x_t + \gamma_1 \lambda x_{t-1} + \cdots + \gamma_1 \lambda^{t-1} x_1 + \eta \lambda^t)]^2 \end{aligned} \tag{17.4.23}$$

Since (17.4.21) is nonlinear in the parameters, numerical procedures have to be employed to minimize the sum of squared errors. A simplifying fact in the present situation is that the model is linear for any fixed λ. For a given λ we get

$$y_t = \alpha_0 + \gamma_1 z_{t1}(\lambda) + \eta z_{t2}(\lambda) + e_t \tag{17.4.24}$$

where

$$z_{t1}(\lambda) = \sum_{i=0}^{t-1} \lambda^i x_{t-i} \qquad \text{and} \qquad z_{t2}(\lambda) = \lambda^t$$

In matrix notation the model can be written as

$$\mathbf{y} = Z(\lambda)\boldsymbol{\beta} + \mathbf{e} \tag{17.4.25}$$

where

$$\mathbf{y} = \begin{bmatrix} y_1 \\ y_2 \\ \vdots \\ y_T \end{bmatrix} \quad Z(\lambda) = \begin{bmatrix} 1 & z_{11}(\lambda) & z_{12}(\lambda) \\ 1 & z_{21}(\lambda) & z_{22}(\lambda) \\ \vdots & \vdots & \vdots \\ 1 & z_{T1}(\lambda) & z_{T2}(\lambda) \end{bmatrix} \quad \boldsymbol{\beta} = \begin{bmatrix} \alpha_0 \\ \gamma_1 \\ \eta \end{bmatrix} \quad \mathbf{e} = \begin{bmatrix} e_1 \\ e_2 \\ \vdots \\ e_T \end{bmatrix}$$

The LS estimator of $\boldsymbol{\beta}$ for a given λ is therefore

$$\hat{\boldsymbol{\beta}}(\lambda) = [Z(\lambda)'Z(\lambda)]^{-1}Z(\lambda)'\mathbf{y}$$

Thus, in order to find the LS estimator of λ we have to minimize

$$\begin{aligned} S(\lambda) &= [\mathbf{y} - Z(\lambda)\hat{\boldsymbol{\beta}}(\lambda)]'[\mathbf{y} - Z(\lambda)\hat{\boldsymbol{\beta}}(\lambda)] \\ &= \{\mathbf{y} - Z(\lambda)[Z(\lambda)'Z(\lambda)]^{-1}Z(\lambda)'\mathbf{y}\}'\{\mathbf{y} - Z(\lambda)[Z(\lambda)'Z(\lambda)]^{-1}Z(\lambda)'\mathbf{y}\} \\ &= \mathbf{y}'\{I - Z(\lambda)[Z(\lambda)'Z(\lambda)]^{-1}Z(\lambda)'\}\mathbf{y} \end{aligned} \tag{17.4.26}$$

Since λ is known to be between 0 and 1 (or perhaps between -1 and 1), a simple grid search procedure can be used to find the minimum of this function. In such a procedure a minimum is first located by taking values of λ at intervals of width 0.1, say. Then, in a second round, a minimum is searched for in a neighborhood of the first-round minimum and values of λ are taken at increments sufficiently small to achieve the desired accuracy. Let us denote the LS (ML) estimator of λ by $\hat{\lambda}$. Then the LS (ML) estimator of $\boldsymbol{\beta}$ is

$$\hat{\boldsymbol{\beta}} = \hat{\boldsymbol{\beta}}(\hat{\lambda}) = [Z(\hat{\lambda})'Z(\hat{\lambda})]^{-1}Z(\hat{\lambda})'\mathbf{y} \tag{17.4.27}$$

We note that the ML estimator of η will not be consistent. An intuitive reason is that it includes the presample values of the x variable. By increasing the sample size T the information about the presample values does not grow sufficiently fast to allow consistent estimation of η. This, however, is of no consequence for the asymptotic distribution of the other parameter estimators. That is, the ML estimators of α_0, γ_1, and λ, which are the parameters of interest, will be consistent and asymptotically efficient under our distributional assumption for the model errors and some weak conditions for the x_t (see Dhrymes, 1971). For five samples generated for the model (17.4.19) we have computed the ML estimates restricting α_0 to zero. The results are given in Table 17.4 where it can be seen that the results from the three estimation methods—LS, instrumental variable, and ML—can be quite different.

Unfortunately, independence of the residuals e_t is a somewhat unrealistic assumption in practice. In dynamic models there is usually no good reason to assume a priori the independence of the errors. Therefore, some procedures for estimating geometric lag models with autoregressive errors are proposed. For a survey see Judge, et al. (1985, Chapter 10).

17.4.3 Other Infinite Distributed Lag Models

In many situations the geometric lag structure is not flexible enough to capture the relationship between an exogenous variable x and a dependent variable y. For instance, there may be an initial increase in the lag weights before they taper off and approach zero. Therefore, other lag models have been proposed. Many of them are generalizations of the simple geometric lag.

One possibility to obtain a more flexible structure is to include more lagged y variables in a model of the type (17.4.12). For instance,

$$y_t = \alpha_0 + \gamma_0 x_t + \lambda_1 y_{t-1} + \cdots + \lambda_p y_{t-p} + e_t$$

is a possible specification. Another possibility to gain flexibility is to include lagged values of the exogenous variables in the model, that is,

$$y_t = \alpha_0 + \gamma_0 x_t + \gamma_1 x_{t-1} + \cdots + \gamma_q x_{t-q} + \lambda y_{t-1} + e_t$$

Finally, both possibilities may be combined giving

$$y_t = \alpha_0 + \gamma_0 x_t + \cdots + \gamma_q x_{t-q} + \lambda_1 y_{t-1} + \cdots + \lambda_p y_{t-p} + e_t$$

or, in lag operator notation,

$$y_t = \alpha_0 + (\gamma_0 + \gamma_1 L + \cdots + \gamma_q L^q)x_t + (\lambda_1 L + \cdots + \lambda_p L^p)y_t + e_t$$

or

$$(1 - \lambda_1 L - \cdots - \lambda_p L^p)y_t = \alpha_0 + (\gamma_0 + \gamma_1 L + \cdots + \gamma_q L^q)x_t + e_t$$

Provided the inverse of the left-hand operator exists, this model can be written as

$$y_t = \alpha + \frac{\gamma_0 + \gamma_1 L + \cdots + \gamma_q L^q}{1 - \lambda_1 L - \cdots - \lambda_p L^p} x_t + u_t$$

where $\alpha = \alpha_0/(1 - \lambda_1 - \cdots - \lambda_p)$ and $u_t = (1 - \lambda_1 L - \cdots - \lambda_p L^p)^{-1} e_t$. This model is called a *rational lag model* because it involves a rational function in the lag operator. To interpret such a model it is often useful to derive the lag weights β_i in the specification

$$y_t = \alpha + \beta_0 x_t + \beta_1 x_{t-1} + \cdots + u_t$$

This can usually be accomplished easily. For example, if $p = 1$ and $q = 1$,

$$\begin{aligned}
\beta_0 + \beta_1 L + \beta_2 L^2 + \cdots &= (\gamma_0 + \gamma_1 L)(1 - \lambda_1 L)^{-1} \\
&= (\gamma_0 + \gamma_1 L)(1 + \lambda_1 L + \lambda_1^2 L^2 + \cdots) \\
&= \gamma_0 + (\gamma_0 \lambda_1 + \gamma_1)L + \cdots + (\gamma_0 \lambda_1^i + \gamma_1 \lambda_1^{i-1})L^i + \cdots
\end{aligned}$$

Thus,

$$\begin{aligned}
\beta_0 &= \gamma_0 \\
\beta_1 &= \gamma_0 \lambda_1 + \gamma_1 \\
&\vdots \\
\beta_i &= \gamma_0 \lambda_1^i + \gamma_1 \lambda_1^{i-1} \\
&\vdots
\end{aligned}$$

The more difficult problem is usually the choice of p and q and the estimation of the parameters $\alpha, \gamma_0, \ldots, \gamma_q, \lambda_1, \ldots, \lambda_p$. Sometimes economic theory may suggest the values of p and q. In other cases statistical procedures are used to determine these quantities. Procedures for estimation and order determination are described in Judge, et al. (1985, Chapter 10).

17.5 Summary and Concluding Remarks

In this chapter we have discussed problems related to certain dynamic models. If no a priori constraints are available, distributed lag models involve an infinite sequence of parameters. To reduce the potentially infinite dimensional parameter space to a feasible finite dimension, we truncate the lag distribution at some finite point or make the infinite sequence of lag weights a function of a finite set of parameters.

Using the first approach, one problem is to determine the truncation point or lag length. In determining the lag length, we have discussed sequential testing procedures and noted some of the statistical consequences of their use. However, a simple truncation may not result in a sufficient reduction of the dimension of the parameter space, because the available data may not be rich enough to provide reasonably precise estimates for the lag weights if the actual lag distribution is fairly long. In other words, there may be multicollinearity or near multicollinearity. We have introduced the Almon polynomial lag model as one solution to this problem.

To make that model operational, the lag length and polynomial degree must be determined. We have presented a sequential testing procedure for selecting the polynomial degree conditional on the lag length being known. In this procedure the model disturbances are assumed to be independently identically normally distributed.

Applying testing procedures for choosing the lag length and polynomial degree means that we actually estimate the lag length and polynomial degree from the data. Unfortunately, the distributions of these estimators are unknown, and, consequently, the resulting estimators of the lag weights have unknown distributions. Only if we know the true lag length and polynomial degree can these distributions be derived in a straightforward manner because the lag weight estimators can be interpreted as linearly restricted LS estimators.

It should be clear now that restrictive assumptions that will usually be violated in practice have to be fulfilled in order to ensure reasonably good estimates if the Almon approach is applied. Although many researchers have attacked these problems, they have not been able to fully solve them to date. Also, other proposed finite lag models give only partial answers to the remaining problems.

Similarly, the practical usefulness of geometric lag models, which we have presented as simple representatives of the class of infinite lag structures, is in many situations questionable. Clearly, its rigid structure, which, for instance, does not permit the lag weights to increase initially and then taper off, leads to constraints that we may not be prepared to impose a priori. Therefore, other infinite distributed lag models, such as rational lags that can generate more flexible lag structures, have been proposed. A more detailed discussion of these and other lag models is given in Judge, et al. (1985).

To impose less structure a priori means, of course, that more information has to be extracted from the data. Consequently, it is not surprising that all lag models are beset with certain problems. Thus to perform a distributed lag analysis it is usually a good idea to base the model choice on both sample information and what economic theory has to say about the data-generating process. The actual implications of a theoretical economic model for a given data set should be carefully checked, however.

Throughout this chapter we have assumed that there is only one dependent variable and one exogenous variable. There are two obvious generalizations of this situation. First, there may be more than one exogenous variable that needs to be included in the model. Some or all exogenous variables may appear in lagged form. In this case methods similar to those described in the foregoing can be used for estimation and specification. Unfortunately, the problems encountered will usually be large in number.

Another generalization of the models discussed in this chapter is required if there is not just one but a set of endogenous, interdependent variables. This situation has been treated in Chapters 14 and 15. In fact, sometimes it is not clear a priori whether any of the variables of interest is exogenous. In that case one would like to treat all variables as endogenous initially and then, in the course of the analysis, decide on the exogeneity of some of them by using statistical tools and the data at hand. In the next chapter such systems will be introduced and analyzed.

There are also a number of other problems that have not been treated in this chapter. For example, if the time series under consideration have strong seasonal components, this may require specific lag distributions. Also, care should be exercised in interpreting lag coefficients that have been obtained with contemporaneously or temporally aggregated data. Furthermore, if important variables are omitted, misleading estimates of the lag coefficients may result. More details and references on these topics are given in Judge, et al. (1985).

17.6 Exercises

17.1 A polynomial lag model with polynomial degree $Q = 2$ and lag length $N = 4$ has been estimated. The estimates of the polynomial coefficients are

$$\hat{\alpha}_0 = 0.3, \quad \hat{\alpha}_1 = 0.5, \quad \hat{\alpha}_2 = -0.1$$

Determine the corresponding estimates of the lag coefficients $\beta_0, \beta_1, \beta_2, \beta_3$, and β_4.

17.2 Fisher (1937) proposed an *arithmetic lag* of length n by defining

$$\beta_i = (n + 1 - i)\alpha, \qquad i = 0, 1, \ldots, n, \tag{17.6.1}$$

where α is a positive constant.

(a) Compute the lag weights β_i for $n = 5$ and $\alpha = 0.1$.

(b) The arithmetic lag can be interpreted as a polynomial lag. What is the degree of the polynomial?

(c) Determine the LS estimator of α.

(d) Write the restrictions for the β_i implied by the arithmetic lag in the form $R\boldsymbol{\beta} = 0$, that is, determine the restriction matrix R.

17.3 Suppose for the finite distributed lag model

$$y_t = \beta_0 x_t + \cdots + \beta_N x_{t-N} + e_t$$

data $(y_1, x_1), \ldots, (y_{24}, x_{24})$ are available. Using only the observations $y_5, y_6, \ldots, y_{24}$ for the dependent variable, models with varying lag lengths are estimated. The resulting LS variance estimates are given in the following table.

Lag length n	0	1	2	3	4
LS variance $\hat{\sigma}_n^2$	1.43	0.918	0.78	0.72	0.736

Using the sequential testing procedure in (17.2.3), determine an estimate $\hat{N}$ for the lag length N. Use a significance level of 0.05 for each individual test and evaluate the overall Type I error in each test.

17.4 The model

$$y_t = \alpha + \beta_0 x_t + \beta_1 x_{t-1} + e_t$$

is estimated using observations $y_1, \ldots, y_{20}$ and $x_0, x_1, \ldots, x_{20}$. The resulting LS estimates are

$$a = 5.0(2.23),$$

$$b_0 = 0.8(2.21),$$

$$b_1 = 0.3(1.86),$$

$$R^2 = 0.86 \quad \text{and} \quad \hat{\sigma}^2 = 25.3$$

where the numbers in parentheses are t values. Because of the low t value of b_1 the model is re-estimated without the lagged regressor x_{t-1}. What is R^2 in that case?

17.5 In country A the following relation between the annual money supply x_t in millions of dollars and income in millions of dollars, holds.

$$y_t = \alpha + 0.3x_t + 0.7y_{t-1} + e_t$$

where e_t satisfies the standard assumptions [i.e., $\mathbf{e} = (e_1, \ldots, e_T)' \sim (\mathbf{0}, \sigma^2 I)$].

(a) If the money supply is expanded by 1 million dollars in year t_0, what is the expected effect on income in year $t_0 + 3$ if everything else is held constant?

(b) What is the expected accumulated effect for the years t_0 through $t_0 + 3$?

17.6 Assume that the considered distributed lag model has the form

$$y_t = \alpha_0 + \gamma_1 x_{t-1} + \gamma_1 \lambda x_{t-2} + \gamma_1 \lambda^2 x_{t-3} + \cdots + e_t$$

Note that there is no x_t in this equation. Write the model in a form similar to (17.4.12). Which instruments would you use to compute the instrumental variable estimates for the parameters?

17.7 For the two time series $x_1, \ldots, x_{20}$ and $y_1, \ldots, y_{20}$ with

$$x_1 = 1, \quad x_{20} = -1, \quad y_1 = 1, \quad \text{and} \quad y_{20} = 2$$

the following sums of squares and cross-products are obtained.

$$\sum_{t=1}^{20} x_t^2 = 21, \quad \sum_{t=1}^{20} y_t^2 = 15, \quad \sum_{t=2}^{20} x_{t-1}y_t = 10, \quad \sum_{t=2}^{20} y_{t-1}x_t = 8,$$

$$\sum_{t=2}^{20} x_{t-1}x_t = 5, \quad \sum_{t=2}^{20} y_{t-1}y_t = 12, \quad \text{and} \quad \sum_{t=1}^{20} x_t y_t = 10$$

Compute the LS and instrumental variable estimates of the parameters α and λ in the model

$$y_t = \alpha x_t + \lambda y_{t-1} + e_t$$

17.8 The infinite distributed lag model

$$y_t = \alpha + \beta_0 x_t + \beta_1 x_{t-1} + \cdots + e_t$$

can be written in the form

$$y_t = \alpha_0 + \gamma_0 x_t + \gamma_1 x_{t-1} + \lambda y_{t-1} + u_t$$

Express α, β_0, β_1, β_2, and β_3 in terms of α_0, γ_0, γ_1, and λ.

The following problems require the use of a computer.

17.9 Use the data in Table 17.1 on capital appropriations and expenditures and assume a lag length of $N = 8$. Impose the constraints that the lag weights fall on a polynomial of degree (*a*) $Q = 7$, (*b*) $Q = 6$, (*c*) $Q = 5$, (*d*) $Q = 4$, (*e*) $Q = 3$, (*f*) $Q = 2$, (*g*) $Q = 1$. Compute for each case the restricted LS estimates for the lag weights.

17.10 For the data of the previous problem set up a sequential scheme for testing for the correct polynomial degree if the lag length is assumed to be $N = 8$. Write down the sequence of test statistics corresponding to the sequential hypotheses and carry out the tests. What is the optimal polynomial degree and what are the corresponding estimates of the lag weights?

17.11 Generate 100 $N(0, 1)$ random numbers to get values $x_1, \ldots, x_{100}$ and use 100 normal random numbers to create a sample $u_1, \ldots, u_{100}$. Given these numbers, generate 100 observations of y_t using the model

$$y_t = \lambda y_{t-1} + \alpha x_t + u_t - \lambda u_{t-1} \tag{17.6.2}$$

with $\lambda = 0.5$ and $\alpha = 1.0$.

(a) Compute LS and instrumental variable estimates for the parameters in (17.6.2) using 20, 50, and 100 observations.

(b) Use the parameter estimates obtained under (*a*) to compute estimates for the lag weights $\beta_0, \beta_1, \ldots, \beta_5$, say. Compute also the true lag weights of (17.6.2).

(c) Do you expect that the LS and instrumental variable estimates for the parameters in (17.6.2) will finally converge to the true parameter values if the sample size tends to infinity? Substantiate your expectations.

17.7 References

Almon, S. (1965) "The Distributed Lag Between Capital Appropriations and Expenditures." *Econometrica*, 33, 178–196.

Dhrymes, P. J. (1971) *Distributed Lags: Problems of Estimation and Formulation*, San Francisco, Holden-Day.

Fisher, I. (1937) "Note on a Short-Cut Method for Calculating Distributed Lags." *Bulletin de l'Institut International de Statistique*, 29, 323–328.

Judge, G. G., W. E. Griffiths, R. C. Hill, H. Lütkepohl, and T. C. Lee (1985), *The Theory and Practice of Econometrics*, 2nd ed. New York, Wiley.

CHAPTER 18

Multiple-Time Series

18.1 Background

In Chapters 14 and 15 the simultaneous nature of the economic data-generation process was recognized. In many instances the relationship between the variables in a dynamic system cannot be described by a single equation model of the type discussed in the previous chapter. Instead, a system of various dynamic equations may be required to describe the data-generation process adequately. For instance, using quarterly variables, the consumption expenditures c_t may be assumed to depend on income y_t and on the consumption expenditures of the previous period c_{t-1}. That is, a consumption function of the form

$$c_t = \eta_1 + \alpha y_t + \beta c_{t-1} + e_{1t} \tag{18.1.1}$$

may be specified. Since increased consumption may stimulate economic growth and thereby generate an increase in future income, an income equation

$$y_t = \eta_2 + \gamma c_{t-1} + \delta y_{t-1} + e_{2t} \tag{18.1.2}$$

may result. Here income is assumed to depend on lagged consumption and in addition on the income of the previous period. Taken together the two equations (18.1.1) and (18.1.2) can be regarded as the structural form of a simultaneous equation system that explicitly specifies an intertemporal relationship between the endogenous variables and is therefore dynamic.

In this chapter the forecasting aspect of a dynamic simultaneous system will be one major topic. It was mentioned in Chapter 15 that for forecasting purposes the reduced form is of interest. For the simple model (18.1.1)-(18.1.2) the reduced form is easily obtained by substituting $\eta_2 + \gamma c_{t-1} + \delta y_{t-1} + e_{2t}$ for y_t in (18.1.1).

$$c_t = (\eta_1 + \alpha\eta_2) + (\beta + \alpha\gamma)c_{t-1} + \alpha\delta y_{t-1} + (e_{1t} + \alpha e_{2t})$$
$$y_t = \eta_2 + \gamma c_{t-1} + \delta y_{t-1} + e_{2t}$$

Now the system involves only predetermined variables on the right side and is therefore a reduced form.

Sometimes it may be reasonable to include more than just one lag of the variables in the model. In that case a more general reduced form would be

$$c_t = v_1 + \theta_1 c_{t-1} + \cdots + \theta_p c_{t-p} + \psi_1 y_{t-1} + \cdots + \psi_q y_{t-q} + v_{1t}$$

$$y_t = v_2 + \gamma_1 c_{t-1} + \cdots + \gamma_p c_{t-p} + \delta_1 y_{t-1} + \cdots + \delta_q y_{t-q} + v_{2t}$$

Writing this model in vector and matrix notation we get

$$\mathbf{y}_t = \mathbf{v} + \Theta_1 \mathbf{y}_{t-1} + \cdots + \Theta_p \mathbf{y}_{t-p} + \mathbf{v}_t \tag{18.1.3}$$

where

$$\mathbf{y}_t = \begin{bmatrix} c_t \\ y_t \end{bmatrix} \qquad \mathbf{v} = \begin{bmatrix} v_1 \\ v_2 \end{bmatrix} \qquad \Theta_i = \begin{bmatrix} \theta_i & \psi_i \\ \gamma_i & \delta_i \end{bmatrix} \qquad \text{and} \quad \mathbf{v}_t = \begin{bmatrix} v_{1t} \\ v_{2t} \end{bmatrix}$$

It is assumed that $p \geq q$ and the ψ_i and δ_i are zero for $i > q$.

The expression in (18.1.3) looks very much like an autoregressive process of order p [AR(p)] that was covered in Section 16.3. The only difference is that the variable y_t investigated in Chapter 16 is now replaced by a vector $\mathbf{y}_t$, the white-noise process e_t is replaced by the vector process $\mathbf{v}_t$, and the AR coefficients θ_i of Chapter 16 are now matrices Θ_i. Moreover, a vector $\mathbf{v}$ of intercept terms is included in the process. Since a vector of variables $\mathbf{y}_t$ is related to lagged vectors $\mathbf{y}_{t-1}, \mathbf{y}_{t-2}, \ldots$ we call the model in (18.1.3) a *vector autoregressive process of order p* [VAR(p)]. Often the supplement "vector" (V) is dropped because it is clear from the context that a vector process rather than a univariate process is considered. We will, however, stick to the "V" in the balance of this chapter.

Note that here and in the following sections we use the same symbol for a random variable and its realization. After having gone through Chapter 16, you should have no difficulties in discriminating between the different meanings of each symbol.

Of course, there is no need to restrict the discussion to a bivariate system involving only two variables. Instead, we will in the following sections investigate systems with M time-series variables, that is, $\mathbf{y}_t = (y_{1t}, \ldots, y_{Mt})'$. Thus, a sample of T observations for each of the variables consists of M time series. The collection $\mathbf{y}_1, \mathbf{y}_2, \ldots, \mathbf{y}_T$ is therefore called a *multiple time-series.*

The generation process of such a multiple time-series may, for instance, be a VAR(p) process of dimension M. In the next section this kind of process with M variables will be specified and some of its properties will be discussed. Estimation and specification of VAR processes will be considered in Section 18.3, and forecasting them is the topic of Section 18.4. In Section 18.5 the concept of Granger-causality is briefly considered. The Granger-causal structure of a relationship between two or more variables is often of interest and, under certain conditions, can be investigated in the framework of vector autoregressive processes. Further possibilities to use VAR models for economic analysis are considered in

Section 18.6. Some extensions of VAR models are discussed in Section 18.7, and a summary of the chapter as well as comments on problems related to the models considered are given in Section 18.8.

Before going through the remainder of this chapter, it is advantageous to be familiar with the basic concepts of univariate time-series analysis given in Chapter 16. Furthermore, much of what is done in this chapter can be regarded as a special case of material on simultaneous equation systems in Chapters 14 and 15. Being acquainted with the contents of these chapters will therefore be beneficial in working through the following sections. A basic difference between structural econometric modeling and multiple time-series analysis lies in the way the models are constructed rather than in the types of models used. The econometrician relies on economic theory in setting up his or her models whereas the time-series analyst tends to prefer the use of statistical tools for model construction.

18.2 Vector Autoregressive Processes

18.2.1 Definition

As we mentioned in the introduction, a vector autoregressive process of order p [VAR(p)] for a system of M variables $\mathbf{y}_t = (y_{1t}, \ldots, y_{Mt})'$ may be defined in the same way as for the bivariate system in (18.1.3),

$$\mathbf{y}_t = \mathbf{v} + \Theta_1 \mathbf{y}_{t-1} + \cdots + \Theta_p \mathbf{y}_{t-p} + \mathbf{v}_t \tag{18.2.1}$$

In this system of M equations $\mathbf{v} = (v_1, \ldots, v_M)'$ is an M-dimensional vector, the

$$\Theta_i = \begin{bmatrix} \theta_{11,i} & \cdots & \theta_{1M,i} \\ \vdots & \ddots & \vdots \\ \theta_{M1,i} & \cdots & \theta_{MM,i} \end{bmatrix}$$

are $(M \times M)$ coefficient matrices and $\mathbf{v}_t = (v_{1t}, \ldots, v_{Mt})'$ has the same stochastic properties as the reduced-form errors in a system of simultaneous equations considered in Chapters 14 and 15. In other words, the $\mathbf{v}_t$ have mean zero, $E[\mathbf{v}_t] = \mathbf{0}$, and the same (nonsingular) covariance matrix $\Sigma_{\mathbf{v}} = E[\mathbf{v}_t \mathbf{v}_t']$ for all t. Furthermore, $\mathbf{v}_t$ and $\mathbf{v}_s$ are uncorrelated for $t \neq s$. A process $\mathbf{v}_t$ with these properties is often called *vector white noise* in analogy with the terminology used for the error process e_t in Chapter 16.

Usually the parameters $\mathbf{v}, \Theta_1, \Theta_2, \ldots, \Theta_p$, and $\Sigma_{\mathbf{v}}$ will be *unknown* in practice and have to be estimated from the available data before the process (18.2.1) can be used for forecasting and analysis purposes. Before considering the estimation of models like (18.2.1) the stationarity of VAR processes will be discussed. This property will be useful in deriving the asymptotic properties of the parameter estimators.

18.2.2 Stationarity

In Section 16.2.3 we defined stationarity of a univariate stochastic process as a property that ensures constancy of the means, variances, and autocovariances through time. In a completely analogous fashion, stationarity may be defined for vector processes. We call a collection of M-dimensional random vectors $\ldots \mathbf{y}_{t-1}, \mathbf{y}_t, \mathbf{y}_{t+1}, \ldots$ a *vector stochastic process.* Thus, for the moment we do not restrict the discussion to VAR processes that are examples of vector stochastic processes.

A vector stochastic process is called *stationary* if

(*i*) All the random vectors have the same mean vector $\boldsymbol{\mu}$, $E[\mathbf{y}_t] = \boldsymbol{\mu}$ for all t

(*ii*) The variances of all involved random variables are finite, $\text{var}(y_{mt}) < \infty$ for $m = 1, \ldots, M$ and all t

(*iii*) The covariance matrices of vectors $\mathbf{y}_t$ and $\mathbf{y}_{t+k}$ that are k periods apart do not depend on t but only on k

$$\text{cov}(\mathbf{y}_t, \mathbf{y}_{t+k}) = E[(\mathbf{y}_t - \boldsymbol{\mu})(\mathbf{y}_{t+k} - \boldsymbol{\mu})'] = \Gamma_k \text{ for all } t$$

The last property implies for $k = 0$ that all vectors $\mathbf{y}_t$ have the same covariance matrix, that is, $E[(\mathbf{y}_t - \boldsymbol{\mu})(\mathbf{y}_t - \boldsymbol{\mu})'] = \Sigma_{\mathbf{y}}$ for all t. *For practical purposes, these conditions imply that the time series under consideration must not have trends, fixed seasonal patterns, or time-varying variances.* Often data transformations will be necessary to ensure these properties (see Chapter 16). Although economic data often do not have these friendly stationarity properties and although nonstationary processes currently receive considerable attention in the literature, it is useful to understand the problems related to the stationary case first. Therefore, we will deal with stationary processes in the following.

It can be shown that a VAR(p) process like (18.2.1) is stationary if it has bounded means and covariance matrices and the polynomial defined by the determinant

$$\det(I - \Theta_1 z - \Theta_2 z^2 - \cdots - \Theta_p z^p) \tag{18.2.2}$$

has all its roots outside the complex unit circle [compare that to the stationarity condition for univariate AR(p) processes given in Section 16.3]. For instance, for a bivariate VAR(1) process

$$\begin{bmatrix} y_{1t} \\ y_{2t} \end{bmatrix} = \begin{bmatrix} v_1 \\ v_2 \end{bmatrix} + \begin{bmatrix} \theta_{11,1} & \theta_{12,1} \\ \theta_{21,1} & \theta_{22,1} \end{bmatrix} \begin{bmatrix} y_{1,t-1} \\ y_{2,t-1} \end{bmatrix} + \begin{bmatrix} v_{1t} \\ v_{2t} \end{bmatrix} \tag{18.2.3}$$

the determinant in (18.2.2) becomes

$$\det\left(\begin{bmatrix} 1 & 0 \\ 0 & 1 \end{bmatrix} - \begin{bmatrix} \theta_{11,1} & \theta_{12,1} \\ \theta_{21,1} & \theta_{22,1} \end{bmatrix} z\right)$$
$$= 1 - (\theta_{11,1} + \theta_{22,1})z + (\theta_{11,1}\theta_{22,1} - \theta_{21,1}\theta_{12,1})z^2 \qquad (18.2.4)$$

which is a polynomial of degree two. The process (18.2.3) will be stationary if this polynomial has no roots in or on the unit circle. For example, if

$$\Theta_1 = \begin{bmatrix} 0.008 & 0.461 \\ 0.232 & 0.297 \end{bmatrix} \qquad (18.2.5)$$

the polynomial in (18.2.4) becomes

$$1 - (0.008 + 0.297)z + (0.008 \cdot 0.297 - 0.232 \cdot 0.461)z^2 = 1 - 0.305z - 0.104576z^2$$

It is easy to check that the roots of this polynomial are $z_1 = -4.877$ and $z_2 = 1.961$, which are both greater than 1 in absolute value. Consequently, the corresponding process is stationary. We have chosen the special matrix Θ_1 in (18.2.5) because it will be of interest in Section 18.3.2.

The stationarity property guarantees for a VAR(1) process that $\lim_{n\to\infty} \Theta_1^n = 0$. This property is just the stability condition used in Section 15.5 in analyzing a system of simultaneous equations.

To appreciate the generality of the VAR processes introduced in the foregoing it may be worth noting that stationary processes, under quite general conditions, can be approximated by finite-order VAR processes. Thus, if the stationarity assumption is justifiable for a given multiple time series, a VAR(p) may be an adequate candidate for modeling the data-generation process. We now turn to the estimation of VAR(p) processes.

18.3 Estimation and Specification of VAR Processes

18.3.1 Estimation of a VAR Process with Known Order *p*

In the introduction we mentioned that a VAR(p) model may be regarded as a reduced form of a simultaneous equation system. This interpretation suggests that parameter estimation in such a model can be done as explained in Chapter 14. Let us write the system (18.2.1) in a form similar to the reduced form in Chapter 14.

For this purpose we consider the mth equation of the system (18.2.1),

$$y_{mt} = \nu_m + \theta_{m1,1}y_{1,t-1} + \cdots + \theta_{mM,1}y_{M,t-1} + \cdots + \theta_{m1,p}y_{1,t-p} + \cdots + \theta_{mM,p}y_{M,t-p} + v_{mt} \tag{18.3.1}$$

Assuming that we have T observations and p presample values for each of the variables, we can set up the vectors

$$\mathbf{y}^m = \begin{bmatrix} y_{m1} \\ y_{m2} \\ \vdots \\ y_{mT} \end{bmatrix}, \quad \mathbf{y}^m_{-i} = \begin{bmatrix} y_{m,1-i} \\ y_{m,2-i} \\ \vdots \\ y_{m,T-i} \end{bmatrix}$$

for $i = 1, \ldots, p$ and $m = 1, \ldots, M$. In other words, $\mathbf{y}^m_{-i}$ contains the variables of the $\mathbf{y}^m$ vector lagged i periods. We also define $\mathbf{v}^m = (v_{m1}, \ldots, v_{mT})'$. Using this notation, (18.3.1) can be written as

$$\mathbf{y}^m = \nu_m\mathbf{j} + \theta_{m1,1}\mathbf{y}^1_{-1} + \cdots + \theta_{mM,1}\mathbf{y}^M_{-1} + \cdots + \theta_{m1,p}\mathbf{y}^1_{-p} + \cdots + \theta_{mM,p}\mathbf{y}^M_{-p} + \mathbf{v}^m$$

where $\mathbf{j}$ is a $(T \times 1)$ vector of ones. Compactly, this system may be written as

$$\mathbf{y}^m = X\boldsymbol{\theta}_m + \mathbf{v}^m \tag{18.3.2}$$

where

$$X = [\mathbf{j}, \mathbf{y}^1_{-1}, \ldots, \mathbf{y}^M_{-1}, \mathbf{y}^1_{-2}, \ldots, \mathbf{y}^M_{-2}, \ldots, \mathbf{y}^1_{-p}, \ldots, \mathbf{y}^M_{-p}]$$

and

$$\boldsymbol{\theta}_m = [\nu_m, \theta_{m1,1}, \ldots, \theta_{mM,1}, \theta_{m1,2}, \ldots, \theta_{mM,2}, \ldots, \theta_{m1,p}, \ldots, \theta_{mM,p}]'$$

is the vector of coefficients in the mth equation of the system. Note that each of the M equations has the same regression matrix X. Writing the M equations as one system, we get as in Chapter 14

$$\mathbf{y} = (I_M \otimes X)\boldsymbol{\theta} + \mathbf{v} \tag{18.3.3}$$

where $\otimes$ denotes the Kronecker product. Under the assumptions of Section 18.2.1 the covariance matrix of $\mathbf{v}$ is $E[\mathbf{v}\mathbf{v}'] = \Sigma_\mathbf{v} \otimes I_T$.

We have seen in Chapters 11 and 14 that in such a system the GLS estimator is identical to the LS estimator. This in turn is equivalent to estimating each equation separately by LS. Thus, without loss of estimation efficiency, we may estimate each equation by LS,

$$\hat{\boldsymbol{\theta}}_m = (X'X)^{-1}X'\mathbf{y}^m \tag{18.3.4}$$

For the complete system the estimator

$$\hat{\boldsymbol{\theta}} = [I_M \otimes (X'X)^{-1}X']\mathbf{y} \tag{18.3.5}$$

is obtained.

To investigate the properties of this estimator we assume that the $\mathbf{v}_t$ have a multivariate normal distribution $N(\mathbf{0}, \Sigma_{\mathbf{v}})$ and $\mathbf{v}_t$ is independent of $\mathbf{v}_s$ for $s \neq t$. If, in addition, $\mathbf{y}_t$ is a stationary process it can be shown that

$$\underset{T\to\infty}{\text{plim}}\ \frac{1}{T}(X'X) = Q \tag{18.3.6}$$

is a nonsingular matrix and

$$\text{plim}\ \frac{1}{T}X'\mathbf{v}^m = \mathbf{0} \qquad m = 1, \ldots, M \tag{18.3.7}$$

Hence,

$$\begin{aligned}
\text{plim}\ \hat{\boldsymbol{\theta}}_m &= \text{plim}(X'X)^{-1}X'\mathbf{y}^m \\
&= \text{plim}[(X'X)^{-1}X'(X\boldsymbol{\theta}_m + \mathbf{v}^m)] \\
&= \boldsymbol{\theta}_m + \text{plim}\left(\frac{X'X}{T}\right)^{-1} \text{plim}\left(\frac{X'\mathbf{v}^m}{T}\right) \\
&= \boldsymbol{\theta}_m
\end{aligned}$$

Consequently, each $\hat{\boldsymbol{\theta}}_m$ is consistent and it follows that

$$\text{plim}\ \hat{\boldsymbol{\theta}} = \boldsymbol{\theta} \tag{18.3.8}$$

Moreover, since the error process $\mathbf{v}_t$ is assumed to be normally distributed, $\hat{\boldsymbol{\theta}}$ is asymptotically equivalent to the ML estimator and is therefore asymptotically efficient and normally distributed,

$$\sqrt{T}(\hat{\boldsymbol{\theta}} - \boldsymbol{\theta}) \xrightarrow{d} N(\mathbf{0}, \Sigma_{\hat{\boldsymbol{\theta}}}) \tag{18.3.9}$$

The covariance matrix of the asymptotic distribution can be shown to be

$$\Sigma_{\hat{\boldsymbol{\theta}}} = \Sigma_{\mathbf{v}} \otimes Q^{-1} \tag{18.3.10}$$

To estimate this matrix consistently, we need a consistent estimator of $\Sigma_{\mathbf{v}}$ and, in view of (18.3.6), we use $(X'X/T)^{-1}$ as a consistent estimator of Q^{-1}. As in Section 14.4 we can estimate the ijth element σ_{ij} of $\Sigma_{\mathbf{v}}$ by

$$\hat{\sigma}_{ij} = \frac{(\mathbf{y}^i - X\hat{\boldsymbol{\theta}}_i)'(\mathbf{y}^j - X\hat{\boldsymbol{\theta}}_j)}{T - Mp - 1} \tag{18.3.11}$$

where in the denominator the number of parameters $Mp + 1$ in each equation is subtracted from the sample size T. Denoting by $\hat{\Sigma}_v$, the matrix with ijth element $\hat{\sigma}_{ij}$, a consistent estimator of $\hat{\Sigma}_{\hat{\theta}}$ is

$$\hat{\Sigma}_{\hat{\theta}} = \hat{\Sigma}_v \otimes (X'X/T)^{-1} \tag{18.3.12}$$

Note that this is an estimator of the asymptotic covariance matrix of $\sqrt{T}(\hat{\boldsymbol{\theta}} - \boldsymbol{\theta})$. Thus, as in the nonstochastic regressor case considered in Section 11.1, an approximation to the covariance matrix of $\hat{\boldsymbol{\theta}}$ is

$$\hat{\Sigma}_v \otimes (X'X)^{-1} \tag{18.3.13}$$

As an example, consider the bivariate system consisting of the quarterly changes of seasonally adjusted U.S. per capita consumption expenditures (y_1) and disposable income (y_2). The data for the second quarter of 1951 to the fourth quarter of 1969 are listed in Table 18.1. The two series are plotted in Figure 18.1 and do not exhibit trends or regular seasonal patterns. Therefore we assume that they are generated by a stationary process. We will only use the first 71 observations for estimation purposes.

Before we can estimate a bivariate VAR model for the two series we must specify the order p because we have assumed in the foregoing that the VAR order is known. Of course, usually we do not know the order. In this case $p = 4$ was selected since this means that the lagged values from one previous year of each of the variables are included in each equation. Since four lags are involved, the first four observations of each of the two variables in Table 18.1 are treated as presample values. Thus, we have an effective sample size of $T = 71 - 4 = 67$ observations (observations 5–71 in Table 18.1). Using the LS approach outlined in the foregoing we obtain the estimated model

$$\begin{bmatrix} y_{1t} \\ y_{2t} \end{bmatrix} = \begin{bmatrix} 8 \\ (3) \\ 9 \\ (4) \end{bmatrix} + \begin{bmatrix} -0.07 & 0.50 \\ (0.15) & (0.12) \\ 0.23 & 0.33 \\ (0.19) & (0.15) \end{bmatrix} \begin{bmatrix} y_{1,t-1} \\ y_{2,t-1} \end{bmatrix} + \begin{bmatrix} 0.15 & -0.03 \\ (0.17) & (0.15) \\ -0.05 & -0.11 \\ (0.20) & (0.18) \end{bmatrix} \begin{bmatrix} y_{1,t-2} \\ y_{2,t-2} \end{bmatrix}$$

$$+ \begin{bmatrix} 0.11 & -0.16 \\ (0.17) & (0.15) \\ 0.04 & 0.01 \\ (0.20) & (0.18) \end{bmatrix} \begin{bmatrix} y_{1,t-3} \\ y_{2,t-3} \end{bmatrix} + \begin{bmatrix} -0.19 & 0.07 \\ (0.12) & (0.13) \\ 0.10 & -0.06 \\ (0.15) & (0.16) \end{bmatrix} \begin{bmatrix} y_{1,t-4} \\ y_{2,t-4} \end{bmatrix} + \begin{bmatrix} \hat{v}_{1t} \\ \hat{v}_{2t} \end{bmatrix}$$

$$\hat{\Sigma}_v = \begin{bmatrix} 284 & 195 \\ 195 & 428 \end{bmatrix} \tag{18.3.14}$$

Here the numbers in parentheses are estimated standard errors obtained from (18.3.13).

Table 18.1 Changes of Quarterly, Seasonally Adjusted U.S. Per Capita Personal Consumption Expenditures (y_1) and Disposable Personal Income (y_2) in 1972 Dollars at Annual Rates, 1951.II–1969. IV

t	y_{1t}	y_{2t}	t	y_{1t}	y_{2t}
1	−61	42	39	−9	−23
2	8	−1	40	−5	13
3	−1	−11	41	23	28
4	−4	−12	42	−3	17
5	30	16	43	37	38
6	−1	41	44	13	14
7	45	14	45	21	16
8	17	17	46	10	3
9	2	26	47	23	1
10	−17	−20	48	8	15
11	−16	−10	49	15	17
12	−4	−11	50	24	19
13	8	−23	51	8	30
14	23	29	52	39	47
15	31	36	53	38	75
16	31	8	54	35	27
17	33	43	55	−3	23
18	14	31	56	46	22
19	26	29	57	17	32
20	−7	8	58	35	76
21	−6	9	59	65	47
22	−4	2	60	29	17
23	13	20	61	−2	6
24	4	−10	62	22	27
25	−6	5	63	0	21
26	5	1	64	15	38
27	−6	−20	65	31	21
28	−37	−35	66	7	16
29	12	6	67	6	17
30	25	45	68	54	36
31	16	25	69	30	43
32	39	6	70	54	−7
33	23	32	71	8	9
34	9	−30	72	21	−2
35	−5	10	73	9	19
36	1	6	74	9	47
37	24	6	75	16	10
38	−19	−12			

Sources: Personal consumption expenditures, disposable personal income: U.S. Department of Commerce, *The National Income and Product Accounts of the United States, 1929–74.* Population data: U.S. Bureau of the Census, *Current Population Reports.*

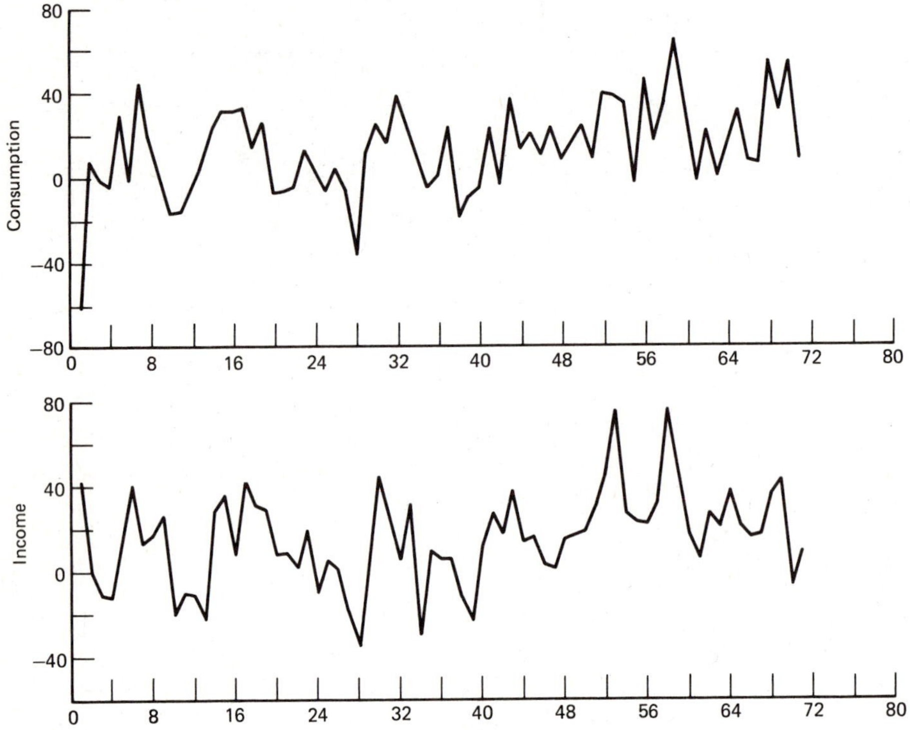

Figure 18.1 Changes of quarterly, seasonally adjusted U.S. per capita personal consumption expenditures and disposable personal income in 1972 dollars at annual rates 1951.II–1969.IV.

There are some obvious problems with this specification. One is that an arbitrary choice of the order is not satisfactory. As a result, there are many parameter estimates that are smaller than their respective standard errors and thus are not significantly different from zero at any common significance level. Hence, we suspect that the model contains some unnecessary parameters. If such is the case, the parameter estimators and forecasts obtained from the model will be inefficient. This problem usually becomes even more severe if more variables ($M > 2$) are involved. It is even possible that insufficient data are available for estimation. For instance, if a five-dimensional system ($M = 5$) is to be estimated with VAR order $p = 10$, then we need at least 13 years of quarterly data for estimation since the number of parameters in each equation is $Mp + 1 = 51$.

Different suggestions have been made for reducing the dimension of the parameter space and increasing the estimation efficiency in VAR models. They all amount to imposing restrictions of some kind on the parameters. The question is then what methods to use for specifying the restrictions and thereby the models. One possibility that has been used in previous chapters is to use prior knowledge based on economic theory and institutional constraints. Unfortunately, these sources of nonsample information are not always rich enough to provide a complete and sufficient set of restrictions for a VAR model. In such a situation one usually has to employ statistical tools and let the data impose restrictions on the VAR parameters. Some ways of doing this in a single equation model have been presented in the previous chapter on distributed lags. In that chapter methods for choosing the lag length were discussed. Similarly, in the present case we can choose the order p by using statistical methods. If this leads to a reduction of the order specified initially, zero restrictions are imposed on the original model. In the following we will present some methods for selecting the VAR order. There are many other ways to reduce the parameter space, and we refer you to Judge, et al. (1985, Chapter 16) for these procedures and references.

18.3.2 VAR Order Selection

In the univariate case we based the choice of an adequate order of an AR process on the partial autocorrelations. For vector processes the partial autocorrelations are matrices; choosing the model order by visual inspection of these matrices requires some experience. Of course, formal tests could be used to decide on their significance. An alternative approach is to use criteria designed to aid in choosing the VAR order. This approach will be followed here, and we remind you that a similar approach was suggested as a possibility for determining the lag length in a distributed lag model (see Section 17.2). In fact, the criteria AIC and SC used in the distributed lags chapter can be generalized for choosing the VAR order.

In the VAR context they are defined as follows:

$$\text{AIC}(n) = \ln \det(\tilde{\Sigma}_n) + \frac{2M^2 n}{T} \tag{18.3.15}$$

and

$$\text{SC}(n) = \ln \det(\tilde{\Sigma}_n) + \frac{M^2 n \ln T}{T} \tag{18.3.16}$$

where M is the number of variables in the system, T is the sample size, and $\tilde{\Sigma}_n$ is an estimate of the residual covariance matrix $\Sigma_{\mathbf{v}}$ obtained with a VAR(n) model. The elements of $\tilde{\Sigma}_n$ are computed as

$$\tilde{\sigma}_{ij} = \frac{(\mathbf{y}^i - X\hat{\boldsymbol{\theta}}_i)'(\mathbf{y}^j - X\hat{\boldsymbol{\theta}}_j)}{T} \tag{18.3.17}$$

that is, in contrast to (18.3.11), the sum of squares or cross-products is divided by the sample size and not by the degrees of freedom. The order p is chosen so that the AIC or SC criterion is minimized. That is, models with order $n = 0, 1, \ldots, P$ are estimated with P being a prespecified upper bound for the VAR order. Then the matrices $\tilde{\Sigma}_n$ for $n = 0, 1, \ldots, P$ and the corresponding values AIC(n) or SC(n) are computed. The value p(AIC) is the order that minimizes AIC(n) over $n = 0, 1, \ldots, P$ and p(SC) is the order minimizing SC(n). In this procedure the sample size T is held fixed. In other words, in each estimation P observations for each variable are treated as presample values.

As an example, consider the U.S. consumption and income data in Table 18.1. The $\tilde{\Sigma}_n$ matrices for $n = 0, 1, 2, 3, 4$ are given in Table 18.2 together with the corresponding AIC and SC values. Observations 1 through 4 have been used as presample values and the sample used for estimation consists of observations 5 through 71 as in the previous subsection. In Table 18.2 it can be seen that both criteria are minimized for order 1, that is, $p(\text{AIC}) = p(\text{SC}) = 1$. In order to use the sample information efficiently, we have re-estimated a VAR(1) process using only the first observation of each of the two series as presample values. The sample size is therefore $T = 70$, and the estimated model is

$$\begin{bmatrix} y_{1t} \\ y_{2t} \end{bmatrix} = \begin{bmatrix} 6.96 \\ (2.51) \\ 7.39 \\ (3.00) \end{bmatrix} + \begin{bmatrix} 0.008 & 0.461 \\ (0.107) & (0.103) \\ 0.232 & 0.297 \\ (0.127) & (0.123) \end{bmatrix} \begin{bmatrix} y_{1,t-1} \\ y_{2,t-1} \end{bmatrix} + \begin{bmatrix} \hat{v}_{1t} \\ \hat{v}_{2t} \end{bmatrix},$$

$$\hat{\Sigma}_v = \begin{bmatrix} 275 & 167 \\ 167 & 390 \end{bmatrix} \tag{18.3.18}$$

In Section 18.2.2 we saw that a VAR(1) with this coefficient matrix is stationary.

Even in the model (18.3.18) there may be too many parameters since two of the parameters are less than twice their respective estimated standard errors. Further reductions of the parameter space could be based on significance tests for individual parameters or groups of parameters. In Section 18.5 we will come back to this point and discuss possible tests.

As in the case of univariate models, it is important to check the adequacy of a multiple time-series model once it has been specified and estimated. It must be remembered that even if the VAR order has been chosen on the basis of a formal criterion, there are chances for model misspecifications. First, the choice of an order selection criterion is often more or less arbitrary and a range of other criteria is available that may select different orders for the same data set. Some of these criteria and further references are given in Lütkepohl (1985) and Judge, et al. (1985, Section 16.6). Second, the given multiple time-series may not be generated by a finite order VAR process, so that choosing the model from this family may be an

Table 18.2 Statistics for Choosing the VAR Order of the Consumption/Income System

VAR order n	$\tilde{\Sigma}_n$	$\det(\tilde{\Sigma}_n)$	$AIC(n) = \ln \det(\tilde{\Sigma}_n) + 8n/67$	$SC(n) = \ln \det(\tilde{\Sigma}_n) + (4n \ln 67)/67$
0	$\begin{bmatrix} 373 & 247 \\ 247 & 465 \end{bmatrix}$	112 669	11.63	11.63
1	$\begin{bmatrix} 266 & 161 \\ 161 & 378 \end{bmatrix}$	74 711	11.34	11.47
2	$\begin{bmatrix} 265 & 162 \\ 162 & 374 \end{bmatrix}$	72 990	11.44	11.70
3	$\begin{bmatrix} 255 & 163 \\ 163 & 373 \end{bmatrix}$	68 644	11.49	11.89
4	$\begin{bmatrix} 246 & 168 \\ 168 & 370 \end{bmatrix}$	62 601	11.52	12.05

inappropriate decision at the outset of the analysis. In this context, it may be worth remembering that stationary processes under general conditions can be approximated quite well by VAR processes. However, the stationarity condition is crucial because many types of nonstationarities cannot be captured by a VAR model. Third, even if the data-generation process is from the class of finite order VAR processes, it is possible that the maximum order P used in the search procedure is chosen to be too small. All these potential sources for misspecifications make checks for model adequacy important. They may involve an examination of the residuals and residual autocorrelations. For details and references see Judge et al. (1985, Section 16.6.3). In the next section we discuss forecasting with VAR processes.

18.4 Forecasting Vector Autoregressive Processes

For the moment let us assume that the generation process for a set of variables is a *known* vector stochastic process. In this situation the optimal forecast is the conditional expectation given all information up to the period in which the forecast is made. Here "optimal" means that the forecast mean square error (MSE) of each variable is minimized. If the generation process is a known VAR(p) of the type (18.2.1) with independent white-noise errors $\mathbf{v}_t$, that is $\mathbf{v}_t$ is independent of $\mathbf{v}_s$ for $s \neq t$, the conditional expectation $\mathbf{y}_T(h)$ of $\mathbf{y}_{T+h}$ given $\mathbf{y}_T, \mathbf{y}_{T-1}, \ldots,$ is easy to determine. Denoting by E_T the conditional expectation operator given $\mathbf{y}_T, \mathbf{y}_{T-1}, \ldots,$

$$\begin{aligned} \mathbf{y}_T(h) &= E_T[\mathbf{y}_{T+h}] = \mathbf{v} + \Theta_1 E_T[\mathbf{y}_{T+h-1}] + \cdots + \Theta_p E_T[\mathbf{y}_{T+h-p}] \\ &= \mathbf{v} + \Theta_1 \mathbf{y}_T(h-1) + \cdots + \Theta_p \mathbf{y}_T(h-p) \end{aligned} \tag{18.4.1}$$

where $\mathbf{y}_T(h-i) = \mathbf{y}_{T+h-i}$ for $i \geq h$ and $E_T[\mathbf{v}_{T+h}] = \mathbf{0}$ has been used. This formula can be applied repeatedly for recursively computing h-step-forecasts for $h = 1, 2, \ldots$. For example, if $p = 1$, so that $\mathbf{y}_t$ is a VAR(1), we get

$$\begin{aligned} \mathbf{y}_T(1) &= \mathbf{v} + \Theta_1 \mathbf{y}_T \\ \mathbf{y}_T(2) &= \mathbf{v} + \Theta_1 \mathbf{y}_T(1) = \mathbf{v} + \Theta_1 \mathbf{v} + \Theta_1^2 \mathbf{y}_T \\ \mathbf{y}_T(3) &= \mathbf{v} + \Theta_1 \mathbf{y}_T(2) = (I + \Theta_1 + \Theta_1^2)\mathbf{v} + \Theta_1^3 \mathbf{y}_T \end{aligned}$$

and so on.

Assuming that the U.S. consumption and income series in Table 18.1 are indeed generated by the VAR(1) process in (18.3.18), we can use these formulas to compute optimal forecasts of $\mathbf{y}_{72}, \mathbf{y}_{73}, \ldots$ starting in period $T = 71$. Note that

$y_{1,71} = 8$ and $y_{2,71} = 9$, so that

$$\begin{bmatrix} \hat{y}_{1,71}(1) \\ \hat{y}_{2,71}(1) \end{bmatrix} = \begin{bmatrix} 6.96 \\ 7.39 \end{bmatrix} + \begin{bmatrix} 0.008 & 0.461 \\ 0.232 & 0.297 \end{bmatrix} \begin{bmatrix} 8 \\ 9 \end{bmatrix} = \begin{bmatrix} 11.173 \\ 11.919 \end{bmatrix}$$

$$\begin{bmatrix} \hat{y}_{1,71}(2) \\ \hat{y}_{2,71}(2) \end{bmatrix} = \begin{bmatrix} 6.96 \\ 7.39 \end{bmatrix} + \begin{bmatrix} 0.008 & 0.461 \\ 0.232 & 0.297 \end{bmatrix} \begin{bmatrix} 11.173 \\ 11.919 \end{bmatrix} = \begin{bmatrix} 12.544 \\ 13.522 \end{bmatrix} \qquad (18.4.2)$$

Of course, the process (18.3.18) involves estimated coefficients and is therefore not the actual data-generation process but just an estimated version. Therefore, the forecasts are estimates and appear with a caret.

The mean square error (MSE) matrix is often used as a measure for the forecast uncertainty. We will denote the MSE matrix of an h-step forecast by $\Sigma(h)$, that is,

$$\Sigma(h) = E[[\mathbf{y}_{T+h} - \mathbf{y}_T(h)][\mathbf{y}_{T+h} - \mathbf{y}_T(h)]'] \qquad (18.4.3)$$

Since the forecast $\mathbf{y}_T(h)$ is unbiased, that is, $E[\mathbf{y}_{T+h} - \mathbf{y}_T(h)] = \mathbf{0}$, $\Sigma(h)$ is the forecast error covariance matrix. It can be shown that the MSE matrix of the VAR(p) in (18.2.1) has the form

$$\Sigma(h) = \Sigma_{\mathbf{v}} + M_1 \Sigma_{\mathbf{v}} M_1' + \cdots + M_{h-1} \Sigma_{\mathbf{v}} M_{h-1}' = \Sigma(h-1) + M_{h-1} \Sigma_{\mathbf{v}} M_{h-1}' \qquad (18.4.4)$$

where the M_i can be computed from the Θ_i using the recursions

$$M_0 = I \text{ and } M_i = \sum_{j=1}^{\min(p,i)} \Theta_j M_{i-j} \qquad i = 1, 2, \ldots \qquad (18.4.5)$$

Thus,

$$M_1 = \Theta_1$$
$$M_2 = \Theta_1 M_1 + \Theta_2 M_0 = \Theta_1^2 + \Theta_2$$
$$M_3 = \Theta_1 M_2 + \Theta_2 M_1 + \Theta_3 M_0 = \Theta_1^3 + \Theta_1 \Theta_2 + \Theta_2 \Theta_1 + \Theta_3$$

and so on. For a VAR(1) it is easy to see that $M_i = \Theta_1^i$.

Assuming that (18.3.18) is the true data-generation process of the U.S. consumption and income data, we get

$$\hat{\Sigma}(1) = \hat{\Sigma}_{\mathbf{v}} = \begin{bmatrix} 275 & 167 \\ 167 & 390 \end{bmatrix} \qquad (18.4.6a)$$

$$\begin{aligned} \hat{\Sigma}(2) &= \hat{\Sigma}_{\mathbf{v}} + \hat{\Theta}_1 \hat{\Sigma}_{\mathbf{v}} \hat{\Theta}_1' \\ &= \begin{bmatrix} 275 & 167 \\ 167 & 390 \end{bmatrix} + \begin{bmatrix} 0.008 & 0.461 \\ 0.232 & 0.297 \end{bmatrix} \begin{bmatrix} 275 & 167 \\ 167 & 390 \end{bmatrix} \begin{bmatrix} 0.008 & 0.232 \\ 0.461 & 0.297 \end{bmatrix} \\ &= \begin{bmatrix} 359 & 240 \\ 240 & 462 \end{bmatrix} \end{aligned} \qquad (18.4.6b)$$

and so on. Here we have not taken into account the fact that the process (18.3.18) is estimated. As in the univariate case (Section 16.7), taking into account the sampling variability due to estimation increases the MSEs by terms that vanish as the sample size T approaches infinity. Thus, for large samples, $\Sigma(h)$ may be used as an approximation to the MSE matrix of an estimated process. Of course, even with this simplification the matrices in (18.4.6) are only estimates of the MSE matrices because they are computed from estimated rather than known quantities. This is the reason for putting the "hat" on top of them.

If the considered VAR process has a known distribution, we can derive probability regions for the forecasts and establish interval forecasts. For instance, if the considered VAR process is normally distributed, the forecast errors are also normally distributed,

$$\mathbf{y}_{T+h} - \mathbf{y}_T(h) \sim N[\mathbf{0}, \Sigma(h)] \tag{18.4.7}$$

Hence,

$$[\mathbf{y}_{T+h} - \mathbf{y}_T(h)]'\Sigma(h)^{-1}[\mathbf{y}_{T+h} - \mathbf{y}_T(h)] \sim \chi^2_M$$

This result can be used to establish a forecast region for the vector $\mathbf{y}_{T+h}$ (see Section 6.3).

An interval forecast for an individual component of $\mathbf{y}_{T+h}$ can be obtained from (18.4.7) since this result implies

$$\frac{y_{m,T+h} - y_{m,T}(h)}{\sigma_m(h)} \sim N(0, 1) \tag{18.4.8}$$

where $y_{m,T+h}$ and $y_{m,T}(h)$ are the mth components of $\mathbf{y}_{T+h}$ and $\mathbf{y}_T(h)$, respectively and $\sigma_m(h)$ is the standard deviation of the corresponding forecast error. This means $\sigma_m(h)$ is the square root of the mth diagonal element of $\Sigma(h)$. Denoting by $z_{(\alpha)}$ the $(1-\alpha)100$ percentage point of the standard normal distribution, we get from (18.4.8)

$$\begin{aligned} 1 - \alpha &= \Pr\left\{ -z_{(\alpha/2)} \le \frac{y_{m,T+h} - y_{m,T}(h)}{\sigma_m(h)} \le z_{(\alpha/2)} \right\} \\ &= \Pr\{ y_{m,T}(h) - z_{(\alpha/2)}\sigma_m(h) \le y_{m,T+h} \le y_{m,T}(h) + z_{(\alpha/2)}\sigma_m(h) \} \end{aligned}$$

Hence a $(1-\alpha)100\%$ forecast interval for the mth variable of the system is

$$y_{m,T}(h) \pm z_{(\alpha/2)}\sigma_m(h) \tag{18.4.9a}$$

or

$$[y_{m,T}(h) - z_{(\alpha/2)}\sigma_m(h),\ y_{m,T}(h) + z_{(\alpha/2)}\sigma_m(h)] \tag{18.4.9b}$$

If forecast intervals of this type are computed repeatedly from a large number of independent realizations of the considered process then, under the aforementioned conditions, about $(1-\alpha)100\%$ of these intervals will contain the true value of $y_{m,T+h}$.

In practice, the unknown quantities in (18.4.9) ($y_{m,T}(h)$ and $\sigma_m(h)$) are replaced by estimates and the obtained forecast intervals are only approximate $(1-\alpha)100\%$ forecast intervals. For the U.S. consumption and income example, using (18.4.2) and (18.4.6), and the assumption of a normally distributed VAR(1) data-generation process, we get the approximate 95% forecast intervals,

$$\begin{aligned}
\hat{y}_{1,71}(1) \pm 1.96\hat{\sigma}_1(1) &= 11.2 \pm 32.5 \text{ or } [-21.3; 43.6] \\
\hat{y}_{2,71}(1) \pm 1.96\hat{\sigma}_2(1) &= 11.9 \pm 38.7 \text{ or } [-26.8; 50.6] \\
\hat{y}_{1,71}(2) \pm 1.96\hat{\sigma}_1(2) &= 12.5 \pm 37.1 \text{ or } [-24.6; 49.7] \\
\hat{y}_{2,71}(2) \pm 1.96\hat{\sigma}_2(2) &= 13.5 \pm 42.1 \text{ or } [-28.6; 55.7]
\end{aligned} \tag{18.4.10}$$

At this point it may be worth emphasizing again that in practice we have to rely on a number of assumptions in order to obtain the foregoing results. For the example data we have assumed that the generation process is a stationary, normally distributed VAR(1). Of course, we actually do not know whether it is stationary or normally distributed or a VAR(1). Furthermore, we have used estimated rather than true parameter values. Therefore, the forecast intervals in (18.4.10) are not exact but just approximate 95% forecast intervals. As in the case of past inference problems, they are conditional on our assumptions being correct. Consequently, it is important to check the assumptions on which an analysis is based. One possible test for checking the model is to compare its forecasts with actually observed values. For our example the actual values from Table 18.1 are $y_{1,72} = 21$, $y_{2,72} = -2$, $y_{1,73} = 9$, and $y_{2,73} = 19$. All these values fall well inside the corresponding forecast intervals in (18.4.10). Therefore, the forecasts from the model do not give rise to concern about the model and assumptions.

From Chapter 15 we know that models for systems of variables are frequently used for purposes other than forecasting. One type of analysis that has been quite popular in recent years is the statistical investigation of causal relations between variables. Such an analysis is often performed in the framework of bivariate vector processes. In the next section we will briefly discuss the concept of Granger causality and how to test for this kind of relationship.

18.5 Granger Causality

Granger (1969) has introduced a concept of causality that, under conditions to be discussed in the following, can be analyzed in the framework of bivariate VAR processes. We first explain the concept of Granger causality and then discuss a test for noncausality.

Broadly speaking, a variable y_{1t} is said to be *Granger-caused* by a variable y_{2t} if the information in past and present y_{2t} helps to improve the forecasts of the y_1 variable. To formalize, suppose Ω_t contains all the relevant information in the universe up to period t and define $\sigma^2[y_{1t}(1)|\Omega_t]$ to be the conditional MSE of the optimal forecast $y_{1t}(1)$ given the information in Ω_t. The variable y_1 is Granger-caused by a variable y_2 if for some t

$$\sigma^2(y_{1t}(1)|\Omega_t) < \sigma^2(y_{1t}(1)|\Omega_t\backslash\{y_{2s}|s \le t\}) \tag{18.5.1}$$

where $\Omega_t\backslash\{y_{2s}|s \le t\}$ denotes all information in Ω_t that is not in $\{y_{2s}|s \le t\}$. In other words, y_1 is Granger-caused by y_2 if it can be predicted more efficiently when the information in past and present y_{2t} is taken into account in addition to all other information in the universe. Granger causality from y_1 to y_2 is defined analogously. A bivariate system where y_1 is caused by y_2 and y_2 is caused by y_1 is called a *feedback system.*

Assuming that $\mathbf{y}_t = (y_{1t}, y_{2t})'$ is generated by a stationary, normally distributed, bivariate VAR(p) process,

$$\begin{bmatrix} y_{1t} \\ y_{2t} \end{bmatrix} = \begin{bmatrix} \nu_1 \\ \nu_2 \end{bmatrix} + \begin{bmatrix} \theta_{11,1} & \theta_{12,1} \\ \theta_{21,1} & \theta_{22,1} \end{bmatrix} \begin{bmatrix} y_{1,t-1} \\ y_{2,t-1} \end{bmatrix} + \cdots + \begin{bmatrix} \theta_{11,p} & \theta_{12,p} \\ \theta_{21,p} & \theta_{22,p} \end{bmatrix} \begin{bmatrix} y_{1,t-p} \\ y_{2,t-p} \end{bmatrix} + \begin{bmatrix} v_{1t} \\ v_{2t} \end{bmatrix} \tag{18.5.2}$$

and assuming in addition that $\mathbf{y}_t$ contains all relevant information in the universe so that

$$\Omega_t = \{\mathbf{y}_s|s \le t\}$$

it can be shown that y_2 does not Granger-cause y_1 if and only if

$$\theta_{12,1} = \theta_{12,2} = \cdots = \theta_{12,p} = 0 \tag{18.5.3}$$

In turn, y_1 does not cause y_2 if and only if

$$\theta_{21,1} = \theta_{21,2} = \cdots = \theta_{21,p} = 0 \tag{18.5.4}$$

In other words, y_2 does not Granger-cause y_1 if y_2 does not appear in the first (y_1) equation of (18.5.2) and y_1 does not cause y_2 if the first variable does not appear in the second equation of the system (18.5.2).

Thus, in the special situation considered here, testing for the lack of causality comes down to testing zero constraints on the coefficients of the VAR(p) in (18.5.2). The null hypothesis (18.5.3) is equivalent to the null hypothesis of no Granger causality from y_2 to y_1. Such a null hypothesis can be tested using an F-test with test statistic

$$\lambda = \frac{\text{SSE}_r - \text{SSE}_u}{p\hat{\sigma}_{11}} \tag{18.5.5}$$

where SSE_r and SSE_u are the sums of squared errors obtained by LS estimation of the first equation in (18.5.2) with and without imposing the restrictions (18.5.3), respectively. The quantity $\hat{\sigma}_{11}$ is the LS estimator of the variance of v_{1t} as defined in (18.3.11). If the null hypothesis is correct the statistic λ has an approximate central F-distribution with p and $T - 2p - 1$ degrees of freedom. The F-distribution is only approximate because the estimation equation involves stochastic regressors. More precisely, $p\lambda$ has an asymptotic ($T \to \infty$) χ_p^2 distribution. In small samples using the F-distribution over the χ_p^2 seems reasonable since F has a fatter upper tail that may account for replacing the actual variance σ_{11} in the denominator by an estimator $\hat{\sigma}_{11}$. The null hypothesis of no Granger causality from y_1 to y_2 may be tested with an analogous statistic for the second equation of (18.5.2).

For our consumption/income example we may test in this way for Granger causality from income to consumption and vice versa if we assume that the data are actually generated by a normally distributed stationary VAR(1)

$$\begin{bmatrix} y_{1t} \\ y_{2t} \end{bmatrix} = \begin{bmatrix} v_1 \\ v_2 \end{bmatrix} + \begin{bmatrix} \theta_{11,1} & \theta_{12,1} \\ \theta_{21,1} & \theta_{22,1} \end{bmatrix} \begin{bmatrix} y_{1,t-1} \\ y_{2,t-1} \end{bmatrix} + \begin{bmatrix} v_{1t} \\ v_{2t} \end{bmatrix}$$

In order to test the null hypothesis

$$H_0\colon \theta_{12,1} = 0 \text{ [income } (y_2) \text{ does not cause consumption} (y_1)]$$

we have also estimated the first equation of the system without $y_{2,t-1}$. The estimation results are

$$\underset{}{y_{1t}} = \underset{(3)}{11} + \underset{(0.106)}{0.237}\, y_{1,t-1} + \hat{v}_{1t}, \qquad \hat{\sigma}_{v_1}^2 = 351 \tag{18.5.6}$$

where $\hat{\sigma}_{v_1}^2$ is the sum of squared errors divided by degrees of freedom. Using the results in (18.3.18) we get

$$\lambda = \frac{\hat{\sigma}_{v_1}^2(T-2) - \hat{\sigma}_{11}(T-3)}{\hat{\sigma}_{11}} = \frac{351 \cdot 68 - 275 \cdot 67}{275} = 20$$

Comparing this with the 1% critical value of the F-distribution with $p = 1$ and $T - 2p - 1 = 67$ degrees of freedom, $F_{(1,67,0.01)} \approx 7$, shows that we can reject the null hypothesis of no causal relation from income to consumption at the 1% significance level.

Note that for the VAR(1) case considered here the F-test is equivalent to a t-test for the significance of $\theta_{12,1}$. Such a test can be performed using the results in (18.3.18). Similarly, the null hypothesis

$$H_0\colon \theta_{21,1} = 0 \text{ [consumption does not cause income]}$$

can be tested with a t-test. From (18.3.18) the value of the test statistic is obtained as $0.232/0.127 = 1.83$. This value is smaller than the 2.5% critical value from the t

distribution with 67 degrees of freedom, $t_{(67, 0.025)} \approx 2$ (see the table at the end of the book). Thus the null hypothesis of *no* Granger causality from consumption to income cannot be rejected at the 5% level in a two-tailed test.

For illustrative purposes we will also test the null hypothesis of no causality from income to consumption on the basis of the VAR(4) model in (18.3.14), that is, we will test

$$H_0\colon \theta_{12,1} = \theta_{12,2} = \theta_{12,3} = \theta_{12,4} = 0$$

To determine the value of the F statistic in this case we have estimated an AR(4) model for y_{1t},

$$\underset{(3)}{y_{1t} = 11} + \underset{(0.125)}{0.220}\, y_{1,t-1} + \underset{(0.131)}{0.219}\, y_{1,t-2} - \underset{(0.131)}{0.017}\, y_{1,t-3} - \underset{(0.119)}{0.162}\, y_{1,t-4} + \hat{v}_{1t},$$

$$\hat{\sigma}_{v_1}^2 = 353 \tag{18.5.7}$$

Note that the effective sample size used for estimation is now $T = 67$ since four presample values are needed for LS estimation. From (18.3.14) $\hat{\sigma}_{11} = 284$ so that

$$\lambda = \frac{\hat{\sigma}_{v_1}^2(T-5) - \hat{\sigma}_{11}(T-9)}{4\hat{\sigma}_{11}} = \frac{353 \cdot 62 - 284 \cdot 58}{4 \cdot 284} = 4.78$$

This value clearly exceeds the 1% critical value $F_{(4, 58, 0.01)} \approx 3.65$, and thus the null hypothesis is rejected. In other words, we reject the hypothesis that there is no causality from income to consumption as we did on the basis of the VAR(1) model. In practice, the outcome of a causality test may depend on the VAR order since the power of the test depends on the order. This, of course, may create problems because the VAR order is usually unknown and must be chosen by the analyst. Noncausality from consumption to income may also be tested on the basis of the VAR(4) model. You are invited to carry out the test (see Exercise 18.7).

In the foregoing model, in order to make Granger's concept of causality operational, some quite restrictive assumptions have been made. First, the information set Ω_t has been reduced to the information in the past and present of the involved variables y_1 and y_2, which is short of some information in the universe. Expanding the information set may change the causal structure. Second, we have assumed that the data-generation process is a normally distributed stationary VAR process with known order p. The violation of any of these assumptions may invalidate the test. It is possible, however, to develop causality tests for more general situations. For some more discussion and references see Judge, et al. (1985, Section 16.2.3). Finally it may be worth noting that Granger's definition has been criticized because it is based on predictability rather than a cause and effect relationship between variables. Other definitions of causality have therefore been suggested.

18.6 Innovation Accounting and Forecast Error Variance Decomposition

Another use of VAR models that has been popularized by Sims (1980, 1981) and others is sometimes called *innovation accounting*. This term usually refers to tracing out the system's reaction to a shock (innovation) in one of the variables. For instance, in the consumption/income example system, the effect of an increase in income may be of interest. To isolate such an effect suppose that both variables are zero prior to time $t = 0$, $y_{1t} = y_{2t} = 0$, for $t < 0$, and income (y_2) increases by one unit in period 0, that is, $v_{20} = 1$. Now we can trace what happens to the system during periods $t = 1, 2, \ldots$ if no further shocks occur, that is, $v_{10} = 0$, $\mathbf{v}_1 = \mathbf{0}$, $\mathbf{v}_2 = \mathbf{0}, \ldots$. Since we are not interested in the mean of the variables in this exercise, but just their variation through time, we eliminate the intercept terms in (18.3.18) and assume that the actual consumption/income system is described by

$$\begin{bmatrix} y_{1t} \\ y_{2t} \end{bmatrix} = \begin{bmatrix} 0.008 & 0.461 \\ 0.232 & 0.297 \end{bmatrix} \begin{bmatrix} y_{1,t-1} \\ y_{2,t-1} \end{bmatrix} + \begin{bmatrix} v_{1t} \\ v_{2t} \end{bmatrix} \qquad \Sigma_{\mathbf{v}} = \begin{bmatrix} 275 & 167 \\ 167 & 390 \end{bmatrix} \tag{18.6.1}$$

Under the aforementioned assumptions we get for this system

$$\begin{bmatrix} y_{10} \\ y_{20} \end{bmatrix} = \begin{bmatrix} 0 \\ 1 \end{bmatrix},$$

$$\begin{bmatrix} y_{11} \\ y_{21} \end{bmatrix} = \begin{bmatrix} 0.008 & 0.461 \\ 0.232 & 0.297 \end{bmatrix} \begin{bmatrix} y_{10} \\ y_{20} \end{bmatrix} = \begin{bmatrix} 0.461 \\ 0.297 \end{bmatrix},$$

$$\begin{bmatrix} y_{12} \\ y_{22} \end{bmatrix} = \begin{bmatrix} 0.008 & 0.461 \\ 0.232 & 0.297 \end{bmatrix} \begin{bmatrix} y_{11} \\ y_{21} \end{bmatrix} = \begin{bmatrix} 0.008 & 0.461 \\ 0.232 & 0.297 \end{bmatrix}^2 \begin{bmatrix} y_{10} \\ y_{20} \end{bmatrix} = \begin{bmatrix} 0.141 \\ 0.195 \end{bmatrix},$$

$$\vdots$$

Continuing this procedure, it turns out that y_{1i} is just the upper right-hand corner element of

$$\begin{bmatrix} 0.008 & 0.461 \\ 0.232 & 0.297 \end{bmatrix}^i \tag{18.6.2}$$

and y_{2i} is the lower right-hand element of this matrix. In accordance with earlier terminology these quantities are called *multipliers*. In other words, the powers of the AR coefficient matrix of a VAR(1) process contain multipliers of the system.

Instead of a unit increase in one variable, a one standard error innovation is sometimes considered. For instance, instead of a unit innovation $v_{20} = 1$, an innovation $v_{20} = \sqrt{\sigma_{22}} = \sqrt{390} = 19.75$ may be traced through the system

(18.6.1). The resulting y_{mi} are obtained by simply multiplying the appropriate elements of (18.6.2) by $\sqrt{\sigma_{22}}$. Hence we obtain

$$\mathbf{y}_0 = \begin{bmatrix} 0 \\ 19.75 \end{bmatrix}, \mathbf{y}_1 = \begin{bmatrix} 9.10 \\ 5.87 \end{bmatrix}, \mathbf{y}_2 = \begin{bmatrix} 2.77 \\ 3.86 \end{bmatrix}, \ldots \tag{18.6.3}$$

More generally, for a higher-order process and a higher-dimensional system it can be shown that the matrices M_i, defined in (18.4.5), contain dynamic multipliers of the system. A stationary VAR(p) process of the type (18.2.1) can be shown to have a moving average (MA) representation

$$\begin{aligned} \mathbf{y}_t &= \boldsymbol{\mu} + \mathbf{v}_t + M_1\mathbf{v}_{t-1} + \cdots \\ &= \boldsymbol{\mu} + \sum_{i=0}^{\infty} M_i\mathbf{v}_{t-i} \end{aligned} \tag{18.6.4}$$

where $\boldsymbol{\mu} = E[\mathbf{y}_t] = (I - \Theta_1 - \cdots - \Theta_p)^{-1}\mathbf{v}$ and M_i is as defined in (18.4.5). The kjth element of M_i represents the reaction of the kth variable to a unit shock experienced by variable j, i periods ago, provided of course that the effect is not contaminated by other shocks to the system.

There are some obvious problems with such a simulation analysis. One of them is that it may be misleading if a model is used for analyzing conditions drastically different from those for which the model is designed. Therefore, it is questionable whether an analysis of this type provides insight into the reactions of the actual economic system. To see the problem, consider again the bivariate system (18.6.1). If $\mathbf{v}_t = (v_{1t}, v_{2t})'$ is actually a white-noise process it may be reasonable to force $\mathbf{v}_t$ to zero for $t \neq 0$ because innovations in different time periods are uncorrelated. Thus $\mathbf{v}_0$ does not imply anything for innovations in other time periods. However, v_{1t} is correlated with v_{2t}. In particular, v_{10} and v_{20} are correlated. Consequently, assuming that $v_{20} \neq 0$ while forcing v_{10} to be zero may be sufficiently unrealistic to obscure the actual reaction of the system. In terms of our example, a unit increase in income is likely to induce an instantaneous increase in consumption. Thus, it is unrealistic to assume that consumption does not increase in period $t = 0$ as we did previously. For this reason, innovation accounting is often performed within a transformed VAR model where the white-noise process has diagonal covariance matrix so that there is no instantaneous correlation among the components.

Since the covariance matrix $\Sigma_{\mathbf{v}}$ of a VAR(p) process is positive definite, there exists a nonsingular matrix P such that $P\Sigma_{\mathbf{v}}P' = I$ (see Appendix A). With this matrix the MA representation of $\mathbf{y}_t$ in (18.6.4) can be rewritten as

$$\mathbf{y}_t = \boldsymbol{\mu} + \sum_{i=0}^{\infty} M_i P^{-1} P\mathbf{v}_{t-i} = \boldsymbol{\mu} + \sum_{i=0}^{\infty} \Psi_i \mathbf{w}_{t-i} \tag{18.6.5}$$

where $\Psi_i = M_i P^{-1}$ and $\mathbf{w}_t = (w_{1t}, \ldots, w_{Mt})' = P\mathbf{v}_t$. The vector $\mathbf{w}_t$ has the convenient property that its components are uncorrelated and all have unit variance,

$$E[\mathbf{w}_t \mathbf{w}_t'] = PE[\mathbf{v}_t \mathbf{v}_t']P' = I$$

The matrices Ψ_i represent the reactions of the system $\mathbf{y}_t$ to unit innovations w_{mt}.

For the example process (18.6.1) one possible choice of the P matrix is

$$P = \begin{bmatrix} 0.070 & -0.030 \\ 0 & 0.051 \end{bmatrix}$$

and the M_i are given in (18.6.2). Using

$$P^{-1} = \begin{bmatrix} 14.286 & 8.403 \\ 0 & 19.608 \end{bmatrix}$$

we get

$$\begin{aligned} \Psi_0 &= M_0 P^{-1} = P^{-1} \\ \Psi_1 &= M_1 P^{-1} = \begin{bmatrix} 0.114 & 9.107 \\ 3.314 & 7.773 \end{bmatrix}, \\ \Psi_2 &= M_2 P^{-1} = \begin{bmatrix} 1.529 & 3.664 \\ 1.014 & 4.420 \end{bmatrix}, \\ &\vdots \qquad\qquad\qquad \vdots \end{aligned} \tag{18.6.6}$$

Hence, if $\mathbf{w}_0 = (0, 1)'$, that is, a unit innovation occurs in income (y_2) in period zero, and $\mathbf{w}_t = 0$ for $t \neq \mathbf{0}$,

$$\mathbf{y}_0 = \Psi_0 \mathbf{w}_0 = \begin{bmatrix} 8.403 \\ 19.608 \end{bmatrix}, \mathbf{y}_1 = \Psi_1 \mathbf{w}_0 = \begin{bmatrix} 9.107 \\ 7.773 \end{bmatrix}, \mathbf{y}_2 = \Psi_2 \mathbf{w}_0 = \begin{bmatrix} 3.664 \\ 4.420 \end{bmatrix}, \ldots$$

Obviously, the effect of an income innovation is now quite different from the effect obtained in (18.6.3). In particular, the income innovation now has an immediate effect on consumption, $y_{10} \neq 0$.

One problem that renders the interpretation of the multipliers difficult is the nonuniqueness of the P matrix and thus the Ψ_i. For instance, for the example process (18.6.1) the matrix

$$P = \begin{bmatrix} 0.060 & 0 \\ -0.036 & 0.059 \end{bmatrix}$$

also has the property that $P\Sigma_{\mathbf{v}}P' = I$ (except for rounding errors). Using the inverse of this matrix in (18.6.6) gives another set of multipliers in which an income innovation has no instantaneous impact on consumption. If a priori information suggests that income affects consumption instantaneously, one would prefer the multipliers in (18.6.6). Unfortunately, a priori information is not always available that suggests a particular form of MA representation. In such a case the multiplier analysis has a certain degree of arbitrariness. Only conclusions robust to the choice of the P matrix or MA representation of the system should be drawn in such a situation.

Recall that we discussed multiplier analysis in Section 15.5 in the context of systems of simultaneous equations. The fundamental difference between the present discussion and that of Chapter 15 is that in Chapter 15 we considered the effect of changes in the exogenous variables, while surprise innovations in the endogenous variables are now under investigation.

The representation (18.6.5) of a VAR(p) process offers another possibility to interpret the interrelationships within a system of variables. From (18.4.4) the MSE or forecast error covariance matrix of an h-step forecast is known to be

$$\begin{aligned}\Sigma(h) &= \Sigma_{\mathrm{v}} + M_1\Sigma_{\mathrm{v}}M_1' + \cdots + M_{h-1}\Sigma_{\mathrm{v}}M_{h-1}' \\ &= P^{-1}P\Sigma_{\mathrm{v}}P'(P^{-1})' + M_1P^{-1}P\Sigma_{\mathrm{v}}P'(P^{-1})'M_1' + \cdots \\ &\quad + M_{h-1}P^{-1}P\Sigma_{\mathrm{v}}P'(P^{-1})'M_{h-1}' \\ &= \Psi_0\Psi_0' + \Psi_1\Psi_1' + \cdots + \Psi_{h-1}\Psi_{h-1}' \end{aligned} \tag{18.6.7}$$

The mth diagonal element of $\Psi_n\Psi_n'$ is just the sum of the squares of the elements in the mth row of Ψ_n. Moreover, the sum of the mth diagonal elements of $\Psi_0\Psi_0', \ldots, \Psi_{h-1}\Psi_{h-1}'$ is the MSE or forecast error variance of the h-step forecast of variable y_m. The contribution of innovations in the jth variable to this MSE is given by

$$\psi_{mj,0}^2 + \psi_{mj,1}^2 + \cdots + \psi_{mj,h-1}^2 \tag{18.6.8}$$

where $\psi_{mj,n}$ is the mjth element of Ψ_n. This way a forecast error variance or MSE decomposition into the components accounted for by innovations in the individual variables can be obtained.

As an example consider again the consumption/income system (18.6.1). Using (18.6.6) the forecast error variance of a two-step forecast of consumption (y_1) is

$$\begin{aligned}\psi_{11,0}^2 + \psi_{11,1}^2 + \psi_{12,0}^2 + \psi_{12,1}^2 &= 14.286^2 + 0.114^2 + 8.403^2 + 9.107^2 \\ &= 357.65\end{aligned}$$

where $\psi_{11,0}^2 + \psi_{11,1}^2 = 204.10$ is the contribution of innovations in y_1 and $\psi_{12,0}^2 + \psi_{12,1}^2 = 153.55$ is the contribution of innovations in y_2. In other words, 57% of the forecast error variance of consumption is accounted for by own innovations and 43% is accounted for by income innovations. In a similar manner the MSE of a forecast of y_2 can be decomposed.

Of course, the interpretation of such a decomposition is difficult because nonuniqueness of the Ψ_i implies that the decomposition is also not unique. Furthermore, if important variables are not included in the system under consideration, the multipliers and forecast error variance components may not reflect the actual characteristics of the system. In small macroeconomic models, like the one used as an example, it seems easy to think of other variables that may have an important impact on the system. We have ignored this problem because it seems useful to begin with a simple example. For more details and references on problems related to the interpretation of VAR systems see Judge, et al. (1985, Chapter 16) and the references given there.

In the foregoing analysis we have assumed that the true data-generation process is known although this is rarely true in practice. At least the coefficients are usually estimated. In such a situation it is useful to consider the sampling variablity of the resulting estimated multipliers and MSE components. Under standard assumptions the asymptotic distribution of these quantities can be derived [see, for example, Schmidt (1973), Yamamoto (1980), and Lütkepohl (1987)].

18.7 Extensions of Vector Autoregressive Models

So far in this chapter we have concentrated on vector autoregressive processes where, a priori, all variables are regarded as endogenous. These models are suitable for forecasting and, to a limited extent, for analyzing the relationship between the involved variables. In the following we note some extensions of the present framework. For details and references you may consult Judge, et al. (1985, Chapter 16).

In some situations, a researcher may prefer a structural form set up with exogenous variables as in Chapters 14 and 15. The fact that all variables, a priori, are regarded as endogenous is not necessarily a shortcoming of the VAR models, however, since information on the exogeneity of some of the variables is often not available or controversial among economists. In such a situation one may want to test for exogeneity. Such tests can be set up in the framework of VAR processes. In fact, the Granger causality tests discussed in the previous section may be regarded as exogeneity tests. For instance, in the consumption/income VAR(1) system we have failed to reject the constraint $\theta_{21,1} = 0$. With this restriction the system (18.3.18) may be written as

$$y_{1t} = \nu_1 + \theta_{11,1} y_{1,t-1} + \theta_{12,1} y_{2,t-1} + v_{1t}$$

$$y_{2t} = \nu_2 + \theta_{22,1} y_{2,t-1} + v_{2t}$$

Assuming independence of v_{1t} and v_{2t}, the income variable y_2 may be regarded as exogenous in this bivariate system.

If a set of variables $\mathbf{x}_t$ is a priori known to be exogenous, these variables can easily be incorporated in a VAR(p) model by writing, for instance,

$$\mathbf{y}_t = B\mathbf{x}_t + \Theta_1\mathbf{y}_{t-1} + \cdots + \Theta_p\mathbf{y}_{t-p} + \mathbf{v}_t$$

where B is the coefficient matrix of the exogenous variables and the intercept terms are also included in $\mathbf{x}_t$. More generally *lagged* exogenous variables may enter the model in addition to the current variables $\mathbf{x}_t$. Models of this type are sometimes called ARX models or systems of dynamic simultaneous equations.

Another extension of the basic VAR(p) model (18.2.1) is obtained by allowing the errors to be intertemporally correlated, that is, $\mathbf{v}_t$ may be correlated with $\mathbf{v}_s$ for $s \neq t$. In considering univariate processes in Chapter 16 we have encountered AR models where the errors were generated by a finite-order moving-average process. Such processes can also be defined for the presently considered multivariate case, and VAR processes with MA error processes are called vector autoregressive moving average (VARMA) processes in analogy with the univariate case. These models may involve fewer parameters than the pure VAR counterparts and therefore may provide more efficient forecasts.

In the previous sections we have concentrated on stationary processes where the means, variances, and autocovariances are constant over time. This assumption excludes, for instance, variables with trends. As we have seen in Chapter 16, sometimes stationarity can be achieved with some initial transformation such as taking differences or logarithms. These transformations are in some cases also useful in multivariable systems. On the other hand, in some situations one may want to analyze the relationship between the original variables rather than transformed variables because transformations may distort or eliminate the original relationship. Possibilities for incorporating nonstationary variables in multiple time-series/dynamic simultaneous equations models have recently been suggested and investigated by Engle and Granger (1987) and others.

18.8 Summary and Comments

In this chapter we have discussed possible dynamic models for systems of variables. In particular we have analyzed vector autoregressive processes of finite order p. In these models all variables may be regarded as endogenous. We have shown that the reduced-form version of a VAR process can be estimated straightforwardly and that the asymptotic properties of the estimators can be derived under common assumptions. We have also shown how to use VAR processes for forecasting, for investigating the Granger causal relationship between variables, and for multiplier analysis.

There are, however, some problems with VAR models that should be kept in mind when using them in applied work. For instance, if the multiple time series under investigation is indeed generated by a stationary vector process it is not obvious that a model from the VAR class provides an optimal representation for all practical purposes. We have argued that under common assumptions stationary processes can be well approximated by finite-order VAR processes. This, of course, does not mean that a finite-order VAR model is always the best choice for a particular analysis. ARX or VARMA models may be advantageous in some situations. In particular, a candidate from the latter class may provide a representation of the generation process of a given multiple time-series that involves fewer parameters than a pure VAR model. More parsimoniously parameterized models may provide more accurate forecasts and are consequently preferable for forecasting purposes. In pure VAR models, parameter restrictions can sometimes help in improving the estimation and forecast efficiency.

Even if, in a particular situation, a pure VAR process is an adequate model for the generation process of a given multiple time-series, in general the order of the process will be unknown. It has to be estimated from the data in addition to the process coefficients. We have presented two criteria for choosing the process order. Many other criteria and procedures have been proposed in the recent literature and, as discussed in Chapter 20, selecting the optimal one for a particular problem at hand is a difficult task.

One of the assumptions underlying the asymptotic estimation theory has been the stationarity of the processes. Many economic time series have trends and regular seasonal components that cannot be captured by a stationary model. The presented models can be applied if the nonstationarities can be removed by transforming the series, for instance by taking differences and/or logarithms. However, initial transformations of the time series of interest are not always acceptable for a researcher investigating a system of variables. Moreover, many types of nonstationarities cannot be removed by transformations. For example, many forms of structural changes belong in this category. If nonstationarities are present, the models of this chapter have to be modified accordingly.

Although, given the critical points raised in the foregoing, you may become pessimistic regarding the usefulness of VAR models for applied work, it must be emphasized that VAR models have been employed extensively in econometric analyses and have proved to be useful analytic and forecasting tools in practice. On the other hand, the applied researcher should be aware of their limitations. For more references on multiple time-series analysis and for an overview of some more general models and alternative methods, refer to Chapter 16 of Judge, et al. (1985).

18.9 Exercises

The first problems will be concerned with the following three bivariate VAR processes.

$$y_{1t} = 0.1y_{2t} + y_{2,t-1} - 0.3y_{2,t-2} + e_{1t} \tag{18.9.1a}$$

$$y_{2t} = 0.5y_{1,t-1} + 0.4y_{2,t-1} + e_{2t} \tag{18.9.1b}$$

$$y_{1t} = 0.5y_{1,t-1} + e_{1t} \tag{18.9.2a}$$

$$y_{2t} = y_{1,t-1} + 0.3y_{2,t-1} + e_{2t} \tag{18.9.2b}$$

$$y_{1t} = 0.5y_{1,t-1} + 0.3y_{2t} + 0.5y_{2,t-1} + e_{1t} \tag{18.9.3a}$$

$$y_{2t} = 0.5y_{2,t-1} + 0.3y_{2,t-2} + e_{2t} \tag{18.9.3b}$$

In all three systems $(e_{1t}, e_{2t})'$ is white noise with unit variance-covariance matrix.

18.1 Rewrite the three processes (18.9.1) through (18.9.3) in reduced form as in (18.2.1) using vector and matrix notation and determine the covariance matrices of the resulting white-noise processes.

18.2 Is the VAR process (18.9.2) stationary?

18.3 In which of the processes (18.9.1), (18.9.2), or (18.9.3) is y_1 Granger-caused by y_2 and in which ones is y_2 caused by y_1?

18.4 Assume that $(y_{1T}, y_{2T})' = (-1.88, -0.10)'$ and compute the forecasts

$$\begin{bmatrix} y_{1T}(1) \\ y_{2T}(1) \end{bmatrix}, \begin{bmatrix} y_{1T}(2) \\ y_{2T}(2) \end{bmatrix}$$

and the corresponding MSE matrices $\Sigma(1)$ and $\Sigma(2)$ for the VAR(1) (18.9.2). Assume that the process is normally distributed, and set up 95% forecast intervals for $y_{1,T+1}$, $y_{2,T+1}$, $y_{1,T+2}$, and $y_{2,T+2}$.

18.5 Assume that the process (18.3.18) is the generation process of the data in Table 18.1 and suppose the process is normally distributed. Compute forecasts $y_{1,73}(1)$, $y_{1,73}(2)$, $y_{2,73}(1)$, and $y_{2,73}(2)$ and the corresponding MSE matrices $\Sigma(1)$ and $\Sigma(2)$. Determine 95% forecast intervals and compare with the actually observed values in Table 18.1.

18.6 Discuss the assumptions underlying the forecasts, MSEs, and forecast intervals in Exercise 18.5.

Table 18.3 First Differences of Quarterly Seasonally Adjusted U.S. Fixed Investment (y_1) and Change in Business Inventories (y_2) in Billions of 1972 Dollars at Annual Rates, 1947.II–1968.IV.

t	y_{1t}	y_{2t}	t	y_{1t}	y_{2t}
1	−2.0	−1.0	45	−2.8	0.6
2	1.9	−2.0	46	0.8	6.5
3	5.2	5.6	47	5.0	5.0
4	2.4	1.4	48	5.3	−0.3
5	0.3	1.5	49	3.3	8.0
6	−0.8	1.3	50	1.0	−13.4
7	−0.5	−1.6	51	−1.2	8.6
8	−4.3	−5.6	52	3.5	5.3
9	−2.9	−6.8	53	−3.1	−8.6
10	−0.4	4.6	54	−3.0	−1.9
11	2.1	−5.2	55	−0.2	−6.9
12	4.8	12.1	56	−0.9	0.1
13	6.9	3.3	57	1.5	5.7
14	5.9	0.3	58	2.1	4.7
15	−1.3	14.1	59	3.3	0.1
16	−3.5	−8.7	60	1.5	3.9
17	−3.1	6.5	61	3.8	−1.4
18	−0.9	−5.3	62	1.2	−1.2
19	−0.8	−7.6	63	−1.0	−3.3
20	0.7	0.3	64	0.6	2.9
21	1.0	−10.0	65	5.3	−0.6
22	−5.0	8.1	66	2.5	2.3
23	5.3	1.8	67	3.5	−2.2
24	3.3	−3.3	68	2.0	−1.0
25	0.3	1.2	69	0.0	1.9
26	0.2	−3.2	70	0.9	−0.7
27	−0.6	−6.9	71	1.5	0.6
28	−1.0	1.6	72	7.0	5.5
29	1.3	−0.7	73	4.5	−2.8
30	2.9	1.4	74	2.2	1.8
31	1.5	4.2	75	3.7	−3.6
32	3.6	4.4	76	3.7	4.7
33	4.0	2.1	77	−1.3	4.3
34	2.2	−0.2	78	−1.2	−2.7
35	0.5	1.4	79	−5.3	5.4
36	−2.2	−1.7	80	−3.3	−5.9
37	0.8	−2.0	81	3.2	−7.1
38	0.2	−0.6	82	1.5	4.7
39	−1.0	0.5	83	4.4	1.6
40	−0.4	−2.9	84	3.4	−7.5
41	−0.9	0.4	85	0.0	5.5
42	1.1	0.8	86	1.8	−2.6
43	−1.5	−6.7	87	4.3	−1.6
44	−4.9	−3.8			

Source: Fixed investment and change in business inventories: U.S. Department of Commerce, *The National Income and Product Accounts of the United States, 1929–74.*

18.7 We have estimated an AR(4) model for the income data in Table 18.1 using observations 5–71 as sample values and observations 1–4 as presample values. The resulting model is

$$\begin{aligned} y_{2t} = \underset{(4)}{10} + \underset{(0.126)}{0.419}\, y_{2,t-1} - \underset{(0.140)}{0.050}\, y_{2,t-2} \\ + \underset{(0.141)}{0.047}\, y_{2,t-3} - \underset{(0.127)}{0.033}\, y_{2,t-4} + \hat{v}_{2t}, \end{aligned}$$

$$\hat{\sigma}_{v2}^2 = 418$$

Use these results and the model in (18.3.14) to test the null hypothesis of no Granger causal relationship from consumption to income.

18.8 Compute the MA coefficient matrices M_3 and M_4 of the process (18.6.1). Interpret the elements of these matrices. Compute also Ψ_3 and Ψ_4 with an upper triangular P matrix as in (18.6.6) and compare the elements of these matrices with those of M_3 and M_4.

The following problems require the use of a computer.

18.9 In Table 18.3 the first differences of seasonally adjusted U.S. quarterly fixed investment (y_1) and change in business inventories (y_2) are given. Plot the data and discuss the stationarity of the series.

18.10 Use observations 1–4 as presample values and observations 5–87 from Table 18.3 as sample values and estimate bivariate VAR(p) models with $p = 0, 1, 2, 3, 4$. Compute the corresponding AIC and SC values and determine the order p(AIC) and p(SC). Interpret the results.

18.11 Reestimate a VAR model for the data in Table 18.3 using the order p(SC). Use the maximum sample size possible for LS estimation.

18.12 Use the model of Problem 18.11 to perform a Granger causality test from fixed investment to change in business inventories.

18.10 References

Engle, R. F., and C. W. J. Granger (1987) "Co-Integration and Error-Correction: Representation, Estimation and Testing." *Econometrica*, 55, 251–276.

Granger, C. W. J. (1969) "Investigating Causal Relations by Econometric Models and Cross-Spectral Methods." *Econometrica*, 37, 424–438.

Judge, G. G., W. E. Griffiths, R. C. Hill, H. Lütkepohl, and T. C. Lee (1985) *The Theory and Practice of Econometrics*, 2nd ed., New York, Wiley.

Lütkepohl, H. (1985) "Comparison of Criteria for Estimating the Order of a Vector Autoregressive Process," *Journal of Time Series Analysis*, 6, 35–52. "Correction," *Journal of Time Series Analysis*, 8 (1987), p. 373.

Lütkepohl, H. (1987) *Forecasting Aggregated Vector ARMA Processes.* Berlin: Springer-Verlag.

Schmidt, P. (1973) "The Asymptotic Distribution of Dynamic Multipliers," *Econometrica*, 41, 161–164.

Sims, C. A. (1980) "Macroeconomics and Reality," *Econometrica*, 48, 1–48.

Sims, C. A. (1981) "An Autoregressive Index Model for the U.S. 1948–1975." In J. Kmenta and J. B. Ramsey, eds. *Large-Scale Macroeconometric Models.* Amsterdam: North-Holland, pp. 283–327.

Yamamoto, T. (1980) "On the Treatment of Autocorrelated Errors in the Multiperiod Prediction of Dynamic Simultaneous Equation Models." *International Economic Review*, 21, 735–748.

PART 6

Additional Econometric Topics

When choice alternatives are limited, the outcomes for economic variables appear in discrete or quantal form. In the first chapter of this part, we consider how to cope with the statistical modeling and estimation in the case of discrete random left-hand side variables. In the second chapter of this part, we consider within a sampling theory and decision theoretic context (1) the problems of inference when both sample and nonsample information is used, (2) the statistical implications of conventional hypothesis-testing schemes, (3) a range of biased estimators that are uniformly superior to the least-squares maximum likelihood estimator, and (4) procedures for choosing the form and content of the design matrix (variable selection). In the third chapter of this part, we consider procedures for coping with situations in which the experimental design is such that the $X'X$ matrix is nearly singular. Finally, in the last chapter of this part, we consider a range of estimators that are robust over a range of distributional assumptions concerning the random errors.

CHAPTER 19

Qualitative and Limited Dependent Variable Models

19.1 Introduction

Economists usually deal with models in which the dependent variable can be assumed to be continuous. Economics, however, as a theory of choice, can deal with much more general situations. In particular, questions about whether to produce or consume, rather than how much to produce or consume, are also of interest. Thus, the econometrician is faced with modeling the behavior of a decision maker who must choose from a finite set of alternatives. Models that are used for such purposes are called models with qualitative dependent variables. Examples of situations in which these models have been used include the household decision of whether to buy or rent a suitable dwelling, a senator's decision on whether to vote yes or no on a piece of legislation, an individual's decision of whether or not to join the labor force, and a consumer's choice of which of several shopping areas to visit. In each case the decision maker must choose an action from a finite set of discrete alternatives, often just two are considered as in a yes–no decision.

To illustrate why these situations require special treatment, suppose we let the binary choice be represented by the dichotomous variable y, which takes the value 1 when one choice is made and 0 when the other is made. If we observe a sample of T choices and wish to explain them using a linear regression model we might write

$$y_i = \mathbf{x}_i'\boldsymbol{\beta} + e_i \qquad i = 1, \ldots, T \tag{19.1.1}$$

in the usual notation. The difficulties with this specification are immediate, however, as we examine the properties the error terms must have if we wish to assume, as usual, that $E[y_i] = \mathbf{x}_i'\boldsymbol{\beta}$. First, given the Bernoulli character of the random variable y_i, it must be the case that $E[y_i] = Pr[y_i = 1] = \mathbf{x}_i'\boldsymbol{\beta}$. Unfortunately, given that $\mathbf{x}_i'\boldsymbol{\beta}$ is unbounded, we face the problem that this model can give probabilities outside the unit interval. Second, since y_i can only take two values, then e_i can only take two values and these with specified probabilities if $E[y_i] = \mathbf{x}_i'\boldsymbol{\beta}$, namely

$$e_i = \begin{cases} 1 - \mathbf{x}_i'\boldsymbol{\beta} \text{ with probability } \mathbf{x}_i'\boldsymbol{\beta} \text{ (when } y_i = 1) \\ -\mathbf{x}_i'\boldsymbol{\beta} \text{ with probability } 1 - \mathbf{x}_i'\boldsymbol{\beta} \text{ (when } y_i = 0) \end{cases}$$

Third, with this probability structure e_i is heteroskedastic since $\text{var}(e_i) = E[y_i](1 - E[y_i])$. One can use the generalized least squares estimation procedure outlined in Chapter 9. However, the drawbacks of such a choice are clear. Consequently, more appropriate models for handling this data-generation process are discussed in Section 19.2.

A related situation leads to consideration of models in which the dependent variable is continuous but only takes a limited range of values. These models are called censored regression models (or frequently Tobit models), and the usual least squares parameter estimator is inconsistent. In Section 19.3 we investigate the problems with the least squares estimator and present and illustrate an appropriate maximum likelihood estimator. Section 19.4 contains a summary and guide to further reading.

19.2 Binary Choice Models

In this section we consider modeling the choice behavior of individuals when two alternatives are available and one must be chosen. This binary choice of the ith individual is conveniently represented by a random variable y_i that takes the value 1 if one choice is made and 0 if the other choice is made. If P_i is the probability that y_i takes the value 1, then $1 - P_i$ is the probability that y_i is 0. This can be summarized by writing the probability function for y_i as

$$f(y_i) = P_i^{y_i}(1 - P_i)^{1-y_i} \qquad y_i = 0, 1 \tag{19.2.1}$$

Economists are typically interested in examining what factors affect the choice probability P_i.

To develop such a model we assume that the average utility derived from a choice by an individual is based on the attributes of the choice, which are specific to the individual, for example, the individual's socioeconomic characteristics. Within this context, consider a decision-maker who must decide whether to commute to work by car or bus. Attributes of the choice that are relevant for an individual include the cost of using a car or riding the bus, the time of the trip using car or bus, the comfort and safety of using car or bus. Attributes of the individual that may affect the choice include income, occupation, and age. Note that these individual characteristics do not vary across alternatives. If we then define the utility derived from the choices as the average utility plus a random disturbance we have

$$U_{i0} = \bar{U}_{i0} + e_{i0} = \mathbf{z}_{i0}'\boldsymbol{\delta} + \mathbf{w}_i'\boldsymbol{\gamma}_0 + e_{i0} \tag{19.2.2a}$$

$$U_{i1} = \bar{U}_{i1} + e_{i1} = \mathbf{z}_{i1}'\boldsymbol{\delta} + \mathbf{w}_i'\boldsymbol{\gamma}_1 + e_{i1} \tag{19.2.2b}$$

where U_{i0} and U_{i1} are the utilities from the two choices, (the subscripts 0 and 1 denote the choice), $\bar{U}_{i0}$ and $\bar{U}_{i1}$ are the average utilities, $\mathbf{z}'_{i0}$ and $\mathbf{z}'_{i1}$ are vectors of characteristics of the alternatives, as perceived by individual i, and $\mathbf{w}'_i$ is a vector of socioeconomic characteristics of the ith individual, and e_{i0} and e_{i1} are random disturbances. Now the utilities U_{i0} and U_{i1} are random, and the ith individual will choose alternative one only if $U_{i1} > U_{i0}$ or if the unobservable, or latent, random variable $y_i^* = U_{i1} - U_{i0} > 0$. Consequently the values of the observable random variable y_i are determined as

$$y_i = \begin{cases} 1 & \text{if } y_i^* > 0 \\ 0 & \text{if } y_i^* \leq 0 \end{cases} \tag{19.2.3a}$$

Let us rewrite y_i^* as

$$\begin{aligned} y_i^* &= (\mathbf{z}_{i1} - \mathbf{z}_{i0})'\boldsymbol{\delta} + \mathbf{w}'_i(\boldsymbol{\gamma}_1 - \boldsymbol{\gamma}_0) + (e_{i1} - e_{i0}) \\ &= [(\mathbf{z}_{i1} - \mathbf{z}_{i0})', \mathbf{w}'_i]\begin{bmatrix} \boldsymbol{\delta} \\ \boldsymbol{\gamma}_1 - \boldsymbol{\gamma}_0 \end{bmatrix} + e_i^* \\ &= \mathbf{x}'_i\boldsymbol{\beta} + e_i^* \end{aligned} \tag{19.2.3b}$$

where $\mathbf{x}'_i$, $\boldsymbol{\beta}$, and e_i^* are explanatory variables, unknown location parameters, and random errors in the linear statistical model for y_i^*. The probability that $y_i = 1$ is

$$P_i = Pr[y_i = 1] = Pr[y_i^* > 0] = Pr[e_i^* > -\mathbf{x}'_i\boldsymbol{\beta}] \tag{19.2.3c}$$

It is clear that to make the model complete a particular probability distribution for e_i^* must be chosen. The two most common choices of distributions are the standard normal and the logistic. The c.d.f. of the standard normal is

$$F(t) = \int_{-\infty}^{t} (2\pi)^{-1/2} \exp\{-x^2/2\}\, dx \tag{19.2.4a}$$

and that of the logistic random variable is

$$F(t) = 1/[1 + \exp(-t)] \tag{19.2.4b}$$

Although more will be said about both these distributions later, for the present we note that both are symmetric with zero means. The standard normal has variance $\sigma^2 = 1$ and the logistic random variable has variance $\sigma^2 = \pi^2/3$. The logistic distribution closely approximates the normal [see Amemiya (1981, p. 1487)] and is easy to work with. See Ben-Akiva and Lerman (1985, pp. 64–72) for a discussion of these error distribution choices. In passing we note that if e_i^* is chosen to have a uniform distribution, then the linear probability model (19.1.1) results. The choice of normal errors leads to the probit statistical model and the choice of the logistic leads to the logit statistical model.

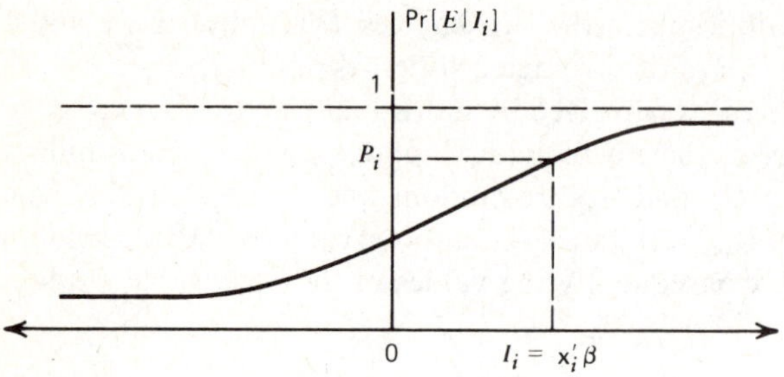

Figure 19.1 The probability model $P_i = F(\mathbf{x}_i'\boldsymbol{\beta})$.

For either the standard normal or logistic distributions, since they are symmetric, $F(-t) = 1 - F(t)$ and we can rewrite (19.2.3c) as

$$\begin{aligned} P_i &= Pr[e_i^* > -\mathbf{x}_i'\boldsymbol{\beta}] \\ &= 1 - Pr[e_i^* \leq -\mathbf{x}_i'\boldsymbol{\beta}] = 1 - F(-\mathbf{x}_i'\boldsymbol{\beta}) \\ &= F(\mathbf{x}_i'\boldsymbol{\beta}) \end{aligned} \tag{19.2.5}$$

This probability model is depicted in Figure 19.1. Note that both the probit model and logit model lead to probabilities that are confined to the unit interval, unlike the linear probability model. The choice between the probit and logit models is usually made on the basis of convenience, with the probit model usually being chosen if the appropriate computer software is available. The differences between the models are, in fact, slight.

The object of estimation in these models is the vector of unknown parameters $\boldsymbol{\beta}$. How the estimation is carried out depends on the type of data that is available. On one hand we sometimes have repeated observations on a particular decision maker. Such a situation arises, for example, if we observe many votes by a particular politician on similar legislative bills or issues. In these cases we can actually estimate P_i using the sample proportion of the occurrences that alternative one was chosen and use this to facilitate the estimation of $\boldsymbol{\beta}$. If sufficient repeated observations on an individual decision maker are not available, then maximum likelihood methods for estimating $\boldsymbol{\beta}$ can be used. We discuss these techniques in turn.

19.2.1 Estimation of Probit and Logit Models When Repeated Observations are Available

In this section we assume that for each individual i, $i = 1, \ldots, T$, we observe a $(1 \times K)$ vector $\mathbf{x}_i'$ of variables measuring attributes of the alternatives and the characteristics of the individual. Furthermore, assume that we observe n_i repetitions of the same choice situation. If p_i is the proportion that alternative one was chosen in n_i trials, then p_i is an estimator of the true probability P_i and we can write

$$p_i = P_i + e_i = F(\mathbf{x}_i'\boldsymbol{\beta}) + e_i \tag{19.2.6}$$

where the random error e_i has mean zero and variance $P_i(1 - P_i)/n_i$, the same mean and variance as the sample proportion. The specification (19.2.6) follows from the fact that p_i is an unbiased (and consistent) estimator of P_i.

19.2.1a The Probit Model

The probit model is derived by letting F be the c.d.f. of a standard normal random variable. The "observed" probit is then defined as $v_i = F^{-1}(p_i)$ so that

$$v_i = F^{-1}(p_i) = F^{-1}(P_i + e_i) \tag{19.2.7}$$

where $F^{-1}(\cdot)$ is the inverse function of the normal c.d.f. If we expand $F^{-1}(P_i + e_i)$ about P_i using a Taylor's series expansion, and retaining only the first-order terms, we have

$$F^{-1}(P_i + e_i) \doteq F^{-1}(P_i) + \frac{e_i}{f[F^{-1}(P_i)]} \tag{19.2.8}$$

where $f(\cdot)$ is the value of the standard normal p.d.f. evaluated at its argument. Then (19.2.7) can be rewritten as

$$v_i = F^{-1}(P_i) + u_i = \mathbf{x}_i'\boldsymbol{\beta} + u_i \qquad i = 1, \ldots, T \tag{19.2.9}$$

since $F^{-1}(P_i) = \mathbf{x}_i'\boldsymbol{\beta}$ (see Fig. 19.1). The random disturbance u_i has zero mean and variance

$$\text{Var}(u_i) = \frac{P_i(1 - P_i)}{n_i\{f[F^{-1}(P_i)]\}^2} \tag{19.2.10}$$

Consequently, if we observe the choices of T independent individuals we can write (19.2.9) in matrix notation as

$$\mathbf{v} = X\boldsymbol{\beta} + \mathbf{u} \tag{19.2.11}$$

where $E[\mathbf{u}] = \mathbf{0}$ and $\text{Cov}(\mathbf{u}) = \boldsymbol{\Phi}$ where $\boldsymbol{\Phi}$ is a diagonal matrix with diagonal elements given by (19.2.10). An EGLS estimator can be obtained as

$$\hat{\hat{\boldsymbol{\beta}}} = (X'\hat{\boldsymbol{\Phi}}^{-1}X)^{-1}X'\hat{\boldsymbol{\Phi}}^{-1}\mathbf{v} \tag{19.2.12}$$

where $\hat{\boldsymbol{\Phi}}$ is constructed using p_i as an estimator for P_i. As a basis for iterating the EGLS estimator note that $\hat{\hat{\boldsymbol{\beta}}}$ could be used to obtain a new estimator of P_i, namely $\hat{P}_i$, leading to a new estimate of $\boldsymbol{\beta}$ and so on. In large samples, the approximate distribution of the EGLS estimator, iterated or not, is $N[\boldsymbol{\beta}, (X'\boldsymbol{\Phi}^{-1}X)^{-1}]$. See Chapter 9 for the conditions under which this result holds.

Finally, we must address several matters of practical importance. First, use of this estimator requires that more than one observation be available on each decision maker. There should be enough observations that the sample proportion p_i provides a reliable estimate of the proportion P_i. In general, to use this procedure a minimum of five or six observations should be available on each decision maker. If fewer observations are available, then the methods described in Section 19.2.2 should be used. Second, the observed probit v_i in (19.2.7) is the value such that

$$p_i = \int_{-\infty}^{v_i} (2\pi)^{-1/2} \exp\{-t^2/2\}\, dt$$

Since the data allow the computation of the estimate p_i, v_i is observed in the sense that it can be solved for. Solving for v_i requires finding the value of a standard normal random variable such that the value of the c.d.f. at this point is p_i. This is not as great a computational burden as it once was, as many computer packages contain the inverse function of the standard normal c.d.f. Third, note that since the covariance matrix $\boldsymbol{\Phi}$ is diagonal, the EGLS estimator can be obtained using weighted least squares. That is, if each observation on the dependent and all explanatory variables is multiplied by the reciprocal of the square root of (19.2.10) with p_i replacing P_i, then the EGLS estimator may be obtained by applying least squares to the resulting transformed model. See Chapter 9 for further discussion of this transformation.

19.2.1b The Logit Model

A frequently used alternative to the probit model is the logit model. The logit model is based on the logistic c.d.f. given by

$$P_i = F(\mathbf{x}_i'\boldsymbol{\beta}) = 1/[1 + \exp(-\mathbf{x}_i'\boldsymbol{\beta})] \tag{19.2.13}$$

This c.d.f. closely approximates that of a normal random variable and has some convenient properties. If the sample proportions are used to form the odds ratio $p_i/(1 - p_i)$, then Zellner and Lee (1965) use a Taylor expansion to show that

$$\ln\left(\frac{p_i}{1 - p_i}\right) \doteq \ln\left(\frac{P_i}{1 - P_i}\right) + \frac{e_i}{P_i(1 - P_i)} = \mathbf{x}_i'\boldsymbol{\beta} + u_i \tag{19.2.14}$$

since $\ln[P_i/(1 - P_i)] = \mathbf{x}_i'\boldsymbol{\beta}$. Once again all T observations can be written as (19.2.11), although $\mathbf{v}$ is now a vector of observed logits, that is, the natural logarithm of the observed odds ratio, and the variance of u_i is $[1/(n_i P_i(1 - P_i))]$. The EGLS estimator for $\boldsymbol{\beta}$ can again be represented as (19.2.12), where $\hat{\boldsymbol{\Phi}}$ and $\mathbf{v}$ are appropriately redefined. The predicted probabilities $\hat{P}_i = F(\mathbf{x}_i'\hat{\hat{\boldsymbol{\beta}}})$ again can be used as a basis for iterative estimation.

19.2.1c An Interpretive Note

Finally, let us add a note on the interpretation of the estimated coefficients in logit and probit models. Estimated coefficients do not indicate the increase in the probability of the event occurring, given a one-unit increase in the corresponding independent variable. Rather, the coefficients reflect the effect of a change in an independent variable on $F^{-1}(P_i)$, for the probit model, and on $\ln[P_i/(1 - P_i)]$, for the logit model. In both cases the amount of the increase in probability depends on the original probability and thus on the initial values of all the independent variables and their coefficients. Specifically, for the probit model

$$\frac{\partial P_i}{\partial x_{ij}} = f(\mathbf{x}_i'\boldsymbol{\beta}) \cdot \beta_j \tag{19.2.15}$$

and for the logit model

$$\frac{\partial P_i}{\partial x_{ij}} = \frac{\beta_j \cdot \exp(-\mathbf{x}_i'\boldsymbol{\beta})}{[1 + \exp(-\mathbf{x}_i'\boldsymbol{\beta})]^2} \tag{19.2.16}$$

where x_{ij} is the jth element of $\mathbf{x}_i$. Having examined binary-dependent variable models with repeated observations, we consider the more usual case in which only one or a few observations are available on each choice maker.

19.2.2 Estimation of Probit and Logit Models When Repeated Observations are Not Available

When there are but a few, or just one, observations on each decision maker, the methods outlined in Section 19.2.1 must be abandoned and maximum likelihood methods may be used. These methods are computationally more burdensome, although not extremely so with modern computing techniques.

Given a sample of T independent observations, where each observation may be on a different individual, the likelihood function is

$$\ell = \prod_{i=1}^{T} f(y_i) = \prod_{i=1}^{T} P_i^{y_i}(1 - P_i)^{(1-y_i)}$$

$$= \prod_{i=1}^{T} F(\mathbf{x}_i'\boldsymbol{\beta})^{y_i}[1 - F(\mathbf{x}_i'\boldsymbol{\beta})]^{(1-y_i)} \tag{19.2.17}$$

where $F(\cdot)$ is either the standard normal or logistic c.d.f., and $y_i = 1$ if alternative one is chosen but is zero otherwise. This likelihood function or its logarithm,

$$\ln \ell = \sum_{i=1}^{T} y_i \ln F(\mathbf{x}_i'\boldsymbol{\beta}) + \sum_{i=1}^{T} (1 - y_i)\ln[1 - F(\mathbf{x}_i'\boldsymbol{\beta})] \tag{19.2.18}$$

must be maximized using numerical methods because the first-order derivatives,

$$\frac{\partial \ln \ell}{\partial \boldsymbol{\beta}} = \sum_{i=1}^{T} y_i \frac{f}{F} \mathbf{x}_i - \sum_{i=1}^{T} (1 - y_i) \frac{f}{1 - F} \mathbf{x}_i \tag{19.2.19}$$

where F and f are the values of the relevant c.d.f. and corresponding density functions at $\mathbf{x}_i'\boldsymbol{\beta}$ are highly nonlinear functions of $\boldsymbol{\beta}$ and cannot be solved directly.

A method for maximizing a nonlinear function in this situation is the iterative procedure called the Newton–Raphson method, or the method of Newton, which is discussed in Chapter 12. In this iterative procedure, the $(t + 1)$st round estimate, say $\hat{\boldsymbol{\beta}}_{t+1}$, is given by

$$\hat{\boldsymbol{\beta}}_{t+1} = \hat{\boldsymbol{\beta}}_t - \left[\frac{\partial^2 \ln \ell}{\partial \boldsymbol{\beta}\, \partial \boldsymbol{\beta}'} \bigg|_{\hat{\boldsymbol{\beta}}_t} \right]^{-1} \left[\frac{\partial \ln \ell}{\partial \boldsymbol{\beta}} \bigg|_{\hat{\boldsymbol{\beta}}_t} \right] \tag{19.2.20}$$

where $[\partial^2 \ln \ell / \partial \boldsymbol{\beta}\, \partial \boldsymbol{\beta}' |_{\hat{\boldsymbol{\beta}}_t}]$ is the $(K \times K)$ matrix of second partials of the log-likelihood function evaluated at the tth round estimate $\hat{\boldsymbol{\beta}}_t$. The properties of the log-likelihood function (19.2.18) for both the normal and logistic c.d.f.'s guarantee that this method will converge to the global maximum based on any set of starting values $\hat{\boldsymbol{\beta}}_0$. Furthermore, we know that the maximum likelihood estimators are consistent, asymptotically efficient, and asymptotically normally distributed. A consistent estimate of the asymptotic covariance matrix that can be used as a basis for hypothesis tests or confidence intervals is

$$-\left[\frac{\partial^2 \ln \ell}{\partial \boldsymbol{\beta}\, \partial \boldsymbol{\beta}'} \right]^{-1}$$

evaluated at the final set of parameter estimates $\tilde{\boldsymbol{\beta}}$.

You may verify that for the probit model, using $f(t) = (2\pi)^{-1/2} e^{-t^2/2}$, $f'(t) = -tf(t)$, and $F(-t) = 1 - F(t)$,

$$\frac{\partial^2 \ln \ell}{\partial \boldsymbol{\beta}\, \partial \boldsymbol{\beta}'} = -\sum_{i=1}^{T} f \left[y_i \frac{f + (\mathbf{x}_i'\boldsymbol{\beta})F}{F^2} + (1 - y_i) \frac{f - (\mathbf{x}_i'\boldsymbol{\beta})(1 - F)}{(1 - F)^2} \right] \mathbf{x}_i \mathbf{x}_i' \tag{19.2.21}$$

and for the logit model, using

$$F(t) = \frac{1}{1 + e^{-t}}, \quad f(t) = \frac{e^{-t}}{(1 + e^{-t})^2}$$

$$1 - F(t) = \frac{e^{-t}}{1 + e^{-t}}, \quad \frac{f(t)}{F(t)} = 1 - F(t)$$

and

$$f'(t) = -f(t) \cdot F(t) \cdot (1 - e^{-t})$$

$$\frac{\partial^2 \ln \ell}{\partial \boldsymbol{\beta}\, \partial \boldsymbol{\beta}'} = -\sum_{i=1}^{T} f(\mathbf{x}_i'\boldsymbol{\beta})\mathbf{x}_i\mathbf{x}_i' \tag{19.2.22}$$

To illustrate the use of these models consider the following example. Using the (20 × 3) design matrix X presented in Chapter 5, Equation (5.10.2) and the parameter values $\boldsymbol{\beta} = (0, 3, -3)'$, 10 sets of values of the dependent variable were generated using the probit structure. (These values appear in the exercise section of this chapter.) That is, the probability P_i of y_i taking the value of 1 is

$$P_i = \int_{-\infty}^{\mathbf{x}_i'\boldsymbol{\beta}} \frac{1}{\sqrt{2\pi}} \exp\left\{-\frac{t^2}{2}\right\} dt$$

The value of y_i was assigned to be 1 or 0 on the basis of whether the value of y_i^*, as defined in (19.2.3b), was greater than 0, or not, respectively.

For this example the first four of the samples in Table 19.4 were combined into a single sample of size 80. The results of estimation of the probit model are presented in Table 19.1. The maximum likelihood estimates of β_2 and β_3 based on this sample of 80 values have the correct signs and are close to the true parameter values. The standard errors are the square roots of the diagonal elements of $-[\partial^2 \ln \ell/\partial\boldsymbol{\beta}\, \partial\boldsymbol{\beta}']^{-1}$, where the matrix of second partial derivatives is given by (19.2.21), after the maximum likelihood estimates were substituted for the unknown parameters. These estimated standard errors of the maximum likelihood estimators have only asymptotic justification. The t-values are values of the test statistics for the hypothesis that the associated parameter is 0. Asymptotically, the test statistic is distributed as an $N(0, 1)$ random variable if the hypothesis is true, so that the relevant critical value for the $\alpha = 0.05$ level of significance is 1.96.

Several other summary measures are often presented with the results of probit and logit models. One measure is the result of a test of hypothesis that the

Table 19.1 Results of Maximum Likelihood Estimation of Probit Model

Parameter	Parameter estimate	Standard error	t-Values
$\beta_1 = 0$	$\tilde{\beta}_1 = 0.115$	0.63	0.18
$\beta_2 = 3$	$\tilde{\beta}_2 = 2.47$	0.58	4.27
$\beta_3 = -3$	$\tilde{\beta}_3 = -2.39$	0.75	−3.18

explanatory variables, other than an intercept, have no impact on choice probabilities P_i, that is, $\beta_2 = \beta_3 = \cdots = \beta_K = 0$. The likelihood ratio test statistic is

$$-2 \ln \lambda = 2[\ln \hat{\ell}(\Omega) - \ln \hat{\ell}(\omega)]$$

where $\hat{\ell}(\Omega)$ is the value of the likelihood function evaluated at the maximum likelihood estimates and $\hat{\ell}(\omega)$ is the maximum value of the likelihood function under the hypothesis that $\beta_2 = \cdots = \beta_K = 0$. If the hypotheses are true, then, asymptotically, the test statistic has a $\chi^2_{(K-1)}$ distribution. For our example, the value of the test statistic is 54.27, and the critical value of a $\chi^2_{(2)}$ distribution for the 0.05 level of significance is 5.99, so that we reject the hypothesis that $\beta_2 = \beta_3 = 0$. A related summary measure is the pseudo-R^2 value computed as

$$1 - \frac{\ln \hat{\ell}(\Omega)}{\ln \hat{\ell}(\omega)}$$

This measure has value 0 when $\tilde{\beta}_2 = \tilde{\beta}_3 = \cdots = \tilde{\beta}_K = 0$ and value 1 when the model is a perfect predictor in the sense that $\hat{P}_i = F(\mathbf{x}_i'\tilde{\boldsymbol{\beta}}) = y_i$. This measure is analogous to the coefficient of determination R^2 in linear regression models. For our sample the pseudo-$R^2 = (1 - 23.31/50.44) = 0.54$.

Another potential use of probit and logit models is to predict whether or not an event will occur given a set of values for the explanatory variables, for example, $\mathbf{x}_*$. The event could be predicted to occur if $\hat{P}_* = F(\mathbf{x}_*'\tilde{\boldsymbol{\beta}}) \geq 0.5$. Based on this usage another summary measure frequently reported is the percent of successful predictions within the given sample. In our sample 68% of the y_i values were correctly predicted using the estimated probit model.

Finally, as indicated earlier, since the estimated coefficients do not indicate changes in probabilities of an event occurring given a unit change in an independent variable, it may be useful to report the values of those partial derivatives, given in (19.2.15) for the probit model. The values of the explanatory variables affect the change in probability, and a set of values must be chosen for the purpose of reporting the results. One approach would be to select the mean values of the explanatory variables. For our example the values chosen were $\mathbf{x}_*' = (1, 0.69, 0.69)$, which was one of the rows of the original X matrix. The values of the partial derivatives for x_2 and x_3 are 0.97 and -0.94, respectively. Thus, starting at the point $\mathbf{x}_*$, an increase in x_2 of one unit is estimated to increase the probability of the event occurring by 0.97. This value is large as a one unit increase in x_2 implies a substantial increase in the value of a variable given $\mathbf{x}_*$.

In Chapter 18 of Judge, et al. (1985) these maximum likelihood methods are applied to models where the decision makers focus on more than two options. Also, the implications of choosing either the logistic or normal c.d.f. in the more general setting are discussed. This problem is important when more than two choices are available. There is also a discussion of summary measures for models with qualitative dependent variables.

19.3 Models with Limited Dependent Variables

Data available to economists are often incomplete in one way or another. For example, values of a dependent variable can often be observed only in a limited way, such as by sign, which is one way of thinking about probit and logit models. As another example, sometimes dependent variables can be observed only in a limited range, as is the case in Tobin's (1958) model of the demand for consumer durables. In this model the utility maximizing amount of expenditures on a durable good (y^*) is taken to be explained by the model

$$y_i^* = \mathbf{x}_i'\boldsymbol{\beta} + e_i \qquad i = 1, \ldots, T \tag{19.3.1}$$

where $\mathbf{x}_i'$ is a $(1 \times K)$ vector of explanatory variables and $e_i \sim N(0, \sigma^2)$ and is independent of other errors. The problem for a household is that there is some minimum level of expenditure required to purchase a durable good, say c. Thus for any household, the amount of expenditure actually observed (y) is

$$y_i = \begin{cases} y_i^* & \text{if } y_i^* > c \\ 0 \text{ or } c & \text{if } y_i^* \leq c \end{cases} \tag{19.3.2}$$

Thus the observed amount of expenditure may be the desired level or it may be 0 or c, which simply reflects that $y_i^* \leq c$. Assuming c is known and the same for all households, it is customary to rewrite the model by subtracting c from both sides of the model. The constant term in the transformed model is then the original constant term minus c, and the standard form of the model, dubbed the "tobit" model, or sometimes the censored regression model, is

$$\begin{aligned} y_i &= \mathbf{x}_i'\boldsymbol{\beta} + e_i && \text{if } \mathbf{x}_i'\boldsymbol{\beta} + e_i > 0 \\ &= 0 && \text{otherwise} \end{aligned} \tag{19.3.3}$$

An important characteristic of this model is that we actually know the values of the explanatory variables $\mathbf{x}_i'$ for the households or individuals who do *not* make a purchase. If no observations are available on the individuals who do not make a purchase, then the sample is said to be *truncated*. The statistical procedures for dealing with a truncated sample are sketched in Exercise 19.6.

19.3.1 Properties of the Least Squares Estimator in the Tobit (Censored) Regression Model

Of the T total sample observations let T_0 be the number of observations for which $y_i = 0$ and T_1 be the number for which $y_i > 0$. To see the statistical problems caused by this censored-sample problem, suppose we consider ignoring the T_0 observations for which $y_i = 0$. For the remaining T_1 observations we have complete observations and we could use the least squares estimator to estimate $\boldsymbol{\beta}$. Unfortunately, the least squares estimator is biased and inconsistent in this context. To see this, write out the expectation of the observed values of y_i *conditional* on the fact that $y_i > 0$. It is

$$E[y_i | y_i > 0] = \mathbf{x}_i'\boldsymbol{\beta} + E(e_i | y_i > 0) \tag{19.3.4}$$

If the conditional expectation of the error term is 0, there is no problem, because a least squares regression on the T_1 available observations will provide an unbiased estimator for $\boldsymbol{\beta}$, but unfortunately, this is not the case. If the e_i are independent and normally distributed random variables, then

$$E[e_i | y_i > 0] = E[e_i | e_i > -\mathbf{x}_i'\boldsymbol{\beta}] > 0 \tag{19.3.5}$$

That the conditional expectation of the error term is nonnegative can be explained as follows. If $e_i \sim N(0, \sigma^2)$, its p.d.f., $f(e_i)$, can be represented as in Figure 19.2. The mean value of e_i is 0 because the p.d.f. is symmetric about 0. If, however, the values of e_i are restricted to be greater than the value of $-\mathbf{x}_i'\boldsymbol{\beta}$, then the p.d.f. would no longer be centered at 0, nor symmetric, and its mathematical expectation would be positive. The p.d.f. of the resulting *truncated normal* random variable is given by

$$f(e_i | e_i \geq -\mathbf{x}_i'\boldsymbol{\beta}) = \frac{f(e_i)}{\int_{-\mathbf{x}_i'\boldsymbol{\beta}}^{\infty} f(t)\, dt} \qquad \text{for } e_i > -\mathbf{x}_i'\boldsymbol{\beta}$$

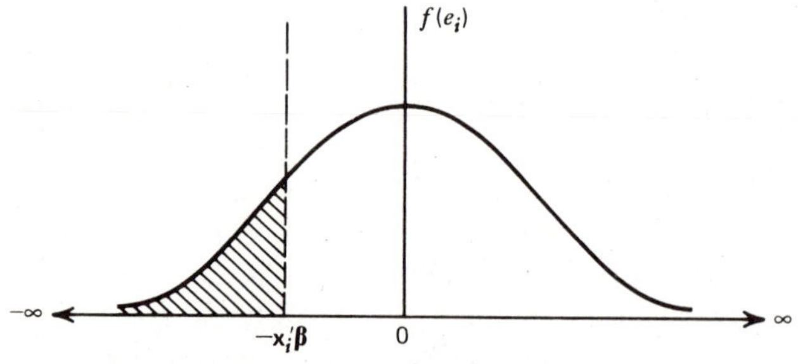

Figure 19.2 The p.d.f. of an $N(0, \sigma^2)$ random variable.

The denominator of this expression is the area under $f(e_i)$, for $e_i > -\mathbf{x}_i'\boldsymbol{\beta}$, which guarantees that the area under the p.d.f. equals 1.

Now, what effect does this result have on least squares estimation of the regression parameters in (19.3.3)? Consider the simple case in which $E[y_i^*] = \mathbf{x}_i'\boldsymbol{\beta} = \beta_1 + \beta_2 x_{i2}$, as illustrated in Figure 19.3. The nonzero values of the dependent variable will be scattered about $E[y_i | y_i > 0]$, not about the population regression function $E[y_i^*]$. Consequently, least squares estimators of β_1 and β_2 will be biased and inconsistent.

In fact it can be shown that the conditional expectation in (19.3.5) is

$$E[e_i | e_i > -\mathbf{x}_i'\boldsymbol{\beta}] = \sigma \cdot f_i / F_i$$

where f_i and F_i are the standard normal p.d.f. and c.d.f. evaluated at $(\mathbf{x}_i'\boldsymbol{\beta}/\sigma)$. Consequently, in the regression model, if $y_i > 0$,

$$\begin{aligned} y_i &= \mathbf{x}_i'\boldsymbol{\beta} + e_i \\ &= \mathbf{x}_i'\boldsymbol{\beta} + \sigma \frac{f_i}{F_i} + u_i \end{aligned}$$

and applying usual LS procedures omits the term $\sigma f_i / F_i$, which is not independent of $\mathbf{x}_i$, leading to the inconsistency and bias of the LS estimators.

It can also be shown that applying OLS to all T observations is an unsatisfactory procedure since the unconditional expectation of y_i is

$$E[y_i] = F_i \cdot (\mathbf{x}_i'\boldsymbol{\beta}) + \sigma f_i$$

Applying least squares to all the observations would not lead to a consistent estimator of the population regression function $E[y_i^*] = \mathbf{x}_i'\boldsymbol{\beta}$.

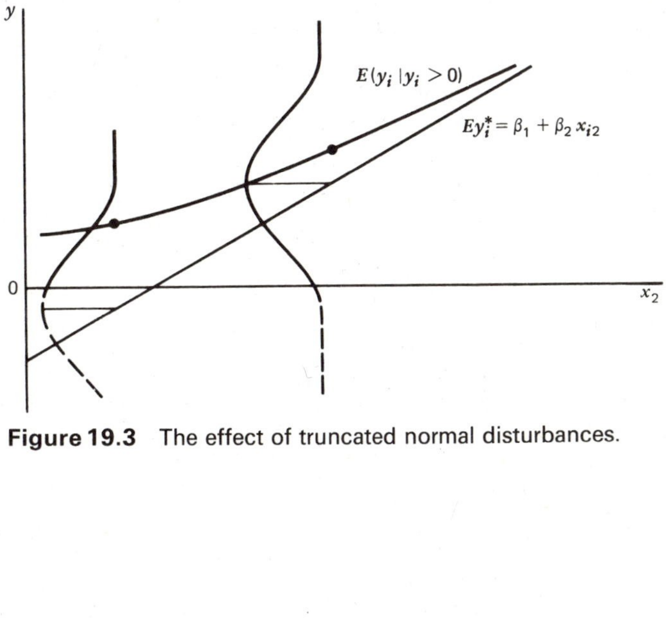

Figure 19.3 The effect of truncated normal disturbances.

19.3.2 Maximum Likelihood Estimation of the Tobit Model

To estimate the parameters $\boldsymbol{\beta}$ and σ^2 consistently, we can apply maximum likelihood procedures. The likelihood of the sample has a component for the observations that are positive and one for those that are 0. Define f_i and F_i to be the p.d.f. and c.d.f., respectively, of a standard normal random variable evaluated at $z_i = \mathbf{x}_i'\boldsymbol{\beta}/\sigma$. For the observations $y_i = 0$ all we know is that $\mathbf{x}_i'\boldsymbol{\beta} + e_i < 0$ or $e_i < -\mathbf{x}_i'\boldsymbol{\beta}$, so

$$Pr[y_i = 0] = Pr[e_i < -x_i'\beta] = Pr\left(\frac{e_i}{\sigma} < -\frac{\mathbf{x}_i'\boldsymbol{\beta}}{\sigma}\right) = 1 - F_i$$

since the normal distribution is symmetric. If $y_i > 0$, the "usual" component of the likelihood function is present. Consequently, denoting the product over the zero observations by Π_0 and the product over positive observations by Π_1, the likelihood function is given by

$$\ell = \Pi_0(1 - F_i)\Pi_1(2\pi\sigma^2)^{-1/2} \exp\{-(y_i - \mathbf{x}_i'\boldsymbol{\beta})^2/2\sigma^2\}$$

The log-likelihood function is

$$L = \ln \ell = \Sigma_0 \ln(1 - F_i) - (T_1/2)\ln 2\pi - (T_1/2)\ln \sigma^2 - \Sigma_1(y_i - \mathbf{x}_i'\boldsymbol{\beta})^2/2\sigma^2 \tag{19.3.6}$$

To maximize this log-likelihood function we can use the Newton–Raphson method. Unfortunately, the expressions for the second derivatives are very cumbersome. A somewhat neater approach is to use the method of scoring, that uses the information matrix in place of the negative of the Hessian. If we denote $\boldsymbol{\theta}' = (\boldsymbol{\beta}', \sigma^2)$, then the iterations of the method of scoring can be written

$$\tilde{\boldsymbol{\theta}}_{n+1} = \tilde{\boldsymbol{\theta}}_n + [I(\tilde{\boldsymbol{\theta}}_n)]^{-1}\left[\left.\frac{\partial L}{\partial \boldsymbol{\theta}}\right|_{\boldsymbol{\theta} = \tilde{\boldsymbol{\theta}}_n}\right] \tag{19.3.7}$$

The necessary first-order derivatives are

$$\frac{\partial L}{\partial \boldsymbol{\beta}} = -\frac{1}{\sigma}\Sigma_0 \frac{f_i \mathbf{x}_i}{1 - F_i} + \frac{1}{\sigma^2}\Sigma_1(y_i - \mathbf{x}_i'\boldsymbol{\beta})\mathbf{x}_i \tag{19.3.7a}$$

$$\frac{\partial L}{\partial \sigma^2} = \frac{1}{2\sigma^3}\Sigma_0 \frac{(\mathbf{x}_i'\boldsymbol{\beta})f_i}{1 - F_i} - \frac{T_1}{2\sigma^2} + \frac{1}{2\sigma^4}\Sigma_1(y_i - \mathbf{x}_i'\boldsymbol{\beta})^2 \tag{19.3.7b}$$

where f_i and F_i are the standard normal p.d.f. and c.d.f. evaluated at $\mathbf{x}_i'\boldsymbol{\beta}/\sigma$. The formulas for the second derivatives are given in Amemiya (1973, p. 1000). The information matrix is also provided by Amemiya (1973, p. 1007) and is

$$I(\boldsymbol{\theta}) = \begin{bmatrix} \sum_{i=1}^{T} a_i \mathbf{x}_i \mathbf{x}_i' & \sum_{i=1}^{T} b_i \mathbf{x}_i \\ \sum_{i=1}^{T} b_i \mathbf{x}_i' & \sum_{i=1}^{T} c_i \end{bmatrix} \tag{19.3.8}$$

where

$$a_i = \frac{-1}{\sigma^2}\left(z_i f_i - \frac{f_i^2}{1 - F_i} - F_i\right)$$

$$b_i = \frac{1}{2\sigma^3}\left(z_i^2 f_i + f_i - \frac{z_i f_i^2}{1 - F_i}\right)$$

$$c_i = -\frac{1}{4\sigma^4}\left(z_i^3 f_i + z_i f_i - \frac{z_i^2 f_i^2}{1 - F_i} - 2F_i\right)$$

and $z_i = \mathbf{x}_i'\boldsymbol{\beta}/\sigma$. Fair (1977) suggests a slightly different approach to obtaining the ML estimates that can be simpler than the method of scoring. However, if the log-likelihood is maximized, Amemiya (1973) has proven that the ML estimators for this model are consistent and asymptotically normal with asymptotic covariance matrix given by the inverse of the information matrix in (19.3.8). It should be pointed out that these properties have been shown to be quite sensitive to specification errors.

As a final note relative to the interpretation and use of this model, one must take care when using the model to predict. Recall that there are three regression functions associated with this model,

$$Ey_i^* = \mathbf{x}_i'\boldsymbol{\beta} \tag{19.3.9a}$$

$$E[y_i | y_i > 0] = \mathbf{x}_i'\boldsymbol{\beta} + \sigma f_i/F_i \tag{19.3.9b}$$

$$E[y_i] = F_i \cdot E[y_i | y_i > 0] \tag{19.3.9c}$$

Also, if one is going to talk about the effects of a unit change of an independent variable x_j (suppressing the observation subscript) on the expected value of the dependent variable this could be

$$\frac{\partial E y_i^*}{\partial x_j} = \beta_j \tag{19.3.10a}$$

$$\frac{\partial E y_i}{\partial x_j} = F_i \beta_j \tag{19.3.10b}$$

$$\frac{\partial E(y_i | y_i > 0)}{\partial x_j} = \beta_j\left[1 - (\mathbf{x}_i'\boldsymbol{\beta}/\sigma) \cdot \frac{f_i}{F_i} - \left(\frac{f_i}{F_i}\right)^2\right] \tag{19.3.10c}$$

19.3.3 An Example

To illustrate the use of the Tobit model $T = 20$ observations were generated from the regression function

$$y_i^* = \beta_1 + \beta_2 x_{i2} + e_i \tag{19.3.11}$$

where $\beta_1 = -9, \beta_2 = 1$ and $e_i \sim N(0, 16)$. The values of y_i^*, the censored variable y_i and x_{i2} are presented in Table 19.2.

There are $T_0 = 6$ "limit" observations ($y^* \leq 0$) and $T_1 = 14$ nonlimit observations ($y = y^* > 0$). In Table 19.3 we report the OLS regression results and the results of the Tobit ML estimation. Column 1 of Table 19.3 contains the LS parameter estimates based on all $T = 20$ observations. Column 2 contains the estimates based only on the $T_1 = 14$ "complete," nonlimit observations. Note that the measured effect of the explanatory variable x_2 is less than the true parameter value, $\beta_2 = 1$. Examining Figure 19.3, this is exactly what we would expect the OLS

Table 19.2 Sample Data for Tobit Example

y^*	y	x_2
−7.228	0	1
−9.0164	0	2
−15.2732	0	3
−3.9712	0	4
3.1348	3.1348	5
3.508	3.508	6
0.8312	0.8312	7
8.0064	8.0064	8
−1.8472	0	9
−4.39	0	10
2.9352	2.9352	11
3.9048	3.9048	12
6.5144	6.5144	13
5.9772	5.9772	14
3.726	3.726	15
10.4124	10.4124	16
16.9064	16.9064	17
9.2968	9.2968	18
7.8916	7.8916	19
14.2164	14.2164	20

Table 19.3 Parameter Estimates for Model (19.3.11)
(t-values in parentheses)

	1	2	3
$\hat{\beta}_1$	−2.153	−1.491	−5.731
	(−1.47)	(−0.57)	(−2.58)
$\hat{\beta}_2$	0.668	0.653	0.901
	(5.48)	(3.46)	(5.30)
$\hat{\sigma}^2$	9.887	11.361	13.184
$\log \ell$	—	—	−41.2552

estimator to do. On the other hand, the maximum likelihood estimates of the Tobit model are reported in column 3 of Table 19.3. These estimates are closer to the true values. The t-values reported with the estimates are often called "asymptotic t's" since they are the ratio of the parameter estimates to their estimated asymptotic standard errors. The asymptotic standard errors are the square roots of the asymptotic covariance matrix, $[I(\boldsymbol{\theta})]^{-1}$ in (19.3.8) where $\boldsymbol{\theta}' = (\beta_1, \beta_2, \sigma^2)$, evaluated at the ML estimates. In this case the covariance matrix is given by

$$[I(\tilde{\boldsymbol{\theta}})]^{-1} = \begin{bmatrix} 4.92 & -0.35 & -3.35 \\ & 0.029 & 0.21 \\ & & 25.94 \end{bmatrix}$$

The estimated parameters of course are those of the regression function (19.3.9a). It is often of interest to know the slopes of the conditional mean regression function (19.3.10c). In order to evaluate these slopes we must choose a set of regressor values to consider since the conditional mean regression function is not linear. A common choice is the mean of the explanatory variables, and the multiplicative factor in (19.3.10c) evaluated there is 0.847, which you are encouraged to verify.

We conclude with two final notes regarding the example. Caution should be exercised when employing computer software packages to estimate Tobit models since not all programs work the same way. For example, in Tobin's original paper he scaled the model by σ before estimation. Although this is perfectly acceptable, the resulting estimates will require "unnormalizing" before being comparable to those preceding. Secondly, not all programs use the information matrix (19.3.8) as a basis for the asymptotic covariance matrix. Some use the inverse of the Hessian matrix as the estimate for the covariance matrix. Although these choices are asymptotically equivalent, there will be differences in finite samples.

19.4 Summary and Guide to Further Reading

In this chapter we have considered the estimation of behavioral models for which we have data that are incomplete in some way. For binary choice situations we only observe what choice is made. Nonetheless, we can estimate the effect that individual explanatory variables have on the probability of a particular choice being made using either a logit or probit model. Binary choice models can be extended to more general situations in which a decision maker must select from a finite set (more than two) of alternatives. Models that are appropriate in these situations are called multinomial choice models or quantal choice models. Surveys of these models and many other references are given in Judge, et al. (1985, pp. 768–778), Amemiya (1981), Hensher and Johnson (1981), Maddala (1983), Train (1986), and Ben-Akiva and Lerman (1985).

The second type of model we considered in this chapter dealt with the situation in which the dependent variable is not necessarily observable for all members of a random sample. In these cases we have shown that it is *not* appropriate to simply delete the observations with missing values and apply the usual least squares estimator. Instead, specific recognition of the process generating the data must be incorporated into the estimation procedure. We presented a maximum likelihood estimation procedure for the situation when the values of the explanatory variables are available for all individuals in the sample whether a value of the dependent variable is observed or not. Other (two-step) estimation procedures and extensions to the truncated sample cases are discussed in Judge, et al. (1985, pp. 779–785), Amemiya (1984), and Maddala (1983).

Finally, there are quite a few computer packages that have programs to estimate a variety of models with qualitative or limited dependent variables. Some of these are listed in Hall (1984).

19.5 Exercises

Table 19.4 lists 10 sets of 20 values on a dependent variable that were generated in a probit context, using the X matrix defined in Chapter 5, Equation (5.10.2) and the parameter vector $\boldsymbol{\beta}' = (0, 3, -3)$. That is, the probability that $y_i = 1$ is

$$P_i = \int_{-\infty}^{\mathbf{x}_i'\boldsymbol{\beta}} \frac{1}{\sqrt{2\pi}} e^{-t^2/2}\, dt$$

Table 19.4 Ten Samples of Observations from a Probit Model

y_1	y_2	y_3	y_4	y_5	y_6	y_7	y_8	y_9	y_{10}
1	0	1	1	0	1	1	0	0	0
1	1	1	1	1	1	1	1	1	1
0	0	0	0	0	0	0	0	0	0
1	0	1	0	1	1	1	0	0	1
0	0	0	0	0	0	0	0	0	0
1	1	1	1	1	1	1	1	1	1
1	0	1	0	1	0	0	0	1	0
1	1	1	1	1	1	1	1	1	1
1	1	1	1	1	1	1	1	1	1
0	1	1	1	0	1	1	0	0	1
0	0	0	0	0	0	0	0	0	0
1	1	1	1	1	1	1	1	1	1
1	1	1	0	1	1	0	1	1	1
0	0	0	0	0	0	0	0	0	0
1	1	1	1	1	1	1	1	1	1
1	1	1	1	0	0	0	0	0	0
1	1	1	1	1	1	1	1	1	1
1	1	1	1	1	1	1	1	1	1
1	1	0	1	1	1	1	0	1	1
1	0	0	1	0	1	1	1	1	1

19.1 For each of the 10 samples apply LS, GLS, and EGLS to estimate the parameters of the model

$$y_i = \beta_1 + \beta_2 x_{i2} + \beta_3 x_{i3} + e_i \tag{19.5.1}$$

19.2 Combine all 10 samples to compute sample proportions p_i and use the EGLS versions of logit and probit to estimate the parameters of (19.5.1).

19.3 Use the first sample of observations and compute the maximum likelihood estimates for the probit and logit models.

19.4 Consider (19.3.11) and the data in Table 19.2 and the empirical results in Table 19.3. Starting from the mean value of the explanatory variable, what is the effect of a one unit increase in x_2 on (*i*) $E[y_i^*]$, (*ii*) $E(y|y > 0)$, (*iii*) Ey_i? Interpret these results.

19.5 To investigate the effects of different degrees of censoring, carry out the following small Monte Carlo experiment. Use the model $y_i = \beta_1 + \beta_2 x_{i2} + e_i$

where $\beta_2 = 1$ and $e_i \sim N(0, 16)$. Let β_1 take the integer values between -9 and $+9$. Generate 10 samples of size $T = 20$ for each of the parameter settings (i.e., values of β_1) using the same set of 200 random disturbances for each. Compute (*i*) the Tobit ML estimates of the parameters and (*ii*) the OLS parameter estimates based only on the complete observations. Compare the average values of the Tobit ML and OLS estimates for each parameter setting. Comment on what you expect to happen and what actually does happen in your experiments.

19.6 A *truncated sample* is one in which the values of the explanatory variables are observed only if the value of the dependent variable is observed. This might arise, for example, if data were gathered *only* on individuals who actually bought a new car in a given time period. If there are T_1 "complete" observations, then the log-likelihood function, apart from constants, is

$$-\sum_{i=1}^{T_1} \ln F_i - \frac{T_1}{2} \ln \sigma^2 - \frac{1}{2\sigma^2} \sum_{i=1}^{T_1} (y_i - \mathbf{x}_i'\boldsymbol{\beta})^2.$$

Use the data on just the complete observations in Table 19.2 to estimate the parameters of (19.3.11) using your favorite numerical optimization procedure or computer package. Compare your ML estimates to the OLS estimates based on the complete observations.

19.6 References

Amemiya, T. (1973) "Regression Analysis When the Dependent Variable is Truncated Normal." *Econometrica*, 42, 999–1012.

Amemiya, T. (1981) "Qualitative Response Models: A Survey." *Journal of Economic Literature*, 19, 1483–1536.

Amemiya, T., ed. (1984) "Censored or Truncated Regression Models." *Journal of Econometrics*, 24, 1–222.

Ben-Akiva, M., and S. Lerman (1985) *Discrete Choice Analysis*. Cambridge, MA, MIT Press.

Fair, R. (1977) "A Note on the Computation of the Tobit Estimator." *Econometrica*, 45, 1723–1727.

Hall, B. (1984) "Software for the Computation of Tobit Model Estimates." *Journal of Econometrics*, 24, 215–222.

Hensher, D., and L. Johnson (1981) *Applied Discrete-Choice Modelling*. New York, Halsted.

Judge, G. G., W. E. Griffiths, R. C. Hill, H. Lütkepohl, and T. C. Lee (1985) *The Theory and Practice of Econometrics*, 2nd ed. New York, Wiley.

Maddala, G. S. (1983) *Limited Dependent and Qualitative Variables in Econometrics.* London, Cambridge University Press.

Tobin, J. (1958) "Estimation of Relationships for Limited Dependent Variables." *Econometrica*, 26, 24–36.

Train, K. (1986) *Qualitative Choice Analysis.* Cambridge, MA, MIT Press.

Zellner, A. and T. H. Lee (1965) "Joint Estimation of Relationships Involving Discrete Random Variables." *Econometrica*, 33, 382–394.

CHAPTER 20

Prior Information, Biased Estimation, and Statistical Model Selection

In the preceding chapters we have specified a wide range of statistical models and proposed and evaluated a large class of sampling theory and Bayesian estimators. In most chapters we have, in a conventional sampling theory sense, focused on the problem of how to make the "best" use of sample information in estimating the unknown parameters. However, in Chapters 4 and 7 on Bayesian inference, we considered how to introduce nonsample information in the form of an informative or noninformative prior probability density function and combine it with the density function for the sample to yield a posterior density function that forms the basis for estimation and inference. In the sampling theory approach to inference, which underlies much of the work in econometrics, attention is focused on statistical properties such as unbiasedness and minimum variance; and estimation rules are evaluated in terms of accuracy within repeated samples or their long-run repetitive precision.

Under this scenario, inferences are generally made without regard to the uses to which they are to be put and little emphasis is placed on the possible consequences of the alternative rules other than whether or not they satisfy certain statistical properties. In addition, classical statistical procedures emphasize the use of sample information in making inferences about the unknown parameters and to a large extent ignore any nonsample information that may exist about the individual parameters or relationships among the unknown parameters. Recognizing the restrictions implied by classical analysis for econometric practice, in this chapter we consider an approach to statistical inference that involves a formal consideration of both sample and nonsample information and the possible loss or statistical consequences of alternative rule choices. This gives a new basis for evaluating the classical estimation rules and permits us to enlarge the set of estimators that may be useful in learning from economic data.

In Section 1 the basic concepts of statistical decision theory are reviewed and alternative decision rules and principles are considered. In Section 2 a range of biased estimators that involve various types of nonsample information are evaluated within a decision theoretic framework. In Section 3 the statistical implications of making a preliminary test of significance based on the data at hand is considered and the corresponding pretest estimator is evaluated. In Section 4 we consider the consequences and possibilities for dealing with uncertainty concerning the specification of the statistical model and consider questions relating to the appropriate functional form and the dimension of the design matrix.

20.1 Statistical Decision Theory

Concern with the implications of scarcity has led economists over time to develop a general theory of choice. Within this context Marschak once remarked, "Information is useful if it helps us make the right decisions." Consequently, as economists, a primary reason for interest in efficient procedures for learning from data is to gain information so that we may (1) better understand economic processes and institutions structurally and quantitatively and (2) use this descriptive information prescriptively as a basis for action or choice. Given these descriptive and prescriptive objectives, it would seem that a decision framework, based on the analysis of losses associated with alternative decision rules should be used.

From the standpoint of classical statistics, where inferences are made without regard to the uses to which they are to be put, any two estimators may have the same precision matrix, but if one is biased while the other is unbiased, then one would choose the unbiased rule, which is right on average. Alternatively, if two rules (estimators) are unbiased but one has a smaller sampling variation than the other, then the more precise estimator would be chosen. The problem, of course, with the classical properties approach to gauging estimator performance comes when one estimator is biased but has a smaller sampling variability than a competing estimator that is unbiased. How, indeed, does the investigator choose? Why should the analyst be interested in a rule that is "right" on average? Is there, in the foregoing example, some trade-off for decision purposes between bias and variance, or in other words could a decision maker tolerate a rule that misses the mark on the average if it brought gains in terms of reduced sampling variability? In many respects, the sampling theorists and much of econometric literature is preoccupied with the concept of unbiasedness and the attainment of this goal in either small or large samples.

In this book, many of the choices between alternative estimators and procedures will be based on decision-theoretic concepts. In the sections to follow, some of the basic definitions and concepts of statistical decision theory are discussed, and the basis for estimator evaluation and choice is specified.

20.1.1 Basic Concepts

Statistical decision theory, as the name implies, is concerned with the problem of making decisions based on statistical knowledge. Since the knowledge is statistical in nature, it involves uncertainties that we will consider to be unknown parameter values. The objective is to combine the sample information with other relevant information in order to make the "best" decision. These other types of nonsample information include (1) knowledge of the possible consequences of the decisions that can be expressed as the loss that would be incurred, over the range of the parameter space, if a particular decision rule is used, and (2) prior or nonsample information that reflects knowledge other than that derived from the statistical investigation.

A problem in decision theory has three ingredients: (1) the parameter space $\mathscr{B}$ that reflects the possible states of nature relative to the unknown parameter vector $\boldsymbol{\beta}$, (2) a set of all possible decisions or actions $\mathscr{A}$ and particular actions a and (3) a loss function $L(\boldsymbol{\beta}, a)$ defined for all $(\boldsymbol{\beta}, a) \in (\mathscr{B} \times \mathscr{A})$.

When we experiment to obtain information about $\boldsymbol{\beta}$, the design is such that the observations $\mathbf{y}$ are distributed according to some probability distribution that has $\boldsymbol{\beta}$ as the unknown parameter vector. In this context, the loss incurred depends on the outcome of an observable random variable $\mathbf{y}$ through the function δ used to assign an action for a given $\mathbf{y}$. As already noted, the distribution of $\mathbf{y}$ depends on $\boldsymbol{\beta}$, the true state of nature. The function $\delta(\mathbf{y})$ is called a decision rule and the loss associated with this rule is denoted as $L(\boldsymbol{\beta}, \delta(\mathbf{y}))$.

Since the T-dimensional sample vector $\mathbf{y}$ is random, it is important for decision purposes to consider the average losses involving actions taken under the various outcomes for $\mathbf{y}$. In other words since the estimator $\delta(\mathbf{y}) = \hat{\boldsymbol{\beta}}$ is random, as it depends on $\mathbf{y}$, the loss incurred in not knowing the parameter vector will also be random. The average losses or the expected value of the loss function $L(\boldsymbol{\beta}, \hat{\boldsymbol{\beta}})$, where $\boldsymbol{\beta}$ is the true parameter is called a risk function $\rho(\boldsymbol{\beta}, \delta(\mathbf{y})) = \rho(\boldsymbol{\beta}, \hat{\boldsymbol{\beta}})$ and is designated by

$$\rho(\boldsymbol{\beta}, \hat{\boldsymbol{\beta}}) = E[L(\boldsymbol{\beta}, \hat{\boldsymbol{\beta}})] = \int_{\mathbf{y}} L(\boldsymbol{\beta}, \hat{\boldsymbol{\beta}}) f(\mathbf{y}|\boldsymbol{\beta}) d\mathbf{y} \tag{20.1.1}$$

where $f(\mathbf{y}|\boldsymbol{\beta})$ is the joint density of $\mathbf{y}$ conditional on $\boldsymbol{\beta}$ and $\int_{\mathbf{y}}$ is the multiple integral over all possible values of the random vector $\mathbf{y}$. Thus for each $\boldsymbol{\beta}$, $\rho(\boldsymbol{\beta}, \hat{\boldsymbol{\beta}})$ is the expected loss over $\mathbf{y}$ that is incurred in using the decision rule or estimator $\delta(\mathbf{y}) = \hat{\boldsymbol{\beta}}$. We assume that the loss function is defined for each possible value of $L(\boldsymbol{\beta}, \hat{\boldsymbol{\beta}})$ and that this function reflects the loss incurred corresponding to each combination of $\boldsymbol{\beta}$ and $\hat{\boldsymbol{\beta}}$. In other words, the value of the loss function of $\hat{\boldsymbol{\beta}}$ at $\boldsymbol{\beta}$ measures the loss incurred if the action (rule) is $\hat{\boldsymbol{\beta}}$ and the state of nature is $\boldsymbol{\beta}$. As an example, we may represent a linear loss function as $L(\boldsymbol{\beta}, \hat{\boldsymbol{\beta}}) = |\boldsymbol{\beta} - \hat{\boldsymbol{\beta}}|$, where the possible states of nature are represented by the set of real numbers.

20.1.2 The Choice of a Decision Rule

Given a framework for defining loss or risk associated with each action and state of nature, the central problem of decision theory is how to choose a decision rule or, alternatively, how to choose among the alternative decision rules. Intuitively, it would seem that we should choose a rule that makes the risk of not knowing $\boldsymbol{\beta}$ as small as possible, that is, as a general criterion we should choose a rule that minimizes the risk for each value of $\boldsymbol{\beta}$ in $\mathscr{B}$. In general, there is no *one* rule with minimum risk for all $\boldsymbol{\beta}$ in $\mathscr{B}$. This means that typically there is no estimator $\hat{\boldsymbol{\beta}}_0$ such that for every other estimator $\hat{\boldsymbol{\beta}}$, $\rho(\boldsymbol{\beta}, \hat{\boldsymbol{\beta}}_0) \leq \rho(\boldsymbol{\beta}, \hat{\boldsymbol{\beta}})$, for every $\boldsymbol{\beta}$. This proposition is expressed graphically in Figure 20.1 for the measure space $\lambda = \boldsymbol{\beta}'\boldsymbol{\beta}$, where each element of the $\boldsymbol{\beta}$ vector may take on values between $-\infty$ and ∞. In Figure 20.1, over the range of the parameter space from the origin to $\lambda = \boldsymbol{\beta}'\boldsymbol{\beta} = a$, the estimator $\hat{\boldsymbol{\beta}}_2$ has the lowest risk. At point a the risk functions for $\hat{\boldsymbol{\beta}}_2$ and $\hat{\boldsymbol{\beta}}_3$ cross and $\hat{\boldsymbol{\beta}}_3$ has the smallest risk over the remaining range of the parameter space.

The situation represented by the alternative risk functions in Figure 20.1 is typical of what happens in practice. Consequently, in order to choose among possible estimators, it is common to add criteria to that of minimizing the risk. The classical approach to estimation consists of a list of desired properties, such as unbiasedness, invariance, minimum variance unbiasedness, and sufficiency. Opinion as to which criteria are most important is not always unanimous. Ideally, imposing new criteria that estimators should satisfy should not result in estimators that are unsatisfactory under the overall criterion of minimizing the risk. In particular, a desirable property of resultant estimators is admissibility.

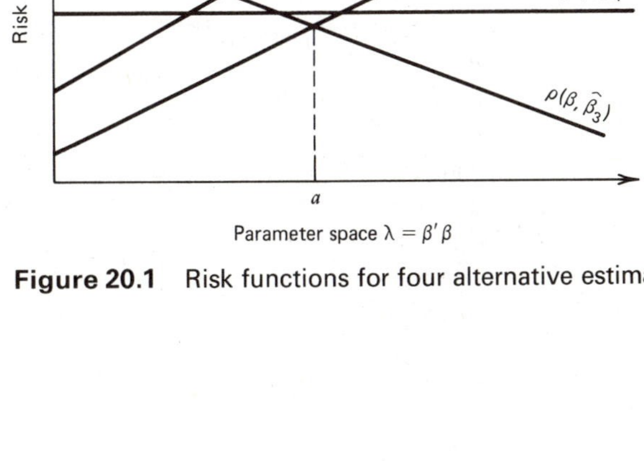

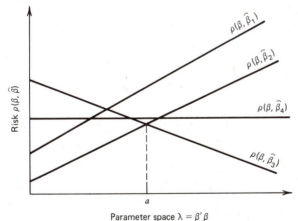

Figure 20.1 Risk functions for four alternative estimators.

In this context an estimator $\hat{\boldsymbol{\beta}}$ is said to *dominate an estimator* $\hat{\boldsymbol{\beta}}_0$ if for all $\boldsymbol{\beta}$,

$$\rho(\boldsymbol{\beta}, \hat{\boldsymbol{\beta}}) \le \rho(\boldsymbol{\beta}, \hat{\boldsymbol{\beta}}_0) \tag{20.1.2}$$

If $\rho(\boldsymbol{\beta}, \hat{\boldsymbol{\beta}}) < \rho(\boldsymbol{\beta}, \hat{\boldsymbol{\beta}}_0)$ for some $\boldsymbol{\beta}$ and $\rho(\boldsymbol{\beta}, \hat{\boldsymbol{\beta}}) \le \rho(\boldsymbol{\beta}, \hat{\boldsymbol{\beta}}_0)$, for all $\boldsymbol{\beta}$, the estimator $\hat{\boldsymbol{\beta}}$ is said to *strictly dominate* $\hat{\boldsymbol{\beta}}_0$. Under this definition the estimator $\hat{\boldsymbol{\beta}}_2$ in Figure 20.1 is said to strictly dominate $\hat{\boldsymbol{\beta}}_1$. However, note that $\hat{\boldsymbol{\beta}}_2$ does not dominate $\hat{\boldsymbol{\beta}}_3$ and $\hat{\boldsymbol{\beta}}_4$ does not dominate $\hat{\boldsymbol{\beta}}_2$.

An estimator is called *admissible* if it is not strictly dominated by any other estimator. We may say that an estimator $\hat{\boldsymbol{\beta}}_1$ is *inadmissible* if there is another estimator, $\hat{\boldsymbol{\beta}}_2$, such that $\rho(\boldsymbol{\beta}, \hat{\boldsymbol{\beta}}_2) \le \rho(\boldsymbol{\beta}, \hat{\boldsymbol{\beta}}_1)$ for all $\boldsymbol{\beta}$ and, for some $\boldsymbol{\beta}$, the strict inequality holds. These results, of course, imply that an inadmissible estimator or rule should not be used. Unfortunately, there is usually a large class of admissible estimators for any one problem.

As we noted in the sampling theory approach, one important way of limiting the class of estimators or rules is to require that the estimator be *unbiased* and thus require that $E[\hat{\boldsymbol{\beta}}] = \boldsymbol{\beta}$. Furthermore, because of tractability, the requirement that $\hat{\boldsymbol{\beta}}$ be a *linear* function of $\mathbf{y}$ is sometimes imposed and in fact many of the estimators used in econometric work are restricted to the *linear unbiased* class. Unfortunately, as we will see in the sections to come, requiring this property sometimes results in *inadmissible* estimators. The question of why one should be interested in a property of unbiasedness that requires absolute accuracy on the average has been asked many times. One might question whether it has been properly answered. Certainly, the typical response—"It is conventional"—is not an adequate reply.

Another restriction sometimes used in estimator choice, which tries to protect against the worst state of nature, is the *minimax criterion.* Under this criterion an estimator $\hat{\boldsymbol{\beta}}_0$ is said to be minimax, within the class of estimators D, if the maximum risk of $\hat{\boldsymbol{\beta}}_0$ is equal to or less than that for all other estimators $\hat{\boldsymbol{\beta}}$, that is,

$$\max_{\boldsymbol{\beta}} \rho(\boldsymbol{\beta}, \hat{\boldsymbol{\beta}}_0) \le \max_{\boldsymbol{\beta}} \rho(\boldsymbol{\beta}, \hat{\boldsymbol{\beta}}) \tag{20.1.3}$$

for all $\hat{\boldsymbol{\beta}}$ in D. In the class of estimators demonstrated in Figure 20.1 the estimator $\hat{\boldsymbol{\beta}}_4$ is a minimax estimator since, for all $\boldsymbol{\beta}$, it minimizes the maximum risk and thus reflects a desire to act conservatively even in the face of nature as a neutral opponent.

Another frequently used basis for choosing among estimators is the Bayes' criterion. As noted in Chapters 4 and 7, in the Bayesian approach the objective is to make proper use of nonsample or prior information $g(\boldsymbol{\beta})$ about the random vector $\boldsymbol{\beta}$. Under this specification the Bayes' solution is to choose the estimator that minimizes the average risk with respect to the prior density $g(\boldsymbol{\beta})$.

20.1.3 The Measure Space

Thus far we have not discussed the specific form of the loss or risk function that is to be used in evaluating estimator performance. Although there are many alternatives, for expository purposes we will at this point discuss only the squared error loss and risk matrix (generalized mean square error) measures.

Within a decision context what we would like is a criterion that takes account of the possible trade-off in estimator selection between bias and variance. Because it seems reasonable for a range of decision problems to penalize outcomes far away from the true parameter $\boldsymbol{\beta}$ more than those close to it, one possible measure of estimator performance that captures these characteristics is the mean squared error criterion, which may be stated as

$$\text{MSE}(\boldsymbol{\beta}, \bar{\boldsymbol{\beta}}) = E[(\bar{\boldsymbol{\beta}} - \boldsymbol{\beta})(\bar{\boldsymbol{\beta}} - \boldsymbol{\beta})'] \tag{20.1.4}$$

where $\bar{\boldsymbol{\beta}}$ is any estimator of the unknown coefficient vector $\boldsymbol{\beta}$. Under this criterion for optimality we would choose the estimator that minimizes, in some sense, the averaged squared deviations of the estimator $\bar{\boldsymbol{\beta}}$ from the true parameter vector. In this context (20.1.4) is called the risk matrix (on the average what do you risk by not knowing the true parameter vector and having to estimate it by $\bar{\boldsymbol{\beta}}$), or the matrix of mean square errors. The diagonal elements of this matrix are the mean square errors $E[(\bar{\beta}_k - \beta_k)^2]$, for $k = 1, 2, \ldots, K$. To see what is implied by the mean square error criterion let us rewrite (20.1.4) as

$$\begin{aligned}
\text{MSE}(\boldsymbol{\beta}, \bar{\boldsymbol{\beta}}) &= E[\{(\bar{\boldsymbol{\beta}} - E[\bar{\boldsymbol{\beta}}]) + (E[\bar{\boldsymbol{\beta}}] - \boldsymbol{\beta})\}\{(\bar{\boldsymbol{\beta}} - E[\bar{\boldsymbol{\beta}}]) + (E[\bar{\boldsymbol{\beta}}] - \boldsymbol{\beta})\}'] \\
&= E[(\bar{\boldsymbol{\beta}} - E[\bar{\boldsymbol{\beta}}])(\bar{\boldsymbol{\beta}} - E[\bar{\boldsymbol{\beta}}])'] + 2E[(\bar{\boldsymbol{\beta}} - E[\bar{\boldsymbol{\beta}}])(E[\bar{\boldsymbol{\beta}}] - \boldsymbol{\beta})'] \\
&\quad + E[(E\bar{\boldsymbol{\beta}}] - \boldsymbol{\beta})(E[\bar{\boldsymbol{\beta}}] - \boldsymbol{\beta})'] \\
&= E[(\bar{\boldsymbol{\beta}} - E[\bar{\boldsymbol{\beta}}])(\bar{\boldsymbol{\beta}} - E[\bar{\boldsymbol{\beta}}])'] \\
&\quad + E[(E[\bar{\boldsymbol{\beta}}] - \boldsymbol{\beta})(E[\bar{\boldsymbol{\beta}}] - \boldsymbol{\beta})'] \\
&= \text{covariance } \bar{\boldsymbol{\beta}} + (\text{bias } \bar{\boldsymbol{\beta}})(\text{bias } \bar{\boldsymbol{\beta}})'
\end{aligned} \tag{20.1.5}$$

which in words means that the mean square error matrix is made up of the covariance matrix for $\bar{\boldsymbol{\beta}}$ and the matrix of squared bias of $\bar{\boldsymbol{\beta}}$. Therefore, we have a criterion that recognizes and takes into account both variance and bias as a performance measure.

The diagonal elements of (20.1.5) are the mean square errors for each element of the $\bar{\boldsymbol{\beta}}$ vector, and this is what we wish to concentrate on. This type of squared error loss can be reduced to a single measure if it is expressed as

$$\rho(\boldsymbol{\beta}, \bar{\boldsymbol{\beta}}) = \text{tr MSE}(\bar{\boldsymbol{\beta}}, \boldsymbol{\beta}) = \text{tr } E[(\bar{\boldsymbol{\beta}} - \boldsymbol{\beta})(\bar{\boldsymbol{\beta}} - \boldsymbol{\beta})'] = E[(\bar{\boldsymbol{\beta}} - \boldsymbol{\beta})'(\bar{\boldsymbol{\beta}} - \boldsymbol{\beta})] \tag{20.1.6}$$

Under this squared error loss criterion an estimator $\bar{\boldsymbol{\beta}}$ is judged equal to or superior to an estimator $\bar{\boldsymbol{\beta}}_0$ if the sum of the mean square errors of $\bar{\boldsymbol{\beta}}$ is equal to or less than the sum of the mean squared errors for $\bar{\boldsymbol{\beta}}_0$, for all values of $\boldsymbol{\beta}$. With this measure the consequences for making an error become more critical in proportion to the square of the error that is made.

It should be noted that if we work with the reparameterized orthonormal statistical model where

$$\mathbf{y} = XS^{-1/2}S^{1/2}\boldsymbol{\beta} + \mathbf{e} = Z\boldsymbol{\theta} + \mathbf{e} \tag{20.1.7}$$

$S^{-1/2}X'XS^{-1/2} = Z'Z = I_K$ and $S^{1/2}\mathbf{b} = \hat{\boldsymbol{\theta}}$, with covariance $\Sigma_{\hat{\boldsymbol{\theta}}} = \sigma^2 I_K$, is the least squares estimator, then under the squared error loss criterion the least squares estimator has risk

$$\rho(\boldsymbol{\theta}, \hat{\boldsymbol{\theta}}) = E[(\hat{\boldsymbol{\theta}} - \boldsymbol{\theta})'(\hat{\boldsymbol{\theta}} - \boldsymbol{\theta})] = \sigma^2 \operatorname{tr} I_K = \sigma^2 K \tag{20.1.8}$$

Furthermore, writing the unweighted, squared error loss risk function in the $\boldsymbol{\theta}$ parameter space as

$$\begin{aligned} \rho(\boldsymbol{\theta}, \hat{\boldsymbol{\theta}}) &= E[(\hat{\boldsymbol{\theta}} - \boldsymbol{\theta})'(\hat{\boldsymbol{\theta}} - \boldsymbol{\theta})] = E[(S^{1/2}\mathbf{b} - S^{1/2}\boldsymbol{\beta})'(S^{1/2}\mathbf{b} - S^{1/2}\boldsymbol{\beta})] \\ &= E[(\mathbf{b} - \boldsymbol{\beta})'S^{1/2}S^{1/2}(\mathbf{b} - \boldsymbol{\beta})] = E[(\mathbf{b} - \boldsymbol{\beta})'S(\mathbf{b} - \boldsymbol{\beta})] \end{aligned} \tag{20.1.9}$$

yields a weighted loss function in the $\boldsymbol{\beta}$ space with weight matrix $X'X = S$. This loss specification is often referred to in the literature as the mean squared prediction error criterion. In the sections that follow, it will sometimes be convenient to assume, for expository purposes, the orthonormal linear statistical model (20.1.7).

20.2 Estimators that Combine Sample and Nonsample Information

In the previous section we noted that in decision theory an attempt is made to combine sample information with at least two other types of information or knowledge. One type deals with knowledge of the possible consequences of the decisions and the other is knowledge other than that derived from the statistical investigation. In this section, we analyze *within a decision theoretic context* the statistical implications of using both sample and various kinds of nonsample information.

20.2.1 Exact Nonsample Information

There may be instances in applied work when the investigator has exact information on a particular parameter or linear combination of parameters. For example, in estimating a log-linear production function, information may be available that the firm is operating under the condition of constant returns to scale. Alternatively, in estimating a demand relation, information may be available from consumer theory on the homogeneity condition or information concerning the income response coefficient may be available from previous empirical work.

If information of this type is available, it may be stated, as in Chapter 6, in the form of the following set of linear relations or linear equality restrictions

$$R\boldsymbol{\beta} = \mathbf{r} \tag{20.2.1}$$

where $\mathbf{r}$ is a $(J \times 1)$ vector of known elements and R is a $(J \times K)$ known prior information design matrix that expresses the structure of the information on the individual parameters β_i or some linear combination of the elements of the $\boldsymbol{\beta}$ vector. Information concerning the parameters such as β_1 equal to some scalar k, the sum of the coefficients equal to unity and β_2 equal to β_3 may be specified in the $R\boldsymbol{\beta} = \mathbf{r}$ format as

$$\begin{bmatrix} 1 & 0 & 0 & 0 & \cdots & 0 \\ 1 & 1 & 1 & 1 & \cdots & 1 \\ 0 & 1 & -1 & 0 & \cdots & 0 \end{bmatrix} \begin{bmatrix} \beta_1 \\ \beta_2 \\ \vdots \\ \beta_K \end{bmatrix} = \begin{bmatrix} k \\ 1 \\ 0 \end{bmatrix} \tag{20.2.2}$$

where $J = 3$. If the first J elements of the coefficient vector were specified to be equal to the vector $\mathbf{k}$, then this information could be specified as

$$[I_J, 0_{(K-J)}] \begin{bmatrix} \boldsymbol{\beta}_J \\ \boldsymbol{\beta}_{K-J} \end{bmatrix} = \mathbf{k} = \mathbf{r} \tag{20.2.3}$$

where I_J is a Jth-order identity matrix and $\mathbf{k}$ is a $(J \times 1)$ known vector.

Given information in the form of (20.2.1), how do we combine it with the information contained in the sample observations $\mathbf{y}$? Because information on the individual parameters and combinations thereof is specified to be known with certainty, that is, no sampling variability from sample to sample, linear equality relations (20.2.1) may be taken as given or restrictions in any estimation process. In the general linear statistical model of Chapter 5, when using the least squares rule, the least squares estimator $\mathbf{b}$ has mean vector $\boldsymbol{\beta}$ and covariance $\Sigma_{\mathbf{b}} = \sigma^2(X'X)^{-1}$. Consequently, the elements of $\mathbf{b}$ are not independent and the restrictions on particular coefficients or their linear combinations reflected by (20.2.1) condition the values that other b_i may take on. Therefore, if one uses the least squares criterion applied to both the sample information and the nonsample information (20.2.1), we are faced with the problem of finding the vector $\mathbf{b}^*$ that minimizes the quadratic form

$$S(\boldsymbol{\beta}) = (\mathbf{y} - X\boldsymbol{\beta})'(\mathbf{y} - X\boldsymbol{\beta}) \tag{20.2.4}$$

subject to

$$R\boldsymbol{\beta} = \mathbf{r} \qquad \text{or} \qquad R\boldsymbol{\beta} - \mathbf{r} = \mathbf{0} \tag{20.2.1}$$

Since (20.2.1) appears as linear equality restrictions, classical Lagrangian procedures used in Section 6.2 may be applied to yield the minimizing solution,

$$\begin{aligned}\mathbf{b}^* &= \mathbf{b} + (X'X)^{-1}R'[R(X'X)^{-1}R']^{-1}(\mathbf{r} - R\mathbf{b}) \\ &= \mathbf{b} + S^{-1}R'(RS^{-1}R')^{-1}(\mathbf{r} - R\mathbf{b})\end{aligned} \tag{20.2.5}$$

which differs from the unrestricted least squares estimator by a linear function of the vector $\mathbf{r} - R\mathbf{b}$. The restricted least squares random vector $\mathbf{b}^*$ has mean

$$\begin{aligned}E[\mathbf{b}^*] &= \boldsymbol{\beta} + S^{-1}R'(RS^{-1}R')^{-1}(\mathbf{r} - R\boldsymbol{\beta}) \\ &= \boldsymbol{\beta} + S^{-1}R'(RS^{-1}R')^{-1}\boldsymbol{\delta}\end{aligned} \tag{20.2.6}$$

and is unbiased if $(\mathbf{r} - R\boldsymbol{\beta}) = \boldsymbol{\delta} = \mathbf{0}$, that is, if the restrictions are correct. If the restrictions are not correct, the restricted least squares estimator is biased by a linear function of the vector $\boldsymbol{\delta} = \mathbf{r} - R\boldsymbol{\beta}$.

The covariance matrix of the restricted least squares estimator is

$$\begin{aligned}E[(\mathbf{b}^* - E[\mathbf{b}^*])(\mathbf{b}^* - E[\mathbf{b}^*])'] = \Sigma_{\mathbf{b}^*} &= \sigma^2[S^{-1} - S^{-1}R'(RS^{-1}R')^{-1}RS^{-1}] \\ &= \sigma^2[S^{-1} - C]\end{aligned} \tag{20.2.7}$$

where $C = S^{-1}R'(RS^{-1}R')^{-1}RS^{-1}$ is a positive semidefinite matrix. Furthermore, the difference between the covariance matrices is $\Sigma_{\mathbf{b}} - \Sigma_{\mathbf{b}^*} = \sigma^2 C$, where C is a nonnegative definite matrix. Therefore, in line with the Gauss-Markoff result of Chapter 5, if $\mathbf{b}^*$ is unbiased, it is the best within the class of unbiased estimators that are a linear function of both types of information $\mathbf{y}$ and $R\boldsymbol{\beta} = \mathbf{r}$.

If the restrictions are incorrect and $E[\mathbf{r} - R\mathbf{b}] = \boldsymbol{\delta} \neq \mathbf{0}$ then the restricted least squares estimator is biased and has a mean squared error or risk matrix

$$\begin{aligned}\text{MSE}(\boldsymbol{\beta}, \mathbf{b}^*) &= E[(\mathbf{b}^* - \boldsymbol{\beta})(\mathbf{b}^* - \boldsymbol{\beta})'] \\ &= \sigma^2[S^{-1} - C] + S^{-1}R'(RS^{-1}R')^{-1}\boldsymbol{\delta}\boldsymbol{\delta}'(RS^{-1}R')^{-1}RS^{-1}\end{aligned} \tag{20.2.8}$$

which in words is equal to the covariance matrix for the restricted least squares estimator plus the bias matrix resulting from the products of the bias vector.

It is apparent from the restricted least squares covariance matrix (20.2.7) and the mean square error matrix (20.2.8) that in the fixed X case if the nonsample information is correct, then using it in conjunction with the sample information will lead to an unbiased estimator that has a precision matrix superior to the unrestricted least squares estimator.

20.2.1a Performance under Squared Error Loss

In applied work we can never be certain that our nonsample information is correct, or in other words we are sometimes not sure that the restrictions we impose are consistent with the real-world parameter system underlying the data-generation process. Therefore, it is important to know the average loss experienced with different degrees of error for the vector $\boldsymbol{\delta} = R\boldsymbol{\beta} - \mathbf{r}$. For expository purposes let us assume the orthonormal linear statistical model, which has a design matrix X such that $X'X = I_K$. We also assume that the information design matrix R is of the form I_K, that is, individual restrictions are placed on each of the elements of the $\boldsymbol{\beta}$ vector. As a basis for evaluating estimator performance, consider the squared error loss criterion

$$\rho(\boldsymbol{\beta}, \mathbf{b}^*) = E[(\mathbf{b}^* - \boldsymbol{\beta})'(\mathbf{b}^* - \boldsymbol{\beta})] = E[\text{tr}(\mathbf{b}^* - \boldsymbol{\beta})(\mathbf{b}^* - \boldsymbol{\beta})'] \qquad (20.2.9)$$

For the orthonormal special case assumed, the risk is

$$\rho(\boldsymbol{\beta}, \mathbf{b}^*) = \sigma^2\text{tr}[I_K - I_K] + \text{tr}[\boldsymbol{\delta}\boldsymbol{\delta}'] = \boldsymbol{\delta}'\boldsymbol{\delta} \qquad (20.2.10)$$

The covariance matrix of the restricted estimator $\mathbf{b}^*$ is a null matrix because each of the parameters of the $\boldsymbol{\beta}$ vector is constrained and the estimates do not vary from sample to sample. Therefore, the risk of the restricted least squares estimator is equal to the sum of squares of the bias or restriction errors $\boldsymbol{\delta}'\boldsymbol{\delta}$. The risk for the unrestricted least-squares estimator under squared error loss is

$$\rho(\boldsymbol{\beta}, \mathbf{b}) = E[(\mathbf{b} - \boldsymbol{\beta})'(\mathbf{b} - \boldsymbol{\beta})] = \sigma^2 \text{ tr } I_K = \sigma^2 K \qquad (20.2.11)$$

a scalar that is unrelated to the information and/or errors contained in the system of linear equality relations, that is, the nonsample information.

Since the least squares risk is $\sigma^2 K$, for every $\boldsymbol{\delta}$ or $\boldsymbol{\delta}'\boldsymbol{\delta}$, and the restricted least squares risk is $\boldsymbol{\delta}'\boldsymbol{\delta}$ and thus a function of $\boldsymbol{\delta}'\boldsymbol{\delta}$, the two risks are equal when

$$\boldsymbol{\delta}'\boldsymbol{\delta} = \sigma^2 K \qquad (20.2.12)$$

or

$$\frac{(\boldsymbol{\beta} - \mathbf{r})'(\boldsymbol{\beta} - \mathbf{r})}{\sigma^2} = \frac{\boldsymbol{\delta}'\boldsymbol{\delta}}{\sigma^2} = K$$

or

$$\frac{\boldsymbol{\delta}'\boldsymbol{\delta}}{2\sigma^2} = \frac{K}{2}$$

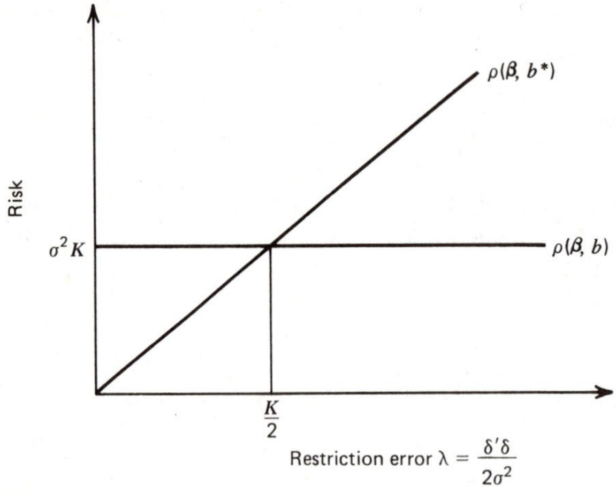

Figure 20.2 Risk functions for the least squares and restricted least squares estimators.

When the nonsample information in the form of restrictions is correct, the risk gain of using the restricted least squares estimator is $\sigma^2 K$. These results are shown in Figure 20.2. As indicated in the figure, under a squared error loss measure of performance, the restricted estimator can be very good or very bad (precisely wrong and unbounded risk). Its performance relative to the least squares estimator depends on the quality of the nonsample information. If the quality of the nonsample information is such that $\boldsymbol{\delta}'\boldsymbol{\delta}/2\sigma^2 < K/2$, then $\rho(\boldsymbol{\beta}, \mathbf{b}^*) < \rho(\boldsymbol{\beta}, \mathbf{b})$ and the restricted least squares estimator is the clear choice. However, if the restrictions are such that $\boldsymbol{\delta}'\boldsymbol{\delta}/2\sigma^2 > K/2$, then the restricted estimator is inferior to the least squares estimator over an infinite range of the parameter space. Unfortunately $\boldsymbol{\beta}$ and thus $\lambda = \boldsymbol{\delta}'\boldsymbol{\delta}/2\sigma^2 = (\boldsymbol{\beta} - \mathbf{r})'(\boldsymbol{\beta} - \mathbf{r})/2\sigma^2$ is unknown. Faced with uncertainty concerning the restriction error, many applied researchers use the hypothesis-testing mechanism discussed in Chapter 6. However, using a hypothesis test to choose the estimator leads to a pretest estimator that will be discussed in Section 20.3.1.

20.2.1b An Example

Consider the sampling model described in Section 6.1.5 and assume nonsample information of the form

$$R\boldsymbol{\beta} = [0 \quad 1 \quad 1]\begin{bmatrix}\beta_1 \\ \beta_2 \\ \beta_3\end{bmatrix} = \beta_2 + \beta_3 = 1 \tag{20.2.1a}$$

Using the sample information given in (6.1.27) and the nonsample information (20.2.1a), the estimates of β_1, β_2, and β_3 consistent with both types of information are

$$\mathbf{b}^* = \begin{bmatrix} 10.06200 \\ 0.46059 \\ 0.53941 \end{bmatrix} \tag{20.2.5a}$$

and the corresponding sample covariance matrix is

$$\hat{\Sigma}_{\mathbf{b}^*} = \begin{bmatrix} 0.004711 & & \\ -0.001958 & 0.006850 & \\ 0.001958 & 0.006850 & 0.006850 \end{bmatrix} \tag{20.2.5b}$$

Both sets of results (location and precision) differ from those obtained in Chapter 6 when only sample information was used.

20.2.2 Stochastic Nonsample Information

There are many situations in applied work when assuming exact prior information is not appropriate or in fact this type of information does not exist. If uncertainty exists about the prior information specifications, one alternative is to make use of stochastic restrictions or hypotheses of the following form

$$\mathbf{r} = R\boldsymbol{\beta} + \mathbf{v} \tag{20.2.13}$$

where R is again a known $(J \times K)$ prior information or hypothesis design matrix, $\mathbf{r}$ is a known or observable $(J \times 1)$ random vector, and $\mathbf{v}$ is a $(J \times 1)$ unobservable, normally distributed random vector with mean vector $\boldsymbol{\delta}$ and covariance $\sigma^2\Omega$, with Ω known. The information in (20.2.13) may come from previous statistical investigations, where an unbiased estimate of a subset of $\boldsymbol{\beta}$ or linear combinations thereof, along with their variances and covariances, are available. Alternatively, prior information may be available that particular coefficients lie between certain upper and lower bounds, for example, in a consumption function the marginal propensity to consume may be thought to lie between 0.6 and 0.9.

Given the existence of this type of information or linear stochastic hypotheses, Theil and Goldberger considered the problem of how to combine this information with the sample information. They assumed that the random vector $\mathbf{e}$ associated with the sampling model $\mathbf{y} = X\boldsymbol{\beta} + \mathbf{e}$ was independent of the random vector $\mathbf{v}$ associated with the prior information and wrote the statistical model containing both types of information as

$$\begin{bmatrix} \mathbf{y} \\ \mathbf{r} \end{bmatrix} = \begin{bmatrix} X \\ R \end{bmatrix} \boldsymbol{\beta} + \begin{bmatrix} \mathbf{e} \\ \mathbf{v} \end{bmatrix} \tag{20.2.14a}$$

where $[\mathbf{e}', \mathbf{v}']'$ is a multivariate normal random vector with mean vector and covariance matrix

$$E\begin{bmatrix}\mathbf{e}\\ \mathbf{v}\end{bmatrix} = \begin{bmatrix}\mathbf{0}\\ \boldsymbol{\delta}\end{bmatrix} \qquad E\left[\begin{pmatrix}\mathbf{e}\\ \mathbf{v}-\boldsymbol{\delta}\end{pmatrix}(\mathbf{e}', \mathbf{v}' - \boldsymbol{\delta}')\right] = \sigma^2\begin{bmatrix}I_T & 0\\ 0 & \Omega\end{bmatrix} \tag{20.2.14b}$$

20.2.2a The Estimator

If the investigator believes that $\boldsymbol{\delta} = \mathbf{0}$, and if the covariance matrix (20.2.14b) for the random vector $(\mathbf{e}', \mathbf{v}')'$ is known; the natural estimator is the Aitken, or generalized least squares estimator

$$\begin{aligned}\tilde{\boldsymbol{\beta}} &= \left[\begin{pmatrix}X\\ R\end{pmatrix}'\begin{pmatrix}I_T & 0\\ 0 & \Omega\end{pmatrix}^{-1}\begin{pmatrix}X\\ R\end{pmatrix}\right]^{-1}\begin{pmatrix}X\\ R\end{pmatrix}'\begin{pmatrix}I_T & 0\\ 0 & \Omega\end{pmatrix}^{-1}\begin{pmatrix}\mathbf{y}\\ \mathbf{r}\end{pmatrix}\\ &= (X'X + R'\Omega^{-1}R)^{-1}(X'\mathbf{y} + R'\Omega^{-1}\mathbf{r})\end{aligned} \tag{20.2.15}$$

with mean

$$E[\tilde{\boldsymbol{\beta}}] = \boldsymbol{\beta} + (S + R'\Omega^{-1}R)^{-1}R'\Omega^{-1}\boldsymbol{\delta} \tag{20.2.16}$$

covariance matrix

$$E[(\tilde{\boldsymbol{\beta}} - E[\tilde{\boldsymbol{\beta}}])(\tilde{\boldsymbol{\beta}} - E[\tilde{\boldsymbol{\beta}}])'] = \sigma^2(S + R'\Omega^{-1}R)^{-1} = \sigma^2W^{-1} \tag{20.2.17}$$

and mean square error or risk matrix

$$\begin{aligned}E[(\tilde{\boldsymbol{\beta}} - \boldsymbol{\beta})(\tilde{\boldsymbol{\beta}} - \boldsymbol{\beta})'] &= \sigma^2W^{-1} + W^{-1}R'\Omega^{-1}\boldsymbol{\delta}\boldsymbol{\delta}'\Omega^{-1}RW^{-1}\\ &= \text{covariance} + \text{square of bias matrix}\end{aligned} \tag{20.2.18}$$

If the stochastic restrictions are unbiased, that is, $E[\mathbf{r} - R\boldsymbol{\beta}] = E[\mathbf{v}] = \boldsymbol{\delta} = \mathbf{0}$, the stochastic restricted estimator is unbiased and the Aitken estimator (20.2.15) is best linear unbiased out of the class of estimators making use of the sample information $\mathbf{y}$ and the stochastic prior information $\mathbf{r}$.

One difficulty with estimator (20.2.15) is that σ^2 is unknown. As it is written (20.2.15) does not depend explicitly on σ^2. However, because the covariance of $\mathbf{v}$ is assumed to be $\sigma^2\Omega$, knowledge of σ^2 is required for proper specification of the prior information. To deal with this problem, Theil (1963) has suggested that σ^2 be replaced by an unbiased estimator based on the sample data, that is, $\hat{\sigma}^2 = (\mathbf{y} - X\mathbf{b})'(\mathbf{y} - X\mathbf{b})/(T - K)$. Now $\hat{\sigma}^2$ is stochastic, but it will differ from σ^2 to the order $1/\sqrt{T}$ in probability when the random vector $\mathbf{e}$ is normally distributed. Therefore, if σ^2 is replaced by $\hat{\sigma}^2$, the estimator is asymptotically unbiased if the stochastic prior information is correct on the average and it has the asymptotic moment matrix given in (20.2.17).

Since $\boldsymbol{\delta}$ is unknown, under a squared error loss or general mean squared error criterion, we can never be sure that the stochastic restricted estimator (20.2.15) is superior to the unrestricted least squares estimator that uses only sample information. Also, assuming the random vector $\mathbf{v}$ has a zero mean and that the covariance matrix Ω is known, seems in most cases unreasonably demanding. You should be alerted that the fixed vector $\boldsymbol{\beta}$ and the random vectors $\mathbf{v}$ and $\mathbf{r}$ do not fit the Bayesian approach to inference and that there does not seem to be a set of principles that would justify this specification.

20.2.2b An Example

Consider again the sampling model presented in Section 6.1.5 and assume nonsample information of the form

$$R\boldsymbol{\beta} + \mathbf{v} = \begin{bmatrix} 0 & 1 & 0 \\ 0 & 0 & 1 \end{bmatrix} \begin{bmatrix} \beta_1 \\ \beta_2 \\ \beta_3 \end{bmatrix} + \begin{bmatrix} v_1 \\ v_2 \end{bmatrix} = \begin{bmatrix} \frac{1}{2} \\ \frac{1}{2} \end{bmatrix} \qquad (20.2.13a)$$

where v_1 and v_2 are normal random variables with mean zero and variance 1/64—that is, $\mathbf{v} \sim N\left(\mathbf{0}, \begin{bmatrix} 1/64 & 0 \\ 0 & 1/64 \end{bmatrix}\right)$. Also assume the scale parameter σ^2 is known and that $\sigma^2 = 0.0625$. For the sample of data given in (6.1.27), the stochastic restricted estimates are

$$\tilde{\boldsymbol{\beta}} = \begin{bmatrix} 10.02983 \\ 0.50427 \\ 0.51166 \end{bmatrix} \qquad (20.2.15a)$$

and the corresponding covariance matrix is

$$\hat{\Sigma}_{\tilde{\boldsymbol{\beta}}} = \begin{bmatrix} 0.006626 & -0.001317 & -0.001152 \\ -0.001317 & 0.000855 & -0.000007 \\ -0.001152 & -0.000007 & 0.000918 \end{bmatrix} \qquad (20.2.17a)$$

20.2.2c Stochastic Linear Hypotheses

We now turn to the question of statistically evaluating the compatibility of sample and stochastic prior information. The sample information is summarized by the estimator $\mathbf{b}$, with mean $\boldsymbol{\beta}$ which is unknown, and covariance $\sigma^2(X'X)^{-1} = \sigma^2 S^{-1}$. The J linear hypotheses about the stochastic prior information are specified as in (20.2.13), and

$$E[\mathbf{r}] = R\boldsymbol{\beta} \qquad (20.2.19)$$

where R is a $(J \times K)$ known matrix of rank J and the $(J \times 1)$ random vector $\mathbf{r}$ has a normal distribution with mean $(R\boldsymbol{\beta} + \boldsymbol{\delta})$ and covariance Ω that is independent of $\mathbf{b}$. Consequently, the hypotheses given in (20.2.19) are equivalent to

$$\boldsymbol{\delta} = \mathbf{0} \tag{20.2.20}$$

where $\boldsymbol{\delta} = E[\mathbf{r}] - R\boldsymbol{\beta}$.

Since the sample information and the stochastic hypotheses provide two independent estimators of $R\boldsymbol{\beta}$, namely, $R\mathbf{b}$ and $\mathbf{r}$, Theil (1963) has suggested the following procedure for developing a compatibility test statistic. The difference between the two estimators is

$$\mathbf{d} = \mathbf{r} - R\mathbf{b} \tag{20.2.21}$$

which, under the null hypothesis of no difference, is normally distributed and has mean $\boldsymbol{\delta} = \mathbf{0}$ and covariance matrix

$$E[(\mathbf{r} - R\mathbf{b} - \boldsymbol{\delta})(\mathbf{r} - R\mathbf{b} - \boldsymbol{\delta})'] = \sigma^2[R(X'X)^{-1}R' + \Omega]$$

In line with the distribution theory of quadratic forms developed in the linear algebra Appendix, in the case where σ^2 and Ω are known, a test statistic for the hypotheses of (20.2.19) is

$$\gamma_0 = (\mathbf{r} - R\mathbf{b})'[R(X'X)^{-1}R' + \Omega]^{-1}(\mathbf{r} - R\mathbf{b})/\sigma^2 \tag{20.2.22}$$

which has a χ^2 distribution with J degrees of freedom. By rejecting the null hypothesis (20.2.19) when γ_0 in (20.2.22) is too large, γ_0 may be used as a test statistic for gauging the compatibility of the sample information $R\mathbf{b}$ and the stochastic prior information $\mathbf{r}$.

When only Ω is known and σ^2 is replaced by an estimate,

$$\hat{\sigma}^2 = (\mathbf{y} - X\mathbf{b})'(\mathbf{y} - X\mathbf{b})/(T - K),$$

the compatibility statistic,

$$\gamma_1 = (\mathbf{r} - R\mathbf{b})'[R(X'X)^{-1}R' + \Omega]^{-1}(\mathbf{r} - R\mathbf{b})/J\hat{\sigma}^2 \tag{20.2.23}$$

is distributed as an F random variable with J and $(T - K)$ degrees of freedom.

Again the reservations expressed at the end of Section 20.2.2a apply to these results. Also, if the compatibility statistic is used with an eye toward estimation, then the pretest estimator sampling results of Section 20.3.1. hold.

20.2.3 Linear Inequality Restrictions

In many situations in economics, information may exist about an unknown parameter or combination of parameters that may be expressed in the form of a general linear inequality restriction or hypothesis. For example, from traditional microtheories and macrotheories of economic processes and institutions, the marginal propensity to consume has an implied upper and lower bound, price and income response coefficients for a superior good have definite signs, and in a production function marginal products are nonnegative. Within the contexts of model validation and parameter estimation the economic researcher faces the problems of estimating the parameters of relevant economic relations when these properties are imposed and/or testing the compatibility of the requirements with the sample data.

When nonsample information in the form of linear inequalities is available, it can be represented in the context of Section 20.2.1 by

$$R\boldsymbol{\beta} \geq \mathbf{r} \tag{20.2.24a}$$

or

$$R\boldsymbol{\beta} - \boldsymbol{\delta} = \mathbf{r} \tag{20.2.24b}$$

where $\boldsymbol{\delta} \geq \mathbf{0}$. The prior information design matrix R and the real vector $\mathbf{r}$ can accommodate individual or linear combinations of inequality restrictions for a mixed system, such as $\mathbf{r}_0 \leq R_1\boldsymbol{\beta} \leq \mathbf{r}_1$, by letting

$$R = \begin{bmatrix} R_1 \\ -R_1 \end{bmatrix} \quad \text{and} \quad \mathbf{r} = \begin{bmatrix} \mathbf{r}_0 \\ -\mathbf{r}_1 \end{bmatrix}$$

20.2.3a The Inequality Restricted Estimator

Given information of this type, we can combine the information contained in both the sample and inequality restrictions and estimate the unknown K-dimensional coefficient vector $\boldsymbol{\beta}$ by minimizing the quadratic form

$$q = (\mathbf{y} - X\boldsymbol{\beta})'(\mathbf{y} - X\boldsymbol{\beta}) = \mathbf{y}'\mathbf{y} - 2\boldsymbol{\beta}'X'\mathbf{y} + \boldsymbol{\beta}'X'X\boldsymbol{\beta} \tag{20.2.25}$$

subject to the system of linear inequality constraints

$$R\boldsymbol{\beta} \geq \mathbf{r} \tag{20.2.26}$$

Because of the inequality structure of the constraint set, the classical Lagrangian approach used in solving for the equality restricted estimator is no longer applicable. However, the optimality conditions for the quadratic programming problem reflected by (20.2.25) and (20.2.26) may be derived by direct application of the Kuhn–Tucker conditions. The first step is to formulate the Lagrangian function

$$q = (\mathbf{y} - X\boldsymbol{\beta})'(\mathbf{y} - X\boldsymbol{\beta}) + 2\boldsymbol{\lambda}'(\mathbf{r} - R\boldsymbol{\beta}) \tag{20.2.27}$$

where $\boldsymbol{\lambda}$ is a J-dimensional vector of Lagrange multipliers. Given (20.2.27), the Kuhn–Tucker conditions are

$$\left.\frac{\partial q}{\partial \boldsymbol{\beta}}\right|_{(\mathbf{b}^+, \boldsymbol{\lambda}^+)} = -2X'(\mathbf{y} - X\mathbf{b}^+) - 2R'\boldsymbol{\lambda}^+ = \mathbf{0} \tag{20.2.28}$$

and

$$\left.\frac{\partial q}{\partial \boldsymbol{\lambda}}\right|_{(\mathbf{b}^+, \boldsymbol{\lambda}^+)} = 2(\mathbf{r} - R\mathbf{b}^+) \leq \mathbf{0} \tag{20.2.29}$$

along with

$$\boldsymbol{\lambda}^{+\prime}(\mathbf{r} - R\mathbf{b}^+) = 0 \tag{20.2.30}$$

and

$$\boldsymbol{\lambda}^+ \geq \mathbf{0} \tag{20.2.31}$$

where $\boldsymbol{\lambda}^+$ is the optimal vector of multipliers associated with the constraints $R\boldsymbol{\beta} \geq \mathbf{r}$. Given these conditions quadratic programming algorithms exist for solving for the inequality restricted estimator $\mathbf{b}^+$ (see Judge & Takayama (1966)).

As an example, consider the sampling model given in Section 6.1.5 and the sample information given in (6.1.27). Assume nonsample in formation of the form

$$R\boldsymbol{\beta} = [0 \quad 1 \quad 1]\begin{bmatrix} \beta_1 \\ \beta_2 \\ \beta_3 \end{bmatrix} \leq 1 \tag{20.2.24a}$$

The unrestricted least squares estimates of $\boldsymbol{\beta}$ are $\tilde{\boldsymbol{\beta}} = [9.7702 \quad 0.5237 \quad 0.6930]'$. Since $\tilde{\beta}_2 + \tilde{\beta}_3 > 1$, the restriction is violated. In this single inequality case, the restriction is binding and the inequality estimates would be exactly the same as the equality restricted estimates (20.2.5a).

20.2.3b The Sampling Properties

Given a rule for combining sample and inequality restricted prior information, it is useful for application and choice purposes to know the sampling properties of the inequality restricted estimator and how its sampling performance compares with other estimators under a squared error-loss criterion. For expository purposes let us simplify the problem and consider the situation in which the sampling information is generated by the orthonormal linear statistical model $\mathbf{y} = X\boldsymbol{\beta} + \mathbf{e}$ where $X'X = I_K$ and the least squares estimator $\mathbf{b} = (X'X)^{-1}X'\mathbf{y}$ is multivariate normal with mean $\boldsymbol{\beta}$ and covariance $\sigma^2 I_K$. Each of the elements of $\mathbf{b}$ is thus a normal random variable with mean β_i, for $i = 1, 2, \ldots, K$ and variance σ^2. Since the elements of **b** are independent random variables we can consider each of the coefficients individually.

Consider the problem of estimating the unknown parameter β_i and assume that the nonsample information that exists for the ith coefficient can be reflected by the inequality constraint

$$\beta_i \geq r_i \qquad \text{for any} \qquad i = 1, 2, \ldots, K \tag{20.2.32a}$$

which can be written using the notation from (20.2.26) as

$$R_i\boldsymbol{\beta} \geq r_i \tag{20.2.32b}$$

where R_i is a $(1 \times K)$ vector with $(K - 1)$ zeros and a 1 as the ith element. For each sample of data, if the inequality restricted estimator b_i^+ is used, this implies either the maximum likelihood estimate b_i violates (20.2.32) and r_i, the restricted estimator, is used to estimate β_i or the maximum likelihood estimate does not violate (20.2.32a), that is, $b_i \geq r_i$, and the maximum likelihood (least squares) estimate is selected. This decision rule or estimator, which combines both the sample and linear inequality prior information in estimating the ith coefficient, may be expressed as

$$b_i^+ = r_i I_{(-\infty, r_i)}(b_i) + b_i I_{[r_i, \infty)}(b_i) \tag{20.2.33}$$

where $I_{(-\infty, r_i)}(b_i)$ and $I_{[r_i, \infty)}(b_i)$ are indicator functions that take the value of 1 if b_i falls within the subscripted interval and are 0 otherwise.

If we let $\delta_i = r_i - \beta_i$, where δ_i is defined over the real line $-\infty < \delta_i < \infty$, then δ_i is the hypothesis or constraint specification error and we can rewrite the inequality restricted estimator for β_i as

$$\begin{aligned}
b_i^+ &= \{I_{(-\infty, \beta_i + \delta_i)}(b_i)\}r_i + \{I_{[\beta_i + \delta_i, \infty)}(b_i)\}b_i \\
&= \{I_{(-\infty, \delta_i)}(b_i - \beta_i)\}r_i + \{I_{[\delta_i, \infty)}(b_i - \beta_i)\}b_i \\
&= \left\{I_{(-\infty, \delta_i/\sigma)}\left(\frac{b_i - \beta_i}{\sigma}\right)\right\}r_i + \left\{I_{[\delta_i/\sigma, \infty)}\left(\frac{b_i - \beta_i}{\sigma}\right)\right\}b_i \\
&= b_i + \left\{I_{(-\infty, \delta_i/\sigma)}\left(\frac{b_i - \beta_i}{\sigma}\right)\right\}\delta_i - \sigma\left\{I_{(-\infty, \delta_i/\sigma)}\left(\frac{b_i - \beta_i}{\sigma}\right)\right\}\left(\frac{b_i - \beta_i}{\sigma}\right)
\end{aligned} \tag{20.2.34}$$

where $(b_i - \beta_i)/\sigma$ is a standard normal random variable with mean 0 and variance 1.

Making use of corrollaries developed by Judge and Yancey (1986), we may, in conjunction with (20.2.34), evaluate the mean $E[b_i^+]$ and risk $\rho(\beta_i, b_i^+) = E[(b_i^+ - \beta_i)^2]$ for different values of the δ_i/σ parameter space (specification error). The characteristics of the resulting bias and risk functions are depicted in Figures 20.3 and 20.4

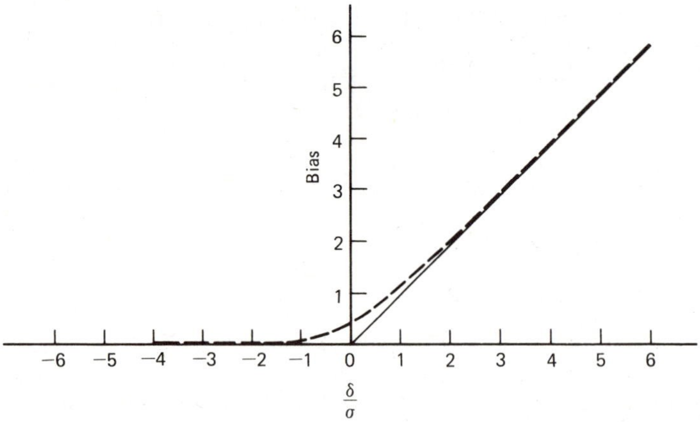

Figure 20.3 Mean of the inequality restricted estimator as a function of the restriction hypothesis specification error δ/σ.

The bias function depicted in Figure 20.3 means that as $\delta_i \to \infty$, the $E[b_i^+] \to \beta_i + \delta_i = r_i$, the equality restricted estimator b_i^*. Alternatively as $\delta_i \to 0$, the $E[b_i^+] \to \beta_i + \sigma/\sqrt{2\pi}$. As the specification error $\delta_i \to -\infty$, the $E[b_i^+] \to \beta_i$. Therefore, in this last case, the inequality restricted estimator is unbiased, since the least squares estimator is always used.

The risk results depicted in Figure 20.4 imply that as the specification error $\delta_i \to 0$ the $\rho(b_i^+, \beta_i) \to \sigma^2/2$. Therefore, when the inequality constraint is specified correctly, in the sense that $r_i = \beta_i$, the inequality restricted estimator risk is one-half that of the maximum likelihood risk. Furthermore, as the specification error $\delta_i \to -\infty$, the $\rho(b_i^+, \beta_i) \to \sigma^2$, the risk of the unrestricted maximum likelihood estimator. These results mean that under squared error loss, when $-\infty < \delta_i < 0$, the inequality restricted estimator b_i^+ is equal to or less than the risk of the maximum likelihood estimator. Alternatively, when $0 \leq \delta_i < \infty$ and as $\delta_i \to \infty$ the $\rho(b_i^+, \beta_i) \to \delta_i^2$, the risk of the equality restricted estimator.

To summarize, these results imply that in applied work, when combining a linear inequality constraint with the linear statistical sampling model, if the hypothesized restriction is indeed correct and thus $-\infty < \delta_i < 0$, the inequality restricted estimator dominates the maximum likelihood estimator under a squared error loss measure of goodness, that is, $\rho(b_i^+, \beta_i) \leq \rho(b_i, \beta_i)$ for every value of the parameter space $-\infty < \delta_i \leq 0$, and for some values of $-\infty < \delta_i < 0$ the strict inequality holds. However, when $0 \leq \delta_i < \infty$, the inequality restricted risk function intersects the maximum likelihood risk function, is unbounded, and is inferior to the maximum likelihood risk over a large range of the δ_i^2/σ^2 parameter space. Thus, if

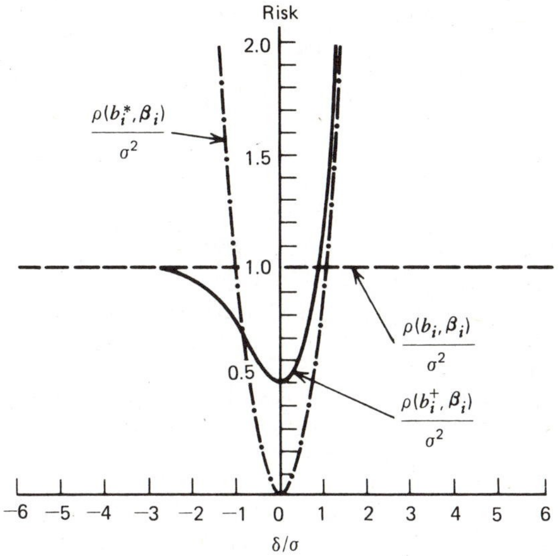

Figure 20.4 Risk functions for the maximum likelihood, equality restricted, and inequality restricted estimators.

we are sure of the direction of the inequality, for example, that the coefficient is nonnegative or nonpositive, then under the squared error loss measure we would always use the inequality restricted estimator.

20.2.3c Hypothesis Testing

In applied work the underlying sampling process by which the data are generated is seldom known, and thus there is uncertainty concerning the appropriate statistical sampling model. Given this uncertainty, the investigator usually proceeds by specifying a hypothesis, for example, about the unknown parameter vector $\boldsymbol{\beta}$, and then making statistical tests concerning the compatibility of the sample information and the linear hypotheses. Within the context of a general linear inequality hypothesis about the coefficient β_i, consider the following null and alternative hypotheses

$$\begin{aligned} H_0&: \beta_i \geq r_i \\ H_a&: \beta_i < r_i \end{aligned} \tag{20.2.35}$$

In contrast to traditional hypothesis testing, this specification reflects the investigator's uncertainty about the position of β_i on the real line and postulates that β_i is contained in the interval $r_i \leq \beta_i < \infty$.

As a basis for checking the compatibility of the sample information and a linear inequality hypothesis for β_i, when σ^2 is known, consider the test statistic

$$\frac{r_i - b_i}{\sigma} = u_i \tag{20.2.36}$$

which is distributed as a normal random variable with mean $\delta_i/\sigma = (r_i - \beta_i)/\sigma$ and variance 1. If it is assumed that $\delta_i = r_i - \beta_i = 0$, then u_i is a standard normal (0, 1) random variable and the test structure could be formulated in terms of δ_i, with H_0: $\delta_i \leq 0$ and H_a: $\delta_i > 0$. Consequently, by using the test statistic (20.2.36), the following test mechanisms may be used.

1. Reject the null hypothesis if $(r_i - b_i)/\sigma = u_i > c_i \geq 0$ and use the maximum likelihood estimator b_i, where c_i is the critical value of the test from the standard normal table.

2. Accept the null hypothesis if $u_i = (r_i - b_i)/\sigma < c_i$ and use the inequality restricted estimator $b_i^+ = I_{(-\infty, r_i)}(b_i)r_i + I_{[r_i, \infty)}(b_i)b_i$.

By accepting the null hypothesis H_0, we take b_i^+ as the estimate of β_i, and by rejecting H_0, the maximum likelihood estimate b_i is used.

When σ^2 is unknown and an unbiased estimate of σ^2 is used, the test statistic (20.2.36) is distributed as a t random variable with $(T - K)$ degrees of freedom.

20.2.3d Bayesian Analysis with Inequality Restrictions

The Bayesian approach introduced in Chapters 4 and 7 provides an alternative inference procedure for estimation with inequality restrictions. Indeed, because of its ability to formally include prior information, the Bayesian approach is well suited for problems that involve prior information in the form of inequality restrictions.

To illustrate the Bayesian approach we will use a simple example, namely, a regression model with only one explanatory variable and no constant term. This model can be written as

$$y_t = x_t\beta + e_t \qquad t = 1, 2, \ldots, T \tag{20.2.37}$$

where the usual variable interpretations hold, and where the e_t are assumed to be independent normally distributed random variables with zero mean and constant variance σ^2. It will be assumed that (20.2.37) represents a long-run consumption function where y_t and x_t denote consumption and income in period t, respectively, and β is the long-run marginal propensity to consume. Furthermore, it is convenient to begin with the assumption that σ^2 is known and equal to 1. The implications of relaxing this assumption will be discussed later. Given these assumptions, the statistical problem is to combine our prior and sample information about β, and to express this combined information in terms of a posterior density function for β.

If no prior information about β exists, the noninformative prior

$$g(\beta) \propto \text{constant} \tag{20.2.38}$$

which was introduced in Chapter 7 can be employed, leading to the following posterior density function, where Σ indicates summation:

$$g(\beta \mid \mathbf{y}) = (2\pi)^{-1/2}(\Sigma x_t^2)^{1/2} \exp\{-\tfrac{1}{2}\Sigma x_t^2(\beta - b)\} \tag{20.2.39}$$

This density function is a normal one, with mean $b = \Sigma x_t y_t / \Sigma x_t^2$, the least squares estimator, and variance $(1/\Sigma x_t^2)$. A likely criticism of any inferences that are made from (20.2.39) is that no provision has been made for the prior information that the marginal propensity to consume must lie between 0 and 1. Such information clearly can be expressed in terms of the linear inequality restrictions $0 < \beta < 1$.

If an investigator wishes to insist that $0 < \beta < 1$, but does not wish to be more specific about what are likely and unlikely values for β, the appropriate prior density function is

$$g(\beta) = \begin{cases} 1 & \text{if } 0 < \beta < 1 \\ 0 & \text{otherwise} \end{cases} \tag{20.2.40}$$

This prior suggests that only values of β between 0 and 1 are feasible, and that all values within this range are equally likely. Few would argue that a value for β of (say) 0.2 is as likely as a value of 0.8. However, if further judgments such as these are quantified, the resulting posterior could be criticized on the grounds that it is too prior-specific. Using Bayes' theorem to combine (20.2.40) with the likelihood function for β given $\mathbf{y}$ yields the posterior density function

$$g(\beta \mid \mathbf{y}) = \begin{cases} c(2\pi)^{-1/2}(\Sigma x_t^2)^{1/2} \exp\{-\tfrac{1}{2}\Sigma x_t^2(\beta - b)^2\} & \text{if } 0 < \beta < 1 \\ 0 & \text{otherwise} \end{cases} \tag{20.2.41}$$

This posterior density function is almost identical to the normal posterior density function given in (20.2.39). The difference is that the density in (20.2.41) cannot take values outside the interval (0, 1); it is a truncated normal distribution, truncated at the points 0 and 1. The constant c is included in (20.2.41) to make the area under the density between 0 and 1 equal to 1; that is, $P(0 < \beta < 1) = 1$.

To describe the differences between the normal and truncated normal posterior distributions, it is convenient to introduce some data. We will consider two cases, one where the least squares estimate lies between 0 and 1, and one where the least squares estimate is greater than 1. For the first case we take

$$b = 0.95 \qquad \text{and} \qquad \Sigma x_t^2 = 196$$

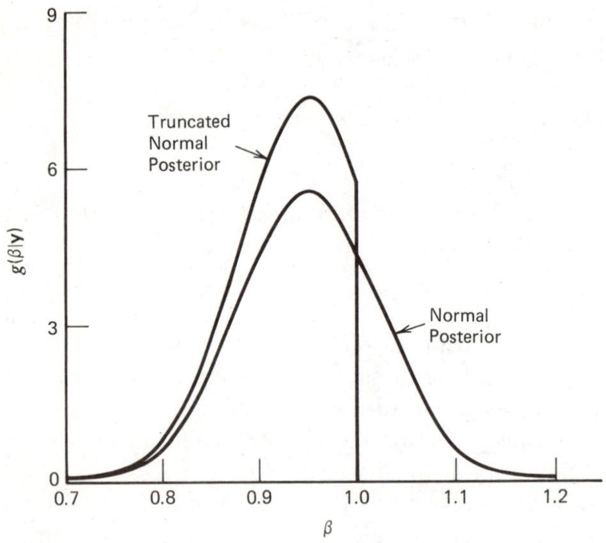

Figure 20.5 Normal and truncated normal posteriors when $0 \leq b < 1$.

Using this data, the normal and truncated normal posteriors that correspond to the noninformative and inequality restricted priors, respectively, are graphed in Figure 20.5. The truncated normal follows the same shape as the normal, but is higher, so as to include the additional area (probability) that is lost when the distribution cuts off at $\beta = 1$. The additional height of the truncated normal is governed by the constant c, which is given by the inverse of the probability that β lies between 0 and 1, taken from the nontruncated posterior. That is, using (20.2.39),

$$c = \{P[0 < \beta < 1]\}^{-1} = (0.758)^{-1} = 1.32$$

Let us consider both point and interval estimates from each of the two posteriors. Assuming quadratic loss, the posterior means are the appropriate Bayesian point estimates. Without the inequality constraints, the posterior mean is the least squares estimate $b = 0.95$. Since this value falls between 0 and 1, it also represents the sampling theory inequality estimate; that is, $b^+ = 0.95$. The Bayesian inequality estimate is different, however. For computation of the mean of the truncated normal posterior, more weight is placed on values of β less than 1, and values of β greater than 1 do not contribute at all. An appropriate formula is given by Johnson and Kotz (1970, pp. 81–83), or, alternatively, numerical integration can be used to compute the mean. These computations yield a posterior mean of $\bar{\bar{\beta}} = 0.921$.

When a noninformative prior is employed, the Bayesian 95% highest posterior density interval for β is identical to the sampling theory 95% confidence interval. In this case, (0.81, 1.09). An obvious difficulty with this interval is that it includes a range (1.00 – 1.09) that is known to be infeasible. The inequality restricted Bayesian posterior overcomes this problem, yielding a 95% highest posterior density interval of (0.82, 1.00). There is no corresponding way of adjusting a sampling theory 95% confidence interval to include the prior information $0 < \beta < 1$.

As a second example, assume we have data such that

$$b = 1.05 \qquad \text{and} \qquad \Sigma x_t^2 = 196$$

The normal and truncated normal posteriors corresponding to these values are graphed in Figure 20.6. Without inequality restrictions, the Bayesian and sampling theory approaches yield identical point and interval estimates, namely, $b = 1.05$ and, for a 95% interval, (0.91, 1.19). When the inequality restrictions are imposed, the sampling theory estimate is the boundary point $b^+ = 1.00$; there is no corresponding 95% confidence interval. The Bayesian inequality restricted results are more interesting. The posterior mean and the 95% highest posterior density interval can be computed as $\bar{\bar{\beta}} = 0.958$ and (0.89, 1.00), respectively.

When a least squares estimate does not satisfy the inequality restrictions, there may be some investigators who query whether the inequality restrictions do in fact

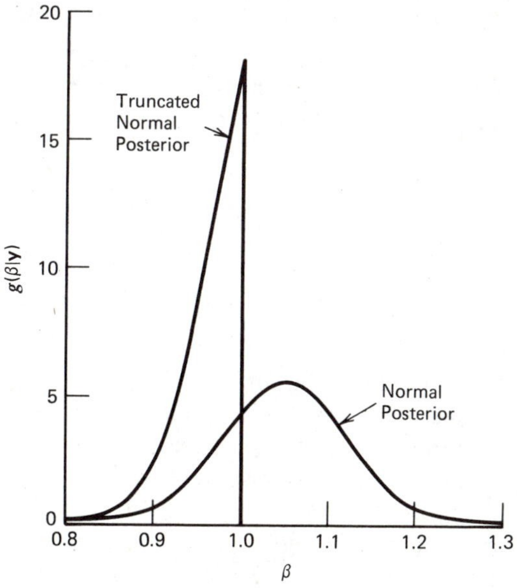

Figure 20.6 Normal and truncated posteriors when $b > 1$.

hold. If these sceptical investigators all have the same noninformative prior, then, using the corresponding posterior density function, they can calculate the probability of the inequality restrictions holding as $P(0 < \beta < 1) = 0.242$.

To make the foregoing analysis more general, it needs to be extended to allow for an unknown σ^2, and for more than one coefficient. When σ^2 is unknown the inequality restricted posterior density function becomes a truncated t-distribution; the introduction of more than one coefficient extends it to a multivariate truncated t-distribution. The same analysis as that just illustrated can be carried out using a multivariate truncated t-posterior, but it becomes more difficult computationally. Posterior means, highest posterior density intervals, and probability statements about regions within the parameter space need to be estimated using Monte Carlo numerical integration.

In this context and as a final example, consider the design matrix and sample of data presented in Section 6.1.5. The maximum likelihood estimates of the unknown parameters based only on the sample observations are $b_1 = 9.7702$, $b_2 = 0.52370$, and $b_3 = 0.69301$. Suppose we introduce a truncated uniform prior density consistent with the inequality $\beta_2 + \beta_3 \leq 1$. Monte Carlo numerical integration procedures yield as the mean of the truncated multivariate t posterior, the Bayes' estimates $\bar{\bar{\beta}}_1 = 10.179$, $\bar{\bar{\beta}}_2 = 0.4387$, and $\bar{\bar{\beta}}_3 = 0.4727$. In 20,000 replications from a multivariate t with no truncation, 2029 satisfied the inequality and formed the basis for computing $\bar{\bar{\boldsymbol{\beta}}}$. Consequently, the posterior probability of the inequality restriction holding for an investigator with an unrestricted uniform prior is $P(\beta_2 + \beta_3 \leq 1) = 0.1014$. The variances of the 2029 estimates that satisfied the prior are $\sigma^2_{\bar{\bar{\beta}}_1} = 0.0179$, $\sigma^2_{\bar{\bar{\beta}}_2} = 0.0093$, and $\sigma^2_{\bar{\bar{\beta}}_3} = 0.1197$. These values are the Monte Carlo based estimates of the marginal posterior variances of the truncated multivariate t p.d.f. For further details and some additional examples, see Geweke (1986).

20.2.4 Summary Statement

In many cases in applied work the investigator has information over and above that contained in the sample observations. Assuming this fortunate event, we have, within a sampling theory context, reviewed in the preceding sections how to take account of three alternative forms of information for the purposes of estimation and inference. Inequality nonsample information was also reviewed within a Bayesian context.

If the investigator is certain of the prior information and can specify it in the form of a system of linear equations, then the restricted least squares rule is best. However, in many instances the prior information is not exact, and we have to consider rules that incorporate this fact. The degree of misspecification error of the prior (nonsample) information affects the performance of the equality restricted estimator. Conventional hypothesis testing provides one basis for checking the compatibility between the sample and prior information.

Alternatively, nonsample information may be available in the form of linear stochastic restrictions. In this case there is a sampling theory estimator available, but this estimator has many of the characteristics of the equality restricted estimator. In addition, one weakness of the stochastic prior information estimator lies in assuming that the random vector representing the uncertainty of the prior information has a mean of zero, that is, the prior information is unbiased. Additional assumptions regarding a known covariance matrix of the stochastic prior information also seem unreasonably demanding.

Inequality restrictions offer another sampling theory alternative for representing nonsample information. If the direction of the inequality restriction(s) is correct, the inequality restricted estimator under squared error loss is uniformly superior to the maximum likelihood estimator. If the direction of the inequality is incorrect, as the specification error grows the risk of the inequality restricted estimator approaches that of the restricted least squares estimator. Therefore, if the applied worker is sure of the direction of the inequality, for example, the parameters are nonnegative or nonpositive, then the inequality estimator not only performs well relative to other alternatives but uniformly dominates the least squares estimator which is used by most applied workers.

20.3 Pretest and Stein Rule Estimators

In the early chapters of the book we were concerned with estimation and inference from a sample of data when the statistical model was correctly specified. In this happy world of perfect knowledge concerning the underlying sampling processes, statistical theory provides techniques for obtaining point and interval estimates of the population parameters and for hypothesis testing. Also in the early chapters much emphasis was placed on developing estimators that were unbiased and efficient or on obtaining estimators that at least had these properties asymptotically. In the preceding section we noted the possible trade-off between bias and variance when evaluating estimator performance, and we suggested the mean square error as a possible measure that could be used that accounts for both types of sampling errors. We also noted that the nonsample information used may be incorrect or false and evaluated the bias and mean square error or risk consequences of its use in such an unfavorable event.

In this section we recognize explicitly that the applied researcher seldom, if ever, knows the true statistical model and thus does not know the specification error parameter $\boldsymbol{\delta}$ when evaluating the risk consequences for alternative estimators. In this context we will specify and evaluate within a decision theory framework (1) a two-stage procedure that yields an estimator after a preliminary test of significance and makes the estimation rule dependent on the outcome of a hypothesis test and (2) a nonlinear biased estimator that makes use of both sample and nonsample information. These estimators, along with the ridge and principal components estimators to be discussed in Chapter 21, fall in the general province of biased estimation.

20.3.1 Pretest Estimators

When the exact content of the true sampling model is unknown the statistical model used in econometric work is sometimes determined by a preliminary hypothesis test using the data at hand. This two-stage procedure, based on a test of hypothesis, provides a rule for choosing between the estimator based on the sample data and the estimator consistent with the hypothesis. Within the context of Chapter 6 and Section 20.2.1 this means that we make a test of the compatibility of the maximum likelihood estimator $\mathbf{b}$, based on the sample information, and the linear hypothesis $R\boldsymbol{\beta} = \mathbf{r}$, and, depending on the outcome, make a choice or take a decision. Consequently under this scenario we choose either the restricted estimator $\mathbf{b}^*$ or unrestricted estimator $\mathbf{b}$. The pretest estimator thereby generated provides a rule for choosing between an unbiased estimator $\mathbf{b}$ and a possibly biased one $\mathbf{b}^*$ that has greater precision and may have smaller risk.

To see the sampling implications of this two-stage procedure let us, for expository purposes, use the orthonormal linear statistical model considered in Section 20.2.1. That is, we consider the statistical model $\mathbf{y} = X\boldsymbol{\beta} + \mathbf{e}$, where the design matrix is such that $X'X = I_K$ and the restriction or hypothesis design matrix $R = I_K$. As a test mechanism we use the likelihood ratio test statistic developed in Chapter 6. To test the null hypothesis that $R\boldsymbol{\beta} = \boldsymbol{\beta} = \mathbf{r}$ against the alternative hypothesis $\boldsymbol{\beta} \neq \mathbf{r}$, it is conventional to use the test statistic

$$\lambda = \frac{(\mathbf{b} - \mathbf{r})'X'X(\mathbf{b} - \mathbf{r})}{K\hat{\sigma}^2} = \frac{(\mathbf{b} - \mathbf{r})'(\mathbf{b} - \mathbf{r})}{K\hat{\sigma}^2} \tag{20.3.1}$$

which is distributed as a central F random variable with K and $(T - K)$ degrees of freedom *if the hypotheses (restrictions) are correct.* If the restrictions are incorrect and $E[\mathbf{b} - \mathbf{r}] = (\boldsymbol{\beta} - \mathbf{r}) = \boldsymbol{\delta} \neq \mathbf{0}$, then λ is distributed as a noncentral F with noncentrality parameter $(\boldsymbol{\beta} - \mathbf{r})'(\boldsymbol{\beta} - \mathbf{r})/2\sigma^2 = \boldsymbol{\delta}'\boldsymbol{\delta}/2\sigma^2$. However, since the noncentrality parameter is unknown when testing, the hypotheses are assumed correct and the central F distribution is used as the test statistic. Consequently, the null hypothesis is rejected if $\lambda \geq F_{(K, T-K, \alpha)} = c$, where the critical value c is determined for a given level of the test α by

$$\int_c^\infty dF_{(K, T-K)} = P[F_{(K, T-K)} \geq c] = \alpha \tag{20.3.2}$$

By accepting the null hypothesis, we take the restricted least squares estimator $\mathbf{b}^* = \mathbf{r}$ as our estimator of $\boldsymbol{\beta}$; by rejecting the null hypothesis $\boldsymbol{\beta} - \mathbf{r} = \boldsymbol{\delta} = \mathbf{0}$, we use the maximum likelihood, unrestricted least squares estimator $\mathbf{b}$. Thus the estimate that results depends on a preliminary test of significance, and the estimator used by an applied worker is therefore of the following form.

$$\hat{\hat{\boldsymbol{\beta}}} = \begin{cases} \mathbf{b}^* & \text{if } \lambda < c \\ \mathbf{b} & \text{if } \lambda \geq c \end{cases} \tag{20.3.3}$$

Alternatively, the estimator may be written as

$$\begin{aligned} \hat{\hat{\boldsymbol{\beta}}} &= I_{(0,c)}(\lambda)\mathbf{b}^* + I_{[c,\infty)}(\lambda)\mathbf{b} \\ &= I_{(0,c)}(\lambda)\mathbf{b}^* + [1 - I_{(0,c)}(\lambda)]\mathbf{b} \\ &= \mathbf{b} - I_{(0,c)}(\lambda)(\mathbf{b} - \mathbf{b}^*) = \mathbf{b} - I_{(0,c)}(\lambda)(\mathbf{b} - \mathbf{r}) \end{aligned} \tag{20.3.4}$$

where $I_{(0,c)}(\lambda)$ and $I_{[c,\infty)}(\lambda)$ are indicator functions that take the values $I_{(0,c)}(\lambda) = 1$ and $I_{[c,\infty)}(\lambda) = 0$ if the argument λ falls within the interval zero to c and take the values $I_{(0,c)}(\lambda) = 0$ and $I_{[c,\infty)}(\lambda) = 1$ when $\lambda \geq c$. Therefore, in a repeated sampling context, the data, the linear hypotheses, and the level of significance all determine the combination of the two estimators that is chosen on the average. From an applied standpoint one thing that becomes apparent from these conditions is the impact of the level of significance on the outcome for the pretest estimator. If the level of significance α is equal to 0, then the pretest estimator in (20.3.4) is

$$\hat{\hat{\boldsymbol{\beta}}} = I_{[0,\infty)}(\lambda)\mathbf{b}^* + I_{(\infty)}(\lambda)\mathbf{b} = \mathbf{b}^* \tag{20.3.5}$$

and the restricted estimator is always chosen. Alternatively, if the level of significance α is equal to 1, then the pretest estimator is

$$\hat{\hat{\boldsymbol{\beta}}} = I_{(0)}(\lambda)\mathbf{b}^* + I_{[0,\infty)}(\lambda)\mathbf{b} = \mathbf{b} \tag{20.3.6}$$

and the least squares estimator is always chosen. Therefore, the choice of α, which is usually made in a cavalier way in applied work, has a crucial role to play in determining the proportion of the time each estimator is used and in determining the sampling performance of the pretest estimator.

20.3.1a Sampling Performance

From (20.3.4), the mean of the pretest estimator is

$$E[\hat{\hat{\boldsymbol{\beta}}}] = \boldsymbol{\beta} - E[I_{(0,c)}(\lambda)(\mathbf{b} - \mathbf{r})] \tag{20.3.7}$$

Consequently, if the null hypothesis is true and $\boldsymbol{\beta} = \mathbf{r}$ or if $\boldsymbol{\delta} = \mathbf{0}$, the pretest estimator is unbiased. For all $\boldsymbol{\delta} \neq \mathbf{0}$, the pretest estimator is biased.

Under the squared error loss criterion, the risk function may be written, using (20.3.4), as

$$\begin{aligned}\rho(\boldsymbol{\beta}, \hat{\hat{\boldsymbol{\beta}}}) &= E[(\hat{\hat{\boldsymbol{\beta}}} - \boldsymbol{\beta})'(\hat{\hat{\boldsymbol{\beta}}} - \boldsymbol{\beta})] \\ &= E[(\mathbf{b} - \boldsymbol{\beta} - I_{(0,c)}(\lambda)(\mathbf{b} - \mathbf{r}))'(\mathbf{b} - \boldsymbol{\beta} - I_{(0,c)}(\lambda)(\mathbf{b} - \mathbf{r}))] \\ &= E[(\mathbf{b} - \boldsymbol{\beta})'(\mathbf{b} - \boldsymbol{\beta})] - E[I_{(0,c)}(\lambda)(\mathbf{b} - \boldsymbol{\beta})'(\mathbf{b} - \boldsymbol{\beta})] + E[I_{(0,c)}(\lambda)]\boldsymbol{\delta}'\boldsymbol{\delta}\end{aligned} \tag{20.3.8}$$

Judge and Bock (1978) have evaluated this risk function, and they reach the following conclusions.

1. If the restrictions are correct and $\boldsymbol{\delta} = \mathbf{0}$, the risk of the pretest estimator is less than that of the least squares estimator, and the decrease in risk depends on the level of significance α and, correspondingly, on the critical value of the test c.
2. As the hypothesis error $\boldsymbol{\beta} - \mathbf{r} = \boldsymbol{\delta}$ increases and approaches infinity, the risk of the pretest estimator approaches $\sigma^2 K$, the risk of the unrestricted least squares estimator.
3. As the hypothesis error grows, the risk of the pretest estimator increases, obtains a maximum after crossing the risk of the least squares estimator, and then monotonically decreases to approach $\sigma^2 K$, the risk of the least squares estimator.

The sampling characteristics of the preliminary test estimator are summarized in Figure 20.7.

From these results we see that the pretest estimator does well relative to the least squares estimator if the hypotheses are correctly specified. However, in the $\boldsymbol{\delta}'\boldsymbol{\delta}/2\sigma^2$ space representing the range of hypothesis errors, the pretest estimator is inferior to the least squares estimator over an infinite range of the parameter space. As also depicted in Figure 20.7 there is a range of the parameter space in which the pretest estimator has risk that is inferior to (greater than) that of both the unrestricted and restricted least squares estimators. No one estimator depicted in Figure 20.7 dominates the other competitors. In addition, in applied problems the hypothesis errors, and thus the correct $\boldsymbol{\delta}$ in the specification error parameter space, are seldom known. Consequently, the choice of the estimator is unresolved.

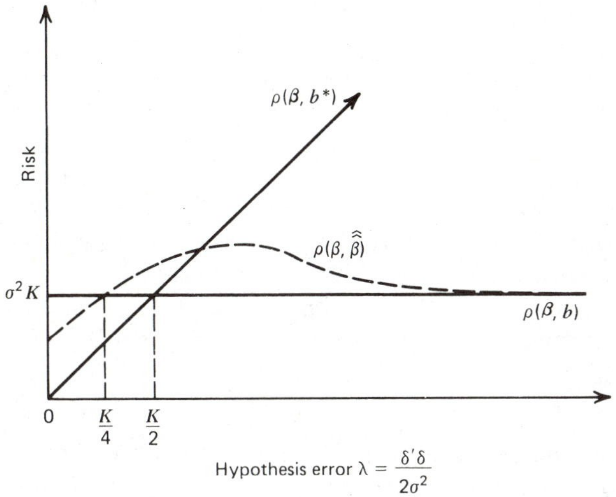

Figure 20.7 Risk functions for the least squares and restricted least squares estimators and a typical risk function for the pretest estimator.

Let us note again that the form of the pretest estimator in (20.3.4) depends on the critical value of the test c or α, the level of statistical significance. Thus, as $\alpha \to 0$, the risk of the pretest estimator approaches that of the restricted least squares estimator $\mathbf{b}^*$. In contrast, as $\alpha \to 1$, the risk of the pretest estimator approaches that of the least squares estimator $\mathbf{b}$. The impact of the choice of c or α, which has a crucial impact on the performance of the pretest estimator, is portrayed in Figure 20.8.

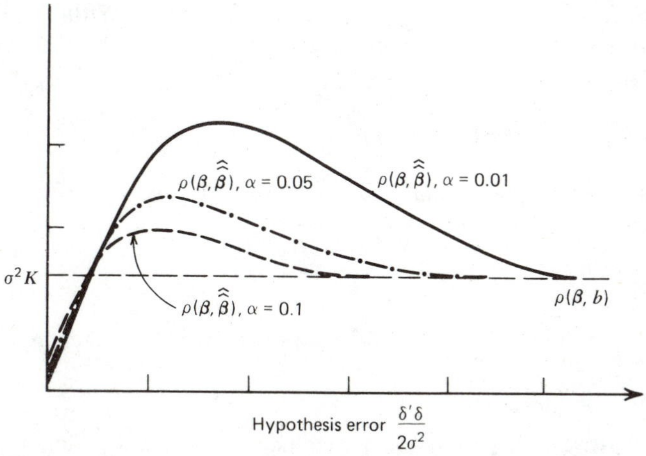

Figure 20.8 Pre-test Estimator Risk Functions for Different Levels of α.

20.3.2 Stein Rules

In the preceding sections of this chapter we have investigated, under a squared error loss measure, the sampling performance of variants of the maximum likelihood estimator and the corresponding pretest estimators and have noted over at least part of the parameter space the unsatisfactory nature of these rules. In this section we consider some nontraditional rules for combining sample and various types of nonsample information. In particular we consider variants of two stage rules that have been proposed by James and Stein (1961). In investigating the sampling performance of these estimators, let us continue to use the orthonormal linear statistical model and a squared error loss measure.

20.3.2a The James and Stein Rule

In a 1955 paper, Stein considered the problem of estimating the unknown coefficient vector $\boldsymbol{\beta}$ for the orthonormal linear statistical model and showed that if the number of parameters was strictly greater than 2, it was possible to uniformly improve on the conventional maximum likelihood (least squares) estimator under a squared error loss measure of performance. Thus Stein was able to prove under squared error loss the inadmissibility of the traditional least squares rule, that is, there is an estimator $\boldsymbol{\beta}^*$ such that $\rho(\boldsymbol{\beta}, \boldsymbol{\beta}^*) \leq \rho(\boldsymbol{\beta}, \mathbf{b})$, for every value of $\boldsymbol{\beta}$, with strict inequality holding for some $\boldsymbol{\beta}$. If for the K-dimensional $\boldsymbol{\beta}$ vector, $K \leq 2$, then the least squares estimator is admissible. Following this work, James and Stein (1961) demonstrated a nonlinear estimator that dominated the least squares-maximum likelihood estimator.

Let us first consider a simple version of the James and Stein estimator based on the orthonormal linear statistical model $\mathbf{y} = X\boldsymbol{\beta} + \mathbf{e}$ or its K mean counterpart $X'\mathbf{y} = \boldsymbol{\beta} + X'\mathbf{e}$, where $X'X = I_K$, $\mathbf{e} \sim N(\mathbf{0}, I_T)$ and $R\boldsymbol{\beta} = I_K\boldsymbol{\beta} = \mathbf{r} = \mathbf{0}$. Within this context the James and Stein estimator, which is a function of the maximum likelihood estimator $\mathbf{b}$, has the form

$$\boldsymbol{\beta}^* = (1 - a/\mathbf{b}'\mathbf{b})\mathbf{b} \tag{20.3.9}$$

where at this point a is an unspecified scalar. The mean of $\boldsymbol{\beta}^*$ is

$$E[\boldsymbol{\beta}^*] = E[\mathbf{b}] - E[(a/\mathbf{b}'\mathbf{b})\mathbf{b}] \tag{20.3.10}$$

Consequently, the James and Stein rule is biased.

The risk of the James and Stein estimator under a squared error loss measure is

$$\begin{aligned}\rho(\boldsymbol{\beta}, \boldsymbol{\beta}^*) &= E[(\boldsymbol{\beta}^* - \boldsymbol{\beta})'(\boldsymbol{\beta}^* - \boldsymbol{\beta})] \\ &= E[(\mathbf{b} - \boldsymbol{\beta})'(\mathbf{b} - \boldsymbol{\beta})] - 2a + 2a\boldsymbol{\beta}'E[\mathbf{b}/\mathbf{b}'\mathbf{b}] + a^2E[1/\mathbf{b}'\mathbf{b}]\end{aligned} \tag{20.3.11}$$

When theorems in Judge and Bock (1978, p. 322) are used in the evaluation of (20.3.11), they demonstrate that $\rho(\boldsymbol{\beta}, \boldsymbol{\beta}^*) \leq \rho(\boldsymbol{\beta}, \mathbf{b})$ for all $\boldsymbol{\beta}$ if $0 \leq a \leq 2(K-2)$ and that the value of a that minimizes the risk of $\boldsymbol{\beta}^*$ is $a = K - 2$. Therefore, the optimal (minimum risk) James and Stein estimator is

$$\boldsymbol{\beta}^* = [1 - (K-2)/\mathbf{b}'\mathbf{b}]\mathbf{b} \tag{20.3.12}$$

and this rule demonstrates the inadmissibility of the maximum likelihood estimator. When $\boldsymbol{\beta} = \mathbf{0}$ the risk of the James and Stein estimator is 2. The risk of $\boldsymbol{\beta}^*$ increases to the risk of the maximum likelihood estimator $[\rho(\boldsymbol{\beta}, \mathbf{b}) = K]$ as $\boldsymbol{\beta}'\boldsymbol{\beta} \to \infty$. Thus for values of $\boldsymbol{\beta}$ close to the origin the gain in risk is considerable. The characteristics of the risk function for the James and Stein estimator are depicted in Figure 20.9.

The James and Stein estimator (20.3.12) shrinks the maximum likelihood estimates toward a null mean vector. A more general formulation that makes the arbitrary origin of the foregoing case more explicit, considers a mean vector $\boldsymbol{\beta}_0 = \mathbf{r} = \mathbf{b}^*$ and an estimator of the form

$$\boldsymbol{\beta}_0^* = [1 - (K-2)/(\mathbf{b} - \mathbf{r})'(\mathbf{b} - \mathbf{r})](\mathbf{b} - \mathbf{r}) + \mathbf{r} \tag{20.3.13}$$

This estimator has bias and risk characteristics consistent with the conventional James and Stein estimator, that is, a risk of 2 when $\boldsymbol{\delta}'\boldsymbol{\delta}/2 = 0$ and a risk of K as $\boldsymbol{\delta}'\boldsymbol{\delta}/2 \to \infty$, where $\boldsymbol{\delta} = \mathbf{r} - \boldsymbol{\beta}$.

20.3.2b Some Remarks

In this chapter we have traced some of the attempts that have been made to combine sample and exact prior information. If squared error loss is used as the

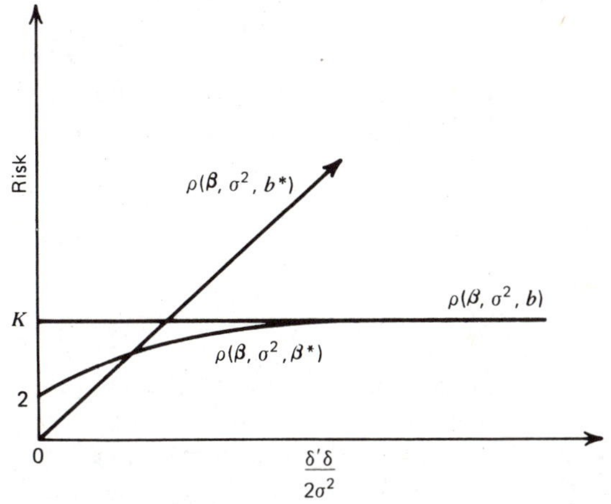

Figure 20.9 The risk characteristics of the Stein rule.

basis for gauging estimator performance, these results clearly point to the unsatisfactory nature of the least squares and restricted least squares estimators and the traditional search rules that involve preliminary tests based on the data at hand. With the estimators specified and evaluated to this point, the Stein rules appear uniformly superior to the conventional estimators normally used in applied work. In addition, the Stein rules, such as (20.3.12) or (20.3.13), are computationally simple to apply.

All these results have been extended by Judge and Bock (1978) to handle a general design matrix X and hypothesis design matrix R. In general, all the hoped for results hold, and only the conditions for superiority change.

Perhaps this is the time to remind you that in this chapter we have specified and analyzed several estimators that resulted from (1) changing the statistical model, (2) changing the amount of information used, and (3) changing the measure of performance.

In the case of the pretest estimator, postdata model-evaluation procedures constitute, to a large degree, a rejection of the concept of a true statistical model for which statistical theory provides a basis for estimation and inference.

The Stein-rule estimators, which shrink the maximum likelihood estimates toward zero or some predetermined coordinate, enjoy good properties from both sampling theory and Bayesian points of view. Since the operating characteristics of the Stein rules depend on means and variances of the observations and the unknown coefficients, the estimators are robust relative to the normality assumption. They also appear to be robust over a range of loss functions. Although there are several known rules for using both sample and nonsample data that satisfy certain decision theory properties, none of the rules dominate the variants of the Stein rule. The Stein estimators thus provide rules that are simple, efficient, and robust.

Finally, we should note that least squares and maximum likelihood estimation of nonlinear statisical models lead, in general, to biased estimators. Some of these results are discussed in Chapter 12. Also, the Bayesian criterion generally leads to biased estimators. The Bayesian basis for estimation and inference is discussed in Chapters 4 and 7.

20.4 Model Specification

Much of the literature concerned with estimation and inference from a sample of economic data deals with a situation when the statistical model is correctly specified. Consequently, in much of econometric practice, it is customary to assume that the parameterized linear statistical model used for purposes of inference is consistent with the sampling process from which the sample observations were generated. In this happy event, statistical theory provides techniques for obtaining point and interval estimators of the population parameters and for hypothesis testing. In practice, however, the possibilities for model misspecification are numerous and false statistical models are the rule rather than the exception.

In many of the previous chapters various types of uncertainty relative to the specification of the statistical model were recognized and procedures were suggested for identifying the misspecification and/or mitigating its statistical impact. Among the various possible sources or false statistical models, the omission of relevant explanatory variables of the inclusion of extraneous explanatory variables, are the most likely and pervasive. Consequently, in this section, within the context of nonexperimental model building and the linear statistical model framework introduced in Chapter 6, we first consider the statistical consequences of and the possibilities for dealing with uncertainty concerning the appropriate column dimension of the design matrix X.

Most model search procedures recognize the importance of econometric theory in narrowing the range of admissible design matrix specifications. Some suggested search procedures have little or no theoretical basis and have, it would appear, solved the problem by making reference to magic, mysticism, or possibly revelation. Others have suggested various criteria or rules of thumb for adding to or deleting explanatory variables from the design matrix. In any event, whatever the choice procedure employed, seldom in a sampling theory context have we known the sampling properties of the estimators thereby generated and in a decision context the risk associated with a particular rule (action).

Our objective in this section is to sort out the statisical implications of using some of the various model selection rules and to provide a guide for choice.

20.4.1 Statistical Consequences of an Incorrect Design Matrix

The problem considered in this section is posed by Efron and Morris as follows:

> "... The statistician wants to estimate the parameters of a linear model that are known to lie in a high dimensional parameter space H_1: but he suspects that they may lie close to a specified lower dimensional parameter space $H_0 \subset H_1$. Then, estimates unbiased for every parameter vector in H_1 may have large variance, while estimates restricted to H_0 have smaller variance but possibly large bias.....

To see the underlying basis for this conclusion for expository purposes let us consider the regressor choice problem within the context of a general two-decision setting and make use of the parameterized linear statistical model

$$\mathbf{y} = X\boldsymbol{\beta} + \mathbf{e} = X_1\boldsymbol{\beta}_1 + X_2\boldsymbol{\beta}_2 + \mathbf{e} \qquad (20.4.1)$$

where $\mathbf{y}$ is a T-dimensional vector of observations; $X = [X_1, X_2]$ is a $(T \times K)$ matrix of constants of rank K; X_1 and X_2 are known matrices of dimension $(T \times K_1)$ and $(T \times K_2)$, respectively, with $K_1 + K_2 = K$; $\boldsymbol{\beta}$ is a K-dimensional vector of unknown parameters that is partitioned conformably into components $\boldsymbol{\beta}_1$ and $\boldsymbol{\beta}_2$; and $\mathbf{e}$ is a $(T \times 1)$ normal random vector with mean vector zero and covariance matrix $\sigma^2 I_T$ with the scalar σ^2 unknown. If we let X_1 contain the included variables and X_2 contain the excluded or omitted variables, where $K_1 \leq K$, the statistical model (20.4.1) can be made to represent all of the possible subsets of X by varying the column dimensions and content of X_1 and X_2. The least squares (maximum likelihood) estimator of $\boldsymbol{\beta}$ and an estimator of σ^2 are

$$\mathbf{b} = \begin{bmatrix} \mathbf{b}_1 \\ \mathbf{b}_2 \end{bmatrix} = (X'X)^{-1}X'\mathbf{y} = \begin{bmatrix} X_1'X_1 & X_1'X_2 \\ X_2'X_1 & X_2'X_2 \end{bmatrix}^{-1} \begin{bmatrix} X_1'\mathbf{y} \\ X_2'\mathbf{y} \end{bmatrix} \tag{20.4.2}$$

and

$$\hat{\sigma}^2 = \frac{(\mathbf{y} - X\mathbf{b})'(\mathbf{y} - X\mathbf{b})}{T - K} = \frac{\mathbf{y}'[I_T - X(X'X)^{-1}X']\mathbf{y}}{T - K} \tag{20.4.3}$$

If the statistical model (20.4.1) is correct; that is, if the column dimension of the design matrix X is K, then $\mathbf{b}$ and $\hat{\sigma}^2$ are minimum variance *unbiased* estimators. The maximum likelihood estimator $\mathbf{b}$ is a normally distributed random vector with mean vector $\boldsymbol{\beta}$ and covariance $E[(\mathbf{b} - \boldsymbol{\beta})(\mathbf{b} - \boldsymbol{\beta})'] = \sigma^2(X'X)^{-1}$. In regard to the unbiased estimator $\hat{\sigma}^2$, the random variable $(T - K)\hat{\sigma}^2/\sigma^2$ is distributed as a central χ^2 random variable with $(T - K)$ degrees of freedom.

Consider only the X_1 subset of X and assume that the X_2 set of variables appears in the equation with a zero coefficient vector. Thus if we assume the X_2 variables are extraneous and are omitted from the statistical model, then we may represent this information by the set of restrictions

$$R\boldsymbol{\beta} = \mathbf{r} = [0, I_{K_2}] \begin{bmatrix} \boldsymbol{\beta}_1 \\ \boldsymbol{\beta}_2 \end{bmatrix} = \mathbf{0}_{K_2} \tag{20.4.4}$$

where R is a $(K_2 \times K)$ known matrix of rank K_2 and $\mathbf{0}_{K_2}$ is a K_2 dimensional zero vector. Under this scenario, the general restricted least squares estimator is

$$\mathbf{b}^* = \mathbf{b} - (X'X)^{-1}R'[R(X'X)^{-1}R']^{-1}(R\mathbf{b} - \mathbf{r}) \tag{20.4.5a}$$

If the elements of $\boldsymbol{\beta}_2$ are restricted to zero, the restricted least squares estimator for this special case becomes

$$\mathbf{b}^* = \begin{bmatrix} \mathbf{b}_1^* \\ \mathbf{0}_{K_2} \end{bmatrix} = \begin{bmatrix} (X_1'X_1)^{-1}X_1'\mathbf{y} \\ \mathbf{0}_{K_2} \end{bmatrix} \tag{20.4.5b}$$

We recognize the fact that some of or possibly all the elements of $\boldsymbol{\beta}_2$ may not be zero by letting $R\boldsymbol{\beta} - \mathbf{r} = \boldsymbol{\delta}$, a vector of parameter specification errors of dimension

K_2. If the restrictions are correct, which for our special case implies $\boldsymbol{\beta}_2 = \mathbf{0}$, then $\boldsymbol{\delta}$ is a null vector. Within this context the mean of the restricted estimator $\mathbf{b}^*$ is

$$E[\mathbf{b}^*] = E[\mathbf{b} - (X'X)^{-1}R'[R(X'X)^{-1}R']^{-1}(R\mathbf{b} - \mathbf{0})]$$

$$= \boldsymbol{\beta} - (X'X)^{-1}R'[R(X'X)^{-1}R']^{-1}\boldsymbol{\delta} = \begin{bmatrix} \boldsymbol{\beta}_1 + (X_1'X_1)^{-1}X_1'X_2\boldsymbol{\beta}_2 \\ \boldsymbol{\beta}_2 - \boldsymbol{\delta} \end{bmatrix} \quad (20.4.6)$$

If $\boldsymbol{\beta}_2 = \mathbf{0}$ and thus $\boldsymbol{\delta} = \mathbf{0}$, then $\mathbf{b}_1^*$ is an unbiased estimator of $\boldsymbol{\beta}_1$. Otherwise, unless the regressor sets X_1 and X_2 are orthogonal, the estimator (20.4.5) is a biased estimator of $\boldsymbol{\beta}_1$ with the bias being proportional to the magnitudes of the $\boldsymbol{\beta}_2$ vector. The covariance matrix of $\mathbf{b}^*$ is

$$E\{[\mathbf{b}^* - E(\mathbf{b}^*)][\mathbf{b}^* - E(\mathbf{b}^*)]'\}$$

$$= \sigma^2\{(X'X)^{-1} - (X'X)^{-1}R'[R(X'X)^{-1}R']^{-1}R(X'X)^{-1}\} \quad (20.4.7a)$$

or

$$E\left[\begin{bmatrix} \mathbf{b}_1^* - E(\mathbf{b}_1^*) \\ \mathbf{b}_2^* - E(\mathbf{b}_2^*) \end{bmatrix}\begin{bmatrix} \mathbf{b}_1^* - E(\mathbf{b}_1^*) \\ \mathbf{b}_2^* - E(\mathbf{b}_2^*) \end{bmatrix}'\right] = \begin{bmatrix} \sigma^2(X_1'X_1)^{-1} & 0 \\ 0 & 0_{K_2} \end{bmatrix} \quad (20.4.7b)$$

The second expression on the right side of (20.4.7a) is a positive semi-definite matrix. Also, the difference between the covariance matrices of the restricted and unrestricted estimators is

$$E\{(\mathbf{b} - \boldsymbol{\beta})(\mathbf{b} - \boldsymbol{\beta})' - [\mathbf{b}^* - E(\mathbf{b}^*)][\mathbf{b}^* - E(\mathbf{b}^*)]'\} = \Delta \quad (20.4.8)$$

where Δ is a positive semidefinite matrix. This implies, among other things, that the covariance matrix (20.4.7a) or (20.4.7b), for the estimator involving restriction (20.4.4), has diagonal elements (sampling variabilities or measures of precision) that are equal to or less than the corresponding unrestricted elements of the least squares estimator $\mathbf{b}$ for the statistical model (20.4.1).

An estimator of σ^2 that uses the restricted least squares estimator $\mathbf{b}^*$ is

$$\overset{*}{\sigma}{}^2 = \frac{(\mathbf{y} - X\mathbf{b}^*)'(\mathbf{y} - X\mathbf{b}^*)}{T - K_1} = \frac{\mathbf{y}'[I_T - X_1(X_1'X_1)^{-1}X_1']\mathbf{y}}{T - K_1} \quad (20.4.9)$$

and has mean

$$E[\overset{*}{\sigma}{}^2] = \sigma^2 + \frac{\boldsymbol{\beta}_2'X_2'[I - X_1(X_1'X_1)^{-1}X_1']X_2\boldsymbol{\beta}_2}{T - K_1} \quad (20.4.10)$$

Therefore, unless $\boldsymbol{\beta}_2 = \mathbf{0}$ and the subset model is correct, $\overset{*}{\sigma}{}^2$ yields a biased estimator of σ^2. Also, when $\boldsymbol{\beta}_2 \neq \mathbf{0}$, the ratio $(T - K_1)\overset{*}{\sigma}{}^2/\sigma^2$ is distributed as a noncentral $\chi^2_{(T-K_1)}$ random variable.

These results are summarized in Table 20.1 as a two-state, two-action structure. The analytical results plus the information contained in Table 20.1 bring out

Table 20.1 Model Alternatives and Statistical Implications

Investigators actions	States of World: True model $\mathbf{y} = X_1\boldsymbol{\beta}_1 + X_2\boldsymbol{\beta}_2 + \mathbf{e}$	States of World: True model $\mathbf{y} = X_1\boldsymbol{\beta}_1 + X_2\boldsymbol{\beta}_2 + \mathbf{e}$, $\boldsymbol{\beta}_2 = \mathbf{0}$
Assume statistical model $\mathbf{y} = X_1\boldsymbol{\beta}_1 + X_2\boldsymbol{\beta}_2 + \mathbf{e}$	$\mathbf{b}$ is minimum variance unbiased	$\mathbf{b}$ is unbiased but not minimum variance
Assume statistical model $\mathbf{y} = X_1\boldsymbol{\beta}_1 + X_2\boldsymbol{\beta}_2 + \mathbf{e}$; $\boldsymbol{\beta}_2 = \mathbf{0}$	$\mathbf{b}^*$ is biased, but its sampling variability is less than that of the unbiased estimator $\mathbf{b}$. $\overset{*}{\sigma}{}^2$ is biased upward	$\mathbf{b}^*$ is minimum variance unbiased

clearly the following statistical consequences of using a subset X_1 of the possible design matrix:

1. The estimator $\mathbf{b}_1^*$ is biased unless $\boldsymbol{\beta}_2 = \mathbf{0}$ or X_1 and X_2 are orthogonal, or $X_1'X_2\boldsymbol{\beta}_2 = \mathbf{0}$.
2. Whether or not $\boldsymbol{\beta}_2 = \mathbf{0}$, the unrestricted least squares estimate of $\mathbf{b}_1$, when both X_1 and X_2 *are included*, has lower precision than the estimate $\mathbf{b}_1^*$ from the subset model, that is, the sampling variability of $\mathbf{b}_1^*$ is equal to or less than the sampling variability of $\mathbf{b}_1$ from the unrestricted model.
3. Unless $\boldsymbol{\beta}_2 = \mathbf{0}$, the subset (restricted) model estimator $\overset{*}{\sigma}{}^2$ has a positive bias.
4. If $\boldsymbol{\beta}_2 \neq \mathbf{0}$, then either $\mathbf{b}_1^*$ or $\overset{*}{\sigma}{}^2$ is biased or both are biased.

20.4.2 Mean Squared Error Norms

The foregoing conclusions cast the incentive for correct model choice in terms of bias and/or variance. The mean squared error measure, which in the case of biased estimators is a composite of the two, provides a basis for reflecting a trade-off between bias and precision (Section 20.1).

Within the context of Section 20.4.1 if $\boldsymbol{\beta}_2 \neq \mathbf{0}$ and thus $\boldsymbol{\delta} \neq \mathbf{0}$, then $\mathbf{b}^*$ is a biased estimator with mean square error (MSE),

$$
\begin{aligned}
\text{MSE}_{\mathbf{b}^*} &= E[(\mathbf{b}^* - \boldsymbol{\beta})(\mathbf{b}^* - \boldsymbol{\beta})'] \\
&= \sigma^2(X'X)^{-1} - \sigma^2(X'X)^{-1}R'[R(X'X)^{-1}R']^{-1}R(X'X)^{-1} \\
&\quad + (X'X)^{-1}R'[R(X'X)^{-1}R']^{-1}\boldsymbol{\delta}\boldsymbol{\delta}'[R(X'X)^{-1}R']^{-1}R(X'X)^{-1}
\end{aligned}
\tag{20.4.11}
$$

which is the sum of the covariance matrix (20.4.7a) and the bias matrix. Of course, if the specification error $\boldsymbol{\delta} = \mathbf{0}$, the restricted estimator is unbiased and (20.4.11) is equal to (20.4.7b).

In particular, the mean squared error matrix for the restricted estimator $\mathbf{b}_1^*$ is from (20.4.6) and (20.4.7),

$$\text{MSE}_{\mathbf{b}_1^*} = \sigma^2(X_1'X_1)^{-1} + (X_1'X_1)^{-1}X_1'X_2\boldsymbol{\beta}_2\boldsymbol{\beta}_2'X_2'X_1(X_1'X_1)^{-1} \quad (20.4.12)$$

Correspondingly, by making use of the partitioned inverse rule (linear algebra Appendix, Section A.7) in regard to the covariance (MSE) matrix of $\mathbf{b}$, the mean squared error of $\mathbf{b}_1$ is

$$\begin{aligned} \text{MSE}_{\mathbf{b}_1} = \sigma^2\{&(X_1'X_1)^{-1} + (X_1'X_1)^{-1}X_1'X_2[X_2'X_2 \\ &- X_2'X_1(X_1'X_1)^{-1}X_1'X_2]^{-1}X_2'X_1(X_1'X_1)^{-1}\} \end{aligned} \quad (20.4.13)$$

The difference in the mean square error matrices for $\mathbf{b}_1^*$ and $\mathbf{b}_1$ is

$$\begin{aligned} \text{MSE}_{\mathbf{b}_1} - \text{MSE}_{\mathbf{b}_1^*} &= \Delta_1 \\ &= (X_1'X_1)^{-1}X_1'X_2\{\sigma^2[X_2'X_2 - X_2'X_1(X_1'X_1)^{-1}X_1'X_2]^{-1} \\ &\quad - \boldsymbol{\beta}_2\boldsymbol{\beta}_2'\}X_2'X_1(X_1'X_1)^{-1} \\ &= (X_1'X_1)^{-1}X_1'X_2\{\Sigma_{\mathbf{b}_2} - \boldsymbol{\delta}\boldsymbol{\delta}'\}X_2'X_1(X_1'X_1)^{-1} \end{aligned} \quad (20.4.14)$$

The expression inside {} is the covariance matrix for $\mathbf{b}_2$ and the bias matrix for $\mathbf{b}_2^*$. The Δ_1 matrix in (20.4.14) will be positive semidefinite if $\Sigma_{\mathbf{b}_2} - \boldsymbol{\beta}_2\boldsymbol{\beta}_2'$ is positive semidefinite.

If in terms of gauging the performance of the estimators $\mathbf{b}$ and $\mathbf{b}^*$ we use the squared error loss measure, where interest centers on the diagonal elements of the mean square or risk matrix, that is, the sum of the variance plus the bias squared for each element of $\boldsymbol{\beta}$, the risk outcome is

$$E[(\mathbf{b} - \boldsymbol{\beta})'(\mathbf{b} - \boldsymbol{\beta})] = \sigma^2 \operatorname{tr}(X'X)^{-1} \quad (20.4.15)$$

for the least squares–maximum likelihood estimator and

$$\begin{aligned} E[(\mathbf{b}^* - \boldsymbol{\beta})'(\mathbf{b}^* - \boldsymbol{\beta})] = \sigma^2 &\operatorname{tr}(X'X)^{-1} \\ &- \sigma^2 \operatorname{tr}(X'X)^{-1}R'[R(X'X)^{-1}R']^{-1}R(X'X)^{-1} \\ &+ \operatorname{tr}\{(X'X)^{-1}R'[R(X'X)^{-1}R']^{-1}\boldsymbol{\delta}\boldsymbol{\delta}' \\ &\times [R(X'X)^{-1}R']^{-1}R(X'X)^{-1}\} \end{aligned} \quad (20.4.16)$$

for the restricted or subset estimator.

As one special case, consider the conditional mean forecasting problem concerned with estimating $X\boldsymbol{\beta}$, the mean values of $\mathbf{y}$ at the sample points X. The risk of the maximum likelihood estimator $X\mathbf{b}$ under mean squared prediction error loss is

$$E[(\mathbf{b}-\boldsymbol{\beta})'X'X(\mathbf{b}-\boldsymbol{\beta})] = \sigma^2 \operatorname{tr} X(X'X)^{-1}X' = \sigma^2 \operatorname{tr} X'X(X'X)^{-1} = \sigma^2 \operatorname{tr} I_K$$
$$= \sigma^2 K \tag{20.4.17}$$

which is an increasing function of the number of variables K. Within the context of Section 20.2, for the restricted estimator $X\mathbf{b}^*$ the risk is

$$E[(\mathbf{b}^*-\boldsymbol{\beta})'X'X(\mathbf{b}^*-\boldsymbol{\beta})] = \operatorname{tr}\{\sigma^2 I_K - \sigma^2(X'X)^{-1}R'[R(X'X)^{-1}R']^{-1}R$$
$$+ (X'X)^{-1}R'[R(X'X)^{-1}R']^{-1}\boldsymbol{\delta}\boldsymbol{\delta}'[R(X'X)^{-1}R']^{-1}R\}$$
$$= \sigma^2 K - \sigma^2 K_2 + \boldsymbol{\delta}'[R(X'X)^{-1}R']^{-1}\boldsymbol{\delta} = \sigma^2(K-K_2) + \boldsymbol{\delta}'[R(X'X)^{-1}R']^{-1}\boldsymbol{\delta}$$
$$= \sigma^2 K_1 + \boldsymbol{\delta}'[R(X'X)^{-1}R']^{-1}\boldsymbol{\delta} = \sigma^2 K_1 + \boldsymbol{\beta}_2'[X_2'X_2 - X_2'X_1(X_1'X_1)^{-1}X_1'X_2]\boldsymbol{\beta}_2$$
$$\tag{20.4.18}$$

where $\sigma^2 K_1$ is the risk penalty for the included variables (complexity) and the second term is the risk penalty for the misspecification (incorrect variable selection). Consequently,

$$E[(\mathbf{b}-\boldsymbol{\beta})'X'X(\mathbf{b}-\boldsymbol{\beta})] - E[(\mathbf{b}^*-\boldsymbol{\beta})'X'X(\mathbf{b}^*-\boldsymbol{\beta})] \geq 0 \tag{20.4.19}$$

if

$$\frac{\boldsymbol{\delta}'[R(X'X)^{-1}R']^{-1}\boldsymbol{\delta}}{2\sigma^2} \leq \frac{K_2}{2} \tag{20.4.20}$$

and one would select the subset model X_1 over the complete model involving X_1, X_2 if the expected loss (20.4.18) is less than the expected loss (20.4.17). However in (20.4.18) the specification error $\boldsymbol{\delta}$ depends on $\boldsymbol{\beta}_2$, which is unknown. Therefore, for variable selection purposes, the rule is not operational. The search for an operational rule is the subject of the next few sections.

20.4.3 Some Alternative Variable Selection Rules

In this section we specify, discuss, and compare a range of sampling theory decision rules that have been proposed for coping with the nested model selection problem. In general, most of these rules rely on discrimination criteria such as maximizing some modified R^2 and each one measures how well the models fit the data after some adjustment for parsimony.

20.4.3a The R^2 and $\bar{R}^2$ Criteria

If one reviews the econometric literature, there appears to have been a strong urge by many to make available some single statistic or index to gauge the "goodness" of an econometric model. One natural competitor for this honor is the coefficient of multiple determination R^2, which is a measure of the proportion of the total variance accounted for by the linear influence of the explanatory variables. For the complete statistical model (20.4.1) the total sum of squares of $\mathbf{y}$ about its mean may be partitioned as follows

$$\begin{array}{ccccc} \text{Total sum} & & \text{Regression} & & \text{Error sum} \\ \text{of squares} & = & \text{sum of squares} & + & \text{of squares} \\ \text{(SST)} & & \text{(SSR)} & & \text{(SSE)} \end{array}$$

$$(\mathbf{y} - \bar{\mathbf{y}})'(\mathbf{y} - \bar{\mathbf{y}}) = (\hat{\mathbf{y}} - \bar{\mathbf{y}})'(\hat{\mathbf{y}} - \bar{\mathbf{y}}) + \hat{\mathbf{e}}'\hat{\mathbf{e}}$$

where $\bar{\mathbf{y}}$ is a vector with elements $\bar{y} = \Sigma_t y_t/T$, and $\hat{\mathbf{y}} = X\mathbf{b}$. Given this decomposition of the sample variation of $\mathbf{y}$ about its mean, the coefficient of determination may be defined as

$$R^2 = 1 - \frac{\text{SSE}}{\text{SST}} = 1 - \frac{(\mathbf{y} - X\mathbf{b})'(\mathbf{y} - X\mathbf{b})}{(\mathbf{y} - \bar{\mathbf{y}})'(\mathbf{y} - \bar{\mathbf{y}})} \tag{20.4.21}$$

As a basis for model choice, the R^2 measure has an obvious fault; it can be increased by increasing the number of explanatory variables, that is, by increasing the column dimension of the design matrix. To take this characteristic of the measure into account, Theil proposed a corrected coefficient of multiple determination $\bar{R}^2$, which uses unbiased estimators of the respective variances. For the subset model involving the design matrix X_1, the corrected or adjusted $\bar{R}_1^2$ may be defined as

$$\bar{R}_1^2 = 1 - \frac{(\mathbf{y} - X_1\mathbf{b}_1^*)'(\mathbf{y} - X_1\mathbf{b}_1^*)/(T - K_1)}{(\mathbf{y} - \bar{\mathbf{y}})'(\mathbf{y} - \bar{\mathbf{y}})/(T - 1)} = 1 - \left(\frac{T-1}{T-K_1}\right)(1 - R_1^2), \tag{20.4.22}$$

where T is the sample size, K_1 is the number of variables included, and $K_1 < K$. Given the measure, Theil's recommendation is to seek that subset of explanatory variables that maximizes the corrected or adjusted R^2. Such a rule, he states, will lead us to the right model "on the average." However, the expectation property alone is no guarantee of high power. Also, the $\bar{R}^2$ criterion need not be the most powerful of the criteria involving the quadratic form of the residuals that have as their property: The expected value is minimized by the true model. Perhaps the most uncomfortable aspect of both the R^2 and adjusted R^2 measures is that they do not include a consideration of the losses associated with choosing an incorrect model; that is, they do not consider within a decision theory context the purpose for which the model is to be used. With the goal of eliminating this deficiency, we now turn to two criteria that are based on the mean square error measure.

20.4.3b The C_p Conditional Mean Squared Error Prediction Criterion

As one solution to the variable selection problem for statistical model (20.4.1), consider a criterion based on conditional mean squared prediction error. For the subset model $\mathbf{y} = X_1\boldsymbol{\beta}_1 + \boldsymbol{\epsilon}$, where $\boldsymbol{\epsilon} = X_2\boldsymbol{\beta}_2 + \mathbf{e}$, this criterion, in line with (20.4.18), may be defined as

$$\begin{aligned}\rho(X\mathbf{b}^*, X\boldsymbol{\beta}) &= E[(X\mathbf{b}^* - X\boldsymbol{\beta})'(X\mathbf{b}^* - X\boldsymbol{\beta})] \\ &= \sigma^2 K_1 + \boldsymbol{\beta}_2' X_2'[I - X_1(X_1'X_1)^{-1}X_1']X_2\boldsymbol{\beta}_2 \\ &= \sigma^2 K_1 + (\text{bias})^2 \end{aligned} \qquad (20.4.23)$$

where the last term on the right side is the sum of squares of the bias and follows from the fact that $\mathbf{b}_1^* = \boldsymbol{\beta}_1 + (X_1'X_1)^{-1}X_1'X_2\boldsymbol{\beta}_2 + (X_1'X_1)^{-1}X_1'\mathbf{e}$, since $\mathbf{y} = X_1\boldsymbol{\beta}_1 + X_2\boldsymbol{\beta}_2 + \mathbf{e}$. Since (20.4.23) contains unknown parameters, one way to proceed is to use an estimate for the unknown parameters and, based on the estimate, choose the model with the smallest estimated risk.

In terms of standardized risk under squared error loss, (20.4.23) can be rewritten as

$$\begin{aligned}\frac{\rho(X_1\mathbf{b}_1^*, X\boldsymbol{\beta})}{\sigma^2} &= \frac{\sigma^2 K_1 + (\text{bias})^2}{\sigma^2} \\ &= K_1 + \frac{(\text{bias})^2}{\sigma^2}\end{aligned} \qquad (20.4.24)$$

Noting that

$$\begin{aligned}E[(\mathbf{y} - X_1\mathbf{b}_1^*)'(\mathbf{y} - X_1\mathbf{b}_1^*)] &= E[(T - K_1)\hat{\sigma}_1^{*2}] \\ &= \boldsymbol{\beta}_2' X_2'[I - X_1(X_1'X_1)^{-1}X_1']X_2\boldsymbol{\beta}_2 + \sigma^2(T - K_1) \\ &= (\text{bias})^2 + \sigma^2(T - K_1)\end{aligned} \qquad (20.4.25)$$

we can express the squared bias as

$$(\text{bias})^2 = E[(T - K_1)\hat{\sigma}_1^{*2}] - (T - K_1)\sigma^2 \qquad (20.4.26)$$

Substituting (20.4.26) in (20.4.24) yields

$$\frac{\rho(X_1\mathbf{b}_1^*, X\boldsymbol{\beta})}{\sigma^2} = \frac{E[(T - K_1)\hat{\sigma}_1^{*2}]}{\sigma^2} + (2K_1 - T) \qquad (20.4.27)$$

If the unknown parameters in (20.4.27) are replaced by unbiased estimators, we can write the estimator of (20.4.24) as

$$\hat{\rho}(X_1\mathbf{b}_1^*, X\boldsymbol{\beta}) = C_p = \frac{(T-K_1)\overset{*}{\sigma}{}_1^2}{\hat{\sigma}^2} + (2K_1 - T)$$

$$= \frac{(T-K_1)(1-\bar{R}_1^2)}{1-\bar{R}^2} + (2K_1 - T) \qquad (20.4.28)$$

where $\hat{\sigma}^2 = (\mathbf{y} - X\mathbf{b})'(\mathbf{y} - X\mathbf{b})/(T-K)$. When the subset model has small bias then $\overset{*}{\sigma}{}_1^2$ is approximately equal to $\hat{\sigma}^2$, and C_p is approximately equal to K_1. Therefore, in the (C_p, K_1) space, C_p values with small bias will tend to cluster about a 45° line, where $C_p = K_1$. In using the C_p criterion, a procedure sometimes recommended is to obtain a C_p value for all the possible 2^K subsets of models and choose the model in which C_p is approximately equal to K_1. No rule such as minimizing C_p is advised in applied work, but the implication is that variable sets with C_p less than K_1 are thought to have smaller prediction error.

20.4.3c An Unconditional Mean Squared Error Criterion

In order to include a consideration of the losses associated with choosing an incorrect model, Amemiya (1980) developed a criterion based on the mean squared prediction error. Amemiya considers the problem of predicting y_0 by $\hat{y}_0 = \mathbf{x}_{01}'(X_1'X_1)^{-1}\mathbf{X}_1'\mathbf{y}$, where $\mathbf{x}_{01}$ is a *vector* of values of X_1 for the prediction period. Using the loss function $(y_0 - \hat{y}_0)^2$, the mean squared prediction error given $\mathbf{x}_{01}$ is for this special case,

$$E[(y_0 - \hat{y}_0)^2] = \sigma^2[1 + \mathbf{x}_{01}'(X_1'X_1)^{-1}\mathbf{x}_{01}] + [\mathbf{x}_0'\boldsymbol{\beta} - \mathbf{x}_{01}'(X_1'X_1)^{-1}X_1'X\boldsymbol{\beta}]^2 \qquad (20.4.29)$$

and involves the unknown parameters $\boldsymbol{\beta}$ and σ^2. Amemiya then regards $\mathbf{x}_0$ as a random vector that satisfies the condition $E[\mathbf{x}_0\mathbf{x}_0'] = (1/T)X'X$. Under this assumption we obtain, by substitution in (20.4.29),

$$E[(y_0 - \hat{y}_0)^2] = \sigma^2\left(1 + \frac{K_1}{T}\right) + \left(\frac{1}{T}\right)\boldsymbol{\beta}_2'X_2'[I - X_1(X_1'X_1)^{-1}X_1']X_2\boldsymbol{\beta}_2 \qquad (20.4.30)$$

and Amemiya calls this the unconditional mean squared prediction error. Unfortunately, (20.4.30) still contains unknown parameters. In typical econometric form, σ^2 is replaced by its unbiased estimator, and $\boldsymbol{\beta}_2$ is made equal to a null (zero) vector. Since $\boldsymbol{\beta}_2$ is assumed zero, the corresponding unbiased estimator of σ^2 is

$$\overset{*}{\sigma}{}_1^2 = \frac{\mathbf{y}'[I - X_1(X_1'X_1)^{-1}X_1']\mathbf{y}}{T-K_1} = \frac{\mathbf{y}'M_1\mathbf{y}}{T-K_1}$$

This sequence of assumptions yields what Amemiya calls the prediction criterion (PC)

$$\mathrm{PC} = \overset{*}{\sigma}{}_1^2\left(1 + \frac{K_1}{T}\right) \tag{20.4.31}$$

which when minimized and expressed in terms of R^2 is

$$\mathrm{PC} = \left(\frac{T + K_1}{T - K_1}\right)(1 - R_1^2)\left(\frac{\mathrm{SST}}{T}\right) \tag{20.4.32}$$

If we compare this with (20.4.22), it is evident that the PC has a higher penalty for adding variables than Theil's adjusted R^2.

20.4.3d The Akaike Information Criterion (AIC)

The information measure or criterion seeks to incorporate in model selection the divergent considerations of accuracy of estimation and the "best" approximation to reality. Thus use of this criterion involves a statistic that incorporates a measure of the precision of the estimate and a measure of the rule of parsimony in the parameterization of a statistical model.

As a basis for discussing the AIC, let $\ell(\boldsymbol{\beta}|\mathbf{y})$ be the likelihood function and consider the statistical model (20.4.1), where the design matrix X is partitioned into components X_1 and X_2 with corresponding partitioning of the $\boldsymbol{\beta}$ vector. Under the hypothesis $R\boldsymbol{\beta} = (0_{(K_2 \times K_1)}, I_{K_2})\boldsymbol{\beta} = \mathbf{0}$; that is, the last $K - K_1 = K_2$ elements of $\boldsymbol{\beta}$ are assumed to be zero, the Akaike information criterion (AIC) is

$$\mathrm{AIC} = -\frac{2}{T}\ln \ell(\mathbf{b}_1^*|\mathbf{y}) + \frac{2K_1}{T} \tag{20.4.33}$$

and under this criterion, (20.4.33) is to be minimized among all the possible linear hypotheses $R\boldsymbol{\beta} = \mathbf{0}$. For the statistical model (20.4.1), this criterion reduces to

$$\mathrm{AIC}_{(R\boldsymbol{\beta}=\mathbf{0})} = \ln \frac{\mathbf{y}'M_1\mathbf{y}}{T} + \frac{2K_1}{T} \tag{20.4.34}$$

where K_1 and thus $M_1 = I - X_1(X_1'X_1)^{-1}X_1'$ is chosen so as to numerically minimize (20.4.34). Therefore, as K_1 increases, $\mathbf{y}'M_1\mathbf{y}$ decreases and the value of the likelihood function increases; thus the trade-off between parsimony and precision is clear, and the penalty for increasing the number of parameters is explicit.

20.4.3e The Schwarz Criterion (SC)

Using Bayesian arguments, Schwarz (1978) derived yet another criterion. Assuming an a priori probability of the true model being K_1 and an a prior conditional

Table 20.2 Model Selection Criteria

Minimize $\text{AIC} = \ln(\mathbf{y}'M_1\mathbf{y}/T) + 2K_1/T$
Minimize $\text{PC} = [\mathbf{y}'M_1\mathbf{y}/(T - K_1)][1 + K_1/T]$
Minimize $\lvert C_p - K_1 \rvert$ where $C_p = (T - K)(\mathbf{y}'M_1\mathbf{y}/\mathbf{y}'M\mathbf{y}) + 2K_1 - T$
Maximize $\bar{R}_1^2 = 1 - ((T-1)/(T-K_1))(1 - R_1^2)$
Minimize $\text{SC} = \ln(\mathbf{y}'M_1\mathbf{y}/T) + \dfrac{K_1 \ln T}{T}$

distribution of the parameters given that K_1 is the true model, Schwarz suggested choosing the a posteriori most probable model. This procedure leads to the criterion, minimize

$$\text{SC} = \ln(\mathbf{y}'M_1\mathbf{y}/T) + \frac{K_1 \ln T}{T} \tag{20.4.35}$$

in order to determine the variables to include in the design matrix.

For your convenience, these model selection criteria are summarized in Table 20.2.

20.4.3f A Monte Carlo Sampling Study

To give some idea of the sampling performance of some of the model selection criteria in this section, a small-scale Monte Carlo experiment was performed using the statistical model discussed in Section 20.5.3. The statistical model corresponding to the design matrix (Section 20.5.2) contains three extraneous variables (X_4, X_5, X_6). The problem is to select a model from the 30 possible models involving the variables $\{X_2, X_3, X_4, X_5, \text{and } X_6\}$.

Using 100 samples of size 20, a model was chosen by maximizing $\bar{R}_1^2$ and minimizing AIC, SC, and PC. Table 20.3 shows the frequency distribution of the models selected when σ^2 is assumed known. In this experiment, each variable selection procedure had a tendency to include too many regressors. This small experiment should only be taken as one indication of the sampling precision of these variable selection procedures.

20.4.3g A Comment

Although there is a certain intuitive appeal and logic to many of the ad hoc, informal model selection rules that have been suggested, we should not forget (1) *their heuristic base,* (2) *the fact that their sampling properties are virtually unknown,*

Table 20.3 Frequency of Models Chosen by $\bar{R}_1^2$, AIC, PC, and SC Selection Procedures

Model	Frequency of model chosen by			
	$\bar{R}_1^2$	AIC	PC	SC
X_2, X_3	27	45	46	65
X_2, X_3, X_4	15	18	18	10
X_2, X_3, X_5	15	16	15	12
X_2, X_3, X_6	17	13	13	9
X_2, X_3, X_4, X_5	8	2	2	2
X_2, X_3, X_4, X_6	9	3	3	1
X_2, X_3, X_5, X_6	9	3	3	1

(3) *that their practical utility is mainly demonstrated by numerical examples*, and (4) *when estimation proceeds conditionally on the model selected, the literature is strangely silent as to the sampling performance of the estimators thereby generated.*

Other selection criteria are, of course, possible, and an exhaustive list of these rules is included in a 1976 review article by Hocking. One example, is the many forward and backward elimination of variables procedures that are based on some form of pretesting.

All the search procedures are functions of the equation error sum of squares. Thus, they are all related; and when used in conjunction with estimation, they lead to pretest estimators (Section 20.3.1) of one form or another. Consequently, inference relative to the estimators that result from these model search processes should be viewed with caution by the applied researcher.

20.4.4 Hypothesis Testing and Model Identification

To a large extent researchers who use hypothesis testing to discriminate among alternative linear statistical models do so within the framework discussed in the introduction to this chapter. An investigator has a set of data and wants to estimate the parameters of a linear statistical model that are known to lie in a K-dimensional parameter space $\boldsymbol{\beta}$, but the investigator suspects that the relationship may be characterized by a lower K_1 dimensional parameter vector $\boldsymbol{\beta}_1$, which is a subvector of $\boldsymbol{\beta}$. Uncertainty relative to the correct dimensions of the parameter space means that investigators may begin with a general or truncated specification and then modify their models, that is, make the variable add or delete decision by using traditional hypothesis-testing procedures to test the statistical significance of individual parameters or linear combinations of some or all of them.

At this point let us distinguish between tests for nested and nonnested models. As an example of a test between nested models we consider whether

$$H_0: \mathbf{y} = X_1\boldsymbol{\beta}_1 + \mathbf{e}_0; \mathbf{e}_0 \sim N(\mathbf{0}, \sigma_0^2 I_T) \tag{20.4.36}$$

or

$$H_1: \mathbf{y} = Z\gamma + \mathbf{e}_1 = X_1\boldsymbol{\beta}_1 + X_2\boldsymbol{\beta}_2 + \mathbf{e}_1; \mathbf{e}_1 \sim N(\mathbf{0}, \sigma_1^2 I_T) \tag{20.4.37}$$

is most compatible with the sampling model underlying the data-generation process. In this case the model H_0 can be obtained from H_1 by imposing the parametric restriction $\boldsymbol{\beta}_2 = \mathbf{0}$ and, therefore, we call the models nested. Parametric tests were presented in Chapter 6 for analyzing this question.

Alternatively, recent econometric research has considered tests for nonnested or separate models. By nonnested models, we mean that one model cannot be obtained from the other by simply imposing constraints on the parameters. One example in the nonnested area that is common in econometric practice is the case where, under H_0, the functional form is specified as linear in natural units and, under H_1, it is specified as linear in logs. Some useful references in the nonnested testing area are McAleer and Pesaran (1986) and Godfrey, McAleer, and McKenzie (1987).

In contrast to conventional procedures used to test a set of parametric restrictions, the Hausman (1978) specification test procedure is designed to test the implications of an hypothesis in terms of inconsistency. The Hausmann specification tests are based on a contrast of an efficient estimator with an inefficient but generally consistent estimator. One example is the test of validity of instrumental variables. The Hausman specification test is an asymptotic test based on the distribution of the quadratic form that results from the difference between an efficient estimator under H_0 and a consistent estimator under H_1. Consequently, it involves the general problem of testing model specifications in the presence of nuisance parameters and does not require that H_0 be given in parametric form.

In most cases hypothesis and specification tests are done with an eye toward estimation. This means estimation proceeds conditionally on the hypothesis (statistical model) that has been selected. This process, which makes the model and thus the estimation procedure dependent on the outcome of the test based on the data at hand, leads to what we referred to in Section 20.3.1 as pretest estimators. In general, what we know about these pretest estimators that come out of conventional testing mechanisms is that they are inadmissible under a squared error loss measure. Little is known of the sampling performance of many of the estimators resulting from nonnested and specification tests. Even less is known when these tests are used sequentially—that is, repeated tests that typically use the same set of data. There is also the corresponding unsolved problem that related to the choice of the optimal level of the test. Because of these and other problems, from a statistical inference point of view, if one is concerned with the sampling properties of the resulting rules, many questions need to be answered before these testing procedures can be recommended as a viable way to handle the model choice problem. Perhaps, if a new hypothesis or specification test is to be proposed and used in an estimation context the originator should be required to demonstrate the sampling performance of the implied estimation rule.

20.5 Exercises

20.5.1 Exercises for Section 20.2

Using the statistical sampling model consistent with the sample observations generated for use in Chapter 6, complete the following exercises involving restricted, stochastic restricted, and inequality restricted estimators.

20.5.1a Individual Exercises for Section 20.2.1

20.1 Using the instructions in the Computer Handbook, generate five samples of data consistent with that used in Chapter 6 and estimate the parameters of the statistical model using a restricted least squares estimator under the restriction

$$R\boldsymbol{\beta} = [0 \quad 1 \quad 1]\begin{bmatrix}\beta_1\\ \beta_2\\ \beta_3\end{bmatrix} = \beta_2 + \beta_3 = 1$$

Compare the sampling characteristics of the unrestricted and restricted least squares estimates and discuss.

20.2 Compute the means and variances of the restricted estimates β_1, β_2, and β_3 and compare these results, over the five samples, with the unrestricted least squares results. Discuss the empirical results and contrast with the theory.

20.3 Test, using two alternative test statistics for each of the five samples of data, the general linear hypothesis that $R\boldsymbol{\beta} = \beta_2 + \beta_3 = 1$. Interpret and comment on the results.

20.5.1b Joint or Class Exercises for Section 20.2.1

20.4 Using the instructions in the Computer Handbook, generate the restricted estimates of β for each of 100 samples of data. Compute the means and variances for the restricted least squares estimates of β_1, β_2, and β_3 and the squared error loss $\sum_{i=1}^{100} (\boldsymbol{\beta}_i^* - \boldsymbol{\beta})'(\boldsymbol{\beta}_i^* - \boldsymbol{\beta})/100$ and compare with the corresponding least squares results in Chapter 6. Repeat the exercise under the restriction $\beta_2 + \beta_3 = 0.75$.

20.5 Using estimates from the 100 samples of data, develop empirical frequency distributions for β_1, β_2, and β_3 and the likelihood ratio test statistic. Compare the empirical distributions with their theoretical counterparts.

20.5.1c Individual Exercises for Section 20.2.2

20.6 With the statistical model, design matrix, and sample observations used in Exercise 20.1, use the stochastic restrictions $R\boldsymbol{\beta} + v = \beta_2 + \beta_3 + v = 1$, where v is assumed to be a normal random variable with mean zero and variance $\frac{1}{64}$, in conjunction with five samples of data, to estimate the unknown parameters for $\boldsymbol{\beta}$ under the assumptions that σ^2 is both known and unknown.

20.7 Compute the compatibility test statistic for the stochastic hypothesis and evaluate the results for the five samples of data under both known and unknown σ^2.

20.5.1d Joint or Class Exercises for Section 20.2.2

20.8 Compute stochastic restricted estimates of the unknown parameters and the compatibility test statistics for 100 samples of data and compute the means and variances of the estimates of β_1, β_2, and β_3 under known and unknown σ^2.

20.9 Develop empirical frequency distributions, using 100 samples of data, for the estimates of β_1, β_2, and β_3 and the compatibility statistic and contrast with their theoretical counterparts.

20.5.1e Individual Exercises for Section 20.2.3

20.10 Using the instructions in the Computer Handbook, generate five samples of data and use the inequality restricted estimator along with the inequality restriction $R\boldsymbol{\beta} = \beta_2 + \beta_3 \geq 1$ to estimate the unknown $\boldsymbol{\beta}$ parameters. Compare and contrast these results with those from the unrestricted and equality restricted estimator results.

20.11 Test the linear inequality hypothesis (under unknown σ^2) that $\beta_2 + \beta_3 \geq 1$, using five samples of data, and contrast the conclusions with those from Exercise 20.3.

20.5.1f Joint or Class Exercises for Section 20.2.3

20.12 Compute inequality restricted estimates of the unknown $\boldsymbol{\beta}$ vector and the test statistic for 100 samples of data. Compute the means and variances of the estimates of β_1, β_2, and β_3 and the squared error loss $\sum_{i=1}^{100} (\hat{\boldsymbol{\beta}}_i - \boldsymbol{\beta})'(\hat{\boldsymbol{\beta}}_i - \boldsymbol{\beta})/100$.

20.13 Develop empirical frequency distributions, using 100 samples of data, for the estimates of β_1, β_2, and β_3 and the test statistic and compare and contrast them to their theoretical counterparts.

20.5.2 Exercises for Section 20.3

Using the statistical sampling model consistent with the exercises in Section 20.5.1 and the corresponding 100 samples of $\mathbf{y}$, complete the following exercises involving pretest and Stein-rule estimators. For the design matrix given in Section 6.1.5 of Chapter 6, there exists a P matrix that will transform the positive definite matrix $X'X$ into an identity matrix I_K. Consequently, by using a procedure such as the Cholesky's decomposition method, there is a P matrix such that $P'X'XP = I_K$.

20.14 Using procedures outlined in the Computer Handbook, reparameterize the statistical model as

$$\mathbf{y} = X\boldsymbol{\beta} + \mathbf{e} = XPP^{-1}\boldsymbol{\beta} + \mathbf{e} = Z\boldsymbol{\theta} + \mathbf{e}$$

where $\boldsymbol{\theta} = P^{-1}\boldsymbol{\beta}$ and $Z = XP$. Using the 100 samples of $\mathbf{y}$ obtained in earlier exercises, compute the unrestricted least squares (maximum likelihood) estimates of $\boldsymbol{\theta}$.

20.15 Under squared error loss and a significance level of $\alpha = 0.05$, develop the empirical risks for the pretest estimator when $H_0: \boldsymbol{\theta} = P^{-1}(10.0\ 0.4\ 0.6)'$, H_0: $\boldsymbol{\theta} = \mathbf{0}$, and $H_0: \boldsymbol{\theta} = P^{-1}(11.0\ 1.4\ 1.4)'$ and compare to the empirical risk of the unrestricted least squares estimator.

20.16 Using the estimator in Equation (20.3.13), develop Stein-rule estimates of θ_1, θ_2, and θ_3 for the 100 samples and compute the empirical risk when $\boldsymbol{\theta} = \mathbf{r} = P^{-1}(10.0\ 0.4\ 0.6)'$ and compare to the empirical risk of the least squares estimator.

20.5.3 Exercises for Section 20.4

To demonstrate the reach of some of the model selection procedures discussed in this chapter, consider the following statistical model and design matrix

$$\mathbf{y} = X\boldsymbol{\beta} + \mathbf{e} = 10\mathbf{x}_1 + 0.4\mathbf{x}_2 + 0.6\mathbf{x}_3 + 0.0\mathbf{x}_4 + 0.0\mathbf{x}_5 + 0.0\mathbf{x}_6 + \mathbf{e} \quad (20.5.1)$$

where $\mathbf{e}$ is a normal random vector with mean vector zero and variance $\sigma^2 = 0.0625$. Assume the (20×6) design matrix is

$$X = \begin{bmatrix} 1 & 0.693 & 0.693 & 0.610 & 1.327 & -2.947 \\ 1 & 1.733 & 0.693 & -1.174 & 2.413 & 0.788 \\ 1 & 0.693 & 1.386 & 0.082 & 3.728 & -0.813 \\ 1 & 1.733 & 1.386 & -0.776 & -0.757 & 1.968 \\ 1 & 0.693 & 1.792 & 1.182 & -0.819 & 3.106 \\ 1 & 2.340 & 0.693 & 3.681 & 2.013 & -3.176 \\ 1 & 1.733 & 1.792 & -1.307 & 0.464 & -2.407 \\ 1 & 2.340 & 1.386 & 0.440 & -2.493 & 0.136 \\ 1 & 2.340 & 1.792 & 1.395 & -1.637 & 3.427 \\ 1 & 0.693 & 0.693 & 0.281 & 0.504 & 0.687 \\ 1 & 0.693 & 1.386 & -1.929 & -0.344 & -2.609 \\ 1 & 1.733 & 0.693 & 1.985 & -0.212 & -0.741 \\ 1 & 1.733 & 1.386 & -2.500 & -0.875 & 0.264 \\ 1 & 0.693 & 1.792 & 0.335 & 2.137 & 0.631 \\ 1 & 2.340 & 0.693 & 0.464 & 1.550 & -1.169 \\ 1 & 1.733 & 1.792 & 4.110 & -1.664 & 1.585 \\ 1 & 2.340 & 1.386 & -2.254 & -0.285 & -0.131 \\ 1 & 2.340 & 1.792 & -1.906 & 1.162 & 0.903 \\ 1 & 1.733 & 1.386 & 0.125 & 0.399 & -1.838 \\ 1 & 0.693 & 0.693 & -2.935 & -2.600 & -2.634 \end{bmatrix} \quad (20.5.2)$$

(columns: $\mathbf{x}_1$, $\mathbf{x}_2$, $\mathbf{x}_3$, $\mathbf{x}_4$, $\mathbf{x}_5$, $\mathbf{x}_6$)

Using the statistical model described by (20.5.1) and (20.5.2) and the sampling process described in Chapter 6, use Monte Carlo procedures described in the Computer Handbook to generate 100 $\mathbf{y}$ samples of size 20.

20.5.3a Individual Exercises

Choose five samples of data and for *each* sample do the following:

20.17 Select a final model using the $\bar{R}^2$ criterion.

20.18 Select a final model using the C_p criterion.

20.19 Select a final model using the PC criterion.

20.20 Select a model using the AIC criterion.

20.6 References and Guide to Further Reading

20.6.1 Section 20.1

Berger, J. O. (1985) *Statistical Decision Theory and Bayesian Analysis.* New York, Springer-Verlag.

DeGroot, M. (1975) *Probability and Statistics.* Reading, MA., Addison-Wesley.

Judge, G. G., W. E. Griffiths, R. C. Hill, H. Lütkepohl, and T. C. Lee (1985). *The Theory and Practice of Econometrics*, 2nd ed. New York, Wiley.

20.6.2 Section 20.2

Geweke, J. (1986) "Exact Inference in the Inequality Constrained Normal Linear Regression Model." *Journal of Applied Econometrics*, 1, 127–141.

Johnson, N. L., and S. Kotz (1970) *Continuous Univariate Distributions.* Boston, Houghton Mifflin.

Judge, G. G., and M. E. Bock (1978) *The Statistical Implications of Pre-Test and Stein-Rule Estimators in Econometrics.* Amsterdam, North Holland.

Judge, G. G., and T. Takayama (1966) "Inequality Restrictions in Regression Analysis." *Journal of the American Statistical Association*, 61:166–181.

Judge, G. G., and T. A. Yancey (1986) *Improved Methods of Inference in Econometrics.* Amsterdam, North Holland.

Theil, H. (1963) "On the Use of Incomplete Prior Information in Regression Analysis." *Journal of the American Statistical Association*, 58:401–414.

Theil, H., and A. S. Goldberger (1961) "Pure and Mixed Statisical Estimation in Economics." *International Economic Review*, 2:65–78.

20.6.3 Section 20.3

Efron, B., and C. Morris (1973) "Stein's Estimation Rule and Its Competitors—An Empirical Bayes Approach." *Journal of the American Statistical Association*, 68:117–130.

James, W., and C. Stein (1961) "Estimation with Quadratic Loss." *Proceedings of the fourth Berkeley Symposium*, pp. 361–379, Berekely, University of California Press.

Judge, G. G., and M. E. Bock (1978) *The Statistical Implications of Pre-Test and Stein-Rule Estimators in Econometrics*, Amsterdam, North-Holland.

Judge, G. G., W. E. Griffiths, R. C. Hill, H. Lütkepohl, and T. C. Lee (1985) *The Theory and Practice of Econometrics*. New York, Wiley.

20.6.4 Section 20.4

Akaike, H. (1981) "Likelihood of a Model and Information Criteria." *Journal of Econometrics*, 16:3–14.

Amemiya, T. (1980) "Selection of Regressors." *International Economic Review*, 21:331–354.

Godfrey, L. G., M. McAleer, and C. R. McKenzie (1987) "Variable Addition and Tests for Linear and Logarithmic Regression Models," Working Paper 136, Australian National University, Canberra.

Hausman, J. A. (1978) "Specification Tests in Econometrics." *Econometrica*, 46:1251–1271.

Hocking, R. R. (1976) "The Analysis and Selection of Variables in Linear Regression." *Biometrics*, 32:1–49.

Judge, G. G., and M. E. Bock (1978) *Statistical Implications of Pre-Test and Stein-Rule Estimators in Econometrics*. Amsterdam: North-Holland.

Leamer, E. E. (1978) *Specification Searches*. New York, Wiley.

Leamer, E. E. (1983) "Model Choice and Specification Analysis." In Z. Griliches and M. Intriligator (eds.) *Handbook of Econometrics*, vol. 1. Amsterdam, North-Holland, pp. 285–332.

McAleer, M. (1985) "Specification Tests for Separate Models: A Survey." In M. L. King and D. E. A. Giles (eds.) *Specification Analysis in the Linear Model: Essays in Honour of Donald Cochrane.* London, Routeledge and Kegor, pp. 146–196.

McAleer, M., and M. H. Pesaran (1986) "Statistical Inference in Non-nested Econometric Models." *Applied Mathematics and Computation,* 20:171–211.

Schwarz, G. (1978) "Estimating the Dimension of a Model." *The Annals of Statistics.* 6, 461–464.

CHAPTER 21

Multicollinearity

21.1 Introduction

Economists, to a large extent, can be described as nonexperimental scientists. Experimental scientists can carefully design controlled experiments to try to ensure that sufficient sample information is present to estimate relevant parameters of the model in question with desired sampling precision. Estimation and inference under these circumstances can be a relatively straightforward procedure. In contrast, in the nonexperimental sciences, much of the data used are passively generated. Consequently, data often are generated by an experimental design proposed by society and collected by agencies for administrative rather than for research purposes. As a result, we are presented in most cases with an implicit experimental design and a data-collection process that are not of our choosing. The number of observations are sometimes limited, variables do not vary over a very wide range, and thus the samples often do not provide enough information to support investigation of the parameter space in question and give us precise responses to all the questions for which we would like answers. In the extreme, not enough information may be present to obtain, for example, unique least squares estimates of all relevant parameters in the model. This lack of sufficient information and the corresponding loss of precision of statistical results based on such data lead to what is commonly called the multicollinearity problem.

The inadequacy of the experimental designs most frequently encountered is reflected by the existence of general interrelationships among the set of explanatory variables in the design matrix. Examples are countless, but one simple illustration comes from the consumption function, which is an attempt to explain household consumption as a function of, among other things, household income and wealth. In a cross-sectional sample we are likely to observe that wealth and income of surveyed households obey a strong positive relationship. Households with small incomes are likely to have a small amount of wealth and those with high incomes are likely to have a large amount of wealth. Thus, in the sample, because we are faced with a poor experimental design, the two variables may be collinear. For a particular sample the consequences of this collinearity, or multicollinearity in the case of several variables, follow.

1. It becomes very difficult to identify the separate effects of the variables involved precisely. In fact, since the regression coefficients are interpreted as reflecting the effects of changes in their corresponding variables, all other things held constant, our ability to interpret the coefficients declines the more persistent and severe the collinearity. The lack of precision is manifested by the existence of potentially large sampling variances for estimators of the unknown parameters and high correlations between affected estimators.

2. Given the foregoing, estimates of unknown parameters may not appear significantly different from zero, and consequently variables may be dropped from the analysis not because they have no effect but simply because the sample is inadequate to isolate the effect precisely. This result obtains despite possibly high R^2 or "F values," indicating "significant" explanatory power of the model.
3. Estimators may be very sensitive to the addition or deletion of a few observations or the deletion of an apparently insignificant variable.
4. Despite the difficulties in isolating the effects of individual variables from such a sample, accurate forecasts may still be possible even outside the sample. This is only true, however, if the pattern of interrelationships among the explanatory variables is the same in the forecast period as in the sample period.

To illustrate these points, we examine data published by Klein and Goldberger (1955), which is reproduced in Table 21.1. These time-series data pertain to the relationship between total U.S. domestic consumption (C) as a function of wage income (W), nonwage–nonfarm income (P), and farm income (A) for the years 1921–1941 and 1945–1950 (the war years 1942–1944 were omitted). Least squares estimates of the parameters of the original model considered by Klein and Goldberger are presented in Table 21.2. The R^2 for the estimated model is 0.95, and the F-statistic for the overall significance of the regression is 107.37, which is large relative to the $\alpha = 0.01$ critical value of the F-statistic, $F_{(0.01, 3, 16)} = 5.29$.

The effects of multicollinearity are readily observed. First, the estimate of the incremental effect of wage income on consumption, 1.059, is too large, in that it is greater than 1, implying that a dollar increase in wage income gives rise to more than a dollar increase in consumption expenditure. Second, the effects of nonwage–nonfarm income and farm income do not appear to be individually statistically different from 0, although theoretically they should be important variables in explaining consumption behavior. The lack of individual coefficient significance occurs despite the overall significance of the regression equation. The imprecision of the parameter estimates is clearly seen by considering their interval estimates. As Klein and Goldberger (1955) state, interrelationships "among the different components of income masks separate contributions of each component toward the explanation of spending behavior."

Table 21.1 The Klein–Goldberger Data

Year	C	W	P	A
1928	58.2	39.21	17.73	4.39
1929	62.2	42.31	20.29	4.60
1930	58.6	40.37	18.83	3.25
1931	56.6	39.15	17.44	2.61
1932	51.6	34.00	14.76	1.67
1933	51.1	33.59	13.39	2.44
1934	54.0	36.88	13.93	2.39
1935	57.2	39.27	14.67	5.00
1936	62.8	45.51	17.20	3.93
1937	65.0	46.06	17.15	5.48
1938	63.9	44.16	15.92	4.37
1939	67.5	47.68	17.59	4.51
1940	71.3	50.79	18.49	4.90
1941	76.6	57.78	19.18	6.37
1945	86.3	78.97	19.12	8.42
1946	95.7	73.54	19.76	9.27
1947	98.3	71.92	17.55	8.87
1948	100.3	74.01	19.17	9.30
1949	103.2	75.51	20.20	6.95
1950	108.9	80.97	22.12	7.15

Since results such as these are common in econometric work, this chapter is devoted to an analysis of the problems caused by the existence of general interrelationships among the explanatory variables and is organized as follows. In Section 21.2 the statistical consequences of multicollinearity are made explicit. Section 21.3 contains a variety of procedures thought to be effective for detecting the degree and/or nature of multicollinearity. In Section 21.4 ways of reducing the ill effects of severe multicollinearity are considered; these include adding additional data, adding nonsample information such as linear restrictions on the parameters, or using a biased estimator.

Table 21.2 Klein and Goldberger's Results

Variable	Constant	W	P	A
Estimated coefficient	8.133	1.059	0.452	0.121
t value	(0.91)	(6.10)	(0.69)	(0.11)
Standard error	8.92	0.17	0.66	1.09
95% confidence interval	(−10.78, 27.04)	(0.69, 1.43)	(−0.94, 1.84)	(−2.18, 2.43)

21.2 The Statistical Consequences of Multicollinearity

In this section we define multicollinearity and investigate its statistical consequences. Let the linear regression model be

$$\mathbf{y} = X\boldsymbol{\beta} + \mathbf{e} \tag{21.2.1}$$

where $\mathbf{y}$ is a $(T \times 1)$ vector of observations, X is a nonstochastic $(T \times K)$ matrix of observations on explanatory variables, $\boldsymbol{\beta}$ is a $(K \times 1)$ vector of unknown regression coefficients, and $\mathbf{e}$ is a $(T \times 1)$ vector of normally and independently distributed random disturbances with zero means and constant variances σ^2. It will be useful to write $X = (\mathbf{x}_1, \mathbf{x}_2, \ldots, \mathbf{x}_K)$ where $\mathbf{x}_i$ is the ith column of X.

21.2.1 Exact or Perfect Multicollinearity

Exact or perfect multicollinearity is said to exist when the X matrix has rank less than K. This occurs when one or more exact relations exist among the columns of X. That is, there are one *or more* relations of the form

$$X\mathbf{c} = \mathbf{x}_1 c_1 + \mathbf{x}_2 c_2 + \cdots + \mathbf{x}_K c_K = \mathbf{0} \tag{21.2.2}$$

where $\mathbf{c} = (c_1, \ldots, c_K)'$ is a vector of constants c_i, not all of which are zero. Alternatively, assuming c_1 is not zero (if it is zero, rearrange the columns of X so it is not)

$$\mathbf{x}_1 = \mathbf{x}_2(-c_2/c_1) + \cdots + \mathbf{x}_K(-c_K/c_1)$$

so that the first variable can be written as an exact linear combination of the rest, and thus the columns of X are linearly dependent. This could happen, for example, if $T < K$, or if too many dummy variables are included with an intercept, or if there are real, physical constraints relating the explanatory variables. An example of the latter case is a production function in which some of the inputs are always used in a fixed proportion.

From the linear algebra appendix we know that if the columns of X are linearly dependent the rank of X is less than K. Consequently, the usual least squares (LS) and maximum likelihood (ML) estimators for $\boldsymbol{\beta}$ do not exist since the normal equations

$$X'X\hat{\boldsymbol{\beta}} = X'\mathbf{y} \tag{21.2.3}$$

cannot be solved *uniquely* for $\hat{\boldsymbol{\beta}}$. This means there is no unique estimator for $\boldsymbol{\beta}$ that minimizes the sum of squared errors or that maximizes the likelihood function. Instead, there are an infinite number of solutions to (21.2.3), but they do not have the usual desirable properties of LS or ML estimators. See Exercise 21.10 for more on this.

On the other hand, just because $\boldsymbol{\beta}$ cannot be estimated does not necessarily mean that all is lost. In particular it is still possible to obtain best linear unbiased estimators of some, but not all, linear combinations of parameters. The point is that, depending on the purposes of the researcher who faces the problem, even the most severe type of collinearity may not be "disastrous." If one wants point estimates of the parameters $\boldsymbol{\beta}$, then exact multicollinearity makes this objective impossible. On the other hand, if one is interested in prediction, then $\mathbf{w}'\boldsymbol{\beta}$ is estimable if $\mathbf{w}$, for example, is the average value of the regressor values or any particular row of X, and BLU forecasts and confidence intervals can be constructed. See Schmidt (1976, pp. 45–47).

Although it is instructive to consider the case of perfect multicollinearity, it does not occur very often in practice. In the next section the usual case is considered where X is of full rank K, but relations like (21.2.2) hold "almost" exactly.

21.2.2 Near Exact Multicollinearity and Auxiliary Regressions

We will now consider the case where the linear relationship between the columns of X is not an exact one, only nearly so, so that there exist one or more relations of the form

$$X\mathbf{c} = \mathbf{x}_1 c_1 + \mathbf{x}_2 c_2 + \cdots + \mathbf{x}_K c_K \doteq \mathbf{0} \tag{21.2.4}$$

where " $\doteq$ " means "almost equal to." Suppose $c_1 \neq 0$ so that

$$\mathbf{x}_1 \doteq \mathbf{x}_2(-c_2/c_1) + \mathbf{x}_3(-c_3/c_1) + \cdots + \mathbf{x}_K(-c_K/c_1) \tag{21.2.5}$$

or

$$\mathbf{x}_1 = \mathbf{x}_2 d_2 + \mathbf{x}_3 d_3 + \cdots + \mathbf{x}_K d_K + \mathbf{v}_1 \tag{21.2.6}$$

where $d_i = -c_i/c_1$ and $\mathbf{v}_1$ is just the difference between the left and right sides of (21.2.5). Relations like (21.2.6), where one regressor is written as a linear function of the other regressors plus the difference (or error) are called "auxiliary regressions," since they do have the form of a regression equation. By examining (21.2.6) it should be intuitively clear that the better the fit (R^2) of this auxiliary regression of $\mathbf{x}_1$ on the other $(K - 1)$ regressors, the more nearly (21.2.4) holds and the more "severe" the multicollinearity. In fact, if (21.2.6) fits *exactly* (so that the SSE is 0), then (21.2.4) would hold exactly, X would not have full rank, and the multicollinearity would be perfect.

To make these notions precise so that we can pinpoint the statistical consequences of multicollinearity, let us make use of the following matrix result. Partition $X = (\mathbf{x}_1 X_2)$ where $\mathbf{x}_1$ is the first column of X (which might be any regressor by rearrangement of the columns of X) and X_2 contains the other $(K-1)$ columns of X. Define $N = I - X_2(X_2'X_2)^{-1}X_2'$, then

$$(X'X)^{-1} = \frac{1}{\mathbf{x}_1'N\mathbf{x}_1} \times \left[\begin{array}{c|c} 1 & -\mathbf{x}_1'X_2(X_2'X_2)^{-1} \\ \hline -(X_2'X_2)^{-1}X_2'\mathbf{x}_1 & \mathbf{x}_1'N\mathbf{x}_1(X_2'X_2)^{-1} + (X_2'X_2)^{-1}X_2'\mathbf{x}_1\mathbf{x}_1'X_2(X_2'X_2)^{-1} \end{array}\right] \tag{21.2.7}$$

This result is useful because as noted in the introductory section the effect of multicollinearity is to make the sampling errors of the LS estimators large. If $\mathbf{b} = (X'X)^{-1}X'\mathbf{y}$ is the LS estimator, then $\text{cov}(\mathbf{b}) = \sigma^2(X'X)^{-1}$ measures the sampling variability of the LS estimator. Using (21.2.7), the variance of b_1, the LS estimator of β_1, is

$$\text{var}(b_1) = \frac{\sigma^2}{\mathbf{x}_1'N\mathbf{x}_1} = \frac{\sigma^2}{\hat{\mathbf{v}}_1'\hat{\mathbf{v}}_1} \tag{21.2.8}$$

where $\hat{\mathbf{v}}_1$ is a vector of LS residuals from the estimation of (21.2.6). See Exercise 21.12. Consequently the variance of b_1 depends on σ^2 and the variation in $\mathbf{x}_1$ *not* explained by the linear influence of the other regressors. Thus the better the fit of the auxiliary regression (21.2.6) the larger $\text{var}(b_1)$, since the better the fit the smaller the SSE $\hat{\mathbf{v}}_1'\hat{\mathbf{v}}_1$.

The covariances between b_1 and the other LS estimators $b_2, \ldots, b_K$ are larger (in absolute value) the greater the estimated effect of x_j on x_1 from (21.2.6) and the better the fit of the auxiliary regression. See Exercise 21.13.

The foregoing exposition, using the notion of auxiliary regressions, is an intuitive one and clearly reveals the nature of "the multicollinearity problem." If $\mathbf{x}_1$ is a near exact function of the other $(K-1)$ regressors, then the associated parameter β_1 will have a LS estimator whose variance is directly proportional to the severity of the multicollinearity as measured by $1/\hat{\mathbf{v}}_1'\hat{\mathbf{v}}_1$. And the larger the variance of b_1, and those of the LS estimators $b_2, \ldots, b_K$, the more likely the negative consequences listed in the introduction of this chapter. This all fits together with the description in the introduction because the fit of the auxiliary regressions measures the degree of linear association between the explanatory variables.

21.2.3 Near Exact Multicollinearity in the Principal Components Model

Although the analysis of near exact multicollinearity just presented is useful, it does not provide a framework for a complete and systematic analysis of multicollinearity and its effects. A more general framework is provided by considering a transformation of the regression model (21.2.1) into the principal components form of the model. This transformation is based on the characteristic vectors of the $X'X$ matrix and is discussed in the matrix appendix, Section A.9.

Let P be the orthogonal $(K \times K)$ matrix whose columns $\mathbf{p}_i$, are the characteristic vectors of $X'X$. Then

$$\mathbf{y} = X\boldsymbol{\beta} + \mathbf{e} = (XP)(P'\boldsymbol{\beta}) + \mathbf{e} = Z\boldsymbol{\theta} + \mathbf{e} \tag{21.2.9}$$

since $PP' = P'P = I$ and where $Z = XP$ and $\boldsymbol{\theta} = P'\boldsymbol{\beta}$. The matrix Z is called the matrix of principal components. Its columns, $\mathbf{z}_i$, are linear combinations of the columns of X with the weights given by the elements of $\mathbf{p}_i$. That is, the ith principal component is

$$\mathbf{z}_i = X\mathbf{p}_i = \mathbf{x}_1 p_{1i} + \mathbf{x}_2 p_{2i} + \cdots + \mathbf{x}_K p_{Ki} \tag{21.2.10}$$

where p_{ji} is the element in the jth row and ith column of P. The principal components have the property that $\mathbf{z}_i'\mathbf{z}_i = \lambda_i$, where λ_i is the ith characteristic root of $X'X$. To see this

$$\mathbf{z}_i'\mathbf{z}_i = \mathbf{p}_i'X'X\mathbf{p}_i = \mathbf{p}_i'(\lambda_i\mathbf{p}_i) = \lambda_i\mathbf{p}_i'\mathbf{p}_i = \lambda_i \tag{21.2.11}$$

since $X'X\mathbf{p}_i = \lambda_i\mathbf{p}_i$, by the definition of characteristic roots and vectors and $\mathbf{p}_i'\mathbf{p}_i = 1$. Also $\mathbf{z}_i'\mathbf{z}_j = 0$ for $i \neq j$ as

$$\mathbf{z}_i'\mathbf{z}_j = \mathbf{p}_i'X'X\mathbf{p}_j = \mathbf{p}_i'(\lambda_j\mathbf{p}_j) = \lambda_j\mathbf{p}_i'\mathbf{p}_j = 0$$

since $\mathbf{p}_i'\mathbf{p}_j = 0$. Thus

$$Z'Z = (XP)'(XP) = P'X'XP = \Lambda = \operatorname{diag}(\lambda_1, \lambda_2, \ldots, \lambda_K) \tag{21.2.12}$$

where the diagonal matrix Λ contains the characteristic roots of $X'X$ on the diagonal, which as a convention are ordered so that $\lambda_1 \geq \lambda_2 \geq \cdots \geq \lambda_K$. The characteristic roots are real since $X'X$ is symmetric and are nonnegative since $X'X$ is positive semidefinite. The number of zero roots is equal to the number of exact linear dependencies among the columns of X. If X is of full rank, K, then $X'X$ is positive definite and all the characteristic roots are positive. The least squares estimator of $\boldsymbol{\theta}$ in the principal components model is

$$\hat{\boldsymbol{\theta}} = (Z'Z)^{-1}Z'\mathbf{y} = \Lambda^{-1}Z'\mathbf{y}$$

and has covariance matrix

$$\operatorname{cov}(\hat{\boldsymbol{\theta}}) = \sigma^2\Lambda^{-1}$$

Consequently,

$$\operatorname{var}(\hat{\theta}_i) = \sigma^2/\lambda_i \tag{21.2.13}$$

Thus the smaller the characteristic root λ_i, the less precisely the ith coefficient θ_i can be estimated. This is important because the size of the characteristic roots of $X'X$ relates directly to the multicollinearity problem. We also see that, in this transformed model, not all the θ_i's can be estimated equally well. Some may be associated with large λ_i's and others with small ones. The latter then can be estimated only relatively imprecisely.

To see how the magnitude of the characteristic roots of $X'X$ relates to the multicollinearity problem, suppose that $\lambda_i = 0$ on the right side of (21.2.11). Then it must be true that

$$X\mathbf{p}_i = p_{1i}\mathbf{x}_1 + p_{2i}\mathbf{x}_2 + \cdots + p_{Ki}\mathbf{x}_K = \mathbf{0} \tag{21.2.14}$$

So that, if any λ_i is zero, we have identified a relation like that in (21.2.2) and perfect multicollinearity exists. If, instead, λ_i is a small nonnegative number, then (21.2.14) holds only approximately, and the variance of $\hat{\theta}_i$ in (21.2.13) may be large. Thus the existence of some relatively small characteristic roots implies the existence of some near exact relations like that in (21.2.4) and therefore implies severe multicollinearity exists. Thus in the transformed model multicollinearity is completely revealed in the magnitudes of the characteristic roots of $X'X$. For every $\lambda_i = 0$, there is an exact linear dependency among the columns of X. For every $\lambda_i \doteq 0$, there is a near exact linear dependency among the columns of X.

Whereas the effects of multicollinearity are easy to see in the transformed model, we must consider the effects on the original model. Since $\mathbf{b} = P\hat{\boldsymbol{\theta}}$, it follows that

$$\operatorname{cov}(\mathbf{b}) = \sigma^2 P\Lambda^{-1}P' = \sigma^2 \sum_{i=1}^{K} \lambda_i^{-1}\mathbf{p}_i\mathbf{p}_i' \tag{21.2.15}$$

and

$$\operatorname{var}(b_j) = \sigma^2 \sum_{i=1}^{K} p_{ji}^2/\lambda_i \tag{21.2.16}$$

This expression shows that the variance of a particular b_j will depend, in general, on all the characteristic roots λ_i and the magnitudes of the elements in the characteristic vectors.

We can be more specific by considering the estimation of linear combinations of parameters, such as

$$\mathbf{w}'\boldsymbol{\beta} = w_1\beta_1 + w_2\beta_2 + \cdots + w_K\beta_K \tag{21.2.17}$$

where the w_i are scalars. If $w_1 = 1$ and $w_2 = w_3 = \cdots = w_K = 0$, then $\mathbf{w}'\boldsymbol{\beta} = \beta_1$. If $w_1 = w_2 = 1$ and $w_3 = w_4 = \cdots = w_K = 0$, then $\mathbf{w}'\boldsymbol{\beta} = \beta_1 + \beta_2$, and so on. It is always possible to express any $\mathbf{w}$ in terms of the $\mathbf{p}_i$ as

$$\mathbf{w} = P\mathbf{k} = k_1\mathbf{p}_1 + k_2\mathbf{p}_2 + \cdots + k_K\mathbf{p}_K \tag{21.2.18}$$

where the k_i are constants, since the columns of P are basis vectors for the K-dimensional space in which the point (vector) $\mathbf{w}$ lies. Also, since P is orthogonal, $\mathbf{k} = P^{-1}\mathbf{w} = P'\mathbf{w}$. An estimator for $\mathbf{w}'\boldsymbol{\beta}$ is $\mathbf{w}'\mathbf{b}$ and has variance

$$\begin{aligned} \operatorname{var}(\mathbf{w}'\mathbf{b}) &= \sigma^2\mathbf{w}'(X'X)^{-1}\mathbf{w} \\ &= \sigma^2\mathbf{k}'P'(P\Lambda^{-1}P')P\mathbf{k} \\ &= \sigma^2\mathbf{k}'\Lambda^{-1}\mathbf{k} \\ &= \sigma^2\sum_{i=1}^{K}\lambda_i^{-1}k_i^2 \end{aligned} \tag{21.2.19}$$

This expression summarizes what we know about how precisely a linear combination of parameters can be estimated. The precision depends on the error variance σ^2, the magnitudes of the constants k_i (recall that $\mathbf{k} = P'\mathbf{w}$), and the magnitudes of the characteristic roots λ_i.

Several observations are now in order. First, if there are several near-exact linear dependencies among the explanatory variables, then there will be several relatively small (near zero) characteristic roots. Thus the data are highly multicollinear, but it may not present a problem. It will not present a problem if the particular linear combinations of parameters $\mathbf{w}'\boldsymbol{\beta}$ of interest result in k_i's that are small when the λ_i's are small. In that case the small λ_i's are effectively canceled out. This will happen when the parameters of interest are attached to variables not involved in any of the strong linear associations between the regressors. Thus simply because the data exhibit multicollinearity, all is not lost.

Second, if we are interested in prediction, multicollinearity again may not pose a problem. To see this let $\mathbf{w}' = \mathbf{x}_t'$, where $\mathbf{x}_t'$ is the tth row of the X matrix. Then

$$\operatorname{var}(\mathbf{x}_t'\mathbf{b}) = \sigma^2\mathbf{x}_t'\left[\sum_{i=1}^{K}\lambda_i^{-1}\mathbf{p}_i\mathbf{p}_i'\right]\mathbf{x}_t$$

If λ_k is small, then $\mathbf{x}_t'\mathbf{p}_k$ may also be small since $X\mathbf{p}_k \doteq \mathbf{0}$, and the ill effects of λ_k will be canceled out. This result explains why an estimated model may predict well, despite the presence of severe multicollinearity, *as long as the values of the explanatory variables for which predictions are desired obey the same near-exact linear dependencies as the original design matrix X.*

21.3 Detecting the Presence, Severity, and Form of Multicollinearity

21.3.1 Methods for Detecting Multicollinearity

Given a model and a set of data, there are a variety of ways of mitigating some of the effects of multicollinearity. Whether or not to pursue alternatives to the usual maximum likelihood estimator, some of which are outlined in the following section, depends on many factors, including whether or not multicollinearity is perceived as a substantial problem. Consequently, methods must be considered that may be used to detect multicollinearity. The detection process has three facets: (1) determining whether or not multicollinearity is present, (2) determining its severity, and (3) determining its form or nature. Although there have been many suggestions about how to detect multicollinearity, most are, unfortunately, ineffective rules of thumb.

Most of the rules of thumb for measuring multicollinearity require that the data be scaled in a certain way so that "benchmark" values can be established. If x_{tk} is the tth observation on the kth explanatory variable, $\mathbf{x}_k$ the kth column of X, $\bar{x}_k = \sum_{t=1}^{T} x_{tk}/T$ and $sd(x_k) = [\sum_{t=1}^{T}(x_{tk} - \bar{x}_k)^2/(T-1)]^{1/2}$, then define

$$x_{tk}^s = \frac{x_{tk} - \bar{x}_k}{sd(x_k)} \tag{21.3.1}$$

$$x_{tk}^c = \frac{x_{tk} - \bar{x}_k}{\sqrt{T-1}\, sd(x_k)} = \frac{x_{tk}^s}{\sqrt{T-1}} \tag{21.3.2}$$

$$x_{tk}^n = \frac{x_{tk}}{(\mathbf{x}_k'\mathbf{x}_k)^{1/2}} \tag{21.3.3}$$

Using x_{tk}^s results in *standardized* explanatory variables with sample mean 0 and sample standard deviation 1. The use of x_{tk}^c converts $X'X$ into a sample correlation matrix, and X is in *correlation matrix form*. Finally, x_{tk}^n *normalizes* the data so that each column of X has unit length, but the data are *not* "centered" by subtracting the mean. See Exercise 21.14 for practice in using these standardizations in a regression context.

Some common measures for the severity of multicollinearity are as follows.

1. *Simple Correlations among Regressors.* A commonly used rule is that if the correlation coefficient between the values of two regressors is greater than 0.8 or 0.9, then multicollinearity is a serious problem. A modification of this rule compares the simple correlation coefficients to R^2; multicollinearity is then

interpreted as harmful if the simple correlation is greater than R^2. The weaknesses of this rule are clear. If a correlation between regressors is unity, then extreme multicollinearity is present. In less extreme situations the determination of when collinearity is severe is arbitrary. Furthermore, pairwise correlations can give no insight into more complex interrelationships among three or more variables.

2. *Determinant of* $X'X$. If the regressor variables are standardized so that $X'X$ contains elements that are the simple correlation coefficients between the regressors, the determinant of $X'X$ falls in the interval [0, 1]. If det $(X'X) = 0$, then one or more exact linear dependencies exist among the columns of X. If $\det(X'X) = 1$, then the columns of X are orthogonal. Given these facts, it has been suggested by some, including Farrar and Glauber (1967) and Willan and Watts (1978), that the position of $\det(X'X)$ in the [0, 1] interval provides an objective measure of multicollinearity and the closer $\det(X'X)$ is to zero, the more severe the problem. Several disadvantages are associated with this measure, the major one being that even if the measure adequately detects multicollinearity, no information is provided about the number or form of exact or near-exact linear dependencies. To be precise, since the determinant of a matrix equals the product of its characteristic roots,

$$\det(X'X) = \prod_{i=1}^{K} \lambda_i$$

a small determinant may result from one or several small characteristic roots.

3. *Variance Inflation Factors.* If the regressor values are standardized so that $X'X$ is the correlation matrix of the regressors, then the variance inflation factors are the diagonal elements of $(X'X)^{-1}$. If any variable is orthogonal to all the other explanatory variables, then its inflation factor is 1.0. Values of the inflation factor greater than 1.0 imply that the variable in question is not orthogonal to the rest and hence multicollinearity is present in some degree. A value of 5.0 or more is used by some as an indication of severe multicollinearity. Marquardt and Snee (1975) illustrate the use of these measures.

We have already considered one form of the inflation factor in the discussion surrounding (21.2.8). The term $1/\hat{\mathbf{v}}_1'\hat{\mathbf{v}}_1$ is a variance inflation factor. The only difference is that the data we used were the original unscaled data. There is actually quite a controversy in the literature regarding whether the data should be centered, by subtracting the mean of each variable, before analyzing the degree of multicollinearity. Belsley (1984) gives a full discussion and points out that if the data are centered before multicollinearity is analyzed then any linear dependence among the regressors that involves the intercept will not be detected. On the other hand, the fact that different variables are measured in different units and have different scales can be misleading, and thus for the purpose of analyzing multicollinearity the regressors should be scaled to unit length by dividing each observation of the ith variable by $\sqrt{\mathbf{x}_i'\mathbf{x}_i}$. We will follow Belsley's recommendation unless noted otherwise.

4. *Auxiliary Regressions.* Another procedure that is sometimes suggested as a way of detecting the presence and nature of multicollinearity is to regress each of the independent variables on the other $(K - 1)$ regressors. If the value of R^2 is high, a near-exact linear dependence among the columns of X is indicated. Also, if the multicollinearity involves only a few variables so that the auxiliary regressions themselves do not suffer from extensive multicollinearity, the estimated coefficients may reveal the nature of the linear dependence among the regressors. Unfortunately, if there are several complex linear associations, this curve-fitting exercise may not prove to be of much value as it will be difficult to identify the separate interrelationships.

5. *Theil's Multicollinearity Effect.* Theil (1971, p. 179) proposes a measure of multicollinearity that is based on the goodness-of-fit of the auxiliary regression equations. He defines the multicollinearity effect to be the difference between R^2 and the incremental contributions to this explanatory power by each of the nonconstant regressor variables as measured by R_h^2, $h = 2, \ldots, K$, where R_h^2 is the "R^2" value for the regression of the dependent variable on $(K - 1)$ explanatory variables with $\mathbf{x}_h$ *deleted.* Specifically, the multicollinearity effect is $R^2 - \sum_{h=2}^{K}(R^2 - R_h^2)$. This measure is zero if all the regressors are orthogonal.

6. *Matrix Decompositions.* It has already been implied that analysis of the characteristic roots and vectors of the $X'X$ matrix can reveal much about the presence and nature of multicollinearity. The number of relatively small characteristic roots (relative to the largest) indicates the number of near-linear dependencies among the columns of X. Furthermore, since λ_i being small implies that $X\mathbf{p}_i \doteq \mathbf{0}$, the near-exact linear dependence is identified by the corresponding characteristic vector. Whether or not the multicollinearity is harmful depends on whether the small characteristic roots contribute a large amount to the variance of $\mathbf{w}'\boldsymbol{\beta}$ in (21.2.19). Whereas this analysis is superior, we feel, to other devices used to explore the nature of multicollinearity, it cannot be considered to be a complete solution to the problem. First, a decision must be made as to what constitutes a small characteristic root. Since simple scaling of variables can affect the magnitudes of the characteristic roots, the question of size is relative. Belsley, Kuh, and Welsch (1980) consider a decomposition similar to the one we have presented called the singular value decomposition. They carry out extensive numerical experiments and

have concluded that if the regressors have been normalized to unit length (but not centered) and if the ratio $(\lambda_1/\lambda_K)^{1/2}$, called the *condition number* of the $X'X$ matrix, is greater than about 30, then a linear dependence among the columns of X exists that may seriously affect the standard errors of the estimated coefficients. This, however, is still just a rule of thumb.

A second weakness of the matrix decomposition approach is that when there are several relatively small characteristic roots, indicating that there are several near-exact linear dependencies, isolation of the separate linear relations is difficult. The characteristic vectors will identify which variables are involved in all the linear dependencies, but that is all.

21.3.2 An Example—The Klein–Goldberger Consumption Function

To illustrate the use of the foregoing multicollinearity measures we examine the Klein–Goldberger consumption function data. The correlation matrix for the regressors is presented in Table 21.3.

The determinant of the correlation matrix, which is the standardized $X'X$ matrix, is 0.078. This evidence seems to indicate that multicollinearity is present, because the simple correlations are high and the determinant of the correlation matrix is at the low end of the interval [0, 1].

The variance inflation factors, which are the diagonal elements of the inverse of the correlation matrix are 7.73, 2.08, and 6.21, corresponding to W, P, and A, respectively. These are "large" relative to the rule of thumb that 5.0 indicates serious multicollinearity.

The results of auxiliary regressions are presented in Table 21.4. The parentheses contain estimated standard errors of the coefficient estimates.

From these results it appears that wage income W and farm income A have a strong linear association. That linear association in the auxiliary regression for

Table 21.3 Regressor Correlation Matrix for Klein–Goldberger Model

	Constant	W	P	A
Constant	1			
W	0	1		
P	0	0.718	1	
A	0	0.915	0.63	1

Table 21.4 Auxiliary Regressions for Klein–Goldberger Model

	Regressors				
Dependent variable	Constant	W	P	A	R^2
W	−6.05		1.71	5.36	0.87
	(12.38)		(0.82)	(0.79)	
P	12.28	0.12		−0.16	0.52
	(1.42)	(0.06)		(0.40)	
A	−0.87	0.14	−0.06		0.84
	(1.98)	(0.02)	(0.15)		

nonwage–nonfarm income P makes those coefficients unreliable, so that little can be inferred about associations of W and A to P. Theil's multicollinearity effect is

$$\begin{aligned} R^2 - \sum_{h=2}^{K} (R^2 - R_h^2) &= R^2 - (R^2 - R_A^2) - (R^2 - R_P^2) - (R^2 - R_W^2) \\ &= 0.9527 - (0.9527 - 0.9526) - (0.9527 - 0.9513) \\ &\quad - (0.9527 - 0.8426) \\ &= 0.8411 \end{aligned}$$

Although no scale of measurement exists for this measure, it says that the effects of multicollinearity leave the sum of individual contributions of the explanatory variables 0.84 short of what their total contribution would have been (0.95) if they were orthogonal.

In Table 21.5 we present the characteristic roots of the $X'X$ matrix in its original form and when the variables have been scaled to unit length, but not centered.

As can be seen from Table 21.5, there are two relatively small characteristic roots with condition numbers that Belsley and associates would classify as moderately

Table 21.5 Characteristic Roots of $X'X$ Matrix

	Original	λ_1/λ_i	Scaled	λ_1/λ_i	$(\lambda_1/\lambda_i)^{1/2}$
λ_1	67316.6		3.88116		
λ_2	300.149	224.277	0.105115	36.9229	6.07
λ_3	16.9518	3971.06	0.00919738	422.445	20.55
λ_4	0.256355	262591	0.00453489	855.844	29.25

large. The associated characteristic vectors (of the scaled $X'X$) define the linear combinations

$$X\mathbf{p}_4 \doteq \mathbf{0} \rightarrow -0.51 \cdot \text{constant} \; -0.37W + 0.77P + 0.11A \doteq 0$$

and

$$X\mathbf{p}_3 \doteq \mathbf{0} \rightarrow 0.38 \cdot \text{constant} \; -0.73W - 0.17P + 0.54A \doteq 0$$

Because all the elements of the characteristic vectors are nonzero, it is indicated that all three variables, W, P, and A, are involved in the linear associations, no separate relations are easily detected. A clearer picture comes from analyzing the proportions of the variances of the estimators associated with each characteristic root. If $\mathbf{w}$ is a vector with one in the jth row and zeros elsewhere, then $\text{var}(\mathbf{w}'\mathbf{b}) = \text{var}(b_j)$, and since $\mathbf{k}$ in (21.2.18) is given by $\mathbf{k} = P'\mathbf{w}$ we see that

$$\text{var}(b_j) = \sigma^2 \sum_{i=1}^{K} \frac{p_{ji}^2}{\lambda_i}$$

The proportion of the variance associated with the ith characteristic root is $(p_{ji}^2/\lambda_i)/(\sum_{i=1}^{K} p_{ji}^2/\lambda_i)$. These values for the scaled X data are given in Table 21.6.

Each column of the table contains the proportions of the variance of the LS coefficient for the variable listed at the top of the column. Each row contains that portion of the total variance (note that the columns sum to 1.0 except for rounding error) associated with the ith characteristic root, and thus the ith near exact linear dependency. Note that the two relatively small characteristic roots here contribute differently to the variances of the coefficients. The near singularity associated with λ_4 severely affects the variances of the estimated constant term and the coefficient of P. The value of the condition number $(\lambda_1/\lambda_4)^{1/2}$ is near 30, which is deemed large by Belsley and associates. Furthermore, the variances of the coefficients on P and the intercept variable are in large part explained by this linear dependence. This result agrees with the auxiliary regression results in Table 21.4, which indicate that there is little variation in P, and is confirmed by examining the coefficient of variation of P, which is only 0.13, as compared to 0.32 and 0.45 for W and A,

Table 21.6 Proportions of Coefficient Variance Associated with Each Characteristic Root

	Constant	W	P	A
λ_1	0.00	0.00	0.00	0.00
λ_2	0.04	0.01	0.01	0.11
λ_3	0.21	0.65	0.02	0.81
λ_4	0.75	0.34	0.97	0.07

respectively. Thus the imprecision in the estimation of the constant term and the coefficient of P can be attributed to the relative lack of variation in P in the sample.

On the other hand, the near singularity associated with λ_3, which is moderately strong based on the condition index of 20.55, contributes substantial proportions to the variances of the estimated coefficients of W and A. The results of the auxiliary regressions confirm the high degree of linear association between these two variables, indicating that the imprecise estimation of these two coefficients is the result of this collinearity. For more examples illustrating the usefulness of the matrix decomposition approach see Belsley, Kuh, and Welsch (1980).

It is important to note that a careful inspection of the characteristic roots and vectors of $X'X$, both scaled and unscaled, and the auxiliary regressions lead to a much fuller understanding of the "problems" with the data than one could obtain by examining any or all the summary measures designed to measure multicollinearity.

21.4 Solutions to the Multicollinearity Problem

Once multicollinearity has been detected and deemed serious enough to warrant additional effort to mitigate some of its ill effects, a variety of alternative strategies may be pursued. In this section four traditional tactics will be considered: obtaining additional sample data, applying exact linear restrictions, applying stochastic linear restrictions, and using biased estimation techniques. Other approaches are considered in Sections 22.4 through 22.6 of Judge, et al. (1985). It should be noted at the outset that none of these alternatives is completely safe; that is, there may be adverse consequences associated with each approach that must be considered as they are used.

21.4.1 Additional Sample Information

Given that multicollinearity is a problem caused by inadequate sample information, the most obvious solution to the problem is to obtain more and better data. Silvey (1969) considered the problem of what values of the independent variables are optimal, in some sense, if one new observation can be added. Suppose that, in the model $\mathbf{y} = X\boldsymbol{\beta} + \mathbf{e}$, there is one exact linear dependency among the columns of X. That means the vector $\mathbf{p}$ is such that $X\mathbf{p} = \mathbf{0}$, and exact multicollinearity exists because every row of X is orthogonal to $\mathbf{p}$. Thus to eliminate the extreme multicollinearity we must choose an observation that is not orthogonal to $\mathbf{p}$ itself. An obvious choice is an observation in the direction of $\mathbf{p}$ itself, say, $\mathbf{x}_{T+1} = l\mathbf{p}$, where l is some scalar. To see this, suppose that $X'X$ has one small root λ, which may be zero, that corresponds to the characteristic vector $\mathbf{p}$. Then the model of the complete set of observations including $\mathbf{x}_{T+1} = l\mathbf{p}$ is

$$\begin{bmatrix} \mathbf{y} \\ y_{T+1} \end{bmatrix} = \begin{bmatrix} X \\ \mathbf{x}'_{T+1} \end{bmatrix} \boldsymbol{\beta} + \begin{bmatrix} \mathbf{e} \\ e_{T+1} \end{bmatrix}$$

or

$$\mathbf{y}_* = X_* \boldsymbol{\beta} + \mathbf{e}_*$$

It is readily shown that

$$X'_* X_* \mathbf{p} = (\lambda + l^2)\mathbf{p}$$

so that $\mathbf{p}$ is a characteristic vector of $X'_* X_*$ corresponding to the root $l^2 + \lambda$. Thus, by choosing a new observation in the direction of $\mathbf{p}$, the smallest characteristic root is increased by the amount of l^2. This result generalizes to the case of more than one small characteristic root.

Silvey also presents an expression that gives the improvement in the precision of estimation of $\mathbf{w}'\boldsymbol{\beta}$ obtained by taking another observation $\mathbf{x}_{T+1}$, not necessarily in the direction of a characteristic vector of $X'X$. If $\mathbf{b}_T$ and $\mathbf{b}_{T+1}$ are the least squares estimates based on T and $T+1$ observations, respectively, then

$$\text{var}(\mathbf{w}'\mathbf{b}_T) - \text{var}(\mathbf{w}'\mathbf{b}_{T+1}) = \frac{\sigma^2 \mathbf{a}'\Lambda^{-1}\mathbf{z}\mathbf{z}'\Lambda^{-1}\mathbf{a}}{1 + \mathbf{z}'\Lambda^{-1}\mathbf{z}}$$

where $\mathbf{a} = P'\mathbf{w}$ and $\mathbf{z} = P\mathbf{x}_{T+1}$. Silvey also proves that the maximum improvement in the precision of estimation of $\mathbf{w}'\boldsymbol{\beta}$ is obtained by adding an observation proportional to the vector $\mathbf{v}$, where $\mathbf{v} = (I + d^{-2}X'X)\mathbf{w}$. Here it is assumed that there is a constraint on the length of $\mathbf{x}_{T+1}$, namely, $\mathbf{x}'_{T+1}\mathbf{x}_{T+1} \leq d^2$. This constraint is necessary because the longer $\mathbf{x}_{T+1}$ can be, the greater the improvement in the precision of estimation.

Unfortunately, economists seldom can obtain additional data without bearing large costs, much less choose the values of the explanatory variables they desire. In addition, when adding new variables in situations that are not controlled, we must be aware of adding observations that were generated by a process other than that associated with the original data set; that is, we must be sure that the economic structure associated with the new observations is the same as the original structure.

21.4.2 Exact Linear Constraints

In Section 6.4 it was shown that the restricted least squares (RLS) estimator that combined J linear and exact constraints $R\boldsymbol{\beta} = \mathbf{r}$ with the sample information has a sampling variance smaller than that of the LS estimator. This result obtains whether the restrictions are true or not. Unless the restrictions are true the RLS estimator is biased. The danger in using exact constraints is that because of this potential bias the estimator has risk that is greater than the least squares estimator over a large portion of the parameter space. In fact, the risk of the RLS estimator can be arbitrarily large if the specification error (information in) the constraints is very incorrect.

To protect against using incorrect exact constraints, investigators often treat the constraints as hypotheses. As shown in Section 20.3.1, a pretest estimator that chooses between the LS and RLS estimator based on the outcome of a hypothesis test has greater risk than the LS estimator over much of the parameter space. However, it does not have unbounded risk. The pretest estimator has a bias no larger than the RLS estimator and a covariance matrix that is smaller than that of the LS estimator. Unfortunately, the covariance matrix of the pretest estimator depends on the unknown parameter vector $\boldsymbol{\beta}$ and thus cannot be used in practice. Investigators frequently ignore the fact that a pretest has been carried out and compute standard errors of the estimated coefficients based on the RLS covariance matrix. This procedure understates the true standard errors, and they must be considered conditional standard errors—conditional on the restrictions being true.

The desirability of using RLS when multicollinearity is present is clear. By augmenting the sample data with nonsample data the sampling variance of the estimator is reduced. The question is, of course, whether the resulting estimator has a sampling distribution that is compactly distributed around the true parameter or not. The answer to that question is unknown, because it depends on the *quality* of the restrictions used, which is also unknown.

As an example of how exact restrictions affect the sampling precision of estimation, let us consider the Klein-Goldberger consumption function data. Suppose that we, like Klein and Goldberger, are willing to assume that the effects of wage income on consumption (β_2) are greater than the effects of nonwage-nonfarm income (β_3) or farm income (β_4). Specifically, suppose that we specify that $\beta_3 = 0.75\beta_2$ and $\beta_4 = 0.625\beta_2$. The effects of these restrictions are summarized in Table 21.7. Model 1 is the original model, which is repeated for convenience. Model 2 results from the imposition of the first restriction only, model 3 from the second restriction only, and model 4 from both restrictions. The F-statistic reported for each model is the usual F-statistic, which is distributed as $F_{(J,T-K)}$ if the restrictions are true. Note that the effect of the restrictions is to lower the standard error of each estimated coefficient as compared to the unrestricted LS estimators. The upper 0.05 critical values for $F_{(1,16)}$ and $F_{(2,16)}$ random variables are 4.49 and 3.63, respectively. Thus, if we were carrying out a conventional pretest, we would choose the restricted estimator in each case on the basis of this test.

There are, of course, other ways to introduce the prior information that are less binding than using exact restricted least squares. One could adopt the Bayesian

Table 21.7 Effect of Exact Restrictions on the Klein–Goldberger Consumption Function (Standard Errors in Parentheses Based on Restricted Sum of Squared Errors)

Parameter/Model	1	2	3	4
Constant	8.133	4.600	8.486	5.605
	(8.92)	(4.75)	(8.68)	(3.68)
W	1.059	1.010	0.989	0.966
	(0.17)	(0.14)	(0.08)	(0.05)
P	0.452	0.758	0.491	0.725
	(0.66)	(0.10)	(0.63)	(0.04)
A	0.121	0.245	0.618	0.604
	(1.09)	(1.03)	(0.05)	(0.03)
F-statistic	—	0.22	0.21	0.17

approach of Chapter 7 and create a prior distribution that incorporates a degree of belief in the linear restrictions.

An alternative is to operate in a sampling theory framework but to weaken the exact linear restrictions $R\boldsymbol{\beta} = \mathbf{r}$ by adding a disturbance term that makes them inexact. This quasi-Bayesian approach is called "mixed-estimation" and is discussed in Section 20.2.2. By specifying the variance of the added disturbance, the degree of belief in the restrictions can be modified by the researcher. This approach is mechanically easier to apply than the Bayesian analysis, but many think it is difficult to interpret. To illustrate the use of this estimator we specify the stochastic linear restrictions of the form

$$\mathbf{r} = R\boldsymbol{\beta} + \mathbf{v} \tag{21.4.1}$$

where the random vector $\mathbf{v}$ has mean $E[\mathbf{v}] = \mathbf{0}$ and covariance $E[\mathbf{v}\mathbf{v}'] = \boldsymbol{\Psi}$. That estimator is given by (20.2.15) and has desirable properties in the context of multicollinearity. The stochastically restricted estimator has a smaller covariance matrix than the LS estimator, implying that the sampling distributions are more compact. As with the exact restrictions, unless (21.4.1) is such that $E[\mathbf{v}] = \mathbf{0}$ so that the stochastic restrictions are unbiased, the stochastically restricted estimator is biased. Consequently, over a large part of the parameter space this estimator has risk that is greater than that of the LS estimator. To prevent the use of an estimator with large risk, the compatibility statistic (20.2.27) is frequently used as a basis for a pretest, if great uncertainty exists about the stochastic restrictions.

In Table 21.8 the results of using the stochastically restricted estimator with two alternative covariance specifications, $\boldsymbol{\Psi}_1 = \text{diag}(1/64,\ 1/64)$ and $\boldsymbol{\Psi}_2 = \text{diag}(1/256,\ 1/256)$ are presented along with their estimated standard errors.

Table 21.8 Effect of Stochastic Restrictions on the Klein–Goldberger Consumption Function (Standard Errors in Parentheses)

Parameter/Model	1	2
Constant	5.683	5.625
	(4.13)	(3.93)
W	0.968	0.967
	(0.06)	(0.05)
P	0.718	0.723
	(0.12)	(0.07)
A	0.600	0.603
	(0.12)	(0.07)

Model 1, which corresponds to the covariance specification $\boldsymbol{\Psi}_1$, and model 2 produce coefficient estimates close to their exact restriction counterpart, model 4 in Table 21.7, but their empirical standard errors are between those of the LS and the restricted LS estimators.

21.4.3 Ridge Regression

Although the best solution to the multicollinearity problem is to introduce additional sample or good nonsample information, this is often very difficult to do. Consequently, attention has turned, in these instances, to the use of biased estimators for $\boldsymbol{\beta}$ in the hope that their smaller variances offset their bias so that the estimator mean square error is reduced below that of LS. One such estimator is the ridge regression estimator proposed by Hoerl and Kennard (1970a,b). The ridge regression estimator is really a family of estimators given by

$$\mathbf{b}(k) = (X'X + kI)^{-1}X'\mathbf{y} \tag{21.4.2}$$

where $k > 0$ is a *constant*, often called the shrinkage or biasing parameter. In order to make ridge regression operational a value for k must be selected. Picking $k = 0$ gives the LS estimator. If $k > 0$ and nonstochastic then

$$E[\mathbf{b}(k)] = (X'X + kI)^{-1}X'X\boldsymbol{\beta} \tag{21.4.3}$$

and

$$\text{cov}[\mathbf{b}(k)] = \sigma^2(X'X + kI)^{-1}X'X(X'X + kI)^{-1} \tag{21.4.4}$$

It is clear that $\mathbf{b}(k)$ is biased, unless $k = 0$ or $\boldsymbol{\beta} = \mathbf{0}$, but it has a smaller covariance matrix than the LS estimator, in the sense that $\text{cov}(\mathbf{b}) - \text{cov}[\mathbf{b}(k)]$ is positive semidefinite for $k > 0$. The mean square error of $\mathbf{b}(k)$, or risk, is

$$E[(\mathbf{b}(k) - \boldsymbol{\beta})'(\mathbf{b}(k) - \boldsymbol{\beta})] = \text{tr}\{\text{cov}[\mathbf{b}(k)]\} + \{E[\mathbf{b}(k)] - \boldsymbol{\beta}\}'\{E[\mathbf{b}(k)] - \boldsymbol{\beta}\} \quad (21.4.5)$$

If P is the orthogonal matrix of characteristic vectors of $X'X$ so that $P'X'XP = \Lambda = \text{diag}(\lambda_1, \ldots, \lambda_K)$, then $Z = XP$ is the principal components matrix and $\boldsymbol{\theta} = P'\boldsymbol{\beta}$ is the vector of parameters associated with the principal components model (21.2.9). If P is the matrix of characteristic vectors of $X'X$, it is also the matrix of characteristic vectors of $(X'X)^{-1}$, $(X'X + kI)$, $(X'X + kI)^{-1}$ and $(X'X + kI)^{-2}$. See the linear algebra appendix, Section A.9, for these results. Then the first term in (21.4.5) can be determined as follows.

$$\begin{aligned}
\text{tr cov}[\mathbf{b}(k)] &= \sigma^2 \, \text{tr}(X'X + kI)^{-1}X'X(X'X + kI)^{-1} \\
&= \sigma^2 \, \text{tr}(X'X + kI)^{-2}X'X \\
&= \sigma^2 \, \text{tr } P(\Lambda + kI)^{-2}P'P\Lambda P' \\
&= \sigma^2 \, \text{tr}(\Lambda + kI)^{-2}\Lambda \\
&= \sigma^2 \sum_{i=1}^{K} \lambda_i/(\lambda_i + k)^2 \qquad (21.4.6)
\end{aligned}$$

In order to determine the bias component of the mean square error we express the bias as

$$\begin{aligned}
\text{bias}[\mathbf{b}(k)] &= E[\mathbf{b}(k) - \boldsymbol{\beta}] \\
&= (X'X + kI)^{-1}X'X\boldsymbol{\beta} - \boldsymbol{\beta} \\
&= [(X'X + kI)^{-1}X'X - I]\boldsymbol{\beta} \\
&= -k(X'X + kI)^{-1}\boldsymbol{\beta} \qquad (21.4.7)
\end{aligned}$$

where we have used the result that

$$(X'X + kI)^{-1}X'X = I - k(X'X + kI)^{-1} \quad (21.4.8)$$

Then the squared bias component of (21.4.5) is

$$\begin{aligned}
\text{tr}[\text{bias } \mathbf{b}(k)][\text{bias } \mathbf{b}(k)]' &= k^2\boldsymbol{\beta}'(X'X + kI)^{-2}\boldsymbol{\beta} \\
&= k^2\boldsymbol{\theta}'(\Lambda + kI)^{-2}\boldsymbol{\theta} \\
&= k^2 \sum_{i=1}^{K} \frac{\theta_i^2}{(\lambda_i + k)^2} \qquad (21.4.9)
\end{aligned}$$

By taking the derivatives of (21.4.6) and (21.4.9) it is easy to show that the larger k is the larger is the bias of $\mathbf{b}(k)$, but the smaller the variance. Furthermore, it is possible to show that there exists a $k > 0$ for which the mean square error of $\mathbf{b}(k)$ is less than that for the LS estimator $\mathbf{b}$. To do so, Hoerl and Kennard differentiate the sum of (21.4.6) and (21.4.9) and show that this derivative is negative at least for the range $0 \leq k \leq \sigma^2/\max(\boldsymbol{\theta})$ where $\max(\boldsymbol{\theta})$ is the maximum element of $\boldsymbol{\theta} = P'\boldsymbol{\beta}$. Since the LS and ridge estimator are identical when $k = 0$, this result shows that the ridge estimator (21.4.2) with nonstochastic k in the given range has lower mean square error than the LS estimator. It is interesting that the way the ridge regression estimator achieves the mean square error gain is by shrinking the LS estimator toward zero. In particular,

$$\mathbf{b}(k) = [I + k(X'X)^{-1}]^{-1}\mathbf{b} \tag{21.4.10}$$

and for $k > 0$, the squared length of $\mathbf{b}(k)$ is less than that of $\mathbf{b}$. That is, for $k > 0$ $\mathbf{b}(k)'\mathbf{b}(k) < \mathbf{b}'\mathbf{b}$ and as $k \to \infty$, $\mathbf{b}(k)'\mathbf{b}(k) \to 0$. Consequently, the ridge regression estimator is called a "shrinkage estimator" and k is interpreted as the parameter that controls the amount of shrinkage. See Exercise 21.4 for another illustration of a shrinkage estimator and also see Section 20.3.2 where the Stein rule, another shrinkage estimator with improved MSE, is discussed.

The problem with this elegant development is that the upper bound on acceptable values for k depends on the unknown parameters $\boldsymbol{\beta}$ and σ^2. If k is based on *estimates* of these unknown parameters, then the resulting ridge estimator, based on $\hat{k}$, which depends on $\mathbf{y}$ and is thus random, will have complicated properties. In particular, a *mean square error gain is no longer guaranteed* and the covariance matrix expression (21.4.6) is no longer correct, and thus usual t- and F-tests and confidence interval statements may be misleading.

Nevertheless, many schemes have been developed for using both X and $\mathbf{y}$ data to choose k. See Judge, et al. (1985, pp. 913–922) for a full discussion of the ridge estimator (21.4.2) and its generalizations. Here we illustrate one of the suggestions that have been made, by Hoerl, Kennard, and Baldwin (HKB) (1975).

Like many who study ridge regression, HKB advocate standardizing the regressor variables so that $X'X$ is a correlation matrix before using ridge regression. Although there is no theoretical reason why this should be done, it is the common practice. To achieve this standardization, the regressors are first "centered" by putting them in deviation from the mean form (i.e., x_{tk} is replaced by $x_{tk} - \bar{x}_k$, where $\bar{x}_k = \sum_{t=1}^{T} x_{tk}/T$) and then divided by $w_k = [\sum_{t=1}^{T} (x_{tk} - \bar{x}_k)^2]^{1/2}$. Centering the explanatory variables eliminates the constant term from the regression but does not affect the values of the slope parameters. Dividing each variable by w_k increases the magnitude of each slope parameter by the multiplicative factor w_k. Eventually we will reverse the process. No standardization of the dependent variable is advocated, but it too will be centered by subtracting the mean of the y's from each observation.

The standardized model then has the form

$$\mathbf{y}_c = X_c\boldsymbol{\beta}_c + \mathbf{e}_c \tag{21.4.11}$$

where $\mathbf{y}_c$ is the centered vector of observations on the dependent variable, X_c is the Tx$(K-1)$ matrix of standardized regressors and has the property that $X_c'X_c$ is the correlation matrix of the explanatory variables. $\boldsymbol{\beta}_c$ is the $(K-1)$x1 vector of slope parameters for the scaled X variables. The HKB estimator of k is

$$\hat{k} = \frac{(K-1)\hat{\sigma}^2}{\hat{\boldsymbol{\beta}}_c'\hat{\boldsymbol{\beta}}_c} \tag{21.4.12}$$

where $\hat{\boldsymbol{\beta}}_c$ is the vector of OLS estimates of $\boldsymbol{\beta}_c$ and

$$\hat{\sigma}^2 = (\mathbf{y}_c - X_c\hat{\boldsymbol{\beta}}_c)'(\mathbf{y}_c - X_c\hat{\boldsymbol{\beta}}_c)/(T-K).$$

Note that the estimator $\hat{\sigma}^2$ is numerically identical to the usual unbiased estimator of σ^2 from the original unstandardized regression model $\mathbf{y} = X\boldsymbol{\beta} + \mathbf{e}$. The divisor is $(T-K)$ instead of $T-(K-1)$ to account for the centering of the y's, which is equivalent to estimating the intercept term. The ridge estimator of $\boldsymbol{\beta}_c$ is thus given by

$$\hat{\boldsymbol{\beta}}_c(\hat{k}) = (X_c'X_c + \hat{k}I)^{-1}X_c'\mathbf{y}_c \tag{21.4.13}$$

Standard practice would lead to (21.4.4) being used to estimate the covariance matrix for $\hat{\boldsymbol{\beta}}_c(\hat{k})$ with $\hat{\sigma}^2$ replacing σ^2 and $\hat{k}$ replacing k.

To transform these results back to the original units of measure, let $W = \text{diag}(w_2, \ldots, w_K)$. Then the ridge estimates of the slopes $\boldsymbol{\beta}_s' = (\beta_2, \ldots, \beta_K)$ are

$$\hat{\boldsymbol{\beta}}_s(\hat{k}) = W^{-1}\hat{\boldsymbol{\beta}}_c(\hat{k})$$

and

$$\text{cov}[\hat{\boldsymbol{\beta}}_s(\hat{k})] = W^{-1}\,\text{cov}[\hat{\boldsymbol{\beta}}_c(\hat{k})]W^{-1}$$

Hoerl and Kennard (1976) suggest iteratively modifying $\hat{k}$ by altering the denominator to be the ridge regression estimator based on the most recent estimate of k and continuing iterations until $\hat{k}$ converges to some value.

For the Klein–Goldberger data the parameter estimates that result from these exercises as well as standard errors based on (21.4.4) are reported in Table 21.9. These standard errors *are not* correct since they are based on the assumption of nonstochastic k. In column 1 we report the OLS results for ease of comparison; column 2 contains the ridge results based on (21.4.12). The results in column 3 were obtained using the iterative scheme for estimating the bias parameter k. It should be re-emphasized that the ridge estimation rule based on $\hat{k}$ does not necessarily have a smaller mean square error than the OLS estimator and the expressions for the bias and covariance matrix, Equations (21.4.3) and (21.4.4), are not correct.

Table 21.9 OLS and Ridge Regression Estimates for Klein–Goldberger Model ("Standard Errors" in Parentheses)

Parameter	1	2	3
W	1.059	0.986	0.975
	(0.17)	(0.15)	(0.15)
P	0.452	0.573	0.591
	(0.66)	(0.63)	(0.63)
A	0.121	0.511	0.566
	(1.09)	(0.97)	(0.95)
$\hat{k}$		0.0104	0.0121

21.5 Summary

In this chapter we have examined some aspects of the multicollinearity problem. Multicollinearity is defined as the existence of one or more near-exact linear relations among the columns of the regressor matrix X. The consequences of multicollinearity are that the sampling distributions of the coefficient estimators may have such large variances that the coefficient estimates are unstable from sample to sample. Thus they may be too unreliable to be useful.

The degree of multicollinearity may be measured in several ways. We advocate the use of the matrix decomposition discussed in this chapter as it can frequently identify both the number and nature of the linear dependencies and what effect they have on the variances of the estimated coefficients.

Methods for improving parameter estimates when multicollinearity is severe involve combining the existing sample information with additional sample information or relevant nonsample information in the form of exact or stochastic restrictions. The statistical consequences of combining sample and uncertain nonsample information are discussed in Chapter 20. There are a variety of more advanced techniques for dealing with multicollinearity, including the use of inequality constraints on the parameters, Bayesian approaches using prior distributions on the parameters, principal components regression, generalized and adaptive ridge regression, and Stein estimators. Also, we have assumed the X matrix is nonstochastic. Consequently analysis is conditional on the values of the explanatory variables that were actually observed. Multicollinearity can be discussed in the stochastic regressor context. Somewhat different diagnostic tools must be used in this case. For a complete discussion of all these topics see Judge, et al. (1985, Chapter 22).

21.6 Exercises

21.1 Let $y_t = \beta_1 x_{t1} + \beta_2 x_{t2} + e_t$ and suppose $\mathbf{y}' = (4 \ -2 \ 4 \ 0)$, $\mathbf{x}_1' = (1 \ 1 \ 2 \ 2)$ and $x_{t2} = 2x_{t1}$. Construct the normal equations and show that there are an infinite number of solutions for b_1 and b_2. Choose any two different solutions and show that they yield the same values of $\hat{\mathbf{y}}$ and thus the same values for the sum of squared errors. Show that the linear combination $5\beta_1 + 10\beta_2$ is estimable but that $\beta_1 + \beta_2$ is not.

21.2 Derive the covariance matrix of the ridge estimator in (21.4.4).

21.3 Use the Klein-Goldberger data to illustrate that the estimated variance of the LS estimator of the parameter on wage income (W) can be written as (21.2.8) with $\hat{\sigma}^2$ replacing σ^2.

21.4 Consider the "shrinkage" estimator $\mathbf{b}(c) = c\mathbf{b}$ where c is a scalar.

(*a*) Show that $\mathbf{b}(c)$ has mean square error (MSE)

$$(c - 1)^2 \boldsymbol{\beta}'\boldsymbol{\beta} + c^2\sigma^2 \operatorname{tr}(X'X)^{-1}$$

(*b*) Show that $\mathbf{b}(c)$ has a lower MSE than $\mathbf{b}$ if

$$\frac{\boldsymbol{\beta}'\boldsymbol{\beta} - \sigma^2 \operatorname{tr}(X'X)^{-1}}{\boldsymbol{\beta}'\boldsymbol{\beta} + \sigma^2 \operatorname{tr}(X'X)^{-1}} \le c \le 1$$

Comment on the usefulness of this estimator.

21.5 Use the Klein-Goldberger data to construct the principal components model $\mathbf{y} = Z\boldsymbol{\theta} + \mathbf{e}$ where $Z = XP$ and $\boldsymbol{\theta} = P'\boldsymbol{\beta}$ as described in Section 21.2.3. Use the unscaled original data.

(*a*) Show that estimating $\boldsymbol{\theta}$ as $\hat{\boldsymbol{\theta}} = (Z'Z)^{-1}Z'\mathbf{y}$ and obtaining estimates of $\boldsymbol{\beta}$ as $\mathbf{b} = P\hat{\boldsymbol{\theta}}$ yields results that are identical to LS. The covariance matrix of $\hat{\boldsymbol{\theta}}$ is estimated by $\hat{\sigma}^2(Z'Z)^{-1} = \hat{\sigma}^2\Lambda^{-1}$. Show that the covariance matrix of $\mathbf{b}$ is obtained as $P(\hat{\sigma}^2\Lambda^{-1})P'$, where $\hat{\sigma}^2$ is estimated as usual in either form of the model.

(*b*) Drop the fourth principal component $\mathbf{z}_4 = X\mathbf{p}_4$ from the model. Apply OLS to the remaining model to estimate θ_1, θ_2, and θ_3 and set the value of θ_4 to zero. Obtain the corresponding estimator of $\boldsymbol{\beta}$ by making the appropriate inverse transformation. Show that these estimates are numerically identical to the restricted least squares estimates obtained by estimating $\boldsymbol{\beta}$ subject to $R\boldsymbol{\beta} = \mathbf{p}_4'\boldsymbol{\beta} = 0$. This procedure is often called principal components regression and is suggested by some as a way to deal with multicollinear data. What are the bias, covariance, and mean square error properties of this estimator? Can you provide a casual justification for the procedure on the basis of the fact that $\mathbf{z}_4'\mathbf{z}_4 = \lambda_4$?

For the next four problems generate a sample of data using the following design. Use the model $y_t = 1 + 3x_{t2} - 3x_{t3} + 0.2x_{t4} - 0.2x_{t5} + e_t$ to generate a sample with $T = 25$ observations on y_t. Let x_{t2} and x_{t3} consist of random numbers from a uniform distribution on $[-1, 1]$ and scaled to unit length. Let $x_{t4} = 0.4x_{t2} + 0.6x_{t3} + u_t$, $u_t \sim N(0, 0.001)$ and $x_{t5} = x_{t2} + v_t$, where $v_t \sim N(0, 0.001)$. Let the random disturbances e_t be generated as a $N(0, 0.0025)$ random variable.

21.6 Estimate the parameters of the above model by least squares and use the techniques in this chapter to analyze the multicollinearity present in the data and their effects on the least squares estimates.

21.7 Impose the exact constraint $\beta_4 + \beta_5 = 0$ and observe the improvement in estimator precision.

21.8 Impose the stochastic constraint that $0 = \beta_4 + \beta_5 + v_t$, where $v_t \sim N(0, 1/64)$, and observe the improvement in estimator precision.

21.9 Using the model just outlined and the values of x_2 and x_3, reduce the variances of the auxiliary relations for x_5 and x_4 to 0.0001 and repeat Exercises 21.6 through 21.8.

21.10 Let $\hat{\boldsymbol{\beta}}$ be any solution to the normal equations (21.2.3) in the case where X is $(T \times K)$ but of rank *less than* K. In this case there is at least one vector of constants $\mathbf{c} \neq \mathbf{0}$ such that $\mathbf{Xc} = \mathbf{0}$ (why?). Define $\tilde{\boldsymbol{\beta}} = \hat{\boldsymbol{\beta}} + \mathbf{c}$ and show that $\tilde{\boldsymbol{\beta}}$ and $\hat{\boldsymbol{\beta}}$ yield identical values of the sum of squares and likelihood function. In the context of Chapter 14 the two estimators are "observationally equivalent" and $\boldsymbol{\beta}$ is not identified on the basis of observational information alone.

21.11 Verify that (21.2.7) is the inverse of $X'X$ when $X = (\mathbf{x}_1 X_2)$ as defined preceding (21.2.7).

21.12 Verify (21.2.8) by showing that $\mathbf{x}_1'N\mathbf{x}_1 = (\mathbf{x}_1 - \hat{\mathbf{x}}_1)'(\mathbf{x}_1 - \hat{\mathbf{x}}_1) = \hat{\mathbf{v}}_1'\hat{\mathbf{v}}_1$ where $\hat{\mathbf{v}}_1 = \mathbf{x}_1 - \hat{\mathbf{x}}_1 = \mathbf{x}_1 - X_2(X_2'X_2)^{-1}X_2'\mathbf{x}_1 = \mathbf{x}_1 - X_2\hat{\mathbf{d}}_1$ where $\hat{\mathbf{d}}_1 = (\hat{d}_2, \ldots, \hat{d}_K)'$ is the vector of LS estimates of (21.2.6).

21.13 Show that the covariances between b_1 and the other $(K-1)$ LS estimators are

$$\begin{bmatrix} \text{cov}(b_1, b_2) \\ \text{cov}(b_1, b_3) \\ \vdots \\ \text{cov}(b_1, b_K) \end{bmatrix} = \frac{-\sigma^2 \hat{\mathbf{d}}_1}{\hat{\mathbf{v}}_1' \hat{\mathbf{v}}_1}$$

where $\hat{\mathbf{d}}_1$ and $\hat{\mathbf{v}}_1$ are defined in Exercise 21.12.

21.14 Let the regression model be

$$y_t = \beta_1 + x_{t2}\beta_2 + \cdots + x_{tK}\beta_K + e_t \qquad t = 1, \ldots, T$$

or in matrix terms

$$\mathbf{y} = \mathbf{j}_T\beta_1 + X_{.}\boldsymbol{\beta}_{.} + \mathbf{e}$$

where $X_{.}$ is $Tx(K-1)$ and $\boldsymbol{\beta}_{.}$ contains the slope parameters $\beta_2, \ldots, \beta_K$

(*a*) Define $A = I_T - \mathbf{jj}'/T$. Show that $\mathbf{y}^* = A\mathbf{y}$ and $X^* = AX_{.}$ contain observations that are "centered" by subtracting the appropriate sample mean from each variable. Show that

$$\mathbf{b}_{.} = (X^{*\prime}X^*)^{-1}X^{*\prime}\mathbf{y}^*$$

and

$$b_1 = \bar{y} - \sum_{k=2}^{K} \bar{x}_k b_k$$

are the usual LS estimators for β_1 and $\boldsymbol{\beta}_{.}$ by using partitioned inversion on the regression model written as

$$\mathbf{y} = [\mathbf{j}_T \quad X_{.}]\begin{bmatrix} \beta_1 \\ \boldsymbol{\beta}_{.} \end{bmatrix} + \mathbf{e}$$

This implies that $\boldsymbol{\beta}_{.}$ can be estimated by applying OLS to the centered model

$$A\mathbf{y} = \mathbf{y}^* = AX\boldsymbol{\beta} + A\mathbf{e} = X^*\boldsymbol{\beta}_{.} + \mathbf{e}^*$$

(*b*) Define $D_s = \text{diag}(\text{sd}(x_2), \ldots, \text{sd}(x_K))$. Show that $X_s = X^*D_s^{-1}$ is the matrix of *standardized* variates using (21.3.1).

Then

$$\mathbf{y}^* = X^*D_s^{-1}D_s\boldsymbol{\beta}_{.} + \mathbf{e}^* = X_s\boldsymbol{\beta}_s + \mathbf{e}^*$$

Show that

$$\mathbf{b}_{.} = (X^{*\prime}X^{*})^{-1}X^{*\prime}\mathbf{y}^{*} = D_s^{-1}\mathbf{b}_s$$

where $\mathbf{b}_s = (X_s'X_s)^{-1}X_s'\mathbf{y}^{*}$.

(c) Define $D_c = \sqrt{T-1} \cdot D_s$. Show that $X_c = X^{*}D_c^{-1}$ is in correlation matrix form.

21.7 References

Belsley, D. (1984) "Demeaning Conditioning Diagnostics Through Centering." *The American Statistician*, 38, 73–93.

Belsley, D. A., E. Kuh, and R. E. Welsch (1980) *Regression Diagnostics.* New York, Wiley.

Farrar, D. E., and R. R. Glauber (1967) "Multicollinearity in Regression Analysis: The Exercise Revisited." *The Review of Economics and Statistics*, 49, 92–107.

Hoerl, A., and R. Kennard (1970a) "Ridge Regression: Biased Estimation for Nonorthogonal Problems." *Technometrics*, 12, 55–67.

Hoerl, A., and R. Kennard (1970b) "Ridge Regression: Applications to Nonorthogonal Problems." *Technometrics*, 12, 69–82.

Hoerl, A., and R. Kennard (1976) "Ridge Regression: Iterative Estimation of the Biasing Parameter," *Communications in Statistics A*, 5, 77–88.

Hoerl, A., R. Kennard, and K. Baldwin (1975) "Ridge Regression: Some Simulations." *Communications in Statistics A*, 4, 105–123.

Judge, G. G., W. E. Griffiths, R. C. Hill, H. Lütkepohl, and T. C. Lee (1985) *The Theory and Practice of Econometrics*, 2nd ed. New York, Wiley.

Klein, L. R., and A. S. Goldberger (1955) *An Econometric Model of the United States*, 1929–1952. Amsterdam, North-Holland.

Marquardt, D., and R. Snee (1975) "Ridge Regression in Practice." *The American Statistician*, 29, 3–19.

Schmidt, P. (1976) *Econometrics.* New York, Dekker.

Silvey, S. D. (1969) "Multicollinearity and Imprecise Estimation." *Journal of the Royal Statistical Society, Series B*, 35, 67–75.

Theil, H. (1971) *Principles of Econometrics.* New York, Wiley.

Willan, A. R., and D. G. Watts (1978) "Meaningful Multicollinearity Measures." *Technometrics* 20, 407–412.

CHAPTER 22

Robust Estimation

The robustness of an estimation procedure refers to the ability of that estimation procedure to produce estimates that are insensitive to model misspecification. Thus, a robust estimator is one that produces estimates that are "good" (in some sense) under a wide variety of possible data-generating processes. For example, in the normal linear statistical model with independent, identically distributed normal random errors, the least squares estimator is the most efficient unbiased estimator. However, when the errors are not normally distributed, it is frequently possible to find estimators that are more efficient than least squares. Recognizing that the underlying distribution of the errors is never known with certainty, the area of robust estimation that has attracted the most attention is concerned with finding estimators that are only slightly less efficient than least squares when the errors are normally distributed, but which can be considerably more efficient than least squares for nonnormal errors. Such estimators are said to be robust with respect to the distribution of the error terms. Other robust developments include estimators and standard errors that are robust under alternative specifications of the error covariance matrix and estimators that are robust with respect to specification of the functional form; in Bayesian inference, choosing an estimator that is robust with respect to specification of the prior is also an issue.

In this chapter we are mainly concerned with robustness and nonnormal errors. We begin in Section 22.1, with a summary of the implications of nonnormal errors. In Section 22.2, under the title Regression Diagnostics, we describe a test for normally distributed errors and methods for detecting influential observations. Alternative estimators for a model with multivariate t error terms are outlined in Section 22.3. In Section 22.4 we consider robust estimators that are based on regression quantiles, including the minimum absolute deviation estimator and trimmed least squares.

22.1 The Consequences of Nonnormal Disturbances

Throughout this book we have, at various times, discussed the implications of normally distributed errors in the linear statistical model and the consequences of relaxing this assumption. It is convenient at this point to summarize the main results. An important issue is whether or not the variance of the errors is finite. Thus, we first consider the finite variance case, then the infinite variance case.

22.1.1 Finite Variance

Consider the general linear model

$$\mathbf{y} = X\boldsymbol{\beta} + \mathbf{e} \tag{22.1.1}$$

where (1) the usual definitions hold, (2) X is nonstochastic of rank K, (3) $\lim_{T\to\infty} T^{-1}X'X$ is a finite nonsingular matrix, and (4) the random vector $\mathbf{e}$ is such that $E[\mathbf{e}] = \mathbf{0}$ and $E[\mathbf{ee}'] = \sigma^2 I$, σ^2 finite. If, in addition, $\mathbf{e}$ is normally distributed

1. The least squares estimator $\mathbf{b} = (X'X)^{-1}X'\mathbf{y}$ is unbiased and has minimum variance from within the class of *all* unbiased estimators. It is also asymptotically efficient and consistent.

2. The variance estimator $\hat{\sigma}^2 = (\mathbf{y} - X\mathbf{b})'(\mathbf{y} - X\mathbf{b})/(T - K)$ is unbiased, minimum variance from within the class of all unbiased estimators, asymptotically efficient, and consistent.

3. The respective distributions for $\mathbf{b}$ and $(T - K)\hat{\sigma}^2/\sigma^2$ are normal and $\chi^2_{(T-K)}$ and, furthermore, they are independent.

4. The F-test on a set of linear restrictions $R\boldsymbol{\beta} = \mathbf{r}$, and t-tests on the individual coefficients, are justified in finite samples.

When $\mathbf{e}$ is not normally distributed, the following occur.

1. The least squares estimator $\mathbf{b}$ is unbiased minimum variance from within the class of *linear* unbiased estimators and consistent.

2. The variance estimator $\hat{\sigma}^2$ is unbiased and consistent.

3. The estimators $\mathbf{b}$ and $\hat{\sigma}^2$ are no longer efficient or asymptotically efficient. If the form of the probability distribution of $\mathbf{e}$ is known, the likelihood function for $\mathbf{y}$ can be used to obtain maximum likelihood estimators for $\boldsymbol{\beta}$ and σ^2. In general, the maximum likelihood estimator for $\boldsymbol{\beta}$ will be *nonlinear* and, under appropriate regularity conditions, the maximum likelihood estimators for both $\boldsymbol{\beta}$ and σ^2 will be asymptotically efficient. If the form of the probability distribution of $\mathbf{e}$ is unknown, one of the nonlinear robust estimators outlined in Section 22.4 can be employed, and, depending on the unknown underlying distribution, such an estimator may be more asymptotically efficient than least squares.

4. The respective distributions of $\mathbf{b}$ and $(T - K)\hat{\sigma}^2/\sigma^2$ are no longer normal and χ^2 and, consequently, the F-tests on $\boldsymbol{\beta}$ are not necessarily valid in finite samples. However, they do have an asymptotic justification. Also, appropriate asymptotic tests such as the Wald test can be constructed. See Chapter 12 for details. These tests may, however, have reduced power under certain departures from normality.

Two of the foregoing results—namely, that (1) **b** is best linear unbiased, and (2) the conventional tests are asymptotically justified in the sense that they have asymptotically correct size—have been used to justify the use of the least squares estimator under conditions of nonnormality. Most econometric textbooks use this argument, either explicitly, or implicitly. However, Koenker (1982) argues that neither of the points is very compelling. He notes that the class of linear estimators is computationally appealing, but it may be drastically restrictive. Also, the power of the asymptotic tests can be extremely sensitive to the hypothesized error distribution. These facts, coupled with the fact that arguments justifying the existence of normally distributed errors are often weak, have led Koenker and others to advocate use of robust estimation techniques (Section 22.4). Such techniques are particularly desirable if the error distribution has infinite variance. We now discuss some aspects of this situation.

22.1.2 Infinite Variance

A large body of literature suggests that many economic data series, particularly prices in financial and commodity markets, are well represented by a class of distributions with infinite variance. One example is the Pareto distribution, with density $f(e) = c(e - e_0)^{-\alpha-1}$, where c, e_0, and α are constants and where the variance does not exist for $\alpha < 2$. Another example is the t-distribution, which has infinite variance if the degrees of freedom parameter is 2 or less, and an infinite mean if the degrees of freedom parameter is 1 or less. Given that such distributions may be good representations of many data series, it is natural to ask whether, in the context of the general linear model, one should assume that the disturbance comes from a distribution with finite variance; and it is worthwhile considering the consequences of an infinite error variance for our usual least squares estimation techniques.

For the variance of a random variable e to be finite, the integral

$$\int_{-\infty}^{\infty} e^2 f(e)\, de \tag{22.1.2}$$

must converge (be finite). Infinite variance distributions typically arise when $f(e)$ does not approach 0 sufficiently quickly to "compensate for" the increase in e^2 as e approaches $\pm\infty$. Thus, distributions with infinite variance tend to have "thick" or "heavy" tails, implying that large values or "outliers" will be relatively frequent.

Because the least squares technique minimizes *squared* deviations, it places a relatively heavy weight on outliers, and their presence can lead to estimates that are extremely sensitive. Thus, in repeated samples, least squares estimates will vary more than in the finite variance case. Also, we will be unable to estimate reliably the variance of the disturbance or the least squares estimates. If the variance does not exist, it is obviously impossible to obtain a meaningful variance estimator and the least squares estimator will not possess its usual minimum variance property. This in turn implies that the conventional F- and t-tests on the coefficients could be very misleading. If the error distribution is so thick-tailed that the mean as well as the variance does not exist, then the least squares estimator cannot be unbiased because its mean also will not exist.

Malinvaud (1980, p. 313) points out that, in practice, one can always assume that the distribution of the disturbances is bounded and hence will have a finite variance. However, he also points out that this will not overcome the problem. A relatively large number of outliers will still lead to variance estimates that are unstable in repeated samples, and the estimates will behave as if the variance was infinite.

The possibility of nonnormal disturbances in general, and infinite variance disturbances in particular, has led to the development of alternative estimation techniques that, relative to least squares, place less weight on outliers. As already mentioned, these techniques come under the general heading of robust estimation; some of them are discussed in Section 22.4. The next questions that we consider are how to test for normally distributed disturbances and how to detect influential observations that can arise because of outliers in the error distribution or because of characteristics of the regressors.

22.2 Regression Diagnostics

22.2.1 A Test for Normal Errors

The literature on testing for normality is vast. For access to this literature see White and MacDonald (1980) and other references listed in Judge, et al. (1985, p. 826). We will concentrate on only one test, that suggested by Bera and Jarque (1981).

Consider the usual linear model $\mathbf{y} = X\boldsymbol{\beta} + \mathbf{e}$ where $E[\mathbf{e}] = \mathbf{0}$ and $E[\mathbf{ee}'] = \sigma^2 I$. If, in addition, $\mathbf{e}$ is normally distributed, then the third and fourth moments for an element in $\mathbf{e}$ are given by

$$\mu_3 = E[e_t^3] = 0 \tag{22.2.1}$$

and

$$\mu_4 = E[e_t^4] = 3\sigma^4 \tag{22.2.2}$$

A large number of tests for normality are based on how far estimates of the third and fourth moments, $\tilde{\mu}_3$ and $\tilde{\mu}_4$, deviate from 0 and $3\tilde{\sigma}^4$, respectively, where $\tilde{\sigma}^2$ is an estimate of $E[e_t^2] = \sigma^2$. In this regard it is conventional to consider scaled versions of μ_3 and μ_4 that are respectively known as measures of skewness and kurtosis. The skewness measure is given by

$$\sqrt{b_1} = \frac{\mu_3}{\sigma^3} \tag{22.2.3}$$

The measure of kurtosis is

$$b_2 = \frac{\mu_4}{\sigma^4}. \tag{22.2.4}$$

The notation $\sqrt{b_1}$ and b_2 is traditional in statistics literature and should not be confused with elements from the least squares estimator $\mathbf{b} = (X'X)^{-1}X'\mathbf{y}$. The skewness of a distribution refers to its degree of symmetry (or lack of it), whereas the kurtosis of a distribution is influenced by the peakness of the distribution and the thickness of its tails. Relative to the normal distribution, a measure of excess kurtosis is given by

$$b_2 - 3 = \frac{\mu_4 - 3\sigma^4}{\sigma^4} \tag{22.2.5}$$

The Bera–Jarque test is a joint test of whether or not estimates of $\sqrt{b_1}$ and/or $(b_2 - 3)$ are significantly different from 0. Since the error vector $\mathbf{e}$ is unobservable, estimates of $\sqrt{b_1}$ and $(b_2 - 3)$ are based on least squares residuals. Specifically, if $\hat{e}_t = y_t - \mathbf{x}_t'\mathbf{b}$ where $\mathbf{b} = (X'X)^{-1}X'\mathbf{y}$, and $\mathbf{x}'_t$ is the tth row of the $(T \times K)$ matrix X, then we have the following estimators

$$\tilde{\sigma}^2 = \frac{1}{T}\sum_{t=1}^{T}\hat{e}_t^2 \qquad \tilde{\mu}_3 = \frac{1}{T}\sum_{t=1}^{T}\hat{e}_t^3 \qquad \tilde{\mu}_4 = \frac{1}{T}\sum_{t=1}^{T}\hat{e}_t^4$$

$$\sqrt{\tilde{b}_1} = \frac{\tilde{\mu}_3}{\tilde{\sigma}^3} \qquad (\tilde{b}_2 - 3) = \frac{\tilde{\mu}_4 - 3\tilde{\sigma}^4}{\tilde{\sigma}^4} \tag{22.2.6}$$

Under the null hypothesis that the errors are normally distributed the Bera–Jarque statistic has an asymptotic $\chi^2_{(2)}$ distribution and is given by

$$\lambda = T\left(\frac{(\sqrt{\tilde{b}_1})^2}{6} + \frac{(\tilde{b}_2 - 3)^2}{24}\right)$$

$$= T\left(\frac{\tilde{\mu}_3^2}{6\tilde{\sigma}^6} + \frac{(\tilde{\mu}_4 - 3\tilde{\sigma}^4)^2}{24\tilde{\sigma}^8}\right) \tag{22.2.7}$$

This statistic will tend to be large if $\sqrt{\tilde{b}_1}$ or $(\tilde{b}_2 - 3)$ or both differ significantly from 0.

There are two ways of developing the statistic λ. Given the null hypothesis is true, and that X contains a constant term, asymptotically it can be shown (Pagan and Hall, 1983) that $\tilde{\mu}_3 \sim N(0, 6\sigma^6/T)$, that $(\tilde{\mu}_4 - 3\tilde{\sigma}^4) \sim N(0, 24\sigma^8/T)$, and that $\tilde{\mu}_3$ and $(\tilde{\mu}_4 - 3\tilde{\sigma}^4)$ are independent. These results imply that λ has an asymptotic $\chi^2_{(2)}$ distribution. Alternatively, Bera and Jarque (1981) show that λ can be viewed as the Lagrange multiplier test statistic when the alternative hypothesis is that the errors come from the Pearson family of distributions. The Pearson family is a very general family of distributions that includes the normal, beta, gamma, t, F, and Pareto distributions as special cases. Other popular tests for normality are the Kolmogorov–Smirnov test (Mood, Graybill, and Boes, 1974, p. 508) and the Shapiro–Wilk test (Shapiro, Wilk, and Chen, 1968; Huang and Bolch, 1974).

22.2.2 Detecting Influential Observations

Influential observations in an estimated regression equation are those observations that make a relatively large contribution to the values of the estimates. Observations can be influential because they result from equation errors that are large in absolute value (outliers) or because of certain characteristics of the regressors. We first consider the effect of the regressors.

22.2.2a Leverage

The regressor values that are most informative in the sense that they have the most influence on the realized values of the coefficient estimates, and they lead to relatively large reductions in the variances of the coefficient estimates, are those regressor values that are far removed from the majority of the X-data. If all regressor values are clustered close to their averages, and hence do not change very much, it is clearly very difficult to get precise estimates of coefficients that describe the effect of changes in the regressors on the dependent variable. On the other hand, regressor values a long way from their averages contribute a great deal to isolation of the effects of changes in the regressors. The most common influence measure for $\mathbf{x}_t' = (1, x_{t2}, \ldots, x_{tK})$, the tth observation on the regressors, is known as the leverage of that observation and is defined by

$$h_t = \mathbf{x}_t'(X'X)^{-1}\mathbf{x}_t \tag{22.2.8}$$

The h_t are the diagonal elements of what is known as the "hat" matrix $H = X(X'X)^{-1}X'$. This terminology comes from the fitted predictions $\hat{\mathbf{y}} = X\mathbf{b}$, or "$y$-hats", which can be written as $\hat{\mathbf{y}} = X(X'X)^{-1}X'\mathbf{y} = H\mathbf{y}$. The leverage h_t will tend to be high for observations that are quite different from the majority of the observations in X. This fact can be illustrated by considering the single regressor model where $\mathbf{x}_t' = (1, x_{t2})$; in this case

$$h_t = \frac{1}{T} + \frac{(x_{t2} - \bar{x}_2)^2}{\sum_{t=1}^{T}(x_{t2} - \bar{x}_2)^2} \tag{22.2.9}$$

where $\bar{x}_2 = T^{-1}\sum_{t=1}^{T} x_{t2}$ is the sample average of the single regressor. Clearly, the further x_{t2} is from the average $\bar{x}_2$, the greater will be h_t.

To see what values of h_t are considered to be large, we note that

$$0 \le h_t \le 1 \tag{22.2.10}$$

and

$$\sum_{t=1}^{T} h_t = \text{tr}[X(X'X)^{-1}X'] = K \tag{22.2.11}$$

Thus, the h_t lie between 0 and 1 and have an average value of K/T. As a general rule of thumb, values of h_t greater than two or three times the average, that is, greater than $2K/T$ or $3K/T$, are regarded as influential and worthy of further investigation.

What are the implications of detecting high leverage observations? First, it should be emphasized that such observations are not necessarily bad and that omitting them can be counterproductive. Indeed, since such observations contribute a lot of information about the coefficient estimates, they could be very useful. On the other hand, for the same reason, it is important that such observations are correct. At the most elementary level, it is important that influential observations are correct in the sense that they have been properly recorded. Incorrect recordings or transcription errors are not uncommon in large data sets collected from cross-sectional surveys. Furthermore, the linear specification $\mathbf{x}_t'\boldsymbol{\beta}$ may be an adequate approximation to reality over a limited part of the data set, but a poor approximation for extreme values of $\mathbf{x}_t'$, which are typically those values that have the greatest influence on the coefficient estimates. Thus, observations with high leverage should be checked not only to see if they are correct but also to see if they are indicative of an incorrect specification; it should always be kept in mind, however, that high leverage observations are not necessarily undesirable.

Krasker, Kuh, and Welsch (1983) argue that model builders are often plagued by occasional unusual events that do not fit adequately into a specified model and that manifest themselves as high leverage points or as outliers. They recommend the use of a robust estimation technique called bounded influence regression; this procedure downweights the influence of potentially influential observations. We will not consider it here, but details can be found in Krasker, Kuh, and Welsch (1983).

22.2.2b Studentized Residuals

Because leverage only measures the influence of the regressors and not the influence of outlying observations that are caused by large absolute errors, it is convenient to consider measures designed to detect large errors. Measures designed to detect the influence of regressors *and* outliers on the coefficient estimates, and on predictions made by the model, are also useful. The least squares residual $\hat{e}_t = y_t - \mathbf{x}_t'\mathbf{b}$ is not always a good indication of whether or not the corresponding error term e_t is large in absolute value. Such is the case because the least squares criterion weights extreme *errors* heavily, a procedure that can lead to *residuals* that are only moderately large in absolute value. This problem can be overcome by considering the tth residual from the least squares fit on all observations except the tth. Specifically, let $\mathbf{b}(t) = [X(t)'X(t)]^{-1}X(t)'\mathbf{y}(t)$ be the least squares estimator obtained when the tth observation has been excluded; $X(t)$ is equal to X with the tth row deleted and $\mathbf{y}(t)$ is equal to $\mathbf{y}$ with the tth element deleted. Then, because y_t is independent of $\mathbf{b}(t)$, the residual $y_t - \mathbf{x}_t'\mathbf{b}(t)$ is likely to be a more accurate reflection of the actual error e_t than is the least squares residual $\hat{e}_t$. Furthermore, the variance of the residual $y_t - \mathbf{x}_t'\mathbf{b}(t)$ is given by $\sigma^2\{1 + \mathbf{x}_t'[X(t)'X(t)]^{-1}\mathbf{x}_t\}$ and, under the assumption of normally distributed errors,

$$e_t^* = \frac{y_t - \mathbf{x}_t'\mathbf{b}(t)}{\hat{\sigma}(t)\{1 + \mathbf{x}_t'[X(t)'X(t)]^{-1}\mathbf{x}_t\}^{1/2}} \tag{22.2.12}$$

follows a t-distribution with $(T - K - 1)$ degrees of freedom. The estimator $\hat{\sigma}^2(t)$ is the variance estimator obtained when the tth observation has been deleted. That is,

$$\hat{\sigma}^2(t) = \frac{[\mathbf{y}(t) - X(t)\mathbf{b}(t)]'[\mathbf{y}(t) - X(t)\mathbf{b}(t)]}{T - K - 1} \tag{22.2.13}$$

The standardized residual e_t^* given in (22.2.12) is frequently called the *studentized residual.*

Studentized residuals that have values that could reasonably have come from a t-distribution, say less than 2 in absolute value, are regarded as acceptable in terms of the model specification. Others are regarded as outliers. Outliers can, of course, arise normally in the course of a model, but they may be worth checking for unmodeled aspects that are peculiar to that particular observation. Alternatively, too many outliers may cast doubt on the normality assumption, in which case robust estimation techniques might be appropriate.

The expressions in (22.2.12) and (22.2.13) are not computationally convenient because they involve as many regressions as there are observations. Alternative, more convenient expressions that only involve one least squares regression on all T observations can be derived. Using the result

$$[X(t)'X(t)]^{-1} = (X'X)^{-1} + \frac{(X'X)^{-1}\mathbf{x}_t\mathbf{x}_t'(X'X)^{-1}}{1 - h_t} \tag{22.2.14}$$

it is possible to show that (see Exercise 22.1)

$$e_t^* = \frac{\hat{e}_t}{\hat{\sigma}(t)(1 - h_t)^{1/2}} \tag{22.2.15}$$

and

$$\hat{\sigma}^2(t) = \frac{(T - K)\hat{\sigma}^2}{T - K - 1} - \frac{\hat{e}_t^2}{(T - K - 1)(1 - h_t)} \tag{22.2.16}$$

Outliers and high leverage points can be an indication of exceptional data points that are worthy of further study. What is likely to be of more importance, however, is whether these points contribute significantly to the values of the coefficient estimates and the model predictions. Diagnostics designed for these two purposes have been suggested by Belsley, Kuh, and Welsch (1980), who called their diagnostics the DFBETAS and DFFITS.

22.2.2c DFBETAS

The contribution of the tth observation to the least squares estimator $\mathbf{b}$ is defined as the difference $\mathbf{b} - \mathbf{b}(t)$, which, using (22.2.14), can be shown to be equal to

$$\mathbf{b} - \mathbf{b}(t) = \frac{(X'X)^{-1}\mathbf{x}_t\hat{e}_t}{1 - h_t} \tag{22.2.17}$$

Since magnitudes of the elements in this vector depend on units of measurement, it is convenient to scale each of them by an appropriate standard deviation. The kth element, denoted by $b_k - b_k(t)$, is scaled by an estimate of the standard deviation of b_k, namely, the square root of the kth diagonal element of $\hat{\sigma}^2(t)(X'X)^{-1}$. If a_{kk} represents the kth diagonal element of $(X'X)^{-1}$, and c_{kt} represents the (k, t)th element in $C = (X'X)^{-1}X'$, then the scaled measure of the contribution of the tth observation to $\mathbf{b}$ is given by

$$\begin{aligned} \text{DFBETAS}_{kt} &= \frac{b_k - b_k(t)}{\hat{\sigma}(t)a_{kk}^{1/2}} \\ &= \frac{c_{kt}\hat{e}_t}{\hat{\sigma}(t)a_{kk}^{1/2}(1 - h_t)} \\ &= \frac{c_{kt}e_t^*}{[a_{kk}(1 - h_t)]^{1/2}} \end{aligned} \tag{22.2.18}$$

Given X, it is clear from (22.2.18) that DFBETAS_{kt} will be large if the studentized residual e_t^* is large and/or the leverage h_t is large.

The critical question when examining the DFBETAS_{kt} is how large does a value need to be before that observation is regarded as influential. Rather than use an "absolute cutoff" of approximately 2, which is the more conventional approach associated with standard hypothesis tests, Belsley, Kuh, and Welsch (1980, p. 28) argue that a "size-adjusted cutoff," which allows for the fact that single observations will have less effect as sample size grows, should be employed. They recommend further investigation of observations where

$$|\text{DFBETAS}_{kt}| > \frac{2}{T^{1/2}} \tag{22.2.19}$$

22.2.2d DFFITS

The final diagnostic that we consider is the contribution of the tth observation to the predictions of the model. Multiplying both sides of (22.2.17) by $\mathbf{x}_t'$, this contribution is given by

$$\hat{y}_t - \hat{y}_t(t) = \mathbf{x}_t'\mathbf{b} - \mathbf{x}_t'\mathbf{b}(t) = \frac{h_t \hat{e}_t}{1 - h_t} \tag{22.2.20}$$

Scaling this factor by the standard deviation of $\hat{y}_t$ estimated as $\hat{\sigma}(t)h_t^{1/2}$ yields the diagnostic

$$\begin{aligned}\text{DFFITS}_t &= \frac{\mathbf{x}_t'\mathbf{b} - \mathbf{x}_t'\mathbf{b}(t)}{\hat{\sigma}(t)h_t^{1/2}} \\ &= \frac{h_t^{1/2}\hat{e}_t}{\hat{\sigma}(t)(1 - h_t)} \\ &= \left(\frac{h_t}{1 - h_t}\right)^{1/2} e_t^*\end{aligned} \tag{22.2.21}$$

Again, it is clear that the contribution of the tth observation will be greater, the greater is h_t and/or e_t^*.

If $\hat{e}_t$ in (22.2.20) is replaced by $y_t - \hat{y}_t$, this expression can be written as

$$\hat{y}_t = (1 - h_t)\hat{y}_t(t) + h_t y_t \tag{22.2.22}$$

Equation 22.2.22 gives another way of viewing the influence of the tth observation. It indicates that the fitted value for y based on all T observations is a weighted average of the actual observation y_t and the fitted value based on the remaining $(T - 1)$ observations. The greater the leverage of the tth observation, the greater is the weight placed on y_t.

As a size-adjusted cutoff that is suggestive of an influential observation, Belsley, Kuh, and Welsch (1980) recommend

$$|\text{DFFITS}_t| > 2\left(\frac{K}{T}\right)^{1/2} \tag{22.2.23}$$

An example illustrating the use of this and the other diagnostics introduced in this section will be given in Section 22.5. For further reading in this area we recommend Hoaglin and Welsch (1978), Belsley, Kuh, and Welsch (1980), Cook and Weisberg (1980), Krasker and Welsch (1982), and Krasker, Kuh, and Welsch (1983). The last two references also deal with the robust estimation technique known as bounded influence regression.

22.3 Estimation under Multivariate *t* Errors

One way of approaching the problem of model specification when outliers are prevalent is to assume the errors follow a distribution with relatively thick tails. In this regard a natural candidate is the *t*-distribution, which is similar in shape to the more traditional normal distribution, except that it has thicker tails. Suppose, therefore, that we are interested in maximum likelihood estimation of $\boldsymbol{\beta}$ in the model

$$\mathbf{y} = X\boldsymbol{\beta} + \mathbf{e} \tag{22.3.1}$$

where the usual notation holds, but where the error vector $\mathbf{e}$ follows a multivariate *t*-distribution. To make more explicit assumptions about $\mathbf{e}$ we need to distinguish between two cases, one where the elements in $\mathbf{e}$ are independent and one where the elements in $\mathbf{e}$ are uncorrelated, but not independent. With the normal distribution the assumption of uncorrelated errors is synonymous with independent errors. That is, $E[e_t e_s] = 0$ $(t \neq s)$ implies $f(e_t, e_s) = f(e_t)f(e_s)$, and vice versa, where $f(.)$ denotes the probability density function. Such is not the case with multivariate t errors, however.

The uncorrelated case has been considered in detail by Zellner (1976). He assumes that the probability density function for $\mathbf{e}$ is given by

$$f_T(\mathbf{e}\,|\,\nu, \sigma) = c_T(\nu\sigma^2 + \mathbf{e}'\mathbf{e})^{-(T+\nu)/2} \tag{22.3.2}$$

where c_T is the normalizing constant, ν is the degrees of freedom parameter, and the mean and covariance matrix for $\mathbf{e}$ are given by $E[\mathbf{e}] = \mathbf{0}$ (for $\nu > 1$) and $E[\mathbf{ee}'] = [\nu/(\nu - 2)]\sigma^2 I_T$ (for $\nu > 2$), respectively. The elements in $\mathbf{e}$ are uncorrelated because $E[\mathbf{ee}']$ is a diagonal matrix; that is, $E[e_t e_s] = 0$ for $t \neq s$. These same elements are not independent, however, because

$$f_T(\mathbf{e}\,|\,\nu, \sigma) \neq \prod_{t=1}^{T} f_1(e_t\,|\,\nu, \sigma) \tag{22.3.3}$$

where $f_1(e_t\,|\,\nu, \sigma)$ is the marginal probability density function for a single element e_t; it is given by

$$f_1(e_t\,|\,\nu, \sigma) = c_1[\nu\sigma^2 + e_t^2]^{-(1+\nu)/2} \tag{22.3.4}$$

Zellner shows that, under these assumptions, the maximum likelihood estimator for $\boldsymbol{\beta}$ is the least squares estimator $\mathbf{b} = (X'X)^{-1}X'\mathbf{y}$, and the maximum likelihood estimator for σ^2 is $\tilde{\sigma}^2 = (\mathbf{y} - X\mathbf{b})'(\mathbf{y} - X\mathbf{b})/T$. The degrees of freedom parameter v is assumed to be known a priori. Furthermore, $\mathbf{b}$ follows a multivariate t-distribution with mean $E[\mathbf{b}] = \boldsymbol{\beta}$ (for $v > 1$) and covariance matrix

$$\Sigma_{\mathbf{b}} = E[(\mathbf{b} - \boldsymbol{\beta})(\mathbf{b} - \boldsymbol{\beta})'] = \frac{v\sigma^2}{v - 2}(X'X)^{-1} \qquad \text{for } v > 2 \tag{22.3.5}$$

Even though the elements of $\mathbf{e}$ are nonnormal and are not independent, tests and intervals based on the usual t- and F-statistics remain valid in finite samples. See Zellner (1976, pp. 401–402) for details.

The case where the elements in $\mathbf{e}$ are independent with marginal density functions given by (22.3.4) has been analyzed by Prucha and Kelejian (1984) and Kelejian and Prucha (1985). Under this set of assumptions the joint density function for $\mathbf{e}$ is given by

$$f_T^*(\mathbf{e}|v, \sigma) = \prod_{t=1}^{T} f_1(e_t|v, \sigma) \tag{22.3.6}$$

To further appreciate the distinction between this density function and that in (22.3.2), it is convenient to describe how the two error vectors might be generated. Let $\mathbf{u}' = (u_1, u_2, \ldots, u_T)$ represent T independent normal random variables with mean zero and variance σ^2, and let z be an independent χ^2 random variable with v degrees of freedom. Then, in (22.3.2), $\mathbf{e}$ is generated as

$$\mathbf{e}' = \frac{\mathbf{u}'}{(z/v)^{1/2}} = \left[\frac{u_1}{(z/v)^{1/2}}, \frac{u_2}{(z/v)^{1/2}}, \ldots, \frac{u_T}{(z/v)^{1/2}}\right] \tag{22.3.7}$$

For (22.3.6) we consider T independent $\chi^2_{(v)}$ random variables $(z_1, z_2, \ldots, z_T)$, that are also independent of $\mathbf{u}$. Then in this case,

$$\mathbf{e}' = \left[\frac{u_1}{(z_1/v)^{1/2}}, \frac{u_2}{(z_2/v)^{1/2}}, \ldots, \frac{u_T}{(z_T/v)^{1/2}}\right] \tag{22.3.8}$$

Prucha and Kelejian show that, when the errors are independent, the maximum likelihood estimator for $\boldsymbol{\beta}$ denoted by $\tilde{\boldsymbol{\beta}}_*$, is the solution to the following four equations

$$\tilde{\boldsymbol{\beta}}_* = (X'\hat{W}X)^{-1}X'\hat{W}\mathbf{y} \tag{22.3.9}$$

$$\hat{W} = \text{diagonal}\,(\hat{w}_1, \hat{w}_2, \ldots, \hat{w}_T) \tag{22.3.10}$$

$$\hat{w}_t = [1 + (y_t - \mathbf{x}_t'\tilde{\boldsymbol{\beta}}_*)^2/v\tilde{\sigma}_*^2]^{-1} \tag{22.3.11}$$

$$v\tilde{\sigma}_*^2 = \frac{(v + 1)(\mathbf{y} - X\tilde{\boldsymbol{\beta}}_*)'(\mathbf{y} - X\tilde{\boldsymbol{\beta}}_*)}{T} \tag{22.3.12}$$

Given that $\lim_{T\to\infty} T^{-1}X'X$ is finite and nonsingular, the limiting distribution of $T^{1/2}(\tilde{\boldsymbol{\beta}}_* - \boldsymbol{\beta})$ is normal with zero mean vector; the "asymptotic covariance matrix" for $\tilde{\boldsymbol{\beta}}_*$ is

$$\Sigma_{\tilde{\boldsymbol{\beta}}*} = \frac{(v+3)\sigma^2}{v+1}(X'X)^{-1} \tag{22.3.13}$$

A comparison of this covariance matrix with that for $\mathbf{b}$ in (22.3.5) yields

$$\Sigma_{\tilde{\boldsymbol{\beta}}*} = \alpha\Sigma_{\mathbf{b}} \tag{22.3.14}$$

where

$$\alpha = \frac{(v-2)(v+3)}{v(v+1)} < 1 \tag{22.3.15}$$

Thus, the vector $\boldsymbol{\beta}$ can be estimated more precisely when the errors are independent rather than just uncorrelated. Also, if we assume the errors are independent when in fact they are just uncorrelated, we will be underestimating the variance of our estimates. For more details, see Kelejian and Prucha (1985).

The performance of Stein and modified Stein-like estimators under multivariate t errors has been investigated by Judge, Miyazaki, and Yancey (1985) and Miyazaki, Judge, and Yancey (1986). Using a quadratic loss criterion, they find that the Stein-like estimators generally dominate the maximum likelihood estimators as well as some more robust procedures such as the minimum absolute deviation estimator and trimmed least squares. These last two estimators form part of the next section.

22.4 Estimation Using Regression Quantiles

In Section 22.1.2 we discussed the effects of nonnormality of the disturbances when the nonnormal distribution has infinite variance or is characterized by a relatively large proportion of outliers. The possible existence of this, or some other type of nonnormal distribution of the disturbances, has led to a search for estimators that are more "robust" than least squares in the sense that they are reasonably efficient irrespective of the form of the underlying distribution. A large number of estimators has been suggested, and a considerable body of literature has developed. The robust estimators developed in this literature can generally be classified as M-estimators, L-estimators, or R-estimators. We will be concerned with a class of estimators that belongs to the category of L-estimators. For a survey of the other estimators and access to the general literature see Judge, et al. (1985, Chapter 20).

To introduce the concept of a regression quantile, let us consider the simple location model

$$y_t = \beta + e_t \tag{22.4.1}$$

where the y_t are independent identically distributed random variables with symmetric distribution function F and median β. It is not necessary to assume that the mean and variance of F exist. The title L-estimators is used for estimators that are linear combinations of the order statistics $y_{(1)}, y_{(2)}, \ldots, y_{(T)}$. Sample quantiles, which are to be defined shortly, are special cases of such linear combinations.

If F is continuous, then its θth quantile $(0 < \theta < 1)$, denoted by ξ_θ, is that value of y for which $P(y < \xi_\theta) = F(\xi_\theta) = \theta$. If θT is not an integer, the θth *sample quantile* is $y_{(n)}$, where $n = [\theta T] + 1$, and the quantity $[\theta T]$ denotes the greatest integer not exceeding θT. If θT is an integer, then the θth sample quantile is not unique and is taken as any value between $y_{(\theta T)}$ and $y_{(\theta T+1)}$. For example, in (22.4.1), $\xi_{0.5} = \beta$ is the median and, if $T = 25$ (say), $y_{(13)}$ is the sample median. For $T = 24$ the sample median is any value between $y_{(12)}$ and $y_{(13)}$, but usually some rule, such as median $= (y_{(12)} + y_{(13)})/2$, is used to obtain a unique value. Thus, the sample quantiles, and any linear function of them, are L-estimators of location. In addition to the median, examples of L-estimators that have been suggested are the Gastwirth (1966)

$$\hat{\beta}_G = 0.3\hat{\xi}_{1/3} + 0.4\hat{\xi}_{0.5} + 0.3\hat{\xi}_{2/3} \tag{22.4.2}$$

where $\hat{\xi}_\theta$ is the θth sample quantile; and the trimmed mean that is the sample mean of all observations lying between two quantiles, say $\hat{\xi}_\alpha$ and $\hat{\xi}_{1-\alpha}$.

When we consider the more general linear model, our usual concept of order statistics is no longer adequate because what constitutes an appropriate ordering depends on the vector $\boldsymbol{\beta}$. One possible approach is to obtain the residuals from a preliminary fit (such as least squares or least absolute values) and to estimate the quantiles of the error distribution on the basis of these residuals. A more appealing approach, however, is that suggested by Koenker and Bassett (1978). They begin by noting that, in the location model, the θth sample quantile can be equivalently defined as any solution to the following minimization problem.

$$\min_{\beta} \left[\sum_{\{t|y_t \geq \beta\}} \theta |y_t - \beta| + \sum_{\{t|y_t < \beta\}} (1-\theta)|y_t - \beta| \right] \tag{22.4.3}$$

To demonstrate the equivalence, consider the following ordered sample

$$\begin{array}{lll} y_{(1)} = 2 & y_{(2)} = 3 & y_{(3)} = 5 \\ y_{(4)} = 8 & y_{(5)} = 9 & y_{(6)} = 9 \\ y_{(7)} = 11 & y_{(8)} = 12 & y_{(9)} = 15 \end{array}$$

To obtain, say, an estimate of the 0.25 quantile, we take

$$n = [\theta T] + 1 = [0.25 \times 9] + 1 = 2 + 1 = 3$$

and our estimate is

$$\hat{\xi}_{0.25} = y_{(3)} = 5$$

Table 22.1 contains values of the objective function specified in (22.4.3) for various values of β and for $\theta = 0.25$. It is clear from this table that 5 is indeed the minimizing value. You are encouraged to verify the entries in this table.

The minimization problem defined in (22.4.3) as a means for finding the θth sample quantile readily extends to the more general case. If we have the linear model

$$y_t = \mathbf{x}_t'\boldsymbol{\beta} + e_t \tag{22.4.4}$$

where the e_t are independent and identically distributed with distribution function F, that is symmetric around zero, and the other notation is identical to that used previously, then the θth *regression quantile* $(0 < \theta < 1)$ is defined as any solution to the minimization problem,

$$\min_{\boldsymbol{\beta}} \left[\sum_{\{t|y_t \geq \mathbf{x}_t'\boldsymbol{\beta}\}} \theta |y_t - \mathbf{x}_t'\boldsymbol{\beta}| + \sum_{\{t|y_t < \mathbf{x}_t'\boldsymbol{\beta}\}} (1-\theta)|y_t - \mathbf{x}_t'\boldsymbol{\beta}| \right] \tag{22.4.5}$$

When $K = 1$ and $x_{t1} \equiv 1$, (22.4.5) reduces to (22.4.3). Also, for $\theta = 1/2$, (22.4.5) is equivalent to minimizing $\Sigma_t|y_t - \mathbf{x}_t'\boldsymbol{\beta}|$, and the resulting estimator is often known as the least absolute value or l_1-estimator. We discuss this estimator in more detail in Section 22.4.1. The minimization problem in (22.4.5) is a linear programming problem whose computational aspects are discussed in Koenker and Bassett (1978), Bassett and Koenker (1982), and Koenker and D'Orey (1987).

Table 22.1 Function Values Associated with the 0.25 Quantile

β	$\sum_{\{t\|y_t \geq \beta\}} \theta\|y_t - \beta\|$	$\sum_{\{t\|y_t < \beta\}} (1-\theta)\|y_t - \beta\|$	Function value
2	14.00	0	14.00
3	12.00	0.75	12.75
4	10.25	2.25	12.50
5	8.50	3.75	12.25
6	7.00	6.00	13.00
7	5.50	8.25	13.75
8	4.00	10.50	14.50
9	2.75	13.50	16.25
10	2.00	18.00	20.00

A number of properties of the estimators $\hat{\boldsymbol{\beta}}^*(\theta)$ that are solutions to (22.4.5) are outlined in Koenker and Bassett (1978), and properties of the empirical quantile functions are studied further in Bassett and Koenker (1982, 1986) and Koenker and Bassett (1982a). We will report just the asymptotic distribution results for $\hat{\boldsymbol{\beta}}^*(\theta)$. It is convenient to define $\boldsymbol{\beta}^*(\theta) = (\beta_1^*(\theta), \beta_2, \beta_3, \ldots, \beta_K)'$, where $\beta_1^*(\theta) = \beta_1 + \xi_\theta$ and $\xi_\theta = F^{-1}(\theta)$ is the θth quantile of the error distribution. We assume that $x_{t1} \equiv 1$, so $\boldsymbol{\beta}^*(\theta)$ is identical to $\boldsymbol{\beta}$ except for an adjustment to the intercept, with the adjustment equal to the θth quantile. Note that, in the case of the median, we have $\xi_{0.5} = 0$ and $\boldsymbol{\beta}^*(0.5) = \boldsymbol{\beta}$. Let $\hat{\boldsymbol{\delta}}' = (\hat{\boldsymbol{\beta}}^{*\prime}(\theta_1), \hat{\boldsymbol{\beta}}^{*\prime}(\theta_2), \ldots, \hat{\boldsymbol{\beta}}^{*\prime}(\theta_M))$ with $0 < \theta_1 < \theta_2 < \cdots < \theta_M < 1$ denote a sequence of unique regression quantile estimates, and, correspondingly, let $\boldsymbol{\delta}' = [\boldsymbol{\beta}^{*\prime}(\theta_1), \boldsymbol{\beta}^{*\prime}(\theta_2), \ldots, \boldsymbol{\beta}^{*\prime}(\theta_M)]$. Then, it can be shown that

$$\sqrt{T}(\hat{\boldsymbol{\delta}} - \boldsymbol{\delta}) \xrightarrow{d} N(\mathbf{0}, \Omega \otimes Q^{-1}) \tag{22.4.6}$$

where

(i) Ω has typical element

$$\omega_{ij} = \frac{\min(\theta_i, \theta_j) - \theta_i\theta_j}{f(\xi_{\theta_i})f(\xi_{\theta_j})} \tag{22.4.7}$$

(ii) F has density function f that is assumed to be continuous and positive at ξ_{θ_i}, $i = 1, 2, \ldots, M$; and

(iii) $\lim T^{-1}X'X = Q$ is a positive definite matrix.

Necessary and sufficient conditions for the uniqueness of $\hat{\boldsymbol{\delta}}$ are given by Koenker and Bassett (1978). Uniqueness can always be achieved by selecting an appropriate design or by using an arbitrary rule to select from any set of multiple solutions. Note that, apart from the intercept term, $\hat{\boldsymbol{\beta}}^*(\theta_1), \hat{\boldsymbol{\beta}}^*(\theta_2), \ldots, \hat{\boldsymbol{\beta}}^*(\theta_M)$ can all be regarded as alternative estimators for the same coefficient vector $\boldsymbol{\beta}$. In the following subsections we use some special cases to indicate how approximate inference procedures can be based on the result in (22.4.6).

22.4.1 l_1 – Estimation

As mentioned previously, when $\theta = 1/2$, the minimization problem in (22.4.5) is equivalent to finding that $\boldsymbol{\beta}$ that minimizes $\Sigma|y_t - \mathbf{x}_t'\boldsymbol{\beta}|$. This estimator, $\hat{\boldsymbol{\beta}}^*(0.5)$, is sometimes referred to as the l_1-estimator since it is a special case of the l_p-estimator that minimizes $\Sigma_t|y_t - \mathbf{x}_t'\boldsymbol{\beta}|^p$. It has also been called the least absolute value (LAV) estimator, the least absolute residual (LAR) estimator, the least absolute error (LAE) estimator, and the minimum absolute deviation (MAD) estimator. See Dielman and Pfaffenberger (1982) for a review of computational algorithms, small-sample (Monte Carlo) properties, and asymptotic properties.

With respect to the statistical properties of $\hat{\boldsymbol{\beta}}^*(0.5)$, we first note [see Blattberg and Sargent (1971)] that, if the disturbances follow a two-tailed exponential distribution with density function

$$f(e_t) = (2\lambda)^{-1} \exp\left\{-\frac{|e_t|}{\lambda}\right\} \tag{22.4.8}$$

then maximization of the likelihood function is equivalent to minimization of $\Sigma_{t=1}^{T}|e_t|$ so $\hat{\boldsymbol{\beta}}^*(0.5)$ will be the maximum likelihood estimator. Relative to the normal distribution this density is more peaked and has fatter tails, but unlike many other distributions with fat tails, it does have a finite variance. The maximum likelihood estimator thus has the usual desirable asymptotic properties. Also, the superiority of $\hat{\boldsymbol{\beta}}^*(0.5)$ over LS in finite samples, when the errors follow the density in (22.4.8) was confirmed in a Monte Carlo study by Smith and Hall (1972).

For the more general case where e_t comes from any distribution, some results on unbiasedness have been provided by Sielken and Hartley (1973) and Taylor (1974). The estimator will be unbiased if it is a unique solution to the minimization problem; alternatively, if multiple solutions exist, unbiasedness can be obtained by using Sielken and Hartley's algorithm.

The limiting distribution of $\hat{\boldsymbol{\beta}}^*(0.5)$ is given by considering the appropriate subvector of $\hat{\boldsymbol{\delta}}$ in (22.4.6). In particular, ω_{ij} becomes $[2f(0)]^{-2}$ and we have

$$\sqrt{T}[\hat{\boldsymbol{\beta}}^*(0.5) - \boldsymbol{\beta}] \xrightarrow{d} N(\mathbf{0}, [2f(0)]^{-2}Q^{-1}) \tag{22.4.9}$$

where $f(0)$ is the value of the density at the median [Bassett and Koenker (1978)]. The term $[2f(0)]^{-2}$ is the asymptotic variance of the sample median from samples with distribution function F. Thus, the l_1-estimator will be more efficient than the least squares estimator for all error distributions where the median is superior to the mean as an estimator of location. This class of error distributions includes the Cauchy, the two-tailed exponential, and a number of other distributions where "outliers" are prevalent.

If the form of the density function $f(.)$ is known, it is straightforward to compute $f(0)$ and hence to obtain an approximation of the covariance matrix for $\hat{\boldsymbol{\beta}}^*(0.5)$. However, the whole point of using the l_1-estimator is to guard against the possibility of some unknown error distribution that yields frequent outliers. Under these circumstances, $f(0)$ needs to be estimated. Such estimation can be troublesome, but one possible consistent estimator [see Cox and Hinkley (1974, p. 470)] is

$$\hat{f}(0) = \frac{2d}{T(\hat{e}_{(m+d)} - \hat{e}_{(m-d)})} \tag{22.4.10}$$

where m and d are integers, $(\hat{e}_{(1)}, \hat{e}_{(2)}, \ldots, \hat{e}_{(T)})$ are the ordered l_1-residuals, and $\hat{e}_{(m)} = 0$ (with $m \approx T/2$) is a central l_1-residual. The best choice of d is not clear; it will depend on the smoothness of the empirical function and the number of observations. Because K of the residuals will be zero, caution must be exercised and the estimator is unlikely to be satisfactory for large (K/T).

Using the result in (22.4.9), and the estimator in (22.4.10), the construction of Wald statistics for testing hypotheses about $\boldsymbol{\beta}$ is straightforward. In addition, Koenker and Bassett (1982b) suggest tests that are analogous to the likelihood ratio (LR) and Lagrange multiplier (LM) tests, and which are also based on l_1-estimation methods. For testing a set of linear restrictions on $\boldsymbol{\beta}$, their LR statistic is

$$\lambda_{\text{LR}} = 2[2f(0)]^{-1}(S_R - S_U) \tag{22.4.11}$$

where S_U and S_R are the sums of the absolute values of the residuals in the unrestricted and restricted models, respectively. For the hypothesis $\boldsymbol{\beta}_2 = \mathbf{0}$ in the partitioning $y_t = \mathbf{x}_{t1}'\boldsymbol{\beta}_1 + \mathbf{x}_{t2}'\boldsymbol{\beta}_2 + e_t$, the LM statistic is

$$\lambda_{\text{LM}} = \mathbf{g}'D\mathbf{g} \tag{22.4.12}$$

where $\mathbf{g} = \Sigma_t \mathbf{x}_{t2} \operatorname{sign}(y_t - \mathbf{x}_{t1}'\tilde{\boldsymbol{\beta}}_1)$, $\tilde{\boldsymbol{\beta}}_1$ is the restricted l_1-estimator for $\boldsymbol{\beta}_1$, and D is the second diagonal block of $(X'X)^{-1}$ corresponding to the foregoing partitioning of $\mathbf{x}_t'\boldsymbol{\beta}$. Under the null hypothesis both statistics have limiting $\chi^2_{(J)}$-distributions, where J is the number of restrictions. The LM test has the advantage that it does not require estimation of $f(0)$. Koenker and Bassett (1982b) compare the asymptotic efficiency of the tests with that of the more conventional ones based on least squares residuals and suggest some finite sample correction factors. As expected, the tests based on l_1-estimation are more powerful for heavytailed distributions.

22.4.2 Linear Functions of Regression Quantiles

The l_1-estimator is, of course, one example of a linear function of regression quantiles where all the weight is placed on $\theta = 0.5$. It is also possible to construct estimators that are more general functions of the regression quantiles and that are analogous to some of the L-estimators suggested for the simple location model (see Equation 22.4.2). Consider the estimator

$$\hat{\boldsymbol{\beta}}(\boldsymbol{\pi}) = \sum_{i=1}^{M} \pi(\theta_i)\hat{\boldsymbol{\beta}}^*(\theta_i) \tag{22.4.13}$$

where $\boldsymbol{\pi} = [\pi(\theta_1), \pi(\theta_2), \ldots, \pi(\theta_M)]'$ is a symmetric weighting scheme, and the assumptions and notation used throughout this section still hold. Because both

$\pi(\theta_i)$ and the distribution of e_t are symmetric, we can treat $\hat{\boldsymbol{\beta}}(\boldsymbol{\pi})$ as an estimator for $\boldsymbol{\beta}$ rather than a particular $\boldsymbol{\beta}^*(\theta)$, and we have the result [Koenker and Bassett (1978)]

$$\sqrt{T}(\hat{\boldsymbol{\beta}}(\boldsymbol{\pi}) - \boldsymbol{\beta}) \xrightarrow{d} N(\mathbf{0}, \boldsymbol{\pi}'\Omega\boldsymbol{\pi}Q^{-1}) \tag{22.4.14}$$

Examples of weighting schemes are the Gastwirth scheme mentioned earlier where $\boldsymbol{\pi}' = [\pi(\frac{1}{3}), \pi(\frac{1}{2}), \pi(\frac{2}{3})] = (0.3, 0.4, 0.3)$, or the trimean suggested by Tukey, where $\boldsymbol{\pi}' = [\pi(\frac{1}{4}), \pi(\frac{1}{2}), \pi(\frac{3}{4})] = (0.25, 0.5, 0.25)$ or a "five quantile estimator" where $\boldsymbol{\pi}' = [\pi(0.1), \pi(0.25), \pi(0.5), \pi(0.75), \pi(0.9)] = (0.05, 0.25, 0.4, 0.25, 0.05)$. The result in (22.4.14) can be used to formulate approximate tests for testing hypotheses about $\boldsymbol{\beta}$, providing we substitute $X'X/T$ for Q and use a consistent estimator for the elements of Ω. For this latter estimator we need an estimator for $f(\xi_{\theta_i})$—see (22.4.7). Along the lines of (22.4.10) such an estimator is given by

$$\hat{f}(\xi_\theta) = \frac{2d}{T(\hat{e}_{(r)} - \hat{e}_{(s)})} \tag{22.4.15}$$

where $r = [T\theta] + d$, $s = [T\theta] - d$, and $\hat{e}_{(1)}, \hat{e}_{(2)}, \ldots, \hat{e}_{(T)}$ are the ordered l_1-residuals.

22.4.3 Trimmed Least Squares

An obvious analog to the trimmed mean of the simple location model is the trimmed least squares estimator suggested by Koenker and Bassett (1978) and studied further by Ruppert and Carroll (1980). To obtain this estimator we first calculate $\hat{\boldsymbol{\beta}}^*(\alpha)$ and $\hat{\boldsymbol{\beta}}^*(1-\alpha)$, where α is the desired trimming proportion ($0 < \alpha < 0.5$). Then, observations where $y_t - \mathbf{x}_t'\hat{\boldsymbol{\beta}}^*(\alpha) \le 0$ or $y_t - \mathbf{x}_t'\hat{\boldsymbol{\beta}}^*(1-\alpha) \ge 0$ are discarded, and least squares is applied to the remaining observations. Denoting this estimator by $\tilde{\boldsymbol{\beta}}_\alpha$, under appropriate conditions it can be shown that

$$\sqrt{T}(\tilde{\boldsymbol{\beta}}_\alpha - \boldsymbol{\beta}) \xrightarrow{d} N(\mathbf{0}, \sigma^2(\alpha, F)Q^{-1}) \tag{22.4.16}$$

where $\sigma^2(\alpha, F)$ denotes the asymptotic variance of the corresponding α-trimmed mean from a population with distribution F. A consistent estimator for $\sigma^2(\alpha, F)$ is given by

$$\hat{\sigma}^2(\alpha, F) = \frac{1}{(1-2\alpha)^2}\left(\frac{S}{T-K} + \alpha(c_1^2 + c_2^2) - \alpha^2(c_1 + c_2)^2\right) \tag{22.4.17}$$

where S is the sum of squares of residuals from the trimmed sample,

$$c_1 = \bar{\mathbf{x}}'[\hat{\boldsymbol{\beta}}^*(\alpha) - \tilde{\boldsymbol{\beta}}_\alpha] \qquad c_2 = \bar{\mathbf{x}}'[\hat{\boldsymbol{\beta}}^*(1-\alpha) - \tilde{\boldsymbol{\beta}}_\alpha] \tag{22.4.18}$$

and $\bar{\mathbf{x}}$ is a K-vector containing the means of the observations on the explanatory variables. Ruppert and Carroll find that $\tilde{\boldsymbol{\beta}}_\alpha$ is preferable to trimmed estimators where the trimming is based on a preliminary estimate such as the least squares or l_1-estimator. A further version of a trimmed least squares estimator that is asymptotically equivalent to $\tilde{\boldsymbol{\beta}}_\alpha$ and that has shown some promise in finite-sample Monte Carlo experiments has been suggested by Welsh (1987).

22.5 An Example

In this section we apply the methods discussed in earlier sections of this chapter to a linear model with independent errors generated from a t-distribution with 1 degree of freedom. In the Exercises at the end of the chapter you are invited to apply the techniques to a model with independent errors from a t-distribution with 3 degrees of freedom.

Consider the linear model

$$y_t = \beta_1 + \beta_2 x_{t2} + \beta_3 x_{t3} + e_t \tag{22.5.1}$$

where $\beta_1 = 0$, $\beta_2 = 1$, $\beta_3 = 1$, and the e_t are independent drawings from the t-distribution

$$f_1(e_t | v, \sigma) = c_1[v\sigma^2 + e_t^2]^{-(1+v)/2} \tag{22.5.2}$$

where the degrees of freedom parameter is $v = 1$, the scale parameter is $\sigma = 2$, and the normalizing constant is

$$\begin{aligned} c_1 &= \frac{\Gamma[(v+1)/2](v\sigma^2)^{v/2}}{\Gamma(\frac{1}{2})\Gamma(v/2)} \\ &= \frac{2}{\pi} \end{aligned} \tag{22.5.3}$$

The density function in (22.5.2) has a median of 0 but, because of its very thick tails, its mean and variance do not exist. A sample of size $T = 40$ was generated using the first 80 standard normal random variables provided in the Computer Handbook. Let $\mathbf{z}_1$ be a (40×1) vector containing the first 40 of these 80 random variables and let $\mathbf{z}_2$ be a (40×1) vector containing the second 40 of the 80 random variables. The tth random error was generated from

$$e_t = \frac{\sigma z_{1t}}{(z_{2t}^2)^{1/2}} \tag{22.5.4}$$

where z_{1t} and z_{2t} are the tth elements in $\mathbf{z}_1$ and $\mathbf{z}_2$ respectively. The values for y_t, x_{t2}, x_{t3}, and e_t are provided in Table 22.2. It is clear that, relative to the normal distribution, it is possible for the errors to take on some extreme values.

Table 22.2 Sample Observations for Model with $t_{(1)}$ Errors

t	y_t	x_{t2}	x_{t3}	e_t
1	106.72470	36.01905	70.52192	0.18368
2	79.27876	21.97229	57.90647	−0.60001
3	12.22471	28.26774	58.50037	−74.54341
4	107.04740	35.06003	63.25390	8.73345
5	147.53440	35.70615	57.61241	54.21581
6	83.86212	28.21484	52.42581	3.22146
7	116.78900	39.08357	75.98202	1.72340
8	96.47288	36.12773	55.71842	4.62673
9	101.73360	39.97100	72.36649	−10.60390
10	76.47594	27.32109	50.56393	−1.40908
11	116.01950	42.19799	73.56165	0.25988
12	65.89518	18.20580	47.04723	0.64216
13	103.27640	33.55657	62.93883	6.78101
14	87.28964	26.26375	56.96774	4.05814
15	76.76136	20.43152	57.69594	−1.36609
16	91.83980	37.83294	51.89209	2.11477
17	84.96762	28.53331	52.22245	4.21186
18	67.29960	17.08261	50.00941	0.20758
19	71.32692	22.43526	49.44603	−0.55438
20	150.22710	40.23658	76.62534	33.36515
21	65.96110	19.62467	52.71374	−6.37732
22	117.65400	46.69020	71.14258	−0.17878
23	105.04080	33.43455	71.00548	0.60074
24	80.47243	24.56063	58.01380	−2.10199
25	126.93280	39.09184	75.71716	12.12385
26	102.34520	36.97122	65.04496	0.32902
27	114.77520	41.26110	77.19905	−3.68500
28	98.09605	31.15756	65.53172	1.40677
29	70.02718	24.16146	49.94260	−4.07688
30	123.61340	42.51484	66.79185	14.30673
31	258.86120	30.68048	59.16228	169.01840
32	87.26062	32.72171	56.67232	−2.13342
33	114.28120	40.60360	71.36273	2.31490
34	112.94040	39.60135	74.99479	−1.65572
35	87.14891	32.41189	60.37341	−5.63638
36	99.64879	34.52499	63.68446	1.43934
37	90.78862	30.03809	59.90063	0.84990
38	92.88983	29.83473	62.41687	0.63823
39	75.47840	23.06305	50.17239	2.24296
40	107.73420	38.81063	69.07652	−0.15294

The parameters $(\beta_1, \beta_2, \beta_3)'$ were estimated using least squares, maximum likelihood estimation for independent t errors, various regression quantiles, and trimmed least squares. Before turning to these various estimates we will discuss some of the regression diagnostics that are based on least squares results. The value obtained for the Bera–Jarque test statistic for normally distributed errors was $\lambda = 671.7$; the 1% critical value from a $\chi^2_{(2)}$ distribution is 9.2. Thus, this test leads us to correctly conclude that the errors are not normally distributed.

Table 22.3 contains the errors, the least squares residuals, the studentized residuals, the leverage, the DFFITS, and the DFBETAS for some selected observations. The observations included in Table 22.3 are those for which at least one of the cutoffs were exceeded plus those that were discarded in the computation of the trimmed least squares estimator. The rule-of-thumb cutoffs described in Section 22.2.2 are

$$h_t > 2K/T = 0.15$$

$$|e_t^*| > 2$$

$$|\text{DFBETAS}_{kt}| > 2/T^{1/2} = 0.316$$

$$|\text{DFFITS}_t| > 2(K/T)^{1/2} = 0.548$$

On the basis of these rules, only four observations would attract more detailed scrutiny. They are observations 3, 5, 16, and 31. Observation 3 has a large residual

Table 22.3 Regression Diagnostics for Model with $t_{(1)}$ Errors[a]

t	e_t	$\hat{e}_t$	e_t^*	h_t	DFBETAS_{2t}	DFBETAS_{3t}	DFFITS_t
3	−74.5	−78.4	−2.72*	0.03	0.159	−0.030	−0.493
5	54.2	43.7	1.46	0.08	0.348*	−0.348*	0.439
9	−10.6	−17.1	−0.55*	0.06	−0.014	−0.052	−0.140
16	2.1	−13.1	−0.47	0.25*	−0.241	0.251	−0.273
18	0.2	1.4	0.05	0.13	−0.012	0.004	0.018
20	33.4	28.8	0.95	0.10	−0.069	0.212	0.316
21	−6.4	−5.9	−0.20	0.10	0.046	−0.018	−0.066
25	12.1	8.0	0.26	0.09	−0.024	0.060	0.084
27	−3.7	−8.8	−0.29	0.10	0.014	−0.061	−0.097
29	−4.1	−8.8	−0.29	0.07	−0.001	0.038	−0.078
30	14.3	2.8	0.09	0.09	0.024	−0.014	0.030
31	169.0	163.5	10.07*	0.03	0.126	−0.391*	1.691*
35	−5.6	−12.0	−0.38	0.03	−0.017	0.020	−0.064

[a] Those entries marked with * exceed the cutoffs $|e_t^*| > 2$, $h_t > 0.15$, $|\text{DFBETAS}_{kt}| > 0.316$, $|\text{DFFITS}_t| > 0.548$.

that, despite its magnitude, does not have an unacceptable influence on the coefficients and predictions. Conversely, the residual for observation 5 is large and has a noticeable effect on the coefficients, but is nevertheless acceptable using the e_t^* criterion. Observation 16 is one of high leverage, but, presumably because its error term is small, its influence on the coefficients and the predictions does not exceed the cutoffs. Finally, the large residual for observation 31 does make that observation influential in terms of both the coefficient values and the predictions.

Various estimates of the parameters and corresponding "standard errors" are presented in Table 22.4. Since the errors possess neither a mean nor a variance, the least squares estimates also have no mean nor variance. It is meaningless to say that the least squares estimates are unbiased; also, the least squares standard errors have no corresponding population parameters for which they are estimates. Similarly, it is not clear that the maximum likelihood estimates that were computed using (22.3.9) through (22.3.12) will possess any of their usual desirable asymptotic properties. Nevertheless, we report standard errors based on (22.3.13) and the estimator for σ^2 given in (22.3.12). In this regard, $v\hat{\sigma}_*^2 = \hat{\sigma}_*^2 = 1893.187$ and

$$\hat{\Sigma}_{\hat{\beta}*} = 3786.374(X'X)^{-1}$$

Coefficient estimates associated with five different regression quantiles, $\theta = \{0.1, 0.25, 0.5, 0.75, 0.9\}$, are also given in Table 22.4. In these cases the slope coefficient estimates are all alternative estimates for β_2 and β_3, but, with the exception of $\theta = 0.5$, the various intercept estimates are not alternative estimates for β_1. We would expect the various intercept estimates to increase as θ increases. Such an increase occurs for the first three quantiles but, for the last two, relatively large estimates for β_2 and β_3 seem to have led to a reduction in the intercept estimate. The estimates for $\theta = 0.5$ are, of course, least absolute deviation estimates. The

Table 22.4 Estimates and Standard Errors for Model with $t_{(1)}$ Errors

Estimator	β_1	β_2	β_3	se_1	se_2	se_3
True values	0.00	1.000	1.000			
Least squares	10.10	1.835	0.489	36.89	1.128	0.950
Maximum likelihood	−1.29	1.448	0.819	71.54	2.187	1.841
0.1 quantile	−2.12	1.373	0.780			
0.25 quantile	−2.07	1.116	0.950			
0.5 quantile	5.59	1.230	0.806	4.58	0.140	0.118
0.75 quantile	5.04	1.519	0.706			
0.9 quantile	−8.27	1.571	0.974			
Trimmed least squares	3.89	1.153	0.878	5.07	0.155	0.131

standard errors that are provided for the least absolute deviation estimator were based on (22.4.9) and (22.4.10). To find a value for the estimator for $f(0)$ given in (22.4.10), we begin by ordering the least absolute deviation residuals. These residuals are given in Table 22.5. Then, using $m = 20$ and $d = 6$, we have

$$\hat{f}(0) = \frac{12}{40[\hat{e}_{(26)} - \hat{e}_{(14)}]} = \frac{12}{40[1.106 - (-1.260)]} = 0.1268$$

If we use our knowledge that $f(.)$ is a t density with 1 degree of freedom we find, from (22.5.2) and (22.5.3), that $f(0) = 0.1592$. For the standard errors in Table 22.4 we assumed that such information is not available and used the estimated covariance matrix

$$[2\hat{f}(0)]^{-2}(X'X)^{-1} = 15.549(X'X)^{-1}$$

The estimates for each of the quantiles could be combined using the five quantile estimator described in Section 22.4.2.

The trimmed least squares estimates were obtained using a trimming proportion of $\alpha = 0.1$. Thus, residuals associated with the 0.1 and 0.9 regression quantiles were considered. The observations discarded were those where the residuals were nonpositive for $\theta = 0.1$ and nonnegative for $\theta = 0.9$. They were observations (3, 9, 21, 27, 29, 35) and (5, 18, 20, 25, 30, 31), from the quantiles $\theta = 0.1$ and $\theta = 0.9$, respectively. An examination of the errors in Tables 22.2 and 22.3 indicates that, with the exception of observation 18, all the discarded observations are, in a relative sense, outliers. The procedure has not picked up some of the "moderately sized outliers," such as observations 4 and 13, but it has certainly picked up all the very large ones. The trimmed least squares estimates are those estimates obtained

Table 22.5 Ordered l_1-residuals for $T = 40$

−75.276	−2.077	0.000	1.895
−11.339	−1.795	0.271	2.197
−6.961	−1.704	0.304	3.488
−6.245	−1.260	0.399	5.691
−5.528	−1.138	1.089	7.359
−4.248	−0.756	1.106	11.903
−3.779	−0.452	1.239	12.242
−3.467	−0.020	1.320	33.396
−2.699	0.000	1.373	51.597
−2.105	0.000	1.542	167.857

by applying least squares to the remaining observations. To obtain the standard errors we need to find $\hat{\sigma}^2(\alpha, F)$ which is given in (22.4.17). Toward this end we have

$$
\begin{aligned}
c_1 &= \bar{\mathbf{x}}'(\hat{\boldsymbol{\beta}}^*(0.1) - \tilde{\boldsymbol{\beta}}_{0.1}) \\
&= (1 \quad 32.157 \quad 61.854)\begin{bmatrix} -2.1209 - 3.8908 \\ 1.3729 - 1.1527 \\ 0.7804 - 0.8781 \end{bmatrix} \\
&= -4.97 \\
c_2 &= \bar{\mathbf{x}}'(\hat{\boldsymbol{\beta}}^*(0.9) - \tilde{\boldsymbol{\beta}}_{0.1}) \\
&= (1 \quad 32.157 \quad 61.854)\begin{bmatrix} -8.2747 - 3.8908 \\ 1.5712 - 1.1527 \\ 0.9745 - 0.8781 \end{bmatrix} \\
&= 7.26 \\
\hat{\sigma}^2(\alpha, F) &= \frac{1}{(0.8)^2}\left(\frac{166.73}{37} + (0.1)(77.371) - (0.1)^2(5.2)\right) \\
&= 19.049
\end{aligned}
$$

The standard errors in Table 22.4 are given by the square roots of the diagonal elements of 19.049 $(X'X)^{-1}$.

The "relative closeness" of the least absolute deviation and trimmed least squares estimates to the true parameter values, when compared with those of least squares and maximum likelihood, suggests that the robust techniques are more efficient. A comparison of the standard errors yields a similar conclusion. Since we are only dealing with one sample, and the standard errors are meaningless when the corresponding variances are infinite, such comparisons must be made with caution. However, it is gratifying when the results of one sample do turn out as expected. In the example considered in the Exercises (Section 22.7), where the errors follow a $t_{(3)}$ distribution, the least squares estimates do possess a finite mean and variance.

22.6 Summary and Guide to Further Reading

Whether the robust estimation techniques in general, or the techniques outlined in this chapter in particular, should be used in preference to the more conventional techniques outlined in the other chapters of this book, is largely an empirical question. The choice depends on whether error distributions with a large number of outliers are the exception or the rule. The proponents of robust estimation argue strongly for its universal adoption. It is more reasonable, however, to regard such techniques as useful under particular circumstances, rather than as an econometric panacea. This view is supported by the relative scarcity of robust estimation in empirical work, although this relative scarcity could be partly explained by the lack of widespread computer programs. Many questions remain. For example, what are the properties of the estimators when the errors are no longer independent and identically distributed? Is the asymptotic theory likely to hold in finite samples of reasonable size? Are suggested covariance matrix estimators satisfactory? If robust techniques are only applied after a preliminary test for outliers, what are the properties of the resulting estimators?

Given the vastness of the literature on nonnormality and robust estimation, the material we have presented only scratches the surface. Nevertheless, what we have presented should serve as a useful introduction to most of the techniques that have gained practical acceptance in econometrics. For further reading and access to the literature we recommend Judge, et al. (1985, Chapter 20) for an overview; White and MacDonald (1980) for tests for normality; Belsley, Kuh, and Welsch (1980), Pagan and Hall (1983), and Pagan (1984) for diagnostic testing and the detection of influential observations; Zellner (1976) and Kelejian and Prucha (1985) for estimation with multivariate t errors; and Huber (1981), Koenker (1982), and Welsch (1987) for robust estimation.

22.7 Exercises

22.1 Prove the results in Equations 22.2.14, 22.2.15, 22.2.16, 22.2.17, and 22.2.22.

Problems 22.2–22.5

Consider the linear model

$$y_t = \beta_1 + \beta_2 x_{t2} + \beta_3 x_{t3} + e_t \tag{22.7.1}$$

where $\beta_1 = 0$, $\beta_2 = 1$, $\beta_3 = 1$, and the e_t are independent drawings from a t-distribution with degrees of freedom $v = 3$ and scale parameter $\sigma = 2$. Table 22.6 contains a sample of $T = 20$ observations on y_t, x_{t2}, x_{t3}, and e_t. The e_t were generated using the first 80 standard normal random variables provided in the Computer Handbook. Let $\mathbf{z}_1$, $\mathbf{z}_2$, $\mathbf{z}_3$, and $\mathbf{z}_4$ be (20×1) vectors containing the first

Table 22.6 Sample Data for Model with $t_{(3)}$ Errors

t	y_t	x_{t2}	x_{t3}	e_t
1	106.79600	36.01905	70.52192	0.25501
2	79.22699	21.97229	57.90647	−0.65178
3	82.40919	28.26774	58.50037	−4.35893
4	98.83046	35.06003	63.25390	0.51653
5	95.63303	35.70615	57.61241	2.31446
6	84.93408	28.21484	52.42581	4.29343
7	116.58020	39.08357	75.98202	1.51463
8	94.88590	36.12773	55.71842	3.03975
9	111.15720	39.97100	72.36649	−1.18030
10	76.07429	27.32109	50.56393	−1.81073
11	116.11700	42.19799	73.56165	0.35740
12	65.92394	18.20580	47.04723	0.67091
13	97.26613	33.55657	62.93883	0.77072
14	83.91416	26.26375	56.96774	0.68266
15	77.41599	20.43152	57.69594	−0.71147
16	92.85494	37.83294	51.89209	3.12991
17	83.95351	28.53331	52.22245	3.19775
18	67.29753	17.08261	50.00941	0.20551
19	71.18548	22.43526	49.44603	−0.69582
20	120.18020	40.23658	76.62534	3.31833

20, second 20, third 20, and fourth 20 normal random variables, respectively. The tth random error was generated from

$$e_t = \frac{\sigma z_{1t}}{[(z_{2t}^2 + z_{3t}^2 + z_{4t}^2)/3]^{1/2}} \tag{22.7.2}$$

where z_{it} is the tth element in $\mathbf{z}_i$.

22.2 Compute the true (asymptotic) covariance matrices for the following estimators.

(a) The least squares estimator.

(b) The maximum likelihood estimator.

(c) The least absolute deviations estimator.

(d) The estimator $\hat{\boldsymbol{\beta}}(\boldsymbol{\pi}) = 0.3\hat{\boldsymbol{\beta}}^*(0.25) + 0.4\hat{\boldsymbol{\beta}}^*(0.5) + 0.3\hat{\boldsymbol{\beta}}^*(0.75)$.

(e) The trimmed least squares estimator with $\alpha = 0.1$. [See Ruppert and Carroll (1980, p. 830).]

Comment on the relative efficiencies of the different estimators.

22.3 Use the Jarque–Bera Lagrange multiplier test to test for normally distributed errors.

22.4 Find the leverage, studentized residuals, DFBETAS, and DFFITS for each observation. Identify any observations that might be influential.

22.5 Find estimates of $(\beta_1, \beta_2, \beta_3)'$ using each of the estimators described in Exercise 22.2. Find also the appropriate standard errors. Comment on the quality of each set of coefficient estimates and on the quality of the standard errors as estimates of quantities computed in Exercise 22.2.

22.8 References

Bassett, G., and R. Koenker (1978) "Asymptotic Theory of Least Absolute Error Regression." *Journal of the American Statistical Association*, 73, 618–622.

Bassett, G., and R. Koenker (1982) "An Empirical Quantile Function for Linear Models with iid Errors." *Journal of the American Statistical Association*, 77, 407–415.

Bassett, G. W. and R. W. Koenker (1986) "Strong Consistency of Regression Quantiles and Related Empirical Processes." *Econometric Theory*, 2, 191–201.

Belsley, D. A., E. Kuh, and R. E. Welsch (1980) *Regression Diagnostics: Identifying Influential Data and Sources of Collinearity*. New York, Wiley.

Bera, A. K., and C. M. Jarque (1981) "An Efficient Large-Sample Test for Normality of Observations and Regression Residuals." Australian National University Working Papers in Econometrics No. 40, Canberra.

Blattberg, R. C., and T. Sargent (1971) "Regression with Non-Gaussian Stable Disturbances: Some Sampling Results." *Econometrica*, 39, 501–510.

Cook, R. D., and S. Weisberg (1980) "Characterizations of an Empirical Influence Function for Detecting Influential Cases in Regression." *Technometrics*, 22, 495–508.

Cox, D. R., and D. V. Hinkley (1974) *Theoretical Statistics*. London, Chapman and Hall.

Dielman, T., and R. Pfaffenberger (1982) "LAV (Least Absolute Value) Estimation in Linear Regression: A Review." *TIMS Studies in the Management Sciences*, 19, 31–52.

Gastwirth, J. L. (1966) "On Robust Procedures." *Journal of the American Statistical Association*, 61, 929–948.

Hoaglin, D. C. and R. E. Welsch (1978) "The Hat Matrix in Regression and ANOVA." *The American Statistician*, 32, 17–22.

Huang, C. J., and B. W. Bolch (1974) "On the Testing of Regression Disturbances for Normality." *Journal of the American Statistical Association*, 69, 330–335.

Huber, P. J. (1981) *Robust Statistics*. New York, Wiley.

Judge, G. G., W. E. Griffiths, R. C. Hill, H. Lütkepohl, and T. C. Lee (1985) *The Theory and Practice of Econometrics*, 2nd ed. New York, Wiley.

Judge, G. G., S. Miyazaki, and T. Yancey (1985) "Minimax Estimators for the Location Vectors of Spherically Symmetric Densities." *Econometric Theory*, 1, 409–418.

Kelejian, H. H., and I. R. Prucha (1985) "Independent or Uncorrelated Disturbances in Linear Regression: An Illustration of the Difference." *Economics Letters*, 19, 35–38.

Koenker, R. W. (1982) "Robust Methods in Econometrics." *Econometric Reviews*, 1, 213–290.

Koenker, R. W., and G. W. Bassett (1978). "Regression Quantiles." *Econometrica*, 46, 33–50.

Koenker, R. W., and G. W. Bassett (1982a) "Robust Tests for Heteroscedasticity Based on Regression Quantiles." *Econometrica*, 50, 43–62.

Koenker, R. W., and G. W. Bassett (1982b) "Tests of Linear Hypotheses and l_1 Estimation." *Econometrica*, 50, 1577–1583.

Koenker, R. W., and V. D'Orey (1987) "Computing Regression Quantiles." *Applied Statistics*, 36, 383–393.

Krasker, W. S., E. Kuh, and R. E. Welsch (1983) "Estimation for Dirty Data and Flawed Models." In Z. Griliches and M. D. Intriligator (eds.) *Handbook of Econometrics*, vol. 1, Amsterdam, North-Holland, pp. 652–698.

Krasker, W. S., and R. E. Welsch (1982) "Efficient Bounded-Influence Regression Estimation." *Journal of the American Statistical Association*, 77, 595–605.

Malinvaud, E. (1980) *Statistical Methods in Econometrics*, 3rd ed. Amsterdam, North-Holland.

Miyazaki, S., G. Judge, and T. Yancey (1986) "Estimation of Location Parameters Under Nonnormal Errors and Quadratic Loss." *Journal of Business and Economic Statistics*, 4, 263–268.

Mood, A. M., F. A. Graybill, and D. C. Boes (1974) *Introduction to the Theory of Statistics*. Tokyo, McGraw-Hill.

Pagan, A. R. (1984) "Model Evaluation by Variable Addition." In D. F. Hendry and K. F. Wallis (eds.) *Econometrics and Quantitative Economics*. Oxford, Basil Blackwell.

Pagan, A. R., and A. D. Hall, (1983) "Diagnostic Tests as Residual Analysis." *Econometric Reviews*, 2, 159–218.

Prucha, I. R., and H. H. Kelejian (1984) "The Structure of Simultaneous Equation Estimators: A Generalization Toward Nonnormal Disturbances." *Econometrica*, 52, 721–736.

Ruppert, D., and J. Carroll (1980) "Trimmed Least Squares Estimation in the Linear Model." *Journal of the American Statistical Association*, 75, 828–838.

Shapiro, S. S., M. B. Wilk, and H. J. Chen (1968) "A Comparative Study of Various Tests of Normality." *Journal of the American Statistical Association*, 63, 1343–1372.

Sielken, R. L., and H. O. Hartley (1973) "Two Linear Programming Algorithms for Unbiased Estimation of Linear Models." *Journal of the American Statistical Association*, 68, 639–641.

Smith, V. K., and T. W. Hall (1972) "A Comparison of Maximum Likelihood Versus BLUE Estimators." *The Review of Economics and Statistics*, 54, 186–190.

Taylor, L. D. (1974) "Estimation by Minimizing the Sum of Absolute Errors." In P. Zarembka (ed.) *Frontiers in Econometrics*, New York, Academic Press.

Welsch, A. H. (1987) "The Trimmed Mean in the Linear Model." *The Annals of Statistics*, 15, 20–36.

White, H., and G. M. MacDonald (1980) "Some Large-Sample Tests for Nonnormality in the Linear Regression Model." *Journal of the American Statistical Association*, 75, 16–28.

Zellner, A. (1976) "Bayesian and Non-Bayesian Analysis of the Regression Model with Multivariate Student-t Error Terms." *Journal of the American Statistical Association*, 71, 400–405.

PART 7

Epilogue

In the preceding chapters we have considered a wide array of statistical models, estimators, and tests that may be used as a basis for learning from a sample of data. We have stressed throughout the book the necessity of the consistency between the sampling process by which the data are generated and the statistical models used as the basis for estimation and inference. We have also emphasized the statistical consequences of alternative ways of modeling economic data, and we have focused on the necessity of evaluating the sampling performance of the alternative rules and tests. We have presented both the sampling theory and Bayesian approaches to inference and have attempted to identify the strong and weak points of each. Although not exhaustive, the topics covered in this book should help give a limited impression of the state of econometrics. However, the statistical models, estimation rules, test statistics, and sets of procedures for learning from economic data that have been covered in this book are but a partial listing of the knowledge boxes on the econometric shelf. New additions to knowledge in the area of econometrics will continue to be brought about by (1) changing the statistical model, (2) changing the amount of information used, and (3) changing the basis by which estimator performance is measured. Thus some of the simplified truths we have discussed will have short lives.

Although the trek we have taken down the sampling model-estimation rule road provides a firm foundation from which to search for quantitative economic knowledge, to analyze many sets of economic data effectively, the models, rules, and inferential bases must be extended or, in some instances, completely revised. In many cases we have suggested or identified sources in the econometric literature where these extensions and revisions may be found. To cope with the other cases, where answers may not be readily available, we have tried to provide you with the econometric background to be a creative participant in the experiment in non-experimental model building and inference.

APPENDIX A

Linear Algebra and Matrix Methods Relevant to Normal Distribution Theory

Econometric theory draws heavily on the mainstream of mathematical statistics, with distinct features of using nonexperimental data and a priori economic knowledge. In many areas of economics, matrix algebra serves as a convenient and powerful notation. In mathematical statistics, matrix algebra is virtually a necessity. It avoids the use of cumbersome summation operation notation and simplifies complex mathematical expressions into neat, compact, and yet comprehensible shorthand expressions. The short and clear expression of matrix algebra enables us to concentrate on the main econometric topics of interest, without being lost in the jungle of mathematics.

The objective of this appendix is to provide some basic definitions and concepts underlying the linear algebra on which we rely in the development of the theory and practice of econometrics. The treatment in this appendix hardly constitutes a rigorous introduction to linear algebra. However, in some cases proofs are included to enhance understanding of basic results and to provide a basis for extensions. For a more rigorous development, see Graybill (1983), Searle (1982), Theil (1984), and others listed in the reference section at the end of this appendix.

A.1 Definition of Matrices and Vectors

A *matrix* is a rectangular array of elements arranged in rows and columns. For example, the following matrix A has m rows and n columns.

$$A = \begin{bmatrix} a_{11} & a_{12} & \cdots & a_{1n} \\ a_{21} & a_{22} & \cdots & a_{2n} \\ \vdots & \vdots & \ddots & \vdots \\ a_{m1} & a_{m2} & \cdots & a_{mn} \end{bmatrix} \tag{A.1.1}$$

All the elements in the matrix can be represented by a typical element a_{ij}, where $i = 1, 2, \ldots, m$ and $j = 1, 2, \ldots, n$. Thus, a simplified representation of A is denoted by

$$A = [a_{ij}] \tag{A.1.2}$$

with the range of i and j specified.

The matrix A that has m rows and n columns is said to be of *order* or *dimension* m by n, which is written $(m \times n)$. A matrix that has a single column is called a *column vector*, whereas a matrix with a single row is a *row vector*. A $(1 \times m)$ row vector and an $(m \times 1)$ column vector are both said to have dimension m or order m. Often they are called m-component or m-dimensional vectors. For example,

$$\begin{bmatrix} 3 \\ 9 \\ 0 \\ -5 \\ 1 \end{bmatrix}$$

is a (5×1) column vector, and

$$(2 \quad -4 \quad 5 \quad 1)$$

is a (1×4) row vector.

The *transpose* of a matrix or vector is formed by interchanging the rows and the columns. That is, if

$$A = \begin{bmatrix} a_{11} & a_{12} & a_{13} \\ a_{21} & a_{22} & a_{23} \end{bmatrix} \tag{A.1.3}$$

then the transpose of A, denoted by A', is

$$A' = \begin{bmatrix} a_{11} & a_{21} \\ a_{12} & a_{22} \\ a_{13} & a_{23} \end{bmatrix} \tag{A.1.4}$$

When a column vector is transposed, it becomes a row vector, and vice versa. If a matrix of order $(m \times n)$ is transposed, the order of the new matrix becomes $(n \times m)$. A useful property of transposes is

$$(A')' = A \tag{A.1.5}$$

In a special case when $A' = A$, the matrix A is called a *symmetric matrix*. Consequently, a symmetric matrix is a square matrix in that it has the same number of rows as it has columns. A special symmetric matrix is the matrix that has

1 on the diagonal positions and 0 on the off-diagonal positions. Such a matrix is called an *identity matrix* and is denoted by I, that is

$$I = \begin{bmatrix} 1 & 0 & \cdots & 0 \\ 0 & 1 & \cdots & 0 \\ \vdots & \vdots & \ddots & \vdots \\ 0 & 0 & \cdots & 1 \end{bmatrix} \tag{A.1.6}$$

The identity matrix is one example of a *diagonal matrix*. A diagonal matrix is often denoted by

$$\text{diag}(a_1, a_2, \ldots, a_n) \tag{A.1.7}$$

where a_i is the ith element on the diagonal position and zeros occur elsewhere. Thus, an identity matrix can be expressed as

$$I = \text{diag}(1, 1, \ldots, 1) \tag{A.1.8}$$

Two matrices or vectors are equal when they are of the same dimensions and are equal element by element. Writing $A = B$ implies that A and B are of the same size and $a_{ij} = b_{ij}$ for all i and j. Equality between matrices is transitive in that if $A = B$ and $B = C$ then $A = C$, where A, B, and C are matrices of the same dimension. For example, if

$$A = \begin{bmatrix} 2 & 4 \\ 6 - c & 8 \end{bmatrix} \qquad B = \begin{bmatrix} 3 + a & 4 + b \\ 5 & 6 + d \end{bmatrix}$$

and $A = B$, then $a = -1$, $b = 0$, $c = 1$, and $d = 2$.

Exercises

1 Let A and B be $(m \times n)$ matrices. If $A = B$, show that $A' = B'$.

2 If $A = B$ and A is symmetric, show that B is also symmetric.

3 If A is symmetric, show that A is a square matrix.

4 If $\mathbf{c} = (2 \quad 5 \quad 8 \quad -1)'$ and $\mathbf{d}' = \mathbf{c}$, find $\mathbf{d}$.

5 If $A = I$ and $B = A$, show that B is symmetric.

A.2 Matrix Addition and Subtraction

The sum (or difference) of two matrices A and B requires that A and B have the same dimensions and is defined to be a new matrix whose elements are the sums (or differences) of the corresponding elements of A and B. Thus $C = A + B$ implies that $c_{ij} = a_{ij} + b_{ij}$ for all i and j. For example, if

$$A = \begin{bmatrix} 6 & 8 \\ -2 & 4 \end{bmatrix} \qquad B = \begin{bmatrix} 0 & -3 \\ 9 & 7 \end{bmatrix}$$

then

$$C = A + B = \begin{bmatrix} 6 & 5 \\ 7 & 11 \end{bmatrix}$$

Note that A and B have the same dimension. The matrices A and B are said to be *conformable for addition.* If there is a matrix D of order (2×3):

$$D = \begin{bmatrix} 3 & -8 & 1 \\ 9 & 2 & 5 \end{bmatrix}$$

then the addition $A + D$ is not operational because of the mismatch of dimensions. The matrices A and D are said to be *not conformable for addition.*

Matrix addition and subtraction are commutative:

$$A \pm B = B \pm A \tag{A.2.1}$$

and associative:

$$(A \pm B) \pm C = A \pm (B \pm C) \tag{A.2.2}$$

The distributive law is true when transposition is applied to the sum (or difference) of matrices in that the transpose of the sum (or difference) of two matrices is the sum (or difference) of the two transposed matrices:

$$(A \pm B)' = A' \pm B' \tag{A.2.3}$$

Exercises

1 Let $\mathbf{a}' = (1 \quad 2 \quad 3 \quad 4)$, $\mathbf{b} = (4 \quad 7 \quad 2 \quad -5)'$. Find $\mathbf{a} + \mathbf{b}$.

2 Let

$$A = \begin{bmatrix} 1 & 2 & 3 & 4 & 5 \\ 0 & 3 & 9 & 8 & 3 \\ 4 & 2 & 7 & 3 & 6 \end{bmatrix} \quad \text{and} \quad B = \begin{bmatrix} 2 & -4 & -9 \\ 0 & 2 & -5 \\ 3 & 4 & 6 \\ 1 & -7 & -8 \\ 2 & 0 & 0 \end{bmatrix}$$

Find $A + B'$.

3 Let $\mathbf{c} = (3 \quad 5 \quad 9 \quad -3 \quad 0 \quad 21)'$, find $\mathbf{c} + \mathbf{c} + \mathbf{c}$.

4 Let A, B, and C be $(m \times n)$ matrices. If $A + B = C + A$, show that $B = C$.

5 Let A and B be the following matrices:

$$A = \begin{bmatrix} 2 & 4 & a \\ 0 & b & 9 \\ 8 & 7 & 1 \end{bmatrix} \qquad B = \begin{bmatrix} 3-a & 5 & -2 \\ 1 & 0 & 7 \\ 8 & b-2 & 6 \end{bmatrix}$$

If

$$A + B = \begin{bmatrix} 6 & c & 0 \\ d & 7 & f \\ e+6 & 0 & 3-g \end{bmatrix}$$

find a, b, c, d, e, f, and g.

A.3 Matrix Multiplication

If k is a scalar constant, and A is a matrix, then the product of k times A is called *scalar multiplication.* The product is a new matrix that is k times each element of A. That is, if $B = kA$, then $b_{ij} = ka_{ij}$ for all i and j. For example, if $k = 2$, then

$$C = kA = 2\begin{bmatrix} 6 & 8 \\ -2 & 4 \end{bmatrix} = \begin{bmatrix} 2 \times 6 & 2 \times 8 \\ 2 \times (-2) & 2 \times 4 \end{bmatrix} = \begin{bmatrix} 12 & 16 \\ -4 & 8 \end{bmatrix}$$

Matrix multiplication, as in $C = AB$ where A is said to premultiply B, or alternatively B is said to postmultiply A, requires that the number of columns in A equals the number of rows in B. If A is of order $(m \times p)$ and B is of order $(p \times n)$, then the product AB is defined to be the matrix of order $(m \times n)$ whose ijth element is

$$c_{ij} = \sum_{k=1}^{p} a_{ik} b_{kj} \tag{A.3.1}$$

That is, the ijth element of the product matrix is found by multiplying the elements of the ith row of A, the first matrix, by the corresponding elements of the jth column of B, the second matrix, and summing the resulting products. For this to be possible, the number of columns in the first matrix must be equal to the number of rows in the second matrix. Such matrices are said to be *conformable for multiplication.* For example, given the matrices A and D above, they can be multiplied to obtain F

$$F = AD = \begin{bmatrix} 6 & 8 \\ -2 & 4 \end{bmatrix} \begin{bmatrix} 3 & -8 & 1 \\ 9 & 2 & 5 \end{bmatrix}$$

$$= \begin{bmatrix} 6 \times 3 + 8 \times 9 & 6 \times (-8) + 8 \times 2 & 6 \times 1 + 8 \times 5 \\ -2 \times 3 + 4 \times 9 & -2 \times (-8) + 4 \times 2 & -2 \times 1 + 4 \times 5 \end{bmatrix}$$

$$= \begin{bmatrix} 90 & -32 & 46 \\ 30 & 24 & 18 \end{bmatrix}$$

According to the definition of matrix multiplication, an $(m \times 1)$ column vector multiplied by a $(1 \times n)$ row vector becomes an $(m \times n)$ matrix, and a $(1 \times m)$ row vector multiplied by a $(m \times 1)$ column vector becomes a scalar. Therefore, generally,

$$AB \neq BA \tag{A.3.2}$$

even if both products exist. In other words, the commutative law does not hold for matrix multiplication. An exception is the product of two diagonal matrices, given conformability; the product is the same diagonal matrix, regardless of the order of multiplication. For example,

$$\begin{bmatrix} a & 0 \\ 0 & b \end{bmatrix} \begin{bmatrix} c & 0 \\ 0 & d \end{bmatrix} = \begin{bmatrix} c & 0 \\ 0 & d \end{bmatrix} \begin{bmatrix} a & 0 \\ 0 & b \end{bmatrix} = \begin{bmatrix} ac & 0 \\ 0 & bd \end{bmatrix}$$

Clearly, the commutative property is true for the algebraic multiplication, $ac = ca$ and $bd = db$. Therefore, in scalar multiplication, it is also true that

$$kA = Ak \tag{A.3.3}$$

where k is a scalar and A is a matrix. Another exception is that $IA = AI$, where I is an identity matrix and A and I are conformable for multiplication.

The product of a row vector and a column vector of the same dimension is often called *inner product*, its value is the sum of products of the components of the vectors. For example, if $\mathbf{j}$ is a $(T \times 1)$ vector with all elements 1, then the inner product $\mathbf{j}'\mathbf{j}$ is equal to a constant T. Two vectors are said to be *orthogonal* if their inner product is 0. For example, $\mathbf{a} = (2 \quad 5)'$ and $\mathbf{b} = (5 \quad -2)'$ are orthogonal, since $\mathbf{a}'\mathbf{b} = (2)(5) + (5)(-2) = 0$. The inner product is commutative in that $\mathbf{a}'\mathbf{b} = \mathbf{b}'\mathbf{a}$. If $\mathbf{c}$ is a $(m \times 1)$ vector, then $\mathbf{c}'\mathbf{c} = 0$ implies that each element of $\mathbf{c}$ is 0, because there is no negative element to offset positive elements in cancellations. In other words, $\mathbf{c}'\mathbf{c} = 0$ if and only if $\mathbf{c} = \mathbf{0}$. The square root of the inner product of the vector with itself is known as the *Euclidean vector norm*. For geometric interpretation of vectors and of the inner product, see for example Wu and Coppins (1981).

Although the commutative law is not true, the distributive law is true for multiplication:

$$A(B + C) = AB + AC \tag{A.3.4}$$

$$(A + B)C = AC + BC \tag{A.3.5}$$

The associative law is also true:

$$A(BC) = (AB)C \tag{A.3.6}$$

The cancellation law is not true, in general: $AB = 0$ does not necessarily imply that either $A = 0$ or $B = 0$. An example is that

$$A = \begin{bmatrix} 1 & 2 \\ 3 & 6 \end{bmatrix} \qquad B = \begin{bmatrix} 2 & -4 \\ -1 & 2 \end{bmatrix} \qquad \text{but } AB = \begin{bmatrix} 0 & 0 \\ 0 & 0 \end{bmatrix}$$

Note that the matrix with elements all zero is called a *null matrix*.

The transpose of the product of two matrices is given by

$$(AB)' = B'A' \tag{A.3.7}$$

which can be used to deduce the formula for the transpose of the product of three matrices:

$$(ABC)' = C'B'A' \tag{A.3.8}$$

and so forth.

The product of two symmetric matrices is not in general symmetric for, if $A' = A$, $B' = B$, we have $(AB)' = B'A' = BA \neq AB$, in general. However, if A is a symmetric matrix of order n, and B is a general $(n \times m)$ matrix, then $B'AB$ is symmetric since $(B'AB)' = B'A'(B')' = B'AB$. A special case is when $A = I$, so that $B'B$ is symmetric. This is a useful property in econometrics in that, for the design matrix X, the cross-product matrix $X'X$ is symmetric of order K, if X is $(T \times K)$.

Exercises

1 Let $\mathbf{a} = (3 \quad 6 \quad -3 \quad 5 \quad 9 \quad 2)'$. Find $\mathbf{a}'\mathbf{a}$ and $\mathbf{aa}'$.

2 Let

$$X = \begin{bmatrix} 1 & 4 & 7 \\ 1 & 4 & 8 \\ 1 & 5 & 8 \\ 1 & 6 & 9 \\ 1 & 8 & 10 \end{bmatrix}$$

Find $X'X$. Is $X'X$ symmetric?

3 If

$$\begin{bmatrix} 1 & 2 \\ 3 & 4 \end{bmatrix}\begin{bmatrix} a & b \\ c & d \end{bmatrix} = \begin{bmatrix} 1 & 0 \\ 0 & 1 \end{bmatrix}$$

find a, b, c, and d.

4 Let

$$A = \begin{bmatrix} 0.5 & a \\ a & 0.5 \end{bmatrix}$$

If $AA = A$, what is the value for a?

5 If

$$\begin{bmatrix} a & b \\ c & d \end{bmatrix}\begin{bmatrix} 8 & 1 \\ 2 & 5 \end{bmatrix} = \begin{bmatrix} 0 & 0 \\ 0 & 0 \end{bmatrix}$$

find a, b, c, and d.

A.4 Trace of a Square Matrix

The trace of a square matrix A, denoted by $\mathrm{tr}(A)$, is defined to be the sum of its diagonal elements. Formally,

$$\mathrm{tr}(A) = a_{11} + a_{22} + \cdots + a_{nn} \tag{A.4.1}$$

By this definition, the trace of a scalar constant k is equal to the scalar constant k itself, that is $\mathrm{tr}(k) = k$. Conversely, any constant k can be expressed as $\mathrm{tr}(k)$. For any square matrix A,

$$\mathrm{tr}(A') = \mathrm{tr}(A) \tag{A.4.2}$$

and

$$\operatorname{tr}(kA) = k \operatorname{tr}(A) \tag{A.4.3}$$

The trace of an identity matrix is equal to its dimension, that is

$$\operatorname{tr}(I_n) = n \tag{A.4.4}$$

where I_n denotes an identity matrix of order $(n \times n)$. Also, if A and B are square, then

$$\operatorname{tr}(A \pm B) = \operatorname{tr}(A) \pm \operatorname{tr}(B) \tag{A.4.5}$$

The trace has the convenient property that if AB and BA exist, then

$$\operatorname{tr}(AB) = \operatorname{tr}(BA) \tag{A.4.6}$$

which can be extended to

$$\operatorname{tr}(ABC) = \operatorname{tr}(BCA) = \operatorname{tr}(CAB) \tag{A.4.7}$$

if ABC, BCA, and CAB exist. Thus, if $CA = I$, then

$$\operatorname{tr}(ABC) = \operatorname{tr}(CAB) = \operatorname{tr}(B) \tag{A.4.8}$$

and

$$\operatorname{tr}(AA') = \operatorname{tr}(A'A) = \sum_{i=1}^{n} \sum_{j=1}^{n} a_{ij}^2 \tag{A.4.9}$$

Properties of the trace are often used in econometrics to simplify seemingly complicated results. For example, if X is $(T \times K)$, and I_T is an identity matrix of order T and $SX'X = I_K$, then $\operatorname{tr}(I_T - XSX')$ can be simplified to equal $T - K$ by the use of the properties listed in this section.

Exercises

1 Let

$$A = \begin{bmatrix} 1 & 2 & 3 \\ 4 & 5 & 6 \\ 7 & 8 & 9 \end{bmatrix}$$

Find $\operatorname{tr}(A)$ and $\operatorname{tr}(5A)$.

2 Let $\mathbf{c} = (1 \quad 2 \quad 3 \quad 4 \quad 5 \quad 6 \quad 7)'$ and $\mathbf{d} = (7 \quad 6 \quad 5 \quad 4 \quad 3 \quad 2 \quad 1)'$. Find $\operatorname{tr}(\mathbf{cc}')$ and $\operatorname{tr}(\mathbf{cd}')$.

3 Let

$$A = \begin{bmatrix} 7 & 5 & 7 \\ 3 & a & 9 \\ 1 & 3 & 2 \end{bmatrix} \qquad B = \begin{bmatrix} 8 & 4 & 2 \\ 87 & -a & 123 \\ 10 & 99 & -2 \end{bmatrix}$$

Find $\mathrm{tr}(A) + \mathrm{tr}(B)$.

4 Let A, B, C, and D be (100×100) matrices. If $DA = I$ and $\mathrm{tr}(CB) = 150$, find $\mathrm{tr}(ABCD)$.

5 Let A and B be (200×200) matrices, C and D be (200×50) matrices, and E and F be (50×50) matrices. If $AB = I$ and $C'DEF = I$, find $\mathrm{tr}(AB - DEFC')$.

A.5 Determinant of a Square Matrix

The determinant of a square matrix A is a uniquely defined scalar number associated with the matrix. It is denoted by det A or $|A|$. The basic definition of the determinant of A is the sum of all the different signed products of the elements selected from the matrix so that one and only one element comes from each row and one and only one element comes from each column, and the algebraic sign attached to each product is positive if the permutation of the subscripts of elements is even, otherwise negative. This basic definition is operationally impractical, so we will adopt the following derived definition. For a single element matrix (a scalar), that is $A = a_{11}$, the determinant of A is just a_{11}. For a (2×2) matrix

$$A = \begin{bmatrix} a_{11} & a_{12} \\ a_{21} & a_{22} \end{bmatrix} \tag{A.5.1}$$

its determinant is defined to be the difference of two terms as follows:

$$|A| = a_{11}a_{22} - a_{21}a_{12} \tag{A.5.2}$$

which is obtained by multiplying the two elements in the principal diagonal (northwest to southeast diagonal) of A and then subtracting the product of the two remaining elements. For a (3×3) matrix

$$A = \begin{bmatrix} a_{11} & a_{12} & a_{13} \\ a_{21} & a_{22} & a_{23} \\ a_{31} & a_{32} & a_{33} \end{bmatrix} \tag{A.5.3}$$

then

$$
\begin{aligned}
|A| &= a_{11}\begin{vmatrix} a_{22} & a_{23} \\ a_{32} & a_{33} \end{vmatrix} - a_{12}\begin{vmatrix} a_{21} & a_{23} \\ a_{31} & a_{33} \end{vmatrix} + a_{13}\begin{vmatrix} a_{21} & a_{22} \\ a_{31} & a_{32} \end{vmatrix} \\
&= a_{11}(a_{22}a_{33} - a_{23}a_{32}) - a_{12}(a_{21}a_{33} - a_{23}a_{31}) \\
&\quad + a_{13}(a_{21}a_{32} - a_{22}a_{31}) \\
&= a_{11}a_{22}a_{33} - a_{11}a_{23}a_{32} + a_{12}a_{23}a_{31} - a_{12}a_{21}a_{33} \\
&\quad + a_{13}a_{21}a_{32} - a_{13}a_{22}a_{31}
\end{aligned} \tag{A.5.4}
$$

For example, if the (3×3) matrix A is

$$
A = \begin{bmatrix} 3 & 5 & 4 \\ 6 & 9 & 7 \\ 2 & 8 & 1 \end{bmatrix}
$$

then the determinant of A is

$$
\begin{aligned}
|A| &= 3 \times \begin{vmatrix} 9 & 7 \\ 8 & 1 \end{vmatrix} - 5 \times \begin{vmatrix} 6 & 7 \\ 2 & 1 \end{vmatrix} + 4 \times \begin{vmatrix} 6 & 9 \\ 2 & 8 \end{vmatrix} \\
&= 3 \times (9 \times 1 - 7 \times 8) - 5 \times (6 \times 1 - 7 \times 2) + 4 \times (6 \times 8 - 9 \times 2) \\
&= 19
\end{aligned}
$$

As shown by (A.5.4) and the foregoing numerical example, the third-order determinant can be written in terms of determinants of order 2. In general, any nth order determinant can be written in terms of determinants of order $n - 1$.

In defining the determinant of a (3×3) matrix, the term $(a_{22}a_{33} - a_{23}a_{32})$, for example, is called the *minor* of the element a_{11}. In general, the minor of the element a_{ij} is the determinant of the submatrix of A that arises when the ith row and jth column are deleted, and is usually denoted by $|A_{ij}|$. The *cofactor* of the element of a_{ij}, which is denoted by c_{ij} is

$$
c_{ij} = (-1)^{i+j}|A_{ij}| \tag{A.5.5}
$$

A cofactor is therefore a signed minor, which explains why $a_{12}(a_{21}a_{33} - a_{23}a_{31})$ is preceded by a minus sign in the summation operation. Thus, the determinant of an $(n \times n)$ matrix A may be defined by the expression

$$
|A| = \det A = \sum_{j=1}^{n} a_{1j}c_{1j} \tag{A.5.6}
$$

In general, the sum of the products of the elements in any row (or column) of a square matrix, and their corresponding cofactors, equals the determinant of the matrix. That is,

$$\det A = \sum_{j=1}^{n} a_{ij}c_{ij} \qquad \text{for any row } i = 1, 2, \ldots, n \tag{A.5.7a}$$

$$= \sum_{i=1}^{n} a_{ij}c_{ij} \qquad \text{for any column } j = 1, 2, \ldots, n \tag{A.5.7b}$$

From the foregoing definition, obviously, if all the elements of any row or any column of a square matrix are 0, then the determinant of the matrix is 0. Note also that the sum of products of the elements in any row of A by the cofactors of the elements of another row (called alien cofactors) is always 0.

The following basic properties of determinants are useful:

1. $|A'| = |A|$, because of the foregoing definition of the determinant.

2. Multiplication of a row or column by a scalar k changes the value of the determinant by a factor k. For example,

$$\begin{vmatrix} a_{11} & ka_{12} \\ a_{21} & ka_{22} \end{vmatrix} = k\begin{vmatrix} a_{11} & a_{12} \\ a_{21} & a_{22} \end{vmatrix} \tag{A.5.8}$$

This is because in each signed product only one element can be chosen from any one column and any one row. In general the following is true.

3. If A is an $(n \times n)$ matrix, then $|kA| = k^n|A|$. As a special case

$$|-A| = (-1)^n|A| \tag{A.5.9}$$

4. If a square matrix has two equal rows (or columns), then its determinant is 0. This is because the sum of products of the elements in one of the identical rows of the matrix by their cofactors is equivalent to the sum of products of the elements of the other identical row by their alien cofactors. From the foregoing two statements, we establish the following: (A.5.10)

5. If any row (or column) of a matrix is a multiple of any other row (or column), then its determinant is 0. (A.5.11)

For example,

$$\begin{vmatrix} a & ka \\ b & kb \end{vmatrix} = k\begin{vmatrix} a & a \\ b & b \end{vmatrix} = k(ab - ab) = 0$$

6. The value of a determinant is unchanged if a multiple of one row (or column) is added to another row (or column). (A.5.12)

This is because the determinant is equal to the sum of the products of the elements of one row (or column) and their cofactors plus the constant multiple of the sum of the products of another row (or column) and their alien cofactors.

7. If A is a diagonal matrix of order n, then

$$|A| = a_{11}a_{22}\cdots a_{nn} \tag{A.5.13}$$

This property follows directly from the evaluation formula for the determinant. For the same reason, the following is also true.

8. A triangular matrix is the matrix that has all elements below or above the diagonal 0. If A is a triangular marix of order n, then

$$|A| = a_{11}a_{22}\cdots a_{nn} \tag{A.5.14}$$

9. If B is the matrix obtained from a square matrix A by interchanging any two rows (columns), then

$$\det B = -\det A \tag{A.5.15}$$

This is due to the change in the permutation of the subscripts of the elements of the matrix in the sum of the signed products as orginally defined for the determinant.

The definition of determinant using expansion with cofactors is actually a special case of a Laplace expansion. Laplace's theorem says that if we select any r rows of A, form all possible r-rowed minors from these r rows, multiply each of these minors by the algebraic complement, and then add the results, we obtain $|A|$. To illustrate the use of the Laplace expansion, consider the matrix P partitioned into four blocks of A, B, C, and 0 n-square matrices, then its determinant can be evaluated as follows:

$$|P| = \begin{vmatrix} A & 0 \\ C & B \end{vmatrix} = |A||B| \tag{A.5.16}$$

because from the first n rows of $|P|$ only one nonzero n-square minor, namely $|A|$, can be formed, and its algebraic complement is $|B|$.

An application of the Laplace expansion is the following:

$$|A||B| = \begin{vmatrix} A & 0 \\ -I_n & B \end{vmatrix} = \begin{vmatrix} A & AB \\ -I_n & 0 \end{vmatrix} = |AB| \tag{A.5.17}$$

where the first block of columns is postmultiplied by B and added to the second block of columns before the Laplace expansion picks $|AB|$ as the only minor for the last block of rows with the algebraic complement of 1. Note that the postmultiplication of a matrix by another matrix is equivalent to adding a constant multiple of columns of the first matrix in forming a new matrix, and its determinant is not changed by the property in 6. Thus, we establish the following rule that the determinant of the product of two square matrices is equal to the product of the determinants of the individual square matrices.

10. If A and B are square matrices of the same order, then

$$|AB| = |A||B| \tag{A.5.18}$$

Again, using the Laplace expansion, it can be shown that the following is also true.

11. If $A_1, A_2, \ldots, A_s$ are square matrices, then

$$|\text{diag}(A_1, A_2, \ldots, A_s)| = |A_1||A_2| \cdots |A_s| \tag{A.5.19}$$

12. $|A + B| \neq |A| + |B|$ in general. (A.5.20)

Exercises

1 Evaluate $|A|$ and $|2A'|$ where

$$|A| = \begin{vmatrix} 1 & 2 & 3 \\ 4 & 5 & 6 \\ 7 & 8 & 9 \end{vmatrix}$$

2 Evaluate $|A|$ using minors of the last column, where

$$A = \begin{bmatrix} 4 & 6 & 9 & 3 \\ 0 & 4 & 5 & 0 \\ 12 & 5 & 8 & 5 \\ 4 & -3 & 9 & 0 \end{bmatrix}$$

3 Let

$$A = \begin{bmatrix} 1 & 2 \\ 8 & 5 \end{bmatrix} \qquad B = \begin{bmatrix} 6 & 8 \\ -3 & 5 \end{bmatrix}$$

Check to see if $|A + B| = |A| + |B|$.

4 Let A, B, and C be (10×10) matrices, and

$$P = \begin{bmatrix} A & 0 \\ C & B \end{bmatrix}$$

If $|A| = 10$, $|B| = 80$, and $|C| = 800$, find $|P|$.

5 Let

$$A = \begin{bmatrix} a_1 & a_2 \\ -a_2 & a_1 \end{bmatrix} \qquad B = \begin{bmatrix} b_1 & b_2 \\ -b_2 & b_1 \end{bmatrix}$$

Use $|AB| = |A||B|$ to show that

$$(a_1^2 + a_2^2)(b_1^2 + b_2^2) = (a_1 b_1 - a_2 b_2)^2 + (a_2 b_1 + a_1 b_2)^2$$

A.6 Rank of a Matrix and Linear Dependency

Consider all square submatrices of A whose determinants are nonzero. The rank of the matrix A is the order of the largest in order of these determinants. A matrix is said to be of rank r if and only if it has one determinant of order r that is not zero, but has no determinant of order more than r that is not zero. A matrix is said to be of rank zero if and only if all its elements are 0. For example, the matrix

$$A = \begin{bmatrix} 4 & 5 & 2 & 14 \\ 3 & 9 & 6 & 21 \\ 8 & 10 & 7 & 28 \\ 1 & 2 & 9 & 5 \end{bmatrix}$$

has rank 3 because $|A| = 0$ but

$$\begin{vmatrix} 4 & 5 & 2 \\ 3 & 9 & 6 \\ 8 & 10 & 7 \end{vmatrix} = 4 \times 9 \times 7 + 3 \times 10 \times 2 + 8 \times 6 \times 5 - 2 \times 9 \times 8$$

$$- 5 \times 3 \times 7 - 4 \times 10 \times 6$$

$$= 63 \neq 0$$

The concept of the rank of a matrix can be viewed in terms of the concept of linear dependency. A set of vectors is said to be *linearly dependent* if there is a nontrivial linear combination of the vectors that is equal to the zero vector. Denote n columns of the matrix A as $\mathbf{a}_1, \mathbf{a}_2, \ldots, \mathbf{a}_n$. The set of these vectors is linearly dependent if and only if there exists a set of scalars $\{c_1, c_2, \ldots, c_n\}$ not all of which are 0, such that

$$c_1\mathbf{a}_1 + c_2\mathbf{a}_2 + \cdots + c_n\mathbf{a}_n = \mathbf{0} \tag{A.6.1}$$

For example, the columns of the foregoing matrix A are linearly dependent, because

$$1\begin{bmatrix}4\\3\\8\\1\end{bmatrix} + 2\begin{bmatrix}5\\9\\10\\2\end{bmatrix} + 0\begin{bmatrix}2\\6\\7\\9\end{bmatrix} - 1\begin{bmatrix}14\\21\\28\\5\end{bmatrix} = \mathbf{0}$$

If the set of vectors is not linearly dependent, it is *linearly independent*. Any subset of a linearly independent set of vectors is linearly independent. For example, the first three columns of A:

$$\begin{bmatrix}4\\3\\8\\1\end{bmatrix} \quad \begin{bmatrix}5\\9\\10\\2\end{bmatrix} \quad \begin{bmatrix}2\\6\\7\\9\end{bmatrix}$$

are independent, so are the first two columns:

$$\begin{bmatrix}4\\3\\8\\1\end{bmatrix} \quad \begin{bmatrix}5\\9\\10\\2\end{bmatrix}$$

If a set contains more than m $(m \times 1)$ vectors, it is linearly dependent. For example, the following two vectors are independent:

$$\begin{bmatrix}1\\2\end{bmatrix} \quad \begin{bmatrix}3\\4\end{bmatrix}$$

If there is a third vector

$$\mathbf{b} = \begin{bmatrix}b_1\\b_2\end{bmatrix}$$

where b_1 and b_2 are any numbers, then the three unknown linear combination constants c_1, c_2, and c_3 can always be found by solving the following two equations:

$$c_1\begin{bmatrix}1\\2\end{bmatrix} + c_2\begin{bmatrix}3\\4\end{bmatrix} + c_3\begin{bmatrix}b_1\\b_2\end{bmatrix} = \begin{bmatrix}0\\0\end{bmatrix}$$

Generalizing, we can state that if there are more than m $(m \times 1)$ vectors, they are always linearly dependent.

From the linear dependency point of view, the *rank of a matrix A* may be defined as the maximum number of linearly independent columns of A. The maximum number of linearly independent columns is equal to the maximum number of linearly independent rows, each being equal to the rank of the matrix. If the maximum number of linearly independent columns (or rows) is equal to the number of columns, we say that the matrix has a *full column rank*. If the maximum number of linearly independent rows (or columns) is equal to the number of rows, then we say that the matrix has a *full row rank*. When a square matrix A does not have a full row (and column) rank, its determinant is 0 and the matrix is said to be *singular*. When a square matrix A has a full row (and column) rank, its determinant is not zero and the matrix is said to be *nonsingular*.

Some useful properties of the rank of a matrix are

1. $\text{rank}(I_n) = n.$ (A.6.2)
2. $\text{rank}(kA) = \text{rank}(A)$, where k is a constant that is not 0. (A.6.3)
3. $\text{rank}(A') = \text{rank}(A).$ (A.6.4)
4. If A is an $(m \times n)$ matrix, then $\text{rank}(A) \leq \min\{m, n\}$. (A.6.5)
5. If A and B are matrices, then $\text{rank}(AB) \leq \min\{\text{rank}(A), \text{rank}(B)\}$. (A.6.6)
6. If A is an $(n \times n)$ matrix, then $\text{rank}(A) = n$ if and only if A is nonsingular; $\text{rank}(A) < n$ if and only if A is singular. (A.6.7)
7. If $\mathbf{u}$ and $\mathbf{v}$ are nonzero $(n \times 1)$ column vectors, then the rank of $\mathbf{uv}'$ is unity. (A.6.8)

There are operations on the rows of a matrix that leave its rank unchanged. These operations are

(*a*) Multiplication of a row of a matrix by a nonzero constant.
(*b*) Addition of a scalar multiple of one row to another row.
(*c*) Interchanging two rows.

These three operations are called *elementary row operations*. The three rules when applied to columns of a matrix are called *elementary column operations*. The elementary row operations are equivalent to premultiplication (or left-multiplication) by some matrix, and the elementary column operations are equivalent to postmultiplication (or right-multiplication) by some matrix. For example, premultiplying the following matrix

$$\begin{bmatrix} 2 & 0 & 0 \\ 1 & 1 & 0 \\ 0 & 0 & 1 \end{bmatrix}$$

to a $(3 \times n)$ matrix A is equivalent to multiplying the first row of A by two, adding the first row to the second row, and leaving the third row unchanged. Elementary operations on a matrix will leave its rank unchanged. It is equivalent to say that premultiplying by a nonsingular matrix will leave its rank unchanged. The elementary row operations are also useful in solving a system of linear equations to be discussed in Section A.8.

If a matrix A can be obtained from a matrix B by elementary row operations, then A is said to be *row-equivalent* to B. Any matrix obtained by performing a single elementary row operation on an identity matrix (also called unit matrix) is known as an *elementary matrix*. For example,

$$\begin{bmatrix} 1 & c \\ 0 & 1 \end{bmatrix}$$

which is obtained by adding a c multiple of the second row of a (2×2) identity matrix to the first row, is an elementary matrix. Elementary matrices are nonsingular since they are row-equivalent to the identity matrix. Without proof, we state the following useful theorems.

8. If two matrices A and B are equivalent, then there exist nonsingular matrices C and D such that $CAD = B$. (A.6.9)

9. Any nonsingular matrix A and the identity matrix of the same dimension have the same rank and are equivalent. (A.6.10)

10. The matrices A, BA, AC, and BAC, where B and C are nonsingular, all have the same rank. (A.6.11)

Exercises

1 Find the rank of the following matrix

$$\begin{bmatrix} 1 & 2 & 3 \\ 3 & 6 & 9 \\ 4 & 8 & 12 \end{bmatrix}$$

2 Show that if $|A|$ and $|B|$ are nonzero, then $|AB|$ and $|BA|$ are also nonzero.

3 If $|P| \neq 0$ and $|Q| \neq 0$, show that A, PA, AQ, and PAQ have the same rank.

4 Let X be a $(T \times K)$ matrix, and Z_i be a $(T \times (m_i - 1 + k_i))$ matrix. If $m_i - 1 + k_i < K < T$, find the rank of $X'Z_i$.

5 Let Γ be an $(M \times M)$ matrix, B be a $(K \times M)$ matrix, D be a $(J \times M)$ matrix, F be a $(J \times K)$ matrix, and I_K be an identity matrix of dimension K. If rank$(\Gamma' D' + B'F') = M - 1$, find the rank of the following matrix

$$\begin{bmatrix} -B' & \Gamma' D' \\ I_K & F' \end{bmatrix}$$

A.7 Inverse Matrix and Generalized Inverse

If A and B are matrices of order n such that $AB = BA = I$, then B is called the $B = A^{-1}$. Premultiplying and postmultiplying A on both sides of $B = A^{-1}$ gives matrix B is the inverse of A if and only if $BA = I = AB$. To see this, suppose that $B = A^{-1}$. Premultiplying and postmultiplying by A on both sides of $B = A^{-1}$ gives $BA = I = AB$ and, conversely, $BA = I = AB$ implies that B is the inverse of A by definition.

A square matrix A has an inverse if and only if it has full row (and column) rank and thus is nonsingular. To prove the statement, suppose that A has an inverse B. Then $AB = I$ implies that $|A||B| = 1$, which in turn implies that $|A| \neq 0$, so A is nonsingular. To see the converse, suppose that A is nonsingular. Then, $|A| \neq 0$ and it enables the creation of a matrix $B = C'/|A|$, which is the inverse of A, where C is the matrix of cofactors of A. To see if B is the inverse of A, check the elements of the product AB. The diagonal elements of AB are all $|A|/|A|$, which is unity, and off-diagonal elements of AB are 0, because they are sums of the products of elements of one row of A and their alien cofactors divided by $|A|$. Thus B is the inverse of A.

From this discussion, the actual inverse of a matrix A in terms of its elements can be obtained by the following formula:

$$A^{-1} = C'/|A| \tag{A.7.1}$$

where $C' = [c_{ij}]'$ is the transpose of the matrix of cofactors of A, as defined in Section A.5. For example, let

$$A = \begin{bmatrix} 1 & 2 \\ 3 & 4 \end{bmatrix}$$

The determinant $|A| = -2$ and cofactors are $c_{11} = 4$, $c_{22} = 1$, $c_{12} = -3$, and $c_{21} = -2$. The inverse is then calculated as

$$A^{-1} = \begin{bmatrix} 4 & -3 \\ -2 & 1 \end{bmatrix}' \frac{1}{-2} = \begin{bmatrix} -2.0 & 1.0 \\ 1.5 & -0.5 \end{bmatrix}$$

The inverse of a nonsingular matrix is unique. Formally, if $AB = I$ and $AC = I$ where A, B, and C are $(n \times n)$ matrices, then $B = C$. This is because $B = BI = B(AC) = (BA)C = IC = C$.

Some useful properties related to inverse matrices are given in the following.

1. The inverse of an identity matrix is the identity matrix itself.

$$I^{-1} = I \tag{A.7.2}$$

2. The inverse of the inverse is the original matrix itself.

$$(A^{-1})^{-1} = A \tag{A.7.3}$$

This is seen from premultiplying by A on both sides of $(A^{-1})(A^{-1})^{-1} = I$.

3. The inverse of the transpose is the transpose of the inverse:

$$(A')^{-1} = (A^{-1})' \tag{A.7.4}$$

This is because transposing both sides of $A'(A')^{-1} = I$ gives $[(A')^{-1}]'A = I$, which implies $[(A')^{-1}]' = A^{-1}$ and then $(A')^{-1} = (A^{-1})'$.

4. A and B are $(n \times n)$ matrices. If $BA = I$, then $AB = I$. (A.7.5)
This is because $BA = I$ implies $|A||B| = 1$, $|A| \neq 0$, $|B| \neq 0$, so that $BA = I$ can be premultiplied by B^{-1} and postmultiplied by B to obtain $AB = I$.

5. If A is nonsingular, then A^{-1} is nonsingular (because $AA^{-1} = I$ and $|A||A^{-1}| = 1$ imply $|A| \neq 0$, $|A^{-1}| \neq 0$), $|A^{-1}| = |A|^{-1}$ (because $|A||A^{-1}| = 1$), and $(A^{-1})^{-1} = A$ (because $(A^{-1})A = I$). (A.7.6)

6. If A and B are nonsingular, then $(AB)^{-1} = B^{-1}A^{-1}$. This can be verified by premultiplying or postmultiplying AB on both sides of the equality. (A.7.7)

7. One of the useful formulas is the inversion of matrices of a special form. If a nonsingular matrix H of order n can be written in the form $H = A + BDC$, where B, D, C are $(n \times r)$, $(r \times r)$, $(r \times n)$, respectively, and A, D are nonsingular, then

$$H^{-1} = A^{-1} - A^{-1}B(D^{-1} + CA^{-1}B)^{-1}CA^{-1} \tag{A.7.8}$$

8. Another useful formula is for a partitioned inverse. Let A be an $(n \times n)$ nonsingular matrix, partitioned as

$$A = \begin{bmatrix} E & F \\ G & H \end{bmatrix}$$

where E is $(p \times p)$, F is $(p \times q)$, G is $(q \times p)$, H is $(q \times q)$, and $p + q = n$. Suppose that E and $D = E - FH^{-1}G$ are nonsingular, then

$$A^{-1} = \begin{bmatrix} D^{-1} & -D^{-1}FH^{-1} \\ -H^{-1}GD^{-1} & H^{-1} + H^{-1}GD^{-1}FH^{-1} \end{bmatrix} \tag{A.7.9}$$

This formula can be verified by direct multiplication of AA^{-1} to obtain I. Alternative forms of A^{-1} can also be formed using the result in (A.7.8).

9. The inverse of a block diagonal matrix is equal to the block diagonal matrix containing the inverses of the blocks. (A.7.10)

There is a broader view of an inverse of a matrix. A *left-inverse* of an $(m \times n)$ matrix A, if it exists, is an $(n \times m)$ matrix B such that $BA = I_n$. A *right-inverse* of an $(m \times n)$ matrix A, if it exists, is an $(n \times m)$ matrix C such that $AC = I_m$. It can be proved that if both left- and right-inverses exist, then they must be the same, and this common inverse must be unique and is called the inverse A^{-1}. The left-inverse and right-inverse can both exist only when A is square $(m = n)$ and nonsingular. Of particular interest in econometrics is the inverse for a $(T \times K)$ design matrix X, where its rank is K, which is less than T. In this case, there exists an infinite number of left-inverses. One of the left-inverses is $(X'X)^{-1}X'$.

Among the left- and right-inverses if they exist, is one called the generalized inverse. Even under a certain situation when the left- and right-inverse do not exist for an $(m \times n)$ matrix A, there always exists a generalized inverse A^+ that has the following properties:

$$A^+AA^+ = A^+ \tag{A.7.11}$$

$$AA^+A = A \tag{A.7.12}$$

and

$$AA^+ \text{ and } A^+A \text{ are symmetric.} \tag{A.7.13}$$

Thus generalized inverses can be defined by means of the foregoing properties. If A is a nonsingular matrix, then $A^+ = A^{-1}$. If A is an $(m \times n)$ matrix that has rank n, then its generalized inverse is $(A'A)^{-1}A'$. If the $(m \times n)$ matrix A has rank m, then its generalized inverse is $A'(AA')^{-1}$. If the $(m \times n)$ matrix A has rank r, which is less than m and n, then its generalized inverse can be found indirectly as

$$A^+ = C'(CC')^{-1}(B'B)^{-1}B' \tag{A.7.14}$$

where $A = BC$ and the $(m \times r)$ matrix B and the $(r \times n)$ matrix C both have rank r. This method of finding A^+ is indirect because there is no systematic way that B and C can be identified from A. A direct calculation of a generalized inverse involves the diagonalization by characteristic roots and will not be presented here. For those who are interested in the method of finding a generalized inverse, see Lee, et al. (1977, pp. 163–173) or Judge, et al. (1985, pp. 499–502).

The indirect formula (A.7.14) is convenient for an $(m \times n)$ matrix A of rank n, because A can be expressed as $A = IA$, so that in the formula $B = I$, $C = A$, and $A^+ = (A'A)^{-1}A'$. Note that the generalized inverse exists for any matrix including singular matrices.

Some other useful properties of generalized inverses are

1. The generalized inverse of the null matrix is the null matrix (not necessarily of the same dimension). (A.7.15)
2. The generalized inverse of a $(T \times k)$ matrix is $(k \times T)$. (A.7.16)
3. The rank of A^+ is the same as the rank of A. (A.7.17)
4. If A is symmetric, then A^+ is symmetric. (A.7.18)
5. $(A^+)^+ = A$ (A.7.19)
6. $(kA)^+ = (1/k)A^+$ (A.7.20)
7. $(A^+)' = (A')^+$ (A.7.21)
8. One of the idiosyncracies of generalized inverses is that $(AB)^+ \neq B^+A^+$ in general. (A.7.22)
9. However, if A is $(m \times r)$, B is $(r \times n)$, and both matrices are of rank r, then $(AB)^+ = B^+A^+$. (A.7.23)
10. If $\mathbf{u}$ is a nonzero column vector, then $\mathbf{u}^+ = (\mathbf{u}'\mathbf{u})^{-1}\mathbf{u}'$. (A.7.24)
11. If an $(m \times n)$ matrix A is diagonal with the first k diagonal elements not equal to 0, and all other elements 0, then A^+ is a diagonal matrix with all elements 0 except for the first k diagonal elements, which are equal to the reciprocals of the original corresponding elements. (A.7.25)
12. The generalized inverse of a (2×2) matrix A of rank one is equal to

$$A^+ = A'/(a_{11}^2 + a_{12}^2 + a_{21}^2 + a_{22}^2) \tag{A.7.26}$$

For example, if A is a (2×2) matrix with all elements 1, then its generalized inverse is a (2×2) matrix with all elements 1/4.

Exercises

1 Find the inverse of the following matrix

$$\begin{bmatrix} -2 & 1 \\ 1.5 & -0.5 \end{bmatrix}$$

2 Find the inverse of the following matrix

$$\begin{bmatrix} 1 & 2 & 3 \\ 2 & 4 & 5 \\ 3 & 5 & 6 \end{bmatrix}$$

3 Show that

$$A = \begin{bmatrix} 1 & 5 & 3 & 4 & 7 \\ 1 & 6 & 4 & 5 & 9 \\ 2 & 7 & 3 & 5 & 8 \end{bmatrix}$$

has neither a right nor a left inverse.

4 Let

$$A = \begin{bmatrix} 8 & 0 & 0 \\ 0 & 5 & 0 \\ 0 & 0 & 0 \end{bmatrix} \qquad B = \begin{bmatrix} 0.125 & 0 & 0 \\ 0 & 0.2 & 0 \\ 0 & 0 & 0 \end{bmatrix}$$

Examine these matrices to see if B is the generalized inverse of A, and vice versa.

5 Let A be an $(n \times n)$ nonsingular matrix. Show that $A^{-1} = (A'A)^{-1}A'$.

A.8 Solutions for Systems of Simultaneous Linear Equations

The concepts of determinant, rank, and inverse are directly applicable to the investigation of the existence and uniqueness of solutions to a system of simultaneous linear equations. In this section the conditions under which the solution may be unique, multiple, trivial, or empty are examined. The concept of the solution unique up to a factor of proportionality will help you understand the argument used for identification of an equation within the context of estimating the parameters of a system of simultaneous linear equations (Chapters 14 and 15). The ability to solve a system of equations is also a prerequisite to the understanding of characteristic roots and vectors to be discussed in the next section.

A system of m simultaneous linear equations in n variables can be written as

$$\begin{aligned} a_{11}x_1 + a_{12}x_2 + \cdots + a_{1n}x_n &= b_1 \\ a_{21}x_1 + a_{22}x_2 + \cdots + a_{2n}x_n &= b_2 \\ \vdots \qquad \vdots \qquad\quad \vdots \qquad & \\ a_{m1}x_1 + a_{m2}x_2 + \cdots + a_{mn}x_n &= b_m \end{aligned} \tag{A.8.1}$$

In view of the definition of matrices and their multiplication, the system can be compactly written as

$$A\mathbf{x} = \mathbf{b} \tag{A.8.2}$$

where

$$A = \begin{bmatrix} a_{11} & a_{12} & \cdots & a_{1n} \\ a_{21} & a_{22} & \cdots & a_{2n} \\ \vdots & \vdots & \ddots & \vdots \\ a_{m1} & a_{m2} & \cdots & a_{mn} \end{bmatrix}, \quad \mathbf{x} = \begin{bmatrix} x_1 \\ x_2 \\ \vdots \\ x_n \end{bmatrix}, \quad \mathbf{b} = \begin{bmatrix} b_1 \\ b_2 \\ \vdots \\ b_m \end{bmatrix}$$

If the matrix A is a square matrix ($m = n$) and nonsingular, then $\mathbf{x} = A^{-1}\mathbf{b}$ is the unique solution to the system of n simultaneous linear equations in n unknowns, $A\mathbf{x} = \mathbf{b}$. The solution is obtained by multiplying both sides of the equations by A^{-1}, and $A^{-1}A\mathbf{x} = A^{-1}\mathbf{b}$ yields $\mathbf{x} = A^{-1}\mathbf{b}$. The solution formula for an individual variable x_i is known as *Cramér's rule.* The rule is derived as follows. Since the solution vector is

$$\begin{aligned} \mathbf{x} &= A^{-1}\mathbf{b} \\ &= |A|^{-1}C'b \end{aligned} \tag{A.8.3}$$

where C is the matrix of cofactors c_{ij} of A as defined in Section A.5, the solution for the ith element of $\mathbf{x}$ is

$$\begin{aligned} x_i &= |A|^{-1} \sum_{j=1}^{n} c_{ji} b_j \\ &= |A_i|/|A| \end{aligned} \tag{A.8.4}$$

where

$$|A_i| = \sum_{j=1}^{n} c_{ji} b_j \tag{A.8.5}$$

$= \text{The determinant of the matrix } A \text{ with the } i\text{th column replaced by } \mathbf{b}.$

For example, consider solving the following system of two linear equations for x_1 and x_2:

$$\begin{aligned} 3x_1 + 5x_2 &= 13 \\ 4x_1 + 2x_2 &= \ \ 8 \end{aligned}$$

Applying Cramér's rule results in

$$x_1 = \begin{vmatrix} 13 & 5 \\ 8 & 2 \end{vmatrix} \Big/ \begin{vmatrix} 3 & 5 \\ 4 & 2 \end{vmatrix} = -14/(-14) = 1$$

$$x_2 = \begin{vmatrix} 3 & 13 \\ 4 & 8 \end{vmatrix} \Big/ \begin{vmatrix} 3 & 5 \\ 4 & 2 \end{vmatrix} = -28/(-14) = 2$$

The foregoing Cramér's rule is possible only when A is nonsingular.

If the matrix A is singular, it is possible that the system is inconsistent or contradictory. For example, the system

$$5x_1 + 8x_2 = 21$$
$$5x_1 + 8x_2 = 24$$

is inconsistent because the same left side of each equation cannot be both equal to 21 and 24 at the same time. If we subtract the first equation from the second equation and write the equivalent system of equations, we have

$$5x_1 + 8x_2 = 21$$
$$0 = 3$$

The inconsistency is obvious because it is not true that 0 and 3 are equal. Note that the 0 on the left side is due to the singularity of matrix A.

If the matrix A is singular and the system is consistent, then some equations can be deleted since they can be obtained from the linear combinations of other equations. When some equations are deleted, the new matrix A will not be a square matrix. There will be more variables than equations ($n > m$). For example, the following system of three linear equations

$$2x_1 + 3x_2 + 4x_3 = 20$$
$$3x_1 + 2x_2 + 5x_3 = 22$$
$$5x_1 + 5x_2 + 9x_3 = 42$$

has a singular A matrix but the system is consistent. The third equation is actually the sum of the first two equations. Thus, by subtracting the first and the second from the third equation, the new consistent system becomes

$$2x_1 + 3x_2 + 4x_3 = 20$$
$$3x_1 + 2x_2 + 5x_3 = 22$$
$$0 = 0$$

where the third equation is *redundant* or *vacuous*. The vacuous equation can be deleted. Then there are only two equations in three unknown variables. The system can be solved for any two variables in terms of the remaining third variable. An iterative procedure can be used: Divide the first equation by 2 (the element is called pivot element) to transform the first equation into

$$x_1 + 1.5x_2 + 2x_3 = 10$$

Multiply this equation by 3 and subtract the result from the second equation in order to eliminate x_1. The result is

$$-2.5x_2 - x_3 = -8$$

Likewise, using -2.5 of the equation as a pivot element, scale the equation, multiply by 1.5 on both sides of the equation, subtract the result from the other equation to obtain the following new system of two equations.

$$\begin{aligned} x_1 \qquad + 1.4x_3 &= 5.2 \\ x_2 + 0.4x_3 &= 3.2 \end{aligned}$$

Or equivalently

$$\begin{aligned} x_1 &= 5.2 - 1.4x_3 \\ x_2 &= 3.2 - 0.4x_3 \end{aligned}$$

Thus, we have solved the system for x_1 and x_2 in terms of x_3. We can write the *complete solution* as

$$\begin{aligned} x_1 &= 5.2 - 1.4t \\ x_2 &= 3.2 - 0.4t \\ x_3 &= t \end{aligned}$$

where t is an arbitrary number. A particular solution can be obtained by assigning a number for t. For example, if $t = 3$, we have a particular solution of $x_1 = 1$, $x_2 = 2$, and $x_3 = 3$. If t is assigned 0 as normally is done in linear programming, then the particular solution is $x_1 = 5.2$, $x_2 = 3.2$, and $x_3 = 0$.

As seen from the previous numerical examples, the system of linear equations (A.8.1) can be reduced, in general, into the following equivalent system:

$$\begin{array}{llllll} x_1 & & & + a'_{1,k+1}x_{k+1} + \cdots + a'_{1,n}x_n = & b'_1 \\ & x_2 & & + a'_{2,k+1}x_{k+1} + \cdots + a'_{2,n}x_n = & b'_2 \\ & & \ddots & \vdots \qquad \ddots \qquad \vdots & \vdots \\ & & x_k & + a'_{k,k+1}x_{k+1} + \cdots + a'_{k,n}x_n = & b'_k \\ & & & \qquad\qquad\qquad 0 = & b'_{k+1} \\ & & & \qquad\qquad\qquad \vdots & \vdots \\ & & & \qquad\qquad\qquad 0 = & b'_m \end{array} \tag{A.8.6}$$

where a''s and b''s are new coefficients. In this system, if any of $b'_{k+1} \ldots b'_m$ is not equal to 0, then the system is inconsistent or contradictory and no solution can be obtained. In this case rank($A \quad \mathbf{b}$) $\neq$ rank(A). If all $b'_{k+1} \ldots b'_m$ are 0, then the system is consistent and rank($A \quad \mathbf{b}$) = rank(A) = k.

Therefore, whether there are solutions to a system of linear equations depends on whether the rank of A is equal to the rank of the augmented matrix ($A \quad \mathbf{b}$). When the system of equations is consistent in the sense that solutions exist, the rank of A is always equal to the rank of the augmented matrix ($A \quad \mathbf{b}$) because $\mathbf{b}$ is a linear combination of the columns of A, the linear combination coefficient vector being $\mathbf{x}$. However, if the system is not consistent so that $\mathbf{b}$ is not a linear combination of the columns of A, then it is possible that the augmented matrix ($A \quad \mathbf{b}$) has a rank larger than rank(A). If $\mathbf{b}$ is not a linear combination of the columns of A, then there exists no linear combination vector $\mathbf{x}$, that is, no solution for $\mathbf{x}$ exists.

In summary, there are three situations.

1. If rank(A) $\neq$ rank($A \quad \mathbf{b}$), then the system of equations is inconsistent or unsolvable.

2. If rank(A) = rank($A \quad \mathbf{b}$) = k and $m > n > k$, then there are at least $m - n$ equations or exactly $m - k$ equations that can be obtained from the linear combination of the remaining k independent equations. In this case, if the solution satisfies the k independent equations, it will satisfy the $m - k$ dependent equations. However, there may be multiple solutions if $k < n$. The solution will be unique if $k = n$.

3. If rank(A) = rank($A \quad \mathbf{b}$) = k and $m < n$, then $k < m < n$ and there are more variables than the number of equations. In this case there will be many solutions if $k < m$, and a unique solution if $k = m$.

Some numerical examples should help build an understanding of these three situations. Consider the following two-equation system:

$$\begin{bmatrix} 2 & 3 \\ 4 & 6 \end{bmatrix} \begin{bmatrix} x_1 \\ x_2 \end{bmatrix} = \begin{bmatrix} 8 \\ 9 \end{bmatrix}$$

The rank of the matrix A is

$$\text{rank}\begin{bmatrix} 2 & 3 \\ 4 & 6 \end{bmatrix} = 1$$

while the rank of ($A \quad \mathbf{b}$) is

$$\text{rank}\begin{bmatrix} 2 & 3 & 8 \\ 4 & 6 & 9 \end{bmatrix} = 2$$

The two-equation system is inconsistent because the equation system $A\mathbf{x} = \mathbf{b}$ says that $\mathbf{b}$ is a linear combination of columns of A, whereas the different ranks of A and

($A \quad \mathbf{b}$) imply that $\mathbf{b}$ is not a linear combination of columns of A, contradicting the equation system. The system is not solvable in this situation.

For situation 2, consider the following example:

$$\begin{bmatrix} 2 & 3 \\ 3 & 5 \\ 4 & 6 \end{bmatrix} \begin{bmatrix} x_1 \\ x_2 \end{bmatrix} = \begin{bmatrix} 7 \\ 11 \\ 14 \end{bmatrix}$$

In this case

$$\text{rank} \begin{bmatrix} 2 & 3 \\ 3 & 5 \\ 4 & 6 \end{bmatrix} = 2$$

and

$$\text{rank} \begin{bmatrix} 2 & 3 & 7 \\ 3 & 5 & 11 \\ 4 & 6 & 14 \end{bmatrix} = 2$$

because

$$\begin{vmatrix} 2 & 3 & 7 \\ 3 & 5 & 11 \\ 4 & 6 & 14 \end{vmatrix} = 0 \qquad \text{and} \qquad \begin{vmatrix} 2 & 3 \\ 3 & 5 \end{vmatrix} = 1$$

Therefore, $\text{rank}(A) = \text{rank}(A \quad \mathbf{b}) = 2$ and there are more rows than columns in A. Since A has a full column rank of 2, the solution can be uniquely solved as $x_1 = 2$ and $x_2 = 1$. Note that there are three equations in two unknowns. Because of the consistency in ranks, any two independent equations can be used to solve for x_1 and x_2. The remaining equation is a linear combination of the other two equations.

Now consider the following system of equations:

$$\begin{bmatrix} 2 & 4 \\ 3 & 6 \\ 4 & 8 \end{bmatrix} \begin{bmatrix} x_1 \\ x_2 \end{bmatrix} = \begin{bmatrix} 8 \\ 12 \\ 16 \end{bmatrix}$$

In this case

$$\text{rank} \begin{bmatrix} 2 & 4 \\ 3 & 6 \\ 4 & 8 \end{bmatrix} = 1$$

and

$$\operatorname{rank}\begin{bmatrix} 2 & 4 & 8 \\ 3 & 6 & 12 \\ 4 & 8 & 16 \end{bmatrix} = 1$$

Thus rank(A) = rank($A \quad \mathbf{b}$) = 1 and the number of rows in A is greater than the number of columns in A, and yet the matrix A does not have a full column rank. In this particular situation, all three equations can be represented by any of the three equations, for example, the first equation:

$$2x_1 + 4x_2 = 8$$

The second equation can be obtained from this equation by multiplying both sides of the equation by 1.5. The third equation can be obtained from this equation by multiplying both sides of the equation by 2. Therefore, the system of equations has infinitely many solutions, just like in situation 3. Some particular solutions are $\mathbf{x} = (4 \quad 0)'$, $(2 \quad 1)'$, and $(0 \quad 2)'$.

If the vector $\mathbf{b} = \mathbf{0}$, then the system of equations becomes $A\mathbf{x} = \mathbf{0}$ and is called a *system of homogeneous linear equations.* In this case rank(A) is always equal to rank($A \quad \mathbf{0}$) and the system is always consistent and possesses at least a solution for $\mathbf{x}$, namely $\mathbf{x} = \mathbf{0}$. If rank(A) = n, then the solution is uniquely the 0 vector and is called the *trivial solution.* If rank(A) = $k < n$, there are more variables than equations, and the system has many nontrivial solutions. It is often but not always the case that the general solution for a set of k (basic) variables can be expressed in terms of the remaining $n - k$ (nonbasic) variables. A particular solution for the k (basic) variables can be obtained by assigning arbitrary values such as 0 for the $n - k$ (nonbasic) variables. If rank(A) = $n - 1$, the solution is unique up to a factor of proportionality. This can be seen as follows: When rank(A) = $n - 1$, the system can be reduced to a system of $n - 1$ homogeneous independent equations with n variables. If one of the variables is assigned an arbitrary value, then the system becomes a system of $n - 1$ *linear equations* with $n - 1$ variables and the solution is unique because rank(A) = $n - 1$. The unique solution conditional on the arbitrary value assigned to a given variable is called the solution unique up to a factor of proportionality.

In general, the rank of A may be only k and is less than n, the number of columns of A or the number of variables. In this case the system of homogeneous equations $A\mathbf{x} = \mathbf{0}$ has an infinite number of nontrivial solutions, because the solutions of k variables can be expressed as functions of $n - k$ other variables, which can take any values arbitrarily. The set of all solutions of $A\mathbf{x} = \mathbf{0}$ is a *vector space* in that if given any two members of the set (two solutions in this case), then the linear combinations of the two members are also members of the set. The vector space consisting of all solutions of the homogeneous equations $A\mathbf{x} = \mathbf{0}$ is called the *null space* (or *kernel*) of A. The dimension of the null space of A is often denoted by $N(A)$. Without proof, we state that if A is an $(m \times n)$ matrix, the null space of A forms a vector space of dimension $n - k$ where k is the rank of A. If $k = n$, then the only solution is the trivial solution $\mathbf{x} = \mathbf{0}$. If $k < n$, k variables in $\mathbf{x}$ can be expressed as functions of the remaining $n - k$ variables.

An example of a system of homogeneous equations that has a unique trivial solution is

$$\begin{bmatrix} 3 & 5 \\ 2 & 4 \end{bmatrix} \begin{bmatrix} x_1 \\ x_2 \end{bmatrix} = \begin{bmatrix} 0 \\ 0 \end{bmatrix}$$

because

$$\begin{vmatrix} 3 & 5 \\ 2 & 4 \end{vmatrix} = 2 \neq 0$$

Another example of a system of homogeneous linear equations that has infinitely many solutions is

$$\begin{bmatrix} 3 & 5 \\ 6 & 10 \end{bmatrix} \begin{bmatrix} x_1 \\ x_2 \end{bmatrix} = \begin{bmatrix} 0 \\ 0 \end{bmatrix}$$

because

$$\begin{vmatrix} 3 & 5 \\ 6 & 10 \end{vmatrix} = 0$$

In this system, the second equation is two times the first equation. Thus, one of the equations can be deleted. The result is one equation with two variables:

$$3x_1 + 5x_2 = 0$$

The complete set of solutions is

$$x_1 = (-5/3)t$$

$$x_2 = t$$

where t is an arbitrary number. If $t = 3$, then a particular solution is

$$x_1 = -5$$

$$x_2 = 3$$

In concluding this section, consider the following system of three equations:

$$\begin{bmatrix} 1 & -1 & 1 \\ 3 & -1 & 2 \\ 3 & 1 & 1 \end{bmatrix} \begin{bmatrix} x_1 \\ x_2 \\ x_3 \end{bmatrix} = \begin{bmatrix} 2 \\ 7 \\ 8 \end{bmatrix}$$

where the augmented matrix

$$(A \quad \mathbf{b}) = \begin{bmatrix} 1 & -1 & 1 & 2 \\ 3 & -1 & 2 & 7 \\ 3 & 1 & 1 & 8 \end{bmatrix}$$

has rank 2, which is equal to the rank of

$$A = \begin{bmatrix} 1 & -1 & 1 \\ 3 & -1 & 2 \\ 3 & 1 & 1 \end{bmatrix}$$

Therefore the system $A\mathbf{x} = \mathbf{b}$ is consistent. Since $|A| = 0$, there are an infinite number of solutions. To find the solutions, we eliminate x_1 from the second and the third equations (by subtracting three times the first equation from the second and the third equations), and then eliminate x_2 from the third equation (by subtracting two times the resulting second equation from the resulting third equation). Or, equivalently premultiply a nonsingular matrix (see Section A.6 for equivalency of premultiplying a nonsingular matrix and elementary row operations)

$$\begin{bmatrix} 1 & 0 & 0 \\ -3 & 1 & 0 \\ -3 & 0 & 1 \end{bmatrix}$$

on both sides of $A\mathbf{x} = \mathbf{b}$ to eliminate x_1 from the second and the third equation. Then, premultiply the following matrix

$$\begin{bmatrix} 1 & 0 & 0 \\ 0 & 1 & 0 \\ 0 & -2 & 1 \end{bmatrix}$$

to eliminate x_2 from the third equation. Multiplying both preceding matrices is the same as multiplying the following matrix

$$P = \begin{bmatrix} 1 & 0 & 0 \\ -3 & 1 & 0 \\ 3 & -2 & 1 \end{bmatrix}$$

on both sides of the system to yield

$$\begin{bmatrix} 1 & -1 & 1 \\ 0 & 2 & -1 \\ 0 & 0 & 0 \end{bmatrix} \begin{bmatrix} x_1 \\ x_2 \\ x_3 \end{bmatrix} = \begin{bmatrix} 2 \\ 1 \\ 0 \end{bmatrix}$$

which can be reduced to

$$\begin{bmatrix} 1 & -1 \\ 0 & 2 \end{bmatrix}\begin{bmatrix} x_1 \\ x_2 \end{bmatrix} - \begin{bmatrix} -1 \\ 1 \end{bmatrix} x_3 = \begin{bmatrix} 2 \\ 1 \end{bmatrix}$$

Solving for x_1 and x_2 in terms of x_3 yields

$$\begin{aligned}
\begin{bmatrix} x_1 \\ x_2 \end{bmatrix} &= \begin{bmatrix} 1 & -1 \\ 0 & 2 \end{bmatrix}^{-1}\begin{bmatrix} -1 \\ 1 \end{bmatrix} x_3 + \begin{bmatrix} 1 & -1 \\ 0 & 2 \end{bmatrix}^{-1}\begin{bmatrix} 2 \\ 1 \end{bmatrix} \\
&= \begin{bmatrix} 1 & 0.5 \\ 0 & 0.5 \end{bmatrix}\begin{bmatrix} -1 \\ 1 \end{bmatrix} x_3 + \begin{bmatrix} 1 & 0.5 \\ 0 & 0.5 \end{bmatrix}\begin{bmatrix} 2 \\ 1 \end{bmatrix} \\
&= \begin{bmatrix} -0.5 \\ 0.5 \end{bmatrix} x_3 + \begin{bmatrix} 2.5 \\ 0.5 \end{bmatrix}
\end{aligned}$$

which is the complete solution. The solution obtained by assigning a particular value to x_3 is a particular solution. For example, a particular solution is that $x_1 = 1$ and $x_2 = 2$ when x_3 is assigned a value of 3.

Exercises

1 Solve the following system of two equations for x_1 and x_2

$$\begin{bmatrix} 1 & 2 \\ 3 & 4 \end{bmatrix}\begin{bmatrix} x_1 \\ x_2 \end{bmatrix} = \begin{bmatrix} 8 \\ 6 \end{bmatrix}$$

2 Show that the following system of equations has no solutions

$$\begin{bmatrix} 3 & 4 & 5 \\ 5 & 9 & 13 \\ 2 & 5 & 8 \end{bmatrix}\begin{bmatrix} x_1 \\ x_2 \\ x_3 \end{bmatrix} = \begin{bmatrix} 12 \\ 15 \\ 8 \end{bmatrix}$$

3 Show that the following homogeneous linear equations possess only the trivial solution

$$\begin{bmatrix} 1 & -1 & 1 \\ 2 & 1 & 3 \\ 1 & 2 & -1 \end{bmatrix}\begin{bmatrix} x_1 \\ x_2 \\ x_3 \end{bmatrix} = \begin{bmatrix} 0 \\ 0 \\ 0 \end{bmatrix}$$

A.9 Characteristic Roots and Vectors of a Square Matrix

Consider a system of n homogeneous equations in n unknowns:

$$(A - \lambda I)\mathbf{x} = \mathbf{0} \tag{A.9.1}$$

This homogeneous set of equations possesses only the trivial solution $\mathbf{x} = \mathbf{0}$ unless $(A - \lambda I)$ is singular and hence the determinant of the coefficients is 0, that is,

$$\det(A - \lambda I) = \begin{vmatrix} a_{11} - \lambda & a_{12} & \cdots & a_{1n} \\ a_{21} & a_{22} - \lambda & \cdots & a_{2n} \\ \vdots & \vdots & \ddots & \vdots \\ a_{n1} & a_{n2} & \cdots & a_{nn} - \lambda \end{vmatrix} = 0 \tag{A.9.2}$$

For example, if A is

$$A = \begin{bmatrix} 1 & 2 \\ 1 & 2 \end{bmatrix}$$

then the characteristic equation of A is

$$\begin{vmatrix} 1 - \lambda & 2 \\ 1 & 2 - \lambda \end{vmatrix} = 0$$

which can be expressed as

$$(1 - \lambda)(2 - \lambda) - 2 = 0$$

or

$$\lambda^2 - 3\lambda = 0$$

In general, this would be a polynomial equation in λ of degree n, known as the *characteristic equation* of A. The roots of this polynomial equation, not necessarily distinct, are called the *characteristic roots* (or eigenvalues, latent roots, or proper values) of the matrix A. Corresponding to each of the characteristic roots, there will be a solution of $(A - \lambda I)\mathbf{x} = \mathbf{0}$ of the form $k_i\mathbf{x}_i$, where $\mathbf{x}_i$ is a nonzero vector, and k_i is an arbitrary constant. These solutions are called the *characteristic vectors* (or eigenvectors, latent vectors, or proper vectors). The solution $k_i\mathbf{x}_i$ is not unique because the system is a homogeneous set of equations. To achieve uniqueness for each of the characteristic vectors, the additional normalizing condition $\mathbf{x}_i'\mathbf{x}_i = 1$ can be imposed.

For example, if A is

$$A = \begin{bmatrix} 5 & -3 \\ 4 & -2 \end{bmatrix}$$

then, the characteristic equation of A is

$$(5-\lambda)(-2-\lambda)+12=0$$

or

$$\lambda^2-3\lambda+2=0$$

The characteristic roots are 1 and 2. When $\lambda=1$, the system of two homogeneous equations in two unknowns

$$\begin{bmatrix} 5-1 & -3 \\ 4 & -2-1 \end{bmatrix}\begin{bmatrix} x_1 \\ x_2 \end{bmatrix}=\mathbf{0}$$

can be reduced to one equation

$$4x_1-3x_2=0$$

which has complete solutions

$$\begin{bmatrix} x_1 \\ x_2 \end{bmatrix}=k_1\begin{bmatrix} 1 \\ 4/3 \end{bmatrix}$$

where k_1 is an arbitrary number. Applying the normalizing condition of a unit length $\mathbf{x}_1'\mathbf{x}_1=1$, or solving

$$4x_1-3x_2=0$$

and

$$x_1^2+x_2^2=1$$

together for x_1 and x_2, we have

$$\begin{bmatrix} x_1 \\ x_2 \end{bmatrix}=\begin{bmatrix} 3/5 \\ 4/5 \end{bmatrix} \quad \text{or} \quad \begin{bmatrix} -3/5 \\ -4/5 \end{bmatrix}$$

Likewise, when $\lambda=2$, the system of two equations with two unknowns can be reduced to one equation

$$x_1-x_2=0$$

which has complete solutions

$$\begin{bmatrix} x_1 \\ x_2 \end{bmatrix}=k_2\begin{bmatrix} 1 \\ 1 \end{bmatrix}$$

When adjusted to unit length, the particular solution is

$$\begin{bmatrix} x_1 \\ x_2 \end{bmatrix}=\begin{bmatrix} 1/\sqrt{2} \\ 1/\sqrt{2} \end{bmatrix}=\begin{bmatrix} 0.7071 \\ 0.7071 \end{bmatrix} \quad \text{or} \quad \begin{bmatrix} -0.7071 \\ -0.7071 \end{bmatrix}$$

Therefore, for this particular example, the characteristic roots are 1 and 2, and the corresponding characteristic vectors, are

$$\begin{bmatrix} 0.6 \\ 0.8 \end{bmatrix} \text{ or } \begin{bmatrix} -0.6 \\ -0.8 \end{bmatrix} \quad \text{and} \quad \begin{bmatrix} 0.7071 \\ 0.7071 \end{bmatrix} \text{ or } \begin{bmatrix} -0.7071 \\ -0.7071 \end{bmatrix}$$

Exercises

1 Find the characteristic roots of the following matrix

$$A = \begin{bmatrix} 1 & 1 \\ 1 & 2 \end{bmatrix}$$

2 Using the matrix A defined in Exercise 1, find the normalized characteristic vectors associated with the characteristic roots.

3 Show that the following matrix

$$A = \begin{bmatrix} 1 & 1 & 2 \\ 1 & 2 & 2 \\ 2 & 2 & 5 \end{bmatrix}$$

has the characteristic roots 6.8541, 1, 0.1459, and the corresponding characteristic vectors

$$\begin{bmatrix} 0.356822 \\ 0.417775 \\ 0.835549 \end{bmatrix}, \quad \begin{bmatrix} 0.000000 \\ -0.894427 \\ 0.447214 \end{bmatrix} \quad \text{and} \quad \begin{bmatrix} -0.934173 \\ 0.159579 \\ 0.319149 \end{bmatrix}$$

A.10 Orthogonal Matrices

An interesting and useful property of characteristic roots and vectors is that if the matrix A is symmetric then all its characteristic roots are real (not complex) and the characteristic vectors corresponding to different characteristic roots are orthogonal in that $\mathbf{x}_i'\mathbf{x}_j = 0$ for $\lambda_i \neq \lambda_j$. Thus, if the n characteristic roots are all different, all the distinct characteristic vectors can be collected to form a matrix $C = (\mathbf{x}_1\mathbf{x}_2 \ldots \mathbf{x}_n)$. The matrix C is called an *orthogonal matrix* since it has the properties $C'C = CC' = I_n$ and $AC = C\Lambda$, where Λ is a diagonal matrix with the characteristic roots of A down the diagonal. Note that $AC = C\Lambda$ is a matrix representation of $A\mathbf{x}_i = \lambda_i\mathbf{x}_i$, for $i = 1, 2, \ldots, n$. The following numerical example will demonstrate the computations and properties: Consider the following symmetric matrix:

$$A = \begin{bmatrix} 4 & 2 \\ 2 & 6 \end{bmatrix}$$

The characteristic polynomial is

$$\begin{vmatrix} 4-\lambda & 2 \\ 2 & 6-\lambda \end{vmatrix} = (4-\lambda)(6-\lambda) - 4 = 0$$

The characteristic roots are real numbers

$$\lambda_1 = 5 + \sqrt{5} = 7.236068 \qquad \text{and} \qquad \lambda_2 = 5 - \sqrt{5} = 2.763932$$

The corresponding characteristic vectors are

$$\mathbf{x}_1 = \begin{bmatrix} 2/(10+2\sqrt{5})^{1/2} \\ (1+\sqrt{5})/(10+2\sqrt{5})^{1/2} \end{bmatrix} = \begin{bmatrix} 0.5257 \\ 0.8507 \end{bmatrix} \quad \text{or} \quad \begin{bmatrix} -0.5257 \\ -0.8507 \end{bmatrix}$$

and

$$\mathbf{x}_2 = \begin{bmatrix} 2/(10-2\sqrt{5})^{1/2} \\ (1-\sqrt{5})/(10-2\sqrt{5})^{1/2} \end{bmatrix} = \begin{bmatrix} 0.8507 \\ -0.5257 \end{bmatrix} \quad \text{or} \quad \begin{bmatrix} -0.8507 \\ 0.5257 \end{bmatrix}$$

The validity of the solutions can be checked by $\mathbf{x}_1'\mathbf{x}_1 = 1$ and $\mathbf{x}_2'\mathbf{x}_2 = 1$. Also, check the orthogonality of $\mathbf{x}_1'\mathbf{x}_2 = 0$. The orthogonal matrix C is then

$$C = \begin{bmatrix} 0.5257 & 0.8507 \\ 0.8507 & -0.5257 \end{bmatrix} \quad \text{or} \quad \begin{bmatrix} -0.5257 & -0.8507 \\ -0.8507 & 0.5257 \end{bmatrix}$$

$$\text{or} \quad \begin{bmatrix} 0.5257 & -0.8507 \\ 0.8507 & 0.5257 \end{bmatrix} \quad \text{or} \quad \begin{bmatrix} -0.5257 & 0.8507 \\ -0.8507 & -0.5257 \end{bmatrix}$$

Note that the matrix C has the properties $C'C = CC' = I_2$. Also note that the matrix A must be symmetric in order to have its characteristic vectors orthogonal. The numerical example in Section A.9 is not symmetric, and its characteristic vectors are not orthogonal.

In general, a square matrix C is said to be orthogonal if and only if its transpose is its inverse. In other words, C is orthogonal if and only if $C'C = CC' = I$. From the numerical example, the inverse of C is

$$C^{-1} = \begin{bmatrix} 0.5257 & 0.8507 \\ 0.8507 & -0.5257 \end{bmatrix}^{-1} = \begin{bmatrix} 0.5257 & 0.8507 \\ 0.8507 & -0.5257 \end{bmatrix} = C'$$

In computing the inverse, the determinant of C is also calculated to be $|C| = (0.5257)(-0.5257) - (0.8506)(0.8506) = -1$.

From the previous discussion, if C is orthogonal and if $\mathbf{c}_i$ and $\mathbf{c}_j$ are columns of the matrix C then $\mathbf{c}_i'\mathbf{c}_j$ equals 1 if $i = j$ and equals 0 if $i \neq j$. In addition, if C is orthogonal, then C' is also orthogonal. In relation to its determinant, if C is orthogonal, then det $C = \pm 1$. This result occurs because $|C'| = |C|$ and $|C'||C| = |C'C| = |I| = 1$, which implies $|C| = \pm 1$.

A simple example of an orthogonal matrix is the identity. Another example is the following matrix.

$$C = \begin{bmatrix} 0 & 1 \\ 1 & 0 \end{bmatrix}$$

since

$$C'C = \begin{bmatrix} 0 & 1 \\ 1 & 0 \end{bmatrix}\begin{bmatrix} 0 & 1 \\ 1 & 0 \end{bmatrix} = \begin{bmatrix} 1 & 0 \\ 0 & 1 \end{bmatrix}$$

Exercises

1 Let

$$C = \begin{bmatrix} -0.8506 & 0.5257 \\ 0.5257 & 0.8506 \end{bmatrix}$$

Find CC' and $C'C$. Is C an orthogonal matrix?

2 Find the determinant of C defined in Exercise 1.

3 Numerically show that the characteristic vectors of the matrix A given by Exercise 3 of Section A.9 form an orthogonal matrix.

A.11 Diagonalization of a Symmetric Matrix

An important application of the use of an orthogonal matrix is the diagonalization of a matrix. Let A be an $(n \times n)$ symmetric matrix. Then, there exists an $(n \times n)$ orthogonal matrix C such that $C'AC$ is diagonal. This result can be seen rather easily for the case where the matrix A has distinct characteristic roots. Because a matrix representation of $A\mathbf{x}_i = \lambda_i \mathbf{x}_i$, for $i = 1, 2, \ldots, n$ is $AC = C\Lambda$, premultiplication by C' leads to the result $C'AC = C'C\Lambda = \Lambda$, a diagonal matrix. For example, if A is

$$A = \begin{bmatrix} 4 & 2 \\ 2 & 6 \end{bmatrix}$$

then an orthogonal matrix C is

$$C = \begin{bmatrix} 0.5257 & 0.8507 \\ 0.8507 & -0.5257 \end{bmatrix}$$

and

$$C'AC = \begin{bmatrix} 0.5257 & 0.8507 \\ 0.8507 & -0.5257 \end{bmatrix} \begin{bmatrix} 4 & 2 \\ 2 & 6 \end{bmatrix} \begin{bmatrix} 0.5257 & 0.8507 \\ 0.8507 & -0.5257 \end{bmatrix}$$
$$= \begin{bmatrix} 7.236068 & 0 \\ 0 & 2.763932 \end{bmatrix}$$

The diagonal elements are the characteristic roots of A and are different. The matrix $C'AC$ can be further diagonalized into an identity matrix by premultiplying and postmultiplying by the following W matrix

$$W = \begin{bmatrix} 0.371748 & 0 \\ 0 & 0.601501 \end{bmatrix}$$

in which the diagonal elements are the reciprocals of the corresponding square roots of the characteristic roots. You should check to see if $WC'ACW = I$. Note that $W'W = WW' = \Lambda^{-1}$. Let $P = CW$, then $P'P = W'C'CW = W'W = \Lambda^{-1}$. Also $PP' = CWW'C' = C\Lambda^{-1}C'$.

If the characteristic roots are not all different for a symmetric matrix, it is still possible to find an orthogonal matrix C such that $C'AC = \Lambda$, but such a C is not unique. For a proof see Hadley (1961, pp. 242–249).

If C is an orthogonal matrix that diagonalizes the symmetric matrix A, then the characteristic roots of A are the diagonal elements of $C'AC$, and the rank of A is the number of nonzero diagonal elements of $C'AC = \Lambda$. Since the choice of an orthogonal matrix that diagonalizes a symmetric matrix is not unique in that the columns of C are interchangeable, a particular order of the columns of C will give the diagonal elements of $C'AC$ in ascending order or descending order. Another interesting observation is that $|\Lambda| = |C'AC| = |C||C||A| = |A|$. This result implies that the determinant of a symmetric matrix is the product of its characteristic roots. For the example given here, $|A| = |\Lambda| = 20$. It follows directly that an $(n \times n)$ symmetric matrix has rank r if and only if it has r nonzero characteristic roots and $(n - r)$ zero characteristic roots.

Exercises

1 Let

$$A = \begin{bmatrix} 1 & 1 \\ 1 & 2 \end{bmatrix} \qquad C = \begin{bmatrix} 0.5257 & 0.8507 \\ 0.8507 & -0.5257 \end{bmatrix} \qquad \Lambda = \begin{bmatrix} 2.6180 & 0 \\ 0 & 0.3820 \end{bmatrix}$$

Calculate $C'AC$. Check to see if $C'AC = \Lambda$.

2 Using the matrices A, C, and Λ, defined in Exercise 1, diagonalize the matrix A into an identity matrix.

3 Diagonalize the matrix A given by Exercise 3 of Section A.9 into a matrix with characteristic roots on the diagonal, then diagonalize the matrix into an identity matrix.

A.12 Idempotent Matrices

A matrix that reproduces itself on multiplication by itself is said to be *idempotent*. Thus,

$$\text{the matrix } A \text{ is idempotent if and only if } AA = A. \tag{A.12.1}$$

For example, the matrix

$$A = \begin{bmatrix} 0.4 & 0.8 \\ 0.3 & 0.6 \end{bmatrix}$$

is idempotent because

$$AA = \begin{bmatrix} 0.4 & 0.8 \\ 0.3 & 0.6 \end{bmatrix}\begin{bmatrix} 0.4 & 0.8 \\ 0.3 & 0.6 \end{bmatrix} = \begin{bmatrix} 0.4 & 0.8 \\ 0.3 & 0.6 \end{bmatrix} = A$$

Note that the foregoing matrix A is not symmetric but singular since $|A| = 0$. In econometrics, we often deal with idempotent matrices that are symmetric. An example of an idempotent matrix that is symmetric and nonsingular is an identity matrix I because $I' = I$ and $II = I$. The most well-known symmetric idempotent matrix used in econometrics is the matrix $M = I - X(X'X)^{-1}X'$ of rank $T - K$. The matrix M is symmetric ($M' = M$) and reproduces itself on multiplication by itself ($MM = M$):

$$\begin{aligned} MM &= [I - X(X'X)^{-1}X'][I - X(X'X)^{-1}X'] \\ &= I - X(X'X)^{-1}X' - X(X'X)^{-1}X' + X(X'X)^{-1}X' \\ &= I - X(X'X)^{-1}X' \\ &= M \end{aligned} \tag{A.12.2}$$

A property of a symmetric idempotent matrix M is that the characteristic roots are all either 1 or 0. This is seen as follows: Let q be a characteristic root of the idempotent matrix A, that is, $A\mathbf{x} = q\mathbf{x}$ for some $\mathbf{x} \neq \mathbf{0}$. Because A is idempotent, $q\mathbf{x} = A\mathbf{x} = AA\mathbf{x} = Aq\mathbf{x} = qA\mathbf{x} = qq\mathbf{x}$ implies that $q\mathbf{x} = qq\mathbf{x}$, or $q(q-1)\mathbf{x} = \mathbf{0}$. The last expression implies that q is either 0 or 1.

Given the property of characteristic roots being 1 and 0 for a symmetric idempotent matrix, if the symmetric idempotent matrix M is diagonalized with its orthogonal matrix C, the result is

$$C'MC = \begin{bmatrix} I_{T-K} & 0 \\ 0 & 0 \end{bmatrix} = \Lambda \qquad \text{(A.12.3)}$$

because the rank of a diagonal matrix is equal to the number of nonzero elements on its diagonal, and the rank of the diagonalized matrix is equal to the rank of M, which is $T - K$. This implies that the idempotent matrix M has $T - K$ characteristic roots equal to 1 and K roots equal to 0. Obviously, the trace of M is also equal to its rank $T - K$. That is,

$$\text{if } M \text{ is symmetric and idempotent, then } \operatorname{rank}(M) = \operatorname{tr}(M). \qquad \text{(A.12.4)}$$

For example,

$$M = \begin{bmatrix} 0.8 & -0.4 \\ -0.4 & 0.2 \end{bmatrix}$$

is a symmetric idempotent matrix. The eigenvalues are 1 and 0. Its orthogonal matrix C is

$$C = \begin{bmatrix} 0.8944272 & 0.4472136 \\ -0.4472136 & 0.8944272 \end{bmatrix}$$

You should check to see if $C'MC = I_2$, $\operatorname{rank}(M) = 1$, and $\operatorname{tr}(M) = 1$.

The foregoing results are useful in deriving a χ^2-distribution from normal distributions. To see its usefulness, we need to first discuss quadratic forms (Section A.13), which then can be expressed as sums of squares.

Exercises

1 Let B be an $(n \times n)$ matrix with $1 - 1/n$ on the diagonal and $-1/n$ on the off-diagonal positions. Show that B is an idempotent matrix.

2 Show that the following nonsymmetric matrix is idempotent

$$\begin{bmatrix} 2 & -2 & -4 \\ -1 & 3 & 4 \\ 1 & -2 & -3 \end{bmatrix}$$

3 Show that the following symmetric matrix is idempotent

$$\begin{bmatrix} 1/6 & -2/6 & 1/6 \\ -2/6 & 4/6 & -2/6 \\ 1/6 & -2/6 & 1/6 \end{bmatrix}$$

4 Find the rank and trace of the matrix in Exercise 3.

A.13 Quadratic Forms

If A is an $(n \times n)$ symmetric matrix, the scalar

$$\mathbf{x}'A\mathbf{x} = \sum_{i=1}^{n} \sum_{j=1}^{n} a_{ij} x_i x_j \tag{A.13.1}$$

which is defined for all $(n \times 1)$ vectors $\mathbf{x}$, is said to be a quadratic form in $\mathbf{x}$, or in the elements of $\mathbf{x}$. For example,

$$\begin{bmatrix} x_1 \\ x_2 \end{bmatrix}' \begin{bmatrix} 1 & 2 \\ 2 & 4 \end{bmatrix} \begin{bmatrix} x_1 \\ x_2 \end{bmatrix} = x_1^2 + 4x_1x_2 + 4x_2^2$$

If $\text{rank}(A) = r$, then $\mathbf{x}'A\mathbf{x}$ is said to be a quadratic form of rank r. If A is symmetric and idempotent, then $\mathbf{x}'A\mathbf{x}$ is said to be a symmetric idempotent quadratic form. A useful property of an idempotent quadratic form is that it can be expressed as a sum of squares. To prove this, let C be the orthogonal matrix that diagonalizes the $(n \times n)$ idempotent matrix A of rank r into the diagonal matrix Λ of characteristic roots, which contain r ones and $n - r$ zeros. Then the idempotent quadratic form $\mathbf{x}'A\mathbf{x}$ can be expressed as a sum of squares:

$$\begin{aligned} \mathbf{x}'A\mathbf{x} &= \mathbf{x}'(CC')A(CC')\mathbf{x} \\ &= (\mathbf{x}'C)(C'AC)(C'\mathbf{x}) \\ &= (C'\mathbf{x})'\Lambda(C'\mathbf{x}) \\ &= \mathbf{y}'\Lambda\mathbf{y} \\ &= (\mathbf{y}_1' \quad \mathbf{y}_2') \begin{bmatrix} I_r & 0 \\ 0 & 0 \end{bmatrix} \begin{bmatrix} \mathbf{y}_1 \\ \mathbf{y}_2 \end{bmatrix} \\ &= \mathbf{y}_1'\mathbf{y}_1 \end{aligned} \tag{A.13.2}$$

where $\mathbf{y} = C'\mathbf{x}$, $\mathbf{y}_1$ is a $(r \times 1)$ vector and $\mathbf{y}_2$ is a $[(n - r) \times 1]$ vector. For example, the symmetric idempotent matrix

$$M = \begin{bmatrix} 0.8 & -0.4 \\ -0.4 & 0.2 \end{bmatrix}$$

has the corresponding matrix of characteristic vectors

$$C = \begin{bmatrix} 0.8944272 & 0.4472136 \\ -0.4472136 & 0.8944272 \end{bmatrix}$$

Let $y_1 = 0.8944272x_1 - 0.4472136x_2$, $y_2 = 0.4472136x_1 + 0.8944272x_2$, then the quadratic form can be expressed as

$$\begin{aligned}\begin{bmatrix} x_1 \\ x_2 \end{bmatrix}' \begin{bmatrix} 0.8 & -0.4 \\ -0.4 & 0.2 \end{bmatrix} \begin{bmatrix} x_1 \\ x_2 \end{bmatrix} &= 0.8x_1^2 - 0.8x_1x_2 + 0.2x_2^2 \\ &= y_1^2 \times 1 + y_2^2 \times 0 \\ &= y_1^2\end{aligned}$$

Exercises

1 Write the following quadratic forms in matrix notations

(*a*) $x_1^2 + 4x_1x_2 + 3x_2^2$

(*b*) $4x_1^2 - 6x_1x_2 + x_3^2$

2 If A is an $(n \times n)$ matrix and $\mathbf{x}$ is an $(n \times 1)$ vector, show that $\mathbf{x}'A\mathbf{x} = \mathbf{x}'B\mathbf{x}$, where $B = (A + A')/2$.

A.14 Definite Matrices

A symmetric matrix A is *positive definite* if and only if $\mathbf{x}'A\mathbf{x} > 0$ for all $\mathbf{x} \neq \mathbf{0}$. A symmetric matrix A is *nonnegative definite* (*positive semidefinite*) if and only if $\mathbf{x}'A\mathbf{x} \geq 0$ for all $\mathbf{x}$. A symmetric matrix A is negative definite if and only if $\mathbf{x}'A\mathbf{x} < 0$ for all $\mathbf{x} \neq \mathbf{0}$. Finally, a symmetric matrix A is *nonpositive definite* (*negative semidefinite*) if and only if $\mathbf{x}'A\mathbf{x} \leq 0$ for all $\mathbf{x}$.

A useful property that can be used to detect a positive definite matrix is the following: A symmetric matrix A is positive definite if and only if all the characteristic roots of A are positive. This follows from the diagonalization of a matrix:

$$\mathbf{x}'A\mathbf{x} = \mathbf{x}'CC'ACC'\mathbf{x} = \mathbf{x}'C\Lambda C'\mathbf{x} = \mathbf{y}'\Lambda\mathbf{y} = \sum_{i=1}^{n} \lambda_i y_i^2 \qquad \text{(A.14.1)}$$

where $\mathbf{y} = C'\mathbf{x}$ or $\mathbf{x} = C\mathbf{y}$. If all the characteristic roots λ_i are positive, then clearly $\mathbf{x}'A\mathbf{x} > 0$ for all $\mathbf{x} \neq \mathbf{0}$ and all $\mathbf{y} \neq \mathbf{0}$. Other properties are

1. If A is an $(n \times n)$ positive definite matrix, then $|A| > 0$, $\text{rank}(A) = n$, and A is nonsingular. (A.14.2)
2. If A is an $(n \times n)$ positive definite matrix and P is an $(n \times m)$ matrix with $\text{rank}(P) = m$, then $P'AP$ is positive definite. (A.14.3)
3. If A is positive definite and P is nonsingular, then $P'AP$ is positive definite. (A.14.4)
4. If A is positive definite, then A^{-1} is positive definite. (A.14.5)
5. If P is an $(n \times m)$ matrix with $\text{rank}(P) = m$, then $P'P$ is positive definite. (A.14.6)
6. If A is positive definite, every principal submatrix of A is positive definite. (A.14.7)
7. If A is positive definite, then every principal minor of A is positive. (A.14.8)
8. If A is positive definite, there exists a nonsingular matrix P such that $PAP' = I$ and $P'P = A^{-1}$. (A.14.9)
9. If A is nonnegative definite but not positive definite, then its smallest characteristic root is 0 and A is singular. (A.14.10)
10. If A is positive definite and B is nonnegative definite but not positive definite, then the smallest root of the equation $|B - \lambda A| = 0$ is zero. (A.14.11)
11. If $A = B + C$ where B is positive definite and C is nonnegative definite, then A is positive definite, $|B| \leq |A|$, and $B^{-1} - A^{-1}$ is nonnegative definite. (A.14.12)
12. If A is negative definite, then the principal minors of A alternate in sign: $a_{ii} < 0$, $a_{ii}a_{jj} - a_{ij}^2 > 0, \ldots$ (A.14.13)
13. A symmetric matrix A is positive semidefinite if and only if all of its characteristic roots are nonnegative. (A.14.14)
14. If A and B are symmetric and $A - B$ is positive definite, then $|A| \geq |B|$, $\mathbf{x}'A\mathbf{x} \geq \mathbf{x}'B\mathbf{x}$ for all $\mathbf{x}$, and $\text{tr}(A) \geq \text{tr}(B)$. (A.14.15)

Exercises

1 Show that

$$\begin{bmatrix} x_1 \\ x_2 \end{bmatrix}' \begin{bmatrix} 1 & 1 \\ 1 & 3 \end{bmatrix} \begin{bmatrix} x_1 \\ x_2 \end{bmatrix}$$

is always positive for all values of x_i except all zero.

2 Show that the matrix

$$\begin{bmatrix} 1 & 2 \\ 2 & 3 \end{bmatrix}$$

is not a positive definite matrix.

3 Let

$$A = \begin{bmatrix} 1 & 1 \\ 1 & 3 \end{bmatrix} \qquad B = \begin{bmatrix} 1 & 2 \\ 2 & 5 \end{bmatrix}$$

Show that $A + B$ is a positive definite matrix and $|B| \leq |A|$. Check to see if $B^{-1} - A^{-1}$ is nonnegative definite or positive definite.

A.15 Kronecker Product of Matrices

Let A be an $(M \times N)$ matrix and B be a $(K \times L)$ matrix. Then the Kronecker product (or direct product) of A and B, written $A \otimes B$, is defined as the $(MK \times NL)$ matrix

$$C = A \otimes B = \begin{bmatrix} a_{11}B & a_{12}B & \cdots & a_{1N}B \\ a_{21}B & a_{22}B & \cdots & a_{2N}B \\ \vdots & \vdots & \ddots & \vdots \\ a_{M1}B & a_{M2}B & \cdots & a_{MN}B \end{bmatrix} \tag{A.15.1}$$

For example, if

$$A = \begin{bmatrix} 1 & 3 \\ 2 & 0 \end{bmatrix} \quad \text{and} \quad B = \begin{bmatrix} 2 & 2 & 0 \\ 1 & 0 & 3 \end{bmatrix}$$

their Kronecker product is

$$A \otimes B = \begin{bmatrix} 1\begin{bmatrix} 2 & 2 & 0 \\ 1 & 0 & 3 \end{bmatrix} & 3\begin{bmatrix} 2 & 2 & 0 \\ 1 & 0 & 3 \end{bmatrix} \\ 2\begin{bmatrix} 2 & 2 & 0 \\ 1 & 0 & 3 \end{bmatrix} & 0\begin{bmatrix} 2 & 2 & 0 \\ 1 & 0 & 3 \end{bmatrix} \end{bmatrix}$$

$$= \begin{bmatrix} 2 & 2 & 0 & 6 & 6 & 0 \\ 1 & 0 & 3 & 3 & 0 & 9 \\ 4 & 4 & 0 & 0 & 0 & 0 \\ 2 & 0 & 6 & 0 & 0 & 0 \end{bmatrix}$$

Note that

$$B \otimes A = \begin{bmatrix} 2 & 6 & 2 & 6 & 0 & 0 \\ 4 & 0 & 4 & 0 & 0 & 0 \\ 1 & 3 & 0 & 0 & 3 & 9 \\ 2 & 0 & 0 & 0 & 6 & 0 \end{bmatrix}$$

and hence

$$B \otimes A \neq A \otimes B \tag{A.15.2}$$

Some other properties of the Kronecker product are

$$(A \otimes B)' = A' \otimes B' \tag{A.15.3}$$

and

$$(A \otimes B)(C \otimes D) = AC \otimes BD \tag{A.15.4}$$

where C and D are $(N \times P)$ and $(L \times Q)$ matrices, respectively. If A and B are nonsingular $(M \times M)$ and $(N \times N)$ matrices respectively, then the foregoing property implies that

$$(A \otimes B)(A^{-1} \otimes B^{-1}) = AA^{-1} \otimes BB^{-1} = I_M \otimes I_N = I_{MN} \tag{A.15.5}$$

The foregoing result, together with the uniqueness of the inverse, imply that

$$(A \otimes B)^{-1} = A^{-1} \otimes B^{-1} \tag{A.15.6}$$

Another useful property of the Kronecker product is that if A is a $(M \times N)$ matrix, B and C are $(K \times L)$ matrices, then

$$A \otimes (B + C) = A \otimes B + A \otimes C \tag{A.15.7}$$

The result holds because

$$\begin{bmatrix} a_{11}(B+C) & a_{12}(B+C) & \cdots & a_{1N}(B+C) \\ a_{21}(B+C) & a_{22}(B+C) & \cdots & a_{2N}(B+C) \\ \vdots & \vdots & \ddots & \vdots \\ a_{M1}(B+C) & a_{M2}(B+C) & \cdots & a_{MN}(B+C) \end{bmatrix}$$

$$= \begin{bmatrix} a_{11}B & \cdots & a_{1N}B \\ \vdots & \ddots & \vdots \\ a_{M1}B & \cdots & a_{MN}B \end{bmatrix} + \begin{bmatrix} a_{11}C & \cdots & a_{1N}C \\ \vdots & \ddots & \vdots \\ a_{M1}C & \cdots & a_{MN}C \end{bmatrix} \tag{A.15.8}$$

The Kronecker product representations of matrices are convenient for simplifying a rather complicated structure of matrices that can be characterized in blocks of submatrices. It is particularly useful in dealing with seemingly unrelated regression and systems of structural and reduced-form eouations.

Exercises

Let

$$A = \begin{bmatrix} 1 & 3 \\ 2 & 4 \end{bmatrix} \quad B = \begin{bmatrix} 5 & 7 \\ 6 & 8 \end{bmatrix} \quad C = \begin{bmatrix} 3 & 4 & 5 \\ 1 & 0 & 2 \end{bmatrix} \quad \text{and} \quad D = \begin{bmatrix} 4 & 0 & 1 \\ 0 & 3 & 9 \end{bmatrix}$$

Using these matrices, show that the following are true.

1 $B \otimes A \neq A \otimes B$

2 $(A \otimes B)' = A' \otimes B'$

3 $(A \otimes B)(C \otimes D) = AC \otimes BD$

4 $(A \otimes B)^{-1} = A^{-1} \otimes B^{-1}$

5 $A \otimes (C + D) = A \otimes C + A \otimes D$

A.16 Vectorization of Matrices

The following vectorization of matrices is designed to simplify notation. The covariance of a zero means vector $\mathbf{e}$ can be expressed as the mathematical expectation of $\mathbf{ee}'$, or $E[\mathbf{ee}']$. However, the covariance of a matrix of random variables cannot be expressed neatly in matrix notation. A convenient way to do it is first to rearrange the elements of the matrix into a vector, such as $\mathbf{e}$, and then apply the mathematical expectation of its cross-product matrix $\mathbf{ee}'$. To rearrange the elements of a matrix A into a vector, we introduce the *stacking operator*, or *vectorization operator*, vec(A), which takes the matrix A into a column vector, $\mathbf{a}$, by stacking the columns of A. That is, let A be an $(m \times n)$ matrix, then vec(A) is an $(mn \times 1)$ vector $\mathbf{a}$:

$$\begin{aligned} \text{vec}(A) &= \text{vec}(\mathbf{a}_1 \quad \mathbf{a}_2 \quad \cdots \quad \mathbf{a}_n) \\ &= \begin{bmatrix} \mathbf{a}_1 \\ \mathbf{a}_2 \\ \vdots \\ \mathbf{a}_n \end{bmatrix} = \mathbf{a} \end{aligned} \tag{A.16.1}$$

where $\mathbf{a}_i$ is the ith column of A.

An obvious result that holds based on the foregoing definition is

$$\text{vec}(A + B) = \text{vec}(A) + \text{vec}(B) \tag{A.16.2}$$

where A and B are of the same dimension. In the area of matrix multiplication, a useful property of the vectorization operation is the following.

If A is an $(m \times n)$ matrix, B is an $(n \times p)$ matrix, and C is a $(p \times q)$ matrix, then the vectorization of ABC can be expressed by

$$\text{vec}(ABC) = [C' \otimes A]\text{vec}(B) \tag{A.16.3}$$

The validity of this result can be seen from the following observation: On the right side of the equation, the jth subvector is $\sum_k c_{kj} A\mathbf{b}_k$, where $\mathbf{b}_k$ is the kth column of B. On the left side, the kth column of AB can be written as $A\mathbf{b}_k$, and the jth column of ABC can therefore be written as $\sum_k c_{kj} A\mathbf{b}_k$, which is the same as the jth subvector of the right side of the equation.

With the application of this basic relation, more useful relations can be generated:

$$\text{vec}(AB) = \text{vec}(IAB) = (B' \otimes I)\text{vec}(A) \tag{A.16.4}$$

$$\text{vec}(AB) = \text{vec}(ABI) = (I \otimes A)\text{vec}(B) \tag{A.16.5}$$

Using these two new results, we can state that

$$\text{vec}(ABC) = \text{vec}(A \cdot BC) = (C'B' \otimes I)\text{vec}(A) \tag{A.16.6}$$

and

$$\text{vec}(ABC) = \text{vec}(AB \cdot C) = (I \otimes AB)\text{vec}(C) \tag{A.16.7}$$

If another matrix D and the product $ABCD$ exist, similar formulas can be extended to expand vec$(ABCD)$ by the recursive use of these relations.

Another useful property of the vectorization operation is that the trace of the product of two matrices AB can be expressed by the inner product of the vectorization of the two matrices in the following manner:

$$\begin{aligned} \text{tr}(AB) = \sum_{k,i} a_{ik} b_{ki} &= [\text{vec}(A')]' \text{ vec}(B) \\ &= [\text{vec}(B)]' \text{ vec}(A') \\ = \text{tr}(BA) \quad &= [\text{vec}(B')]' \text{ vec}(A) \\ &= [\text{vec}(A)]' \text{ vec}(B') \end{aligned} \tag{A.16.8}$$

We will conclude this section by showing a popular application of vectorization in the estimation of reduced-form parameters of a system of simultaneous equations (see Chapters 14 and 15). Let Y be a $(T \times M)$ matrix, X be a $(T \times K)$ matrix, Π be a $(K \times M)$ matrix, and V be a $(T \times M)$ matrix. Assume that the following relation holds

$$Y = X\Pi + V \tag{A.16.9}$$

This relation represents a set of regression equations and is often considered as regressions in a block. Expressing the covariance matrix for the matrix of equation errors, V, is cumbersome. If we apply the vectorization operator to both sides of the equation, we obtain

$$\text{vec}(Y) = \text{vec}(X\Pi) + \text{vec}(V) \tag{A.16.10}$$

which can be reduced to

$$\mathbf{y} = (I \otimes X)\text{vec}(\Pi) + \mathbf{v} \tag{A.16.11}$$

where $\mathbf{y} = \text{vec}(Y)$ and $\mathbf{v} = \text{vec}(V)$. Let $\boldsymbol{\pi} = \text{vec}(\Pi)$, then we have the conventional regression format

$$\mathbf{y} = (I \otimes X)\boldsymbol{\pi} + \mathbf{v} \tag{A.16.12}$$

For details, see Chapters 14 and 15 on the estimation of the parameters of a system of simultaneous equations.

Exercises

1 Let

$$A = \begin{bmatrix} 3 & 5 & 8 \\ 2 & 1 & 0 \\ 6 & 4 & 7 \end{bmatrix} \qquad B = \begin{bmatrix} 0 & 3 & 1 \\ 4 & 0 & 2 \\ 5 & 6 & 0 \end{bmatrix}$$

Find vec(A) and vec(B).

2 Using the numbers in Exercise 1, show that

$$\text{vec}(AB) = (I_3 \otimes A)\text{vec}(B)$$

3 Using the numbers in Exercise 1, show that

$$\text{tr}(AB) = [\text{vec}(A)]' \, \text{vec}(B')$$

4 Let $\mathbf{c} = (1 \quad 1 \quad 1)'$. Using the numbers in $\mathbf{c}$ and those numbers defined for A and B in Exercise 1, show that

$$\text{vec}(AB\mathbf{c}) = (I_1 \otimes AB)\text{vec}(\mathbf{c})$$

5 Let $\hat{\Pi} = (X'X)^{-1}X'Y$, where X is a $(T \times K)$ matrix, Y is a $(T \times M)$ matrix, and $\hat{\Pi}$ is a $(K \times M)$ matrix. Show $\text{vec}(\hat{\Pi}) = (I \otimes (X'X)^{-1}X')\mathbf{y}$, where $\mathbf{y} = \text{vec}(Y)$.

A.17 Vector and Matrix Differentiation

In least squares and maximum likelihood estimation of regression parameters, we need to take the derivatives of the objective function with respect to a vector of parameters. This requires a basic definition of vector differentiation. The basic rules of vector differentiation can be defined, derived, and extended to the case of matrix differentiation.

Let a function relating y to a set of variables $x_1, x_2, \ldots, x_n$ be

$$y = f(x_1, x_2, \ldots, x_n) \tag{A.17.1a}$$

or, in a simplified matrix notation,

$$y = f(\mathbf{x}) \tag{A.17.1b}$$

where $\mathbf{x}$ is an $(n \times 1)$ column vector. We need to take the derivatives of y with respect to each of the elements of $\mathbf{x}$ and write the results in a vector form. Therefore, we define the following column vector of derivatives:

$$\partial y/\partial \mathbf{x} = \begin{bmatrix} \partial y/\partial x_1 \\ \partial y/\partial x_2 \\ \vdots \\ \partial y/\partial x_n \end{bmatrix} \tag{A.17.2}$$

This is known as the *gradient* of y. The operations defined in (A.17.2) can be extended to the derivatives of y with respect to the elements of an $(m \times n)$ matrix X.

$$\begin{aligned} \partial y/\partial X &= [\partial y/\partial \mathbf{x}_1 \quad \cdots \quad \partial y/\partial \mathbf{x}_n] \\ &= \begin{bmatrix} \partial y/\partial x_{11} & \partial y/\partial x_{12} & \cdots & \partial y/\partial x_{1n} \\ \partial y/\partial x_{21} & \partial y/\partial x_{22} & \cdots & \partial y/\partial x_{2n} \\ \vdots & \vdots & \ddots & \vdots \\ \partial y/\partial x_{m1} & \partial y/\partial x_{m2} & \cdots & \partial y/\partial x_{mn} \end{bmatrix} \end{aligned} \tag{A.17.3}$$

where $\mathbf{x}_1, \ldots, \mathbf{x}_n$ are columns of X.

Let $\mathbf{y}$ be an $(m \times 1)$ column vector of y_i, $i = 1, 2, \ldots, m$, and $\mathbf{x}$ be an $(n \times 1)$ column vector of $x_j, j = 1, 2, \ldots, n$. We define the derivatives of $\mathbf{y}$ with respect to $\mathbf{x}'$ as an $(m \times n)$ matrix:

$$\begin{aligned} \partial \mathbf{y}/\partial \mathbf{x}' &= [\partial y_i/\partial x_j] \\ &= \begin{bmatrix} \partial y_1/\partial x_1 & \cdots & \partial y_1/\partial x_n \\ \vdots & \ddots & \vdots \\ \partial y_m/\partial x_1 & \cdots & \partial y_m/\partial x_n \end{bmatrix} \end{aligned} \tag{A.17.4}$$

This matrix is also known as the Jacobian matrix of $\mathbf{y}$ with respect to $\mathbf{x}'$.

The second derivatives of y with respect to the column vector $\mathbf{x}$ are defined as the following matrix:

$$\begin{aligned}\partial^2 y/\partial \mathbf{x}\partial \mathbf{x}' &= \partial(\partial y/\partial \mathbf{x})/\partial \mathbf{x}' \\ &= [\partial^2 y/\partial x_i\, \partial x_j] \\ &= \begin{bmatrix} \partial^2 y/\partial x_1\, \partial x_1 & \cdots & \partial^2 y/\partial x_1\, \partial x_n \\ \vdots & \ddots & \vdots \\ \partial^2 y/\partial x_n\, \partial x_1 & \cdots & \partial^2 y/\partial x_n\, \partial x_n \end{bmatrix}\end{aligned} \tag{A.17.5}$$

which is a symmetric matrix. It is called the *Hessian matrix* of y.

Based on the foregoing basic definitions, the rules of derivatives in matrix notation can be established for reference. Consider the following function: $z = \mathbf{c}'\mathbf{x}$, where $\mathbf{c}$ is an $(n \times 1)$ vector and does not depend on $\mathbf{x}$, $\mathbf{x}$ is an $(n \times 1)$ vector, and z is a scalar. Then

$$\partial z/\partial \mathbf{x} = \partial \mathbf{c}'\mathbf{x}/\partial \mathbf{x} = \partial \mathbf{x}'\mathbf{c}/\partial \mathbf{x} = \begin{bmatrix} \partial z/\partial x_1 \\ \vdots \\ \partial z/\partial x_n \end{bmatrix} = \begin{bmatrix} c_1 \\ \vdots \\ c_n \end{bmatrix} = \mathbf{c} \tag{A.17.6}$$

If $z = C'\mathbf{x}$, where C is an $(n \times n)$ matrix and $\mathbf{x}$ is an $(n \times 1)$ vector, then

$$\partial z'/\partial \mathbf{x} = \partial \mathbf{x}'C/\partial \mathbf{x} = (\mathbf{c}_1 \quad \mathbf{c}_2 \quad \cdots \quad \mathbf{c}_n) = C \tag{A.17.7}$$

where $\mathbf{c}_i$ is the ith column of C.

The following formula for the quadratic form $z = \mathbf{x}'A\mathbf{x}$ is also useful:

$$\partial z/\partial \mathbf{x} = \partial \mathbf{x}'A\mathbf{x}/\partial \mathbf{x} = A'\mathbf{x} + A\mathbf{x} = (A' + A)\mathbf{x} \tag{A.17.8a}$$

because $z = \sum_{j=1}^{n} \sum_{i=1}^{n} a_{ij}x_i x_j$ and the differentiation with respect to the kth element of $\mathbf{x}$ is

$$\partial z/\partial x_k = \sum_{j=1}^{n} a_{kj}x_j + \sum_{i=1}^{n} a_{ik}x_i, \qquad k = 1, 2, \ldots, n \tag{A.17.8b}$$

If A is an $(n \times n)$ symmetric matrix, that is, $A = A'$, then

$$\partial \mathbf{x}'A\mathbf{x}/\partial \mathbf{x} = 2A\mathbf{x} \tag{A.17.9}$$

Based on the derivatives of linear and quadratic forms, the second derivatives are

$$\partial^2(\mathbf{x}'A\mathbf{x})/\partial\mathbf{x}\,\partial\mathbf{x}' = A + A' \tag{A.17.10}$$

and if $A = A'$

$$\partial^2(\mathbf{x}'A\mathbf{x})/\partial\mathbf{x}\,\partial\mathbf{x}' = 2A \tag{A.17.11}$$

Finally, consider the expression $\mathbf{x}'B\mathbf{y}$, where $\mathbf{x}$ and $\mathbf{y}$ are $(n \times 1)$ vectors and B is an $(n \times n)$ matrix. The derivatives of this form with respect to the elements of B are

$$\partial\mathbf{x}'B\mathbf{y}/\partial b_{ij} = x_i y_j \tag{A.17.12}$$

because $\mathbf{x}'B\mathbf{y} = \sum_i \sum_j x_i b_{ij} y_j$. Assembling all the elements for B yields

$$\partial\mathbf{x}'B\mathbf{y}/\partial B = [x_i y_j] = \mathbf{x}\mathbf{y}' \tag{A.17.13}$$

Without elaborating, the following rules are also useful:

$$\partial\,\mathrm{tr}\,(A)/\partial A = I \tag{A.17.14}$$

$$\partial|A|/\partial A = |A|(A')^{-1} \tag{A.17.15}$$

$$\partial\ln|A|/\partial A = (A')^{-1} \tag{A.17.16}$$

$$\partial AB/\partial x = A(\partial B/\partial x) + (\partial A/\partial x)B \tag{A.17.17}$$

$$\partial A^{-1}/\partial x = -A^{-1}(\partial A/\partial x)A^{-1} \tag{A.17.18}$$

where x is a scalar.

Exercises

1 Let $\mathbf{x}$ be an $(n \times 1)$ vector and A be an $(n \times n)$ matrix. Show that the quadratic form $\mathbf{x}'A\mathbf{x}$ is equivalent to $\mathbf{x}'B\mathbf{x}$ where $B = (A + A')/2$.

2 Show that $\partial(\mathbf{y} - X\boldsymbol{\beta})'(\mathbf{y} - X\boldsymbol{\beta})/\partial\boldsymbol{\beta} = -2X'(\mathbf{y} - X\boldsymbol{\beta})$, where $\mathbf{y}$ is a $(T \times 1)$ vector, X is a $(T \times K)$ matrix, and $\boldsymbol{\beta}$ is a $(K \times 1)$ vector.

3 Show that $\partial(\mathbf{y} - X\boldsymbol{\beta})'\Sigma^{-1}(\mathbf{y} - X\boldsymbol{\beta})/\partial\boldsymbol{\beta} = -2X'\Sigma^{-1}(\mathbf{y} - X\boldsymbol{\beta})$, where $\mathbf{y}$, X, and $\boldsymbol{\beta}$ are defined in Exercise 2, and Σ is a $(T \times T)$ matrix.

4 Let $z = -\mathbf{y}'X\boldsymbol{\beta} + (1/2)\boldsymbol{\beta}'X'X\boldsymbol{\beta}$, where $\mathbf{y}$ is a $(T \times 1)$ vector, X is a $(T \times K)$ matrix, and $\boldsymbol{\beta}$ is a $(K \times 1)$ vector. Find $\partial z/\partial\boldsymbol{\beta}$, set it to $\mathbf{0}$, and solve for $\boldsymbol{\beta}$.

5 Let $z = (\mathbf{y} - X\boldsymbol{\beta})'(\mathbf{y} - X\boldsymbol{\beta}) + \boldsymbol{\lambda}'(R\boldsymbol{\beta} - \mathbf{r})$, where $\mathbf{y}$ is a $(T \times 1)$ vector, X is a $(T \times K)$ matrix, $\boldsymbol{\beta}$ is a $(K \times 1)$ vector, $\boldsymbol{\lambda}$ and $\mathbf{r}$ are $(J \times 1)$ vectors, and R is a $(J \times K)$ matrix. Find $\partial z/\partial\boldsymbol{\beta}$.

A.18 Normal Vectors and Multivariate Normal Distribution

An $(n \times 1)$ random vector $\mathbf{x}$ is a normal vector if its probability density function is

$$f(\mathbf{x}) = (2\pi)^{-n/2}|\Sigma|^{-1/2} \exp\{-(1/2)(\mathbf{x} - \mu)'\Sigma^{-1}(\mathbf{x} - \mu)\} \qquad \text{(A.18.1)}$$

where $\boldsymbol{\mu} = (\mu_1 \quad \mu_2 \quad \cdots \quad \mu_n)'$ and the positive definite matrix

$$\Sigma = \begin{bmatrix} \sigma_{11} & \cdots & \sigma_{1n} \\ \vdots & \ddots & \vdots \\ \sigma_{n1} & \cdots & \sigma_{nn} \end{bmatrix} \qquad \text{(A.18.2)}$$

are parameters. We say that $\mathbf{x}$ is multivariate normally distributed with mean $\boldsymbol{\mu}$ and variance-covariance matrix Σ. An abbreviated notation is

$$\mathbf{x} \sim N(\boldsymbol{\mu}, \Sigma) \qquad \text{(A.18.3)}$$

The normal distribution has the following properties. If

$$\mathbf{x} \sim N(\boldsymbol{\mu}, \Sigma), \text{ then } \mathbf{x} - \boldsymbol{\mu} \sim N(\mathbf{0}, \Sigma) \qquad \text{(A.18.4)}$$

which can be thought of as an "additive property."

Let $\mathbf{c}$ be an $(n \times 1)$ vector of constants. The distribution of the inner product $\mathbf{c}'\mathbf{x}$, which is a scalar, is univariate normally distributed:

$$\mathbf{c}'\mathbf{x} \sim N(\mathbf{c}'\boldsymbol{\mu}, \mathbf{c}'\Sigma\mathbf{c}) \qquad \text{(A.18.5)}$$

which can be thought of as a "multiplicative property." If C is an $(m \times n)$ matrix, then the $(m \times 1)$ vector $C\mathbf{x}$ is also normally distributed:

$$C\mathbf{x} \sim N(C\boldsymbol{\mu}, C\Sigma C') \qquad \text{(A.18.6)}$$

Thus, $C\mathbf{x}$ is a linear transformation of n normal variables to m normal variables, where m cannot exceed n. When $m = n$, C becomes a square matrix and is required to have rank m so that $C\Sigma C'$ is positive definite as required for positive values of variances. The problem with $m > n$ is that the matrices C and $C\Sigma C'$ cannot have full rank and the singular covariance matrix possesses no inverse, which is required in the expression of the probability density function.

The univariate variable $z = \mathbf{c}'(\mathbf{x} - \boldsymbol{\mu})$ is also normally distributed:

$$\mathbf{c}'(\mathbf{x} - \boldsymbol{\mu}) \sim N(0, \mathbf{c}'\Sigma\mathbf{c}) \qquad \text{(A.18.7)}$$

Also the $(m \times 1)$ vector $C(\mathbf{x} - \boldsymbol{\mu})$ is a multivariate normal:

$$C(\mathbf{x} - \boldsymbol{\mu}) \sim N(\mathbf{0}, C\Sigma C') \qquad \text{(A.18.8)}$$

If we choose $C = P'$, where P is the matrix that diagonalizes Σ into an identity matrix I ($P'\Sigma P = I$) of dimension n (see Section A.11), then $\mathbf{z} = P'(\mathbf{x} - \boldsymbol{\mu})$ is an $(n \times 1)$ standard multivariate normal vector:

$$P'(\mathbf{x} - \boldsymbol{\mu}) \sim N(\mathbf{0}, I) \tag{A.18.9}$$

which has the probability density function

$$f(\mathbf{z}) = (2\pi)^{-(n/2)} \exp\{-\mathbf{z}'\mathbf{z}/2\} \tag{A.18.10}$$

Thus a normal vector can be transformed into a standard normal vector by subtracting out its mean vector and applying a certain nonsingular transformation. The elements of the standard normal vector have zero means, unit variance, and zero covariances. The marginal distribution of each element of the standard normal vector is a univariate normal with mean zero and variance unity. This can be seen as follows: Without loss of generality, let $\mathbf{c}$ be an $(n \times 1)$ unit vector with 1 on the first position, that is, $\mathbf{c} = (1 \quad 0 \quad \cdots \quad 0)'$. Then $\mathbf{c}'\mathbf{x} = x_1$, and

$$\begin{aligned} \mathbf{c}'\mathbf{x} = x_1 &\sim N(\mathbf{c}'\boldsymbol{\mu}, \mathbf{c}'\Sigma\mathbf{c}) \\ &\sim N(\mu_1, \sigma_{11}) \end{aligned} \tag{A.18.11}$$

where $\mathbf{c}'\boldsymbol{\mu} = \mu_1$, and $\mathbf{c}'\Sigma\mathbf{c} = \sigma_{11}$ because of the unit vector $\mathbf{c}$.

For example, in this book, we often deal with the model

$$\mathbf{y} = X\boldsymbol{\beta} + \mathbf{e} \tag{A.18.12}$$

where $\mathbf{y}$ is a $(T \times 1)$ vector, X is a $(T \times K)$ matrix of fixed nonstochastic observations, $\boldsymbol{\beta}$ is a $(K \times 1)$ vector of unknown parameters, and $\mathbf{e}$ is a $(T \times 1)$ vector of normal random errors with a mean vector

$$E[\mathbf{e}] = \mathbf{0} \tag{A.18.13}$$

and a variance-covariance matrix

$$E[\mathbf{e}\mathbf{e}'] = \sigma^2 I \tag{A.18.14}$$

Given that $\mathbf{e} \sim N(\mathbf{0}, \sigma^2 I)$, we would like to find the distribution of the least squares estimator $\mathbf{b} = (X'X)^{-1}X'\mathbf{y}$. Applying the properties of linear transformations, we can derive the distributions of $\mathbf{y}$ and $\mathbf{b}$:

$$\mathbf{y} \sim N(X\boldsymbol{\beta}, \sigma^2 I) \tag{A.18.15}$$

and

$$\begin{aligned} \mathbf{b} &\sim N((X'X)^{-1}X'X\boldsymbol{\beta}, (X'X)^{-1}X'\sigma^2 IX(X'X)^{-1}) \\ &\sim N(\boldsymbol{\beta}, \sigma^2(X'X)^{-1}) \end{aligned} \tag{A.18.16}$$

Also, the marginal distribution of the elements of **b** can be obtained by finding the distribution of $\mathbf{c}'\mathbf{b}$ with $\mathbf{c} = (0 \quad \cdots \quad 1 \quad \cdots \quad 0)'$, a unit vector with 1 on the ith position and 0 elsewhere. The distribution is

$$\begin{aligned} b_i = \mathbf{c}'\mathbf{b} &\sim N(\mathbf{c}'\boldsymbol{\beta}, \mathbf{c}'\sigma^2(X'X)^{-1}\mathbf{c}) \\ &\sim N(\beta_i, \sigma^2(X'X)_{ii}^{-1}) \end{aligned} \tag{A.18.17}$$

where $(X'X)_{ii}^{-1}$ denotes the ith diagonal element of $(X'X)^{-1}$.

Instead of (A.18.14), if the covariance matrix of **e** is

$$E[\mathbf{e}\mathbf{e}'] = \sigma^2\boldsymbol{\Psi} \tag{A.18.18}$$

then the distributions of **y** and **b** would be

$$\mathbf{y} \sim N(X\boldsymbol{\beta}, \sigma^2\boldsymbol{\Psi}) \tag{A.18.19}$$

and

$$\begin{aligned} \mathbf{b} &\sim N[(X'X)^{-1}X'X\boldsymbol{\beta}, (X'X)^{-1}X'\sigma^2\boldsymbol{\Psi}X(X'X)^{-1}] \\ &\sim N[\boldsymbol{\beta}, \sigma^2(X'X)^{-1}X'\boldsymbol{\Psi}X(X'X)^{-1}] \end{aligned} \tag{A.18.20}$$

The distributions of other estimators such as generalized least squares estimators can be derived in a similar way. These properties are linear properties in that the transformations involve linear combinations of the elements of the normal vector and the addition of constants. There are other quadratic properties that will be discussed in Section A.19.

Exercises

Let $\mathbf{x} = (x_1 \quad x_2)'$, and **x** is bivariate normally distributed with mean vector

$$\boldsymbol{\mu} = (1 \quad 2)'$$

and covariance matrix

$$\Sigma = \begin{bmatrix} 1 & 1 \\ 1 & 2 \end{bmatrix}$$

1 Find the mean vector and covariance matrix of $\mathbf{c}'\mathbf{x}$, where $\mathbf{c} = (4 \quad 5)'$.

2 Find the mean vector and covariance matrix of $C'\mathbf{x}$, where

$$C = \begin{bmatrix} 2 & 3 \\ 5 & 8 \end{bmatrix}$$

3 Find the (2×2) matrix P such that $P'(\mathbf{x} - \boldsymbol{\mu})$ is $N(\mathbf{0}, I)$.

4 Find the (2×2) matrix Q such that $Q'(\mathbf{x} - \boldsymbol{\mu})$ is $N(\mathbf{0}, \sigma^2 I)$.

5 Find the (2×2) matrix R such that $R'\mathbf{x}$ is $N(R'\boldsymbol{\mu}, I)$.

A.19 Linear, Quadratic, and Other Nonlinear Functions of Normal Vectors

Some linear properties of the normal random vector are discussed in the previous section. Now we examine more properties of linear, quadratic, and other nonlinear functions of the normal random vector.

Before considering transformations of a standard normal random vector, consider a transformation of a standard normal random variable. If z_i is $N(0, 1)$, the squared transformation of z_i, $y = z_i^2$, becomes a χ^2 random variable with 1 degree of freedom. It has a mean of 1 and variance of 2. (The mathematical proof is omitted here. It would involve a variable transformation on the probability density function corrected with the Jacobian.) The χ^2 probability density function with n degrees of freedom is

$$f(\chi^2) = [2^{n/2}\Gamma(n/2)]^{-1}(\chi^2)^{n/2-1}\exp(-\chi^2/2)$$

where $\chi^2 > 0$, n is the degrees of freedom, and $\Gamma(n)$ is the gamma function given by

$$\Gamma(n) = \int_0^\infty x^{n-1}e^{-x}\,dx \qquad n > 0$$

The χ^2 distribution has a mean equal to its degrees of freedom, n, and variance equal to twice the degrees of freedom, $2n$. The χ^2 distribution has the property that the sum of two independent χ^2 random variables is also a χ^2 random variable with the degrees of freedom equal to the sum of the respective degrees of freedom. In general, the sum of n independent χ^2 random variables is also a χ^2 random variable with degrees of freedom equal to the sum of the respective degrees of freedom.

If $\mathbf{z}$ is an $(n \times 1)$ standard normal random vector, that is,

$$\mathbf{z} \sim N(\mathbf{0}, I) \tag{A.19.1}$$

then

$$\mathbf{z}'\mathbf{z} \sim \chi^2(n) \tag{A.19.2}$$

where $\chi^2(n)$ denotes a χ^2 variable with n degrees of freedom. This is because $\mathbf{z}'\mathbf{z} = \sum_i z_i^2$ and $z_1, z_2, \ldots, z_n$ are independent standard normal variables. Now we can establish some results for future reference:

$$\mathbf{z}'\mathbf{z} = \mathbf{z}'I_n\mathbf{z} \sim \chi^2(n) \tag{A.19.3}$$

Let J_r be

$$J_r = \begin{bmatrix} I_r & 0 \\ 0 & 0_{n-r} \end{bmatrix} \tag{A.19.4}$$

where I_r is a $(r \times r)$ identity matrix and 0_{n-r} is an $(n-r) \times (n-r)$ matrix of zeros, then

$$\mathbf{z}'J_r\mathbf{z} = \sum_{i=1}^{n} z_i^2 \sim \chi^2(r) \tag{A.19.5}$$

Let M be an $(n \times n)$ symmetric idempotent matrix of rank r, then

$$\mathbf{z}'M\mathbf{z} = \mathbf{z}'C'CMC'C\mathbf{z} = \mathbf{y}'J_r\mathbf{y} \sim \chi^2(r) \tag{A.19.6}$$

where $C'C = I_n$, $CMC' = J_r$, $\mathbf{y} = C\mathbf{z}$, and $\mathbf{y} \sim N(\mathbf{0}, C'I_nC) = N(\mathbf{0}, I_n)$. Let $\mathbf{x}$ be a spherical normal random vector, that is,

$$\mathbf{x} \sim N(\mathbf{0}, \sigma^2 I_n) \tag{A.19.7}$$

then

$$\mathbf{x}'\mathbf{x} \sim \sigma^2\chi^2(n) \tag{A.19.8}$$

$$\mathbf{x}'M\mathbf{x} \sim \sigma^2\chi^2(r) \tag{A.19.9}$$

Before we proceed to derive more results of combining linear and quadratic transformations, we need a way to check independence of two random variables. Let

$$F = (C_r \quad 0) \tag{A.19.10}$$

be an $(n \times n)$ marix with the last $n - r$ columns all zero. Let

$$G = (0 \quad C_s) \tag{A.19.11}$$

be an $(n \times n)$ matrix with the first $n - s$ columns all zero, where $s \leq n - r$. Then $F\mathbf{z}$ and $G\mathbf{z}$ are independent because the former is a linear combination of the first r elements of $\mathbf{z}$ and the latter is a linear combination of the last s elements of $\mathbf{z}$ and both have no common elements of $\mathbf{z}$. Also $F\mathbf{z}$ and $\mathbf{z}'L_s\mathbf{z}$ and $G\mathbf{z}$ and $\mathbf{z}'J_r\mathbf{z}$ are independent. The independence is characterized by the relations

$$FL_s = (C_r \quad 0)\begin{bmatrix} 0 & 0 \\ 0 & I_s \end{bmatrix} = \begin{bmatrix} 0 & 0 \\ 0 & 0 \end{bmatrix} \tag{A.19.12}$$

and

$$GJ_r = (0 \quad C_s)\begin{bmatrix} I_r & 0 \\ 0 & 0 \end{bmatrix} = \begin{bmatrix} 0 & 0 \\ 0 & 0 \end{bmatrix} \tag{A.19.13}$$

Let L_s be

$$L_s = \begin{bmatrix} 0 & 0 & 0 \\ 0 & 0 & 0 \\ 0 & 0 & I_s \end{bmatrix} \tag{A.19.14}$$

where s is less than or equal to $n - r$. The quadratic form $\mathbf{z}'L_s\mathbf{z}$ is independent of $\mathbf{z}'J_r\mathbf{z}$ because the former is a quadratic function of the last s elements of $\mathbf{z}$ and the latter is a quadratic function of the first r elements of $\mathbf{z}$, and the two functions have none of these elements in common. They are characterized by the relation

$$J_r L_s = 0_n \tag{A.19.15}$$

Therefore, if $\mathbf{y}$ is an $(n \times 1)$ standard normal random vector, A is a $(k \times n)$ matrix, and M is an $(n \times n)$ symmetric idempotent matrix, then the linear form $A\mathbf{y}$ is distributed independently of the quadratic form $\mathbf{y}'M\mathbf{y}$ when $AM = 0$. Also if N is an $(n \times n)$ symmetric idempotent matrix of rank s, and $NM = 0$, then the quadratic form $\mathbf{y}'M\mathbf{y}$ is distributed independently of the quadratic form $\mathbf{y}'N\mathbf{y}$. This statement is also true for $\mathbf{x} = \sigma\mathbf{y}$, a spherical normal random vector, that is, distributed as $N(0, \sigma^2 I)$. That is,

$$A\mathbf{x} \text{ and } \mathbf{x}'M\mathbf{x} \text{ are independent if } AM = 0 \tag{A.19.16}$$

Also,

$$\mathbf{x}'M\mathbf{x} \text{ and } \mathbf{x}'N\mathbf{x} \text{ are independent if } MN = 0 \tag{A.19.17}$$

Given the independent random variables, the F- and t-distributions can be defined:

$$F(r, s) = [(\mathbf{x}'M\mathbf{x}/\sigma^2)/r]/[\mathbf{x}'N\mathbf{x}/\sigma^2)/s] \tag{A.19.18}$$

is distributed as an F random variable. The F-distribution is not symmetric and has a mean equal to $s/(s-2)$ for $s > 2$, and variance equal to $2(r + s - 2)s^2/[(s-2)^2(s-4)r]$ for $s > 4$. The F-distribution is a two-parameter family of distributions and has the property that its reciprocal is also an F-distribution with the numerator degrees of freedom and denominator degrees of freedom reversed, that is

$$1/F(r, s) = F(s, r) \tag{A.19.19}$$

Also, when s approaches infinity, $rF(r, s)$ approaches the $\chi^2(r)$.

Similarly, if the elements of $A\mathbf{z}$ are distributed as standard normal independent of $\mathbf{z}'M\mathbf{z}$ that is distributed as a χ^2 with r degrees of freedom, by a variable transformation, the following ratio of the standard normal to the square root of the χ^2 adjusted (divided) by its degrees of freedom is a vector of Student t random variables, that is

$$[t_1(r) \quad t_2(r) \quad \cdots \quad t_k(r)]' = A\mathbf{z}/(\mathbf{z}'M\mathbf{z}/r)^{1/2} \tag{A.19.20}$$

where $t_i(r)$, $i = 1, 2, \ldots, k$, are the Student t variables. The t-distribution, denoted as $t(r)$ where r is its degrees of freedom, is symmetric, has mean 0 and variance $r/(r-2)$ for $r > 2$, and approaches the standard normal distribution $N(0, 1)$ when r approaches infinity. The t-distribution has the property that its square becomes an F distribution, that is,

$$t^2(r) = F(1, r) \tag{A.19.21}$$

There are some distributions that can be derived from a normal vector that is not necessarily standard or spherical. For example, if the $(T \times 1)$ vector $\mathbf{x}$ is distributed as $N(\mathbf{d}, A)$, then $\mathbf{x}'A^{-1}\mathbf{x}$ can be shown to be distributed as a noncentral χ^2 with T degrees of freedom and noncentrality parameter

$$\lambda = \mathbf{d}'A^{-1}\mathbf{d}/2 \tag{A.19.22}$$

The noncentral χ^2 is a two-parameter family of distributions. Another example is that if the random vectors $\mathbf{x}$ and $\mathbf{y}$ are distributed $N(\mathbf{d}, \sigma^2 I_T)$ and $N(0, \sigma^2 I_T)$, respectively, and A and B are symmetric idempotent matrices of rank K and J, respectively, where $BA = 0$, then the ratio

$$u = [(\mathbf{x}'A\mathbf{x}/\sigma^2)/(\mathbf{y}'B\mathbf{y}/\sigma^2)]/(J/K) \tag{A.19.23}$$

is distributed as a noncentral $F(K, J, \lambda)$ random variable with the noncentrality parameter

$$\lambda = \mathbf{d}'A\mathbf{d}/(2\sigma^2) \tag{A.19.24}$$

The noncentral F-distribution is a three-parameter family of distributions.

Exercises

1 Let $\mathbf{z}$ be a $(K \times 1)$ standard normal vector, $A = (X'X)^{-1}X'$, $M = I - XA$, where X is a $(T \times K)$ matrix and I is a $(T \times T)$ identity matrix. Show that $A\mathbf{z}$ is distributed independently of $\mathbf{z}'M\mathbf{z}$.

2 Given the notations defined in Exercise 1, show that $A\mathbf{y}$ is distributed independently of $\mathbf{y}'M\mathbf{y}$, where $\mathbf{y}$ is a $(K \times 1)$ vector distributed as $N(\mathbf{0}, \sigma^2 I)$.

3 Let $\mathbf{x}$ be a $(K \times 1)$ vector distributed as $N(\mathbf{u}, \sigma^2 I)$. Identify the distributions of the following statistics

$$(\mathbf{x} - \mathbf{u})'(\mathbf{x} - \mathbf{u})/\sigma^2 \qquad \text{and} \qquad (\mathbf{x} - \mathbf{u})/\sigma$$

and examine them to see if they are distributed independently.

4 Let $\mathbf{x}$ be an $(n \times 1)$ normal vector distributed as $N(\mathbf{u}, \sigma^2 I)$, $\mathbf{a}$ is an $(n \times 1)$ vector with each element equal to $1/n$, M is an $(n \times n)$ matrix with $1 - 1/n$ on the diagonal and $-1/n$ elsewhere. Show that $\mathbf{a}'\mathbf{x}$ is distributed independently of $\mathbf{x}'M\mathbf{x}$.

5 If the $(K \times 1)$ vector $\mathbf{b}$ is distributed as $N[\boldsymbol{\beta}, \sigma^2(X'X)^{-1}]$, where X is $(T \times K)$ and $K < T$, show that

$$(R\mathbf{b} - R\boldsymbol{\beta})'[R(X'X)^{-1}R']^{-1}(R\mathbf{b} - R\boldsymbol{\beta})$$

is distributed as χ^2 with J degrees of freedom, where R is $(J \times K)$ and of rank $J < K$.

6 Let $\mathbf{z}$ be an $(n \times 1)$ standard normal vector, A an $(n \times n)$ idempotent matrix of rank r, and B an $(n \times n)$ idempotent matrix of rank s. Show that $A\mathbf{z}$ and $\mathbf{z}'B\mathbf{z}$ and $\mathbf{z}'A\mathbf{z}$ and $\mathbf{z}'B\mathbf{z}$ are not independent if $r + s > n$. Also show that if $r + s < n$, it is not necessary that $A\mathbf{z}$ and $\mathbf{z}'B\mathbf{z}$, and $\mathbf{z}'A\mathbf{z}$ and $\mathbf{z}'B\mathbf{z}$ are independent.

A.20 Summation and Product Operators

For convenience and reference purposes, only the summation and product operators will be discussed in this section. The operators discussed herein are for simplification of mathematical derivations that involve a series of numbers. Without the convenience of the mathematical operators, some mathematical inductions and deductions would be unmanageable.

We will start with the summation operator, which is denoted by the Greek capital sigma, $\sum$, with a range of summation specified. For example

$$\sum_{x=1}^{n} x = 1 + 2 + \cdots + n \tag{A.20.1}$$

where x, in this case, serves as an index of the summation ranging from 1 to n in a discrete increment of 1. The summation sign is similar to the integration sign of long S with the lower limit of integration and upper limit of integration indicated.

Thus the summation operation is the discrete version of the definite integrals from the lower limit (of normally 0 or 1) to the upper limit (of n, say) by the increment of 1 instead of infinitesimal change of dx. Like integration, the summation operation has the property of breaking into segments:

$$\sum_{x=1}^{n} x = \sum_{x=1}^{r} x + \sum_{x=r+1}^{n} x \tag{A.20.2}$$

Also, the summation of the total is the summation of components:

$$\sum_{x=5}^{9} (a + bx) = \sum_{x=5}^{9} a + \sum_{x=5}^{9} bx \tag{A.20.3}$$

Summation of a constant is the constant multiplied by the difference of the upper limit and the lower limit plus 1:

$$\sum_{x=5}^{9} a = (9 - 5 + 1)a = 5a \tag{A.20.4}$$

Summation of a constant multiple of a variable is the constant multiplied by the summation of the variable:

$$\sum_{x=5}^{9} bx = b \sum_{x=5}^{9} x = b(5 + 6 + 7 + 8 + 9) = 35b$$

There are useful formulas that are often associated with series of numbers: The sum of numbers from 1 to n can be expressed as

$$\sum_{x=1}^{n} x = n(n + 1)/2 \tag{A.20.5}$$

because there are $n/2$ pairs of the numbers that sum up to $n + 1$, for a series of numbers from 1, 2, ..., to n. The often-used sum of a geometric series with the increment rate of r can be expressed as

$$\begin{aligned} \sum_{i=1}^{n} ar^i &= a + ar + ar^2 + \cdots + ar^n \\ &= a(1 - r^{n+1})/(1 - r) \end{aligned} \tag{A.20.6}$$

For $0 < |r| < 1$ when n approaches infinity, (A.20.6) can be simplified to $a/(1 - r)$. In the power series, the following is a polynomial function of x

$$\sum_{i=0}^{\infty} a_i x^i = a_0 + a_1 x^1 + a_2 x^2 + \cdots + a_n x^n + \cdots \tag{A.20.7}$$

If $a_i = 1$, for all $i = 1, 2, \ldots$, then the following basic series can be used to generate many interesting other series:

$$\sum_{i=0}^{\infty} x^i = 1 + x + x^2 + \cdots = 1/(1-x) \qquad \text{if } |x| < 1 \tag{A.20.8}$$

Taking the derivatives with respect to x on both sides of (A.20.8), we obtain

$$1 + 2x + 3x^2 + \cdots = 1/(1-x)^2 \tag{A.20.9}$$

or

$$\sum_{i=1}^{\infty} ix^{i-1} = 1/(1-x)^2 \tag{A.20.10}$$

If we take the derivatives of both sides of (A.20.8) with respect to x again, we obtain

$$1 \cdot 2 + 3 \cdot 2x + 4 \cdot 3x^2 + \cdots + i(i-1)x^{i-2} + \cdots = 2(1-x)^{-3} \tag{A.20.11}$$

or in summation notation

$$\sum_{i=1}^{\infty} i(i-1)x^{i-2} = 2/(1-x)^3 \tag{A.20.12}$$

More formulas for summations can be generated by taking derivatives of the foregoing relation, but they will be omitted here.

The formulas of summations for a finite series can be generated by taking derivatives of the binomial expansion:

$$\begin{aligned}(1+x)^n &= C_0^n + C_1^n x + \cdots + C_n^n x^n \\ &= \sum_{r=0}^{n} C_r^n x^r \end{aligned} \tag{A.20.13}$$

where $C_r^n = n!/[r!(n-r)!]$, and $n! = n \cdot (n-1) \cdots 2 \cdot 1$. Taking the derivatives of both sides of (A.20.13) results in

$$\begin{aligned} n(1+x)^{n-1} &= C_1^n + 2C_2^n x + \cdots + nC_n^n x^{n-1} \\ &= \sum_{r=1}^{n} rC_r^n x^{r-1} \end{aligned} \tag{A.20.14}$$

More formulas can be generated from (A.20.14). For example, let $x = 1$, we obtain

$$\sum_{r=1}^{n} rC_r^n = n2^{n-1} \tag{A.20.15}$$

Other formulas can be obtained by taking further derivatives and letting x be some other constants, and so on.

For a quadratic series of the sum of squared numbers, the following formula is useful

$$\sum_{x=1}^{n} x^2 = n(n+1)(2n+1)/6 \tag{A.20.16}$$

This formula is derived as follows:

$$\begin{aligned}\sum_{x=1}^{n} x^2 &= 1^2 + 2^2 + 3^2 \cdots + n^2\\ &= 1 + (1+3) + (1+3+5) + \cdots + (1+3+5+\cdots+2n-1)\\ &= n\cdot 1 + (n-1)3 + (n-2)5 + \cdots + 1\cdot(2n-1)\\ &= \sum_{x=1}^{n} (n-x+1)(2x-1)\\ &= 2n\sum_{x=1}^{n} x - 2\sum_{x=1}^{n} x^2 + 3\sum_{x=1}^{n} x - \sum_{x=1}^{n} (n+1)\end{aligned} \tag{A.20.17}$$

Collecting x^2 to the left side results in

$$\begin{aligned}3\sum_{x=1}^{n} x^2 &= (2n+3)\sum_{x=1}^{n} x - n(n+1)\\ &= n(n+1)(2n+3)/2 - n(n+1)\end{aligned} \tag{A.20.18}$$

Dividing both sides by 3 and simplifying yields

$$\sum_{x=1}^{n} x^2 = n(n+1)(2n+1)/6 \tag{A.20.19}$$

This formula can be used to generate the following formula

$$\begin{aligned}\sum_{x=1}^{n} x(x-1) &= \sum_{x=1}^{n} x^2 - \sum_{x=1}^{n} x\\ &= n(n+1)(2n+1)/6 - n(n+1)/2\\ &= n(n-1)(n+1)/3\end{aligned} \tag{A.20.20}$$

Also,

$$\sum_{x=1}^{n} x(x+1) = n(n+1)(n+2)/3 \tag{A.20.21}$$

The proof is left for you to do as an exercise.

The summation operator is also used to express a typical element of the matrix multiplication. For example, if A is an $(m \times q)$ matrix and B is a $(q \times n)$ matrix, then the typical element of the product $C = AB$ can be expressed as

$$c_{ij} = \sum_{k=1}^{q} a_{ik} b_{kj} \tag{A.20.22}$$

Double summation operations are often used to denote the expansion of a quadratic form $\mathbf{x}'B\mathbf{x}$:

$$\mathbf{x}'B\mathbf{x} = \sum_{i=1}^{n} \sum_{j=1}^{n} x_i b_{ij} x_j \tag{A.20.23}$$

where $\mathbf{x}$ is an $(n \times 1)$ column vector and B is an $(n \times n)$ matrix. If this B matrix is symmetric, then $\mathbf{x}'B\mathbf{x}$ can be expressed as

$$\mathbf{x}'B\mathbf{x} = \sum_{i=1}^{n} b_{ii} x_i^2 + 2 \sum_{\substack{i=1 \\ i \neq j}}^{n} \sum_{j=1}^{n} x_i b_{ij} x_j \tag{A.20.24}$$

The following formula, which expresses the sum of the elements on and below the diagonal of an $(n \times n)$ matrix A, also uses double summations:

$$\sum_{j=1}^{n} \sum_{i=j}^{n} a_{ij} = \sum_{i=1}^{n} \sum_{j=1}^{i} a_{ij} \tag{A.20.25}$$

The left side of the equality sums over the elements columns by column whereas the right side sums over the elements row wise.

Similar to the summation operator, the capital Greek letter pi, $\prod$ is used to denote the product operator, which is defined as follows:

$$\prod_{x=1}^{n} x = 1 \cdot 2 \cdot 3 \cdots n = n! \tag{A.20.26}$$

If x_i denotes a number, then

$$\prod_{i=1}^{n} x_i = x_1 x_2 x_3 \cdots x_n \tag{A.20.27}$$

Thus, the geometric mean can be expressed as

$$G = \left(\prod_{i=1}^{n} x_i \right)^{1/n} \tag{A.20.28}$$

By taking the logarithm, the product operator can be transformed into the summation operator:

$$\log G = \log\left(\prod_{i=1}^{n} x_i\right)^{1/n} = \sum_{i=1}^{n} \log x_i/n \qquad \text{(A.20.29)}$$

The product operator is often used in denoting the likelihood function, which is the product of the probability density functions under the assumption that data are observed independently of each other. For example

$$\prod_{i=1}^{n} (2\pi\sigma)^{-1/2} \exp\{-(x_i - \mu)^2/(2\sigma^2)\} \qquad \text{(A.20.30)}$$

is the likelihood function of the parameters μ, and σ^2, given the data x_i, $i = 1, 2, \ldots, n$.

Exercises

1 Show that $\sum_{i=1}^{2} \sum_{j=1}^{3} a_{ij} = \sum_{j=1}^{3} \sum_{i=1}^{2} a_{ij}$

2 Show $\sum_{x=1}^{n} x(x+1) = n(n+1)(n+2)/3$

3 Let $\bar{x} = \sum_{t=1}^{T} x_t/T$, show that

$$\begin{vmatrix} T & \sum_{t=1}^{T} x_t \\ \sum_{t=1}^{T} x_t & \sum_{t=1}^{T} x_t^2 \end{vmatrix} = T \sum_{t=1}^{T} (x_t - \bar{x})^2$$

4 Let $\bar{x} = \sum_{t=1}^{T} x_t/T$ and $\bar{y} = \sum_{t=1}^{T} y_t/T$, show that

$$\begin{vmatrix} T & \sum_{t=1}^{T} y_t \\ \sum_{t=1}^{T} x_t & \sum_{i=1}^{T} x_t y_t \end{vmatrix} = T \sum_{t=1}^{T} (x_t - \bar{x})(y_t - \bar{y})$$

A.21 References

Graybill, F. A. (1976) *Theory and Application of the Linear Model.* North Scituate, MA, Duxbury Press.

Graybill, F. A. (1983) *Introduction to Matrices with Applications in Statistics, 2nd ed.* Belmont, CA, Wadsworth.

Hadley, G. (1961) *Linear Algebra.* Reading, MA, Addison-Wesley.

Johnston, J. (1984) *Econometric Methods,* 3rd ed. New York, McGraw-Hill.

Judge, G. G., W. E. Griffiths, R. C. Hill, H. Lütkepohl, and T. C. Lee (1985) *The Theory and Practice of Econometrics,* 2nd ed. New York, Wiley.

Kolman, B. (1984) *Introductory Linear Algebra With Applications.* New York, Macmillan.

Lee, T. C., G. G. Judge, and A. Zellner (1977) *Estimating the Parameters of the Markov Probability Model from Aggregate Economic Data,* 2nd ed. Amsterdam, North-Holland.

Noble, B., and J. W. Daniel (1977) *Applied Linear Algebra.* Englewood Cliffs, NJ, Prentice-Hall.

Searle, S. R. (1982) *Matrix Algebra Useful for Statistics.* New York, Wiley.

Strang, G. (1980) *Linear Algebra and Its Applications,* 2nd ed. New York, Academic Press.

Theil, H. (1983) "Mathematical and Statistical Methods in Econometrics." In Z. Griliches and M. D. Intriligator (eds). *Handbook of Econometrics,* vol. 1. Part 1. Amsterdam, North-Holland, pp. 5-66.

Wu, N., and R. Coppins (1981) *Linear Programming and Extensions.* New York, McGraw-Hill.

Tables Included

Table 1. Area under the Standard Normal Distribution
Table 2. Percentage Points for the t-Distribution
Table 3. Percentage Points for the χ^2 Distribution
Table 4. Percentage Points for the F-Distribution
Table 5. Critical Values for the Durbin-Watson Test: 5% Significance Level
Table 6. Mean (E) and Variance (V) of the Durbin-Watson Upper Bound

Table 1 Area under the Standard Normal Distribution

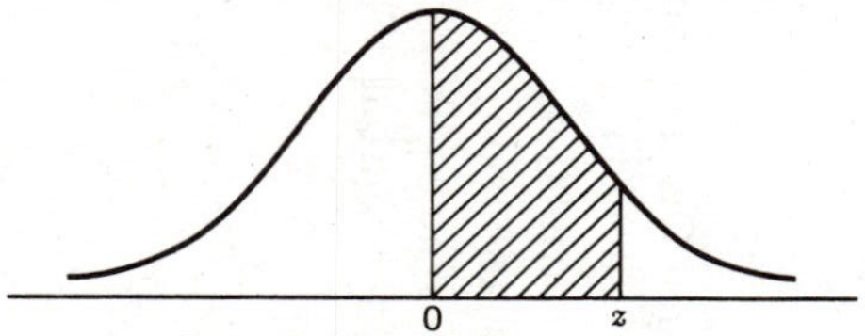

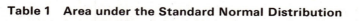

Example for $z = 0.64$
$P\{0 \leqslant N(0, 1) \leqslant 0.64\} = 0.2389$

z	0.00	0.01	0.02	0.03	0.04	0.05	0.06	0.07	0.08	0.09
0.0	0.0000	0.0040	0.0080	0.0120	0.0160	0.0199	0.0239	0.0279	0.0319	0.0359
0.1	0.0398	0.0438	0.0478	0.0517	0.0557	0.0596	0.0636	0.0675	0.0714	0.0753
0.2	0.0793	0.0832	0.0871	0.0910	0.0948	0.0987	0.1026	0.1064	0.1103	0.1141
0.3	0.1179	0.1217	0.1255	0.1293	0.1331	0.1368	0.1406	0.1443	0.1480	0.1517
0.4	0.1554	0.1591	0.1628	0.1664	0.1700	0.1736	0.1772	0.1808	0.1844	0.1879
0.5	0.1915	0.1950	0.1985	0.2019	0.2054	0.2088	0.2123	0.2157	0.2190	0.2224
0.6	0.2257	0.2291	0.2324	0.2357	0.2389	0.2422	0.2454	0.2486	0.2517	0.2549
0.7	0.2580	0.2611	0.2642	0.2673	0.2704	0.2734	0.2764	0.2794	0.2823	0.2852
0.8	0.2881	0.2910	0.2939	0.2967	0.2995	0.3023	0.3051	0.3078	0.3106	0.3133
0.9	0.3159	0.3186	0.3212	0.3238	0.3264	0.3289	0.3315	0.3340	0.3365	0.3389
1.0	0.3413	0.3438	0.3461	0.3485	0.3508	0.3531	0.3554	0.3577	0.3599	0.3621

1.1	0.3643	0.3665	0.3686	0.3708	0.3729	0.3749	0.3770	0.3790	0.3810	0.3830
1.2	0.3849	0.3869	0.3888	0.3907	0.3925	0.3944	0.3962	0.3980	0.3997	0.4015
1.3	0.4032	0.4049	0.4066	0.4082	0.4099	0.4115	0.4131	0.4147	0.4162	0.4177
1.4	0.4192	0.4207	0.4222	0.4236	0.4251	0.4265	0.4279	0.4292	0.4306	0.4319
1.5	0.4332	0.4345	0.4357	0.4370	0.4382	0.4394	0.4406	0.4418	0.4429	0.4441
1.6	0.4452	0.4463	0.4474	0.4484	0.4495	0.4505	0.4515	0.4525	0.4535	0.4545
1.7	0.4554	0.4564	0.4573	0.4582	0.4591	0.4599	0.4608	0.4616	0.4625	0.4633
1.8	0.4641	0.4649	0.4656	0.4664	0.4671	0.4678	0.4686	0.4693	0.4699	0.4706
1.9	0.4713	0.4719	0.4726	0.4732	0.4738	0.4744	0.4750	0.4756	0.4761	0.4767
2.0	0.4772	0.4778	0.4783	0.4788	0.4793	0.4798	0.4803	0.4804	0.4812	0.4817
2.1	0.4821	0.4826	0.4830	0.4834	0.4838	0.4842	0.4846	0.4850	0.4854	0.4857
2.2	0.4861	0.4864	0.4868	0.4871	0.4875	0.4878	0.4881	0.4884	0.4887	0.4890
2.3	0.4893	0.4896	0.4898	0.4901	0.4904	0.4906	0.4909	0.4911	0.4913	0.4916
2.4	0.4918	0.4920	0.4922	0.4925	0.4927	0.4929	0.4931	0.4932	0.4934	0.4936
2.5	0.4938	0.4940	0.4941	0.4943	0.4945	0.4946	0.4948	0.4949	0.4951	0.4952
2.6	0.4953	0.4955	0.4956	0.4957	0.4959	0.4960	0.4961	0.4962	0.4963	0.4964
2.7	0.4965	0.4966	0.4967	0.4968	0.4969	0.4970	0.4971	0.4972	0.4973	0.4974
2.8	0.4974	0.4975	0.4976	0.4977	0.4977	0.4978	0.4979	0.4979	0.4980	0.4981
2.9	0.4981	0.4982	0.4982	0.4983	0.4984	0.4984	0.4985	0.4985	0.4986	0.4986
3.0	0.4987	0.4987	0.4987	0.4988	0.4988	0.4989	0.4989	0.4989	0.4990	0.4990

Table 2 Percentage Points for the t-Distribution

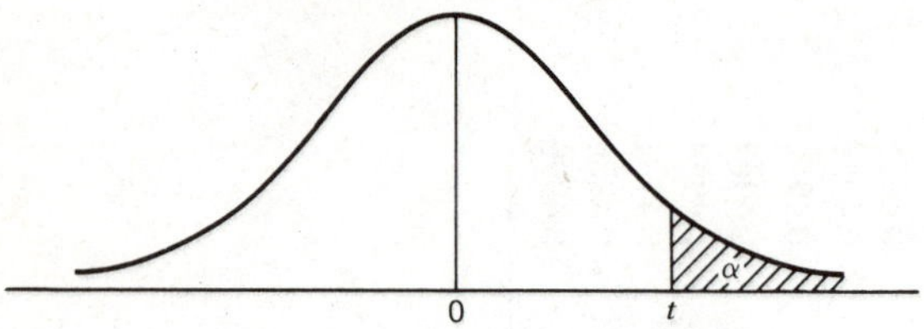

DF	$\alpha = 0.05$	$\alpha = 0.025$	$\alpha = 0.005$
1	6.314	12.706	63.657
2	2.920	4.303	9.925
3	2.353	3.182	5.841
4	2.132	2.776	4.604
5	2.015	2.571	4.032
6	1.943	2.447	3.707
7	1.895	2.365	3.499
8	1.860	2.306	3.355
9	1.833	2.262	3.250
10	1.812	2.228	3.169
11	1.796	2.201	3.106
12	1.782	2.179	3.055
13	1.771	2.160	3.012
14	1.761	2.145	2.977
15	1.753	2.131	2.947
16	1.746	2.120	2.921
17	1.740	2.110	2.898
18	1.734	2.101	2.878
19	1.729	2.093	2.861
20	1.725	2.086	2.845
21	1.721	2.080	2.831
22	1.717	2.074	2.819
23	1.714	2.069	2.807
24	1.711	2.064	2.797
25	1.708	2.060	2.787
26	1.706	2.056	2.779
27	1.703	2.052	2.771
28	1.701	2.048	2.763
29	1.699	2.045	2.756
30	1.697	2.042	2.750
40	1.684	2.021	2.704
60	1.671	2.000	2.660
120	1.658	1.980	2.617
∞	1.645	1.960	2.576

Source: This table is based on Table 12 of *Biometrika Tables for Statisticians*. Vol. I, edited by E. S. Pearson and H. O. Hartley (1970). By permission of the *Biometrika* trustees.

Table 3 Percentage Points for the χ^2 Distribution

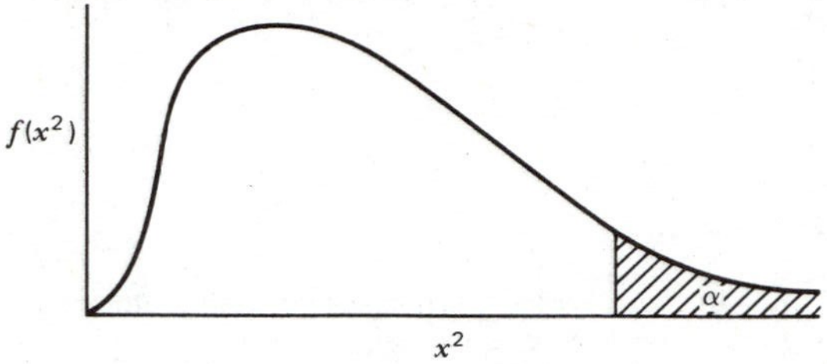

DF	$\alpha = 0.995$	$\alpha = 0.975$	$\alpha = 0.950$	$\alpha = 0.500$	$\alpha = 0.100$	$\alpha = 0.050$	$\alpha = 0.025$	$\alpha = 0.010$	$\alpha = 0.005$
1	392704.10^{-10}	982069.10^{-9}	393214.10^{-8}	0.454936	2.70554	3.84146	5.02389	6.63490	7.87944
2	0.0100251	0.0506356	0.102587	1.38629	4.60517	5.99146	7.37776	9.21034	10.5966
3	0.0717218	0.215795	0.351846	2.36597	6.25139	7.81473	9.34840	11.3449	12.8382
4	0.206989	0.484419	0.710723	3.35669	7.77944	9.48773	11.1433	13.2767	14.8603
5	0.411742	0.831212	1.145476	4.35146	9.23635	11.0705	12.8325	15.0863	16.7496
6	0.675727	1.23734	1.63538	5.34812	10.6446	12.5916	14.4494	16.8119	18.5476
7	0.989256	1.68987	2.16735	6.34581	12.0170	14.0671	16.0128	18.4753	20.2777
8	1.34441	2.17973	2.73264	7.34412	13.3616	15.5073	17.5345	20.0902	21.9550
9	1.73493	2.70039	3.32511	8.34283	14.6837	16.9190	19.0228	21.6660	23.5894
10	2.15586	3.24697	3.94030	9.34182	15.9871	18.3070	20.4832	23.2093	25.1882
11	2.60322	3.81575	4.57481	10.3410	17.2750	19.6751	21.9200	24.7250	26.7568
12	3.07382	4.40379	5.22603	11.3403	18.5494	21.0261	23.3367	26.2170	28.2995
13	3.56503	5.00875	5.89186	12.3398	19.8119	22.3620	24.7356	27.6883	29.8195
14	4.07467	5.62873	6.57063	13.3393	21.0642	23.6848	26.1189	29.1413	31.3194
15	4.60092	6.26214	7.26094	14.3389	22.3072	24.9958	27.4884	30.5779	32.8013
16	5.14221	6.90766	7.96165	15.3385	23.5418	26.2962	28.8454	31.9999	34.2672
17	5.69722	7.56419	8.67176	16.3382	24.7690	27.5871	30.1910	33.4087	35.7185
18	6.26480	8.23075	9.39046	17.3379	25.9894	28.8693	31.5264	34.8053	37.1565
19	6.84397	8.90652	10.1170	18.3377	27.2036	30.1435	32.8523	36.1908	38.5823

(continued)

Table 3 *(continued)*

DF	$\alpha = 0.995$	$\alpha = 0.975$	$\alpha = 0.950$	$\alpha = 0.500$	$\alpha = 0.100$	$\alpha = 0.050$	$\alpha = 0.025$	$\alpha = 0.010$	$\alpha = 0.005$
20	7.43384	9.59078	10.8508	19.3374	28.4120	31.4104	34.1696	37.5662	39.9968
21	8.03365	10.28293	11.5913	20.3372	29.6151	32.6706	35.4789	38.9321	41.4011
22	8.64272	10.9823	12.3380	21.3370	30.8133	33.9244	36.7807	40.2984	42.7957
23	9.26043	11.6886	13.0905	22.3369	32.0069	35.1725	38.0756	41.6384	44.1813
24	9.88623	12.4012	13.8484	23.3367	33.1963	36.4150	39.3641	42.9798	45.5585
25	10.5197	13.1197	14.6114	24.3366	34.3816	37.6525	40.6465	44.3141	46.9279
26	11.1602	13.8439	15.3792	25.3365	35.5631	38.8851	41.9232	45.6417	48.2899
27	11.8076	14.5734	16.1514	26.3363	36.7412	40.1133	43.1945	46.9630	49.6449
28	12.4613	15.3079	16.9279	27.3362	37.9159	41.3371	44.4608	48.2782	50.9934
29	13.1211	16.0471	17.7084	28.3361	39.0875	42.5570	45.7223	49.5879	52.3356
30	13.7867	16.7908	18.4927	29.3360	40.2560	43.7730	46.9792	50.8922	53.6720
40	20.7065	24.4330	26.5093	39.3353	51.8050	55.7585	59.3417	63.6907	66.7660
50	27.9907	32.3574	34.7643	49.3349	63.1671	67.5048	71.4202	76.1539	79.4900
60	35.5345	40.4817	43.1880	59.3347	74.3970	79.0819	83.2977	88.3794	91.9517
70	43.2752	48.7576	51.7393	69.3345	85.5271	90.5312	95.0232	100.425	104.215
80	51.1719	57.1532	60.3915	79.3343	96.5782	101.879	106.629	112.329	116.321
90	59.1963	65.6466	69.1260	89.3342	107.565	113.145	118.136	124.116	128.299
100	67.3276	74.2219	77.9295	99.3341	118.494	124.342	129.561	135.807	140.169

Source: This table is based on Table 8 of *Biometrika Tables for Statisticians*, Vol. I, edited by E. S. Pearson and H. O. Hartley (1970). By permission of the *Biometrika* trustees.

Table 4 Percentage Points for the F-Distribution

Upper 1% Points

ν_2 \ ν_1	1	2	3	4	5	6	7	8	9	10	12	15	20	24	30	40	60	120	∞
1	4052	4999.5	5403	5625	5764	5859	5928	5981	6022	6056	6106	6157	6209	6235	6261	6287	6313	6339	6366
2	98.50	99.00	99.17	99.25	99.30	99.33	99.36	99.37	99.39	99.40	99.42	99.43	99.45	99.46	99.47	99.47	99.48	99.49	99.50
3	34.12	30.82	29.46	28.71	28.24	27.91	27.67	27.49	27.35	27.23	27.05	26.87	26.69	26.60	26.50	26.41	26.32	26.22	26.13
4	21.20	18.00	16.69	15.98	15.52	15.21	14.98	14.80	14.66	14.55	14.37	14.20	14.02	13.93	13.84	13.75	13.65	13.56	13.46
5	16.26	13.27	12.06	11.39	10.97	10.67	10.46	10.29	10.16	10.05	9.89	9.72	9.55	9.47	9.38	9.29	9.20	9.11	9.02
6	13.75	10.92	9.78	9.15	8.75	8.47	8.26	8.10	7.98	7.87	7.72	7.56	7.40	7.31	7.23	7.14	7.06	6.97	6.88
7	12.25	9.55	8.45	7.85	7.46	7.19	6.99	6.84	6.72	6.62	6.47	6.31	6.16	6.07	5.99	5.91	5.82	5.47	5.65
8	11.26	8.65	7.59	7.01	6.63	6.37	6.18	6.03	5.91	5.81	5.67	5.52	5.36	5.28	5.20	5.12	5.03	4.95	4.86
9	10.56	8.02	6.99	6.42	6.06	5.80	5.61	5.47	5.35	5.26	5.11	4.96	4.81	4.73	4.65	4.57	4.48	4.40	4.31
10	10.04	7.56	6.55	5.99	5.64	5.39	5.20	5.06	4.94	4.85	4.71	4.56	4.41	4.33	4.25	4.17	4.08	4.00	3.91
11	9.65	7.21	6.22	5.67	5.32	5.07	4.89	4.74	4.63	4.54	4.40	4.25	4.10	4.02	3.94	3.86	3.78	3.69	3.60
12	9.33	6.93	5.95	5.41	5.06	4.82	4.64	4.50	4.39	4.30	4.16	4.01	3.86	3.78	3.70	3.62	3.54	3.45	3.36
13	9.07	6.70	5.74	5.21	4.86	4.62	4.44	4.30	4.19	4.10	3.96	3.82	3.66	3.59	3.51	3.43	3.34	3.25	3.17
14	8.86	6.51	5.56	5.04	4.69	4.46	4.28	4.14	4.03	3.94	3.80	3.66	3.51	3.43	3.35	3.27	3.18	3.09	3.00
15	8.68	6.36	5.42	4.89	4.56	4.32	4.14	4.00	3.89	3.80	3.67	3.52	3.37	3.29	3.21	3.13	3.05	2.96	2.87
16	8.53	6.23	5.29	4.77	4.44	4.20	4.03	3.89	3.78	3.69	3.55	3.41	3.26	3.18	3.10	3.02	2.93	2.84	2.75
17	8.40	6.11	5.18	4.67	4.34	4.10	3.93	3.79	3.68	3.59	3.46	3.31	3.16	3.08	3.00	2.92	2.83	2.75	2.65
18	8.29	6.01	5.09	4.58	4.25	4.01	3.84	3.71	3.60	3.51	3.37	3.23	3.08	3.00	2.92	2.84	2.75	2.66	2.57
19	8.18	5.93	5.01	4.50	4.17	3.94	3.77	3.63	3.52	3.43	3.30	3.15	3.00	2.92	2.84	2.76	2.67	2.58	2.49
20	8.10	5.85	4.94	4.43	4.10	3.87	3.70	3.56	3.46	3.37	3.23	3.09	2.94	2.86	2.78	2.69	2.61	2.52	2.42
21	8.02	5.78	4.87	4.37	4.04	3.81	3.64	3.51	3.40	3.31	3.17	3.03	2.88	2.80	2.72	2.64	2.55	2.46	2.36
22	7.95	5.72	4.82	4.31	3.99	3.76	3.59	3.45	3.35	3.26	3.12	2.98	2.83	2.75	2.67	2.58	2.50	2.40	2.31
23	7.88	5.66	4.76	4.26	3.94	3.71	3.54	3.41	3.30	3.21	3.07	2.93	2.78	2.70	2.62	2.54	2.45	2.35	2.26
24	7.82	5.61	4.72	4.22	3.90	3.67	3.50	3.36	3.26	3.17	3.03	2.89	2.74	2.66	2.58	2.49	2.40	2.31	2.21
25	7.77	5.57	4.68	4.18	3.85	3.63	3.46	3.32	3.22	3.13	2.99	2.85	2.70	2.62	2.54	2.45	2.36	2.27	2.17
26	7.72	5.53	4.64	4.14	3.82	3.59	3.42	3.29	3.18	3.09	2.96	2.81	2.66	2.58	2.50	2.42	2.33	2.23	2.13
27	7.68	5.49	4.60	4.11	3.78	3.56	3.39	3.26	3.15	3.06	2.93	2.78	2.63	2.55	2.47	2.38	2.29	2.20	2.10
28	7.64	5.45	4.57	4.07	3.75	3.53	3.36	3.23	3.12	3.03	2.90	2.75	2.60	2.52	2.44	2.35	2.26	2.17	2.06
29	7.60	5.42	4.54	4.04	3.73	3.50	3.33	3.20	3.09	3.00	2.87	2.73	2.57	2.49	2.41	2.33	2.23	2.14	2.03
30	7.56	5.39	4.51	4.02	3.70	3.47	3.30	3.17	3.07	2.98	2.84	2.70	2.55	2.47	2.39	2.30	2.21	2.11	2.01
40	7.31	5.18	4.31	3.83	3.51	3.29	3.12	2.99	2.89	2.80	2.66	2.52	2.37	2.29	2.20	2.11	2.02	1.92	1.80
60	7.08	4.98	4.13	3.65	3.34	3.12	2.95	2.82	2.72	2.63	2.50	2.35	2.20	2.12	2.03	1.94	1.84	1.73	1.60
120	6.85	4.79	3.95	3.48	3.17	2.96	2.79	2.66	2.56	2.47	2.34	2.19	2.03	1.95	1.86	1.76	1.66	1.53	1.38
∞	6.63	4.61	3.78	3.32	3.02	2.80	2.64	2.51	2.41	2.32	2.18	2.04	1.88	1.79	1.70	1.59	1.47	1.32	1.00

(continued)

Table 4 *(continued)*

Upper 5% Points

ν_2 \ ν_1	1	2	3	4	5	6	7	8	9	10	12	15	20	25	30	40	60	120	∞
1	161.4	199.5	215.7	224.6	230.2	234.0	236.8	238.9	240.5	241.9	243.9	245.9	248.0	249.1	250.1	251.1	252.2	253.3	254.3
2	18.51	19.00	19.16	19.25	19.30	19.33	19.35	19.37	19.38	19.40	19.41	19.43	19.45	19.45	19.46	19.47	19.48	19.49	19.50
3	10.13	9.55	9.28	9.12	9.01	8.94	8.89	8.85	8.81	8.79	8.74	8.70	8.66	8.64	8.62	8.59	8.57	8.55	8.53
4	7.71	6.94	6.59	6.39	6.26	6.16	6.09	6.04	6.00	5.96	5.91	5.86	5.80	5.77	5.75	5.72	5.69	5.66	5.63
5	6.61	5.79	5.41	5.19	5.05	4.95	4.88	4.82	4.77	4.74	4.68	4.62	4.56	4.53	4.50	4.46	4.43	4.40	4.36
6	5.99	5.14	4.76	4.53	4.39	4.28	4.21	4.15	4.10	4.06	4.00	3.94	3.87	3.84	3.81	3.77	3.74	3.70	3.67
7	5.59	4.74	4.35	4.12	3.97	3.87	3.79	3.73	3.68	3.64	3.57	3.51	3.44	3.41	3.38	3.34	3.30	3.27	3.23
8	5.32	4.46	4.07	3.84	3.69	3.58	3.50	3.44	3.39	3.35	3.28	3.22	3.15	3.12	3.08	3.04	3.01	2.97	2.93
9	5.12	4.26	3.86	3.63	3.48	3.37	3.29	3.23	3.18	3.14	3.07	3.01	2.94	2.90	2.86	2.83	2.79	2.75	2.71
10	4.96	4.10	3.71	3.48	3.33	3.22	3.14	3.07	3.02	2.98	2.91	2.85	2.77	2.74	2.70	2.66	2.62	2.58	2.54
11	4.84	3.98	3.59	3.36	3.20	3.09	3.01	2.95	2.90	2.85	2.79	2.72	2.65	2.61	2.57	2.53	2.49	2.45	2.40
12	4.75	3.89	3.49	3.26	3.11	3.00	2.91	2.85	2.80	2.75	2.69	2.62	2.54	2.51	2.47	2.43	2.38	2.34	2.30
13	4.67	3.81	3.41	3.18	3.03	2.92	2.83	2.77	2.71	2.67	2.60	2.53	2.46	2.42	2.38	2.34	2.30	2.25	2.21
14	4.60	3.74	3.34	3.11	2.96	2.85	2.76	2.70	2.65	2.60	2.53	2.46	2.39	2.35	2.31	2.27	2.22	2.18	2.13
15	4.54	3.68	3.29	3.06	2.90	2.79	2.71	2.64	2.59	2.54	2.48	2.40	2.33	2.29	2.25	2.20	2.16	2.11	2.07
16	4.49	3.63	3.24	3.01	2.85	2.74	2.66	2.59	2.54	2.49	2.42	2.35	2.28	2.24	2.19	2.15	2.11	2.06	2.01
17	4.45	3.59	3.20	2.96	2.81	2.70	2.61	2.55	2.49	2.45	2.38	2.31	2.23	2.19	2.15	2.10	2.06	2.01	1.96
18	4.41	3.55	3.16	2.93	2.77	2.66	2.58	2.51	2.46	2.41	2.34	2.27	2.19	2.15	2.11	2.06	2.02	1.97	1.92
19	4.38	3.52	3.13	2.90	2.74	2.63	2.54	2.48	2.42	2.38	2.31	2.23	2.16	2.11	2.07	2.03	1.98	1.93	1.88
20	4.35	3.49	3.10	2.87	2.71	2.60	2.51	2.45	2.39	2.35	2.28	2.20	2.12	2.08	2.04	1.99	1.95	1.90	1.84
21	4.32	3.47	3.07	2.84	2.68	2.57	2.49	2.42	2.37	2.32	2.25	2.18	2.10	2.05	2.01	1.96	1.92	1.87	1.81
22	4.30	3.44	3.05	2.82	2.66	2.55	2.46	2.40	2.34	2.30	2.23	2.15	2.07	2.03	1.98	1.94	1.89	1.84	1.78
23	4.28	3.42	3.03	2.80	2.64	2.53	2.44	2.37	2.32	2.27	2.20	2.12	2.05	2.01	1.96	1.91	1.86	1.81	1.76
24	4.26	3.40	3.01	2.78	2.62	2.51	2.42	2.36	2.30	2.25	2.18	2.11	2.03	1.98	1.94	1.89	1.84	1.79	1.73
25	4.24	3.39	2.99	2.76	2.60	2.49	2.40	2.34	2.28	2.24	2.16	2.09	2.01	1.96	1.92	1.87	1.82	1.77	1.71
26	4.23	3.37	2.98	2.74	2.59	2.47	2.39	2.32	2.27	2.22	2.15	2.07	1.99	1.95	1.90	1.85	1.80	1.75	1.69
27	4.21	3.35	2.96	2.73	2.57	2.46	2.37	2.31	2.25	2.20	2.13	2.06	1.97	1.93	1.88	1.84	1.79	1.73	1.67
28	4.20	3.34	2.95	2.71	2.56	2.45	2.36	2.29	2.24	2.19	2.12	2.04	1.96	1.91	1.87	1.82	1.77	1.71	1.65
29	4.18	3.33	2.93	2.70	2.55	2.43	2.35	2.28	2.22	2.18	2.10	2.03	1.94	1.90	1.85	1.81	1.75	1.70	1.64
30	4.17	3.32	2.92	2.69	2.53	2.42	2.33	2.27	2.21	2.16	2.09	2.01	1.93	1.89	1.84	1.79	1.74	1.68	1.62
40	4.08	3.23	2.84	2.61	2.45	2.34	2.25	2.18	2.12	2.08	2.00	1.92	1.84	1.79	1.74	1.69	1.64	1.58	1.51
60	4.00	3.15	2.76	2.53	2.37	2.25	2.17	2.10	2.04	1.99	1.92	1.84	1.75	1.70	1.65	1.59	1.53	1.47	1.39
120	3.92	3.07	2.68	2.45	2.29	2.17	2.09	2.02	1.96	1.91	1.83	1.75	1.66	1.61	1.55	1.50	1.43	1.35	1.25
∞	3.84	3.00	2.60	2.37	2.21	2.10	2.01	1.94	1.88	1.83	1.75	1.67	1.57	1.52	1.46	1.39	1.32	1.22	1.00

Source: This table is based on Table 18 of *Biometrika Tables for Statisticians*, Vol. I, edited by E. S. Pearson and H. O. Hartley (1970). By permission of the *Biometrika* trustees. ν_1 = numerator degrees of freedom; ν_2 = denominator degrees of freedom.

Table 5 Critical Values for the Durbin–Watson Test: 5% Significance Level[a]

T	$K = 2$ d_L^*	$K = 2$ d_U^*	$K = 3$ d_L^*	$K = 3$ d_U^*	$K = 4$ d_L^*	$K = 4$ d_U^*	$K = 5$ d_L^*	$K = 5$ d_U^*	$K = 6$ d_L^*	$K = 6$ d_U^*	$K = 7$ d_L^*	$K = 7$ d_U^*	$K = 8$ d_L^*	$K = 8$ d_U^*	$K = 9$ d_L^*	$K = 9$ d_U^*	$K = 10$ d_L^*	$K = 10$ d_U^*	$K = 11$ d_L^*	$K = 11$ d_U^*
6	0.610	1.400																		
7	0.700	1.356	0.467	1.896																
8	0.763	1.332	0.559	1.777	0.368	2.287														
9	0.824	1.320	0.629	1.699	0.455	2.128	0.296	2.588												
10	0.879	1.320	0.697	1.641	0.525	2.016	0.376	2.414	0.243	2.822										
11	0.927	1.324	0.758	1.604	0.595	1.928	0.444	2.283	0.316	2.645	0.203	3.005								
12	0.971	1.331	0.812	1.579	0.658	1.864	0.512	2.177	0.379	2.506	0.268	2.832	0.171	3.149						
13	1.010	1.340	0.861	1.562	0.715	1.816	0.574	2.094	0.445	2.390	0.328	2.692	0.230	2.985	0.147	3.266				
14	1.045	1.350	0.905	1.551	0.767	1.779	0.632	2.030	0.505	2.296	0.389	2.572	0.286	2.848	0.200	3.111	0.127	3.360		
15	1.077	1.361	0.946	1.543	0.814	1.750	0.685	1.977	0.562	2.220	0.447	2.472	0.343	2.727	0.251	2.979	0.175	3.216	0.111	3.438
16	1.106	1.371	0.982	1.539	0.857	1.728	0.734	1.935	0.615	2.157	0.502	2.388	0.398	2.624	0.304	2.860	0.222	3.090	0.155	3.304
17	1.133	1.381	1.015	1.536	0.897	1.710	0.779	1.900	0.664	2.104	0.554	2.318	0.451	2.537	0.356	2.757	0.272	2.975	0.198	3.184
18	1.158	1.391	1.046	1.535	0.933	1.696	0.820	1.872	0.710	2.060	0.603	2.257	0.502	2.461	0.407	2.667	0.321	2.873	0.244	3.073
19	1.180	1.401	1.074	1.536	0.967	1.685	0.859	1.848	0.752	2.023	0.649	2.206	0.549	2.396	0.456	2.589	0.369	2.783	0.290	2.974
20	1.201	1.411	1.100	1.537	0.998	1.676	0.894	1.828	0.792	1.991	0.692	2.162	0.595	2.339	0.502	2.521	0.416	2.704	0.336	2.885
21	1.221	1.420	1.125	1.538	1.026	1.669	0.927	1.812	0.829	1.964	0.732	2.124	0.637	2.290	0.547	2.460	0.461	2.633	0.380	2.806
22	1.239	1.429	1.147	1.541	1.053	1.664	0.958	1.797	0.863	1.940	0.769	2.090	0.677	2.246	0.588	2.407	0.504	2.571	0.424	2.734
23	1.257	1.437	1.168	1.543	1.078	1.660	0.986	1.785	0.895	1.920	0.804	2.061	0.715	2.208	0.628	2.360	0.545	2.514	0.465	2.670
24	1.273	1.446	1.188	1.546	1.101	1.656	1.013	1.775	0.925	1.902	0.837	2.035	0.751	2.174	0.666	2.318	0.584	2.464	0.506	2.613
25	1.288	1.454	1.206	1.550	1.123	1.654	1.038	1.767	0.953	1.886	0.868	2.012	0.784	2.144	0.702	2.280	0.621	2.419	0.544	2.560
26	1.302	1.461	1.224	1.553	1.143	1.652	1.062	1.759	0.979	1.873	0.897	1.992	0.816	2.117	0.735	2.246	0.657	2.379	0.581	2.513
27	1.316	1.469	1.240	1.556	1.162	1.651	1.084	1.753	1.004	1.861	0.925	1.974	0.845	2.093	0.767	2.216	0.691	2.342	0.616	2.470
28	1.328	1.476	1.255	1.560	1.181	1.650	1.104	1.747	1.028	1.850	0.951	1.958	0.874	2.071	0.798	2.188	0.723	2.309	0.650	2.431
29	1.341	1.483	1.270	1.563	1.198	1.650	1.124	1.743	1.050	1.841	0.975	1.944	0.900	2.052	0.826	2.164	0.753	2.278	0.682	2.396
30	1.352	1.489	1.284	1.567	1.214	1.650	1.143	1.739	1.071	1.833	0.998	1.931	0.926	2.034	0.854	2.141	0.782	2.251	0.712	2.363
31	1.363	1.496	1.297	1.570	1.229	1.650	1.160	1.735	1.090	1.825	1.020	1.920	0.950	2.018	0.879	2.120	0.810	2.226	0.741	2.333

[a] K refers to the number of columns in X, including the constant term.

(continued)

Table 5 *(continued)*

T	K = 2		K = 3		K = 4		K = 5		K = 6		K = 7		K = 8		K = 9		K = 10		K = 11	
	d_L^*	d_U^*	d_L^*	d_U^*	d_L^*	d_U^*	d_L^*	d_U^*	d_L^*	d_U^*	d_L^*	d_U^*	d_L^*	d_U^*	d_L^*	d_U^*	d_L^*	d_U^*	d_L^*	d_U^*
32	1.373	1.502	1.309	1.574	1.244	1.650	1.177	1.732	1.109	1.819	1.041	1.909	0.972	2.004	0.904	2.102	0.836	2.203	0.769	2.306
33	1.383	1.508	1.321	1.577	1.258	1.651	1.193	1.730	1.127	1.813	1.061	1.900	0.994	1.991	0.927	2.085	0.861	2.181	0.795	2.281
34	1.393	1.514	1.333	1.580	1.271	1.652	1.208	1.728	1.144	1.808	1.080	1.891	1.015	1.979	0.950	2.069	0.885	2.162	0.821	2.257
35	1.402	1.519	1.343	1.584	1.283	1.653	1.222	1.726	1.160	1.803	1.097	1.884	1.034	1.967	0.971	2.054	0.908	2.144	0.845	2.236
36	1.411	1.525	1.354	1.587	1.295	1.654	1.236	1.724	1.175	1.799	1.114	1.877	1.053	1.957	0.991	2.041	0.930	2.127	0.868	2.216
37	1.419	1.530	1.364	1.590	1.307	1.655	1.249	1.723	1.190	1.795	1.131	1.870	1.071	1.948	1.011	2.029	0.951	2.112	0.891	2.198
38	1.427	1.535	1.373	1.594	1.318	1.656	1.261	1.722	1.204	1.792	1.146	1.864	1.088	1.939	1.029	2.017	0.970	2.098	0.912	2.180
39	1.435	1.540	1.382	1.597	1.328	1.658	1.273	1.722	1.218	1.789	1.161	1.859	1.104	1.932	1.047	2.007	0.990	2.085	0.932	2.164
40	1.442	1.544	1.391	1.600	1.338	1.659	1.285	1.721	1.230	1.786	1.175	1.854	1.120	1.924	1.064	1.997	1.008	2.072	0.945	2.149
45	1.475	1.566	1.430	1.615	1.383	1.666	1.336	1.720	1.287	1.776	1.238	1.835	1.189	1.895	1.139	1.958	1.089	2.022	1.038	2.088
50	1.503	1.585	1.462	1.628	1.421	1.674	1.378	1.721	1.335	1.771	1.291	1.822	1.246	1.875	1.201	1.930	1.156	1.986	1.110	2.044
55	1.528	1.601	1.490	1.641	1.452	1.681	1.414	1.724	1.374	1.768	1.334	1.814	1.294	1.861	1.253	1.909	1.212	1.959	1.170	2.010
60	1.549	1.616	1.514	1.652	1.480	1.689	1.444	1.727	1.408	1.767	1.372	1.808	1.335	1.850	1.298	1.894	1.260	1.939	1.222	1.984
65	1.567	1.629	1.536	1.662	1.503	1.696	1.471	1.731	1.438	1.767	1.404	1.805	1.370	1.843	1.336	1.882	1.301	1.923	1.266	1.964
70	1.583	1.641	1.554	1.672	1.525	1.703	1.494	1.735	1.464	1.768	1.433	1.802	1.401	1.837	1.369	1.873	1.337	1.910	1.305	1.948
75	1.598	1.652	1.571	1.680	1.543	1.709	1.515	1.739	1.487	1.770	1.458	1.801	1.428	1.834	1.399	1.867	1.369	1.901	1.339	1.935
80	1.611	1.662	1.586	1.688	1.560	1.715	1.534	1.743	1.507	1.772	1.480	1.801	1.453	1.831	1.425	1.861	1.397	1.893	1.369	1.925
85	1.624	1.671	1.600	1.696	1.575	1.721	1.550	1.747	1.525	1.774	1.500	1.801	1.474	1.829	1.448	1.857	1.422	1.886	1.396	1.916
90	1.635	1.679	1.612	1.703	1.589	1.726	1.566	1.751	1.542	1.776	1.518	1.801	1.494	1.827	1.469	1.854	1.445	1.881	1.420	1.909
95	1.645	1.687	1.623	1.709	1.602	1.732	1.579	1.755	1.557	1.778	1.535	1.802	1.512	1.827	1.489	1.852	1.465	1.877	1.442	1.903
100	1.654	1.694	1.634	1.715	1.613	1.736	1.592	1.758	1.571	1.780	1.550	1.803	1.528	1.826	1.506	1.850	1.484	1.874	1.462	1.898
150	1.720	1.746	1.706	1.760	1.693	1.774	1.679	1.788	1.665	1.802	1.651	1.817	1.637	1.832	1.622	1.847	1.608	1.862	1.594	1.877
200	1.758	1.778	1.748	1.789	1.738	1.799	1.728	1.810	1.718	1.820	1.707	1.831	1.697	1.841	1.686	1.852	1.675	1.863	1.665	1.874

(continued)

Table 5 (continued)

T	K = 12 d_L^*	K = 12 d_U^*	K = 13 d_L^*	K = 13 d_U^*	K = 14 d_L^*	K = 14 d_U^*	K = 15 d_L^*	K = 15 d_U^*	K = 16 d_L^*	K = 16 d_U^*	K = 17 d_L^*	K = 17 d_U^*	K = 18 d_L^*	K = 18 d_U^*	K = 19 d_L^*	K = 19 d_U^*	K = 20 d_L^*	K = 20 d_U^*	K = 21 d_L^*	K = 21 d_U^*
16	0.098	3.503																		
17	0.138	3.378	0.087	3.557																
18	0.177	3.265	0.123	3.441	0.078	3.603														
19	0.220	3.159	0.160	3.335	0.111	3.496	0.070	3.642												
20	0.263	3.063	0.200	3.234	0.145	3.395	0.100	3.542	0.063	3.676										
21	0.307	2.976	0.240	3.141	0.182	3.300	0.132	3.448	0.091	3.583	0.058	3.705								
22	0.349	2.897	0.281	3.057	0.220	3.211	0.166	3.358	0.120	3.495	0.083	3.619	0.052	3.731						
23	0.391	2.826	0.322	2.979	0.259	3.128	0.202	3.272	0.153	3.409	0.110	3.535	0.076	3.650	0.048	3.753				
24	0.431	2.761	0.362	2.908	0.297	3.053	0.239	3.193	0.186	3.327	0.141	3.454	0.101	3.572	0.070	3.678	0.044	3.773		
25	0.470	2.702	0.400	2.844	0.335	2.983	0.275	3.119	0.221	3.251	0.172	3.376	0.130	3.494	0.094	3.604	0.065	3.702	0.041	3.790
26	0.508	2.649	0.438	2.784	0.373	2.919	0.312	3.051	0.256	3.179	0.205	3.303	0.160	3.420	0.120	3.531	0.087	3.632	0.060	3.724
27	0.544	2.600	0.475	2.730	0.409	2.859	0.348	2.987	0.291	3.112	0.238	3.233	0.191	3.349	0.149	3.460	0.112	3.563	0.081	3.658
28	0.578	2.555	0.510	2.680	0.445	2.805	0.383	2.928	0.325	3.050	0.271	3.168	0.222	3.283	0.178	3.392	0.138	3.495	0.104	3.592
29	0.612	2.515	0.544	2.634	0.479	2.755	0.418	2.874	0.359	2.992	0.305	3.107	0.254	3.219	0.208	3.327	0.166	3.431	0.129	3.528
30	0.643	2.477	0.577	2.592	0.512	2.708	0.451	2.823	0.392	2.937	0.337	3.050	0.286	3.160	0.238	3.266	0.195	3.368	0.156	3.465
31	0.674	2.443	0.608	2.553	0.545	2.665	0.484	2.776	0.425	2.887	0.370	2.996	0.317	3.103	0.269	3.208	0.224	3.309	0.183	3.406
32	0.703	2.411	0.638	2.517	0.576	2.625	0.515	2.733	0.457	2.840	0.401	2.946	0.349	3.050	0.299	3.153	0.253	3.252	0.211	3.348
33	0.731	2.382	0.668	2.484	0.606	2.588	0.546	2.692	0.488	2.796	0.432	2.899	0.379	3.000	0:329	3.100	0.283	3.198	0.239	3.293
34	0.758	2.355	0.695	2.454	0.634	2.554	0.575	2.654	0.518	2.754	0.462	2.854	0.409	2.954	0.359	3.051	0.312	3.147	0.267	3.240
35	0.783	2.330	0.722	2.425	0.662	2.521	0.604	2.619	0.547	2.716	0.492	2.813	0.439	2.910	0.388	3.005	0.340	3.099	0.295	3.190
36	0.808	2.306	0.748	2.398	0.689	2.492	0.631	2.586	0.575	2.680	0.520	2.774	0.467	2.868	0.417	2.961	0.369	3.053	0.323	2.142
37	0.831	2.285	0.772	2.374	0.714	2.464	0.657	2.555	0.602	2.646	0.548	2.738	0.495	2.829	0.445	2.920	0.397	3.009	0.351	3.097
38	0.854	2.265	0.796	2.351	0.739	2.438	0.683	2.526	0.628	2.614	0.575	2.703	0.522	2.792	0.472	2.880	0.424	2.968	0.378	3.054

(continued)

Table 5 (*continued*)

T	$K = 12$ d_L^*	$K = 12$ d_U^*	$K = 13$ d_L^*	$K = 13$ d_U^*	$K = 14$ d_L^*	$K = 14$ d_U^*	$K = 15$ d_L^*	$K = 15$ d_U^*	$K = 16$ d_L^*	$K = 16$ d_U^*	$K = 17$ d_L^*	$K = 17$ d_U^*	$K = 18$ d_L^*	$K = 18$ d_U^*	$K = 19$ d_L^*	$K = 19$ d_U^*	$K = 20$ d_L^*	$K = 20$ d_U^*	$K = 21$ d_L^*	$K = 21$ d_U^*
39	0.875	2.246	0.819	2.329	0.763	2.413	0.707	2.499	0.653	2.585	0.600	2.671	0.549	2.757	0.499	2.843	0.451	2.929	0.404	3.013
40	0.896	2.228	0.840	2.309	0.785	2.391	0.731	2.473	0.678	2.557	0.626	2.641	0.575	2.724	0.525	2.808	0.477	2.892	0.430	2.974
45	0.988	2.156	0.938	2.225	0.887	2.296	0.838	2.367	0.788	2.439	0.740	2.512	0.692	2.586	0.644	2.659	0.598	2.733	0.553	2.807
50	1.064	2.103	1.019	2.163	0.973	2.225	0.927	2.287	0.882	2.350	0.836	2.414	0.792	2.479	0.747	2.544	0.703	2.610	0.660	2.675
55	1.129	2.062	1.087	2.116	1.045	2.170	1.003	2.225	0.961	2.281	0.919	2.338	0.877	2.396	0.836	2.454	0.795	2.512	0.754	2.571
60	1.184	2.031	1.145	2.079	1.106	2.127	1.068	2.177	1.029	2.227	0.990	2.278	0.951	2.330	0.913	2.382	0.874	2.434	0.836	2.487
65	1.231	2.006	1.195	2.049	1.160	2.093	1.124	2.138	1.088	2.183	1.052	2.229	1.016	2.276	0.980	2.323	0.944	3.371	0.908	2.419
70	1.272	1.986	1.239	2.026	1.206	2.066	1.172	2.106	1.139	2.148	1.105	2.189	1.072	2.232	1.038	2.275	1.005	2.318	0.971	2.362
75	1.308	1.970	1.277	2.006	1.247	2.043	1.215	2.080	1.184	2.118	1.153	2.156	1.121	2.195	1.090	2.235	1.058	2.275	1.027	2.315
80	1.340	1.957	1.311	1.991	1.283	2.024	1.253	2.059	1.224	2.093	1.195	2.129	1.165	2.165	1.136	2.201	1.106	2.238	1.076	2.275
85	1.369	1.946	1.342	1.977	1.315	2.009	1.287	2.040	1.260	2.073	1.232	2.105	1.205	2.139	1.177	2.172	1.149	2.206	1.121	2.241
90	1.395	1.937	1.369	1.966	1.344	1.995	1.318	2.025	1.292	2.055	1.266	2.085	1.240	2.116	1.213	2.148	1.187	2.179	1.160	2.211
95	1.418	1.929	1.394	1.956	1.370	2.984	1.345	2.012	1.321	2.040	1.296	2.068	1.271	2.097	1.247	2.126	1.222	2.156	1.197	2.186
100	1.439	1.923	1.416	1.948	1.393	1.974	1.371	2.000	1.347	2.026	1.324	2.053	1.301	2.080	1.277	2.108	1.253	2.135	1.229	2.164
150	1.579	1.892	1.564	1.908	1.550	1.924	1.535	1.940	1.519	1.956	1.504	1.972	1.489	1.989	1.474	2.006	1.458	2.023	1.443	2.040
200	1.654	1.885	1.643	1.896	1.632	1.908	1.621	1.919	1.610	1.931	1.599	1.943	1.588	1.955	1.576	1.967	1.565	1.979	1.554	1.991

Source: This table is reproduced from N. E. Savin, and K. J. White, "The Durbin–Watson Test for Serial Correlation with Extreme Sample Sizes or Many Regressors." *Econometrica*, 45; 1989–1996, 1977. With permission from The Econometric Society.

Table 6 Mean (*E*) and Variances (*V*) of the Durbin–Watson Upper Bound

	$K = 2$		$K = 3$		$K = 4$		$K = 5$		$K = 6$	
T	E	V	E	V	E	V	E	V	E	V
6	2.433	0.35417								
7	2.360	0.34878	2.762	0.23951						
8	2.308	0.33403	2.652	0.25473	3.007	0.16209				
9	2.268	0.31630	2.569	0.25754	2.882	0.18448	3.190	0.11154		
10	2.238	0.29824	2.503	0.25377	2.783	0.19613	3.063	0.13445	3.328	0.07842
11	2.213	0.28098	2.450	0.24663	2.702	0.20081	2.957	0.14941	3.205	0.09919
12	2.193	0.26491	2.407	0.23791	2.635	0.20111	2.868	0.15842	3.099	0.11456
13	2.177	0.25016	2.371	0.22857	2.579	0.19871	2.793	0.16318	3.008	0.12531
14	2.162	0.23668	2.341	0.21918	2.532	0.19468	2.729	0.16497	2.929	0.13243
15	2.150	0.22440	2.315	0.21002	2.491	0.18971	2.674	0.16472	2.860	0.13676
16	2.140	0.21319	2.293	0.20125	2.456	0.18425	2.626	0.16310	2.800	0.13903
17	2.131	0.20296	2.274	0.19294	2.425	0.17859	2.584	0.16056	2.747	0.13977
18	2.123	0.19360	2.257	0.18510	2.399	0.17289	2.547	0.15743	2.700	0.13941
19	2.116	0.18501	2.242	0.17776	2.375	0.16728	2.514	0.15394	2.658	0.13825
20	2.110	0.17712	2.228	0.17087	2.354	0.16182	2.485	0.15024	2.621	0.13652
21	2.104	0.16984	2.216	0.16442	2.335	0.15656	2.459	0.14645	2.587	0.13440
22	2.099	0.16311	2.205	0.15839	2.318	0.15151	2.435	0.14264	2.557	0.13201
23	2.094	0.15688	2.195	0.15274	2.302	0.14669	2.414	0.13887	2.530	0.12945
24	2.090	0.15110	2.186	0.14744	2.288	0.14210	2.394	0.13517	2.505	0.12679
25	2.086	0.14571	2.178	0.14247	2.275	0.13773	2.377	0.13156	2.482	0.12408
26	2.083	0.14069	2.171	0.13780	2.264	0.13357	2.360	0.12806	2.461	0.12136
27	2.079	0.13599	2.164	0.13340	2.253	0.12962	2.345	0.12468	2.441	0.11866
28	2.076	0.13159	2.157	0.12927	2.243	0.12587	2.332	0.12142	2.424	0.11599
29	2.074	0.12746	2.152	0.12537	2.233	0.12230	2.319	0.11829	2.407	0.11337
30	2.071	0.12358	2.146	0.12169	2.225	0.11891	2.307	0.11527	2.392	0.11081

(*continued*)

Table 6 (*continued*)

T	$K = 2$ E	V	$K = 3$ E	V	$K = 4$ E	V	$K = 5$ E	V	$K = 6$ E	V
31	2.069	0.11992	2.141	0.11821	2.217	0.11569	2.296	0.11238	2.378	0.10832
32	2.066	0.11647	2.136	0.11491	2.209	0.11262	2.286	0.10960	2.365	0.10590
33	2.064	0.11321	2.132	0.11179	2.203	0.10969	2.276	0.10694	2.352	0.10355
34	2.062	0.11013	2.128	0.10882	2.196	0.10691	2.267	0.10439	2.341	0.10128
35	2.060	0.10721	2.124	0.10601	2.190	0.10425	2.259	0.10194	2.330	0.09908
36	2.059	0.10443	2.120	0.10333	2.184	0.10172	2.251	0.09958	2.320	0.09695
37	2.057	0.10180	2.117	0.10079	2.179	0.09929	2.243	0.09733	2.310	0.09490
38	2.055	0.09929	2.113	0.09836	2.174	0.09698	2.236	0.09516	2.301	0.09292
39	2.054	0.09691	2.110	0.09604	2.169	0.09476	2.230	0.09308	2.292	0.09100
40	2.052	0.09463	2.107	0.09383	2.164	0.09264	2.223	0.09108	2.284	0.08915
45	2.046	0.08468	2.095	0.08411	2.145	0.08328	2.196	0.08218	2.250	0.08082
50	2.042	0.07661	2.085	0.07620	2.129	0.07559	2.175	0.07479	2.222	0.07379
55	2.038	0.06994	2.077	0.06963	2.117	0.06917	2.158	0.06857	2.200	0.06782
60	2.034	0.06433	2.070	0.06410	2.106	0.06374	2.144	0.06328	2.182	0.06270
65	2.032	0.05956	2.064	0.05937	2.098	0.05909	2.132	0.05873	2.167	0.05827
70	2.029	0.05544	2.060	0.05529	2.090	0.05507	2.122	0.05477	2.155	0.05441
75	2.027	0.05185	2.055	0.05173	2.084	0.05155	2.114	0.05131	2.144	0.05101
80	2.026	0.04870	2.052	0.04860	2.079	0.04845	2.106	0.04826	2.134	0.04801
85	2.024	0.04591	2.049	0.04583	2.074	0.04570	2.099	0.04554	2.126	0.04534
90	2.023	0.04342	2.046	0.04335	2.070	0.04325	2.094	0.04311	2.118	0.04294
95	2.021	0.04119	2.043	0.04113	2.066	0.04104	2.089	0.04092	2.112	0.04078
100	2.020	0.03918	2.041	0.03912	2.062	0.03905	2.084	0.03895	2.106	0.03882
150	2.014	0.02630	2.027	0.02629	2.041	0.02627	2.055	0.02624	2.069	0.02620
200	2.010	0.01980	2.020	0.01979	2.031	0.01978	2.041	0.01977	2.051	0.01975

(*continued*)

	K = 7		K = 8		K = 9		K = 10		K = 11	
T	E	V	E	V	E	V	E	V	E	V
11	3.436	0.05635								
12	3.319	0.07424	3.520	0.04135						
13	3.216	0.08865	3.411	0.05639	3.586	0.03093				
14	3.125	0.09968	3.313	0.06931	3.486	0.04345	3.641	0.02354		
15	3.045	0.10781	3.224	0.07987	3.393	0.05477	3.548	0.03393	3.685	0.01821
16	2.974	0.11354	3.144	0.08819	3.308	0.06449	3.460	0.04373	3.600	0.02683
17	2.911	0.11736	3.073	0.09454	3.230	0.07255	3.379	0.05249	3.518	0.03526
18	2.854	0.11969	3.008	0.09924	3.159	0.07904	3.304	0.06004	3.440	0.04306
19	2.804	0.12087	2.950	0.10258	3.094	0.08415	3.234	0.06639	3.368	0.05001
20	2.759	0.12118	2.898	0.10481	3.036	0.08807	3.171	0.07161	3.301	0.05604
21	2.718	0.12081	2.850	0.10616	2.982	0.09098	3.112	0.07581	3.238	0.06116
22	2.681	0.11994	2.807	0.10682	2.933	0.09306	3.058	0.07912	3.180	0.06544
23	2.648	0.11870	2.768	0.10691	2.889	0.09445	3.008	0.08167	3.126	0.06896
24	2.617	0.11718	2.732	0.10658	2.848	0.09527	2.963	0.08357	3.077	0.07179
25	2.589	0.11546	2.699	0.10590	2.810	0.09564	2.921	0.08493	3.030	0.07404
26	2.564	0.11361	2.669	0.10497	2.775	0.09564	2.881	0.08583	2.987	0.07577
27	2.540	0.11167	2.641	0.10384	2.743	0.09534	2.845	0.08635	2.948	0.07706
28	2.518	0.10966	2.615	0.10256	2.713	0.09480	2.812	0.08656	2.910	0.07798
29	2.498	0.10763	2.591	0.10116	2.685	0.09408	2.780	0.08651	2.876	0.07858
30	2.479	0.10559	2.569	0.09969	2.659	0.09320	2.751	0.08624	2.843	0.07892
31	2.462	0.10356	2.548	0.09817	2.635	0.09222	2.724	0.08580	2.813	0.07903
32	2.446	0.10155	2.529	0.09661	2.613	0.09114	2.699	0.08523	2.785	0.07896
33	2.430	0.09957	2.511	0.09503	2.592	0.08999	2.675	0.08453	2.758	0.07873
34	2.416	0.09762	2.494	0.09344	2.572	0.08880	2.652	0.08375	2.733	0.07836
35	2.403	0.09571	2.478	0.09186	2.554	0.08757	2.631	0.08290	2.710	0.07789
36	2.390	0.09385	2.463	0.09029	2.537	0.08632	2.612	0.08199	2.688	0.07733

(*continued*)

Table 6 (*continued*)

	$K = 7$		$K = 8$		$K = 9$		$K = 10$		$K = 11$	
T	E	V	E	V	E	V	E	V	E	V
37	2.378	0.09203	2.449	0.08874	2.520	0.08506	2.593	0.08103	2.667	0.07670
38	2.367	0.09026	2.435	0.08721	2.505	0.08379	2.575	0.08005	2.647	0.07601
39	2.357	0.08854	2.423	0.08570	2.490	0.08253	2.559	0.07904	2.628	0.07527
40	2.347	0.08686	2.411	0.08423	2.476	0.08127	2.543	0.07802	2.610	0.07450
45	2.304	0.07919	2.360	0.07732	2.417	0.07520	2.475	0.07286	2.535	0.07031
50	2.271	0.07260	2.320	0.07122	2.371	0.06966	2.422	0.06792	2.475	0.06602
55	2.244	0.06692	2.288	0.06588	2.334	0.06470	2.380	0.06338	2.427	0.06193
60	2.222	0.06200	2.262	0.06120	2.303	0.06028	2.345	0.05926	2.387	0.05813
65	2.203	0.05772	2.240	0.05709	2.277	0.05637	2.315	0.05556	2.354	0.05466
70	2.188	0.05397	2.221	0.05346	2.256	0.05288	2.291	0.05223	2.326	0.05151
75	2.174	0.05066	2.205	0.05024	2.237	0.04977	2.269	0.04924	2.302	0.04866
80	2.162	0.04772	2.191	0.04738	2.221	0.04699	2.251	0.04655	2.281	0.04606
85	2.152	0.04509	2.179	0.04481	2.207	0.04448	2.235	0.04412	2.263	0.04371
90	2.143	0.04273	2.169	0.04249	2.194	0.04222	2.221	0.04191	2.247	0.04157
95	2.135	0.04060	2.159	0.04040	2.183	0.04016	2.208	0.03990	2.233	0.03961
100	2.128	0.03867	2.151	0.03850	2.174	0.03830	2.197	0.03807	2.220	0.03782
150	2.084	0.02615	2.098	0.02610	2.113	0.02604	2.128	0.02598	2.143	0.02590
200	2.062	0.01973	2.073	0.01971	2.084	0.01969	2.094	0.01966	2.105	0.01963

(*continued*)

Table 6 (*continued*)

	K = 12		K = 13		K = 14		K = 15		K = 16	
T	E	V	E	V	E	V	E	V	E	V
16	3.722	0.01429								
17	3.643	0.02147	3.752	0.01135						
18	3.566	0.02870	3.680	0.01736	3.778	0.00913				
19	3.493	0.03559	3.608	0.02357	3.711	0.01418	3.800	0.00742		
20	3.424	0.04190	3.539	0.02963	3.645	0.01952	3.738	0.01168	3.819	0.00609
21	3.359	0.04753	3.473	0.03532	3.579	0.02484	3.676	0.01628	3.762	0.00971
22	3.298	0.05245	3.411	0.04052	3.517	0.02995	3.615	0.02097	3.704	0.01369
23	3.241	0.05668	3.352	0.04517	3.457	0.03471	3.555	0.02554	3.646	0.01780
24	3.188	0.06025	3.296	0.04925	3.400	0.03905	3.498	0.02987	3.589	0.02189
25	3.138	0.06324	3.244	0.05279	3.345	0.04294	3.443	0.03390	3.534	0.02583
26	3.092	0.06569	3.195	0.05582	3.294	0.04639	3.390	0.03757	3.481	0.02954
27	2.049	0.06767	3.149	0.05839	3.246	0.04940	3.340	0.04088	3.430	0.03298
28	3.009	0.06925	3.106	0.06053	3.200	0.05200	3.293	0.04382	3.382	0.03612
29	2.971	0.07046	3.065	0.06230	3.158	0.05423	3.248	0.04641	3.336	0.03896
30	2.935	0.07137	3.027	0.06373	3.117	0.05611	3.205	0.04867	3.292	0.04150
31	2.902	0.07202	2.991	0.06486	3.079	0.05769	3.165	0.05062	3.250	0.04375
32	2.871	0.07243	2.957	0.06574	3.043	0.05900	3.127	0.05229	3.210	0.04573
33	2.842	0.07265	2.926	0.06640	3.009	0.06005	3.091	0.05371	3.172	0.04746
34	2.814	0.07271	2.896	0.06686	2.977	0.06090	3.057	0.05490	3.136	0.04895
35	2.788	0.07262	2.867	0.06715	2.946	0.06155	3.024	0.05588	3.102	0.05024
36	2.764	0.07242	2.841	0.06729	2.917	0.06203	2.994	0.05668	3.069	0.05132
37	2.741	0.07211	2.815	0.06731	2.890	0.06236	2.964	0.05732	3.038	0.05224
38	2.719	0.07172	2.792	0.06722	2.864	0.06257	2.937	0.05781	3.009	0.05299

(*continued*)

Table 6 *(continued)*

	K = 12		K = 13		K = 14		K = 15		K = 16	
T	E	V	E	V	E	V	E	V	E	V
39	2.698	0.07126	2.769	0.06704	2.840	0.06266	2.910	0.05817	2.981	0.05361
40	2.679	0.07074	2.747	0.06678	2.816	0.06266	2.885	0.05842	2.954	0.05410
45	2.594	0.06756	2.655	0.06464	2.716	0.06157	2.777	0.05837	2.838	0.05507
50	2.528	0.06397	2.581	0.06177	2.636	0.05944	2.690	0.05699	2.745	0.05444
55	2.474	0.06036	2.522	0.05867	2.571	0.05687	2.620	0.05497	2.669	0.05297
60	2.430	0.05691	2.474	0.05558	2.518	0.05417	2.562	0.05267	2.607	0.05109
65	2.393	0.05369	2.433	0.05264	2.473	0.05151	2.514	0.05031	2.555	0.04904
70	2.362	0.05073	2.398	0.04988	2.435	0.04896	2.473	0.04799	2.510	0.04696
75	2.335	0.04801	2.369	0.04732	2.403	0.04657	2.438	0.04577	2.472	0.04492
80	2.312	0.04553	2.343	0.04496	2.375	0.04434	2.407	0.04367	2.439	0.04297
85	2.292	0.04327	2.321	0.04278	2.351	0.04226	2.380	0.04171	2.411	0.04111
90	2.274	0.04119	2.301	0.04079	2.329	0.04035	2.357	0.03987	2.385	0.03937
95	2.258	0.03929	2.284	0.03895	2.310	0.03857	2.336	0.03817	2.363	0.03774
100	2.244	0.03755	2.269	0.03725	2.293	0.03693	2.318	0.03658	2.343	0.03621
150	2.158	0.02582	2.173	0.02573	2.189	0.02564	2.204	0.02553	2.220	0.02542
200	2.116	0.01959	2.127	0.01956	2.139	0.01952	2.150	0.01947	2.161	0.01943

(continued)

Table 6 (*continued*)

	$K = 17$		$K = 18$		$K = 19$		$K = 20$		$K = 21$	
T	E	V	E	V	E	V	E	V	E	V
21	3.836	0.00505								
22	3.782	0.00813	3.850	0.00421						
23	3.728	0.01158	3.800	0.00686	3.863	0.00355				
24	3.673	0.01520	3.749	0.00986	3.816	0.00582	3.874	0.00300		
25	3.620	0.01886	3.698	0.01306	3.768	0.00844	3.830	0.00497	3.883	0.00256
26	3.567	0.02243	3.647	0.01632	3.720	0.01127	3.785	0.00727	3.843	0.00427
27	3.516	0.02584	3.597	0.01956	3.671	0.01419	3.739	0.00978	3.800	0.00629
28	3.467	0.02905	3.548	0.02269	3.623	0.01712	3.693	0.01240	3.757	0.00852
29	3.420	0.03201	3.500	0.02566	3.576	0.01999	3.647	0.01505	3.713	0.01087
30	3.375	0.03473	3.455	0.02845	3.531	0.02275	3.602	0.01767	3.669	0.01328
31	3.332	0.03719	3.411	0.03103	3.487	0.02536	3.559	0.02022	3.626	0.01568
32	3.290	0.03941	3.369	0.03340	3.444	0.02780	3.516	0.02266	3.584	0.01803
33	3.251	0.04138	3.328	0.03556	3.403	0.03007	3.474	0.02496	3.543	0.02030
34	3.214	0.04313	3.289	0.03751	3.363	0.03215	3.434	0.02712	3.502	0.02246
35	3.178	0.04467	3.252	0.03925	3.325	0.03405	3.395	0.02912	3.463	0.02451
36	3.144	0.04601	3.217	0.04081	3.288	0.03578	3.358	0.03097	3.425	0.02643
37	3.111	0.04717	3.183	0.04219	3.253	0.03733	3.322	0.03266	3.389	0.02821
38	3.080	0.04817	3.151	0.04340	3.220	0.03873	3.288	0.03419	3.354	0.02985

(*continued*)

Table 6 *(continued)*

	$K = 17$		$K = 18$		$K = 19$		$K = 20$		$K = 21$	
T	E	V	E	V	E	V	E	V	E	V
39	3.051	0.04902	3.120	0.04446	3.188	0.03997	3.254	0.03559	3.320	0.03136
40	3.022	0.04974	3.090	0.04538	3.157	0.04107	3.223	0.03684	3.287	0.03274
45	2.899	0.05169	2.960	0.04825	3.021	0.04479	3.081	0.04133	3.141	0.03790
50	2.800	0.05181	2.855	0.04910	2.910	0.04634	2.965	0.04355	3.020	0.04074
55	2.719	0.05090	2.769	0.04875	2.819	0.04655	2.869	0.04429	2.919	0.04200
60	2.652	0.04944	2.698	0.04722	2.743	0.04594	2.789	0.04411	2.835	0.04224
65	2.596	0.04771	2.638	0.04632	2.680	0.04487	2.722	0.04338	2.764	0.04184
70	2.548	0.04587	2.587	0.04473	2.625	0.04355	2.664	0.04231	2.703	0.04104
75	2.508	0.04402	2.543	0.04308	2.579	0.04210	2.615	0.04108	2.651	0.04001
80	2.472	0.04222	2.505	0.04143	2.538	0.04061	2.572	0.03975	2.605	0.03886
85	2.441	0.04049	2.472	0.03982	2.503	0.03913	2.534	0.03840	2.565	0.03765
90	2.414	0.03884	2.443	0.03828	2.472	0.03769	2.501	0.03707	2.530	0.03642
95	2.390	0.03728	2.417	0.03680	2.444	0.03630	2.471	0.03577	2.499	0.03521
100	2.368	0.03582	2.393	0.03541	2.419	0.03497	2.445	0.03451	2.471	0.03403
150	2.236	0.02530	2.252	0.02518	2.268	0.02505	2.284	0.02491	2.300	0.02476
200	2.173	0.01938	2.184	0.01932	2.196	0.01927	2.208	0.01921	2.220	0.01915

INDEX